▪ For Students

MyAccountingLab provides students with a personalized interactive learning environment, where they can learn at their own pace and measure their progress.

Interactive Tutorial Exercises ▼

MyAccountingLab's homework and practice questions are correlated to the textbook, and they regenerate algorithmically to give students unlimited opportunity for practice and mastery. Questions include guided solutions, DemoDoc examples, and learning aids for extra help at point-of-use, and they offer helpful feedback when students enter incorrect answers.

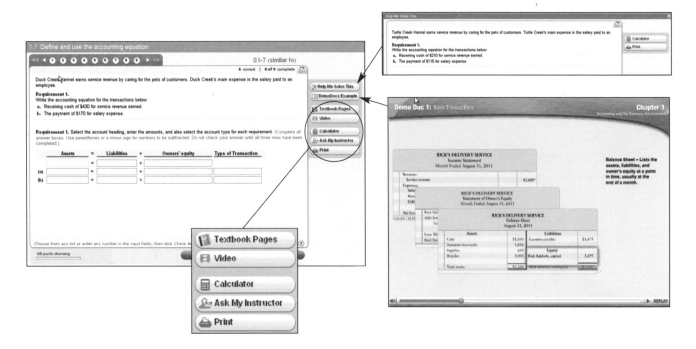

Study Plan for Self-Paced Learning ▶

MyAccountingLab's study plan helps students monitor their own progress, letting them see at a glance exactly which topics they need to practice. MyAccountingLab generates a personalized study plan for each student based on his or her test results, and the study plan links directly to interactive, tutorial exercises for topics the student hasn't yet mastered. Students can regenerate these exercises with new values for unlimited practice, and the exercises include guided solutions and multimedia learning aids to give students the extra help they need.

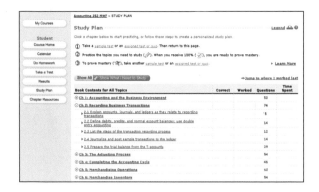

View a guided tour of MyAccountingLab at http://www.myaccountinglab.com/support/tours.

FINANCIAL
ACCOUNTING
Eighth Edition

Walter T. Harrison Jr.
Baylor University

Charles T. Horngren
Stanford University

C. William (Bill) Thomas
Baylor University

Pearson Education

Boston   Columbus   Indianapolis   New York   San Francisco   Upper Saddle River
Amsterdam   Cape Town   Dubai   London   Madrid   Milan   Munich   Paris   Montreal   Toronto
Delhi   Mexico City   Sao Paulo   Sydney   Hong Kong   Seoul   Singapore   Taipei   Tokyo

AVP/Executive Editor: Jodi McPherson
VP/Publisher: Natalie E. Anderson
Acquisitions Editor: Jodi Bolognese
Director of Marketing, Intro Markets: Kate Valentine
AVP/Executive Editor, Media: Richard Keaveny
AVP/Executive Producer, Media: Lisa Strite
Director, Product Development: Pamela Hersperger
Editorial Project Manager: Rebecca Knauer
Editorial Media Project Manager: Allison Longley
Editorial Assistant: Terenia McHenry
Development Editor: Karen Misler
Supplements Development Editor: Claire Hunter
Marketing Manager: Maggie Moylan
Marketing Assistant: Justin Jacob
Senior Managing Editor, Production: Cynthia Zonneveld
Production Project Manager: Carol O'Rourke
Production Media Project Manager: John Cassar

Permissions Coordinator: Charles Morris
Senior Operations Specialist: Diane Peirano
Senior Art Director: Jonathan Boylan
Cover Design: Jonathan Boylan
Director, Image Resource Center: Melinda Patelli
Manager, Rights and Permissions: Zina Arabia
Manager, Visual Research: Beth Brenzel
Manager, Cover Visual Research & Permissions:
    Karen Sanatar
Image Permission Coordinator: Jan Marc Quisumbing
Photo Researcher: Kathy Ringrose
Composition: GEX Publishing Services
Full-Service Project Management: GEX Publishing
    Services
Printer/Binder: Courier
Typeface: Berkley Book 11/13.5

NOTICE:
This work is protected by U.S. copyright laws and is provided solely for the use of college instructors in reviewing course materials for classroom use. Dissemination or sale of this work, or any part (including on the World Wide Web) is not permitted.

Credits and acknowledgments borrowed from other sources and reproduced, with permission, in this textbook appear on appropriate page within text.

Chapter 1: Alamy Images, p. 1; Chapter 2: Jupiter Images/Comstock Images, p. 63; Chapter 3: James Leynse/CORBIS, p. 137; Chapter 4: iStockPhoto, pp. 231, 256; David R. Frazier/Photolibrary, Inc./Photo Researchers, Inc., p. 242; Chapter 5: Jean Claude Moschetti/REA Agency, p. 289; Chapter 6: Getty Images, p. 341; Chapter 7: Alamy Images, p. 409; Chapter 8: Southwest Airlines Co., p. 467; Chapter 9: Alamy Images, p. 533; Chapter 10: Robert Clare/Photographer's Choice/Getty Images, Inc., p. 603; Chapter 11: Alamy Images, p. 653; Chapter 12: David Grossman/Photo Researchers, Inc., p. 701; Chapter 13: Ken James/Landov Media, p. 775.

All real company financial data presented in chapters 1–13 has been based on the most recent information reported by each company.

Copyright © 2010, 2008, 2006, 2004, 2001 by Pearson Education, Inc., publishing as Pearson Prentice Hall, Upper Saddle River, New Jersey, 07458.
All rights reserved. Manufactured in the United States of America. This publication is protected by Copyright, and permission should be obtained from the publisher prior to any prohibited reproduction, storage in a retrieval system, or transmission in any form or by any means, electronic, mechanical, photocopying, recording, or likewise. To obtain permission(s) to use material from this work, please submit a written request to Pearson Education, Inc., Permissions Department, Upper Saddle River, New Jersey 07458.

Many of the designations by manufacturers and seller to distinguish their products are claimed as trademarks. Where those designations appear in this book, and the publisher was aware of a trademark claim, the designations have been printed in initial caps or all caps.

Library of Congress Cataloging-in-Publication Data
Harrison, Walter T.
    Financial accounting / Walter T. Harrison Jr., Charles T.
Horngren, C. William (Bill) Thomas. — 8th ed.
        p. cm.
    Includes index.
    ISBN-13: 978-0-13-610886-3
    ISBN-10: 0-13-610886-5
    1. Accounting. I. Horngren, Charles T., – II. Thomas, C. William. III. Title.
HF5636.H37 2010
657--dc22   2009020390

10 9 8 7 6 5 4 3 2 1

Prentice Hall
is an imprint of

www.pearsonhighered.com

ISBN-13: 978-0-13-610886-3
ISBN-10: 0-13-610886-5

For our wives,

Nancy, Joan, and Mary Ann

About the Authors

Walter T. Harrison, Jr. is professor emeritus of accounting at the Hankamer School of Business, Baylor University. He received his BBA from Baylor University, his MS from Oklahoma State University, and his PhD from Michigan State University.

Professor Harrison, recipient of numerous teaching awards from student groups as well as from university administrators, has also taught at Cleveland State Community College, Michigan State University, the University of Texas, and Stanford University.

A member of the American Accounting Association and the American Institute of Certified Public Accountants, Professor Harrison has served as chairman of the Financial Accounting Standards Committee of the American Accounting Association, on the Teaching/Curriculum Development Award Committee, on the Program Advisory Committee for Accounting Education and Teaching, and on the Notable Contributions to Accounting Literature Committee.

Professor Harrison has lectured in several foreign countries and published articles in numerous journals, including *Journal of Accounting Research*, *Journal of Accountancy*, *Journal of Accounting and Public Policy*, *Economic Consequences of Financial Accounting Standards*, *Accounting Horizons*, *Issues in Accounting Education*, and *Journal of Law and Commerce*.

He is co-author of *Financial & Managerial Accounting*, second edition, 2009 and *Accounting*, eighth edition, 2009 (with Charles T. Horngren and M. Suzanne Oliver), published by Pearson Prentice Hall. Professor Harrison has received scholarships, fellowships, and research grants or awards from PricewaterhouseCoopers, Deloitte & Touche, the Ernst & Young Foundation, and the KPMG Foundation.

Charles T. Horngren is the Edmund W. Littlefield professor of accounting, emeritus, at Stanford University. A graduate of Marquette University, he received his MBA from Harvard University and his PhD from the University of Chicago. He is also the recipient of honorary doctorates from Marquette University and DePaul University.

A certified public accountant, Horngren served on the Accounting Principles Board for six years, the Financial Accounting Standards Board Advisory Council for five years, and the Council of the American Institute of Certified Public Accountants for three years. For six years he served as a trustee of the Financial Accounting Foundation, which oversees the Financial Accounting Standards Board and the Government Accounting Standards Board.

Horngren is a member of the Accounting Hall of Fame.

A member of the American Accounting Association, Horngren has been its president and its director of research. He received its first annual Outstanding Accounting Educator Award.

The California Certified Public Accountants Foundation gave Horngren its Faculty Excellence Award and its Distinguished Professor Award. He is the first person to have received both awards.

The American Institute of Certified Public Accountants presented its first Outstanding Educator Award to Horngren.

Horngren was named Accountant of the Year, in Education, by the national professional accounting fraternity, Beta Alpha Psi.

Professor Horngren is also a member of the Institute of Management Accountants, from whom he has received its Distinguished Service Award. He was a member of the institute's Board of Regents, which administers the Certified Management Accountant examinations.

Horngren is the author of these other accounting books published by Pearson Prentice Hall: *Cost Accounting: A Managerial Emphasis*, thirteenth edition, 2008 (with Srikant Datar and George Foster); *Introduction to Financial Accounting*, ninth edition, 2006 (with Gary L. Sundem and John A. Elliott); *Introduction to Management Accounting*, fourteenth edition, 2008 (with Gary L. Sundem and William Stratton); *Financial & Managerial Accounting*, second edition, 2009 and *Accounting*, eighth edition, 2009 (with Walter T. Harrison, Jr. and M. Suzanne Oliver).

Horngren is the consulting editor for Pearson Prentice Hall's Charles T. Horngren Series in Accounting.

Charles William (Bill) Thomas is the KPMG/Thomas L. Holton Chair, the J. E. Bush Professor of Accounting, and a Master Teacher at Baylor University. A Baylor University alumnus, he received both his BBA and MBA there and went on to earn his PhD from The University of Texas at Austin.

With primary interests in the areas of financial accounting and auditing, Bill Thomas has served as the J.E. Bush Professor of Accounting since 1995 and the KPMG/Thomas L. Holton Chair since 2006. He has been a member of the faculty of the Accounting and Business Law Department of the Hankamer School of Business since 1971, and served as chair of the department from 1983 until 1995. He was recognized as an Outstanding Faculty Member of Baylor University in 1984 and Distinguished Professor for the Hankamer School of Business in 2002. Dr. Thomas has received several awards for outstanding teaching, including the Outstanding Professor in the Executive MBA Programs in 2001, 2002, and 2006. In 2004, he received the designation as Master Teacher, an honor that has only been bestowed on 21 persons since the University's inception in 1845.

Thomas is the author of textbooks in auditing and financial accounting, as well as many articles in auditing, financial accounting and reporting, taxation, ethics and accounting education. His scholarly work focuses on the subject of fraud prevention and detection, as well as ethical issues among accountants in public practice. His most recent publication of national prominence is "The Rise and Fall of the Enron Empire" which appeared in the April 2002 *Journal of Accountancy*, and which was selected by Encyclopedia Britannica for inclusion in its *Annals of American History*. He presently serves as both technical and accounting and auditing editor of *Today's CPA*, the journal of the Texas Society of Certified Public Accountants, with a circulation of approximately 28,000.

Thomas is a certified public accountant in Texas. Prior to becoming a professor, Thomas was a practicing accountant with the firms of KPMG, LLP, and BDO Seidman, LLP. He is a member of the American Accounting Association, the American Institute of Certified Public Accountants, and the Texas Society of Certified Public Accountants.

Brief Contents

Contents

Chapter 4

Internal Control & Cash   231

Chapter 5

Short-Term Investments &
Receivables   289

Chapter 6

Inventory & Cost of Goods Sold   341

Chapter 12
The Statement of Cash Flows   701

Chapter 13
Financial Statement Analysis   775

With
Financial Accounting
Student Text, Study Resources,
and MyAccountingLab
students will have more
"I get it!"
moments!

Students understand (or "get it") right after you do a problem in class. Once they leave the classroom, however, students often struggle to complete the homework on their own. This frustration can cause students to quit on the material altogether and fall behind in the course, resulting in an entire class falling behind as the instructor attempts to keep everyone on the same page.

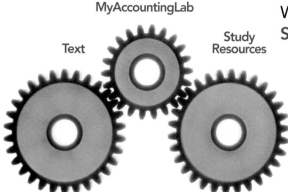

MyAccountingLab

Text

Study Resources

With the *Financial Accounting*, Eighth Edition, **Student Learning System**, all the features of the student textbook, study resources, and online homework system are designed to work together to provide students with the consistency, repetition, and high level of detail that will keep both instructors and students on track, providing more "I get it!" moments inside and outside the classroom.

Replicating the Classroom Experience with Demo Doc Examples

The Demo Doc examples consist of entire problems, worked through step-by-step, from start to finish, narrated with the kind of comments that instructors would say in class. The Demo Docs are available in the accounting cycle chapters of the text and in the study guide. In addition to the printed Demo Docs, Flash-animated versions are available so that students can watch the problems as they are worked through while listening to the explanations and details. Demo Docs will aid students when they are trying to solve exercises and problems on their own, duplicating the classroom experience outside of class.

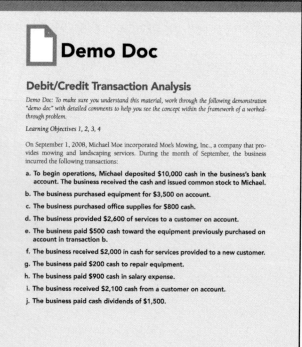

Demo Doc

Debit/Credit Transaction Analysis

Demo Doc: To make sure you understand this material, work through the following demonstration "demo doc" with detailed comments to help you see the concept within the framework of a worked-through problem.

Learning Objectives 1, 2, 3, 4

On September 1, 2008, Michael Moe incorporated Moe's Mowing, Inc., a company that provides mowing and landscaping services. During the month of September, the business incurred the following transactions:

a. To begin operations, Michael deposited $10,000 cash in the business's bank account. The business received the cash and issued common stock to Michael.

b. The business purchased equipment for $3,500 on account.

c. The business purchased office supplies for $800 cash.

d. The business provided $2,600 of services to a customer on account.

e. The business paid $500 cash toward the equipment previously purchased on account in transaction b.

f. The business received $2,000 in cash for services provided to a new customer.

g. The business paid $200 cash to repair equipment.

h. The business paid $900 cash in salary expense.

i. The business received $2,100 cash from a customer on account.

j. The business paid cash dividends of $1,500.

with the Student Learning System!

Consistency, Repetition, and a High Level of Detail Throughout the Learning Process
The concepts, materials, and practice problems are presented with clarity and consistency across all mediums—textbook, study resources, and online homework system. No matter which platform students use they will continually experience the same look, feel, and language, minimizing confusion and ensuring clarity.

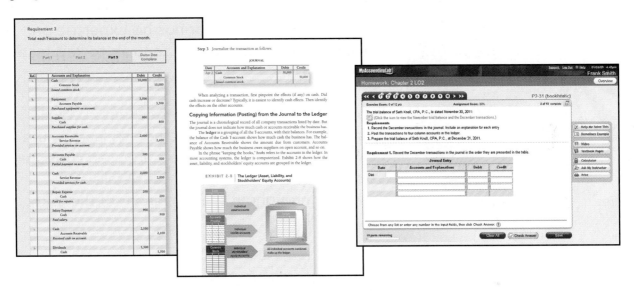

Experiencing the Power of Practice with MyAccountingLab: www.myaccountinglab.com
MyAccountingLab is an online homework system that gives students more "I get it!" moments through the power of practice. With MyAccountingLab, students can

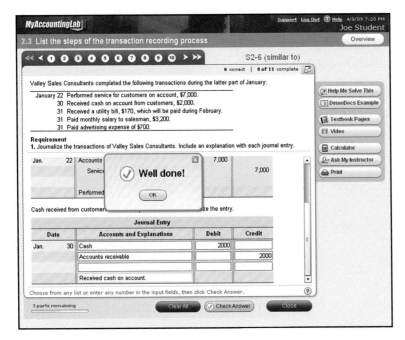

- Work on problems assigned by the instructor that are either exact matches or algorithmic versions of the end-of-chapter material.
- Use the Study Plan for self-assessment and customized study outlines.
- Use the Help Me Solve This for a step-by-step tutorial.
- View the Demo Docs example to see an animated demonstration of where the numbers came from.
- Watch a video to see additional information pertaining to the lecture.
- Open textbook pages to find the material they need to get help on specific problems.

Financial Accounting helps students

Financial Accounting helps students "nail" the accounting cycle up front in order to increase success and retention later on.

The Eighth Edition features new coauthor Bill Thomas of Baylor University who brings his expertise on auditing, ethics, and internal controls to key sections of the book.

Helping Students "Nail" the Accounting Cycle

The concepts and mechanics students learn in the critical accounting cycle chapters are used consistently and repetitively—and with clear-cut details and explanations—throughout the remainder of the text, minimizing confusion.

Better Coverage of the Accounting Cycle from Start to Finish

Chapter 1 introduces the accounting cycle with a brief financial statement overview, using the financial statements of J.Crew Group, Inc. This first exposure to accounting explores financial statements in depth, familiarizes students with using real business data, and points out basic relationships between the different types of statements.

Chapter 2 continues the discussion of the accounting cycle by explaining how to analyze and record basic transactions, and builds in repetition to ensure that students understand the fundamentals when they prepare the trial balance.

Chapter 3 concludes the discussion of the accounting cycle with adjusting and closing entries, and preparation of the related trial balances to close the loop for students.

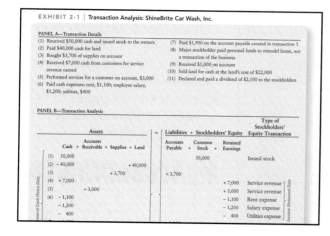

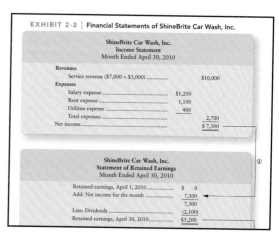

"nail" the accounting cycle!

Consistency, Repetition, and a High Level of Detail

Throughout the text, the core concepts and mechanics are brought together using consistent language, format, and formulas. Students also receive thorough explanations and details that show the meaning behind each concept and how to do the computation following it, providing an in-depth understanding of the fundamentals.

Whether it's the first transaction or the last, students perform the analysis in the same way, thus reinforcing their understanding, reducing the level of confusion and frustration, and helping them capture those "I get it!" moments.

For example, in Chapter 2 students see the impact of transactions and how the transactions are eventually summarized into the income statement, statement of retained earnings, and balance sheet.

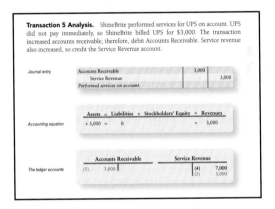

A **Mid-Chapter Summary Problem** provides a stopping point for students—it gives them an opportunity to repeat the entire process again, using data from a different company, to make sure they've "got it." The **End-of-Chapter Summary Problem** closes out the chapter and allows students to practice the process again and really "nail" these fundamental skills.

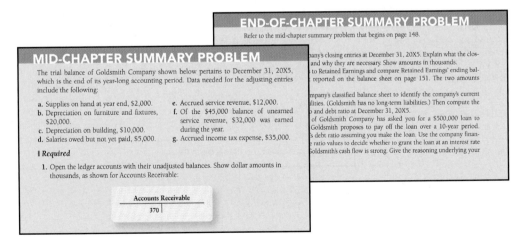

www.pearsonhighered.com/harrison

New to the Eighth Edition

New International Financial Reporting Standards (IFRS)

In order to increase student awareness of the most important potential shift in the future of financial accounting, information on IFRS is introduced in Chapter 1, where appropriate throughout chapters in the new Global View feature, and in a new appendix.

 One of the most significant differences between U.S. GAAP and International Financial Reporting Standards (IFRS) is the permitted reported carrying values of property, plant, and equipment. Recall from Chapter 1 that U.S. GAAP has long advocated the historical cost principle as most appropriate for plant assets because it results in a more objective (non-biased) and therefore a more reliable (auditable) figure. It also supports the continuity assumption, which states that we expect the entity to remain in business long enough to recover the cost of its plant assets through depreciation.

In contrast, while historical cost is the primary basis of accounting under IFRS, it permits the periodic revaluation of plant assets to fair market value. The primary justification for this position is that the historical cost of plant assets pur-

When students practice or complete their homework in **MyAccountingLab**, they will also be exposed to IFRS. The content is designed to raise student awareness of IFRS and to be a companion for the IFRS text coverage.

New and Updated Content on Ethics

Sound ethical judgment is important for every major financial decision—which is why this text provides consistent ethical reinforcement in every chapter. And, with new coauthor Bill Thomas's expertise, a new decision-making model is introduced in Chapter 1 and applied to each of the end-of-chapter cases.

Ethical Issues in Accrual Accounting

Accrual accounting provides some ethical challenges that cash accounting avoids. For example, suppose that in 2008, Starbucks Corporation prepays a $3 million advertising campaign to be conducted by a large advertising agency. The advertisements are scheduled to run during December, January, and February. In this case, Starbucks is buying an asset, a prepaid expense.

Suppose Starbucks pays for the advertisements on December 1 and the ads start running immediately. Starbucks should record one-third of the expense ($1 million) during the year ended December 31, 2008, and two-thirds ($2 million) during 2009.

Suppose 2008 is a great year for Starbucks—net income is better than expected. Starbucks' top managers believe that 2009 will not be as profitable. In this case, the company has a strong incentive to expense the full $3 million during 2008 in order to report all the advertising expense in the 2008 income statement. This unethical action would keep $2 million of advertising expense off the 2009 income statement and make 2009's net income look better.

Enhanced Coverage of Cash Flows

The current economy has created a shift in how we view money—specifically, cash. Cash flow is the lifeblood of any business, so in the Eighth Edition of *Financial Accounting*, coverage of Cash Flows has been increased and highlighted in Chapters 4–10 so that students can easily see the connections and understand the significance.

IMPACT OF REPORTING STOCKHOLDER FINANCING ACTIVITIES ON CASH FLOWS

At the end of the period, the business reports its financial statements. This process begins with the trial balance introduced in Chapter 2. We refer to this trial balance as unadjusted because the accounts are not yet ready for the financial statements. In most cases the simple label "Trial Balance" means "unadjusted."

Which Accounts Need to Be Updated (Adjusted)?

The stockholders need to know how well Genie Car Wash is performing. The financial statements report this information, and all accounts must be up-to-date. That

New Fraud Coverage

In an age of public scandals, understanding fraud is a key component of *Financial Accounting*. Chapter 4 now includes the concept of fraud, and introduces students to the "fraud triangle" (motivation, opportunity, and rationalization) and a discussion of internal controls as the primary way companies prevent fraud.

For example, **Cooking the Books** sections highlight real fraud cases in relevant sections throughout the text, giving students real-life business context. Examples include the following:

- Crazy Eddie (Chapters 6 and 8)
- WorldCom and Waste Management (Chapter 7)
- Enron (Chapters 8, 9, and 10)

COOKING THE BOOKS
by Improper Capitalization
WorldCom

It is one thing to accidentally capitalize a plant asset but quite another to do it intentionally, thus deliberately understating expenses and overstating net income. One well-known company committed one of the biggest financial statement frauds in history.

In 2002, WorldCom, Inc., was one of the largest telecommunications service providers in the world. The company had grown rapidly from a small, regional telephone company in 1983 to a giant corporation in 2002 by acquiring an ever-increasing number of other such companies. But 2002 was a bad year for WorldCom, as well as for many others in the "telecom" industry. The United States was reeling from the effects of a deep economic recession spawned by the "bursting dot-com bubble" in 2000 and intensified by the terrorist attacks on the World Trade Center and the U.S. Pentagon in 2001. Wall Street was looking high and low for positive signs, pressuring public companies to keep profits trending upward in order to support share prices, without much success, at least for the honest companies.

www.pearsonhighered.com/harrison

Hallmark Features

Summary Problems and Solutions appear in both the middle and end-of-chapter sections, providing students with additional guided learning. By presenting these problems and solutions twice in one chapter, this text breaks up the information, enabling students to absorb and master the material in more manageable pieces.

END-OF-CHAPTER SUMMARY PROBLEM

Refer to the mid-chapter summary problem that begins on page 148.

Required
1. Make Goldsmith Company's closing entries at December 31, 20X5. Explain what the closing entries accomplish and why they are necessary. Show amounts in thousands.
2. Post the closing entries to Retained Earnings and compare Retained Earnings' ending balance with the amount reported on the balance sheet on page 151. The two amounts should be the same.

MID-CHAPTER SUMMARY PROBLEM

The trial balance of Goldsmith Company shown below pertains to December 31, 20X5, which is the end of its year-long accounting period. Data needed for the adjusting entries include the following:

a. Supplies on hand at year end, $2,000.
b. Depreciation on furniture and fixtures, $20,000.
c. Depreciation on building, $10,000.
d. Salaries owed but not yet paid, $5,000.

e. Accrued service revenue, $12,000.
f. Of the $45,000 balance of unearned service revenue, $32,000 was earned during the year.
g. Accrued income tax expense, $35,000.

Required
1. Open the ledger accounts with their unadjusted balances. Show dollar amounts in thousands, as shown for Accounts Receivable:

Accounts Receivable
370	

STOP & THINK...

1. A customer pays Starbucks $100 on March 15 for coffee to be served at a party in April. Has Starbucks earned revenue on March 15? When will Starbucks earn the revenue?
2. Starbucks pays $4,500 on July 1 for store rent for the next 3 months. Has Starbucks incurred an expense on July 1?

Answers:

1. No. Starbucks has received the cash but will not deliver the coffee until later. Starbucks earns the revenue when it gives the goods to the customer.

Stop & Think sections relate concepts to everyday life so that students can see the immediate relevance.

Demo Docs in the accounting cycle chapters offer fully worked-through problems that weave computation and concepts together in a step-by-step format, helping students understand the "how" and "why." Additional Demo Docs, including animated versions, are available in the study guide and in **MyAccountingLab**.

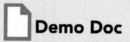 **Demo Doc**

Debit/Credit Transaction Analysis

Demo Doc: To make sure you understand this material, work through the following demonstration "demo doc" with detailed comments to help you see the concept within the framework of a worked-through problem.

Learning Objectives 1, 2, 3, 4

On September 1, 2008, Michael Moe incorporated Moe's Mowing, Inc., a company that provides mowing and landscaping services. During the month of September, the business incurred the following transactions.

a. To begin operations, Michael deposited $10,000 cash in the business's bank account. The business received the cash and issued common stock to Michael.
b. The business purchased equipment for $3,500 on account.
c. The business purchased office supplies for $800 cash.
d. The business provided $2,600 of services to a customer on account.
e. The business paid $500 cash toward the equipment previously purchased on account in transaction b.
f. The business received $2,000 in cash for services provided to a new customer.
g. The business paid $200 cash to repair equipment.
h. The business paid $900 cash in salary expense.
i. The business received $2,100 cash from a customer on account.
j. The business paid cash dividends of $1,500.

Decision Guidelines in the end-of-chapter material summarize the chapter's key terms, concepts, and formulas in the context of business decisions. Not only does this help students read more actively in the question and answer format, but it also reinforces how the accounting information they are learning is used to make decisions in business.

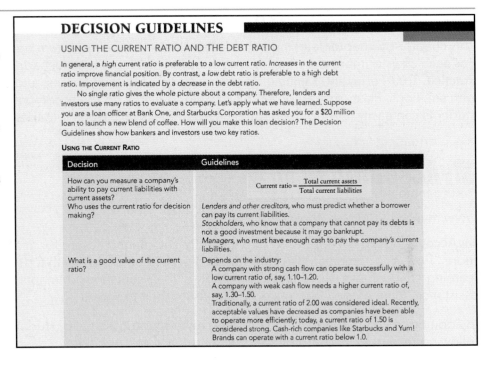

DECISION GUIDELINES

USING THE CURRENT RATIO AND THE DEBT RATIO

In general, a *high* current ratio is preferable to a low current ratio. *Increases* in the current ratio improve financial position. By contrast, a *low* debt ratio is preferable to a high debt ratio. Improvement is indicated by a *decrease* in the debt ratio.

No single ratio gives the whole picture about a company. Therefore, lenders and investors use many ratios to evaluate a company. Let's apply what we have learned. Suppose you are a loan officer at Bank One, and Starbucks Corporation has asked you for a $20 million loan to launch a new blend of coffee. How will you make this loan decision? The Decision Guidelines show how bankers and investors use two key ratios.

USING THE CURRENT RATIO

Decision	Guidelines
How can you measure a company's ability to pay current liabilities with current assets?	$\text{Current ratio} = \dfrac{\text{Total current assets}}{\text{Total current liabilities}}$
Who uses the current ratio for decision making?	*Lenders and other creditors,* who must predict whether a borrower can pay its current liabilities. *Stockholders,* who know that a company that cannot pay its debts is not a good investment because it may go bankrupt. *Managers,* who must have enough cash to pay the company's current liabilities.
What is a good value of the current ratio?	Depends on the industry: A company with strong cash flow can operate successfully with a low current ratio of, say, 1.10–1.20. A company with weak cash flow needs a higher current ratio of, say, 1.30–1.50. Traditionally, a current ratio of 2.00 was considered ideal. Recently, acceptable values have decreased as companies have been able to operate more efficiently; today, a current ratio of 1.50 is considered strong. Cash-rich companies like Starbucks and Yum! Brands can operate with a current ratio below 1.0.

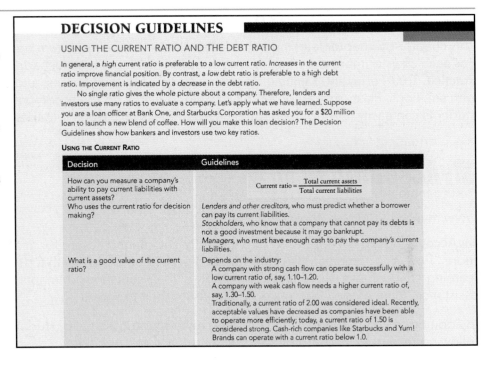

MyAccountingLab ®

NEW! End-of-Chapter Material Integrated with MyAccountingLab at www.myaccountinglab.com

Students need practice and repetition in order to successfully learn the fundamentals of financial accounting. *Financial Accounting,* Eighth Edition, now contains an additional set of exercises in the text for professors to choose from. Also available in **MyAccountingLab** are three static alternatives for all exercises and problems, as well as algorithmic versions, providing students with unlimited practice. In addition, IFRS coverage has been added so students can see how IFRS will impact decisions in accounting. (For more information, visit **www.myaccountinglab.com**.)

End-of-Chapter Materials include Quick Check multiple-choice review questions, short exercises, A and B exercises and problems, serial and challenge exercises, multiple-choice quiz questions, decision cases, ethical cases, Focus on Financials (with real financial statement analysis), Focus on Analysis (with real financial statement analysis), and group projects.

www.pearsonhighered.com/harrison

Student Resources

Study Guide and Study Guide CD with Demo Docs and Working Papers

This chapter-by-chapter learning aid helps students get the maximum benefit from their study time. For each chapter there is an explanation of each Learning Objective; additional Demo Docs; Quick Practice, True/False, and Multiple Choice questions; Quick Exercises; and a Do It Yourself question, all with solutions. Flash-animated Demo Docs are available on the accompanying study guide CD so students can easily refer to them when needed. Electronic working papers are also included.

www.myaccountinglab.com

MyAccountingLab is Web-based tutorial and assessment software for accounting that gives students more "I get it!" moments. **MyAccountingLab** provides students with a personalized interactive learning environment where they can complete their course assignments with immediate tutorial assistance, learn at their own pace, and measure their progress.

In addition to completing assignments and reviewing tutorial help, students have access to the following resources in **MyAccountingLab**:

- The Flash-based eBook
- Study Guide
- Animated Demo Docs
- General Ledger Student Data Files
- Excel in Practice
- Videos and MP3 files
- Audio and Student PowerPoints
- Working Papers
- Flashcards

Student Resource Web site: www.pearsonhighered.com/harrison

- General Ledger Student Data Files
- Working Papers
- Excel in Practice

Student Reference Cards

 International Financial Reporting Standards Student Reference Card

This four-page laminated reference card includes an overview of IFRS, why they matter and how they compare to U.S. standards, and highlights key differences between IFRS and U.S. GAAP.

 Math for Accounting Student Reference Card

This six-page laminated reference card provides students with a study tool for the basic math they will need to be successful in accounting, such as rounding, fractions, converting decimals, calculating interest, break-even analysis, and more!

 Accounting Tips Student Reference Card

This four-page laminated reference card illustrates the key steps in the accounting cycle.

Instructor Resources

The primary goal of the Instructor Resources is to help instructors deliver their course with ease, using any delivery method—traditional, self-paced, or online.

www.myaccountinglab.com

MyAccountingLab is Web-based tutorial and assessment software for accounting that not only gives students more "I get it!" moments, but also provides instructors the flexibility to make technology an integral part of their course. And, because practice makes perfect, **MyAccountingLab** offers exactly the same end-of-chapter material found in the text with algorithmic options that instructors can assign for homework. **MyAccountingLab** also replicates the text's exercises and problems with journal entries and financial statements so that students are familiar and comfortable working with the material.

Instructor's Manual

The Instructor's Manual, available electronically or in print, offers course-specific content including a guide to available resources, a road map for using **MyAccountingLab**, a first-day handout for students, sample syllabi, and guidelines for teaching an online course, as well as content-specific material including chapter overviews, teaching outlines, student summary handouts, lecture outline tips, assignment grids, ten-minute quizzes, and more!

Instructor Resource Center: www.pearsonhighered.com/harrison

For your convenience, many of our instructor supplements are available for download from the textbook's catalog page or your **MyAccountingLab** account. Available resources include the following:

- Solutions Manual containing the fully worked-through and accuracy-checked solutions for every question, exercise, and problem in the text
- Test Item File with TestGen Software providing over 1,600 multiple choice, true/false, and problem-solving questions correlated by Learning Objective and difficulty level as well as AACSB and AICPA standards
- Four sets of PowerPoint presentations give instructors flexibility and choices for their courses. There are 508 Compliant Instructor PowerPoints with extensive notes for on-campus or online classes, Student PowerPoints, Clicker Response System (CRS) PowerPoints, and Audio Narrated PowerPoints.
- Data and Solution Files—General Ledger
- Working Papers and Solutions
- Instructor's Manual
- Excel in Practice
- Image Library

Course Cartridges

Course Cartridges for BlackBoard, WebCT, CourseCompass, and other learning management systems are available upon request.

www.pearsonhighered.com/harrison

Changes to the Eighth Edition

Students and instructors will benefit from a variety of new content and features in the Eighth Edition of *Financial Accounting*. To reflect the most recent developments in the economy and in the accounting industry, the following content additions or changes have been made:

The first chapter has been rewritten to introduce the new **Joint Conceptual Framework for Accounting** from the Financial Accounting Standards Board (FASB) and the International Accounting Standards Board (IASB).

In order to increase student awareness of the most important potential shift in the future of financial accounting, **International Financial Reporting Standards (IFRS)** have been integrated into the Eighth Edition. Chapter 1 introduces the topic and summarizes the current plan for U.S. adoption of IFRS by 2014. This discussion lays the foundation for integration of IFRS in appropriate chapters throughout the book, including highlighting key differences between U.S. GAAP and IFRS. A new appendix (F) was added with a table highlighting the IFRS coverage topic by topic. A Global View feature was added in relevant chapters to specifically explain how IFRS integration will impact financial accounting. IFRS Student Study Guide by Marlene Plumlee at the University of Utah is a chapter long supplement that discusses the general context of U.S. GAAP and IFRS, providing background information about the use of U.S. GAAP and IFRS and "players" that will ultimately affect how and when IFRS will be adopted internationally. Included also is an overview of the conceptual frameworks that underlie the formation of U.S. GAAP and IFRS. A comparison of two companies is offered, one that employs U.S. GAAP to prepare its financial report and one that employs IFRS to prepare its financial report.

With the recent changes and events in the economy, educating students on the importance of **ethics and ethical decision making** is critical. The discussion of ethics in accounting has been updated and moved to Chapter 1, placing greater emphasis on the importance of ethics at the very beginning of the text. The Eighth Edition also introduces an expanded decision-making model in Chapter 1 and integrates the model throughout the entire text with economic, legal, and ethical dimensions. The Ethical Cases in the end-of-chapter material have been rewritten to unify and better integrate coverage on this important topic so that the material is reinforced consistently in every chapter.

In an age of public scandals, understanding **fraud** is a key component of financial accounting. Chapter 4 now includes the concept of fraud, and introduces students to the "fraud triangle" (motivation, opportunity, and rationalization) that leads to the discussion of internal controls as the primary way that companies prevent fraud—which has also been updated. The discussion of fraud in Chapter 4 also lays the foundation for the new Cooking the Books sections (found in appropriate chapters later on in the book), which add real-life relevance and interest to otherwise dry accounting concepts by presenting real-world fraud cases such as Crazy Eddie (Chapters 6 and 8), WorldCom and Waste Management (Chapter 7), and Enron (Chapters 8, 9, and 10).

To help students understand accounting topics that are currently impacting **the global economy**, Chapter 11 includes a new discussion on quality of earnings, revenue recognition, and fraud. The quality of earnings section focuses on evaluating a company's financial position to help in decision making, which students will need when they enter the workforce. There is also an expanded discussion on the elements of the income statement and revenue recognition. The revenue recognition and extraordinary items sections are key points that highlight the difference between IFRS and U.S. GAAP, and are critical to understanding the convergence of global accounting standards. The new Cooking the Books feature uses Bristol-Myers Squibb to highlight improper revenue recognition.

To keep examples and data current and accurate, all **financial statements** for the companies covered have been updated. All real company financial data now refers to 2007 or 2008.

Both of the **focus companies are new** (Amazon.com, Inc., and Foot Locker, Inc.) so that students see examples of statements and accounting practices that are as current as possible. As a result, the annual reports in the book's appendices are new, and all the Focus on Financials and Focus on Analysis questions in the end-of-chapter material have been updated throughout the text.

Understanding cash flows is a critical concept for students in today's economy, which is why there is a new and increased emphasis on the use of **cash flow information** in selected chapters. By highlighting this coverage from chapter to chapter, this edition helps students make the connection between cash and other accounting concepts so they understand the significance of cash flow as the lifeblood of a business.

To provide students with more opportunities to practice important concepts, and to provide instructors with additional choices of material to assign, all of the **end-of-chapter content** has been revised, including the following:

- 100% of values and dates in the end-of-chapter questions are new.
- A new set of "B" exercises has been added in every chapter, giving students more opportunities to practice important concepts.
- Every end-of-chapter question in the Assess Your Progress sections is now available in **MyAccountingLab** for students to complete and receive immediate tutorial feedback and help when they need it. Alternative, static exercises and problems were also added in **MyAccountingLab** (**www.myaccountinglab.com**) to give students and instructors more options for assignments and practice.

www.pearsonhighered.com/harrison

ACKNOWLEDGMENTS

In revising previous editions of *Financial Accounting*, we had the help of instructors from across the country who have participated in online surveys, chapter reviews, and focus groups. Their comments and suggestions for both the text and the supplements have been a great help in planning and carrying out revisions, and we thank them for their contributions.

Financial Accounting, Eighth Edition

Revision Plan Reviewers

Elizabeth Ammann, Lindenwood University
Brenda Anderson, Brandeis University
Patrick Bauer, DeVry University, Kansas City
Amy Bourne, Oregon State University
Elizabeth Brown, Keene State College
Scott Bryant, Baylor University
Marci Butterfield, University of Utah
Dr. Paul Clikeman, University of Richmond
Sue Counte, Saint Louis Community College-Meramec
Julia Creighton, American University
Sue Cullers, Buena Vista University
Betty David, Francis Marion University
Peter DiCarlo, Boston College
Allan Drebin, Northwestern University
Carolyn Dreher, Southern Methodist University
Emily Drogt, Grand Valley State University
Dr. Andrew Felo, Penn State Great Valley
Dr. Caroline Ford, Baylor University
Clayton Forester, University of Minnesota
Timothy Gagnon, Northeastern University
Marvin Gordon, University of Illinois at Chicago
Anthony Greig, Purdue University
Dr. Heidi Hansel, Kirkwood Community College
Michael Haselkorn, Bentley University
Mary Hollars, Vincennes University
Grace Johnson, Marietta College
Celina Jozsi, University of South Florida
John Karayan, Woodbury University
Robert Kollar, Duquesne University
Elliott Levy, Bentley University
Joseph Lupino, Saint Mary's College of California
Anthony Masino, Queens University / NC Central
Lizbeth Matz, University of Pittsburgh, Bradford
Mary Miller, University of New Haven
Scott Miller, Gannon University
Dr. Birendra (Barry) K. Mishra, University of California, Riverside
Lisa Nash, Vincennes University

Rosemary Nurre, College of San Mateo
Stephen Owen, Hamilton College
Rama Ramamurthy, College of William and Mary
Barb Reeves, Cleary University
Anwar Salimi, California State Polytechnic University, Pomona
Philippe Sammour, Eastern Michigan University
Albert A Schepanski, University of Iowa
Lily Sieux, California State University, East Bay
Vic Stanton, Stanford University
Martin Taylor, University of Texas at Arlington
Vincent Turner, California State Polytechnic University, Pomona
Craig Weaver, University of California, Riverside
Betsy Willis, Baylor University
Dr. Jia Wu, University of Massachusetts, Dartmouth
Barbara Yahvah, University of Montana-Helena

Chapter Reviewers

Florence Atiase, University of Texas at Austin
Amy Bourne, Oregon State University
Rada Brooks, University of California, Berkeley
Marci Butterfield, University of Utah
Carolyn Dreher, Southern Methodist University
Lisa Gillespie, Loyola University, Chicago
Mary Hollars, Vincennes University
Constance Malone Hylton, George Mason University
Barry Mishra, University of California, Riverside
Virginia Smith, Saint Mary's College of California
Betsy Willis, Baylor University

Supplements Authors

Excel in Practice Templates: Jennie Mitchell, Saint Mary-of-the-Woods College
Excel Data Files: Jennie Mitchell, Saint Mary-of-the-Woods College
General Ledger Templates: Jamie McCracken, Saint Mary-of-the-Woods College

Instructor's Manual: Denise Wooten, Erie Community College–North
PowerPoints: Courtney Baillie, Nebraska Wesleyan University
Study Guide: Helen Brubeck, San Jose State University
Solutions Manual: Richard J. Pettit, Mountain View College
Test Item File: Sandra Augustine, Hilbert College

Supplements Reviewers

Linda Abernathy, Kirkwood Community College
Brenda Bindschatel, Green River Community College
Allan Sheets, International Business College
Richard J. Pettit, Mountain View College

Previous Edition

Online Reviewers

Lucille Berry, Webster University, MO
Patrick Bouker, North Seattle Community College
Michael Broihahn, Barry University, FL
Kam Chan, Pace University
Hong Chen, Northeastern Illinois University
Charles Coate, St. Bonaventure University, NY
Bryan Church, Georgia Tech at Atlanta
Terrie Gehman, Elizabethtown College, PA
Brian Green, University of Michigan at Dearborn
Chao-Shin Liu, Notre Dame
Herb Martin, Hope College, MI
Bruce Maule, College of San Mateo
Michelle McEacharn, University of Louisiana at Monroe
Bettye Rogers-Desselle, Prairie View A&M University, TX
Norlin Rueschhoff, Notre Dame
William Schmul, Notre Dame
Arnie Schnieder, Georgia Tech at Atlanta
J. B. Stroud, Nicholls State Univesity, LA
Bruce Wampler, Louisiana State University, Shreveport
Myung Yoon, Northeastern Illinois University
Lin Zeng, Northeastern Illinois University

Focus Group Participants

Ellen D. Cook, University of Louisiana at Lafayette
Theodore D. Morrison III, Wingate University, NC
Alvin Gerald Smith, University of Northern Iowa

Carolyn R. Stokes, Frances Marion University, SC
Suzanne Ward, University of Louisiana at Lafayette

Chapter Reviewers

Kim Anderson, Indiana University of Pennsylvania
Peg Beresewski, Robert Morris College, IL
Helen Brubeck, San Jose State University, CA
Mark Camma, Atlantic Cape Community College, NJ
Freddy Choo, San Francisco State University, CA
Laurie Dahlin, Worcester State College, MA
Ronald Guidry, University of Louisiana at Monroe
Ellen Landgraf, Loyola University, Chicago
Nick McGaughey, San Jose State University, CA
Mark Miller, University of San Francisco, CA
Craig Reeder, Florida A&M University
Brian Stanko, Loyola University, Chicago
Marcia Veit, University of Central Florida
Ronald Woan, Indiana University of Pennsylvania

Online Supplement Reviewers

Shawn Abbott, College of the Siskiyous, CA
Sol Ahiarah, SUNY College at Buffalo (Buffalo State)
M. J. Albin, University of Southern Mississippi
Gary Ames, Brigham Young University, Idaho
Walter Austin, Mercer University, Macon GA
Brad Badertscher, University of Iowa
Sandra Bailey, Oregon Institute of Technology
Barbara A. Beltrand, Metropolitan State University, MN
Jerry Bennett, University of South Carolina–Spartanburg
John Bildersee, New York University, Stern School
Candace Blankenship, Belmont University, TN
Charlie Bokemeier, Michigan State University
Scott Boylan, Washington and Lee University, VA
Robert Braun, Southeastern Louisiana University
Linda Bressler, University of Houston Downtown
Carol Brown, Oregon State University
Marcus Butler, University of Rochester, NY
Kay Carnes, Gonzaga University, WA
Brian Carpenter, University of Scranton, PA
Sandra Cereola, James Madison University, VA
Hong Chen, Northeastern Illinois University
Shifei Chung, Rowan University, NJ
Bryan Church, Georgia Tech

Charles Christy, Delaware Tech and Community College, Stanton Campus

Carolyn Clark, Saint Joseph's University, PA

Dianne Conry, University of California State College Extension–Cupertino

John Coulter, Western New England College

Donald Curfman, McHenry County College, IL

Alan Czyzewski, Indiana State University

Bonita Daly, University of Southern Maine

Patricia Derrick, George Washington University

Charles Dick, Miami University

Barbara Doughty, New Hampshire Community Technical College

Carol Dutton, South Florida Community College

James Emig, Villanova University, PA

Ellen Engel, University of Chicago

Alan Falcon, Loyola Marymount University, CA

Janet Farler, Pima Community College, AZ

Andrew Felo, Penn State Great Valley

Ken Ferris, Thunderbird College, AZ

Lou Fowler, Missouri Western State College

Lucille Genduso, Nova Southeastern University, FL

Frank Gersich, Monmouth College, IL

Bradley Gillespie, Saddleback College, CA

Brian Green, University of Michigan–Dearborn

Konrad Gunderson, Missouri Western State College

William Hahn, Southeastern College, FL

Jack Hall, Western Kentucky University

Gloria Halpern, Montgomery College, MD

Kenneth Hart, Brigham Young University, Idaho

Al Hartgraves, Emory University

Thomas Hayes, University of North Texas

Larry Hegstad, Pacific Lutheran University, WA

Candy Heino, Anoka-Ramsey Community College, MN

Anit Hope, Tarrant County College, TX

Thomas Huse, Boston College

Fred R. Jex, Macomb Community College, MI

Beth Kern, Indiana University, South Bend

Hans E. Klein, Babson College, MA

Willem Koole, North Carolina State University

Emil Koren, Hillsborough Community College, FL

Dennis Kovach, Community College of Allegheny County–North Campus

Ellen Landgraf, Loyola University Chicago

Howard Lawrence, Christian Brothers University, TN

Barry Leffkov, Regis College, MA

Chao Liu, Notre Dame University

Barbara Lougee, University of California, Irvine

Heidemarie Lundblad, California State University, Northridge

Anna Lusher, West Liberty State College, WV

Harriet Maccracken, Arizona State University

Carol Mannino, Milwaukee School of Engineering

Aziz Martinez, Harvard University, Harvard Business School

Cathleen Miller, University of Michigan–Flint

Frank Mioni, Madonna University, MI

Bruce L. Oliver, Rochester Institute of Technology

Charles Pedersen, Quinsigamond Community College, MA

George Plesko, Massachusetts Institute of Technology

David Plumlee, University of Utah

Gregory Prescott, University of South Alabama

Craig Reeder, Florida A&M University

Darren Roulstone, University of Chicago

Angela Sandberg, Jacksonville State University, AL

George Sanders, Western Washington University, WA

Betty Saunders, University of North Florida

Arnie Schneider, Georgia Tech

Gim Seow, University of Connecticut

Itzhak Sharav, CUNY–Lehman Graduate School of Business

Gerald Smith, University of Northern Iowa

James Smith, Community College of Philadelphia

Beverly Soriano, Framingham State College, MA

J. B. Stroud, Nicholls State University, LA

Al Taccone, Cuyamaca College, CA

Diane Tanner, University of North Florida

Howard Toole, San Diego State University

Bruce Wampler, Louisiana State University, Shreveport

Frederick Weis, Claremont McKenna College, CA

Frederick Weiss, Virginia Wesleyan College

Allen Wright, Hillsborough Community College, FL

Tony Zordan, University of St. Francis, IL

Supplement Authors and Preparers

Excel templates: Al Fisher, Community College of Southern Nevada
General Ledger templates: Lanny Nelms, the Landor Group
Instructor's Edition: Helen Brubeck, San Jose State University
Interactive Powerpoints: Courtney Baillie
Solutions Manual preparer: Diane Colwyn
Study Guide: Helen Brubeck, San Jose State University
Test Item File: Calvin Fink
Working Papers, Essentials of Excel: Dr. L. Murphy Smith, Texas A&M University; Dr. Katherine T. Smith
Videos: Beverly Amer, Northern Arizona University; Lanny Nelms, The Landor Group

The author would like to thank the following faculty members at Baylor University who provided valuable input for improvements in various sections of the eighth edition of this text: Suzanne Abbe, Jane Baldwin, Scott Bryant, Gia Chevis, Carie Ford, David Hurtt, Becky Jones, and Betsy Willis. The author would like to extend special thanks to Dr. Marty Stuebs, who helped develop the model for ethical decision-making introduced in Chapter 1 and used in problems throughout the remainder of the eighth edition.

Prologue

Accounting Careers: Much More Than Counting Things

What kind of career can you have in accounting? Almost any kind you want. A career in accounting lets you use your analytical skills in a variety of ways, and it brings both monetary and personal rewards. According to the Jobs Rated Almanac, "accountant" was the fifth best job in terms of low stress, high compensation, lots of autonomy, and tremendous hiring demand.[1]

Accounting as an art is widely believed to have been invented by Fra Luca Bartolomeo de Pacioli, an Italian mathematician and Franciscan friar in the 16th Century. Pacioli was a close friend of Leonardo da Vinci, and collaborated with him on many projects.

Accounting as the profession we know today has its roots in the Industrial Revolution during the 18th and 19th centuries, mostly in England. However, accounting did not attain the stature of other professions such as law, medicine, or engineering until early in the 20th Century. Professions are distinguished from trades by the following characteristics: (1) a unifying body of technical literature; (2) standards of competence; (3) codes of professional conduct; and (4) dedication to service to the public.

Today's accountants obtain years of formal education at the college level which, for most, culminates in taking a very rigorous professional exam that qualifies them to hold the designation *certified public accountant* (CPA). There are other professional designations that accountants may obtain as well, each with its own professional exam and set of professional standards. Examples are certified management accountant (CMA), certified internal auditor (CIA), and certified fraud examiner (CFE).

WHERE ACCOUNTANTS WORK

Where can you work as an accountant? There are four kinds of employers.

Public Practice

You can work for a public accounting firm, which could be a large international firm or a variety of medium to small-sized firms. Within the CPA firm, you can specialize in areas such as audit, tax, or consulting. In this capacity, you'll be serving as an external accountant to many different clients. At present, the largest six international firms are Deloitte, Ernst & Young, KPMG, PricewaterhouseCoopers, Grant Thornton, and RSM McGladrey. However, there are many other firms with international and national scope of practice. Most CPAs start their career at a large CPA firm. From there, they move on to obtain positions of leadership in the corporate finance world, industry, or just about anywhere there is a demand for persons who like solving complex problems.

Managerial Accounting

Instead of working for a wide variety of clients, you can work within one corporation or nonprofit enterprise. Your role may be to analyze financial information and communicate that information to managers, who use it to plot strategy and make decisions. You may be called upon to help allocate corporate resources or improve financial performance. For example, you might do a cost-benefit analysis to help decide whether to acquire a company or build a factory. Or you might describe the financial implications of choosing one strategy over another. You might work in areas such as internal auditing, financial management, financial reporting, treasury management, and tax planning. The highest position in management accounting is the chief financial officer (CFO) position, with some CFOs rising to become chief executive officers (CEOs).

Government and Not-for-Profit Entities

As an accountant, you might work for the government—federal, state, or local. Like your counterparts in public accounting and business, your role as a government accountant includes responsibilities in the areas of auditing, financial reporting, and management accounting. You'll evaluate how government agencies are being managed. You may advise decision makers on how to allocate resources to promote efficiency. The FBI hires CPAs to investigate the financial aspects of white-collar crime. You might find yourself working for the IRS, the Securities and Exchange Commission, the Department of Treasury, or even the White House.

The Government Accountability Office (GAO)—formerly called the General Accounting Office—is an agency that works for Congress and the American people. Congress asks GAO to study federal government programs and expenditures. GAO studies how the federal government spends taxpayer dollars and advises Congress and the heads of executive agencies (such as the Environmental Protection Agency, Department of Defense, and Health and Human Services) about ways to make government more effective and responsive.

As an accountant, you might also decide to work in the not-for-profit sector. Colleges, universities, public and private primary and secondary schools, hospitals, and charitable organizations such as churches and the United Way all have accounting functions. Accountants for these types of entities prepare financial statements as well as budgets and projections. Most have special training in accounting standards specially designed for work in the not-for-profit sector.

Education

Finally, you can work at a college or university, advancing the thought and theory of accounting and teaching future generations of new accountants. On the research side of education, you might study how companies use accounting information. You might develop new ways of categorizing financial data, or study accounting practices in different countries. You then publish your ideas in journals and books and present them to colleagues at meetings around the world. On the education side, you can help others learn about accounting and give them the tools they need to be their best.

CPA: THREE LETTERS THAT SPEAK VOLUMES

When employers see the CPA designation, they know what to expect about your education, knowledge, abilities, and personal attributes. They value your analytic skills and extensive training. Your CPA credential gives you a distinct advantage in the job market and instant credibility and respect in the workplace. It's a plus when dealing with other professionals such as bankers, attorneys, auditors, and federal regulators. In addition, your colleagues in private industry tend to defer to you when dealing with complex business matters, particularly those involving financial management.[2]

THE HOTTEST GROWTH AREAS IN ACCOUNTING

Recent legislation, such as the Sarbanes-Oxley Act of 2002, has brought rising demand for accountants of all kinds. In addition to strong overall demand, certain areas of accounting are especially hot.[3]

Sustainability Reporting

Sustainability reporting involves reporting on an organization's performance with respect to health, safety, and environmental (HSE) issues. As businesses take a greater interest in environmental issues, CPAs are getting involved in reporting on such matters as employee health, on-the-job accident rates, emissions of certain pollutants, spills, volumes of waste generated, and initiatives to reduce and minimize such incidents and releases. Utilities, manufacturers, and chemical companies are particularly affected by environmental issues. As a result, they turn to CPAs to set up a preventive system to ensure compliance and avoid future claims or disputes or to provide assistance once legal implications have arisen.

Corporate social responsibility reporting (CSR) is similar to HSE reporting but with a broadened emphasis on social matters such as ethical labor practices, training, education, and diversity of workforce and corporate philanthropic initiatives. Most of the world's largest corporations have extensive CSR initiatives.

Assurance Services

Assurance services are services provided by a CPA that improve the quality of information, or its context, for decision makers. Such information can be financial or non-financial, and it can be about past events or about ongoing processes or systems. This broad concept includes audit and attestation services and is distinct from consulting because it focuses primarily on improving information rather than on providing advice or installing systems. You can use your analytical and information-processing expertise by providing assurance services in areas ranging from electronic commerce to elder care, comprehensive risk assessment, business valuations, entity performance measurement, and information systems quality assessment.

Information Technology Services

Companies can't compete effectively if their information technology systems don't have the power or flexibility to perform essential functions. Companies need accountants with strong computer skills who can design and implement advanced systems to fit a company's specific needs and to find ways to protect and insulate data. CPAs skilled in software research and development (including multimedia technology) are also highly valued.

International Accounting

Globalization means that cross-border transactions are becoming commonplace. Countries in Eastern Europe and Latin America, which previously had closed economies, are opening up and doing business with new trading partners. The passage of the North American Free Trade Agreement (NAFTA) and the General Agreement on Tariffs and Trade (GATT) facilitates trade, and the economic growth in areas such as the Pacific Rim further brings greater volumes of trade and financial flows. Organizations need accountants who understand international trade rules, accords, and laws; cross-border merger and acquisition issues; and foreign business customs, languages, cultures, and procedures.

Forensic Accounting

Forensic accounting is in growing demand after scandals such as the collapse of Enron and WorldCom, which are featured in this text. Forensic accountants look at a company's financial records for evidence of criminal activity. This could be anything from securities fraud to overvaluation of inventory to money laundering and improper capitalization of expenses.

Whether you seek a career in business, government, the not-for-profit sector, or a charity, **accounting** has a career for you. Every organization, from the smallest mom-and-pop music retailer to the biggest government in the world, needs accountants to help manage its resources. Global trade demands accountability, and ever-more complex tax laws mean an ever-increasing need for the skills and services of accountants.

ENDNOTES

[1]Alba, Jason, and Manisha Bathija. *Vault Career Guide to Accounting*. (New York: Vault, 2002).

[2]http://www.startheregoplaces.com/news/news_half5.asp.

[3]AICPA, the American Institute of Certified Public Accountants, http://www.aicpa.org.

1

The Financial Statements

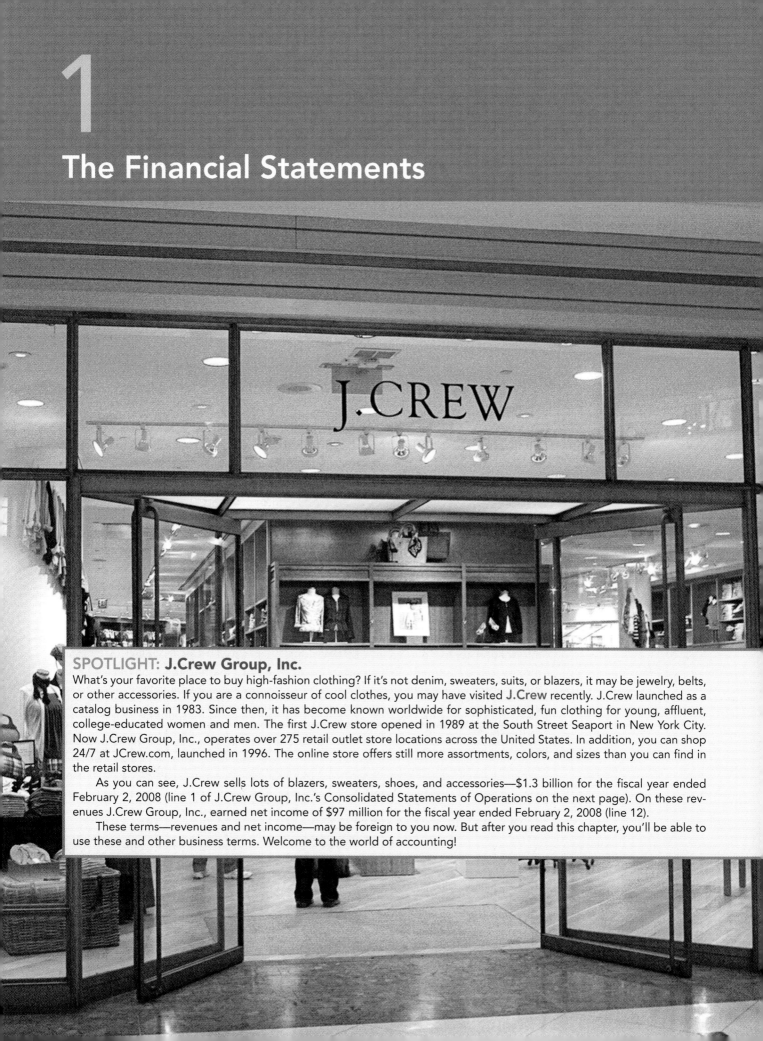

SPOTLIGHT: J.Crew Group, Inc.

What's your favorite place to buy high-fashion clothing? If it's not denim, sweaters, suits, or blazers, it may be jewelry, belts, or other accessories. If you are a connoisseur of cool clothes, you may have visited **J.Crew** recently. J.Crew launched as a catalog business in 1983. Since then, it has become known worldwide for sophisticated, fun clothing for young, affluent, college-educated women and men. The first J.Crew store opened in 1989 at the South Street Seaport in New York City. Now J.Crew Group, Inc., operates over 275 retail outlet store locations across the United States. In addition, you can shop 24/7 at JCrew.com, launched in 1996. The online store offers still more assortments, colors, and sizes than you can find in the retail stores.

As you can see, J.Crew sells lots of blazers, sweaters, shoes, and accessories—$1.3 billion for the fiscal year ended February 2, 2008 (line 1 of J.Crew Group, Inc.'s Consolidated Statements of Operations on the next page). On these revenues J.Crew Group, Inc., earned net income of $97 million for the fiscal year ended February 2, 2008 (line 12).

These terms—revenues and net income—may be foreign to you now. But after you read this chapter, you'll be able to use these and other business terms. Welcome to the world of accounting!

J.Crew Group, Inc.
Consolidated Statements of Operations (adapted)

(In millions)	Year Ended February 3, 2007	Year Ended February 2, 2008
Revenues		
1 Net sales..	$1,117	$1,292
2 Other revenue	35	43
3 Total revenues..	1,152	1,335
4 Cost of goods sold	652	746
5 Gross profit	500	589
6 Selling, general and administrative expense...............	375	416
7 Income from operations.................................	125	173
8 Interest expense, net......................................	44	11
9 Loss on debt refinancing................................	10	
10 Income before income taxes............................	71	162
11 Income tax expense.......................................	(7)	65
12 Net income	$ 78	$ 97

Each chapter of this book begins with an actual financial statement.
In this chapter, it's the income statements (or Consolidated Statements of
Operations) of J.Crew Group, Inc. The core of financial accounting revolves around
the basic financial statements:

- Income statement (the statement of operations)
- Statement of retained earnings
- Balance sheet (the statement of financial position)
- Statement of cash flows

Financial statements are the business documents that companies use to report
the results of their activities to various user groups, which can include managers,
investors, creditors, and regulatory agencies. In turn, these parties use the reported
information to make a variety of decisions, such as whether to invest in or loan
money to the company. To learn accounting, you must learn to focus on decisions. In
this chapter we explain generally accepted accounting principles, their underlying
assumptions, principles, and concepts, and the bodies responsible for issuing
accounting standards. We discuss the judgment process that is necessary to make
good accounting decisions. We also discuss the contents of the four basic financial
statements that report the results of those decisions. In later chapters, we will
explain in more detail how to construct the financial statements, as well as how user
groups typically use the information contained in them to make business decisions.

LEARNING OBJECTIVES

1 **Use** accounting vocabulary

2 **Learn** underlying concepts, assumptions, and principles of accounting

3 **Apply** the accounting equation to business organizations

4 **Evaluate** business operations

5 **Use** information in financial statements to make business decisions, which are informed
by economic, legal, and ethical guidelines

> **ac/t** For more practice and review of accounting cycle concepts, use ACT, the Accounting Cycle Tutorial, online at www.myaccountinglab.com. Margin logos like this one, directing you to the appropriate ACT section and material, appear throughout Chapters 1, 2, and 3. When you enter the tutorial, you'll find three buttons on the opening page of each chapter module. Here's what the buttons mean: **Tutorial** gives you a review of the major concepts, **Application** gives you practice exercises, and **Glossary** reviews important terms.

BUSINESS DECISIONS

J.Crew Group, Inc., managers make lots of decisions. Which is selling faster—pants, suits, blazers, or shoes? Are jeans bringing in more profits than blazers? Should J.Crew expand into Europe or Asia? Accounting information helps companies make these decisions.

Take a look at J.Crew Group, Inc.'s Consolidated Statement of Operations on page 2. Focus on net income (line 12). Net income (profit) is the excess of revenues over expenses. You can see that J.Crew Group, Inc., earned a $97 million profit in the year ended February 2, 2008. That's good news because it means that J.Crew had $97 million more revenues than expenses for the year.

J.Crew's Consolidated Statement of Operations conveys more good news. Net income for fiscal 2007 (year ended February 2, 2008) increased by 24% over net income for the previous year (about $78 million). J.Crew is growing, and investors buy stocks of growing companies.

Suppose you have $5,000 to invest. What information would you need before deciding to invest that money in J.Crew Group, Inc.? Let's see how accounting works.

ACCOUNTING IS THE LANGUAGE OF BUSINESS

Accounting is an information system. It measures business activities, processes data into reports, and communicates results to decision makers. Accounting is "the language of business." The better you understand the language, the better you can manage your finances as well as those of your business.

OBJECTIVE

1 **Use** accounting vocabulary

Accounting produces financial statements, which report information about a business entity. The financial statements measure performance and communicate where a business stands in financial terms. In this chapter we focus on J.Crew Group, Inc. After completing this chapter, you'll begin to understand financial statements.

Don't confuse bookkeeping and accounting. Bookkeeping is a mechanical part of accounting, just as arithmetic is a part of mathematics. Exhibit 1-1 on the following page illustrates the flow of accounting information and helps illustrate accounting's role in business. The accounting process begins and ends with people making decisions.

EXHIBIT 1-1 | **The Flow of Accounting Information**

1. People make decisions.   2. Business transactions occur.   3. Companies report their results.

Who Uses Accounting Information?

Decision makers use many types of information. A banker decides who gets a loan. J.Crew Group, Inc., decides where to locate a new store. Let's see how decision makers use accounting information.

- *Individuals.* People like you manage their personal bank accounts, decide whether to rent an apartment or buy a house, and budget the monthly income and expenditures of their businesses. Accounting provides the necessary information to allow individuals to make these decisions.
- *Investors and Creditors.* Investors and creditors provide the money to finance J.Crew Group, Inc. Investors want to know how much income they can expect to earn on an investment. Creditors want to know when and how J.Crew Group, Inc., is going to pay them back. These decisions also require accounting information.
- *Regulatory Bodies.* All kinds of regulatory bodies use accounting information. For example, the Internal Revenue Service (IRS) and various state and local governments require businesses, individuals, and other types of organizations to pay income, property, excise, and other taxes. The U.S. Securities and Exchange Commission (SEC) requires companies whose stock is traded publicly to provide it with many kinds of periodic financial reports. All of these reports contain accounting information.
- *Nonprofit Organizations.* Nonprofit organizations—churches, hospitals, and charities such as Habitat for Humanity and the Red Cross—base many of their operating decisions on accounting data. In addition, these organizations have to file periodic reports of their activities with the IRS and state governments, even though they may owe no taxes.

Two Kinds of Accounting: Financial Accounting and Management Accounting

Both *external* and *internal users* of accounting information exist. We can therefore classify accounting into two branches.

Financial accounting provides information for decision makers outside the entity, such as investors, creditors, government agencies, and the public. This information must be relevant for the needs of decision makers and must faithfully give an accurate picture of the entity's economic activities. This textbook focuses on financial accounting.

Management accounting provides information for managers of J.Crew Group, Inc. Examples of management accounting information include budgets, forecasts, and projections that are used in making strategic decisions of the entity. Internal information must still be accurate and relevant for the decision needs of managers. Management accounting is covered in a separate course that usually follows this one.

Organizing a Business

Accounting is used in every type of business. A business generally takes one of the following forms:

- proprietorship
- partnership
- limited-liability company (LLC)
- corporation

Exhibit 1-2 compares ways to organize a business.

EXHIBIT 1-2 | The Various Forms of Business Organization

	Proprietorship	Partnership	LLC	Corporation
1. *Owner(s)*	Proprietor—one owner	Partners—two or more owners	Members	Stockholders—generally many owners
2. *Personal liability of owner(s) for business debts*	Proprietor is personally liable	General partners are personally liable; limited partners are not	Members are *not* personally liable	Stockholders are *not* personally liable

Proprietorship. A **proprietorship** has a single owner, called the proprietor. Dell Computer started out in the college dorm room of Michael Dell, the owner. Proprietorships tend to be small retail stores or solo providers of professional services— physicians, attorneys, or accountants. Legally, the business *is* the proprietor, and the proprietor is personally liable for all the business's debts. But for accounting purposes, a proprietorship is a distinct entity, separate from its proprietor. Thus, the business records should not include the proprietor's personal finances.

Partnership. A **partnership** has two or more parties as co-owners, and each owner is a partner. Individuals, corporations, partnerships, or other types of entities can be partners. Income and loss of the partnership "flows through" to the partners and they recognize it based on their agreed-upon percentage interest in the business. The partnership is not a taxpaying entity. Instead, each partner takes a proportionate share of the entity's taxable income and pays tax according to that partner's individual or corporate rate. Many retail establishments, professional service firms (law, accounting, etc.), real estate, and oil and gas exploration companies operate as partnerships. Many partnerships are small or medium-sized, but some are gigantic, with thousands of partners. Partnerships are governed by agreement, usually spelled out in writing in the form of a contract between the partners. General partnerships have mutual agency and unlimited liability, meaning that each partner may conduct business in the name of the entity and can make agreements that legally bind all partners without limit for the partnership's debts. Partnerships are therefore quite risky, because an irresponsible partner can create large debts for the other general partners without their knowledge or permission. This feature of general partnerships has spawned the creation of limited-liability partnerships (LLPs).

A *limited-liability partnership* is one in which a wayward partner cannot create a large liability for the other partners. In LLPs, each partner is liable for partnership debts only up to the extent of his or her investment in the partnership, plus his or her proportionate share of the liabilities. Each LLP, however, must have one general partner with unlimited liability for all partnership debts.

Limited-Liability Company (LLC). A **limited-liability company** is one in which the business (and not the owner) is liable for the company's debts. An LLC may have one owner or many owners, called *members*. Unlike a proprietorship or a general partnership, the members of an LLC do *not* have unlimited liability for the LLC's debts. An LLC pays no business income tax. Instead, the LLC's income "flows through" to the members, and they pay income tax at their own tax rates, just as they would if they were partners. Today, many multiple-owner businesses are organized as LLCs, because members of an LLC effectively enjoy limited liability while still being taxed like members of a partnership.

Corporation. A **corporation** is a business owned by the **stockholders**, or **shareholders**, who own **stock** representing shares of ownership in the corporation. One of the major advantages of doing business in the corporate form is the ability to raise large sums of capital from issuance of stock to the public. All types of entities (individuals, partnerships, corporations, or other types) may be shareholders in a corporation. Even though proprietorships and partnerships are more numerous, corporations transact much more business and are larger in terms of assets, income, and number of employees. Most well-known companies, such as J.Crew Group, Inc., Google, Toyota, and Apple, Inc., are corporations. Their full names include *Corporation* or *Incorporated* (abbreviated *Corp.* and *Inc.*) to indicate that they are corporations—for example, J.Crew Group, Inc., and Starbucks Corporation. Some bear the name *Company*, such as Ford Motor Company.

A corporation is formed under state law. Unlike proprietorships and partnerships, a corporation is legally distinct from its owners. The corporation is like an artificial person and possesses many of the same rights that a person has. The stockholders have no personal obligation for the corporation's debts. So, stockholders of a corporation have limited liability, as do limited partners and members of an LLC. However, unlike partnerships or LLCs, a corporation pays a business income tax as well as many other types of taxes. Furthermore, the shareholders of a corporation are effectively taxed twice on distributions received from the corporation (called dividends). Thus, one of the major disadvantages of the corporate form of business is *double taxation of distributed profits*.

Ultimate control of a corporation rests with the stockholders, who generally get one vote for each share of stock they own. Stockholders elect the **board of directors**, which sets policy and appoints officers. The board elects a chairperson, who holds the most power in the corporation and often carries the title chief executive officer (CEO). The board also appoints the president as chief operating officer (COO). Corporations also have vice presidents in charge of sales, accounting, and finance (called the chief financial officer or CFO), and other key areas.

ACCOUNTING PRINCIPLES, ASSUMPTIONS, AND CONCEPTS

Accountants follow professional guidelines for measurement and disclosure of financial information. These are called **generally accepted accounting principles (GAAP)**. In the United States, the **Financial Accounting Standards Board (FASB)** formulates GAAP. The **International Accounting Standards Board (IASB)** sets global—or International—Financial Reporting Standards (IFRS), as discussed in a later section.

OBJECTIVE

2 **Learn** underlying concepts, assumptions, and principles of accounting

Exhibit 1-3 gives an overview of the joint conceptual framework of accounting developed by the FASB and the IASB. Financial reporting standards (whether U.S. or international), at the bottom, follow the conceptual framework. The overall *objective* of accounting is to provide financial information that is useful to present and potential capital providers in making investment and lending decisions. In this sense, *capital* means resources (usually cash). The two basic types of external providers of capital include investors (who exchange cash for stock) and creditors (who loan cash) to the entity.

EXHIBIT 1-3 | **Conceptual Foundations of Accounting**

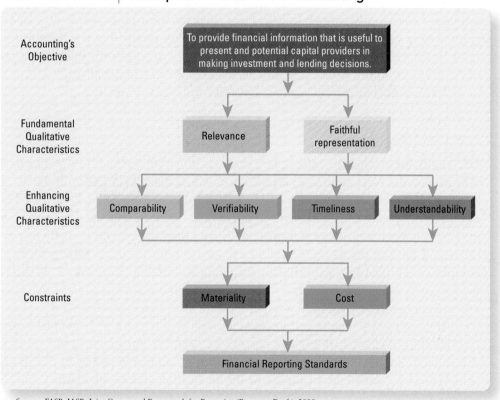

Source: FASB, IASB, Joint Conceptual Framework for Reporting (Exposure Draft). 2008.

To be useful, information must have the fundamental qualitative characteristics. Those include:

- Relevance; and
- Faithful representation

To be relevant, information must be capable of making a difference to the decision maker, having predictive or confirming value. To faithfully represent, the information must be complete, neutral (free from bias), and without material error (accurate). Accounting information must focus on the *economic substance* of a transaction, event, or circumstance, which may or may not always be the same as its legal form. Faithful representation makes the information *reliable* to users.

Accounting information must also have a number of *enhancing qualitative characteristics*. These include

- Comparability;
- Verifiability;
- Timeliness; and
- Understandability.

Comparability means that the accounting information for a company must be prepared in such a way as to be capable of being both compared with information from other companies in the same period, and *consistent* with similar information for that company in previous periods. *Verifiability* means that the information must be capable of being checked for accuracy, completeness, and reliability. The process of verifying information is often done by *internal* as well as *external auditors*. Verifiability enhances the reliability of information, and thus makes the information more representative of economic reality. *Timeliness* means that the information must be made available to users early enough to help them make decisions, thus making the information more relevant to their needs. *Understandability* means that the information must be sufficiently transparent so that it makes sense to reasonably informed users of the information (investors, creditors, regulatory agencies, and managers).

Accounting information is also subject to constraints. These include

- Materiality; and
- Cost

Materiality means that the information must be important enough to the informed user so that, if it were omitted or erroneous, it would make a difference in the user's decision. Only information that is material needs to be separately *disclosed* (listed or discussed) in the financial statements. If not, it does not need separate disclosure, but may be combined with other information. Accounting information is costly to produce, and the *cost should not exceed the expected benefits* to users. Management of companies is primarily responsible for preparing accounting information. Managers must exercise judgment in determining whether the information is sufficiently material and not excessively costly to warrant separate disclosure.

This course will expose you to GAAP as well as to relevant international financial reporting standards (IFRS). We summarize GAAP in Appendix E and IFRS in Appendix F. In the following section, we briefly summarize some of the basic assumptions and principles that underlie the application of these standards.

The Entity Assumption

The most basic accounting assumption (underlying idea) is the **entity**, which is any organization that stands apart as a separate economic unit. Sharp boundaries are drawn around each entity so as not to confuse its affairs with those of others.

Consider Millard S. Drexler, chairman of the board and CEO of J.Crew Group, Inc. Mr. Drexler owns a home and several automobiles. In addition, he may owe money on some personal loans. All these assets and liabilities belong to Mr. Drexler and have nothing to do with J.Crew Group, Inc. Likewise, J.Crew Group, Inc.'s cash, computers, and inventories belong to the company and not to Drexler. Why? Because the entity assumption draws a sharp boundary around each entity; in this case J.Crew Group, Inc., is one entity, and Millard S. Drexler is a second, separate entity.

Let's consider the various types of stores that make up J.Crew Group, Inc. Top managers evaluate the retail stores separately from the outlet stores. If retail-store sales were dropping, J.Crew should identify the reason. But if sales figures from all the retail and outlet stores were combined in a single total, managers couldn't tell how differently each unit was performing. To correct the problem, managers need accounting information for each division (entity) in the company. Thus, each store, both retail and outlet, keeps its own records in order to be evaluated separately.

The Continuity (Going-Concern) Assumption

In measuring and reporting accounting information, we assume that the entity will continue to operate long enough to use existing assets—land, buildings, equipment, and supplies—for its intended purposes. This is called the **continuity (going-concern) assumption**.

Consider the alternative to the **going-concern assumption**: the quitting concern, or going out of business. An entity that is not continuing would have to sell all of its assets in the process. In that case, the most *relevant* measure of the value of the assets would be their current fair market values (the amount the company would receive for the assets when sold). But going out of business is the exception rather than the rule. Therefore, the continuity assumption says that a business should stay in business long enough to recover the cost of those assets by allocating that cost through a process called *depreciation* to business operations over the assets' economic lives.

The Historical Cost Principle

The **historical cost principle** states that assets should be recorded at their *actual cost,* measured on the date of purchase as the amount of cash paid plus the dollar value of all non-cash consideration (other assets, privileges, or rights) also given in exchange. For example, suppose J.Crew Group, Inc., purchases a building for a new store. The building's current owner is asking for $600,000 for the building. The management of J.Crew believes the building is worth $585,000, and offers the present owner that amount. Two real estate professionals appraise the building at $610,000. The two parties compromise and agree on a price of $590,000 for the building. The historical cost principle requires J.Crew to initially record the building at its actual cost of $590,000, not at $585,000, $600,000 or $610,000, even though those amounts were what some people believed the building was worth. At the point of purchase, $590,000 is both the *relevant* amount for the building's worth and the amount that *faithfully represents* a reliable figure for the price the company paid for it.

The *historical cost principle*, and the *continuity assumption* (discussed above), also maintain that J.Crew's accounting records should continue to use historical cost to value the asset for as long as the business holds it. Why? Because cost is a *verifiable* measure that is relatively *free from bias*. Suppose that J.Crew Group, Inc., owns the building for six years. Real estate prices increase during this period. As a result, at the end of the period, the building can be sold for $650,000. Should J.Crew increase the carrying value of the building on the company's books to $650,000? No. According to the historical cost principle, the building remains on J.Crew Group, Inc.'s books at its historical cost of $590,000. According to the continuity assumption, J.Crew intends to stay in business and keep the building, not to sell it, so its historical cost is the most relevant and the most faithful representation of its carrying value. It is also the most easily verifiable (auditable) amount. Should the company decide to sell the building later at a price above or below its carrying value, it will record the cash received, remove the carrying value of the building from the books, and record a gain or a loss for the difference at that time.

The historical cost principle is not used as pervasively in the United States as it once was. Accounting is moving in the direction of reporting more and more assets and liabilities at their fair values. **Fair value** is the amount that the business could sell the asset for, or the amount that the business could pay to settle the liability. The FASB has issued guidance for companies to report many assets and liabilities at fair values. Moreover, in recent years, the FASB has agreed to align GAAP with International Financial Reporting Standards (IFRS). These standards generally allow for more liberal measurement of different types of assets with fair values than GAAP, which may cause more assets to be re-valued periodically to fair market values. We will discuss the trend toward globalization of accounting standards in a later part of this chapter, and illustrate it in later chapters throughout the book.

The Stable-Monetary-Unit Assumption

In the United States, we record transactions in dollars because that is our medium of exchange. British accountants record transactions in pounds sterling, Japanese in yen, and Europeans in euros.

Unlike a liter or a mile, the value of a dollar changes over time. A rise in the general price level is called *inflation*. During inflation, a dollar will purchase less food, less toothpaste, and less of other goods and services. When prices are stable—there is little inflation—a dollar's purchasing power is also stable.

Under the **stable-monetary-unit assumption**, accountants assume that the dollar's purchasing power is stable over time. We ignore inflation, and this allows us to add and subtract dollar amounts as though dollars over successive years have a consistent amount of purchasing power. This is important because businesses that report their financial information publicly usually report comparative financial information (that is, the current year along with one or more prior years). If we could not assume a stable monetary unit, assets and liabilities denominated in prior years' dollars would have to be adjusted to current year price levels. Since inflation is considered to be relatively minor over time, those adjustments do not have to be made.

GLOBAL VIEW

INTERNATIONAL FINANCIAL REPORTING STANDARDS (IFRS)

We live in a global economy! The global credit crisis of 2008 originated in the United States but rapidly spread throughout the world. U.S. investors can easily trade stocks on the Hong Kong, London, and Brussels stock exchanges over the Internet. Each year, American companies such as Starbucks, The Gap, McDonald's, Microsoft, and Disney conduct billions of dollars of business around the globe. Conversely, foreign companies such as Nokia, Samsung, Toyota, and Nestlé conduct billions of dollars of business in the United States. American companies have merged with foreign companies to create international conglomerates such as Pearson (publisher of this textbook) and Anheuser-Busch InBev. No matter where your career starts, it is very likely that it will eventually take you into global markets.

Until recently, one of the major challenges of conducting global business has been the fact that different countries have adopted different accounting standards for business transactions. Historically, the major developed countries in the world (United States, U.K., Japan, Germany, etc.) have all had their own versions of GAAP. As investors seek to compare financial results across entities from different countries, they have had to re-state and convert accounting data from one country to the next in order to make them comparable. This takes time and can be expensive.

The solution to this problem lies with the IASB, which has developed International Financial Reporting Standards (IFRS). These standards are now being used by most countries around the world. For years, accountants in the United States did not pay much attention to IFRS because our GAAP was considered to be the strongest single set of accounting standards in the world. In addition, the application of GAAP for public companies in the United States is overseen carefully by the U.S. Securities and Exchange Commission (SEC), a body which at present has no global counterpart.

Nevertheless, in order to promote consistency in global financial reporting, the SEC announced in November 2008 that it intends to require all U.S. public companies to adopt IFRS within the next few years. Some companies can choose to begin implementing IFRS by the end of 2009. Mandatory U.S. adoption of IFRS is currently slated to begin in stages from 2014 through 2016, beginning with the largest companies.

The advantage to adopting IFRS is that financial statements from a U.S. company (say, Hershey Corporation in Pennsylvania) will be comparable to those of a foreign company (say, Nestlé in Switzerland). It will be far easier for investors and businesspeople to evaluate information of various companies in the same industries from across the globe, and companies will only have to prepare one set of financial statements, instead of multiple versions. Thus, in the long run, global use of IFRS should significantly reduce costs of doing global business.

These are impressive goals, but what do these changes mean for U.S. GAAP? It could mean that U.S. GAAP will no longer exist, being replaced by international standards within the next decade. Alternatively, it could mean that U.S. GAAP will remain, and will become a domestic interpretation of IFRS for businesses operating solely within the United States.

Does this mean that the accounting information you are studying in this textbook will soon become outdated? Fortunately, no. For one thing, the vast majority of the material you learn from this textbook, including the underlying conceptual framework outlined in the previous section, is *already* part of IFRS. The most commonly used accounting practices are essentially the same under both U.S. GAAP and IFRS. Additionally, the FASB is working hand-in-hand with the IASB toward *convergence* of standards: that is, gradually adjusting both sets of standards to more closely align them over time so that, when transition to IFRS in the United States occurs, it will occur smoothly. Over the past few years, all newly-issued U.S. accounting standards have conformed U.S. practices to IFRS.

As of the publication of this text, there are still some areas of disagreement between GAAP and IFRS. For example, certain widely accepted U.S. practices, such as the use of the last-in, first-out (LIFO) inventory costing method (discussed in Chapter 6), are disallowed under IFRS. Other differences exist as well. These differences must be resolved before IFRS can be fully adopted in the United States.

In general, the main difference between U.S. GAAP and IFRS is that U.S. GAAP has become rather "rules-based" over its long history, while IFRS (not in existence as long) allows more professional judgment on the part of companies. In many areas, the international regulations allow accountants and managers to apply the rules in ways they think is best. For example, revenue recognition is one area where IFRS provides significantly less guidance and allows more judgment than U.S. GAAP. We will discuss this concept further in Chapters 3 and 11.

The other major difference between IFRS and U.S. GAAP lies in the valuation of long-term assets (plant assets and intangibles) and liabilities. In U.S. GAAP, the historical cost principle tells us to value assets at historical cost. In contrast, IFRS prefers more of a fair-value approach, which reports assets and liabilities on the balance sheet at their up-to-date values, rather than at historical cost. This may seem like a big difference, but U.S. GAAP already allows for a partial fair-value approach with rules such as lower-of-cost-or-market, accounting for the impairment of long-term assets, and adjusting certain investments to fair values. We cover these concepts in more depth in later chapters.

In past years, there have been many more lawsuits over accounting disputes in the United States than in other countries. This has led to more detailed U.S. accounting rules, so that American accountants and managers have clear guidelines to follow. Once IFRS is adopted, U.S. GAAP may be used as "secondary" guidance, in instances where IFRS is vague. As of the date of this text, it's unclear exactly how the eventual interaction between IFRS and U.S. GAAP will play out.

There are also terminology differences between IFRS and GAAP. Americans may have to get used to some new words that replace old familiar ones. The underlying concepts probably won't change, but there will probably be new terms and phrasings. Portions of the income statement and balance sheet may also be rearranged, as IFRS presentation is slightly different than the financial statements of U.S. GAAP. The information would still be on the same financial statement, but might appear in a new location.

Of course, everyone focuses on what is different, not on what stays the same. What will we have to adjust as the United States adopts international standards? Throughout the remainder of this textbook, in chapters that cover concepts where major differences between GAAP and IFRS exist, we will discuss those differences. Because this is an introductory textbook in financial accounting, our discussion will be brief, in order to focus on the changes that are relevant for this course. Appendix F includes a table, cross-referenced by chapter, that summarizes all of these differences, as well as their impacts on financial statements once IFRS is fully adopted.

You can expect to hear more about the adoption of IFRS, as well as global harmonization of accounting standards, in the future. When you do, the most important things to remember will be that these changes will be beneficial for financial statement users in the long run, and that most of what you learned in this accounting course will still apply. Remember that there are far more areas of common ground than of disagreement. Whatever may come, your knowledge of international accounting principles will benefit you in the future. The globalization of the world economy provides a wonderful opportunity for you to succeed in the business world.

THE ACCOUNTING EQUATION

J.Crew Group, Inc.'s financial statements tell us how the business is performing and where it stands. But how do we arrive at the financial statements? Let's examine the *elements of financial statements*, which are the building blocks on which these statements rest.

OBJECTIVE

3 **Apply** the accounting equation to business organizations

Assets and Liabilities

The financial statements are based on the **accounting equation**. This equation presents the resources of a company and the claims to those resources.

- **Assets** are economic resources that are expected to produce a benefit in the future. J.Crew Group, Inc.'s cash, merchandise inventory, and equipment are examples of assets.

  Claims on assets come from two sources:

- **Liabilities** are "outsider claims." They are debts that are payable to outsiders, called *creditors*. For example, a creditor who has loaned money to J.Crew Group, Inc., has a claim—a legal right—to a part of J.Crew's assets until J.Crew repays the debt.
- **Owners' equity** (also called **capital**, or **stockholders' equity for a corporation**) represents the "insider claims" of a business. Equity means ownership, so J.Crew Group, Inc.'s stockholders' equity is the stockholders' interest in the assets of the corporation.

The accounting equation shows the relationship among assets, liabilities, and owners' equity. Assets appear on the left side and liabilities and owners' equity on the right. As Exhibit 1-4 shows, the two sides must be equal:

EXHIBIT 1-4 | The Accounting Equation

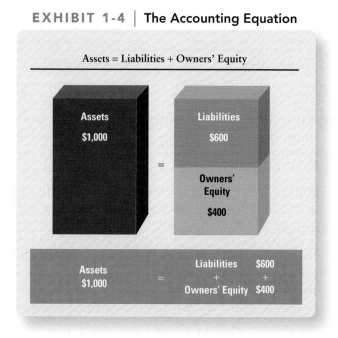

What are some of J.Crew Group, Inc.'s assets? The first asset is **cash** and cash equivalents, the liquid assets that are the medium of exchange. Another important asset is **merchandise inventory** (often called inventories)—the clothing and accessory items—that J.Crew's stores sell. J.Crew also has assets in the form of **property, plant, and equipment**, or **fixed assets**. These are the long-lived assets the company uses to do business—store equipment, buildings, computers, and so on.

J.Crew Group, Inc.'s liabilities include a number of payables, such as accounts payable and federal and state income taxes payable. The word *payable* always signifies a liability. An **account payable** is a liability for goods or services purchased on credit and supported by the credit standing of the purchaser. A **note payable** is a written promise to pay on a certain date. **Long-term debt** is a liability that's payable beyond one year from the date of the financial statements.

Owners' Equity

The owners' equity of any business is its assets minus its liabilities. We can write the accounting equation to show that owners' equity is what's left over when we subtract liabilities from assets.

$$\text{Assets} - \text{Liabilities} = \text{Owners' Equity}$$

A corporation's equity—called **stockholders' equity**—has two main subparts:

- paid-in capital and
- retained earnings

The accounting equation can be written as

$$\text{Assets} = \text{Liabilities} + \text{Stockholders' Equity}$$
$$\text{Assets} = \text{Liabilities} + \text{Paid-in Capital} + \text{Retained Earnings}$$

Paid-in capital is the amount the stockholders have invested in the corporation. The basic component of paid-in capital is **common stock**, which the corporation issues to the stockholders as evidence of their ownership. All corporations have common stock.

Retained earnings is the amount earned by income-producing activities and kept for use in the business. Three major types of transactions affect retained earnings: revenues, expenses, and dividends.

- **Revenues** are inflows of resources that increase retained earnings by delivering goods or services to customers. For example, a J.Crew store's sale of a blazer brings in cash revenue and increases J.Crew Group, Inc.'s retained earnings.
- **Expenses** are resource outflows that decrease retained earnings due to operations. For example, the wages that J.Crew pays employees are an expense and

decrease retained earnings. Expenses represent the costs of doing business; they are the opposite of revenues. Expenses include cost of goods sold, building rent, salaries, and utility payments. Expenses also include the depreciation of display cases, racks, shelving, and other equipment.

- **Dividends** decrease retained earnings, because they are distributions to stock-holders of assets (usually cash) generated by net income, A successful business may pay dividends to shareholders as a return on their investments. Remember: **Dividends are not expenses. Dividends never affect net income. Instead of being subtracted from revenues to compute net income, dividends are recorded as direct reductions of retained earnings.**

Businesses strive for **profits**, the excess of revenues over expenses.

- When total revenues exceed total expenses, the result is called **net income**, **net earnings**, or **net profit**.
- When expenses exceed revenues, the result is a **net loss**.
- Net income or net loss is the "bottom line" on an income statement. J.Crew Group, Inc.'s bottom line reports net income for the year ended February 2, 2008, of $97 million (line 12 on the Consolidated Statement of Operations on page 2).

Exhibit 1-5 shows the relationships among

- Retained earnings
- Revenues – Expenses = Net income (or net loss)
- Dividends

EXHIBIT 1-5 | The Components of Retained Earnings

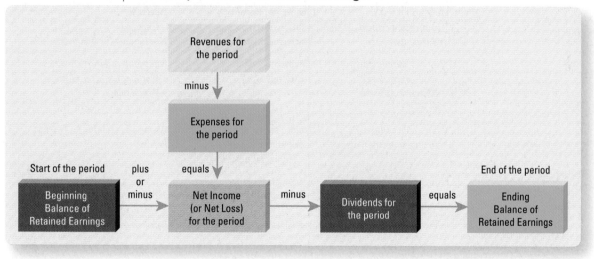

The owners' equity of proprietorships and partnerships is different from that of corporations. Proprietorships and partnerships don't identify paid-in capital and retained earnings separately. Instead, they use a single heading—Capital. Examples include: Randall Waller, Capital, for a proprietorship; and Powers, Capital, and Salazar, Capital, for a partnership.

STOP & THINK...

1. If the assets of a business are $240,000 and the liabilities are $80,000, how much is the owners' equity?
2. If the owners' equity in a business is $160,000 and the liabilities are $130,000, how much are the assets?
3. A company reported monthly revenues of $129,000 and expenses of $85,000. What is the result of operations for the month?
4. If the beginning balance of retained earnings is $100,000, revenue is $75,000, expenses total $50,000, and the company pays a $10,000 dividend, what is the ending balance of retained earnings?

Answers:

1. $160,000 ($240,000 − $80,000)
2. $290,000 ($160,000 + $130,000)
3. Net income of $44,000 ($129,000 − $85,000); revenues minus expenses
4. $115,000 [$100,000 beginning balance + net income $25,000 ($75,000 − $50,000) − dividends $10,000]

THE FINANCIAL STATEMENTS

OBJECTIVE

4 **Evaluate** business operations

The financial statements present a company to the public in financial terms. Each financial statement relates to a specific date or time period. What would investors want to know about J.Crew Group, Inc., at the end of its fiscal year? Exhibit 1-6 lists four questions decision makers may ask. Each answer comes from one of the financial statements.

EXHIBIT 1-6 | **Information Reported in the Financial Statements**

Question	Financial Statement	Answer
1. How well did the company perform during the year?	Income statement (also called the Statement of operations)	Revenues − Expenses ————————— Net income (or Net loss)
2. Why did the company's retained earnings change during the year?	Statement of retained earnings	Beginning retained earnings + Net income (or − Net loss) − Dividends ————————— Ending retained earnings
3. What is the company's financial position at December 31?	Balance sheet (also called the Statement of financial position)	Assets = Liabilities + Owners' Equity
4. How much cash did the company generate and spend during the year?	Statement of cash flows	Operating cash flows ± Investing cash flows ± Financing cash flows ————————— Increase (decrease) in cash

To learn how to use financial statements, let's work through J.Crew Group, Inc.'s statements for 2007 fiscal year (year ended February 2, 2008). The following diagram shows how the data flow from one financial statement to the next. The order is important.

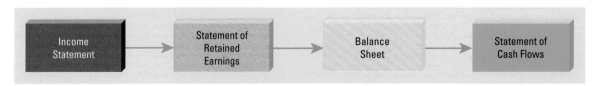

We begin with the income statement in Exhibit 1-7.

EXHIBIT 1-7 | **J.Crew Group, Inc., Consolidated Statements of Operations**

J.Crew Group, Inc.
Consolidated Statements of Operations (adapted)

(In millions)	Year Ended February 3, 2007	Year Ended February 2, 2008
Revenues		
1 Net sales..	$1,117	$1,292
2 Other revenue	35	43
3 Total revenues..	1,152	1,335
4 Cost of goods sold	652	746
5 Gross profit	500	589
6 Selling, general and administrative expense...............	375	416
7 Income from operations...........................	125	173
8 Interest expense, net...............................	44	11
9 Loss on debt refinancing........................	10	
10 Income before income taxes....................	71	162
11 Income tax expense.................................	(7)	65
12 Net income	$ 78	$ 97

The Income Statement Measures Operating Performance

The **income statement**, or **statement of operations**, reports revenues and expenses for the period. The bottom line is net income or net loss *for the period*. At the top of Exhibit 1-7 is the company's name, J.Crew Group, Inc. On the second line is the term "Consolidated Statements of Operations." J.Crew Group, Inc., is actually made up of several corporations that are owned by a common group of shareholders. Commonly controlled corporations like this are required to combine, or consolidate, all of their revenues, expenses, assets, liabilities, and stockholders' equity, and to report them all as one.

The dates of J.Crew Group, Inc.'s Consolidated Statements of Operations are "Years Ended February 3, 2007 (fiscal year 2006) and February 2, 2008 (fiscal year 2007)." J.Crew uses a *fiscal year* consisting of 52 (or 53) weeks ending on the closest day to January 31 as its accounting year. This is because the holiday season is the busiest time of the year and includes Christmas, when the company typically earns the largest amount of revenue. In contrast, January is typically the slowest month of the year for retailers, allowing the company time to get its books in order. Companies often adopt a fiscal year that ends at the low point of their operations. Wal-Mart uses the same fiscal year as J.Crew. Whole Foods Markets, Inc., uses a fiscal year consisting of the 52 weeks ending closest to September 30. FedEx's year-end falls on May 31. About 60% of the largest companies use a fiscal year ending on December 31.

J.Crew Group, Inc.'s Consolidated Statements of Operations in Exhibit 1-7 report operating results for two fiscal years: 2006 (53 weeks ended February 3, 2007); and 2007 (52 weeks ended February 2, 2008), to show trends for revenues, expenses, and net income. To avoid clutter, J.Crew reports in millions of dollars. During fiscal 2007, J.Crew increased total revenues (line 3) from $1,152 million to

$1,335 million. Net income rose from $78 million to $97 million (line 12). J.Crew Group, Inc., stores sold more pants, coats, and accessories in 2007, and that boosted profits. Focus on fiscal 2007. (We show 2006 for comparative purposes.) An income statement reports two main categories:

- Revenues and gains
- Expenses and losses

We measure net income as follows:

> **Net Income = Total Revenues and Gains – Total Expenses and Losses**

In accounting, the word *net* refers to an amount after a subtraction. *Net* income is the profit left over after subtracting expenses and losses from revenues and gains. **Net income is the single most important item in the financial statements.**

Revenues. J.Crew Group, Inc., has two kinds of revenue: Net sales and Other revenue. Revenues (lines 1, 2, and 3) do not always carry the term *revenue* in their titles. For example, net sales revenue is often abbreviated as *net sales*. *Net* sales means sales revenue after subtracting all the goods customers have returned to the company. J.Crew, Wal-Mart, Best Buy, and The Gap get some goods back from customers due to product defects, or items that customers do not want for other reasons. Other revenue consists principally of shipping and handling fees from catalog and Internet sales.

Expenses. Not all expenses have the word *expense* in their title. For example, J.Crew Group, Inc.'s largest expense is for Cost of goods sold (line 4). Another title of this expense is *cost of sales*. This expense represents the direct cost of making sales. This includes J.Crew's cost of the merchandise it sold to customers, as well as occupancy costs (rent and maintenance) for leased stores. For example, suppose a sweater costs J.Crew $30. Assume J.Crew sells the sweater for $75. Sales revenue is $75, and cost of goods sold is $30. Cost of goods sold is the major expense of merchandising entities such as J.Crew, Best Buy, Wal-Mart, and Whole Foods Markets.

J.Crew has some other expenses:

- Selling, general and administrative expenses (line 6) are the costs of everyday operations that are not directly related to merchandise purchases and occupancy. Many expenses may be included in this category, including sales commissions paid to employees, catalog production, mailing costs, warehousing expenses, depreciation, credit card fees, executive salaries, and other home-office expenses. These expenses amounted to $416 million in fiscal 2007.
- Interest expense (line 8) was $11 million for 2007. This is J.Crew's cost of borrowing money. For J.Crew Group, Inc., interest revenue has been *netted* against interest expense. Companies are allowed to offset items like interest income and interest expense against each other and show only the difference (in this case the larger item is interest expense, and so the net amount appears as an expense).
- Income tax expense (line 11) is the expense levied on J.Crew Group, Inc.'s income by the government. This is often one of a corporation's largest expenses.

J.Crew's income tax expense for fiscal 2007 is a whopping $65 million (40% of its net income before taxes)! Compare this to fiscal 2006 when J. Crew had a tax benefit (income) of $7 million. The tax benefit occurred because, before 2006, J.Crew had reported net operating *losses* rather than net operating *income*, for tax purposes. Corporations are allowed a 20-year carry-forward for net operating losses, and are allowed to offset those losses against taxable income in profitable years. In fiscal 2006, the second year of profitable operations, the company used up the last of its net operating loss carry-forward, and showed net income, rather than expense, from income taxes.

J.Crew Group, Inc., reports Income from operations (line 7) of $173 million and Net income (line 12) of $97 million in fiscal 2007. Some investors use operating income to measure operating performance. Others use the "bottom-line" net income. A company whose net income from operations is consistently growing is regarded by the financial markets as a healthy and growing company. In the long run, that company's stock price should increase. We will explain this trend in greater detail in Chapter 11.

Now let's examine the statement of retained earnings (accumulated deficit) in Exhibit 1-8.

The Statement of Retained Earnings Shows What a Company Did with Its Net Income

Retained earnings means exactly what the term implies, that portion of net income the company has kept over a period of years. If, historically, revenue exceeds expenses, the result will be a positive balance in retained earnings. On the other hand, if, historically, expenses have exceeded sales revenues, the accumulation of these losses will result in an accumulated **deficit** in retained earnings (usually shown in parentheses). Net income or net loss flows from the income statement to the **statement of retained earnings** (lines 3 and 5 in Exhibit 1-8).

Net income increases retained earnings, and net losses and dividends decrease retained earnings.

*ac
t*

Accounting Cycle Tutorial Income Statement Accounts

EXHIBIT 1-8 | **J.Crew Group, Inc., Consolidated Statement of Retained Earnings**

J.Crew Group, Inc.
Consolidated Statement of Retained Earnings (adapted)

(In millions)	Accumulated deficit
1 Balance 28-Jan-06...............	$(583)
2 Reclassifications...................	(3)
3 Net income 2006	78
4 Balance 3-Feb-07	$(508)
5 Net income 2007	97
6 Balance 2-Feb-08	$(411)

J.Crew Group, Inc.'s Consolidated Statements of Retained Earnings need explanation. Start with fiscal 2006. At the beginning of 2006 (January 28, 2006), J.Crew Group, Inc., had an accumulated deficit of $583 million (line 1) caused by the company's accumulated losses during its early years of operation (not uncommon for a young company). However, as the company turned profitable in more recent years, those deficits have been shrinking. During fiscal 2006, J.Crew earned net income of $78 million (line 3) and made another adjustment of $3 million (line 2). J.Crew ended fiscal 2006 with an accumulated deficit of $508 million (–$583 + $78 – $3, line 4). That deficit carried over and became the beginning balance of retained earnings in fiscal 2007.

In fiscal 2007, the company earned net income of $97 million (line 5) to end fiscal 2007 (February 2, 2008) with an accumulated deficit of about $411 million (line 6). If the company remains profitable for a few more years, it will erase the accumulated deficit, and retained earnings will start to show a positive balance (one of the signs of a maturing healthy company).

Which item on the statement of retained earnings comes directly from the income statement? It's net income. Lines 3 and 5 of the retained earnings statement come directly from line 12 of the income statement for fiscal years 2006 and 2007, respectively. Take a moment to trace this amount from one statement to the other.

Give yourself a pat on the back. You're already learning how to analyze financial statements!

After a company earns net income, the board of directors decides whether to pay a dividend to the stockholders. Corporations are not obligated to pay dividends unless their boards decide to pay (i.e., declare) them. Usually, companies who are in development stages or growth mode (like J.Crew Group, Inc.) elect not to pay dividends, opting instead to plow the money back into the company to expand operations or purchase property, plant, and equipment. Established companies usually have enough accumulated retained earnings (and cash) to pay dividends. Dividends decrease retained earnings because they represent a distribution of a company's assets (usually cash) to its stockholders.

The Balance Sheet Measures Financial Position

A company's **balance sheet**, also called the **statement of financial position**, reports three items: assets (line 9), liabilities (line 16), and stockholders' equity, (line 21). J.Crew Group, Inc.'s Consolidated Balance Sheets, shown in Exhibit 1-9, are dated at the *moment in time* when the accounting periods end (February 3, 2007, for fiscal 2006, and February 2, 2008, for fiscal 2007).

EXHIBIT 1-9 | J.Crew, Group, Inc., Consolidated Balance Sheets (Adapted)

J.Crew Group, Inc.
Consolidated Balance Sheets (adapted)

(In millions)	February 3, 2007	February 2, 2008
Assets		
1 Cash and cash equivalents	$ 89	$ 131
2 Merchandise inventories	141	159
3 Prepaid expenses	47	43
4 **Total current assets**	277	333
5 Property and equipment at cost	252	305
6 Less accumulated depreciation and amoritzation	(130)	(137)
7 Net property and equipment	122	168
8 Other assets	29	34
9 **Total assets**	$ 428	$ 535
Liabilities and Stockholders' Equity		
10 Accounts payable	$ 78	$ 101
11 Other current liabilities	77	92
12 Federal and state income taxes payable	5	2
13 **Total current liabilities**	160	195
14 Long-term debt	200	125
15 Other liabilities	62	75
16 **Total liabilities**	422	395
Stockholders' equity:		
17 Common stock	1	1
18 Additional paid-in capital	516	553
19 Accumulated deficit	(508)	(411)
20 Treasury stock, at cost	(3)	(3)
21 **Total stockholders' equity**	6	140
22 Total liabilities and stockholders' equity	$ 428	$ 535

Assets.   There are two main categories of assets: current and long-term. **Current assets** are assets that are expected to be converted to cash, sold, or consumed during the next 12 months or within the business's operating cycle if longer than a year. Current assets include Cash, Short-term investments, Accounts and Notes receivable, Merchandise inventory, and Prepaid expenses. J.Crew's current assets at

February 2, 2008, total $333 million (line 4). Let's examine each current asset that J.Crew Group, Inc., holds.

- All companies have cash. Cash is the liquid asset that's the medium of exchange, and *cash equivalents* include money-market accounts or other financial instruments that are easily convertible to cash. J.Crew owns $131 million in cash and cash equivalents at February 2, 2008 (line 1).
- *Short-term investments* include stocks and bonds of other companies that J.Crew intends to sell within the next year. J.Crew's only short-term investments as of February 2, 2008, are counted as cash equivalents.
- *Accounts receivable* are amounts the company expects to collect from customers. J.Crew doesn't have any accounts receivable. That's because, as a retailer, all of J.Crew's sales are made either in cash or with credit cards, which are treated like cash sales. We'll discuss accounts receivable further in Chapter 5.
- *Notes receivable* are amounts a company expects to collect from a party who has signed a promissory note to that company and therefore owes it money. J.Crew doesn't own any notes receivable.
- Cash, short-term investments, and current receivables are the most liquid assets, in that order.
- *Merchandise inventory* (line 2) is the company's most important, and probably the largest, current asset. For J.Crew, merchandise inventory at February 2, 2008, totals $159 million (about 48% of total current assets and 30% of total assets). *Inventory* is a common abbreviation for *merchandise inventory*, and the two terms are used interchangeably.
- *Prepaid expenses* (line 3) represent amounts paid in advance for advertisements, rent, insurance, and supplies. Prepaid expenses are current assets because J.Crew Group, Inc., will benefit from these expenditures in the next fiscal year. J.Crew owns $43 million in prepaid expenses and other current assets as of February 2, 2008.
- An asset always represents a future benefit.

The main categories of *long-term assets* are Property, Plant, and Equipment (also called **plant assets**, lines 5–7), and other assets (line 8). Long-term assets may also include intangibles and other investments that are expected to benefit the company for long periods of time.

- *Property, plant, and equipment (PP&E)* includes J.Crew Group, Inc.'s land, buildings, computers, store fixtures, and equipment. J.Crew reports PP&E on three lines. Line 5 shows the company's cost of PP&E, which is $305 million through February 2, 2008. Cost means the historical acquisition price of these assets to J.Crew. It does not mean that J.Crew could sell its PP&E for $305 million. After all, the company may have acquired the assets several years ago.
- Line 6 shows how much *accumulated depreciation* J.Crew has recorded on its PP&E. *Depreciation* reallocates an asset's cost from the balance sheet to expense in the income statement over time as the asset is used in producing revenue. Accumulated depreciation ($137 million) is the total amount of depreciation recorded on PP&E from acquisition (perhaps years ago) through the end of the most recent year. Thus, accumulated depreciation represents the used-up portion of the asset. We subtract accumulated depreciation from the cost of PP&E to determine its book value ($168 million on line 7).

- *Intangibles* are assets with no physical form, such as patents, trademarks, and goodwill. J.Crew doesn't own any of these assets.
- *Long-term investments* are those investments the company does not intend to sell within the next year. J.Crew doesn't own any long-term investments.
- *Other assets* (line 8) is a catchall category for assets that are difficult to classify. J.Crew owns about $34 million of these assets. For J.Crew Group, Inc., these primarily represent long-term tax benefits, due to differences between the way the company keeps its books for financial reporting purposes and the way it keeps its books for tax purposes.
- Overall, J.Crew Group, Inc., reports total assets of $535 million at February 2, 2008 (line 9).

Liabilities.　Liabilities are also divided into current and long-term categories. **Current liabilities** (lines 10–13) are debts payable within one year or within J.Crew's operating cycle if longer than a year. Chief among the current liabilities are Accounts payable, Federal and state income taxes payable, and other liabilities like short-term notes payable, and accrued salaries and wages payable. *Long-term liabilities* are payable after one year.

- *Accounts payable* (line 10) of $101 million represents amounts owed to J.Crew's vendors and suppliers for purchases of inventory.
- *Income taxes payable* are tax debts owed to the government. J.Crew owes $2 million of federal and state income taxes as of February 2, 2008 (line 12).
- *Short-term notes payable* are amounts that a company has promised to pay back within one year or less. J.Crew doesn't owe any of these as of February 2, 2008.
- *Other current liabilities* (line 11). Included in this $92 million are interest payable on borrowed money, accrued liabilities for salaries, utilities, and other expenses that J.Crew has not yet paid.
- At February 2, 2008, J.Crew's current liabilities total $195 million (line 13). J.Crew also owes $125 million in long-term liabilities (line 14). These liabilities include long-term debt and other payables due after one year.
- At the end of fiscal 2007, total liabilities are $395 million (line 16). This is high relative to total assets of $535 million (about 74% of line 9) and indicates a not-so-strong financial position.

Stockholders' Equity.　The accounting equation states that

$$\text{Assets} - \text{Liabilities} = \text{Owners' Equity}$$

The assets (resources) and the liabilities (debts) of J.Crew Group, Inc., are fairly easy to understand. Owners' equity is harder to pin down. Owners' equity is simple to calculate, but what does it *mean*?

J.Crew Group, Inc., calls its owners' equity *Stockholders' equity* (line 21), and this title is descriptive. Remember that a company's owners' equity represents the stockholders' ownership of the business's assets. J.Crew's equity consists of

- *Common Stock* (line 17), represented by shares issued to stockholders for about $1 million through February 2, 2008. This amount represents the face amount (par value) of the stock. Par value is an artificial amount set by the company for the stock. Par value is explained in Chapter 9.

- *Additional paid-in capital* (line 18) represents amounts of cash received on initial sale of the company's stock in excess of the par value. This amounts to about $553 million at February 2, 2008.

- *Retained earnings* at February 2, 2008, is negative, or a *deficit* of $411 million (line 19). A year earlier J.Crew Group, Inc., had a deficit of $508 million. We saw these figures on the statement of retained earnings in Exhibit 1-8 (line 6). Retained earnings' final resting place is the balance sheet.

Accounting Cycle Tutorial Balance Sheet Accounts

- J.Crew Group, Inc.'s stockholders' equity holds another item, Treasury Stock (line 20), which represents amounts paid by the company to repurchase its own stock. We will discuss the reasons for this in Chapter 9. For now, focus on the two main components of stockholders' equity: common stock and retained earnings.

- At February 2, 2008, J.Crew Group, Inc., has Total stockholders' equity of $140 million (line 21). We can now prove that J.Crew's total assets equal total liabilities and equity (amounts in millions):

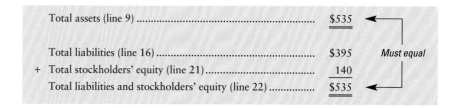

Total assets (line 9)	$535
Total liabilities (line 16)	$395
+ Total stockholders' equity (line 21)	140
Total liabilities and stockholders' equity (line 22)	$535

Must equal

The statement of cash flows is the fourth required financial statement.

THE STATEMENT OF CASH FLOWS MEASURES CASH RECEIPTS AND PAYMENTS

Companies engage in three basic types of activities:

1. **Operating activities**

2. **Investing activities**

3. **Financing activities**

The **statement of cash flows** reports cash flows under each of these activities. Think about the cash flows (receipts and payments) in each category:

- *Companies operate by selling goods and services to customers.* **Operating activities** result in net income or net loss, and they either increase or decrease cash. The income statement tells whether the company is profitable. The statement of cash flows reports whether operations increased cash. Operating activities are most important, and they should be the company's main source of cash. Continuing negative cash flow from operations can lead to bankruptcy.

- *Companies invest in long-term assets.* J.Crew Group, Inc., buys store fixtures and equipment, and when these assets wear out, the company sells them. Both purchases and sales of long-term assets are investing cash flows. Investing cash flows are the next most important after operations.

- *Companies need money for financing.* Financing includes both issuing stock and borrowing. J.Crew Group, Inc., issues stock to its shareholders and borrows from banks. These are cash receipts. The company may also pay loans and repurchase its own stock. These payments are financing cash flows.

Overview.   Each category of cash flows—operating, investing, and financing—either increases or decreases cash. In Exhibit 1-10, which shows J.Crew Group, Inc.'s Consolidated Statements of Cash Flows, operating activities provided cash of $168 million in fiscal 2007 (line 4). This signals strong cash flow from operations. 2007's investing activities (purchase of property, plant, and equipment) used cash of about $81 million (line 6). That signals expansion. Financing activities used another $45 million (line 14). J.Crew paid off some debt and also issued some stock during the year. On a statement of cash flows, cash receipts appear as positive amounts. Cash payments are negative and enclosed by parentheses.

EXHIBIT 1-10 | J.Crew Group, Inc., Consolidated Statements of Cash Flows

J.Crew Group, Inc.
Consolidated Statements of Cash Flows (adapted)

	Years Ended	
(In millions)	February 3, 2007	February 2, 2008
1 Cash flows from operating activities:		
2 Net income	$ 78	$ 97
3 Adjustments to reconcile to cash provided by operations	43	71
4 Net cash provided by operating activities	121	168
5 Cash flows from investing activities:		
6 Purchases of property, plant and equipment	(46)	(81)
7 Cash flows from financing activities:		
8 Costs incurred in connection with amended credit agreement		(1)
9 Repayments and redemption of long-term debt	(386)	(75)
10 Redemption of preferred stock	(358)	
11 Proceeds from issuance of long-term debt	276	
12 Proceeds from issuance of common stock	421	32
13 Repurchase of common stock		(1)
14 Net cash provided by (used in) financing activities	(47)	(45)
15 Increase in cash and cash equivalents	28	42
16 Cash and cash equivalents, beginning of year	61	89
17 Cash and cash equivalents, end of year	$ 89	$131

Overall, J.Crew's cash increased by about $42 million during 2007 (line 15) and ended the year at $131 million (line 17). Trace ending cash back to the balance sheet in Exhibit 1-9 (line 1). Cash links the statement of cash flows to the balance sheet. You've just performed more financial-statement analysis!

Let's now summarize the relationships that link the financial statements.

RELATIONSHIPS AMONG THE FINANCIAL STATEMENTS

OBJECTIVE

5 **Use** information in financial statements to make business decisions, which are informed by economic, legal, and ethical guidelines

Exhibit 1-11 summarizes the relationships among the financial statements of ABC Company for 2010. These statements are summarized with all amounts assumed for the illustration. Study the exhibit carefully because these relationships apply to all organizations. Specifically, note the following:

1. The income statement for the year ended December 31, 2010
   a. Reports revenues and expenses of the year. Revenues and expenses are reported *only* on the income statement.
   b. Reports net income if total revenues exceed total expenses. If expenses exceed revenues, there is a net loss.

2. The statement of retained earnings for the year ended December 31, 2010
   a. Opens with the beginning retained earnings balance.
   b. Adds net income (or subtracts net loss). Net income comes directly from the income statement (arrow ① in Exhibit 1-11).
   c. Subtracts dividends.
   d. Reports the retained earnings balance at the end of the year.

3. The balance sheet at December 31, 2010, end of the accounting year
   a. Reports assets, liabilities, and stockholders' equity at the end of the year. Only the balance sheet reports assets and liabilities.
   b. Reports that assets equal the sum of liabilities plus stockholders' equity. This balancing feature follows the accounting equation and gives the balance sheet its name.
   c. Reports retained earnings, which comes from the statement of retained earnings (arrow ② in Exhibit 1-11).

4. The statement of cash flows for the year ended December 31, 2010
   a. Reports cash flows from operating, investing, and financing activities. Each category results in net cash provided (an increase) or used (a decrease).
   b. Reports whether cash increased (or decreased) during the year. The statement shows the ending cash balance, as reported on the balance sheet (arrow ③ in Exhibit 1-11).

Accounting Cycle Tutorial Glossary

Accounting Cycle Tutorial Glossary Quiz

EXHIBIT 1-11 | **Relationships Among the Financial Statements**

ABC Company
Income Statement
Year Ended December 31, 2010

Revenues....................	$700,000
Expenses	670,000
Net income................	$ 30,000

①

ABC Company
Statement of Retained Earnings
Year Ended December 31, 2010

Beginning retained earnings................	$180,000
Net income...	30,000
Cash dividends...................................	(10,000)
Ending retained earnings....................	$200,000

②

ABC Company
Balance Sheet
December 31, 2010

Assets
Cash	$ 35,000
All other assets...	265,000
Total assets	$300,000

Liabilities
Total liabilities..	$120,000

Stockholders' Equity
Common stock	40,000
Retained earnings	200,000
Other equity..	(60,000)
Total stockholders' equity....................................	180,000
Total liabilities and stockholders' equity...............	$300,000

③

ABC Company
Statement of Cash Flows
Year Ended December 31, 2010

Net cash provided by operating activities...............	$ 90,000
Net cash used for investing activities.......................	(100,000)
Net cash provided by financing activities	40,000
Net increase in cash...	30,000
Cash balance, December 31, 2009	5,000
Cash balance, December 31, 2010	$ 35,000

$ac \atop t$

Accounting Cycle Tutorial Applications
Cottage Kitchen

$ac \atop t$

Accounting Cycle Tutorial Applications
Marwood Homes

DECISION GUIDELINES

IN EVALUATING A COMPANY, WHAT DO DECISION MAKERS LOOK FOR?

These Decision Guidelines illustrate how people use financial statements. Decision Guidelines appear throughout the book to show how accounting information aids decision making.

Suppose you are considering an investment in J.Crew Group, Inc., stock. How do you proceed? Where do you get the information you need? What do you look for?

Decision	Guidelines
1. Can the company sell its products?	1. Sales revenue on the income statement. Are sales growing or falling?
2. What are the main income measures to watch for trends?	2. a. Gross profit (Sales – Cost of goods sold) b. Operating income (Gross profit – Operating expenses) c. Net income (bottom line of the income statement) All three income measures should be increasing over time.
3. What percentage of sales revenue ends up as profit?	3. Divide net income by sales revenue. Examine the trend of the net income percentage from year to year.
4. Can the company collect its receivables?	4. From the balance sheet, compare the percentage increase in accounts receivable to the percentage increase in sales. If receivables are growing much faster than sales, collections may be too slow, and a cash shortage may result.
5. Can the company pay its a. Current liabilities? b. Current and long-term liabilities?	5. From the balance sheet, compare a. Current assets to current liabilities. Current assets should be somewhat greater than current liabilities. b. Total assets to total liabilities. Total assets must be somewhat greater than total liabilities.
6. Where is the company's cash coming from? How is cash being used?	6. On the cash-flows statement, operating activities should provide the bulk of the company's cash during most years. Otherwise, the business will fail. Examine investing cash flows to see if the company is purchasing long-term assets—property, plant, and equipment and intangibles (this signals growth).

ETHICS IN BUSINESS AND ACCOUNTING DECISIONS

Good business requires decision making, which in turn requires the exercise of good judgment, both at the individual and corporate levels. For example, you may work for or eventually run a company like **Starbucks** that has decided to devote 5 cents from every cup of coffee sold to helping save the lives of AIDS victims in Africa. Can that be profitable in the long run?

Perhaps as an accountant, you may have to decide whether to record a $50,000 expenditure for a piece of equipment as an asset on the balance sheet or an expense on the income statement. Alternatively, as a sales manager for a company like IBM, you may have to decide whether $25 million of goods and services delivered to customers in 2010 would be more appropriately recorded as revenue in 2010 or 2011.

As mentioned earlier, the transition from U.S. GAAP to IFRS *will require increased emphasis on judgment*, because IFRS contains fewer rules than U.S. GAAP. Depending on the type of business, the facts and circumstances surrounding accounting decisions may not always make them clear cut, and yet the decision may determine whether the company shows a profit or a loss in a particular period! What are the factors that influence business and accounting decisions, and how should these factors be weighed? Generally, three factors influence business and accounting decisions: **economic, legal, and ethical**.

The *economic* factor states that the decision being made should *maximize the economic benefits* to the decision maker. Based on most economic theory, every rational person faced with a decision will choose the course of action that maximizes his or her own welfare, without regard to how that decision impacts others. In summary, the combined outcome of each person acting in his or her own self-interest will maximize the benefits to society as a whole.

The *legal* factor is based on the proposition that free societies are governed by laws. Laws are written to provide clarity and to prevent abuse of the rights of individuals or society. Democratically enacted laws both contain and express society's collective moral standards. Legal analysis involves applying the relevant laws to each decision, and then choosing the action that complies with those laws. A complicating factor for a global business may be that what is legal in one country might not be legal in another. In that case, it is usually best to abide by the laws of the most restrictive country.

The *ethical* factor recognizes that while certain actions might be both economically profitable and legal, they may still not be right. Therefore, most companies, and many individuals, have established standards for themselves to enforce a higher level of conduct than that imposed by law. These standards govern how we treat others and the way we restrain our selfish desires. This behavior and its underlying beliefs are the essence of ethics. **Ethics** are shaped by our cultural, socioeconomic, and religious backgrounds. An *ethical analysis* is needed to guide judgment for making decisions.

The decision rule in an ethical analysis is to choose the action that fulfills ethical duties—responsibilities of the members of society to each other. The challenge in an ethical analysis is to identify specific ethical duties and stakeholders to whom you owe these duties. As with legal issues, a complicating factor in making global ethical decisions may be that what is considered ethical in one country is not considered ethical in another.

Among the questions you may ask in making an ethical analysis are:

- *Which options are most honest, open, and truthful?*

- *Which options are most kind, compassionate, and build a sense of community?*

- *Which options create the greatest good for the greatest number of stakeholders?*

- *Which options result in treating others as I would want to be treated?*

Ethical training starts at home and continues throughout our lives. It is reinforced by the teaching that we receive in our church, synagogue, or mosque; the schools we attend; and by the persons and companies we associate with.

A thorough understanding of ethics requires more study than we can accomplish in this book. However, remember that, when making accounting decisions, do not check your ethics at the door!

DECISION GUIDELINES

DECISION FRAMEWORK FOR MAKING ETHICAL JUDGMENTS

Weighing tough ethical judgments in business and accounting requires a decision framework. Answering the following four questions will guide you through tough decisions:

Decision	Guidelines
1. What is the issue?	1. The issue will usually deal with making a judgment about an accounting measurement or disclosure that results in economic consequences, often to numerous parties.
2. Who are the stakeholders, and what are the consequences of the decision to each?	2. Stakeholders are anyone who might be impacted by the decision—you, your company, and potential users of the information (investors, creditors, regulatory agencies). Consequences can be economic, legal, or ethical in nature.
3. Weigh the alternatives.	3. Analyze the impact of the decision on all stakeholders, using economic, legal, and ethical criteria. Ask "Who will be helped or hurt, whose rights will be exercised or denied, and in what way?"
4. Make the decision and be prepared to deal with the consequences.	4. Exercise the courage to either defend the decision or to change it, depending on its positive or negative impact. How does your decision make you feel afterward?

To simplify, we might ask three questions:

1. Is the action legal? If not, steer clear, unless you want to go to jail or pay monetary damages to injured parties. If the action is legal, go on to questions (2) and (3).
2. Who will be affected by the decision and how? Be as thorough about this analysis as possible, and analyze it from all three standpoints (economic, legal, and ethical).
3. How will this decision make me feel afterward? How would it make me feel if my family reads about it in the newspaper?

In later chapters throughout the book, we will apply this model to different accounting decisions.

In the business setting, ethics work best when modeled "from the top." Ethisphere Institute (www.ethisphere.com) has recently established the Business Ethics Leadership Alliance (BELA), aimed at "reestablishing ethics as the foundation of everyday business practices." BELA members agree to embrace and uphold four core values that incorporate ethics and integrity into all their practices: (1) Legal compliance; (2) Transparency; (3) Conflict identification; and (4) Accountability. Each year, Ethisphere Institute publishes a list of the World's Most Ethical Companies. The 2008 list includes corporations like UPS, Starbucks, McDonald's, The Gap, Target, and Pearson (the publisher of this textbook). Excerpts from many of these companies' financial statements will be featured in later chapters of this text. As you begin to make your decisions about future employers, put these companies on your list! It's easier to act ethically when those you work for recognize the importance of ethics in business practices. These companies have learned from experience that, in the long run, ethical conduct pays big rewards, not only socially, morally, and spiritually, but economically as well!

END-OF-CHAPTER SUMMARY PROBLEM

ShineBrite Car Wash, Inc., began operations on April 1, 2010. During April, the business provided services for customers. It is now April 30, and investors wonder how well ShineBrite performed during its first month. The investors also want to know the company's financial position at the end of April and its cash flows during the month.

The following data are listed in alphabetical order. Prepare the ShineBrite financial statements at the end of April 2010.

Accounts payable	$ 1,800	Land	$18,000
Accounts receivable	2,000	Payments of cash:	
Adjustments to reconcile net		Acquisition of land	40,000
income to net cash provided		Dividends	2,100
by operating activities	(3,900)	Rent expense	1,100
Cash balance at beginning of April	0	Retained earnings at beginning	
Cash balance at end of April	?	of April	0
Cash receipts:		Retained earnings at end of April	?
Issuance (sale) of stock to owners	50,000	Salary expense	1,200
Sale of land	22,000	Service revenue	10,000
Common stock	50,000	Supplies	3,700
		Utilities expense	400

Requirements

1. Prepare the income statement, the statement of retained earnings, and the statement of cash flows for the month ended April 30, 2010, and the balance sheet at April 30, 2010. Draw arrows linking the statements.
2. Answer the following questions:
   a. How well did ShineBrite perform during its first month of operations?
   b. Where does ShineBrite stand financially at the end of April?

Answers

Requirement 1

Financial Statements of ShineBrite Car Wash, Inc.

ShineBrite Car Wash, Inc.
Income Statement
Month Ended April 30, 2010

Revenue:		
Service revenue		$10,000
Expenses:		
Salary expense	$1,200	
Rent expense	1,100	
Utilities expense	400	
Total expenses		2,700
Net income		$ 7,300

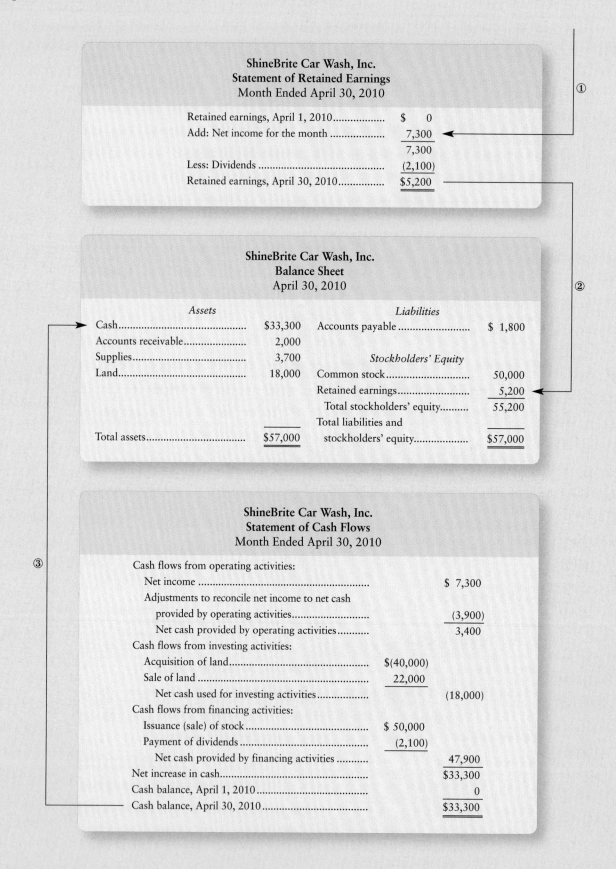

①

ShineBrite Car Wash, Inc.
Statement of Retained Earnings
Month Ended April 30, 2010

Retained earnings, April 1, 2010..................	$ 0
Add: Net income for the month	7,300
	7,300
Less: Dividends	(2,100)
Retained earnings, April 30, 2010...............	$5,200

②

ShineBrite Car Wash, Inc.
Balance Sheet
April 30, 2010

Assets		Liabilities	
Cash..	$33,300	Accounts payable	$ 1,800
Accounts receivable.....................	2,000		
Supplies.......................................	3,700	*Stockholders' Equity*	
Land..	18,000	Common stock..............................	50,000
		Retained earnings.........................	5,200
		Total stockholders' equity..........	55,200
		Total liabilities and	
Total assets..................................	$57,000	stockholders' equity..................	$57,000

③

ShineBrite Car Wash, Inc.
Statement of Cash Flows
Month Ended April 30, 2010

Cash flows from operating activities:		
Net income		$ 7,300
Adjustments to reconcile net income to net cash		
provided by operating activities............................		(3,900)
Net cash provided by operating activities...........		3,400
Cash flows from investing activities:		
Acquisition of land..	$(40,000)	
Sale of land	22,000	
Net cash used for investing activities.................		(18,000)
Cash flows from financing activities:		
Issuance (sale) of stock	$ 50,000	
Payment of dividends	(2,100)	
Net cash provided by financing activities		47,900
Net increase in cash...		$33,300
Cash balance, April 1, 2010.......................................		0
Cash balance, April 30, 2010......................................		$33,300

Requirement 2

   a. ShineBrite performed rather well in April. Net income was $7,300—very good in relation to service revenue of $10,000. The company was able to pay cash dividends of $2,100.

   b. ShineBrite ended April with cash of $33,300. Total assets of $57,000 far exceed total liabilities of $1,800. Stockholders' equity of $55,200 provides a good cushion for borrowing. The business's financial position at April 30, 2010, is strong.

REVIEW THE FINANCIAL STATEMENTS

Quick Check (Answers are given on page 58.)

1. All of the following statements are true except one. Which statement is false?
   a. The organization that formulates generally accepted accounting principles is the Financial Accounting Standards Board.
   b. A proprietorship is a business with several owners.
   c. Professional accountants are held to a high standard of ethical conduct.
   d. Bookkeeping is only a part of accounting.

2. The valuation of assets on the balance sheet is generally based on:
   a. current fair market value as established by independent appraisers.
   b. historical cost.
   c. selling price.
   d. what it would cost to replace the asset.

3. The accounting equation can be expressed as:
   a. Assets = Liabilities – Owners' Equity
   b. Assets + Liabilities = Owners' Equity
   c. Assets – Liabilities = Owners' Equity
   d. Owners' Equity - Assets = Liabilities

4. The nature of an asset is best described as:
   a. an economic resource that's expected to benefit future operations.
   b. something with physical form that's valued at cost in the accounting records.
   c. something owned by a business that has a ready market value.
   d. an economic resource representing cash or the right to receive cash in the future.

5. Which financial statement covers a period of time?
   a. Balance sheet   c. Statement of cash flows
   b. Income statement   d. Both b and c

6. How would net income be most likely to affect the accounting equation?
   a. Increase assets and increase liabilities
   b. Decrease assets and decrease liabilities
   c. Increase liabilities and decrease stockholders' equity
   d. Increase assets and increase stockholders' equity

7. During the year, EcoWash, Inc., has $120,000 in revenues, $50,000 in expenses, and $4,000 in dividend payments. Stockholders' equity changed by:
   a. +$66,000   c. –$66,000
   b. +$70,000   d. +$74,000

8. EcoWash in question 7 had net income (or net loss) of
   a. net loss of $50,000.
   c. net income of $66,000.
   b. net income of $70,000.
   d. net income of $120,000.

9. Rochester Corporation holds cash of $11,000 and owes $27,000 on accounts payable. Rochester has accounts receivable of $40,000, inventory of $34,000, and land that cost $55,000. How much are Rochester's total assets and liabilities?

	Total assets	Liabilities
a.	$129,000	$27,000
b.	$27,000	$140,000
c.	$140,000	$27,000
d.	$140,000	$93,000

10. Which item(s) is (are) reported on the balance sheet?
    a. Inventory
    c. Retained earnings
    b. Accounts payable
    d. All of the above

11. During the year, McKenna Company's stockholders' equity increased from $38,000 to $50,000. McKenna earned net income of $18,000. How much in dividends did McKenna declare during the year?
    a. $-0-
    c. $12,000
    b. $6,000
    d. $7,000

12. Javis Company had total assets of $340,000 and total stockholders' equity of $130,000 at the beginning of the year. During the year assets increased by $70,000 and liabilities increased by $25,000. Stockholders' equity at the end of the year is:
    a. $95,000.
    c. $200,000.
    b. $175,000.
    d. $155,000.

13. Which of the following is a true statement about International Financial Reporting Standards?
    a. They are more exact (contain more rules) than U.S. generally accepted accounting principles.
    b. They are not being applied anywhere in the world yet, but soon will be.
    c. They are converging gradually with U.S. standards.
    d. They are not needed for U.S. businesses since the United States already has the strongest accounting standards in the world.

14. Which of the following is the most accurate statement regarding ethics as applied to decision making in accounting?
    a. Ethics involves making difficult choices under pressure, and should be kept in mind in making every decision, including those involving accounting.
    b. Ethics has no place in accounting, since accounting deals purely with numbers.
    c. It is impossible to learn ethical decision making, since it is just something you decide to do or not to do.
    d. Ethics is becoming less and less important as a field of study in business.

Accounting Vocabulary

account payable (p. 14) A liability backed by the general reputation and credit standing of the debtor.

accounting (p. 3) The information system that measures business activities, processes that information into reports and financial statements, and communicates the results to decision makers.

accounting equation (p. 13) The most basic tool of accounting: Assets = Liabilities + Owners' Equity.

asset (p. 13) An economic resource that is expected to be of benefit in the future.

balance sheet (p. 20) List of an entity's assets, liabilities, and owners' equity as of a specific date. Also called the *statement of financial position.*

board of directors (p. 6) Group elected by the stockholders to set policy for a corporation and to appoint its officers.

capital (p. 13) Another name for the *owners' equity* of a business.

cash (p. 14) Money and any medium of exchange that a bank accepts at face value.

common stock (p. 14) The most basic form of capital stock.

continuity assumption (p. 9) See going-concern assumption.

corporation (p. 6) A business owned by stockholders. A corporation is a legal entity, an "artificial person" in the eyes of the law.

current asset (p. 21) An asset that is expected to be converted to cash, sold, or consumed during the next 12 months, or within the business's normal operating cycle if longer than a year.

current liability (p. 23) A debt due to be paid within one year or within the entity's operating cycle if the cycle is longer than a year.

deficit (p. 19) Negative balance in retained earnings caused by net losses over a period of years.

dividends (p. 15) Distributions (usually cash) by a corporation to its stockholders.

entity (p. 8) An organization or a section of an organization that, for accounting purposes, stands apart from other organizations and individuals as a separate economic unit.

ethics (p. 29) Standards of right and wrong that transcend economic and legal boundaries. Ethical standards deal with the way we treat others and restrain our own actions because of the desires, expectations, or rights of others, or with our obligations to them.

expenses (p. 14) Decrease in retained earnings that results from operations; the cost of doing business; opposite of revenues.

fair value (p. 10) The amount that a business could sell an asset for, or the amount that a business could pay to settle a liability.

financial accounting (p. 4) The branch of accounting that provides information to people outside the firm.

financial statements (p. 2) Business documents that report financial information about a business entity to decision makers.

financing activities (p. 24) Activities that obtain from investors and creditors the cash needed to launch and sustain the business; a section of the statement of cash flows.

fixed assets (p. 14) Another name for *property, plant, and equipment.*

generally accepted accounting principles (GAAP) (p. 7) Accounting guidelines, formulated by the Financial Accounting Standards Board, that govern how accounting is practiced.

going-concern assumption (p. 9) Holds that the entity will remain in operation for the foreseeable future.

historical cost principle (p. 9) Principle that states that assets and services should be recorded at their actual cost.

income statement (p. 17) A financial statement listing an entity's revenues, expenses, and net income or net loss for a specific period. Also called the *statement of operations.*

International Financial Reporting Standards (IFRS) (p. 7) Accounting guidelines, formulated by the International Accounting Standards Board (IASB). By 2014, U.S. GAAP is expected to be harmonized with IFRS. At that time, U.S. companies are expected to adopt these principles for their financial statements, so that they can be compared with those of companies from other countries.

investing activities (p. 24) Activities that increase or decrease the long-term assets available to the business; a section of the statement of cash flows.

liability (p. 13) An economic obligation (a debt) payable to an individual or an organization outside the business.

limited liability company (p. 6) A business organization in which the business (not the owner) is liable for the company's debts.

long-term debt (p. 14) A liability that falls due beyond one year from the date of the financial statements.

management accounting (p. 5) The branch of accounting that generates information for the internal decision makers of a business, such as top executives.

merchandise inventory (p. 14) The merchandise that a company sells to customers, also called *inventory.*

net earnings (p. 15) Another name for *net income.*

net income (p. 15) Excess of total revenues over total expenses. Also called *net earnings* or *net profit.*

net loss (p. 15) Excess of total expenses over total revenues.

net profit (p. 15) Another name for *net income.*

note payable (p. 14) A liability evidenced by a written promise to make a future payment.

operating activities (p. 24) Activities that create revenue or expense in the entity's major line of business; a section of the statement of cash flows. Operating activities affect the income statement.

owners' equity (p. 13) The claim of the owners of a business to the assets of the business. Also called *capital, stockholders' equity,* or *net assets.*

paid-in capital (p. 14) The amount of stockholders' equity that stockholders have contributed to the corporation. Also called *contributed capital.*

partnership (p. 5) An association of two or more persons who co-own a business for profit.

plant assets (p. 22) Another name for *property, plant, and equipment*.

property, plant, and equipment (p. 14) Long-lived assets, such as land, buildings, and equipment, used in the operation of the business. Also called *plant assets* or *fixed assets*.

proprietorship (p. 5) A business with a single owner.

retained earnings (p. 14) The amount of stockholders' equity that the corporation has earned through profitable operation and has not given back to stockholders.

revenues (p. 14) Increase in retained earnings from delivering goods or services to customers or clients.

shareholder (p. 6) Another name for *stockholder*.

stable-monetary-unit assumption (p. 10) The reason for ignoring the effect of inflation in the accounting records, based on the assumption that the dollar's purchasing power is relatively stable.

statement of cash flows (p. 24) Reports cash receipts and cash payments classified according to the entity's major activities: operating, investing, and financing.

statement of financial position (p. 20) Another name for the *balance sheet*.

statement of operations (p. 17) Another name for the *income statement*.

statement of retained earnings (p. 19) Summary of the changes in the retained earnings of a corporation during a specific period.

stock (p. 6) Shares into which the owners' equity of a corporation is divided.

stockholder (p. 6) A person who owns stock in a corporation. Also called a *shareholder*.

stockholders' equity (p. 13) The stockholders' ownership interest in the assets of a corporation.

ASSESS YOUR PROGRESS

Short Exercises

S1-1 (*Learning Objective 3: Using the accounting equation*) Suppose you manage a Pizza Sauce restaurant. Identify the missing amount for each situation:

	Total Assets	=	Total Liabilities	+	Stockholders' Equity
a.	$?		$130,000		$210,000
b.	250,000		70,000		?
c.	190,000		?		80,000

S1-2 (*Learning Objective 5: Making ethical judgments*) Good business and accounting practices require the exercise of good judgment. How should ethics be incorporated into making accounting judgments? Why is ethics important?

S1-3 (*Learning Objective 1: Organizing a business*) A Healthy Planet, Inc., needs funds, and Mary Barry, the president, has asked you to consider investing in the business. Answer the following questions about the different ways that Barry might organize the business. Explain each answer.

    a. What forms of organization will enable the owners of A Healthy Planet to limit their risk of loss to the amounts they have invested in the business?

    b. What form of business organization will give Barry the most freedom to manage the business as she wishes?

    c. What form of organization will give creditors the maximum protection in the event that A Healthy Planet fails and cannot pay its debts?

S1-4 (*Learning Objective 2: Applying accounting assumptions*) Daniel Newman is chairman of the board of Quality Food Brands, Inc. Suppose Mr. Newman has just founded Quality Food Brands, and assume that he treats his home and other personal assets as part of Quality Food Brands. Answer these questions about the evaluation of Quality Food Brands, Inc.

    1. Which accounting assumption governs this situation?

    2. How can the proper application of this accounting concept give Newman and others a realistic view of Quality Food Brands, Inc.? Explain in detail.

S1-5 (*Learning Objective 2: Applying accounting concepts, assumptions, and principles*)
Identify the accounting concept, assumption or principle that best applies to each of the following situations:

a. Arby's, the restaurant chain, sold a store location to McDonald's. How can Arby's determine the sale price of the store—by a professional appraisal, Arby's cost, or the amount actually received from the sale?

b. Inflation has been around 6.25% for some time. Ridgeview Realtors is considering measuring its land values in inflation-adjusted amounts.

c. Honda wants to determine which division of the company—Honda or Acura—is more profitable.

d. You get an especially good buy on a television, paying only $1,100 for a television that normally costs $1,900. What is your accounting value for this television?

S1-6 (*Learning Objective 3: Using the accounting equation*)

1. Use the accounting equation to show how to determine the amount of a company's owners' equity. How would your answer change if you were analyzing your own household or a single Denny's restaurant?

2. If you know the assets and the owners' equity of a business, how can you measure its liabilities? Give the equation.

S1-7 (*Learning Objective 1: Defining key accounting terms*) Accounting definitions are precise, and you must understand the vocabulary to properly use accounting. Sharpen your understanding of key terms by answering the following questions:

1. How do the assets and owners' equity of Microsoft Corporation differ from each other? Which one (assets or owners' equity) must be at least as large as the other? Which one can be smaller than the other?

2. How are Microsoft's liabilities and owners' equity similar? Different?

S1-8 (*Learning Objective 1: Classifying assets, liabilities, and owners' equity*) Consider Target, a large retailer. Classify the following items as an Asset (A), a Liability (L), or Stockholders' Equity (S) for Target:

a. ____ Accounts payable
b. ____ Common stock
c. ____ Supplies
d. ____ Retained earnings
e. ____ Land
f. ____ Prepaid expenses

g. ____ Accounts receivable
h. ____ Long-term debt
i. ____ Merchandise inventory
j. ____ Notes payable
k. ____ Expenses payable
l. ____ Equipment

S1-9 (*Learning Objectives 1, 4: Using accounting vocabulary; using the income statement*)

1. Identify the two basic categories of items on an income statement.

2. What do we call the bottom line of the income statement?

S1-10 (*Learning Objective 4: Preparing an income statement*) Call Anywhere Wireless, Inc., began 2010 with total assets of $130 million and ended 2010 with assets of $165 million. During 2010 Call Anywhere earned revenues of $94 million and had expenses of $23 million. Call Anywhere paid dividends of $13 million in 2010. Prepare the company's income statement for the year ended December 31, 2010, complete with an appropriate heading.

S1-11 (*Learning Objective 4: Preparing a statement of retained earnings*) Roam Corp. began 2010 with retained earnings of $210 million. Revenues during the year were $380 million and expenses totaled $250 million. Roam declared dividends of $43 million. What was the company's ending balance of retained earnings? To answer this question, prepare Roam's statement of retained earnings for the year ended December 31, 2010, complete with its proper heading.

S1-12 (*Learning Objective 4: Preparing a balance sheet*) At December 31, 2010, Tommer Products has cash of $12,000, receivables of $5,000, and inventory of $42,000. The company's equipment totals $82,000. Tommer owes accounts payable of $17,000, and long-term notes payable of $78,000. Common stock is $14,800.

Prepare Tommer's balance sheet at December 31, 2010, complete with its proper heading. Use the accounting equation to compute retained earnings.

S1-13 (*Learning Objective 4: Preparing a statement of cash flows*) Lanos Medical, Inc., ended 2009 with cash of $25,000. During 2010, Lanos earned net income of $95,000 and had adjustments to reconcile net income to net cash provided by operations totaling $20,000 (this is a negative amount).

Lanos paid $35,000 to purchase equipment during 2010. During 2010, the company paid dividends of $15,000.

Prepare Lanos' statement of cash flows for the year ended December 31, 2010, complete with its proper heading.

S1-14 (*Learning Objectives 1, 4: Using accounting vocabulary; identifying items with the appropriate financial statement*) Suppose you are analyzing the financial statements of Murphy Radiology, Inc. Identify each item with its appropriate financial statement, using the following abbreviations: Income statement (IS), Statement of retained earnings (SRE), Balance sheet (BS), and Statement of cash flows (SCF). Three items appear on two financial statements, and one item shows up on three statements.

a. ____ Dividends
b. ____ Salary expense
c. ____ Inventory
d. ____ Sales revenue
e. ____ Retained earnings
f. ____ Net cash provided by operating activities
g. ____ Net income

h. ____ Cash
i. ____ Net cash used for financing activities
j. ____ Accounts payable
k. ____ Common stock
l. ____ Interest revenue
m. ____ Long-term debt
n. ____ Increase or decrease in cash

S1-15 (*Learning Objectives 2, 4: Applying accounting concepts, assumptions and principles to explain business activity*) Apply your understanding of the relationships among the financial statements to answer these questions.

a. How can a business earn large profits but have a small balance of retained earnings?
b. Give two reasons why a business can have a steady stream of net income over a six-year period and still experience a cash shortage.
c. If you could pick a single source of cash for your business, what would it be? Why?
d. How can a business lose money several years in a row and still have plenty of cash?

Exercises

All of the A and B exercises can be found within MyAccountingLab, an online homework and practice environment. Your instructor may ask you to complete these exercises using MyAccountingLab.

(Group A)

E1-16A (*Learning Objective 3, 4: Using the accounting equation; evaluating business operations*) Compute the missing amount in the accounting equation for each company (amounts in billions):

	Assets	Liabilities	Owners' Equity
Fresh Produce	$?	$ 9	$17
Hudson Bank	29	?	15
Pet Lovers	21	10	?

Which company appears to have the strongest financial position? Explain your reasoning.

E1-17A (*Learning Objectives 3, 4: Using the accounting equation; evaluating business operations*)   Hombran Doughnuts has current assets of $290 million; property, plant, and equipment of $490 million; and other assets totaling $150 million. Current liabilities are $150 million and long-term liabilities total $310 million.

❙ Requirements

1. Use these data to write Hombran Doughnuts' accounting equation.
2. How much in resources does Hombran have to work with?
3. How much does Hombran owe creditors?
4. How much of the company's assets do the Hombran stockholders actually own?

E1-18A (*Learning Objectives 3, 4: Using the accounting equation; evaluating business operations*)   Nelson, Inc.'s comparative balance sheet at January 31, 2011, and 2010, reports (in millions):

	2011	2010
Total assets	$39	$31
Total liabilities	10	9

❙ Requirements

Three situations about Nelson's issuance of stock and payment of dividends during the year ended January 31, 2011, follow. For each situation, use the accounting equation and the statement of retained earnings to compute the amount of Nelson's net income or net loss during the year ended January 31, 2011.

1. Nelson issued $11 million of stock and paid no dividends.
2. Nelson issued no stock but paid dividends of $11 million.
3. Nelson issued $55 million of stock and paid dividends of $32 million.

E1-19A (*Learning Objective 3: Using the accounting equation*) Answer these questions about two companies.

1. Clay, Inc., began the year with total liabilities of $50,000 and total stockholders' equity of $80,000. During the year, total assets increased by 35%. How much are total assets at the end of the year?
2. EastWest Airlines Ltd. began the year with total assets of $100,000 and total liabilities of $7,000. Net income for the year was $25,000, and dividends were zero. How much is stockholders' equity at the end of the year?

E1-20A (*Learning Objectives 4, 5: Evaluating business operations; making business decisions*) Assume Facebook is expanding into Ireland. The company must decide where to locate and how to finance the expansion. Identify the financial statement where these decision makers can find the following information about Facebook, Inc. In some cases, more than one statement will report the needed data.

a. Common stock
b. Income tax payable
c. Dividends
d. Income tax expense
e. Ending balance of retained earnings
f. Total assets
g. Long-term debt
h. Revenue

i. Cash spent to acquire the building
j. Selling, general, and administrative expenses
k. Adjustments to reconcile net income to net cash provided by operations
l. Ending cash balance
m. Current liabilities
n. Net income

■ spreadsheet

E1-21A (*Learning Objectives 3, 4: Using the accounting equation; preparing a balance sheet*) Amounts of the assets and liabilities of Ellen Samuel Banking Company, as of January 31, 2010, are given as follows. Also included are revenue and expense figures for the year ended on that date (amounts in millions):

Total revenue	$ 37.8	Investment assets	$169.6
Receivables	0.9	Property and equipment, net	1.9
Current liabilities	151.1	Other expenses	6.9
Common stock	14	Retained earnings, beginning	8.6
Interest expense	0.8	Retained earnings, ending	?
Salary and other employee expenses	17.7	Cash	2.1
Long-term liabilities	2.8	Other assets	14.4

❙ Requirement

1. Prepare the balance sheet of Ellen Samuel Banking Company at January 31, 2010. Use the accounting equation to compute ending retained earnings.

■ spreadsheet

E1-22A (*Learning Objective 4: Preparing an income statement and a statement of retained earnings*) This exercise should be used with Exercise 1-21A. Refer to the data of Ellen Samuel Banking Company in Exercise 1-21A.

❙ Requirements

1. Prepare the income statement of Ellen Samuel Banking Company, for the year ended January 31, 2010.
2. What amount of dividends did Ellen Samuel declare during the year ended January 31, 2010? Hint: Prepare a statement of retained earnings.

E1-23A (*Learning Objective 4: Preparing a statement of cash flows*) Lucky, Inc., began 2010 with $87,000 in cash. During 2010, Lucky earned net income of $410,000, and adjustments to reconcile net income to net cash provided by operations totaled $70,000, a positive amount. Investing activities used cash of $420,000, and financing activities provided cash of $72,000. Lucky ended 2010 with total assets of $260,000 and total liabilities of $115,000.

❙ Requirement

1. Prepare Lucky, Inc.'s statement of cash flows for the year ended December 31, 2010. Identify the data items given that do not appear on the statement of cash flows. Also identify the financial statement that reports the unused items.

E1-24A (*Learning Objective 4: Preparing an income statement and a statement of retained earnings*) Assume an Earl Copy Center ended the month of July 2010 with these data:

Payments of cash:			
Acquisition of equipment	$420,000	Cash balance, June 30, 2010	$ 0
Dividends	4,800	Cash balance, July 31, 2010	10,900
Retained earnings		Cash receipts:	
June 30, 2010	0	Issuance (sale) of stock	
Retained earnings		to owners	69,500
July 31, 2010	?	Rent expense	2,200
Utilities expense	10,000	Common stock	69,500
Adjustments to reconcile		Equipment	420,000
net income to net cash		Office supplies	14,800
provided by operations	2,200	Accounts payable	17,000
Salary expense	167,000	Service revenue	543,200

▮ Requirement

1. Prepare the income statement and the statement of retained earnings of Earl Copy Center, Inc., for the month ended July 31, 2010.

E1-25A (*Learning Objective 4: Preparing a balance sheet*) Refer to the data in Exercise 1-24A.

▮ Requirement

1. Prepare the balance sheet of Earl Copy Center, Inc., for July 31, 2010.

E1-26A (*Learning Objective 4: Preparing a statement of cash flows*) Refer to the data in Exercises 1-24A and 1-25A.

▮ Requirement

1. Prepare the statement of cash flows of Earl Copy Center, Inc., for the month ended July 31, 2010. Also explain the relationship among income statement, statement of retained earnings, balance sheet, and statement of cash flows.

E1-27A (*Learning Objectives 4, 5: Evaluating a business; advising a business*) This exercise should be used in conjunction with Exercises 1-24A through 1-26A.

<u>**writing assignment ▮**</u>

The owner of Earl Copy Center seeks your advice as to whether he should cease operations or continue the business. Complete the report giving him your opinion of net income, dividends, financial position, and cash flows during his first month of operations. Cite specifics from the financial statements to support your opinion. Conclude your memo with advice on whether to stay in business or cease operations.

(Group B)

E1-28B (*Learning Objectives 3, 4: Using the accounting equation; evaluating business operations*) Compute the missing amount in the accounting equation for each company (amounts in billions):

	Assets	Liabilities	Owners' Equity
DJ Video Rentals	$?	$ 8	$18
Ernie's Bank	34	?	14
Hudson Gift and Cards	20	12	?

Which company appears to have the strongest financial position? Explain your reasoning.

E1-29B (*Learning Objectives 3, 4: Using the accounting equation; evaluating business operations*) Tinman Doughnuts has current assets of $270 million; property, plant, and equipment of $470 million; and other assets totaling $110 million. Current liabilities are $110 million and long-term liabilities total $370 million.

▮ Requirements

1. Use these data to write Tinman's accounting equation.
2. How much in resources does Tinman have to work with?
3. How much does Tinman owe creditors?
4. How much of the company's assets do the Tinman stockholders actually own?

E1-30B (*Learning Objectives 3, 4: Using the accounting equation; evaluating business operations*) Winkler, Inc.'s comparative balance sheet at January 31, 2011, and 2010, reports (in millions):

	2011	2010
Total assets	$38	$24
Total liabilities	11	1

❚ Requirements

Three situations about Winkler's issuance of stock and payment of dividends during the year ended January 31, 2011, follow. For each situation, use the accounting equation and the statement of retained earnings to compute the amount of Winkler's net income or net loss during the year ended January 31, 2011.

1. Winkler issued $15 million of stock and paid no dividends.
2. Winkler issued no stock but paid dividends of $11 million.
3. Winkler issued $90 million of stock and paid dividends of $35 million.

E1-31B *(Learning Objective 3: Applying the accounting equation)* Answer these questions about two companies.

1. Sapphire, Inc., began the year with total liabilities of $90,000 and total stockholders' equity of $35,000. During the year, total assets increased by 30%. How much are total assets at the end of the year?
2. Southbound Airlines Ltd. began the year with total assets of $95,000 and total liabilities of $47,000. Net income for the year was $26,000, and dividends were zero. How much is stockholders' equity at the end of the year?

E1-32B *(Learning Objectives 4, 5: Evaluating business operations; making business decisions)* Assume Lesley, Inc., is expanding into Sweden. The company must decide where to locate and how to finance the expansion. Identify the financial statement where these decision makers can find the following information about Lesley, Inc. In some cases, more than one statement will report the needed data.

a. Income tax expense	**i.** Dividends
b. Net income	**j.** Total Assets
c. Current liabilities	**k.** Long-term debt
d. Common stock	**l.** Selling, general, and administrative expenses
e. Income tax payable	**m.** Cash spent to acquire the building
f. Ending balance of retained earnings	**n.** Adjustments to reconcile net income to net cash provided by operations
g. Revenue	
h. Ending cash balance	

■ **spreadsheet**

E1-33B *(Learning Objectives 3, 4: Using the accounting equation; preparing a balance sheet)* Amounts of the assets and liabilities of Eliza Bennet Banking Company, as of May 31, 2010, are given as follows. Also included are revenue and expense figures for the year ended on that date (amounts in millions):

Total revenue	$ 33.5		Investment assets	$169.8
Receivables	0.2		Property and equipment, net	1.6
Current liabilities	155.1		Other expenses	6.6
Common stock	14.9		Retained earnings, beginning	8.6
Interest expense	0.4		Retained earnings, ending	?
Salary and other employee expenses	17.5		Cash	2.7
Long-term liabilities	2.3		Other assets	14.9

❚ Requirement

1. Prepare the balance sheet of Eliza Bennet Banking Company at May 31, 2010. Use the accounting equation to compute ending retained earnings

■ **spreadsheet**

E1-34B *(Learning Objective 4: Preparing an income statement and a statement of retained earnings)* This exercise should be used with Exercise 1-33B.

❚ Requirements

1. Prepare the income statement of Eliza Bennet Banking Company, for the year ended May 31, 2010.

2. What amount of dividends did Eliza Bennet declare during the year ended May 31, 2010? Hint: Prepare a statement of retained earnings.

E1-35B (*Learning Objective 4: Preparing a statement of cash flows*) Fortune, Inc., began 2010 with $83,000 in cash. During 2010, Fortune earned net income of $440,000, and adjustments to reconcile net income to net cash provided by operations totaled $60,000, a positive amount. Investing activities used cash of $390,000, and financing activities provided cash of $65,000. Fortune ended 2010 with total assets of $300,000 and total liabilities of $120,000.

I Requirement

1. Prepare Fortune, Inc.'s statement of cash flows for the year ended December 31, 2010. Identify the data items given that do not appear on the statement of cash flows. Also identify the financial statement that reports each unused items.

E1-36B (*Learning Objective 4: Preparing an income statement and a statement of retained earnings*) Assume a Carson Copy Center ended the month of July 2011 with these data:

Payments of cash:				
Acquisition of equipment.......	$410,000		Cash balance, June 30, 2011......	$ 0
Dividends..............................	4,100		Cash balance, July 31, 2011.......	9,500
Retained earnings			Cash receipts:	
June 30, 2011........................	0		Issuance (sale) of stock	
Retained earnings			to owners..........................	54,200
July 31, 2011	?		Rent expense.............................	2,900
Utilities expense	10,800		Common stock..........................	54,200
Adjustments to reconcile			Equipment................................	410,000
net income to net cash			Office supplies..........................	15,000
provided by operations...........	2,900		Accounts payable	17,900
Salary expense..........................	162,000		Service revenue.........................	542,200

I Requirement

1. Prepare the income statement and the statement of retained earnings of Carson Copy Center, Inc., for the month ended July 31, 2011.

E1-37B (*Learning Objective 4: Preparing a balance sheet*) Refer to the data in Exercise 1-36B.

I Requirement

1. Prepare the balance sheet of Carson Copy Center, Inc., at July 31, 2011.

E1-38B (*Learning Objective 4: Preparing a statement of cash flows*) Refer to the data in Exercises 1-36B and 1-37B.

I Requirement

1. Prepare the statement of cash flows of Carson Copy Center, Inc., for the month ended July 31, 2011. Also explain the relationship among income statement, statement of retained earnings, balance sheet, and statement of cash flows.

E1-39B (*Learning Objectives 4, 5: Evaluating a business; advising a business*) This exercise should be used in conjunction with Exercises 1-36B through 1-38B.

writing assignment ■

The owner of Carson Copy Center now seeks your advice as to whether he should cease operations or continue the business. Complete the report giving him your opinion of net income, dividends, financial position, and cash flows during his first month of operations. Cite specifics from the financial statements to support your opinion. Conclude your memo with advice on whether to stay in business or cease operations.

Quiz

Test your understanding of the financial statements by answering the following questions. Select the best choice from among the possible answers given.

Q1-40 The *primary* objective of financial reporting is to provide information
a. useful for making investment and credit decisions.
b. about the profitability of the enterprise.
c. to the federal government.
d. on the cash flows of the company.

Q1-41 Which type of business organization provides the least amount of protection for bankers and other creditors of the company?
a. Partnership   c. Corporation
b. Proprietorship   d. Both a and b

Q1-42 Assets are usually reported at their
a. historical cost.   c. appraised value.
b. current market value.   d. none of the above (fill in the blank).

Q1-43 During March, assets increased by $19,000 and liabilities increased by $6,000. Stockholders' equity must have
a. increased by $13,000.   c. increased by $25,000.
b. decreased by $13,000.   d. decreased by $25,000.

Q1-44 The amount a company expects to collect from customers appears on the
a. statement of cash flows.
b. balance sheet in the current assets section.
c. income statement in the expenses section.
d. balance sheet in the stockholders' equity section.

Q1-45 All of the following are current assets except
a. Inventory.   c. Cash.
b. Sales Revenue.   d. Accounts Receivable.

Q1-46 Revenues are
a. decreases in liabilities resulting from paying off loans.
b. increases in paid-in capital resulting from the owners investing in the business.
c. increases in retained earnings resulting from selling products or performing services.
d. all of the above.

Q1-47 The financial statement that reports revenues and expenses is called the
a. statement of cash flows.   c. statement of retained earnings.
b. income statement.   d. balance sheet.

Q1-48 Another name for the balance sheet is the
a. statement of financial position   c. statement of profit and loss.
b. statement of operations.   d. statement of earnings.

Q1-49 Pinker Corporation began the year with cash of $30,000 and a computer that cost $25,000. During the year Pinker earned sales revenue of $135,000 and had the following expenses: salaries, $57,000; rent, $11,000; and utilities, $4,000. At year-end Pinker's cash balance was down to $18,000. How much net income (or net loss) did Pinker experience for the year?
a. ($12,000)   c. $63,000
b. $135,000   d. $123,000

Q1-50 Advanced Instruments had retained earnings of $155,000 at December 31, 2009. Net income for 2010 totaled $100,000, and dividends for 2010 were $25,000. How much retained earnings should Advanced report at December 31, 2010?

a. $255,000   c. $230,000
b. $180,000   d. $155,000

Q1-51 Net income appears on which financial statement(s)?

a. Income statement   c. Balance sheet
b. Statement of retained earnings   d. Both a and b

Q1-52 Cash paid to purchase a building appears on the statement of cash flows among the

a. Stockholders' equity.   c. Financing activities.
b. Investing activities.   d. Operating activities.

Q1-53 The stockholders' equity of Diakovsky Company at the beginning and end of 2010 totaled $15,000 and $20,000, respectively. Assets at the beginning of 2010 were $27,000. If the liabilities of Diakovsky Company increased by $9,000 in 2010, how much were total assets at the end of 2010? Use the accounting equation.

a. $45,000   c. $50,000
b. $34,000   d. $41,000

Q1-54 Robbin Company had the following on the dates indicated:

	12/31/10	12/31/09
Total assets	$740,000	$510,000
Total liabilities	290,000	190,000

Robbin had no stock transactions in 2010 and, thus, the change in stockholders' equity for 2010 was due to net income and dividends. If dividends were $55,000, how much was Robbin's net income for 2010? Use the accounting equation and the statement of retained earnings.

a. $185,000   c. $155,000
b. $245,000   d. $215,000

Problems

All of the following A and B problems can be found within MyAccountingLab, an online homework and practice environment. Your instructor may ask you to complete these problems using MyAccountingLab.

(Group A)

P1-55A (*Learning Objectives 1, 2, 4: Applying accounting vocabulary, concepts, and principles; evaluating business operations*) Assume that the A division of Smith Corporation experienced the following transactions during the year ended December 31, 2011:

   a. Suppose division A supplied copy products for a customer for the discounted price of $252,000. Under normal conditions they would have provided these services for $300,000. Other revenues totaled $52,000.

   b. Salaries cost the division $21,000 to provide these services. The division had to pay employees overtime occasionally. Ordinarily the salary cost for these services would have been $18,000.

c. All other expenses totaled $247,000 for the year. Income tax expense was 35% of income before tax.

d. The A division has two operating subdivisions: basic retail and special contracts. Each subdivision is accounted for separately to indicate how well each is performing. However the A division combines the statements of all subdivisions to show results for the A division as a whole.

e. Inflation affects the amounts that the A division must pay for copy machines. To show the effects of inflation, net income would drop by $4,000.

f. If the A division were to go out of business, the sale of its assets would bring in $147,000 in cash.

▌ Requirements

1. Prepare the A division's income statement for the year ended December 31, 2011.
2. For items a through f, identify the accounting concept, assumption, or principle that provides guidance in accounting for the item. State how you have applied the concept or principle in preparing the income statement.

P1-56A (*Learning Objectives 3, 4: Using the accounting equation; evaluating business operations*) Compute the missing amount (?) for each company—amounts in millions.

	Sapphire Corp.	Lance Co.	Branch Inc.
Beginning			
Assets.................................	$83	$35	$?
Liabilities	47	23	2
Common stock...................	2	2	1
Retained earnings..............	?	10	4
Ending			
Assets.................................	$?	$54	$8
Liabilities	49	34	?
Common stock...................	2	?	1
Retained earnings..............	33	?	?
Income statement			
Revenues............................	$221	$?	$18
Expenses	213	152	?
Net income........................	?	?	?
Statement of retained earnings			
Beginning RE	$34	$10	$ 4
+ Net income......................	?	10	3
− Dividends..........................	(9)	(2)	(3)
= Ending RE........................	$33	$18	$ 4

At the end of the year, which company has the

- Highest net income?
- Highest percent of net income to revenues?

P1-57A (*Learning Objectives 3, 4, 5: Using the accounting equation; preparing a balance sheet; making decisions*) The manager of Headlines, Inc., prepared the company's balance sheet while the accountant was ill. The balance sheet contains numerous errors. In particular, the manager knew that the balance sheet should balance, so he plugged in the stockholders' equity amount needed to achieve this balance. The stockholders' equity amount is *not* correct. All other amounts are accurate.

Headlines, Inc.				
Balance Sheet				
For the Month Ended June 30, 2010				
Assets		**Liabilities**		
Cash..	$ 8,000	Notes receivable......................	$ 13,000	
Equipment...............................	39,500	Interest expense.......................	1,800	
Accounts payable	5,000	Office supplies.........................	1,000	
Utilities expense	1,700	Accounts receivable................	2,600	
Advertising expense................	500	Note payable...........................	55,500	
Land...	77,000	Total	73,900	
Salary expense..........................	4,000	**Stockholders' Equity**		
		Stockholders' equity	61,800	
Total assets..............................	$135,700	Total liabilities	$135,700	

▌ Requirements

1. Prepare the correct balance sheet and date it properly. Compute total assets, total liabilities, and stockholders' equity.
2. Is Headlines actually in better (or worse) financial position than the erroneous balance sheet reports? Give the reason for your answer.
3. Identify the accounts listed on the incorrect balance sheet that should not be reported on the balance sheet. State why you excluded them from the correct balance sheet you prepared for Requirement 1. On which financial statement should these accounts appear?

P1-58A (*Learning Objectives 2, 4, 5: Preparing a balance sheet; applying the entity assumption; making business decisions*) Sandy Healey is a realtor. She organized the business as a corporation on April 16, 2011. The business received $95,000 cash from Healey and issued common stock. Consider the following facts as of April 30, 2011.

a. Healey has $16,000 in her personal bank account and $71,000 in the business bank account.
b. Healey owes $1,000 on a personal charge account with The Loft.
c. Healey acquired business furniture for $41,000 on April 25. Of this amount, the business owes $33,000 on accounts payable at April 30.
d. Office supplies on hand at the real estate office total $11,000.
e. Healey's business owes $36,000 on a note payable for some land acquired for a total price of $110,000.
f. Healey's business spent $24,000 for a Realty Universe franchise, which entitles her to represent herself as an agent. Realty Universe is a national affiliation of independent real estate agents. This franchise is a business asset.
g. Healey owes $140,000 on a personal mortgage on her personal residence, which she acquired in 2003 for a total price of $340,000.

▌ Requirements

1. Prepare the balance sheet of the real estate business of Sandy Healey Realtor, Inc., at April 30, 2011.
2. Does it appear that the realty business can pay its debts? How can you tell?
3. Identify the personal items given in the preceding facts that should not be reported on the balance sheet of the business.

■ **spreadsheet**

P1-59A (*Learning Objectives 4, 5: Preparing an income statement, a statement of retained earnings and a balance sheet; using accounting information to make decisions*) The assets and liabilities of Post Maple, Inc., as of December 31, 2010, and revenues and expenses for the year ended on that date follow.

Land	$ 8,200	Equipment	$ 33,000
Note payable	28,000	Interest expense	4,200
Property tax expense	1,900	Interest payable	1,200
Rent expense	14,000	Accounts payable	11,000
Accounts receivable	24,000	Salary expense	34,000
Service revenue	145,000	Building	126,000
Supplies	2,200	Cash	15,000
Utilities expense	3,000	Common stock	1,300

Beginning retained earnings was $117,000, and dividends totaled $38,000 for the year.

❙ Requirements

1. Prepare the income statement of Post Maple, Inc., for the year ended December 31, 2010.
2. Prepare the company's statement of retained earnings for the year.
3. Prepare the company's balance sheet at December 31, 2010.
4. Analyze Post Maple, Inc., by answering these questions:
   a. Was Post Maple profitable during 2010? By how much?
   b. Did retained earnings increase or decrease? By how much?
   c. Which is greater, total liabilities or total equity? Who owns more of Post Maple's assets, creditors of the company or the Post Maple's stockholders?

P1-60A (*Learning Objective 4: Preparing a statement of cash flows*) The following data come from the financial statements of The Water Sport Company for the year ended May 31, 2011 (in millions):

Purchases of property, plant, and equipment	$ 3,515	Other investing cash payments	$ 180
Net income	3,030	Accounts receivable	500
Adjustments to reconcile net income to net cash provided		Payment of dividends	290
		Common stock	4,850
by operating activities	2,370	Issuance of common stock	170
Revenues	59,200	Sales of property, plant,	
Cash, beginning of year	275	and equipment	30
end of year	1,890	Retained earnings	12,990
Cost of goods sold	37,450		

❙ Requirements

1. Prepare a cash flows statement for the year ended May 31, 2011. Not all items given appear on the cash flows statement.
2. What activities provided the largest source amount of cash? Is this a sign of financial strength or weakness?

P1-61A (*Learning Objective 4: Analyzing a company's financial statements*) Summarized versions of Cora Corporation's financial statements are given for two recent years.

	2010	2009
Income Statement	**(In Thousands)**	
Revenues..	$ k	$15,750
Cost of goods sold...	11,030	a
Other expenses..	1,220	1,170
Income before income taxes	1,580	1,830
Income taxes (35% tax rate)	l	641
Net income..	$ m	$ b
Statement of Retained Earnings		
Beginning balance	$ n	$ 2,660
Net income..	o	c
Dividends...	(98)	(120)
Ending balance...	$ p	$ d
Balance Sheet		
Assets:		
Cash..	$ q	$ e
Property, plant, and equipment.........................	1,600	1,725
Other assets..	r	10,184
Total assets	$ s	$13,239
Liabilities:		
Current liabilities	$ t	$ 5,650
Notes payable and long-term debt......................	4,350	3,380
Other liabilities	50	70
Total liabilities	$ 9,350	$ f
Stockholders' Equity:		
Common stock..	$ 250	$ 250
Retained earnings...	u	g
Other stockholders' equity	140	160
Total stockholders' equity	v	4,139
Total liabilities and stockholders' equity	$ w	$ h
Cash Flow Statement		
Net cash provided by operating activities................	$ x	$ 950
Net cash used in investing activities........................	(230)	(300)
Net cash used in financing activities........................	(560)	(540)
Increase (decrease) in cash...................................	(90)	i
Cash at beginning of year......................................	y	1,220
Cash at end of year	$ z	$ j

❙ Requirement

1. Determine the missing amounts denoted by the letters.

(Group B)

P1-62B (*Learning Objectives 1, 2, 4: Applying accounting vocabulary, concepts, and principles to the income statement; evaluating business operations*) Assume that the A division of Perez Corporation experienced the following transactions during the year ended December 31, 2011:

  a. Suppose division A supplied copy products for a customer for the discounted price of $263,000. Under normal conditions they would have provided these services for $296,000. Other revenues totaled $55,000.

b. Salaries cost the division $24,000 to provide these services. The division had to pay employees overtime occasionally. Ordinarily the salary cost for these services would have been $18,100.

c. All other expenses, excluding income taxes, totaled $235,000 for the year. Income tax expense was 33% of income before tax.

d. The A division has two operating subdivisions: basic retail and special contracts. Each division is accounted for separately to indicate how well each is performing. However, the A division combines the statements of all subdivisions to show results for the A division as a whole.

e. Inflation affects the amounts that the A division must pay for copy machines. To show the effects of inflation, net income would drop by $1,000.

f. If A division were to go out of business, the sale of its assets would bring in $145,000 in cash.

❙ Requirements

1. Prepare the A division's income statement for the year ended December 31, 2011.

2. For items a through f, identify the accounting concept or principle that provides guidance in accounting for the item described. State how you have applied the concept or principle in preparing the income statement.

P1-63B (*Learning Objective 3, 4: Using the accounting equation; evaluating business operations*) Compute the missing amount (?) for each company—amounts in millions.

	Diamond Corp.	Lally Co.	Bryant Inc.
Beginning			
Assets	$82	$25	$?
Liabilities	48	21	5
Common stock	3	2	1
Retained earnings	?	2	2
Ending			
Assets	$?	$43	$10
Liabilities	50	34	?
Common stock	3	?	1
Retained earnings	30	?	?
Income statement			
Revenues	$223	$?	$26
Expenses	215	159	?
Net income	?	?	?
Statement of retained earnings			
Beginning RE	$31	$ 2	$ 2
+ Net income	?	7	4
− Dividends	(9)	(2)	(3)
= Ending RE	$30	$ 7	$ 3

Which company has the

- Highest net income?
- Highest percent of net income to revenues?

P1-64B (*Learning Objectives 3, 4, 5: Using the accounting equation; preparing a balance sheet; making decisions*) The manager of News Maker, Inc., prepared the company's balance sheet while the accountant was ill. The balance sheet contains numerous errors. In particular, the manager knew that the balance sheet should balance, so he plugged in the stockholders' equity amount needed to achieve this balance. The stockholders' equity amount is *not* correct. All other amounts are accurate.

News Maker, Inc.
Balance Sheet
For the Month Ended November 30, 2010

Assets		Liabilities	
Cash..	$ 7,500	Notes receivable......................	$ 14,500
Equipment...............................	39,000	Interest expense.......................	1,600
Accounts payable....................	4,000	Office supplies.........................	900
Utilities expense	1,700	Accounts receivable................	3,400
Advertising expense................	400	Note payable...........................	55,000
Land..	82,000	Total	75,400
Salary expense.........................	4,500	**Stockholders' Equity**	
		Stockholders' equity	63,700
Total assets.............................	$139,100	Total liabilities	$139,100

I Requirements

1. Prepare the correct balance sheet and date it properly. Compute total assets, total liabilities, and stockholders' equity.
2. Is News Maker in better (or worse) financial position than the erroneous balance sheet reports? Give the reason for your answer.
3. Identify the accounts that should *not* be reported on the balance sheet. State why you excluded them from the correct balance sheet you prepared for Requirement 1. On which financial statement should these accounts appear?

P1-65B (*Learning Objectives 2, 4, 5: Preparing a balance sheet; applying the entity assumption; making business decisions*) Jeana Hart is a realtor. She organized her business as a corporation on September 16, 2011. The business received $95,000 from Hart and issued common stock. Consider these facts as of September 30, 2011.

   a. Hart has $15,000 in her personal bank account and $70,000 in the business bank account.
   b. Hart owes $2,000 on a personal charge account with The Gap.
   c. Hart acquired business furniture for $45,000 on September 25. Of this amount, the business owes $31,000 on accounts payable at September 30.
   d. Office supplies on hand at the real estate office total $7,000.
   e. Hart's business owes $36,000 on a note payable for some land acquired for a total price of $116,000.
   f. Hart's business spent $29,000 for a Realty Region franchise, which entitles her to represent herself as an agent. Realty Region is a national affiliation of independent real estate agents. This franchise is a business asset.
   g. Hart owes $140,000 on a personal mortgage on her personal residence, which she acquired in 2003 for a total price of $360,000.

I Requirements

1. Prepare the balance sheet of the real estate business of Jeana Hart Realtor, Inc., at September 30, 2011.
2. Does it appear that the realty business can pay its debts? How can you tell?
3. Identify the personal items given in the preceding facts that should not be reported on the balance sheet of the business.

■ spreadsheet

P1-66B (*Learning Objectives 4, 5: Preparing an income statement, a statement of retained earnings, and a balance sheet; using accounting information to make decisions*) The assets and liabilities of Post Shrub as of December 31, 2010, and revenues and expenses for the year ended on that date follow.

Land..................................	$ 9,000	Equipment..........................	$ 36,000
Note payable......................	33,000	Interest expense.................	4,950
Property tax expense...........	1,900	Interest payable.................	1,100
Rent expense......................	13,500	Accounts payable...............	14,000
Accounts receivable............	26,000	Salary expense...................	38,000
Service revenue...................	144,000	Building............................	129,000
Supplies.............................	2,000	Cash.................................	15,000
Utilities expense	3,200	Common stock..................	16,450

Beginning retained earnings was $112,000, and dividends totaled $42,000 for the year.

Requirements

1. Prepare the income statement of Post Shrub, Inc., for the year ended December 31, 2010.
2. Prepare the company's statement of retained earnings for the year.
3. Prepare the company's balance sheet at December 31, 2010.
4. Analyze Post Shrub, Inc., by answering these questions:
   a. Was Post Shrub profitable during 2010? By how much?
   b. Did retained earnings increase or decrease? By how much?
   c. Which is greater, total liabilities or total equity? Who owns more of Post Shrub's assets, creditors of the company or Post Shrub's stockholders?

P1-67B (*Learning Objective 4: Preparing a statement of cash flows*) The following data come from the financial statements of The High Tide Company at the year ended May 31, 2011 (in millions).

Purchases of property, plant, and equipment	$ 3,480	Other investing cash payments...........................	$ 170
Net income..........................	3,030	Accounts receivable..............	500
Adjustments to reconcile net income to net cash provided by operating activities	2,390	Payment of dividends............	285
		Common stock......................	4,830
Revenues.............................	59,400	Issuance of common stock......	190
Cash, beginning of year........	200	Sales of property, plant, and equipment	25
end of year	1,900	Retained earnings.................	13,000
Cost of goods sold...............	37,550		

Requirements

1. Prepare a cash flows statement for the year ended May 31, 2011. Not all the items given appear on the cash flows statement.
2. Which activities provided the largest amount of cash? Is this a sign of financial strength or weakness?

P1-68B (*Learning Objective 4: Analyzing a company's financial statements*) Summarized versions of Espinola Corporation's financial statements follow for two recent years.

	2011	2010
Income Statement	**(In Thousands)**	
Revenues..	$ k	$15,250
Cost of goods sold...	11,070	a
Other expenses..	1,280	1,230
Income before income taxes	1,500	1,830
Income taxes (35% tax rate)	l	641
Net income...	$ m	$ b
Statement of Retained Earnings		
Beginning balance	$ n	$ 2,720
Net income...	o	c
Dividends...	(84)	(140)
Ending balance..	$ p	$ d
Balance Sheet		
Assets:		
Cash...	$ q	$ e
Property, plant, and equipment..........................	2,100	1,750
Other assets..	r	10,404
Total assets	$ s	$13,419
Liabilities:		
Current liabilities	$ t	$ 5,690
Notes payable and long-term debt......................	4,300	3,340
Other liabilities	60	80
Total liabilities...	$ 9,250	$ f
Stockholders' Equity:		
Common stock...	$ 350	$ 350
Retained earnings..	u	g
Other stockholders' equity	110	190
Total stockholders' equity............................	v	4,309
Total liabilities and stockholders' equity	$ w	$ h
Cash Flows Statement		
Net cash provided by operating activities............	$ x	$ 850
Net cash used in investing activities..................	(240)	(325)
Net cash used in financing activities..................	(560)	(490)
Increase (decrease) in cash...............................	(90)	i
Cash at beginning of year.................................	y	1,230
Cash at end of year	$ z	$ j

❙ Requirement

1. Complete Espinola Corporation's financial statements by determining the missing amounts denoted by the letters.

APPLY YOUR KNOWLEDGE

Decision Cases

Case 1. *(Learning Objectives 1, 2, 5: Using financial statements to evaluate a loan request)* Two businesses, Blue Skies Corp., and Open Road, Inc., have sought business loans from you. To decide whether to make the loans, you have requested their balance sheets.

Blue Skies Corp.
Balance Sheet
August 31, 2011

Assets		Liabilities	
Cash	$ 5,000	Accounts payable	$ 50,000
Accounts receivable	10,000	Notes payable	80,000
Furniture	15,000	Total liabilities	130,000
Land	75,000	**Owners' Equity**	
Equipment	45,000	Owners' equity	20,000
		Total liabilities and	
Total assets	$150,000	owners' equity	$150,000

Open Road, Inc.
Balance Sheet
August 31, 2011

Assets		Liabilities	
Cash	$ 5,000	Accounts payable	$ 6,000
Accounts receivable	10,000	Note payable	9,000
Merchandise inventory	15,000	Total liabilities	15,000
Building	35,000	**Stockholders' Equity**	
		Stockholders' equity	50,000
		Total liabilities and	
Total assets	$65,000	stockholders' equity	$65,000

❙ *Requirement*

1. Using only these balance sheets, to which entity would you be more comfortable lending money? Explain fully, citing specific items and amounts from the respective balance sheets. (Challenge)

Case 2. *(Learning Objectives 2, 5: Analyzing a company as an investment)* A year out of college, you have $10,000 to invest. A friend has started GrandPrize Unlimited, Inc., and she asks you to invest in her company. You obtain the company's financial statements, which are summarized at the end of the first year as follows:

Grand Prize Unlimited, Inc. Income Statement Year Ended Dec. 31, 2010	
Revenues....................	$100,000
Expenses	80,000
Net income................	$ 20,000

Grand Prize Unlimited, Inc. Balance Sheet Dec. 31, 2010			
Cash........................	$ 6,000	Liabilities	$ 60,000
Other assets.............	100,000	Equity	46,000
		Total liabilities	
Total assets..............	$106,000	and equity	$106,000

Visits with your friend turn up the following facts:

a. Revenues and receivables of $40,000 were overlooked and omitted.

b. Software costs of $50,000 were recorded as assets. These costs should have been expenses. GrandPrize Unlimited paid cash for these expenses and recorded the cash payment correctly.

c. The company owes an additional $10,000 for accounts payable.

❙ *Requirements*

1. Prepare corrected financial statements.
2. Use your corrected statements to evaluate GrandPrize Unlimited's results of operations and financial position. (Challenge)
3. Will you invest in Grand Prize Unlimited? Give your reason. (Challenge)

Ethical Issue

You are studying frantically for an accounting exam tomorrow. You are having difficulty in this course, and the grade you make on this exam can make the difference between receiving a final grade of B or C. If you receive a C, it will lower your grade point average to the point that you could lose your academic scholarship. An hour ago, a friend, also enrolled in the course but in a different section under the same professor, called you with some unexpected news. In her sorority test files, she has just found a copy of an old exam from the previous year. In looking at the exam, it appears to contain questions that come right from the class notes you have taken, even the very same numbers. She offers to make a copy for you and bring it over.

You glance at your course syllabus and find the following: "You are expected to do your own work in this class. Although you may study with others, giving, receiving, or obtaining information pertaining to an examination is considered an act of academic dishonesty, unless such action is authorized by the instructor giving the examination. Also, divulging the contents of an essay or objective examination designated by the instructor as an examination is considered an act of academic dishonesty. Academic dishonesty is considered a violation of the student honor code, and will subject the student to disciplinary procedures, which can include suspension from the University." Although you have heard a rumor that fraternities and sororities have cleared their exam files with professors, you are not sure.

▌ *Requirements*

1. What is the ethical issue in this situation?
2. Who are the stakeholders? What are the possible consequences to each?
3. Analyze the alternatives from the following standpoints: (a) economic, (b) legal, and (c) ethical.
4. What would you do? How would you justify your decision? How would your decision make you feel afterward?
5. How is this similar to a business situation?

Focus on Financials: ■ Amazon.com, Inc.

(Learning Objective 4: Identifying items from a company's financial statements) This and similar cases in succeeding chapters are based on the consolidated financial statements of **Amazon.com, Inc.** As you work with Amazon.com, Inc., throughout this course, you will develop the ability to use the financial statements of actual companies.

▌ *Requirements*

Refer to the Amazon.com, Inc., consolidated financial statements in Appendix A at the end of the book.

1. Suppose you own stock in Amazon.com, Inc. If you could pick one item on the company's Consolidated Statements of Operations to increase year after year, what would it be? Why is this item so important? Did this item increase or decrease during fiscal 2008? Is this good news or bad news for the company?
2. What was Amazon.com, Inc.'s largest expense each year? In your own words, explain the meaning of this item. Give specific examples of items that make up this expense. The chapter gives another title for this expense. What is it?
3. Use the Consolidated Balance Sheets of Amazon.com, Inc., in Appendix A to answer these questions: At the end of fiscal 2008, how much in total resources did Amazon.com, Inc., have to work with? How much did the company owe? How much of its assets did the company's stockholders actually own? Use these amounts to write Amazon.com, Inc.'s accounting equation at December 31, 2008.
4. How much cash did Amazon.com, Inc., have at the beginning of the most recent year? How much cash did Amazon.com have at the end of the year?

Focus on Analysis: ■ Foot Locker, Inc.

(Learning Objectives 3, 4: Evaluating a leading company) This and similar cases in each chapter are based on the consolidated financial statements of **Foot Locker, Inc.**, given in Appendix B at the end of this book. As you work with Foot Locker, Inc., you will develop the ability to analyze the financial statements of actual companies.

▌ *Requirements*

1. Write Foot Locker, Inc.'s accounting equation at February 2, 2008, the end of fiscal 2007 (express all items in millions and round to the nearest $1 million). Does Foot Locker, Inc.'s financial condition look strong or weak? How can you tell?
2. What was the result of Foot Locker, Inc.'s operations during fiscal 2007? Identify both the name and the dollar amount of the result of operations for fiscal 2007. Does an increase (decrease) signal good news or bad news for the company and its stockholders?
3. Examine retained earnings in the Consolidated Statements of Shareholders' Equity. What caused retained earnings to increase during fiscal 2007?
4. Which statement reports cash as part of Foot Locker, Inc.'s financial position? Which statement tells *why* cash increased (or decreased) during the year? What two individual items caused Foot Locker, Inc.'s cash to change the most during fiscal 2007?

Group Projects

Project 1. As instructed by your professor, obtain the annual report of a well-known company.

❙ *Requirements*

1. Take the role of a loan committee of Bank of America, a large banking company head-quartered in Charlotte, North Carolina. Assume the company has requested a loan from Bank of America. Analyze the company's financial statements and any other information you need to reach a decision regarding the largest amount of money you would be willing to lend. Go as deeply into the analysis and the related decision as you can. Specify the following:

   a. The length of the loan period—that is, over what period will you allow the company to pay you back?

   b. The interest rate you will charge on the loan. Will you charge the prevailing interest rate, a lower rate, or a higher rate? Why?

   c. Any restrictions you will impose on the borrower as a condition for making the loan.

Note: The long-term debt note to the financial statements gives details of the company's existing liabilities.

2. Write your group decision in a report addressed to the bank's board of directors. Limit your report to two double-spaced word-processed pages.

3. If your professor directs, present your decision and your analysis to the class. Limit your presentation to 10 to 15 minutes.

Project 2. You are the owner of a company that is about to "go public"—that is, issue its stock to outside investors. You wish to make your company look as attractive as possible to raise $1 million of cash to expand the business. At the same time, you want to give potential investors a realistic picture of your company.

❙ *Requirements*

1. Design a booklet to portray your company in a way that will enable outsiders to reach an informed decision as to whether to buy some of your stock. The booklet should include the following:

   a. Name and location of your company.

   b. Nature of the company's business (be as detailed as possible).

   c. How you plan to spend the money you raise.

   d. The company's comparative income statement, statement of retained earnings, balance sheet, and statement of cash flows for two years: the current year and the preceding year. Make the data as realistic as possible with the intent of receiving $1 million.

2. Word-process your booklet, not to exceed five pages.

3. If directed by your professor, make a copy for each member of your class. Distribute copies to the class and present your case with the intent of interesting your classmates in investing in the company. Limit your presentation to 10 to 15 minutes.

Quick Check Answers

1. *b*
2. *b*
3. *c [This is not the typical way the accounting equation is expressed (Assets = Liabilities + Owners' Equity), but it may be rearranged this way].*
4. *a*
5. *d*
6. *d*
7. *a ($120,000 – $50,000 – $4,000 = $66,000)*
8. *b ($120,000 – $50,000 = $70,000)*
9. *c Total assets = $140,000 ($11,000 + $40,000 + $34,000 + $55,000). Liabilities = $27,000.*
10. *d*
11. *b $38,000 + Net income ($18,000) – Dividends = $50,000; Dividends = $6,000*
12. *b*

	Assets =	Liabilities +	Equity
Beginning	$340,000 =	$210,000* +	$130,000
Increase	70,000 =	25,000 +	45,000*
Ending	$410,000* =	$235,000* +	$175,000*

*Must solve for these amounts.

13. *c*
14. *a*

Demo Doc

The Accounting Equation and Financial Statement Preparation

To make sure you understand this material, work through the following demonstration "Demo Doc" with detailed comments to help you see the concept within the framework of a worked-through problem.

Learning Objectives 3, 4, 5

David Richardson is the only shareholder of DR Painting, Inc., a painting business near a historical housing district. At March 31, 2010, DR Painting had the following information:

Cash	$27,300
Accounts receivable	1,400
Supplies	1,800
Truck	20,000
Accounts payable	1,000
Common stock	40,000
Retained earnings (March 1)	5,000
Retained earnings (March 31)	?
Dividends	1,500
Service revenue	7,000
Salary expense	1,000

Requirements

1. Prepare the income statement and statement of retained earnings for the month of March 2010 and the balance sheet of the business at March 31, 2010. Use Exhibits 1-7, 1-8, and 1-9 (pp. 17, 19, and 21) in the text as a guide.

2. Write the accounting equation of the business.

Demo Doc Solutions

Requirement 1

Prepare the income statement, statement of retained earnings, and balance sheet of the business. Use Exhibits 1-7, 1-8, and 1-9 (pp. 17, 19, and 21) in the text as a guide.

Part 1	Part 2	Demo Doc Complete

Income Statement

The income statement is the first statement to prepare because the other financial statements rely upon the net income number calculated on the income statement.

The income statement reports the profitability of the business. To prepare an income statement, begin with the proper heading. A proper heading includes the name of the company (DR Painting, Inc.), the name of the statement (Income Statement), and the time period covered (Month Ended March 31, 2010). Notice that we are reporting income for a period of time, rather than at a single date.

The income statement lists all revenues and expenses. It uses the following formula to calculate net income:

$$\text{Revenues} - \text{Expenses} = \text{Net income}$$

First, you should list revenues. Second, list the expenses. After you have listed and totaled the revenues and expenses, subtract the total expenses from total revenues to determine net income or net loss. A positive number means you earned net income (revenues exceeded expenses). A negative number indicates that expenses exceeded revenues, and this is a net loss.

DR Painting's total Service Revenue for the month was $7,000. The only expense is Salary Expense of $1,000. On the income statement, these would be reported as follows:

DR Painting, Inc.
Income Statement
Month Ended March 31, 2010

Revenue:		
Service revenue		$7,000
Expenses:		
Salary expense	$1,000	
Total expenses		1,000
Net income		$6,000

Note that the result is a net income of $6,000 ($7,000 − $1,000 = $6,000). You will also report net income on the statement of retained earnings, which comes next.

Statement of Retained Earnings

The statement of retained earnings shows the changes in Retained Earnings for a period of time. To prepare a statement of retained earnings, begin with the proper heading. A proper heading includes the name of the company (DR Painting, Inc.), the name of the statement (Statement of Retained Earnings), and the time period covered (Month Ended March 31, 2010). As with the income statement, we are reporting the changes in Retained Earnings for a period of time, rather than at a single date.

Net income is used on the statement of retained earnings to calculate the new balance in Retained Earnings. This calculation uses the following formula:

$$
\begin{array}{l}
\text{Beginning Retained Earnings} \\
+ \text{ Net Income (or } - \text{Net Loss)} \\
\underline{- \text{ Dividends}} \\
= \text{Ending Retained Earnings}
\end{array}
$$

Start the body of the statement of retained earnings with the Retained Earnings at the beginning of the period (March 1). Then list net income. Observe that the amount of net income comes directly from the income statement. Following net income you will list the dividends declared and paid, which reduce Retained Earnings. Finally, total all amounts and compute the Retained Earnings at the end of the period.

The beginning Retained Earnings of $5,000 was given in the problem. Net income of $6,000 comes from the income statement and is added. Dividends of $1,500 are deducted. On the statement of retained earnings, these amounts are reported as follows:

DR Painting, Inc. Statement of Retained Earnings Month Ended March 31, 2010	
Beginning retained earnings	$ 5,000
Add: Net income	6,000
	11,000
Less: Dividends	(1,500)
Retained earnings, March 31, 2010	$ 9,500

Note that Retained Earnings has a balance of $9,500 at March 31, 2010. You will also report Retained Earning's ending balance on the balance sheet, which you prepare last.

Balance Sheet

The balance sheet reports the financial position of the business at a moment in time. To prepare a balance sheet, begin with the proper heading. A proper heading includes the name of the company (DR Painting, Inc.), the name of the statement (Balance Sheet), and the time of the ending balances (March 31, 2010). Unlike the income statement and statement of retained earnings, we are reporting the financial position of the company at a specific date rather than for a period of time.

The balance sheet lists all assets, liabilities, and equity of the business, with the accounting equation verified at the bottom.

To prepare the body of the balance sheet, begin by listing assets. Then list all the liabilities and stockholders' equity. Notice that the balance sheet is organized in the same order as the accounting equation. The amount of Retained Earnings comes directly from the ending balance on your statement of retained earnings. You should then total both sides of the balance sheet to make sure that they are equal. If they are not equal, then you must correct an error.

In this case, assets accounts include cash of $27,300, accounts receivable of $1,400, $1,800 worth of supplies, and the truck, valued at $20,000. The only liability is accounts payable of $1,000. Stockholders' equity consists of common stock of $40,000, and the updated retained earnings of $9,500, from the statement of retained earnings.

DR Painting, Inc.
Balance Sheet
March 31, 2010

Assets		Liabilities	
Cash	$27,300	Accounts payable	$ 1,000
Accounts receivable	1,400		
Supplies	1,800	**Stockholders' Equity**	
Truck	20,000	Common stock	40,000
		Retained earnings	9,500
		Total stockholders' equity	49,500
		Total liabilities and	
Total assets	$50,500	stockholders' equity	$50,500

Assets   = **Liabilities + Stockholders' Equity**

Requirement 2

Write the accounting equation of the business

Part 1	**Part 2**	Demo Doc Complete

In this case, asset accounts total $50,500. Liabilities total $1,000—the balance of Accounts Payable, and stockholder's equity is $49,500. This gives us a total for liabilities and equity of $50,500 ($1,000 + $49,500).

The accounting equation is:

Assets of $50,500 = Liabilities of $1,000 + Stockholders' Equity of $49,500

Part 1	Part 2	**Demo Doc Complete**

2

Transaction Analysis

SPOTLIGHT: Apple, Inc.

How do you manage your messages? You may use Apple's iPhone for text messaging or surfing the Internet when you're on the go. The iPhone and iPod, in addition to the company's popular notebook computers, have generated billions of dollars in profits for the company.

Apple, Inc., is an American multinational corporation that designs and manufactures consumer electronics. The company started out 30 years ago with the name Apple Computer, Inc., but because the company has expanded its product line so much in the last few years, it dropped the "computer" from its name in 2007. The company's best-known hardware products include Macintosh computers, the iPod, and the iPhone. Apple software includes the Mac OS X operating system, the iTunes media browser, the iLife suite of multimedia and creativity software, the iWork suite of productivity software, and Final Cut Studio, a suite of professional audio and film-industry software products. The company operates more than 250 retail stores in nine countries and an online store where hardware and software products are sold.

How does Apple determine the amount of its revenues, expenses, and net income? Like all other companies, Apple has a comprehensive accounting system. Apple's income statement (statement of operations) is given at the start of this chapter. The income statement shows that during fiscal year 2008, Apple made over $32 billion of sales and earned net income of $4.8 billion. Where did those figures come from? In this chapter, we'll show you.

Apple, Inc. Statement of Operations (Adapted) Fiscal Year Ended September 30, 2008	
(In billions)	2008
Net sales..	$32.4
Cost of goods sold...	21.3
Gross profit..	11.1
Operating expenses:	
Research and development expense...........................	1.1
Selling, general, and administrative expense.............	3.7
Total operating expenses..	4.8
Operating income (loss)...	6.3
Other income...	.6
Income before income taxes.......................................	6.9
Income tax expense..	2.1
Net income..	$ 4.8

Chapter 1 introduced the financial statements. Chapter 2 will show you how companies actually record the transactions that eventually become part of the financial statements.

LEARNING OBJECTIVES

1 **Analyze** transactions

2 **Understand** how accounting works

3 **Record** transactions in the journal

4 **Use** a trial balance

5 **Analyze** transactions using only T-accounts

---

ac
t

For more practice and review of accounting cycle concepts, use ACT, the Accounting Cycle Tutorial, online at www.myaccountinglab.com. Margin logos like this one, directing you to the appropriate ACT section and material, appear throughout Chapters 1, 2, and 3. When you enter the tutorial, you'll find three buttons on the opening page of each chapter module. Here's what the buttons mean: **Tutorial** gives you a review of the major concepts, **Application** gives you practice exercises, and **Glossary** reviews important terms.

TRANSACTIONS

Business activity is all about transactions. A **transaction** is any event that has a financial impact on the business and can be measured reliably. For example, Apple, Inc., pays programmers to create iTunes® software. Apple sells computers, borrows money, and repays the loan—three separate transactions.

But not all events qualify as transactions. iTunes® may be featured in *Showtime Magazine* and motivate you to buy an Apple iPod. The magazine article may create lots of new business for Apple. But no transaction occurs until someone actually buys an Apple product. A transaction must occur before Apple records anything.

Transactions provide objective information about the financial impact on a company. Every transaction has two sides:

- You give something.
- You receive something.

In accounting we always record both sides of a transaction. And we must be able to measure the financial impact of the event on the business before recording it as a transaction.

THE ACCOUNT

As we saw in Chapter 1, the accounting equation expresses the basic relationships of accounting:

$$\text{Assets} = \text{Liabilities} + \text{Stockholders' (Owners') Equity}$$

For each asset, each liability, and each element of stockholders' equity, we use a record called the account. An **account** is the record of all the changes in a particular asset, liability, or stockholders' equity during a period. The account is the basic summary device of accounting. Before launching into transaction analysis, let's review the accounts that a company such as Apple, Inc., uses.

Assets

Assets are economic resources that provide a future benefit for a business. Most firms use the following asset accounts:

Cash.   Cash means money and any medium of exchange including bank account balances, paper currency, coins, certificates of deposit, and checks.

Accounts Receivable.   Apple, Inc., like most other companies, sells its goods and services and receives a promise for future collection of cash. The Accounts Receivable account holds these amounts.

Notes Receivable.   Apple may receive a note receivable from a customer, who signed the note promising to pay Apple. A note receivable is similar to an account receivable, but a note receivable is more binding because the customer signed the note. Notes receivable usually specify an interest rate.

Inventory.   Apple's most important asset is its inventory—the hardware and software Apple sells to customers. Other titles for this account include *Merchandise* and *Merchandise Inventory*.

Prepaid Expenses.   Apple pays certain expenses in advance, such as insurance and rent. A prepaid expense is an asset because the payment provides a *future* benefit for the business. Prepaid Rent, Prepaid Insurance, and Supplies are prepaid expenses.

Land.   The Land account shows the cost of the land Apple uses in its operations.

Buildings.   The costs of Apple's office building, manufacturing plant, and the like appear in the Buildings account.

Equipment, Furniture, and Fixtures.   Apple has a separate asset account for each type of equipment, for example, Manufacturing Equipment and Office Equipment. The Furniture and Fixtures account shows the cost of these assets, which are similar to equipment.

Liabilities

Recall that a *liability* is a debt. A payable is always a liability. The most common types of liabilities include:

Accounts Payable.   The Accounts Payable account is the direct opposite of Accounts Receivable. Apple's promise to pay a debt arising from a credit purchase of inventory or from a utility bill appears in the Accounts Payable account.

Notes Payable.   A note payable is the opposite of a note receivable. The Notes Payable account includes the amounts Apple must *pay* because Apple signed notes promising to pay a future amount. Notes payable, like notes receivable, also carry interest.

Accrued Liabilities.   An **accrued liability** is a liability for an expense you have not yet paid. Interest Payable and Salary Payable are accrued liability accounts for most companies. Income Tax Payable is another accrued liability.

Stockholders' (Owners') Equity

The owners' claims to the assets of a corporation are called *stockholders' equity, shareholders' equity*, or simply *owners' equity*. A corporation such as Apple, Inc., uses Common Stock, Retained Earnings, and Dividends accounts to record in the company's stockholders' equity. In a proprietorship, there is a single capital account. For a partnership, each partner has a separate owner equity account.

Common Stock.   The Common Stock account shows the owners' investment in the corporation. Apple, Inc., receives cash and issues common stock to its stockholders. A company's common stock is its most basic element of equity. All corporations have common stock.

STOP & THINK. . .

Name two things that (1) increase Apple, Inc.'s stockholders' equity and (2) decrease Apple's stockholders' equity.

Answer:
(1) Increases in equity: Sale of stock and net income (revenue greater than expenses).
(2) Decreases in equity: Dividends and net loss (expenses greater than revenue).

Retained Earnings.   The Retained Earnings account shows the cumulative net income earned by Apple, Inc., over the company's lifetime, minus its cumulative net losses and dividends.

Dividends.   Dividends are optional; they are decided (declared) by the board of directors. After profitable operations, the board of directors of Apple, Inc., may (or may not) declare and pay a cash dividend. The corporation may keep a separate account titled *Dividends*, which indicates a decrease in Retained Earnings.

Revenues.   The increase in stockholders' equity from delivering goods or services to customers is called *revenue*. The company uses as many revenue accounts as needed. Apple, Inc., uses a Sales Revenue account for revenue earned by selling its products. Apple has a Service Revenue account for the revenue it earns by providing services to customers. A lawyer provides legal services for clients and also uses a Service Revenue account. A business that loans money to an outsider needs an Interest Revenue account. If the business rents a building to a tenant, the business needs a Rent Revenue account.

Expenses.   The cost of operating a business is called *expense*. Expenses *decrease* stockholders' equity, the opposite effect of revenues. A business needs a separate account for each type of expense, such as Cost of Goods Sold, Salary Expense, Rent Expense, Advertising Expense, Insurance Expense, Utilities Expense, and Income Tax Expense. Businesses strive to minimize expenses and thereby maximize net income.

ACCOUNTING FOR BUSINESS TRANSACTIONS
Example: ShineBrite Car Wash, Inc.

To illustrate the accounting for transactions, let's return to ShineBrite Car Wash, Inc. In Chapter 1's End-of-Chapter Problem, Van Gray opened ShineBrite Car Wash, Inc., in April 2010.

OBJECTIVE

1 **Analyze** transactions

We consider 11 events and analyze each in terms of its effect on ShineBrite Car Wash. We begin by using the accounting equation. In the second half of the chapter, we record transactions using the journal and ledger of the business.

Transaction 1.   Gray and a few friends invest $50,000 to open ShineBrite Car Wash, and the business issues common stock to the stockholders. The effect of this transaction on the accounting equation of ShineBrite Car Wash, Inc., is a receipt of cash and issuance of common stock, as follows:

Assets		=		Liabilities	+	Stockholders' Equity	Type of Stockholders' Equity Transaction
Cash						Common Stock	
(1) + 50,000						+ 50,000	Issued stock

Every transaction's net amount on the left side of the equation must equal the net amount on the right side. The first transaction increases both the cash and the common stock of the business. To the right of the transaction we write "Issued stock" to show the reason for the increase in stockholders' equity.

Every transaction affects the financial statements of the business, and we can prepare financial statements after one, two, or any number of transactions. For example, ShineBrite Car Wash could report the company's balance sheet after its first transaction, shown here.

ShineBrite Car Wash, Inc.
Balance Sheet
April 1, 2010

Assets		Liabilities	
Cash..........................	$50,000	None	
		Stockholders' Equity	
		Common stock.................................	$50,000
		Total stockholders' equity.............	50,000
		Total liabilities and	
Total assets................	$50,000	stockholders' equity......................	$50,000

This balance sheet shows that the business holds cash of $50,000 and owes no liabilities. The company's equity (ownership) is denoted as *Common Stock* on the balance sheet. A bank would look favorably on this balance sheet because the business has $50,000 cash and no debt—a strong financial position.

As a practical matter, most entities report their financial statements at the end of the accounting period—not after each transaction. But an accounting system can produce statements whenever managers need to know where the business stands.

Transaction 2. ShineBrite purchases land for a new location and pays cash of $40,000. The effect of this transaction on the accounting equation is:

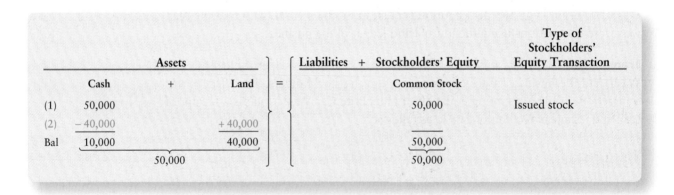

The purchase increases one asset (Land) and decreases another asset (Cash) by the same amount. After the transaction is completed, ShineBrite has cash of $10,000, land of $40,000, and no liabilities. Stockholders' equity is unchanged at $50,000. Note that total assets must always equal total liabilities plus equity.

Transaction 3. The business buys supplies on account, agreeing to pay $3,700 within 30 days. This transaction increases both the assets and the liabilities of the business. Its effect on the accounting equation follows.

	Assets				Liabilities	+	Stockholders' Equity
	Cash	+	Supplies	+	Land	Accounts Payable	+	Common Stock
Bal	10,000				40,000			50,000
(3)			+ 3,700			+ 3,700		
Bal	10,000		3,700		40,000	3,700		50,000
			53,700				53,700	

The new asset is Supplies, and the liability is an Account Payable. ShineBrite signs no formal promissory note, so the liability is an account payable, not a note payable.

Transaction 4.   ShineBrite earns $7,000 of service revenue by providing services for customers. The business collects the cash. The effect on the accounting equation is an increase in the asset Cash and an increase in Retained Earnings, as follows:

	Assets						Liabilities	+	Stockholders' Equity			Type of Stockholders' Equity Transaction
	Cash	+	Supplies	+	Land		Accounts Payable	+	Common Stock	+	Retained Earnings	
Bal	10,000		3,700		40,000	=	3,700		50,000			
(4)	+ 7,000										+ 7,000	Service revenue
Bal	17,000		3,700		40,000		3,700		50,000		7,000	
			60,700						60,700			

To the right we record "Service revenue" to show where the $7,000 of increase in Retained Earnings came from.

Transaction 5.   ShineBrite performs service on account, which means that ShineBrite lets some customers pay later. ShineBrite earns revenue but doesn't receive the cash immediately. In transaction 5, ShineBrite cleans a fleet of UPS delivery trucks, and UPS promises to pay ShineBrite $3,000 within one month. This promise is an account receivable—an asset—of ShineBrite Car Wash. The transaction record follows.

	Assets								Liabilities	+	Stockholders' Equity			Type of Stockholders' Equity Transaction
	Cash	+	Accounts Receivable	+	Supplies	+	Land		Accounts Payable	+	Common Stock	+	Retained Earnings	
Bal	17,000				3,700		40,000	=	3,700		50,000		7,000	
(5)			+ 3,000										+ 3,000	Service revenue
Bal	17,000		3,000		3,700		40,000		3,700		50,000		10,000	
			63,700								63,700			

It's performing the service that earns the revenue—not collecting the cash. Therefore, ShineBrite records revenue when it performs the service—regardless of whether ShineBrite receives cash now or later.

Transaction 6.   During the month, ShineBrite Car Wash pays $2,700 for the following expenses: equipment rent, $1,100; employee salaries, $1,200; and utilities, $400. The effect on the accounting equation is as follows:

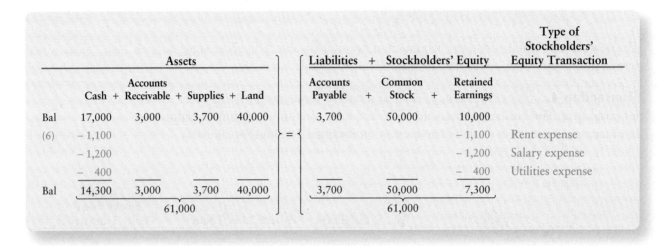

		Assets					Liabilities	+	Stockholders' Equity		Type of Stockholders' Equity Transaction
	Cash	+ Accounts Receivable	+ Supplies	+ Land			Accounts Payable	+ Common Stock	+ Retained Earnings	
Bal	17,000	3,000	3,700	40,000			3,700	50,000	10,000	
(6)	– 1,100				=				– 1,100	Rent expense
	– 1,200								– 1,200	Salary expense
	– 400								– 400	Utilities expense
Bal	14,300	3,000	3,700	40,000			3,700	50,000	7,300	
		61,000							61,000	

The expenses decrease ShineBrite's Cash and Retained Earnings. List each expense separately to keep track of its amount.

Transaction 7.   ShineBrite pays $1,900 on account, which means to pay off an account payable. In this transaction ShineBrite pays the store from which it purchased supplies in transaction 3. The transaction decreases Cash and also decreases Accounts Payable as follows:

			Assets						Liabilities	+	Stockholders' Equity		
	Cash	+	Accounts Receivable	+	Supplies	+	Land			Accounts Payable	+ Common Stock	+ Retained Earnings	
Bal	14,300		3,000		3,700		40,000	=		3,700	50,000	7,300	
(7)	– 1,900									– 1,900			
Bal	12,400		3,000		3,700		40,000			1,800	50,000	7,300	
			59,100								59,100		

Transaction 8.   Van Gray, the major stockholder of ShineBrite Car Wash, paid $30,000 to remodel his home. This event is a personal transaction of the Gray family. It is not recorded by the ShineBrite Car Wash business. We focus solely on the business entity, not on its owners. This transaction illustrates the entity assumption from Chapter 1.

Transaction 9.   In transaction 5, ShineBrite performed services for UPS on account. The business now collects $1,000 from UPS. We say that ShineBrite *collects the cash on account*, which means that ShineBrite will record an increase in Cash and a decrease in

Accounts Receivable. This is not service revenue because ShineBrite already recorded the revenue in transaction 5. The effect of collecting cash on account is:

	Assets						Liabilities	+	Stockholders' Equity		
	Cash	+	Accounts Receivable	+	Supplies	+	Land		Accounts Payable	+	Common Stock	+	Retained Earnings
Bal	12,400		3,000		3,700		40,000	=	1,800		50,000		7,300
(9)	+ 1,000		− 1,000										
Bal	13,400		2,000		3,700		40,000		1,800		50,000		7,300
				59,100							59,100		

Transaction 10.   ShineBrite sells some land for $22,000, which is the same amount that ShineBrite paid for the land. ShineBrite receives $22,000 cash, and the effect on the accounting equation is as follows:

	Assets						Liabilities	+	Stockholders' Equity		
	Cash	+	Accounts Receivable	+	Supplies	+	Land		Accounts Payable	+	Common Stock	+	Retained Earnings
Bal	13,400		2,000		3,700		40,000	=	1,800		50,000		7,300
(10)	+ 22,000						− 22,000						
Bal	35,400		2,000		3,700		18,000		1,800		50,000		7,300
				59,100							59,100		

Note that the company did not sell all its land; ShineBrite still owns $18,000 worth of land.

Transaction 11.   ShineBrite Car Wash declares a dividend and pays the stockholders $2,100 cash. The effect on the accounting equation is as follows:

	Assets				Liabilities	+	Stockholders' Equity			Type of Stockholders' Equity Transaction
	Cash	+ Accounts Receivable	+ Supplies	+ Land	Accounts Payable	+	Common Stock	+	Retained Earnings	
Bal	35,400	2,000	3,700	18,000	= 1,800		50,000		7,300	
(11)	− 2,100								− 2,100	Dividends
Bal	33,300	2,000	3,700	18,000	1,800		50,000		5,200	
			57,000					57,000		

The dividend decreases both the Cash and the Retained Earnings of the business. *But dividends are not an expense.*

Transactions and Financial Statements

Exhibit 2-1 summarizes the 11 preceding transactions. Panel A gives the details of the transactions, and Panel B shows the transaction analysis. As you study the exhibit, note that every transaction maintains the equality:

Assets = Liabilities + Stockholders' Equity

Exhibit 2-1 provides the data for ShineBrite Car Wash's financial statements:

EXHIBIT 2-1 | Transaction Analysis: ShineBrite Car Wash, Inc.

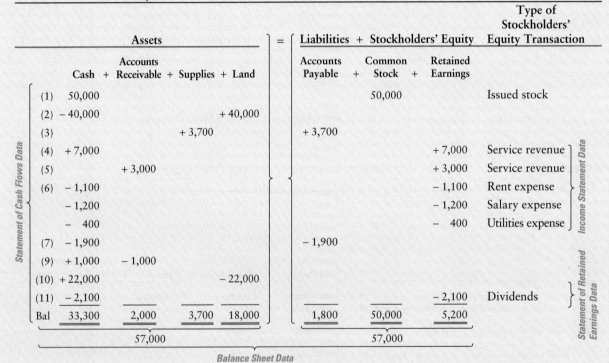

PANEL A—Transaction Details

(1) Received $50,000 cash and issued stock to the owners
(2) Paid $40,000 cash for land
(3) Bought $3,700 of supplies on account
(4) Received $7,000 cash from customers for service revenue earned
(5) Performed services for a customer on account, $3,000
(6) Paid cash expenses: rent, $1,100; employee salary, $1,200; utilities, $400

(7) Paid $1,900 on the account payable created in transaction 3
(8) Major stockholder paid personal funds to remodel home, *not* a transaction of the business
(9) Received $1,000 on account
(10) Sold land for cash at the land's cost of $22,000
(11) Declared and paid a dividend of $2,100 to the stockholders

PANEL B—Transaction Analysis

	Assets				=	Liabilities +	Stockholders' Equity		Type of Stockholders' Equity Transaction
	Cash +	Accounts Receivable +	Supplies +	Land		Accounts Payable +	Common Stock +	Retained Earnings	
(1)	50,000						50,000		Issued stock
(2)	− 40,000			+ 40,000					
(3)			+ 3,700			+ 3,700			
(4)	+ 7,000							+ 7,000	Service revenue
(5)		+ 3,000						+ 3,000	Service revenue
(6)	− 1,100							− 1,100	Rent expense
	− 1,200							− 1,200	Salary expense
	− 400							− 400	Utilities expense
(7)	− 1,900					− 1,900			
(9)	+ 1,000	− 1,000							
(10)	+ 22,000			− 22,000					
(11)	− 2,100							− 2,100	Dividends
Bal	33,300	2,000	3,700	18,000		1,800	50,000	5,200	
		57,000					57,000		

Statement of Cash Flows Data

Income Statement Data

Statement of Retained Earnings Data

Balance Sheet Data

- *Income statement* data appear as revenues and expenses under Retained Earnings. The revenues increase retained earnings; the expenses decrease retained earnings.
- The *balance sheet* data are composed of the ending balances of the assets, liabilities, and stockholders' equities shown at the bottom of the exhibit. The accounting equation shows that total assets ($57,000) equal total liabilities plus stockholders' equity ($57,000).
- The *statement of retained earnings* repeats net income (or net loss) from the income statement. Dividends are subtracted. Ending retained earnings is the final result.
- Data for the *statement of cash flows* are aligned under the Cash account. Cash receipts increase cash, and cash payments decrease cash.

Exhibit 2-2 on the following page shows the ShineBrite Car Wash financial statements at the end of April, the company's first month of operations. Follow the flow of data to observe the following:

1. The income statement reports revenues, expenses, and either a net income or a net loss for the period. During April, ShineBrite earned net income of $7,300. Compare ShineBrite's income statement with that of Apple, Inc., at the beginning of the chapter. The income statement includes only two types of accounts: revenues and expenses.

2. The statement of retained earnings starts with the beginning balance of retained earnings, (zero for a new business). Add net income for the period (arrow ①), subtract dividends, and compute the ending balance of retained earnings ($5,200).

3. The balance sheet lists the assets, liabilities, and stockholders' equity of the business at the end of the period. Included in stockholders' equity is retained earnings, which comes from the statement of retained earnings (arrow ②).

EXHIBIT 2-2 | **Financial Statements of ShineBrite Car Wash, Inc.**

ShineBrite Car Wash, Inc.
Income Statement
Month Ended April 30, 2010

Revenues		
Service revenue ($7,000 + $3,000)		$10,000
Expenses		
Salary expense...	$1,200	
Rent expense..	1,100	
Utilities expense	400	
Total expenses...		2,700
Net income...		$ 7,300

ShineBrite Car Wash, Inc.
Statement of Retained Earnings
Month Ended April 30, 2010

Retained earnings, April 1, 2010....................	$ 0
Add: Net income for the month	7,300
	7,300
Less: Dividends	(2,100)
Retained earnings, April 30, 2010.................	$5,200

①

②

ShineBrite Car Wash, Inc.
Balance Sheet
April 30, 2010

Assets		**Liabilities**	
Cash..	$33,300	Accounts payable	$ 1,800
Accounts receivable................	2,000	**Stockholders' Equity**	
Supplies...................................	3,700	Common stock.................................	50,000
Land..	18,000	Retained earnings............................	5,200
		Total stockholders' equity.............	55,200
Total assets.............................		Total liabilities and	
	$57,000	stockholders' equity......................	$57,000

Let's put into practice what you have learned thus far.

MID-CHAPTER SUMMARY PROBLEM

Shelly Herzog opens a research service near a college campus. She names the corporation Herzog Researchers, Inc. During the first month of operations, July 2010, the business engages in the following transactions:

a. Herzog Researchers, Inc., issues its common stock to Shelly Herzog, who invests $25,000 to open the business.

b. The company purchases on account office supplies costing $350.

c. Herzog Researchers pays cash of $20,000 to acquire a lot next to the campus. The company intends to use the land as a building site for a business office.

d. Herzog Researchers performs research for clients and receives cash of $1,900.

e. Herzog Researchers pays $100 on the account payable it created in transaction b.

f. Herzog pays $2,000 of personal funds for a vacation.

g. Herzog Researchers pays cash expenses for office rent ($400) and utilities ($100).

h. The business sells a small parcel of the land for its cost of $5,000.

i. The business declares and pays a cash dividend of $1,200.

Requirements

1. Analyze the preceding transactions in terms of their effects on the accounting equation of Herzog Researchers, Inc. Use Exhibit 2-1, Panel B as a guide.

2. Prepare the income statement, statement of retained earnings, and balance sheet of Herzog Researchers, Inc., after recording the transactions. Draw arrows linking the statements.

Answers

Requirement 1

PANEL B—Analysis of Transactions

	Cash	+	Office Supplies	+	Land	=	Accounts Payable	+	Common Stock	+	Retained Earnings	Type of Stockholders' Equity Transaction
(a)	+ 25,000								+ 25,000			Issued stock
(b)			+ 350				+ 350					
(c)	− 20,000				+ 20,000							
(d)	+ 1,900										+ 1,900	Service revenue
(e)	− 100						− 100					
(f)	Not a transaction of the business											
(g)	− 400										− 400	Rent expense
	− 100										− 100	Utilities expense
(h)	+ 5,000				− 5,000							
(i)	− 1,200										− 1,200	Dividends
Bal	10,100		350		15,000		250		25,000		200	
			25,450						25,450			

Herzog Researchers, Inc.
Income Statement
Month Ended July 31, 2010

Revenues		
Service revenue.................		$1,900
Expenses		
Rent expense....................	$400	
Utilities expense	100	
Total expenses.................		500
Net income..............................		$1,400

Herzog Researchers, Inc.
Statement of Retained Earnings
Month Ended July 31, 2010

Retained earnings, July 1, 2010.................	$ 0
Add: Net income for the month	1,400
	1,400
Less: Dividends	(1,200)
Retained earnings, July 31, 2010...............	$ 200

Herzog Researchers, Inc.
Balance Sheet
July 31, 2010

Assets		Liabilities	
Cash..............................	$10,100	Accounts payable	$ 250
Office supplies...............	350	**Stockholders' Equity**	
Land..............................	15,000	Common stock................................	25,000
		Retained earnings...........................	200
		Total stockholders' equity.............	25,200
		Total liabilities and	
Total assets....................	$25,450	stockholders' equity.....................	$25,450

The analysis in the first half of this chapter can be used, but it is cumbersome. Apple, Inc., has hundreds of accounts and millions of transactions. The spreadsheet to account for Apple's transactions would be huge! In the second half of this chapter we discuss double-entry accounting as it is actually used in business.

DOUBLE-ENTRY ACCOUNTING

All business transactions include two parts:

- You give something.
- You receive something.

OBJECTIVE

2 **Understand** how accounting works

Accounting is, therefore, based on a double-entry system, which records the *dual effects* on the entity. *Each transaction affects at least two accounts.* For example, ShineBrite Car Wash's receipt of $50,000 cash and issuance of stock increased both Cash and Common Stock. It would be incomplete to record only the increase in Cash or only the increase in Common Stock.

The T-Account

An account can be represented by the letter T. We call them *T-accounts*. The vertical line in the letter divides the account into its two sides: left and right. The account title appears at the top of the T. For example, the Cash account can appear as follows:

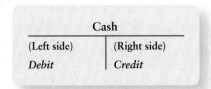

The left side of each account is called the **debit** side, and the right side is called the **credit** side. Often, students are confused by the words *debit* and *credit*. To become comfortable using these terms, remember that for every account

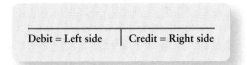

Every business transaction involves both a debit and a credit. The debit side of an account shows what you received. The credit side shows what you gave.

Increases and Decreases in the Accounts: The Rules of Debit and Credit

The type of account determines how we record increases and decreases. *The rules of debit and credit follow* in Exhibit 2-3 on the next page.

- Increases in *assets* are recorded on the left (debit) side of the account. Decreases in *assets* are recorded on the right (credit) side. You receive cash and debit the Cash account. You pay cash and credit the Cash account.
- Conversely, increases in *liabilities* and *stockholders' equity* are recorded by credits. Decreases in *liabilities* and *stockholders' equity* are recorded by debits.

EXHIBIT 2-3 | **Accounting Equation and the Rules of Debit and Credit**

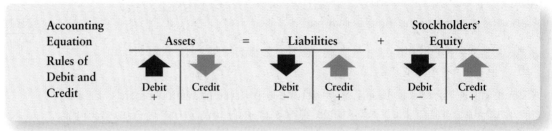

To illustrate the ideas diagrammed in Exhibit 2-3, let's review the first transaction. ShineBrite Car Wash received $50,000 and issued (gave) stock. Which accounts are affected? The Cash account and the Common Stock account will hold these amounts:

EXHIBIT 2-4 | **The Accounting Equation after ShineBrite Car Wash's First Transaction**

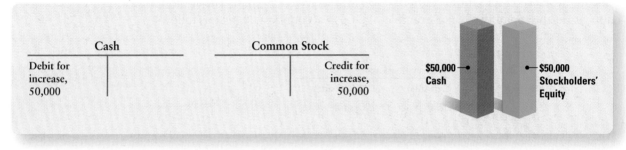

The amount remaining in an account is called its *balance*. This first transaction gives Cash a $50,000 debit balance and Common Stock a $50,000 credit balance. Exhibit 2-4 shows this relationship.

ShineBrite's second transaction is a $40,000 cash purchase of land. This transaction decreases Cash with a credit and increases Land with a debit, as shown in the following T-accounts (focus on Cash and Land):

Cash				Common Stock	
Bal	50,000	Credit for decrease, 40,000		Bal	50,000
Bal	10,000				

Land	
Debit for increase, 40,000	
Bal	40,000

After this transaction, Cash has a $10,000 debit balance, Land has a debit balance of $40,000, and Common Stock has a $50,000 credit balance, as shown in Exhibit 2-5.

EXHIBIT 2-5 | **The Accounting Equation after ShineBrite Car Wash's First Two Transactions**

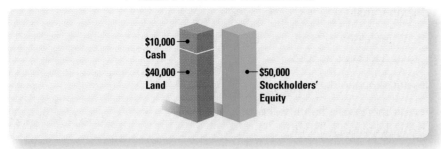

Additional Stockholders' Equity Accounts: Revenues and Expenses

Stockholders' equity also includes the two categories of income statement accounts, Revenues and Expenses:

- *Revenues* are increases in stockholders' equity that result from delivering goods or services to customers.
- *Expenses* are decreases in stockholders' equity due to the cost of operating the business.

Therefore, the accounting equation may be expanded as shown in Exhibit 2-6. Revenues and expenses appear in parentheses because their net effect—revenues minus expenses—equals net income, which increases stockholders' equity. If expenses exceed revenues, there is a net loss, which decreases stockholders' equity.

EXHIBIT 2-6 | **Expansion of the Accounting Equation**

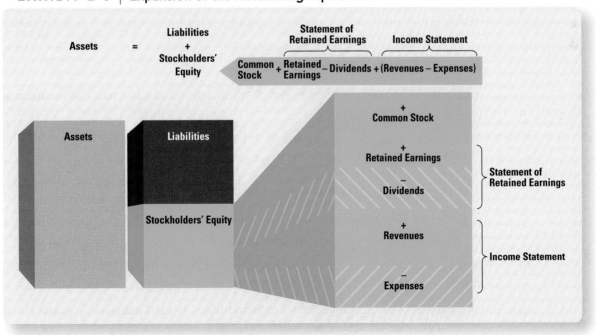

We can now express the final form of the rules of debit and credit, as shown in Exhibit 2-7. *You should not proceed until you have learned these rules.* For example, you must remember that

- A debit increases an asset account.
- A credit decreases an asset.

Liabilities and stockholders' equity are the opposite.

- A credit increases a liability account.
- A debit decreases a liability.

Dividends and Expense accounts are exceptions to the rule. Dividends and Expenses are equity accounts that are increased by a debit. Dividends and Expense accounts are negative (or *contra*) equity accounts.

Revenues and Expenses are often treated as separate account categories because they appear on the income statement. Exhibit 2-7 shows Revenues and Expenses below the other equity accounts.

EXHIBIT 2-7 | **Final Form of the Rules of Debit and Credit**

ASSETS	=	LIABILITIES	+		STOCKHOLDERS' EQUITY		

Assets		Liabilities		Common Stock		Retained Earnings		Dividends	
Debit	Credit	Debit	Credit	Debit	Credit	Debit	Credit	Debit	Credit
+	−	−	+	−	+	−	+	+	−

						Revenues		Expenses	
						Debit	Credit	Debit	Credit
						−	+	+	−

RECORDING TRANSACTIONS

OBJECTIVE

3 **Record** transactions in the journal

Accountants use a chronological record of transactions called a **journal**. The journalizing process follows three steps:

1. Specify each account affected by the transaction and classify each account by type (asset, liability, stockholders' equity, revenue, or expense).

2. Determine whether each account is increased or decreased by the transaction. Use the rules of debit and credit to increase or decrease each account.

3. Record the transaction in the journal, including a brief explanation. The debit side is entered on the left margin, and the credit side is indented to the right.

Step 3 is also called "making the journal entry" or "journalizing the transaction." Let's apply the steps to journalize the first transaction of ShineBrite Car Wash.

Step 1 The business receives cash and issues stock. Cash and Common Stock are affected. Cash is an asset, and Common Stock is equity.

Step 2 Both Cash and Common Stock increase. Debit Cash to record an increase in this asset. Credit Common Stock to record an increase in this equity account.

Step 3 Journalize the transaction as follows:

JOURNAL

Date	Accounts and Explanation	Debit	Credit
Apr 2	Cash	50,000	
	Common Stock		50,000
	Issued common stock.		

When analyzing a transaction, first pinpoint the effects (if any) on cash. Did cash increase or decrease? Typically, it is easiest to identify cash effects. Then identify the effects on the other accounts.

Copying Information (Posting) from the Journal to the Ledger

The journal is a chronological record of all company transactions listed by date. But the journal does not indicate how much cash or accounts receivable the business has.

The **ledger** is a grouping of all the T-accounts, with their balances. For example, the balance of the Cash T-account shows how much cash the business has. The balance of Accounts Receivable shows the amount due from customers. Accounts Payable shows how much the business owes suppliers on open account, and so on.

In the phrase "keeping the books," *books* refers to the accounts in the ledger. In most accounting systems, the ledger is computerized. Exhibit 2-8 shows how the asset, liability, and stockholders' equity accounts are grouped in the ledger.

EXHIBIT 2-8 | **The Ledger (Asset, Liability, and Stockholders' Equity Accounts)**

Entering a transaction in the journal does not get the data into the ledger. Data must be copied to the ledger—a process called **posting**. Debits in the journal are always posted as debits in the accounts, and likewise for credits. Exhibit 2-9 shows how ShineBrite Car Wash's stock issuance transaction is posted to the accounts.

EXHIBIT 2-9 | **Journal Entry and Posting to the Accounts**

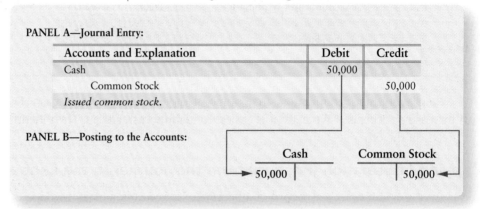

PANEL A—Journal Entry:

Accounts and Explanation	Debit	Credit
Cash	50,000	
Common Stock		50,000
Issued common stock.		

PANEL B—Posting to the Accounts:

Cash	Common Stock
50,000		50,000

The Flow of Accounting Data

Exhibit 2-10 summarizes the flow of accounting data from the business transaction to the ledger.

EXHIBIT 2-10 | **Flow of Accounting Data**

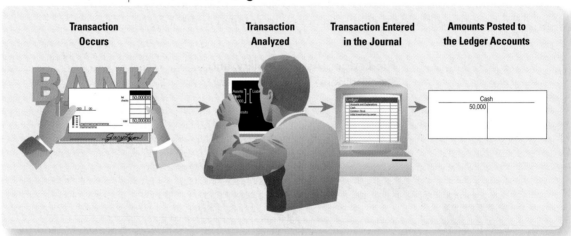

Let's continue the example of ShineBrite Car Wash, Inc., and account for the same 11 transactions we illustrated earlier. Here we use the journal and the accounts. Each journal entry posted to the accounts is keyed by date or by transaction number. This linking allows you to locate any information you may need.

Transaction 1 Analysis. ShineBrite Car Wash, Inc., received $50,000 cash from the stockholders and in turn issued common stock to them. The journal entry, accounting equation, and ledger accounts follow.

Journal entry	Cash	50,000	
	Common Stock		50,000
	Issued common stock.		

	Assets	=	Liabilities	+	Stockholders' Equity
Accounting equation	50,000	=	0	+	50,000

	Cash		Common Stock	
The ledger accounts	(1)	50,000	(1)	50,000

Transaction 2 Analysis.   The business paid $40,000 cash for land. The purchase decreased cash; therefore, credit Cash. The purchase increased the asset land; to record this increase, debit Land.

Journal entry	Land		40,000	
	Cash			40,000
	Paid cash for land.			

	Assets	=	Liabilities	+	Stockholders' Equity
Accounting equation	+ 40,000	=	0	+	0
	− 40,000				

	Cash			Land	
The ledger accounts	(1) 50,000	(2) 40,000	(2) 40,000	

Transaction 3 Analysis.   The business purchased supplies for $3,700 on account payable. The purchase increased Supplies, an asset, and Accounts Payable, a liability.

Journal entry	Supplies		3,700	
	Accounts Payable			3,700
	Purchased office supplies on account.			

	Assets	=	Liabilities	+	Stockholders' Equity
Accounting equation	+ 3,700	=	+ 3,700	+	0

	Supplies		Accounts Payable	
The ledger accounts	(3) 3,700		(3) 3,700	

Transaction 4 Analysis.   The business performed services for clients and received cash of $7,000. The transaction increased cash and service revenue. To record the revenue, credit Service Revenue.

Journal entry

Cash	7,000	
Service Revenue		7,000
Performed services for cash.		

Accounting equation

Assets	=	Liabilities	+	Stockholders' Equity	+	Revenues
+ 7,000	=	0			+	7,000

The ledger accounts

	Cash				Service Revenue	
(1)	50,000	(2)	40,000		(4)	7,000
(4)	7,000					

Transaction 5 Analysis. ShineBrite performed services for UPS on account. UPS did not pay immediately, so ShineBrite billed UPS for $3,000. The transaction increased accounts receivable; therefore, debit Accounts Receivable. Service revenue also increased, so credit the Service Revenue account.

Journal entry

Accounts Receivable	3,000	
Service Revenue		3,000
Performed services on account.		

Accounting equation

Assets	=	Liabilities	+	Stockholders' Equity	+	Revenues
+ 3,000	=	0			+	3,000

The ledger accounts

	Accounts Receivable		Service Revenue	
(5)	3,000		(4)	7,000
			(5)	3,000

Transaction 6 Analysis. The business paid $2,700 for the following expenses: equipment rent, $1,100; employee salary, $1,200; and utilities, $400. Credit Cash for the sum of the expense amounts. The expenses increased, so debit each expense account separately.

Journal entry

Rent Expense	1,100	
Salary Expense	1,200	
Utilities Expense	400	
Cash		2,700
Paid expenses.		

	Assets	=	Liabilities	+	Stockholders' Equity	−	Expenses
Accounting equation	− 2,700	=	0			−	2,700

		Cash					Rent Expense	
The ledger accounts	(1)	50,000	(2)	40,000	(6)	1,100		
	(4)	7,000	(6)	2,700				

		Salary Expense					Utilities Expense	
	(6)	1,200			(6)	400		

Transaction 7 Analysis.   The business paid $1,900 on the account payable created in transaction 3. Credit Cash for the payment. The payment decreased a liability, so debit Accounts Payable.

Journal entry	Accounts Payable	1,900	
	Cash		1,900
	Paid cash on account.		

	Assets	=	Liabilities	+	Stockholders' Equity
Accounting equation	− 1,900	=	− 1,900	+	0

		Cash				Accounts Payable	
The ledger accounts	(1)	50,000	(2)	40,000	(7)	1,900	(3)	3,700
	(4)	7,000	(6)	2,700			
			(7)	1,900			

Transaction 8 Analysis.   Van Gray, the major stockholder of ShineBrite Car Wash, remodeled his personal residence. This is not a transaction of the car-wash business, so the business does not record the transaction.

Transaction 9 Analysis.   The business collected $1,000 cash on account from the clients in transaction 5. Cash increased so debit Cash. The asset accounts receivable decreased; therefore, credit Accounts Receivable.

Journal entry	Cash	1,000	
	Accounts Receivable		1,000
	Collected cash on account.		

	Assets	=	Liabilities	+	Stockholders' Equity
Accounting equation	+ 1,000	=	0	+	0
	− 1,000				

	Cash			Accounts Receivable	
The ledger accounts	(1) 50,000	(2) 40,000	(5) 3,000	(9) 1,000	
	(4) 7,000	(6) 2,700			
	(9) 1,000	(7) 1,900			

Transaction 10 Analysis.   The business sold land for its cost of $22,000, receiving cash. The asset cash increased; debit Cash. The asset land decreased; credit Land.

Journal entry	Cash	22,000	
	Land		22,000
	Sold land.		

	Assets	=	Liabilities	+	Stockholders' Equity
Accounting equation	+ 22,000	=	0	+	0
	− 22,000				

	Cash			Land	
The ledger accounts	(1) 50,000	(2) 40,000	(2) 40,000	(10) 22,000	
	(4) 7,000	(6) 2,700			
	(9) 1,000	(7) 1,900			
	(10) 22,000				

Transaction 11 Analysis.   ShineBrite Car Wash paid its stockholders cash dividends of $2,100. Credit Cash for the payment. The transaction also decreased stockholders' equity and requires a debit to an equity account. Therefore, debit Dividends.

Journal entry	Dividends	2,100	
	Cash		2,100
	Declared and paid dividends.		

	Assets	=	Liabilities	+	Stockholders' Equity	−	Dividends
Accounting equation	− 2,100	=	0			−	2,100

	Cash				Dividends	
The ledger accounts	(1)	50,000	(2)	40,000	(11)	2,100
	(4)	7,000	(6)	2,700		
	(9)	1,000	(7)	1,900		
	(10)	22,000	(11)	2,100		

Accounts After Posting to the Ledger

Exhibit 2-11 shows the accounts after all transactions have been posted to the ledger. Group the accounts under assets, liabilities, and equity.

Each account has a balance, denoted as Bal, which is the difference between the account's total debits and its total credits. For example, the Accounts Payable's balance of $1,800 is the difference between the credit ($3,700) and the debit ($1,900). Cash has a debit balance of $33,300.

A horizontal line separates the transaction amounts from the account balance. If an account's debits exceed its total credits, that account has a debit balance, as for Cash. If the sum of the credits is greater, the account has a credit balance, as for Accounts Payable.

Accounting Cycle Tutorial Application 1—Xpert Driving School

Accounting Cycle Tutorial Application 2—Small Business Services

EXHIBIT 2-11 | **ShineBrite Car Wash's Ledger Accounts After Posting**

	Assets			=	Liabilities		+		Stockholders' Equity		

	Cash				Accounts Payable				Common Stock			Dividends	
(1)	50,000	(2)	40,000	(7)	1,900	(3)	3,700		(1)	50,000	(11)	2,100
(4)	7,000	(6)	2,700			Bal	1,800		Bal	50,000	Bal	2,100
(9)	1,000	(7)	1,900									
(10)	22,000	(11)	2,100									
Bal	33,300											

Revenue   **Expenses**

Service Revenue   **Rent Expense**

	Accounts Receivable				Service Revenue			Rent Expense	
(5)	3,000	(9)	1,000		(4)	7,000	(6)	1,100
Bal	2,000				(5)	3,000	Bal	1,100
				Bal	10,000			

Salary Expense

	Supplies			Salary Expense	
(3)	3,700		(6)	1,200
Bal	3,700		Bal	1,200

Utilities Expense

	Land				Utilities Expense	
(2)	40,000	(10)	22,000		(6)	400
Bal	18,000				Bal	400

THE TRIAL BALANCE

A **trial balance** lists all accounts with their balances—assets first, then liabilities and stockholders' equity. The trial balance summarizes all the account balances for the financial statements and shows whether total debits equal total credits. A trial balance

OBJECTIVE

4 Use a trial balance

may be taken at any time, but the most common time is at the end of the period. Exhibit 2-12 is the trial balance of ShineBrite Car Wash, Inc., after all transactions have been journalized and posted at the end of April.

ac↗t

Accounting Cycle Tutorial Glossary

ac↗t

Accounting Cycle Tutorial Glossary Quiz

EXHIBIT 2-12 | Trial Balance

ShineBrite Car Wash, Inc.
Trial Balance
April 30, 2010

Account Title	Balance Debit	Balance Credit
Cash..................................	$33,300	
Accounts receivable...............	2,000	
Supplies................................	3,700	
Land....................................	18,000	
Accounts payable		$ 1,800
Common stock.......................		50,000
Dividends.............................	2,100	
Service revenue......................		10,000
Rent expense.........................	1,100	
Salary expense.......................	1,200	
Utilities expense	400	
Total	$61,800	$61,800

Analyzing Accounts

You can often tell what a company did by analyzing its accounts. This is a powerful tool for a manager who knows accounting. For example, if you know the beginning and ending balance of Cash, and if you know total cash receipts, you can compute your total cash payments during the period.

In our chapter example, suppose ShineBrite Car Wash began May with cash of $1,000. During May ShineBrite received cash of $8,000 and ended the month with a cash balance of $3,000. You can compute total cash payments by analyzing ShineBrite's Cash account as follows:

Cash			
Beginning balance	1,000		
Cash receipts	8,000	Cash payments	$x = 6,000$
Ending balance	3,000		

Or, if you know Cash's beginning and ending balances and total payments, you can compute cash receipts during the period—for any company!

You can compute either sales on account or cash collections on account by analyzing the Accounts Receivable account as follows (using assumed amounts):

Accounts Receivable			
Beginning balance	6,000		
Sales on account	10,000	Collections on account	11,000
Ending balance	5,000		

Also, you can determine how much you paid on account by analyzing Accounts Payable as follows (using assumed amounts):

Accounts Payable			
		Beginning balance	9,000
Payments on account	4,000	Purchases on account	6,000
		Ending balance	11,000

Please master this powerful technique. It works for any company and for your own personal finances! You will find this tool very helpful when you become a manager.

Correcting Accounting Errors

Accounting errors can occur even in computerized systems. Input data may be wrong, or they may be entered twice or not at all. A debit may be entered as a credit, and vice versa. You can detect the reason or reasons behind many out-of-balance conditions by computing the difference between total debits and total credits. Then perform one or more of the following actions:

1. Search the records for a missing account. Trace each account back and forth from the journal to the ledger. A $200 transaction may have been recorded incorrectly in the journal or posted incorrectly to the ledger. Search the journal for a $200 transaction.

2. Divide the out-of-balance amount by 2. A debit treated as a credit, or vice versa, doubles the amount of error. Suppose ShineBrite Car Wash added $300 to Cash instead of subtracting $300. The out-of-balance amount is $600, and dividing by 2 identifies $300 as the amount of the transaction. Search the journal for the $300 transaction and trace to the account affected.

3. Divide the out-of-balance amount by 9. If the result is an integer (no decimals), the error may be a

   - *slide* (writing $400 as $40). The accounts would be out of balance by $360 ($400 − $40 = $360). Dividing $360 by 9 yields $40. Scan the trial balance in Exhibit 2-12 for an amount similar to $40. Utilities Expense (balance of $400) is the misstated account.

- *transposition* (writing $2,100 as $1,200). The accounts would be out of balance by $900 ($2,100 − $1,200 = $900). Dividing $900 by 9 yields $100. Trace all amounts on the trial balance back to the T-accounts. Dividends (balance of $2,100) is the misstated account.

Chart of Accounts

As you know, the ledger contains the accounts grouped under these headings:

1. **Balance sheet accounts: Assets, Liabilities, and Stockholders' Equity**
2. **Income statement accounts: Revenues and Expenses**

Organizations use a **chart of accounts** to list all their accounts and account numbers. Account numbers usually have two or more digits. Asset account numbers may begin with 1, liabilities with 2, stockholders' equity with 3, revenues with 4, and expenses with 5. The second, third, and higher digits in an account number indicate the position of the individual account within the category. For example, Cash may be account number 101, which is the first asset account. Accounts Payable may be number 201, the first liability. All accounts are numbered by using this system.

Organizations with many accounts use lengthy account numbers. For example, the chart of accounts of Apple, Inc., may use five-digit account numbers. The chart of accounts for ShineBrite Car Wash appears in Exhibit 2-13. The gap between account numbers 111 and 141 leaves room to add another category of receivables, for example, Notes Receivable, which may be numbered 121.

EXHIBIT 2-13 | **Chart of Accounts—ShineBrite Car Wash, Inc.**

Balance Sheet Accounts		
Assets	**Liabilities**	**Stockholders' Equity**
101 Cash	201 Accounts Payable	301 Common Stock
111 Accounts Receivable	231 Notes Payable	311 Dividends
141 Office Supplies		312 Retained Earnings
151 Office Furniture		
191 Land		

Income Statement Accounts (Part of Stockholders' Equity)	
Revenues	**Expenses**
401 Service Revenue	501 Rent Expense
	502 Salary Expense
	503 Utilities Expense

Appendix D to this book gives two expanded charts of accounts that you will find helpful as you work through this course. The first chart lists the typical accounts that a *service* corporation, such as ShineBrite Car Wash, would have after a period of growth. The second chart is for a *merchandising* corporation, one that sells a product instead of a service.

The Normal Balance of an Account

An account's *normal balance* falls on the side of the account—debit or credit—where increases are recorded. The normal balance of assets is on the debit side, so assets are *debit-balance accounts*. Conversely, liabilities and stockholders' equity usually have a credit balance, so these are *credit-balance accounts*. Exhibit 2-14 illustrates the normal balances of all the assets, liabilities, and stockholders' equities, including revenues and expenses.

EXHIBIT 2-14 | **Normal Balances of the Accounts**

Assets	Debit	
Liabilities		Credit
Stockholders' Equity—overall		Credit
Common stock		Credit
Retained earnings		Credit
Dividends	Debit	
Revenues		Credit
Expenses	Debit	

As explained earlier, stockholders' equity usually contains several accounts. Dividends and expenses carry debit balances because they represent decreases in stockholders' equity. In total, the equity accounts show a normal credit balance.

Account Formats

So far we have illustrated accounts in a two-column T-account format, with the debit column on the left and the credit column on the right. Another format has four *amount* columns, as illustrated for the Cash account in Exhibit 2-15. The first pair of amount columns are for the debit and credit amounts of individual transactions. The last two columns are for the account balance. This four-column format keeps a running balance in the two right columns.

ac
t

**Accounting Cycle Tutorial
The Journal, the Ledger, and the
Trial Balance**

EXHIBIT 2-15 | **Account in Four-Column Format**

Account: Cash					Account No. 101
				Balance	
Date	Item	Debit	Credit	Debit	Credit
2010					
Apr 2		50,000		50,000	
3			40,000	10,000	

Analyzing Transactions Using Only T-Accounts

OBJECTIVE

5 **Analyze** transactions using only T-accounts

Businesspeople must often make decisions without the benefit of a complete accounting system. For example, the managers of Apple, Inc., may consider borrowing $100,000 to buy equipment. To see how the two transactions [(a) borrowing cash and (b) buying equipment] affect Apple, the manager can go directly to T-accounts, as follows:

T-accounts:

Cash		Note Payable	
(a) 100,000			(a) 100,000

T-accounts:

Cash		Equipment		Note Payable	
(a) 100,000	(b) 100,000	(b) 100,000			(a) 100,000

This informal analysis shows immediately that Apple will add $100,000 of equipment and a $100,000 note payable. Assuming that Apple began with zero balances, the equipment and note payable transactions would result in the following balance sheet (date assumed for illustration only):

Apple, Inc.
Balance Sheet
September 12, 2010

Assets		Liabilities	
Cash.............................	$ 0	Note payable...........................	$100,000
Equipment.....................	100,000		
		Stockholders' Equity	0
		Total liabilities and	
Total assets....................	$100,000	stockholders' equity..............	$100,000

Accounting Cycle Tutorial Application
Constanza Architect

Companies don't actually keep records in this shortcut fashion. But a decision maker who needs information quickly may not have time to journalize, post to the accounts, take a trial balance, and prepare the financial statements. A manager who knows accounting can analyze the transaction and make the decision quickly.

Now apply what you've learned. Study the Decision Guidelines, which summarize the chapter.

DECISION GUIDELINES

HOW TO MEASURE RESULTS OF OPERATIONS AND FINANCIAL POSITION

Any entrepreneur must determine whether the venture is profitable. To do this, he or she needs to know its results of operations and financial position. If Steve Jobs, who founded Apple, Inc., wants to know whether the business is making money, the Guidelines that follow will help him.

Decision	Guidelines
Has a transaction occurred?	If the event affects the entity's financial position and can be reliably recorded—Yes. If either condition is absent—No.
Where to record the transaction?	In the *journal*, the chronological record of transactions
How to record an increase or decrease in the following accounts?	Rules of *debit* and *credit*:

	Increase	Decrease
Assets	Debit	Credit
Liabilities	Credit	Debit
Stockholders' equity...............	Credit	Debit
Revenues	Credit	Debit
Expenses	Debit	Credit

Decision	Guidelines
Where to store all the information for each account?	In the *ledger*, the book of accounts
Where to list all the accounts and their balances?	In the *trial* balance
Where to report the:	
Results of operations?	In the *income* statement (Revenues – Expenses = Net income or net loss)
Financial position?	In the balance sheet (Assets = Liabilities + Stockholders' equity)

END-OF-CHAPTER SUMMARY PROBLEM

The trial balance of Calderon Service Center, Inc., on March 1, 2010, lists the entity's assets, liabilities, and stockholders' equity on that date.

| | Balance | |
Account Title	Debit	Credit
Cash	$26,000	
Accounts receivable	4,500	
Accounts payable		$ 2,000
Common stock		10,000
Retained earnings		18,500
Total	$30,500	$30,500

During March, the business completed the following transactions:

a. Borrowed $45,000 from the bank, with Calderon signing a note payable in the name of the business.

b. Paid cash of $40,000 to a real estate company to acquire land.

c. Performed service for a customer and received cash of $5,000.

d. Purchased supplies on credit, $300.

e. Performed customer service and earned revenue on account, $2,600.

f. Paid $1,200 on account.

g. Paid the following cash expenses: salaries, $3,000; rent, $1,500; and interest, $400.

h. Received $3,100 on account.

i. Received a $200 utility bill that will be paid next week.

j. Declared and paid dividend of $1,800.

I Requirements

1. Open the following accounts, with the balances indicated, in the ledger of Calderon Service Center, Inc. Use the T-account format.
   - Assets—Cash, $26,000; Accounts Receivable, $4,500; Supplies, no balance; Land, no balance
   - Liabilities—Accounts Payable, $2,000; Note Payable, no balance
   - Stockholders' Equity—Common Stock, $10,000; Retained Earnings, $18,500; Dividends, no balance
   - Revenues—Service Revenue, no balance
   - Expenses—(none have balances) Salary Expense, Rent Expense, Interest Expense, Utilities Expense
2. Journalize the preceding transactions. Key journal entries by transaction letter.
3. Post to the ledger and show the balance in each account after all the transactions have been posted.
4. Prepare the trial balance of Calderon Service Center, Inc., at March 31, 2010.
5. To determine the net income or net loss of the entity during the month of March, prepare the income statement for the month ended March 31, 2010. List expenses in order from the largest to the smallest.

Answers

Requirement 1

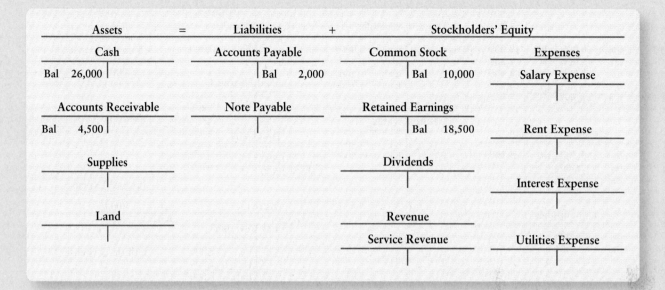

Requirement 2

Accounts and Explanation	Debit	Credit	Accounts and Explanation	Debit	Credit
a. Cash..	45,000		**g.** Salary Expense	3,000	
Note Payable		45,000	Rent Expense	1,500	
Borrowed cash on note payable.			Interest Expense	400	
b. Land..	40,000		Cash		4,900
Cash		40,000	Paid cash expenses.		
Purchased land for cash.			**h.** Cash..	3,100	
c. Cash..	5,000		Accounts Receivable		3,100
Service Revenue		5,000	Received on account.		
Performed service and received cash.			**i.** Utilities Expense..........................	200	
d. Supplies.....................................	300		Accounts Payable...................		200
Accounts Payable...............		300	Received utility bill.		
Purchased supplies on account.			**j.** Dividends...................................	1,800	
e. Accounts Receivable.................	2,600		Cash		1,800
Service Revenue		2,600	Declared and paid dividends.		
Performed service on account.					
f. Accounts Payable	1,200				
Cash		1,200			
Paid on account.					

▎Requirement 3

Assets		=	Liabilities		+	Stockholders' Equity	

Cash			
Bal	26,000	(b)	40,000
(a)	45,000	(f)	1,200
(c)	5,000	(g)	4,900
(h)	3,100	(j)	1,800
Bal	31,200		

Accounts Payable			
(f)	1,200	Bal	2,000
		(d)	300
		(i)	200
		Bal	1,300

Common Stock	
Bal	10,000

Retained Earnings	
Bal	18,500

Expenses	

Salary Expense		
(g)	3,000	
Bal	3,000	

Accounts Receivable			
Bal	4,500	(h)	3,100
(e)	2,600		
Bal	4,000		

Note Payable			
		(a)	45,000
		Bal	45,000

Dividends		
(j)	1,800	
Bal	1,800	

Rent Expense		
(g)	1,500	
Bal	1,500	

Supplies		
(d)	300	
Bal	300	

Revenue	

Service Revenue		
	(c)	5,000
	(e)	2,600
	Bal	7,600

Interest Expense		
(g)	400	
Bal	400	

Utilities Expense		
(i)	200	
Bal	200	

Land		
(b)	40,000	
Bal	40,000	

▎Requirement 4

Calderon Service Center, Inc.
Trial Balance
March 31, 2010

Account Title	Balance	
	Debit	Credit
Cash...	$31,200	
Accounts receivable................	4,000	
Supplies...................................	300	
Land...	40,000	
Accounts payable		$ 1,300
Note payable...........................		45,000
Common stock........................		10,000
Retained earnings...................		18,500
Dividends................................	1,800	
Service revenue.......................		7,600
Salary expense........................	3,000	
Rent expense	1,500	
Interest expense......................	400	
Utilities expense	200	
Total	$82,400	$82,400

Requirement 5

Calderon Service Center, Inc.
Income Statement
Month Ended March 31, 2010

Revenue		
Service revenue..................		$7,600
Expenses		
Salary expense..................	$3,000	
Rent expense...................	1,500	
Interest expense..............	400	
Utilities expense	200	
Total expenses.....................		5,100
Net income..........................		$2,500

REVIEW TRANSACTION ANALYSIS

Quick Check (Answers are given on page 122.)

1. A debit entry to an account
   a. increases liabilities.
   b. increases assets.
   c. increases stockholders' equity.
   d. both a and c.

2. Which account types normally have a credit balance?
   a. Revenues
   b. Liabilities
   c. Expenses
   d. Both a and b

3. An attorney performs services of $900 for a client and receives $100 cash with the remainder on account. The journal entry for this transaction would
   a. debit Cash, debit Service Revenue, credit Accounts Receivable.
   b. debit Cash, debit Accounts Receivable, credit Service Revenue.
   c. debit Cash, credit Service Revenue.
   d. debit Cash, credit Accounts Receivable, credit Service Revenue.

4. Accounts Payable had a normal beginning balance of $1,600. During the period, there were debit postings of $300 and credit postings of $900. What was the ending balance?
   a. $1,000 credit
   b. $2,200 debit
   c. $2,200 credit
   d. $1,000 debit

5. The list of all accounts with their balances is the
   a. balance sheet.
   b. journal.
   c. trial balance.
   d. chart of accounts.

6. The basic summary device of accounting is the
   a. account.
   b. ledger.
   c. trial balance.
   d. journal.

7. The beginning Cash balance was $9,000. At the end of the period, the balance was $11,000. If total cash paid out during the period was $25,000, the amount of cash receipts was
   a. $27,000.
   c. $23,000.
   b. $45,000.
   d. $5,000.

8. In a double-entry accounting system
   a. half of all the accounts have a normal credit balance.
   b. liabilities, owners' equity, and revenue accounts all have normal debit balances.
   c. a debit entry is recorded on the left side of a T-account.
   d. both a and c are correct.

9. Which accounts appear on which financial statement?

Balance sheet	*Income statement*
a. Receivables, land, payables	Revenues, supplies
b. Cash, revenues, land	Expenses, payables
c. Cash, receivables, payables	Revenues, expenses
d. Expenses, payables, cash	Revenues, receivables, land

10. A doctor purchases medical supplies of $760 and pays $380 cash with the remainder on account. The journal entry for this transaction would be which of the following?
    a. Supplies
       Cash
          Accounts Payable
    c. Supplies
          Accounts Payable
          Cash
    b. Supplies
       Accounts Payable
       Cash
    d. Supplies
       Accounts Receivable
          Cash

11. Which is the correct sequence for recording transactions and preparing financial statements?
    a. Ledger, trial balance, journal, financial statements
    b. Financial statements, trial balance, ledger, journal
    c. Ledger, journal, trial balance, financial statements
    d. Journal, ledger, trial balance, financial statements

12. The error of posting $300 as $30 can be detected by
    a. totaling each account's balance in the ledger.
    b. dividing the out-of-balance amount by 2.
    c. examining the chart of accounts.
    d. dividing the out-of-balance amount by 9.

Accounting Vocabulary

account (p. 65) The record of the changes that have occurred in a particular asset, liability, or stockholders' equity during a period. The basic summary device of accounting.

accrued liability (p. 66) A liability for an expense that has not yet been paid by the company.

cash (p. 65) Money and any medium of exchange that a bank accepts at face value.

chart of accounts (p. 90) List of a company's accounts and their account numbers.

credit (p. 77) The right side of an account.

debit (p. 77) The left side of an account.

journal (p. 80) The chronological accounting record of an entity's transactions.

ledger (p. 81) The book of accounts and their balances.

posting (p. 81) Copying amounts from the journal to the ledger.

transaction (p. 64) Any event that has a financial impact on the business and can be measured reliably.

trial balance (p. 87) A list of all the ledger accounts with their balances.

ASSESS YOUR PROGRESS

Short Exercises

S2-1 (*Learning Objective 1: Explaining an asset versus an expense*) Brian Horton opened a software consulting firm that immediately paid $8,000 for a computer. Was Horton's computer an expense of the business? If not, explain.

S2-2 (*Learning Objective 1: Analyzing the effects of transactions*) Young Software began with cash of $13,000. Young then bought supplies for $1,800 on account. Separately, Young paid $4,000 for a computer. Answer these questions.

    a. How much in total assets does Young have?

    b. How much in liabilities does Young owe?

S2-3 (*Learning Objectives 1, 2: Analyzing transactions; understanding how accounting works*) Hannah Lyle, MD, opened a medical practice. The business completed the following transactions:

Aug 1	Lyle invested $31,000 cash to start her medical practice. The business issued common stock to Lyle.
1	Purchased medical supplies on account totaling $9,200.
2	Paid monthly office rent of $3,000.
3	Recorded $10,000 revenue for service rendered to patients, received cash of $2,000, and sent bills to patients for the remainder.

After these transactions, how much cash does the business have to work with? Use a T-account to show your answer.

S2-4 (*Learning Objective 1: Analyzing transactions*) Refer to Short Exercise 2-3. Which of the transactions of Hannah Lyle, MD, increased the total assets of the business? For each transaction, identify the asset that was increased.

S2-5 (*Learning Objective 1: Analyzing transactions*) Capri Design specializes in imported clothing. During May, Capri completed a series of transactions. For each of the following items, give an example of a transaction that has the described effect on the accounting equation of Capri Design.

    a. Increase one asset and decrease another asset.

    b. Decrease an asset and decrease owners' equity.

    c. Decrease an asset and decrease a liability.

    d. Increase an asset and increase owners' equity.

    e. Increase an asset and increase a liability.

S2-6 (*Learning Objectives 2, 3: Understanding how accounting works; journalizing transactions*) After operating for several months, architect Gwen Markum completed the following transactions during the latter part of July:

Jul 15	Borrowed $34,000 from the bank, signing a note payable.
22	Performed service for clients on account totaling $8,500.
28	Received $6,500 cash on account from clients.
29	Received a utility bill of $700, an account payable that will be paid during August.
31	Paid monthly salary of $3,100 to employee.

Journalize the transactions of Gwen Markum, Architect. Include an explanation with each journal entry.

S2-7 (*Learning Objectives 2, 3: Understanding how accounting works; journalizing transactions; posting*) Architect David Delorme purchased supplies on account for $2,000. Later Delorme paid $500 on account.

1. Journalize the two transactions on the books of David Delorme, architect. Include an explanation for each transaction.
2. Open a T-account for Accounts Payable and post to Accounts Payable. Compute the balance and denote it as Bal.
3. How much does the Delorme business owe after both transactions? In which account does this amount appear?

S2-8 (*Learning Objectives 2, 3: Understanding how accounting works; journalizing transactions; posting*) Orman Unlimited performed service for a client who could not pay immediately. Orman expected to collect the $5,200 the following month. A month later, Orman received $2,400 cash from the client.

1. Record the two transactions on the books of Orman Unlimited. Include an explanation for each transaction.
2. Post to these T-accounts: Cash, Accounts Receivable, and Service Revenue. Compute each account balance and denote as Bal.

S2-9 (*Learning Objective 4: Preparing and using a trial balance*) Assume that Old Boardwalk reported the following summarized data at December 31, 2010. Accounts appear in no particular order; dollar amounts are in millions.

Other liabilities	$ 5	Revenues	$37
Cash	6	Other assets	13
Expenses	27	Accounts payable	1
Stockholders' equity	3		

Prepare the trial balance of Old Boardwalk at December 31, 2010. List the accounts in their proper order. How much was Old Boardwalk's net income or net loss?

S2-10 (*Learning Objective 4: Using a trial balance*) Redberry's trial balance follows.

Redberry, Inc.
Trial Balance
December 31, 2010

	Balance	
Account Title	Debit	Credit
Cash	$ 7,500	
Accounts receivable	12,000	
Supplies	5,000	
Equipment	24,000	
Land	52,000	
Accounts payable		$ 21,000
Note payable		32,000
Common stock		7,000
Retained earnings		9,000
Service revenue		63,000
Salary expense	23,000	
Rent expense	7,500	
Utilities expense	1,000	
Total	$132,000	$132,000

Compute these amounts for the business:

1. Total assets
2. Total liabilities
3. Net income or net loss during December

S2-11 *(Learning Objective 4: Using a trial balance)* Refer to Redberry's trial balance in Short Exercise 2-10. The purpose of this exercise is to help you learn how to correct three common accounting errors.

Error 1. Slide. Suppose the trial balance lists Land as $5,200 instead of $52,000. Recompute column totals, take the difference, and divide by 9. The result is an integer (no decimals), which suggests that the error is either a transposition or a slide.

Error 2. Transposition. Assume the trial balance lists Accounts Receivable as $21,000 instead of $12,000. Recompute column totals, take the difference, and divide by 9. The result is an integer (no decimals), which suggests that the error is either a transposition or a slide.

Error 3. Mislabeling an item. Assume that Redberry accidentally listed Accounts Receivable as a credit balance instead of a debit. Recompute the trial balance totals for debits and credits. Then take the difference between total debits and total credits, and divide the difference by 2. You get back to the original amount of Accounts Receivable.

S2-12 *(Learning Objective 2: Using key accounting terms)* Accounting has its own vocabulary and basic relationships. Match the accounting terms at left with the corresponding definition or meaning at right.

____ **1.** Debit	**A.** The cost of operating a business; a decrease in
____ **2.** Expense	stockholders' equity
____ **3.** Net income	**B.** Always a liability
____ **4.** Ledger	**C.** Revenues – Expenses
____ **5.** Posting	**D.** Grouping of accounts
____ **6.** Normal balance	**E.** Assets – Liabilities
____ **7.** Payable	**F.** Record of transactions
____ **8.** Journal	**G.** Always an asset
____ **9.** Receivable	**H.** Left side of an account
____ **10.** Owners' equity	**I.** Side of an account where increases are recorded
	J. Copying data from the journal to the ledger

S2-13 *(Learning Objective 5: Analyzing transactions without a journal)* Seventh Investments, Inc., began by issuing common stock for cash of $140,000. The company immediately purchased computer equipment on account for $100,000.

1. Set up the following T-accounts of Seventh Investments, Inc.: Cash, Computer Equipment, Accounts Payable, Common Stock.
2. Record the first two transactions of the business directly in the T-accounts without using a journal.
3. Show that total debits equal total credits.

Exercises

All of the A and B exercises can be found within MyAccountingLab, an online homework and practice environment. Your instructor may ask you to complete these exercises using MyAccountingLab.

MyAccountingLab

(Group A)

E2-14A *(Learning Objectives 1, 2: Analyzing transactions)* Assume M. Crew opened a store in Dallas, starting with cash and common stock of $94,000. Melissa Farino, the store manager, then signed a note payable to purchase land for $88,000 and a building for $123,000. Farino also paid $60,000 for equipment and $8,000 for supplies to use in the business.

writing assignment ■

Suppose the home office of M. Crew requires a weekly report from store managers. Write Farino's memo to the home office to report on her purchases. Include the store's balance sheet as the final part of your memo. Prepare a T-account to compute the balance for Cash.

E2-15A (*Learning Objective 1: Analyzing transactions*) The following selected events were experienced by either Solution Seekers, Inc., a corporation, or Paul Flynn, the major stockholder. State whether each event (1) increased, (2) decreased, or (3) had no effect on the total assets of the business. Identify any specific asset affected.

  a. Received $9,200 cash from customers on account.
  b. Flynn used personal funds to purchase a swimming pool for his home.
  c. Sold land and received cash of $65,000 (the land was carried on the company's books at $65,000).
  d. Borrowed $60,000 from the bank.
  e. Made cash purchase of land for a building site, $90,000.
  f. Received $25,000 cash and issued stock to a stockholder.
  g. Paid $70,000 cash on accounts payable.
  h. Purchased equipment and signed a $101,000 promissory note in payment.
  i. Purchased merchandise inventory on account for $17,000.
  j. The business paid Flynn a cash dividend of $5,000.

E2-16A (*Learning Objective 1: Analyzing transactions; using the accounting equation*) Harry Samson opened a medical practice specializing in surgery. During the first month of operation (March), the business, titled Harry Samson, Professional Corporation (P.C.), experienced the following events:

Mar	6	Samson invested $42,000 in the business, which in turn issued its common stock to him.
	9	The business paid cash for land costing $25,000. Samson plans to build an office building on the land.
	12	The business purchased medical supplies for $16,000 on account.
	15	Harry Samson, P.C., officially opened for business.
	15–31	During the rest of the month, Samson treated patients and earned service revenue of $7,700, receiving cash for half the revenue earned.
	15–31	The business paid cash expenses: employee salaries, $900; office rent, $900; utilities, $200.
	31	The business sold supplies to another physician for cost of $200.
	31	The business borrowed $18,000, signing a note payable to the bank.
	31	The business paid $1,100 on account.

❙ Requirements

  1. Analyze the effects of these events on the accounting equation of the medical practice of Harry Samson, P.C.
  2. After completing the analysis, answer these questions about the business.
    a. How much are total assets?
    b. How much does the business expect to collect from patients?
    c. How much does the business owe in total?
    d. How much of the business's assets does Samson really own?
    e. How much net income or net loss did the business experience during its first month of operations?

E2-17A (*Learning Objectives 2, 3: Understanding how accounting works; journalizing transactions*) Refer to Exercise 2-16A.

❙ Requirement

  1. Record the transactions in the journal of Harry Samson, P.C. List the transactions by date and give an explanation for each transaction.

E2-18A (*Learning Objectives 2, 3: Understanding how accounting works; journalizing transactions*) Harris Tree Cellular, Inc., completed the following transactions during April 2010, its first month of operations:

■ **general ledger**

Apr	1	Received $19,100 and issued common stock.
	2	Purchased $300 of office supplies on account.
	4	Paid $14,700 cash for land to use as a building site.
	6	Performed service for customers and received cash of $2,700.
	9	Paid $200 on accounts payable.
	17	Performed service for ShipEx on account totaling $1,000.
	23	Collected $200 from ShipEx on account.
	30	Paid the following expenses: salary, $1,300; rent, $500.

❙ Requirement

1. Record the transactions in the journal of Harris Tree Cellular, Inc. Key transactions by date and include an explanation for each entry.

E2-19A (*Learning Objectives 3, 4: Posting to the ledger; preparing and using a trial balance*) Refer to Exercise 2-18A.

■ **general ledger**

❙ Requirements

1. After journalizing the transactions of Exercise 2-18A, post the entries to the ledger, using T-accounts. Key transactions by date. Date the ending balance of each account April 30.
2. Prepare the trial balance of Harris Tree Cellular, Inc., at April 30, 2010.
3. How much are total assets, total liabilities, and total stockholders' equity on April 30?

E2-20A (*Learning Objectives 2, 3: Understanding how accounting works; journalizing transactions*) The first seven transactions of Fournier Advertising, Inc., have been posted to the company's accounts as follows:

	Cash				Supplies			Equipment			Land	
(1)	10,200	(3)	6,000	(4)	500	(5)	150	(6)	5,100	(3)	30,000	
(2)	6,900	(6)	5,100									
(5)	150	(7)	100									

	Accounts Payable				Note Payable			Common Stock	
(7)	100	(4)	500		(2)	6,900		(1)	10,200
					(3)	24,000			

❙ Requirement

1. Prepare the journal entries that served as the sources for the seven transactions. Include an explanation for each entry. As Fournier moves into the next period, how much cash does the business have? How much does Fournier owe in total liabilities?

E2-21A (*Learning Objective 4: Preparing and using a trial balance*) The accounts of Deluxe Deck Service, Inc., follow with their normal balances at June 30, 2010. The accounts are listed in no particular order.

Account	Balance	Account	Balance
Common stock..................	$ 8,400	Dividends..........................	$ 6,100
Accounts payable..............	4,400	Utilities expense	2,100
Service revenue.................	22,400	Accounts receivable...........	15,900
Land.................................	29,800	Delivery expense	700
Note payable....................	10,500	Retained earnings..............	25,600
Cash.................................	8,500	Salary expense..................	8,200

❘ Requirements

1. Prepare the company's trial balance at June 30, 2010, listing accounts in proper sequence, as illustrated in the chapter. For example, Accounts Receivable comes before Land. List the expense with the largest balance first, the expense with the next largest balance second, and so on.

2. Prepare the financial statement for the month ended June 30, 2010, that will tell the company the results of operations for the month.

E2-22A (*Learning Objective 4: Correcting errors in a trial balance*) The trial balance of Carver, Inc., at September 30, 2010, does not balance:

Cash	$ 4,500	
Accounts receivable	13,100	
Inventory	16,600	
Supplies	200	
Land	52,000	
Accounts payable		$11,900
Common stock		47,500
Service revenue		30,500
Salary expense	1,700	
Rent expense	1,100	
Utilities expense	900	
Total	$90,100	$89,900

The accounting records hold the following errors:

a. Recorded a $400 cash revenue transaction by debiting Accounts Receivable. The credit entry was correct.
b. Posted a $3,000 credit to Accounts Payable as $300.
c. Did not record utilities expense or the related account payable in the amount of $500.
d. Understated Common Stock by $500.
e. Omitted Insurance Expense of $3,000, from the trial balance.

❘ Requirement

1. Prepare the correct trial balance at September 30, 2010, complete with a heading. Journal entries are not required.

E2-23A (*Learning Objective 5: Recording transactions without a journal*) Set up the following T-accounts: Cash, Accounts Receivable, Office Supplies, Office Furniture, Accounts Payable, Common Stock, Dividends, Service Revenue, Salary Expense, and Rent Expense. Record the following transactions directly in the T-accounts without using a journal. Use the letters to identify the transactions.

a. Linda Oxford opened a law firm by investing $12,000 cash and office furniture valued at $8,600. Organized as a professional corporation, the business issued common stock to Oxford.
b. Paid monthly rent of $1,000.
c. Purchased office supplies on account, $700.
d. Paid employees' salaries of $2,000.
e. Paid $300 of the account payable created in Transaction c.
f. Performed legal service on account, $8,100.
g. Declared and paid dividends of $2,900.

writing assignment ■

E2-24A (*Learning Objective 4: Preparing and using a trial balance*) Refer to Exercise 2-23A.

1. After recording the transactions in Exercise 2-23A, prepare the trial balance of Linda Oxford, Attorney, at May 31, 2010. Use the T-accounts that have been prepared for the business.
2. How well did the business perform during its first month? Compute net income (or net loss) for the month.

(Group B)

E2-25B (*Learning Objectives 1, 2: Analyzing transactions*) Assume T. Crew opened a store in San Diego, starting with cash and common stock of $90,000. Barbara Breen, the store manager, then signed a note payable to purchase land for $91,000 and a building for $120,000. Breen also paid $62,000 for equipment and $13,000 for supplies to use in the business.

writing assignment ■

Suppose the home office of T. Crew requires a weekly report from store managers. Write Breen's memo to the head office to report on her purchases. Include the store's balance sheet as the final part of your memo. Prepare a T-account to compute the balance for Cash.

E2-26B (*Learning Objective 1: Analyzing transactions*) The following selected events were experienced by either Simple Solutions, Inc., a corporation, or Bob Gallagher, the major stockholder. State whether each event (1) increased, (2) decreased, or (3) had no effect on the total assets of the business. Identify any specific asset affected.

 a. Received $30,000 cash and issued stock to a stockholder.
 b. Purchased equipment for $75,000 cash.
 c. Paid $10,000 cash on accounts payable.
 d. Gallagher used personal funds to purchase a flat screen TV for his home.
 e. Purchased land for a building site and signed an $80,000 promissory note to the bank.
 f. Received $17,000 cash from customers for services performed.
 g. Sold land and received a note receivable of $55,000 (the land was carried on the company's books at $55,000).
 h. Earned $25,000 in revenue for services performed. The customer promises to pay Simple Solutions in one month.
 i. Purchased supplies on account for $5,000.
 j. The business paid Gallagher a cash dividend of $4,000.

E2-27B (*Learning Objective 1: Analyzing transactions; using the accounting equation*) Kyle Cohen opened a medical practice specializing in surgery. During the first month of operation (July), the business, titled Kyle Cohen, Professional Corporation (P.C.), experienced the following events:

Jul	6	Cohen invested $44,000 in the business, which in turn issued its common stock to him.
	9	The business paid cash for land costing $31,000. Cohen plans to build an office building on the land.
	12	The business purchased medical supplies for $1,700 on account.
	15	Kyle Cohen, P.C., officially opened for business.
	15–31	During the rest of the month, Cohen treated patients and earned service revenue of $7,600, receiving cash for half the revenue earned.
	15–31	The business paid cash expenses: employee salaries, $800; office rent, $800; utilities, $300.
	31	The business sold supplies to another physician for cost of $400.
	31	The business borrowed $16,000, signing a note payable to the bank.
	31	The business paid $700 on account.

▌Requirements

 1. Analyze the effects of these events on the accounting equation of the medical practice of Kyle Cohen, P.C.
 2. After completing the analysis, answer these questions about the business.
    a. How much are total assets?
    b. How much does the business expect to collect from patients?
    c. How much does the business owe in total?
    d. How much of the business's assets does Cohen really own?
    e. How much net income or net loss did the business experience during its first month of operations?

E2-28B (*Learning Objectives 2, 3: Understanding how accounting works; journalizing transactions*) Refer to Exercise 2-27B.

I Requirement

1. Record the transactions in the journal of Kyle Cohen, P.C. List the transactions by date and give an explanation for each transaction.

E2-29B (*Learning Objectives 2, 3: Understanding how accounting works; journalizing transactions*) Green Tree Cellular, Inc., completed the following transactions during April 2010, its first month of operations:

Apr	1	Received $19,600 and issued common stock.
	2	Purchased $900 of office supplies on account.
	4	Paid $14,600 cash for land to use as a building site.
	6	Performed service for customers and received cash of $2,500.
	9	Paid $200 on accounts payable.
	17	Performed service for **UPS** on account totaling $1,200.
	23	Collected $900 from **UPS** on account.
	30	Paid the following expenses: salary, $1,900; rent, $1,400.

I Requirement

1. Record the transactions in the journal of Green Tree Cellular, Inc. Key transactions by date and include an explanation for each entry.

E2-30B (*Learning Objectives 3, 4: Posting to the ledger; preparing and using a trial balance*) Refer to Exercise 2-29B.

I Requirements

1. Post the entries to the ledger, using T-accounts. Key transactions by date. Date the ending balance of each account April 30.
2. Prepare the trial balance of Green Tree Cellular, Inc., at April 30, 2010.
3. How much are total assets, total liabilities, and total shareholders' equity on April 30?

E2-31B (*Learning Objectives 2, 3: Understanding how accounting works; journalizing transactions*) The first seven transactions of Portman Advertising, Inc., have been posted to the company's accounts as follows:

Cash				Supplies				Equipment				Land		
(1)	9,700	(3)	5,000	(4)	500	(5)	80	(6)	6,000			(3)	30,000	
(2)	6,700	(6)	6,000											
(5)	80	(7)	90											

Accounts Payable				Note Payable				Common Stock		
(7)	90	(4)	500			(2)	6,700		(1)	9,700
						(3)	25,000			

I Requirement

1. Prepare the journal entries that served as the sources for the seven transactions. Include an explanation for each entry. As Portman moves into the next period, how much cash does the business have? How much does Portman owe in total liabilities?

E2-32B (*Learning Objective 4: Preparing and using a trial balance*) The accounts of Grand Pool Service, Inc., follow with their normal balances at June 30, 2010. The accounts are listed in no particular order.

Account	Balance	Account	Balance
Common stock.................	$ 8,000	Dividends..........................	$ 6,300
Accounts payable	4,500	Utilities expense	1,600
Service revenue.................	22,800	Accounts receivable...........	15,300
Land...............................	29,400	Delivery expense	200
Note payable....................	10,500	Retained earnings.............	24,600
Cash...............................	9,400	Salary expense..................	8,200

Requirements

1. Prepare the company's trial balance at June 30, 2010, listing accounts in proper sequence, as illustrated in the chapter. For example, Accounts Receivable comes before Land. List the expense with the largest balance first, the expense with the next largest balance second, and so on.
2. Prepare the financial statement for the month ended June 30, 2010, that will tell the company the results of operations for the month.

E2-33B (*Learning Objective 4: Correcting errors in a trial balance*) The trial balance of Farris, Inc., at June 30, 2010, does not balance.

Cash......................................	$ 4,100	
Accounts receivable..............	13,300	
Inventory.............................	16,500	
Supplies...............................	700	
Land.....................................	53,000	
Accounts payable		$12,400
Common stock......................		47,800
Service revenue......................		31,900
Salary expense......................	2,200	
Rent expense.......................	600	
Utilities expense	300	
Total.....................................	$90,700	$92,100

The accounting records hold the following errors:

    a. Recorded a $200 cash revenue transaction by debiting Accounts Receivable. The credit entry was correct.
    b. Posted a $2,000 credit to Accounts Payable as $200.
    c. Did not record utilities expense or the related account payable in the amount of $300.
    d. Understated Common Stock by $100.
    e. Omitted Insurance Expense of $3,300, from the trial balance.

Requirement

1. Prepare the correct trial balance at June 30, 2010, complete with a heading. Journal entries are not required.

E2-34B (*Learning Objective 5: Recording transactions without a journal*) Set up the following T-accounts: Cash, Accounts Receivable, Office Supplies, Office Furniture, Accounts Payable, Common Stock, Dividends, Service Revenue, Salary Expense, and Rent Expense. Record the following transactions directly in the T-accounts without using a journal. Use the letters to identify the transactions.

a. Linda Conway opened a law firm by investing $11,000 cash and office furniture valued at $9,100. Organized as a professional corporation, the business issued common stock to Conway.

b. Paid monthly rent of $1,200.

c. Purchased office supplies on account, $700.

d. Paid employee salaries of $2,200.

e. Paid $300 of the accounts payable created in Transaction c.

f. Performed legal service on account, $8,300.

g. Declared and paid dividends of $2,100.

E2-35B (*Learning Objective 4: Preparing and using a trial balance*) Refer to Exercise 2-34B.

❙ *Requirements*

1. Prepare the trial balance of Linda Conway, Attorney, at January 31, 2010. Use the T-accounts that have been prepared for the business.

2. How well did the business perform during its first month? Compute net income (or net loss) for the month.

Serial Exercise

Exercise 2-36 begins an accounting cycle that is completed in Chapter 3.

■ **general ledger**

E2-36 (*Learning Objectives 2, 3, 4: Recording transactions; preparing a trial balance*) Jerome Smith, Certified Public Accountant, operates as a professional corporation (P.C.). The business completed these transactions during the first part of March, 2010:

Mar 2	Received $7,000 cash from Smith, and issued common stock to him.	
2	Paid monthly office rent, $600.	
3	Paid cash for a Dell computer, $2,400, with the computer expected to remain in service for five years.	
4	Purchased office furniture on account, $7,500, with the furniture projected to last for five years.	
5	Purchased supplies on account, $500.	
9	Performed tax service for a client and received cash for the full amount of $1,200.	
12	Paid utility expenses, $300.	
18	Performed consulting service for a client on account, $2,100.	

❙ *Requirements*

1. Journalize the transactions. Explanations are not required.

2. Post to the T-accounts. Key all items by date and denote an account balance on March 18, 2010, as Bal.

3. Prepare a trial balance at March 18, 2010. In the Serial Exercise of Chapter 3, we add transactions for the remainder of March and will require a trial balance at March 31.

Challenge Exercises

E2-37 (*Learning Objective 5: Computing financial statement amounts*) The manager of Pierce Furniture needs to compute the following amounts.

a. Total cash paid during October.

b. Cash collections from customers during October. Analyze Accounts Receivable.

c. Cash paid on a note payable during October. Analyze Notes Payable.

Here's the additional data you need to analyze the accounts:

	Balance		Additional Information
Account	Sep 30	Oct 31	for the Month of October
1. Cash..............................	$11,000	$ 6,000	Cash receipts, $83,000
2. Accounts Receivable.......	28,000	26,000	Sales on account, $47,000
3. Notes Payable	15,000	23,000	New borrowing, $24,000

❙ Requirement

1. Prepare a T-account to compute each amount, *a* through *c*.

E2-38 (*Learning Objectives 1, 4: Analyzing transactions; using a trial balance*) The trial balance of Circle 360, Inc., at October 31, 2010, does not balance.

Cash..................................	$ 4,400	Common stock....................	$20,700
Accounts receivable.............	6,800	Retained earnings................	7,800
Land...................................	34,000	Service revenue....................	9,000
Accounts payable	6,300	Salary expense.....................	3,200
Note payable......................	5,400	Advertising expense.............	1,000

❙ Requirements

1. How much out of balance is the trial balance? Determine the out-of-balance amount. The error lies in the Accounts Receivable account. Add the out-of-balance amount to, or subtract it from, Accounts Receivable to determine the correct balance of Accounts Receivable.

2. After correcting Accounts receivable, advise the top management of Circle 360, Inc., on the company's
   a. total assets.
   b. total liabilities.
   c. net income or net loss for October.

E2-39 (*Learning Objective 1: Analyzing transactions*) This question concerns the items and the amounts that two entities, Nashua Co., and Ditka Hospital, should report in their financial statements.

During September, Ditka provided Nashua with medical exams for Nashua employees and sent a bill for $46,000. On October 7, Nashua sent a check to Ditka for $34,000. Nashua began September with a cash balance of $57,000; Ditka began with cash of $0.

❙ Requirements

1. For this situation, show everything that both Nashua and Ditka will report on their September and October income statements and on their balance sheets at September 30 and October 31.

2. After showing what each company should report, briefly explain how the Nashua and Ditka data relate to each other.

Quiz

Test your understanding of transaction analysis by answering the following questions. Select the best choice from among the possible answers.

Q2-40 An investment of cash into the business will
a. decrease total liabilities.
b. decrease total assets.
c. have no effect on total assets.
d. increase stockholders' equity.

Q2-41 Purchasing a laptop computer on account will
a. increase total liabilities.
b. have no effect on stockholders' equity.
c. increase total assets.
d. all of the above.

Q2-42 Performing a service on account will
a. increase stockholders' equity.
b. increase total assets.
c. increase total liabilities.
d. both a and b.

Q2-43 Receiving cash from a customer on account will
a. increase total assets.
b. decrease liabilities.
c. increase stockholders equity.
d. have no effect on total assets.

Q2-44 Purchasing computer equipment for cash will
a. decrease both total assets and stockholders' equity.
b. increase both total assets and total liabilities.
c. have no effect on total assets, total liabilities, or stockholders' equity.
d. decrease both total liabilities and stockholders' equity.

Q2-45 Purchasing a building for $110,000 by paying cash of $15,000 and signing a note payable for $95,000 will
a. increase both total assets and total liabilities by $95,000.
b. increase both total assets and total liabilities by $110,000.
c. decrease both total assets and total liabilities by $15,000.
d. decrease total assets and increase total liabilities by $15,000.

Q2-46 What is the effect on total assets and stockholders' equity of paying the telephone bill as soon as it is received each month?

Total assets	Stockholders' equity
a. No effect	No effect
b. Decrease	No effect
c. No effect	Decrease
d. Decrease	Decrease

Q2-47 Which of the following transactions will increase an asset and increase a liability?
a. Purchasing office equipment for cash
b. Issuing stock
c. Payment of an account payable
d. Buying equipment on account

Q2-48 Which of the following transactions will increase an asset and increase stockholders' equity?
a. Borrowing money from a bank
b. Purchasing supplies on account
c. Performing a service on account for a customer
d. Collecting cash from a customer on an account receivable

Q2-49 Where do we first record a transaction?
a. Journal
b. Trial balance
c. Account
d. Ledger

Q2-50 Which of the following is not an asset account?

a. Salary Expense

b. Service Revenue

c. Common Stock

d. None of the above accounts is an asset.

Q2-51 Which statement is false?

a. Assets are increased by debits.

b. Revenues are increased by credits.

c. Liabilities are decreased by debits.

d. Dividends are increased by credits.

Q2-52 The journal entry to record the receipt of land and a building and issuance of common stock

a. debits Land and credits Common Stock.

b. debits Land and Building and credits Common Stock.

c. debits Land, Building, and Common Stock.

d. debits Common Stock and credits Land and Building.

Q2-53 The journal entry to record the purchase of supplies on account

a. debits Supplies and credits Accounts Payable.

b. credits Supplies and debits Cash.

c. credits Supplies and debits Accounts Payable.

d. debits Supplies Expense and credits Supplies.

Q2-54 If the credit to record the purchase of supplies on account is not posted,

a. expenses will be overstated.

b. liabilities will be understated.

c. stockholders' equity will be understated.

d. assets will be understated.

Q2-55 The journal entry to record a payment on account will

a. debit Cash and credit Expenses.

b. debit Accounts Payable and credit Retained Earnings.

c. debit Accounts Payable and credit Cash.

d. debit Expenses and credit Cash.

Q2-56 If the credit to record the payment of an account payable is not posted,

a. expenses will be understated.

b. liabilities will be understated.

c. cash will be understated.

d. cash will be overstated.

Q2-57 Which statement is false?

a. A trial balance is the same as a balance sheet.

b. A trial balance can verify the equality of debits and credits.

c. A trial balance can be taken at any time.

d. A trial balance lists all the accounts with their current balances.

Q2-58 A business's receipt of a $120,000 building, with a $60,000 mortgage payable, and issuance of $60,000 of common stock will

a. increase stockholders' equity by $60,000.

b. increase assets by $60,000.

c. decrease assets by $60,000.

d. increase stockholders' equity by $120,000.

Q2-59 Gartex, a new company, completed these transactions. What will Gartex's total assets equal?

(1) Stockholders invested $54,000 cash and inventory worth $27,000.

(2) Sales on account, $15,000.

a. $66,000

b. $69,000

c. $96,000

d. $81,000

Problems

MyAccountingLab | All of the A and B problems can be found within MyAccountingLab, an online homework and practice environment. Your instructor may ask you to complete these problems using MyAccountingLab.

(Group A)

writing assignment ■ **P2-60A** (*Learning Objective 4: Analyzing a trial balance*) The trial balance of Luxury Specialties, Inc., follows.

Luxury Specialties
Trial Balance
December 31, 2010

Cash	$ 11,000	
Accounts receivable	48,000	
Prepaid expenses	5,000	
Equipment	239,000	
Building	105,000	
Accounts payable		$108,000
Note payable		90,000
Common stock		35,000
Retained earnings		38,000
Dividends	19,000	
Service revenue		257,000
Rent expense	28,000	
Advertising expense	4,000	
Wage expense	61,000	
Supplies expense	8,000	
Total	$528,000	$528,000

Ashley Richards, your best friend, is considering investing in Luxury Specialties, Inc. Ashley seeks your advice in interpreting this information. Specifically, she asks how to use this trial balance to compute the company's total assets, total liabilities, and net income or net loss for the year.

▌Requirement

1. Write a short note to answer Ashley's questions. In your note, state the amounts of Luxury Specialties' total assets, total liabilities, and net income or net loss for the year. Also show how you computed each amount.

P2-61A (*Learning Objective 1: Analyzing transactions with the accounting equation; preparing the financial statements*) The following amounts summarize the financial position of Mason Resources, Inc., on May 31, 2010:

	Assets					=	Liabilities	+	Stockholders' Equity		
	Cash	+	Accounts Receivable	+ Supplies +	Land	=	Accounts Payable	+	Common Stock	+	Retained Earnings
Bal	1,150		1,350		11,900		7,600		4,400		2,400

During June 2010, Mason Resources completed these transactions:

a. The business received cash of $9,200 and issued common stock.

b. Performed services for a customer and received cash of $6,700.

c. Paid $4,500 on accounts payable.

d. Purchased supplies on account, $600.

e. Collected cash from a customer on account, $700.

f. Consulted on the design of a computer system and billed the customer for services rendered, $2,900.

g. Recorded the following business expenses for the month: (1) paid office rent—$1,100; (2) paid advertising—$1,000.

h. Declared and paid a cash dividend of $1,500.

❙ Requirements

1. Analyze the effects of the preceding transactions on the accounting equation of Mason Resources, Inc.

2. Prepare the income statement of Mason Resources, Inc., for the month ended June 30, 2010. List expenses in decreasing order by amount.

3. Prepare the entity's statement of retained earnings for the month ended June 30, 2010.

4. Prepare the balance sheet of Mason Resources, Inc., at June 30, 2010.

P2-62A (*Learning Objectives 2, 3: Recording transactions; posting*) This problem can be used in conjunction with Problem 2-61A. Refer to Problem 2-61A.

■ general ledger

❙ Requirements

1. Journalize the June transactions of Mason Resources, Inc. Explanations are not required.

2. Prepare T-Accounts for each account. Insert in each T-account its May 31 balance as given (example: Cash $1,150). Then, post the June transactions to the T-Accounts.

3. Compute the balance in each account.

P2-63A (*Learning Objectives 1, 2, 3: Analyzing transactions; understanding how accounting works; journalizing transactions*) Demers Real Estate Co. experienced the following events during the organizing phase and its first month of operations. Some of the events were personal for the stockholders and did not affect the business. Others were transactions of the business.

Nov	4	David Demers, the major stockholder of real estate company, received $100,000 cash from an inheritance.
	5	Demers deposited $57,000 cash in a new business bank account titled Demers Real Estate Co. The business issued common stock to Demers.
	6	The business paid $600 cash for letterhead stationery for the new office.
	7	The business purchased office equipment. The company paid cash of $12,000 and agreed to pay the account payable for the remainder, $8,000, within three months.
	10	Demers sold EVN stock, which he had owned for several years, receiving $76,500 cash from his stockbroker.
	11	Demers deposited the $76,500 cash from sale of the EVN stock in his personal bank account.
	12	A representative of a large company telephoned Demers and told him of the company's intention to transfer $15,500 of business to Demers.
	18	Demers finished a real estate deal for a client and submitted his bill for services, $3,500. Demers expects to collect from the client within two weeks.
	21	The business paid half its account payable on the equipment purchased on November 7.
	25	The business paid office rent of $1,300.
	30	The business declared and paid a cash dividend of $1,900.

❙ Requirements

1. Classify each of the preceding events as one of the following:
    a. A business-related event but not a transaction to be recorded by Demers Real Estate Co.
    b. A business transaction for a stockholder, not to be recorded by Demers Real Estate Co.
    c. A business transaction to be recorded by Demers Real Estate Co.
2. Analyze the effects of the preceding events on the accounting equation of Demers Real Estate Co.
3. Record the transactions of the business in its journal. Include an explanation for each entry.

■ **general ledger**

P2-64A *(Learning Objectives 2, 3: Understanding how accounting works; analyzing and recording transactions)* During December, Smith Auction Co. completed the following transactions:

Dec	1	Smith received $26,000 cash and issued common stock to the stockholders.
	5	Paid monthly rent, $1,100.
	9	Paid $8,500 cash and signed a $30,000 note payable to purchase land for an office site.
	10	Purchased supplies on account, $1,700.
	19	Paid $600 on account.
	22	Borrowed $20,000 from the bank for business use. Smith signed a note payable to the bank in the name of the business.
	31	Service revenue earned during the month included $12,000 cash and $8,000 on account.
	31	Paid employees' salaries ($2,400), advertising expense ($1,500), and utilities expense ($1,400).
	31	Declared and paid a cash dividend of $6,500.

Smith's business uses the following accounts: Cash, Accounts Receivable, Supplies, Land, Accounts Payable, Notes Payable, Common Stock, Dividends, Service Revenue, Salary Expense, Advertising Expense, and Utilities Expense.

❙ Requirements

1. Journalize each transaction of Smith Auction Co. Explanations are not required.
2. Post to these T-accounts: Cash, Accounts Payable, and Notes Payable.
3. After these transactions, how much cash does the business have? How much in total liabilities does it owe?

■ **general ledger**

P2-65A *(Learning Objectives 2, 3, 4: Understanding how accounting works; journalizing transactions; posting; preparing and using a trial balance)* During the first month of operations, Simmons Heating and Air Conditioning, Inc., completed the following transactions:

Jan	2	Simmons received $39,000 cash and issued common stock to the stockholders.
	3	Purchased supplies, $200, and equipment, $3,100, on account.
	4	Performed service for a customer and received cash, $1,600.
	7	Paid cash to acquire land, $27,000.
	11	Performed service for a customer and billed the customer, $900. We expect to collect within one month.
	16	Paid for the equipment purchased January 3 on account.
	17	Paid the telephone bill, $170.
	18	Received partial payment from customer on account, $450.
	22	Paid the water and electricity bills, $190.
	29	Received $1,400 cash for servicing the heating unit of a customer.
	31	Paid employee salary, $2,400.
	31	Declared and paid dividends of $3,000.

Requirements

1. Record each transaction in the journal. Key each transaction by date. Explanations are not required.
2. Post the transactions to the T-accounts, using transaction dates as posting references. Label the ending balance of each account Bal, as shown in the chapter.
3. Prepare the trial balance of Simmons Heating and Air Conditioning, Inc., at January 31 of the current year.
4. The manager asks you how much in total resources the business has to work with, how much it owes, and whether January was profitable (and by how much).

P2-66A (*Learning Objectives 4, 5: Recording transactions directly in T-accounts; preparing and using a trial balance*) During the first month of operations (November 2010), Stein Services Corporation completed the following selected transactions:

■ **general ledger**

    a. The business received cash of $28,000 and a building valued at $52,000. The corporation issued common stock to the stockholders.
    b. Borrowed $37,300 from the bank; signed a note payable.
    c. Paid $33,000 for music equipment.
    d. Purchased supplies on account, $500.
    e. Paid employees' salaries, $2,500.
    f. Received $1,600 for music service performed for customers.
    g. performed service for customers on account, $3,200.
    h. Paid $100 of the account payable created in Transaction d.
    i. Received an $800 bill for utility expense that will be paid in the near future.
    j. Received cash on account, $1,200.
    k. Paid the following cash expenses: (1) rent, $1,200; (2) advertising, $700.

Requirements

1. Record each transaction directly in the T-accounts without using a journal. Use the letters to identify the transactions.
2. Prepare the trial balance of Stein Services Corporation at November 30, 2010.

(Group B)

P2-67B (*Learning Objective 4: Analyzing a trial balance*) The trial balance of Advantage Specialties, Inc., follows:

writing assignment ■

Advantage Specialties, Inc.
Trial Balance
December 31, 2010

Cash	$ 11,000	
Accounts receivable	49,000	
Prepaid expenses	5,000	
Equipment	234,000	
Building	96,000	
Accounts payable		$102,000
Note payable		95,000
Common stock		34,000
Retained earnings		36,000
Dividends	23,000	
Service revenue		252,000
Rent expense	25,000	
Advertising expense	4,000	
Wage expense	65,000	
Supplies expense	7,000	
Total	$519,000	$519,000

Rebecca Smith, your best friend, is considering making an investment in Advantage Specialties, Inc. Rebecca seeks your advice in interpreting the company's information. Specifically, she asks how to use this trial balance to compute the company's total assets, total liabilities, and net income or net loss for the year.

I Requirement

1. Write a short note to answer Rebecca's questions. In your note, state the amounts of Advantage Specialties' total assets, total liabilities, and net income or net loss for the year. Also show how you computed each amount.

P2-68B (*Learning Objective 1: Analyzing transactions with the accounting equation; preparing the financial statements*) The following amounts summarize the financial position of Rodriguez Resources on May 31, 2010:

			Assets					=	Liabilities	+	Stockholders' Equity		
	Cash	+	Accounts Receivable	+	Supplies	+	Land	=	Accounts Payable	+	Common Stock	+	Retained Earnings
Bal	1,450		1,650				11,500		7,800		4,000		2,800

During June, 2010, the business completed these transactions:

    a. Rodriguez Resources received cash of $8,600 and issued common stock.
    b. Performed services for a customer and received cash of $6,500.
    c. Paid $4,700 on accounts payable.
    d. Purchased supplies on account, $600.
    e. Collected cash from a customer on account, $200.
    f. Consulted on the design of a computer system and billed the customer for services rendered, $2,700.
    g. Recorded the following expenses for the month: (1) paid office rent—$900; (2) paid advertising—$800.
    h. Declared and paid a cash dividend of $2,300.

I Requirements

1. Analyze the effects of the preceding transactions on the accounting equation of Rodriguez Resources, Inc.
2. Prepare the income statement of Rodriguez Resources, Inc., for the month ended June 30, 2010. List expenses in decreasing order by amount.
3. Prepare the statement of retained earnings of Rodriguez Resources, Inc., for the month ended June 30, 2010.
4. Prepare the balance sheet of Rodriguez Resources, Inc., at June 30, 2010.

■ general ledger

P2-69B (*Learning Objectives 2, 3: Understanding how accounting works; journalizing transactions; posting*) This problem can be used in conjunction with Problem 2-68B. Refer to Problem 2-68B.

I Requirements

1. Journalize the transactions of Rodriguez Resources, Inc. Explanations are not required.
2. Prepare T-accounts for each account. Insert in each T-account its May 31 balance as given (example: Cash $1,450). Then, post the June transactions to the T-accounts.
3. Compute the balance in each account.

P2-70B (*Learning Objectives 1, 2, 3: Analyzing transactions; understanding how accounting works; journalizing transactions*) Smith Real Estate Co. experienced the following events during the organizing phase and its first month of operations. Some of the events were personal for the stockholders and did not affect the business. Others were transactions of the business.

Nov	4	John Smith, the major stockholder of real estate company, received $108,000 cash from an inheritance.
	5	Smith deposited $59,000 cash in a new business bank account titled Smith Real Estate Co. The business issued common stock to Smith.
	6	The business paid $500 cash for letterhead stationery for the new office.
	7	The business purchased office equipment. The company paid cash of $12,000 and agreed to pay the account payable for the remainder, $8,500, within three months.
	10	Smith sold DLD stock, which he owned for several years, receiving $74,000 cash from his stockbroker.
	11	Smith deposited the $74,000 cash from sale of the DLD stock in his personal bank account.
	12	A representative of a large company telephoned Smith and told him of the company's intention to transfer $12,500 of business to Smith.
	18	Smith finished a real estate deal for a client and submitted his bill for services, $3,000. Smith expects to collect from the client within two weeks.
	21	The business paid half its account payable for the equipment purchased on November 7.
	25	The business paid office rent of $500.
	30	The business declared and paid a cash dividend of $1,700.

▌*Requirements*

1. Classify each of the preceding events as one of the following:
   a. A business-related event but not a transaction to be recorded by Smith Real Estate Co.
   b. A business transaction for a stockholder, not to be recorded by Smith Real Estate Co.
   c. A business transaction to be recorded by the Smith Real Estate Co.
2. Analyze the effects of the preceding events on the accounting equation of Smith Real Estate Co.
3. Record the transactions of the business in its journal. Include an explanation for each entry.

P2-71B (*Learning Objectives 2, 3: Analyzing and recording transactions*) During December, Swanson Auction Co. completed the following transactions:

■ **general ledger**

Dec	1	Swanson received $28,000 cash and issued common stock to the stockholders.
	5	Paid monthly rent, $2,000.
	9	Paid $11,500 cash and signed a $33,000 note payable to purchase land for an office site.
	10	Purchased supplies on account, $1,700.
	19	Paid $800 on account.
	22	Borrowed $18,500 from the bank for business use. Swanson signed a note payable to the bank in the name of the business.
	31	Service revenue earned during the month included $14,500 cash and $4,500 on account.
	31	Paid employees' salaries ($2,100), advertising expense ($1,000), and utilities expense ($1,100).
	31	Declared and paid a cash dividend of $2,000.

Swanson's business uses the following accounts: Cash, Accounts Receivable, Supplies, Land, Accounts Payable, Notes Payable, Common Stock, Dividends, Service Revenue, Salary Expense, Rent Expense, Advertising Expense, and Utilities Expense.

❙ Requirements

1. Journalize each transaction of Swanson Auction Co. Explanations are not required.
2. Post to these T-accounts: Cash, Accounts Payable, and Notes Payable.
3. After these transactions, how much cash does the business have? How much does it owe in total liabilities?

■ general ledger

P2-72B (*Learning Objectives 2, 3, 4: Understanding how accounting works; journalizing transactions; posting; preparing and using a trial balance*) During the first month of operations, O'Shea Plumbing, Inc., completed the following transactions:

Jan	2	O'Shea received $33,000 cash and issued common stock to the stockholders.
	3	Purchased supplies, $400, and equipment, $2,900, on account.
	4	Performed service for a client and received cash, $1,700.
	7	Paid cash to acquire land, $22,000.
	11	Performed service for a customer and billed the customer, $1,100. We expect to collect within one month.
	16	Paid for the equipment purchased January 3 on account.
	17	Paid the telephone bill, $130.
	18	Received partial payment from customer on account, $550.
	22	Paid the water and electricity bills, $150.
	29	Received $1,100 cash for servicing the heating unit of a customer.
	31	Paid employee salary, $2,300.
	31	Declared and paid dividends of $2,900.

❙ Requirements

1. Record each transaction in the journal. Key each transaction by date. Explanations are not required.
2. Post the transactions to the T-accounts, using transaction dates as posting references.
3. Prepare the trial balance of O'Shea Plumbing, Inc., at January 31 of the current year.
4. The manager asks you how much in total resources the business has to work with, how much it owes, and whether January was profitable (and by how much).

P2-73B (*Learning Objectives, 4, 5: Recording transactions directly in T-accounts; preparing and using a trial balance*) During the first month of operations (March 2010), Silver Entertainment Corporation completed the following selected transactions:

    a. The business received cash of $32,000 and a building valued at $52,000. The corporation issued common stock to the stockholders.
    b. Borrowed $35,800 from the bank; signed a note payable.
    c. Paid $32,000 for music equipment.
    d. Purchased supplies on account, $200.
    e. Paid employees' salaries, $2,300.
    f. Received $1,700 for music service performed for customers.
    g. Performed service for customers on account, $2,800.
    h. Paid $100 of the account payable created in Transaction d.
    i. Received a $900 bill for advertising expense that will be paid in the near future.
    j. Received cash on account, $1,600.
    k. Paid the following cash expenses: (1) rent, $1,200; (2) advertising, $800.

❙ Requirements

1. Record each transaction directly in the T-accounts without using a journal. Use the letters to identify the transactions.
2. Prepare the trial balance of Silver Entertainment Corporation, at March 31, 2010.

APPLY YOUR KNOWLEDGE

Decision Cases

Case 1. *(Learning Objectives 4, 5: Recording transactions directly in T-accounts; preparing a trial balance; measuring net income or loss)* A friend named Jay Barlow has asked what effect certain transactions will have on his company. Time is short, so you cannot apply the detailed procedures of journalizing and posting. Instead, you must analyze the transactions without the use of a journal. Barlow will continue the business only if he can expect to earn monthly net income of at least $5,000. The following transactions occurred this month:

  a. Barlow deposited $5,000 cash in a business bank account, and the corporation issued common stock to him.
  b. Borrowed $5,000 cash from the bank and signed a note payable due within 1 year.
  c. Paid $1,300 cash for supplies.
  d. Purchased advertising in the local newspaper for cash, $1,800.
  e. Purchased office furniture on account, $4,400.
  f. Paid the following cash expenses for 1 month: employee salary, $2,000; office rent, $1,200.
  g. Earned revenue on account, $7,000.
  h. Earned revenue and received $2,500 cash.
  i. Collected cash from customers on account, $1,200.
  j. Paid on account, $1,000.

Requirements

  1. Set up the following T-accounts: Cash, Accounts Receivable, Supplies, Furniture, Accounts Payable, Notes Payable, Common Stock, Service Revenue, Salary Expense, Advertising Expense, and Rent Expense.
  2. Record the transactions directly in the accounts without using a journal. Key each transaction by letter.
  3. Prepare a trial balance for Barlow Networks, Inc., at the current date. List expenses with the largest amount first, the next largest amount second, and so on.
  4. Compute the amount of net income or net loss for this first month of operations. Why or why not would you recommend that Barlow continue in business?

Case 2. *(Learning Objective 2: Correcting financial statements; deciding whether to expand a business)* Sophia Loren opened an Italian restaurant. Business has been good, and Loren is considering expanding the restaurant. Loren, who knows little accounting, produced the following financial statements for Little Italy, Inc., at December 31, 2011, end of the first month of operations:

Little Italy, Inc. Income Statement Month Ended December 31, 2011	
Sales revenue	$42,000
Common stock	10,000
Total revenue	52,000
Accounts payable	$ 8,000
Advertising expense	5,000
Rent expense	6,000
Total expenses	19,000
Net income	$33,000

Little Italy, Inc. Balance Sheet December 31, 2011	
Assets	
Cash	$12,000
Cost of goods sold (expense)	22,000
Food inventory	5,000
Furniture	10,000
Total Assets	$49,000
Liabilities	
None	
Owners' Equity	$49,000

In these financial statements all *amounts* are correct, except for Owners' Equity. Loren heard that total assets should equal total liabilities plus owners' equity, so she plugged in the amount of owners' equity at $49,000 to make the balance sheet come out even.

I *Requirement*

1. Sophia Loren has asked whether she should expand the restaurant. Her banker says Loren may be wise to expand if (a) net income for the first month reached $10,000 and (b) total assets are at least $35,000. It appears that the business has reached these milestones, but Loren doubts whether her financial statements tell the true story. She needs your help in making this decision. Prepare a corrected income statement and balance sheet. (Remember that Retained Earnings, which was omitted from the balance sheet, should equal net income for the first month; there were no dividends.) After preparing the statements, give Sophia Loren your recommendation as to whether she should expand the restaurant.

Ethical Issues

Issue 1. Scruffy Murphy is the president and principal stockholder of Scruffy's Bar & Grill, Inc. To expand, the business is applying for a $250,000 bank loan. To get the loan, Murphy is considering two options for beefing up the owners' equity of the business:

> *Option 1.* Issue $100,000 of common stock for cash. A friend has been wanting to invest in the company. This may be the right time to extend the offer.
>
> *Option 2.* Transfer $100,000 of Murphy's personal land to the business, and issue common stock to Murphy. Then, after obtaining the loan, Murphy can transfer the land back to himself and zero out the common stock.

I *Requirements*

Use the ethical decision model in Chapter 1 to answer the following questions:

1. What is the ethical issue?
2. Who are the stakeholders? What are the possible consequences to each?
3. Analyze the alternatives from the following standpoints (a) economic, (b) legal, and (c) ethical
4. What would you do? How would you justify your decision? How would your decision make you feel afterward?

Issue 2. Part a. You have received your grade in your first accounting course, and to your amazement, it is an A. You feel the instructor must have made a big mistake. Your grade was a B going into the final, but you are sure that you really "bombed" the exam, which is worth 30% of the final grade. In fact, you walked out after finishing only 50% of the exam, and the grade report says you made 99% on the exam!

I *Requirements*

1. What is the ethical issue?
2. Who are the stakeholders? What are the possible consequences to each?
3. Analyze the alternatives from the following standpoints: (a) economic, (b) legal, and (c) ethical.
4. What would you do? How would you justify your decision? How would it make you feel afterward?

Part b. Now assume the same facts as above, except that you have received your final grade for the course and the grade is a B. You are confident that you "aced" the final. In fact, you stayed to the very end of the period, and checked every figure twice! You are confident that the instructor must have made a mistake grading the final.

I *Requirements*

1. What is the ethical issue?
2. Who are the stakeholders and what are the consequences to each?

3. Analyze the alternatives from the following standpoints: (a) economic, (b) legal, and (c) ethical.
4. What would you do? How would you justify your decision? How would it make you feel?

Part c. How is this situation like a financial accounting misstatement? How is it different?

Focus on Financials: ■ Amazon.com, Inc.

(*Learning Objectives 3, 4: Recording transactions; computing net income*) Refer to **Amazon.com, Inc.'s** financial statements in Appendix A at the end of the book. Assume that Amazon.com completed the following selected transactions during 2008.

   a. Made company sales (revenue) of $19,166 million, all on account (debit accounts receivable).
   b. Collected cash on accounts receivable $19,044.
   c. Purchased inventories, paying cash of $15,095 million.
   d. Incurred cost of sales in the amount of $14,896 million. Debit the Cost of sales (expense) account. Credit the Inventories account.
   e. Paid operating expenses of $3,428 million.
   f. Collected non-operating income (net) in cash, $59 million.
   g. Paid income taxes $247 million (debit provision for income taxes).
   h. Accounted for other investment activity net of taxes in the amount of $9 million. Debit equity method investment activity, net of taxes. Credit other assets.
   i. Paid cash for other assets, $103 million.

▌Requirements

1. Set up T-accounts for: Cash (beginning debit balance of $2,539 million); Accounts Receivable, net and other (debit balance of $705 million); Inventories (debit balance $1,200 million); Other Assets ($0 balance); Net Sales ($0 balance); Cost of Sales ($0 balance); Operating expenses ($0 balance); Non-operating income (expense), net ($0 balance); Provision for income taxes ($0 balance); Equity method investment activity, net of tax ($0 balance).
2. Journalize Amazon.com's transactions a–i. Explanations are not required.
3. Post to the T-accounts, and compute the balance for each account. Key postings by transaction letters a–i.
4. For each of the following accounts, compare your computed balance to Amazon.com, Inc.'s actual balance as shown on its 2008 Consolidated Statement of Operations or Consolidated Balance Sheet in Appendix A. Your amounts should agree to the actual figures.

   a. Cash
   b. Accounts Receivable, net and other
   c. Inventories
   d. Net Sales
   e. Cost of sales
   f. Operating expenses
   g. Non-operating income (expenses), net
   h. Provision for income taxes
   i. Equity method investment activity, net of tax

5. Use the relevant accounts from requirement 4 to prepare a summary income statement for Amazon.com, Inc., for 2008. Compare the net income you computed to Amazon.com, Inc.'s actual net income. The two amounts should be equal.

Focus on Analysis: ■ Foot Locker, Inc.

(*Learning Objectives 1, 2: Analyzing a leading company's financial statements*) Refer to the **Foot Locker, Inc.**, financial statements in Appendix B at the end of the book. Suppose you are an investor considering buying Foot Locker, Inc., common stock. The following questions are important: **Show amounts in millions and round to the nearest $1 million.**

1. Explain whether Foot Locker, Inc., had more sales revenue, or collected more cash from customers, during 2007. Why is accounts receivable missing from its balance sheet? (Challenge)

2. Investors are vitally interested in a company's sales and profits, and its trends of sales and profits over time. Consider Foot Locker's sales and net income (net loss) during the period from 2005 through 2007. Compute the percentage increase or decrease in net sales and also in net income (net loss) from 2005 to 2007. Which item grew faster during this two-year period, net sales or net income (net loss)? Can you offer a possible explanation for these changes? (Challenge)

Group Projects

Project 1. You are promoting a rock concert in your area. Your purpose is to earn a profit, so you need to establish the formal structure of a business entity. Assume you organize as a corporation.

▍*Requirements*

1. Make a detailed list of 10 factors you must consider as you establish the business.
2. Describe 10 of the items your business must arrange to promote and stage the rock concert.
3. Identify the transactions that your business can undertake to organize, promote, and stage the concert. Journalize the transactions, and post to the relevant T-accounts. Set up the accounts you need for your business ledger. Refer to Appendix D at the end of the book if needed.
4. Prepare the income statement, statement of retained earnings, and balance sheet immediately after the rock concert, that is, before you have had time to pay all the business bills and to collect all receivables.
5. Assume that you will continue to promote rock concerts if the venture is successful. If it is unsuccessful, you will terminate the business within three months after the concert. Discuss how to evaluate the success of your venture and how to decide whether to continue in business.

Project 2. Contact a local business and arrange with the owner to learn what accounts the business uses.

▍*Requirements*

1. Obtain a copy of the business's chart of accounts.
2. Prepare the company's financial statements for the most recent month, quarter, or year. You may use either made-up account balances or balances supplied by the owner.

If the business has a large number of accounts within a category, combine related accounts and report a single amount on the financial statements. For example, the company may have several cash accounts. Combine all cash amounts and report a single Cash amount on the balance sheet.

You will probably encounter numerous accounts that you have not yet learned. Deal with these as best you can. The charts of accounts given in Appendix D at the end of the book can be helpful.

For online homework, exercises, and problems that provide you with immediate feedback, please visit www.myaccountinglab.com.

Quick Check Answers

1. *b*	5. *c*	8. *c*	11. *d*
2. *d*	6. *a*	9. *c*	12. *d*
3. *b*	7. *a* ($9,000 + x −	10. *c*	
4. *c* ($1,600 +	25,000 = 11,000;		
900 − 300)	x = 27,000)		

Demo Doc

Debit/Credit Transaction Analysis

To make sure you understand this material, work through the following demonstration "Demo Doc" with detailed comments to help you see the concept within the framework of a worked-through problem.

Learning Objectives 1, 2, 3, 4

On September 1, 2010, Michael Moe incorporated Moe's Mowing, Inc., a company that provides mowing and landscaping services. During the month of September, the business incurred the following transactions:

a. To begin operations, Michael deposited $10,000 cash in the business's bank account. The business received the cash and issued common stock to Michael.

b. The business purchased equipment for $3,500 on account.

c. The business purchased office supplies for $800 cash.

d. The business provided $2,600 of services to a customer on account.

e. The business paid $500 cash toward the equipment previously purchased on account in transaction b.

f. The business received $2,000 in cash for services provided to a new customer.

g. The business paid $200 cash to repair equipment.

h. The business paid $900 cash in salary expense.

i. The business received $2,100 cash from a customer on account.

j. The business paid cash dividends of $1,500.

Requirements

1. Create blank T-accounts for the following accounts: Cash, Accounts Receivable, Supplies, Equipment, Accounts Payable, Common Stock, Dividends, Service Revenue, Salary Expense, Repair Expense.

2. Journalize the transactions and then post to the T-accounts. Use the table in Exhibit 2-16 to help with the journal entries.

EXHIBIT 2-16 | **The Rules of Debit and Credit**

	Increase	Decrease
Assets	debit	credit
Liabilities	credit	debit
Stockholders' Equity	credit	debit
Revenues	credit	debit
Expenses	debit	credit
Dividends	debit	credit

3. Total each T-account to determine its balance at the end of the month.

4. Prepare the trial balance of Moe's Mowing, Inc., at September 30, 2010.

Demo Doc Solutions

Requirement 1

Create blank T-accounts for the following accounts: Cash, Accounts Receivable, Supplies, Equipment, Accounts Payable, Common Stock, Dividends, Service Revenue, Salary Expense, Repair Expense.

Part 1	Part 2	Part 3	Part 4	Demo Doc Complete

Opening a T-account means drawing a blank account that looks like a capital "T" and putting the account title across the top. T-accounts show the additions and subtractions made to each account. For easy reference, the accounts are grouped into assets, liabilities, stockholders' equity, revenue, and expenses (in that order).

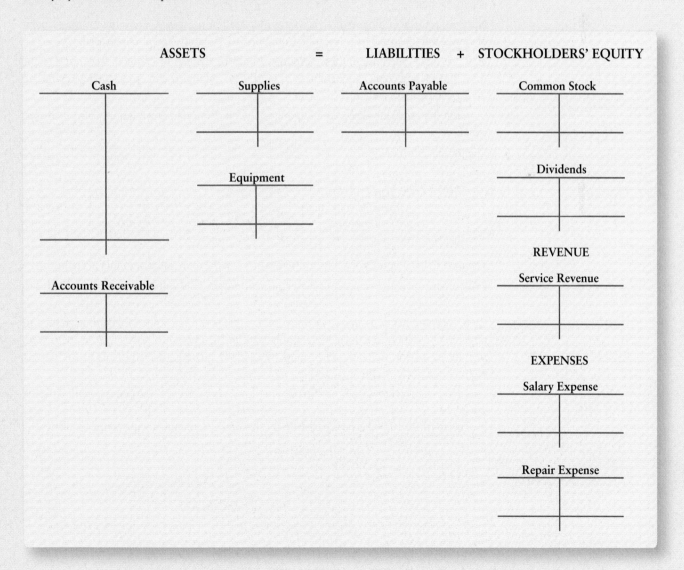

Requirement 2

Journalize the transactions and show how they are recorded in T-accounts.

Part 1	**Part 2**	Part 3	Part 4	Demo Doc Complete

a. To begin operations, Michael deposited $10,000 cash in the business's bank account. The business received the cash and issued common stock to Michael.

First, we must determine which accounts are affected by the transaction.

The business received $10,000 cash from its principal stockholder (Michael Moe). In exchange, the business issued common stock to Michael. So, the accounts involved are Cash and Common Stock.

Remember that we are recording the transactions of Moe's Mowing, Inc., not the transactions of Michael Moe, the person. Michael and his business are two entirely separate accounting entities.

The next step is to determine what type of accounts these are. Cash is an asset, Common Stock is part of equity.

Next, we must determine if these accounts increased or decreased. From the business's point of view, Cash (an asset) has increased. Common Stock (equity) has also increased.

Now we must determine if these accounts should be debited or credited. According to the rules of debit and credit (see Exhibit 2-16 on p. 124), an increase in assets is a debit, while an increase in equity is a credit.

So, Cash (an asset) increases, which requires a debit. Common Stock (equity) also increases, which requires a credit.

The journal entry follows.

a.	Cash (Asset ↑; debit)	10,000	
	Common Stock (Equity ↑; credit)		10,000
	Issued common stock.		

The total dollar amounts of debits must always equal the total dollar amounts of credits.

Remember to use the transaction letters as references. This will help as we post entries to the T-accounts.

Each T-account has two sides—one for recording debits and the other for recording credits. To post the transaction to a T-account, simply transfer the amount of each debit to the correct account as a debit (left-side) entry, and transfer the amount of each credit to the correct account as a credit (right-side) entry.

This transaction includes a debit of $10,000 to cash. This means that $10,000 is posted to the left side of the Cash T-account. The transaction also includes a credit of $10,000 to Common Stock. This means that $10,000 is posted to the right side of the Common Stock account, as follows:

Cash		Common Stock	
a. 10,000			**a.** 10,000

Now the first transaction has been journalized and posted. We repeat this process for every journal entry. Let's proceed to the next transaction.

b. The business purchased equipment for $3,500 on account.

The business received equipment in exchange for a promise to pay for the $3,500 cost at a future date. So the accounts involved in the transaction are Equipment and Accounts Payable.

Equipment is an asset and Accounts Payable is a liability.

The asset Equipment has increased. The liability Accounts Payable has also increased.

Looking at Exhibit 2-16, an increase in assets (in this case, the increase in Equipment) is a debit, while an increase in liabilities (in this case, Accounts Payable) is a credit.

The journal entry follows.

b.	Equipment (Asset ↑; debit)	3,500	
	Accounts Payable (Liability ↑; credit)		3,500
	Purchased equipment on account.		

$3,500 is then posted to the debit (left) side of the Equipment T-account. $3,500 is posted to the credit (right) side of Accounts Payable, as follows:

Equipment		Accounts Payable	
b. 3,500			**b.** 3,500

c. The business purchased office supplies for $800 cash.

The business purchased supplies, paying cash of $800. So the accounts involved in the transaction are Supplies and Cash.

Supplies and Cash are both assets.

Supplies (an asset) has increased. Cash (an asset) has decreased.

Looking at Exhibit 2-16, an increase in assets is a debit, while a decrease in assets is a credit.

So the increase to Supplies (an asset) is a debit, while the decrease to Cash (an asset) is a credit.

The journal entry follows:

c.	Supplies (Asset ↑; debit)	800	
	Cash (Asset ↓; credit)		800
	Purchased supplies for cash.		

$800 is then posted to the debit (left) side of the Supplies T-account. $800 is posted to the credit (right) side of the Cash account, as follows:

Cash		Supplies	
a. 10,000		**c.** 800	
	c. 800		

Notice the $10,000 already on the debit side of the Cash account. This came from transaction a.

d. The business provided $2,600 of services to a customer on account.

The business rendered service for a customer and received a promise from the customer to pay us $2,600 cash next month. So the accounts involved in the transaction are Accounts Receivable and Service Revenue.

Accounts Receivable is an asset and Service Revenue is revenue.

Accounts Receivable (an asset) has increased. Service Revenue (revenue) has also increased.

Looking at Exhibit 2-16, an increase in assets is a debit, while an increase in revenue is a credit.

So the increase to Accounts Receivable (an asset) is a debit, while the increase to Service Revenue (revenue) is a credit.

The journal entry follows.

d.	Accounts Receivable (Asset ↑; debit)	2,600	
	Service Revenue (Revenue ↑; credit)		2,600
	Provided services on account.		

$2,600 is posted to the debit (left) side of the Accounts Receivable T-account. $2,600 is posted to the credit (right) side of the Service Revenue account, as follows:

Accounts Receivable		Service Revenue	
d. 2,600		d. 2,600	

e. The business paid $500 cash toward the equipment previously purchased on account in transaction b.

The business paid some of the money that it owed on the purchase of equipment in transaction b. The accounts involved in the transaction are Accounts Payable and Cash.

Accounts Payable is a liability that has decreased. Cash is an asset that has also decreased.

Remember that Accounts Payable shows the amount the business must pay in the future (a liability). When the business pays these creditors, Accounts Payable will decrease because the business will then owe less (in this case, Accounts Payable drops from $3,500—in transaction b—to $3,000).

Looking at Exhibit 2-16, a decrease in liabilities is a debit, while a decrease in assets is a credit.

So Accounts Payable (a liability) decreases, which is a debit. Cash (an asset) decreases, which is a credit.

e.	Accounts Payable (Liability ↓; debit)	500	
	Cash (Asset ↓; credit)		500
	Partial payment on account.		

$500 is posted to the debit (left) side of the Accounts Payable T-account. $500 is posted to the credit (right) side of the Cash account, as follows:

	Cash				Accounts Payable	
a.	10,000					b.	3,500
		c.	800	e.	500		
		e.	500				

Again notice the amounts already in the T-accounts from previous transactions. The reference letters show which transaction caused each amount to appear in the T-account.

f. The business received $2,000 in cash for services provided to a new customer.

The business received $2,000 cash in exchange for mowing and landscaping services rendered to a customer. The accounts involved in the transaction are Cash and Service Revenue.

Cash is an asset that has increased and Service Revenue is revenue, which has also increased.

Looking at Exhibit 2-16, an increase in assets is a debit, while an increase in revenue is a credit.

So the increase to Cash (an asset) is a debit. The increase to Service Revenue (revenue) is a credit.

f.			
	Cash (Asset ↑; debit)	2,000	
	Service Revenue (Revenue ↑; credit)		2,000
	Provided services for cash.		

$2,000 is then posted to the debit (left) side of the Cash T-account. $2,000 is posted to the credit (right) side of the Service Revenue account, as follows:

	Cash				Service Revenue	
a.	10,000					d.	2,600
		c.	800			f.	2,000
		e.	500				
f.	2,000						

Notice how we keep adding onto the T-accounts. The values from previous transactions remain in their places.

g. The business paid $200 cash to repair equipment.

The business paid $200 cash to have equipment repaired. Because the benefit of the repairs has already been used, the repairs are recorded as Repair Expense. Because the repairs were paid in cash, the Cash account is also involved.

Repair Expense is an expense that has increased and Cash is an asset that has decreased.

Looking at Exhibit 2-16, an increase in expenses calls for a debit, while a decrease in an asset requires a credit.

So Repair Expense (an expense) increases, which is a debit. Cash (an asset) decreases, which is a credit.

g.	Repair Expense (Expense ↑ ; debit)	200	
	Cash (Asset ↓; credit)		200
	Paid for repairs.		

$200 is then posted to the debit (left) side of the Repair Expense T-account. $200 is posted to the credit (right) side of the Cash account, as follows:

	Cash					Repair Expense	
a.	10,000				g.	200	
		c.	800				
		e.	500				
f.	2,000						
		g.	200				

h. The business paid $900 cash for salary expense.

The business paid employees $900 in cash. Because the benefit of the employees' work has already been used, their salaries are recorded as Salary Expense. Because the salaries were paid in cash, the Cash account is also involved.

Salary Expense is an expense that has increased and Cash is an asset that has decreased.

Looking at Exhibit 2-16, an increase in expenses is a debit, while a decrease in an asset is a credit.

In this case, Salary Expense (an expense) increases, which is a debit. Cash (an asset) decreases, which is a credit.

h.	Salary Expense (Expense ↑; debit)	900	
	Cash (Asset ↓; credit)		900
	Paid salary.		

$900 is posted to the debit (left) side of the Salary Expense T-account. $900 is posted to the credit (right) side of the Cash account, as follows:

Cash				Salary Expense	
a.	10,000			h.	900
		c.	800		
		e.	500		
f.	2,000				
		g.	200		
		h.	900		

i. The business received $2,100 cash from a customer on account.

The business received cash of $2,100 from a customer for services previously provided in transaction d. The accounts affected by this transaction are Cash and Accounts Receivable.

Cash and Accounts Receivable are both assets.

The asset Cash has increased, and the asset Accounts Receivable has decreased.

Remember, Accounts Receivable shows the amount of cash the business has coming from customers. When the business receives cash from these customers, Accounts Receivable will decrease, because the business will have less to receive in the future (in this case, it reduces from $2,600—in transaction d—to $500).

Looking at Exhibit 2-16, an increase in assets is a debit, while a decrease in assets is a credit.

So Cash (an asset) increases, which is a debit. Accounts Receivable (an asset) decreases, which is a credit.

i.	Cash (Asset ↑; debit)	2,100	
	Accounts Receivable (Asset ↓; credit)		2,100
	Received cash on account.		

$2,100 is posted to the debit (left) side of the Cash T-account. $2,100 is posted to the credit (right) side of the Accounts Receivable account, as follows:

Cash				Accounts Receivable			
a.	10,000			d.	2,600		
		c.	800			i.	2,100
		e.	500				
f.	2,000						
		g.	200				
		h.	900				
i.	2,100						

j. The business declared and paid cash dividends of $1,500.

The business paid Michael dividends from the earnings it had retained on his behalf. This caused Michael's ownership interest (equity) to decrease. The accounts involved in this transaction are Dividends and Cash.

Dividends have increased and Cash is an asset that has decreased.

Looking at Exhibit 2-16, an increase in dividends is a debit, while a decrease in an asset is a credit.

Remember that Dividends are a negative element of stockholders' equity. Therefore, when Dividends increase, stockholders' equity decreases. So in this case, Dividends decrease equity with a debit. Cash (an asset) decreases with a credit.

j.	Dividends (Dividends ↑; debit) ↓SE	1,500	
	Cash (Asset ↓; credit)		1,500
	Paid dividends.		

$1,500 is posted to the debit (left) side of the Dividends T-account. $1,500 is posted to the credit (right) side of the Cash account, as follows:

	Cash					Dividends	
a.	10,000				j.	1,500	
		c.	800				
		e.	500				
f.	2,000						
		g.	200				
		h.	900				
i.	2,100						
		j.	1,500				

Now we can summarize all of the journal entries during the month.

Ref.		Accounts and Explanation	Debit	Credit
a.		Cash	10,000	
		Common Stock		10,000
		Issued common stock.		
b.		Equipment	3,500	
		Accounts Payable		3,500
		Purchased equipment on account.		
c.		Supplies	800	
		Cash		800
		Purchased supplies for cash.		
d.		Accounts Receivable	2,600	
		Service Revenue		2,600
		Provided services on account.		
e.		Accounts Payable	500	
		Cash		500
		Partial payment on account.		
f.		Cash	2,000	
		Service Revenue		2,000
		Provided services for cash.		
g.		Repair Expense	200	
		Cash		200
		Paid for repairs.		
h.		Salary Expense	900	
		Cash		900
		Paid salary.		
i.		Cash	2,100	
		Accounts Receivable		2,100
		Received cash on account.		
j.		Dividends	1,500	
		Cash		1,500
		Paid dividends.		

Requirement 3

Total each T-account to determine its balance at the end of the month.

Part 1	Part 2	**Part 3**	Part 4	Demo Doc Complete

To compute the balance in a T-account (total the T-account), add up the numbers on the debit/left side of the account and (separately) add the credit/right side of the account. The difference between the total debits and the total credits is the account's balance, which is placed on the side that holds the larger total. This gives the balance in the T-account.

For example, for the Cash account, the numbers on the debit/left side total $10,000 + $2,000 + $2,100 = $14,100. The credit/right side = $800 + $500 + $200 + $900 + $1,500 = $3,900. The difference is $14,100 − $3,900 = $10,200. At the end of the period Cash has a debit balance of $10,200. We put the $10,200 at the bottom of the debit side because that was the side that showed the bigger total ($14,100). This is called a debit balance.

An easy way to think of totaling T-accounts is:

> Beginning balance in a T-account
>
> + Increases to the T-account
>
> − Decreases to the T-account
>
> T-account balance (net total)

T-accounts after posting all transactions and totaling each account are as follows:

ASSETS		=	LIABILITIES	+	STOCKHOLDERS' EQUITY

Cash

a.	10,000		
		c.	800
		e.	500
f.	2,000		
		g.	200
		h.	900
i.	2,100		
		j.	1,500
Bal	10,200		

Accounts Receivable

d.	2,600		
		i.	2,100
Bal	500		

Supplies

c.	800		
Bal	800		

Equipment

b.	3,500		
Bal	3,500		

Accounts Payable

		b.	3,500
e.	500		
		Bal	3,000

Common Stock

		a.	10,000
		Bal	10,000

Dividends

j.	1,500		
Bal	1,500		

REVENUE

Service Revenue

		d.	2,600
		f.	2,000
		Bal	4,600

EXPENSES

Salary Expense

h.	900		
Bal	900		

Repair Expense

g.	200		
Bal	200		

Requirement 4

| Part 1 | Part 2 | Part 3 | **Part 4** | Demo Doc Complete |

The trial balance lists all the accounts along with their balances. This listing is helpful because it summarizes all the accounts in one place. Otherwise one must plow through all the T-accounts to find the balance of Accounts Payable, Salary Expense, or any other account.

The trial balance is an *internal* accounting document that accountants and managers use to prepare the financial statements. It's not like the income statement and balance sheet, which are presented to the public.

Data for the trial balance come directly from the T-accounts that we prepared in Requirement 3. A debit balance in a T-account remains a debit in the trial balance, and likewise for credits. For example, the T-account for Cash shows a debit balance of $10,200, and the trial balance lists Cash the same way. The Accounts Payable T-account shows a $3,000 credit balance, and the trial balance lists Accounts Payable correctly.

The trial balance for Moe's Mowing at September 30, 2010, appears as follows. Notice that we list the accounts in their proper order—assets, liabilities, stockholder's equity, revenues, and expenses.

Moe's Mowing, Inc.
Trial Balance
September 30, 2010

		Balance	
		Debit	Credit
Assets	Cash	$10,200	
	Accounts receivable	500	
	Supplies	800	
	Equipment	3,500	
Liabilities	Accounts payable		$ 3,000
Equity	Common stock		10,000
	Dividends	1,500	
Revenues	Service revenue		4,600
Expenses	Salary expense	900	
	Repair expense	200	
	Total	$17,600	$17,600

You should trace each account from the T-accounts to the trial balance.

| Part 1 | Part 2 | Part 3 | Part 4 | **Demo Doc Complete** |

3

Accrual Accounting & Income

SPOTLIGHT: Starbucks Corporation

Starbucks has changed coffee from a breakfast drink to an experience. The corporation began in Seattle, Washington, in 1985 and now has over 10,000 locations in the United States alone, with almost 2,000 more abroad.

As you can see from Starbucks' Consolidated Statement of Earnings on the next page, the company sold over $10 billion of coffee and related products during the 2008 fiscal year. The company translated that revenue into about $316 million in profits. That's a lot of coffee!

But at Starbucks, the motto is "it's bigger than coffee." *Ethisphere* magazine has named Starbucks one of the 100 most ethical companies in the world. During the holiday season each year, the company donates five cents from every cup of certain specialty drinks to help feed starving HIV patients in Africa, where some of its coffee is grown. Through its Web site, the company also provides ways for customers to partner with Starbucks in donating to this and other worthy causes. The company sponsors community improvement projects for its coffee farmers in Central America and Africa. It has also developed standards for environmentally, socially, and economically responsible coffee-buying guidelines to help assure better prices for farmers who do business with it. Starbucks works with Conservation International to encourage coffee growers to use sustainable farming practices that help protect the environment. The company is developing reusable and recyclable cups. It also sponsors employee programs that contribute hundreds of thousands of service hours to the communities where Starbucks stores operate. All of these ethical practices cost money, which can be hard to justify during difficult economic times. But Starbucks is committed to using its resources for good as well as for gain. Think about that when you buy that next latte.

Starbucks Corporation
Consolidated Statement of Earnings (Adapted)
Year Ended September 28, 2008

	(In millions)
Revenues:	
Net operating revenues	$10,383
Other income	70
Total net revenues	10,453
Expenses:	
Cost of sales (cost of goods sold)	4,646
Store operating expenses	3,745
Other operating expenses	597
Depreciation and amortization expenses	549
General and administrative expenses	456
Total operating expenses	9,993
Income before income tax	460
Income tax expense	144
Net income	$ 316

This chapter completes our coverage of the accounting cycle. It gives the basics of what you need before tackling individual topics such as receivables, inventory, and cash flows.

LEARNING OBJECTIVES

1 **Relate** accrual accounting and cash flows

2 **Apply** the revenue and matching principles

3 **Adjust** the accounts

4 **Prepare** the financial statements

5 **Close** the books

6 **Use** two new ratios to evaluate a business

For more practice and review of accounting cycle concepts, use ACT, the accounting Cycle Tutorial, online at www.myaccountinglab.com. Margin logos like this one, directing you to the appropriate ACT section and material, appear throughout Chapters 1, 2, and 3. When you enter the tutorial, you'll find three buttons on the opening page of each chapter module. Here's what the buttons mean: **Tutorial** gives you a review of the major concepts, **Application** gives you practice exercises, and **Glossary** reviews important terms.

ACCRUAL ACCOUNTING VERSUS CASH-BASIS ACCOUNTING

Managers want to earn a profit. Investors search for companies whose stock prices will increase. Banks seek borrowers who'll pay their debts. Accounting provides the information these people use for decision making. Accounting can be based on either the

- accrual basis, or the
- cash basis.

Accrual accounting records the impact of a business transaction as it occurs. When the business performs a service, makes a sale, or incurs an expense, the accountant records the transaction even if it receives or pays no cash.

Cash-basis accounting records only cash transactions—cash receipts and cash payments. Cash receipts are treated as revenues, and cash payments are handled as expenses.

Generally accepted accounting principles (GAAP) require accrual accounting. The business records revenues as the revenues are earned and expenses as the expenses are incurred—not necessarily when cash changes hands. Consider a sale on account. Which transaction increases your wealth—making an $800 sale on account, or collecting the $800 cash? Making the sale increases your wealth by $300 because you gave up inventory that cost you $500 and you got a receivable worth $800. Collecting cash later merely swaps your $800 receivable for $800 cash—no gain on this transaction. Making the sale—not collecting the cash—increases your wealth.

The basic defect of cash-basis accounting is that the cash basis ignores important information. That makes the financial statements incomplete. The result? People using the statements make decisions based on incomplete information, which can lead to mistakes.

Suppose your business makes a sale *on account*. The cash basis does not record the sale because you received no cash. You may be thinking, "Let's wait until we collect cash and then record the sale. After all, we pay the bills with cash, so ignore transactions that don't affect cash."

What's wrong with this argument? There are two defects—one on the balance sheet and the other on the income statement.

Balance-Sheet Defect.   If we fail to record a sale on account, the balance sheet reports no account receivable. Why is this so bad? The receivable represents a claim to receive cash in the future, which is a real asset, and it should appear on the balance sheet. Without this information, assets are understated on the balance sheet.

Income-Statement Defect.   A sale on account provides revenue that increases the company's wealth. Ignoring the sale understates revenue and net income on the income statement.

The take-away lessons from this discussion are as follows:

- Companies that use the cash basis of accounting do not follow GAAP. Their financial statements omit important information.
- All but the smallest businesses use the accrual basis of accounting.

Accrual Accounting and Cash Flows

Accrual accounting is more complex—and, in terms of the Conceptual Foundations of Accounting (Exhibit 1-3), is a more faithful representation of economic reality—than cash-basis accounting. To be sure, accrual accounting records cash transactions, such as

- Collecting cash from customers
- Receiving cash from interest earned
- Paying salaries, rent, and other expenses
- Borrowing money
- Paying off loans
- Issuing stock

But accrual accounting also records *noncash* transactions, such as

- Sales on account
- Purchases of inventory on account
- Accrual of expenses incurred but not yet paid
- Depreciation expense
- Usage of prepaid rent, insurance, and supplies
- Earning of revenue when cash was collected in advance

Accrual accounting is based on a framework of additional concepts and principles to those we discussed in Chapter 1. We turn now to the time-period concept, the revenue principle, and the matching principle.

The Time-Period Concept

The only way for a business to know for certain how well it performed is to shut down, sell the assets, pay the liabilities, and return any leftover cash to the owners. This process, called liquidation, means going out of business. Ongoing companies can't wait until they go out of business to measure income! Instead, they need regular progress reports. Accountants, therefore, prepare financial statements for specific periods. The **time-period concept** ensures that accounting information is reported at regular intervals.

The basic accounting period is one year, and virtually all businesses prepare annual financial statements. Around 60% of large companies—including Amazon.com, eBay, and YUM! Brands—use the calendar year from January 1 through December 31.

A *fiscal* year ends on a date other than December 31. Most retailers, including Wal-Mart, J.Crew, and JCPenney, use a fiscal year that ends on or near January 31 because the low point in their business activity falls in January, after Christmas. Starbucks Corporation uses a fiscal year that ends on September 30.

Companies also prepare financial statements for interim periods of less than a year, such as a month, a quarter (three months), or a semiannual period (six months). Most of the discussions in this text are based on an annual accounting period.

The Revenue Principle

The **revenue principle** deals with two issues:

1. When to record revenue (make a journal entry); and

2. The amount of revenue to record.

When should you record revenue? After it has been earned—and not before. In most cases, revenue is earned when the business has delivered a good or service to a customer. It has done everything required to earn the revenue by transferring the good or service to the customer.

 **GLOBAL VIEW** Revenue recognition is one of the areas in which a number of differences exist between U.S. GAAP and IFRS. Those differences deal with the two issues listed previously. U.S. GAAP is highly detailed and varies by industry. For example, the rules for timing and amount of revenue in the computer software industry differ from those in the construction industry. By contrast, IFRS is less detailed, leaving more room for interpretation on the part of the company. We will touch on these differences again in Chapter 11, where we discuss revenue in more detail. This book deals with retail businesses selling goods and services. Fortunately, in this industry, U.S. GAAP and IFRS are consistent with respect to general principles of revenue recognition.

Exhibit 3-1 shows two situations that provide guidance on when to record revenue for Starbucks Corporation. Situation 1 illustrates when not to record revenue. No transaction has occurred, so Starbucks Corporation records nothing. Situation 2 illustrates when revenue should be recorded—after a transaction has occurred.

EXHIBIT 3-1 | **When to Record Revenue**

Situation 1—Do Not Record Revenue
No transaction has occurred.

Customer: I plan to start drinking Starbucks drinks.

Joe Starbucks: Great! We'll welcome you as a customer.

Situation 2—Record Revenue
Starbucks sells a cup of coffee.

Customer: A latte, please!

Joe Starbucks: I appreciate your business. Here's your latte.

The *amount* of revenue to record is the cash value of the goods or services transferred to the customer. Suppose that in order to promote business, Starbucks runs a promotion and sells lattes for the discount price of $2 per cup. Ordinarily Starbucks would charge $4 for this drink. How much revenue should Starbucks record? The answer is $2—the cash value of the transaction. The amount of the sale, $2, is the amount of revenue earned—not the regular price of $4.

The Matching Principle

The **matching principle** is the basis for recording expenses. Expenses are the costs of assets used up, and of liabilities created, in the earning of revenue. Expenses have no future benefit to the company. The matching principle includes two steps:

1. Identify all the expenses incurred during the accounting period.
2. Measure the expenses, and match expenses against the revenues earned.

To *match* expenses against revenues means to subtract expenses from revenues to compute net income or net loss. Exhibit 3-2 illustrates the matching principle.

EXHIBIT 3-2 | **The Matching Principle**

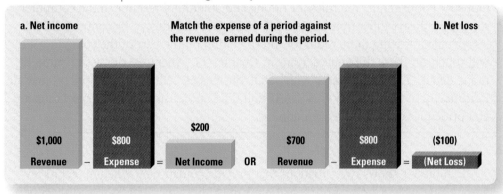

Some expenses are paid in cash. Other expenses arise from using up an asset such as supplies. Still other expenses occur when a company creates a liability. For example, Starbucks' salary expense occurs when employees work for the company. Starbucks may pay the salary expense immediately, or Starbucks may record a liability for the salary to be paid later. In either case, Starbucks has salary expense. The critical event for recording an expense is the employees' working for the company, not the payment of cash.

STOP & THINK...

1. A customer pays Starbucks $100 on March 15 for coffee to be served at a party in April. Has Starbucks earned revenue on March 15? When will Starbucks earn the revenue?
2. Starbucks pays $4,500 on July 1 for store rent for the next three months. Has Starbucks incurred an expense on July 1?

Answers:

1. No. Starbucks has received the cash but will not deliver the coffee until later. Starbucks earns the revenue when it gives the goods to the customer.
2. No. Starbucks has paid cash for rent in advance. There is no expense. This prepaid rent is an asset because Starbucks has the use of a store location in the future.

Ethical Issues in Accrual Accounting

Accrual accounting provides some ethical challenges that cash accounting avoids. For example, suppose that in 2010, Starbucks Corporation prepays a $3 million advertising campaign to be conducted by a large advertising agency. The advertisements are scheduled to run during September, October, and November. In this case, Starbucks is buying an asset, a prepaid expense.

Suppose Starbucks pays for the advertisements on September 1 and the ads start running immediately. Under accrual accounting, Starbucks should record one-third of the expense ($1 million) during the year ended September 30, 2010, and two-thirds ($2 million) during 2011.

Suppose fiscal 2010 is a great year for Starbucks—net income is better than expected. Starbucks' top managers believe that fiscal 2011 will not be as profitable.

In this case, the company has a strong incentive to expense the full $3 million during fiscal 2010 in order to report all the advertising expense in the fiscal 2010 income statement. This unethical action would keep $2 million of advertising expense off the fiscal 2011 income statement and make 2011's net income look $2 million better.

UPDATING THE ACCOUNTS: THE ADJUSTING PROCESS

At the end of the period, the business reports its financial statements. This process begins with the trial balance introduced in Chapter 2. We refer to this trial balance as unadjusted because the accounts are not yet ready for the financial statements. In most cases the simple label "Trial Balance" means "unadjusted."

OBJECTIVE

3 **Adjust** the accounts

Which Accounts Need to Be Updated (Adjusted)?

The stockholders need to know how well ShineBrite Car Wash is performing. The financial statements report this information, and all accounts must be up-to-date. That means some accounts must be adjusted. Exhibit 3-3 gives the trial balance of ShineBrite Car Wash, Inc., at June 30, 2010.

EXHIBIT 3-3 | **Unadjusted Trial Balance**

ShineBrite Car Wash, Inc. Unadjusted Trial Balance June 30, 2010		
Cash	$24,800	
Accounts receivable	2,200	
Supplies	700	
Prepaid rent	3,000	
Equipment	24,000	
Accounts payable		$13,100
Unearned service revenue		400
Common stock		20,000
Retained earnings		18,800
Dividends	3,200	
Service revenue		7,000
Salary expense	900	
Utilities expense	500	
Total	$59,300	$59,300

This trial balance is unadjusted. That means it's not completely up-to-date. It's not quite ready for preparing the financial statements for presentation to the public.

Cash, Equipment, Accounts Payable, Common Stock, and Dividends are up-to-date and need no adjustment at the end of the period. Why? Because the day-to-day transactions provide all the data for these accounts.

Accounts Receivable, Supplies, Prepaid Rent, and the other accounts are another story. These accounts are not yet up-to-date on June 30. Why? Because certain transactions have not yet been recorded. Consider Supplies. During June, ShineBrite Car Wash used cleaning supplies to wash cars. But ShineBrite didn't make a journal entry for supplies used every time it washed a car. That would waste time and money. Instead, ShineBrite waits until the end of the period and then records the supplies used up during the entire month.

The cost of supplies used up is an expense. An adjusting entry at the end of June updates both Supplies (an asset) and Supplies Expense. We must adjust all accounts whose balances are not yet up-to-date.

Categories of Adjusting Entries

Accounting adjustments fall into three basic categories: deferrals, depreciation, and accruals.

Deferrals. A **deferral** is an adjustment for an item that the business paid or received cash in advance. Starbucks purchases supplies for use in its operations. During the period, some supplies (assets) are used up and become expenses. At the end of the period, an adjustment is needed to decrease the Supplies account for the supplies used up. This is Supplies Expense. Prepaid rent, prepaid insurance, and all other prepaid expenses require deferral adjustments.

There are also deferral adjustments for liabilities. Companies such as Starbucks may collect cash from a grocery-store chain in advance of earning the revenue. When Starbucks receives cash up front, Starbucks has a liability to provide coffee for the customer. This liability is called Unearned Sales Revenue. Then, when Starbucks delivers the goods to the customer, it earns Sales Revenue. This earning process requires an adjustment at the end of the period. The adjustment decreases the liability and increases the revenue for the revenue earned. Publishers such as Time, Inc., and your cell-phone company collect cash in advance. They too must make adjusting entries for revenues earned later.

Depreciation. **Depreciation** allocates the cost of a plant asset to expense over the asset's useful life. Depreciation is the most common long-term deferral. Starbucks buys buildings and equipment. As Starbucks uses the assets, it records depreciation for wear-and-tear and obsolescence. The accounting adjustment records Depreciation Expense and decreases the asset's book value over its life. The process is identical to a deferral-type adjustment; the only difference is the type of asset involved.

Accruals. An **accrual** is the opposite of a deferral. For an accrued *expense*, Starbucks records the expense before paying cash. For an accrued *revenue*, Starbucks records the revenue before collecting cash.

Salary Expense can create an accrual adjustment. As employees work for Starbucks Corporation, the company's salary expense accrues with the passage of time. At September 30, 2008, Starbucks owed employees some salaries to be paid after year end. At September 30, Starbucks recorded Salary Expense and Salary Payable for the amount owed. Other examples of expense accruals include interest expense and income tax expense.

An accrued revenue is a revenue that the business has earned and will collect next year. At year end Starbucks must accrue the revenue. The adjustment debits a receivable and credits a revenue. For example, accrual of interest revenue debits Interest Receivable and credits Interest Revenue.

Let's see how the adjusting process actually works for ShineBrite Car Wash at June 30. We start with prepaid expenses.

Prepaid Expenses

A **prepaid expense** is an expense paid in advance. Therefore, prepaid expenses are assets because they provide a future benefit for the owner. Let's do the adjustments for prepaid rent and supplies.

Prepaid Rent.   Companies pay rent in advance. This prepayment creates an asset for the renter, who can then use the rented item in the future. Suppose ShineBrite Car Wash prepays three months' store rent ($3,000) on June 1. The entry for the prepayment of three months' rent debits Prepaid Rent as follows:

Jun 1	Prepaid Rent ($1,000 × 3)	3,000	
	Cash		3,000
	Paid three months' rent in advance.		

The accounting equation shows that one asset increases and another decreases. Total assets are unchanged.

Assets	=	Liabilities	+	Stockholders' Equity
3,000	=	0	+	0
− 3,000				

After posting, the Prepaid Rent account appears as follows:

Prepaid Rent	
Jun 1 3,000	

Throughout June, the Prepaid Rent account carries this beginning balance, as shown in Exhibit 3-3 (p. 143). The adjustment transfers $1,000 from Prepaid Rent to Rent Expense as follows:*

Adjusting entry a

Jun 30	Rent Expense ($3,000 × 1/3)	1,000	
	Prepaid Rent		1,000
	To record rent expense.		

Both assets and stockholders' equity decrease.

Assets	=	Liabilities	+	Stockholders' Equity	−	Expenses
− 1,000	=	0				− 1,000

---

*See Exhibit 3-8, page 155, for a summary of adjustments a–g.

After posting, Prepaid Rent and Rent Expense appear as follows:

Prepaid Rent				Rent Expense		
Jun 1	3,000	Jun 30	1,000 →	Jun 30	1,000	
Bal	2,000			Bal	1,000	

This expense illustrates the matching principle. We record an expense in order to measure net income.

Supplies. Supplies are another type of prepaid expense. On June 2, ShineBrite Car Wash paid cash of $700 for cleaning supplies:

Jun 2	Supplies	700	
	Cash		700
	Paid cash for supplies.		

Assets	=	Liabilities	+	Stockholders' Equity
700	=	0	+	0
– 700				

The cost of the supplies ShineBrite used is supplies expense. To measure June's supplies expense, the business counts the supplies on hand at the end of the month. The count shows that $400 of supplies remain. Subtracting the $400 of supplies on hand from the supplies available ($700) measures supplies expense for the month ($300), as follows:

Asset Available During the Period	–	Asset on Hand at the End of the Period	=	Asset Used (Expense) During the Period
$700	–	$400	=	$300

The June 30 adjusting entry debits the expense and credits the asset, as follows:

Adjusting entry b

Jun 30	Supplies Expense ($700 – $400)	300	
	Supplies		300
	To record supplies expense.		

Assets	=	Liabilities	+	Stockholders' Equity	–	Expenses
– 300	=	0				– 300

After posting, the Supplies and Supplies Expense accounts appear as follows. The adjustment is highlighted for emphasis.

Supplies				Supplies Expense		
Jun 2	700	Jun 30	300 →	Jun 30	300	
Bal	400			Bal	300	

At the start of July, Supplies has this $400 balance, and the adjustment process is repeated each month.

STOP & THINK...

At the beginning of the month, supplies were $5,000. During the month, $7,000 of supplies were purchased. At month's end, $3,000 of supplies are still on hand. What is the

- adjusting entry?
- ending balance in the Supplies account?

Answer:

Supplies Expense ($5,000 + $7,000 − $3,000)	9,000	
Supplies		9,000
Ending balance of supplies = $3,000 (the supplies still on hand)		

Depreciation of Plant Assets

Plant assets are long-lived tangible assets, such as land, buildings, furniture, and equipment. All plant assets but land decline in usefulness, and this decline is an expense. Accountants spread the cost of each plant asset, except land, over its useful life. Depreciation is the process of allocating cost to expense for a long-term plant asset.

To illustrate depreciation, consider ShineBrite Car Wash. Suppose that on June 2 ShineBrite purchased car-washing equipment on account for $24,000:

Jun 3	Equipment	24,000	
	Accounts Payable		24,000
	Purchased equipment on account.		

Assets	=	Liabilities	+	Stockholders' Equity
24,000	=	24,000	+	0

After posting, the Equipment account appears as follows:

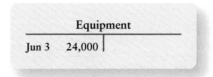

	Equipment
Jun 3	24,000

ShineBrite records an asset when it purchases equipment. Then, as the asset is used, a portion of the asset's cost is transferred to Depreciation Expense. Accounting matches the expense against revenue—this is the matching principle. Computerized systems program the depreciation for automatic entry each period.

ShineBrite's equipment will remain useful for five years and then be worthless. One way to compute the amount of depreciation for each year is to divide the cost of the asset ($24,000 in our example) by its expected useful life (five years). This procedure—called the straight-line depreciation method—gives annual depreciation of $4,800. The depreciation amount is an estimate. (Chapter 7 covers plant assets and depreciation in more detail.)

$$\text{Annual Depreciation} = \$24{,}000/5 \text{ years} = \$4{,}800 \text{ per year}$$

Depreciation for June is $400.

$$\text{Monthly Depreciation} = \$4{,}800/12 \text{ months} = \$400 \text{ per month}$$

The Accumulated Depreciation Account. Depreciation expense for June is recorded as follows:

Adjusting entry c

Jun 30	Depreciation Expense—Equipment	400	
	Accumulated Depreciation—Equipment		400
	To record depreciation.		

Total assets decrease by the amount of the expense:

Assets	=	Liabilities	+	Stockholders' Equity	–	Expenses
– 400	=	0				– 400

The Accumulated Depreciation account, (not Equipment) is credited to preserve the original cost of the asset in the Equipment account. Managers can then refer to the Equipment account if they ever need to know how much the asset cost.

The **Accumulated Depreciation** account shows the sum of all depreciation expense from using the asset. Therefore, the balance in the Accumulated Depreciation account increases over the asset's life.

Accumulated Depreciation is a contra asset account—an asset account with a normal credit balance. A **contra account** has two distinguishing characteristics:

1. It always has a companion account.

2. Its normal balance is opposite that of the companion account.

In this case, Accumulated Depreciation is the contra account to Equipment, so Accumulated Depreciation appears directly after Equipment on the balance sheet. A business carries an accumulated depreciation account for each depreciable asset, for example, Accumulated Depreciation—Building and Accumulated Depreciation—Equipment.

After posting, the plant asset accounts of ShineBrite Car Wash are as follows— with the adjustment highlighted:

Equipment		Accumulated Depreciation—Equipment		Depreciation Expense—Equipment	
Jun 3 24,000		Jun 30 400		Jun 30 400	
Bal 24,000		Bal 400		Bal 400	

Book Value.   The net amount of a plant asset (cost minus accumulated depreciation) is called that asset's **book value (of a plant asset)**, or carrying amount. Exhibit 3-4 shows how ShineBrite would report the book value of its equipment and building at June 30 (the building data are assumed for this illustration).

EXHIBIT 3-4 | **Plant Assets on the Balance Sheet of ShineBrite Car Wash**

ShineBrite Car Wash Plant Assets at June 30		
Equipment...	$24,000	
Less: Accumulated Depreciation	(400)	$23,600
Building...	$50,000	
Less: Accumulated Depreciation	(200)	49,800
Book value of plant assets		$73,400

At June 30, the book value of equipment is $23,600; the book value of the building is $49,800.

STOP & THINK...

What will be the book value of ShineBrite's equipment at the end of July?

Answer:
$24,000 – $400 – $400 = $23,200.

Exhibit 3-5 shows how Starbucks Corporation reports property, plant, and equipment in its annual report. Lines 1 to 6 list specific assets and their cost. Line 7 shows the cost of all Starbucks plant assets. Line 8 gives the amount of accumulated depreciation, and line 9 shows the assets' book value of $2,956 million.

EXHIBIT 3-5 | **Starbucks Corporation's Reporting of Property, Plant, and Equipment (Adapted, in millions)**

1	Land...	$ 59
2	Buildings	218
3	Leasehold improvements......................................	3,363
4	Store equipment	1,045
5	Roasting equipment	220
6	Furniture, fixtures, and other	812
7	Property, plant, and equipment, at cost..............	5,717
8	Less: Accumulated depreciation	(2,761)
9	Property, plant, and equipment, net	$ 2,956

Accrued Expenses

Businesses incur expenses before they pay cash. Consider an employee's salary. Starbucks' expense and payable grow as the employee works, so the liability is said to accrue. Another example is interest expense on a note payable. Interest accrues as the clock ticks. The term **accrued expense** refers to a liability that arises from an expense that has not yet been paid.

Companies don't record accrued expenses daily or weekly. Instead, they wait until the end of the period and use an adjusting entry to update each expense (and related liability) for the financial statements. Let's look at salary expense.

Most companies pay their employees at set times. Suppose ShineBrite Car Wash pays its employee a monthly salary of $1,800, half on the 15th and half on the last day of the month. The following calendar for June has the paydays circled:

			June			
Sun.	Mon.	Tue.	Wed.	Thur.	Fri.	Sat.
						1
2	3	4	5	6	7	8
9	10	11	12	13	14	(15)
16	17	18	19	20	21	22
23	24	25	26	27	28	29
(30)						

Assume that if a payday falls on a Sunday, ShineBrite pays the employee on the following Monday. During June, ShineBrite paid its employees the first half-month salary of $900 and made the following entry:

Jun 15	Salary Expense	900	
	Cash		900
	To pay salary.		

Assets	=	Liabilities	+	Stockholders' Equity	−	Expenses
− 900	=	0				− 900

After posting, the Salary Expense account is

Salary Expense	
Jun 15	900

The trial balance at June 30 (Exhibit 3-3, p. 143) includes Salary Expense with its debit balance of $900. Because June 30, the second payday of the month, falls on a Sunday, the second half-month amount of $900 will be paid on Monday, July 1. At June 30, therefore, ShineBrite adjusts for additional salary expense and salary payable of $900 as follows:

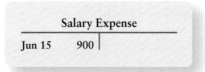

		Adjusting entry d	
Jun 30	Salary Expense	900	
	Salary Payable		900
	To accrue salary expense.		

An accrued expense increases liabilities and decreases stockholders' equity:

Assets	=	Liabilities	+	Stockholders' Equity	−	Expenses
0	=	900				− 900

After posting, the Salary Payable and Salary Expense accounts appear as follows (adjustment highlighted):

Salary Payable				Salary Expense		
	Jun 30	900		Jun 15	900	
	Bal	900		Jun 30	900	
				Bal	1,800	

The accounts now hold all of June's salary information. Salary Expense has a full month's salary, and Salary Payable shows the amount owed at June 30. All accrued expenses are recorded this way—debit the expense and credit the liability.

Computerized systems contain a payroll module. Accrued salaries can be automatically journalized and posted at the end of each period.

Accrued Revenues

Businesses often earn revenue before they receive the cash. A revenue that has been earned but not yet collected is called an **accrued revenue**.

Assume that FedEx hires ShineBrite on June 15 to wash FedEx delivery trucks each month. Suppose FedEx will pay ShineBrite $600 monthly, with the first payment on July 15. During June, ShineBrite will earn half a month's fee, $300, for work done June 15 through June 30. On June 30, ShineBrite makes the following adjusting entry:

Adjusting entry e

Jun 30	Accounts Receivable ($600 × 1/2)	300	
	Service Revenue		300
	To accrue service revenue.		

Revenue increases both total assets and stockholders' equity:

Assets	=	Liabilities	+	Stockholders' Equity	+	Revenues
300	=	0				+ 300

Recall that Accounts Receivable has an unadjusted balance of $2,200, and Service Revenue's unadjusted balance is $7,000 (Exhibit 3-3, p. 143). This June 30 adjusting entry has the following effects (adjustment highlighted):

Accounts Receivable			**Service Revenue**	
	2,200			7,000
Jun 30	300		Jun 30	300
Bal	2,500		Bal	7,300

All accrued revenues are accounted for similarly—debit a receivable and credit a revenue.

STOP & THINK...

Suppose ShineBrite Car Wash holds a note receivable as an investment. At the end of June, $100 of interest revenue has been earned. Journalize the accrued revenue adjustment at June 30.

Answer:

Jun 30	Interest Receivable	100	
	Interest Revenue		100
	To accrue interest revenue.		

Unearned Revenues

Some businesses collect cash from customers before earning the revenue. This creates a liability called **unearned revenue**. Only when the job is completed does the business earn the revenue. Suppose **Home Depot** engages ShineBrite Car Wash to wash

Home Depot trucks, agreeing to pay ShineBrite $400 monthly, beginning immediately. If ShineBrite collects the first amount on June 15, then ShineBrite records this transaction as follows:

Jun 15	Cash	400	
	Unearned Service Revenue		400
	Received cash for revenue in advance.		

	Assets	=	Liabilities	+	Stockholders' Equity
	400	=	400	+	0

After posting, the liability account appears as follows:

Unearned Service Revenue

| | Jun 15 | 400 |

Unearned Service Revenue is a liability because ShineBrite is obligated to perform services for Home Depot. The June 30 unadjusted trial balance (Exhibit 3-3, p. 143) lists Unearned Service Revenue with a $400 credit balance. During the last 15 days of the month, ShineBrite will earn one-half of the $400, or $200. On June 30, ShineBrite makes the following adjustment:

Adjusting entry f

Jun 30	Unearned Service Revenue ($400 × 1/2)	200	
	Service Revenue		200
	To record unearned service revenue that has been earned.		

	Assets	=	Liabilities	+	Stockholders' Equity	+	Revenues
	0	=	− 200	+			+ 200

This adjusting entry shifts $200 of the total amount received ($400) from liability to revenue. After posting, Unearned Service Revenue is reduced to $200, and Service Revenue is increased by $200, as follows (adjustment highlighted):

Unearned Service Revenue

| Jun 30 | 200 | Jun 15 | 400 |
| | | Bal | 200 |

Service Revenue

			7,000
		Jun 30	300
		Jun 30	200
		Bal	7,500

All revenues collected in advance are accounted for this way. An unearned revenue is a liability, not a revenue.

One company's prepaid expense is the other company's unearned revenue. For example, Home Depot's prepaid expense is ShineBrite Car Wash's liability for unearned revenue.

Exhibit 3-6 diagrams the distinctive timing of prepaids and accruals. Study prepaid expenses all the way across. Then study unearned revenues across, and so on.

EXHIBIT 3-6 | Prepaid and Accrual Adjustments

PREPAIDS—Cash First

	First			Later		
Prepaid expenses	*Pay cash and record an asset:* Prepaid Expense ...... XXX Cash		XXX	*Record an expense and decrease the asset:* Expense .... XXX Prepaid Expense		XXX
Unearned revenues	*Receive cash and record unearned revenue:* Cash .... XXX Unearned Revenue		XXX	*Record revenue and decrease unearned revenue:* Unearned Revenue .... XXX Revenue		XXX

ACCRUALS—Cash Later

	First			Later		
Accrued expenses	*Accrue expense and a payable:* Expense .... XXX Payable		XXX	*Pay cash and decrease the payable:* Payable .... XXX Cash		XXX
Accrued revenues	*Accrue revenue and a receivable:* Receivable .... XXX Revenue		XXX	*Receive cash and decrease the receivable:* Cash .... XXX Receivable		XXX

The authors thank Professors Darrel Davis and Alfonso Oddo for suggesting this exhibit.

Summary of the Adjusting Process

Two purposes of the adjusting process are to

- measure income, and
- update the balance sheet.

Therefore, every adjusting entry affects at least one of the following:

- Revenue or expense—to measure income
- Asset or liability—to update the balance sheet

Exhibit 3-7 summarizes the standard adjustments.

EXHIBIT 3-7 | **Summary of Adjusting Entries**

	Type of Account	
Category of Adjusting Entry	Debit	Credit
Prepaid expense..................	Expense	Asset
Depreciation......................	Expense	Contra asset
Accrued expense.................	Expense	Liability
Accrued revenue.................	Asset	Revenue
Unearned revenue...............	Liability	Revenue

Adapted from material provided by Beverly Terry.

Exhibit 3-8 summarizes the adjustments of ShineBrite Car Wash, Inc., at June 30—the adjusting entries we've examined over the past few pages.

- Panel A repeats the data for each adjustment.
- Panel B gives the adjusting entries.
- Panel C on the following page shows the accounts after posting the adjusting entries. The adjustments are keyed by letter.

EXHIBIT 3-8 | **The Adjusting Process of ShineBrite Car Wash, Inc.**

PANEL A—Information for Adjustments at June 30, 2010	PANEL B—Adjusting Entries
(a) Prepaid rent expired, $1,000.	(a) Rent Expense .... 1,000 Prepaid Rent .... 1,000 To record rent expense.
(b) Supplies used, $300.	(b) Supplies Expense .... 300 Supplies... 300 To record supplies used.
(c) Depreciation on equipment, $400.	(c) Depreciation Expense—Equipment .... 400 Accumulated Depreciation—Equipment 400 To record depreciation.
(d) Accrued salary expense, $900.	(d) Salary Expense .... 900 Salary Payable...................................... 900 To accrue salary expense.
(e) Accrued service revenue, $300.	(e) Accounts Receivable................................. 300 Service Revenue.................................... 300 To accrue service revenue.
(f) Amount of unearned service revenue that has been earned, $200.	(f) Unearned Service Revenue......................... 200 Service Revenue.................................... 200 To record unearned revenue that has been earned.
(g) Accrued income tax expense, $600.	(g) Income Tax Expense .... 600 Income Tax Payable.............................. 600 To accrue income tax expense.

PANEL C—Ledger Accounts

Assets	Liabilities	Stockholders' Equity

Assets

Cash

Bal 24,800 |

Accounts Receivable

	2,200	
(e)	300	
Bal	2,500	

Supplies

| | 700 | (b) | 300 |
| Bal | 400 | | |

Prepaid Rent

| | 3,000 | (a) | 1,000 |
| Bal | 2,000 | | |

Equipment

Bal 24,000 |

Accumulated Depreciation— Equipment

| | (c) | 400 |
| | Bal | 400 |

Liabilities

Accounts Payable

| | Bal | 13,100 |

Salary Payable

| | (d) | 900 |
| | Bal | 900 |

Unearned Service Revenue

| (f) | 200 | | 400 |
| | | Bal | 200 |

Income Tax Payable

| | (g) | 600 |
| | Bal | 600 |

Stockholders' Equity

Common Stock

| | Bal | 20,000 |

Retained Earnings

| | Bal | 18,800 |

Dividends

Bal 3,200 |

Revenue

Service Revenue

		7,000
	(e)	300
	(f)	200
	Bal	7,500

Expenses

Rent Expense

| (a) | 1,000 | |
| Bal | 1,000 | |

Salary Expense

	900	
(d)	900	
Bal	1,800	

Supplies Expense

| (b) | 300 | |
| Bal | 300 | |

Depreciation Expense—Equipment

| (c) | 400 | |
| Bal | 400 | |

Utilities Expense

Bal 500 |

Income Tax Expense

| (g) | 600 | |
| Bal | 600 | |

Exhibit 3-8 includes an additional adjusting entry that we have not yet discussed—the accrual of income tax expense. Like individual taxpayers, corporations are subject to income tax. They typically accrue income tax expense and the related income tax payable as the final adjusting entry of the period. ShineBrite Car Wash accrues income tax expense with adjusting entry g, as follows:

			Adjusting entry g
Jun 30	Income Tax Expense	600	
	Income Tax Payable		600
	To accrue income tax expense.		

The income tax accrual follows the pattern for accrued expenses.

The Adjusted Trial Balance

This chapter began with the unadjusted trial balance (see Exhibit 3-3, p. 143). After the adjustments are journalized and posted, the accounts appear as shown in Exhibit 3-8, Panel C. A useful step in preparing the financial statements is to list the accounts, along with their adjusted balances, on an **adjusted trial balance**. This document lists all the accounts and their final balances in a single place. Exhibit 3-9 shows the adjusted trial balance of ShineBrite Car Wash.

EXHIBIT 3-9 | **Adjusted Trial Balance**

ShineBrite Car Wash, Inc.
Preparation of Adjusted Trial Balance
June 30, 2010

Account Title	Trial Balance Debit	Trial Balance Credit	Adjustments Debit		Adjustments Credit		Adjusted Trial Balance Debit	Adjusted Trial Balance Credit	
Cash	24,800						24,800		⎫
Accounts receivable	2,200		(e)	300			2,500		
Supplies	700				(b)	300	400		
Prepaid rent	3,000				(a)	1,000	2,000		
Equipment	24,000						24,000		
Accumulated depreciation—equipment					(c)	400		400	**Balance Sheet**
Accounts payable		13,100						13,100	(*Exhibit 3-12*)
Salary payable					(d)	900		900	
Unearned service revenue		400	(f)	200				200	
Income tax payable					(g)	600		600	
Common stock		20,000						20,000	
Retained earnings		18,800						18,800	⎫ **Statement of**
Dividends	3,200						3,200		⎬ **Retained Earnings**
Service revenue		7,000			(e)	300		7,500	⎭ (*Exhibit 3-11*)
					(f)	200			⎫
Rent expense			(a)	1,000			1,000		
Salary expense	900		(d)	900			1,800		**Income Statement**
Supplies expense			(b)	300			300		(*Exhibit 3-10*)
Depreciation expense			(c)	400			400		
Utilities expense	500						500		
Income tax expense			(g)	600			600		⎭
	59,300	59,300		3,700		3,700	61,500	61,500	

Note how clearly the adjusted trial balance presents the data. The Account Title and the Trial Balance data come from the trial balance. The two Adjustments columns summarize the adjusting entries. The Adjusted Trial Balance columns then give the final account balances. Each adjusted amount in Exhibit 3-9 is the unadjusted balance plus or minus the adjustments. For example, Accounts Receivable starts with a balance of $2,200. Add the $300 debit adjustment to get Accounts Receivable's ending balance of $2,500. Spreadsheets are designed for this type of analysis.

ac ↗t

**Accounting Cycle
Tutorial Glossary**

PREPARING THE FINANCIAL STATEMENTS

The June financial statements of ShineBrite Car Wash can be prepared from the adjusted trial balance. At the far right, Exhibit 3-9 shows how the accounts are distributed to the financial statements.

OBJECTIVE

4 Prepare the financial statements

- The income statement (Exhibit 3-10) lists the revenue and expense accounts.
- The statement of retained earnings (Exhibit 3-11) shows the changes in retained earnings.
- The balance sheet (Exhibit 3-12) reports assets, liabilities, and stockholders' equity.

The arrows in Exhibits 3-10, 3-11, and 3-12 (all on the following page) show the flow of data from one statement to the next.

EXHIBIT 3-10 | **Income Statement**

ShineBrite Car Wash, Inc.
Income Statement
Month Ended June 30, 2010

Revenues:		
Service revenue		$7,500
Expenses:		
Salary expense	$1,800	
Rent expense...........................	1,000	
Utilities expense......................	500	
Depreciation expense	400	
Supplies expense	300	4,000
Income before tax		3,500
Income tax expense.....................		600
Net income..................................		$2,900

①

EXHIBIT 3-11 | **Statement of Retained Earnings**

ShineBrite Car Wash, Inc.
Statement of Retained Earnings
Month Ended June 30, 2010

Retained earnings, May 31, 2010................	$18,800
Add: Net income...	2,900
	21,700
Less: Dividends	(3,200)
Retained earnings, June 30, 2010................	$18,500

EXHIBIT 3-12 | **Balance Sheet**

ShineBrite Car Wash, Inc.
Balance Sheet
June 30, 2010

Assets			Liabilities		
Cash...............................		$24,800	Accounts payable		$13,100
Accounts receivable........		2,500	Salary payable		900
Supplies..........................		400	Unearned service revenue		200
Prepaid rent...................		2,000	Income tax payable		600
Equipment.....................	$24,000		Total liabilities		14,800
Less: Accumulated					
depreciation	(400)	23,600	**Stockholders' Equity**		
			Common stock.........................		20,000
			Retained earnings....................		18,500
			Total stockholders' equity........		38,500
			Total liabilities and		
Total assets....................		$53,300	stockholders' equity..............		$53,300

②

Why is the income statement prepared first and the balance sheet last?

1. The income statement reports net income or net loss, the result of revenues minus expenses. Revenues and expenses affect stockholders' equity, so net income is then transferred to retained earnings. The first arrow tracks net income.

2. Retained Earnings is the final balancing element of the balance sheet. To solidify your understanding, trace the $18,500 retained earnings figure from Exhibit 3-11 to Exhibit 3-12. Arrow ❷ tracks retained earnings.

MID-CHAPTER SUMMARY PROBLEM

The trial balance of Goldsmith Company shown below pertains to December 31, 2010, which is the end of its year-long accounting period. Data needed for the adjusting entries include the following:

a. Supplies on hand at year end, $2,000.

b. Depreciation on furniture and fixtures, $20,000.

c. Depreciation on building, $10,000.

d. Salaries owed but not yet paid, $5,000.

e. Accrued service revenue, $12,000.

f. Of the $45,000 balance of unearned service revenue, $32,000 was earned during the year.

g. Accrued income tax expense, $35,000.

❚ Requirements

1. Open the ledger accounts with their unadjusted balances. Show dollar amounts in thousands, as shown for Accounts Receivable:

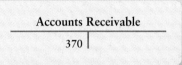

Accounts Receivable

370 |

2. Journalize the Goldsmith Company adjusting entries at December 31, 2010. Key entries by letter, as in Exhibit 3-8, page 155.
3. Post the adjusting entries.
4. Prepare an adjusted trial balance, as shown in Exhibit 3-9, page 157.
5. Prepare the income statement, the statement of retained earnings, and the balance sheet. (At this stage, it is not necessary to classify assets or liabilities as current or long term.) Draw arrows linking these three financial statements.

Goldsmith Company
Trial Balance
December 31, 2010

Cash	$ 198,000	
Accounts receivable	370,000	
Supplies	6,000	
Furniture and fixtures	100,000	
Accumulated depreciation—furniture and fixtures		$ 40,000
Building	250,000	
Accumulated depreciation—building		130,000
Accounts payable		380,000
Salary payable		
Unearned service revenue		45,000
Income tax payable		
Common stock		100,000
Retained earnings		193,000
Dividends	65,000	
Service revenue		286,000
Salary expense	172,000	
Supplies expense		
Depreciation expense—furniture and fixtures		
Depreciation expense—building		
Income tax expense		
Miscellaneous expense	13,000	
Total	$1,174,000	$1,174,000

Answers

❙ *Requirements 1 and 3*

(Amounts in thousands)

| Assets | | Stockholders' Equity | |

Cash

| Bal | 198 | |

Accounts Receivable

	370	
(e)	12	
Bal	382	

Supplies

| | 6 | (a) | 4 |
| Bal | 2 | | |

Furniture and Fixtures

| Bal | 100 | |

Accumulated Depreciation—Furniture and Fixtures

			40
		(b)	20
		Bal	60

Building

| Bal | 250 | |

Accumulated Depreciation—Building

			130
		(c)	10
		Bal	140

Liabilities

Accounts Payable

| | | Bal | 380 |

Salary Payable

| | | (d) | 5 |
| | | Bal | 5 |

Unearned Service Revenue

| (f) | 32 | | 45 |
| | | Bal | 13 |

Income Tax Payable

| | | (g) | 35 |
| | | Bal | 35 |

Common Stock

| | | Bal | 100 |

Retained Earnings

| | | Bal | 193 |

Dividends

| Bal | 65 | |

Revenues

Service Revenue

			286
		(e)	12
		(f)	32
		Bal	330

Expenses

Salary Expense

	172	
(d)	5	
Bal	177	

Supplies Expense

| (a) | 4 | |
| Bal | 4 | |

Depreciation Expense—Furniture and Fixtures

| (b) | 20 | |
| Bal | 20 | |

Depreciation Expense—Building

| (c) | 10 | |
| Bal | 10 | |

Income Tax Expense

| (g) | 35 | |
| Bal | 35 | |

Miscellaneous Expense

| Bal | 13 | |

▌*Requirement 2*

(a)	Dec 31	Supplies Expense ($6,000 − $2,000)	4,000	
		Supplies		4,000
		To record supplies used.		
(b)	31	Depreciation Expense—Furniture and Fixtures	20,000	
		Accumulated Depreciation—Furniture and Fixtures		20,000
		To record depreciation expense on furniture and fixtures.		
(c)	31	Depreciation Expense—Building	10,000	
		Accumulated Depreciation—Building		10,000
		To record depreciation expense on building.		
(d)	31	Salary Expense	5,000	
		Salary Payable		5,000
		To accrue salary expense.		
(e)	31	Accounts Receivable	12,000	
		Service Revenue		12,000
		To accrue service revenue.		
(f)	31	Unearned Service Revenue	32,000	
		Service Revenue		32,000
		To record unearned service revenue that has been earned.		
(g)	31	Income Tax Expense	35,000	
		Income Tax Payable		35,000
		To accrue income tax expense.		

Requirement 4

Goldsmith Company
Preparation of Adjusted Trial Balance
December 31, 2010

(Amounts in thousands) Account Title	Trial Balance Debit	Trial Balance Credit	Adjustments Debit		Adjustments Credit		Adjusted Trial Balance Debit	Adjusted Trial Balance Credit
Cash	198						198	
Accounts receivable	370		(e)	12			382	
Supplies	6				(a)	4	2	
Furniture and fixtures	100						100	
Accumulated depreciation— furniture and fixtures		40			(b)	20		60
Building	250						250	
Accumulated depreciation—building		130			(c)	10		140
Accounts payable		380						380
Salary payable					(d)	5		5
Unearned service revenue		45	(f)	32				13
Income tax payable					(g)	35		35
Common stock		100						100
Retained earnings		193						193
Dividends	65						65	
Service revenue		286			(e)	12		330
					(f)	32		
Salary expense	172		(d)	5			177	
Supplies expense			(a)	4			4	
Depreciation expense— furniture and fixtures			(b)	20			20	
Depreciation expense—building			(c)	10			10	
Income tax expense			(g)	35			35	
Miscellaneous expense	13						13	
	1,174	1,174	118		118		1,256	1,256

▌*Requirement 5*

Goldsmith Company
Income Statement
Year Ended December 31, 2010

(Amounts in thousands)

Revenue:		
Service revenue		$330
Expenses:		
Salary expense	$177	
Depreciation expense—furniture and fixtures	20	
Depreciation expense—building............................	10	
Supplies expense	4	
Miscellaneous expense	13	224
Income before tax		106
Income tax expense		35
Net income...		$ 71

①

Goldsmith Company
Statement of Retained Earnings
Year Ended December 31, 2010

(Amounts in thousands)

Retained earnings, December 31, 2009	$193
Add: Net income....................................	71
	264
Less: Dividends	(65)
Retained earnings, December 31, 2010	$199

Goldsmith Company
Balance Sheet
December 31, 2010

(Amounts in thousands)

②

Assets			Liabilities		
Cash..		$198	Accounts payable		$380
Accounts receivable.................		382	Salary payable		5
Supplies....................................		2	Unearned service revenue		13
Furniture and fixtures	$100		Income tax payable		35
Less: Accumulated			Total liabilities		433
depreciation................	(60)	40			
			Stockholders' Equity		
Building..................................	$250		Common stock............................		100
Less: Accumulated			Retained earnings........................		199
depreciation................	(140)	110	Total stockholders' equity		299
			Total liabilities and		
Total assets.............................		$732	stockholders' equity..................		$732

Which Accounts Need to Be Closed?

It is now June 30, the end of the month. Van Gray, the manager, will continue ShineBrite Car Wash into July, August, and beyond. But wait—the revenue and the expense accounts still hold amounts for June. At the end of each accounting period, it is necessary to close the books.

Closing the books means to prepare the accounts for the next period's transactions. The **closing entries** set the revenue, expense, and dividends balances back to zero at the end of the period. The idea is the same as setting the scoreboard back to zero after a game.

Closing is easily handled by computers. Recall that the income statement for a particular year reports only one year's income. For example, net income for Starbucks 2008 relates exclusively to the year ended September 28, 2008. At each year end, Starbucks accountants close the company's revenues and expenses for that year.

Temporary Accounts. Because revenues and expenses relate to a limited period, they are called **temporary accounts**. The Dividends account is also temporary. The closing process applies only to temporary accounts (revenues, expenses, and dividends).

Permanent Accounts. Let's contrast the temporary accounts with the **permanent accounts**: assets, liabilities, and stockholders' equity. The permanent accounts are not closed at the end of the period because they carry over to the next period. Consider Cash, Receivables, Equipment, Accounts Payable, Common Stock, and Retained Earnings. Their ending balances at the end of one period become the beginning balances of the next period.

Closing entries transfer the revenue, expense, and dividends balances to Retained Earnings. Here are the steps to close the books of a company such as Starbucks Corporation or ShineBrite Car Wash:

① Debit each revenue account for the amount of its credit balance. Credit Retained Earnings for the sum of the revenues. Now the sum of the revenues is in Retained Earnings.

② Credit each expense account for the amount of its debit balance. Debit Retained Earnings for the sum of the expenses. The sum of the expenses is now in Retained Earnings.

③ Credit the Dividends account for the amount of its debit balance. Debit Retained Earnings. This entry places the dividends amount in the debit side of Retained Earnings. Remember that dividends are not expenses. Dividends never affect net income.

After closing the books, the Retained Earnings account of ShineBrite Car Wash appears as follows (data from page 158):

Retained Earnings			
		Beginning balance	18,800
Expenses	4,600	Revenues	7,500
Dividends	3,200		
		Ending balance	18,500

Assume that ShineBrite Car Wash closes the books at the end of June. Exhibit 3-13 presents the complete closing process for the business. Panel A gives the closing journal entries, and Panel B shows the accounts after closing.

EXHIBIT 3-13 | **Journalizing and Posting the Closing Entries**

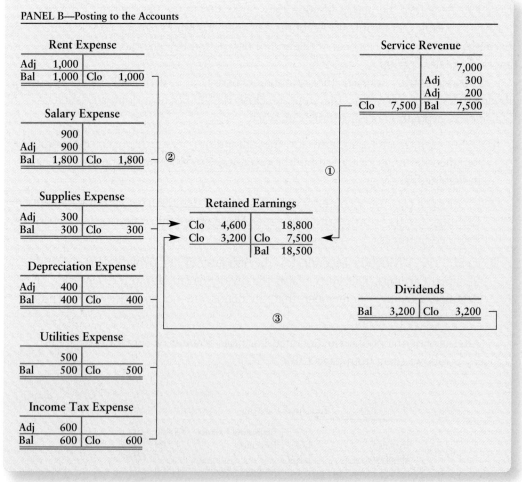

PANEL A—Journalizing the Closing Entries | Page 5

Closing Entries

①	Jun 30	Service Revenue...............................		7,500	
		Retained Earnings			7,500
②	30	Retained Earnings		4,600	
		Rent Expense			1,000
		Salary Expense			1,800
		Supplies Expense			300
		Depreciation Expense..............			400
		Utilities Expense......................			500
		Income Tax Expense			600
③	30	Retained Earnings		3,200	
		Dividends..................................			3,200

Accounting Cycle Tutorial Adjusting & Closing the Books

Accounting Cycle Tutorial Application—Cottage Kitchen

Accounting Cycle Tutorial Application—Cottage Kitchen 2

PANEL B—Posting to the Accounts

Rent Expense

Adj	1,000		
Bal	1,000	Clo	1,000

Salary Expense

	900		
Adj	900		
Bal	1,800	Clo	1,800

Supplies Expense

Adj	300		
Bal	300	Clo	300

Depreciation Expense

Adj	400		
Bal	400	Clo	400

Utilities Expense

	500		
Bal	500	Clo	500

Income Tax Expense

Adj	600		
Bal	600	Clo	600

②

Retained Earnings

Clo	4,600		18,800
Clo	3,200	Clo	7,500
		Bal	18,500

Service Revenue

			7,000
		Adj	300
		Adj	200
Clo	7,500	Bal	7,500

①

Dividends

Bal	3,200	Clo	3,200

③

Adj = Amount posted from an adjusting entry
Clo = Amount posted from a closing entry
Bal = Balance
As arrow ② in Panel B shows, we can make a compound closing entry for all the expenses.

Classifying Assets and Liabilities Based on Their Liquidity

On the balance sheet, assets and liabilities are classified as current or long term to indicate their relative liquidity. **Liquidity** measures how quickly an item can be converted to cash. Cash is the most liquid asset. Accounts receivable are relatively liquid because cash collections usually follow quickly. Inventory is less liquid than accounts receivable because the company must first sell the goods. Equipment and buildings are even less liquid because these assets are held for use and not for sale. A balance sheet lists assets and liabilities in the order of relative liquidity.

Current Assets. As we saw in Chapter 1, **current assets** are the most liquid assets. They will be converted to cash, sold, or consumed during the next 12 months or within the business's normal operating cycle if longer than a year. The **operating cycle** is the time span during which cash is paid for goods and services and these goods and services are sold to bring in cash.

For most businesses, the operating cycle is a few months. Cash, Short-Term Investments, Accounts Receivable, Merchandise Inventory, and Prepaid Expenses are the current assets.

Long-Term Assets. **Long-term assets** are all assets not classified as current assets. One category of long-term assets is plant assets, often labeled Property, Plant, and Equipment. Land, Buildings, Furniture and Fixtures, and Equipment are plant assets. Of these, ShineBrite Car Wash has only Equipment. Long-Term Investments, Intangible Assets, and Other Assets (a catchall category for assets that are not classified more precisely) are also long-term.

Current Liabilities. As we saw in Chapter 1, **current liabilities** are debts that must be paid within one year or within the entity's operating cycle if longer than a year. Accounts Payable, Notes Payable due within one year, Salary Payable, Unearned Revenue, Interest Payable, and Income Tax Payable are current liabilities.

Bankers and other lenders are interested in the due dates of an entity's liabilities. The sooner a liability must be paid, the more pressure it creates. Therefore, the balance sheet lists liabilities in the order in which they must be paid. Balance sheets usually report two liability classifications, current liabilities and long-term liabilities.

Long-Term Liabilities. All liabilities that are not current are classified as **long-term liabilities**. Many notes payable are long term. Some notes payable are paid in installments, with the first installment due within one year, the second installment due the second year, and so on. The first installment is a current liability and the remainder is long term.

Let's see how Starbucks Corporation reports these asset and liability categories on its balance sheet.

Reporting Assets and Liabilities: Starbucks Corporation

Exhibit 3-14 on the following page shows a classified balance sheet: The Consolidated Balance Sheet of Starbucks Corporation. A **classified balance sheet** separates current assets from long-term assets and current liabilities from long-term liabilities. You should be familiar with most of Starbucks' accounts. Study the Starbucks balance sheet all the way through—line by line.

EXHIBIT 3-14 | **Classified Balance Sheet of Starbucks Corporation (Adapted, in millions)**

Starbucks Corporation
Consolidated Balance Sheet (Adapted)
September 28, 2008

(In millions)

Assets

Current assets:	
Cash and cash equivalents	$ 270
Short-term investments	53
Accounts receivable	329
Inventories	693
Prepaid expenses and other current assets	403
Total current assets	1,748
Long-term investments	374
Property, plant, and equipment, net	2,956
Intangible assets	333
Other assets	262
Total assets	$5,673

Liabilities and Shareholders' Equity

Current liabilities:	
Accounts payable	$ 325
Accrued expenses payable	783
Short-term notes payable	713
Current portion of long-term	1
Unearned revenue	368
Total current liabilities	2,190
Long-term debt	550
Other long-term liabilities	442
Total liabilities	3,182
Shareholders' equity:	
Common stock	40
Retained earnings	2,402
Other equity	49
Total shareholders' equity	2,491
Total liabilities and shareholders' equity	$5,673

FORMATS FOR THE FINANCIAL STATEMENTS

Companies can format their financial statements in different ways. Both the balance sheet and the income statement can be formatted in two basic ways.

Balance Sheet Formats

The **report format** lists the assets at the top, followed by the liabilities and stockholders' equity below. The Consolidated Balance Sheet of Starbucks Corporation in Exhibit 3-14 illustrates the report format. The report format is more popular, with approximately 60% of large companies using it.

The **account format** lists the assets on the left and the liabilities and stockholders' equity on the right in the same way that a T-account appears, with assets (debits) on the left and liabilities and equity (credits) on the right. Exhibit 3-12 (p. 158) shows an account-format balance sheet for ShineBrite Car Wash. Either format is acceptable.

Income Statement Formats

A **single-step income statement** lists all the revenues together under a heading such as Revenues, or Revenues and Gains. The expenses are listed together in a single category titled Expenses, or Expenses and Losses. There is only one step, the subtraction of Expenses and Losses from the sum of Revenues and Gains, in arriving at net income. Starbucks' income statement (p. 138) appears in single-step format.

A **multi-step income statement** reports a number of subtotals to highlight important relationships between revenues and expenses. Exhibit 3-15 shows Starbucks' income statement in multi-step format. Gross profit, income from operations, income before tax, and net income are highlighted for emphasis.

EXHIBIT 3-15 | **Starbucks Corporation Income Statement in Multi-Step Format**

Starbucks Corporation
Consolidated Statement of Earnings (Adapted)
Year Ended September 28, 2008

		Millions
Net operating revenues		$10,383
Cost of sales (Cost of goods sold)		4,646
Gross profit		5,737
Store operating expenses	$3,745	
Other operating expenses	597	
Depreciation and amortization expenses	549	
General and administrative expenses	456	
Total operating expenses		5,347
Income from operations		390
Other income		70
Income before income taxes		460
Income tax expense		144
Net income		$ 316

In particular, income from operations ($390 million) is separated from "Other income," which Starbucks did not earn by selling coffee. The other income was mainly interest revenue and other investment income. Most companies consider it important to report their operating income separately from nonoperating income such as interest and dividends.

Most companies' income statements do not conform to either a pure single-step format or a pure multi-step format. Business operations are too complex for all companies to conform to rigid reporting formats. We will discuss the components of the income statement in more detail in Chapter 11.

USING ACCOUNTING RATIOS

As we've seen, accounting provides information for decision making. A bank considering lending money must predict whether the borrower can repay the loan. If the borrower already has a lot of debt, the probability of repayment may be low. If the borrower owes little, the loan may go through. To analyze a company's financial position, decision makers use ratios computed from various items in the financial statements. Let's see how this process works.

OBJECTIVE

6 **Use** two new ratios to evaluate a business

Current Ratio

One of the most widely used financial ratios is the **current ratio**, which divides total current assets by total current liabilities, taken from the balance sheet.

$$\text{Current ratio} = \frac{\text{Total current assets}}{\text{Total current liabilities}}$$

For Starbucks Corporation (amounts in millions on page 168) is as follows:

$$\text{Current ratio} = \frac{\text{Total current assets}}{\text{Total current liabilities}} = \frac{\$1,748}{\$2,190} = 0.80$$

The current ratio measures the company's ability to pay current liabilities with current assets. A company prefers a high current ratio, which means that the business has plenty of current assets to pay current liabilities. An increasing current ratio from period to period indicates improvement in financial position.

As a rule of thumb, a strong current ratio is 1.50, which indicates that the company has $1.50 in current assets for every $1.00 in current liabilities. A company with a current ratio of 1.50 would probably have little trouble paying its current liabilities. Most successful businesses operate with current ratios between 1.20 and 1.50. A current ratio of 1.00 is considered quite low.

Starbucks' current ratio of 0.80 is very low and indicates a relatively weak current position. How does Starbucks survive with so low a current ratio? The company makes most sales for cash, enough to pay off its accounts payable, accrued expenses, and the current portion of its long-term debt, which are the liabilities that must be met with cash immediately. In recent years, the company has borrowed increasing amounts on both a short-term and long-term basis to finance operations and expansion, which has somewhat weakened its debt position. However, in comparison to other companies in the retail business, Starbucks' level of total debt is still relatively low. That leads us to the next ratio.

Debt Ratio

A second aid to decision making is the **debt ratio**, which is the ratio of total liabilities to total assets.

$$\text{Debt ratio} = \frac{\text{Total liabilities}}{\text{Total assets}}$$

For Starbucks (amounts in millions on page 168),

$$\text{Debt ratio} = \frac{\text{Total liabilities}}{\text{Total assets}} = \frac{\$3,182}{\$5,673} = 0.56$$

The debt ratio indicates the proportion of a company's assets that is financed with debt. This ratio measures a business's ability to pay both current and long-term debts (total liabilities).

A low debt ratio is safer than a high debt ratio. Why? Because a company with few liabilities has low required debt payments. This company is unlikely to get into financial difficulty. By contrast, a business with a high debt ratio may have trouble paying its liabilities, especially when sales are low and cash is scarce.

Starbucks' debt ratio of 56% (0.56) is low compared to most companies in the United States. The norm for the debt ratio ranges from 60% to 70%. Starbucks' debt ratio indicates low risk for the company, and that partly offsets Starbucks' risky current ratio.

When a company fails to pay its debts, some of its creditors might be in a position to take the company away from its owners. Most bankruptcies result from high debt ratios. Companies that continue in this pattern are often forced out of business.

How Do Transactions Affect the Ratios?

Companies such as Starbucks are keenly aware of how transactions affect their ratios. Lending agreements often require that a company's current ratio not fall below a certain level. Another loan requirement is that the company's debt ratio may not rise above a threshold, such as 0.70. When a company fails to meet one of these conditions, it is said to default on its lending agreements. The penalty can be severe: The lender can require immediate payment of the loan. Starbucks has little enough debt that the company is not in much danger. But many companies are.

Let's use Starbucks Corporation to examine the effects of some transactions on the company's current ratio and debt ratio. As shown in the preceding section, Starbucks' ratios are as follows (dollar amounts in millions):[1]

$$\text{Current ratio} = \frac{\$1,748}{\$2,190} = 0.80 \qquad \text{Debt ratio} = \frac{\$3,182}{\$5,673} = 0.561$$

The managers of any company would be concerned about how inventory purchases, payments on account, expense accruals, and depreciation would affect its ratios. Let's see how Starbucks would be affected by some typical transactions. For each transaction, the journal entry helps identify the effects on the company.

a. Issued stock and received cash of $50 million.

Journal entry:			
Cash		50	
Common Stock			50

Cash, a current asset, affects both the current ratio and the debt ratio as follows:

$$\text{Current ratio} = \frac{\$1,748 + \$50}{\$2,190} = 0.82 \qquad \text{Debt ratio} = \frac{\$3,182}{\$5,673 + \$50} = 0.556$$

---

[1]Because of the relatively small amounts of these particular illustrative transactions compared to the original components, we have chosen to carry debt ratio computations to three decimals in order to illustrate the impact of individual transactions on the debt ratio. The larger the individual transaction in comparison with the original components (for example, see the End-of-Chapter Summary Problem) the less necessary this will be.

The issuance of stock improves both ratios.

    b. Paid cash to purchase buildings for $20 million.

Journal entry:

Buildings	20	
Cash		20

Cash, a current asset, decreases, but total assets stay the same. Liabilities are unchanged.

$$\text{Current ratio} = \frac{\$1,748 - \$20}{\$2,190} = 0.79 \qquad \text{Debt ratio} = \frac{\$3,182}{\$5,673 + \$20 - \$20} = 0.561; \text{ no change}$$

A cash purchase of a building hurts the current ratio, but doesn't affect the debt ratio.

    c. Made a $30 million sale on account to a grocery chain.

Journal entry:

Accounts Receivable	30	
Sales Revenue		30

The increase in Accounts Receivable increases current assets and total assets, as follows:

$$\text{Current ratio} = \frac{\$1,748 + \$30}{\$2,190} = 0.81 \qquad \text{Debt ratio} = \frac{\$3,182}{\$5,673 + \$30} = 0.558$$

A sale on account improves both ratios.

    d. Collected the account receivable, $30 million.

Journal entry:

Cash	30	
Accounts Receivable		30

This transaction has no effect on total current assets, total assets, or total liabilities. Both ratios are unaffected.

    e. Accrued expenses at year end, $40 million.

Journal entry:

Expenses	40	
Expenses Payable		40

$$\text{Current ratio} = \frac{\$1,748}{\$2,190 + \$40} = 0.78 \qquad \text{Debt ratio} = \frac{\$3,182 + \$40}{\$5,673} = 0.568$$

Most expenses hurt both ratios.

f. Recorded depreciation, $80 million.

Journal entry:

Depreciation Expense	80	
Accumulated Depreciation		80

No current accounts are affected, so only the debt ratio is affected.

$$\text{Current ratio} = \frac{\$1,748}{\$2,190} = 0.80 \qquad \text{Debt ratio} = \frac{\$3,182}{\$5,673 - \$80} = 0.569$$

Depreciation decreases total assets and therefore hurts the debt ratio.

g. Earned interest revenue and collected cash, $40 million.

Journal entry:

Cash	40	
Interest Revenue		40

Cash, a current asset, affects both the current ratio and the debt ratio as follows:

$$\text{Current ratio} = \frac{\$1,748 + \$40}{\$2,190} = 0.82 \qquad \text{Debt ratio} = \frac{\$3,182}{\$5,673 + \$40} = 0.557$$

A revenue improves both ratios.

Now, let's wrap up the chapter by seeing how to use the current ratio and the debt ratio for decision making. The Decision Guidelines feature offers some clues.

DECISION GUIDELINES

USING THE CURRENT RATIO AND THE DEBT RATIO

In general, a *high* current ratio is preferable to a low current ratio. *Increases* in the current ratio improve financial position. By contrast, a *low* debt ratio is preferable to a high debt ratio. Improvement is indicated by a *decrease* in the debt ratio.

No single ratio gives the whole picture about a company. Therefore, lenders and investors use many ratios to evaluate a company. Let's apply what we have learned. Suppose you are a loan officer at Bank of America, and Starbucks Corporation has asked you for a $20 million loan to launch a new blend of coffee. How will you make this loan decision? The Decision Guidelines show how bankers and investors use two key ratios.

USING THE CURRENT RATIO

Decision	Guidelines
How can you measure a company's ability to pay current liabilities with current assets?	$$\text{Current ratio} = \frac{\text{Total current assets}}{\text{Total current liabilities}}$$
Who uses the current ratio for decision making?	*Lenders and other creditors*, who must predict whether a borrower can pay its current liabilities. *Stockholders*, who know that a company that cannot pay its debts is not a good investment because it may go bankrupt. *Managers*, who must have enough cash to pay the company's current liabilities.
What is a good value of the current ratio?	Depends on the industry: A company with strong cash flow can operate successfully with a low current ratio of, say, 1.10–1.20. A company with weak cash flow needs a higher current ratio of, say, 1.30–1.50. Traditionally, a current ratio of 2.00 was considered ideal. Recently, acceptable values have decreased as companies have been able to operate more efficiently; today, a current ratio of 1.50 is considered strong. Cash-rich companies like Starbucks can operate with a current ratio below 1.0.

USING THE DEBT RATIO

Decision	Guidelines
How can you measure a company's ability to pay total liabilities?	$$\text{Debt ratio} = \frac{\text{Total liabilities}}{\text{Total assets}}$$
Who uses the debt ratio for decision making?	*Lenders and other creditors*, who must predict whether a borrower can pay its debts. *Stockholders*, who know that a company that cannot pay its debts is not a good investment because it may go bankrupt. *Managers*, who must have enough assets to pay the company's debts.
What is a good value of the debt ratio?	Depends on the industry: A company with strong cash flow can operate successfully with a high debt ratio of, say, 0.70–0.80 A company with weak cash flow needs a lower debt ratio of, say, 0.50–0.60. Traditionally, a debt ratio of 0.50 was considered ideal. Recently, values have increased as companies have been able to operate more efficiently; today, a normal value of the debt ratio is around 0.60–0.65.

END-OF-CHAPTER SUMMARY PROBLEM

Refer to the Mid-Chapter Summary Problem that begins on page 160. The adjusted trial balance appears on page 163.

| Requirements

1. Make Goldsmith Company's closing entries at December 31, 2010. Explain what the closing entries accomplish and why they are necessary. Show amounts in thousands.
2. Post the closing entries to Retained Earnings and compare Retained Earnings' ending balance with the amount reported on the balance sheet on page 164. The two amounts should be the same.
3. Prepare Goldsmith Company's classified balance sheet to identify the company's current assets and current liabilities. (Goldsmith has no long-term liabilities.) Then compute the company's current ratio and debt ratio at December 31, 2010.
4. The top management of Goldsmith Company has asked you for a $500,000 loan to expand the business. Goldsmith proposes to pay off the loan over a 10-year period. Recompute Goldsmith's debt ratio assuming you make the loan. Use the company financial statements plus the ratio values to decide whether to grant the loan at an interest rate of 8%, 10%, or 12%. Goldsmith's cash flow is strong. Give the reasoning underlying your decision.

Answers

| Requirement 1

2010		(In thousands)	
Dec 31	Service Revenue...	330	
	Retained Earnings		330
31	Retained Earnings	259	
	Salary Expense		177
	Depreciation Expense—		
	Furniture and Fixtures............................		20
	Depreciation Expense—Building		10
	Supplies Expense		4
	Income Tax Expense		35
	Miscellaneous Expense...............................		13
31	Retained Earnings	65	
	Dividends..		65

| Explanation of Closing Entries

The closing entries set the balance of each revenue, expense, and Dividends account back to zero for the start of the next accounting period. We must close these accounts because their balances relate only to one accounting period.

| Requirement 2

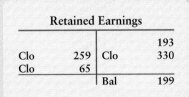

		Retained Earnings		
				193
Clo	259	Clo		330
Clo	65			
		Bal		199

The balance in the Retained Earnings account agrees with the amount reported on the balance sheet, as it should.

Requirement 3

Goldsmith Company
Balance Sheet
December 31, 2010

(Amounts in thousands)

Assets			Liabilities	
Current assets:			Current liabilities:	
Cash		$198	Accounts payable	$380
Accounts receivable		382	Salary payable	5
Supplies		2	Unearned service revenue	13
Total current assets...............		582	Income tax payable	35
Furniture and			Total current liabilities..............	433
fixtures	$100			
Less: Accumulated			*Stockholders' Equity*	
depreciation..................	(60)	40	Common stock.............................	100
Building...................................	$250		Retained earnings........................	199
Less: Accumulated			Total stockholders' equity	299
depreciation..................	(140)	110	Total liabilities and	
Total assets.............................		$732	stockholders' equity..................	$732

$$\text{Current ratio} = \frac{\$582}{\$433} = 1.34 \qquad \text{Debt ratio} = \frac{\$433}{\$732} = 0.59$$

Requirement 4

$$\text{Debt ratio assuming the loan is made} = \frac{\$433 + \$500}{\$732 + \$500} = \frac{\$933}{\$1,232} = .76$$

Decision: Make the loan at 10%.

Reasoning: Prior to the loan, the company's financial position and cash flow are strong. The current ratio is in a middle range, and the debt ratio is not too high. Net income (from the income statement) is high in relation to total revenue. Therefore, the company should be able to repay the loan.

The loan will increase the company's debt ratio from 59% to 76%, which is more risky than the company's financial position at present. On this basis, a midrange interest rate appears reasonable—at least as the starting point for the negotiation between Goldsmith Company and the bank.

REVIEW ACCRUAL ACCOUNTING & INCOME

Quick Check (Answers are given on page 216.)

1. On October 1, River Place Apartments received $5,200 from a tenant for four months' rent. The receipt was credited to Unearned Rent Revenue. What adjusting entry is needed on December 31?

   a. Unearned Rent Revenue   1,300
          Rent Revenue   1,300
   b. Cash   1,300
          Rent Revenue   1,300
   c. Rent Revenue   1,300
          Unearned Rent Revenue   1,300
   d. Unearned Rent Revenue   3,900
          Rent Revenue   3,900

2. The following normal balances appear on the *adjusted* trial balance of Greenville National Company:

Equipment...	$110,000
Accumulated depreciation, equipment...............	22,000
Depreciation expense, equipment......................	5,500

   The book value of the equipment is
   a. $82,500.   c. $88,000.
   b. $66,000.   d. $104,500.

3. Details, Inc., purchased supplies for $1,300 during 2010. At year end Details had $800 of supplies left. The adjusting entry should
   a. debit Supplies $800.   c. debit Supplies $500.
   b. credit Supplies $800.   d. debit Supplies Expense $500.

4. The accountant for Exeter Corp. failed to make the adjusting entry to record depreciation for the current year. The effect of this error is which of the following?
   a. Assets, net income, and stockholders' equity are all overstated.
   b. Assets and expenses are understated; net income is understated.
   c. Net income is overstated and liabilities are understated.
   d. Assets are overstated, stockholders' equity and net income are understated.

5. Interest earned on a note receivable at December 31 equals $375. What adjusting entry is required to accrue this interest?

   a. Interest Expense   375
          Interest Payable   375
   b. Interest Receivable   375
          Interest Revenue   375
   c. Interest Payable   375
          Interest Expense   375
   d. Interest Expense   375
          Cash   375

6. If a real estate company fails to accrue commission revenue,
    a. revenues are understated and net income is overstated.
    b. assets are understated and net income is understated.
    c. net income is understated and stockholders' equity is overstated.
    d. liabilities are overstated and owners' equity is understated.

7. All of the following statements are true except one. Which statement is false?
    a. A fiscal year ends on some date other than December 31.
    b. The matching principle directs accountants to identify and measure all expenses incurred and deduct them from revenues earned during the same period.
    c. Adjusting entries are required for a business that uses the cash basis.
    d. Accrual accounting produces better information than cash-basis accounting.

8. The account Unearned Revenue is a(n)
    a. asset.   c. revenue.
    b. expense.   d. liability.

9. Adjusting entries
    a. update the accounts.
    b. are needed to measure the period's net income or net loss.
    c. do not debit or credit cash.
    d. all of the above.

10. An adjusting entry that debits an expense and credits a liability is which type?
    a. Depreciation expense   c. Accrued expense
    b. Cash expense   d. Prepaid expense

Use the following data for questions 11 and 12.
Here are key figures from the balance sheet of Geneva, Inc., at the end of 2010 (amounts in thousands):

	December 31, 2010
Total assets (of which 50% are current)	$5,000
Current liabilities	500
Bonds payable (long-term)	1,400
Common stock	1,000
Retained earnings	2,100
Total liabilities and stockholders' equity	5,000

11. Geneva's current ratio at the end of 2010 is
    a. 10.00.   c. 1.32.
    b. 1.19.   d. 5.00.

12. Geneva's debt ratio at the end of 2010 is (all amounts are rounded)
    a. 1.32%.   c. 10.00%.
    b. 16%.   d. 38%.

13. On a trial balance, which of the following would indicate that an error has been made?
    a. Accumulated Depreciation has a credit balance.
    b. Salary Expense has a debit balance.
    c. Service Revenue has a debit balance.
    d. All of the above indicate errors.

14. The entry to close Management Fee Revenue would be which of the following?
    a. Management Fee Revenue
            Retained Earnings
    b. Management Fee Revenue does not need to be closed.
    c. Retained Earnings
            Management Fee Revenue
    d. Management Fee Revenue
            Service Revenue

15. Which of the following accounts is not closed?
    a. Dividends
    c. Interest Revenue
    b. Depreciation Expense
    d. Accumulated Depreciation
16. UPS earns service revenue of $800,000. How does this transaction affect UPS's ratios?
    a. Improves the current ratio and doesn't affect the debt ratio
    b. Hurts the current ratio and improves the debt ratio
    c. Hurts both ratios
    d. Improves both ratios
17. Suppose Green Mountain Corporation borrows $20 million on a 20-year note payable. How does this transaction affect Green Mountain's current ratio and debt ratio?
    a. Hurts both ratios
    b. Improves both ratios
    c. Improves the current ratio and hurts the debt ratio
    d. Hurts the current ratio and improves the debt ratio

Accounting Vocabulary

account format (p. 168) A balance-sheet format that lists assets on the left and liabilities and stockholders' equity on the right.

accrual (p. 144) An expense or a revenue that occurs before the business pays or receives cash. An accrual is the opposite of a deferral.

accrual accounting (p. 139) Accounting that records the impact of a business event as it occurs, regardless of whether the transaction affected cash.

accrued expense (p. 150) An expense incurred but not yet paid in cash.

accrued revenue (p. 151) A revenue that has been earned but not yet received in cash.

accumulated depreciation (p. 148) The cumulative sum of all depreciation expense from the date of acquiring a plant asset.

adjusted trial balance (p. 156) A list of all the ledger accounts with their adjusted balances.

book value (of a plant asset) (p. 149) The asset's cost minus accumulated depreciation.

cash-basis accounting (p. 139) Accounting that records only transactions in which cash is received or paid.

classified balance sheet (p. 167) A balance sheet that shows current assets separate from long-term assets, and current liabilities separate from long-term liabilities.

closing the books (p. 165) The process of preparing the accounts to begin recording the next period's transactions. Closing the accounts consists of journalizing and posting the closing entries to set the balances of the revenue, expense, and dividends accounts to zero. Also called closing the accounts.

closing entries (p. 165) Entries that transfer the revenue, expense, and dividends balances from these respective accounts to the Retained Earnings account.

contra account (p. 149) An account that always has a companion account and whose normal balance is opposite that of the companion account.

current asset (p. 167) An asset that is expected to be converted to cash, sold, or consumed during the next 12 months, or within the business's normal operating cycle if longer than a year.

current liability (p. 167) A debt due to be paid within one year or within the entity's operating cycle if the cycle is longer than a year.

current ratio (p. 170) Current assets divided by current liabilities. Measures a company's ability to pay current liabilities with current assets.

debt ratio (p. 170) Ratio of total liabilities to total assets. States the proportion of a company's assets that is financed with debt.

deferral (p. 144) An adjustment for which the business paid or received cash in advance. Examples include prepaid rent, prepaid insurance, and supplies.

depreciation (p. 144) Allocation of the cost of a plant asset to expense over its useful life.

liquidity (p. 167) Measure of how quickly an item can be converted to cash.

long-term asset (p. 167) An asset that is not a current asset.

long-term liability (p. 167) A liability that is not a current liability.

matching principle (p. 141) The basis for recording expenses. Directs accountants to identify all expenses incurred during the period, to measure the expenses, and to match them against the revenues earned during that same period.

multi-step income statement (p. 169) An income statement that contains subtotals to highlight important relationships between revenues and expenses.

operating cycle (p. 167) Time span during which cash is paid for goods and services that are sold to customers who pay the business in cash.

permanent accounts (p. 165) Asset, liability, and stockholders' equity accounts that are not closed at the end of the period.

plant assets (p. 147) Long-lived assets, such as land, buildings, and equipment, used in the operation of the business. Also called fixed assets.

prepaid expense (p. 145) A category of miscellaneous assets that typically expire or get used up in the near future. Examples include prepaid rent, prepaid insurance, and supplies.

report format (p. 168) A balance-sheet format that lists assets at the top, followed by liabilities and stockholders' equity below.

revenue principle (p. 140) The basis for recording revenues; tells accountants when to record revenue and the amount of revenue to record.

single-step income statement (p. 169) An income statement that lists all the revenues together under a heading such as Revenues or Revenues and Gains. Expenses appear in a separate category called Expenses or perhaps Expenses and Losses.

temporary accounts (p. 165) The revenue and expense accounts that relate to a limited period and are closed at the end of the period are temporary accounts. For a corporation, the Dividends account is also temporary.

time-period concept (p. 140) Ensures that accounting information is reported at regular intervals.

unearned revenue (p. 152) A liability created when a business collects cash from customers in advance of earning the revenue. The obligation is to provide a product or a service in the future.

ASSESS YOUR PROGRESS

Short Exercises

S3-1 *(Learning Objective 1: Linking accrual accounting and cash flows)* St. Pierre Corporation made sales of $960 million during 2010. Of this amount, St. Pierre collected cash for all but $25 million. The company's cost of goods sold was $270 million, and all other expenses for the year totaled $300 million. Also during 2010, St. Pierre paid $370 million for its inventory and $285 million for everything else. Beginning cash was $105 million. St. Pierre's top management is interviewing you for a job and they ask two questions:

    a. How much was St. Pierre's net income for 2010?

    b. How much was St. Pierre's cash balance at the end of 2010?

You will get the job only if you answer both questions correctly.

S3-2 *(Learning Objective 1: Linking accrual accounting and cash flows)* Capeside Corporation began 2010 owing notes payable of $3.9 million. During 2010 Capeside borrowed $2.3 million on notes payable and paid off $2.0 million of notes payable from prior years. Interest expense for the year was $1.8 million, including $0.1 million of interest payable accrued at December 31, 2010.

Show what Capeside should report for these facts on the following financial statements:

    1. Income statement

        a. Interest expense

    2. Balance sheet

        a. Notes payable

        b. Interest payable

writing assignment ■

S3-3 *(Learning Objectives 1, 2: Linking accrual accounting and cash flows; applying accounting principles)* As the controller of Eden Consulting, you have hired a new employee, whom you must train. She objects to making an adjusting entry for accrued salaries at the end of the period. She reasons, "We will pay the salaries soon. Why not wait until payment to record the expense? In the end, the result will be the same." Write a reply to explain to the employee why the adjusting entry is needed for accrued salary expense.

S3-4 (*Learning Objective 2: Applying the revenue and the matching principles*) A large auto manufacturer sells large fleets of vehicles to auto rental companies, such as Acme and Harris. Suppose Acme is negotiating with the auto manufacturer to purchase 950 vehicles. Write a short paragraph to explain to the auto manufacturer when the company should, and should not, record this sales revenue and the related expense for cost of goods sold. Mention the accounting principles that provide the basis for your explanation.

writing assignment ■

S3-5 (*Learning Objective 2: Applying accounting concepts and principles*) Write a short paragraph to explain in your own words the concept of depreciation as used in accounting.

writing assignment ■

S3-6 (*Learning Objective 2: Applying accounting concepts and principles*) Identify the accounting concept or principle that gives the most direction on how to account for each of the following situations:

a. Salary expense of $35,000 is accrued at the end of the period to measure income properly.

b. May has been a particularly slow month, and the business will have a net loss for the second quarter of the year. Management is considering not following its customary practice of reporting quarterly earnings to the public.

c. A physician performs a surgical operation and bills the patient's insurance company. It may take four months to collect from the insurance company. Should the physician record revenue now or wait until cash is collected?

d. A construction company is building a highway system, and construction will take five years. When should the company record the revenue it earns?

e. A utility bill is received on December 28 and will be paid next year. When should the company record utility expense?

S3-7 (*Learning Objective 3: Adjusting prepaid expenses*) Answer the following questions about prepaid expenses:

a. On March 1, Blue & Green Travel prepaid $4,800 for six months' rent. Give the adjusting entry to record rent expense at March 31. Include the date of the entry and an explanation. Then post all amounts to the two accounts involved, and show their balances at March 31. Blue & Green Travel adjusts the accounts only at March 31, the end of its fiscal year.

b. On December 1, Blue & Green Travel paid $900 for supplies. At March 31, Blue & Green Travel has $700 of supplies on hand. Make the required journal entry at March 31. Then post all amounts to the accounts and show their balances at March 31.

S3-8 (*Learning Objectives 1, 3: Recording depreciation; linking accrual accounting and cash flows*) Suppose that on January 1 Georgetown Golf Company paid cash of $80,000 for computers that are expected to remain useful for four years. At the end of four years, the computers' values are expected to be zero.

1. Make journal entries to record (a) purchase of the computers on January 1 and (b) annual depreciation on December 31. Include dates and explanations, and use the following accounts: Computer Equipment; Accumulated Depreciation—Computer Equipment; and Depreciation Expense—Computer Equipment.

2. Post to the accounts and show their balances at December 31.

3. What is the computer equipment's book value at December 31?

S3-9 (*Learning Objective 2: Applying the matching principle and the time-period concept*) During 2010, Northwest Airlines paid salary expense of $38.3 million. At December 31, 2010, Northwest accrued salary expense of $2.8 million. Northwest then paid $1.8 million to its employees on January 3, 2011, the company's next payday after the end of the 2010 year. For this sequence of transactions, show what Northwest would report on its 2010 income statement and on its balance sheet at the end of 2010.

S3-10 (*Learning Objective 3: Accruing and paying interest expense*) Resort Travel borrowed $80,000 on October 1 by signing a note payable to Texas First Bank. The interest expense for each month is $500. The loan agreement requires Resort to pay interest on December 31.

1. Make Resort's adjusting entry to accrue monthly interest expense at October 31, at November 30, and at December 31. Date each entry and include its explanation.
2. Post all three entries to the Interest Payable account. You need not take the balance of the account at the end of each month.
3. Record the payment of three months' interest at December 31.

S3-11 (*Learning Objective 3: Accruing and receiving cash from interest revenue*) Return to the situation in Short Exercise 3-10. Here you are accounting for the same transactions on the books of Texas First Bank, which lent the money to Resort Travel.

1. Make Texas First Bank's adjusting entry to accrue monthly interest revenue at October 31, at November 30, and at December 31. Date each entry and include its explanation.
2. Post all three entries to the Interest Receivable account. You need not take the balance of the account at the end of each month.
3. Record the receipt of three months' interest at December 31.

writing assignment ■

S3-12 (*Learning Objectives 1, 3: Relating accrual accounting to cash flows; adjusting the accounts*) Write a paragraph to explain why unearned revenues are liabilities instead of revenues. In your explanation, use the following actual example: *The Globe and Trail*, a national newspaper, collects cash from subscribers in advance and later delivers newspapers to subscribers over a one-year period. Explain what happens to the unearned revenue over the course of a year as *The Globe and Trail* delivers papers to subscribers. Into what account does the earned subscription revenue go as *The Globe and Trail* delivers papers? Give the journal entries that The Globe and Trail would make to (a) collect $50,000 of subscription revenue in advance and (b) record earning $50,000 of subscription revenue. Include an explanation for each entry, as illustrated in the chapter.

S3-13 (*Learning Objective 3, 4: Adjusting the accounts; reporting prepaid expenses*) Crow Golf Co. prepaid three years' rent ($24,000) on January 1, 2010. At December 31, 2010, Crow prepared a trial balance and then made the necessary adjusting entry at the end of the year. Crow adjusts its accounts once each year—on December 31.

What amount appears for Prepaid Rent on

  a. Crow's *unadjusted* trial balance at December 31, 2010?
  b. Crow's *adjusted* trial balance at December 31, 2010?

What amount appears for Rent Expense on

  a. Crow's *unadjusted* trial balance at December 31?
  b. Crow's *adjusted* trial balance at December 31?

S3-14 (*Learning Objective 3: Adjusting the accounts*) Bryson, Inc., collects cash from customers two ways:

  a. **Accrued revenue**. Some customers pay Bryson after Bryson has performed service for the customer. During 2010, Bryson made sales of $60,000 on account and later received cash of $45,000 on account from these customers.
  b. **Unearned revenue**. A few customers pay Bryson in advance, and Bryson later performs the service for the customer. During 2010 Bryson collected $7,500 cash in advance and later earned $3,500 of this amount.

Journalize for Bryson

  a. Earning service revenue of $60,000 on account and then collecting $45,000 on account.
  b. Receiving $7,500 in advance and then earning $3,500 as service revenue.

S3-15 (*Learning Objective 4: Preparing the financial statements*) Suppose Vulture Sporting Goods Company reported the following data at March 31, 2010, with amounts in thousands:

Retained earnings,		Cost of goods sold.................	$136,800
March 31, 2009........	$ 2,000	Cash.......................................	1,300
Accounts receivable.......	28,200	Property and equipment, net ...	6,000
Net revenues	174,000	Common stock......................	27,000
Total current liabilities..	53,000	Inventories	37,000
All other expenses.........	26,000	Long-term liabilities	12,500
Other current assets	5,200	Dividends.............................	0
Other assets...................	28,000		

Use these data to prepare Vulture Sporting Goods Company's income statement for the year ended March 31, 2010; statement of retained earnings for the year ended March 31, 2010; and classified balance sheet at March 31, 2010. Use the report format for the balance sheet. Draw arrows linking the three statements.

S3-16 (*Learning Objective 5: Making closing entries*) Use the Vulture Sporting Goods Company data in Short Exercise 3-15 to make the company's closing entries at March 31, 2010.

Then set up a T-account for Retained Earnings and post to that account. Compare Retained Earnings' ending balance to the amount reported on Vulture's statement of retained earnings and balance sheet. What do you find?

S3-17 (*Learning Objective 6: Computing the current ratio and the debt ratio*) Vulture Sporting Goods reported the following data at March 31, 2010, with amounts adapted in thousands:

Vulture Sporting Goods Company
Income Statement
For the Year Ended March 31, 2010

(Amounts in thousands)

Net revenues	$174,000
Cost of goods sold...............	136,800
All other expenses	26,000
Net income..........................	$ 11,200

Vulture Sporting Goods Company
Statement of Retained Earnings
For the Year Ended March 31, 2010

(Amounts in thousands)

Retained earnings, March 31, 2009	$ 2,000
Add: Net income..	11,200
Retained earnings, March 31, 2010	$13,200

Vulture Sporting Goods Company
Balance Sheet
March 31, 2010

(Amounts in thousands)

ASSETS

Current:

Cash...	$ 1,300
Accounts receivable..............................	28,200
Inventories	37,000
Other current assets	5,200
Total current assets	71,700
Property and equipment, net.....................	6,000
Other assets	28,000
Total assets...	$105,700

LIABILITIES

Total current liabilites	$ 53,000
Long-term liabilities..................................	12,500
Total liabilities	65,500

STOCKHOLDERS' EQUITY

Common stock..	27,000
Retained earnings.....................................	13,200
Total stockholders' equity..........................	40,200
Total liabilities and stockholders' equity............	$105,700

1. Compute Vulture's current ratio. Round to two decimal places.
2. Compute Vulture's debt ratio. Round to two decimal places.

Do these ratio values look strong, weak, or middle-of-the-road?

S3-18 (*Learning Objective 6: Using the current ratio and the debt ratio*) Refer to the Vulture Sporting Goods Company data in Short Exercise 3-17.

At March 31, 2010, Vulture Sporting Goods Company's current ratio was 1.35 and their debt ratio was 0.62. Compute Vulture's (a) current ratio and (b) debt ratio after each of the following transactions (all amounts in thousands, as in the Vulture financial statements):

1. Vulture earned revenue of $8,000 on account.
2. Vulture paid off accounts payable of $8,000.

When calculating the revised ratios, treat each of the above scenarios independently. Round ratios to two decimal places.

Exercises

All of the A and B exercises can be found within MyAccountingLab, an online homework and practice environment. Your instructor may ask you to complete these exercises using MyAccountingLab.

MyAccountingLab

(Group A)

E3-19A (*Learning Objective 1: Linking accrual accounting and cash flows*) During 2010 Galaxy Corporation made sales of $4,100 (assume all on account) and collected cash of $4,900 from customers. Operating expenses totaled $1,400, all paid in cash. At year end, 2010, Galaxy customers owed the company $700. Galaxy owed creditors $1,300 on account. All amounts are in millions.

1. For these facts, show what Galaxy reported on the following financial statements:
   - Income statement
   - Balance sheet
2. Suppose Galaxy had used the cash basis of accounting. What would Galaxy have reported for these facts?

E3-20A (*Learning Objective 1: Linking accrual accounting and cash flows*) During 2010 Prairie Sales, Inc., earned revenues of $580,000 on account. Prairie collected $590,000 from customers during the year. Expenses totaled $480,000, and the related cash payments were $460,000. Show what Prairie would report on its 2010 income statement under the

a. cash basis.
b. accrual basis.

Compute net income under both bases of accounting. Which basis measures net income better? Explain your answer.

E3-21A (*Learning Objectives 1, 2: Using the accrual basis of accounting; applying accounting principles*) During 2010, Carson Network, Inc., which designs network servers, earned revenues of $800 million. Expenses totaled $590 million. Carson collected all but $28 million of the revenues and paid $610 million on its expenses. Carson's top managers are evaluating 2010, and they ask you the following questions:

a. Under accrual accounting, what amount of revenue should Carson Network report for 2010? Is the revenue the $800 million earned or is it the amount of cash actually collected? How does the revenue principle help to answer these questions?
b. Under accrual accounting, what amount of total expense should Carson Network report for 2010—$590 million or $610 million? Which accounting principle helps to answer this question?
c. Which financial statement reports revenues and expenses? Which statement reports cash receipts and cash payments?

■ **general ledger**

E3-22A (*Learning Objectives 1, 3: Journalizing adjusting entries and analyzing their effects on net income; comparing accrual and cash basis*) An accountant made the following adjustments at December 31, the end of the accounting period:

   a. Prepaid insurance, beginning, $500. Payments for insurance during the period, $1,500. Prepaid insurance, ending, $1,000.
   b. Interest revenue accrued, $1,100.
   c. Unearned service revenue, beginning, $1,200. Unearned service revenue, ending, $400.
   d. Depreciation, $4,900.
   e. Employees' salaries owed for three days of a five-day work week; weekly payroll, $14,000.
   f. Income before income tax, $22,000. Income tax rate is 25%.

I *Requirements*

   1. Journalize the adjusting entries.
   2. Suppose the adjustments were not made. Compute the overall overstatement or understatement of net income as a result of the omission of these adjustments.

■ **spreadsheet**

E3-23A (*Learning Objectives 2, 3: Applying the revenue and matching principles; allocating supplies cost between the asset and the expense*) Bird-Bath, Inc., experienced four situations for its supplies. Compute the amounts that have been left blank for each situation. For situations 1 and 2, journalize the needed transaction. Consider each situation separately.

	Situation			
	1	**2**	**3**	**4**
Beginning supplies..	$ 100	$ 600	$ 1,400	$ 900
Payments for supplies during the year.......	?	600	?	700
Total amount to account for	1,400	?	?	1,600
Ending supplies..	(200)	(200)	(1,000)	?
Supplies Expense.......................................	$1,200	$?	$ 1,200	$1,300

■ **general ledger**

E3-24A (*Learning Objective 3: Journalizing adjusting entries*) Jenkins Motor Company faced the following situations. Journalize the adjusting entry needed at December 31, 2010, for each situation. Consider each fact separately.

   a. The business has interest expense of $9,500 that it must pay early in January 2011.
   b. Interest revenue of $4,500 has been earned but not yet received.
   c. On July 1, when we collected $13,600 rent in advance, we debited Cash and credited Unearned Rent Revenue. The tenant was paying us for two years' rent.
   d. Salary expense is $1,800 per day—Monday through Friday—and the business pays employees each Friday. This year, December 31 falls on a Wednesday.
   e. The unadjusted balance of the Supplies account is $3,300. The total cost of supplies on hand is $1,200.
   f. Equipment was purchased at the beginning of this year at a cost of $100,000. The equipment's useful life is five years. There is no residual value. Record depreciation for this year and then determine the equipment's book value.

E3-25A (*Learning Objective 3: Making adjustments in T-accounts*) The accounting records of Fletcher Publishing Company include the following unadjusted balances at May 31: Accounts Receivable, $1,600; Supplies, $600; Salary Payable, $0; Unearned Service Revenue, $900; Service Revenue, $4,800; Salary Expense, $2,500; Supplies Expense, $0.

Fletcher's accountant develops the following data for the May 31 adjusting entries:

   a. Supplies on hand, $100
   b. Salary owed to employees, $300
   c. Service revenue accrued, $800
   d. Unearned service revenue that has been earned, $200

Open the foregoing T-accounts with their beginning balances. Then record the adjustments directly in the accounts, keying each adjustment amount by letter. Show each account's adjusted balance. Journal entries are not required.

E3-26A (*Learning Objective 4: Preparing the financial statements*) The adjusted trial balance of Delicious Hams, Inc., follows.

Delicious Hams, Inc.
Adjusted Trial Balance
December 31, 2010

(Amounts in thousands)	Adjusted Trial Balance	
Account	**Debit**	**Credit**
Cash..	$ 3,800	
Accounts receivable..	1,500	
Inventories	1,100	
Prepaid expenses...	1,700	
Property, plant and equipment	6,500	
Accumulated depreciation..		$ 2,300
Other assets...	9,300	
Accounts payable		7,600
Income tax payable		600
Other liabilities		2,200
Common stock...		4,700
Retained earnings (beginning, December 31, 2009)...............		4,700
Dividends...	1,500	
Sales revenue...		41,400
Cost of goods sold...	25,100	
Selling, administrative, and general expenses..........................	10,700	
Income tax expense	2,300	
Total	$63,500	$63,500

▌Requirement

1. Prepare Delicious Hams, Inc.'s income statement and statement of retained earnings for the year ended December 31, 2010, and its balance sheet on that date.

E3-27A (*Learning Objectives 3, 4: Measuring financial statement amounts; preparing financial statement amounts*) The adjusted trial balances of Dickens Corporation at March 31, 2010, and March 31, 2009, include these amounts (in millions):

	2010	2009
Receivables...	$390	$270
Prepaid insurance...	190	160
Accrued liabilities payable (for other operating expenses)	730	610

Dickens completed these transactions during the year ended March 31, 2010.

Collections from customers...	$20,200
Payment of prepaid insurance	420
Cash payments for other operating expenses...............	4,100

Compute the amount of sales revenue, insurance expense, and other operating expenses to report on the income statement for the year ended March 31, 2010.

E3-28A (*Learning Objective 4: Reporting on the financial statements*) This question deals with the items and the amounts that two entities, Mother Meghan Hospital (Mother Meghan) and City of Boston (Boston) should report in their financial statements. Fill in the blanks.

❙ Requirements

1. On July 1, 2010, Mother Meghan collected $6,000 in advance from Boston, a client. Under the contract, Mother Meghan is obligated to perform medical exams for City of Boston employees evenly during the 12 months ending June 30, 2011. Assume you are Mother Meghan.

   Mother Meghan's income statement for the year ended December 31, 2010, will report _____ of $ _____.

   Mother Meghan's balance sheet at December 31, 2010, will report _____ of $ _____.

2. Assume now that you are Boston.

   Boston's income statement for the year ended December 31, 2010, will report _____ of $ _____.

   Boston's balance sheet at December 31, 2010, will report _____ of $ _____.

E3-29A (*Learning Objectives 1, 3: Linking deferrals and cash flows*) Nanofone, the British wireless phone service provider, collects cash in advance from customers. All amounts are in millions of pounds sterling (£), the British monetary unit. Assume Nanofone collected £460 in advance during 2010 and at year end still owed customers phone service worth £110.

❙ Requirements

1. Show what Nanofone will report for 2010 on its income statement and balance sheet.
2. Use the same facts for Nanofone as in Requirement 1. Further, assume Nanofone reported unearned service revenue of £55 back at the end of 2009. Show what Nanofone will report for 2010 on the same financial statements. Explain why your answer here differs from your answer to Requirement 1.

E3-30A (*Learning Objective 5: Closing the accounts*) Prepare the closing entries from the following selected accounts from the records of Sunnydale Corporation at December 31, 2010:

Cost of services sold	$11,300	Service revenue	$24,000
Accumulated depreciation	40,900	Depreciation expense	4,800
Selling, general, and		Other revenue	300
administrative expenses	6,700	Dividends	600
Retained earnings,		Income tax expense	800
December 31, 2009	2,100	Income tax payable	300

How much net income did Sunnydale earn during 2010? Prepare a T-account for Retained Earnings to show the December 31, 2010, balance of Retained Earnings.

E3-31A (*Learning Objectives 3, 5: Identifying and recording adjusting and closing entries*)
The unadjusted trial balance and income statement amounts from the December 31 adjusted
trial balance of Draper Production Company follow.

Draper Production Company

Account	Unadjusted Trial Balance		From the Adjusted Trial Balance	
Cash...................................	14,800			
Prepaid rent........................	1,000			
Equipment..........................	44,000			
Accumulated depreciation...............		3,100		
Accounts payable............................		5,100		
Salary payable................................				
Unearned service revenue.................		9,300		
Income tax payable.........................				
Notes payable, long-term.................		13,000		
Common stock..............................		8,500		
Retained earnings...........................		14,100		
Dividends......................................	1,300			
Service revenue..............................		13,600		20,100
Salary expense...............................	4,600		5,100	
Rent expense.................................	1,000		1,300	
Depreciation expense......................			400	
Income tax expense........................			1,000	
Total	66,700	66,700	7,800	20,100

❙ Requirement

1. Journalize the adjusting and closing entries of Draper Production Company at
   December 31. There was only one adjustment to Service Revenue.

E3-32A (*Learning Objectives 4, 6: Preparing a classified balance sheet; using the ratios*)
Refer to Exercise 3-31A.

❙ Requirements

1. Use the data in the partial worksheet to prepare Draper Production Company's classified
   balance sheet at December 31 of the current year. Use the report format. First you must
   compute the adjusted balance for several of the balance-sheet accounts.
2. Compute Draper Production Company's current ratio and debt ratio at December 31. A
   year ago, the current ratio was 1.70 and the debt ratio was 0.30. Indicate whether the
   company's ability to pay its debts—both current and total—improved or deteriorated
   during the current year.

E3-33A (*Learning Objective 6: Measuring the effects of transactions on the ratios*) Ben Williams Company reported these ratios at December 31, 2010 (dollar amounts in millions):

$$\text{Current ratio} = \frac{\$30}{\$20} = 1.50$$

$$\text{Debt ratio} = \frac{\$30}{\$60} = 0.50$$

Ben Williams Company completed these transactions during 2011:

   a. Purchased equipment on account, $8
   b. Paid long-term debt, $11
   c. Collected cash from customers in advance, $6
   d. Accrued interest expense, $3
   e. Made cash sales, $11

Determine whether each transaction improved or hurt Williams' current ratio and debt ratio.

(Group B)

E3-34B (*Learning Objective 1: Linking accrual accounting and cash flows*) During 2010 Nebula Corporation made sales of $4,800 (assume all on account) and collected cash of $4,900 from customers. Operating expenses totaled $1,100, all paid in cash. At year end, 2010, Nebula customers owed the company $300. Nebula owed creditors $500 on account. All amounts are in millions.

   1. For these facts, show what Nebula reported on the following financial statements:

   • Income statement   • Balance sheet

   2. Suppose Nebula had used the cash basis of accounting. What would Nebula have reported for these facts?

E3-35B (*Learning Objective 1: Linking accrual accounting and cash flows*) During 2010 Mountain Sales, Inc., earned revenues of $510,000 on account. Mountain collected $580,000 from customers during the year. Expenses totaled $470,000, and the related cash payments were $440,000. Show what Mountain would report on its 2010 income statement under the

   a. cash basis.
   b. accrual basis.

Compute net income under both bases of accounting. Which basis measures net income better? Explain your answer.

E3-36B (*Learning Objectives 1, 2: Using the accrual basis of accounting; applying accounting principles*) During 2010 Carlton Network, Inc., which designs network servers, earned revenues of $740 million. Expenses totaled $560 million. Carlton collected all but $24 million of the revenues and paid $580 million on its expenses. Carlton's top managers are evaluating 2010, and they ask you the following questions:

   a. Under accrual accounting, what amount of revenue should Carlton Network report for 2010? Is it the revenue of $740 million earned or is it the amount of cash actually collected? How does the revenue principle help to answer these questions?
   b. Under accrual accounting, what amount of total expense should Carlton report for 2010—$560 million or $580 million? Which accounting principle helps to answer this question?
   c. Which financial statement reports revenues and expenses? Which statement reports cash receipts and cash payments?

E3-37B *(Learning Objectives 1, 3: Journalizing adjusting entries and analyzing their effects on net income; comparing accrual and cash basis)* An accountant made the following adjustments at December 31, the end of the accounting period:

■ **general ledger**

a. Prepaid insurance, beginning, $800. Payments for insurance during the period, $2,400. Prepaid insurance, ending, $1,600.
b. Interest revenue accrued, $1,000.
c. Unearned service revenue, beginning, $1,500. Unearned service revenue, ending, $400.
d. Depreciation, $4,600.
e. Employees' salaries owed for three days of a five-day work week; weekly payroll, $16,000.
f. Income before income tax, $21,000. Income tax rate is 25%.

❚ Requirements

1. Journalize the adjusting entries.
2. Suppose the adjustments were not made. Compute the overall overstatement or understatement of net income as a result of the omission of these adjustments.

E3-38B *(Learning Objectives 2, 3: Applying the revenue and matching principles; allocating supplies cost between the asset and the expense)* Bird-Brain, Inc., experienced four situations for its supplies. Compute the amounts that have been left blank for each situation. For situations 1 and 2, journalize the needed transaction. Consider each situation separately.

■ **spreadsheet**

	Situation			
	1	**2**	**3**	**4**
Beginning supplies	$ 100	$ 400	$ 1,200	$ 800
Payments for supplies during the year	?	1,000	?	800
Total amount to account for	1,500	?	?	1,600
Ending supplies	(400)	(500)	(700)	?
Supplies Expense	$1,100	$?	$ 1,300	$1,100

E3-39B *(Learning Objective 3: Journalizing adjusting entries)* Folton Motor Company faced the following situations. Journalize the adjusting entry needed at December 31, 2010, for each situation. Consider each fact separately.

■ **general ledger**

a. The business has interest expense of $9,200 that it must pay early in January 2011.
b. Interest revenue of $4,200 has been earned but not yet received.
c. On July 1, when we collected $12,600 rent in advance, we debited Cash and credited Unearned Rent Revenue. The tenant was paying us for two years' rent.
d. Salary expense is $1,900 per day—Monday through Friday—and the business pays employees each Friday. This year, December 31 falls on a Wednesday.
e. The unadjusted balance of the Supplies account is $2,600. The total cost of supplies on hand is $1,200.
f. Equipment was purchased at the beginning of this year at a cost of $160,000. The equipment's useful life is five years. There is no residual value. Record depreciation for this year and then determine the equipment's book value.

E3-40B *(Learning Objective 3: Making adjustments in T-accounts)* The accounting records of Harris Publishing Company include the following unadjusted balances at May 31: Accounts Receivable, $1,200; Supplies, $300; Salary Payable, $0; Unearned Service Revenue, $800; Service Revenue, $4,400; Salary Expense, $1,900; Supplies Expense, $0.

Harris' accountant develops the following data for the May 31 adjusting entries:

a. Supplies on hand, $200
b. Salary owed to employees, $600
c. Service revenue accrued, $800
d. Unearned service revenue that has been earned, $100

Open the foregoing T-accounts with their beginning balances. Then record the adjustments directly in the accounts, keying each adjustment amount by letter. Show each account's adjusted balance. Journal entries are not required.

E3-41B (*Learning Objective 4: Preparing the financial statements*) The adjusted trial balance of Holiday Hams, Inc., follows.

Holiday Hams, Inc. Adjusted Trial Balance December 31, 2010		
(Amounts in thousands)	**Adjusted Trial Balance**	
Account	**Debit**	**Credit**
Cash..	$ 3,500	
Accounts receivable..	1,700	
Inventories	1,200	
Prepaid expenses	1,600	
Property, plant and equipment	6,700	
Accumulated depreciation....................................		$ 2,700
Other assets...	9,500	
Accounts payable..		7,900
Income tax payable		900
Other liabilities		2,700
Common stock...		4,800
Retained earnings (beginning, December 31, 2009)...............		4,700
Dividends...	1,200	
Sales revenue		39,900
Cost of goods sold...	25,400	
Selling, administrative, and general expenses.........................	10,400	
Income tax expense	2,400	
Total	$63,600	$63,600

Requirement

1. Prepare Holiday Hams, Inc.'s income statement and statement of retained earnings for the year ended December 31, 2010, and its balance sheet on that date. Draw the arrows linking the three statements.

E3-42B (*Learning Objectives 3, 4: Measuring financial statement amounts; preparing financial statement amounts*) The adjusted trial balances of Victory Corporation at March 31, 2010, and March 31, 2009, include these amounts (in millions):

	2010	2009
Receivables..	$330	$250
Prepaid insurance	140	130
Accrued liabilities payable (for other operating expenses).....	760	600

Victory completed these transactions during the year ended March 31, 2010.

Collections from customers...	$20,600
Payment of prepaid insurance	450
Cash payments for other operating expenses...............	4,100

Compute the amount of sales revenue, insurance expense, and other operating expenses to report on the income statement for the year ended March 31, 2010.

E3-43B (*Learning Objective 4: Reporting on the financial statements*) This question deals with the items and the amounts that two entities, Mother Elizabeth Hospital (Mother Elizabeth) and City of Portland (Portland) should report in their financial statements. Fill in the blanks.

❙ *Requirements*

1. On July 1, 2010, Mother Elizabeth collected $9,600 in advance from Portland, a client. Under the contract, Mother Elizabeth is obligated to perform medical exams for City of Portland employees evenly during the 12 months ending June 30, 2011. Assume you are Mother Elizabeth.

 Mother Elizabeth's income statement for the year ended December 31, 2010, will report ___ of $ ___.

 Mother Elizabeth's balance sheet at December 31, 2010, will report ___ of $ ___

2. Assume now that you are Portland.

 Portland's income statement for the year ended December 31, 2010, will report ___ of $ ___.

 Portland's balance sheet at December 31, 2010, will report ___ of $ ___.

E3-44B (*Learning Objectives 1, 3: Linking deferrals and cash flows*) Direct, the British wireless phone service provider, collects cash in advance from customers. All amounts are in millions of pounds sterling (£), the British monetary unit. Assume Direct collected £400 in advance during 2010 and at year end still owed customers phone service worth £105.

❙ *Requirements*

1. Show what Direct will report for 2010 on its income statement balance sheet.
2. Use the same facts for Direct as in Requirement 1. Further, assume Direct reported unearned service revenue of £95 back at the end of 2009. Show what Direct will report for 2010 on the same financial statements. Explain why your answer here differs from your answer to Requirement 1.

E3-45B (*Learning Objective 5: Closing the accounts*) Prepare the closing entries from the following selected accounts from the records of East Shore Corporation at December 31, 2010:

Cost of services sold............	$11,200	Service revenue........................	$24,100
Accumulated depreciation...	41,800	Depreciation expense	4,800
Selling, general, and		Other revenue	500
administrative expenses....	6,100	Dividends..............................	900
Retained earnings,		Income tax expense................	400
December 31, 2009.........	2,400	Income tax payable................	900

How much net income did East Shore earn during 2010? Prepare a T-account for Retained Earnings to show the December 31, 2010, balance of Retained Earnings.

E3-46B (*Learning Objectives 3, 5: Identifying and recording adjusting and closing entries*)
The unadjusted trial balance and income statement amounts from the December 31 adjusted
trial balance of Wallace Production Company follow.

Wallace Production Company

Account	Unadjusted Trial Balance		From the Adjusted Trial Balance	
Cash...	$13,600			
Prepaid rent.....................................	1,100			
Equipment..	48,000			
Accumulated depreciation................		$ 3,600		
Accounts payable		4,400		
Salary payable...................................				
Unearned service revenue		8,500		
Income tax payable				
Notes payable, long-term		10,000		
Common stock..................................		8,400		
Retained earnings.............................		20,800		
Dividends..	1,000			
Service revenue................................		13,400		$19,900
Salary expense.................................	4,500		$4,900	
Rent expense....................................	900		1,400	
Depreciation expense			600	
Income tax expense..........................			1,700	
Total	$69,100	$69,100	$8,600	$19,900

❙ Requirement

1. Journalize the adjusting and closing entries of Wallace Production Company at
   December 31. There was only one adjustment to Service Revenue.

E3-47B (*Learning Objectives 4, 6: Preparing a classified balance sheet; using the ratios*)
Refer to Exercise 3-46B.

❙ Requirements

1. Use the data in the partial worksheet to prepare Wallace Production Company's classified
   balance sheet at December 31 of the current year. Use the report format. First you must
   compute the adjusted balance for several of the balance-sheet accounts.
2. Compute Wallace Production Company's current ratio and debt ratio at December 31. A
   year ago, the current ratio was 1.45 and the debt ratio was 0.35. Indicate whether the
   company's ability to pay its debts—both current and total—improved or deteriorated
   during the current year.

E3-48B (*Learning Objective 6: Measuring the effects of transactions on the ratios*) Brent
Landry Company reported these ratios at December 31, 2010 (dollar amounts in millions):

$$\text{Current ratio} = \frac{\$40}{\$30} = 1.33$$

$$\text{Debt ratio} = \frac{\$30}{\$60} = 0.50$$

Brent Landry Company completed these transactions during 2011:

a. Purchased equipment on account, $6
b. Paid long-term debt, $11
c. Collected cash from customers in advance, $8
d. Accrued interest expense, $7
e. Made cash sales, $11

Determine whether each transaction improved or hurt Landry's current ratio and debt ratio.

Serial Exercise

Exercise 3-49 continues the Jerome Smith, Certified Public Accountant, P.C., situation begun in Exercise 2-36 of Chapter 2.

E3-49 (*Learning Objectives 3, 4, 5, 6: Adjusting the accounts; preparing the financial statements; closing the accounts; evaluating the business*) Refer to Exercise 2-36 of Chapter 2. Start from the trial balance and the posted T-accounts that Jerome Smith, Certified Public Accountant, Professional Corporation (P.C.), prepared for his accounting practice at March 18. A professional corporation is not subject to income tax. Later in March, the business completed these transactions:

■ **general ledger**

Mar 21	Received $1,800 in advance for tax work to be performed over the next 30 days.
	21	Hired a secretary to be paid on the 15th day of each month.
	26	Paid $500 for the supplies purchased on March 5.
	28	Collected $2,100 from the client on March 18.
	31	Declared and paid dividends of $1,400.

❚ *Requirements*

1. Journalize the transactions of March 21 through 31.
2. Post the March 21 to 31 transactions to the T-accounts, keying all items by date.
3. Prepare a trial balance at March 31.
4. At March 31, gathers the following information for the adjusting entries:
   a. Accrued service revenue, $1,600
   b. Earned $600 of the service revenue collected in advance on March 21
   c. Supplies on hand, $100
   d. Depreciation expense equipment, $40; furniture, $125
   e. Accrued expense for secretary's salary, $600

   Make these adjustments in the adjustments columns and complete the adjusted trial balance at January 31.

5. Journalize and post the adjusting entries. Denote each adjusting amount as Adj and an account balance as Bal.
6. Prepare the income statement and statement of retained earnings of Jerome Smith Certified Public Accountant, P.C., for the month ended March 31 and the classified balance sheet at that date.
7. Journalize and post the closing entries at March 31. Denote each closing amount as Clo and an account balance as Bal.
8. Compute the current ratio and the debt ratio of Jerome Smith Certified Public Accountant, P.C., and evaluate these ratio values as indicative of a strong or weak financial position.

Challenge Exercises

E3-50 (*Learning Objective 6: Evaluating the current ratio*) Worthy Hills Corporation reported the following current accounts at December 31, 2010 (amounts in thousands):

Cash	$1,800
Receivables	5,300
Inventory	2,300
Prepaid expenses	1,100
Accounts payable	2,800
Unearned revenue	1,100
Accrued expenses payable	2,000

During 2011, Worthy Hills completed these selected transactions:

- Sold services on account, $8,700
- Depreciation expense, $700
- Paid for expenses, $7,400
- Collected from customers on account, $7,500
- Accrued expenses, $300
- Paid on account, $1,500
- Used up prepaid expenses, $400

Compute Worthy Hills's current ratio at December 31, 2010, and again at December 31, 2011. Did the current ratio improve or deteriorate during 2011? Comment on the level of the company's current ratio.

E3-51 (*Learning Objectives 3, 4: Computing financial statement amounts*) The accounts of Greatbrook Company prior to the year-end adjustments follow.

Cash	$ 16,600	Common stock	$ 14,000
Accounts receivable	7,000	Retained earnings	45,000
Supplies	4,200	Dividends	12,000
Prepaid insurance	3,400	Service revenue	160,000
Building	107,000	Salary expense	34,000
Accumulated depreciation—		Depreciation expense—	
building	15,000	building	
Land	52,000	Supplies expense	
Accounts payable	6,500	Insurance expense	
Salary payable		Advertising expense	7,600
Unearned service revenue	5,400	Utilities expense	2,100

Adjusting data at the end of the year include which of the following?

a. Unearned service revenue that has been earned, $1,620
b. Accrued service revenue, $32,000
c. Supplies used in operations, $3,600
d. Accrued salary expense, $3,200
e. Prepaid insurance expired, $1,200
f. Depreciation expense—building, $2,500

Rorie Lacourse, the principal stockholder, has received an offer to sell Greatbrook Company. He needs to know the following information within one hour:

a. Net income for the year covered by these data

b. Total assets

c. Total liabilities

d. Total stockholders' equity

e. Prove that Total assets = Total liabilities + Total stockholders' equity after all items are updated.

❙ *Requirement*

1. Without opening any accounts, making any journal entries, or using a work sheet, provide Mr. Lacourse with the requested information. The business is not subject to income tax.

Practice Quiz

Test your understanding of accrual accounting by answering the following questions. Select the best choice from among the possible answers given.

Questions 52–54 are based on the following facts:

Frank Dunn began a music business in January 2010. Dunn prepares monthly financial statements and uses the accrual basis of accounting. The following transactions are Dunn Company's only activities during January through April:

Jan	14	Bought music on account for $23, with payment to the supplier due in 90 days.
Feb	3	Performed a job on account for Jimmy Jones for $38, collectible from Jones in 30 days. Used up all the music purchased on Jan 14.
Mar	16	Collected the $38 receivable from Jones.
Apr	22	Paid the $23 owed to the supplier from the January 14 transaction.

Q3-52 In which month should Dunn record the cost of the music as an expense?

a. January   **c.** March

b. February   **d.** April

Q3-53 In which month should Dunn report the $38 revenue on its income statement?

a. January   **c.** March

b. February   **d.** April

Q3-54 If Dunn Company uses the *cash* basis of accounting instead of the accrual basis, in what month will Dunn report revenue and in what month will it report expense?

	Revenue	Expense
a.	March	February
b.	February	April
c.	February	February
d.	March	April

Q3-55 In which month should revenue be recorded?

a. In the month that cash is collected from the customer

b. In the month that goods are shipped to the customer

c. In the month that goods are ordered by the customer

d. In the month that the invoice is mailed to the customer

Q3-56 On January 1 of the current year, Bambi Company paid $1,200 rent to cover six months (January–June). Bambi recorded this transaction as follows:

	Journal Entry		
Date	**Accounts**	**Debit**	**Credit**
Jan 1	Prepaid Rent	1,200	
	Cash		1,200

Bambi adjusts the accounts at the end of each month. Based on these facts, the adjusting entry at the end of January should include
a. a credit to Prepaid Rent for $1,000.
b. a credit to Prepaid Rent for $200.
c. a debit to Prepaid Rent for $1,000.
d. a debit to Prepaid Rent for $200.

Q3-57 Assume the same facts as in question 3-56. Bambi's adjusting entry at the end of February should include a debit to Rent Expense in the amount of
a. $200.   **c.** $400.
b. $1,000.   **d.** $0.

Q3-58 What effect does the adjusting entry in question 3-57 have on Bambi's net income for February?
a. Increase by $200   **c.** Increase by $400
b. Decrease by $200   **d.** Decrease by $400

Q3-59 An adjusting entry recorded April salary expense that will be paid in May. Which statement best describes the effect of this adjusting entry on the company's accounting equation?
a. Assets are decreased, liabilities are increased, and stockholders' equity is decreased.
b. Assets are not affected, liabilities are increased, and stockholders' equity is decreased.
c. Assets are decreased, liabilities are not affected, and stockholders' equity is decreased.
d. Assets are not affected, liabilities are increased, and stockholders' equity is increased.

Q3-60 On April 1, 2010, Rural Insurance Company sold a one-year insurance policy covering the year ended April 1, 2011. Rural collected the full $2,700 on April 1, 2010. Rural made the following journal entry to record the receipt of cash in advance:

	Journal Entry		
Date	**Accounts**	**Debit**	**Credit**
Apr 1	Cash	2,700	
	Unearned Revenue		2,700

Nine months have passed, and Rural has made no adjusting entries. Based on these facts, the adjusting entry needed by Rural at December 31, 2010, is

a.	Insurance Revenue	675	
	Unearned Revenue		675
b.	Unearned Revenue	2,025	
	Insurance Revenue		2,025
c.	Insurance Revenue	2,025	
	Unearned Revenue		2,025
d.	Unearned Revenue	675	
	Insurance Revenue		675

Q3-61 The Unearned Revenue account of Super Incorporated began 2010 with a normal balance of $2,000 and ended 2010 with a normal balance of $17,000. During 2010, the Unearned Revenue account was credited for $26,000 that Super will earn later. Based on these facts, how much revenue did Super earn in 2010?

a. $11,000

b. $28,000

c. $2,000

d. $26,000

Q3-62 What is the effect on the financial statements of *recording* depreciation on equipment?

a. Net income is not affected, but assets and stockholders' equity are decreased.

b. Net income and assets are decreased, but stockholders' equity is not affected.

c. Net income, assets, and stockholders' equity are all decreased.

d. Assets are decreased, but net income and stockholders' equity are not affected.

Q3-63 For 2010, Matthews Company had revenues in excess of expenses. Which statement describes Matthews' closing entries at the end of 2010?

a. Revenues will be credited, expenses will be debited, and retained earnings will be credited.

b. Revenues will be debited, expenses will be credited, and retained earnings will be debited.

c. Revenues will be credited, expenses will be debited, and retained earnings will be debited.

d. Revenues will be debited, expenses will be credited, and retained earnings will be credited.

Q3-64 Which of the following accounts would *not* be included in the closing entries?

a. Depreciation Expense

b. Accumulated Depreciation

c. Retained Earnings

d. Service Revenue

Q3-65 A major purpose of preparing closing entries is to

a. zero out the liability accounts.

b. close out the Supplies account.

c. adjust the asset accounts to their correct current balances.

d. update the Retained Earnings account.

Q3-66 Selected data for the Blossom Company follow:

Current assets..............	$ 29,333	Current liabilities	$ 24,800
Long-term assets	187,430	Long-term liabilities	112,738
Total revenues.............	196,651	Total expenses................	169,015

Based on these facts, what are Blossom's current ratio and debt ratio?

	Current ratio	Debt ratio
a.	1.633 to 1	0.742 to 1
b.	0.694 to 1	6.815 to 1
c.	1.183 to 1	0.635 to 1
d.	1.633 to 1	0.601 to 1

Q3-67 Unadjusted net income equals $7,500. Calculate what net income will be after the following adjustments:

1. Salaries payable to employees, $660

2. Interest due on note payable at the bank, $100

3. Unearned revenue that has been earned, $950

4. Supplies used, $300

Q3-68 Salary Payable at the beginning of the month totals $28,000. During the month salaries of $126,000 were accrued as expense. If ending Salary Payable is $15,000, what amount of cash did the company pay for salaries during the month?

a. $124,000

b. $139,000

c. $126,000

d. $154,000

Problems

> All of the A and B problems can be found within MyAccountingLab, an online home-work and practice environment. Your instructor may ask you to complete these problems using MyAccountingLab.

(Group A)

P3-69A (*Learning Objective 1: Linking accrual accounting and cash flows*) Labear Corporation earned revenues of $41 million during 2011 and ended the year with net income of $5 million. During 2011, Labear collected $23 million from customers and paid cash for all of its expenses plus an additional $5 million for amounts payable at December 31, 2010. Answer these questions about Labear's operating results, financial position, and cash flows during 2011:

❚ *Requirements*

1. How much were Labear's total expenses? Show your work.
2. Identify all the items that Labear will report on its 2011 income statement. Show each amount.
3. Labear began 2011 with receivables of $4 million. All sales are on account. What was the company's receivables balance at the end of 2011? Identify the appropriate financial statement, and show how Labear will report ending receivables in the 2011 annual report.
4. Labear began 2011 owing accounts payable of $8 million. All expenses are incurred on account. During 2011 Labear paid $41 million on account. How much in accounts payable did the company owe at the end of 2011? Identify the appropriate financial statement and show how Labear will report accounts payable in its 2011 annual report.

P3-70A (*Learning Objective 1: Comparing cash basis and accrual basis*) Elders Consulting had the following selected transactions in August:

Aug	1	Prepaid insurance for August through December, $500.
	4	Purchased software for cash, $800.
	5	Performed services and received cash, $700.
	8	Paid advertising expense, $500.
	11	Performed service on account, $3,500.
	19	Purchased computer on account, $1,700.
	24	Collected for August 11 service.
	26	Paid account payable from August 19.
	29	Paid salary expense, $800.
	31	Adjusted for August insurance expense (see Aug 1).
	31	Earned revenue of $600 that was collected in advance back in July.

❚ *Requirements*

1. Show how each transaction would be handled using the cash basis and the accrual basis.
2. Compute August income (loss) before tax under each accounting method.
3. Indicate which measure of net income or net loss is preferable. Use the transactions on August 11 and August 24 to explain.

writing assignment ■

P3-71A (*Learning Objective 3: Making accounting adjustments*) Journalize the adjusting entry needed on December 31, end of the current accounting period, for each of the following independent cases affecting Rowling Corp. Include an explanation for each entry.

a. Details of Prepaid Insurance are shown in the account:

Prepaid Insurance		
Jan 1 Bal	900	
Mar 31	3,600	

Rowling prepays insurance on March 31 each year. At December 31, $1,300 is still prepaid.

b. Rowling pays employees each Friday. The amount of the weekly payroll is $6,100 for a five-day work week. The current accounting period ends on Tuesday.

c. Rowling has a note receivable. During the current year, Rowling has earned accrued interest revenue of $400 that it will collect next year.

d. The beginning balance of supplies was $2,700. During the year, Rowling purchased supplies costing $6,400, and at December 31 supplies on hand total $2,200.

e. Rowling is providing services for Orca Investments, and the owner of Orca paid Rowling $12,000 as the annual service fee. Rowling recorded this amount as Unearned Service Revenue. Rowling estimates that it has earned 70% of the total fee during the current year.

f. Depreciation for the current year includes Office Furniture, $3,000, and Equipment, $5,400. Make a compound entry.

P3-72A (*Learning Objectives 3, 4: Preparing an adjusted trial balance and the financial statements*) Consider the unadjusted trial balance of London, Inc., at December 31, 2010, and the related month-end adjustment data.

London, Inc.
Trial Balance Work Sheet
December 31, 2010

Account	Trial Balance Debit	Trial Balance Credit	Adjustments Debit	Adjustments Credit	Adjusted Trial Balance Debit	Adjusted Trial Balance Credit
Cash	8,900					
Accounts receivable	1,200					
Prepaid rent	2,400					
Supplies	2,500					
Furniture	72,000					
Accumulated depreciation		3,900				
Accounts payable		3,300				
Salary payable						
Common stock		12,000				
Retained earnings		63,110				
Dividends	3,500					
Service revenue		11,000				
Salary expense	2,300					
Rent expense						
Utilities expense	510					
Depreciation expense						
Supplies expense						
Total	93,310	93,310				

Adjustment data December 31, 2010:

    a. Accrued service revenue at December 31, $2,100.

    b. Prepaid rent expired during the month. The unadjusted prepaid balance of $2,400 relates to the period December 1, 2010 through February, 2011.

    c. Supplies used during December, $2,170.

    d. Depreciation on furniture for the month. The estimated useful life of the furniture is three years.

    e. Accrued salary expense at December 31 for Monday, Tuesday, and Wednesday. The five-day weekly payroll of $4,800 will be paid on Friday.

▌ *Requirements*

1. Using Exhibit 3-9 as an example, prepare the adjusted trial balance of London, Inc., at December 31, 2010. Key each adjusting entry by letter.

2. Prepare the monthly income statement, the statement of retained earnings, and the classified balance sheet. Draw arrows linking the three statements.

■ **general ledger**

P3-73A *(Learning Objective 3: Analyzing and recording adjustments)* Peachtree Apartments, Inc.'s unadjusted and adjusted trial balances at April 30, 2010, follow.

Peachtree Apartments, Inc.
Adjusted Trial Balance
April 30, 2010

Account	Trial Balance Debit	Trial Balance Credit	Adjusted Trial Balance Debit	Adjusted Trial Balance Credit
Cash	$ 8,900		$ 8,900	
Accounts receivable	5,900		6,810	
Interest receivable			200	
Note receivable	4,400		4,400	
Supplies	1,800		600	
Prepaid insurance	2,300		600	
Building	70,000		70,000	
Accumulated depreciation		$ 7,400		$ 8,800
Accounts payable		6,700		6,700
Wages payable				1,000
Unearned rental revenue		2,100		1,600
Common stock		17,000		17,000
Retained earnings		40,000		40,000
Dividends	3,300		3,300	
Rental revenue		25,100		26,510
Interest revenue		400		600
Depreciation expense			1,400	
Supplies expense			1,200	
Utilities expense	400		400	
Wage expense	1,300		2,300	
Property tax expense	400		400	
Insurance expense			1,700	
Total	$98,700	$98,700	$102,210	$102,210

Requirements

1. Make the adjusting entries that account for the differences between the two trial balances.
2. Compute Peachtree's total assets, total liabilities, total equity, and net income.

P3-74A (*Learning Objectives 4, 6: Preparing the financial statements; using the debt ratio*)   The adjusted trial balance of Schneider Corporation at July 31, 2010, follows.

■ spreadsheet

Schneider Corporation
Adjusted Trial Balance
July 31, 2010

Account	Debit	Credit
Cash	$ 2,000	
Accounts receivable	9,400	
Supplies	2,400	
Prepaid rent	1,200	
Equipment	36,600	
Accumulated depreciation		$ 4,200
Accounts payable		3,400
Interest payable		200
Unearned service revenue		700
Income tax payable		2,000
Note payable		18,900
Common stock		4,000
Retained earnings		5,000
Dividends	21,000	
Service revenue		102,100
Depreciation expense	1,700	
Salary expense	39,800	
Rent expense	10,300	
Interest expense	3,300	
Insurance expense	3,500	
Supplies expense	2,800	
Income tax expense	6,500	
Total	$140,500	$140,500

Requirements

1. Prepare Schneider Corporation's 2010 income statement, statement of retained earnings, and balance sheet. List expenses (except for income tax) in decreasing order on the income statement and show total liabilities on the balance sheet. Draw arrows linking the three financial statements.
2. Schneider's lenders require that the company maintain a debt ratio no higher than 0.60. Compute Schneider's debt ratio at July 31, 2010, to determine whether the company is in compliance with this debt restriction. If not, suggest a way that Schneider could have avoided this difficult situation.

P3-75A (*Learning Objective 5: Closing the books; evaluating retained earnings*) The accounts of Spa View Service, Inc., at March 31, 2010, are listed in alphabetical order.

Accounts payable	$14,400	Interest expense	$ 900
Accounts receivable	16,100	Note payable, long term	6,100
Accumulated depreciation—		Other assets	14,400
equipment	6,900	Prepaid expenses	6,000
Advertising expense	10,900	Retained earnings,	
Cash	7,900	March 31, 2009	22,000
Common stock	5,600	Salary expense	17,800
Current portion of note		Salary payable	2,900
payable	1,000	Service revenue	95,000
Depreciation expense	1,700	Supplies	3,600
Dividends	31,200	Supplies expense	4,400
Equipment	41,700	Unearned service revenue	2,700

❚ Requirements

1. All adjustments have been journalized and posted, but the closing entries have not yet been made. Journalize Spa View's closing entries at March 31, 2010.
2. Set up a T-account for Retained Earnings and post to that account. Then compute Spa View's net income for the year ended March 31, 2010. What is the ending balance of Retained Earnings?
3. Did Retained Earnings increase or decrease during the year? What caused the increase or the decrease?

P3-76A (*Learning Objectives 4, 6: Preparing a classified balance sheet; using the ratios to evaluate the business*)   Refer back to Problem 3-75A.

❚ Requirements

1. Use the Spa View data in Problem 3-75A to prepare the company's classified balance sheet at March 31, 2010. Show captions for total assets, total liabilities, and total liabilities and stockholders' equity.
2. Compute Spa View's current ratio and debt ratio at March 31, 2010, rounding to two decimal places. At March 31, 2009, the current ratio was 1.25 and the debt ratio was 0.20. Did Spa View's ability to pay both current and total debts improve or deteriorate during 2010? Evaluate Spa View's debt position as strong or weak and give your reason.

P3-77A (*Learning Objective 6: Analyzing financial ratios*)   This problem demonstrates the effects of transactions on the current ratio and the debt ratio of Hartford Company. Hartford's condensed and adapted balance sheet at December 31, 2010, follows.

	(In millions)
Total current assets	$15.6
Properties, plant, equipment, and other assets	16.1
	$31.7
Total current liabilities	$ 9.6
Total long-term liabilities	5.8
Total stockholders' equity	16.3
	$31.7

Assume that during the first quarter of the following year, 2011, Hartford completed the following transactions:

a. Paid half the current liabilities.
b. Borrowed $6.0 million on long-term debt.
c. Earned revenue, $2.5 million, on account.
d. Paid selling expense of $0.6 million.
e. Accrued general expense of $0.7 million. Credit General Expense Payable, a current liability.
f. Purchased equipment for $4.2 million, paying cash of $1.5 million and signing a long-term note payable for $2.7 million.
g. Recorded depreciation expense of $0.8 million.

❙ *Requirements*

1. Compute Hartford's current ratio and debt ratio at December 31, 2010. Round to two decimal places.
2. Consider each transaction separately. Compute Hartford's current ratio and debt ratio after each transaction during 2011, that is, seven times. Round ratios to two decimal places.
3. Based on your analysis, you should be able to readily identify the effects of certain transactions on the current ratio and the debt ratio. Test your understanding by completing these statements with either "increase" or "decrease":
   a. Revenues usually _____ the current ratio.
   b. Revenues usually _____ the debt ratio.
   c. Expenses usually _____ the current ratio. (*Note:* Depreciation is an exception to this rule.)
   d. Expenses usually _____ the debt ratio.
   e. If a company's current ratio is greater than 1.0, as it is for Hartford, paying off a current liability will always _____ the current ratio.
   f. Borrowing money on long-term debt will always the current ratio and _____ the debt ratio.

(Group B)

P3-78B (*Learning Objective 1: Linking accrual accounting and cash flows*) Gauge Corporation earned revenues of $33 million during 2010 and ended the year with net income of $6 million. During 2010 Gauge collected cash of $24 million from customers and paid cash for all of its expenses plus an additional $1 million on account for amounts payable at December 31, 2009. Answer these questions about Gauge's operating results, financial position, and cash flows during 2010:

❙ *Requirements*

1. How much were Gauge's total expenses? Show your work.
2. Identify all the items that Gauge will report on its 2010 income statement. Show each amount.
3. Gauge began 2010 with receivables of $9 million. All sales are on account. What was Gauge's receivables balance at the end of 2010? Identify the appropriate financial statement and show how Gauge will report its ending receivables balance in the company's 2010 annual report.
4. Gauge began 2010 owing accounts payable of $11 million. All expenses are incurred on account. During 2010, Gauge paid $28 million on account. How much in accounts payable did Gauge owe at the end of 2010? Identify the appropriate financial statement and show how Gauge will report accounts payable in its 2010 annual report.

P3-79B (*Learning Objective 1: Comparing cash basis and accrual basis*) Kings Consulting had the following selected transactions in May:

May	1	Prepaid insurance for May through September, $500.
	4	Purchased software for cash, $600.
	5	Performed services and received cash, $1,000.
	8	Paid advertising expense, $400.
	11	Performed service on account, $3,100.
	19	Purchased computer on account, $2,000.
	24	Collected for May 11 service.
	26	Paid account payable from May 19.
	29	Paid salary expense, $1,500.
	31	Adjusted for May insurance expense (see May 1).
	31	Earned revenue of $500 that was collected in advance back in April.

❚ Requirements

1. Show how each transaction would be handled using the cash basis and the accrual basis.
2. Compute May income (loss) before tax under each accounting method.
3. Indicate which measure of net income or net loss is preferable. Use the transactions on May 11 and May 24 to explain.

writing assignment ■

P3-80B (*Learning Objective 3: Making accounting adjustments*) Journalize the adjusting entry needed on December 31, the end of the current accounting period, for each of the following independent cases affecting Irons Corp. Include an explanation for each entry.

a. Details of Prepaid Insurance are shown in the account:

Prepaid Insurance		
Jan 1 Bal	500	
Mar 31	3,800	

Irons prepays insurance on March 31 each year. At December 31, $900 is still prepaid.

b. Irons pays employees each Friday. The amount of the weekly payroll is $5,800 for a five-day work week. The current accounting period ends on Wednesday.

c. Irons has a note receivable. During the current year, has earned accrued interest revenue of $700 that it will collect next year.

d. The beginning balance of supplies was $2,700. During the year, Irons purchased supplies costing $6,100, and at December 31 supplies on hand total $2,200.

e. Irons is providing services for Orca Investments, and the owner of Orca paid Irons $12,100 as the annual service fee. Irons recorded this amount as Unearned Service Revenue. Irons estimates that it has earned 60% of the total fee during the current year.

f. Depreciation for the current year includes Office Furniture, $3,500, and Equipment, $5,400. Make a compound entry.

P3-81B (*Learning Objectives 3, 4: Preparing an adjusted trial balance and the financial statements*) Consider the unadjusted trial balance of Kings, Inc., at August 31, 2010, and the related month-end adjustment data.

Kings, Inc.
Trial Balance Work Sheet
August 31, 2010

Account	Trial Balance Debit	Trial Balance Credit	Adjustments Debit	Adjustments Credit	Adjusted Trial Balance Debit	Adjusted Trial Balance Credit
Cash	9,200					
Accounts receivable	1,500					
Prepaid rent	2,400					
Supplies	2,200					
Furniture	81,000					
Accumulated depreciation		3,900				
Accounts payable		3,500				
Salary payable						
Common stock		15,000				
Retained earnings		71,020				
Dividends	3,600					
Service revenue		10,000				
Salary expense	3,000					
Rent expense						
Utilities expense	520					
Depreciation expense						
Supplies expense						
Total	103,420	103,420				

Adjustment data at August 31, 2010 include the following:
a. Accrued advertising revenue at August 31, $2,000
b. Prepaid rent expired during the month. The unadjusted prepaid balance of $2,400 relates to the period August 2010 through October 2010.
c. Supplies used during August, $1,820
d. Depreciation on furniture for the month. The furniture's expected useful life is five years.
e. Accrued salary expense at August 31 for Monday, Tuesday, and Wednesday. The five-day weekly payroll is $5,200 and will be paid on Friday.

❙ *Requirements*

1. Using Exhibit 3-9 as an example, prepare the adjusted trial balance of Kings, Inc., at August 31, 2010. Key each adjusting entry by letter.
2. Prepare the monthly income statement, the statement of retained earnings, and the classified balance sheet. Draw arrows linking the three statements.

■ **general ledger**

P3-82B *(Learning Objective 3: Analyzing and recording adjustments)* Fairview Apartments, Inc.'s unadjusted and adjusted trial balances at April 30, 2010, follow:

Fairview Apartments, Inc.
Adjusted Trial Balance
April 30, 2010

Account	Trial Balance Debit	Trial Balance Credit	Adjusted Trial Balance Debit	Adjusted Trial Balance Credit
Cash	$ 7,900		$ 7,900	
Accounts receivable	6,000		6,880	
Interest receivable			500	
Note receivable	5,000		5,000	
Supplies	1,500		600	
Prepaid insurance	2,500		800	
Building	67,000		67,000	
Accumulated depreciation		$ 8,800		$10,300
Accounts payable		6,500		6,500
Wages payable				800
Unearned rental revenue		1,500		1,200
Common stock		17,000		17,000
Retained earnings		43,300		43,300
Dividends	3,200		3,200	
Rental revenue		18,300		19,480
Interest revenue		200		700
Depreciation expense			1,500	
Supplies expense			900	
Utilities expense	300		300	
Wage expense	1,900		2,700	
Property tax expense	300		300	
Insurance expense			1,700	
Total	$95,600	$95,600	$99,280	$99,280

❙ Requirements

1. Make the adjusting entries that account for the differences between the two trial balances.
2. Compute Fairview's total assets, total liabilities, total equity, and net income.

P3-83B (*Learning Objectives 4, 6: Preparing the financial statements; using the debt ratio*) The adjusted trial balance of Sneed Corporation at October 31, 2010, follows:

■ spreadsheet

Sneed Corporation
Adjusted Trial Balance
October 31, 2010

Account	Debit	Credit
Cash...	$ 1,600	
Accounts receivable.........................	8,800	
Supplies..	2,100	
Prepaid rent....................................	1,000	
Equipment......................................	36,700	
Accumulated depreciation...............		$ 4,400
Accounts payable............................		3,800
Interest payable..............................		400
Unearned service revenue		900
Income tax payable		2,500
Note payable...................................		18,600
Common stock................................		8,000
Retained earnings...........................		4,000
Dividends.......................................	25,000	
Service revenue...............................		101,700
Depreciation expense	1,200	
Salary expense................................	40,500	
Rent expense..................................	10,200	
Interest expense..............................	3,200	
Insurance expense	3,600	
Supplies expense.............................	2,900	
Income tax expense.........................	7,500	
Total	$144,300	$144,300

I Requirements

1. Prepare Sneed's 2010 income statement, statement of retained earnings, and balance sheet. List expenses (except for income tax) in decreasing order on the income statement and show total liabilities on the balance sheet.
2. Sneed's lenders require that the company maintain a debt ratio no higher than 0.60. Compute Sneed's debt ratio at October 31, 2010, to determine whether the company is in compliance with this debt restriction. If not, suggest a way Sneed could have avoided this difficult situation.

P3-84B (*Learning Objective 5: Making closing entries; evaluating retained earnings*) The accounts of Sunny Stream Service, Inc., at March 31, 2010, are listed in alphabetical order.

Accounts payable	$14,300	Interest expense	$ 800
Accounts receivable	16,400	Note payable, long term	5,900
Accumulated depreciation—		Other assets	14,500
equipment	7,300	Prepaid expenses	5,700
Advertising expense	11,100	Retained earnings,	
Cash	7,300	March 31, 2009	22,000
Common stock	6,700	Salary expense	18,100
Current portion of note		Salary payable	2,600
payable	500	Service revenue	94,100
Depreciation expense	2,000	Supplies	3,300
Dividends	30,000	Supplies expense	4,300
Equipment	42,500	Unearned service revenue	2,600

Requirements

1. All adjustments have been journalized and posted, but the closing entries have not yet been made. Journalize Sunny Stream's closing entries at March 31, 2010.
2. Set up a T-account for Retained Earnings and post to that account. Then compute Sunny Stream's net income for 2010. What is the ending balance of Retained Earnings?
3. Did Retained Earnings increase or decrease during the year? What caused the increase or decrease?

P3-85B (*Learning Objectives 4, 6: Preparing a classified balance sheet; using the ratios*)   Refer back to Problem 3-84B.

Requirements

1. Prepare the company's classified balance sheet in report form at March 31, 2010. Show captions for total assets, total liabilities, and total liabilities and stockholders' equity.
2. Compute Sunny Stream's current ratio and debt ratio at March 31, 2010, rounding to two decimal places. At March 31, 2009, the current ratio was 1.40 and the debt ratio was 0.25. Did Sunny Stream's ability to pay both current and total liabilities improve or deteriorate during 2010? Evaluate Sunny Stream's debt position as strong or weak and give your reason.

P3-86B (*Learning Objective 6: Analyzing financial ratios*)   This problem demonstrates the effects of transactions on the current ratio and the debt ratio of Hillsboro Company. Hillsboro's condensed and adapted balance sheet at December 31, 2009, follows.

	(In millions)
Total current assets	$15.3
Properties, plant, equipment, and other assets	16.4
	$31.7
Total current liabilities	$ 8.6
Total long-term liabilities	5.4
Total shareholders' equity	17.7
	$31.7

Assume that during the first quarter of the following year 2010, Hillsboro completed the following transactions:

   a. Paid half of the current liabilities.
   b. Borrowed $7.0 million on long-term debt.
   c. Earned revenue of $2.5 million, on account.
   d. Paid selling expense of $3.0 million.
   e. Accrued general expense of $0.7 million. Credit General Expense Payable, a current liability.
   f. Purchased equipment for $4.7 million, paying cash of $1.9 million and signing a long-term note payable for $2.8 million.
   g. Recorded depreciation expense of $0.6 million.

❚ Requirements

1. Compute Hillsboro's current ratio and debt ratio at December 31, 2009. Round to two decimal places.
2. Consider each transaction separately. Compute Hillsboro's current ratio and debt ratio after each transaction during 2010, that is, seven times. Round ratios to two decimal places.
3. Based on your analysis, you should be able to readily identify the effects of certain transactions on the current ratio and the debt ratio. Test your understanding by completing these statements with either "increase" or "decrease."
   a. Revenues usually _____ the current ratio.
   b. Revenues usually _____ the debt ratio.
   c. Expenses usually _____ the current ratio. (*Note:* Depreciation is an exception to this rule.)
   d. Expenses usually _____ the debt ratio.
   e. If a company's current ratio is greater than 1.0, as for Hillsboro, paying off a current liability will always _____ the current ratio.
   f. Borrowing money on long-term debt will always _____ the current ratio and _____ the debt ratio.

APPLY YOUR KNOWLEDGE

Decision Cases

Case 1. (*Learning Objectives 3, 6: Adjusting and correcting the accounts; computing and evaluating the current ratio*) The unadjusted trial balance of Good Times, Inc., at January 31, 2010, does not balance. In addition, the trial balance needs to be adjusted before the financial statements at January 31, 2010 can be prepared. The manager of Good Times needs to know the business's current ratio.

Cash	$ 8,000
Accounts receivable	4,200
Supplies	800
Prepaid rent	1,200
Land	43,000
Accounts payable	12,000
Salary payable	0
Unearned service revenue	700
Note payable, due in three years	23,400
Common stock	5,000
Retained earnings	9,300
Service revenue	9,100
Salary expense	3,400
Rent expense	0
Advertising expense	900
Supplies expense	0

❚ Requirements

1. How much *out of balance* is the trial balance? Notes Payable (the only error) is understated.
2. Good Times needs to make the following adjustments at January 31:
   a. Supplies of $400 were used during January.
   b. The balance of Prepaid Rent was paid on January 1 and covers the whole year 2010. No adjustment was made on January 31.
   c. At January 31, Good Times owes employees $1,000.
   d. Unearned service revenue of $500 was earned during January.
   Prepare a corrected, adjusted trial balance. Give Notes Payable its correct balance.

3. After the error is corrected and after these adjustments are made, compute the current ratio of Good Times, Inc. If your business had this current ratio, could you sleep at night?

Case 2. *(Learning Objectives 4: Preparing financial statements; deciding to continue or shut down the business)* On October 1, Lou Marks opened Eagle Restaurant, Inc. Marks is now at a crossroads. The October financial statements paint a glowing picture of the business, and Marks has asked you whether he should expand the business. To expand the business, Marks wants to be earning net income of $10,000 per month and have total assets of $50,000. Marks believes he is meeting both goals.

To start the business, Marks invested $25,000, not the $15,000 amount reported as "Common stock" on the balance sheet. The business issued $25,000 of common stock to Marks. The bookkeeper plugged the $15,000 "Common stock" amount into the balance sheet to make it balance. The bookkeeper made some other errors too. Marks shows you the following financial statements that the bookkeeper prepared:

Eagle Restaurant, Inc.
Income Statement
Month Ended October 31, 2011

Revenues:		
Investments by owner	$25,000	
Unearned banquet sales revenue	3,000	
		$28,000
Expenses:		
Wages expense	$ 5,000	
Rent expense	4,000	
Dividends	3,000	
Depreciation expense—fixtures	1,000	
		13,000
Net income		$15,000

Eagle Restaurant, Inc.
Balance Sheet
October 31, 2011

Assets:		Liabilities:	
Cash	$ 8,000	Accounts payable	$ 7,000
Prepaid insurance	1,000	Sales revenue	32,000
Insurance expense	1,000	Acuumulated depreciation—	
Food inventory	5,000	fixtures	1,000
Cost of goods sold (expense)	12,000		40,000
Fixtures (tables, chairs, etc.)	24,000	**Owners' equity:**	
Dishes and silverware	4,000	Common stock	15,000
	$55,000		$55,000

❙ Requirement

1. Prepare corrected financial statements for Eagle Restaurant, Inc.: Income Statement, Statement of Retained Earnings, and Balance Sheet. Then, based on Marks' goals and your corrected statements, recommend to Marks whether he should expand the restaurant.

Case 3. (*Learning Objectives 3, 4: Valuing a business on the basis of its net income*) Stanley Williams has owned and operated SW Advertising, Inc., since its beginning 10 years ago. Recently, Williams mentioned that he would consider selling the company for the right price.

Assume that you are interested in buying this business. You obtain its most recent monthly trial balance, which follows. Revenues and expenses vary little from month to month, and June is a typical month. Your investigation reveals that the trial balance does not include the effects of monthly revenues of $4,000 and expenses totaling $1,100. If you were to buy SW Advertising, you would hire a manager so you could devote your time to other duties. Assume that your manager would require a monthly salary of $5,000.

SW Advertising, Inc.
Trial Balance
June 30, 2010

Cash...	$ 12,000	
Accounts receivable..............................	6,900	
Prepaid expenses	3,200	
Plant assets..	125,000	
Accumulated depreciation.....................		$ 81,500
Land...	158,000	
Accounts payable		13,800
Salary payable......................................		
Unearned advertising revenue...............		58,700
Common stock......................................		50,000
Retained earnings.................................		93,000
Dividends...	9,000	
Advertising revenue..............................		22,000
Rent expense..		
Salary expense......................................	4,000	
Utilities expense	900	
Depreciation expense		
Supplies expense..................................		
Total	$319,000	$319,000

❙ Requirements

1. Assume that the most you would pay for the business is 16 times the amount of monthly net income *you could expect to earn* from it. Compute this possible price.
2. Williams states that the least he will take for the business is two times its stockholders' equity on June 30. Compute this amount.
3. Under these conditions, how much should you offer Williams? Give your reason. (Challenge)

Ethical Issues

Issue 1. Cross Timbers Energy Co. is in its third year of operations, and the company has grown. To expand the business, Cross Timbers borrowed $15 million from Bank of Fort Worth. As a condition for making this loan, the bank required that Cross Timbers maintain a current ratio of at least 1.50 and a debt ratio of no more than 0.50.

Business recently has been worse than expected. Expenses have brought the current ratio down to 1.47 and the debt ratio up to 0.51 at December 15. Lane Collins, the general manager, is considering the result of reporting this current ratio to the bank. Collins is considering recording this year some revenue on account that Cross Timbers will earn next year. The contract for this job has been signed, and Cross Timbers will deliver the natural gas during January of next year.

❚ *Requirements*

1. Journalize the revenue transaction (without dollar amounts), and indicate how recording this revenue in December would affect the current ratio and the debt ratio.
2. Analyze this transaction according to the decision framework for making ethical judgments in Chapter 1:
   a. What is the issue?
   b. Who are the stakeholders and what are the alternatives? Weigh them from the standpoint of economic, legal, and ethical implications.
   c. What decision would you make?
3. Propose for Cross Timbers a course of action that is ethical.

Issue 2. The net income of Solas Photography Company decreased sharply during 2010. Lisa Almond, owner of the company, anticipates the need for a bank loan in 2011. Late in 2010, Almond instructed Brad Lail, the accountant and a personal friend of yours, to record a $10,000 sale of portraits to the Almond family, even though the photos will not be shot until January 2011. Almond also told Lail *not* to make the following December 31, 2010, adjusting entries:

> Salaries owed to employees $10,000
> Prepaid insurance that has expired 1,000

❚ *Requirements*

1. Compute the overall effect of these transactions on the company's reported income for 2010. Is reported net income overstated or understated?
2. Why did Almond take these actions? Are they ethical? Give your reason, identifying the parties helped and the parties harmed by Almond's action. Consult the Decision Framework for Making Ethical Judgments in Chapter 1. Which factor (economic, legal, or ethical) seems to be taking precedence? Identify the stakeholders and the potential consequences to each.
3. As a personal friend of Brad's, what advice would you give him?

Focus on Financials: ■ Amazon.com, Inc.

(Learning Objectives 3, 6: Tracing account balances to the financial statements) **Amazon.com, Inc.**—like all other businesses—adjusts accounts prior to year end to get correct amounts for the financial statements. Examine Amazon.com, Inc.'s Consolidated Balance Sheets in Appendix A, and pay particular attention to "accrued expenses and other."

❚ *Requirements*

1. Why does a company have accrued expenses payable at year end?
2. Open a T-account for "accrued expenses and other." Insert Amazon.com, Inc.'s balance (in millions) at December 31, 2007.
3. Journalize the following transactions for the year ended December 31, 2008. Key entries by letter, and show amounts in millions. Explanations are not required.
   a. Paid off the beginning balance of "accrued expenses and other"
   b. Recorded operating expenses of $3,428 million, paying $2,335 million in cash and accruing the remainder
4. Post these entries to "accrued expenses and other" and show that the ending balance of the account agrees with the corresponding amount reported in Amazon.com, Inc.'s December 31, 2008, Consolidated Balance Sheets.
5. Compute the current ratios and debt ratios for Amazon.com, Inc., at December 31, 2007, and December 31, 2008. Did the ratio values improve, deteriorate, or hold steady during 2008? Do Amazon.com, Inc.'s ratio values indicate relative financial strength or weakness?

Focus on Analysis: ▪ Foot Locker, Inc.

(Learning Objective 3: Explaining accruals and deferrals) During 2007, **Foot Locker, Inc.**, had numerous accruals and deferrals. As a new member of Foot Locker, Inc.'s accounting staff, it is your job to explain the effects of accruals and deferrals on net income for 2007. The accrual and deferral data follow, along with questions that Foot Locker, Inc.'s stockholders have raised (all amounts in millions):

1. Examine Footnote 8 to Foot Locker's consolidated financial statements (Other Current Assets) in Appendix B. Notice that included in this total are "net receivables." Ending net receivables for 2006 (beginning balance of 2007) were $59 million. Ending net receivables for 2007 were $50 million. Which of these amounts did Foot Locker, Inc., earn in 2006? Which amount is included in Foot Locker, Inc.'s 2007 net income?

2. In Footnote 8, examine the line entitled "prepaid rent." The beginning balance is $62 million and the ending balance is $65 million. Which of these amounts impacted Foot Locker, Inc.'s 2007 net income? Which amount impacted Foot Locker, Inc.'s 2008 net income?

3. Examine Footnote 9 (Property and Equipment, Net). Notice that accumulated depreciation stood at $870 million at the end of 2006 and at $903 million at year end 2007. Assume that depreciation expense for 2007 was $100. Explain what must have happened to account for the remainder of the change in the accumulated depreciation account during 2007. (Challenge)

4. Examine Footnote 13 (Accrued and Other Liabilities). Foot Locker, Inc., reports an account titled Customer deposits. The attached footnote states that customer deposits include unredeemed gift cards and certificates, merchandise credits. and deferred revenue related to undelivered merchandise, including layaway sales. This account carried credit balances of $33 million at the end of 2006 and $34 million at the end of 2007. What type of account is Customer deposits? Make a single journal entry to show how this account could have increased its balance during 2007. Then explain the event in your own words.

Group Project

Mark Davis formed a lawn service company as a summer job. To start the business on May 1, he deposited $2,000 in a new bank account in the name of the corporation. The $2,000 consisted of a $1,600 loan from his father and $400 of his own money. The corporation issued 200 shares of common stock to Davis.

Davis rented lawn equipment, purchased supplies, and hired high school students to mow and trim his customers' lawns. At the end of each month, Davis mailed bills to his customers. On August 31, Davis was ready to dissolve the business and return to Rutgers University for the fall semester. Because he had been so busy, he had kept few records other than his checkbook and a list of amounts owed by customers.

At August 31, Davis' checkbook shows a balance of $2,040, and his customers still owe him $600. During the summer, he collected $5,600 from customers. His checkbook lists payments for supplies totaling $400, and he still has gasoline, weedeater cord, and other supplies that cost a total of $50. He paid his employees wages of $1,900, and he still owes them $200 for the final week of the summer.

Davis rented some equipment from Ludwig Tool Company. On May 1, he signed a six-month lease on mowers and paid $600 for the full lease period. Ludwig will refund the unused portion of the prepayment if the equipment is in good shape. To get the refund, Davis has kept the mowers in excellent condition. In fact, he had to pay $300 to repair a mower that ran over a hidden tree stump.

To transport employees and equipment to jobs, Davis used a trailer that he bought for $300. He figures that the summer's work used up one-third of the trailer's service potential. The business checkbook lists an expenditure of $460 for dividends paid to Davis during the summer. Also, Davis paid his father back during the summer.

▌Requirements

1. Prepare the income statement of Davis Lawn Service, Inc., for the four months May through August. The business is not subject to income tax.
2. Prepare the classified balance sheet of Davis Lawn Service, Inc., at August 31.

For online homework, exercises, and problems that provide you with immediate feedback, please visit www.myaccountinglab.com.

Quick Check Answers

1. *d*	6. *b*	10. *c*	14. *a*
2. *c*	7. *c*	11. *d*	15. *d*
3. *d*	8. *d*	12. *d*	16. *d*
4. *a*	9. *d*	13. *c*	17. *c*
5. *b*			

Demo Doc

Preparation of Adjusting Entries, Closing Entries, and Financial Statements

To make sure you understand this material, work through the following demonstration "Demo Doc" with detailed comments to help you see the concept within the framework of a worked-through problem.

Learning Objectives 2–5

Cloud Break Consulting, Inc., has the following information at June 30, 2010:

		Account Title	Debit	Credit
		Cloud Break Consulting, Inc.		
		Unadjusted Trial Balance		
		June 30, 2010		
			Balance	
		Account Title	**Debit**	**Credit**
		Cash	$131,000	
		Accounts receivable	104,000	
		Supplies	4,000	
		Prepaid rent	27,000	
		Land	45,000	
		Building	300,000	
		Accumulated depreciation—building		$155,000
		Accounts payable		159,000
		Unearned service revenue		40,000
		Common stock		50,000
		Retained earnings		52,000
		Dividends	7,000	
		Service revenue		450,000
		Salary expense	255,000	
		Rent expense	25,000	
		Miscellaneous expense	8,000	
		Total	$906,000	$906,000

June 30 is Cloud Break's fiscal year end; accordingly, it must make adjusting entries for the following items:

a. **Supplies on hand at year-end, $1,000.**

b. **Nine months of rent totaling $27,000 were paid in advance on April 1, 2010. Cloud Break has recorded no rent expense yet.**

c. **Depreciation expense has not been recorded on the building for the 2010 fiscal year. The building has a useful life of 25 years.**

d. **Employees work Monday through Friday. The weekly payroll is $5,000 and is paid every Friday. June 30, 2010, falls on a Thursday.**

e. Service revenue of $15,000 must be accrued.

f. Cloud Break received $40,000 in advance for consulting services to be provided evenly from January 1, 2010 through August 31, 2010. Cloud Break has recorded none of this revenue.

Requirements

1. Open the T-accounts with their unadjusted balances.

2. Journalize Cloud Break's adjusting entries at June 30, 2010, and post the entries to the T-accounts.

3. Total each T-account in the ledger.

4. Journalize and post Cloud Break's closing entries.

5. Prepare Cloud Break's income statement and statement of retained earnings for the year ended June 30, 2010, and the balance sheet at June 30, 2010. Draw arrows linking the three financial statements.

Demo Doc Solutions

Requirement 1

Open the T-accounts with their unadjusted balances.

Part 1	Part 2	Part 3	Part 4	Part 5	Demo Doc Complete

Remember from Chapter 2 that opening a T-account means drawing a blank account that looks like a capital "T" and putting the account title across the top. To help find the accounts later, they are grouped into assets, liabilities, stockholders' equity, revenues, and expenses (in that order). If the account has a starting balance, it **must** appear on the correct side.

Remember that debits are always on the left side of the T-account and credits are always on the right side. This is true for *every* account.

The correct side to enter each account's starting balance is the side of *increase* in the account. This is because we expect all accounts to have a *positive* balance (that is, more increases than decreases).

For assets, an increase is a debit, so we would expect all assets (except contra assets such as Accumulated Depreciation) to have a debit balance. For liabilities and stockholders' equity, an increase is a credit, so we would expect all liabilities and equities (except Dividends) to have a credit balance. By the same reasoning, we expect revenues to have credit balances and expenses and dividends to have debit balances.

The unadjusted balances appearing in the T-accounts are simply the amounts from the starting trial balance.

ASSETS	STOCKHOLDERS' EQUITY	EXPENSES

ASSETS

Cash		Building		Common Stock		Salary Expense
Bal 131,000		Bal 300,000		Bal 50,000		Bal 255,000

Accounts Receivable		Accumulated Depreciation—Building		Retained Earnings		Rent Expense
Bal 104,000		Bal 155,000		Bal 52,000		Bal 25,000

Supplies				Dividends		Miscellaneous Expense
Bal 4,000		**LIABILITIES**		Bal 7,000		Bal 8,000

		Accounts Payable	
Prepaid Rent		Bal 159,000	
Bal 27,000			

REVENUE

		Unearned Service Revenue		Service Revenue
Land		Bal 40,000		Bal 450,000
Bal 45,000				

Requirement 2

Journalize Cloud Break's adjusting entries at June 30, 2010, and post the entries to the T-accounts.

| Part 1 | **Part 2** | Part 3 | Part 4 | Part 5 | Demo Doc Complete |

a. Supplies on hand at year-end, $1,000.

On June 30, 2010, the unadjusted balance in the Supplies account was $4,000. However, a count shows that only $1,000 of supplies actually remains on hand. The supplies that are no longer there have been used. When assets/benefits are used, an expense is created.

Cloud Break will need to make an adjusting journal entry in order to report the correct amount of supplies on the balance sheet.

Looking at the Supplies T-account:

	Supplies		
	4,000		
		Used up	X
Bal	1,000		

The supplies have decreased because they have been used up. The amount of the decrease is **X**. **X** = $4,000 − $1,000 = $3,000.

$3,000 of supplies expense must be recorded to show the value of supplies that have been used.

a.	Jun 30	Supplies Expense ($4,000 − $1,000) (Expense ↑; debit)	3,000	
		Supplies (Asset ↓; credit)		3,000
		To record supplies expense.		

After posting, Supplies and Supplies Expense hold their correct ending balances:

	ASSETS				EXPENSES	
	Supplies				Supplies Expense	
	4,000			a.	3,000	
		a.	3,000	Bal	3,000	
Bal	1,000					

b. Nine months of rent (totalling $27,000) were paid in advance on April 1, 2010. Cloud Break has recorded no rent expense yet.

A prepayment for something, such as for rent or insurance, creates a *future* benefit (an asset) because the business is now entitled to receive the prepaid goods or services. Once those goods or services are received (in this case, once Cloud Break has occupied the building being rented), the benefit expires, and the prepaid cost becomes an expense.

4

Internal Control & Cash

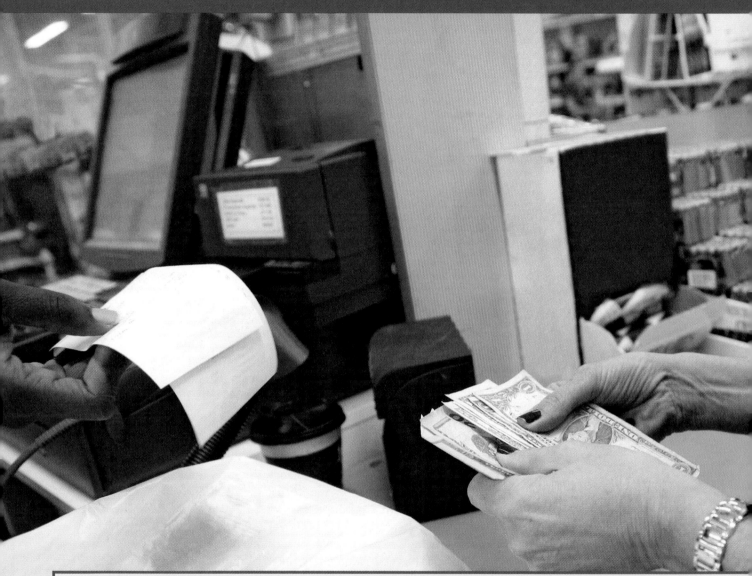

SPOTLIGHT: Cooking the Books: AMEX Products Takes a Hit

The following is adapted from a true story:

"I've never been so shocked in my life!" exclaimed Lee Riffe, manager of the **AMEX Products** office in Palo Alto, California. "I never thought this could happen to us. We are such a close-knit organization where everyone trusts everyone else. Why, people at AMEX feel like family! I feel betrayed, violated."

Riffe had just returned from the trial of Melissa Price, who had been convicted of embezzling over $600,000 from AMEX over a six-year period. Price had been one of AMEX's most trusted employees for 10 years. A single mom with two teenage daughters, Price had pulled herself up by her own bootstraps, putting herself through community college where she had obtained an associate's degree in accounting. Riffe had hired her as a part-time bookkeeper at AMEX while Price was in college to help her out. She had done such a good job that, when she completed her degree, Riffe asked her to stay on and assigned her the additional role of cashier, in charge of accumulating the daily cash receipts from customers and taking them to the night depository at the bank each day after work. Through the years, he also awarded her what he considered good raises, compensating her at a rate that was generally higher than other employees with her education and experience levels.

(continued on next page)

Price rapidly became the company's "go-to" financial employee. She was eager to learn, dependable, responsible. In 10 years she never took a day of vacation, choosing instead to take advantage of the company's policy that allowed employees to draw additional compensation for vacation accrued but not taken at the end of each year. Riffe grew to depend on Price more and more each month, as the business grew to serve over 1,000 customers. Price's increased involvement on the financial side of the business freed Riffe to spend his time working on new business, spending less and less time on financial matters. Riffe had noticed that, in the past few years, Price had begun to wear better clothes and drive a shiny late-model convertible around town. Both of her teenagers also drove late-model automobiles, and the family had recently moved into a new home in an upscale subdivision of the city. Riffe had been pleased that he had contributed to Price's success. But in recent months, Riffe was becoming worried because, in spite of increasing revenues, the cash balances and cash flows from operations at AMEX had been steadily deteriorating, sometimes causing the company difficulty in paying its bills on time.

Price, on the other hand, had felt underappreciated and underpaid for all of her hard work. Having learned the system well, and observing that no one was monitoring her, Price fell into a simple but deadly trap. As cashier, she was in charge of receiving customer payments that came in by mail. Unknown to Riffe, Price had been **lapping** accounts receivable, an embezzlement scheme nicknamed "robbing Peter to pay Paul." Price began by misappropriating (stealing) some of the customers' checks, endorsing them, and depositing them to her own bank account. To cover up the shortage in a particular customer's account, Price would apply the collections received later from another customer's account. She would do this just before the monthly statements were mailed to the first customer, so that the customer wouldn't notice when he or she received the statement that someone else's payment was being applied to the amount owed AMEX. Of course, this left the second customer's account short, so Price had to misapply the collection from a third customer to straighten out the discrepancy in the second customer's account. She did this for many customers, over a period of many months, boldly stealing more and more each month. With unlimited access to both cash and customer accounts, and with careful planning and constant diligence, Price became very proficient at juggling entries in the books to keep anyone from discovering her scheme. This embezzlement went on for six years, allowing Price to misappropriate $622,000 from the company. The customer accounts that were misstated due to the fraud eventually had to be written off.

What tipped off Riffe to the embezzlement? Price was involved in an automobile accident and couldn't work for two weeks. The employee covering for Price was swamped with telephone calls from customers wanting to discuss unexplained differences in their billing statements for amounts they could prove had been paid. The ensuing investigation pointed straight to Price, and Riffe turned the case over to the authorities.

The excerpt from the AMEX Products balance sheet on the following page reports the company's assets. Focus on the top line, Cash and cash equivalents. At December 31, 2010, AMEX reported cash of $6,260. Due to Price's scheme, the company had been cheated of $622,000 over several years that it could have used to buy new equipment, expand operations, or pay off debts.

AMEX Products has now revamped its internal controls. The company has hired a separate person, with no access to cash, to keep customer accounts receivable records. The company now uses a **lock-box system** for all checks received by mail. They are sent to AMEX's bank lock box, where they are gathered by a bank employee and immediately deposited. The remittance advices accompanying the checks are electronically scanned and forwarded to AMEX's accounts receivable bookkeeper where they are used as the source documents for posting amounts collected from customers. A summary of cash received goes to Riffe, who reviews it for reasonableness and compares it with the daily bank deposit total. Another employee, who has neither cash handling nor customer bookkeeping responsibilities, reconciles AMEX's monthly bank statement, and reconciles the total cash deposited per the daily listings with the total credits to customer accounts receivable. Now Riffe requires every employee to take time off for earned vacation, and rotates other employees through those positions while those employees are away.

AMEX Products, Inc.
Balance Sheet (Partial, Adapted)

Assets	December 31, 2010
Cash and cash equivalents......................................	$ 6,260
Cash pledged as collateral	2,000
Accounts receivable...	8,290
Inventories	36,200
Prepaid expenses	1,400
Investments	10,000
Equipment and facilities (net of accumulated depreciation of ($2,400)...............	13,170
Other assets..	3,930
Total assets...	$81,250

Lapping is a type of fraud known as misappropriation of assets. Although it doesn't take a genius to accomplish, lapping requires some *motivation*, and is usually *rationalized* by distorted and unethical thinking. The *opportunity* to commit this type and other types of frauds arises through a weak internal control system. In this case, the fact that Price had access to cash and the customer accounts receivable, along with the fact that Riffe failed to monitor Price's activities, proved to be the deadly combination that provided the opportunity for this fraud.

This chapter begins with a discussion of fraud, its types, and common characteristics. We then discuss internal controls, which are the primary means by which fraud as well as unintentional financial statement errors are prevented. We also discuss how to account for cash. These three topics—fraud, internal control, and cash—go together. Internal controls help prevent fraud. Cash is probably the asset that is most often misappropriated through fraud.

LEARNING OBJECTIVES

1 **Learn** about fraud and how much it costs

2 **Set up** an internal control system

3 **Prepare** and **use** a bank reconciliation

4 **Apply** internal controls to cash receipts and cash payments

5 **Use** a budget to manage cash

FRAUD AND ITS IMPACT

Fraud is an intentional misrepresentation of facts, made for the purpose of persuading another party to act in a way that causes injury or damage to that party. For example, in the chapter opening story, Melissa Price intentionally misappropriated money from AMEX and covered it up by making customer accounts look different than they actually were. In the end, her actions caused $622,000 in damages to AMEX.

OBJECTIVE

1 **Learn** about fraud and how much it costs

Fraud is a huge problem and is getting bigger, not only in the United States, but across the globe. Recent surveys of large and medium-sized companies in the United States and Canada revealed the following:

- Over 75% of businesses surveyed had experienced fraud;
- Over 50% of companies had experienced six or more instances of fraud in only one year;
- In 2007, companies lost an average of $2.4 million each to fraud (up from $1.7 million each in 2005);
- One out of every five American workers indicated personal awareness of fraud in the workplace.

Since small businesses and those in countries outside the United States and Canada were omitted from these surveys, we can be sure that the actual incidence of fraud is even higher! Another recent survey taken by the Association for Certified Fraud Examiners (ACFE) reveals that occupational fraud and abuse in America alone results in losses equal to about 6% of total business revenue. When applied to the U.S. gross domestic product, this means that about $600 billion per year is lost due to fraud, an astonishing $4,500 per employee! If you think that fraud occurs only in the for-profit sector, think again. About 13.4% of the ACFE survey cases are not-for-profit organizations, amounting to about $50 billion in fraud through not-for-profit organizations each year.

Fraud has literally exploded with the expansion of e-commerce via the Internet. In addition, studies have shown that the percentage of losses related to fraud from transactions originating in "third world" or developing countries via the Internet is even higher than in economically-developed countries.

What are the most common types of fraud? What causes fraud? What can be done to prevent it?

There are many types of fraud. Some of the most common types are insurance fraud, check forgery, Medicare fraud, credit card fraud, and identity theft. The two most common types of fraud that impact financial statements are:

- **Misappropriation of assets.**   *This type of fraud is committed by employees of an entity who steal money from the company and cover it up* through erroneous entries in the books. The AMEX case is an example. Other examples of asset misappropriation include employee theft of inventory, bribery or kickback schemes in the purchasing function, or employee overstatement of expense reimbursement requests.
- **Fraudulent financial reporting.**   *This type of fraud is committed by company managers who make false and misleading entries in the books*, making financial results of the company appear to be better than they actually are. The purpose of this type of fraud is to deceive investors and creditors into investing or loaning money to the company that they might not otherwise have invested or loaned.

Both of these types of fraud involve making false or misleading entries in the books of the company. We call this *cooking the books*. Of these two types, asset misappropriation is the most common, but fraudulent financial reporting is by far the most expensive. Perhaps the two most notorious recent cases involving fraudulent financial reporting in the United States involved **Enron Corporation** in 2001 and **WorldCom Corporation** in 2002. These two scandals alone rocked the U.S. economy and impacted financial markets across the world. Enron (discussed in Chapter 10) committed fraudulent financial reporting by overstating profits through bogus sales of nonexistent assets with inflated values.

When Enron's banks found out, they stopped loaning the company money to operate, causing it to go out of business almost overnight. WorldCom (discussed in Chapter 7) reported expenses as plant assets and overstated both profits and assets. The company's internal auditor blew the whistle on WorldCom, resulting in the company's eventual collapse. Sadly, the same international accounting firm, Arthur Andersen, LLP, had audited both companies' financial statements. Because of these and other failed audits, the once mighty firm of Arthur Andersen was forced to close its doors in 2002.

Each of these frauds, and many others revealed about the same time, involved losses in the billions of dollars and thousands of jobs when the companies went out of business. Widespread media coverage sparked adverse market reaction, loss of confidence in the financial reporting system, and losses through declines in stock values that ran in the trillions of dollars! We will discuss some of these cases throughout the remaining chapters of the text as examples of how accounting principles were deliberately misapplied, through cooking the books, in environments characterized by *weak internal controls*.

Exhibit 4-1 explains in graphic form the elements that make up virtually every fraud. We call it the **fraud triangle**.

EXHIBIT 4-1 | The Fraud Triangle

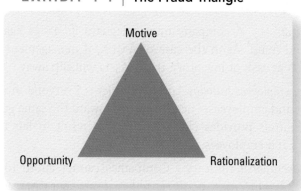

The first element in the fraud triangle is *motive*. This usually results from either critical need or greed on the part of the person who commits the fraud (the perpetrator). Sometimes it is a matter of just never having enough (because some persons who commit fraud are already rich by most people's standards). Other times the perpetrator of the fraud might have a legitimate financial need, such as a medical emergency, but he or she uses illegitimate means to meet that need. A recent article in the *Wall Street Journal* indicated that employee theft was on the rise due to economic hard times. In any case, the prevailing attitude on the part of the perpetrator is, "I want it, and someone else has it, so I'm going to do whatever I have to do to get it."

The second element in the fraud triangle is *opportunity*. As in the case of AMEX, the opportunity to commit fraud usually arises through weak internal controls. It might be a breakdown in a key element of controls, such as improper *segregation of duties* and/or *improper access to assets*. Or it might result from a weak *control environment*, such as a domineering CEO, a weak or conflicted board of directors, or lax ethical practices, allowing top management to override whatever controls the company has placed in operation for other transactions.

The third element in the triangle is *rationalization*. The perpetrator engages in distorted thinking, such as: "I deserve this;" "Nobody treats me fairly;" "No one will ever know;" "Just this once, I won't let it happen again;" or "Everyone else is doing it."

Fraud and Ethics

As we pointed out in our decision model for making ethical accounting and business judgments introduced in Chapter 1, the decision to engage in fraud is an act with economic, legal, and ethical implications. The perpetrators of fraud usually do so for their own short-term *economic gain*, while others incur *economic losses* that may far outstrip the gains of the fraudsters. Moreover, fraud is defined by state, federal, and international law as *illegal*. Those who are caught and found guilty of fraud ultimately face penalties which include imprisonment, fines, and monetary damages. Finally, from an *ethical* standpoint, fraud violates the rights of many for the temporary betterment of a few, and for the ultimate betterment of no one. At the end of the day, everyone loses! **Fraud is the ultimate unethical act in business!**

INTERNAL CONTROL

The primary way that fraud, as well as unintentional errors, is prevented, detected, or corrected in an organization is through a proper system of internal control. **Internal control** is a plan of organization and a system of procedures implemented by company management and the board of directors, and designed to accomplish the following five objectives:

1. *Safeguard assets.* A company must safeguard its assets against waste, inefficiency, and fraud. As in the case of AMEX, if management fails to safeguard assets such as cash or inventory, those assets will slip away.

2. *Encourage employees to follow company policy.* Everyone in an organization—managers and employees—needs to work toward the same goals. A proper system of controls provides clear policies that result in fair treatment of both customers and employees.

3. *Promote operational efficiency.* Companies cannot afford to waste resources. They work hard to make a sale, and they don't want to waste any of the benefits. If the company can buy something for $30, why pay $35? Effective controls minimize waste, which lowers costs and increases profits.

4. *Ensure accurate, reliable accounting records.* Accurate records are essential. Without proper controls, records may be unreliable, making it impossible to tell which part of the business is profitable and which part needs improvement. A business could be losing money on every product it sells—unless it keeps accurate records for the cost of its products.

5. *Comply with legal requirements.* Companies, like people, are subject to laws, such as those of regulatory agencies like the SEC, the IRS, and state, local, and international governing bodies. When companies disobey the law, they are subject to fines, or in extreme cases, their top executives may even go to prison. Effective internal controls help ensure compliance with the law and avoidance of legal difficulties.

How critical are internal controls? They're so important that the U.S. Congress has passed a law to require public companies—those that sell their stock to the public—to maintain a system of internal controls and to require that their auditors examine those controls and issue audit reports as to their reliability. Exhibit 4-2 is AMEX Products' Management Discussion of Financial Responsibility.

EXHIBIT 4-2 | **AMEX Products, Inc., Management's Discussion of Financial Responsibility**

Management's Discussion of Financial Responsibility

AMEX Products regularly reviews its framework of internal controls, which includes the company's policies, procedures and organizational structure. Corrective actions are taken to address any control deficiencies, and improvements are implemented as appropriate.

The Sarbanes-Oxley Act (SOX)

As the Enron and WorldCom scandals unfolded, many people asked, "How can these things happen? If such large companies that we have trusted commit such acts, how can we trust any company to be telling the truth in its financial statements? Where were the auditors?" To address public concerns, Congress passed the Sarbanes-Oxley Act of 2002 (SOX). SOX revamped corporate governance in the United States and profoundly affected the way that accounting and auditing is done in public companies. Here are some of the SOX provisions:

1. Public companies must issue an internal control report, and the outside auditor must evaluate and report on the soundness of the company's internal controls.

2. A new body, the Public Company Accounting Oversight Board, has been created to oversee the audits of public companies.

3. An accounting firm may not both audit a public client and also provide certain consulting services for the same client.

4. Stiff penalties await violators—25 years in prison for securities fraud; 20 years for an executive making false sworn statements.

The former CEO of WorldCom was convicted of securities fraud and sentenced to 25 years in prison. The top executives of Enron were also sent to prison. You can see that internal controls and related matters can have serious consequences.

Exhibit 4-3 diagrams the shield that internal controls provide for an organization. Protected by this shield, which provides protection from fraud, waste, and inefficiency, companies can do business in a trustworthy manner that ensures public confidence, an extremely important element in maintaining the stability of financial markets around the world.

EXHIBIT 4-3 | **The Shield of Internal Control**

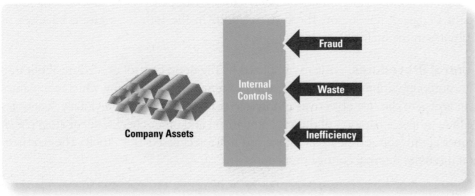

How does a business achieve good internal controls? The next section identifies the components of internal control.

The Components of Internal Control

Internal control can be broken down into five components:

- Control environment
- Risk assessment
- Information system
- Control procedures
- Monitoring of controls

Exhibit 4-4 (p. 239) diagrams the components of internal control.

Control Environment. The control environment, symbolized by the roof over the building in Exhibit 4-4, is the "tone at the top" of the business. It starts with the owner and the top managers. They must behave honorably to set a good example for company employees. The owner must demonstrate the importance of internal controls if he or she expects employees to take the controls seriously. A key ingredient in the control environment of many companies is a corporate code of ethics, modeled by top management, which includes such provisions as prohibition against giving or taking bribes or kickbacks from customers or suppliers, prohibition of transactions that involve conflicts of interest, and provisions that encourage good citizenship and corporate social responsibility.

Risk Assessment. Symbolized by the smoke rising from the chimney, assessment of risks that a company faces offers hints of where mistakes or fraud might arise. A company must be able to identify its business risks, as well as to establish procedures for dealing with those risks to minimize their impacts on the company. For example, Kraft Foods faces the risk that its food products may harm people. American Airlines planes may crash. And all companies face the risk of bankruptcy. The managements of companies, supported by their boards, have to identify these risks and do what they can to prevent those risks from causing financial or other harm to the company, its employees, its owners, and its creditors.

Information System. Symbolized by the door of the building, the information system is the means by which accounting information enters and exits. The owner of a business needs accurate information to keep track of assets and measure profits and losses. Every system within the business that processes accounting data should have the ability to capture transactions as they occur, record (journalize) those transactions in an accurate and timely manner, summarize (post) those transactions in the books (ledgers), and report those transactions in the form of account balances or footnotes in the financial statements.

Control Procedures. Also symbolized by the door, control procedures built into the control environment and information system are the means by which companies gain access to the five objectives of internal controls discussed previously. Examples include proper separation of duties, comparison and other checks, adequate records, proper approvals, and physical safeguards to protect assets from theft. The next section discusses internal control procedures.

Monitoring of Controls.   Symbolized by the windows of the building, monitoring provides "eyes and ears," so that no one person or group of persons can process a transaction completely without being seen and checked by another person or group. With modern computerized systems, much of the monitoring of day-to-day activity is done through controls programmed into a company's information technology. Computer programs dealing with such systems as cash receipts and cash disbursements can be automatically programmed to generate *exception reports* for transactions that exceed certain pre-defined guidelines (such as disbursements in excess of $15,000 in a payroll) for special management scrutiny. In addition, companies hire auditors to monitor their controls. Internal auditors monitor company controls from the inside to safeguard the company's assets, and external auditors test the controls from the outside to ensure that the accounting records are accurate and reliable. Audits are discussed more thoroughly in the next section.

EXHIBIT 4-4 | The Components of Internal Control

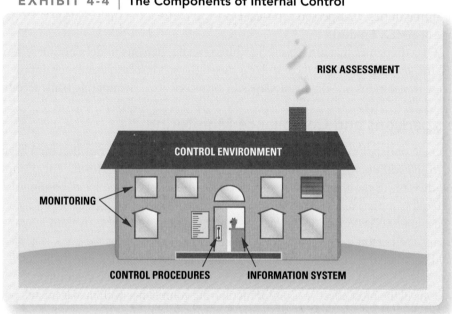

INTERNAL CONTROL PROCEDURES

Whether the business is AMEX Products, Microsoft, or a Starbucks store, every major class of transactions needs to have the following *internal control procedures*.

Smart Hiring Practices and Separation of Duties

In a business with good internal controls, no important duty is overlooked. Each person in the information chain is important. The chain should start with hiring. Background checks should be conducted on job applicants. Proper training and supervision, as well as paying competitive salaries, helps ensure that all employees are sufficiently competent for their jobs. Employee responsibilities should be clearly laid out in position descriptions. For example, the **treasurer**'s department should be in charge of cash handling, as well as signing and approving checks. Warehouse personnel should be in charge of storing and keeping track of inventory. With clearly assigned responsibilities, all important jobs get done.

In processing transactions, smart management *separates three key duties: asset handling, record keeping, and transaction approval.* For example, in the case of AMEX Products, separation of the duties of cash handling from record keeping for customer accounts receivable would have removed Melissa Price's incentive to engage in fraud, because it would have made it impossible for her to have lapped accounts receivable if another employee had been keeping the books. Ideally, someone else should also review customer accounts for collectability and be in charge of writing them off if they become completely uncollectible.

The accounting department should be completely separate from the operating departments, such as production and sales. What would happen if sales personnel, who were compensated based on a percentage of the amount of sales they made, approved the company's sales transactions to customers? Sales figures could be inflated and might not reflect the eventual amount collected from customers.

At all costs, accountants must not handle cash, and cash handlers must not have access to the accounting records. If one employee has both cash-handling and accounting duties, that person can steal cash and conceal the theft. This is what happened at AMEX Products.

For companies that are *too small* to hire separate persons to do all of these functions, the key to good internal control is *getting the owner involved*, usually by approving all large transactions, making bank deposits, or reconciling the monthly bank account.

Comparisons and Compliance Monitoring

No person or department should be able to completely process a transaction from beginning to end without being cross-checked by another person or department. For example, some division of the treasurer's department should be responsible for depositing daily cash receipts in the bank. The **controller**'s department should be responsible for recording customer collections to individual customer accounts receivable. A third employee (perhaps the person in the controller's department who reconciles the bank statement) should compare the treasurer department's daily records of cash deposited with totals of collections posted to individual customer accounts by the accounting department.

One of the most effective tools for monitoring compliance with management's policies is the use of **operating budgets** and **cash budgets**. A **budget** is a quantitative financial plan that helps control day-to-day management activities. Management may prepare these budgets on a yearly, quarterly, monthly, or more frequent basis. Operating budgets are budgets of future periods' net income. They are prepared by line item of the income statement. Cash budgets, discussed in depth later in this chapter, are budgets of future periods' cash receipts and cash disbursements. Often these budgets are "rolling," being constantly updated by adding a time period a year away while dropping the time period that has just passed. Computer systems are programmed to prepare exception reports for data that are out of line with expectations. This data can include variances for each account from budgeted amounts. Department managers are required to explain the variances, and to take corrective actions in their operating plans to keep the budgets in line with expectations. This is an example of the use of **exception reporting**.

To validate the accounting records and monitor compliance with company policies, most companies have an audit. An **audit** is an examination of the company's financial statements and its accounting system, including its controls.

Audits can be internal or external. *Internal auditors* are employees of the business. They ensure that employees are following company policies and operations are running efficiently. Internal auditors also determine whether the company is following legal requirements.

External auditors are completely independent of the business. They are hired to determine whether or not the company's financial statements agree with generally accepted accounting principles. Auditors examine the client's financial statements and the underlying transactions in order to form a professional opinion on the accuracy and reliability of the company's financial statements.

Adequate Records

Accounting records provide the details of business transactions. The general rule is that all major groups of transactions should be supported by either hard copy documents or electronic records. Examples of documents include sales invoices, shipping records, customer remittance advices, purchase orders, vendor invoices, receiving reports, and canceled (paid) checks. Documents should be pre-numbered to assure completeness of processing and proper transaction cutoff, and to prevent theft and inefficiency. A gap in the numbered document sequence draws attention to the possibility that transactions might have been omitted from processing.

Limited Access

To complement segregation of duties, company policy should limit access to assets only to those persons or departments that have custodial responsibilities. For example, access to cash should be limited to persons in the treasurer's department. Cash receipts might be processed through a lock-box system. Access to inventory should be limited to persons in the company warehouse where inventories are stored, or to persons in the shipping and receiving functions. Likewise, the company should limit access to records to those persons who have record keeping responsibilities. All manual records of the business should be protected by lock and key and electronic records should be protected by passwords. Only authorized persons should have access to certain records. Individual computers in the business should be protected by user identification and password. Electronic data files should be encrypted (processed through a special code) to prevent their recognition if accessed by a "hacker" or other unauthorized person.

Proper Approvals

No transaction should be processed without management's general or specific approval. The bigger the transaction, the more specific approval it should have. For individual small transactions, management might delegate approval to a specific department. For example:

- Sales to customers on account should all be approved by a separate *credit department* that reviews all customers for creditworthiness before goods are shipped to customers on credit. This helps assure that the company doesn't make sales to customers who cannot afford to pay their bills.
- Purchases of all items on credit should be approved by a separate *purchasing department* that specializes in that function. Among other things, a purchasing department should only buy from approved vendors, on the basis of competitive bids, to assure that the company gets the highest quality products for the most competitive prices.
- All personnel decisions, including hiring, firing, and pay adjustments, should be handled by a separate *human resources (HR) department* that specializes in personnel-related matters.

Very large (material) transactions should generally be approved by top management, and may even go to the board of directors.

What's an easy way to remember the basic control procedures for any class of transactions? Look at the first letters of each of the headings in this section:

Smart hiring practices and **S**egregation of duties

Comparisons and compliance monitoring

Adequate records

Limited access to both assets and records

Proper approvals (either general or specific) for each class of transaction

So, if you can remember SCALP and how to apply each of these attributes, you can have great controls in your business!

Information Technology

Accounting systems are relying less on manual procedures and more on information technology (IT) than ever before for record keeping, asset handling, approval, and monitoring, as well as physically safeguarding the assets. For example, retailers such as Target Stores and Macy's control inventory by attaching an *electronic sensor* to merchandise. The cashier must remove the sensor before the customer can walk out of the store. If a customer tries to leave the store with the sensor attached, an alarm sounds. According to Checkpoint Systems, these devices reduce theft by as much as 50%. *Bar codes* speed checkout at retail stores, performing multiple operations in a single step. When the sales associate scans the merchandise at the register, the computer records the sale, removes the item from inventory, and computes the amount of cash tendered.

When a company employs sophisticated IT, the basic attributes of internal control (SCALP) do not change, but the procedures by which these attributes are implemented change substantially. For example, segregation of duties is often accomplished by separating mainframe computer departments from other user departments (i.e., controller, sales, purchasing, receiving, credit, HR, treasurer) and restricting access to the IT department only to authorized personnel. Within the computer department, programmers should be separated from computer operators and data librarians. Access to sensitive data files is protected by **password** and data encryption. Electronic records must be saved routinely, or they might be written over or erased. Comparisons of data (such as cash receipts with total credits to customer accounts) that might otherwise be done by hand are performed by the computer. Computers can monitor inventory levels by item, generating a purchase order for inventory when it reaches a certain level.

The use of computers has the advantage of speed and accuracy (when programmed correctly). However, a computer that is *not* programmed correctly can corrupt *all* the data, making it unusable. It is therefore important to hire experienced and competent people to run the IT department, to restrict access to sensitive data and the IT department only to authorized personnel, to check data entered into and retrieved from the computer for accuracy and completeness, and to test and retest programs on a regular basis to assure data integrity and accuracy.

Safeguard Controls

Businesses keep important documents in *fireproof vaults*. *Burglar alarms* safeguard buildings, and *security cameras* safeguard other property. *Loss-prevention specialists* train employees to spot suspicious activity.

Employees who handle cash are in a tempting position. Many businesses purchase **fidelity bonds** on cashiers. The bond is an insurance policy that reimburses the company for any losses due to employee theft. Before issuing a fidelity bond, the insurance company investigates the employee's background.

Mandatory vacations and *job rotation* improve internal control. Companies move employees from job to job. This improves morale by giving employees a broad view of the business. Also, knowing someone else will do your job next month keeps you honest. AMEX Products didn't rotate employees to different jobs, and it cost the company $622,000.

INTERNAL CONTROLS FOR E-COMMERCE

E-commerce creates its own risks. Hackers may gain access to confidential information such as account numbers and passwords.

Pitfalls

E-commerce pitfalls include the following:

- Stolen credit card numbers
- Computer viruses and Trojan Horses
- Phishing expeditions

Stolen Credit Card Numbers. Suppose you buy CDs from EMusic.com. To make the purchase, your credit card number must travel through cyberspace. Wireless networks (Wi-Fi) are creating new security hazards.

Amateur hacker Carlos Salgado, Jr., used his home computer to steal 100,000 credit card numbers with a combined limit exceeding $1 billion. Salgado was caught when he tried to sell the numbers to an undercover FBI agent.

Computer Viruses and Trojan Horses. A **computer virus** is a malicious program that (a) enters program code without consent and (b) performs destructive actions in the victim's computer files or programs. A **Trojan Horse** is a malicious computer program that hides inside a legitimate program and works like a virus. Viruses can destroy or alter data, make bogus calculations, and infect files. Most firms have found a virus in their system at some point.

Suppose the U.S. Department of Defense takes bids for a missile system. Raytheon and Lockheed-Martin are competing for the contract. A hacker infects Raytheon's system and alters Raytheon's design. Then the government labels the Raytheon design as flawed and awards the contract to Lockheed.

Phishing Expeditions.   Thieves **phish** by creating bogus Web sites, such as AOL4Free.com and BankAmerica.com. The neat-sounding Web site attracts lots of visitors, and the thieves obtain account numbers and passwords from unsuspecting people. The thieves then use the data for illicit purposes.

Security Measures

To address the risks posed by e-commerce, companies have devised a number of security measures, including

- encryption
- firewalls

Encryption.   The server holding confidential information may not be secure. One technique for protecting customer data is encryption. **Encryption** rearranges messages by a mathematical process. The encrypted message can't be read by those who don't know the code. An accounting example uses check-sum digits for account numbers. Each account number has its last digit equal to the sum of the previous digits. For example, consider Customer Number 2237, where $2 + 2 + 3 = 7$. Any account number that fails this test triggers an error message.

Firewalls.   **Firewalls** limit access into a local network. Members can access the network but nonmembers can't. Usually several firewalls are built into the system. Think of a fortress with multiple walls protecting the company's computerized records in the center. At the point of entry, passwords, PINs (personal identification numbers), and signatures are used. More sophisticated firewalls are used deeper in the network. Start with Firewall 1, and work toward the center.

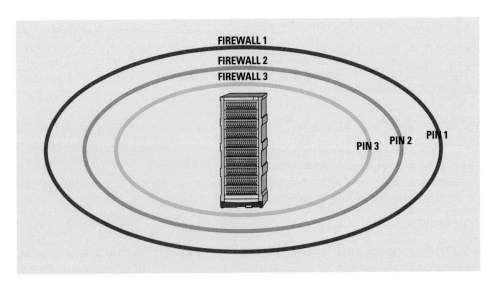

The Limitations of Internal Control—Costs and Benefits

Unfortunately, most internal controls can be overcome. Collusion—two or more people working together—can beat internal controls. Consider AMEX Products, discussed in the chapter opening. Even if Riffe were to hire a new person to keep the books, if that person had a relationship with Price and if they conspired with each other, they could design a scheme to lap accounts receivable, the same as Price did, and split the take. Other ways to circumvent a good system of internal controls include management override, human limitations such as fatigue and negligence, and gradual deterioration over time due to neglect. Because of the cost/benefit principle, discussed in the next paragraph, internal controls are not generally designed to detect these types of breakdowns. The best a company can do in this regard is to exercise care in hiring honest persons who have no conflicts of interest with existing employees, and to exercise constant diligence in monitoring the system to assure it continues to work properly.

The stricter the internal control system, the more it costs. An overly complex system of internal control can strangle the business with red tape. How tight should the controls be? Internal controls must be judged in light of their costs and benefits. An example of a good cost/benefit relationship: A part-time security guard at a **Wal-Mart** store costs about $28,000 a year. On average, each part-time guard prevents about $50,000 of theft. The net savings to Wal-Mart is $22,000. Most people would say the extra guard is well worth the cost!

THE BANK ACCOUNT AS A CONTROL DEVICE

Cash is the most liquid asset because it's the medium of exchange. Cash is easy to conceal and relatively easy to steal. As a result, most businesses create specific controls for cash.

Keeping cash in a bank account helps control cash because banks have established practices for safeguarding customers' money. The documents used to control a bank account include the following:

- Signature card
- Bank statement
- Deposit ticket
- Bank reconciliation
- Check

Signature Card

Banks require each person authorized to sign on an account to provide a *signature card*. This protects against forgery.

Deposit Ticket

Banks supply standard forms such as *deposit tickets*. The customer fills in the amount of each deposit. As proof of the transaction, the customer keeps a deposit receipt.

Check

To pay cash, the depositor can write a **check**, which tells the bank to pay the designated party a specified amount. There are three parties to a check:

- The maker, who signs the check
- The payee, to whom the check is paid
- The bank on which the check is drawn

Exhibit 4-5 shows a check drawn by AMEX Products, the maker. The check has two parts, the check itself and the **remittance advice** below. This optional attachment, which may often be scanned electronically, tells the payee the reason for the payment and is used as the source document for posting to proper accounts.

EXHIBIT 4-5 | **Check with Remittance Advice**

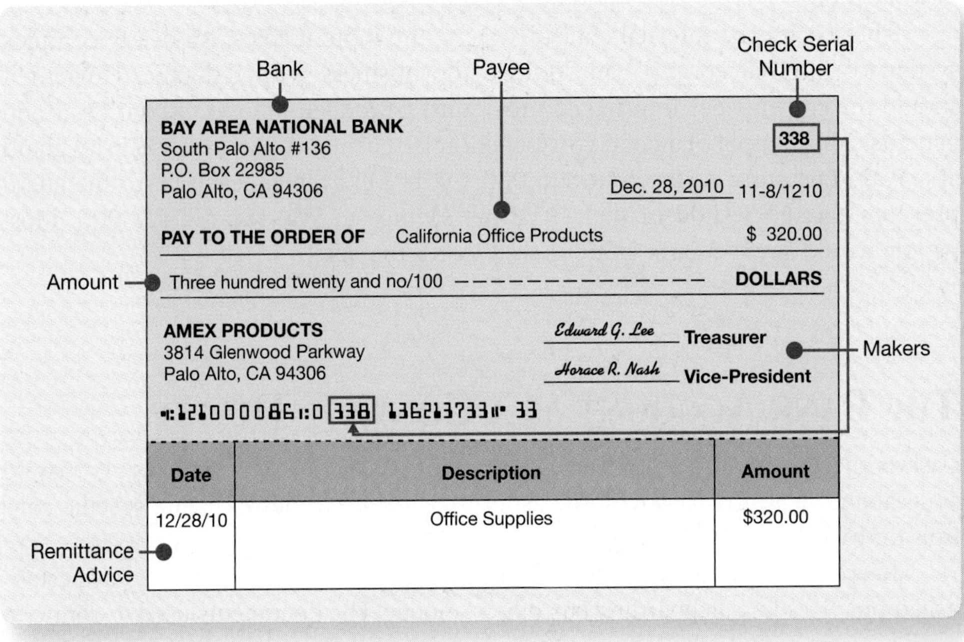

Bank Statement

Banks send monthly statements to customers. A **bank statement** reports what the bank did with the customer's cash. The statement shows the account's beginning and ending balances, cash receipts, and payments. Included with the statement are copies of the maker's *canceled checks* (or the actual paid checks). Exhibit 4-6 is the December bank statement of the Palo Alto office of AMEX Products.

EXHIBIT 4-6 | **Bank Statement**

BANK STATEMENT

BAY AREA NATIONAL BANK
SOUTH PALO ALTO #136 P.O. BOX 22985 PALO ALTO, CA 94306

AMEX Products
3814 Glenwood Parkway
Palo Alto, CA 94306

CHECKING ACCOUNT 136–213733

DECEMBER 31, 2010

BEGINNING BALANCE	TOTAL DEPOSITS	TOTAL WITHDRAWALS	SERVICE CHARGES	ENDING BALANCE
6,550	4,370	5,000	20	5,900

— TRANSACTIONS —

DEPOSITS	DATE	AMOUNT
Deposit	12/04	1,150
Deposit	12/08	190
EFT—Receipt of cash dividend	12/17	900
Bank Collection	12/26	2,100
Interest	12/31	30

CHARGES	DATE	AMOUNT
Service Charge	12/31	20

CHECKS

Number	Amount	Number	Amount	Number	Amount
307	100	333	150	335	100
332	3,000	334	100	336	1,100

OTHER DEDUCTIONS	DATE	AMOUNT
NSF	12/04	50
EFT—Insurance	12/20	400

Electronic funds transfer (EFT) moves cash by electronic communication. It is cheaper to pay without having to mail a check, so many people pay their mortgage, rent, utilities, and insurance by EFT.

Bank Reconciliation

There are two records of a business's cash:

1. The Cash account in the company's general ledger. Exhibit 4-7 on the following page shows that AMEX Products' ending cash balance is $3,340.

EXHIBIT 4-7 | **Cash Records of AMEX Products**

General Ledger:

ACCOUNT Cash

Date	Item	Debit	Credit	Balance
2010				
Dec 1	Balance			6,550
2	Cash receipt	1,150		7,700
7	Cash receipt	190		7,890
31	Cash payments		6,150	1,740
31	Cash receipt	1,600		3,340

Cash Payments:

Check No.	Amount	Check No.	Amount
332	$3,000	337	$ 280
333	510	338	320
334	100	339	250
335	100	340	490
336	1,100	Total	$6,150

2. The bank statement, which shows the cash receipts and payments transacted through the bank. In Exhibit 4-6 the bank shows an ending balance of $5,900 for AMEX.

The books and the bank statement usually show different cash balances. Differences arise because of a time lag in recording transactions—two examples follow:

- When you write a check, you immediately deduct it in your checkbook. But the bank does not subtract the check from your account until the bank pays the check a few days later. And you immediately add the cash receipt for all your deposits. But it may take a day or two for the bank to add deposits to your balance.
- Your EFT payments and cash receipts are recorded by the bank before you learn of them.

To ensure accurate cash records, you need to update your cash record—either online or after you receive your bank statement. The result of this updating process creates a **bank reconciliation**, which you must prepare. The bank reconciliation explains all differences between your cash records and your bank balance. The person who prepares the bank reconciliation should have no other cash duties. Otherwise, he or she can steal cash and manipulate the reconciliation to conceal the theft.

Preparing the Bank Reconciliation

OBJECTIVE

3 **Prepare** and use a bank reconciliation

Here are the items that appear on a bank reconciliation. They all cause differences between the bank balance and the book balance. We call your cash record (also known as a "checkbook") the "Books."

Bank Side of the Reconciliation

1. Items to show on the *Bank* side of the bank reconciliation include the following:

   a. **Deposits in transit** (outstanding deposits). You have recorded these deposits, but the bank has not. Add deposits in transit on the bank reconciliation.

   b. **Outstanding checks**. You have recorded these checks, but the bank has not yet paid them. Subtract outstanding checks.

   c. **Bank errors.** Correct all bank errors on the Bank side of the reconciliation. For example, the bank may erroneously subtract from your account a check written by someone else.

Book Side of the Reconciliation

2. Items to show on the *Book* side of the bank reconciliation include the following:

   a. **Bank collections.** Bank collections are cash receipts that the bank has recorded for your account. But you haven't recorded the cash receipt yet. Many businesses have their customers pay directly to their bank. This is called a *lock-box system* and reduces theft. An example is a bank collecting an account receivable for you. Add bank collections on the bank reconciliation.

   b. **Electronic funds transfers.** The bank may receive or pay cash on your behalf. An EFT may be a cash receipt or a cash payment. Add EFT receipts and subtract EFT payments.

   c. **Service charge.** This cash payment is the bank's fee for processing your transactions. Subtract service charges.

   d. **Interest revenue on your checking account.** On certain types of bank accounts, you earn interest if you keep enough cash in your account. The bank statement tells you of this cash receipt. Add interest revenue.

   e. **Nonsufficient funds (NSF) checks.** These are cash receipts from customers for which there are not sufficient funds in the bank to cover the amount. NSF checks (sometimes called hot checks) are treated as cash payments on your bank reconciliation. Subtract NSF checks.

   f. **The cost of printed checks.** This cash payment is handled like a service charge. Subtract this cost.

   g. **Book errors.** Correct all book errors on the Book side of the reconciliation. For example, you may have recorded a $150 check that you wrote as $510.

Bank Reconciliation Illustrated. The bank statement in Exhibit 4-6 shows that the December 31 bank balance of AMEX Products is $5,900 (upper right corner). However, the company's Cash account has a balance of $3,340, as shown in Exhibit 4-7. This situation calls for a bank reconciliation. Exhibit 4-8, panel A, on the following page, lists the reconciling items for easy reference, and panel B shows the completed reconciliation.

EXHIBIT 4-8 | Bank Reconciliation

PANEL A—Reconciling Items

Bank side:	Book side:
1. Deposit in transit, $1,600.	4. EFT receipt of your dividend revenue earned on an investment, $900.
2. Bank error: The bank deducted $100 for a check written by another company. Add $100 to the bank balance.	5. Bank collection of your account receivable, $2,100.
3. Outstanding checks—total of $1,340.	6. Interest revenue earned on your bank balance, $30.
	7. Book error: You recorded check no. 333 for $510. The amount you actually paid on account was $150. Add $360 to your book balance.
	8. Bank service charge, $20.
	9. NSF check from a customer, $50. Subtract $50 from your book balance.
	10. EFT payment of insurance expense, $400.

Check No.	Amount
337	$280
338	320
339	250
340	490

PANEL B—Bank Reconciliation

AMEX Products
Bank Reconciliation
December 31, 2010

Bank			Books		
Balance, December 31		$5,900	Balance, December 31		$3,340
Add:			Add:		
1. Deposit in transit		1,600	4. EFT receipt of dividend revenue		900
2. Correction of bank error		100	5. Bank collection of account		
		7,600	receivable		2,100
			6. Interest revenue earned on		
			bank balance		30
			7. Correction of book error—		
			overstated our check no. 333		360
					6,730
Less:					
3. Outstanding checks					
No. 337	$280		Less:		
No. 338	320		8. Service charge	$ 20	
No. 339	250		9. NSF check	50	
No. 340	490	(1,340)	10. EFT payment of insurance expense	400	(470)
Adjusted bank balance		**$6,260**	**Adjusted bank balance**		**$6,260**

These amounts should agree.

SUMMARY OF THE VARIOUS RECONCILING ITEMS:

BANK BALANCE—ALWAYS	BOOK BALANCE—ALWAYS
• *Add* deposits in transit.	• *Add* bank collections, interest revenue, and EFT receipts.
• *Subtract* outstanding checks.	• *Subtract* service charges, NSF checks, and EFT payments.
• *Add* or *subtract* corrections of bank errors.	• *Add* or *subtract* corrections of book errors.

Journalizing Transactions from the Bank Reconciliation. The bank reconciliation is an accountant's tool separate from the journals and ledgers. It does *not* account for transactions in the journal. To get the transactions into the accounts, we must make journal entries and post to the ledger. All items on the *Book* side of the bank reconciliation require journal entries.

The bank reconciliation in Exhibit 4-8 requires AMEX Products to make journal entries to bring the Cash account up-to-date. The numbers in red correspond to the reconciling items listed in Exhibit 4-8, Panel A.

4.	Dec 31	Cash	900	
		Dividend Revenue		900
		Receipt of dividend revenue earned on investment.		
5.	31	Cash	2,100	
		Accounts Receivable		2,100
		Account receivable collected by bank.		
6.	31	Cash	30	
		Interest Revenue		30
		Interest earned on bank balance.		
7.	31	Cash	360	
		Accounts Payable		360
		Correction of check no. 333.		
8.	31	Miscellaneous Expense[1]	20	
		Cash		20
		Bank service charge.		
9.	31	Accounts Receivable	50	
		Cash		50
		NSF check returned by bank.		
10.	31	Insurance Expense	400	
		Cash		400
		Payment of monthly insurance.		

[1]Miscellaneous Expense is debited for the bank service charge because the service charge pertains to no particular expense category.

The entry for the NSF check (entry 9) needs explanation. Upon learning that a customer's $50 check to us was not good, we must credit Cash to update the Cash account. Unfortunately, we still have a receivable from the customer, so we must debit Accounts Receivable to reinstate our receivable.

Online Banking

Online banking allows you to pay bills and view your account electronically. You don't have to wait until the end of the month to get a bank statement. With online banking you can reconcile transactions at any time and keep your account current whenever you wish. Exhibit 4-9 shows a page from the account history of Toni Anderson's bank account.

EXHIBIT 4-9 | **Online Banking—Account History (like a Bank Statement)**

Account History for Toni Anderson Checking # 5401-632-9 as of Close of Business 07/27/2010

Account Details

Current Balance $4,136.08

Date ↓	Description	Withdrawals	Deposits	Balance
	Current Balance			**$4,136.08**
07/27/10	DEPOSIT		1,170.35	
07/26/10	28 DAYS INTEREST		2.26	
07/25/10	Check #6131 View Image	443.83		
07/24/10	Check #6130 View Image	401.52		
07/23/10	EFT PYMT CINGULAR	61.15		
07/22/10	EFT PYMT CITICARD PAYMENT	3,172.85		
07/20/10	Check #6127 View Image	550.00		
07/19/10	Check #6122 View Image	50.00		
07/16/10	Check #6116 View Image	2,056.75		
07/15/10	Check #6123 View Image	830.00		
07/13/10	Check #6124 View Image	150.00		
07/11/10	ATM 4900 SANGER AVE	200.00		
07/09/10	Check #6119 View Image	30.00		
07/05/10	Check #6125 View Image	2,500.00		
07/04/10	ATM 4900 SANGER AVE	100.00		
07/01/10	DEPOSIT		9,026.37	

FDIC Each depositor insured to $100,000.00 FEDERAL DEPOSIT INSURANCE CORPORATION   EQUAL HOUSING LENDER   E-Mail

The account history—like a bank statement—lists deposits, checks, EFT payments, ATM withdrawals, and interest earned on your bank balance.

But the account history doesn't show your beginning balance, so you can't work from your beginning balance to your ending balance.

STOP & THINK...

The bank statement balance is $4,500 and shows a service charge of $15, interest earned of $5, and an NSF check for $300. Deposits in transit total $1,200; outstanding checks are $575. The bookkeeper recorded as $152 a check of $125 in payment of an account payable. This created a book error of $27 (positive amount to correct the error).

1. What is the adjusted bank balance?
2. What was the book balance of cash before the reconciliation?

Answers:

1. $5,125 ($4,500 + $1,200 − $575).
2. $5,408 ($5,125 + $15 − $5 + $300 − $27). The adjusted book and bank balances are the same. The answer can be determined by working backward from the adjusted balance.

Using the Bank Reconciliation to Control Cash.   The bank reconciliation can be a powerful control device. Randy Vaughn is a CPA in Houston, Texas. He owns several apartment complexes that are managed by his aunt. His aunt signs up tenants, collects the monthly rents, arranges maintenance work, hires and fires employees, writes the checks, and performs the bank reconciliation. In short, she does it all. This concentration of duties in one person is evidence of weak internal control. Vaughn's aunt could be stealing from him, and as a CPA he is aware of this possibility.

Vaughn trusts his aunt because she is a member of the family. Nevertheless, Vaughn exercises some controls over his aunt's management of his apartments. Vaughn periodically drops by the apartments to see whether the maintenance staff is keeping the property in good condition. To control cash, Vaughn occasionally examines the bank reconciliation that his aunt has performed. Vaughn would know immediately if his aunt were writing checks to herself. By examining the copy of each check, Vaughn establishes control over cash payments.

Vaughn has a simple method for controlling cash receipts. He knows the occupancy level of his apartments. He also knows the monthly rent he charges. Vaughn multiplies the number of apartments—say 20—by the monthly rent (which averages $500 per unit) to arrive at expected monthly rent revenue of $10,000. By tracing the $10,000 revenue to the bank statement, Vaughn can tell if all his rent money went into his bank account. To keep his aunt on her toes, Vaughn lets her know that he periodically audits her work.

Control activities such as these are critical. If there are only a few employees, separation of duties may not be feasible. The manager must control operations, or the assets will slip away.

MID-CHAPTER SUMMARY PROBLEM

The cash account of Baylor Associates at February 28, 2011, follows.

Cash			
Feb 1	Bal 3,995	Feb 3	400
6	800	12	3,100
15	1,800	19	1,100
23	1,100	25	500
28	2,400	27	900
Feb 28	Bal 4,095		

Baylor Associates received the bank statement on February 28, 2011 (negative amounts are in parentheses):

Bank Statement for February 2011			
Beginning balance			$3,995
Deposits:			
Feb 7		$ 800	
15		1,800	
24		1,100	3,700
Checks (total per day):			
Feb 8		$ 400	
16		3,100	
23		1,100	(4,600)
Other items:			
Service charge			(10)
NSF check from M. E. Crown			(700)
Bank collection of note receivable for the company			1,000
EFT—monthly rent expense			(330)
Interest revenue earned on account balance			15
Ending balance			$3,070

Additional data:
Baylor deposits all cash receipts in the bank and makes all payments by check.

❚ Requirements

1. Prepare the bank reconciliation of Baylor Associates at February 28, 2011.
2. Journalize the entries based on the bank reconciliation.

Answers

Requirement 1

Baylor Associates
Bank Reconciliation
February 28, 2011

Bank:		
Balance, February 28, 2011		$3,070
Add: Deposit of February 28 in transit		2,400
		5,470
Less: Outstanding checks issued on Feb 25 ($500)		
and Feb 27 ($900)		(1,400)
Adjusted bank balance, February 28, 2011		$4,070 ◄
Books:		
Balance, February 28, 2011		$4,095
Add: Bank collection of note receivable		1,000
Interest revenue earned on bank balance		15
		5,110
Less: Service charge	$ 10	
NSF check	700	
EFT—Rent expense	330	(1,040)
Adjusted book balance, February 28, 2011		$4,070 ◄

Requirement 2

Feb 28	Cash	1,000	
	Note Receivable		1,000
	Note receivable collected by bank.		
28	Cash	15	
	Interest Revenue		15
	Interest earned on bank balance.		
28	Miscellaneous Expense	10	
	Cash		10
	Bank service charge.		
28	Accounts Receivable	700	
	Cash		700
	NSF check returned by bank.		
28	Rent Expense	330	
	Cash		330
	Monthly rent expense.		

INTERNAL CONTROL OVER CASH RECEIPTS

OBJECTIVE

4 **Apply** internal controls to cash receipts and cash payments

Cash requires some specific internal controls because cash is relatively easy to steal and it's easy to convert to other forms of wealth. Moreover, all transactions ultimately affect cash. That's why cash is called the "eye of the needle." Let's see how to control cash receipts.

All cash receipts should be deposited for safekeeping in the bank—quickly. Companies receive cash over the counter and through the mail. Each source of cash has its own security measures.

Cash Receipts over the Counter

Exhibit 4-10 illustrates the purchase of products in a grocery store. The point-of-sale terminal provides control over the cash receipts, while also recording the sale and relieving inventory for the appropriate cost of the goods sold. Consider a **Whole Foods Market** store. For each transaction, the Whole Foods sales associate issues a receipt to the customer as proof of purchase. The cash drawer opens when the sales associate enters a transaction, and the machine electronically transmits a record of the sale to the store's main computer. At the end of each shift, the sales associate delivers his or her cash drawer to the office, where it is combined with cash from all other terminals and delivered by armored car to the bank for deposit, as explained in the next section. Later, a separate employee in the accounting department reconciles the electronic record of the sales per terminal to the record of the cash turned in. These measures, coupled with oversight by a manager, discourage theft.

EXHIBIT 4-10 | **Cash Receipts over the Counter**

Point-of-sale terminals also provide effective control over inventory. For example, in a restaurant, these devices track sales by menu item and total sales by cash, type of credit card, gift card redeemed, etc. They create the daily sales journal for that store, which, in turn, interfaces with the general ledger. Managers can use records produced by point-of-sale terminals to check inventory levels and compare them against sales records for accuracy. For example, in a restaurant, an effective way to monitor sales of expensive wine is for a manager to perform a quick count of the bottles on hand at the end of the day and compare it with the count at the end of the previous day, plus the record of any purchased. The count at the end of the previous day, plus the record of bottles purchased, minus the count at the end of the current day should equal the amount sold as recorded by the point-of-sale terminals in the restaurant.

An effective control for many chain retail businesses, such as restaurants, grocery stores, or clothing stores, to prevent unauthorized access to cash as well as to allow for more efficient management of cash, is the use of "depository bank accounts." Cash receipts for an individual store are deposited into a local bank account (preferably delivered by armored car for security reasons) on a daily basis. The corporate headquarters arranges for its centralized bank to draft the local depository accounts on a frequent (perhaps daily) basis to get the money concentrated into the company's centralized account, where it can be used to pay the corporation's bills. Depository accounts are "one-way" accounts where the local management may only make deposits. They have no authority to write checks on the account or take money out of the store's account.

Cash Receipts by Mail

Many companies receive cash by mail. Exhibit 4-11 shows how companies control cash received by mail. All incoming mail is opened by a mailroom employee. The mailroom then sends all customer checks to the treasurer, who has the cashier deposit the money in the bank. The remittance advices go to the accounting department for journal entries to Cash and customer accounts receivable. As a final step, the controller compares the following records for the day:

- Bank deposit amount from the treasurer
- Debit to Cash from the accounting department

The debit to Cash should equal the amount deposited in the bank. All cash receipts are safe in the bank, and the company books are up-to-date.

EXHIBIT 4-11 | **Cash Receipts by Mail**

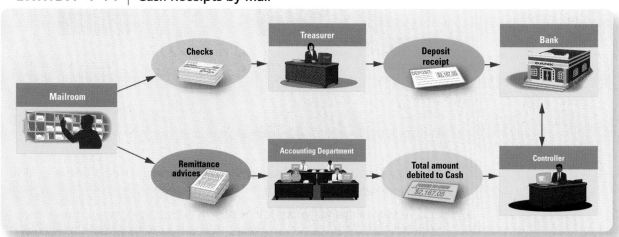

To prevent unauthorized access to cash, many companies use a bank lock-box system, rather than risk processing checks through the mailroom. Customers send their checks by return mail directly to a post office box controlled by the company's bank. The bank sends a detailed record of cash received, by customer, to the company for use in posting collections to accounts receivable. Internal control is tight because company personnel never touch incoming cash. The lock-box system also gets the cash to the bank in a more timely manner, allowing the company to put the cash to work faster than would be possible if it were processed by the company's mailroom.

INTERNAL CONTROL OVER CASH PAYMENTS

Companies make most payments by check. Let's see how to control cash payments by check.

Controls over Payment by Check

As we have seen, you need a good separation of duties between (a) operations and (b) writing checks for cash payments. Payment by check is an important internal control, as follows:

- The check provides a record of the payment.
- The check must be signed by an authorized official.
- Before signing the check, the official should study the evidence supporting the payment.

Controls over Purchase and Payment. To illustrate the internal control over cash payments by check, suppose AMEX Products buys some of its inventory from Hanes Textiles. The purchasing and payment process follows these steps, as shown in Exhibit 4-12. Start with the box for AMEX Products on the left side.

EXHIBIT 4-12 | Cash Payments by Check

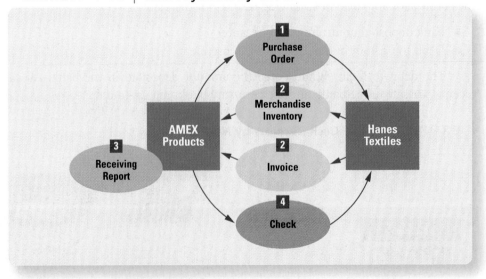

1 AMEX faxes or e-mails an electronic *purchase order* to Hanes Textiles. AMEX says, "Please send us 100 T-shirts."

2 Hanes Textiles ships the goods and sends an electronic or paper *invoice* back to AMEX. Hanes sent the goods.

3 AMEX receives the *inventory* and prepares a *receiving report* to list the goods received. AMEX got its T-shirts.

4 After approving all documents, AMEX sends a *check* to Hanes, or authorizes an electronic funds transfer (EFT) directly from its bank to Hanes' bank. By this action, AMEX says, "Okay, we'll pay you."

For good internal control, the purchasing agent should neither receive the goods nor approve the payment. If these duties aren't separated, a purchasing agent can buy goods and have them shipped to his or her home. Or a purchasing agent can spend too much on purchases, approve the payment, and split the excess with the supplier. To avoid these problems, companies split the following duties among different employees:

- Purchasing goods
- Receiving goods
- Approving and paying for goods

Exhibit 4-13 shows AMEX's payment packet of documents. Before signing the check or approving the EFT, the treasurer's department should examine the packet to prove that all the documents agree. Only then does the company know that

1. it received the goods ordered.

2. it is paying only for the goods received.

EXHIBIT 4-13 | **Payment Packet**

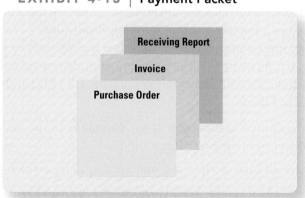

After payment, the person in the treasurer's department who has authorized the disbursement stamps the payment packet "paid" or punches a hole through it to prevent it from being submitted a second time. Dishonest people have tried to run a bill through twice for payment. The stamp or hole shows that the bill has been paid. If checks are used, they should then be mailed directly to the payee without being allowed to return to the department that prepared them. To do so would violate separation of the duties of cash handling and record keeping, as well as unauthorized access to cash.

Petty Cash. It would be wasteful to write separate checks for an executive's taxi fare, name tags needed right away, or delivery of a package across town. Therefore, companies keep a **petty cash** fund on hand to pay such minor amounts. The word "petty" means small. That's what petty cash is—a small cash fund kept by a single employee for the purpose of making such on-the-spot minor purchases.

The petty cash fund is opened with a particular amount of cash. A check for that amount is then issued to the custodian of the petty cash fund, who is solely responsible for accounting for it. Assume that on February 28 **Cisco Systems**, the worldwide leader in networks for the Internet, establishes a petty cash fund of $500 in a sales department by writing a check to the designated custodian. The custodian of the petty cash fund cashes the check and places $500 in the fund, which may be a cash box or other device.

For each petty cash payment, the custodian prepares a petty cash voucher to list the item purchased. The sum of the cash in the petty cash fund plus the total of the paid vouchers in the cash box should equal the opening balance at all times—in this case, $500. The Petty Cash account keeps its $500 balance at all times. Maintaining the Petty Cash account at this balance, supported by the fund (cash plus vouchers), is how an **imprest system** works. The control feature is that it clearly identifies the amount for which the custodian is responsible.

Using a Budget to Manage Cash

OBJECTIVE

5 **Use** a budget to manage cash

As mentioned earlier in the chapter, a budget is a financial plan that helps coordinate business activities. Managers control operations with an operating budget. They also control cash receipts and cash payments, as well as ending cash balances, through use of a cash budget.

How, for example, does AMEX Products decide when to invest in new inventory-tracking technology? How will AMEX decide how much to spend? Will borrowing be needed, or can AMEX finance the purchase with internally generated cash? What do ending cash balances need to be in order to provide a "safety margin" so the company won't unexpectedly run out of cash? A cash budget for a business works on roughly the same concept as a personal budget. By what process do you decide how much to spend on your education? On an automobile? On a house? All these decisions depend to some degree on the information that a cash budget provides.

A *cash budget helps a company or an individual manage cash by planning receipts and payments during a future period.* The company must determine how much cash it will need and then decide whether or not operations will bring in the needed cash. Managers proceed as follows:

1. Start with the entity's cash balance at the beginning of the period. This is the amount left over from the preceding period.

2. Add the budgeted cash receipts and subtract the budgeted cash payments.

3. The beginning balance plus receipts and minus payments equals the expected cash balance at the end of the period.

4. Compare the cash available before new financing to the budgeted cash balance at the end of the period. Managers know the minimum amount of cash they need (the budgeted balance). If the budget shows excess cash, managers can invest the excess. But if the cash available falls below the budgeted balance, the company will need additional financing. The company may need to borrow the shortfall amount. The budget is a valuable tool for helping the company plan for the future.

The budget period can span any length of time—a day, a week, a month, or a year. Exhibit 4-14 shows a cash budget for AMEX Products, Inc., for the year ended December 31, 2011. Study it carefully, because at some point you will use a cash budget.

AMEX Products' cash budget in Exhibit 4-14 begins with $6,260 of cash at the end of the previous year (line 1). Then add budgeted cash receipts and subtract budgeted payments for the current year. In this case, AMEX expects to have $3,900 of cash available at year-end (line 10). AMEX managers need to maintain a cash balance of at least $5,000 (line 11). Line 12 shows that AMEX must arrange $1,100 of financing in order to achieve its goals for 2011.

EXHIBIT 4-14 | Cash Budget

AMEX Products, Inc.
Cash Budget
For the Year Ended December 31, 2011

(1)	Cash balance, December 31, 2010....................................		$ 6,260
	Budgeted cash receipts:		
(2)	Collections from customers		55,990
(3)	Dividends on investments		1,200
(4)	Sale of store fixtures		5,700
			69,150
	Budgeted cash payments:		
(5)	Purchases of inventory...	$33,720	
(6)	Operating expenses...	11,530	
(7)	Expansion of store...	12,000	
(8)	Payment of long-term debt	5,000	
(9)	Payment of dividends..	3,000	65,250
(10)	Cash available (needed) before new financing...............		$ 3,900
(11)	Budgeted cash balance, December 31, 2011..................		(5,000)
(12)	Cash available for additional investments, or		
	(New financing needed)		$ (1,100)

Reporting Cash on the Balance Sheet

Most companies have numerous bank accounts, but they usually combine all cash amounts into a single total called "Cash and Cash Equivalents." **Cash equivalents** include liquid assets such as time deposits, certificates of deposit, and high-grade government securities. These are interest-bearing accounts that can be withdrawn with no penalty, or interest-bearing securities. Slightly less liquid than cash, cash equivalents are sufficiently similar to be reported along with cash. The balance sheet of AMEX Products reported the following:

AMEX Products, Inc.
Balance Sheet (Excerpts, adapted)
For the Year Ended December 31, 2010

Assets	
Cash and cash equivalents................	$ 6,260
Cash pledged as collateral	2,000

Compensating Balance Agreements

The Cash account on the balance sheet reports the liquid assets available for day-to-day use. None of the Cash balance is restricted in any way.

Any restricted amount of cash should *not* be reported as Cash on the balance sheet. For example, on the AMEX Products balance sheet, *cash pledged as collateral* is reported separately because that cash is not available for day-to-day use. Instead, AMEX has pledged the cash as security (collateral) for a loan. If AMEX fails to pay the loan, the lender can take the pledged cash. For this reason, the pledged cash is less liquid.

Also, banks often lend money under a compensating balance agreement. The borrower agrees to maintain a minimum balance in a checking account at all times. This minimum balance becomes a long-term asset and is therefore not cash in the normal sense.

Suppose AMEX Products borrowed $10,000 at 8% from First Interstate Bank and agreed to keep 20% ($2,000) on deposit at all times. The net result of the compensating balance agreement is that AMEX actually borrowed only $8,000. And by paying 8% interest on the full $10,000, AMEX's actual interest rate is really 10%, as shown here:

$$\$10,000 \times .08 = \$800 \text{ interest}$$
$$\$800/\$8,000 = .10 \text{ interest rate}$$

END-OF-CHAPTER SUMMARY PROBLEM

Assume the following situation for PepsiCo, Inc.: PepsiCo ended 2010 with cash of $200 million. At December 31, 2010, Bob Detmer, the CFO of PepsiCo, is preparing the budget for 2011.

During 2011, Detmer expects PepsiCo to collect $26,400 million from customers and $80 million from interest earned on investments. PepsiCo expects to pay $12,500 million for its inventories and $5,400 million for operating expenses. To remain competitive, PepsiCo plans to spend $2,200 million to upgrade production facilities and an additional $350 million to acquire other companies. PepsiCo also plans to sell older assets for approximately $300 million and to collect $220 million of this amount in cash. PepsiCo is budgeting dividend payments of $550 million during the year. Finally, the company is scheduled to pay off $1,200 million of long-term debt plus the $6,600 million of current liabilities left over from 2010.

Because of the growth planned for 2011, Detmer budgets the need for a minimum cash balance of $300 million.

❙ Requirement

1. How much must PepsiCo borrow during 2011 to keep its cash balance from falling below $300 million? Prepare the 2011 cash budget to answer this important question.

Answer

PepsiCo, Inc.
Cash Budget
For the Year Ended December 31, 2011

(In millions)		
Cash balance, December 31, 2010		$ 200
Estimated cash receipts:		
Collections from customers		26,400
Receipt of interest		80
Sales of assets		220
		26,900
Estimated cash payments:		
Purchases of inventory	$12,500	
Payment of operating expenses	5,400	
Upgrading of production facilities	2,200	
Acquisition of other companies	350	
Payment of dividends	550	
Payment of long-term debt and other		
liabilities ($1,200 + $6,600)	7,800	(28,800)
Cash available (needed) before new financing		$ (1,900)
Budgeted cash balance, December 31, 2011		(300)
Cash available for additional investments, or		
(New financing needed)		$ (2,200)

PepsiCo. must borrow $2,200 million.

REVIEW INTERNAL CONTROL AND CASH

Quick Check (Answers are given on page 287.)

1. Internal control has its own terminology. On the left are some key internal control concepts. On the right are some key terms. Match each internal control concept with its term by writing the appropriate letter in the space provided. Not all letters are used.

___ This procedure limits access to sensitive data.	**a.** Competent personnel
___ This type of insurance policy covers losses due to employee theft.	**b.** Encryption
	c. Separation of duties
___ Trusting your employees can lead you to overlook this procedure.	**d.** Safeguarding assets
	e. Fidelity bond
___ The most basic purpose of internal control.	**f.** Collusion
___ Internal control cannot always safeguard against this problem.	**g.** Firewalls
	h. Supervision
___ Often mentioned as the cornerstone of a good system of internal control.	**i.** External audits
___ Pay employees enough to require them to do a good job.	

2. Each of the following is an example of a control procedure, *except*
   a. sound personnel procedures.
   b. a sound marketing plan.
   c. separation of duties.
   d. limited access to assets.

3. Which of the following is an example of poor internal control?
   a. Employees must take vacations.
   b. Rotate employees through various jobs.
   c. The accounting department compares goods received with the related purchase order.
   d. The mailroom clerk records daily cash receipts in the journal.

Lowell Corporation has asked you to prepare its bank reconciliation at the end of the current month. Answer questions 4–8 using the following code letters to indicate how the item described would be reported on the bank reconciliation.
   a. Deduct from the book balance
   b. Does not belong on the bank reconciliation
   c. Add to the bank balance
   d. Deduct from the bank balance
   e. Add to the book balance

4. A check for $835 written by Lowell during the current month was erroneously recorded as a $358 payment.

5. A $400 deposit made on the last day of the current month did not appear on this month's bank statement.

6. The bank statement showed interest earned of $65.

7. The bank statement included a check from a customer that was marked NSF.

8. The bank statement showed the bank had credited Lowell's account for an $800 deposit made by Lawrence Company.

9. Which of the following reconciling items does not require a journal entry?
   a. Bank service charge   c. NSF check
   b. Bank collection of note receivable   d. Deposit in transit

10. A check was written for $754 to purchase supplies. The check was recorded in the journal as $745. The entry to correct this error would
    a. increase Supplies, $9.   c. decrease Cash, $9.
    b. decrease Supplies, $9.   d. both a. and c.

11. A cash budget helps control cash by
    a. helping to determine whether additional cash is available for investments or new financing is needed.
    b. developing a plan for increasing sales.
    c. ensuring accurate cash records.
    d. all of the above.

Accounting Vocabulary

audit (p. 240) A periodic examination of a company's financial statements and the accounting systems, controls, and records that produce them. Audits may be either external or internal. External audits are usually performed by certified public accountants (CPAs).

bank collections (p. 249) Collection of money by the bank on behalf of a depositor.

bank reconciliation (p. 248) A document explaining the reasons for the difference between a depositor's records and the bank's records about the depositor's cash.

bank statement (p. 246) Document showing the beginning and ending balances of a particular bank account listing the month's transactions that affected the account.

budget (p. 240) A quantitative expression of a plan that helps managers coordinate the entity's activities.

cash budget (p. 240) A budget that projects the entity's future cash receipts and cash disbursements.

cash equivalent (p. 261) Investments such as time deposits, certificates of deposit, or high-grade government securities that are considered so similar to cash that they are combined with cash for financial disclosure purposes on the balance sheet.

check (p. 246) Document instructing a bank to pay the designated person or business the specified amount of money.

computer virus (p. 243) A malicious program that enters a company's computer system by e-mail or other means and destroys program and data files.

controller (p. 240) The chief accounting officer of a business.

deposits in transit (p. 249) A deposit recorded by the company but not yet by its bank.

electronic fund transfer (EFT) (p. 247) System that transfers cash by electronic communication rather than by paper documents.

encryption (p. 244) Mathematical rearranging of data within an electronic file to prevent unauthorized access to information.

exception reporting (p. 240) Identifying data that is not within "normal limits" so that managers can follow up and take corrective action. Exception reporting is used in operating and cash budgets to keep company profits and cash flow in line with management's plans.

fidelity bond (p. 243) An insurance policy taken out on employees who handle cash.

firewall (p. 244) An electronic barrier, usually provided by passwords, around computerized data files to protect local area networks of computers from unauthorized access.

fraud (p. 233) An intentional misrepresentation of facts, made for the purpose of persuading another party to act in a way that causes injury or damage to that party.

fraud triangle (p. 235) The three elements that are present in almost all cases of fraud. These elements are motive, opportunity, and rationalization on the part of the perpetrator.

fraudulent financial reporting (p. 234) Fraud perpetrated by management by preparing misleading financial statements.

imprest system (p. 260) A way to account for petty cash by maintaining a constant balance in the petty cash account, supported by the fund (cash plus payment tickets) totaling the same amount.

internal control (p. 236) Organizational plan and related measures adopted by an entity to safeguard assets, encourage adherence to company policies, promote operational efficiency, and ensure accurate and reliable accounting records.

lapping (p. 232) A fraudulent scheme to steal cash through misappropriating certain customer payments and posting payments from other customers to the affected accounts to cover it up. Lapping is caused by weak internal controls (i.e., not segregating the duties of cash handling and accounts receivable bookkeeping, allowing the bookkeeper improper access to cash, and not appropriately monitoring the activities of those who handle cash).

lock-box system (p. 232) A system of handling cash receipts by mail whereby customers remit payment directly to the bank, rather than through the entity's mail system.

misappropriation of assets (p. 234) Fraud committed by employees by stealing assets from the company.

nonsufficient funds (NSF) check (p. 249) A "hot" check, one for which the payer's bank account has insufficient money to pay the check. NSF checks are cash receipts that turn out to be worthless.

operating budget (p. 240) A budget of future net income. The operating budget projects a company's future revenue and expenses. It is usually prepared by line item of the company's income statement.

outstanding checks (p. 249) A check issued by the company and recorded on its books but not yet paid by its bank.

password (p. 242) A special set of characters that must be provided by the user of computerized program or data files to prevent unauthorized access to those files.

petty cash (p. 259) Fund containing a small amount of cash that is used to pay minor amounts.

phishing (p. 244) Creating bogus Web sites for the purpose of stealing unauthorized data, such as names, addresses, social security numbers, bank account, and credit card numbers.

remittance advice (p. 246) An optional attachment to a check (sometimes a perforated tear-off document and sometimes capable of being electronically scanned) that indicates the payer, date, and purpose of the cash payment. The remittance advice is often used as the source documents for posting cash receipts or payments.

treasurer (p. 239) In a large company, the department that has total responsibility for cash handling and cash management. This includes cash budgeting, cash collections, writing checks, investing excess funds, and making proposals for raising additional cash when needed.

Trojan Horse (p. 243) A malicious program that hides within legitimate programs and acts like a computer virus.

ASSESS YOUR PROGRESS

Short Exercises

S4-1 (*Learning Objective 1: Defining fraud*) Define "fraud." List and briefly discuss the three major components of the "fraud triangle."

S4-2 (*Learning Objective 2: Listing components of internal control*) List the components of internal control. Briefly describe each component.

writing assignment ■

S4-3 (*Learning Objective 2: Explaining and describing characteristics of an effective system of internal control*) Explain why separation of duties is often described as the cornerstone of internal control for safeguarding assets. Describe what can happen if the same person has custody of an asset and also accounts for the asset.

S4-4 (*Learning Objective 2: Identifying internal control characteristics*) Identify the other control procedures usually found in a company's system of internal control besides separation of duties, and tell why each is important.

S4-5 (*Learning Objective 2: Explaining e-commerce internal control pitfalls*) How do computer viruses, Trojan Horses, and phishing expeditions work? How can these e-commerce pitfalls hurt you? Be specific.

S4-6 (*Learning Objective 2: Explaining the role of internal control*) Cash may be a small item on the financial statements. Nevertheless, internal control over cash is very important. Why is this true?

S4-7 (*Learning Objectives 2, 4: Explaining the role of internal control; identifying controls over cash payments*) Crow Company requires that all documents supporting a check be cancelled by punching a hole through the packet. Why is this practice required? What might happen if it were not?

S4-8 (*Learning Objective 3: Preparing a bank reconciliation*) The Cash account of Randell Corp. reported a balance of $2,400 at October 31. Included were outstanding checks totaling $500 and an October 31 deposit of $200 that did not appear on the bank statement. The bank statement, which came from Park Bank, listed an October 31 balance of $3,180. Included in the bank balance was an October 30 collection of $530 on account from a customer who pays the bank directly. The bank statement also shows a $20 service charge, $10 of interest revenue that Randell earned on its bank balance, and an NSF check for $40.

Prepare a bank reconciliation to determine how much cash Randell actually has at October 31.

S4-9 *(Learning Objective 3: Recording transactions from a bank reconciliation)* After preparing Randell Corp.'s bank reconciliation in Short Exercise 4-8, make the company's journal entries for transactions that arise from the bank reconciliation. Date each transaction October 31, and include an explanation with each entry.

S4-10 *(Learning Objective 3: Using a bank reconciliation as a control device)* Barbara Smith manages Jones Advertising. Smith fears that a trusted employee has been stealing from the company. This employee receives cash from clients and also prepares the monthly bank reconciliation. To check up on the employee, Smith prepares her own bank reconciliation, as follows:

writing assignment ■

Jones Advertising				
Bank Reconciliation				
October 31, 2010				
Bank		**Books**		
Balance, October 31.....................	$4,400	Balance, October 31....................	$3,920	
Add:		Add:		
Deposits in transit	500	Bank collections	900	
		Interest revenue	20	
Less:		Less:		
Outstanding checks	(900)	Service charge..........................	(40)	
Adjusted bank balance	$4,000	Adjusted book balance..............	$4,800	

Does it appear that the employee has stolen from the company? If so, how much? Explain your answer. Which side of the bank reconciliation shows the company's true cash balance?

S4-11 *(Learning Objective 4: Applying internal controls over cash receipts)* Greta Cassidy sells memberships to the Phoenix Symphony Association in Phoenix, Arizona. The Symphony's procedure requires Cassidy to write a patron receipt for all memberships sold. The receipt forms are prenumbered. Cassidy is having personal financial problems and she stole $400 received from a customer. To hide her theft, Cassidy destroyed the company copy of the receipt that she gave the patron. What will alert manager Stephanie Stevens that something is wrong?

S4-12 *(Learning Objective 4: Applying internal control over cash payments by check)* Answer the following questions about internal control over cash payments:

1. Payment by check carries three controls over cash. What are they?
2. Suppose a purchasing agent receives the goods that he purchases and also approves payment for the goods. How could a dishonest purchasing agent cheat his company? How do companies avoid this internal control weakness?

S4-13 *(Learning Objective 5: Using a cash budget)* Briefly explain how a cash budget works and what it accomplishes with its last few lines of data.

writing assignment ■

S4-14 *(Learning Objective 5: Preparing a cash budget)* Crescent Artichoke Growers (CAG) is a major food cooperative. Suppose CAG begins 2010 with cash of $11 million. CAG estimates cash receipts during 2010 will total $104 million. Planned payments will total $93 million. To meet daily cash needs next year, CAG must maintain a cash balance of at least $17 million. Prepare the organization's cash budget for 2010.

writing assignment ■

S4-15 (*Learning Objectives 1, 5: Learning about fraud; making an ethical judgment related to internal controls*) Gretchen Rourke, an accountant for Dublin Limited, discovers that her supervisor, Billy Dunn, made several errors last year. In total, the errors overstated the company's net income by 25%. It is not clear whether the errors were deliberate or accidental. What should Rourke do?

Exercises

MyAccountingLab

> All of the Group A and Group B exercises can be found within MyAccountingLab, an online homework and practice environment. Your instructor may ask you to complete these exercises using MyAccountingLab.

(Group A)

writing assignment ■

E4-16A (*Learning Objectives 1, 2: Learning about fraud; identifying internal control weaknesses*) Identify the internal control weakness in the following situations. State how the person can hurt the company.

a. James Mason works as a security guard at SAFETY parking in Detroit. Mason has a master key to the cash box where customers pay for parking. Each night Mason prepares the cash report that shows (a) the number of cars that parked on the lot and (b) the day's cash receipts. Louise Carrington, the SAFETY treasurer, checks Mason's figures by multiplying the number of cars by the parking fee per car. Carrington then deposits the cash in the bank.

b. Elizabeth Fleming is the purchasing agent for Marshfield Golf Equipment. Fleming prepares purchase orders based on requests from division managers of the company. Fleming faxes the purchase order to suppliers who then ship the goods to Marshfield. Fleming receives each incoming shipment and checks it for agreement with the purchase order and the related invoice. She then routes the goods to the respective division managers and sends the receiving report and the invoice to the accounting department for payment.

E4-17A (*Learning Objective 2: Identifying internal control strengths and weaknesses*) The following situations describe two cash payment situations and two cash receipt situations. In each pair, one set of internal controls is better than the other. Evaluate the internal controls in each situation as strong or weak, and give the reason for your answer.

Cash payments:

a. Tim McDermott Construction policy calls for construction supervisors to request the equipment needed for their jobs. The home office then purchases the equipment and has it shipped to the construction site.

b. Gravel & Sand, Inc., policy calls for project supervisors to purchase the equipment needed for jobs. The supervisors then submit the paid receipts to the home office for reimbursement. This policy enables supervisors to get the equipment quickly and keep construction jobs moving.

Cash receipts:

a. At Carlisle Auto Parts, cash received by mail goes straight to the accountant, who debits Cash and credits Accounts Receivable to record the collections from customers. The Carlisle accountant then deposits the cash in the bank.

b. Cash received by mail at Sole Orthopedic Clinic goes to the mail room, where a mail clerk opens envelopes and totals the cash receipts for the day. The mail clerk forwards customer checks to the cashier for deposit in the bank and forwards the remittance advices to the accounting department for posting credits to customer accounts.

writing assignment ■

E4-18A (*Learning Objectives 1, 2: Learning about fraud; correcting an internal control weakness*) Bobby Flynn served as executive director of Downtown Kalamazoo, an organization created to revitalize Kalamazoo, Michigan. Over the course of 13 years Flynn embezzled

$333,000. How did Flynn do it? By depositing subscriber cash receipts in his own bank account, writing Downtown Kalamazoo checks to himself, and creating phony entities that Downtown Kalamazoo wrote checks to.

Downtown Kalamazoo was led by a board of directors comprised of civic leaders. Flynn's embezzlement went undetected until Downtown Kalamazoo couldn't pay its bills.

Give four ways Flynn's embezzlement could have been prevented.

E4-19A (*Learning Objective 3: Classifying bank reconciliation items*) The following items appear on a bank reconciliation:

1. ___ Outstanding checks
2. ___ Bank error: The bank credited our account for a deposit made by another bank customer.
3. ___ Service charge
4. ___ Deposits in transit
5. ___ NSF check
6. ___ Bank collection of a note receivable on our behalf
7. ___ Book error: We debited Cash for $200. The correct debit was $2,000.

Classify each item as (a) an addition to the bank balance, (b) a subtraction from the bank balance, (c) an addition to the book balance, or (d) a subtraction from the book balance.

E4-20A (*Learning Objective 3: Preparing a bank reconciliation*) D. J. Hunter's checkbook lists the following:

Date	Check No.	Item	Check	Deposit	Balance
6/1					$ 525
4	622	Art Cafe	$ 30		495
9		Dividends received		$ 110	605
13	623	General Tire Co.	35		570
14	624	QuickMobil	68		502
18	625	Cash	55		447
26	626	Woodway Baptist Church	85		362
28	627	Bent Tree Apartments	285		77
30		Paycheck		1,210	1,287

The June bank statement shows

Balance				$525
Add: Deposits				110
Debit checks:	No.	Amount		
	622	$30		
	623	35		
	624	86*		
	625	55	(206)	
Other charges:				
NSF check......................................		$20		
Service charge		10	(30)	
Balance				$399

*This is the correct amount for check number 624.

❙ Requirement

1. Prepare Hunter's bank reconciliation at June 30.

E4-21A (*Learning Objective 3: Preparing a bank reconciliation*) Evan Root operates a bowling alley. He has just received the monthly bank statement at April 30 from City National Bank, and the statement shows an ending balance of $565. Listed on the statement are an EFT rent collection of $320, a service charge of $7, two NSF checks totaling $115, and an $11 charge for printed checks. In reviewing his cash records, Root identifies outstanding checks totaling $602 and an April 30 deposit in transit of $1,790. During April, he recorded a $290 check for the salary of a part-time employee as $29. Root's Cash account shows an April 30 cash balance of $1,827. How much cash does Root actually have at April 30?

E4-22A (*Learning Objective 3: Making journal entries from a bank reconciliation*) Use the data from Exercise 4-21 to make the journal entries that Root should record on April 30 to update his Cash account. Include an explanation for each entry.

writing assignment ■

E4-23A (*Learning Objective 4: Evaluating internal control over cash receipts*) McCall stores use point-of-sale terminals as cash registers. The register shows the amount of each sale, the cash received from the customer, and any change returned to the customer. The machine also produces a customer receipt but keeps no record of transactions. At the end of the day, the clerk counts the cash in the register and gives it to the cashier for deposit in the company bank account.

Write a memo to convince the store manager that there is an internal control weakness over cash receipts. Identify the weakness that gives an employee the best opportunity to steal cash and state how to prevent such a theft.

E4-24A (*Learning Objective 4: Evaluating internal control over cash payments*) Green Grass Golf Company manufactures a popular line of golf clubs. Green Grass Golf employs 188 workers and keeps their employment records on time sheets that show how many hours the employee works each week. On Friday the shop foreman collects the time sheets, checks them for accuracy, and delivers them to the payroll department for preparation of paychecks. The treasurer signs the paychecks and returns the checks to the payroll department for distribution to the employees.

Identify the main internal control weakness in this situation, state how the weakness can hurt Green Grass Golf, and propose a way to correct the weakness.

■ spreadsheet

E4-25A (*Learning Objective 5: Preparing a cash budget*) Cole Communications, Inc., is preparing its cash budget for 2011. Cole ended 2010 with cash of $86 million, and managers need to keep a cash balance of at least $82 million for operations.

Collections from customers are expected to total $11,305 million during 2011, and payments for the cost of services and products should reach $6,167 million. Operating expense payments are budgeted at $2,544 million.

During 2011, Cole expects to invest $1,826 million in new equipment and sell older assets for $118 million. Debt payments scheduled for 2011 will total $603 million. The company forecasts net income of $885 million for 2011 and plans to pay dividends of $347 million.

Prepare Cole Communications' cash budget for 2011. Will the budgeted level of cash receipts leave Cole with the desired ending cash balance of $82 million, or will the company need additional financing? If so, how much?

E4-26A (*Learning Objective 5: Compensating balance agreement*) Assume Lenny's Lanes borrowed $14 million from Greenback Bank and agreed to (a) pay an interest rate of 7.7% and (b) maintain a compensating balance amount equal to 5.7% of the loan. Determine Lenny's Lanes' actual effective interest rate on this loan.

(Group B)

E4-27B (*Learning Objectives 1, 2: Learning about fraud; identifying internal control weaknesses*) Identify the internal control weakness in the following situations. State how the person can hurt the company.

writing assignment ■

a. Jason Monroe works as a security guard at CITY parking in Dayton. Monroe has a master key to the cash box where customers pay for parking. Each night Monroe prepares the cash report that shows (a) the number of cars that parked on the lot and (b) the day's cash receipts. Linda Cooper, the CITY treasurer, checks Monroe's figures by multiplying the number of cars by the parking fee per car. Cooper then deposits the cash in the bank.

b. Ashley Adams is the purchasing agent for Superior Golf Equipment. Adams prepares purchase orders based on requests from division managers of the company. Adams faxes the purchase order to suppliers who then ship the goods to Superior. Adams receives each incoming shipment and checks it for agreement with the purchase order and the related invoice. She then routes the goods to the respective division managers and sends the receiving report and the invoice to the accounting department for payment.

E4-28B (*Learning Objective 2: Identifying internal control strengths and weaknesses*) The following situations describe two cash payment situations and two cash receipt situations. In each pair, one set of internal controls is better than the other. Evaluate the internal controls in each situation as strong or weak, and give the reason for your answer.

Cash payments:

a. Mike Milford Construction policy calls for construction supervisors to request the equipment needed for their jobs. The home office then purchases the equipment and has it shipped to the construction site.

b. Superior Structures, Inc., policy calls for project supervisors to purchase the equipment needed for jobs. The supervisors then submit the paid receipts to the home office for reimbursement. This policy enables supervisors to get the equipment quickly and keep construction jobs moving.

Cash receipts:

a. At Cramer Auto Parts, cash received by mail goes straight to the accountant, who debits Cash and credits Accounts Receivable to record the collections from customers. The Cramer accountant then deposits the cash in the bank.

b. Cash received by mail at Better Vision Eye Clinic goes to the mail room, where a mail clerk opens envelopes and totals the cash receipts for the day. The mail clerk forwards customer checks to the cashier for deposit in the bank and forwards the remittance slips to the accounting department for posting credits to customer accounts.

E4-29B (*Learning Objectives 1, 2: Learning about fraud; correcting an internal control weakness*) Sam Smith served as executive director of Downtown Scanlon, an organization created to revitalize Scanlon, Minnesota. Over the course of 11 years Smith embezzled $297,000. How did Smith do it? He did it by depositing subscriber cash receipts in his own bank account, writing Downtown Scanlon checks to himself, and creating phony entities that Downtown Scanlon wrote checks to.

writing assignment ■

Downtown Scanlon was led by a board of directors comprised of civic leaders. Smith's embezzlement went undetected until Downtown Scanlon couldn't pay its bills.

Give four ways Smith's embezzlement could have been prevented.

E4-30B (*Learning Objective 3: Classifying bank reconciliation items*) The following items appear on a bank reconciliation.

Classify each item as (a) an addition to the bank balance, (b) a subtraction from the bank balance, (c) an addition to the book balance, or (d) a subtraction from the book balance.

1. ___ Outstanding checks
2. ___ Bank error: The bank credited our account for a deposit made by another bank customer.
3. ___ Service charge
4. ___ Deposits in transit
5. ___ NSF check
6. ___ Bank collection of a note receivable on our behalf
7. ___ Book error: We debited Cash for $300. The correct debit was $3,000.

E4-31B (*Learning Objective 3: Preparing a bank reconciliation*) D. J. Hill's checkbook and February bank statement show the following:

Date	Check No.	Item	Check	Deposit	Balance
2/1					$ 515
4	622	Art Cafe	$ 15		500
9		Dividends received		$ 115	615
13	623	General Tire Co.	40		575
14	624	QuickMobil	78		497
18	625	Cash	70		427
26	626	Woodway Baptist Church	85		342
28	627	Bent Tree Apartments	275		67
28		Paycheck		1,215	1,282

Balance				$515	
Add: Deposits				115	
Debit checks:	No.	Amount			
	622	$15			
	623	40			
	624	87*			
	625	70		(212)	
Other charges:					
NSF check			$20		
Service charge			15	(35)	
Balance				$383	

*This is the correct amount for check number 624.

Requirement

1. Prepare Hill's bank reconciliation at February 28.

E4-32B (*Learning Objective 3: Preparing a bank reconciliation*) Harry Smith operates a bowling alley. He has just received the monthly bank statement at September 30 from City National Bank, and the statement shows an ending balance of $545. Listed on the statement are an EFT rent collection of $325, a service charge of $8, two NSF checks totaling $125, and a $10 charge for printed checks. In reviewing his cash records, Smith identifies outstanding checks totaling $609 and a September 30 deposit in transit of $1,790. During September, he recorded a $310 check for the salary of a part-time employee as $31. Smith's Cash account shows a September 30 cash balance of $1,823. How much cash does Smith actually have at September 30?

E4-33B (*Learning Objective 3: Making journal entries from a bank reconciliation*) Use the data from Exercise 4-32B to make the journal entries that Smith should record on September 30 to update his Cash account. Include an explanation for each entry.

writing assignment ■

E4-34B (*Learning Objective 4: Evaluating internal control over cash receipts*) Radley stores use point-of-sale terminals as cash registers. The register shows the amount of each sale, the cash received from the customer, and any change returned to the customer. The machine also produces a customer receipt but keeps no record of transactions. At the end of the day, the clerk counts the cash in the register and gives it to the cashier for deposit in the company bank account.

Write a memo to convince the store manager that there is an internal control weakness over cash receipts. Identify the weakness that gives an employee the best opportunity to steal cash and state how to prevent such a theft.

E4-35B (*Learning Objective 4: Evaluating internal control over cash payments*) Beautiful Meadows Golf Company manufactures a popular line of golf clubs. Beautiful Meadows Golf employs 173 workers and keeps their employment records on time sheets that show how many hours the employee works each week. On Friday the shop foreman collects the time sheets, checks them for accuracy, and delivers them to the payroll department for preparation of paychecks. The treasurer signs the paychecks and returns the checks to the payroll department for distribution to the employees.

Identify the main internal control weakness in this situation, state how the weakness can hurt Beautiful Meadows Golf, and propose a way to correct the weakness.

E4-36B (*Learning Objective 5: Preparing a cash budget*) Fallon Communications, Inc., is preparing its cash budget for 2011. Fallon ended 2010 with cash of $82 million, and managers need to keep a cash balance of at least $81 million for operations.

■ spreadsheet

Collections from customers are expected to total $11,307 million during 2011, and payments for the cost of services and products should reach $6,174 million. Operating expense payments are budgeted at $2,545 million.

During 2011, Fallon expects to invest $1,831 million in new equipment and sell older assets for $121 million. Debt payments scheduled for 2011 will total $604 million. The company forecasts net income of $883 million for 2011 and plans to pay dividends of $341 million.

Prepare Fallon Communications' cash budget for 2011. Will the budgeted level of cash receipts leave Fallon with the desired ending cash balance of $81 million, or will the company need additional financing? If so, how much?

E4-37B (*Learning Objective 5: Compensating balance agreement*) Assume Dan's Drums borrowed $19 million from Need It Now Bank and agreed to (a) pay an interest rate of 7.1% and (b) maintain a compensating balance amount equal to 5.8% of the loan. Determine Dan's Drums' actual effective interest rate on this loan.

Challenge Exercises

E4-38 (*Learning Objectives 1, 2, 4: Learning about fraud; evaluating internal controls over cash payments; focusing on ethical considerations*) Susan Healey, the owner of Susan's Perfect Presents, has delegated management of the business to Louise Owens, a friend. Healey drops by to meet customers and check up on cash receipts, but Owens buys the merchandise and handles cash payments. Business has been very good lately, and cash receipts have kept pace with the apparent level of sales. However, for a year or so, the amount of cash on hand has been too low. When asked about this, Owens explains that suppliers are charging more for goods than in the past. During the past year, Owens has taken two expensive vacations, and Healey wonders how Owens can afford these trips on her $59,000 annual salary and commissions.

List at least three ways Owens could be defrauding Healey of cash. In each instance also identify how Healey can determine whether Owens' actions are ethical. Limit your answers to the store's cash payments. The business pays all suppliers by check (no EFTs).

E4-39 (*Learning Objective 5: Preparing and using a cash budget*) Dan Davis, the chief financial officer, is responsible for The Furniture Mart's cash budget for 2010. The budget will help Davis determine the amount of long-term borrowing needed to end the year with a cash balance of $130,000. Davis's assistants have assembled budget data for 2010, which the computer printed in alphabetical order. Not all the data items reproduced below are used in preparing the cash budget.

(Assumed Data)	(In thousands)
Actual cash balance, December 31, 2009	$ 130
Budgeted total assets	22,377
Budgeted total current assets	7,976
Budgeted total current liabilities	4,260
Budgeted total liabilities	11,088
Budgeted total stockholders' equity	7,197
Collections from customers	21,800
Dividend payments	317
Issuance of stock	647
Net income...	1,183
Payment of long-term and short-term debt...............	980
Payment of operating expenses	2,349
Purchases of inventory items	14,545
Purchase of property and equipment........................	1,528

❙ Requirements

1. Prepare the cash budget of The Furniture Mart, Inc.
2. Compute The Furniture Mart's budgeted current ratio and debt ratio at December 31, 2010. Based on these ratio values, and on the cash budget, would you lend $100,000 to The Furniture Mart? Give the reason for your decision.

Quiz

Test your understanding of internal control and cash by answering the following questions. Answer each question by selecting the best choice from among the answers given.

Q4-40 All of the following are objectives of internal control except
a. to comply with legal requirements.
b. to maximize net income.
c. to ensure accurate and reliable accounting records.
d. to safeguard assets.

Q4-41 All of the following are internal control procedures except
a. Sarbanes-Oxley reforms.
b. electronic devices.
c. assignment of responsibilities.
d. internal and external audits.

Q4-42 Requiring that an employee with no access to cash do the accounting is an example of which characteristic of internal control?

a. Assignment of responsibility
b. Competent and reliable personnel
c. Monitoring of controls
d. Separation of duties

Q4-43 All of the following are controls for cash received over the counter except
a. the cash drawer should open only when the salesclerk enters an amount on the keys.
b. a printed receipt must be given to the customer.
c. the customer should be able to see the amounts entered into the cash register.
d. the sales clerk must have access to the cash register tape.

Q4-44 In a bank reconciliation, an outstanding check is

a. deducted from the book balance.
b. added to the bank balance.
c. added to the book balance.
d. deducted from the bank balance.

Q4-45 In a bank reconciliation, a bank collection of a note receivable is

a. deducted from the bank balance.
b. added to the book balance.
c. added to the bank balance.
d. deducted from the book balance.

Q4-46 In a bank reconciliation, an EFT cash payment is

a. deducted from the bank balance.
b. deducted from the book balance.
c. added to the book balance.
d. added to the bank balance.

Q4-47 If a bookkeeper mistakenly recorded a $35 deposit as $53, the error would be shown on the bank reconciliation as a

a. $53 deduction from the book balance.
b. $53 addition to the book balance.
c. $18 deduction from the book balance.
d. $18 addition to the book balance.

Q4-48 If a bank reconciliation included a deposit in transit of $880, the entry to record this reconciling item would include a

a. credit to cash for $880.
b. debit to cash for $880.
c. credit to prepaid insurance for $880.
d. no entry is required.

Q4-49 In a bank reconciliation, interest revenue earned on your bank balance is

a. deducted from the book balance.
b. deducted from the bank balance.
c. added to the bank balance.
d. added to the book balance.

Q4-50 Before paying an invoice for goods received on account, the controller or treasurer should ensure that
a. the company has not already paid this invoice.
b. the company is paying for the goods it ordered.
c. the company is paying for the goods it actually received.
d. all of the above.

Q4-51 The Little French Bakery is budgeting cash for 2011. The cash balance at December 31, 2010, was $6,000. The Little French Bakery budgets 2011 cash receipts at $83,000. Estimated cash payments include $36,000 for inventory, $26,000 for operating expenses, and $19,000 to expand the store. The Little French Bakery needs a minimum cash balance of $15,000 at all times. The Little French Bakery expects to earn net income of $78,000 during 2011. What is the final result of the company's cash budget for 2011?
a. Pay off $14,000 of debt.
b. $7,000 available for additional investments.
c. Must arrange new financing for $7,000.
d. $14,000 available for additional investments.

Problems

All of the Group A and Group B problems can be found within MyAccountingLab, an online homework and practice environment. Your instructor may ask you to complete these problems using MyAccountingLab.

(Group A)

writing assignment ■

P4-52A (*Learning Objectives 1, 2: Learning about fraud; identifying internal control weaknesses*) Celtic Imports is an importer of silver, brass, and furniture items from Ireland. Eileen Sullivan is the general manager of Celtic Imports. Sullivan employs two other people in the business. Mary McNicholas serves as the buyer for Celtic Imports. In her work McNicholas travels throughout Ireland to find interesting new products. When McNicholas finds a new product, she arranges for Celtic Imports to purchase and pay for the item. She helps the Irish artisans prepare their invoices and then faxes the invoices to Sullivan in the company office.

Sullivan operates out of an office in Boston, Massachusetts. The office is managed by Margaret Sweeney, who handles the mail, keeps the accounting records, makes bank deposits, and prepares the monthly bank reconciliation. Virtually all of Celtic Imports' cash receipts arrive by mail—from sales made to Target, Pier 1 Imports, and Macy's.

Sweeney also prepares checks for payment based on invoices that come in from the suppliers who have been contacted by McNicholas. To maintain control over cash payments, Sullivan examines the paperwork and signs all checks.

❚ Requirement

1. Identify all the major internal control weaknesses in Celtic Imports' system and how the resulting action could hurt Celtic Imports. Also state how to correct each weakness.

writing assignment ■

P4-53A (*Learning Objectives 1, 4: Learning about fraud; identifying internal control weakness*) Each of the following situations reveals an internal control weakness:

 a. In evaluating the internal control over cash payments of Framingham Manufacturing, an auditor learns that the purchasing agent is responsible for purchasing diamonds for use in the company's manufacturing process, approving the invoices for payment, and signing the checks. No supervisor reviews the purchasing agent's work.

 b. Leslie Joyce owns an architectural firm. Joyce's staff consists of 18 professional architects, and Joyce manages the office. Often, Joyce's work requires her to travel to meet with clients. During the past six months, Joyce has observed that when she returns from a business trip, the architecture jobs in the office have not progressed satisfactorily. Joyce learns that when she is away, two of her senior architects take over office management and neglect their normal duties. One employee could manage the office.

 c. J. T. Durfee has been an employee of the City of Maron for many years. Because the city is small, Durfee performs all accounting duties, plus opening the mail, preparing the bank deposit, and preparing the bank reconciliation.

❚ Requirements

1. Identify the missing internal control characteristic in each situation.
2. Identify each firm's possible problem.
3. Propose a solution to the problem.

P4-54A *(Learning Objective 3: Using the bank reconciliation as a control device)* The cash data of Dunlap Automotive for July 2010 follow:

writing assignment ■

■ **spreadsheet**

Cash					Account No. 101
Date	Item	Jrnl. Ref.	Debit	Credit	Balance
Jul 1	Balance				7,900
31		CR6	9,124		17,024
31		CP11		9,087	7,937

Cash Receipts (CR)		Cash Payments (CP)	
Date	Cash Debit	Check No.	Cash Credit
Jul 2	$2,771	3113	$1,503
8	516	3114	1,149
10	1,682	3115	1,630
16	871	3116	19
22	352	3117	825
29	924	3118	91
30	2,008	3119	440
Total	$9,124	3120	965
		3121	205
		3122	2,260
		Total	$9,087

Dunlap received the following bank statement on July 31, 2010:

Bank Statement for July 2010

Beginning balance		$ 7,900
Deposits and other additions:		
Jul 1.............................	$ 750 EFT	
4.............................	2,771	
9.............................	516	
12.............................	1,682	
17.............................	871	
22.............................	352	
23.............................	1,250 BC	8,192
Checks and other deductions:		
Jul 7.............................	$1,503	
13.............................	1,360	
14.............................	407 US	
15.............................	1,149	
18.............................	19	
21.............................	334 EFT	
26.............................	825	
30.............................	91	
30.............................	25 SC	(5,713)
Ending balance....................		$10,379

Explanation: BC—bank collection, EFT—electronic funds transfer, US—unauthorized signature, SC—service charge

Additional data for the bank reconciliation include the following:

 a. The EFT deposit was a receipt of monthly rent. The EFT debit was a monthly insurance payment.
 b. The unauthorized signature check was received from a customer.
 c. The correct amount of check number 3115, a payment on account, is $1,360. (Dunlap's accountant mistakenly recorded the check for $1,630.)

Requirements

1. Prepare the Dunlap Automotive bank reconciliation at July 31, 2010.
2. Describe how a bank account and the bank reconciliation help the general manager control Dunlap's cash.

■ spreadsheet

P4-55A (*Learning Objective 3: Preparing a bank reconciliation and the related journal entries*) The August 31 bank statement of Dickson Engineering Associates has just arrived from Carolina First Bank. To prepare the Dickson bank reconciliation, you gather the following data:

 a. Dickson's Cash account shows a balance of $8,152.71 on August 31.
 b. The August 31 bank balance is $8,879.24.
 c. The bank statement shows that Dickson earned $15.85 of interest on its bank balance during August. This amount was added to Dickson's bank balance.
 d. Dickson pays utilities ($730) and insurance ($280) by EFT.
 e. The following Dickson checks did not clear the bank by August 31:

Check No.	Amount
237	$401.00
288	74.82
291	33.25
293	165.55
294	236.00
295	47.75
296	107.85

 f. The bank statement includes a deposit of $899.15, collected on account by the bank on behalf of Dickson.
 g. The bank statement lists a $5.50 bank service charge.
 h. On August 31, the Dickson treasurer deposited $383.54, which will appear on the September bank statement.
 i. The bank statement includes a $398.00 deposit that Dickson did not make. The bank added $398.00 to Dickson's account for another company's deposit.
 j. The bank statement includes two charges for returned checks from customers. One is a $185.50 check received from a customer with the imprint "Unauthorized Signature." The other is a nonsufficient funds check in the amount of $68.15 received from another customer.

Requirements

1. Prepare the bank reconciliation for Dickson Engineering Associates.
2. Journalize the August 31 transactions needed to update Dickson's Cash account. Include an explanation for each entry.

writing assignment ■

P4-56A (*Learning Objectives 2, 4: Identifying internal control weakness in sales and cash receipts*) Fresh Skin Care makes all sales on credit. Cash receipts arrive by mail, usually within 30 days of the sale. Kate Martin opens envelopes and separates the checks from the accompanying remittance advices. Martin forwards the checks to another employee, who makes the daily bank deposit but has no access to the accounting records. Martin sends the remittance advices, which show the amount of cash received, to the accounting department for entry in the accounts receivable. Martin's only other duty is to grant allowances to customers. (An *allowance* decreases the amount that the customer must pay.) When Martin receives a customer check for less than the full amount of the invoice, she records the allowance in the accounting records and forwards the document to the accounting department.

▌Requirement

1. You are a new employee of Fresh Skin Care. Write a memo to the company president identifying the internal control weakness in this situation. State how to correct the weakness.

P4-57A (*Learning Objective 5: Preparing a cash budget and using cash-flow information*) John Watson, chief financial officer of Jasper Wireless, is responsible for the company's budgeting process. Watson's staff is preparing the Jasper cash budget for 2011. A key input to the budgeting process is last year's statement of cash flows, which follows (amounts in thousands):

Jasper Wireless Statement of Cash Flows 2010	
(In thousands)	
Cash Flows from Operating Activities	
Collections from customers	$ 64,000
Interest received	300
Purchases of inventory	(49,000)
Operating expenses	(13,500)
Net cash provided by operating activities	1,800
Cash Flows from Investing Activities	
Purchases of equipment	(4,800)
Purchases of investments	(400)
Sales of investments	500
Net cash used for investing activities	(4,700)
Cash Flows from Financing Activities	
Payment of long-term debt	(400)
Issuance of stock	1,700
Payment of cash dividends	(300)
Net cash provided by financing activities	1,000
Cash	
Increase (decrease) in Cash	(1,900)
Cash, beginning of year	3,400
Cash, end of year	$ 1,500

▌Requirements

1. Prepare the Jasper Wireless cash budget for 2011. Date the budget simply "2011" and denote the beginning and ending cash balances as "beginning" and "ending." Assume the company expects 2011 to be the same as 2010, but with the following changes:
   a. In 2011, the company expects a 10% increase in collections from customers and a 20% increase in purchases of inventory.
   b. There will be no sales of investments in 2011.
   c. Jasper plans to issue no stock in 2011.
   d. Jasper plans to end the year with a cash balance of $3,800.
2. Does the company's cash budget for 2011 suggest that Jasper is growing, holding steady, or decreasing in size? (Challenge)

(Group B)

writing assignment ■

P4-58B (*Learning Objectives 1, 2: Learning about fraud; identifying internal control weaknesses*) International Imports is an importer of silver, brass, and furniture items from France. Elaine Spencer is the general manager of International Imports. Spencer employs two other people in the business. Marie Walsh serves as the buyer for International Imports. In her work Walsh travels throughout France to find interesting new products. When Walsh finds a new product, she arranges for International Imports to purchase and pay for the item. She helps the French artisans prepare their invoices and then faxes the invoices to Spencer in the company office.

Spencer operates out of an office in Brooklyn, New York. The office is managed by Donna Durkin, who handles the mail, keeps the accounting records, makes bank deposits, and prepares the monthly bank reconciliation. Virtually all of International Imports' cash receipts arrive by mail—from sales made to Target, Crate and Barrel, and Williams-Sonoma.

Durkin also prepares checks for payment based on invoices that come in from the suppliers who have been contacted by Walsh. To maintain control over cash payments, Spencer examines the paperwork and signs all checks.

❙ Requirement

1. Identify all the major internal control weaknesses in International Imports' system and how the resulting action could hurt International Imports. Also state how to correct each weakness.

writing assignment ■

P4-59B (*Learning Objectives 1, 4: Learning about fraud; identifying internal control weakness*) Each of the following situations reveals an internal control weakness:

Situation a. In evaluating the internal control over cash payments of York Manufacturing, an auditor learns that the purchasing agent is responsible for purchasing diamonds for use in the company's manufacturing process, approving the invoices for payment, and signing the checks. No supervisor reviews the purchasing agent's work.

Situation b. Rita White owns an architectural firm. White's staff consists of 16 professional architects, and White manages the office. Often, White's work requires her to travel to meet with clients. During the past six months, White has observed that when she returns from a business trip, the architecture jobs in the office have not progressed satisfactorily. White learns that when she is away, two of her senior architects take over office management and neglect their normal duties. One employee could manage the office.

Situation c. M. J. Dowd has been an employee of the City of Northport for many years. Because the city is small, Dowd performs all accounting duties, plus opening the mail, preparing the bank deposit, and preparing the bank reconciliation.

❙ Requirements

1. Identify the missing internal control characteristic in each situation.
2. Identify each firm's possible problem.
3. Propose a solution to the problem.

P4-60B *(Learning Objective 3: Using the bank reconciliation as a control device)* The cash data of Donald Automotive for January 2010 follow:

writing assignment ■

■ **spreadsheet**

Cash					Account No. 101
Date	Item	Jrnl. Ref.	Debit	Credit	Balance
Jan 1	Balance				7,200
31		CR 6	9,127		16,327
31		CP 11		9,983	6,344

Cash Receipts (CR)		Cash Payments (CP)	
Date	Cash Debit	Check No.	Cash Credit
Jan 2	$2,726	3113	$1,475
8	572	3114	1,925
10	1,647	3115	1,530
16	837	3116	32
22	436	3117	870
29	856	3118	132
30	2,053	3119	493
Total	$9,127	3120	985
		3121	219
		3122	2,322
		Total	$9,983

Donald received the following bank statement on January 31, 2010:

Bank Statement for January 2010

Beginning balance		$ 7,200
Deposits and other additions:		
Jan 1............................	$ 650 EFT	
4............................	2,726	
9............................	572	
12............................	1,647	
17............................	837	
22............................	436	
23............................	1,350 BC	8,218
Checks and other deductions:		
Jan 7............................	$1,475	
13............................	1,350	
14............................	466 US	
15............................	1,925	
18............................	32	
21............................	331 EFT	
26............................	870	
30............................	132	
30............................	20 SC	(6,601)
Ending balance..................		$ 8,817

Explanation: BC—bank collection, EFT—electronic funds transfer, US—unauthorized signature, SC—service charge

Additional data for the bank reconciliation include the following:

a. The EFT deposit was a receipt of monthly rent. The EFT debit was a monthly insurance expense.

b. The unauthorized signature check was received from a customer.

c. The correct amount of check number 3115, a payment on account, is $1,350. (Donald's accountant mistakenly recorded the check for $1,530.)

❚ Requirements

1. Prepare the Donald Automotive bank reconciliation at January 31, 2010.
2. Describe how a bank account and the bank reconciliation help the general manager control Donald's cash.

■ spreadsheet

P4-61B (*Learning Objective 3: Preparing a bank reconciliation and the related journal entries*) The October 31 bank statement of Dunlap Engineering Associates has just arrived from Carolina First Bank. To prepare the Dunlap bank reconciliation, you gather the following data:

a. Dunlap's Cash account shows a balance of $7,605.86 on October 31.

b. The October 31 bank balance is $8,343.87.

c. The bank statement shows that Dunlap earned $15.45 of interest on its bank balance during October. This amount was added to Dunlap's bank balance.

d. Dunlap pays utilities ($770) and insurance ($250) by EFT.

e. The following Dunlap checks did not clear the bank by October 31:

Check No.	Amount
237	$403.15
288	78.98
291	36.39
293	155.45
294	234.00
295	47.50
296	106.79

f. The bank statement includes a deposit of $915.20, collected on account by the bank on behalf of Dunlap.

g. The bank statement lists a $6.25 bank service charge.

h. On October 31, the Dunlap treasurer deposited $380.50, which will appear on the November bank statement.

i. The bank statement includes a $405.00 deposit that Dunlap did not make. The bank added $405.00 to Dunlap's account for another company's deposit.

j. The bank statement includes two charges for returned checks from customers. One is a $185.50 check received from a customer with the imprint "Unauthorized Signature." The other is a nonsufficient funds check in the amount of $67.65 received from another customer.

❚ Requirements

1. Prepare the bank reconciliation for Dunlap Engineering Associates.
2. Journalize the October 31 transactions needed to update Dunlap's Cash account. Include an explanation for each entry.

writing assignment ■

P4-62B (*Learning Objective 4: Identifying internal control weakness in sales and cash receipts*) Flawless Skin Care makes all sales on credit. Cash receipts arrive by mail, usually within 30 days of the sale. Elizabeth Nelson opens envelopes and separates the checks from the accompanying remittance advices. Nelson forwards the checks to another employee, who makes the daily bank deposit but has no access to the accounting records. Nelson sends the remittance advices, which show the amount of cash received, to the accounting department for entry in the accounts receivable. Nelson's only other duty is to grant allowances to customers. (An *allowance* decreases the amount that the customer must pay.) When Nelson receives a customer check for less than the full amount of the invoice, she records the allowance in the accounting records and forwards the document to the accounting department.

❙ Requirement

1. You are a new employee of Flawless Skin Care. Write a memo to the company president identifying the internal control weakness in this situation. State how to correct the weakness.

P4-63B *(Learning Objective 5: Preparing a cash budget and using cash-flow information)* Don Beecher, chief financial officer of Carvel Wireless, is responsible for the company's budgeting process. Beecher's staff is preparing the Carvel cash budget for 2011. A key input to the budgeting process is last year's statement of cash flows, which follows (amount in thousands):

Carvel Wireless
Statement of Cash Flows
2010

(In thousands)

Cash Flows from Operating Activities	
Collections from customers	$ 62,000
Interest received	700
Purchases of inventory	(47,000)
Operating expenses	(13,700)
Net cash provided by operating activities	2,000
Cash Flows from Investing Activities	
Purchases of equipment	(4,100)
Purchases of investments	(300)
Sales of investments	900
Net cash used for investing activities	(3,500)
Cash Flows from Financing Activities	
Payment of long-term debt	(500)
Issuance of stock	1,500
Payment of cash dividends	(400)
Net cash provided by financing activities	600
Cash	
Increase (decrease) in Cash	(900)
Cash, beginning of year	2,800
Cash, end of year	$ 1,900

❙ Requirements

1. Prepare the Carvel Wireless cash budget for 2011. Date the budget simply "2011" and denote the beginning and ending cash balances as "beginning" and "ending." Assume the company expects 2011 to be the same as 2010, but with the following changes:
   a. In 2011, the company expects a 14% increase in collections from customers and a 25% increase in purchases of inventory.
   b. There will be no sales of investments in 2011.
   c. Carvel plans to issue no stock in 2011.
   d. Carvel plans to end the year with a cash balance of $3,550.
2. Does the company's cash budget for 2011 suggest that Carvel is growing, holding steady, or decreasing in size?

APPLY YOUR KNOWLEDGE

Decision Cases

Case 1. *(Learning Objectives 1, 2, 3: Learning about fraud; using a bank reconciliation to detect a theft)* Environmental Concerns, Inc., has poor internal control. Recently, Oscar Benz, the manager, has suspected the bookkeeper of stealing. Details of the business's cash position at September 30 follow.

    a. The Cash account shows a balance of $10,402. This amount includes a September 30 deposit of $3,794 that does not appear on the September 30 bank statement.

    b. The September 30 bank statement shows a balance of $8,224. The bank statement lists a $200 bank collection, an $8 service charge, and a $36 NSF check. The accountant has not recorded any of these items.

    c. At September 30, the following checks are outstanding:

Check No.	Amount
154	$116
256	150
278	853
291	990
292	206
293	145

    d. The bookkeeper receives all incoming cash and makes the bank deposits. He also reconciles the monthly bank statement. Here is his September 30 reconciliation:

Balance per books, September 30...............		$10,402
Add: Outstanding checks		1,460
Bank collection...................................		200
Subtotal...		12,062
Less: Deposits in transit............................	$3,794	
Service charge	8	
NSF check..	36	(3,838)
Balance per bank, September 30................		$ 8,224

❙ *Requirement*

    1. Benz has requested that you determine whether the bookkeeper has stolen cash from the business and, if so, how much. He also asks you to explain how the bookkeeper attempted to conceal the theft. To make this determination, you perform a proper bank reconciliation. There are no bank or book errors. Benz also asks you to evaluate the internal controls and to recommend any changes needed to improve them.

Case 2. *(Learning Objectives 1, 2: Learning about fraud; correcting an internal control weakness)* This case is based on an actual situation experienced by one of the authors. Gilead Construction, headquartered in Topeka, Kansas, built a motel in Kansas City. The construction foreman, Slim Pickins, hired the workers for the project. Pickins had his workers fill out the necessary tax forms and sent the employment documents to the home office.

Work on the motel began on May 1 and ended in December. Each Thursday evening, Pickins filled out a time card that listed the hours worked by each employee during the five-day work-week ended at 5 p.m. on Thursday. Pickins faxed the time sheets to the home office, which prepared the payroll checks on Friday morning. Pickins drove to the home office after lunch on Friday, picked up the payroll checks, and returned to the construction site. At 5 p.m. on Friday, Pickins distributed the paychecks to the workers.

    a. Describe in detail the internal control weakness in this situation. Specify what negative result could occur because of the internal control weakness.

    b. Describe what you would do to correct the internal control weakness.

Ethical Issues

For each of the following situations, answer the following questions:

1. What is the ethical issue in this situation?

2. What are the alternatives?

3. Who are the stakeholders? What are the possible consequences to each? Analyze from the following standpoints: (a) economic, (b) legal, and (c) ethical.

4. Place yourself in the role of the decision maker. What would you do? How would you justify your decision?

Issue 1. Sunrise Bank recently appointed the accounting firm of Smith, Godfroy, and Hannaford as the bank's auditor. Sunrise quickly became one of Smith, Godfroy, and Hannaford's largest clients. Subject to banking regulations, Sunrise must provide for any expected losses on notes receivable that Sunrise may not collect in full.

During the course of the audit, Smith, Godfroy, and Hannaford determined that three large notes receivable of Sunrise seem questionable. Smith, Godfroy, and Hannaford discussed these loans with Susan Carter, controller of Sunrise. Carter assured the auditors that these notes were good and that the makers of the notes will be able to pay their notes after the economy improves.

Smith, Godfroy, and Hannaford stated that Sunrise must record a loss for a portion of these notes receivable to account for the likelihood that Sunrise may never collect their full amount. Carter objected and threatened to dismiss Smith, Godfroy, and Hannaford if the auditor demands that the bank record the loss. Smith, Godfroy, and Hannaford want to keep Sunrise as a client. In fact, Smith, Godfroy, and Hannaford were counting on the revenue from the Sunrise audit to finance an expansion of the firm.

Issue 2. Barry Galvin is executive vice president of Community Bank. Active in community affairs, Galvin serves on the board of directors of The Salvation Army. The Salvation Army is expanding rapidly and is considering relocating. At a recent meeting, The Salvation Army decided to buy 250 acres of land on the edge of town. The owner of the property is Olga Nadar, a major depositor in Community Bank. Nadar is completing a bitter divorce, and Galvin knows that Nadar is eager to sell her property. In view of Nadar's difficult situation, Galvin believes Nadar would accept a low offer for the land. Realtors have appraised the property at $3.6 million.

Issue 3. Community Bank has a loan receivable from IMS Chocolates. IMS is six months late in making payments to the bank, and Jan French, a Community Bank vice president, is assisting IMS to restructure its debt.

French learns that IMS is depending on landing a contract with Snicker Foods, another Community Bank client. French also serves as Snicker Foods' loan officer at the bank. In this capacity, French is aware that Snicker is considering bankruptcy. No one else outside Snicker Foods knows this. French has been a great help to IMS and IMS's owner is counting on French's expertise in loan workouts to advise the company through this difficult process. To help the bank collect on this large loan, French has a strong motivation to alert IMS of Snicker's financial difficulties.

Focus on Financials: ■ Amazon.com, Inc.

(*Learning Objectives 2, 3: Cash and internal control*) Refer to the **Amazon.com, Inc.**, consolidated financial statements in Appendix A at the end of this book. The cash and cash equivalents section of the Consolidated Balance Sheet shows a balance of $2,769 as of December 31, 2008, and is made up of many different bank accounts, as well as time deposits, certificates of deposit, and perhaps government securities that are equivalent to cash. Suppose Amazon.com's year-end bank statement for the operating bank account, dated December 31, 2008, has just arrived at company headquarters. Further assume the bank statement shows Amazon.com's cash balance at $324 million and that Amazon.com, Inc.'s operating bank account has a balance of $316 million on the books (since this is only one of many bank accounts, it will not be possible to match it to the $2,769 that is shown.)

1. You must determine the correct balance for cash in the operating bank account on December 31, 2008. Suppose you uncover the following reconciling items (all amounts are assumed and are stated in millions):

   a. Interest earned on bank balance, $1
   b. Outstanding checks, $8
   c. Bank collections of various items, $2
   d. Deposits in transit, $3
      Prepare a bank reconciliation to show how Amazon.com, Inc., arrived at the correct amount of cash in the operating bank account at December 31, 2008. Journal entries are not required.

2. Study Amazon.com, Inc.'s Management's Report on Internal Control over Financial Reporting in Item 9A of its annual report, paragraph two. Indicate how that report links to specific items of internal control discussed in this chapter. (Challenge)

Focus on Analysis: ■ Foot Locker, Inc.

(*Learning Objectives 2, 5: Analyzing internal control and cash flows*) Refer to the **Foot Locker, Inc.**, Consolidated Financial Statements in Appendix B at the end of this book.

1. Focus on cash and cash equivalents. Why did cash change during 2007? The statement of cash flows holds the answer to this question. Analyze the seven largest *individual* items on the statement of cash flows (not the summary subtotals such as "net cash provided by operating activities"). For each of the seven individual items, state how Foot Locker, Inc.'s action affected cash. Show amounts in millions and round to the nearest $1 million. (Challenge)

2. Foot Locker, Inc.'s Report of Management describes the company's internal controls. Show how the management report corresponds to three of the five objectives of internal control included in this chapter. (Challenge)

Group Project

You are promoting a rock concert in your area. Assume you organize as a corporation, with each member of your group purchasing $10,000 of the corporation's stock. Therefore, each of you is risking some hard-earned money on this venture. Assume it is April 1 and that the concert will be performed on June 30. Your promotional activities begin immediately, and ticket sales start on May 1. You expect to sell all of the firm's assets, pay all the liabilities, and distribute all remaining cash to the group members by July 31.

❙ *Requirements*

Write an internal control manual that will help to safeguard the assets of the business. The manual should address the following aspects of internal control:

1. Assign responsibilities among the group members.
2. Authorize individuals, including group members and any outsiders that you need to hire to perform specific jobs.

3. Separate duties among the group and any employees.

4. Describe all documents needed to account for and safeguard the business's assets.

For online homework, exercises, and problems that provide you with immediate feedback, please visit www.myaccountinglab.com

---

Quick Check Answers

1. *g, e, h, d, f, c, a*	3. *d*	6. *e*	9. *d*
Unused: *b, i*	4. *a*	7. *a*	10. *d*
2. *b*	5. *c*	8. *d*	11. *a*

5
Short-Term Investments & Receivables

SPOTLIGHT: Receivables and Investments Account for Over Half of PepsiCo's Current Assets!

What comes to mind when you think of PepsiCo? Do you think of a soft drink or a snack chip? PepsiCo's two main products are soft drinks and snack foods. PepsiCo also owns Frito Lay, the snack-food company. That might lead you to believe that inventories are the company's largest current asset. However, as of December 31, 2007, short-term investments and receivables account for about 59% of PepsiCo's current assets.

Take a look at PepsiCo's comparative balance sheets for 2007 and 2006 on the following page. Does it surprise you that receivables are PepsiCo's largest current asset? It turns out that receivables are the largest current asset for lots of companies, including FedEx and The Boeing Company.

Another important current asset is short-term investments. As you can see from PepsiCo's 2007 balance sheet, PepsiCo had about $1.5 billion of short-term investments at the end of 2007. You'll notice that short-term investments are listed on the balance sheet immediately after cash and before receivables. Let's see why.

> **PepsiCo, Inc.**
> **Balance Sheets (Excerpt, Adapted)**
> December 31, 2007 and 2006
>
> | (In millions) | 2007 | 2006 |
> |---|---|---|
> | **ASSETS** | | |
> | **Current Assets** | | |
> | Cash and cash equivalents... | $ 910 | $1,651 |
> | Short-term investments... | 1,571 | 1,171 |
> | Accounts receivable, net of allowance for doubtful | | |
> | accounts of $75 in 2007 and $64 in 2006................ | 4,389 | 3,725 |
> | Inventories .... | 2,290 | 1,926 |
> | Prepaid expenses and other current assets .... | 991 | 657 |
> | Total Current Assets .... | $10,151 | $9,130 |

This chapter shows how to account for short-term investments and receivables. We cover short-term investments along with receivables to emphasize their relative liquidity. Short-term investments are the next-most-liquid current assets after cash. (Recall that liquid means close to cash.) We begin our discussion with short-term investments.

LEARNING OBJECTIVES

1 **Account** for short-term investments

2 **Account** for, and control, accounts receivable

3 **Use** the allowance method for uncollectible receivables

4 **Account** for notes receivable

5 **Use** two new ratios to evaluate a business

SHORT-TERM INVESTMENTS

OBJECTIVE

1 **Account** for short-term investments

Short-term investments are also called **marketable securities**. These are investments in marketable securities easily convertible to cash that a company plans to hold for one year or less. They allow the company to invest cash for a short period of time and earn a return until the cash is needed.

Short-term investments are the next-most-liquid asset after cash. This is why we report short-term investments in marketable securities immediately after cash and before receivables on the balance sheet. Short-term investments in marketable securities falls into one of three categories:

Three Categories of Short-Term Investments		
Trading Securities	**Available-for-Sale Securities**	**Held-to-Maturity Securities**
Covered in this section of the chapter	Covered in Chapter 10	Same as accounting for a note receivable, starting on page 307

The investor, such as PepsiCo, expects to sell a trading security within a very short time—a few months at most. Therefore, all trading securities are included in current assets. The other two categories of securities can be either current or long-term, depending on how long management intends to hold them. Let's begin with trading securities.

Trading Securities

The purpose of owning a **trading security** is to hold it for a short time and then sell it for more than its cost. Trading securities can be in the form of stock or debt securities of another company. Suppose PepsiCo purchases **IBM** stock, intending to sell the stock within a few months. If the market value of the IBM stock increases, PepsiCo will have a gain; if IBM's stock price drops, PepsiCo will have a loss. Along the way, PepsiCo will receive dividend revenue from IBM.

Suppose PepsiCo buys the IBM stock on November 18, paying $100,000 cash. PepsiCo records the purchase of the investment at cost:

2010			
Nov 18	Investment in IBM stock	100,000	
	Cash		100,000
	Purchased investment.		

Investment in IBM Stock
100,000

Assume that PepsiCo receives a cash dividend of $4,000 from IBM. PepsiCo records the dividend revenue as follows:

2010			
Nov 27	Cash	4,000	
	Dividend Revenue		4,000
	Received cash dividend.		

Assets	=	Liabilities	+	Stockholders' Equity	+	Revenues
+ 4,000	=				+	4,000

Unrealized Gains and Losses.   PepsiCo's fiscal year ends on December 31, and PepsiCo prepares financial statements. The IBM stock has risen in value, and on December 31 PepsiCo's investment has a current market value of $102,000. Market value is the amount the owner can sell the securities for. PepsiCo has an *unrealized gain* on the investment:

- *Gain* because the market value ($102,000) of the securities is greater than PepsiCo's cost of the securities ($100,000). A gain has the same effect as a revenue.
- *Unrealized gain* because PepsiCo has not yet sold the securities.

Trading securities are reported on the balance sheet at their current market value, because market value is the amount the investor can receive by selling the securities. Prior to preparing financial statements on December 31, PepsiCo adjusts the investment in IBM securities to its current market value with this year-end journal entry:

2010			
Dec 31	Investment in IBM stock	2,000	
	Unrealized Gain on Investments		2,000
	Adjusted investment to market value.		

Investment in IBM Stock		Unrealized Gain on Investments	
100,000			2,000
2,000			
102,000			

After the adjustment, PepsiCo's Short-Term Investments account is ready to be reported on the balance sheet—at current market value of $102,000.

If PepsiCo's investment in IBM stock had decreased in value, say to $95,000, then PepsiCo would have reported an unrealized loss. A *loss* has the same effect as an expense. In that case, PepsiCo would have made a different entry at December 31. For an *unrealized* loss of $5,000, the entry would have been as follows:

Unrealized Loss on Investments		5,000	
Investment in IBM Stock			5,000
Adjusted investment to market value.			

Investment in IBM Stock		Unrealized Loss on Investments	
100,000	5,000	5,000	
95,000			

Reporting on the Balance Sheet and the Income Statement

The Balance Sheet.   Short-term investments are current assets. They appear on the balance sheet immediately after cash because short-term investments are almost as liquid as cash. Report **trading investments** at their *current market value.*

Income Statement.   Investments in debt and equity securities earn interest revenue and dividend revenue. Investments also create gains and losses. For trading investments these items are reported on the income statement as Other revenue, gains, and (losses), as shown in Exhibit 5-1.

EXHIBIT 5-1 | **Reporting Short-Term Investments and the Related Revenues, Gains, and Losses**

Balance sheet		Income statement	
Current assets:........................		Revenues...........................	$ XXX
Cash....................................	$ XXX	Expenses	XXX
Short-term investments, at		Other revenue, gains	
market value	102,000	and (losses):	
Accounts receivable...............	XXX	Interest revenue.............	XXX
		Dividend revenue	4,000
		Unrealized gain on	
		investment..............	2,000
		Net income...................	$ XXX

Realized Gains and Losses. A *realized* gain or loss occurs only when the investor sells an investment. This gain or loss is different from the unrealized gain that we reported for PepsiCo above. The result may be a

- Realized gain = Sale price is *greater than* the Investment carrying amount
- Realized loss = Sale price is *less than* the Investment carrying amount

Suppose PepsiCo sells its IBM stock during 2011. The sale price is $98,000, and PepsiCo makes this journal entry:

2011			
Jan 19	Cash	98,000	
	Loss on Sale of Investments	4,000	
	Investment in IBM Stock		102,000
	Sold investments at a loss.		

Investment in IBM Stock		Loss on Sale of Investments	
100,000		4,000	
2,000	102,000		

Accountants rarely use the word "Realized" in the account title. A gain (or a loss) is understood to be a realized gain (or loss) arising from a sale transaction. Unrealized gains and losses are clearly labeled as *unrealized*. PepsiCo would report Gain (or Loss) on Sale of Investments among the "Other" items of the income statement, as shown in Exhibit 5-1.

Lending Agreements and the Current Ratio

Lending agreements often require the borrower to maintain a current ratio at some specified level, say 1.50 or greater. What happens when the borrower's current ratio falls below 1.50? The consequences can be severe:

- The lender can call the loan for immediate payment.
- If the borrower cannot pay, then the lender may take over the company.

Suppose it's December 10 and it looks like Health Corporation of America's (HCA's) current ratio will end the year at a value of 1.48. That would put HCA in default on the lending agreement and create a bad situation. With three weeks remaining in the year, how can HCA improve its current ratio?

Recall that the current ratio is computed as

$$\text{Current ratio} = \frac{\text{Total current assets}}{\text{Total current liabilities}}$$

There are several strategies for increasing the current ratio, such as:

1. Launch a major sales effort. The increase in cash and receivables will more than offset the decrease in Inventory, total current assets will increase, and the current ratio will improve.

2. Pay off some current liabilities before year end. Both current assets in the numerator and current liabilities in the denominator will decrease by the same amount. The proportionate impact on current liabilities in the denominator will be greater than the impact on current assets in the numerator, and the current ratio will increase. This strategy increases the current ratio when the current ratio is already above 1.0, as for HCA and PepsiCo.

3. A third strategy is questionable, and we wish to alert you to one of the accounting games that companies sometimes play. Suppose HCA has some long-term investments (investments that HCA plans to hold for longer than a year—these are long-term assets). Before year end HCA might choose to reclassify these long-term investments as current assets. The reclassification of these investments increases HCA's current assets, and that increases the current ratio. This strategy would be okay if HCA does in fact plan to sell the investments within the next year. But the strategy would be unethical and dishonest if HCA in fact plans to keep the investments for longer than a year.

From this example you can see that accounting is not cut-and-dried or all black-and-white. It takes good judgment—which includes ethics—to become a successful accountant.

MID-CHAPTER SUMMARY PROBLEM

The largest current asset on Waverly Corporation's balance sheet is Short-Term Investments. The investments consist of stock in other corporations and cost Waverly $8,660. At the balance sheet date, the fair market value of these securities is $9,000 (amounts in millions).

Suppose Waverly holds the stock investments in the hope of selling at a profit within a few months. How will Waverly classify the investments? What will Waverly report on the balance sheet at December 31, 2010? What will Waverly report on its 2010 income statement? Show a T-account for Short-Term Investments.

Answer

These investments in trading securities are *current assets* as reported on the 2010 balance sheet, and Waverly's 2010 income statement will report as follows (amounts in millions):

Balance sheet		Income statement	
Current assets:		Other revenue and expense:	
Cash.....................................	$ XX	Unrealized gain on investments	
Short-term investments,		($9,000 – $8,660).................	$ 340
at market value	9,000		

Short-Term Investments	
8,660	
340	

Suppose Waverly sells the investment in securities for $8,700 in 2011. Journalize the sale and then show the Short-Term Investments T-account as it appears after the sale.

Answer

	(In millions)
Cash..	8,700
Loss on Sale of Investments.........	300
Short-Term Investments	9,000
Sold investments at a loss.	

Short-Term Investments	
8,660	
340	9,000

ACCOUNTS AND NOTES RECEIVABLE

OBJECTIVE

2 **Account** for, and control, accounts receivable

Receivables are the third most liquid asset—after cash and short-term investments. Most of the remainder of this chapter shows how to account for receivables.

Types of Receivables

Receivables are monetary claims against others. Receivables are acquired mainly by selling goods and services (accounts receivable) and by lending money (notes receivable). The journal entries to record the receivables can be shown as follows:

Performing a Service on Account		Lending Money on a Note Receivable	
Accounts Receivable...................	XXX	Note Receivable	XXX
Service Revenue......................	XXX	Cash..	XXX
Performed a service on account.		*Loaned money to another company.*	

The two major types of receivables are accounts receivable and notes receivable. A business' *accounts receivable* are the amounts collectible from customers from the sale of goods and services. Accounts receivable, which are *current assets*, are sometimes called *trade receivables* or merely *receivables*.

The Accounts Receivable account in the general ledger serves as a *control account* that summarizes the total amount receivable from all customers. Companies also keep a *subsidiary record* of accounts receivable with a separate account for each customer, illustrated as follows:

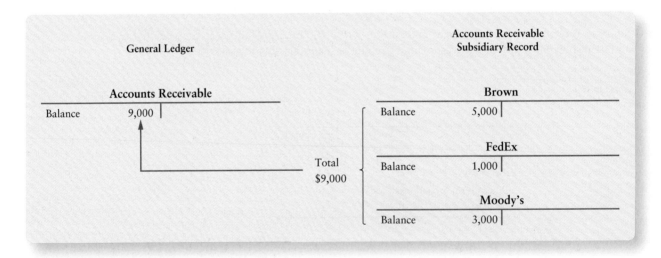

Notes receivable are more formal contracts than accounts receivable. For a note, the borrower signs a written promise to pay the lender a definite sum at the **maturity** date, plus interest. This is why notes are also called promissory notes. The note may require the borrower to pledge *security* for the loan. This means that the borrower gives the lender permission to claim certain assets, called *collateral*, if the borrower fails to pay the amount due. We cover the details of notes receivable starting on page 306.

Other receivables is a miscellaneous category for all receivables other than accounts receivable and notes receivable. Examples include loans to employees and to related companies.

Internal Controls over Cash Collections on Account

Businesses that sell on credit receive most of their cash receipts from collections of accounts receivable. Internal control over collections on account is important. Chapter 4 discusses control procedures for cash receipts, but another element of internal control deserves emphasis here—the separation of cash-handling and cash-accounting duties. Consider the following case:

> **Central Paint Company is a small, family-owned business that takes pride in the loyalty of its workers. Most employees have been with Central for 10 or more years. The company makes 90% of its sales on account and receives most of its cash by mail.**
>
> **The office staff consists of a bookkeeper and an office supervisor. The bookkeeper maintains the general ledger and a subsidiary record of individual customer accounts receivable. The bookkeeper also makes the daily bank deposit.**
>
> **The supervisor prepares monthly financial statements and any special reports the company needs. The supervisor also takes sales orders from customers and serves as office manager.**

Can you identify the internal control weakness here? The problem is that the bookkeeper makes the bank deposit. Remember the AMEX case in Chapter 4? With this cash-handling duty, the bookkeeper could lap accounts receivable. Alternatively, he or she could steal an incoming customer check and write off the customer's account as uncollectible. The customer doesn't complain because the bookkeeper wrote off the customer's account, and Central therefore stops pursuing collection.

How can this weakness be corrected? The supervisor—not the bookkeeper—could open incoming mail and make the daily bank deposit. The bookkeeper should *not* be allowed to handle cash. Only the remittance advices should be forwarded to the bookkeeper to credit customer accounts receivable. Removing cash handling from the bookkeeper and keeping the accounts away from the supervisor separates duties and strengthens internal control.

Using a bank lockbox achieves the same separation of duties. Customers send their payments directly to Central Paint Company's bank, which records cash as the cash goes into Central's bank account. The bank then forwards the remittance advice to Central's bookkeeper, who credits the customer account. No Central Paint employee even touches incoming cash.

How Do We Manage the Risk of Not Collecting?

In Chapters 1 to 4, we use many different companies to illustrate how to account for a business. Chapter 1 began with J.Crew Group, Inc., a high fashion clothing retailer. J.Crew, like other exclusively retail businesses, doesn't own any receivables, because it makes all of its sales in cash, which includes credit card sales. However, for most types of businesses, strictly cash sales are the exception rather than the rule. Chapter 2 featured Apple, Inc., Chapter 3 Starbucks Corporation, and Chapter 4 AMEX Products. This chapter features PepsiCo. All of these companies hold substantial amounts of receivables.

By selling on credit, companies run the risk of not collecting some receivables. Unfortunately, some customers don't pay their debts. The prospect of failing to collect from a customer provides the biggest challenge in accounting for receivables. The Decision Guidelines address this challenge.

DECISION GUIDELINES

MANAGING AND ACCOUNTING FOR RECEIVABLES

Here are the management and accounting issues a business faces when the company extends credit to customers. For each issue, the Decision Guidelines propose a plan of action. Let's look at a business situation: Suppose you open a health club near your college. Assume you will let customers use the club and bill them for their monthly dues. What challenges will you encounter by extending credit to customers?

The main issues in *managing* receivables, along with plans of action, are

Issues	Plan of Action
1. What are the benefits and the costs of extending credit to customers?	1. Benefit—Increase in sales. Cost—Risk of not collecting.
2. Extend credit only to creditworthy customers.	2. Run a credit check on prospective customers.
3. Separate cash-handling and accounting duties to keep employees from stealing the cash collected from customers.	3. Design the internal control system to separate duties.
4. Pursue collection from customers to maximize cash flow.	4. Keep a close eye on customer pay habits. Send second and third statements to slow-paying customers, if necessary.

The main issues in accounting for receivables, and the related plans of action, are (amounts are assumed)

Issues	Plan of Action
1. Measure and report receivables on the balance sheet at their net realizable value, the amount we expect to collect. This is the appropriate amount to report for receivables.	Report receivables at their net realizable value: **Balance sheet** Receivables... $1,000 Less: Allowance for uncollectibles............... (80) Receivables, net.. $ 920
2. Measure and report the expense associated with failure to collect receivables. This expense is called *uncollectible-account expense* and is reported on the income statement.	Measure the expense of not collecting from customers: **Income statement** Sales (or service) revenue............................. $8,000 Expenses: Uncollectible-account expense................. 190

These guidelines lead to our next topic, Accounting for Uncollectible Receivables.

ACCOUNTING FOR UNCOLLECTIBLE RECEIVABLES

A company gets an account receivable only when it sells its product or service on credit (on account). You'll recall that the entry to record the earning of revenue on account is (amount assumed)

Accounts Receivable	1,000	
Sales Revenue (or Service Revenue)		1,000
Earned revenue on account.		

Ideally, the company would collect cash for all of its receivables. But unfortunately the entry to record cash collections on account is for only $950.

Cash	950	
Accounts Receivable		950
Collections on account.		

You can see that companies rarely collect all of their accounts receivables. So companies must account for their uncollectible accounts—$50 in this example. Selling on credit creates both a benefit and a cost:

- *Benefit*: Customers who cannot pay cash immediately can buy on credit, so sales and profits increase.
- *Cost*: The company cannot collect from some customers. Accountants label this cost **uncollectible-account expense**, **doubtful-account expense**, or **bad-debt expense**.

PepsiCo reports receivables as follows on its 2007 balance sheet (in millions):

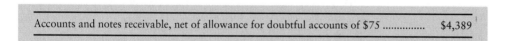

Accounts and notes receivable, net of allowance for doubtful accounts of $75 .... $4,389

The allowance ($75) represents the amount that PepsiCo does *not* expect to collect. The net amount of the receivables ($4,389) is the amount that PepsiCo *does* expect to collect. This is called the *net realizable value* because it's the amount of cash PepsiCo expects to realize in cash receipts.

Uncollectible-account expense is an operating expense along with salaries, depreciation, rent, and utilities. To measure uncollectible-account expense, accountants use the allowance method or, in certain limited cases, the direct write-off method (p. 305).

Allowance Method

The best way to measure bad debts is by the **allowance method**. This method records collection losses based on estimates developed from the company's collection experience. PepsiCo doesn't wait to see which customers will not pay. Instead, PepsiCo records the estimated amount as Uncollectible-Account Expense and also sets up **Allowance for Uncollectible Accounts**. Other titles for this account are **Allowance for Doubtful Accounts** and *Allowance for Bad Debts*. This is a contra

OBJECTIVE

3 **Use** the allowance method for uncollectible receivables

account to Accounts Receivable. The allowance shows the amount of the receivables the business expects *not* to collect.

In Chapter 3 we used the Accumulated Depreciation account to show the amount of a plant asset's cost that has been expensed—the portion of the asset that's no longer a benefit to the company. Allowance for Uncollectible Accounts serves a similar purpose for Accounts Receivable. The allowance shows how much of the receivable has been expensed. You'll find this diagram helpful (amounts are assumed):

Equipment........................	$100,000	Accounts receivable..................	$10,000
Less: Accumulated		Less: Allowance for	
depreciation	(40,000)	uncollectible accounts	(900)
Equipment, net...................	60,000	Accounts receivable, net............	9,100

Focus on Accounts Receivable. Customers owe this company $10,000, but it expects to collect only $9,100. The *net realizable value* of the receivables is therefore $9,100. Another way to report these receivables is

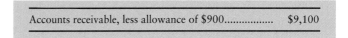

Accounts receivable, less allowance of $900.................	$9,100

You can work backward to determine the full amount of the receivable, $10,000 (net realizable value of $9,100 plus the allowance of $900).

The income statement reports Uncollectible-Account Expense among the operating expenses, as follows (using assumed figures):

Income statement (partial):

Expenses:
  Uncollectible-account expense:................ $2,000

STOP & THINK...

Refer to the PepsiCo balance sheet on page 290. At December 31, 2007, how much in total did customers owe PepsiCo? How much did PepsiCo expect *not* to collect? How much did PepsiCo expect to collect? What was the net realizable value of PepsiCo's receivables?

Answer:

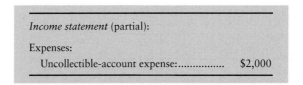

	Millions
Customers owed PepsiCo...	$4,464 ($4,389 + 75)
PepsiCo expected not to collect the allowance of	(75)
PepsiCo expected to collect—net realizable value........	$4,389

Notice that, to determine the *total* (*gross*) amount customers owed, you have to add the amount of the allowance back to the "net realizable value" ($4,389 + $75 = $4,464). Although this amount is not shown in the financial statements, it is useful for analysis purposes, as shown in the following section.

The best way to estimate uncollectibles uses the company's history of collections from customers. There are two basic ways to estimate uncollectibles:

- Percent-of-sales method
- Aging-of-receivables method

Percent-of-Sales. The **percent-of-sales method** computes uncollectible-account expense as a percent of revenue. This method takes an *income-statement approach* because it focuses on the amount of expense to be reported on the income statement. Assume it is December 31, 2007, and PepsiCo's accounts have these balances *before the year-end adjustments* (amounts in millions):

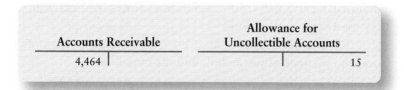

Customers owe PepsiCo $4,464, and the Allowance amount on the books is $15. But PepsiCo's top managers know that the company will fail to collect more than $15. Suppose PepsiCo's credit department estimates that uncollectible-account expense is 1/10 of 1% (0.001) of total revenues, which were $46,000. The entry that records uncollectible-account expense for the year also updates the allowance as follows (using PepsiCo figures):

2007			
Dec 31	Uncollectible-Account Expense		
	($46,000 × .001)	46	
	Allowance for Uncollectible Accounts		46
	Recorded expense for the year.		

The expense decreases PepsiCo's assets, as shown by the accounting equation.

Assets	=	Liabilities	+	Stockholders' Equity	−	Expenses
− 46	=	0			−	46

The percentage-of-sales method employs the matching concept to estimate, probably on a monthly or quarterly basis, the amount of cost that has been incurred in order to earn a certain amount of revenue, and to recognize both in the same time period.

Accounts Receivable	Allowance for Uncollectible Accounts		Uncollectible-Account Expense
4,464		15	46
	Adj	46	
	End Bal	61	

Net accounts receivable, $4,403

Using the percentage-of-sales method, the net realizable value of accounts receivable, or the amount ultimately expected to be collected from customers, would be $4,403 ($4,464 − $61). This method will usually result in a different amount of estimated uncollectible accounts expense and net realizable value than the aging method, discussed next.

Aging-of-Receivables. The other popular method for estimating uncollectibles is called **aging-of-receivables**. The aging method is a *balance-sheet approach* because it focuses on what should be the most relevant and faithful representation of accounts receivable as of the balance sheet date. In the aging method, individual receivables from specific customers are analyzed based on how long they have been outstanding.

Suppose it is December 31, 2007, and PepsiCo's receivables accounts show the following before the year-end adjustment (amounts in millions):

Accounts Receivable		Allowance for Uncollectible Accounts	
$4,464			15

These accounts are not yet ready for the financial statements because the allowance balance is not realistic.

PepsiCo's computerized accounting package ages the company's accounts receivable. Exhibit 5-2 shows a representative aging schedule at December 31, 2007. PepsiCo's receivables total $4,464. Of this amount, the aging schedule shows that the company will *not* collect $75 (lower right corner).

EXHIBIT 5-2 | **Aging the Accounts Receivable of PepsiCo.**

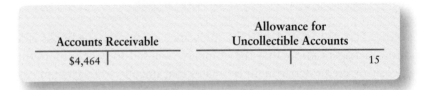

	Age of Account (Dollar amounts rounded to the nearest million)				
Customer	1–30 Days	31–60 Days	61–90 Days	Over 90 Days	Total Balance
Taco Bell					
Pizza Hut					
Totals.................................	$3,600	$ 600	$ 200	$ 64	$4,464
Estimated percent uncollectible.................	× 1%	× 2%	× 7%	× 20%	
Allowance for Uncollectible Accounts balance should be	$ 36 +	$ 12 +	$ 14 +	$ 13* =	$ 75

*Rounded to the nearest million

The aging method will bring the balance of the allowance account ($15) to the needed amount as determined by the aging schedule ($75). The lower right corner of the aging schedule gives the needed balance in the allowance account. To update the allowance, PepsiCo would make this adjusting entry at year end:

2007			
Dec 31	Uncollectible-Account Expense	60	
	Allowance for Uncollectible Accounts		
	($75 – $15)		60
	Recorded expense for the year.		

The expense decreases PepsiCo's assets and net income, as shown by the accounting equation.

Assets	=	Liabilities	+	Stockholders' Equity	–	Expenses
– 60	=	0			–	60

Now the balance sheet can report the amount that PepsiCo actually expects to collect from customers: $4,389 ($4,464 – $75). This is the net realizable value of PepsiCo's accounts receivable.

Accounts Receivable		Allowance for Uncollectible Accounts		Uncollectible-Account Expense
4,464		Beg Bal	15	60
		Adj	60	
		End Bal	75	

Net accounts receivable, $4,389

Writing Off Uncollectible Accounts.   Assume that at the beginning of 2010 a division of PepsiCo had these accounts receivable (amounts in thousands):

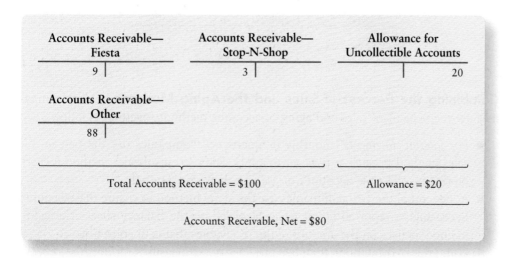

Accounts Receivable—Fiesta	Accounts Receivable—Stop-N-Shop	Allowance for Uncollectible Accounts
9	3	20

Accounts Receivable—Other		
88		

Total Accounts Receivable = $100   Allowance = $20

Accounts Receivable, Net = $80

Suppose that early in 2010, PepsiCo's credit department determines that PepsiCo cannot collect from customers Fiesta and Stop–N–Shop. PepsiCo then writes off the receivables from these customers with the following entry:

2010			
Jan 31	Allowance for Uncollectible Accounts	12	
	Accounts Receivable—Fiesta		9
	Accounts Receivable—Stop-N-Shop		3
	Wrote off uncollectible receivables.		

After the write-off, PepsiCo's accounts show these amounts:

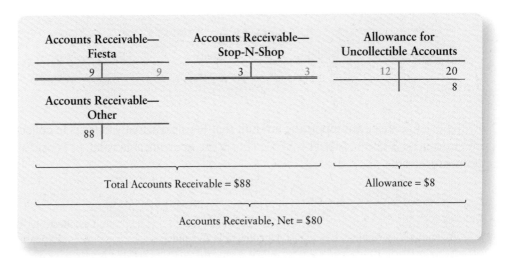

The accounting equation shows that the write-off of uncollectibles has no effect on PepsiCo's total assets, no effect on current assets, and no effect on net accounts receivable. Notice that Accounts Receivable, Net is still $80. There is no effect on net income either. Why is there no effect on net income? Net income is unaffected because the write-off of uncollectibles affects no expense account. If the company uses the allowance method as discussed in the previous section, expenses would have been properly recognized in the period they were incurred, which is the same period in which the related sales took place.

Assets	=	Liabilities	+	Stockholders' Equity
+ 12 – 12	=	0	+	0

Combining the Percent-of-Sales and the Aging Methods. Most companies use the percent-of-sales and aging-of-accounts methods together, as follows:

- For *interim statements* (monthly or quarterly), companies use the percent-of-sales method because it is easier to apply. The percent-of-sales method focuses on the uncollectible-account *expense*, but that is not enough.
- At the end of the year, companies use the aging method to ensure that Accounts Receivable is reported at *net realizable value* on the balance sheet. The aging method focuses on the amount of the receivables that is uncollectible.
- Using the two methods together provides good measures of both the *expense* and the *asset*. Exhibit 5-3 compares the two methods.

EXHIBIT 5-3 | **Comparing the Percent-of-Sales and Aging Methods for Estimating Uncollectibles**

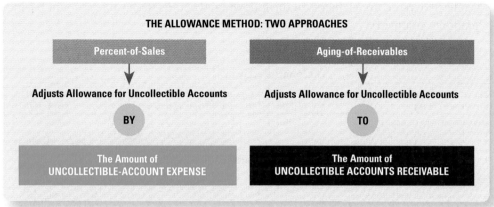

Direct Write-Off Method

There is another, less preferable, way to account for uncollectible receivables. Under the **direct write-off method**, the company waits until a specific customer's receivable proves uncollectible. Then the accountant writes off the customer's account and records Uncollectible-Account Expense, as follows (using assumed data):

2010			
Jan 2	Uncollectible-Account Expense	12	
	Accounts Receivable—Fiesta		9
	Accounts Receivable—Stop-N-Shop		3
	Wrote off bad accounts by direct write-off method.		

The direct write-off method is not considered generally accepted accounting for financial statement purposes. It is considered defective for two reasons:

1. It uses no allowance for uncollectibles. As a result, receivables are always reported at their full amount, which is more than the business expects to collect. *Assets on the balance sheet may be overstated.*

2. It causes a poor matching of uncollectible-account expense against revenue. In this example, PepsiCo made the sales to Fiesta and Stop–N–Shop in 2009 and should have recorded the uncollectible-account expense during 2009, not in 2010 when it wrote off the accounts.

Because of these deficiencies, PepsiCo and virtually all other large companies use the allowance method for preparing their financial statements.

The direct write-off method is the *required* method of accounting for uncollectible accounts for federal income tax purposes. It is one of several sources of timing differences that may arise between net income for financial reporting purposes and net income for federal income tax purposes. We will discuss other differences between book and taxable income in later chapters.

Computing Cash Collections from Customers

A company earns revenue and then collects the cash from customers. For PepsiCo and most other companies, there is a time lag between earning the revenue and collecting the cash. Collections from customers are the single most important source of cash for any business. You can compute a company's collections from customers by analyzing its Accounts Receivable account. Receivables typically hold only five items, as reflected in the five elements of the following Accounts Receivable account balance (amounts assumed):

Accounts Receivable			
Beg Bal (left over from last period)	200	Write-offs of uncollectibles	100**
Sales (or service) revenue	1,800*	Collections from customers	X = 1,500†
End Bal (carries over to next period)	400		

*The journal entry that places revenue into the receivable account is

Accounts Receivable	1,800	
Sales (or Service) Revenue		1,800

**The journal entry for write-offs is

Allowance for Uncollectibles	100	
Accounts Receivable		100

†The journal entry that places collections into the receivable account is

Cash	1,500	
Accounts Receivable		1,500

Suppose you know all these amounts *except* collections from customers. You can compute collections by solving for X in the T-account.[1] Often write-offs are unknown and must be omitted. Then the computation of collections becomes an approximation.

Notes Receivable

OBJECTIVE

4 **Account** for notes receivable

As stated earlier, notes receivable are more formal than accounts receivable. Notes receivable due within one year or less are current assets. Notes due beyond one year are *long-term receivables* and are reported as long-term assets. Some notes receivable are collected in installments. The portion due within one year is a current asset and the remainder is long term. PepsiCo may hold a $20,000 note receivable from a customer, but only the $6,000 the customer must pay within one year is a current asset of PepsiCo.

Before launching into the accounting for notes receivable, let's define some key terms:

Creditor. The party to whom money is owed. The creditor is also called the *lender*.

Debtor. The party that borrowed and owes money on the note. The debtor is also called the *maker* of the note or the *borrower*.

Interest. Interest is the cost of borrowing money. The interest is stated in an annual percentage rate.

Maturity date. The date on which the debtor must pay the note.

Maturity value. The sum of principal and interest on the note.

---

[1]An equation may help you solve for X. The equation is $200 + $1,800 − X − $100 = $400. X = $1,500.

Principal. The amount of money borrowed by the debtor.

Term. The length of time from when the note was signed by the debtor to when the debtor must pay the note.

There are two parties to a note:

- The *creditor* has a note receivable.
- The *debtor* has a note payable.

Exhibit 5-4 is a typical promissory note.

EXHIBIT 5-4 | A Promissory Note

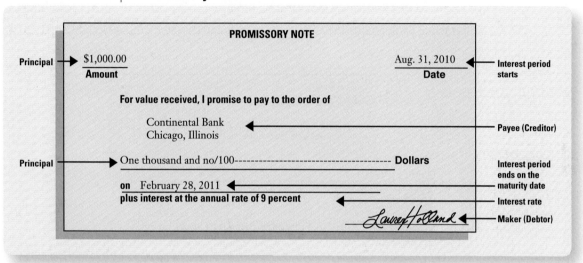

The **principal** amount of the note ($1,000) is the amount borrowed by the debtor, lent by the creditor. This six-month note receivable runs from August 31, 2010, to February 28, 2011, when Lauren Holland (the maker) promises to pay Continental Bank (the creditor) the principal of $1,000 plus 9% interest. Interest is revenue to the creditor (Continental Bank, in this case).

Accounting for Notes Receivable

Consider the promissory note in Exhibit 5-4. After Lauren Holland signs the note, Continental Bank gives her $1,000 cash. The bank's entries follow, assuming a December 31 year end for Continental Bank:

2010			
Aug 31	Note Receivable—L. Holland	1,000	
	Cash		1,000
	Made a loan.		

Note Receivable— L. Holland	
1,000	

The bank gave one asset, cash, in return for another asset, a note receivable, so total assets did not change.

Continental Bank earns interest revenue during September, October, November, and December. At December 31, the bank accrues 9% interest revenue for four months as follows:

2010			
Dec 31	Interest Receivable ($1,000 × .09 × 4/12)	30	
	Interest Revenue		30
	Accrued interest revenue.		

The bank's assets and revenues increase.

Continental Bank reports these amounts in its financial statements at December 31, 2010:

Balance sheet	
Current assets:	
Note receivable	$1,000
Interest receivable................	30
Income statement	
Interest revenue	$ 30

The bank collects the note on February 28, 2011, and records

2011			
Feb 28	Cash	1,045	
	Note Receivable—L. Holland		1,000
	Interest Receivable		30
	Interest Revenue ($1,000 × .09 × 2/12)		15
	Collected note at maturity.		

This entry zeroes out Note Receivable and Interest Receivable and also records the interest revenue earned in 2011.

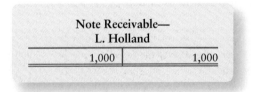

In its 2011 financial statements the only item that Continental Bank will report is the interest revenue of $15 that was earned in 2011. There's no note receivable or interest receivable on the balance sheet because those items were zeroed out when the bank collected the note at maturity.

Three aspects of the interest computation deserve mention:

1. Interest rates are always for an annual period, unless stated otherwise. In this example, the annual interest rate is 9%. At December 31, 2010, Continental Bank accrues interest revenue for four months. The interest computation is

Principal	×	Interest Rate	×	Time	=	Amount of Interest
$1,000	×	.09	×	4/12	=	$30

2. The time element (4/12) is the fraction of the year that the note has been in force during 2010.

3. Interest is often completed for a number of days. For example, suppose you loaned out $10,000 on April 10. The note receivable runs for 90 days and specifies interest at 8%.

   a. Interest starts accruing on April 11 and runs for 90 days, ending on the due date, July 9, as follows:

Month	Number of Days That Interest Accrues
April	20
May	31
June	30
July	9
Total	90

   b. The interest computation is

   $10,000 × .08 × 90/365 = $197

Some companies sell goods and services on notes receivable (versus selling on accounts receivable). This often occurs when the payment term extends beyond the customary accounts receivable period of 30 to 60 days.

Suppose that on March 20, 2011, PepsiCo sells a large amount of food to Wal-Mart. PepsiCo gets Wal-Mart's three-month promissory note plus 10% annual interest. At the outset, PepsiCo would debit Notes Receivable and credit Sales Revenue.

A company may also accept a note receivable from a trade customer whose account receivable is past due. The company then debits Notes Receivable and credits Accounts Receivable. We would say the company "received a note receivable on account." Now let's examine some strategies to speed up cash flow.

How to Speed Up Cash Flow

All companies want speedy cash receipts. Rapid cash flow finances new products, research, and development. Thus, companies such as PepsiCo find ways to collect cash quickly. Two common strategies generate cash quickly.

Credit Card or Bankcard Sales

The merchant sells merchandise and lets the customer pay with a credit card, such as Discover or American Express, or with a bankcard, such as VISA or MasterCard. This strategy may dramatically increase sales, but the added revenue comes at a cost, which is typically about 2% to 3% of the total amount of the sale. Let's see how credit cards and bankcards work from the seller's perspective.

Suppose Dell, Inc., sells computers for $5,000, and the customer pays with a VISA card. Dell records the sale as follows:

Cash	4,900	
Credit Card Discount Expense	100	
Sales Revenue		5,000
Recorded bankcard sales.		

Assets	=	Liabilities	+	Stockholders' Equity	+	Revenues	−	Expenses
+ 4,900	=	0	+			+ 5,000		− 100

Dell enters the transaction in the credit card machine. The machine, linked to a VISA server, automatically credits Dell's account for a discounted portion, say $4,900, of the $5,000 sale amount. Two percent ($100) goes to VISA. To Dell, the credit card discount expense is an operating expense similar to interest expense.

Selling (Factoring) Receivables

PepsiCo makes some large sales to grocery chains on account, debiting Accounts Receivable and crediting Sales Revenue. PepsiCo might then sell these accounts receivable to another business, called a *factor*. The factor earns revenue by paying a discounted price for the receivable and then hopefully collecting the full amount from the customer. The benefit to PepsiCo is the immediate receipt of cash. The biggest disadvantage of factoring is that it is often quite expensive, when compared to the costs of retaining the receivable on the books and ultimately collecting the full amount. In addition, the company that factors its receivables loses control over the collection process. For these reasons, factoring is often not used by companies who have other less costly means to raise cash, such as short-term borrowing from banks. Factoring may be used by start-up companies with insufficient credit history to obtain loans at a reasonable cost, by companies with weak credit history, or by companies that are already saddled with a significant amount of debt.

To illustrate selling, or *factoring*, accounts receivable, suppose a company wishes to speed up cash flow and therefore sells $100,000 of accounts receivables, receiving cash of $95,000. The company would record the sale of the receivables as follows:

Cash	95,000	
Financing Expense	5,000	
Accounting Receivable		100,000
Sold accounts receivable.		

Again, Financing Expense is an operating expense, with the same effect as a loss. Some companies may debit a Loss account. Discounting a note receivable is similar to selling an account receivable. However, the credit is to Notes Receivable (instead of Accounts Receivable).

Notice the high price (5% of the face amount, or $5,000) the company has had to pay in order to collect the cash immediately, as opposed to waiting 30 to 60 days to collect the full amount. Therefore, if the company can afford to wait, it will probably not engage in factoring in order to collect the full amount of the receivables.

Reporting on the Statement of Cash Flows

Receivables and short-term investments appear on the balance sheet as assets. We saw these in PepsiCo's balance sheet at the beginning of the chapter. We've also seen how to report the related revenues, expenses, gains, and losses on the income statement. Because receivable and investment transactions affect cash, their effects must also be reported on the statement of cash flows.

Receivables bring in cash when the business collects from customers. These transactions are reported as *operating activities* on the statement of cash flows because they result from sales. Investment transactions show up as *investing activities* on the statement of cash flows. Chapter 12 shows how companies report their cash flows on the statement of cash flows. In that chapter we will see exactly how to report cash flows related to receivables and investment transactions.

USING TWO KEY RATIOS TO MAKE DECISIONS

Investors and creditors use ratios to evaluate the financial health of a company. We introduced the current ratio in Chapter 3. Other ratios, including the **quick** (or *acid-test*) **ratio** and the number of days' sales in receivables, help investors measure liquidity.

OBJECTIVE

5 **Use** two new ratios to evaluate a business

Acid-Test (or Quick) Ratio

The balance sheet lists assets in the order of relative liquidity:

1. Cash and cash equivalents

2. Short-term investments

3. Accounts (or notes) receivable

PepsiCo's balance sheet in the chapter-opening story lists these accounts in order.

Managers, stockholders, and creditors care about the liquidity of a company's assets. The current ratio measures ability to pay current liabilities with current assets. A more stringent measure of ability to pay current liabilities is the **acid-test** (or *quick*) **ratio**:

PepsiCo 2007

(Dollars in millions, taken from PepsiCo balance sheet)

$$\text{Acid-test ratio} = \frac{\text{Cash} + \frac{\text{Short-term}}{\text{investments}} + \frac{\text{Net current}}{\text{receivables}}}{\text{Total current liabilities}} = \frac{\$910 + \$1,571 + \$4,389}{\$7,753} = 0.89$$

The higher the acid-test ratio, the easier it is to pay current liabilities. PepsiCo's acid-test ratio of 0.89 means that it has 89 cents of quick assets to pay each $1 of current liabilities. This ratio value is considered reasonably good, but not excellent. Traditionally, companies have wanted an acid-test ratio of at least 1.0 to be safe. The ratio needs to be high enough for safety, but not too high. After all, cash and the other liquid assets don't earn very high rates of return, as inventory and plant assets do.

What is an acceptable acid-test ratio? The answer depends on the industry. Auto dealers can operate smoothly with an acid-test ratio of 0.20, roughly one-fourth of PepsiCo's ratio value. How can auto dealers survive with so low an acid-test ratio? The auto manufacturers help finance their dealers' inventory. Most dealers, therefore, have a financial safety net provided through the manufacturers. During the recent business recession, General Motors' sales slumped and the company ran dangerously low of cash. One of the many consequences of GM's cash shortage was that it deprived dealerships of these safety nets and put them in jeopardy of bankruptcy and insolvency as well as the company. You can see the "domino effect" of arrangements like this, and why a number of GM dealerships were forced to close, even after GM received about $25 billion in "bailout money" from the United States government.

Days' Sales in Receivables

After a business makes a credit sale, the *next* step is collecting the receivable. **Days' sales in receivables**, also called the *collection period*, tells a company how long it takes to collect its average level of receivables. Shorter is better because cash is coming in quickly. The longer the collection period, the less cash is available to pay bills and expand.

Days' sales in receivables can be computed in two logical steps. First, compute one day's sales (or total revenues). Then divide one day's sales into average receivables for the period. We show days' sales in receivables for PepsiCo.

(Dollars in millions, taken from PepsiCo's financial statements)

Days' Sales in Receivables		PepsiCo

$$1. \quad \frac{\text{One}}{\text{day's sales}} = \frac{\text{Net sales}}{365 \text{ days}} \qquad\qquad \frac{\$39{,}474}{365 \text{ days}} = \$108 \text{ per day}$$

$$2. \quad \frac{\text{Days' sales in average receivables}}{=} \frac{\text{Average receivables *}}{\text{One day's sales}} \qquad\qquad \frac{\$4{,}057*}{\$108 \text{ per day}} = 38 \text{ days}$$

$$\begin{array}{l} *\text{Average} \\ \text{net} \\ \text{receivables} \end{array} = \frac{\text{Beginning net receivables} + \text{Ending net receivables}}{2} = \frac{\$3{,}725 + \$4{,}389}{2} = \$4{,}057$$

Net sales come from the income statement, and the receivables amounts are taken from the balance sheet. Average receivables is the simple average of the beginning and ending balance.

It takes PepsiCo 38 days to collect its average level of receivables. To evaluate PepsiCo's collection period of 38 days, we need to compare 38 days to the credit terms that PepsiCo offers customers when the company makes a sale, as well as the number of days on average that creditors typically allow PepsiCo to pay them without penalty.

Suppose PepsiCo makes sales on "net 30" terms, which means that customers should pay PepsiCo within 30 days of the sale. PepsiCo's collection period of 38 days is pretty good in comparison to the ideal measure of 30 days. After all, some customers drag out their payments. And, as we've seen, some customers don't pay at all. On the other hand, if PepsiCo's short-term creditors expect payment of their accounts payable within 30 days, PepsiCo might be forced to borrow cash at banks in order to pay its creditors on time, which could prove to be expensive.

Companies watch their collection periods closely. Whenever collections slow down, the business must find other sources of financing, such as borrowing or selling receivables. During recessions, customers pay more slowly, and a longer collection period may be unavoidable.[2]

---

[2]Another ratio, **accounts receivable turnover**, captures the same information as days' sales in receivables. Receivable turnover is computed as follows: Net sales/Average net accounts receivable. During 2007, PepsiCo had a receivable turnover rate of 9.7 times ($39,474/$4,057 = 9.7). Days sales in average receivables can then be computed by dividing 365 by the receivable turnover (365/9.7 = 37.63). You can see that this method merely rearranges the equations in the body of the text, "going through the back door" to achieve the same result. The authors prefer days' sales in receivables to receivables turnover because days' sales in receivable can be compared directly to the company's credit sale terms.

END-OF-CHAPTER SUMMARY PROBLEM

Superior Technical Resources' (STR's) balance sheet at December 31, 2010, reported

	(In millions)
Accounts receivable..	$382
Allowance for doubtful accounts................	(52)

STR uses both the percent-of-sales and the aging approaches to account for uncollectible receivables.

Requirements

1. How much of the December 31, 2010, balance of accounts receivables did STR expect to collect? Stated differently, what was the net realizable value of STR's receivables?
2. Journalize, without explanations, 2011 entries for STR:
   a. Estimated doubtful-account expense of $40 million, based on the percent-of-sales method, all during the year.
   b. Write-offs of uncollectible accounts receivable totaling $58 million. Prepare a T-account for Allowance for Doubtful Accounts and post to this account. Show its unadjusted balance at December 31, 2011.
   c. December 31, 2011, aging of receivables, which indicates that $47 million of the total receivables of $409 million is uncollectible at year end. Post to Allowance for Doubtful Accounts, and show its adjusted balance at December 31, 2011.
3. Show how STR's receivables and the related allowance will appear on the December 31, 2011, balance sheet.
4. Show what STR's income statement will report for the foregoing transactions.

Answers

Requirement 1

	(In millions)
Net realizable value of receivables ($382 – $52)	$330

Requirement 2

		(In millions)	
a.	Doubtful-Account Expense	40	
	Allowance for Doubtful Accounts		40
b.	Allowance for Doubtful Accounts	58	
	Accounts Receivable		58

Allowance for Doubtful Accounts

		Dec 31, 2010	52	
2011 Write-offs	58	2011 Expense	40	
		Unadjusted balance at Dec 31, 2011	34	

c.	Doubtful-Account Expense ($47 – $34)	13	
	Allowance for Doubtful Accounts		13

Allowance for Doubtful Accounts

	Dec 31, 2011 Unadj bal	34
	2011 Expense	13
	Dec 31, 2011 Adj bal	47

▮ Requirement 3

	(In millions)
Accounts receivable.....................................	$409
Allowance for doubtful accounts...............	(47)

▮ Requirement 4

	(In millions)
Expenses: Doubtful-account expense for 2011 ($40 + $13)	$53

REVIEW RECEIVABLES AND INVESTMENTS

Quick Check (Answers are given on page 340.)

1. Henry Funaro Golf Academy held investments in trading securities valued at $40,000 at December 31, 2010. These investments cost Henry Funaro $33,000. What is the appropriate amount for Henry Funaro to report for these investments on the December 31, 2010, balance sheet?
   a. $40,000
   b. $7,000 gain
   c. 33,000
   d. Cannot be determined from the data given

2. Return to Henry Funaro Golf Academy in question 1. What should appear on the Henry Funaro income statement for the year ended December 31, 2010, for the trading securities?
   a. $7,000 unrealized gain
   b. $33,000
   c. $40,000
   d. Cannot be determined from the data given

Use the following information to answer questions 3–7.
Anderson Company had the following information relating to credit sales in 2010.

Accounts receivable 12/31/10...	$10,000
Allowance for uncollectible accounts 12/31/10 (before adjustment)...........	600
Credit sales during 2010	40,000
Cash sales during 2010	15,000
Collections from customers on account during 2010.................................	44,000

3. Uncollectible accounts are determined by the percent-of-sales method to be 4% of credit sales. How much is uncollectible-account expense for 2010?
   a. $2,200   c. $1,600
   b. $400   d. $1,760

4. Uncollectible-account expense for 2010 is $1,600. What is the adjusted balance in the Allowance account at year-end 2010?
   a. $3,800   c. $1,600
   b. $2,200   d. $600

5. If uncollectible accounts are determined by the aging-of-receivables method to be $1,030, the uncollectible account expense for 2010 would be
   a. $1,630.   c. $430.
   b. $600.   d. $1,030.

6. Using the aging-of-receivables method, the balance of the Allowance account after the adjusting entry would be
   a. $600.   c. $1,630.
   b. $1,030.   d. $430.

7. Using the aging-of-receivables method, the net realizable value of accounts receivable on the 12/31/10 balance sheet would be
   a. $8,370.   c. $8,400.
   b. $10,000.   d. $8,970.

8. Accounts Receivable has a debit balance of $2,800, and the Allowance for Uncollectible Accounts has a credit balance of $400. A $90 account receivable is written off. What is the amount of net receivables (net realizable value) after the write-off?
   a. $2,490   c. $2,310
   b. $2,710   d. $2,400

9. Magnolia Corporation began 2010 with Accounts Receivable of $575,000. Sales for the year totaled $2,200,000. Magnolia ended the year with accounts receivable of $725,000. Magnolia's bad-debt losses are minimal. How much cash did Magnolia collect from customers in 2010?
   a. $2,925,000   c. $2,200,000
   b. $2,050,000   d. $2,350,000

10. Neptune Company received a four-month, 9%, $2,800 note receivable on December 1. The adjusting entry on December 31 will
   a. debit Interest Receivable $21.   c. both a and b.
   b. credit Interest Revenue $21.   d. credit Interest Revenue $252.

11. What is the maturity value of a $70,000, 12%, six-month note?
   a. $70,000   c. $65,800
   b. $78,400   d. $74,200

12. If the adjusting entry to accrue interest on a note receivable is omitted, then
   a. assets, net income, and stockholders' equity are understated.
   b. assets are overstated, net income is understated, and stockholders' equity is understated.
   c. liabilities are understated, net income is overstated, and stockholders' equity is overstated.
   d. assets, net income, and stockholders' equity are overstated.

13. Net sales total $803,000. Beginning and ending accounts receivable are $80,000 and $74,000, respectively. Calculate days' sales in receivables.
   a. 35 days
   b. 36 days
   c. 30 days
   d. 34 days

14. From the following list of accounts, calculate the quick ratio.

Cash	$ 6,000	Accounts payable	$10,000
Accounts receivable	9,000	Salary payable	4,000
Inventory	11,000	Notes payable (due in two years)	13,000
Prepaid insurance	1,000	Short-term note investments	3,000

   a. 1.3
   b. 2.1
   c. 1.1
   d. 1.8

Accounting Vocabulary

acid-test ratio (p. 311) Ratio of the sum of cash plus short-term investments plus net current receivables to total current liabilities. Tells whether the entity can pay all its current liabilities if they come due immediately. Also called the *quick ratio*.

accounts receivable turnover (p. 313) Net sales divided by average net accounts receivable.

aging-of-receivables (p. 302) A way to estimate bad debts by analyzing individual accounts receivable according to the length of time they have been receivable from the customer.

Allowance for Doubtful Accounts (p. 299) Another name for *Allowance for Uncollectible Accounts*.

Allowance for Uncollectible Accounts (p. 299) The estimated amount of collection losses. Another name for *Allowance for Doubtful Accounts*.

allowance method (p. 299) A method of recording collection losses based on estimates of how much money the business will not collect from its customers.

bad-debt expense (p. 299) Another name for *uncollectible-account expense*.

creditor (p. 306) The party to whom money is owed.

days' sales in receivables (p. 312) Ratio of average net accounts receivable to one day's sales. Indicates how many days' sales remain in Accounts Receivable awaiting collection. Also called the *collection period*.

debtor (p. 306) The party who owes money.

direct write-off method (p. 305) A method of accounting for bad debts in which the company waits until a customer's account receivable proves uncollectible and then debits

Uncollectible-Account Expense and credits the customer's Account Receivable.

doubtful-account expense (p. 299) Another name for *uncollectible-account expense*.

interest (p. 306) The borrower's cost of renting money from a lender. Interest is revenue for the lender and expense for the borrower.

marketable securities (p. 290) Another name for *short-term investments*.

maturity (p. 296) The date on which a debt instrument must be paid.

maturity date (p. 306) The date on which the debtor must pay the note.

maturity value (p. 306) The sum of principal and interest on the note.

percent-of-sales method (p. 301) Computes uncollectible-account expense as a percentage of net sales. Also called the income statement approach because it focuses on the amount of expense to be reported on the income statement.

principal (p. 307) The amount borrowed by a debtor and lent by a creditor.

quick ratio (p. 311) Another name for *acid-test ratio*.

receivables (p. 296) Monetary claims against a business or an individual, acquired mainly by selling goods or services and by lending money.

short-term investments (p. 290) Investments that a company plans to hold for one year or less. Also called *marketable securities*.

term (p. 307) The length of time from inception to maturity.

trading securities (p. 291) Stock investments that are to be sold in the near future with the intent of generating profits on the sale.

uncollectible-account expense (p. 299) Cost to the seller of extending credit. Arises from the failure to collect from credit customers. Also called doubtful-account expense or bad-debt expense.

ASSESS YOUR PROGRESS

Short Exercises

S5-1 (*Learning Objective 1: Reporting trading investments*) Answer these questions about investments.

1. What is the amount to report on the balance sheet for a trading security?
2. Why is a trading security always a current asset? Explain.

S5-2 (*Learning Objective 1: Accounting for a trading investment*) Newsome Corp. holds a portfolio of trading securities. Suppose that on November 1, Newsome paid $87,000 for an investment in Quark shares to add to its portfolio. At December 31, the market value of Quark shares is $98,000. For this situation, show everything that Newsome would report on its December 31 balance sheet and on its income statement for the year ended December 31.

S5-3 (*Learning Objective 1: Accounting for a trading investment*) McCarver Investments purchased Hoffman shares as a trading security on December 18 for $103,000.

1. Suppose the Hoffman shares decreased in value to $96,000 at December 31. Make the McCarver journal entry to adjust the Short-Term Investment account to market value.
2. Show how McCarver would report the short-term investment on its balance sheet and the unrealized gain or loss on its income statement.

S5-4 (*Learning Objective 2: Applying internal controls over the collection of receivables*) Susan Perry keeps the Accounts Receivable T-account of Abraham & Paige, a partnership. What duty will a good internal control system withhold from Perry? Why?

writing assignment ■

S5-5 (*Learning Objective 2: Controlling cash receipts from customers*) As a recent college graduate, you land your first job in the customer collections department of Countryroads Publishing. Zach Peters, the manager, asked you to propose a system to ensure that cash received from customers by mail is handled properly. Draft a short memorandum to explain the essential element in your proposed plan. State why this element is important.

writing assignment ■

S5-6 (*Learning Objective 3: Applying the allowance method [percent-of-sales] to account for uncollectibles*) During its first year of operations, Turning Leaves Furniture Restoration, Inc., had sales of $312,000, all on account. Industry experience suggests that Turning Leaves Furniture Restoration's uncollectibles will amount to 4% of credit sales. At December 31, 2010, accounts receivable total $38,000. The company uses the allowance method to account for uncollectibles.

1. Make Turning Leaves Furniture Restoration's journal entry for uncollectible-account expense using the percent-of-sales method.
2. Show how Turning Leaves Furniture Restoration should report accounts receivable on its balance sheet at December 31, 2010.

S5-7 (*Learning Objective 3: Applying the allowance method [percent-of-sales] to account for uncollectibles*) During 2011, Turning Leaves Furniture Restoration completed these transactions:

1. Sales revenue on account, $1,000,000
2. Collections on account, $870,000
3. Write-offs of uncollectibles, $12,000
4. Uncollectible-account expense, 4% of sales revenue

Journalize Turning's 2011 transactions. Explanations are not required

S5-8 (*Learning Objective 3: Applying the allowance method to account for uncollectibles*) Use the information from the following journal entries of Turning Leaves Furniture Restoration to answer the questions below:

	Journal Entry		
	Accounts	Debit	Credit
1.	Accounts Receivable	1,000,000	
	Sales Revenue		1,000,000
2.	Cash	870,000	
	Accounts Receivable		870,000
3.	Allowance for Uncollectible Accounts	12,000	
	Accounts Receivable		12,000
4.	Uncollectible-Account Expense	40,000	
	Allowance for Uncollectible Accounts		40,000

❙ Requirements

1. Start with Accounts Receivable's beginning balance ($38,000) and then post to the Accounts Receivable T-account. How much do Turning Leaves Furniture Restoration's customers owe the company at December 31, 2011?
2. Start with the Allowance account's beginning credit balance ($12,480) and then post to the Allowance for Uncollectible Accounts T-account. How much of the receivables at December 31, 2011, does Turning Leaves Furniture Restoration expect *not* to collect?
3. At December 31, 2011, how much cash does Turning Leaves Furniture Restoration expect to collect on its accounts receivable?

S5-9 (*Learning Objective 3: Applying the allowance method [aging-of-accounts-receivable] to account for uncollectibles*)   Gray and Dumham, a law firm, started 2010 with accounts receivable of $31,000 and an allowance for uncollectible accounts of $4,000. The 2010 service revenues on account totaled $175,000, and cash collections on account totaled $128,000. During 2010, Gray and Dumham wrote off uncollectible accounts receivable of $2,800. At December 31, 2010, the aging of accounts receivable indicated that Gray and Dumham will not collect $1,850 of its accounts receivable.

Journalize Gray and Dumham's (a) service revenue, (b) cash collections on account, (c) write-offs of uncollectible receivables, and (d) uncollectible-account expense for the year. Explanations are not required. Prepare a T-account for Allowance for Uncollectible Accounts to show your computation of uncollectible-account expense for the year.

S5-10 (*Learning Objective 3: Applying the allowance method to account for uncollectibles*) Perform the following accounting for the receivables of Evans and Tanner, a law firm, at December 31, 2010.

❙ Requirements

1. Start with the beginning balances for these T-accounts:

   • Accounts Receivable, $97,000   • Allowance for Uncollectible Accounts, $5,000

   Post the following 2010 transactions to the T-accounts:
   a. Service revenue of $698,000, all on account
   b. Collections on account, $722,000
   c. Write-offs of uncollectible accounts, $8,000
   d. Uncollectible-account expense (allowance method), $14,000
2. What are the ending balances of Accounts Receivable and Allowance for Uncollectible Accounts?
3. Show how Evans and Tanner will report accounts receivable on its balance sheet at December 31, 2010.

S5-11 (*Learning Objectives 3, 4: Answering practical questions about receivables*) Answer these questions about receivables and uncollectibles. For the true-false questions, explain any answers that turn out to be false.

1. True or false? Credit sales increase receivables. Collections and write-offs decrease receivables.
2. Which receivables figure, the *total* amount that customers *owe* the company, or the *net* amount the company expects to collect, is more interesting to investors as they consider buying the company's stock? Give your reason.
3. Show how to determine net accounts receivable.
4. True or false? The direct write-off method of accounting for uncollectibles understates assets.
5. California Bank lent $200,000 to Sacramento Company on a six-month, 8% note. Which party has interest receivable? Which party has interest payable? Interest expense? Interest revenue? How much interest will these organizations record one month after Sacramento Company signs the note?
6. When California Bank accrues interest on the Sacramento Company note, show the directional effects on the bank's assets, liabilities, and equity (increase, decrease, or no effect).

S5-12 (*Learning Objective 4: Accounting for a note receivable*)   Northend Bank & Trust Company lent $130,000 to Sylvia Peters on a six-month, 9% note. Record the following for bank (explanations are not required):

  a. Lending the money on May 6.
  b. Collecting the principal and interest at maturity. Specify the date.

S5-13 (*Learning Objective 4: Computing note receivable amounts*)

1. Compute the amount of interest during 2010, 2011, and 2012 for the following note receivable: On April 30, 2010, BCDE Bank lent $170,000 to Carl Abbott on a two-year, 7% note.
2. Which party has a (an)
  a. note receivable?
  b. note payable?
  c. interest revenue?
  d. interest expense?
3. How much in total would BCDE Bank collect if Carl Abbott paid off the note early—say, on November 30, 2010?

S5-14 (*Learning Objective 4: Accruing interest receivable and collecting a note receivable*) On August 31, 2010, Nancy Thompson borrowed $2,000 from Green Interstate Bank. Thompson signed a note payable, promising to pay the bank principal plus interest on August 31, 2011. The interest rate on the note is 10%. The accounting year of Green Interstate Bank ends on June 30, 2011. Journalize Green Interstate Bank's (a) lending money on the note receivable at August 31, 2010, (b) accrual of interest at June 30, 2011, and (c) collection of principal and interest August 31, 2011, the maturity date of the note.

S5-15 (*Learning Objective 4: Reporting receivables amounts*)   Using your answers to Short Exercise 5-14, show how the Green Interstate Bank will report the following:

  a. Whatever needs to be reported on its classified balance sheet at June 30, 2011.
  b. Whatever needs to be reported on its income statement for the year ended June 30, 2011.
  c. Whatever needs to be reported on its classified balance sheet at June 30, 2012. Ignore Cash.
  d. Whatever needs to be reported on its income statement for the year ended June 30, 2012.

S5-16 (*Learning Objective 5: Evaluating the acid-test ratio and days' sales in receivables*) West Highland Clothiers reported the following amounts in its 2011 financial statements. The 2010 amounts are given for comparison.

		2011		2010
Current assets:				
Cash..		$ 9,700		$ 9,700
Short-term investments................		17,000		14,000
Accounts receivable.....................	$84,000		$77,000	
Less: Allowance for				
uncollectibles........................	(7,100)	76,900	(6,100)	70,900
Inventory.......................................		189,000		190,500
Prepaid insurance.........................		2,300		2,300
Total current assets.....................		294,900		287,400
Total current liabilities....................		99,000		111,000
Net sales...		802,000		736,000

❚ *Requirements*

1. Compute West Highland's acid-test ratio at the end of 2011. Round to two decimal places.
   How does the acid-test ratio compare with the industry average of 0.97?
2. Compare days' sales in receivables measure for 2011 with the company's credit terms of net 30 days.

S5-17 (*Learning Objectives 2, 3, 5: Reporting receivables and other accounts in the financial statements; using ratios to evaluate a business*)   Norbert Medical Service reported the following items, (amounts in thousands):

Unearned revenues (current)...............	$ 607	Service revenue..................................		$23,653
Allowance for		Other assets...		1,707
doubtful accounts...........................	309	Property, plant, and equipment..........		25,376
Other expenses....................................	12,559	Operating expense.............................		11,610
Accounts receivable............................	4,467	Cash..		289
Accounts payable	2,255	Notes payable (long term).................		18,729

❚ *Requirements*

1. Classify each item as (a) income statement or balance sheet and as (b) debit balance or credit balance.
2. How much net income (or net loss) did Norbert report for the year?
3. Compute Norbert's quick (acid-test) ratio. Round to two decimal places. Evaluate Norbert Medical Service's liquidity position.

Exercises

All of A and B exercises can be found within MyAccountingLab, an online homework and practice environment. Your instructor may ask you to complete these exercises using MyAccountingLab.

(Group A)

E5-18A (*Learning Objective 1: Accounting for a trading investment*)   Northern Corporation, the investment banking company, often has extra cash to invest. Suppose Northern buys 800 shares of Andy, Inc., stock at $54 per share. Assume Northern expects to hold the Andy stock for one month and then sell it. The purchase occurs on December 15, 2010. At December 31, the market price of a share of Andy stock is $66 per share.

❚ *Requirements*

1. What type of investment is this to Northern? Give the reason for your answer.
2. Record Northern's purchase of the Andy stock on December 15 and the adjustment to market value on December 31.
3. Show how Northern would report this investment on its balance sheet at December 31 and any gain or loss on its income statement for the year ended December 31, 2010.

E5-19A *(Learning Objective 1: Reporting a trading investment)* On November 16, ACA, Inc., paid $95,000 for an investment in the stock of American Pacific Railway (APR). ACA plans to account for these shares as trading securities. On December 12, ACA received a $400 cash dividend from APR. It is now December 31, and the market value of the APR stock is $92,000. For this investment, show what ACA should report in its income statement and balance sheet.

E5-20A *(Learning Objective 1: Accounting for a trading investment)* Sponsor Corporation reports short-term investments on its balance sheet. Suppose a division of Sponsor completed the following short-term investment transactions during 2010:

2010	
Dec 12	Purchased 600 shares of Disc, Inc., stock for $21,600. Sponsor plans to sell the stock at a profit in the near future.
21	Received a cash dividend of $0.81 per share on the Disc, Inc., stock.
31	Adjusted the investment in Disc, Inc., stock. Current market value is $27,000. Sponsor still plans to sell the stock in early 2011.
2011	
Jan 16	Sold the Disc, Inc., stock for $35,670.

❚ *Requirement*

1. Prepare T-accounts for Cash, Short-Term Investment, Dividend Revenue, Unrealized Gain (Loss) on Investment, and Gain on Sale of Investment. Show the effects of Sponsor's investment transactions. Start with a cash balance of $97,000; all the other accounts start at zero.

E5-21A *(Learning Objective 3: Reporting bad debts by the allowance method)* At December 31, 2010, Darci's Travel has an accounts receivable balance of $88,000. Allowance for Doubtful Accounts has a credit balance of $900 before the year-end adjustment. Service revenue for 2010 was $900,000. Darci's Travel estimates that doubtful-account expense for the year is 3% of sales. Make the year-end entry to record doubtful-account expense. Show how the accounts receivable and the allowance for doubtful accounts are reported on the balance sheet.

E5-22A *(Learning Objective 3: Using the allowance method for bad debts)* On September 30, Hilly Mountain Party Planners had a $30,000 balance in Accounts Receivable and a $2,000 credit balance in Allowance for Uncollectible Accounts. During October, the store made credit sales of $161,000. October collections on account were $137,000, and write-offs of uncollectible receivables totaled $2,300. Uncollectible-account expense is estimated as 4% of revenue.

❚ *Requirements*

1. Journalize sales, collections, write-offs of uncollectibles, and uncollectible-account expense by the allowance method during October. Explanations are not required.
2. Show the ending balances in Accounts Receivable, Allowance for Uncollectible Accounts, and *Net* Accounts Receivable at October 31. How much does the store expect to collect?
3. Show how the store will report Accounts Receivable on its October 31 balance sheet.

E5-23A (*Learning Objective 3: Using the direct write-off method for bad debts*) Refer to Exercise 5-22A.

▌Requirements

1. Record uncollectible-account expense for October by the direct write-off method.
2. What amount of accounts receivable would Hilly Mountain report on its October 31 balance sheet under the direct write-off method? Does it expect to collect the full amount?

E5-24A (*Learning Objective 3: Using the aging approach to estimate bad debts*) At December 31, 2010, before any year-end adjustments, the Accounts Receivable balance of Alpha Company is $210,000. The Allowance for Doubtful Accounts has a $13,500 credit balance. Alpha Company prepares the following aging schedule for Accounts Receivable:

■ spreadsheet

	Age of Accounts			
Total Balance	1–30 Days	31–60 Days	61–90 Days	Over 90 Days
$210,000	$80,000	$60,000	$40,000	$30,000
Estimated uncollectible	0.6%	4.0%	5.0%	40.0%

▌Requirements

1. Based on the aging of accounts receivable, is the unadjusted balance of the allowance account adequate? Too high? Too low?
2. Make the entry required by the aging schedule. Prepare a T-account for the allowance.
3. Show how Alpha Company will report Accounts Receivable on its December 31 balance sheet.

E5-25A (*Learning Objective 3: Measuring and accounting for uncollectibles*) Assume Dogwood Leaf Foods, Inc., experienced the following revenue and accounts receivable write-offs:

	Service	Accounts Receivable Write-Offs in Month			
Month	Revenue	January	February	March	Totals
January	$ 6,700	$54	$ 89		$143
February	6,900		101	$ 34	135
March	7,000			112	112
	$20,600	$54	$190	$146	$390

Suppose Dogwood Leaf estimates that 1% of revenues will become uncollectible.

▌Requirement

1. Journalize service revenue (all on account), bad-debt expense, and write-offs during March. Include explanations.

E5-26A (*Learning Objective 4: Recording notes receivable and accruing interest revenue*) Record the following note receivable transactions in the journal of Aegean Realty. How much interest revenue did Aegean earn this year? Use a 365-day year for interest computations, and round interest amounts to the nearest dollar.

Sep 1	Loaned $15,000 cash to Carroll Fadal on a one-year, 10% note.
Nov 6	Performed service for Turf Masters, receiving a 90-day, 8% note for $12,000.
16	Received a $4,000, six-month, 11% note on account from Voleron, Inc.
30	Accrued interest revenue for the year.

E5-27A (*Learning Objective 4: Reporting the effects of note receivable transactions on the balance sheet and income statement*) Assume Port City Credit Union completed these transactions:

2010		
Apr	1	Loaned $125,000 to Lee Franz on a one-year, 12% note.
Dec	31	Accrued interest revenue on the Franz note.
2011		
Apr	1	Collected the maturity value of the note from Franz (principal plus interest).

Show what the company would report for these transactions on its 2010 and 2011 balance sheets and income statements.

E5-28A (*Learning Objective 5: Using the acid-test ratio and days' sales in receivables to evaluate a company*) Cherokee, Inc., reported the following items at December 31, 2010 and 2009:

Balance Sheets (Summarized)

	Year End				Year End	
	2010	2009			2010	2009
Current assets:				**Current liabilities:**		
Cash..	$ 3,000	$ 9,000		Accounts payable.........................	$ 19,000	$ 20,500
Marketable securities.................	20,000	9,000		Other current liabilities...............	103,000	105,000
Accounts receivable, net..............	55,000	69,000		Long-term liabilities.......................	15,000	16,000
Inventory....................................	192,000	188,000				
Other current assets..................	2,000	2,000		Stockholders' equity.......................	135,000	135,500
Long-term assets						
Total assets....................................	$272,000	$277,000		Total liabilities and equity..............	$272,000	$277,000
Income Statement (partial):	2010					
Sales revenue.............................	$730,000					

Requirement

1. Compute Cherokee's (a) acid-test ratio and (b) days' sales in average receivables for 2010. Evaluate each ratio value as strong or weak. Cherokee sells on terms of net 30 days.

E5-29A (*Learning Objective 5: Analyzing a company's financial statements*) Modern Co., Inc., the electronics and appliance chain, reported these figures in millions of dollars:

	2011	2010
Net sales...	$573,000	$604,000
Receivables at end of year..............	3,910	4,710

Requirements

1. Compute Modern's average collection period during 2011.
2. Is Modern's collection period long or short? Viflex Networks takes 40 days to collect its average level of receivables. Domarko, the overnight shipper, takes 34 days. What causes Modern's collection period to be so different?

(Group B)

E5-30B (*Learning Objective 1: Accounting for a trading investment*) River Corporation, the investment banking company, often has extra cash to invest. Suppose River buys 600 shares of Eathen, Inc., stock at $40 per share. Assume River expects to hold the Eathen stock for one month and then sell it. The purchase occurs on December 15, 2010. At December 31, the market price of a share of Eathen stock is $48 per share.

Requirements

1. What type of investment is this to River? Give the reason for your answer.
2. Record River's purchase of the Eathen stock on December 15 and the adjustment to market value on December 31.
3. Show how River would report this investment on its balance sheet at December 31 and any gain or loss on its income statement for the year ended December 31, 2010.

E5-31B (*Learning Objective 1: Reporting a trading investment*) On November 16, SRO, Inc., paid $98,000 for an investment in the stock of Northwest Pacific Railway (NPR). SRO intends to account for these shares as trading securities. On December 12, SRO received a $700 cash dividend from NPR. It is now December 31, and the market value of the NPR stock is $94,000. For this investment, show what SRO should report in its income statement and balance sheet.

E5-32B (*Learning Objective 1: Accounting for a trading investment*) Eastern Corporation reports short-term investments on its balance sheet. Suppose a division of Eastern completed the following short-term investment transactions during 2010:

2010	
Dec 12	Purchased 600 shares of Music, Inc., stock for $46,800. Eastern plans to sell the stock at a profit in the near future.
21	Received a cash dividend of $0.52 per share on the Music, Inc., stock.
31	Adjusted the investment in Music, Inc., stock. Current market value is $48,600. Eastern still plans to sell the stock in early 2011.
2011	
Jan 16	Sold the Music, Inc., stock for $66,465.

Requirement

1. Prepare T-accounts for Cash, Short-Term Investment, Dividend Revenue, Unrealized Gain (Loss) on Investment, and Gain on Sale of Investment. Show the effects of Eastern's investment transactions. Start with a cash balance of $94,000; all the other accounts start at zero.

E5-33B (*Learning Objective 3: Reporting bad debts by the allowance method*) At December 31, 2010, White's Travel has an accounts receivable balance of $92,000. Allowance for Doubtful Accounts has a credit balance of $820 before the year-end adjustment. Service revenue for 2010 was $500,000. White's Travel estimates that doubtful-account expense for the year is 4% of sales. Make the December 31 entry to record doubtful-account expense. Show how the Accounts Receivable and the Allowance for Doubtful Accounts are reported on the balance sheet.

E5-34B (*Learning Objective 3: Using the allowance method for bad debts*)   On April 30, Hilltop Party Planners had a $33,000 balance in Accounts Receivable and a $4,000 credit balance in Allowance for Uncollectible Accounts. During May, the store made credit sales of $156,000. May collections on account were $132,000, and write-offs of uncollectible receivables totaled $2,300. Uncollectible-account expense is estimated as 2% of revenue.

❙ Requirements

1. Journalize sales, collections, write-offs of uncollectibles, and uncollectible-account expense by the allowance method during May. Explanations are not required.
2. Show the ending balances in Accounts Receivable, Allowance for Uncollectible Accounts, and *Net* Accounts Receivable at May 31. How much does the store expect to collect?
3. Show how the store will report Accounts Receivable on its May 31 balance sheet.

E5-35B (*Learning Objective 3: Using the direct write-off method for bad debts*)   Refer to Exercise 5-34B.

❙ Requirements

1. Record uncollectible-account expense for May by the direct write-off method.
2. What amount of accounts receivable would Hilltop report on its May 31 balance sheet under the direct write-off method? Does it expect to collect the full amount?

❙ spreadsheet

E5-36B (*Learning Objective 3: Using the aging approach to estimate bad debts*)   At December 31, 2010, before any year-end adjustments, the accounts receivable balance of Digital Electronics Company is $150,000. The allowance for doubtful accounts has a $6,800 credit balance. Digital Electronics Company prepares the following aging schedule for accounts receivable:

		Age of Accounts		
Total Balance	**1–30 Days**	**31–60 Days**	**61–90 Days**	**Over 90 Days**
$150,000	$60,000	$50,000	$30,000	$10,000
Estimated uncollectible	0.6%	4.0%	7.0%	40.0%

❙ Requirements

1. Based on the aging of accounts receivable, is the unadjusted balance of the allowance account adequate? Too high? Too low?
2. Make the entry required by the aging schedule. Prepare a T-account for the allowance.
3. Show how Digital Electronics Company will report Accounts Receivable on its December 31 balance sheet.

E5-37B (*Learning Objective 3: Measuring and accounting for uncollectibles*)   Assume Birch Leaf Foods, Inc., experienced the following revenue and accounts receivable write-offs:

Month	Service Revenue	Accounts Receivable Write-Offs in Month			
		January	February	March	Totals
January	$ 6,550	$53	$ 85		$138
February	6,750		100	$ 35	135
March	6,850			110	110
	$20,150	$53	$185	$145	$383

Suppose Birch Leaf estimates that 1% of revenues will become uncollectible.

Ⅰ Requirement

1. Journalize service revenue (all on account), bad-debt expense, and write-offs during March. Include explanations.

E5-38B *(Learning Objective 4: Recording notes receivable and accruing interest revenue)* Record the following note receivable transactions in the journal of Celtic Realty. How much interest revenue did Celtic earn this year? Use a 365-day year for interest computations, and round interest amounts to the nearest dollar.

Apr 1	Loaned $11,000 cash to Britt Durant on a one-year, 6% note.	
Jun 6	Performed service for Putt Masters, receiving a 90-day, 7% note for $14,000.	
16	Received a $3,000, six-month, 12% note on account from Voleron, Inc.	
30	Accrued interest revenue for the year.	

E5-39B *(Learning Objective 4: Reporting the effects of note receivable transactions on the balance sheet and income statement)* Assume Tradesmen Credit Union completed these transactions:

2010		
Apr 1	Loaned $50,000 to Leanne Harold on a one-year, 7% note.	
Dec 31	Accrued interest revenue on the Harold note.	
2011		
Apr 1	Collected the maturity value of the note from Harold (principal plus interest).	

Show what the company would report for these transactions on its 2010 and 2011 balance sheets and income statements.

E5-40B *(Learning Objective 5: Using the acid-test ratio and days' sales in receivables to evaluate a company)* Navajo, Inc., reported the following items at December 31, 2010 and 2009:

Balance Sheets (Summarized)

	Year End 2010	Year End 2009		Year End 2010	Year End 2009
Current assets:			**Current liabilities:**		
Cash..	$ 4,000	$ 10,000	Accounts payable	$ 15,000	$ 16,500
Marketable securities	23,000	12,000	Other current liabilities	105,000	107,000
Accounts receivable, net	56,000	70,000	Long-term liabilities	15,000	16,000
Inventory	192,000	188,000			
Other current assets	6,000	6,000	Stockholders' equity......................	146,000	146,500
Long-term assets					
Total assets....................................	$281,000	$286,000	Total liabilities and equity..............	$281,000	$286,000

Income Statement (partial):	2010
Sales revenue.............................	$727,000

Requirement

1. Compute Navajo's (a) acid-test ratio and (b) days' sales in average receivables for 2010. Evaluate each ratio value as strong or weak. Navajo sells on terms of net 30 days.

E5-41B (*Learning Objective 5: Analyzing a company's financial statements*)
Contemporary Co., Inc., the electronics and appliance chain, reported these figures in millions of dollars:

	2011	2010
Net sales..	$572,000	$601,000
Receivables at end of year..............	3,880	4,810

Requirements

1. Compute Contemporary's average collection period during 2011.
2. Is Contemporary's collection period long or short? Kurzwel Networks takes 36 days to collect its average level of receivables. Damascus, the overnight shipper, takes 35 days. What causes Contemporary's collection period to be so different?

Challenge Exercises

E5-42 (*Learning Objective 2: Determining whether to sell on bankcards*)   Radical Shirt Company sells on credit and manages its own receivables. Average experience for the past three years has been as follows:

	Cash	Credit	Total
Sales...	$350,000	$350,000	$700,000
Cost of goods sold............................	192,500	192,500	385,000
Uncollectible-account expense...........	—	18,000	18,000
Other expenses..................................	87,500	87,500	175,000

Jack Ryan, the owner, is considering whether to accept bankcards (VISA, MasterCard). Ryan expects total sales to increase by 12% but cash sales to remain unchanged. If Ryan switches to bankcards, the business can save $9,000 on other expenses, but VISA and MasterCard charge 2% on bankcard sales. Ryan figures that the increase in sales will be due to the increased volume of bankcard sales.

Requirement

1. Should Radical Shirt Company start selling on bankcards? Show the computations of net income under the present plan and under the bankcard plan.

E5-43 (*Learning Objective 3: Reconstructing receivables and bad-debt amounts*)
Suppose Diamond, Inc., reported net receivables of $2,586 million and $2,268 million at January 31, 2011, and 2010, after subtracting allowances of $70 million and $64 million at these respective dates. Diamond earned total revenue of $53,333 million (all on account) and recorded doubtful-account expense of $16 million for the year ended January 31, 2011.

Requirement

1. Use this information to measure the following amounts for the year ended January 31, 2011:
   a. Write-offs of uncollectible receivables
   b. Collections from customers

Quiz

Test your understanding of receivables by answering the following questions. Select the best choice from among the possible answers given.

Q5-44 United First Bank, the nationwide banking company, owns many types of investments. Assume that United First Bank paid $700,000 for trading securities on December 3. Two weeks later United First Bank received a $37,000 cash dividend. At December 31, these trading securities were quoted at a market price of $705,000. United First Bank's December income statement should report:

a. unrealized loss of $5,000.
b. unrealized loss of $3,000.
c. both a and b.
d. none of the above.

Q5-45 Refer to the United First Bank data in Quiz question 5-44. At December 31, United First Bank's balance sheet should report:

a. dividend revenue of $37,000.
b. short-term investment of $700,000.
c. short-term investment of $705,000.
d. unrealized gain of $5,000.

Q5-46 Under the allowance method for uncollectible receivables, the entry to record uncollectible-account expense has what effect on the financial statements?

a. Decreases owners' equity and increases liabilities
b. Increases expenses and increases owners' equity
c. Decreases assets and has no effect on net income
d. Decreases net income and decreases assets

Q5-47 Vincent Company uses the aging method to adjust the allowance for uncollectible accounts at the end of the period. At December 31, 2010, the balance of accounts receivable is $200,000 and the allowance for uncollectible accounts has a credit balance of $4,000 (before adjustment). An analysis of accounts receivable produced the following age groups:

Current	$160,000
60 days past due.........................	32,000
Over 60 days past due................	8,000
	$200,000

Based on past experience, Vincent estimates that the percentage of accounts that will prove to be uncollectible within the three age groups is 4%, 10%, and 21%, respectively. Based on these facts, the adjusting entry for uncollectible accounts should be made in the amount of

a. $7,280.
b. $11,280.
c. $16,280.
d. $2,000.

Q5-48 Refer to Question 5-47. The net receivables on the balance sheet is _____.

Q5-49 Graham Company uses the percent-of-sales method to estimate uncollectibles. Net credit sales for the current year amount to $130,000 and management estimates 3% will be uncollectible. Allowance for doubtful accounts prior to adjustment has a credit balance of $2,000. The amount of expense to report on the income statement will be

a. $3,900.
b. $5,200.
c. $1,000.
d. $5,900.

Q5-50 Refer to question 5-49. The balance of Allowance for Doubtful Accounts, after adjustment, will be

a. $7,900.
b. $1,000.
c. $5,900.
d. $5,200.
e. Cannot be determined from the information given.

Q5-51 Refer to Quiz questions 5-49 and 5-50. The following year, Graham Company wrote off $3,900 of old receivables as uncollectible. What is the balance in the Allowance account now?

Questions 5-52 through 5-56 use the following data:

On August 1, 2010, Botores, Inc., sold equipment and accepted a six-month, 12%, $50,000 note receivable. Botores' year-end is December 31.

Q5-52 How much interest revenue should Botores accrue on December 31, 2010?
a. $6,000   c. $2,500
b. $3,000   d. Some other amount

Q5-53 If Botores, Inc., fails to make an adjusting entry for the accrued interest,
a. net income will be overstated and liabilities will be understated.
b. net income will be overstated and assets will be overstated.
c. net income will be understated and liabilities will be overstated.
d. net income will be understated and assets will be understated.

Q5-54 How much interest does Botores, Inc., expect to collect on the maturity date (February 1, 2011)?
a. $3,000   c. $2,500
b. $6,000   d. Some other amount

Q5-55 Which of the following accounts will Botores credit in the journal entry at maturity on February 1, 2011, assuming collection in full?
a. Cash   c. Note Payable
b. Interest Payable   d. Interest Receivable

Q5-56 Write the journal entry on the maturity date (February 1, 2011).

Q5-57 Which of the following is included in the calculation of the acid-test ratio?
a. Prepaid expenses and cash   c. Inventory and prepaid expenses
b. Cash and accounts receivable   d. Inventory and short-term investment

Q5-58 A company with net sales of $1,017,000, beginning net receivables of $110,000, and ending net receivables of $120,000, has days' sales in accounts receivable of
a. 38 days.   c. 41 days.
b. 47 days.   d. 44 days.

Q5-59 A company sells on credit terms of "net 30 days" and has days' sales in account receivable of 30 days. Its days' sales in receivables is
a. too high.   c. about right.
b. too low.   d. cannot be evaluated from the data given.

Problems

MyAccountingLab | All of the A and B problems can be found within MyAccountingLab, an online homework and practice environment. Your instructor may ask you to complete these problems using MyAccountingLab.

(Group A)

P5-60A (*Learning Objective 1: Accounting for a trading investment*)   During the fourth quarter of 2010, Cable, Inc., generated excess cash, which the company invested in trading securities as follows:

2010	
Nov 18	Purchased 900 common shares as an investment in trading securities, paying $12 per share.
Dec 15	Received cash dividend of $0.48 per share on the trading securities.
Dec 31	Adjusted the trading securities to their market value of $8 per share.

❙ *Requirements*

1. Open T-accounts for Cash (including its beginning balance of $15,000), Short-Term Investments, Dividend Revenue, and Unrealized Gain (Loss) on Investment.
2. Journalize the foregoing transactions and post to the T-accounts.
3. Show how to report the short-term investment on Cable's balance sheet at December 31.
4. Show how to report whatever should appear on Cable's income statement for the year ended December 31, 2010.
5. Cable sold the trading securities for $8,388 on January 12, 2011. Journalize the sale.

P5-61A (*Learning Objective 2: Controlling cash receipts from customers*) Laptop Delivery, Inc., makes all sales on account. Sarah Carter, accountant for the company, receives and opens incoming mail. Company procedure requires Carter to separate customer checks from the remittance slips, which list the amounts that Carter posts as credits to customer accounts receivable. Carter deposits the checks in the bank. At the end of each day she computes the day's total amount posted to customer accounts and matches this total to the bank deposit slip. This procedure ensures that all receipts are deposited in the bank.

writing assignment ■

❙ *Requirement*

1. As a consultant hired by Laptop Delivery, Inc., write a memo to management evaluating the company's internal controls over cash receipts from customers. If the system is effective, identify its strong features. If the system has flaws, propose a way to strengthen the controls.

P5-62A (*Learning Objective 3: Accounting for revenue, collections, and uncollectibles; percent-of-sales method*)   This problem takes you through the accounting for sales, receivables, and uncollectibles for Mail Time Corp., the overnight shipper. By selling on credit, the company cannot expect to collect 100% of its accounts receivable. At May 31, 2010, and 2011, respectively, Mail Time Corp. reported the following on its balance sheet (in millions of dollars):

writing assignment ■

	May 31,	
	2011	2010
Accounts receivable..	$3,697	$3,434
Less: Allowance for uncollectible accounts...............	(126)	(155)
Accounts receivable, net..	$3,571	$3,279

During the year ended May 31, 2011, Mail Time Corp. earned service revenue and collected cash from customers. Assume uncollectible-account expense for the year was 1% of service revenue and that Mail Time wrote off uncollectible receivables. At year-end Mail Time ended with the foregoing May 31, 2011, balances.

❙ *Requirements*

1. Prepare T-accounts for Accounts Receivable and Allowance for Uncollectibles and insert the May 31, 2010, balances as given.
2. Journalize the following assumed transactions of Mail Time Corp. for the year ended May 31, 2011 (explanations are not required):
   a. Service revenue on account, $32,481 million
   b. Collections from customers on account, $31,864 million
   c. Uncollectible-account expense, 2% of service revenue
   d. Write-offs of uncollectible accounts receivable, $354 million
3. Post your entries to the Accounts Receivable and the Allowance for Uncollectibles T-accounts.
4. Compute the ending balances for the two T-accounts and compare your balances to the actual May 31, 2011, amounts. They should be the same.
5. Show what Mail Time would report on its income statement for the year ended May 31, 2011.

■ general ledger

P5-63A (*Learning Objective 3: Using the aging approach for uncollectibles*) The September 30, 2011, records of Perfecto Communications include these accounts:

Accounts Receivable....................................	$250,000
Allowance for Doubtful Accounts..............	(8,200)

During the year, Perfecto Communications estimates doubtful-account expense at 1% of credit sales. At year-end (December 31), the company ages its receivables and adjusts the balance in Allowance for Doubtful Accounts to correspond to the aging schedule. During the last quarter of 2011, the company completed the following selected transactions:

Nov 30	Wrote off as uncollectible the $1,400 account receivable from Black Carpets and the $600 account receivable from Old Timer Antiques.
Dec 31	Adjusted the Allowance for Doubtful Accounts and recorded doubtful-account expense at year-end, based on the aging of receivables, which follows.

	Age of Accounts			
Accounts Receivable	**1–30 Days**	**31–60 Days**	**61–90 Days**	**Over 90 Days**
$232,000	$140,000	$45,000	$18,000	$29,000
Estimated percent uncollectible	0.1%	1%	10%	30%

❙ *Requirements*

1. Record the transactions in the journal. Explanations are not required.
2. Prepare a T-account for Allowance for Doubtful Accounts and post to that account.
3. Show how Perfecto Communications will report its accounts receivable in a comparative balance sheet for 2010 and 2011. Use the three-line reporting format. At December 31, 2010, the company's Accounts Receivable balance was $214,000 and the Allowance for Doubtful Accounts stood at $4,600.

P5-64A (*Learning Objectives 1, 3, 5: Correcting current asset accounts and recomputing ratios*) Assume Smith & Jones, the accounting firm, advises Ocean Mist Seafood that its financial statements must be changed to conform to GAAP. At December 31, 2010, Ocean Mist's accounts include the following:

Cash..	$ 53,000
Short-term investment in trading securities, at cost	24,000
Accounts receivable...	36,000
Inventory..	63,000
Prepaid expenses	10,000
Total current assets	$186,000
Accounts payable..	$ 67,000
Other current liabilities	39,000
Total current liabilities................................	$106,000

The accounting firm advised Ocean Mist that

- Cash includes $17,000 that is deposited in a compensating balance account that is tied up until 2012.

- The market value of the trading securities is $10,000. Ocean Mist purchased the investments a couple of weeks ago.
- Ocean Mist has been using the direct write-off method to account for uncollectible receivables. During 2010, Ocean Mist wrote off bad receivables of $7,500. Smith & Jones determines that uncollectible-account expense should be 3% of sales revenue, which totaled $600,000 in 2010. The aging of Ocean Mist's receivables at year-end indicated uncollectibles of $10,500.
- Ocean Mist reported net income of $92,000 in 2010.

I Requirements

1. Restate Ocean Mist's current accounts to conform to GAAP. (Challenge)
2. Compute Ocean Mist's current ratio and acid-test ratio both before and after your corrections.
3. Determine Ocean Mist's correct net income for 2010. (Challenge)

P5-65A (*Learning Objective 4: Accounting for notes receivable and accrued interest revenue*)   Healthy Meal completed the following selected transactions.

■ **general ledger**

2010	
Oct 31	Sold goods to Buy Low Foods, receiving a $34,000, three-month, 5.25% note.
Dec 31	Made an adjusting entry to accrue interest on the Buy Low Foods note.
2011	
Jan 31	Collected the Buy Low Foods note.
Feb 18	Received a 90-day, 7.75%, $7,600 note from Dutton Market on account.
19	Sold the Dutton Market note to Amherst Bank, receiving cash of $7,400. (Debit the difference to financing expense.)
Nov 11	Lent $14,600 cash to Street Provisions, receiving a 90-day, 10.00% note.
Dec 31	Accrued the interest on the Street Provisions note.

I Requirements

1. Record the transactions in Healthy Meal's journal. Round interest amounts to the nearest dollar. Explanations are not required.
2. Show what Healthy Meal will report on its comparative classified balance sheet at December 31, 2011, and December 31, 2010.

P5-66A (*Learning Objective 5: Using ratio data to evaluate a company's financial position*) The comparative financial statements of Highland Pools, Inc., for 2011, 2010, and 2009 included the following select data:

■ **spreadsheet**

	(In millions)		
	2011	**2010**	**2009**
Balance sheet			
Current assets:			
Cash...	$ 80	$ 70	$ 60
Short-term investments	145	170	120
Receivables, net of allowance for doubtful accounts of $7, $6, and $4, respectively	270	250	240
Inventories	355	345	300
Prepaid expenses.........................	60	30	55
Total current assets.....................	$ 910	$ 865	$ 775
Total current liabilities....................	$ 580	$ 620	$ 690
Income statement			
Net sales	$5,880	$5,130	$4,220

❙ *Requirements*

1. Compute these ratios for 2011 and 2010:
   a. Current ratio
   b. Acid-test ratio
   c. Days' sales in receivables
2. Which ratios improved from 2010 to 2011 and which ratios deteriorated? Is this trend favorable or unfavorable?

(Group B)

P5-67B (*Learning Objective 1: Accounting for a trading investment*)   During the fourth quarter of 2010, Main St., Inc., generated excess cash, which the company invested in trading securities, as follows:

2010	
Nov 13	Purchased 1,200 common shares as an investment in trading securities, paying $10 per share.
Dec 14	Received cash dividend of $0.48 per share on the trading securities.
Dec 31	Adjusted the securities to their market value of $7 per share.

❙ *Requirements*

1. Open T-accounts for Cash (including its beginning balance of $22,000), Short-Term Investment, Dividend Revenue, and Unrealized Gain (Loss) on Investment.
2. Journalize the foregoing transactions and post to the T-accounts.
3. Show how to report the short-term investment on Main St.'s balance sheet at December 31.
4. Show how to report whatever should appear on Main St.'s income statement for the year ended December 31, 2010.
5. Main St. sold the trading securities for $10,512 on January 21, 2011. Journalize the sale.

writing assignment ■

P5-68B (*Learning Objective 2: Controlling cash receipts from customers*)   Lakeview Software Solutions makes all sales on account, so virtually all cash receipts arrive in the mail. Larry Higgins, the company president, has just returned from a trade association meeting with new ideas for the business. Among other things, Higgins plans to institute stronger internal controls over cash receipts from customers.

❙ *Requirement*

1. Take the role of Larry Higgins, the company president. Write a memo to employees outlining procedures to ensure that all cash receipts are deposited in the bank and that the total amounts of each day's cash receipts are posted to customer accounts receivable.

writing assignment ■

P5-69B (*Learning Objective 3: Accounting for revenue, collections, and uncollectibles; percent-of-sales method*)   This problem takes you through the accounting for sales, receivables, and uncollectibles for Dependable Delivery Corp, the overnight shipper. By selling on credit, the company cannot expect to collect 100% of its accounts receivable. At May 31, 2010, and 2011, respectively, Dependable Delivery Corp. reported the following on its balance sheet (in millions of dollars):

	May 31,	
	2011	**2010**
Accounts receivable..	$3,693	$3,435
Less: Allowance for uncollectible accounts..............	(129)	(156)
Accounts receivable, net...	$3,564	$3,279

During the year ended May 31, 2011, Dependable Delivery Corp. earned sales revenue and collected cash from customers. Assume uncollectible-account expense for the year was 1% of service revenue and Dependable Delivery wrote off uncollectible receivables. At year end, Dependable Delivery ended with the foregoing May 31, 2011 balances.

❚ Requirements

1. Prepare T-accounts for Accounts Receivable and Allowance for Uncollectibles, and insert the May 31, 2010, balances as given.
2. Journalize the following transactions of Dependable Delivery for the year ended May 31, 2011. (Explanations are not required.)
   a. Service revenue on account, $32,487 million.
   b. Collections from customers on account, $31,877 million.
   c. Uncollectible-account expense, 1% of service revenue.
   d. Write-offs of uncollectible accounts receivable, $352 million.
3. Post to the Accounts Receivable and Allowance for Uncollectibles T-accounts.
4. Compute the ending balances for the two T-accounts and compare your balances to the actual May 31, 2011, amounts. They should be the same.
5. Show what Dependable Delivery should report on its income statement for the year ended May 31, 2011.

P5-70B (*Learning Objective 3: Using the aging approach for uncollectibles*) The September 30, 2011, records of Image Communications include these accounts:

■ **general ledger**

Accounts Receivable..................................	$260,000
Allowance for Doubtful Accounts..............	(8,100)

During the year, Image Communications estimates doubtful-account expense at 1% of credit sales. At year-end, the company ages its receivables and adjusts the balance in Allowance for Doubtful Accounts to correspond to the aging schedule. During the last quarter of 2011, the company completed the following selected transactions:

Dec 28	Wrote off as uncollectible the $1,500 account receivable from Blue Carpets and the $400 account receivable from Show-N-Tell Antiques.
Dec 31	Adjusted the Allowance for Doubtful Accounts and recorded doubtful-account expense at year-end, based on the aging of receivables, which follows.

	Age of Accounts			
Accounts Receivable	1–30 Days	31–60 Days	61–90 Days	Over 90 Days
$230,000	$160,000	$35,000	$14,000	$21,000
Estimated percent uncollectible	0.2%	1%	5%	30%

❚ Requirements

1. Record the transactions in the journal. Explanations are not required.
2. Prepare a T-account for Allowance for Doubtful Accounts and post to that account.
3. Show how Image Communications will report its accounts receivable in a comparative balance sheet for 2011 and 2010. Use the three line reporting format. At December 31, 2010, the company's Accounts Receivable balance was $213,000 and the Allowance for Doubtful Accounts stood at $4,200.

P5-71B (*Learning Objectives 1, 3, 5: Correcting current asset accounts and recomputing ratios*)   Assume Smith & Jones, the accounting firm, advises Catch of the Day Seafood that its financial statement must be changed to conform to GAAP. At December 31, 2010, Catch of the Day's accounts include the following:

Cash	$ 56,000
Short-term trading securities, at cost	18,000
Accounts receivable	44,000
Inventory	55,000
Prepaid expenses	16,000
Total current assets	$189,000
Accounts payable	$ 58,000
Other current liabilities	38,000
Total current liabilities	$ 96,000

The accounting firm advised Catch of the Day that

- Cash includes $24,000 that is deposited in a compensating balance account that will be tied up until 2012.
- The market value of the trading securities is $11,000. Catch of the Day purchased the trading securities a couple of weeks ago.
- Catch of the Day has been using the direct write-off method to account for uncollectible receivables. During 2010, Catch of the Day wrote off bad receivables of $5,500. Smith & Jones determines that uncollectible-account expense should be 3% of service revenue, which totaled $670,000 in 2010. The aging of Catch of the Day's receivables at year-end indicated uncollectibles of $14,600.
- Catch of the Day reported net income of $99,000 for 2010.

❙ Requirements

1. Restate Catch of the Day's current accounts to conform to GAAP. (Challenge)
2. Compute Catch of the Day's current ratio and acid-test ratio both before and after your corrections.
3. Determine Catch of the Day's correct net income for 2010. (Challenge)

■ general ledger

P5-72B (*Learning Objective 4: Accounting for notes receivable and accrued interest revenue*)   Quick Meals completed the following selected transactions:

2010	
Nov 30	Sold goods to Bragg Market, receiving a $32,000, three-month, 4.00% note.
Dec 31	Made an adjusting entry to accrue interest on the Bragg Market note.
2011	
Feb 28	Collected the Bragg Market note.
Mar 1	Received a 90-day, 8.00%, $7,200 note from Don's Market on account.
1	Sold the Don's Market note to Chelmsford Bank, receiving cash of $7,000. (Debit the difference to financing expense.)
Dec 16	Lent $15,400 cash to Stratford Provisions, receiving a 90-day, 9.50% note.
Dec 31	Accrued the interest on the Stratford Provisions note.

❙ Requirements

1. Record the transactions in Quick Meals' journal. Round all amounts to the nearest dollar. Explanations are not required.
2. Show what Quick Meals will report on its comparative classified balance sheet at December 31, 2011, and December 31, 2010.

P5-73B (*Learning Objective 5: Using ratio data to evaluate a company's financial position*) The comparative financial statements of Gold Pools, Inc., for 2011, 2010, and 2009 included the following select data:

■ spreadsheet

	(In millions)		
	2011	2010	2009
Balance sheet			
Current assets:			
Cash...	$ 70	$ 80	$ 50
Short-term investments	145	160	110
Receivables, net of allowance for doubtful accounts of $7, $6, and $4, respectively	290	260	230
Inventories	360	345	310
Prepaid expenses........................	70	10	40
Total current assets....................	$ 935	$ 855	$ 740
Total current liabilities...................	$ 560	$ 610	$ 680
Income statement			
Net sales	$5,890	$5,150	$4,200

Requirements

1. Compute these ratios for 2011 and 2010:
   a. Current ratio
   b. Acid-test ratio
   c. Days' sales in receivables
2. Which ratios improved from 2010 to 2011 and which ratios deteriorated? Is this trend favorable or unfavorable?

APPLY YOUR KNOWLEDGE

Decision Cases

Case 1. (*Learning Objective 3: Using accounts receivable data to reconstruct revenues, collections, and bad debts on receivables*) A fire during 2010 destroyed most of the accounting records of Clearview Cablevision, Inc. The only accounting data for 2010 that Clearview can come up with are the following balances at December 31, 2010. The general manager also knows that bad-debt expense should be 5% of service revenue.

Accounts receivable	$180,000
Less: Allowance for bad debts...............................	(22,000)
Total expenses, excluding bad-debt expense............	670,000
Collections from customers...................................	840,000
Write-offs of bad receivables.................................	30,000
Accounts receivable, December 31, 2009	110,000

Prepare a summary income statement for Clearview Cablevision, Inc., for the year ended December 31, 2010. The stockholders want to know whether the company was profitable in 2010. Use a T-account for Accounts Receivable to compute service revenue.

Case 2. *(Learning Objective 3: Estimating the collectibility of accounts receivable)*
Suppose you work in the loan department of Superior Bank. Dean Young, owner of Dean Young Beauty Aids, has come to you seeking a loan for $500,000 to expand operations. Young proposes to use accounts receivable as collateral for the loan and has provided you with the following information from the company's most recent financial statements:

	2011	2010	2009
	(In thousands)		
Sales	$1,475	$1,001	$902
Cost of goods sold	876	647	605
Gross profit	599	354	297
Other expenses	518	287	253
Net profit or (loss) before taxes	$ 81	$ 67	$ 44
Accounts receivable	$ 128	$ 107	$ 94
Allowance for doubtful accounts	13	11	9

❙ Requirement

1. Analyze the trends of sales, days' sales in receivables, and cash collections from customers for 2011 and 2010. Would you make the loan to Young? Support your decision with facts and figures.

Ethical Issue

Sunnyvale Loan Company is in the consumer loan business. Sunnyvale borrows from banks and loans out the money at higher interest rates. Sunnyvale's bank requires Sunnyvale to submit quarterly financial statements to keep its line of credit. Sunnyvale's main asset is Notes Receivable. Therefore, Uncollectible-Account Expense and Allowance for Uncollectible Accounts are important accounts for the company.

Kimberly Burnham, the company's owner, prefers that net income reflect a steady increase in a smooth pattern, rather than increase in some periods and decrease in other periods. To report smoothly increasing net income, Burnham underestimates Uncollectible-Account Expense in some periods. In other periods, Burnham overestimates the expense. She reasons that the income overstatements roughly offset the income understatements over time.

❙ Requirements

1. What is the ethical issue in this situation?
2. Who are the stakeholders? What are the possible consequences to each?
3. Analyze the alternatives from the following standpoints: (a) economic, (b) legal, (c) ethical.
4. What would you do? How would you justify your decision?

Focus on Financials: ■ Amazon.com, Inc.

(Learning Objectives 2, 3: Accounting for receivables) Refer to **Amazon.com, Inc.'s** Consolidated Balance Sheets as well as Note 1—Description of Business and Accounting Policies, in Appendix A at the end of this book.

1. The fourth account listed on Amazon.com's Consolidated Balance Sheet is called "accounts receivable, net and other." What does the "net" mean? The "other"?
2. Refer to Note 1. What kinds of accounts receivable are included in Amazon.com, Inc.'s receivables?
3. How much is the allowance for doubtful accounts in 2008 and 2007?

Focus on Analysis: ■ Foot Locker, Inc.

(Learning Objective 1: Analyzing short-term investments) This case is based on the **Foot Locker, Inc.'s** consolidated balance sheets, consolidated statements of cash flows, and Footnote 6 of its financial statements in Appendix B at the end of this book.

1. What securities are included in Foot Locker's Short-term investments? What type of securities are they?
2. Make a T-account for Short-term investments. Record $249 as the balance in the account as of the end of 2006. Using the information in the investments section of the Consolidated Statement of Cash Flows, record the cash purchases and sales of short-term investments during 2007. Why doesn't the ending balance equal the amount shown on the balance sheet as of the end of 2007?

Group Project

Jillian Michaels and Dee Childress worked for several years as sales representatives for Xerox Corporation. During this time, they became close friends as they acquired expertise with the company's full range of copier equipment. Now they see an opportunity to put their expertise to work and fulfill lifelong desires to establish their own business. Navarro Community College, located in their city, is expanding, and there is no copy center within five miles of the campus. Business in the area is booming, office buildings and apartments are springing up, and the population of the Navarro section of the city is growing.

Michaels and Childress want to open a copy center, similar to FedEx Kinko's, near the Navarro campus. A small shopping center across the street from the college has a vacancy that would fit their needs. Michaels and Childress each have $35,000 to invest in the business, but they forecast the need for $200,000 to renovate the store and purchase some of the equipment they will need. Xerox Corporation will lease two large copiers to them at a total monthly rental of $6,000. With enough cash to see them through the first six months of operation, they are confident they can make the business succeed. The two women work very well together, and both have excellent credit ratings. Michaels and Childress must borrow $130,000 to start the business, advertise its opening, and keep it running for its first six months.

▌*Requirements*

Assume two roles: (1) Michaels and Childress, the partners who will own Navarro Copy Center; and (2) loan officers at Synergy Bank.

1. As a group, visit a copy center to familiarize yourselves with its operations. If possible, interview the manager or another employee. Then write a loan request that Michaels and Childress will submit to Synergy Bank with the intent of borrowing $130,000 to be paid back over three years. The loan will be a personal loan to the partnership of Michaels and Childress, not to Navarro Copy Center. The request should specify all the details of Michaels' and Childress' plan that will motivate the bank to grant the loan. Include a budget for each of the first six months of operation of the proposed copy center.
2. As a group, interview a loan officer in a bank. Write Synergy Bank's reply to the loan request. Specify all the details that the bank should require as conditions for making the loan.
3. If necessary, modify the loan request or the bank's reply in order to reach agreement between the two parties.

For online homework, exercises, and problems that provide you with immediate feedback, please visit www.myaccountinglab.com.

Quick Check Answers

1. *a*
2. *a*
3. *c* ($40,000 × .04)
4. *b* ($600 + $1,600)
5. *c* ($1,030 − $600)
6. *b*
7. *d* ($10,000 − $1,030)
8. *d* ($2,800 − $90) − ($400 − $90)
9. *b* ($575,000 + $2,200,000 − $725,000)
10. *c* ($2,800 × .09 × 4/12 × 1/4)
11. *d* $70,000 + ($70,000 × .12 × 6/12)
12. *a*
13. *a* [($80,000 + $74,000)/2] ÷ ($803,000/365)
14. *a* ($6,000 + $3,000 + $9,000) ÷ ($10,000 + $4,000)

6

Inventory & Cost of Goods Sold

SPOTLIGHT: Williams-Sonoma, Inc.

You've just graduated from college, taken a job, and you're moving into an apartment. The place is unfurnished, so you'll need everything: furniture, rugs, dishes, pots, pans, and everything that goes with them. Where will you find these things? Williams-Sonoma, Inc., stores, its subsidiaries (Pottery Barn, Pottery Barn Bed and Bath, West Elm, Williams-Sonoma Home), and its e-commerce Web sites may get some of your business.

Williams-Sonoma, Inc., is a specialty retailer of high-style products for the home. As of February 3, 2008, the company operated 600 stores in 44 states, Washington, D.C., and Canada.

Williams-Sonoma, Inc.'s Consolidated Balance Sheets are summarized on the following page. You can see that the merchandise inventory is Williams-Sonoma's largest current asset. That's not surprising since Williams-Sonoma, like other retailers, attracts customers with the latest styles in home furnishings that they can purchase and take home immediately.

We also present Williams-Sonoma's Consolidated Statements of Earnings for the comparative fiscal years 2008 and 2007. As of the fiscal year ended 2008, a difficult economic recession was beginning to hit the company, as it did virtually all retail businesses. A few quick computations will show that, while net revenues increased by $217 million, total costs (cost of goods sold and selling, general, and administrative expenses) went up by a total of $231 million, causing the company's pre-tax earnings to decline by $21 million year-over-year.

Williams-Sonoma, Inc.
Consolidated Balance Sheets (Adapted)
Fiscal years 2008 and 2007

(in thousands)	2008	2007
ASSETS		
Current assets		
Cash and cash equivalents....................................	$ 118,950	$ 275,429
Accounts receivable...	48,052	48,821
Merchandise inventories	693,661	610,599
Prepaid expenses	87,183	88,180
Other current assets	101,929	77,934
Total current assets	1,049,775	1,100,963
Property and equipment, net	981,075	912,582
Other non-current assets	63,004	34,786
Total assets...	$2,093,854	$2,048,331
LIABILITIES AND STOCKHOLDERS' EQUITY		
Current liabilities	$ 611,534	$ 627,734
Long-term liabilities	316,597	269,166
Total liabilities	928,131	896,900
Stockholders' equity...	1,165,723	1,151,431
Total liabilities and stockholders' equity	$2,093,854	$2,048,331

Williams-Sonoma, Inc.
Consolidated Statements of Earnings (Adapted)
Fiscal years 2008 and 2007

(in thousands)	2008	2007
Net revenues	$3,944,934	$3,727,513
Cost of goods sold..	2,408,963	2,240,226
Gross margin (gross profit)	1,535,971	1,487,287
Selling, general, and administrative expenses..............	1,222,573	1,159,786
Interest (income), net......................................	(2,942)	(9,685)
Earnings before income taxes.............................	316,340	337,186
Income taxes...	120,583	128,318
Net earnings..	$ 195,757	$ 208,868

You can see that cost of goods sold is by far Williams-Sonoma's largest expense. The title *Cost of Goods Sold* perfectly describes that expense. In short,

- Williams-Sonoma buys inventory, an asset carried on the books at cost.
- The goods that Williams-Sonoma sells are no longer Williams-Sonoma's assets. The cost of inventory that's sold gets shifted into the expense account, Cost of Goods Sold.

Merchandise inventory is the heart of a merchandising business, and cost of goods sold is the most important expense for a company that sells goods rather than services. Gross profit (or gross margin) is the difference between net sales and cost of goods sold. This chapter covers the accounting for inventory and cost of goods sold. It also shows you how to analyze financial statements. Here we focus on inventory, cost of goods sold, and gross profit.

LEARNING OBJECTIVES

1 **Account** for inventory

2 **Understand** the various inventory methods

3 **Use** gross profit percentage and inventory turnover to evaluate operations

4 **Estimate** inventory by the gross profit method

5 **Show** how inventory errors affect the financial statements

ACCOUNTING FOR INVENTORY

We begin by showing how the financial statements of a merchandiser such as Williams-Sonoma, Inc., or The Gap, Inc., differ from those of service entities such as FedEx and Century 21 Real Estate. The financial statements in Exhibit 6-1 (p. 344) highlight how service entities differ from merchandisers (dollar amounts are assumed).

The basic concept of accounting for merchandise inventory can be illustrated with an example. Suppose Pottery Barn (a subsidiary company of Williams-Sonoma, Inc.) has in stock three chairs that cost $300 each. Pottery Barn marks the chairs up by $200 and sells two of the chairs for $500 each.

- Pottery Barn's balance sheet reports the one chair that the company still holds in inventory.
- The income statement reports the cost of the two chairs sold, as shown in Exhibit 6-2 (p. 344).

Here is the basic concept of how we identify **inventory**, the asset, from **cost of goods sold**, the expense.

OBJECTIVE

1 **Account** for inventory

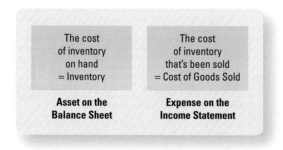

EXHIBIT 6-1 | **Contrasting a Service Company with a Merchandiser**

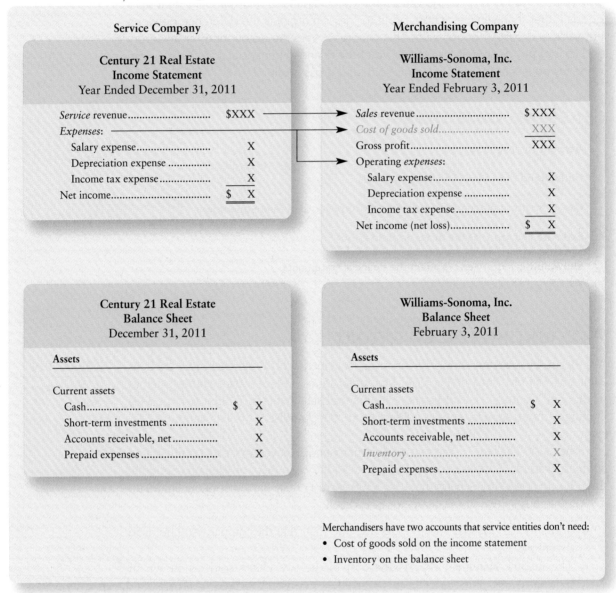

Merchandisers have two accounts that service entities don't need:

- Cost of goods sold on the income statement
- Inventory on the balance sheet

EXHIBIT 6-2 | **Inventory and Cost of Goods Sold When Inventory Cost Is Constant**

Balance Sheet (partial)		Income Statement (partial)	
Current assets		Sales revenue	
Cash..	$XXX	(2 chairs @ sale price of $500 each)	$1,000
Short-term investments	XXX	Cost of goods sold	
Accounts receivable..............................	XXX	(2 chairs @ cost of $300 each)...............	600
Inventory (1 chair @ cost of $300).........	300	Gross profit.......................................	$ 400
Prepaid expenses	XXX		

The cost of the inventory sold shifts from asset to expense when the seller delivers the goods to the buyer.

Sale Price vs. Cost of Inventory

Note the difference between the sale price of inventory and the cost of inventory. In our example,

- Sales revenue is based on the *sale price* of the inventory sold ($500 per chair).
- Cost of goods sold is based on the *cost* of the inventory sold ($300 per chair).
- Inventory on the balance sheet is based on the *cost* of the inventory still on hand ($300 per chair).

Exhibit 6-2 shows these items.

Gross profit, also called **gross margin**, is the excess of sales revenue over cost of goods sold. It is called *gross* profit because operating expenses have not yet been subtracted. Exhibit 6-3 shows actual inventory and cost of goods sold data adapted from the financial statements of Williams-Sonoma.

EXHIBIT 6-3 | **Williams-Sonoma, Inc., Inventory and Cost of Goods Sold (Cost of Sales)**

Williams-Sonoma, Inc.
Consolidated Balance Sheet (Adapted)
February 3, 2008

Assets (In millions)

Current assets

Cash and cash equivalents...............	$119
Receivables, net..............................	48
Inventories	694

Williams-Sonoma, Inc.
Consolidated Statement of Income (Adapted)
Year Ended February 3, 2008

(In millions)

Net sales	$3,945
Cost of sales (same as Cost of goods sold)...............	2,409
Gross profit...	$1,536

Williams-Sonoma, Inc.'s inventory of $694 million represents

$$\text{Inventory (balance sheet)} = \text{Number of units of inventory } on\ hand \times \text{Cost per unit of inventory}$$

Williams-Sonoma's cost of goods sold ($2,409 million) represents

$$\begin{array}{l} \text{Cost of goods sold} \\ \text{(income statement)} \end{array} = \begin{array}{l} \text{Number of units of} \\ \text{inventory } \textit{sold} \end{array} \times \begin{array}{l} \text{Cost per unit} \\ \text{of inventory} \end{array}$$

Let's see what "units of inventory" and "cost per unit" mean.

Number of Units of Inventory. The number of inventory units on hand is determined from the accounting records, backed up by a physical count of the goods at year end. Companies do not include in their inventory any goods they hold on **consignment** because those goods belong to another company. But they do include their own inventory that is out on consignment and held by another company. Companies include inventory in transit from suppliers or in transit to customers that, according to shipping terms, legally belong to them as of the year end. Shipping terms, otherwise known as *FOB terms*, indicate who owns the goods at a particular time and, therefore, who must pay for the shipping costs. The term **FOB** stands for *free on board*. When the vendor invoice specifies *FOB shipping point* (the most common business practice), legal title to the goods passes from the seller to the purchaser when the inventory leaves the seller's place of business. The purchaser therefore owns the goods while they are in transit and must pay the transportation costs. In the case of goods purchased FOB shipping point, the company purchasing the goods must include goods in transit from suppliers as units in inventory as of the year end. In the case of goods purchased *FOB destination*, title to the goods does not pass from the seller to the purchaser until the goods arrive at the purchaser's receiving dock. Therefore, these goods are not counted in year-end inventory of the purchasing company. Rather, the cost of these goods is included in inventory of the seller until the goods reach their destination.

Cost Per Unit of Inventory. The cost per unit of inventory poses a challenge because companies purchase goods at different prices throughout the year. Which unit costs go into ending inventory? Which unit costs go to cost of goods sold?

The next section shows how different accounting methods determine amounts on the balance sheet and the income statement. First, however, you need to understand how inventory accounting systems work.

Accounting for Inventory in the Perpetual System

There are two main types of inventory accounting systems: the periodic system and the perpetual system. The **periodic inventory system**, discussed in more detail in Appendix 6A, is used for inexpensive goods. A fabric store or a lumber yard won't keep a running record of every bolt of fabric or every two-by-four. Instead, these stores count their inventory periodically—at least once a year—to determine the quantities on hand. Businesses such as restaurants and hometown nurseries also use the periodic system because the accounting cost of a periodic system is low.

A **perpetual inventory system** uses computer software to keep a running record of inventory on hand. This system achieves control over goods such as Pottery Barn furniture, automobiles, jewelry, apparel, and most other types of inventory. Most businesses use the perpetual inventory system.

Even with a perpetual system, the business still counts the inventory on hand annually. The physical count establishes the correct amount of ending inventory for the financial statements and also serves as a check on the perpetual records. Here is a quick summary of the two main inventory accounting systems.

Perpetual Inventory System	Periodic Inventory System
• Used for all types of goods	• Used for inexpensive goods
• Keeps a running record of all goods bought, sold, and on hand	• Does *not* keep a running record of all goods bought, sold, and on hand
• Inventory counted at least once a year	• Inventory counted at least once a year

How the Perpetual System Works.   Let's use an everyday situation to show how a perpetual inventory system works. When you check out of a Foot Locker, a Best Buy, or a Pottery Barn store, the clerk scans the bar codes on the labels of the items you buy. Exhibit 6-4 illustrates a typical bar code. Suppose you are buying a desk lamp from Pottery Barn. The bar code on the product label holds lots of information. The optical scanner reads the bar code, and the computer records the sale and updates the inventory records.

EXHIBIT 6-4 | Bar Code for Electronic Scanner

0 72512 06581 5

Recording Transactions in the Perpetual System.   All accounting systems record each purchase of inventory. When Pottery Barn makes a sale, two entries are needed in the perpetual system:

- The company records the sale—debits Cash or Accounts Receivable and credits Sales Revenue for the sale price of the goods.
- Pottery Barn also debits Cost of Goods Sold and credits Inventory for the cost of the inventory sold.

Exhibit 6-5, on the following page, shows the accounting for inventory in a perpetual system. Panel A gives the journal entries and the T-accounts, and Panel B shows the income statement and the balance sheet. All amounts are assumed. (Appendix 6A illustrates the accounting for these same transactions for a periodic inventory system.)

In Exhibit 6-5, the first entry to Inventory summarizes a lot of detail. The cost of the inventory, $560,000, is the *net* amount of the purchases, determined as follows (using assumed amounts):

Purchase price of the inventory	$600,000
+ **Freight-in** (the cost to transport the goods from the seller to the buyer)	4,000
− **Purchase returns** for unsuitable goods returned to the seller	(25,000)
− **Purchase allowances** granted by the seller	(5,000)
− **Purchase discounts** for early payment by the buyer	(14,000)
= Net purchases of inventory—Cost to the buyer	$560,000

EXHIBIT 6-5 | **Recording and Reporting Inventory—Perpetual System (Amounts Assumed)**

PANEL A—Recording Transactions and the T-accounts (All amounts are assumed)

Journal Entry

1.	Inventory	560,000	
	Accounts Payable		560,000
	Purchased inventory on account.		
2.	Accounts Receivable	900,000	
	Sales Revenue		900,000
	Sold inventory on account.		
	Cost of Goods Sold	540,000	
	Inventory		540,000
	Recorded cost of goods sold.		

Inventory

Beginning balance	100,000*		
Purchases	560,000	Cost of goods sold	540,000
Ending balance	120,000		

*Beginning inventory was $100,000

Cost of Goods Sold

Cost of goods sold	540,000

PANEL B—Reporting in the Financial Statements

Income Statement (partial)	
Sales revenue	$900,000
Cost of goods sold	540,000
Gross profit	$360,000

Ending Balance Sheet (partial)	
Current assets:	
Cash	$ XXX
Short-term investments	XXX
Accounts receivable	XXX
Inventory	120,000
Prepaid expenses	XXX

Freight-in is the transportation cost, paid by the buyer, under terms FOB shipping point, to move goods from the seller to the buyer. Freight-in is accounted for as part of the cost of inventory. A **purchase return** is a decrease in the cost of inventory because the buyer returned the goods to the seller (vendor). A **purchase allowance** also decreases the cost of inventory because the buyer got an allowance (a deduction) from the amount owed. To document approval of purchase returns, management issues a **debit memorandum**, meaning that accounts payable are reduced (debited) for the amount of the return. The offsetting credit is to inventory as the goods are shipped back to the seller (vendor). Purchase discounts and allowances are usually documented on the final invoice received from the vendor. Throughout this book, we often refer to net purchases simply as Purchases.

A **purchase discount** is a decrease in the buyer's cost of inventory earned by paying quickly. Many companies offer payment terms of "2/10 n/30." This means the buyer can take a 2% discount for payment within 10 days, with the final amount due within 30 days. Another common credit term is "net 30," which tells the customer to pay the full amount within 30 days. In summary,

Net purchases = Purchases
    – Purchase returns and allowances
    – Purchase discounts
    + Freight-in

Net sales are computed exactly the same as net purchases, but with no freight-in, as follows:

$$
\begin{aligned}
\text{Net sales} = &\ \text{Sales revenue} \\
&- \text{Sales returns and allowances} \\
&- \text{Sales discounts}
\end{aligned}
$$

Freight-out paid by the *seller*, under shipping terms FOB destination, is not part of the cost of inventory. Instead, freight-out is delivery expense. It's the seller's expense of delivering merchandise to customers.

INVENTORY COSTING

Inventory is the first asset for which a manager can decide which accounting method to use. The accounting method selected affects the profits to be reported, the amount of income tax to be paid, and the values of the ratios derived from the balance sheet.

What Goes into Inventory Cost?

The cost of inventory on Williams-Sonoma, Inc.'s balance sheet represents all the costs that the company incurred to bring its inventory to the point of sale. The following cost principle applies to all assets:

> **The cost of any asset, such as inventory, is the sum of all the costs incurred to bring the asset to its intended use, less any discounts.**

As we have seen, inventory's cost includes its basic purchase price, plus freight-in, insurance while in transit, and any fees or taxes paid to get the inventory ready to sell, less returns, allowances, and discounts.

After a Pottery Barn chair is sitting in the showroom, other costs, such as advertising and sales commissions, are *not* included as the cost of inventory. Advertising, sales commissions, and delivery costs are selling expenses that go in the income statement, rather than in the balance sheet.

The Various Inventory Costing Methods

Determining the cost of inventory is easy when the unit cost remains constant, as in Exhibit 6-2. But the unit cost usually changes. For example, prices often rise. The desk lamp that cost Pottery Barn $10 in January may cost $14 in June and $18 in October. Suppose Pottery Barn sells 1,000 lamps in November. How many of those lamps cost $10, how many cost $14, and how many cost $18?

OBJECTIVE

2 **Understand** the various inventory methods

To compute cost of goods sold and the cost of ending inventory still on hand, we must assign unit cost to the items. Accounting uses four generally accepted inventory methods:

1. **Specific unit cost**
2. **Average cost**
3. **First-in, first-out (FIFO) cost**
4. **Last-in, first-out (LIFO) cost**

A company can use any of these methods. The methods can have very different effects on reported profits, income taxes, and cash flow. Therefore, companies select their inventory method with great care.

Specific Unit Cost. Some businesses deal in unique inventory items, such as automobiles, antique furniture, jewels, and real estate. These businesses cost their inventories at the specific cost of the particular unit. For instance, a Toyota dealer may have two vehicles in the showroom—a "stripped-down" model that cost the dealer $19,000 and a "loaded" model that cost the dealer $24,000. If the dealer sells the loaded model, the cost of goods sold is $24,000. The stripped-down auto will be the only unit left in inventory, and so ending inventory is $19,000.

The **specific-unit-cost method** is also called the *specific identification method.* This method is too expensive to use for inventory items that have common characteristics, such as bushels of wheat, gallons of paint, or auto tires.

The other inventory accounting methods—average, FIFO, and LIFO—are fundamentally different. These other methods do not use the specific cost of a particular unit. Instead, they assume different flows of inventory costs. To illustrate average, FIFO, and LIFO costing, we use a common set of data, given in Exhibit 6-6.

EXHIBIT 6-6 | **Inventory Data Used to Illustrate the Various Inventory Costing Methods**

	Inventory				
Beg bal	(10 units @ $10)	100			
Purchases:			Cost of goods sold		
No. 1	(25 units @ $14)	350	(40 units @ ?)		?
No. 2	(25 units @ $18)	450			
End bal	(20 units @ ?)	?			

In Exhibit 6-6, Pottery Barn began the period with 10 lamps that cost $10 each; the beginning inventory was therefore $100. During the period Pottery Barn bought 50 more lamps, sold 40 lamps, and ended the period with 20 lamps, summarized in the T-account as follows:

Goods Available		Number of Units	Total Cost
Goods available	=	10 + 25 + 25 = 60 units	$100 + $350 + $450 = $900
Cost of goods sold	=	40 units	?
Ending inventory	=	20 units	?

The big accounting questions are

1. What is the cost of goods sold for the income statement?

2. What is the cost of the ending inventory for the balance sheet?

It all depends on which inventory method Pottery Barn uses. Pottery Barn, like other Williams-Sonoma, Inc., companies, actually uses the average-cost method, so let's look at average costing first.

Average Cost.   The **average-cost method**, sometimes called the **weighted-average method**, is based on the average cost of inventory during the period. Average cost per unit is determined as follows (data from Exhibit 6-6):

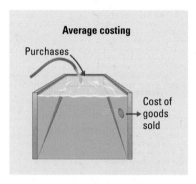

Average costing

$$\text{Average cost per unit} = \frac{\text{Cost of goods available}^*}{\text{Number of units available}^*} = \frac{\$900}{60} = \$15$$

*Goods available = Beginning inventory + Purchases

Cost of goods sold =	Number of units sold	× Average cost per unit	
=	40 units	× $15	= $600

Ending inventory =	Number of units on hand	× Average cost per unit	
=	20 units	× $15	= $300

The following T-account shows the effects of average costing:

Inventory (at Average Cost)

Beg bal	(10 units @ $10)	100		
Purchases:				
No. 1	(25 units @ $14)	350		
No. 2	(25 units @ $18)	450	Cost of goods sold (40 units @ average cost of $15 per unit)	600
End bal	(20 units @ average cost of $15 per unit)	300		

FIFO Cost.   Under the FIFO method, the first costs into inventory are the first costs assigned to cost of goods sold—hence, the name *first-in, first-out*. The diagram near the bottom of the page shows the effect of FIFO costing. The following T-account shows how to compute FIFO cost of goods sold and ending inventory for the Pottery Barn lamps (data from Exhibit 6-6):

Inventory (at FIFO cost)					
Beg bal	(10 units @ $10)	100			
Purchases:			Cost of goods sold (40 units):		
No. 1	(25 units @ $14)	350	(10 units @ $10)	100	
No. 2	(25 units @ $18)	450	(25 units @ $14)	350	} 540
			(5 units @ $18)	90	
End bal	(20 units @ $18)	360			

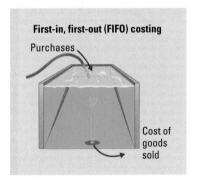

First-in, first-out (FIFO) costing

Under FIFO, the cost of ending inventory is always based on the latest costs incurred—in this case $18 per unit.

LIFO Cost.   LIFO costing is the opposite of FIFO. Under LIFO, the last costs into inventory go immediately to cost of goods sold, as shown in the diagram on the following page. Compare LIFO and FIFO, and you will see a vast difference.

The following T-account shows how to compute the LIFO inventory amounts for the Pottery Barn lamps (data from Exhibit 6-6):

Inventory (at LIFO cost)					
Beg bal	(10 units @ $10)	100			
Purchases:			Cost of goods sold (40 units):		
No. 1	(25 units @ $14)	350	(25 units @ $18)	450	} 660
No. 2	(25 units @ $18)	450	(15 units @ $14)	210	
End bal	(10 units @ $10) (10 units @ $14)	} 240			

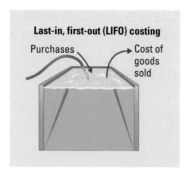

Under LIFO, the cost of ending inventory is always based on the oldest costs—from beginning inventory plus the early purchases of the period—$10 and $14 per unit.

The Effects of FIFO, LIFO and Average Cost on Cost of Goods Sold, Gross Profit, and Ending Inventory

In our Pottery Barn example, the cost of inventory rose from $10 to $14 to $18. When inventory unit costs change this way, the various inventory methods produce different cost-of-goods sold figures. Exhibit 6-7 summarizes the income effects (sales – cost of goods sold = gross profit) of the three inventory methods (remember that prices are rising). Study Exhibit 6-7 carefully, focusing on cost of goods sold and gross profit.

EXHIBIT 6-7 | **Income Effects of the FIFO, LIFO, and Average Inventory Methods**

	FIFO	LIFO	Average
Sales revenue (assumed)	$1,000	$1,000	$1,000
Cost of goods sold.........................	540 (lowest)	660 (highest)	600
Gross profit...................................	$ 460 (highest)	$ 340 (lowest)	$ 400

Exhibit 6-8 on the following page shows the impact of both FIFO and LIFO costing methods on cost of goods sold and inventories during both increasing costs (Panel A) and decreasing costs (Panel B). Study this exhibit carefully; it will help you *really* understand FIFO and LIFO.

EXHIBIT 6-8 | Cost of Goods Sold and Ending Inventory—FIFO and LIFO; Increasing Costs and Decreasing Costs

Panel A—When Inventory Costs Are Increasing

	Cost of Goods Sold (COGS)	**Ending Inventory (EI)**
FIFO	FIFO COGS is lowest because it's based on the oldest costs, which are low. Gross profit is, therefore, the highest.	FIFO EI is highest because it's based on the most recent costs, which are high.
LIFO	LIFO COGS is highest because it's based on the most recent costs, which are high. Gross profit is, therefore, the lowest.	LIFO EI is lowest because it's based on the oldest costs, which are low.

Panel B—When Inventory Costs Are Decreasing

	Cost of Goods Sold (COGS)	**Ending Inventory (EI)**
FIFO	FIFO COGS is highest because it's based on the oldest costs, which are high. Gross profit is, therefore, the lowest.	FIFO EI is lowest because it's based on the most recent costs, which are low.
LIFO	LIFO COGS is lowest because it's based on the most recent costs, which are low. Gross profit is, therefore, the highest.	LIFO EI is highest because it's based on the oldest costs, which are high.

Financial analysts search the stock markets for companies with good prospects for income growth. Analysts sometimes need to compare the net income of a company that uses LIFO with the net income of a company that uses FIFO. Appendix 6B, pages 407-408, shows how to convert a LIFO company's net income to the FIFO basis in order to compare the companies.

The Tax Advantage of LIFO

The Internal Revenue Service requires all U.S. companies to use the same method of pricing inventories for tax purposes that they use for financial reporting purposes. Thus, the choice of inventory methods directly affects income taxes, which must be paid in cash. When prices are rising, LIFO results in the *lowest taxable income* and thus the *lowest income taxes*. Let's use the gross profit data of Exhibit 6-7 to illustrate.

	FIFO	LIFO
Gross profit (from Exhibit 6-7)	$460	$340
Operating expenses (assumed)	260	260
Income before income tax	$200	$ 80
Income tax expense (40%)	$ 80	$ 32

Income tax expense is lowest under LIFO ($32). **This is the most attractive feature of LIFO—low income tax payments**, which is why about one-third of all U.S. companies use LIFO. During periods of inflation, many companies switch to LIFO for its tax and cash-flow advantage. Exhibit 6-9, based on an American Institute of Certified Public Accountants (AICPA) survey of 600 companies, indicates that FIFO remains the most popular inventory method.

EXHIBIT 6-9 | **Use of the Various Inventory Methods**

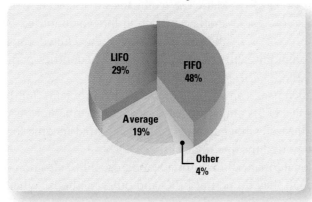

Comparison of the Inventory Methods

Let's compare the average, FIFO, and LIFO inventory methods.

1. **Measuring Cost of Goods Sold.** How well does each method match inventory expense—cost of goods sold—against revenue? LIFO results in the most realistic net income figure because LIFO assigns the most recent inventory costs to expense. In contrast, FIFO matches old inventory costs against revenue—a poor measure of expense. FIFO income is therefore less realistic than LIFO income.

2. **Measuring Ending Inventory.** Which method reports the most up-to-date inventory cost on the balance sheet? FIFO. LIFO can value inventory at very old costs because LIFO leaves the oldest prices in ending inventory.

LIFO and Managing Reported Income.   LIFO allows managers to manipulate net income by timing their purchases of inventory. When inventory prices are rising rapidly and a company wants to show less income (in order to pay less taxes), managers can buy a large amount of inventory near the end of the year. Under LIFO, these high inventory costs go straight to cost of goods sold. As a result, net income is decreased.

If the business is having a bad year, management may wish to report higher income. The company can delay the purchase of high-cost inventory until next year. This avoids decreasing current-year income. In the process, the company draws down inventory quantities, a practice known as *LIFO inventory liquidation*.

LIFO Liquidation.   When LIFO is used and inventory quantities fall below the level of the previous period, the situation is called a *LIFO liquidation*. To compute cost of goods sold, the company must dip into older layers of inventory cost. Under LIFO, and when prices are rising, that action shifts older, lower costs into cost of goods sold. The result is higher net income. Managers try to avoid a LIFO liquidation because it increases income taxes.

INTERNATIONAL PERSPECTIVE

Many U.S. companies that currently use LIFO must use another method in foreign countries. Why? LIFO is not allowed in Australia, the United Kingdom, and some other British commonwealth countries. Virtually all countries permit FIFO and the average cost method.

These differences can create comparability problems for financial analysts when comparing a U.S. company against a foreign competitor. As discussed earlier, Appendix 6B illustrates how analysts convert reported income for a company that uses LIFO to reported income under FIFO.

International Financial Reporting Standards (IFRS) also do not permit the use of LIFO, although they do permit FIFO and other methods. When U.S. GAAP and IFRS are fully integrated in a few years, U.S. companies that use LIFO will be forced to convert their inventory pricing to another method. As we discussed earlier in the chapter, in periods of rising prices, the use of LIFO inventories results in the lowest amount of reported income and, thus, the lowest amount of income taxes. If the statistics in Figure 6-9 continue to hold through the next few years, conversion of inventories to methods other than LIFO may substantially increase reported income for up to 30 percent of U.S. companies. This change has potentially far-reaching implications. For example, if the Internal Revenue Service continues to require companies to use the same inventory pricing methods for income tax purposes and financial statement purposes, conversion of LIFO inventories to another method will greatly increase the tax burden on many U.S. companies, including small and medium-sized businesses that can least afford it.

The disallowance of LIFO inventories under IFRS is only one of several rather thorny issues that must be resolved before the United States can adopt IFRS. Resolution of these differences will likely have political as well as financial implications. We will cover other key differences between GAAP and IFRS in later chapters. Appendix F to the book summarizes all of these differences.

MID-CHAPTER SUMMARY PROBLEM

Suppose a division of **Texas Instruments** that sells computer microchips has these inventory records for January 2011:

Date		Item	Quantity	Unit Cost	Total cost
Jan	1	Beginning inventory	100 units	$ 8	$ 800
	6	Purchase	60 units	9	540
	21	Purchase	150 units	9	1,350
	27	Purchase	90 units	10	900

Company accounting records show sales of 310 units for revenue of $6,770. Operating expense for January was $1,900.

Requirements

1. Prepare the January income statement, showing amounts for LIFO, average, and FIFO cost. Label the bottom line "Operating income." Round average cost per unit to three decimal places and all other figures to whole-dollar amounts. Show your computations.

2. Suppose you are the financial vice president of Texas Instruments. Which inventory method will you use if your motive is to
   a. Minimize income taxes?
   b. Report the highest operating income?
   c. Report operating income between the extremes of FIFO and LIFO?
   d. Report inventory on the balance sheet at the most current cost?
   e. Attain the best measure of net income for the income statement?
   State the reason for each of your answers.

Answers

Requirement 1

Texas Instruments Incorporated
Income Statement for Microchip
Month Ended January 31, 2011

	LIFO	Average	FIFO
Sales revenue............................	$6,770	$6,770	$6,770
Cost of goods sold.................	2,870	2,782	2,690
Gross profit............................	3,900	3,988	4,080
Operating expenses	1,900	1,900	1,900
Operating income..................	$2,000	$2,088	$2,180

Cost of goods sold computations:

LIFO: (90 @ $10) + (150 @ $9) + (60 @ $9) + (10 @ $8) = $2,870

Average: 310 × $8.975* = $2,782

FIFO: (100 @ $8) + (60 @ $9) + (150 @ $9) = $2,690

$$*\frac{(\$800 + \$540 + \$1,350 + \$900)}{(100 + 60 + 150 + 90)} = \$8.975$$

❙ *Requirement 2*

a. Use LIFO to minimize income taxes. Operating income under LIFO is lowest when inventory unit costs are increasing, as they are in this case (from $8 to $10). (If inventory costs were decreasing, income under FIFO would be lowest.)

b. Use FIFO to report the highest operating income. Income under FIFO is highest when inventory unit costs are increasing, as in this situation.

c. Use the average cost method to report an operating income amount between the FIFO and LIFO extremes. This is true in this situation and in others when inventory unit costs are increasing or decreasing.

d. Use FIFO to report inventory on the balance sheet at the most current cost. The oldest inventory costs are expensed as cost of goods sold, leaving in ending inventory the most recent (most current) costs of the period.

e. Use LIFO to attain the best measure of net income. LIFO produces the best matching of current expense with current revenue. The most recent (most current) inventory costs are expensed as cost of goods sold.

Accounting Principles Related to Inventory

Several accounting principles have special relevance to inventories:

- Consistency   ■ Disclosure   ■ Conservatism

Consistency Principle

The **consistency principle** states that businesses should use the same accounting methods and procedures from period to period. Consistency enables investors to compare a company's financial statements from one period to the next.

Suppose you are analyzing Interfax Corporation's net income pattern over a two-year period. Interfax switched from LIFO to FIFO during that time. Its net income increased dramatically but only because of the change in inventory method. If you did not know of the accounting change, you might believe that Interfax's income increased due to improved operations, but that's not the case.

The consistency principle does not mean that a company is not permitted to change its accounting methods. However, a company making an accounting change must disclose the effect of the change on net income. American-Saudi Oil Company, Inc., disclosed the following in a note to its annual report:

> **EXCERPT FROM NOTE 6 OF THE FINANCIAL STATEMENTS**
> . . . American-Saudi changed its method of accounting for the cost of crude oil . . . from the FIFO method to the LIFO method. The company believes that the LIFO method better matches current costs with current revenues. . . . The change decreased the Company's 2007 net income . . . by $3 million. . . .

Disclosure Principle

The **disclosure principle** holds that a company's financial statements should report enough information for outsiders to make informed decisions about the company. The company should report *relevant* and *representationally faithful* information about itself. That means properly disclosing inventory accounting methods, as well as the substance of all material transactions impacting the existence and proper valuation of inventory, using *comparable* methods from period to period. The financial statements typically contain a footnote describing the inventory pricing method used, as well as the fact that inventory was valued at the lower of that method or market. The lower-of-cost-or-market rule is described later. Without knowledge of the accounting method and without clear, complete disclosures in the financial statements, a banker could make an unwise lending decision. Suppose the banker is comparing two companies—one using LIFO and the other, FIFO. The FIFO company reports higher net income but only because it uses FIFO. Without knowing this, the banker could loan money to the wrong business.

Accounting Conservatism

Conservatism in accounting means reporting financial statement amounts that paint the most cautious or moderate immediate picture of the company. If faced with a choice of overstatement or understatement, accounting chooses to err on the side of caution in order to protect investors from inflated or overly positive results. However, this should not be interpreted to mean that companies must deliberately understate assets or profits, or overstate liabilities. These are still misstatements! What advantage does conservatism give a business? Many accountants regard conservatism as a brake on management's optimistic tendencies. The goal of accounting conservatism is representational faithfulness.

Conservatism appears in accounting guidelines such as "anticipate no gains, but provide for all probable losses" and "if in doubt, record an asset at the lowest reasonable amount and report a liability at the highest reasonable amount." Conservatism directs accountants to decrease the accounting value of an asset if it appears unrealistically high. Assume that **Texas Instruments** paid $35,000 for inventory that has become outdated and whose current value is only $12,000. Conservatism dictates that Texas Instruments must record a $23,000 loss immediately and write the inventory down to $12,000.

Lower-of-Cost-or-Market Rule

The **lower-of-cost-or-market rule** (abbreviated as **LCM**) is based on accounting conservatism. LCM requires that inventory be reported in the financial statements at whichever is lower—the inventory's historical cost or its market value. Applied to inventories, *market value* generally means *current replacement cost* (that is, how much the business would have to pay now to replace its inventory). If the replacement cost of inventory falls below its historical cost, the business must write down the value of its goods to market value. **The business reports ending inventory at its LCM value on the balance sheet**. All this can be done automatically by a computerized accounting system. How is the write-down accomplished?

Suppose Williams-Sonoma, Inc., paid $3,000 for inventory on September 26. By February 3, its fiscal year-end, the inventory can be replaced for $2,000. Williams-Sonoma's year-end balance sheet must report this inventory at LCM value of $2,000. Exhibit 6-10 on the following page presents the effects of LCM on the balance sheet and the income statement. Before any LCM effect, cost of goods sold is $9,000. An LCM write-down decreases Inventory and increases Cost of Goods Sold, as follows:

Cost of Goods Sold		1,000	
Inventory			1,000
Wrote inventory down to market value.			

EXHIBIT 6-10 | **Lower-of-Cost-or-Market (LCM) Effects on Inventory and Cost of Goods Sold**

Balance Sheet

Current assets:

Cash	$ XXX
Short-term investments	XXX
Accounts receivable	XXX
Inventories, at market (which is lower than $3,000 cost)	2,000
Prepaid expenses	XXX
Total current assets	$X,XXX

Income Statement

Sales revenue	$21,000
Cost of goods sold ($9,000 + $1,000)	10,000
Gross profit	$11,000

If the market value of Williams-Sonoma's inventory had been above cost, it would have made no adjustment for LCM. In that case, simply report the inventory at cost, which is the lower of cost or market.

Companies disclose LCM in notes to their financial statements, as shown below for Williams-Sonoma, Inc.:

> **NOTE 1: ACCOUNTING POLICIES**
> - *Inventories.* Inventories are . . . stated at the *lower of average cost or market.* [Emphasis added.]

LCM is not optional. It is required by GAAP.

GLOBAL VIEW

ANOTHER IFRS DIFFERENCE

IFRS defines "market" differently than U.S. GAAP. Under IFRS, "market" is always defined as "net realizable value," which, for inventories, is current market value. Once IFRS is adopted in the United States, inventory write-downs may become less common than they are now, due to the fact that selling prices are usually greater than replacement cost.

Under U.S. GAAP, once the LCM rule is applied to write inventories down to replacement cost, the write-downs may never be reversed. In contrast, under IFRS, some LCM write-downs may be reversed, and inventory may be subsequently written up again, not to exceed original cost. This may cause more fluctuation in the reported incomes of companies that sell inventories than we currently see.

INVENTORY AND THE FINANCIAL STATEMENTS

Detailed Income Statement

Exhibit 6-11 provides an example of a detailed income statement, complete with all the discounts and expenses in their proper places. Study it carefully.

EXHIBIT 6-11 | **Detailed Income Statement**

New Jersey Technology, Inc.
Income Statement
Year Ended December 31, 2011

Sales revenue..	$100,000	
Less: Sales discounts.....................................	(2,000)	
Sales returns and allowances.................	(3,000)	
Net sales..		$95,000*
Cost of goods sold..		45,000
Gross profit..		50,000
Operating expenses:		
Selling:		
Sales commission expense	$ 5,000	
Freight-out (delivery expense)	1,000	
Other expenses (detailed)	6,000	12,000
Administrative:		
Salary expense..	$ 2,000	
Depreciation expense	2,000	
Other expenses (detailed)	4,000	8,000
Income before income tax		30,000
Income tax expense (40%).........................		12,000
Net income..		$18,000

*Most companies report only the net sales figure, $95,000.

Analyzing Financial Statements

Owners, managers, and investors use ratios to evaluate a business. Two ratios relate directly to inventory: gross profit percentage and the rate of inventory turnover.

Gross Profit Percentage.   Gross profit—sales minus cost of goods sold—is a key indicator of a company's ability to sell inventory at a profit. Merchandisers strive to increase **gross profit percentage**, also called the **gross margin percentage**. Gross profit percentage is markup stated as a percentage of sales. Gross profit percentage is computed as follows for Williams-Sonoma, Inc. Data (in millions) for 2008 are taken from Exhibit 6-3, page 345.

$$\text{Gross profit percentage} = \frac{\text{Gross profit}}{\text{Net sales revenue}} = \frac{\$1,536}{\$3,945} = 0.389 = 38.9\%$$

OBJECTIVE

3 **Use** gross profit percentage and inventory turnover to evaluate operations

The gross profit percentage is watched carefully by managers and investors. A 38.9% gross margin means that each dollar of sales generates about $0.39 of gross profit. On average, cost of goods sold consumes $0.61 of each sales dollar for Williams-Sonoma, Inc. For most firms, the gross profit percentage changes little from year to year, so a small downturn may signal trouble. Williams-Sonoma's gross profit in 2007 was 39.8%, so the company experienced almost a 1% decline in gross margin year over year. In 2008 and 2009, a severe economic recession hit retail sales hard. In order to sell inventories, many retailers have had to cut selling prices, thus reducing gross margins.

Williams-Sonoma's gross profit percentage of 39% is greater than that of Wal-Mart Stores, Inc. (23%), but similar to the gross profit percentage of Nordstrom, Inc. (37.4%). Both Williams-Sonoma and Nordstrom handle higher-priced merchandise than Wal-Mart, thus resulting in higher gross profit. Exhibit 6-12 graphs the gross profit percentages for these three companies.

EXHIBIT 6-12 | **Gross Profit Percentages of Three Leading Retailers**

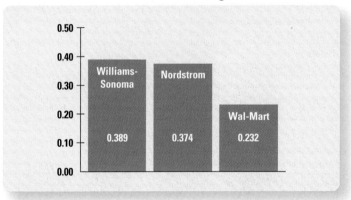

Inventory Turnover. Williams-Sonoma, Inc., strives to sell its inventory as quickly as possible because the goods generate no profit until they're sold. The faster the sales, the higher the income, and vice versa, for slow-moving goods. Ideally, a business could operate with zero inventory, but most businesses, especially retailers, must keep some goods on hand. **Inventory turnover**, the ratio of cost of goods sold to average inventory, indicates how rapidly inventory is sold. The 2008 computation for Williams-Sonoma, Inc., follows (data in millions from the Consolidated Balance Sheets and Statements of Income, page 342):

$$\text{Inventory turnover} = \frac{\text{Cost of goods sold}}{\text{Average inventory}} = \frac{\text{Cost of goods sold}}{\left(\dfrac{\text{Beginning}}{\text{inventory}} + \dfrac{\text{Ending}}{\text{inventory}}\right) \div 2}$$

$$= \frac{\$2,409}{(\$611 + \$694)/2} = \frac{3.7 \text{ times per year}}{(\text{every 99 days})}$$

The inventory turnover statistic shows how many times the company sold (or turned over) its average level of inventory during the year. Inventory turnover varies from industry to industry.

Exhibit 6-13 graphs the rates of inventory turnover for the same three companies. Let's compare Williams-Sonoma's turnover with that of Nordstrom and Wal-Mart department stores. You can see that both Nordstrom and Wal-Mart turn inventory over faster than Williams-Sonoma. Both Nordstrom and Wal-Mart are department stores. They sell a variety of products (Nordstrom sells clothing and Wal-Mart sells virtually every kind of consumer item) that sell faster than the specialty home furnishings of Williams-Sonoma, Inc. Thus, both Nordstrom and Wal-Mart, Inc., report higher gross profit and net income than Williams-Sonoma.

EXHIBIT 6-13 | **Inventory Turnover of Three Leading Retailers**

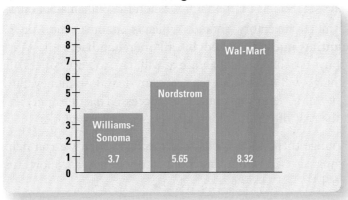

STOP & THINK...

Examine Exhibits 6-12 and 6-13. What do those ratio values say about the merchandising (pricing) strategies of Nordstrom, Inc., and Wal-Mart Stores, Inc.?

Answer:
It's obvious that Nordstrom sells high-end merchandise. Nordstrom's profit percentage is higher than Wal-Mart's. Wal-Mart has a much faster rate of inventory turnover. The lower the price, the faster the turnover, and vice versa.

ADDITIONAL INVENTORY ISSUES
Using the Cost-of-Goods-Sold Model

Exhibit 6-14 presents the **cost-of-goods-sold model.** Some may view this model as related to the periodic inventory system. But the cost-of-goods-sold model is used by all companies, regardless of their accounting system. The model is extremely powerful because it captures all the inventory information for an entire accounting period. Study this model carefully (all amounts are assumed).

EXHIBIT 6-14 | **The Cost-of-Goods-Sold Model**

Cost of goods sold:	
Beginning inventory	$1,200
+ Purchases	6,300
= Goods available	7,500
− Ending inventory	(1,500)
= Cost of goods sold	$6,000

Williams-Sonoma, Inc., uses a perpetual inventory accounting system. Let's see how the company can use the cost-of-goods-sold model to manage the business effectively.

1. What's the single most important question for Williams-Sonoma, Inc., to address?
   - What merchandise should Williams-Sonoma, Inc., offer to its customers? This is a *marketing* question that requires market research. If Williams-Sonoma and its affiliated stores continually stock up on the wrong merchandise, sales will suffer and profits will drop.

2. What's the second most important question for Williams-Sonoma, Inc.?
   - How much inventory should Williams-Sonoma, Inc., buy? **This is an accounting question faced by all merchandisers**. If Williams-Sonoma, Inc., buys too much merchandise, it will have to lower prices, the gross profit percentage will suffer, and the company may lose money. Buying the right quantity of inventory is critical for success. This question can be answered with the cost-of-goods-sold model. Let's see how it works.

We must rearrange the cost-of-goods-sold formula. Then we can help a Williams-Sonoma store manager know how much inventory to buy, as follows (using amounts from Exhibit 6-14):

1	Cost of goods sold (based on the plan for the next period)....................	$6,000
2	+ Ending inventory (based on the plan for the next period)......................	1,500
3	= Goods available as planned...	7,500
4	− Beginning inventory (actual amount left over from the prior period)......	(1,200)
5	= Purchases (how much inventory the manager needs to buy)...................	$6,300

In this case the manager should buy $6,300 of merchandise to work his plan for the upcoming period.

Estimating Inventory by the Gross Profit Method

Often a business must *estimate* the value of its goods. A fire may destroy inventory, and the insurance company requires an estimate of the loss. In this case, the business must estimate the cost of ending inventory because it was destroyed.

The **gross profit method**, also known as the **gross margin method**, is widely used to estimate ending inventory. This method uses the familiar cost-of-goods-sold model (amounts are assumed):

Beginning inventory	$ 4,000
+ Purchases	16,000
= Goods available.......................................	20,000
− Ending inventory......................................	(5,000)
= Cost of goods sold...................................	$15,000

For the gross-profit method, we rearrange *ending inventory* and *cost of goods sold* as follows:

Beginning inventory	$ 4,000
+ Purchases	16,000
= Goods available......................................	20,000
− Cost of goods sold.................................	(15,000)
= Ending inventory....................................	$ 5,000

Suppose a fire destroys some of Williams-Sonoma's inventory. To collect insurance, the company must estimate the cost of the ending inventory lost. Using its *actual gross profit rate* of 39%, you can estimate the cost of goods sold. Then subtract cost of goods sold from goods available to estimate the amount of ending inventory. Exhibit 6-15 shows the calculations for the gross profit method, with new amounts assumed for the illustration.

EXHIBIT 6-15 | **Gross Profit Method of Estimating Inventory**

Beginning inventory		$ 38,000
Purchases		72,000
Goods available..		110,000
Estimated cost of goods sold:		
Net sales revenue	$100,000	
Less estimated gross profit of 39%	(39,000)	
Estimated cost of goods sold........................		61,000
Estimated cost of *ending inventory* lost............		$ 49,000

You can also use the gross profit method to test the overall reasonableness of an ending inventory amount. This method also helps to detect large errors.

STOP & THINK...

Beginning inventory is $70,000, net purchases total $365,000, and net sales are $500,000. With a normal gross profit rate of 40% of sales (cost of goods sold = 60%), how much is ending inventory?

Answer:

$$\$135,000 = [\$70,000 + \$365,000 - (0.60 \times \$500,000)]$$

Effects of Inventory Errors

Inventory errors sometimes occur. An error in ending inventory creates errors for two accounting periods. In Exhibit 6-16 on the following page, start with period 1 in which ending inventory is *overstated* by $5,000 and cost of goods sold is therefore *understated* by $5,000. Then compare period 1 with period 3, which is correct. *Period 1 should look exactly like period 3.*

OBJECTIVE

5 **Show** how inventory errors affect the financial statements

Inventory errors counterbalance in two consecutive periods. Why? Recall that period 1's ending inventory becomes period 2's beginning amount. Thus, the period 1 error carries over into period 2. Trace the ending inventory of $15,000 from period 1 to period 2. Then compare periods 2 and 3. *All three periods should look exactly like period 3.* The Exhibit 6-16 amounts in color are incorrect.

EXHIBIT 6-16 | Inventory Errors: An Example

	Period 1	Period 2	Period 3
	Ending Inventory Overstated by $5,000	Beginning Inventory Overstated by $5,000	Correct
Sales revenue...............................	$100,000	$100,000	$100,000
Cost of goods sold:			
Beginning inventory.....................	$10,000	$15,000	$10,000
Purchases..................................	50,000	50,000	50,000
Cost of goods available...............	60,000	65,000	60,000
Ending inventory.........................	(15,000)	(10,000)	(10,000)
Cost of goods sold	45,000	55,000	50,000
Gross profit.................................	$ 55,000	$ 45,000	$ 50,000
		100,000	

The authors thank Professor Carl High for this example.

Beginning inventory and ending inventory have opposite effects on cost of goods sold (beginning inventory is added; ending inventory is subtracted). Therefore, after two periods, an inventory error washes out (counterbalances). Notice that total gross profit is correct for periods 1 and 2 combined ($100,000) even though each year's gross profit is off by $5,000. The correct gross profit is $50,000 for each period, as shown in Period 3.

We must have accurate information for all periods. Exhibit 6-17 summarizes the effects of inventory accounting errors.

EXHIBIT 6-17 | Effects of Inventory Errors

	Period 1		Period 2	
Inventory Error	Cost of Goods Sold	Gross Profit and Net Income	Cost of Goods Sold	Gross Profit and Net Income
Period 1				
Ending inventory **overstated**	Understated	Overstated	Overstated	Understated
Period 1				
Ending inventory **understated**	Overstated	Understated	Understated	Overstated

COOKING THE BOOKS
with Inventory
Crazy Eddie

It is one thing to make honest mistakes in accounting for inventory, but quite another to use inventory to commit fraud. The two most common ways to "cook the books" with inventory are:

1. inserting fictitious inventory, thus overstating quantities; and

2. deliberately overstating unit prices used in the computation of ending inventory amounts.

Either one of these tricks has exactly the same effect on income as inventory errors, discussed in the previous section. The difference is that honest inventory errors are often corrected as soon as they are detected, thus minimizing their impact on income. In contrast, deliberate overstatement of inventories tends to be repeated over and over again throughout the course of months, or even years, thus causing the misstatement to grow ever higher until it is discovered. By that time, it can be too late for the company.

Crazy Eddie, Inc.[1] was a retail consumer electronics store in 1987, operating 43 retail outlets in the New York City area, with $350 million in reported sales and reported profits of $10.5 million. Its stock was a Wall Street "darling," with a collective market value of $600 million. The only problem was that the company's reported profits had been grossly overstated since 1984, the year that the company went public.

Eddie Antar, the company's founder and major stockholder, became preoccupied with the price of his company's stock in 1984. Antar realized that the company, in an extremely competitive retail market in the largest city in the United States, had to keep posting impressive operating profits in order to maintain the upward trend in the company's stock price.

Within the first six months, Antar ordered a subordinate to double count about $2 million of inventory in the company's stores and warehouses. Using Exhibits 6-16 and 6-17, you can see that the impact of this inventory overstatement went straight to the "bottom line," overstating profits by the same amount. Unfortunately, the company's auditors failed to detect the inventory overstatement. The following year, emboldened by the audit error, Antar ordered subordinates (now accomplices) to bump the overstatement to $9 million. In addition, he ordered employees to destroy incriminating documents to conceal the inventory shortage. When auditors asked for these documents, employees told them they had been lost. Antar also ordered that the company scrap its sophisticated computerized perpetual inventory system and return to an outdated manual system that was easier to manipulate. The auditors made the mistake of telling Antar which company stores and warehouses they were going to visit in order to observe the year-end physical count of inventory. Antar shifted sufficient inventory to those locations just before the counts to conceal the shortages. By 1988, when the fraud was discovered, the inventory shortage (overstatement) was larger than the total profits the company had reported since it went public in 1984.

In June 1989, Crazy Eddie, Inc., filed for Chapter 11 bankruptcy protection. Later that year, the company closed its stores and sold off its assets. Eddie Antar became a fugitive from justice, moved to Israel, and took an assumed name. He was arrested in 1992, extradited to the United States, and convicted on 17 counts of fraudulent financial reporting in 1993. He was ordered to pay $121 million in restitution to former stockholders and creditors.

A series of missteps by the courts led to a plea bargain agreement in 1996, a condition of which Antar admitted, for the first time, that he had defrauded investors by manipulating the company's accounting records. One of the prosecuting attorneys was quoted as saying, "Crazy Eddie wasn't crazy, just crooked." ▲

The following Decision Guidelines summarize the situations that call for (a) a particular inventory system and (b) the motivation for using each costing method.

---

[1]Michael C. Knapp, *Contemporary Auditing: Real Issues and Cases*, 6th edition, Mason, Ohio: Thomson Southwestern, 2009.

DECISION GUIDELINES

ACCOUNTING FOR INVENTORY

Suppose a Williams-Sonoma store stocks two basic categories of merchandise:

- Furniture pieces, such as tables and chairs
- Small items of low value, near the checkout stations, such as cupholders and bottle openers

Jacob Stiles, the store manager, is considering how accounting will affect the business. Let's examine several decisions Stiles must make to properly account for the store's inventory.

Decision	Guidelines	System or Method
Which inventory system to use?	■ Expensive merchandise ■ Cannot control inventory by visual inspection	Perpetual system for the furniture
	■ Can control inventory by visual inspection	Periodic system for the small, low value items
Which costing method to use?	■ Unique inventory items	Specific unit cost for art objects because they are unique
	■ Most current cost of ending inventory ■ Maximizes reported income when costs are rising	FIFO
	■ Most current measure of cost of goods sold and net income ■ Minimizes income tax when costs are rising	LIFO
	■ Middle-of-the-road approach for income tax and reported income	Average

END-OF-CHAPTER SUMMARY PROBLEM

Town & Country Gift Ideas began 2010 with 60,000 units of inventory that cost $36,000. During 2010, Town & Country purchased merchandise on account for $352,500 as follows:

Purchase 1	(100,000 units costing)	$ 65,000
Purchase 2	(270,000 units costing)	175,500
Purchase 3	(160,000 units costing)	112,000

Cash payments on account totaled $326,000 during the year.

Town & Country's sales during 2010 consisted of 520,000 units of inventory for $660,000, all on account. The company uses the FIFO inventory method.

Cash collections from customers were $630,000. Operating expenses totaled $240,500, of which Town & Country paid $211,000 in cash. Town & Country credited Accrued Liabilities for the remainder. At December 31, Town & Country accrued income tax expense at the rate of 35% of income before tax.

Requirements

1. Make summary journal entries to record Town & Country's transactions for the year, assuming the company uses a perpetual inventory system.
2. Determine the FIFO cost of Town & Country's ending inventory at December 31, 2010 two ways:
   a. Use a T-account.
   b. Multiply the number of units on hand by the unit cost.
3. Show how Town & Country would compute cost of goods sold for 2010. Follow the FIFO example on page 352.
4. Prepare Town & Country's income statement for 2010. Show totals for the gross profit and income before tax.
5. Determine Town & Country's gross profit percentage, rate of inventory turnover, and net income as a percentage of sales for the year. In Town & Country's industry, a gross profit percentage of 40%, an inventory turnover of six times per year, and a net income percentage of 7% are considered excellent. How well does Town & Country compare to these industry averages?

Answers

Requirement 1

Inventory ($65,000 + $175,500 + $112,000)	$352,500	
Accounts Payable		352,500
Accounts Payable	326,000	
Cash		326,000
Accounts Receivable	660,000	
Sales Revenue		660,000
Cost of Goods Sold (see Requirement 3)	339,500	
Inventory		339,500
Cash	630,000	
Accounts Receivable		630,000
Operating Expenses	240,500	
Cash		211,000
Accrued Liabilities		29,500
Income Tax Expense (see Requirement 4)	28,000	
Income Tax Payable		28,000

Requirement 2

Inventory			
Beg bal	36,000		
Purchases	352,500	Cost of goods sold	339,500
End bal	49,000		

Number of units in ending inventory (60,000 + 100,000 + 270,000 + 160,000 − 520,000)		70,000
Unit cost of ending inventory at FIFO ($112,000 ÷ 160,000 from Purchase 3).....	×	$ 0.70
FIFO cost of ending inventory......................		$49,000

❙ Requirement 3

Cost of goods sold (520,000 units):	
60,000 units costing...	$ 36,000
100,000 units costing...	65,000
270,000 units costing...	175,500
90,000 units costing $0.70 each*.................................	63,000
Cost of goods sold...	$339,500

*From Purchase 3: $112,000/160,000 units = $0.70 per unit.

❙ Requirement 4

Town & Country Gift Ideas
Income Statement
Year Ended December 31, 2010

Sales revenue	$660,000
Cost of goods sold..	339,500
Gross profit..	320,500
Operating expenses	240,500
Income before tax	80,000
Income tax expense (35%)...	28,000
Net income..	$ 52,000

❙ Requirement 5

		Industry Average
Gross profit percentage:	$320,500 ÷ $660,000 = 48.6%	40%
Inventory turnover:	$\dfrac{\$339,500}{(\$36,000 + \$49,000)/2} = 8$ times	6 times
Net income as a percent of sales:	$52,000 ÷ $660,000 = 7.9%	7%

Town & Country's statistics are better than the industry averages.

REVIEW INVENTORY & COST OF GOODS SOLD

Quick Check (Answers are given on page 400.)

1. Which statement is true?
   a. The invoice is the purchaser's request for collection from the customer.
   b. Gross profit is the excess of sales revenue over cost of goods sold.
   c. The Sales account is used to record only sales on account.
   d. A service company purchases products from suppliers and then sells them.

2. Sales discounts should appear in the financial statements:
   a. as a deduction from sales.
   b. among the current liabilities.
   c. as an addition to inventory.
   d. as an addition to sales.
   e. as an operating expense.

3. How is inventory classified in the financial statements?
   a. As a contra account to Cost of Goods Sold
   b. As an expense
   c. As a liability
   d. As a revenue
   e. As an asset

Questions 4–6 use the following data of Tortoise, Inc.:

	Units	Unit Cost	Total Cost	Units Sold
Beginning inventory	15	$5	$ 75	
Purchase on Apr 25	40	8	320	
Purchase on Nov 13	10	9	90	
Sales	40	?	?	

4. Tortoise uses a FIFO inventory system. Cost of goods sold for the period is:
   a. $360.   c. $275.
   b. $298.   d. $330.

5. Tortoise's LIFO cost of ending inventory would be:
   a. $187.   c. $210.
   b. $155.   d. $200.

6. Tortoise's average cost of ending inventory is:
   a. $210.   c. $187.
   b. $155.   d. $200.

7. When applying lower-of-cost-or-market to inventory, "market" generally means
   a. original cost, less physical deterioration.
   b. original cost.
   c. replacement cost.
   d. resale value.

8. During a period of rising prices, the inventory method that will yield the highest net income and asset value is:
   a. FIFO.   c. average cost.
   b. LIFO.   d. specific identification.

9. Which statement is true?
   a. When prices are rising, the inventory method that results in the lowest ending inventory value is FIFO.
   b. The inventory method that best matches current expense with current revenue is FIFO.
   c. Application of the lower-of-cost-or-market rule often results in a lower inventory value.
   d. An error overstating ending inventory in 2010 will understate 2010 net income.
10. The ending inventory of Misty Harbor Co. is $57,000. If beginning inventory was $68,000 and goods available totaled $117,000, the cost of goods sold is:
    a. $60,000.
    b. $128,000.
    c. $68,000.
    d. $49,000.
    e. none of the above.
11. Lantern Company had cost of goods sold of $145,000. The beginning and ending inventories were $15,000 and $25,000, respectively. Purchases for the period must have been:
    a. $136,000.
    b. $160,000.
    c. $155,000.
    d. $170,000.
    e. $185,000.

Use the following information for questions 12–14.
Fairway Company had a $28,000 beginning inventory and a $35,000 ending inventory. Net sales were $184,000; purchases, $93,000; purchase returns and allowances, $7,000; and freight-in, $3,000.
12. Cost of goods sold for the period is
    a. $98,000.
    b. $82,000.
    c. $96,000.
    d. $81,000.
    e. none of the above.
13. What is Fairway's gross profit percentage (rounded to the nearest percentage)?
    a. 55%
    b. 15%
    c. 45%
    d. None of the above
14. What is Fairway's rate of inventory turnover?
    a. 5.3 times
    b. 2.6 times
    c. 2.3 times
    d. 3.0 times
15. Beginning inventory is $110,000, purchases are $260,000 and sales total $470,000. The normal gross profit is 40%. Using the gross profit method, how much is ending inventory?
    a. $210,000
    b. $132,000
    c. $188,000
    d. $88,000
    e. None of the above
16. An overstatement of ending inventory in one period results in:
    a. an understatement of net income of the next period.
    b. no effect on net income of the next period.
    c. an understatement of the beginning inventory of the next period.
    d. an overstatement of net income of the next period.

Accounting Vocabulary

average-cost method (p. 351) Inventory costing method based on the average cost of inventory during the period. Average cost is determined by dividing the cost of goods available by the number of units available. Also called the *weighted-average method.*

consignment (p. 346) An inventory arrangement where the seller sells inventory that belongs to another party. The seller does not include consigned merchandise on hand in its balance sheet, because the seller does not own this inventory.

conservatism (p. 359) The accounting concept by which the least favorable figures are presented in the financial statements.

consistency principle (p. 358) A business must use the same accounting methods and procedures from period to period.

cost of goods sold (p. 343) Cost of the inventory the business has sold to customers.

cost-of-goods-sold model (p. 363) Formula that brings together all the inventory data for the entire accounting period: Beginning inventory + Purchases = Goods available. Then, Goods available – Ending inventory = Cost of goods sold.

debit memorandum (p. 348) A document issued to the seller (vendor) when an item of inventory that is unwanted or damaged is returned. This document authorizes a reduction (debit) to accounts payable for the amount of the goods returned.

disclosure principle (p. 358) A business's financial statements must report enough information for outsiders to make knowledgeable decisions about the business. The company should report relevant, reliable, and comparable information about its economic affairs.

first-in, first-out (FIFO) cost (method) (p. 352) Inventory costing method by which the first costs into inventory are the first costs out to cost of goods sold. Ending inventory is based on the costs of the most recent purchases.

FOB (p. 346) Stands for *free on board*, a legal term that designates the point at which title passes for goods sold. FOB shipping point means that the buyer owns, and therefore is legally obligated to pay for goods at the point of shipment, including transportation costs. In this case, the buyer owns the goods while they are in transit from the seller and must include their costs, including freight, in inventory at that point. FOB destination means that the seller pays the transportation costs, so the goods do not belong to the buyer until they reach the buyer's place of business.

gross margin (p. 345) Another name for *gross profit*.

gross margin method (p. 364) Another name for the *gross profit method*.

gross margin percentage (p. 361) Another name for the *gross profit percentage*.

gross profit (p. 345) Sales revenue minus cost of goods sold. Also called *gross margin*.

gross profit method (p. 364) A way to estimate inventory based on a rearrangement of the cost-of-goods-sold model: Beginning inventory + Net purchases = Goods available – Cost of goods sold = Ending inventory. Also called the *gross margin method*.

gross profit percentage (p. 361) Gross profit divided by net sales revenue. Also called the *gross margin percentage*.

inventory (p. 343) The merchandise that a company sells to customers.

inventory turnover (p. 362) Ratio of cost of goods sold to average inventory. Indicates how rapidly inventory is sold.

last-in, first-out (LIFO) cost (method) (p. 352) Inventory costing method by which the last costs into inventory are the first costs out to cost of goods sold. This method leaves the oldest costs—those of beginning inventory and the earliest purchases of the period—in ending inventory.

lower-of-cost-or-market (LCM) rule (p. 359) Requires that an asset be reported in the financial statements at whichever is lower—its historical cost or its market value (current replacement cost for inventory).

periodic inventory system (p. 346) An inventory system in which the business does not keep a continuous record of the inventory on hand. Instead, at the end of the period, the business makes a physical count of the inventory on hand and applies the appropriate unit costs to determine the cost of the ending inventory.

perpetual inventory system (p. 346) An inventory system in which the business keeps a continuous record for each inventory item to show the inventory on hand at all times.

purchase allowance (p. 348) A decrease in the cost of purchases because the seller has granted the buyer a subtraction (an allowance) from the amount owed.

purchase discount (p. 348) A decrease in the cost of purchases earned by making an early payment to the vendor.

purchase return (p. 348) A decrease in the cost of purchases because the buyer returned the goods to the seller.

specific-unit-cost method (p. 350) Inventory cost method based on the specific cost of particular units of inventory.

weighted-average method (p. 351) Another name for the *average-cost method*.

ASSESS YOUR PROGRESS

Short Exercises

S6-1 (*Learning Objective 1: Accounting for inventory transactions*) Journalize the following assumed transactions for The Pepson Company. Show amounts in billions.

    a. Cash purchases of inventory, $3.8 billion
    b. Sales on account, $19.7 billion
    c. Cost of goods sold (perpetual inventory system), $4.5 billion
    d. Collections on account, $18.8 billion

S6-2 (*Learning Objective 1: Accounting for inventory transactions*) Summer Kluxon, Inc., purchased inventory costing $120,000 and sold 75% of the goods for $150,000. All purchases and sales were on account. Kluxon later collected 30% of the accounts receivable.

1. Journalize these transactions for Kluxon, which uses the perpetual inventory system.

2. For these transactions, show what Kluxon will report for inventory, revenues, and expenses on its financial statements. Report gross profit on the appropriate statement.

S6-3 (*Learning Objective 2: Applying the average, FIFO, and LIFO methods*)   Continental Sporting Goods started April with an inventory of nine sets of golf clubs that cost a total of $1,260. During April Continental purchased 25 sets of clubs for $4,000. At the end of the month, Continental had 8 sets of golf clubs on hand. The store manager must select an inventory costing method, and he asks you to tell him both cost of goods sold and ending inventory under these three accounting methods:

    a. Average cost (round average unit cost to the nearest cent)

    b. FIFO

    c. LIFO

S6-4 (*Learning Objective 2: Applying the average, FIFO, and LIFO methods*)   Jefferson's Copy Center uses laser printers. Assume Jefferson started the year with 92 containers of ink (average cost of $9.00 each, FIFO cost of $8.90 each, LIFO cost of $8.05 each). During the year, Jefferson purchased 680 containers of ink at $9.80 and sold 580 units for $20.25 each. Jefferson paid operating expenses throughout the year, a total of $3,750. Jefferson is not subject to income tax.

Prepare Jefferson's income statement for the current year ended December 31 under the average, FIFO, and LIFO inventory costing methods. Include a complete statement heading.

S6-5 (*Learning Objective 2: Computing income tax effects of the inventory costing methods*)   This exercise should be used in conjunction with Short Exercise 6-4. Jefferson is a corporation subject to a 30% income tax. Compute Jefferson's income tax expense under the average, FIFO, and LIFO inventory costing methods. Which method would you select to (a) maximize income before tax and (b) minimize income tax expense?

S6-6 (*Learning Objective 2: Computing income and income tax effects of LIFO*)   Microdata.com uses the LIFO method to account for inventory. Microdata is having an unusually good year, with net income well above expectations. The company's inventory costs are rising rapidly. What can Microdata do immediately before the end of the year to decrease net income? Explain how this action decreases reported income, and tell why Microdata might want to decrease its net income.

writing assignment ◼

S6-7 (*Learning Objective 2: Applying the lower-of-cost-or-market rule to inventory*)   It is December 31, end of the year, and the controller of Reed Corporation is applying the lower-of-cost-or-market (LCM) rule to inventories. Before any year-end adjustments Reed reports the following data:

Cost of goods sold..	$440,000
Historical cost of ending inventory,	
as determined by a physical count..............	57,000

Reed determines that the replacement cost of ending inventory is $42,000. Show what Reed should report for ending inventory and for cost of goods sold. Identify the financial statement where each item appears.

S6-8 (*Learning Objective 2: Managing income taxes under the LIFO method*)   Smith Saxophone Company is nearing the end of its worst year ever. With two weeks until year-end, it appears that net income for the year will have decreased by 25% from last year. Joe Smith, the president and principal stockholder, is distressed with the year's results. Smith asks you, the financial vice president, to come up with a way to increase the business's net income. Inventory quantities are a little higher than normal because sales have been slow during the last few months. Smith uses the LIFO inventory method, and inventory costs have risen dramatically during the latter part of the year.

writing assignment ◼

Complete the memorandum to Joe Smith to explain how the company can increase its net income for the year. Explain your reasoning in detail. Smith is a man of integrity, so your plan must be completely ethical.

S6-9 (*Learning Objective 2: Identifying income, tax, and other effects of the inventory methods*)   This exercise tests your understanding of the four inventory methods. List the name of the inventory method that best fits the description. Assume that the cost of inventory is rising.

1. _____ Generally associated with saving income taxes.
2. _____ Results in a cost of ending inventory that is close to the current cost of replacing the inventory.
3. _____ Used to account for automobiles, jewelry, and art objects.
4. _____ Provides a middle-ground measure of ending inventory and cost of goods sold.
5. _____ Maximizes reported income.
6. _____ Matches the most current cost of goods sold against sales revenue.
7. _____ Results in an old measure of the cost of ending inventory.
8. _____ Writes inventory down when replacement cost drops below historical cost.
9. _____ Enables a company to buy high-cost inventory at year end and thereby decrease reported income and income tax.
10. _____ Enables a company to keep reported income from dropping lower by liquidating older layers of inventory.

S6-10 (*Learning Objective 3: Using ratio data to evaluate operations*)   Mountain Company made sales of $35,482 million during 2010. Cost of goods sold for the year totaled $15,333 million. At the end of 2009, Mountain's inventory stood at $1,641 million, and Mountain ended 2010 with inventory of $1,945 million.

Compute Mountain's gross profit percentage and rate of inventory turnover for 2010.

S6-11 (*Learning Objective 4: Estimating ending inventory by the gross profit method*)   City Technology began the year with inventory of $244,000 and purchased $1,540,000 of goods during the year. Sales for the year are $4,000,000, and City's gross profit percentage is 60% of sales. Compute City's estimated cost of ending inventory by using the gross profit method.

S6-12 (*Learning Objective 5: Assessing the effect of an inventory error—one year only*)   ABC, Inc., reported these figures for its fiscal year (amounts in millions):

Net sales.............................	$ 1,900
Cost of goods sold...............	1,130
Ending inventory..................	450

Suppose ABC later learns that ending inventory was overstated by $14 million. What are the correct amounts for (a) net sales, (b) ending inventory, (c) cost of goods sold, and (d) gross profit?

S6-13 (*Learning Objective 5: Assessing the effect of an inventory error on 2 years*)   Binder's $5.8 million cost of inventory at the end of last year was understated by $1.7 million.

1. Was last year's reported gross profit of $3.8 million overstated, understated, or correct? What was the correct amount of gross profit last year?
2. Is this year's gross profit of $5.5 million overstated, understated, or correct? What is the correct amount of gross profit for the current year?

S6-14 (*Learning Objectives 2, 4: Considering ethical implications of inventory actions*)   Determine whether each of the following actions in buying, selling, and accounting for inventories is ethical or unethical. Give your reason for each answer.

1. In applying the lower-of-cost-or-market rule to inventories, Tewksbury Financial Industries recorded an excessively low market value for ending inventory. This allowed the company to pay less income tax for the year.

2. Livingston Pharmaceuticals purchased lots of inventory shortly before year-end to increase the LIFO cost of goods sold and decrease reported income for the year.
3. Mulberry, Inc., delayed the purchase of inventory until after December 31, 2010, to keep 2010's cost of goods sold from growing too large. The delay in purchasing inventory helped net income of 2010 to reach the level of profit demanded by the company's investors.
4. Dunn Sales Company deliberately overstated ending inventory in order to report higher profits (net income).
5. Burke Corporation deliberately overstated purchases to produce a high figure for cost of goods sold (low amount of net income). The real reason was to decrease the company's income tax payments to the government.

Exercises

All of the A and B exercises can be found within MyAccountingLab, an online homework and practice environment. Your instructor may ask you to complete these exercises using MyAccountingLab.

(Group A)

E6-15A (*Learning Objectives 1, 2: Accounting for inventory transactions under FIFO costing*) Accounting records for Richmond Corporation yield the following data for the year ended December 31, 2010:

Inventory, December 31, 2009	$ 8,000
Purchases of inventory (on account).......................................	47,000
Sales of inventory—79% on account; 21% for cash (cost $41,000)	79,000
Inventory at FIFO, December 31, 2010....................................	14,000

❙ Requirements

1. Journalize Richmond's inventory transactions for the year under the perpetual system.
2. Report ending inventory, sales, cost of goods sold, and gross profit on the appropriate financial statement.

E6-16A (*Learning Objectives 1, 2: Analyzing inventory transactions under FIFO costing*) Ken's, Inc.'s inventory records for a particular development program show the following at December 31:

Dec 1	Beginning inventory	5 units @ $150 =	$ 750
15	Purchase.............................	4 units @ 150 =	$ 600
26	Purchase.............................	12 units @ 160 =	$1,920

At December 31, nine of these programs are on hand. Journalize for Ken's:

1. Total December purchases in one summary entry. All purchases were on credit.
2. Total December sales and cost of goods sold in two summary entries. The selling price was $550 per unit, and all sales were on credit. Assume that Ken's uses the FIFO inventory method.
3. Under FIFO, how much gross profit would Ken's earn on these transactions? What is the FIFO cost of Ken's ending inventory?

E6-17A (*Learning Objective 2: Determining ending inventory and cost of goods sold by four methods*) Use the data for Ken's in Exercise 6-16A to answer the following:

▌*Requirements*

1. Compute cost of goods sold and ending inventory, using each of the following methods:
    a. Specific unit cost, with three $150 units and six $160 units still on hand at the end.
    b. Average cost.
    c. First-in, first-out.
    d. Last-in, first-out.
2. Which method produces the highest cost of goods sold? Which method produces the lowest cost of goods sold? What causes the difference in cost of goods sold?

E6-18A (*Learning Objective 2: Computing the tax advantage of LIFO over FIFO*) Use the data for Ken's in Exercise 6-16A to illustrate Ken's income tax advantage from using LIFO over FIFO. Sales revenue is $6,600, operating expenses are $1,500, and the income tax rate is 35%. How much in taxes would Ken's save by using the LIFO method versus FIFO?

E6-19A (*Learning Objective 2: Determining ending inventory and cost of goods sold— FIFO vs. LIFO*) MusicPlace.net specializes in sound equipment. Because each inventory item is expensive, MusicPlace uses a perpetual inventory system. Company records indicate the following data for a line of speakers:

Date		Item	Quantity	Unit Cost	Sale Price
Apr	1	Balance..................	16	$32	
Apr	2	Purchase................	5	63	
Apr	7	Sale	7		$112
Apr	13	Sale	5		112

▌*Requirements*

1. Determine the amounts that MusicPlace should report for cost of goods sold and ending inventory two ways:
    a. FIFO
    b. LIFO
2. MusicPlace uses the FIFO method. Prepare MusicPlace's income statement for the month ended April 30, 2010, reporting gross profit. Operating expenses totaled $260, and the income tax rate was 35%.

E6-20A (*Learning Objective 2: Measuring gross profit—FIFO vs. LIFO; Falling prices*) Suppose a Waldorf store in Atlanta, Georgia, ended November 2010 with 900,000 units of merchandise that cost an average of $5 each. Suppose the store then sold 800,000 units for $4.8 million during December. Further, assume the store made two large purchases during December as follows:

Dec 11	200,000 units @ $4.00 =	$ 800,000
24	500,000 units @ $3.00 =	$1,500,000

▌*Requirements*

1. At December 31, the store manager needs to know the store's gross profit under both FIFO and LIFO. Supply this information.
2. What caused the FIFO and LIFO gross profit figures to differ?
3. Assume that the store uses FIFO to value inventories, and that the store manager, whose bonus is based on profits, decides to change the unit cost on inventory to $5 for all units. What impact will this have on gross profit and net income? Does GAAP allow this?

E6-21A (*Learning Objective 2: Applying the lower-of-cost-or-market rule to inventories*) Thames Garden Supplies uses a perpetual inventory system. Thames Garden Supplies has these account balances at July 31, 2010, prior to making the year-end adjustments:

Inventory	Cost of Goods Sold	Sales Revenue
Beg bal 11,500		
End bal 15,000	Bal 67,000	Bal 116,000

A year ago, the replacement cost of ending inventory was $12,000, which exceeded cost of $11,500. Thames Garden Supplies has determined that the replacement cost of the July 31, 2010, ending inventory is $10,800.

❙ *Requirement*

1. Prepare Thames Garden Supplies' 2010 income statement through gross profit to show how the company would apply the lower-of-cost-or-market rule to its inventories.

E6-22A (*Learning Objective 2: Using the cost-of-goods-sold model*) Supply the missing income statement amounts for each of the following companies (amounts adapted, in millions or billions):

Company	Net Sales	Beginning Inventory	Net Purchases	Ending Inventory	Cost of Goods Sold	Gross Profit
Crane	$105,000	$19,000	$65,000	$18,000	(a)	(b)
Foster	138,000	27,000	(c)	28,000	(d)	45,000
Allen	(e)	(f)	56,000	21,000	60,000	32,000
Matthews	84,000	11,000	30,000	(g)	36,000	(h)

❙ *Requirement*

1. Prepare the income statement for Crane Company, for the year ended December 31, 2010. Use the cost-of-goods-sold model to compute cost of goods sold. Crane's operating and other expenses, as adapted, for the year were $41,000. Ignore income tax.

Note: Exercise E6-23A builds on Exercise 6-22A with a profitability analysis of these actual companies.

E6-23A (*Learning Objective 3: Measuring profitability*) Refer to the data in Exercise 6-22A. Compute all ratio values to answer the following questions:

■ **general ledger**

- ■ Which company has the highest, and which company has the lowest, gross profit percentage?
- ■ Which company has the highest, and the lowest rate of inventory turnover?

Based on your figures, which company appears to be the most profitable?

E6-24A (*Learning Objective 3: Computing gross profit percentage and inventory turnover*) Thurston & Talty, a partnership, had the following inventory data:

	2009	2010
Ending inventory at:		
FIFO Cost	$21,000	$ 23,000
LIFO Cost	8,000	17,000
Cost of goods sold at:		
FIFO Cost		$ 85,200
LIFO Cost		92,800
Sales revenue		144,000

Thurston & Talty need to know the company's gross profit percentage and rate of inventory turnover for 2010 under

1. FIFO   **2.** LIFO

Which method makes the business look better on

3. Gross profit percentage?   **4.** Inventory turnover?

E6-25A (*Learning Objective 2: Budgeting inventory purchases*) Toys Plus prepares budgets to help manage the company. Toys Plus is budgeting for the fiscal year ended January 31, 2010. During the preceding year ended January 31, 2009, sales totaled $9,300 million and cost of goods sold was $6,500 million. At January 31, 2009, inventory stood at $2,100 million. During the upcoming 2010 year, suppose Toys Plus expects cost of goods sold to increase by 10%. The company budgets next year's ending inventory at $2,400 million.

❙ Requirement

  1. One of the most important decisions a manager makes is how much inventory to buy. How much inventory should Toys Plus purchase during the upcoming year to reach its budgeted figures?

■ **spreadsheet**

E6-26A (*Learning Objective 4: Estimating inventory by the gross profit method*) J R Company began May with inventory of $47,500. The business made net purchases of $30,900 and had net sales of $62,100 before a fire destroyed the company's inventory. For the past several years, J R's gross profit percentage has been 35%. Estimate the cost of the inventory destroyed by the fire. Identify another reason owners and managers use the gross profit method to estimate inventory.

E6-27A (*Learning Objective 5: Correcting an inventory error*) Big Blue Sea Marine Supply reported the following comparative income statement for the years ended September 30, 2010, and 2009:

Big Blue Sea Marine Supply Income Statements For the Years Ended September 30, 2010, and 2009		
	2010	**2009**
Sales revenue	$143,000	$120,000
Cost of goods sold:		
Beginning inventory	$ 14,500	$ 9,000
Net purchases	74,000	67,000
Cost of goods available	88,500	76,000
Ending inventory.........................	(19,000)	(14,500)
Cost of goods sold	69,500	61,500
Gross profit..................................	73,500	58,500
Operating expenses	28,000	24,000
Net income..................................	$ 45,500	$ 34,500

Big Blue Sea's president and shareholders are thrilled by the company's boost in sales and net income during 2010. Then the accountants for the company discover that ending 2009 inventory was understated by $6,500. Prepare the corrected comparative income statement for the 2-year period, complete with a heading for the statement. How well did Big Blue Sea really perform in 2010, as compared with 2009?

(Group B)

E6-28B (*Learning Objectives 1, 2: Accounting for inventory transactions under FIFO costing*) Accounting records for Rockford Corporation yield the following data for the year ended December 31, 2010:

■ **general ledger**

Inventory, December 31, 2009...	$ 8,000
Purchases of inventory (on account)...	49,000
Sales of inventory—76% on account; 24% for cash (cost $40,000).........	74,000
Inventory at FIFO, December 31, 2010..	17,000

▮ Requirements

1. Journalize Rockford's inventory transactions for the year under the perpetual system.
2. Report ending inventory, sales, cost of goods sold, and gross profit on the appropriate financial statement.

E6-29B (*Learning Objectives 1, 2: Analyzing inventory transactions under FIFO costing*) Ron's, Inc.'s inventory records for a particular development program show the following at May 31:

May	1	Beginning inventory	7 units @	$160	=	$1,120
	15	Purchase................................	6 units @	160	=	960
	26	Purchase................................	11 units @	170	=	1,870

At May 31, 10 of these programs are on hand. Journalize for Ron's:

1. Total May purchases in one summary entry. All purchases were on credit.
2. Total May sales and cost of goods sold in two summary entries. The selling price was $625 per unit and all sales were on credit. Assume that Ron's uses the FIFO inventory method.
3. Under FIFO, how much gross profit would Ron's earn on these transactions? What is the FIFO cost of Ron's, Inc.'s ending inventory?

E6-30B (*Learning Objective 2: Determining ending inventory and cost of goods sold by four methods*) Use the data for Ron's, Inc., in Exercise 6-29B to answer the following.

■ **spreadsheet**

▮ Requirements

1. Compute cost of goods sold and ending inventory using each of the following methods:
   a. Specific unit cost, with five $160 units and five $170 units still on hand at the end.
   b. Average cost.
   c. FIFO.
   d. LIFO.
2. Which method produces the highest cost of goods sold? Which method produces the lowest cost of goods sold? What causes the difference in cost of goods sold?

E6-31B (*Learning Objective 2: Computing the tax advantage of LIFO over FIFO*) Use the data for Ron's, Inc., in Exercise 6-29B to illustrate Ron's income tax advantage from using LIFO over FIFO. Sales revenue is $8,750, operating expenses are $2,000, and the income tax rate is 32%. How much in taxes would Ron's save by using the LIFO method versus FIFO?

E6-32B *(Learning Objective 2: Determining ending inventory and cost of goods sold—FIFO vs. LIFO)* MusicLife.net specializes in sound equipment. Because each inventory item is expensive, MusicLife uses a perpetual inventory system. Company records indicate the following data for a line of speakers:

Date		Item	Quantity	Unit Cost	Sale Price
Apr	1	Balance..................	16	$39	
Apr	2	Purchase................	6	66	
Apr	7	Sale	7		$105
Apr	13	Sale	6		96

❙ Requirements

1. Determine the amounts that MusicLife should report for cost of goods sold and ending inventory two ways:
   a. FIFO
   b. LIFO
2. MusicLife uses the FIFO method. Prepare MusicLife's income statement for the month ended April 30, 2010, reporting gross profit. Operating expenses totaled $340, and the income tax rate was 30%.

E6-33B *(Learning Objective 2: Measuring gross profit—FIFO vs. LIFO; falling prices)* Suppose a Williams store in Cleveland, Ohio, ended September 2010 with 1,100,000 units of merchandise that cost an average of $9.00 each. Suppose the store then sold 1,000,000 units for $9.7 million during October. Further, assume the store made two large purchases during October as follows:

Oct 12	100,000 units @ $8.00 =	$ 800,000
24	600,000 units @ $7.00 =	$4,200,000

❙ Requirements

1. At October 31, the store manager needs to know the store's gross profit under both FIFO and LIFO. Supply this information.
2. What caused the FIFO and LIFO gross profit figures to differ?
3. Assume that the store uses FIFO, and that the store manager, whose bonus is based on profits, decides to value all units in ending inventory at $9 per unit. What impact will this action have on gross profit and net income? Does GAAP allow this?

E6-34B *(Learning Objective 2: Applying the lower-of-cost-or-market rule to inventories)* Ontario Garden Supplies uses a perpetual inventory system. Ontario Garden Supplies has these account balances at May 31, 2010, prior to making the year-end adjustments:

Inventory		Cost of Goods Sold		Sales Revenue	
Beg bal 12,500					
End bal 13,500		Bal 73,000		Bal 115,000	

A year ago, the replacement cost of ending inventory was $13,400, which exceeded the cost of $12,500. Ontario Garden Supplies has determined that the replacement cost of the May 31, 2010, ending inventory is $13,000.

❚ Requirement

1. Prepare Ontario Garden Supplies' 2010 income statement through gross profit to show how the company would apply the lower-of-cost-or-market rule to its inventories.

E6-35B (*Learning Objective 2: Using the cost-of-goods-sold model*)   Supply the missing amounts for each of the following companies:

Company	Net Sales	Beginning Inventory	Net Purchases	Ending Inventory	Cost of Goods Sold	Gross Profit
Fisher	$101,000	$22,000	$61,000	$17,000	(a)	(b)
Hults	132,000	26,000	(c)	27,000	(d)	40,000
Franklin	(e)	(f)	56,000	20,000	65,000	30,000
Ogden	86,000	8,000	37,000	(g)	39,000	(h)

❚ Requirement

1. Prepare the income statement for Fisher Company, for the year ended December 31, 2010. Use the cost-of-goods-sold model to compute cost of goods sold. Fisher's operating and other expenses for the year were $46,000. Ignore income tax.

Note: Exercise E6-36B builds on Exercise E6-35B with a profitability analysis of these actual companies.

E6-36B (*Learning Objective 3: Measuring profitability*)   Refer to the data in Exercise 6-35B. Compute all ratio values to answer the following questions:

general ledger ■

- Which company has the highest, and which company has the lowest, gross profit percentage?
- Which company has the highest, and the lowest rate of inventory turnover?

Based on your figures, which company appears to be the most profitable?

E6-37B (*Learning Objective 3: Computing gross profit percentage and inventory turnover*)   Durkin & Davis, a partnership, had these inventory data:

	2009	2010
Ending inventory at:		
FIFO Cost	$17,000	$ 21,000
LIFO Cost..............	15,000	23,000
Cost of goods sold at:		
FIFO Cost		$ 85,700
LIFO Cost..............		92,500
Sales revenue..............		141,000

Durkin & Davis need to know the company's gross profit percentage and rate of inventory turnover for 2010 under

1. FIFO   2. LIFO

Which method makes the business look better on

3. Gross profit percentage?   4. Inventory turnover?

E6-38B (*Learning Objective 2: Budgeting inventory purchases*)   Toyland prepares budgets to help manage the company. Toyland is budgeting for the fiscal year ended January 31, 2010. During preceding year ended January 31, 2009, sales totaled $9,700 million and cost of goods sold was $6,200 million. At January 31, 2009, inventory stood at $1,800 million. During the upcoming 2010 year, suppose Toyland expects cost of goods sold to increase by 10%. The company budgets next year's inventory at $2,100 million.

I Requirement

1. One of the most important decisions a manager makes is how much inventory to buy. How much inventory should Toyland purchase during the upcoming year to reach its budgeted figures?

■ spreadsheet

E6-39B (*Learning Objective 4: Estimating inventory by the gross profit method*) R B Company began June with inventory of $45,800. The business made net purchases of $31,900 and had net sales of $64,500 before a fire destroyed the company's inventory. For the past several years, R B's gross profit percentage has been 45%. Estimate the cost of the inventory destroyed by the fire. Identify another reason owners and managers use the gross profit method to estimate inventory.

E6-40B (*Learning Objective 5: Correcting an inventory error*)   Harbour Master Marine Supply reported the following comparative income statement for the years ended September 30, 2010, and 2009:

Harbour Master Marine Supply Income Statements For the Years Ended September 30, 2010, and 2009				
	2010		**2009**	
Sales revenue		$139,000		$121,000
Cost of goods sold:				
Beginning inventory	$ 13,000		$ 12,000	
Net purchases	74,000		69,000	
Cost of goods available	87,000		81,000	
Ending inventory	(18,500)		(13,000)	
Cost of goods sold		68,500		68,000
Gross profit		70,500		53,000
Operating expenses		26,000		19,000
Net income		$ 44,500		$ 34,000

Harbour Master's president and shareholders are thrilled by the company's boost in sales and net income during 2010. Then the accountants for the company discover that ending 2009 inventory was understated by $7,000. Prepare the corrected comparative income statement for the two-year period, complete with a heading for the statement. How well did Harbour Master really perform in 2010, as compared with 2009?

Challenge Exercises

E6-41 (*Learning Objective 2: Making inventory policy decisions*)   For each of the following situations, identify the inventory method that you would use or, given the use of a particular method, state the strategy that you would follow to accomplish your goal:

a. Inventory costs are increasing. Your company uses LIFO and is having an unexpectedly good year. It is near year-end, and you need to keep net income from increasing too much in order to save on income tax.

b. Suppliers of your inventory are threatening a labor strike, and it may be difficult for your company to obtain inventory. This situation could increase your income taxes.

c. Company management, like that of IBM and Pier 1 Imports, prefers a middle-of-the-road inventory policy that avoids extremes.

d. Inventory costs are *decreasing*, and your company's board of directors wants to minimize income taxes.

e. Inventory costs are *increasing*, and the company prefers to report high income.

f. Inventory costs have been stable for several years, and you expect costs to remain stable for the indefinite future. (Give the reason for your choice of method.)

E6-42 (*Learning Objective 2: Measuring the effect of a LIFO liquidation*) Suppose Trendy Now Fashions, a specialty retailer, had these records for ladies' evening gowns during 2010.

Beginning inventory (40 @ $1,075)	$ 43,000
Purchase in February (22 @ $1,200)	26,400
Purchase in June (53 @ $1,275)	67,575
Purchase in December (26 @ $1,325)	34,450
Goods available for sale	$171,425

Assume sales of evening gowns totaled 130 units during 2010 and that Trendy Now uses the LIFO method to account for inventory. The income tax rate is 40%.

❙ Requirements

1. Compute Trendy Now's cost of goods sold for evening gowns in 2010.
2. Compute what cost of goods sold would have been if Trendy Now had purchased enough inventory in December—at $1,325 per evening gown—to keep year-end inventory at the same level it was at the beginning of the year.

E6-43 (*Learning Objective 3: Evaluating a company's profitability*) T Mart, Inc., declared bankruptcy. Let's see why. T Mart reported these figures:

T Mart, Inc.
Statement of Income
Years Ended December 31

Millions	2010	2009	2008	2007
Sales	$36.1	$36.0	$34.6	
Cost of sales	28.7	27.9	26.9	
Selling expenses	7.6	6.7	6.1	
Other expenses	0.1	0.9	0.7	
Net income (net loss)	$ (0.3)	$ 0.5	$ 0.9	
Additional data:				
Ending inventory	$ 8.8	$ 7.4	$ 7.6	$ 6.6

❙ Requirement

1. Evaluate the trend of T Mart's results of operations during 2008 through 2010. Consider the trends of sales, gross profit, and net income. Track the gross profit percentage (to three decimal places) and the rate of inventory turnover (to one decimal place) in each year. Also discuss the role that selling expenses must have played in T Mart's difficulties.

Quiz

Test your understanding of accounting for inventory by answering the following questions. Select the best choice from among the possible answers given.

Q6-44 Oceanview Software began January with $3,200 of merchandise inventory. During January, Oceanview made the following entries for its inventory transactions:

Inventory	6,400	
Accounts Payable		6,400
Accounts Receivable	7,400	
Sales Revenue		7,400
Cost of Goods Sold	5,400	
Inventory		5,400

How much was Oceanview's inventory at the end of January?

a. $5,200   c. $4,200

b. Zero   d. $4,700

Q6-45 What is Oceanview's gross profit for January?

a. Zero   c. $5,400

b. $7,400   d. $2,000

Q6-46 When does the cost of inventory become an expense?

a. When inventory is purchased from the supplier.

b. When cash is collected from the customer.

c. When payment is made to the supplier.

d. When inventory is delivered to a customer.

The next two questions use the following facts. Perfect Corner Frame Shop wants to know the effect of different inventory costing methods on its financial statements. Inventory and purchases data for April follow:

			Units	Unit Cost	Total Cost
Apr 1	Beginning inventory		2,700	$14.00	$37,800
4	Purchase		1,500	$14.40	21,600
9	Sale		(1,600)		

Q6-47 If Perfect Corner uses the FIFO method, the *cost of the ending inventory* will be

a. $37,000.   c. $22,400.

b. $22,700.   d. $21,600.

Q6-48 If Perfect Corner uses the LIFO method, *cost of goods sold* will be

a. $22,700.   c. $22,400.

b. $23,000.   d. $21,600.

Q6-49 In a period of rising prices,

a. Net income under LIFO will be higher than under FIFO.

b. Gross profit under FIFO will be higher than under LIFO.

c. LIFO inventory will be greater than FIFO inventory.

d. Cost of goods sold under LIFO will be less than under FIFO.

Q6-50 The income statement for Feel Good Health Foods shows gross profit of $151,000, operating expenses of $126,000, and cost of goods sold of $215,000. What is the amount of net sales revenue?

a. $277,000
b. $366,000
c. $492,000
d. $341,000

Q6-51 The word "market" as used in "the lower of cost or market" generally means

a. retail market price.
b. Replacement cost.
c. Retail market price.
d. Liquidation price.

Q6-52 The sum of (a) ending inventory and (b) cost of goods sold is

a. beginning inventory.
b. goods available.
c. net purchases.
d. gross profit.

Q6-53 The following data come from the inventory records of Draper Company:

Net sales revenue	$623,000
Beginning inventory	64,000
Ending inventory	45,000
Net purchases	460,000

Based on these facts, the gross profit for Draper Company is

a. $130,000.
b. $163,000.
c. $134,000.
d. Some other amount.

Q6-54 Eleanor Barker Cosmetics ended the month of May with inventory of $25,000. Eleanor Barker expects to end June with inventory of $12,000 after cost of goods sold of $102,000. How much inventory must Eleanor Barker purchase during June in order to accomplish these results?

a. $89,000
b. $114,000
c. $115,000
d. Cannot be determined from the data given

Q6-55 Two financial ratios that clearly distinguish a discount chain such as Kmart from a high-end retailer such as Saks Fifth Avenue are the gross profit percentage and the rate of inventory turnover. Which set of relationships is most likely for Saks Fifth Avenue?

Gross profit percentage	Inventory turnover
a. High	Low
b. High	High
c. Low	Low
d. Low	High

Q6-56 Sales are $540,000 and cost of goods sold is $330,000. Beginning and ending inventories are $29,000 and $34,000, respectively. How many times did the company turn its inventory over during this period?

a. 17.1 times
b. 6.7 times
c. 7.2 times
d. 10.5 times

Q6-57 Trigger, Inc., reported the following data:

Freight in	$ 25,000	Sales returns	$ 7,000
Purchases	208,000	Purchase returns	6,200
Beginning inventory	57,000	Sales revenue	450,000
Purchase discounts	4,300	Ending inventory	46,000

Trigger's gross profit percentage is

a. 46.3.

c. 47.3.

b. 52.7.

d. 57.4.

Q6-58 Shipley Tank Company had the following beginning inventory, net purchases, net sales, and gross profit percentage for the first quarter of 2010:

Beginning inventory, $52,000	Net purchases, $73,000
Net sales revenue, $94,000	Gross profit rate, 50%

By the gross profit method, the ending inventory should be

a. $80,000.

c. $81,000.

b. $78,000.

d. $79,000.

Q6-59 An error understated Regan Corporation's December 31, 2010, ending inventory by $42,000. What effect will this error have on total assets and net income for 2010?

Assets	**Net income**
a. Understate	No effect
b. No effect	No effect
c. Understate	Understate
d. No effect	Overstate

Q6-60 An error understated Regan Corporation's December 31, 2010, ending inventory by $42,000. What effect will this error have on net income for 2011?

a. Overstate

b. Understate

c. No effect

Problems

All of the A and B problems can be found within MyAccountingLab, an online homework and practice environment. Your instructor may ask you to complete these problems using MyAccountingLab.

(Group A)

■ **general ledger**

P6-61A (*Learning Objectives 1, 2: Accounting for inventory in a perpetual system using average costing method*)   Nice Buy purchases inventory in crates of merchandise; each crate of inventory is a unit. The fiscal year of Nice Buy ends each February 28. Assume you are dealing with a single Nice Buy store in Dallas, Texas. The Dallas store began 2010 with an inventory of 21,000 units that cost a total of $1,050,000. During the year, the store purchased merchandise on account as follows:

April (31,000 units at $51).................................	$1,581,000
August (51,000 units at $55)...............................	2,805,000
November (61,000 units at $61)	3,721,000
Total purchases...	$8,107,000

Cash payments on account totaled $7,707,000. During fiscal year 2010, the store sold 148,000 units of merchandise for $14,208,000, of which $4,900,000 was for cash and the balance was on account. Nice Buy uses the average cost method for inventories. Operating expenses for the year were $3,750,000. Nice Buy paid 70% in cash and accrued the rest as accrued liabilities. The store accrued income tax at the rate of 30%.

❙ Requirements

1. Make summary journal entries to record the store's transactions for the year ended February 28, 2010. Nice Buy uses a perpetual inventory system.
2. Prepare a T-account to show the activity in the Inventory account.
3. Prepare the store's income statement for the year ended February 28, 2010. Show totals for gross profit, income before tax, and net income.

P6-62A (*Learning Objective 2: Measuring cost of goods sold and ending inventory—perpetual system*)   Assume a Tiger Sports outlet store began October 2010 with 48 pairs of running shoes that cost the store $34 each. The sale price of these shoes was $69. During October, the store completed these inventory transactions:

		Units	Unit Cost	Units Sales Price
Oct 3	Sale	11	$34	$69
8	Purchase	83	35	
11	Sale	37	34	69
19	Sale	6	35	71
24	Sale	38	35	71
30	Purchase	25	36	

❙ Requirements

1. The preceding data are taken from the store's perpetual inventory records. Which cost method does the store use? Explain how you arrived at your answer.
2. Determine the store's cost of goods sold for October. Also compute gross profit for October.
3. What is the cost of the store's October 31 inventory of running shoes?

P6-63A (*Learning Objective 2: Computing inventory by three methods—perpetual system*)   Fatigues Surplus began October with 72 tents that cost $17 each. During the month, Fatigues Surplus made the following purchases at cost:

Oct 4	103 tents @ $19 = $1,957
19	158 tents @ $21 = 3,318
25	43 tents @ $22 = 946

Fatigues Surplus sold 324 tents and at October 31 the ending inventory consists of 52 tents. The sale price of each tent was $51.

❙ Requirements

1. Determine the cost of goods sold and ending inventory amounts for October under the average cost, FIFO cost, and LIFO cost. Round average cost per unit four decimal places, and round all other amounts to the nearest dollar.
2. Explain why cost of goods sold is highest under LIFO. Be specific.
3. Prepare Fatigues Surplus' income statement for October. Report gross profit. Operating expenses totaled $5,000. Fatigues Surplus uses average costing for inventory. The income tax rate is 40%.

writing assignment ■

P6-64A (*Learning Objective 2: Applying the different inventory costing methods—perpetual system*)   The records of Bell Aviation include the following accounts for inventory of aviation fuel at December 31 of the current year:

Inventory			
Jan 1	Balance	790 units @ $7.70	$ 6,083
Mar 6	Purchase	320 units @ $7.80	2,496
Jun 22	Purchase	8,350 units @ $8.20	68,470
Oct 4	Purchase	530 units @ $9.20	4,876

Sales Revenue		
Dec 31	9,010 units	$132,447

❙ Requirements

1. Prepare a partial income statement through gross profit under the average, FIFO, and LIFO methods. Round average cost per unit to four decimal places and all other amounts to the nearest dollar.
2. Which inventory method would you use to minimize income tax? Explain why this method causes income tax to be the lowest.

writing assignment ■

P6-65A (*Learning Objective 2: Applying the lower-of-cost-or-market rule to inventories—perpetual system*)   ELV Trade Mart has recently had lackluster sales. The rate of inventory turnover has dropped, and the merchandise is gathering dust. At the same time, competition has forced ELV's suppliers to lower the prices that ELV will pay when it replaces its inventory. It is now December 31, 2010, and the current replacement cost of ELV's ending inventory is $75,000 below what ELV actually paid for the goods, which was $220,000. Before any adjustments at the end of the period, the Cost of Goods Sold account has a balance of $770,000.

a. What accounting action should ELV take in this situation?
b. Give any journal entry required.
c. At what amount should ELV report Inventory on the balance sheet?
d. At what amount should the company report Cost of Goods Sold on the income statement?
e. Discuss the accounting principle or concept that is most relevant to this situation.

P6-66A (*Learning Objective 3: Using gross profit percentage and inventory turnover to evaluate two companies*)   Sprinkle Top and Coffee Shop are both specialty food chains. The two companies reported these figures, in millions:

Sprinkle Top, Inc. Income Statement (Adapted) Years Ended December 31		
(Amounts in millions)	2010	2009
Revenues:		
Net sales	$544	$707
Costs and Expenses:		
Cost of goods sold...	478	594
Selling, general, and administrative expenses...............	60	55

Sprinkle Top, Inc.
Balance Sheet (Adapted)
December 31

(Amounts in millions)	2010	2009
Assets		
Current assets:		
Cash and cash equivalents................	$12	$27
Receivables......................................	28	40
Inventories	26	36

Coffee Shop Corporation
Income Statement (Adapted)
Years Ended December 31

(Amounts in millions)	2010	2009
Net sales	$7,700	$6,300
Cost of goods sold...	3,160	2,604
Selling, general, and administrative expenses.......	2,950	2,390

Coffee Shop Corporation
Balance Sheet (Adapted)
December 31

(Amounts in millions)	2010	2009
Assets		
Current assets:		
Cash and temporary investments................	$313	$172
Receivables, net...	230	188
Inventories	627	544

Requirements

1. Compute the gross profit percentage and the rate of inventory turnover for Sprinkle Top and Coffee Shop for 2010.
2. Based on these statistics, which company looks more profitable? Why? What other expense category should we consider in evaluating these two companies?

P6-67A (*Learning Objectives 1, 4: Estimating inventory by the gross profit method; preparing the income statement*)   Assume Thompson Company, a copy center, lost some inventory in a fire. To file an insurance claim, Thompson Company must estimate its inventory by the gross profit method. Assume that for the past two years that Thompson

■ spreadsheet

Company's gross profit has averaged 41% of net sales. Suppose the Thompson Company's inventory records reveal the following data:

Inventory, October 1	$ 57,100
Transactions during October:	
Purchases	490,200
Purchase discounts	11,000
Purchase returns	70,900
Sales	667,000
Sales returns	11,000

I Requirements

1. Estimate the cost of the lost inventory, using the gross profit method.
2. Prepare the October income statement for this product through gross profit. Show the detailed computations of cost of goods sold in a separate schedule.

P6-68A (*Learning Objective 3: Determining the amount of inventory to purchase*)   Maroney's Convenience Store's income statement and balance sheet reported the following.

Maroney's Convenience Stores
Income Statement
Year Ended December 31, 2009

Sales	$957,000
Cost of sales	720,000
Gross profit	237,000
Operating expenses	114,000
Net income	$123,000

Maroney's Convenience Stores
Balance Sheet
December 31, 2009

Assets		Liabilities	
Cash	$ 44,000	Accounts payable	$ 31,000
Inventories	68,000	Note payable	187,000
Land and		Total liabilities	218,000
buildings, net	273,000	Owner, capital	167,000
		Total liabilities	
Total assets	$385,000	and capital	$385,000

The business is organized as a proprietorship, so it pays no corporate income tax. The owner is budgeting for 2010. He expects sales and cost of goods sold to increase by 6%. To meet customer demand, ending inventory will need to be $76,000 at December 31, 2010. The owner hopes to earn a net income of $154,000 next year.

I Requirements

1. One of the most important decisions a manager makes is the amount of inventory to purchase. Show how to determine the amount of inventory to purchase in 2010.
2. Prepare the store's budgeted income statement for 2010 to reach the target net income of $154,000. To reach this goal, operating expenses must decrease by $16,780.

P6-69A (*Learning Objective 5: Correcting inventory errors over a three-year period*)   The accounting records of R.B. Video Sales show the data on the following page (in millions). The shareholders are very happy with R.B.'s steady increase in net income.

Auditors discovered that the ending inventory for 2008 was understated by $3 million and that the ending inventory for 2009 was also understated by $3 million. The ending inventory at December 31, 2010, was correct.

	2010	2009	2008
Net sales revenue..........................	$39	$36	$33
Cost of goods sold:			
Beginning inventory.................	$ 5	$ 4	$ 3
Net purchases	27	25	23
Cost of goods available.............	32	29	26
Less ending inventory...............	(6)	(5)	(4)
Cost of goods sold	26	24	22
Gross profit..................................	13	12	11
Operating expenses	6	6	6
Net income...................................	$ 7	$ 6	$ 5

Requirements

1. Show corrected income statements for each of the three years.
2. How much did these assumed corrections add to or take away from R.B.'s total net income over the three-year period? How did the corrections affect the trend of net income?
3. Will R.B.'s shareholders still be happy with the company's trend of net income? Give the reason for your answer.

(Group B)

P6-70B (*Learning Objectives 1, 2: Accounting for inventory in a perpetual system using average costing method*)   Best Guy purchases inventory in crates of merchandise; each crate of inventory is a unit. The fiscal year of Best Guy ends each February 28. Assume you are dealing with a single Best Guy store in Denver, Colorado. The Denver store began 2010 with an inventory of 17,000 units that cost a total of $850,000. During the year, the store purchased merchandise on account as follows:

■ **general ledger**

April (33,000 units at $60)...................................	$1,980,000
August (53,000 units at $64)..............................	3,392,000
November (63,000 units at $70)	4,410,000
Total purchases...	$9,782,000

Cash payments on account totaled $9,382,000. During fiscal 2010, the store sold 152,000 units of merchandise for $14,592,000, of which $4,500,000 was for cash and the balance was on account. Best Guy uses the average cost method for inventories. Operating expenses for the year were $2,750,000. Best Guy paid 60% in cash and accrued the rest as accrued liabilities. The store accrued income tax at the rate of 35%.

Requirements

1. Make summary journal entries to record the store's transactions for the year ended February 28, 2010. Best Guy uses a perpetual inventory system.
2. Prepare a T-account to show the activity in the Inventory account.
3. Prepare the store's income statement for the year ended February 28, 2010. Show totals for gross profit, income before tax, and net income.

P6-71B (*Learning Objective 2: Measuring cost of goods sold and ending inventory—perpetual system*) Assume a Championship Sports outlet store began March 2010 with 46 pairs of running shoes that cost the store $39 each. The sale price of these shoes was $65. During March the store completed these inventory transactions:

		Units	Unit Cost	Units Sale Price
Mar 3	Sale	17	$39	$65
8	Purchase......	78	40	
11	Sale	29	39	65
19	Sale	11	40	67
24	Sale	36	40	67
30	Purchase......	19	41	

❚ Requirements

1. The preceding data are taken from the store's perpetual inventory records. Which cost method does the store use? Explain how you arrived at your answer.
2. Determine the store's cost of goods sold for March. Also compute gross profit for March.
3. What is the cost of the store's March 31 inventory of running shoes?

P6-72B (*Learning Objective 2: Computing inventory by three methods—perpetual system*) SWAT Team Surplus began July with 66 tents that cost $23 each. During the month, SWAT Team Surplus made the following purchases at cost:

Jul 4	105 tents @ $25 =	$2,625
19	157 tents @ $27 =	4,239
25	37 tents @ $28 =	1,036

SWAT Team Surplus sold 310 tents, and at July 31 the ending inventory consists of 55 tents. The sale price of each tent was $53.

❚ Requirements

1. Determine the cost of goods sold and ending inventory amounts for July under the average cost, FIFO cost, and LIFO cost. Round average cost per unit four decimal places, and round all other amounts to the nearest dollar.
2. Explain why cost of goods sold is highest under LIFO. Be specific.
3. Prepare SWAT Team Surplus income statement for July. Report gross profit. Operating expenses totaled $3,000. SWAT Team Surplus uses average costing for inventory. The income tax rate is 32%.

writing assignment ■

P6-73B (*Learning Objective 2: Applying the different inventory costing methods—perpetual system*) The records of Buzz Aviation include the following accounts for inventory of aviation fuel at December 31 of the current year:

Inventory				
Jan 1	Balance	730 units @ $7.60	$ 5,548	
Mar 6	Purchase	310 units @ $7.70	2,387	
Jun 22	Purchase	8,370 units @ $8.10	67,797	
Oct 4	Purchase	520 units @ $9.10	4,732	

Sales Revenue			
	Dec 31	9,030 units	$128,226

Requirements

1. Prepare a partial income statement through gross profit under the average, FIFO, and LIFO methods. Round average cost per unit to four decimal places and all other amounts to the nearest whole dollar.

2. Which inventory method would you use to minimize income tax? Explain why this method causes income tax to be the lowest.

P6-74B (*Learning Objective 2: Applying the lower-of-cost-or-market rule to inventories— perpetual system*)   Aquarium Trade Mart has recently had lackluster sales. The rate of inventory turnover has dropped, and the merchandise is gathering dust. At the same time, competition has forced Aquarium's suppliers to lower the prices that Aquarium will pay when it replaces its inventory. It is now December 31, 2010, and the current replacement cost of Aquarium's ending inventory is $70,000 below what Aquarium actually paid for the goods, which was $280,000. Before any adjustments at the end of the period, the Cost of Goods Sold account has a balance of $800,000.

writing assignment ■

   a. What accounting action should Aquarium take in this situation?
   b. Give any journal entry required.
   c. At what amount should Aquarium report Inventory on the balance sheet?
   d. At what amount should the company report Cost of Goods Sold on the income statement?
   e. Discuss the accounting principle or concept that is most relevant to this situation.

P6-75B (*Learning Objective 3: Using gross profit percentage and inventory turnover to evaluate two companies*)   Pastry People and Coffee Grind are both specialty food chains. The two companies reported these figures, in millions:

Pastry People, Inc.
Income Statement (Adapted)
Years Ended December 31

(Amounts in millions)	2010	2009
Revenues:		
Net sales	$548	$701
Costs and Expenses:		
Cost of goods sold...	477	593
Selling, general, and administrative expenses..............	61	51

Pastry People, Inc.
Balance Sheet (Adapted)
December 31

(Amounts in millions)	2010	2009
Assets		
Current assets:		
Cash and cash equivalents................	$17	$22
Receivables.......................................	21	34
Inventories	17	33

Coffee Grind Corporation
Income Statement (Adapted)
Years Ended December 31

(Amounts in millions)	2010	2009
Net sales	$7,171	$6,369
Cost of goods sold	3,190	2,603
Selling, general, and administrative expenses	2,955	2,360

Coffee Grind Corporation
Balance Sheet (Adapted)
December 31

(Amounts in millions)	2010	2009
Assets		
Current assets:		
Cash and temporary investments	$310	$171
Receivables, net	227	193
Inventories	631	546

❘ Requirements

1. Compute the gross profit percentage and the rate of inventory turnover for Pastry People and Coffee Grind for 2010.
2. Based on these statistics, which company looks more profitable? Why? What other expense category should we consider in evaluating these two companies?

■ spreadsheet

P6-76B (*Learning Objectives 1, 4: Estimating inventory by the gross profit method; preparing the income statement*) Assume Ross Company, a sporting goods store, lost some inventory in a fire. To file an insurance claim, Ross Company must estimate its ending inventory by the gross profit method. Assume that for the past two years, Ross Company's gross profit has averaged 43% of net sales. Suppose Ross Company's inventory records reveal the following data:

Inventory, January 1	$ 57,500
Transactions during January:	
Purchases	490,500
Purchase discounts	12,000
Purchase returns	70,300
Sales	664,000
Sales returns	16,000

❘ Requirements

1. Estimate the cost of the lost inventory, using the gross profit method.
2. Prepare the January income statement for this product through gross profit. Show the detailed computation of cost of goods sold in a separate schedule.

P6-77B (*Learning Objective 3: Determining the amount of inventory to purchase*) Dave's Convenience Store's income statement and balance sheet reported the following. The business is organized as a proprietorship, so it pays no corporate income tax. The owner is budgeting for 2010. He expects sales and cost of goods sold to increase by 9%. To meet customer demand, ending inventory will need to be $78,000 at December 31, 2010. The owner hopes to earn a net income of $156,000 next year.

Dave's Convenience Stores Income Statement Year Ended December 31, 2009	
Sales	$964,000
Cost of sales	722,000
Gross profit	242,000
Operating expenses.............	110,000
Net income	$132,000

Dave's Convenience Stores Balance Sheet December 31, 2009			
Assets		**Liabilities**	
Cash	$ 35,000	Accounts payable	$ 28,000
Inventories	65,000	Note payable.................	193,000
Land and		Total liabilities	221,000
buildings, net	268,000	Owner, capital..............	147,000
		Total liabilities	
Total assets....................	$368,000	and capital	$368,000

Requirements

1. One of the most important decisions a manager makes is the amount of inventory to purchase. Show how to determine the amount of inventory to purchase in 2010.
2. Prepare the store's budgeted income statement for 2010 to reach the target net income of $156,000. To reach this goal, operating expenses must decrease by $2,220.

P6-78B (*Learning Objective 5: Correcting inventory errors over a three-year period*) The accounting records of Waterville Video Sales show these data (in millions). The shareholders are very happy with Waterville's steady increase in net income.

	2010		2009		2008	
Net sales revenue............................		$42		$39		$36
Cost of goods sold:						
Beginning inventory...................	$ 10		$ 9		$ 8	
Net purchases	33		31		29	
Cost of goods available..............	43		40		37	
Less ending inventory.................	(11)		(10)		(9)	
Cost of goods sold		32		30		28
Gross profit.....................................		10		9		8
Operating expenses		5		5		5
Net income.......................................		$ 5		$ 4		$ 3

Auditors discovered that the ending inventory for 2008 was understated by $2 million and that the ending inventory for 2009 was also understated by $2 million. The ending inventory at December 31, 2010 was correct.

Requirements

1. Show corrected income statements for each of the three years.
2. How much did these assumed corrections add to or take away from Waterville's total net income over the three-year period? How did the corrections affect the trend of net income?
3. Will Waterville's shareholders still be happy with the company's trend of net income? Give the reason for your answer.

APPLY YOUR KNOWLEDGE

Decision Cases

writing assignment ■

Case 1. *(Learning Objectives 1, 2: Assessing the impact of a year-end purchase of inventory)* Duracraft Corporation is nearing the end of its first year of operations. Duracraft made inventory purchases of $745,000 during the year, as follows:

January	1,000 units @	$100.00 =	$100,000
July	4,000	121.25	485,000
November	1,000	160.00	160,000
Totals	6,000		$745,000

Sales for the year are 5,000 units for $1,200,000 of revenue. Expenses other than cost of goods sold and income taxes total $200,000. The president of the company is undecided about whether to adopt the FIFO method or the LIFO method for inventories. The income tax rate is 40%.

▎*Requirements*

1. To aid company decision making, prepare income statements under FIFO and under LIFO.
2. Compare the net income under FIFO with net income under LIFO. Which method produces the higher net income? What causes this difference? Be specific.

writing assignment ■

Case 2. *(Learning Objective 2: Assessing the impact of the inventory costing method on the financial statements)* The inventory costing method a company chooses can affect the financial statements and thus the decisions of the people who use those statements.

▎*Requirements*

1. Company A uses the LIFO inventory method and discloses its use of the LIFO method in notes to the financial statements. Company B uses the FIFO method to account for its inventory. Company B does *not* disclose which inventory method it uses. Company B reports a higher net income than Company A. In which company would you prefer to invest? Give your reason.
2. Conservatism is an accepted accounting concept. Would you want management to be conservative in accounting for inventory if you were a shareholder or a creditor of a company? Give your reason.

Ethical Issue

During 2010, Vanguard, Inc., changed to the LIFO method of accounting for inventory. Suppose that during 2011, Vanguard changes back to the FIFO method and the following year Vanguard switches back to LIFO again.

▎*Requirements*

1. What would you think of a company's ethics if it changed accounting methods every year?
2. What accounting principle would changing methods every year violate?
3. Who can be harmed when a company changes its accounting methods too often? How?

Focus on Financials: ■ Amazon.com, Inc.

(Learning Objectives 2, 3: Analyzing inventories) The notes are part of the financial statements. They give details that would clutter the statements. This case will help you learn to use a

company's inventory notes. Refer to **Amazon.com, Inc.'s** consolidated financial statements and related notes in Appendix A at the end of the book and answer the following questions:

1. How much was Amazon.com, Inc.'s merchandise inventory at December 31, 2008? At December 31, 2007? Does Amazon.com, Inc., include all inventory that it handles in the inventory account on its balance sheet?
2. How does Amazon.com, Inc., *value* its inventories? Which *cost* method does the company use?
3. How much were Amazon.com, Inc.'s purchases of inventory during the year ended December 31, 2008?
4. Did Amazon.com, Inc.'s gross profit percentage on company sales improve or deteriorate in the year ended February 2, 2008, compared to the previous year?
5. Would you rate Amazon.com, Inc.'s rate of inventory turnover for the years ended February 2, 2008, and February 3, 2007, as fast or slow in comparison to most other companies in its industry? Explain your answer.
6. Go to the SEC's Web site (www.sec.gov). Find Amazon.com, Inc.'s most recent consolidated balance sheet and consolidated statement of operations. What has happened to the company's inventory turnover and gross profit percentages since December 31, 2008? Can you explain the reasons? Where would you find the company's explanations for these changes? (Challenge)

Focus on Analysis: ■ Foot Locker, Inc.

(Learning Objectives 1, 2, 3: Measuring critical inventory amounts) Refer to the **Foot Locker, Inc.**, consolidated financial statements in Appendix B at the end of this book. Show amounts in millions and round to the nearest $1 million.

1. Three important pieces of inventory information are (a) the cost of inventory on hand, (b) the cost of sales, and (c) the cost of inventory purchases. Identify or compute each of these items for Foot Locker, Inc., at the end of its fiscal 2007 year.
2. Which item in requirement 1 is most directly related to cash flow? Why? (Challenge)
3. Assume that all inventory purchases were made on account, and that only inventory purchases increased Accounts Payable. Compute Foot Locker, Inc.'s cash payments for inventory during fiscal 2007.
4. How does Foot Locker, Inc., *value* its inventories? Which *costing* method does Foot Locker, Inc., use?
5. Did Foot Locker, Inc.'s gross profit percentage and rate of inventory turnover improve or deteriorate in fiscal 2007 (versus fiscal 2006)? Consider the overall effect of these two ratios. Did Foot Locker, Inc., improve during fiscal 2007? How did these factors affect the net income for fiscal 2007? Foot Locker, Inc.'s inventories totaled $1,254 million at the end of fiscal 2005. Round decimals to three places.

Group Project

(Learning Objective 3: Comparing companies' inventory turnover ratios) Obtain the annual reports of 10 companies, two from each of five different industries. Most companies' financial statements can be downloaded from their Web sites.

writing assignment ■

1. Compute each company's gross profit percentage and rate of inventory turnover for the most recent two years. If annual reports are unavailable or do not provide enough data for multiple-year computations, you can gather financial statement data from *Moody's Industrial Manual*.
2. For the industries of the companies you are analyzing, obtain the industry averages for gross profit percentage and inventory turnover from Robert Morris Associates, *Annual Statement Studies*; Dun and Bradstreet, *Industry Norms and Key Business Ratios*; or Leo Troy, *Almanac of Business and Industrial Financial Ratios*.

3. How well does each of your companies compare to the other company in its industry? How well do your companies compare to the average for their industry? What insight about your companies can you glean from these ratios?
4. Write a memo to summarize your findings, stating whether your group would invest in each of the companies it has analyzed.

For online homework, exercises, and problems that provide you with immediate feedback, please visit www.myaccountinglab.com.

Quick Check Answers

1. *b*
2. *a*
3. *e*
4. *c* [(15 × $5) + (25 × $8)]
5. *b* (15 × $5) + ($10 × $8)
6. *c* 25 × [($75 + $320 + $90) ÷ 65]
7. *c*
8. *a*
9. *c*

10. *a* ($117,000 − $57,000)
11. *c* ($145,000 + $25,000 − $15,000)
12. *b* ($28,000 + $93,000 + $3,000 − $7,000 − $35,000)
13. *a* ($184,000 − $82,000)/$184,000
14. *b* [$82,000 ÷ ($28,000 + $35,000)/2]
15. *d* $110,000 + $260,000 − [$470,000 × (1 − .40)]
16. *a*

APPENDIX 6A

Accounting for Inventory in the Periodic System

In the periodic inventory system, the business keeps no running record of the merchandise. Instead, at the end of the period, the business counts inventory on hand and applies the unit costs to determine the cost of ending inventory. This inventory figure appears on the balance sheet and is used to compute cost of goods sold.

Recording Transactions in the Periodic System

In the periodic system, throughout the period the Inventory account carries the beginning balance left over from the preceding period. The business records purchases of inventory in the Purchases account (an expense). Then, at the end of the period, the Inventory account must be updated for the financial statements. A journal entry removes the beginning balance by crediting Inventory and debiting Cost of Goods Sold. A second journal entry sets up the ending inventory balance, based on the physical count. The final entry in this sequence transfers the amount of Purchases to Cost of Goods Sold. These end-of-period entries can be made during the closing process.

Exhibit 6A-1 illustrates the accounting in the periodic system. After the process is complete, Inventory has its correct ending balance of $120,000, and Cost of Goods Sold shows $540,000.

EXHIBIT 6-A1 | **Recording and Reporting Inventories—Periodic System (Amounts Assumed)**

PANEL A—Recording Transactions and the T-accounts (All amounts are assumed)

1.	Purchases	560,000	
	Accounts Payable		560,000
	Purchased inventory on account.		
2.	Accounts Receivable	900,000	
	Sales Revenue		900,000
	Sold inventory on account.		
3.	End-of-period entries to update Inventory and record Cost of Goods Sold:		
a.	Cost of Goods Sold	100,000	
	Inventory (beginning balance)		100,000
	Transferred beginning inventory to COGS.		
b.	Inventory (ending balance)	120,000	
	Cost of Goods Sold		120,000
	Set up ending inventory based on physical count.		
c.	Cost of Goods Sold	560,000	
	Purchases		560,000
	Transferred purchases to COGS.		

The T-accounts show the following:

Inventory			Cost of Goods Sold	
100,000*	100,000		100,000	120,000
120,000			560,000	
			540,000	

*Beginning inventory was $100,000

PANEL B—Reporting in the Financial Statements

Income Statement (Partial)			Ending Balance Sheet (Partial)	
Sales revenue		$900,000	Current assets:	
Cost of goods sold:			Cash	$ XXX
Beginning inventory	$ 100,000		Short-term investments	XXX
Purchases	560,000		Accounts receivable	XXX
Goods available	660,000		Inventory	120,000
Ending inventory	(120,000)		Prepaid expenses	XXX
Cost of goods sold		540,000		
Gross profit		$360,000		

Appendix Assignments

Short Exercises

S6A-1 (*Recording inventory transactions in the periodic system*) Saxton Technologies began the year with inventory of $480. During the year, Saxton purchased inventory costing $1,180 and sold goods for $3,200, with all transactions on account. Saxton ended the year with inventory of $610. Journalize all the necessary transactions under the periodic inventory system.

S6A-2 (*Computing cost of goods sold and preparing the income statement—periodic system*)   Use the data in Short Exercise 6A-1 to do the following for Saxton Technologies:

❚ *Requirements*

1. Post to the Inventory and Cost of Goods Sold accounts.
2. Compute cost of goods sold by the cost-of-goods-sold model.
3. Prepare the income statement of Saxton Technologies through gross profit.

Exercises

> All of these exercises can be found within MyAccountingLab, an online homework and practice environment. Your instructor may ask you to complete these exercises using MyAccountingLab.

(Group A)

E6A-3A (*Computing amounts for the GAAP inventory methods—periodic system*)   Suppose Halton Corporation's inventory records for a particular computer chip indicate the following at July 31:

Jul	1	Beginning inventory	5 units @ $59 =	$295
	8	Purchase................................	3 units @ $59 =	177
	15	Purchase................................	13 units @ $69 =	897
	26	Purchase................................	1 units @ $79 =	79

The physical count of inventory at July 31 indicates that seven units of inventory are on hand.

❚ *Requirements*

Compute ending inventory and cost of goods sold, using each of the following methods:

1. Specific unit cost, assuming two $59 units and five $69 units are on hand
2. Average cost (round average unit cost to the nearest cent)
3. First-in, first-out
4. Last-in, first-out

E6A-4A (*Journalizing inventory transactions in the periodic system; computing cost of goods sold*)   Use the data in Exercise 6A-3A.

❚ *Requirements*

Journalize the following for the periodic system:

1. Total July purchases in one summary entry. All purchases were on credit.
2. Total July sales in a summary entry. Assume that the selling price was $295 per unit and that all sales were on credit.
3. July 31 entries for inventory. Halton uses LIFO. Post to the Cost of Goods Sold T-account to show how this amount is determined. Label each item in the account.
4. Show the computation of cost of goods sold by the cost-of-goods-sold model.

(Group B)

E6A-5B (*Computing amounts for the GAAP inventory methods—periodic system*) Suppose Saxton Corporation's inventory records for a particular computer chip indicate the following at December 31:

Dec	1	Beginning inventory	6 units @ $60 = $360
	8	Purchase.................................	4 units @ $60 = 240
	15	Purchase.................................	13 units @ $70 = 910
	26	Purchase.................................	2 units @ $80 = 160

The physical count of inventory at December 31 indicates that nine units of inventory are on hand.

▌ Requirements

Compute ending inventory and cost of goods sold, using each of the following methods:

1. Specific unit cost, assuming four $60 units and five $70 units are on hand
2. Average cost (round average unit cost to the nearest cent)
3. First-in, first-out
4. Last-in, first-out

E6A-6B (*Journalizing inventory transactions in the periodic system; computing cost of goods sold*) Use the data in Exercise 6A-5B.

▌ Requirements

Journalize the following for the periodic system:

1. Total December purchases in one summary entry. All purchases were on credit.
2. Total December sales in a summary entry. Assume that the selling price was $315 per unit and that all sales were on credit.
3. December 31 entries for inventory. Saxton uses LIFO. Post to the Cost of Goods Sold T-account to show how this amount is determined. Label each item in the account.
4. Show the computation of cost of goods sold by the cost-of-goods-sold model.

Problems

All of these problems can be found within MyAccountingLab, an online homework and practice environment. Your instructor may ask you to complete these problems using MyAccountingLab.

MyAccountingLab

(Group A)

P6A-7A (*Computing cost of goods sold and gross profit on sales—periodic system*)   Assume a Watercrest outlet store began July 2010 with 48 units of inventory that cost $16 each. The sale price of these units was $69. During July, the store completed these inventory transactions:

		Units	Unit Cost	Units Sale Price
Jul 3	Sale	19	$16	$69
8	Purchase......	80	17	71
11	Sale	29	16	69
19	Sale	3	17	71
24	Sale	35	17	71
30	Purchase......	22	18	72
31	Sale	4	17	71

❚ Requirements

1. Determine the store's cost of goods sold for July under the periodic inventory system. Assume the FIFO method.
2. Compute gross profit for July.

P6A-8A (*Recording transactions in the periodic system; reporting inventory items in the financial statements*)   Accounting records for Halton Desserts, Inc., yield the following data for the year ended December 31, 2010 (amounts in thousands):

Inventory, December 31, 2009..	$ 560
Purchases of inventory (on account)..	2,040
Sales of inventory—70% on account; 30% for cash.......................................	3,400
Inventory at the lower of FIFO cost or market, December 31, 2010	680

❚ Requirements

1. Journalize Halton Desserts' inventory transactions for the year under the periodic system. Show all amounts in thousands.
2. Report ending inventory, sales, cost of goods sold, and gross profit on the appropriate financial statement (amounts in thousands). Show the computation of cost of goods sold.

(Group B)

P6A-9B (*Computing cost of goods sold and gross profit on sales—periodic system*)   Assume a Championship outlet store began January 2010 with 50 units of inventory that cost $19 each. The sale price of these units was $71. During January the store completed these inventory transactions:

		Units	Unit Cost	Units Sale Price
Jan 3	Sale	17	$19	$71
8	Purchase......	77	20	73
11	Sale	33	19	71
19	Sale	2	20	73
24	Sale	39	20	73
30	Purchase......	19	21	74
31	Sale	5	20	73

❚ Requirements

1. Determine the store's cost of goods sold for January under the periodic inventory system. Assume the FIFO method.
2. Compute gross profit for January.

P6A-10B (*Recording transactions in the periodic system; reporting inventory items in the financial statements*)   Accounting records for Just Desserts, Inc., yield the following data for the year ended December 31, 2010 (amounts in thousands):

Inventory, December 31, 2009	$ 530
Purchases of inventory (on account)..	2,000
Sales of inventory—75% on account, 25% for cash......................................	3,800
Inventory at the lower of FIFO cost or market, December 31, 2010	650

❚ Requirements

1. Journalize Just Desserts' inventory transactions for the year under the periodic system. Show all amounts in thousands.
2. Report ending inventory, sales, cost of goods sold, and gross profit on the appropriate financial statement (amounts in thousands). Show the computation of cost of goods sold.

APPENDIX 6B

The LIFO Reserve—Converting a LIFO Company's Net Income to the FIFO Basis

Suppose you are a financial analyst, and it is your job to recommend stocks for your clients to purchase as investments. You have narrowed your choice to **Wal-Mart Stores, Inc.**, and **Gap, Inc.** Wal-Mart uses the LIFO method for inventories and the GAP uses FIFO. The two companies' net incomes are not comparable because they use different inventory methods. To compare the two companies, you need to place them on the same footing.

The Internal Revenue Service allows companies to use LIFO for income tax purposes only if they use LIFO for financial reporting, but companies may also report an alternative inventory amount in the financial statements. Doing so presents a rare opportunity to convert a company's net income from the LIFO basis to what the income would have been if the business had used FIFO. Fortunately, you can convert Wal-Mart's income from the LIFO basis, as reported in the company's financial statements, to the FIFO basis. Then you can compare Wal-Mart and Gap.

Like many other companies that use LIFO, Wal-Mart reports the FIFO cost, a LIFO Reserve, and the LIFO cost of ending inventory. The LIFO Reserve[1] is the difference between the LIFO cost of an inventory and what the cost of that inventory would be under FIFO. Assume that Wal-Mart reported the following amounts:

Wal-Mart Uses LIFO		
	(In millions)	
	2011	2010
From the Wal-Mart balance sheet:		
Inventories (approximate FIFO cost)...............	$ 25,056	$22,749
Less LIFO reserve..	(165)	(135)
LIFO cost..	24,891	22,614
From the Wal-Mart income statement:		
Cost of goods sold..	$191,838	
Net income..	8,039	
Income tax rate	35%	

Converting Wal-Mart's 2011 net income to the FIFO basis focuses on the LIFO Reserve because the reserve captures the difference between Wal-Mart's ending inventory costed at LIFO and at FIFO. Observe that during each year, the FIFO cost of ending inventory exceeded the LIFO cost. During 2011, the LIFO Reserve increased by $30 million ($165 million – $135 million). *The LIFO Reserve can increase only when inventory costs are rising.* Recall that during a period of rising costs, LIFO produces the highest cost of goods sold and the lowest net income. Therefore, for 2011, Wal-Mart's cost of goods sold would have been lower if the company had used the FIFO method for inventories. Wal-Mart's net income would have been higher, as the following computations show:

---

[1]The LIFO Reserve account is widely used in practice even though the term "reserve" is poor terminology.

If Wal-Mart Had Used FIFO in 2011	
	(In millions)
Cost of goods sold, as reported under LIFO..	$191,838
− Increase in LIFO Reserve ($165 − $135)	(30)
= Cost of goods sold, if Wal-Mart had used FIFO.......................................	$191,808
Lower cost of goods sold → Higher pretax income by...............................	$ 30
Minus income taxes (35%)	11
Higher net income under FIFO.......................	19
Net income as reported under LIFO...............	8,039
Net income Wal-Mart would have reported for 2011 if using FIFO.....................................	$ 8,058

Now you can compare Wal-Mart's net income with that of The Gap, Inc. All the ratios used for the analysis—current ratio, inventory turnover, and so on—can be compared between the two companies as though they both used the FIFO inventory method.

The LIFO Reserve provides another opportunity for managers and investors to answer a key question about a company.

How much income tax has the company saved over its lifetime by using the LIFO method to account for inventory?

Using Wal-Mart as an example, the computation at the end of 2011 is (amounts in millions):

Income tax saved by using LIFO = LIFO Reserve × Income tax rate
$$\$58 \quad = \quad \$165 \quad \times \quad .35$$

With these price changes, by the end of 2011 Wal-Mart has saved a total of $58 million by using the LIFO method to account for its merchandise inventory. Had Wal-Mart used the FIFO method, Wal-Mart would have almost $58 million less cash to invest in the opening of new stores.

In recent years many companies have experienced decreases in the cost of their inventories. When prices decline, cost of goods sold under FIFO is greater (LIFO cost of goods sold is less). This makes gross profit and net income less under FIFO.

7

Plant Assets & Intangibles

SPOTLIGHT: FedEx Corporation

If you need a document delivered across the country overnight, FedEx can handle it. FedEx Corporation sets the standard for quick delivery. As you can see from the company's Consolidated Balance Sheets on the following page, FedEx moves packages using aircraft, package-handling equipment, computers, and vehicles. These are FedEx's most important assets (lines 8–16).

This chapter covers long-term plant assets to complete our coverage of assets, except for long-term investments in Chapter 10. Let's begin by examining the various types of long-term assets.

FedEx Corporation
Consolidated Balance Sheets (Partial, Adapted)

(In millions)	May 31, 2008	May 31, 2007
1 ASSETS		
2 CURRENT ASSETS		
3 Cash and cash equivalents....................................	$ 1,539	$ 1,569
4 Receivables, less allowances of $158 and $136	4,359	3,942
5 Spare parts, supplies and fuel	435	338
6 Prepaid expenses and other	911	780
7 Total current assets..	7,244	6,629
8 PROPERTY AND EQUIPMENT, AT COST		
9 Aircraft and related equipment...........................	10,165	9,593
10 Package handling and ground support equipment....	4,817	3,889
11 Computer and electronic equipment....................	5,040	4,685
12 Vehicles..	2,754	2,561
13 Facilities and other..	6,529	6,362
14 Total cost..	29,305	27,090
15 Less: Accumulated depreciation	(15,827)	(14,454)
16 Net property and equipment..........................	13,478	12,636
17 OTHER LONG-TERM ASSETS		
18 Goodwill..	3,165	3,497
19 Prepaid pension cost...	827	—
20 Intangible and other assets	919	1,238
21 Total other long-term assets..........................	4,911	4,735
22 TOTAL ASSETS	$ 25,633	$ 24,000

LEARNING OBJECTIVES

1 **Determine** the cost of a plant asset

2 **Account** for depreciation

3 **Select** the best depreciation method

4 **Analyze** the effect of a plant asset disposal

5 **Account** for natural resources and depletion

6 **Account** for intangible assets and amortization

7 **Report** plant asset transactions on the statement of cash flows

TYPES OF ASSETS

Businesses use several types of long-lived assets, as shown in Exhibit 7-1. We also show the expense that applies to each asset. For example, buildings, airplanes, and equipment depreciate. Natural resources deplete, and intangible assets are amortized.

- **Plant assets**, or *fixed assets*, are long-lived assets that are tangible—for instance, land, buildings, and equipment. The expense associated with plant assets is called *depreciation*. Of the plant assets, land is unique. Land is not expensed over time because its usefulness does not decrease. Most companies report plant assets as property, plant, and equipment on the balance sheet. **FedEx** uses the heading Property and Equipment (lines 8–16).

- **Intangible assets** are useful because of the special rights they carry. They have no physical form. Patents, copyrights, and trademarks are intangible assets; so is goodwill. Accounting for intangibles is similar to accounting for plant assets. FedEx reports Goodwill and Intangible Assets on its balance sheet (lines 18 and 20). Prepaid pension cost (line 19) is a type of long-term prepaid expense that's covered in later courses.

Accounting for plant assets and intangibles has its own terminology. Different names apply to the individual plant assets and their corresponding expenses, as shown in Exhibit 7-1.

EXHIBIT 7-1 | **Plant Assets Terminology**

Asset Account (Balance Sheet)	Related Expense Account (Income Statement)
Plant Assets	
Land	None
Buildings, Machinery and Equipment	Depreciation
Furniture and Fixtures	Depreciation
Land Improvements	Depreciation
Natural Resources	Depletion
Intangibles	Amortization

Unless stated otherwise, we describe accounting that follows generally accepted accounting principles (GAAP) for the financial statements. Later, we cover depreciation for income-tax purposes. Before examining the various types of plant assets, let's see how to value them.

Measuring the Cost of a Plant Asset

Here is a basic working rule for determining the cost of an asset:

The cost of any asset is the sum of all the costs incurred to bring the asset to its intended use. The cost of a plant asset includes purchase price, plus any taxes, commissions, and other amounts paid to make the asset ready for use. Because the specific costs differ for the various types of plant assets, we discuss the major groups individually.

OBJECTIVE

1 **Determine** the cost of a plant asset

Land

The cost of land includes its purchase price (cash plus any note payable given), brokerage commission, survey fees, legal fees, and any back property taxes that the purchaser pays. Land cost also includes expenditures for grading and clearing the land and for removing unwanted buildings.

The cost of land does *not* include the cost of fencing, paving, security systems, and lighting. These are separate plant assets—called *land improvements*—and they are subject to depreciation.

Suppose FedEx signs a $300,000 note payable to purchase 20 acres of land for a new shipping site. FedEx also pays $10,000 for real estate commission,

$8,000 of back property tax, $5,000 for removal of an old building, a $1,000 survey fee, and $260,000 to pave the parking lot—all in cash. What is FedEx's cost of this land?

Purchase price of land		$300,000
Add related costs:		
Real estate commission	$10,000	
Back property tax.......................	8,000	
Removal of building...................	5,000	
Survey fee...................................	1,000	
Total related costs......................		24,000
Total cost of land..........................		$324,000

Note that the cost to pave the parking lot, $260,000, is *not* included in the land's cost, because the pavement is a land improvement. FedEx would record the purchase of this land as follows:

Land	324,000	
Note Payable		300,000
Cash		24,000

Assets	=	Liabilities	+	Stockholders' Equity
+ 324,000 − 24,000	=	+ 300,000	+	0

This purchase of land increases both assets and liabilities. There is no effect on equity.[1]

Buildings, Machinery, and Equipment

The cost of constructing a building includes architectural fees, building permits, contractors' charges, and payments for material, labor, and overhead. If the company constructs its own building, the cost will also include the cost of interest on money borrowed to finance the construction.

When an existing building (new or old) is purchased, its cost includes the purchase price, brokerage commission, sales and other taxes paid, and all expenditures to repair and renovate the building for its intended purpose.

The cost of FedEx's package-handling equipment includes its purchase price (less any discounts), plus transportation from the seller to FedEx, insurance while in transit, sales and other taxes, purchase commission, installation costs, and any expenditures to test the asset before it's placed in service. The equipment cost will also include the cost of any special platforms. Then after the asset is up and running, insurance, taxes, and maintenance costs are recorded as expenses, not as part of the asset's cost.

---

[1]We show the accounting equation along with each journal entry—where the accounting equation aids your understanding of the transaction.

Land Improvements and Leasehold Improvements

For a FedEx shipping terminal, the cost to pave a parking lot ($260,000) would be recorded in a separate account entitled Land Improvements. This account includes costs for such other items as driveways, signs, fences, and sprinkler systems. Although these assets are located on the land, they are subject to decay, and their cost should therefore be depreciated.

FedEx may lease some of its airplanes and other assets. The company customizes these assets for its special needs. For example, FedEx paints its logo on delivery trucks. These improvements are assets of FedEx even though the company may not own the truck. The cost of leasehold improvements should be depreciated over the term of the lease. Most companies call the depreciation on leasehold improvements *amortization*, which is the same concept as *depreciation*.

Lump-Sum (or Basket) Purchases of Assets

Businesses often purchase several assets as a group, or a "basket," for a single lump-sum amount. For example, FedEx may pay one price for land and a building. The company must identify the cost of each asset. The total cost is divided among the assets according to their relative sales (or market) values. This technique is called the *relative-sales-value method*.

Suppose FedEx purchases land and a building in Denver. The building sits on two acres of land, and the combined purchase price of land and building is $2,800,000. An appraisal indicates that the land's market value is $300,000 and that the building's market value is $2,700,000.

FedEx first figures the ratio of each asset's market value to the total market value. Total appraised value is $2,700,000 + $300,000 = $3,000,000. Thus, the land, valued at $300,000, is 10% of the total market value. The building's appraised value is 90% of the total. These percentages are then used to determine the cost of each asset, as follows:

Asset	Market (Sales) Value		Total Market Value		Percentage of Total Market Value		Total Cost	Cost of Each Asset
Land	$ 300,000	÷	$3,000,000	=	10%	×	$2,800,000	$ 280,000
Building	2,700,000	÷	3,000,000	=	90%	×	$2,800,000	2,520,000
Total	$3,000,000				100%			$2,800,000

If FedEx pays cash, the entry to record the purchase of the land and building is

Land		280,000	
Building		2,520,000	
Cash			2,800,000

Assets	=	Liabilities	+	Stockholders' Equity
+ 280,000	=			
+ 2,520,000	=	0	+	0
− 2,800,000	=			

Total assets don't change—merely the makeup of FedEx's assets.

STOP & THINK...

How would FedEx divide a $120,000 lump-sum purchase price for land, building, and equipment with estimated market values of $40,000, $95,000, and $15,000, respectively?

Answer:

	Estimated Market Value	Percentage of Total Market Value	×	Total Cost	=	Cost of Each Asset
Land..................	$ 40,000	26.7%*	×	$120,000	=	$ 32,040
Building.............	95,000	63.3%	×	$120,000	=	75,960
Equipment.........	15,000	10.0%	×	$120,000	=	12,000
Total	$150,000	100.0%				$120,000

*$40,000/$150,000 = 0.267, and so on

Capital Expenditure vs. Immediate Expense

When a company spends money on a plant asset, it must decide whether to record an asset or an expense. Examples of these expenditures range from FedEx's purchase of an airplane to replacing the tires on a FedEx truck.

Expenditures that increase the asset's capacity or extend its useful life are called **capital expenditures**. For example, the cost of a major overhaul that extends the useful life of a FedEx truck is a capital expenditure. Capital expenditures are said to be *capitalized, which means the cost is added to an asset account* and not expensed immediately. A major decision in accounting for plant assets is whether to capitalize or to expense a certain cost.

Costs that do not extend the asset's capacity or its useful life, but merely maintain the asset or restore it to working order, are recorded as expenses. For example, Repair Expense is reported on the income statement and matched against revenue. The costs of repainting a FedEx delivery truck, repairing a dented fender, and replacing tires are also expensed immediately. Exhibit 7-2 shows the distinction between capital expenditures and immediate expenses for delivery truck expenditures.

EXHIBIT 7-2 | **Capital Expenditure or Immediate Expense for Costs Associated with a Delivery Truck**

Record an Asset for Capital Expenditures	Record Repair and Maintenance Expense (Not an Asset) for an Expense
Extraordinary repairs:	**Ordinary repairs:**
Major engine overhaul	Repair of transmission or other mechanism
Modification of body for new use of truck	Oil change, lubrication, and so on
	Replacement of tires and windshield,
Addition to storage capacity of truck	or a paint job

The distinction between a capital expenditure and an expense requires judgment: Does the cost extend the asset's usefulness or its useful life? If so, record an asset. If the cost merely repairs the asset or returns it to its prior condition, then record an expense.

Most companies expense all small costs, say, below $1,000. For higher costs, they follow the rule we gave above: capitalize costs that extend the asset's usefulness or its useful life, and expense all other costs. A conservative policy is one that avoids overstating assets and profits. A company that overstates its assets may get into trouble and have to defend itself in court. Whenever investors lose money because a company overstated its profits or its assets, the investors file a lawsuit. The courts tend to be sympathetic to investor losses caused by shoddy accounting.

Accounting errors sometimes occur for plant asset costs. For example, a company may

- expense a cost that should have been capitalized. This error overstates expenses and understates net income in the year of the error.
- capitalize a cost that should have been expensed. This error understates expenses and overstates net income in the year of the error.

COOKING THE BOOKS
by Improper Capitalization

WorldCom

It is one thing to accidentally capitalize a plant asset but quite another to do it intentionally, thus deliberately overstating assets, understating expenses, and overstating net income. One well-known company committed one of the biggest financial statement frauds in U.S. history in this way.

In 2002, WorldCom, Inc., was one of the largest telecommunications service providers in the world. The company had grown rapidly from a small, regional telephone company in 1983 to a giant corporation in 2002 by acquiring an ever-increasing number of other such companies. But 2002 was a bad year for WorldCom, as well as for many others in the "telecom" industry. The United States was reeling from the effects of a deep economic recession spawned by the "bursting dot-com bubble" in 2000 and intensified by the terrorist attacks on U.S. soil in 2001. Wall Street was looking high and low for positive signs, pressuring public companies to keep profits trending upward in order to support share prices, without much success, at least for the honest companies.

Bernard J. ("Bernie") Ebbers, WorldCom's chief executive officer, was worried. He began to press his chief financial officer, Scott Sullivan, to find a way to make the company's income statement look healthier. After all legitimate attempts to improve earnings failed, Sullivan concocted a scheme to cook the books.

Like all telecommunications companies, WorldCom had signed contracts with other telephone companies, paying them fees so that WorldCom customers could use their lines for telephone calls and Internet usage. GAAP require such fees to be expensed as incurred, rather than capitalized. Overestimating the growth of its business, WorldCom had incurred billions of dollars in such costs, about 15% more than its customers would ever use.

In direct violation of GAAP, Sullivan rationalized that the excessive amounts WorldCom had spent on line costs would eventually lead to the company's recognizing revenue in future years (thus extending their usefulness and justifying, in his mind, their classification as assets). Sullivan directed the accountants working under him to reclassify line costs as property, plant, and equipment assets, rather than as expenses, and to amortize (spread) the costs over several years rather than to expense them in the periods in which they were incurred. Over several quarters, Mr. Sullivan and his assistants transferred a total of $3.1 billion in such charges from operating expense accounts to property, plant, and equipment, resulting in the transformation of what would have been a net loss for all of 2001 and the first quarter of 2002 into a sizeable profit. It was the largest single fraud in U.S. history to that point.

Sullivan's fraudulent scheme was discovered by the company's internal audit staff during a routine spot-check of the company's records for capital expenditures. The staff members reported Sullivan's (and his staff's) fraudulent activities to the head of the company's audit committee and its external auditor, setting in motion a chain of events that resulted in Ebbers' and Sullivan's firing, and the company's eventual bankruptcy. Ebbers, Sullivan, and several of their assistants went to prison for their participation in this fraudulent scheme.

Shareholders of WorldCom lost billions of dollars in share value when the company went down, and more than 500,000 people lost their jobs.

The WorldCom scandal rocked the financial world, causing global stock markets to plummet from lack of confidence. This prompted action on the part of the U.S. Congress and President George W. Bush that eventually led to the passage of the Sarbanes-Oxley Act, the most significant piece of shareholder protection legislation since the Great Depression in the 1930s.

MEASURING DEPRECIATION ON PLANT ASSETS

As we've seen in previous chapters, plant assets are reported on the balance sheet at book value, which is

> Book Value of a Plant Asset = Cost − Accumulated Depreciation

Plant assets wear out, grow obsolete, and lose value over time. To account for this process we allocate a plant asset's cost to expense over its life—a process called *depreciation*. The depreciation process matches the asset's expense against revenue to measure income, as the matching principle directs. Exhibit 7-3 illustrates the accounting for a Boeing 737 jet by FedEx.

EXHIBIT 7-3 | Depreciation and the Matching of Expense with Revenue

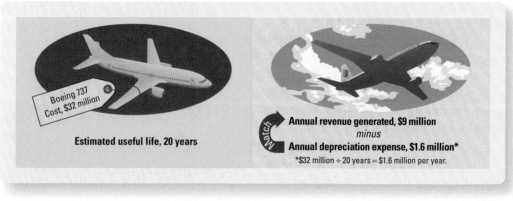

Boeing 737
Cost, $32 million

Estimated useful life, 20 years

Match

Annual revenue generated, $9 million
minus
Annual depreciation expense, $1.6 million*

*$32 million ÷ 20 years = $1.6 million per year.

Recall that depreciation expense (not accumulated depreciation) is reported on the income statement.

Only land has an unlimited life and is not depreciated for accounting purposes. For most plant assets, depreciation is caused by:

- *Physical wear and tear.* For example, physical deterioration takes its toll on the usefulness of FedEx airplanes, equipment, delivery trucks, and buildings.
- *Obsolescence.* Computers and other electronic equipment may become *obsolete* before they deteriorate. An asset is obsolete when another asset can do the job more efficiently. An asset's useful life may be shorter than its physical life. FedEx and other companies depreciate their computers over a short period of time—perhaps four years—even though the computers will remain in working condition much longer.

Suppose FedEx buys a computer for use in tracking packages. FedEx believes it will get four years of service from the computer, which will then be worthless. Under straight-line depreciation, FedEx expenses one-quarter of the asset's cost in each of its four years of use.

You've just seen what depreciation is. Let's see what depreciation is *not*.

1. **Depreciation is not a process of valuation.** Businesses do *not* record depreciation based on changes in the market value of their plant assets. Instead, businesses allocate the asset's *cost* to the period of its useful life.

2. **Depreciation does not mean setting aside cash to replace assets as they wear out.** Any cash fund is entirely separate from depreciation.

How to Measure Depreciation

To measure depreciation for a plant asset, we must know three things about the asset:

1. Cost   2. Estimated useful life   3. Estimated residual value

We have discussed cost, which is a known amount. The other two factors must be estimated.

Estimated useful life is the length of service expected from using the asset. Useful life may be expressed in years, units of output, miles, or some other measure. For example, the useful life of a building is stated in years. The useful life of a FedEx airplane or delivery truck may be expressed as the number of miles the vehicle is expected to travel. Companies base estimates on their experience and trade publications.

Estimated residual value—also called *scrap value* or *salvage value*—is the expected cash value of an asset at the end of its useful life. For example, FedEx may believe that a package-handling machine will be useful for seven years. After that time, FedEx may expect to sell the machine as scrap metal. The amount FedEx believes it can get for the machine is the estimated residual value. In computing depreciation, the estimated residual value is *not* depreciated because FedEx expects to receive this amount from selling the asset. If there's no expected residual value, the full cost of the asset is depreciated. A plant asset's **depreciable cost** is measured as follows:

> Depreciable Cost = Asset's cost − Estimated residual value

Depreciation Methods

There are three main depreciation methods:

- Straight-line
- Units-of-production
- Double-declining-balance—an accelerated depreciation method

These methods allocate different amounts of depreciation to each period. However, they all result in the same total amount of depreciation, which is the asset's depreciable cost. Exhibit 7-4 presents the data we use to illustrate depreciation computations for a FedEx truck.

EXHIBIT 7-4 | **Data for Depreciation Computations—A FedEx Truck**

Data Item	Amount
Cost of truck...............................	$41,000
Less: Estimated residual value..............	(1,000)
Depreciable cost..................................	$40,000
Estimated useful life:	
Years	5 years
Units of production	100,000 units [miles]

Straight-Line Method. In the **straight-line (SL) method**, an equal amount of depreciation is assigned to each year (or period) of asset use. Depreciable cost is divided by useful life in years to determine the annual depreciation expense. Applied to the FedEx truck data from Exhibit 7-4, SL depreciation is

$$\text{Straight-line depreciation per year} = \frac{\text{Cost} - \text{Residual value}}{\text{Useful life, in years}}$$

$$= \frac{\$41,000 - \$1,000}{5}$$

$$= \$8,000$$

The entry to record depreciation is

Depreciation Expense	8,000	
Accumulated Depreciation		8,000

Assets	=	Liabilities	+	Stockholders' Equity	−	Expenses
− 8,000	=	0				− 8,000

Observe that depreciation decreases the asset (through Accumulated Depreciation) and also decreases equity (through Depreciation Expense). Let's assume that FedEx purchased this truck on January 1, 2009. Assume that FedEx's accounting year ends on December 31. Exhibit 7-5 gives a *straight-line depreciation schedule* for the truck. The final column of the exhibit shows the *asset's book value*, which is cost less accumulated depreciation.

EXHIBIT 7-5 | Straight-Line Depreciation for a FedEx Truck

Date	Asset Cost	Depreciation for the Year				Accumulated Depreciation	Asset Book Value
		Depreciation Rate	Depreciable Cost	Depreciation Expense			
1- 1-2009	$41,000						$41,000
12-31-2009		0.20* ×	$40,000 =	$8,000		$ 8,000	33,000
12-31-2010		0.20 ×	40,000 =	8,000		16,000	25,000
12-31-2011		0.20 ×	40,000 =	8,000		24,000	17,000
12-31-2012		0.20 ×	40,000 =	8,000		32,000	9,000
12-31-2013		0.20 ×	40,000 =	8,000		40,000	1,000

*⅕ year = .20 per year

As an asset is used in operations,

- accumulated depreciation increases.
- the book value of the asset decreases.

An asset's final book value is its *residual value* ($1,000 in Exhibit 7-5). At the end of its useful life, the asset is said to be *fully depreciated*.

STOP & THINK...

A FedEx sorting machine that cost $10,000, has a useful life of five years, and residual value of $2,000, was purchased on January 1. What is SL depreciation for each year?

Answer:

$1,600 = ($10,000 − $2,000)/5

Units-of-Production Method. In the **units-of-production (UOP) method**, a fixed amount of depreciation is assigned to each *unit of output*, or service, produced by the asset. Depreciable cost is divided by useful life—in units of production—to determine this amount. This per-unit depreciation expense is then multiplied by the number of units produced each period to compute depreciation. The UOP depreciation for the FedEx truck data in Exhibit 7-4 (p. 418) is

$$\text{Units-of-production depreciation per unit of output} = \frac{\text{Cost} - \text{Residual value}}{\text{Useful life, in units of production}}$$

$$= \frac{\$41,000 - \$1,000}{100,000 \text{ miles}} = \$0.40 \text{ per mile}$$

Assume that FedEx expects to drive the truck 20,000 miles during the first year, 30,000 during the second, 25,000 during the third, 15,000 during the fourth, and 10,000 during the fifth. Exhibit 7-6 on the following page shows the UOP depreciation schedule.

EXHIBIT 7-6 | **Units-of-Production Depreciation for a FedEx Truck**

Date	Asset Cost	Depreciation for the Year			Accumulated Depreciation	Asset Book Value
		Depreciation Per Unit	Number of Units	Depreciation Expense		
1- 1-2009	$41,000					$41,000
12-31-2009		$0.40* ×	20,000 =	$ 8,000	$ 8,000	33,000
12-31-2010		0.40 ×	30,000 =	12,000	20,000	21,000
12-31-2011		0.40 ×	25,000 =	10,000	30,000	11,000
12-31-2012		0.40 ×	15,000 =	6,000	36,000	5,000
12-31-2013		0.40 ×	10,000 =	4,000	40,000	1,000

*($41,000 – $1,000)/100,000 miles = $0.40 per mile.

The amount of UOP depreciation varies with the number of units the asset produces. In our example, the total number of units produced is 100,000. UOP depreciation does not depend directly on time, as do the other methods.

Double-Declining-Balance Method. An **accelerated depreciation method** writes off a larger amount of the asset's cost near the start of its useful life than the straight-line method does. Double-declining-balance is the main accelerated depreciation method. **Double-declining-balance (DDB) depreciation** computes annual depreciation by multiplying the asset's declining book value by a constant percentage, which is two times the straight-line depreciation rate. DDB amounts are computed as follows:

- *First*, compute the straight-line depreciation rate per year. A 5-year truck has a straight-line depreciation rate of 1/5, or 20% each year. A 10-year asset has a straight-line rate of 1/10, or 10%, and so on.
- *Second*, multiply the straight-line rate by 2 to compute the DDB rate. For a 5-year asset, the DDB rate is 40% (20% × 2). A 10-year asset has a DDB rate of 20% (10% × 2).
- *Third*, multiply the DDB rate by the period's beginning asset book value (cost less accumulated depreciation). Under the DDB method, ignore the residual value of the asset in computing depreciation, except during the last year. The DDB rate for the FedEx truck in Exhibit 7-4 (p. 418) is

$$\text{DDB depreciation rate per year} = \frac{1}{\text{Useful life, in years}} \times 2$$

$$= \frac{1}{5 \text{ years}} \times 2$$

$$= 20\% \times 2 = 40\%$$

- *Fourth*, determine the final year's depreciation amount—that is, the amount needed to reduce asset book value to its residual value. In Exhibit 7-7, the fifth and final year's DDB depreciation is $4,314—book value of $5,314 less the $1,000 residual value. *The residual value should not be depreciated* but should remain on the books until the asset is disposed of.

EXHIBIT 7-7 | **Double-Declining-Balance Depreciation for a FedEx Truck**

Date	Asset Cost	Depreciation for the Year			Accumulated Depreciation	Asset Book Value
		DDB Rate	Asset Book Value	Depreciation Expense		
1- 1-2009	$41,000					$41,000
12-31-2009		0.40 ×	$41,000 =	$16,400	$16,400	24,600
12-31-2010		0.40 ×	24,600 =	9,840	26,240	14,760
12-31-2011		0.40 ×	14,760 =	5,904	32,144	8,856
12-31-2012		0.40 ×	8,856 =	3,542	35,686	5,314
12-31-2013				4,314*	40,000	1,000

*Last-year depreciation is the "plug" amount needed to reduce asset book value (far right column) to the residual amount ($5,314 − $1,000 = $4,314).

The DDB method differs from the other methods in two ways:

1. Residual value is ignored initially; first-year depreciation is computed on the asset's full cost.

2. Depreciation expense in the final year is the "plug" amount needed to reduce the asset's book value to the residual amount.

STOP & THINK...

What is the DDB depreciation each year for the asset in the Stop & Think on page 419?

Answers:

Yr. 1: $4,000 ($10,000 × 40%)
Yr. 2: $2,400 ($6,000 × 40%)
Yr. 3: $1,440 ($3,600 × 40%)
Yr. 4: $160 ($10,000 − $4,000 − $2,400 − $1,440 − $2,000 = $160)*
Yr. 5: $0

*The asset is not depreciated below residual value of $2,000.

Comparing Depreciation Methods

Let's compare the three methods in terms of the yearly amount of depreciation. The yearly amount varies by method, but the total $40,000 depreciable cost is the same under all methods.

	Amount of Depreciation per Year		
Year	Straight-Line	Units-of-Production	Accelerated Method Double-Declining Balance
1	$ 8,000	$ 8,000	$16,400
2	8,000	12,000	9,840
3	8,000	10,000	5,904
4	8,000	6,000	3,542
5	8,000	4,000	4,314
Total	$40,000	$40,000	$40,000

GAAP say to match an asset's depreciation against the revenue the asset produces. For a plant asset that generates revenue evenly over time, the straight-line method best meets the matching principle. The units-of-production method best fits those assets that wear out because of physical use rather than obsolescence. The accelerated method (DDB) applies best to assets that generate more revenue earlier in their useful lives and less in later years.

Exhibit 7-8 graphs annual depreciation amounts for the straight-line, units-of-production, and accelerated depreciation (DDB) methods. The graph of straight-line depreciation is flat through time because annual depreciation is the same in all periods. Units-of-production depreciation follows no particular pattern because annual depreciation depends on the use of the asset. Accelerated depreciation is greatest in the first year and less in the later years.

EXHIBIT 7-8 | **Depreciation Patterns Through Time**

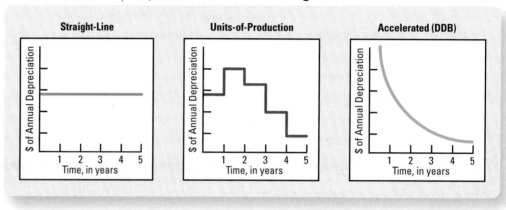

Exhibit 7-9 shows the percentage of companies that use each depreciation method from a survey of 600 companies by the American Institute of Certified Public Accountants (AICPA).

EXHIBIT 7-9 | **Depreciation Methods Used by 600 Companies**

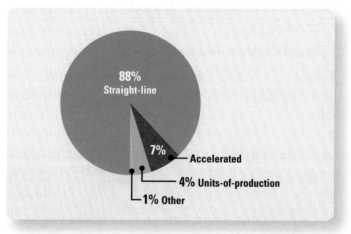

For reporting in the financial statements, straight-line depreciation is most popular. As we shall see, however, accelerated depreciation is most popular for income-tax purposes.

MID-CHAPTER SUMMARY PROBLEM

Suppose FedEx purchased equipment on January 1, 2010, for $44,000. The expected useful life of the equipment is 10 years or 100,000 units of production, and its residual value is $4,000. Under three depreciation methods, the annual depreciation expense and the balance of accumulated depreciation at the end of 2010 and 2011 are as follows:

	Method A		Method B		Method C	
Year	Annual Depreciation Expense	Accumulated Depreciation	Annual Depreciation Expense	Accumulated Depreciation	Annual Depreciation Expense	Accumulated Depreciation
2010	$4,000	$4,000	$8,800	$ 8,800	$1,200	$1,200
2011	4,000	8,000	7,040	15,840	5,600	6,800

▌Requirements

1. Identify the depreciation method used in each instance, and show the equation and computation for each. (Round to the nearest dollar.)
2. Assume continued use of the same method through year 2012. Determine the annual depreciation expense, accumulated depreciation, and book value of the equipment for 2010 through 2012 under each method, assuming 12,000 units of production in 2012.

Answers

▌Requirement 1

Method A: Straight-Line

Depreciable cost = $40,000($44,000 − $4,000)

Each year: $40,000/10 years = $4,000

Method B: Double-Declining-Balance

$$\text{Rate} = \frac{1}{10 \text{ years}} \times 2 = 10\% \times 2 = 20\%$$

2010: 0.20 × $44,000 = $8,800

2011: 0.20 × ($44,000 − $8,800) = $7,040

Method C: Units-of-Production

$$\text{Depreciation per unit} = \frac{\$44,000 - \$4,000}{100,000 \text{ units}} = \$0.40$$

2010: $0.40 × 3,000 units = $1,200

2011: $0.40 × 14,000 units = $5,600

| *Requirement 2*

		Method A: Straight-Line	
Year	Annual Depreciation Expense	Accumulated Depreciation	Book Value
Start			$44,000
2010	$4,000	$ 4,000	40,000
2011	4,000	8,000	36,000
2012	4,000	12,000	32,000

		Method B: Double-Declining-Balance	
Year	Annual Depreciation Expense	Accumulated Depreciation	Book Value
Start			$44,000
2010	$8,800	$ 8,800	35,200
2011	7,040	15,840	28,160
2012	5,632	21,472	22,528

		Method C: Units-of-Production	
Year	Annual Depreciation Expense	Accumulated Depreciation	Book Value
Start			$44,000
2010	$1,200	$ 1,200	42,800
2011	5,600	6,800	37,200
2012	4,800	11,600	32,400

Computations for 2012	
Straight-line	$40,000/10 years = $4,000
Double-declining-balance	$28,160 × 0.20 = $5,632
Units-of-production	12,000 units × $0.40 = $4,800

OTHER ISSUES IN ACCOUNTING FOR PLANT ASSETS

OBJECTIVE

3 **Select** the best depreciation method

Plant assets are complex because

- they have long lives.
- depreciation affects income taxes.
- companies may have gains or losses when they sell plant assets.
- international accounting changes in the future may affect the recognition as well as the carrying values of assets.

Depreciation for Tax Purposes

FedEx and most other companies use straight-line depreciation for reporting to stockholders and creditors on their financial statements. But for their income taxes they also keep a separate set of depreciation records. For tax purposes, FedEx and most other companies use an accelerated depreciation method. This is legal, ethical, and honest. U.S. law permits it.

Suppose you are a business manager, and the IRS allows an accelerated depreciation method. Why do FedEx managers prefer accelerated over straight-line depreciation for income-tax purposes? Accelerated depreciation provides the fastest tax deductions, thus decreasing immediate tax payments. FedEx can reinvest the tax savings back into the business. FedEx has a choice—pay taxes or buy equipment. This choice is easy.

To understand the relationships between cash flow, depreciation, and income tax, recall our depreciation example of a FedEx truck:

- First-year depreciation is $8,000 under straight-line and $16,400 under double-declining-balance (DDB).
- DDB is permitted for income tax purposes.

Assume that this FedEx office has $400,000 in revenue and $300,000 in cash operating expenses during the truck's first year and an income tax rate of 30%. The cash-flow analysis appears in Exhibit 7-10.

EXHIBIT 7-10 | **The Cash-Flow Advantage of Accelerated Depreciation over Straight-Line Depreciation for Income Tax Purposes**

		SL	Accelerated
1	Cash revenue	$400,000	$400,000
2	Cash operating expenses	300,000	300,000
3	Cash provided by operations before income tax	100,000	100,000
4	Depreciation expense (a noncash expense)	8,000	16,400
5	Income before income tax	$ 92,000	$ 83,600
6	Income tax expense (30%)	$ 27,600	$ 25,080
	Cash-flow analysis:		
7	Cash provided by operations before tax	$100,000	$100,000
8	Income tax expense	27,600	25,080
9	Cash provided by operations	$ 72,400	$ 74,920
10	Extra cash available for investment		
	if DDB is used ($74,920 – $72,400)		$ 2,520

You can see that, for income-tax purposes, accelerated depreciation helps conserve cash for the business. That's why virtually all companies use accelerated depreciation to compute their income tax.

There is a special depreciation method—used only for income tax purposes—called the **Modified Accelerated Cost Recovery System (MACRS)**. Under MACRS each fixed asset is classified into one of eight classes identified by asset life (Exhibit 7-11 on the following page). Depreciation for the first four classes is computed by the double-declining-balance method. Depreciation for 15-year assets and 20-year assets is computed by the 150%-declining-balance method. Under 150% DB, annual depreciation is computed by multiplying the straight-line rate by 1.50 (instead of 2.00, as for DDB). For a 20-year asset, the straight-line rate is 0.05 per year (1/20 = 0.05), so the annual MACRS depreciation rate is 0.075 (0.05 × 1.50 = 0.075). The taxpayer computes annual depreciation by multiplying asset book value by 0.075, in a manner similar to how DDB works.

Most real estate is depreciated by the straight-line method (see the last two categories in Exhibit 7-11).

EXHIBIT 7-11 | MACRS Depreciation Method

Class Identified by Asset Life (years)	Representative Assets	Depreciation Method
3	Race horses	DDB
5	Automobiles, light trucks	DDB
7	Equipment	DDB
10	Equipment	DDB
15	Sewage-treatment plants	150% DDB
20	Certain real estate	150% DDB
27½	Residential rental property	SL
39	Nonresidential rental property	SL

Depreciation for Partial Years

Companies purchase plant assets whenever they need them, not just at the beginning of the year. Therefore, companies must compute *depreciation for partial years*. Suppose UPS purchases a warehouse building on April 1 for $500,000. The building's estimated life is 20 years, and its estimated residual value is $80,000. UPS's accounting year ends on December 31. Let's consider how UPS computes depreciation for April through December:

- First, compute depreciation for a full year.
- Second, multiply full-year depreciation by the fraction of the year that you held the asset—in this case, 9/12. Assuming the straight-line method, the year's depreciation for this UPS building is $15,750, as follows:

$$\text{Full-year depreciation} \qquad \frac{\$500,000 - \$80,000}{20} = \$21,000$$

$$\text{Partial year depreciation} \qquad \$21,000 \times 9/12 = \$15,750$$

What if UPS bought the asset on April 18? Many businesses record no monthly depreciation on assets purchased after the 15th of the month, and they record a full month's depreciation on an asset bought on or before the 15th.

Most companies use computerized systems to account for fixed assets. Each asset has a unique identification number, and the system will automatically calculate the asset's depreciation expense. Accumulated Depreciation is automatically updated.

Changing the Useful Life of a Depreciable Asset

After an asset is in use, managers may change its useful life on the basis of experience and new information. **Disney Enterprises, Inc.**, made such a change, called a *change in accounting estimate*. Disney recalculated depreciation on the basis of revised useful lives of several of its theme park assets. The following note in Disney Enterprises, Inc.'s financial statements reports this change in accounting estimate:

> **Note 5**
> ...[T]he Company extended the estimated useful lives of certain theme park ride and attraction assets based upon historical data and engineering studies. The effect of this change was to decrease depreciation by approximately $8 million (an increase in net income of approximately $4.2 million...).

Assume that a Disney hot dog stand cost $50,000 and that the company originally believed the asset had a 10-year useful life with no residual value. Using the straight-line method, the company would record $5,000 depreciation each year ($50,000/10 years = $5,000). Suppose Disney used the asset for four years. Accumulated depreciation reached $20,000, leaving a remaining depreciable book value (cost less accumulated depreciation less residual value) of $30,000 ($50,000 – $20,000). From its experience, management believes the asset will remain useful for an *additional* 10 years. The company would spread the remaining depreciable book value over the asset's remaining life as follows:

Asset's remaining depreciable book value	÷	(New) Estimated useful life remaining	=	(New) Annual depreciation
$30,000	÷	10 years	=	$3,000

The yearly depreciation entry based on the new estimated useful life is

Depreciation Expense—Hot Dog Stand	3,000	
Accumulated Depreciation—Hot Dog Stand		3,000

Depreciation decreases both assets and equity.

Assets	=	Liabilities	+	Stockholders' Equity	–	Expenses
– 3,000	=	0		– 3,000		

COOKING THE BOOKS
Through Depreciation

Waste Management

Since plant assets usually involve relatively large amounts and relatively large numbers of assets, sometimes a seemingly subtle change in the way they are accounted for can have a tremendous impact on the financial statements. When these changes are made in order to cook the books, the results can be devastating.

Waste Management, Inc., is North America's largest integrated waste service company, providing collection, transfer, recycling, disposal, and waste-to-energy services for commercial, industrial, municipal, and residential customers from coast to coast.

Starting in 1992, six top executives of the company, including its founder and chairman of the board, its chief financial officer, its corporate controller, its top lawyer, and its vice president of finance, decided that the company's profits were not growing fast enough to meet "earnings targets," which were tied to their executive bonuses. Among several fraudulent financial tactics these top executives employed to cook the books were: (1) assigning unsupported and inflated salvage values to garbage trucks; (2) unjustifiably extending the estimated useful lives of their garbage trucks; and (3) assigning arbitrary salvage values to other fixed assets that previously had no salvage values. All of these tactics had the effect of decreasing the amount of depreciation expense in the income statements and increasing net income by a corresponding amount. While practices like this might seem relatively subtle and even insignificant when performed on an individual asset, remember that there were thousands of trash trucks and dumpsters involved, so the dollar amount grew huge in a short time. In addition, the company continued these practices for five years, overstating earnings by $1.7 billion.

The Waste Management fraud was the largest of its kind in history until the WorldCom scandal, discussed earlier in this chapter. In 1997, the company fired the officers involved and hired a new CEO who ordered a review of these practices, which uncovered the fraud. In the meantime, these dishonest executives had profited handsomely, receiving performance-based bonuses based on the company's inflated earnings, retaining their high-paying jobs, and receiving enhanced retirement benefits. One of the executives took the fraud to another level. Just 10 days before the fraud was disclosed, he enriched himself with a tax benefit by donating inflated company stock to his alma mater to fund a building in his name! Although the men involved were sued for monetary damages, none of them ever went to jail.

When the fraud was disclosed, Waste Management shareholders lost over $6 billion in the market value of their investments when the stock price plummeted by more than 33%. The company and these officers eventually settled civil lawsuits for approximately $700 million because of the fraud.

You might ask, "Where were the auditors while this was occurring?" The company's auditor was Arthur Andersen, LLP, whose partners involved on the audit engagement were eventually found to be complicit in the scheme. In fact, a few of the Waste Management officers who perpetrated the scheme had been ex-partners of the audit firm. As it turns out, the auditors actually identified many of the improper accounting practices of Waste Management. However, rather than insisting that the company fix the errors, or risk exposure, they merely "persuaded" management to agree not to repeat these practices in the future, and entered into an agreement with them to write off the accumulated balance sheet overstatement over a period of 10 years. In June 2001, the SEC fined Arthur Andersen $7 million for "knowingly and recklessly issuing false and misleading audit reports" for Waste Management from 1993 through 1996.

In October 2001, immediately on the heels of these disclosures, the notorious Enron scandal broke. Enron, as well as WorldCom, were Arthur Andersen clients at the time. The Enron scandal finally put the firm out of business. Many people feel that, had it not been for Andersen's involvement in the Waste Management affair, the SEC might have been more lenient toward the company in the Enron scandal.

The Enron scandal is discussed in Chapter 10.

Fully Depreciated Assets

A *fully depreciated asset* is one that has reached the end of its estimated useful life. Suppose FedEx has fully depreciated equipment with zero residual value (cost was $60,000). FedEx accounts will appear as follows:

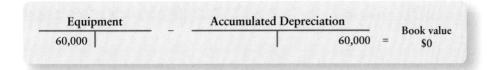

Equipment	−	Accumulated Depreciation		Book value
60,000			60,000	= $0

The equipment's book value is zero, but that doesn't mean the equipment is worthless. FedEx may use the equipment for a few more years, but FedEx will not record any more depreciation on a fully depreciated asset.

When FedEx disposes of the equipment, FedEx will remove both the asset's cost ($60,000) and its accumulated depreciation ($60,000) from the books. The next section shows how to account for plant asset disposals.

Accounting for Disposal of Plant Assets

Eventually, a plant asset ceases to serve a company's needs. The asset may wear out or become obsolete. Before accounting for the disposal of the asset, the business should bring depreciation up to date to

OBJECTIVE

4 **Analyze** the effect of a plant asset disposal

- measure the asset's final book value and
- record the expense up to the date of sale.

To account for disposal, remove the asset and its related accumulated depreciation from the books. Suppose the final year's depreciation expense has just been recorded for a machine that cost $60,000 and is estimated to have zero residual value. The machine's accumulated depreciation thus totals $60,000. Assuming that this asset is junked, the entry to record its disposal is:

Accumulated Depreciation—Machinery	60,000	
Machinery		60,000
To dispose of a fully depreciated machine.		

Assets	=	Liabilities	+	Stockholders' Equity
+ 60,000 − 60,000	=	0	+	0

There is no gain or loss on this disposal, and there's no effect on total assets, liabilities, or equity.

If assets are junked before being fully depreciated, the company incurs a loss on the disposal. Suppose FedEx disposes of equipment that cost $60,000. This asset's accumulated depreciation is $50,000, and book value is, therefore, $10,000. Junking this equipment results in a loss equal to the book value of the asset, as follows:

Accumulated Depreciation—Equipment	50,000	
Loss on Disposal of Equipment	10,000	
Equipment		60,000
To dispose of equipment.		

Assets	=	Liabilities	+	Stockholders' Equity	−	Losses
+ 50,000 − 60,000	=	0				− 10,000

FedEx got rid of an asset with $10,000 book value and received nothing. The result is a $10,000 loss, which decreases both total assets and equity.

The Loss on Disposal of Equipment is reported as Other income (expense) on the income statement. Losses decrease net income exactly as expenses do. Gains increase net income the same as revenues.

Selling a Plant Asset.   Suppose FedEx sells equipment on September 30, 2012, for $7,300 cash. The equipment cost $10,000 when purchased on January 1, 2009, and has been depreciated straight-line. FedEx estimated a 10-year useful life and no residual value. Prior to recording the sale, FedEx accountants must update the asset's depreciation. Assume that FedEx uses the calendar year as its accounting period. Partial-year depreciation must be recorded for the asset's depreciation from January 1, 2012, to the sale date. The straight-line depreciation entry at September 30, 2012, is

Sep 30	Depreciation Expense ($10,000/10 years × 9/12)	750	
	Accumulated Depreciation—Equipment		750
	To update depreciation.		

The Equipment account and the Accumulated Depreciation account appear as follows. Observe that the equipment's book value is $6,250 ($10,000 – $3,750).

Equipment			Accumulated Depreciation		
Jan 1, 2009	10,000		Dec 31, 2009	1,000	
		−	Dec 31, 2010	1,000	= Book value
			Dec 31, 2011	1,000	$6,250
			Sep 30, 2012	750	
			Balance	3,750	

The gain on the sale of the equipment for $7,300 is $1,050, computed as follows:

Cash received from sale of the asset		$7,300
Book value of asset sold:		
Cost	$10,000	
Less: Accumulated depreciation	(3,750)	6,250
Gain on sale of the asset................................		$1,050

The entry to record sale of the equipment is

Sep 30	Cash	7,300	
	Accumulated Depreciation—Equipment	3,750	
	Equipment		10,000
	Gain on Sale of Equipment		1,050
	To sell equipment.		

Total assets increase, and so does equity—by the amount of the gain.

Assets	=	Liabilities	–	Stockholders' Equity	+	Gains
+ 7,300						
+ 3,750	=	0			+	1,050
– 10,000						

Gains are recorded as credits, as revenues are. Gains and losses on asset disposals appear on the income statement as Other income (expense), or Other gains (losses).

Exchanging Plant Assets.   Managers often trade in old assets for new ones. This is called a *nonmonetary exchange*. The accounting for nonmonetary exchanges is based on the *fair values of the assets involved*. Thus, the cost of an asset like plant and equipment received in a nonmonetary exchange is equal to the fair values of the assets given up (including the old asset and any cash paid). Any difference between the fair value of the old asset from its book value is recognized as gain (fair value of old asset exceeds book value) or loss (book value of old asset exceeds fair value) on the exchange. For example, assume Papa John's Pizza's

- old delivery car cost $9,000 and has accumulated depreciation of $8,000. Thus, the old car's book value is $1,000.

Assume Papa John's trades in the old automobile for a new one with a fair market value of $15,000 and pays cash of $10,000. Thus, the implied fair value of the old car is $5,000 ($15,000 − $10,000). This amount is treated as cash paid by the seller for the old vehicle.

- The cost of the new delivery car is $15,000 (fair value of the old asset, $5,000, plus cash paid, $10,000).

The pizzeria records the exchange transaction as follows:

Delivery Auto (new)	15,000	
Accumulated Depreciation (old)	8,000	
Delivery Auto (old)		9,000
Cash		10,000
Gain on Exchange of Delivery Auto		4,000
Traded in old delivery car for new auto.		

Assets	=	Liabilities	+	Stockholders' Equity
+15,000				
+ 8,000	=	0	+	4,000
− 9,000				
−10,000				

There was a net increase in total assets of $4,000 and a corresponding increase in stockholders' equity, to reflect the gain on the exchange. Notice that this amount represents the excess of the fair value of the old asset over its book value. Some special rules may apply here, but they are reserved for more advanced courses.

T-Accounts for Analyzing Plant Asset Transactions

You can perform quite a bit of analysis if you know how transactions affect the plant asset accounts. Here are the accounts with descriptions of the activity in each account.

Building (or Equipment)			Accumulated Depreciation		
Beg bal			Accum deprec	Beg bal	
Cost of assets purchased	Cost of assets disposed of		of assets disposed of	Depreciation expense for the current period	
End bal				End bal	

Depreciation Expense		Gain on Sale of Building (or Equipment)	
Depreciation expense for the current period			Gain on sale
		Loss on Sale of Building (or Equipment)	
		Loss on sale	

Example: Suppose you started the year with buildings that cost $100,000. During the year you bought another building for $150,000 and ended the year with buildings that cost $180,000. What was the cost of the building you sold?

Building			
Beg bal	100,000		
Cost of assets purchased	150,000	Cost of assets sold	? = $70,000*
End bal	180,000		

*100,000 + 150,000 – $180,000

You can perform similar analyses to answer other interesting questions about what the business did during the period.

GLOBAL VIEW

One of the most significant differences between U.S. GAAP and International Financial Reporting Standards (IFRS) is the permitted reported carrying values of property, plant, and equipment. Recall from Chapter 1 that U.S. GAAP has long advocated the historical cost principle as most appropriate for plant assets because it results in a more objective (nonbiased) and therefore a more reliable (auditable) figure. It also supports the continuity assumption, which states that we expect the entity to remain in business long enough to recover the cost of its plant assets through depreciation.

In contrast, while historical cost is the primary basis of accounting under IFRS, it permits the periodic revaluation of plant assets to fair market value. The primary justification for this position is that the historical cost of plant assets purchased years ago does not properly reflect their current values. Thus, the amounts shown on the balance sheet for these assets do not reflect a relevant measure of what these assets are worth. For example, suppose a business bought a building in downtown Orlando, Florida, in 1960 for $1 million. Assume that this year that building has been appraised for $20 million. IFRS would permit the company to revalue the building on its balance sheet.

The primary objection to use of fair values on the balance sheet for plant assets is that these values are subjective, and subject to change, sometimes quite rapidly. Consider, for example, residential and commercial real estate in California during the credit crisis of 2008 and 2009. The fair market values of these assets dropped by double-digit percentages in a period of less than one year. If these assets had been valued at fair market values on the books of the companies that held them, assets would have to have been adjusted accordingly, causing the balance sheet amounts to fluctuate wildly. Furthermore, if the assets had been depreciated, it is likely that both the depreciation expense and the allowance for depreciation would also have had to be adjusted more frequently.

ACCOUNTING FOR NATURAL RESOURCES

OBJECTIVE

5 **Account** for natural resources and depletion

Natural resources are plant assets of a special type, such as iron ore, petroleum (oil), and timber. As plant assets are expensed through depreciation, so natural resource assets are expensed through *depletion*. **Depletion expense** is that portion of the cost of a natural resource that is used up in a particular period. Depletion expense is computed in the same way as units-of-production depreciation.

An oil lease may cost **ExxonMobil** $100,000 and contain an estimated 10,000 barrels of oil. The depletion rate would be $10 per barrel ($100,000/10,000 barrels). If 3,000 barrels are extracted, depletion expense is $30,000 (3,000 barrels × $10 per barrel). The depletion entry is

Depletion Expense (3,000 barrels × $10)	30,000	
Accumulated Depletion—Oil		30,000

This entry is almost identical to a depreciation entry using the units-of-production method.

If 4,500 barrels are removed the next year, that period's depletion is $45,000 (4,500 barrels × $10 per barrel). Accumulated Depletion is a contra account similar to Accumulated Depreciation.

Natural resource assets can be reported on ExxonMobil's balance sheet as follows (amounts assumed):

Property, Plant, and Equipment:		
Equipment..	$960,000	
Less: Accumulated depreciation	(410,000)	$550,000
Oil...	$340,000	
Less: Accumulated depletion	(140,000)	200,000
Total property, plant, and equipment...............		$750,000

ACCOUNTING FOR INTANGIBLE ASSETS

OBJECTIVE

6 **Account** for intangible assets and amortization

As we've seen, *intangible assets* are long-lived assets with no physical form. Intangibles are valuable because they carry special rights from patents, copyrights, trademarks, franchises, leaseholds, and goodwill. Like buildings and equipment, an intangible asset is recorded at its acquisition cost. Intangibles are the most valuable assets of high-tech companies and those that depend on research and development. The residual value of most intangibles is zero.

Intangible assets fall into two categories:

- Intangibles with *finite lives* that can be measured. We record amortization for these intangibles. **Amortization** expense is the title of the expense associated with intangibles. Amortization works like depreciation and is usually computed on a straight-line basis. Amortization can be credited directly to the asset account, as we shall see.
- Intangibles with *indefinite lives*. Record no amortization for these intangibles. Instead, check them annually for any loss in value (impairment), and record a loss when it occurs. Goodwill is the most prominent example of an intangible asset with an indefinite life.

In the following discussions, we illustrate the accounting for both categories of intangibles.

Accounting for Specific Intangibles

Each type of intangible asset is unique, and the accounting can vary from one asset to another.

Patents.   Patents are federal government grants that give the holder the exclusive right for 20 years to produce and sell an invention. The invention may be a product or a process—for example, Sony compact disc players and the Dolby noise-reduction process. Like any other asset, a patent may be purchased. Suppose **Sony** pays $170,000 to acquire a patent on January 1, and the business believes the expected useful life of the patent is five years—not the entire 20-year period. Amortization expense is $34,000 per year ($170,000/5 years). Sony records the acquisition and amortization for this patent as follows:

Jan 1	Patents	170,000	
	Cash		170,000
	To acquire a patent.		

Dec 31	Amortization Expense—Patents ($170,000/5)	34,000	
	Patents		34,000
	To amortize the cost of a patent.		

You can see that we credited the Patents account directly (no Accumulated Amortization account).

Assets	=	Liabilities	+	Stockholders' Equity	−	Expenses
− 34,000	=	0				− 34,000

Amortization for an intangible decreases both assets and equity exactly as depreciation does for equipment or a building.

Copyrights.   Copyrights are exclusive rights to reproduce and sell a book, musical composition, film, or other work of art. Copyrights also protect computer software programs, such as **Microsoft**'s Windows® and Excel. Issued by the federal government, copyrights extend 70 years beyond the author's (composer's, artist's, or programmer's) life. The cost of obtaining a copyright from the government is low, but a company may pay a large sum to purchase an existing copyright from the owner. For example, a publisher may pay the author of a popular novel $1 million or more for the book copyright. Because the useful life of a copyright is usually no longer than two or three years, each period's amortization amount is a high proportion of the copyright cost.

Trademarks and Trade Names.   **Trademarks** and **trade names** (or *brand names*) are distinctive identification of a product or service. The "eye" symbol that flashes across our television screens is the trademark that identifies the **CBS** television network. You are probably also familiar with **NBC**'s peacock. Advertising slogans that are legally protected include **United Airlines'** "Fly the friendly skies®" and **Avis Rental Car's** "We try harder®." These are distinctive identifications of products or services, marked with the symbol ™ or ®.

Some trademarks may have a definite useful life set by contract. We should amortize the cost of this type of trademark over its useful life. But a trademark or a trade name may have an indefinite life and not be amortized.

Franchises and Licenses. **Franchises** and **licenses** are privileges granted by a private business or a government to sell a product or service in accordance with specified conditions. The Chicago Cubs baseball organization is a franchise granted to its owner by the National League. **McDonald's** restaurants and **Holiday Inns** are popular franchises. The useful lives of many franchises and licenses are indefinite and, therefore, are not amortized.

Goodwill. In accounting, **goodwill** has a very specific meaning.

> **Goodwill is defined as the excess of the cost of purchasing another company over the sum of the market values of the acquired company's net assets (assets minus liabilities).**

A purchaser is willing to pay for goodwill when the purchaser buys another company that has abnormal earning power.

FedEx operates in several foreign countries. Suppose FedEx acquires Europa Company at a cost of $10 million. Europa's assets have a market value of $9 million, and its liabilities total $2 million so Europa's net assets total $7 million at current market value. In this case, FedEx paid $3 million for goodwill, computed as follows:

Purchase price paid for Europa Company		$10 million
Sum of the market values of Europa Company's assets	$9 million	
Less: Europa Company's liabilities	(2 million)	
Market value of Europa Company's net assets		7 million
Excess is called *goodwill*		$ 3 million

FedEx's entry to record the acquisition of Europa Company, including its goodwill, would be

	Assets (Cash, Receivables, Inventories, Plant Assets, all at market value)		9,000,000	
	Goodwill		3,000,000	
	Liabilities			2,000,000
	Cash			10,000,000

Goodwill in accounting has special features, as follows:

1. Goodwill is recorded *only* when it is purchased in the acquisition of another company. A purchase transaction provides objective evidence of the value of goodwill. Companies never record goodwill that they create for their own business.

2. According to GAAP, goodwill is not amortized because the goodwill of many entities increases in value.

Accounting for the Impairment of an Intangible Asset

Some intangibles—such as goodwill, licenses, and some trademarks—have indefinite lives and therefore are not subject to amortization. But all intangibles are subject to a write-down when their value decreases. The decline in value of an asset is called an **impairment**.

PepsiCo is a major company with vast amounts of purchased goodwill due to its acquisition of other companies. Each year, PepsiCo determines whether the goodwill it has purchased has increased or decreased in value. If PepsiCo's goodwill is worth more at the end of the year than at the beginning, no increase in the asset is permitted. But if PepsiCo's goodwill has decreased in value, say from $500 million to $470 million, then PepsiCo will record a $30 million impairment loss and write down the book value of the goodwill, as follows (in millions):

2011			
Dec 31	Impairment Loss on Goodwill ($500 – $470)	30	
	Goodwill		30

Both assets (Goodwill) and equity decrease (through the Loss account). Under U.S. GAAP, once a long-term asset like goodwill has been written down because of impairment, it may never again be written back up, should it increase in value.

Assets	=	Liabilities	+	Stockholders' Equity	–	Losses
– 30	=	0				– 30

PepsiCo's financial statements will report the following (in millions):

	2011	2010
Balance sheet		
Intangible assets:		
Goodwill.................................	$470	$500
Income statement		
Impairment (Loss) on goodwill	(30)	—

Accounting for Research and Development Costs

Accounting for research and development (R&D) costs is one of the most difficult issues in accounting. R&D is the lifeblood of companies such as **Procter & Gamble**, **General Electric**, **Intel**, and **Boeing**. R&D is one of these companies' most valuable (intangible) assets. But, in general, U.S. companies do not report R&D assets on their balance sheets.

GAAP requires companies to expense R&D costs as they incur them. Only in limited circumstances may the company capitalize R&D cost as an asset and amortize it over future periods as sales revenue from the product is earned. For example, a computer software company may incur R&D cost under a contract whereby the company will recover R&D costs through future sales revenue. This R&D cost is an asset, and the company records an intangible R&D asset when it incurs the cost. But this is the exception to the general rule.

Accounting for research and development costs represents another prominent difference between U.S. GAAP and IFRS. Whereas under GAAP, in general, both research and development costs are expensed as incurred, under IFRS, costs associated with the creation of intangible assets are classified into research phase costs and development phase costs. Costs in the research phase are always expensed. However, costs in the development phase are capitalized if the company can demonstrate meeting all of the following six criteria:

- the technical feasibility of completing the intangible asset;
- the intention to complete the intangible asset;
- the ability to use or sell the intangible asset;
- the future economic benefits (e.g., the existence of a market or, if for internal use, the usefulness of the intangible asset);
- the availability of adequate resources to complete development of the asset; and
- the ability to reliably measure the expenditure attributable to the intangible asset during its development.

Thus, IFRS are generally more permissive than U.S. GAAP toward capitalization of research and development costs. Adoption of IFRS should result in generally higher reported incomes for companies that incur research and development costs in periods in which these costs are incurred.

The Financial Accounting Standards Board (FASB) is currently working on a new accounting standard aimed at eliminating the differences between U.S. GAAP and IFRS in the area of research and development costs.

Still another difference between IFRS and U.S. GAAP lies in the capitalization of internally-generated intangible assets such as brand names and patents. U.S. GAAP only permits capitalization when they are purchased from a source outside the company. The cost of internally-generated brand names and patents must be expensed on the income statement. In contrast, IFRS allows the capitalization of internally-generated intangible assets like these as long as it is probable (i.e., more likely than not) that the company will receive future benefits from them. Adoption of IFRS by U.S. companies is therefore expected to result in the recognition of more intangible assets on their balance sheets than presently exist. These assets may be either amortized over the assets' estimated useful lives or tested for impairment as they are held, depending on the asset.

REPORTING PLANT ASSET TRANSACTIONS ON THE STATEMENT OF CASH FLOWS

OBJECTIVE

7 **Report** plant asset transactions on the statement of cash flows

Three main types of plant asset transactions appear on the statement of cash flows:

- acquisitions,
- sales, and
- depreciation (including amortization and depletion).

Acquisitions and sales are *investing* activities. A company invests in plant assets. The payments for equipment and buildings are investing activities that appear on the statement of cash flows. The sale of plant assets results in a cash receipt, as illustrated in Exhibit 7-12, which excerpts data from the cash-flow statement of FedEx Corporation. Depreciation, acquisitions, and sales of plant assets are denoted in color (lines 2, 5, and 6).

EXHIBIT 7-12 | **Reporting Plant Asset Transactions on FedEx's Statement of Cash Flows**

FedEx Corporation
Statement of Cash Flows (partial, adapted)
Year Ended May 31, 2008

		(In millions)
Cash Flows from Operating Activities:		
1	Net income...	$1,125
	Adjustments to reconcile net income	
	to net cash provided by operating activities:	
2	Depreciation and amortization.............................	1,946
3	Other items (summarized).....................................	413
4	Cash provided by operating activities....................	3,484
Cash Flows from Investing Activities:		
5	Capital expenditures	(2,947)
6	Proceeds from asset dispositions...........................	50
7	Cash (used in) investing activities.........................	(2,897)
Cash Flows from Financing Activities:		
8	Cash (used in) financing activities	(617)
9	Net (decrease) in cash and cash equivalents......................	(30)
10	Cash and cash equivalents, beginning of period	1,569
11	Cash and cash equivalents, end of period........................	$1,539

Let's examine FedEx's investing activities first. During 2008, FedEx paid $2,947 million for plant assets (line 5). FedEx also sold property and equipment, receiving cash of $50 million (line 6). FedEx labels the cash received as Proceeds from asset dispositions.

FedEx's statement of cash flows reports Depreciation and amortization (line 2). Observe that "Depreciation and amortization" is listed as a positive item under Adjustments to reconcile net income to Cash provided by operating activities. Since depreciation does not affect cash, you may be wondering why depreciation appears on the Statement of Cash Flows. In this format, the operating activities section of the Statement of Cash Flows starts with net income (line 1) and reconciles to cash provided by operating activities (line 4). Depreciation decreases net income but does not affect cash. Depreciation is therefore added back to net income to measure cash flow from operations. The add-back of depreciation to net income offsets the earlier subtraction of the expense. The sum of net income plus depreciation, therefore, helps to reconcile net income (on the accrual basis) to cash flow from operations (a cash-basis amount). We revisit this topic in the full context of the statement of cash flows in Chapter 12.

FedEx's cash flows are strong, but you can tell from reading the Statement of Cash Flows that the recession of 2008 and 2009 has taken its toll on FedEx. Cash flows from operations has declined over the past two fiscal years (not shown). Capital expenditures have grown, signaling that the company has invested much of its cash in the plant and equipment needed to run its business. However, the company has also had to borrow money to help finance these purchases. The company's debt payments ($617) have grown substantially over the past two years as well. This has resulted in a decline in cash and cash equivalents of $30 million in 2008. However, the company's cash position at the end of the year, in the amount of $1,539, is still very strong.

DECISION GUIDELINES

PLANT ASSETS AND RELATED EXPENSES

FedEx Corporation, like all other companies, must make some decisions about how to account for its plant assets and intangibles. Let's review some of these decisions.

Decision	Guidelines
Capitalize or expense a cost?	General rule: Capitalize all costs that provide *future* benefit for the business such as a new package-handling system. Expense all costs that provide no *future* benefit, such as a repair to an airplane.
Capitalize or expense:	
• Cost associated with a new asset?	Capitalize all costs that bring the asset to its intended use, including asset purchase price, transportation charges, and taxes paid to acquire the asset.
• Cost associated with an existing asset?	Capitalize only those costs that add to the asset's usefulness or to its useful life. Expense all other costs as maintenance or repairs.
Which depreciation method to use:	
• For financial reporting?	Use the method that best matches depreciation expense against the revenues produced by the asset. Most companies use the straight-line method.
• For income tax?	Use the method that produces the fastest tax deductions (MACRS). A company can use different depreciation methods for financial reporting and for income-tax purposes. In the United States, this practice is both legal and ethical.
• How to account for natural resources?	Capitalize the asset's acquisition cost and all later costs that add to the natural resource's future benefit. Then record depletion expense, as computed by the units-of-production method.
• How to account for intangibles?	Capitalize acquisition cost and all later costs that add to the asset's future benefit. For intangibles with finite lives, record amortization expense. For intangibles with indefinite lives, do not record amortization. But if an intangible asset loses value, then record a loss in the amount of the decrease in asset value.

END-OF-CHAPTER SUMMARY PROBLEM

The figures that follow appear in the *Answers to the Mid-Chapter Summary Problem*, Requirement 2, on page 424.

	Method A: Straight-Line			Method B: Double-Declining-Balance		
Year	Annual Depreciation Expense	Accumulated Depreciation	Book Value	Annual Depreciation Expense	Accumulated Depreciation	Book Value
Start			$44,000			$44,000
2009	$4,000	$ 4,000	40,000	$8,800	$ 8,800	35,200
2010	4,000	8,000	36,000	7,040	15,840	28,160
2011	4,000	12,000	32,000	5,632	21,472	22,528

I Requirements

1. Suppose the income tax authorities permitted a choice between these two depreciation methods. Which method would FedEx select for income-tax purposes? Why?
2. Suppose FedEx purchased the equipment described in the table on January 1, 2009. Management has depreciated the equipment by using the double-declining-balance method. On July 1, 2011, FedEx sold the equipment for $27,000 cash.

Record depreciation for 2011 and the sale of the equipment on July 1, 2011.

Answers

I Requirement 1

For tax purposes, most companies select the accelerated method because it results in the most depreciation in the earliest years of the asset's life. Accelerated depreciation minimizes income tax payments in the early years of the asset's life. That maximizes the business's cash at the earliest possible time.

I Requirement 2

Entries to record depreciation to date of sale, and then the sale of the equipment, follow:

2011			
Jul 1	Depreciation Expense—Equipment ($5,632 × 1/2 year)	2,816	
	Accumulated Depreciation—Equipment		2,816
	To update depreciation.		
Jul 1	Cash	27,000	
	Accumulated Depreciation—Equipment		
	($15,840 + $2,816)	18,656	
	Equipment		44,000
	Gain on Sale of Equipment		1,656
	To record sale of equipment.		

REVIEW PLANT ASSETS AND INTANGIBLES

Quick Check (**Answers are given on page 466.**)

1. Bartman, Inc., purchased a tract of land, a small office building, and some equipment for $1,900,000. The appraised value of the land was $1,380,000, the building $575,000, and the equipment $345,000. What is the cost of the land?
   - a. $633,333
   - b. $1,140,000
   - c. $1,380,000
   - d. None of the above

2. Which statement is false?
   - a. Depreciation is a process of allocating the cost of a plant asset over its useful life.
   - b. Depreciation is based on the matching principle because it matches the cost of the asset with the revenue generated over the asset's useful life.
   - c. The cost of a plant asset minus accumulated depreciation equals the asset's book value.
   - d. Depreciation creates a fund to replace the asset at the end of its useful life.

Use the following data for questions 3–6.

On July 1, 2010, Horizon Communications purchased a new piece of equipment that cost $45,000. The estimated useful life is 10 years and estimated residual value is $5,000.

3. What is the depreciation expense for 2010 if Horizon uses the straight-line method?
   - a. $4,000
   - b. $2,000
   - c. $4,500
   - d. $2,250

4. Assume Horizon Communications purchased the equipment on January 1, 2010. If Horizon uses the straight-line method for depreciation, what is the asset's book value at the end of 2011?
   - a. $42,000
   - b. $36,000
   - c. $32,000
   - d. $37,000

5. Assume Horizon Communications purchased the equipment on January 1, 2010. If Horizon uses the double-declining-balance method, what is depreciation for 2011?
   - a. $9,000
   - b. $6,400
   - c. $16,200
   - d. $7,200

6. Return to Horizon's original purchase date of July 1, 2010. Assume that Horizon uses the straight-line method of depreciation and sells the equipment for $36,500 on July 1, 2014. The result of the sale of the equipment is a gain (loss) of
   - a. ($3,500).
   - b. $7,500.
   - c. $2,500.
   - d. $0.

7. A company bought a new machine for $24,000 on January 1. The machine is expected to last five years and have a residual value of $4,000. If the company uses the double-declining-balance method, accumulated depreciation at the end of year 2 will be:
   - a. $12,800.
   - b. $15,360.
   - c. $19,200.
   - d. $16,000.

8. Which of the following is *not* a capital expenditure?
   - a. The addition of a building wing
   - b. A tune-up of a company vehicle
   - c. A complete overhaul of an air-conditioning system
   - d. Replacement of an old motor with a new one in a piece of equipment
   - e. The cost of installing a piece of equipment

9. Which of the following assets is *not* subject to a decreasing book value through depreciation, depletion, or amortization?
   - a. Land improvements
   - b. Goodwill
   - c. Intangibles
   - d. Natural resources

10. Why would a business select an accelerated method of depreciation for tax purposes?
   - a. MACRS depreciation follows a specific pattern of depreciation.
   - b. Accelerated depreciation generates higher depreciation expense immediately, and therefore lowers tax payments in the early years of the asset's life.
   - c. Accelerated depreciation is easier to calculate because salvage value is ignored.
   - d. Accelerated depreciation generates a greater amount of depreciation over the life of the asset than does straight-line depreciation.

11. A company purchased an oil well for $270,000. It estimates that the well contains 90,000 barrels, has an eight-year life, and no salvage value. If the company extracts and sells 10,000 barrels of oil in the first year, how much depletion expense should be recorded?

a. $33,750		**c.** $27,000	
b. $135,000		**d.** $30,000	

12. Which item among the following is not an intangible asset?

a. A copyright	**d.** Goodwill
b. A patent	**e.** All of the above are intangible assets.
c. A trademark	

Accounting Vocabulary

accelerated depreciation method (p. 420) A depreciation method that writes off a relatively larger amount of the asset's cost nearer the start of its useful life than the straight-line method does.

amortization (p. 434) The systematic reduction of a lump-sum amount. Expense that applies to intangible assets in the same way depreciation applies to plant assets and depletion applies to natural resources.

capital expenditure (p. 414) Expenditure that increases an asset's capacity or efficiency or extends its useful life. Capital expenditures are debited to an asset account.

copyright (p. 435) Exclusive right to reproduce and sell a book, musical composition, film, other work of art, or computer program. Issued by the federal government, copyrights extend 70 years beyond the author's life.

depletion expense (p. 434) That portion of a natural resource's cost that is used up in a particular period. Depletion expense is computed in the same way as units-of-production depreciation.

depreciable cost (p. 417) The cost of a plant asset minus its estimated residual value.

double-declining-balance (DDB) method (p. 420) An accelerated depreciation method that computes annual depreciation by multiplying the asset's decreasing book value by a constant percentage, which is two times the straight-line rate.

estimated residual value (p. 417) Expected cash value of an asset at the end of its useful life. Also called *residual value, scrap value,* or *salvage value.*

estimated useful life (p. 417) Length of service that a business expects to get from an asset. May be expressed in years, units of output, miles, or other measures.

franchises and licenses (p. 436) Privileges granted by a private business or a government to sell a product or service in accordance with specified conditions.

goodwill (p. 436) Excess of the cost of an acquired company over the sum of the market values of its net assets (assets minus liabilities).

impairment (p. 437) The condition that exists when the carrying amount of a long-lived asset exceeds its fair value. Whenever long-term assets have been impaired, they have to be written down to fair market values. Under U.S. GAAP, once impaired, the carrying value of a long-lived asset may never again be increased. Under IFRS, if the fair value of impaired assets recovers in the future, the values may be increased.

intangible assets (p. 411) An asset with no physical form, a special right to current and expected future benefits.

Modified Accelerated Cost Recovery System (MACRS) (p. 425) A special depreciation method used only for income-tax purposes. Assets are grouped into classes, and for a given class depreciation is computed by the double-declining-balance method, the 150%-declining balance method, or, for most real estate, the straight-line method.

patent (p. 435) A federal government grant giving the holder the exclusive right for 20 years to produce and sell an invention.

plant assets (p. 410) Long-lived assets, such as land, buildings, and equipment, used in the operation of the business. Also called *fixed assets.*

straight-line (SL) method (p. 418) Depreciation method in which an equal amount of depreciation expense is assigned to each year of asset use.

trademark, trade name (p. 435) A distinctive identification of a product or service. Also called a *brand name.*

units-of-production (UOP) method (p. 419) Depreciation method by which a fixed amount of depreciation is assigned to each unit of output produced by the plant asset.

ASSESS YOUR PROGRESS

Short Exercises

S7-1 (*Learning Objective 1: Determining cost and book value of a company's plant assets*)   Examine Round Rock's assets.

Round Rock Corporation
Consolidated Balance Sheets (Partial, Adapted)

	May 31,	
(In millions)	2011	2010
1 Assets		
2 Current assets		
3 Cash and cash equivalents..	$ 2,098	$ 246
4 Receivables, less allowances of $144 and $125	2,772	2,610
5 Spare parts, supplies, and fuel	4,670	4,510
6 Prepaid expenses and other..	468	411
7 Total current assets	10,008	7,777
8 Property and equipment, at cost		
9 Aircraft	2,394	2,394
10 Package handling and ground support equipment..............	12,225	12,139
11 Computer and electronic equipment...................................	28,165	26,115
12 Vehicles...	586	453
13 Facilities and other..	1,435	1,594
14 Total cost..	44,805	42,695
15 Less: Accumulated depreciation	(14,903)	(12,942)
16 Net property and equipment...	29,902	29,753
17 Other long-term assets		
18 Goodwill..	724	724
19 Prepaid pension cost..	1,341	1,275
20 Intangible and other assets	324	329
21 Total other long-term assets..	2,389	2,328
22 Total assets	$ 42,299	$ 39,858

1. What is Round Rock's largest category of assets? List all 2011 assets in the largest category and their amounts as reported by Round Rock.
2. What was Round Rock's cost of property and equipment at May 31, 2011? What was the book value of property and equipment on this date? Why is book value less than cost?

S7-2 (*Learning Objective 1: Measuring the cost of a plant asset*)   This chapter lists the costs included for the acquisition of land on pages 411–412. First is the purchase price of the land, which is obviously included in the cost of the land. The reasons for including the other costs are not so obvious. For example, property tax is ordinarily an expense, not part of the cost of an asset. State why the other costs listed are included as part of the cost of the land. After the land is ready for use, will these related costs be capitalized or expensed?

S7-3 (*Learning Objective 1: Determining the cost of individual assets in a lump-sum purchase of assets*) Foley Distribution Service pays $140,000 for a group purchase of land, building, and equipment. At the time of acquisition, the land has a current market value of $75,000, the building's current market value is $45,000, and the equipment's current market value is $30,000. Journalize the lump-sum purchase of the three assets for a total cost of $140,000. You sign a note payable for this amount.

S7-4 (*Learning Objective 1: Capitalizing versus expensing plant asset costs*) Assume Nation Airlines repaired a Boeing 777 aircraft at a cost of $1.5 million, which Nation paid in cash. Further, assume the Nation accountant erroneously capitalized this expense as part of the cost of the plane.

Show the effects of the accounting error on Nation Airlines' income statement. To answer this question, determine whether revenues, total expenses, and net income were overstated or understated by the accounting error.

S7-5 (*Learning Objective 2: Computing depreciation by three methods—first year only*) Assume that at the beginning of 2010, Northeast USA, a FedEx competitor, purchased a used Boeing 737 aircraft at a cost of $53,000,000. Northeast USA expects the plane to remain useful for five years (six million miles) and to have a residual value of $5,000,000. Northeast USA expects to fly the plane 775,000 miles the first year, 1,275,000 miles each year during the second, third, and fourth years, and 1,400,000 miles the last year.

1. Compute Northeast USA's first-year depreciation on the plane using the following methods:
   a. Straight-line
   b. Units-of-production
   c. Double-declining-balance
2. Show the airplane's book value at the end of the first year under each depreciation method.

S7-6 (*Learning Objective 2: Computing depreciation by three methods—third year only*) Use the Northeast USA data in Short Exercise 7-5 to compute Northeast USA's third-year depreciation on the plane using the following methods:

   a. Straight-line
   b. Units-of-production
   c. Double-declining balance

S7-7 (*Learning Objective 3: Selecting the best depreciation method for income tax purposes*) This exercise uses the assumed Northeast USA data from Short Exercise 7-5. Assume Northeast USA is trying to decide which depreciation method to use for income tax purposes. The company can choose from among the following methods: (a) straight-line, (b) units of production, or (c) double-declining-balance.

1. Which depreciation method offers the tax advantage for the first year? Describe the nature of the tax advantage.
2. How much income tax will Northeast USA save for the first year of the airplane's use under the method you selected above as compared with using the straight-line depreciation method? The income tax rate is 32%. Ignore any earnings from investing the extra cash.

S7-8 (*Learning Objectives 2, 3: Computing partial year depreciation; selecting the best depreciation method*) Assume that on September 30, 2010, LoganAir, the national airline of Switzerland, purchased an Airbus aircraft at a cost of €45,000,000 (€ is the symbol for the euro). LoganAir expects the plane to remain useful for six years (4,500,000 miles) and to have a residual value of €5,400,000. LoganAir will fly the plane 410,000 miles during the remainder of 2010.

Compute LoganAir's depreciation on the plane for the year ended December 31, 2010, using the following methods:

    a. Straight-line
    b. Units-of-production
    c. Double-declining-balance

Which method would produce the highest net income for 2010? Which method produces the lowest net income?

S7-9 (*Learning Objectives 2, 3: Computing and recording depreciation after a change in useful life of the asset*)   Ten Flags over Georgia paid $100,000 for a concession stand. Ten Flags started out depreciating the building straight-line over 20 years with zero residual value. After using the concession stand for three years, Ten Flags determines that the building will remain useful for only six more years. Record Ten Flags' depreciation on the concession stand for year 4 by the straight-line method.

S7-10 (*Learning Objectives 2, 4: Computing depreciation; recording a gain or loss on disposal*)   On January 1, 2010, ABC Airline Service purchased an airplane for $37,700,000. ABC Airline Service expects the plane to remain useful for six years and to have a residual value of $2,900,000. ABC Airline Service uses the straight-line method to depreciate its airplanes. ABC Airline Service flew the plane for three years and sold it on January 1, 2013, for $8,300,000.

    1. Compute accumulated depreciation on the airplane at January 1, 2013 (same as December 31, 2012).
    2. Record the sale of the plane on January 1, 2013.

S7-11 (*Learning Objective 5: Accounting for the depletion of a company's natural resources*)   North Coast Petroleum, the giant oil company, holds reserves of oil and gas assets. At the end of 2010, assume the cost of North Coast Petroleum's mineral assets totaled $120 billion, representing 10 billion barrels of oil in the ground.

    1. Which depreciation method is similar to the depletion method that North Coast Petroleum and other oil companies use to compute their annual depletion expense for the minerals removed from the ground?
    2. Suppose North Coast Petroleum removed 0.4 billion barrels of oil during 2011. Record depletion expense for the year. Show amounts in billions.
    3. At December 31, 2010, North Coast Petroleum's Accumulated Depletion account stood at $38 billion. Report Mineral Assets and Accumulated Depletion at December 31, 2011. Do North Coast Petroleum's Mineral Assets appear to be plentiful or mostly used up? Give your reason.

S7-12 (*Learning Objective 6: Measuring and recording goodwill*)   Vector, Inc., dominates the snack-food industry with its Tangy-Chip brand. Assume that Vector, Inc., purchased Concord Snacks, Inc., for $8.8 million cash. The market value of Concord Snacks' assets is $15 million, and Concord Snacks has liabilities of $8 million.

❙ Requirements

    1. Compute the cost of the goodwill purchased by Vector.
    2. Explain how Vector will account for goodwill in future years.

S7-13 (*Learning Objective 6: Accounting for patents and research and development cost*)   This exercise summarizes the accounting for patents, which like copyrights, trademarks, and franchises, provide the owner with a special right or privilege. It also covers research and development costs.

Suppose Solar Automobiles Limited paid $600,000 to research and develop a new global positioning system. Solar also paid $350,000 to acquire a patent on a new motor. After readying the motor for production, Solar's sales revenue for the first year totaled

$5,200,000. Cost of goods sold was $3,800,000, and selling expenses totaled $480,000. All these transactions occurred during 2010. Solar expects the patent to have a useful life of seven years.

Prepare Solar Automobiles' income statement for the year ended December 31, 2010, complete with a heading. Ignore income tax.

S7-14 (*Learning Objective 7: Reporting investing activities on the statement of cash flows*) During 2010, Northern Satellite Systems, Inc., purchased two other companies for $16 million. Also during 2010, Northern made capital expenditures of $7 million to expand its market share. During the year, Northern sold its North American operations, receiving cash of $14 million. Overall, Northern reported a net income of $2 million during 2010.

Show what Northern would report for cash flows from investing activities on its statement of cash flows for 2010. Report a total amount for net cash provided by (used in) investing activities.

Exercises

All of the A and B exercises can be found within MyAccountingLab, an online homework and practice environment. Your instructor may ask you to complete these exercises using MyAccountingLab.

(Group A)

E7-15A (*Learning Objective 1: Determining the cost of plant assets*) Ayer Self Storage purchased land, paying $175,000 cash as a down payment and signing a $190,000 note payable for the balance. Ayer also had to pay delinquent property tax of $3,500, title insurance costing $3,000, and $9,000 to level the land and remove an unwanted building. The company paid $59,000 to add soil for the foundation and then constructed an office building at a cost of $650,000. It also paid $55,000 for a fence around the property, $14,000 for the company sign near the property entrance, and $8,000 for lighting of the grounds. Determine the cost of Ayer's land, land improvements, and building.

E7-16A (*Learning Objectives 1, 4: Allocating costs to assets acquired in a lump-sum purchase; disposing of a plant asset*) Deadwood Manufacturing bought three used machines in a $167,000 lump-sum purchase. An independent appraiser valued the machines as shown in the table.

Machine No.	Appraised Value
1	$38,250
2	73,100
3	58,650

What is each machine's individual cost? Immediately after making this purchase, Deadwood sold machine 2 for its appraised value. What is the result of the sale? (Round decimals to three places when calculating proportions, and use your computed percentages throughout.)

E7-17A (*Learning Objective 1: Distinguishing capital expenditures from expenses*) Assume Candy Corner, Inc., purchased conveyor-belt machinery. Classify each of the following expenditures as a capital expenditure or an immediate expense related to machinery:

  a. Sales tax paid on the purchase price
  b. Transportation and insurance while machinery is in transit from seller to buyer
  c. Purchase price
  d. Installation

e. Training of personnel for initial operation of the machinery
f. Special reinforcement to the machinery platform
g. Income tax paid on income earned from the sale of products manufactured by the machinery
h. Major overhaul to extend the machinery's useful life by three years
i. Ordinary repairs to keep the machinery in good working order
j. Lubrication of the machinery before it is placed in service
k. Periodic lubrication after the machinery is placed in service

E7-18A (*Learning Objectives 1, 2: Measuring, depreciating, and reporting plant assets*)   During 2010, Chun Book Store paid $487,000 for land and built a store in Akron. Prior to construction, the city of Akron charged Chun $1,400 for a building permit, which Chun paid. Chun also paid $15,320 for architect's fees. The construction cost of $690,000 was financed by a long-term note payable, with interest cost of $28,300 paid at completion of the project. The building was completed September 30, 2010. Chun depreciates the building by the straight-line method over 35 years, with estimated residual value of $337,000.

1. Journalize transactions for
   a. Purchase of the land
   b. All the costs chargeable to the building in a single entry
   c. Depreciation on the building

Explanations are not required.

2. Report Chun Book Store's plant assets on the company's balance sheet at December 31, 2010.
3. What will Chun's income statement for the year ended December 31, 2010, report for this situation?

writing assignment ■

■ spreadsheet

E7-19A (*Learning Objectives 2, 3: Determining depreciation amounts by three methods*) West Side's Pizza bought a used Nissan delivery van on January 2, 2010, for $19,000. The van was expected to remain in service for four years (36,000 miles). At the end of its useful life, West Side's officials estimated that the van's residual value would be $2,800. The van traveled 11,000 miles the first year, 13,000 miles the second year, 5,000 miles the third year, and 7,000 miles in the fourth year. Prepare a schedule of *depreciation expense* per year for the van under the three depreciation methods. (For units-of-production and double-declining-balance, round to the nearest two decimals after each step of the calculation.)

Which method best tracks the wear and tear on the van? Which method would West Side's prefer to use for income tax purposes? Explain in detail why West Side's prefers this method.

E7-20A (*Learning Objectives 1, 2, 7: Reporting plant assets, depreciation, and investing cash flows*)   Assume that in January 2010, an Oatmeal House restaurant purchased a building, paying $56,000 cash and signing a $107,000 note payable. The restaurant paid another $61,000 to remodel the building. Furniture and fixtures cost $53,000, and dishes and supplies—a current asset—were obtained for $9,200.

Oatmeal House is depreciating the building over 20 years by the straight-line method, with estimated residual value of $55,000. The furniture and fixtures will be replaced at the end of five years and are being depreciated by the double-declining-balance method, with zero residual value. At the end of the first year, the restaurant still has dishes and supplies worth $1,700.

Show what the restaurant will report for supplies, plant assets, and cash flows at the end of the first year on its

   ■ Income statement
   ■ Balance sheet
   ■ Statement of cash flows (investing only)

Note: The purchase of dishes and supplies is an operating cash flow because supplies are a current asset.

E7-21A *(Learning Objective 3: Selecting the best depreciation method for income tax purposes)*   On June 30, 2010, Rockwell Corp. paid $220,000 for equipment that is expected to have an eight-year life. In this industry, the residual value of equipment is approximately 10% of the asset's cost. Rockwell's cash revenues for the year are $115,000 and cash expenses total $75,000.

Select the appropriate MACRS depreciation method for income tax purposes. Then determine the extra amount of cash that Rockwell can invest by using MACRS depreciation, versus straight-line, for the year ended December 31, 2010. The income tax rate is 40%.

E7-22A *(Learning Objectives 2, 3: Changing a plant asset's useful life)*   Assume G-1 Designing Consultants purchased a building for $400,000 and depreciated it on a straight-line basis over 40 years. The estimated residual value was $55,000. After using the building for 20 years, G-1 realized that the building will remain useful only 15 more years. Starting with the 21st year, G-1 began depreciating the building over a revised total life of 35 years and decreased the residual value to $10,000. Record depreciation expense on the building for years 20 and 21.

E7-23A *(Learning Objectives 2, 3, 4: Analyzing the effect of a sale of a plant asset; DDB depreciation)*   Assume that on January 2, 2010, Maxwell of Michigan purchased fixtures for $8,800 cash, expecting the fixtures to remain in service for five years. Maxwell has depreciated the fixtures on a double-declining-balance basis, with $1,300 estimated residual value. On August 31, 2011, Maxwell sold the fixtures for $2,900 cash. Record both the depreciation expense on the fixtures for 2011 and the sale of the fixtures. Apart from your journal entry, also show how to compute the gain or loss on Maxwell' disposal of these fixtures.

E7-24A *(Learning Objectives 1, 2, 4: Measuring a plant asset's cost; using UOP depreciation; trading in a used asset)*   Honest Truck Company is a large trucking company that operates throughout the United States. Honest Truck Company uses the units-of-production (UOP) method to depreciate its trucks.

Honest Truck Company trades in trucks often to keep driver morale high and to maximize fuel economy. Consider these facts about one Mack truck in the company's fleet: When acquired in 2010, the tractor-trailer rig cost $380,000 and was expected to remain in service for 10 years or 1,000,000 miles. Estimated residual value was $100,000. During 2010, the truck was driven 76,000 miles; during 2011, 116,000 miles; and during 2012, 156,000 miles. After 37,000 miles in 2013, the company traded in the Mack truck for a less-expensive Freightliner with a sticker price of $300,000. Honest Truck Company paid cash of $28,000. Determine Honest's gain or loss on the transaction. Prepare the journal entry to record the trade-in of the old truck on the new one.

E7-25A *(Learning Objective 5: Recording natural resource assets and depletion)*   Rocky Mines paid $426,000 for the right to extract ore from a 275,000-ton mineral deposit. In addition to the purchase price, Rocky Mines also paid a $120 filing fee, a $2,100 license fee to the state of Colorado, and $64,030 for a geologic survey of the property. Because the company purchased the rights to the minerals only, it expects the asset to have zero residual value when fully depleted. During the first year of production, Rocky Mines removed 40,000 tons of ore. Make journal entries to record (a) purchase of the mineral rights, (b) payment of fees and other costs, and (c) depletion for first-year production. What is the mineral asset's book value at the end of the year?

E7-26A *(Learning Objectives 3, 6: Recording intangibles, amortization, and a change in the asset's useful life)*

1. Morris Printers purchased for $900,000 a patent for a new laser printer. Although the patent gives legal protection for 20 years, it is expected to provide Morris Printers with a competitive advantage for only 10 years. Assuming the straight-line method of amortization, make journal entries to record (a) the purchase of the patent and (b) amortization for year 1.
2. After using the patent for five years, Morris Printers learns at a industry trade show that Super Printers is designing a more-efficient printer. On the basis of this new information, Morris Printers determines that the patent's total useful life is only seven years. Record amortization for year 6.

E7-27A (*Learning Objective 6: Computing and accounting for goodwill*) Assume Haledan paid $16 million to purchase Northshore.com. Assume further that Northshore had the following summarized data at the time of the Haledan acquisition (amounts in millions):

Northshore.com			
Assets		**Liabilities and Equity**	
Current assets	$13	Total liabilities	$25
Long-term assets	23	Stockholders' equity............	11
	$36		$36

Northshore's long-term assets had a current market value of only $18 million.

▌Requirements

1. Compute the cost of goodwill purchased by Haledan.
2. Journalize Haledan's purchase of Northshore.
3. Explain how Haledan will account for goodwill in the future.

E7-28A (*Learning Objective 7: Reporting cash flows for property and equipment*) Assume Shoe Warehouse Corporation completed the following transactions:

a. Sold a store building for $650,000. The building had cost Shoe Warehouse $1,700,000, and at the time of the sale its accumulated depreciation totaled $1,050,000.

b. Lost a store building in a fire. The building cost $380,000 and had accumulated depreciation of $190,000. The insurance proceeds received by Shoe Warehouse totaled $130,000.

c. Renovated a store at a cost of $160,000.

d. Purchased store fixtures for $70,000. The fixtures are expected to remain in service for 10 years and then be sold for $20,000. Shoe Warehouse uses the straight-line depreciation method.

For each transaction, show what Shoe Warehouse would report for investing activities on its statement of cash flows. Show negative amounts in parentheses.

(Group B)

E7-29B (*Learning Objective 1: Determining the cost of plant assets*) Lavallee Self Storage purchased land, paying $155,000 cash as a down payment and signing a $195,000 note payable for the balance. Lavallee also had to pay delinquent property tax of $4,000, title insurance costing $3,500, and $5,000 to level the land and remove an unwanted building. The company paid $53,000 to add soil for the foundation and then constructed an office building at a cost of $600,000. It also paid $45,000 for a fence around the property, $20,000 for the company sign near the property entrance, and $3,000 for lighting of the grounds. Determine the cost of Lavallee's land, land improvements, and building.

E7-30B (*Learning Objectives 1, 4: Allocating costs to assets acquired in a lump-sum purchase; disposing of a plant asset*) Eastwood Manufacturing bought three used machines in a $216,000 lump-sum purchase. An independent appraiser valued the machines as shown in the table.

Machine No.	Appraised Value
1	$ 77,000
2	116,600
3	26,400

What is each machine's individual cost? Immediately after making this purchase, Eastwood sold machine 2 for its appraised value. What is the result of the sale? (Round decimals to three places when calculating proportions, and use your computed percentages throughout.)

E7-31B (*Learning Objective 1: Distinguishing capital expenditures from expenses*)   Assume Delicious Desserts, Inc., purchased conveyor-belt machinery. Classify each of the following expenditures as a capital expenditure or an immediate expense related to machinery:

    a. Sales tax paid on the purchase price
    b. Transportation and insurance while machinery is in transit from seller to buyer
    c. Purchase price
    d. Installation
    e. Training of personnel for initial operation of the machinery
    f. Special reinforcement to the machinery platform
    g. Income tax paid on income earned from the sale of products manufactured by the machinery
    h. Major overhaul to extend the machinery's useful life by three years
    i. Ordinary repairs to keep the machinery in good working order
    j. Lubrication of the machinery before it is placed in service
    k. Periodic lubrication after the machinery is placed in service

E7-32B (*Learning Objectives 1, 2: Measuring, depreciating, and reporting plant assets*)   During 2010, Tao Book Store paid $488,000 for land and built a store in Detroit. Prior to construction, the city of Detroit charged Tao $1,800 for a building permit, which Tao paid. Tao also paid $15,800 for architect's fees. The construction cost of $710,000 was financed by a long-term note payable, with interest cost of $30,180 paid at completion of the project. The building was completed September 30, 2010. Tao depreciates the building by the straight-line method over 35 years, with estimated residual value of $341,000.

    1. Journalize transactions for
        a. Purchase of the land
        b. All the costs chargeable to the building in a single entry
        c. Depreciation on the building

Explanations are not required.

    2. Report Tao Book Store's plant assets on the company's balance sheet at December 31, 2010.
    3. What will Tao's income statement for the year ended December 31, 2010, report for this situation?

E7-33B (*Learning Objectives 2, 3: Determining depreciation amounts by three methods*)   Southern's Pizza bought a used Nissan delivery van on January 2, 2010, for $19,200. The van was expected to remain in service four years (30,000 miles). At the end of its useful life, Southern's officials estimated that the van's residual value would be $2,400. The van traveled 8,000 miles the first year, 8,500 miles the second year, 5,500 miles the third year, and 8,000 miles in the fourth year. Prepare a schedule of *depreciation expense* per year for the van under the three depreciation methods. (For units-of-production and double-declining-balance, round to the nearest two decimals after each step of the calculation.)

writing assignment ■

■ **spreadsheet**

Which method best tracks the wear and tear on the van? Which method would Southern's prefer to use for income tax purposes? Explain in detail why Southern's prefers this method.

E7-34B (*Learning Objectives 1, 2, 7: Reporting plant assets, depreciation, and investing cash flows*)   Assume that in January 2010, an International Eatery restaurant purchased a building, paying $52,000 cash and signing a $106,000 note payable. The restaurant paid another $62,000 to remodel the building. Furniture and fixtures cost $57,000, and dishes and supplies—a current asset—were obtained for $8,800.

International Eatery is depreciating the building over 20 years by the straight-line method, with estimated residual value of $54,000. The furniture and fixtures will be replaced at the end of five years and are being depreciated by the double-declining-balance method, with zero residual value. At the end of the first year, the restaurant still has dishes and supplies worth $1,600.

Show what the restaurant will report for supplies, plant assets, and cash flows at the end of the first year on its

- Income statement
- Balance sheet
- Statement of cash flows (investing only)

Note: The purchase of dishes and supplies is an operating cash flow because supplies are a current asset.

E7-35B (*Learning Objective 3: Selecting the best depreciation method for income tax purposes*) On June 30, 2010, Roy Corp. paid $200,000 for equipment that is expected to have an eight-year life. In this industry, the residual value is approximately 10% of the asset's cost. Roy's cash revenues for the year are $140,000 and cash expenses total $100,000.

Select the appropriate MACRS depreciation method for income tax purposes. Then determine the extra amount of cash that Roy can invest by using MACRS depreciation, versus straight-line, for the year ended December 31, 2010. The income tax rate is 30%.

E7-36B (*Learning Objectives 2, 3: Changing a plant asset's useful life*) Assume B − 1 Accounting Consultants purchased a building for $435,000 and depreciated it on a straight-line basis over 40 years. The estimated residual value was $73,000. After using the building for 20 years, B − 1 realized that the building will remain useful only 15 more years. Starting with the 21st year, B − 1 began depreciating the building over the newly revised total life of 35 years and decreased the estimated residual value to $14,000. Record depreciation expense on the building for years 20 and 21.

E7-37B (*Learning Objectives 2, 3, 4: Analyzing the effect of a sale of a plant asset; DDB depreciation*) Assume that on January 2, 2010, McKnight of Wyoming purchased fixtures for $8,300 cash, expecting the fixtures to remain in service for five years. McKnight has depreciated the fixtures on a double-declining-balance basis, with $1,700 estimated residual value. On September 30, 2011, McKnight sold the fixtures for $2,300 cash. Record both the depreciation expense on the fixtures for 2011 and then the sale of the fixtures. Apart from your journal entry, also show how to compute the gain or loss on McKnight's disposal of these fixtures.

E7-38B (*Learning Objectives 1, 2, 4: Measuring a plant asset's cost; using UOP depreciation; trading in a used asset*) Trusty Truck Company is a large trucking company that operates throughout the United States. Trusty Truck Company uses the units-of-production (UOP) method to depreciate its trucks.

Trusty Truck Company trades in trucks often to keep driver morale high and to maximize fuel economy. Consider these facts about one Mack truck in the company's fleet: When acquired in 2010, the rig cost $370,000 and was expected to remain in service for 10 years or 1,000,000 miles. Estimated residual value was $100,000. During 2010, the truck was driven 77,000 miles; during 2011, 117,000 miles; and during 2012, 157,000 miles. After 42,000 miles in 2013, the company traded in the Mack truck for a less-expensive Freightliner with a sticker price of $300,000. Trusty Truck Company paid cash of $25,000. Determine Trusty's gain or loss on the transaction. Prepare the journal entry to record the trade-in of the old truck on the new one.

E7-39B (*Learning Objective 5: Recording natural resource assets and depletion*) Mighty Mines paid $432,000 for the right to extract ore from a 425,000-ton mineral deposit. In addition to the purchase price, Mighty Mines also paid a $150 filing fee, a $2,700 license fee to the state of Colorado, and $92,150 for a geologic survey of the property. Because the company purchased the rights to the minerals only, it expected the asset to have zero residual value when fully depleted. During the first year of production, Mighty Mines removed 70,000 tons of ore. Make journal entries to record (a) purchase of the mineral rights, (b) payment of fees and other costs, and (c) depletion for first-year production. What is the mineral asset's book value at the end of the year?

E7-40B (*Learning Objectives 3, 6: Recording intangibles, amortization, and a change in the asset's useful life*)

1. Miracle Printers purchased for $700,000 a patent for a new laser printer. Although the patent gives legal protection for 20 years, it is expected to provide Miracle Printers with a competitive advantage for only eight years. Assuming the straight-line method of amortization, make journal entries to record (a) the purchase of the patent and (b) amortization for year 1.

2. After using the patent for four years, Miracle Printers learns at an industry trade show that Speedy Printers is designing a more-efficient printer. On the basis of this new information, Miracle Printers determines that the patent's total useful life is only six years. Record amortization for year 5.

E7-41B (*Learning Objective 6: Computing and accounting for goodwill*)   Assume Kaledan paid $18 million to purchase Southwest.com. Assume further that Southwest had the following summarized data at the time of the Kaledan acquisition (amounts in millions):

Southwest.com			
Assets		**Liabilities and Equity**	
Current assets	$10	Total liabilities	$25
Long-term assets	22	Stockholders' equity	7
	$32		$32

Southwest's long-term assets had a current market value of only $17 million.

❙ Requirements

1. Compute the cost of goodwill purchased by Kaledan.
2. Journalize Kaledan's purchase of Southwest.
3. Explain how Kaledan will account for goodwill in the future.

E7-42B (*Learning Objective 7: Reporting cash flows for property and equipment*)   Assume Shoes-R-Us Corporation completed the following transactions:

a. Sold a store building for $610,000. The building had cost Shoes-R-Us $1,300,000, and at the time of the sale its accumulated depreciation totaled $690,000.

b. Lost a store building in a fire. The building cost $350,000 and had accumulated depreciation of $170,000. The insurance proceeds received by Shoes-R-Us totaled $110,000.

c. Renovated a store at a cost of $120,000.

d. Purchased store fixtures for $90,000. The fixtures are expected to remain in service for 10 years and then be sold for $10,000. Shoes-R-Us uses the straight-line depreciation method.

For each transaction, show what Shoes-R-Us would report for investing activities on its statement of cash flows. Show negative amounts in parentheses.

Challenge Exercises

E7-43 (*Learning Objective 2: Computing units-of-production depreciation*)   Buff Gym purchased exercise equipment at a cost of $107,000. In addition, Buff paid $3,000 for a special platform on which to stabilize the equipment for use. Freight costs of $1,600 to ship the equipment were borne by the seller. Buff will depreciate the equipment by the units-of-production method, based on an expected useful life of 55,000 hours of exercise. The estimated residual value of the equipment is $11,000. How many hours did Buff Gym use the machine if depreciation expense is $4,320?

E7-44 (*Learning Objective 4: Determining the sale price of property and equipment*)   Wilson Corporation reported the following for property and equipment (in millions, adapted):

	Year End	
	2011	**2010**
Property and equipment....................	$24,073	$22,011
Accumulated depreciation................	(13,306)	(12,087)

During 2011, Wilson paid $2,510 million for new property and equipment. Depreciation for the year totaled $1,546 million. During 2011, Wilson sold property and equipment for cash of $48 million. How much was Wilson's gain or loss on the sale of property and equipment during 2011?

E7-45 (*Learning Objectives 2, 3: Determining net income after a change in depreciation method*)   Norzani, Inc., has a popular line of sunglasses. Norzani reported net income of $66 million for 2010. Depreciation expense for the year totaled $32 million. Norzani, Inc., depreciates plant assets over eight years using the straight-line method and no residual value.

Norzani, Inc., paid $256 million for plant assets at the beginning of 2010. Then at the start of 2011, Norzani switched over to double-declining-balance (DDB) depreciation. 2011 is expected to be the same as 2010 except for the change in depreciation method. If Norzani had been using DDB depreciation all along, how much net income can Norzani, Inc., expect to earn during 2011? Ignore income tax.

E7-46 (*Learning Objective 1: Capitalizing versus expensing; measuring the effect of an error*)   All French Press (AFP) is a major French telecommunication conglomerate. Assume that early in year 1, AFP purchased equipment at a cost of 8 million euros (€8 million). Management expects the equipment to remain in service for four years and estimated residual value to be negligible. AFP uses the straight-line depreciation method. *Through an accounting error, AFP expensed the entire cost of the equipment at the time of purchase.* Because AFP is operated as a partnership, it pays no income tax.

I *Requirements*

Prepare a schedule to show the overstatement or understatement in the following items at the end of each year over the four-year life of the equipment:

1. Total current assets
2. Equipment, net
3. Net income

Quiz

Test your understanding of accounting for plant assets, natural resources, and intangibles by answering the following questions. Select the best choice from among the possible answers given.

Q7-47 A capital expenditure
a. adds to an asset.
b. is expensed immediately.
c. is a credit like capital (owners' equity).
d. records additional capital.

Q7-48 Which of the following items should be accounted for as a capital expenditure?
a. The monthly rental cost of an office building
b. Taxes paid in conjunction with the purchase of office equipment
c. Maintenance fees paid with funds provided by the company's capital
d. Costs incurred to repair leaks in the building roof

Q7-49 Suppose you buy land for $2,900,000 and spend $1,200,000 to develop the property. You then divide the land into lots as follows:

Catergory	Sale Price per Lot
10 Hilltop lots...............	$525,000
10 Valley lots................	350,000

How much did each hilltop lot cost you?
a. $246,000   c. $234,285
b. $175,715   d. $410,000

Q7-50 Which statement about depreciation is false?
a. Depreciation should not be recorded in years that the market value of the asset has increased.
b. Depreciation is a process of allocating the cost of an asset to expense over its useful life.
c. A major objective of depreciation accounting is to match the cost of using an asset with the revenues it helps to generate.
d. Obsolescence as well as physical wear and tear should be considered when determining the period over which an asset should be depreciated.

Q7-51 Boston Corporation acquired a machine for $33,000 and has recorded depreciation for two years using the straight-line method over a five-year life and $6,000 residual value. At the start of the third year of use, Boston revised the estimated useful life to a total of 10 years. Estimated residual value declined to $0.

What is the book value of the machine at the end of two full years of use?
a. $13,200   c. $10,800
b. $16,800   d. $22,200

Q7-52 Boston Corporation acquired a machine for $33,000 and has recorded depreciation for two years using the straight-line method over a five-year life and $6,000 residual value. At the start of the third year of use, Boston revised the estimated useful life to a total of 10 years. Estimated residual value declined to $0.

How much depreciation should Boston record in each of the asset's last eight years (that is, year 3 through year 10), following the revision?
a. $13,200   c. $2,775
b. $3,300   d. Some other amount

Q7-53 King Company failed to record depreciation of equipment. How does this omission affect King's financial statements?

a. Net income is overstated and assets are understated.
b. Net income is overstated and assets are overstated.
c. Net income is understated and assets are overstated.
d. Net income is understated and assets are understated.

Q7-54 Jimmy's DVD, Inc., uses the double-declining-balance method for depreciation on its computers. Which item is not needed to compute depreciation for the first year?

a. Original cost   c. Estimated residual value
b. Expected useful life in years   d. All the above are needed.

Q7-55 Which of the following costs is reported on a company's income statement?
a. Land   c. Depreciation expense
b. Accumulated depreciation   d. Accounts payable

Q7-56 Which of the following items is reported on the balance sheet?
a. Gain on disposal of equipment
b. Accumulated depreciation
c. Cost of goods sold
d. Net sales revenue

Use the following information to answer questions 7-57 through 7-59.

Hill Company purchased a machine for $8,600 on January 1, 2010. The machine has been depreciated using the straight-line method over a 10-year life and $600 residual value. Hill sold the machine on January 1, 2012, for $7,700.

Q7-57 What gain or loss should Hill record on the sale?
a. Gain, $1,300   c. Gain, $300
b. Loss, $900   d. Gain, $700

Q7-58 Journalize Hill's sale of the machine.

Q7-59 What is straight-line depreciation for the year ended December 31, 2010, and what is the book value on December 31, 2011?

Q7-60 A company purchased mineral assets costing $840,000, with estimated residual value of $30,000, and holding approximately 300,000 tons of ore. During the first year, 48,000 tons are extracted and sold. What is the amount of depletion for the first year?
a. $114,500
b. $129,600
c. $109,400
d. Cannot be determined from the data given

Q7-61 Suppose Timely Delivery pays $64 million to buy Guaranteed Overnight. Guaranteed's assets are valued at $74 million, and its liabilities total $16 million. How much goodwill did Timely Delivery purchase in its acquisition of Guaranteed Overnight?
a. $48 million   c. $26 million
b. $16 million   d. $6 million

Problems

> All of the A and B problems can be found within MyAccountingLab, an online homework and practice environment. Your instructor may ask you to complete these problems using MyAccountingLab.

(Group A)

P7-62A (*Learning Objectives 1, 2, 3: Identifying the elements of a plant asset's cost*) Assume Online, Inc., opened an office in Clearwater, Florida. Further assume that Online incurred the following costs in acquiring land, making land improvements, and constructing and furnishing the new sales building:

a.	Purchase price of land, including an old building that will be used for a garage (land market value is $315,000; building market value is $85,000)..	$360,000
b.	Landscaping (additional dirt and earth moving).....................................	8,500
c.	Fence around the land..	31,800
d.	Attorney fee for title search on the land	900
e.	Delinquent real estate taxes on the land to be paid by Online	5,600
f.	Company signs at entrance to the property	1,200
g.	Building permit for the sales building..	400
h.	Architect fee for the design of the sales building....................................	19,600
i.	Masonry, carpentry, and roofing of the sales building............................	515,000
j.	Renovation of the garage building...	41,200
k.	Interest cost on construction loan for sales building...............................	9,100
l.	Landscaping (trees and shrubs)	6,600
m.	Parking lot and concrete walks on the property	52,100
n.	Lights for the parking lot and walkways..	7,500
o.	Salary of construction supervisor (86% to sales building; 11% to land improvements; and 3% to garage building renovations)..............	44,000
p.	Office furniture for the sales building..	79,400
q.	Transportation and installation of furniture...	1,900

Assume Online depreciates buildings over 40 years, land improvements over 20 years, and furniture over 10 years, all on a straight-line basis with zero residual value.

▌Requirements

1. Show how to account for each of Online's costs by listing the cost under the correct account. Determine the total cost of each asset.
2. All construction was complete and the assets were placed in service on May 2. Record depreciation for the year ended December 31. Round to the nearest dollar.
3. How will what you learned in this problem help you manage a business?

P7-63A (*Learning Objectives 2, 3: Recording plant asset transactions; reporting on the balance sheet*)   Romano Lakes Resort reported the following on its balance sheet at December 31, 2010:

▌ **general ledger**

Property, plant, and equipment, at cost:	
Land...	$ 146,000
Buildings..	709,000
Less: Accumulated depreciation	(342,000)
Equipment..	405,000
Less: Accumulated depreciation	(265,000)

In early July 2011, the resort expanded operations and purchased additional equipment at a cost of $102,000. The company depreciates buildings by the straight-line method over 20 years with residual value of $89,000. Due to obsolescence, the equipment has a useful life of only 10 years and is being depreciated by the double-declining-balance method with zero residual value.

▌Requirements

1. Journalize Romano Lakes Resort's plant asset purchase and depreciation transactions for 2011.
2. Report plant assets on the December 31, 2011, balance sheet.

■ **general ledger**

P7-64A (*Learning Objectives 1, 2, 3, 4: Recording plant asset transactions, exchanges, and changes in useful life*)   Carr, Inc., has the following plant asset accounts: Land, Buildings, and Equipment, with a separate accumulated depreciation account for each of these except land. Carr completed the following transactions:

Jan 2	Traded in equipment with accumulated depreciation of $65,000 (cost of $136,000) for similar new equipment with a cash cost of $175,000. Received a trade-in allowance of $75,000 on the old equipment and paid $100,000 in cash.
Jun 30	Sold a building that had a cost of $655,000 and had accumulated depreciation of $130,000 through December 31 of the preceding year. Depreciation is computed on a straight-line basis. The building has a 40-year useful life and a residual value of $275,000. Carr received $115,000 cash and a $405,250 note receivable.
Oct 29	Purchased land and a building for a single price of $390,000. An independent appraisal valued the land at $221,100 and the building at $180,900.
Dec 31	Recorded depreciation as follows:
Equipment has an expected useful life of 5 years and an estimated residual value of 6% of cost. Depreciation is computed on the double-declining-balance method.
Depreciation on buildings is computed by the straight-line method. The new building carries a 40-year useful life and a residual value equal to 20% of its cost.

I *Requirement*

1. Record the transactions in Carr, Inc.'s journal

writing assignment ■

P7-65A (*Learning Objective 2: Explaining the concept of depreciation*)   The board of directors of Gold Structures, Inc., is reviewing the 2010 annual report. A new board member—a wealthy woman with little business experience—questions the company accountant about the depreciation amounts. The new board member wonders why depreciation expense has decreased from $220,000 in 2008 to $204,000 in 2009 to $196,000 in 2010. She states that she could understand the decreasing annual amounts if the company had been disposing of properties each year, but that has not occurred. Further, she notes that growth in the city is increasing the values of company properties. Why is the company recording depreciation when the property values are increasing?

■ **spreadsheet**

P7-66A (*Learning Objectives 1, 2, 3: Computing depreciation by three methods; identifying the cash-flow advantage of accelerated depreciation for tax purposes*)   On January 9, 2010, J.T. Outtahe Co. paid $230,000 for a computer system. In addition to the basic purchase price, the company paid a setup fee of $1,000, $6,000 sales tax, and $28,000 for a special platform on which to place the computer. J.T. Outtahe management estimates that the computer will remain in service for five years and have a residual value of $15,000. The computer will process 30,000 documents the first year, with annual processing decreasing by 2,500 documents during each of the next four years (that is, 27,500 documents in year 2011; 25,000 documents in year 2012; and so on). In trying to decide which depreciation method to use, the company president has requested a depreciation schedule for each of the three depreciation methods (straight-line, units-of-production, and double-declining-balance).

I *Requirements*

1. For each of the generally accepted depreciation methods, prepare a depreciation schedule showing asset cost, depreciation expense, accumulated depreciation, and asset book value.
2. J.T. Outtahe reports to stockholders and creditors in the financial statements using the depreciation method that maximizes reported income in the early years of asset use. For income tax purposes, the company uses the depreciation method that minimizes income tax payments in those early years. Consider the first year J.T. Outtahe Co. uses the computer. Identify the depreciation methods that meet Outtahe's objectives, assuming the income tax authorities permit the use of any of the methods.

3. Cash provided by operations before income tax is $156,000 for the computer's first year. The income tax rate is 28%. For the two depreciation methods identified in Requirement 2, compare the net income and cash provided by operations (cash flow). Show which method gives the net-income advantage and which method gives the cash-flow advantage.

P7-67A *(Learning Objectives 2, 4, 7: Analyzing plant asset transactions from a company's financial statements)* Floral, Inc., sells electronics and appliances. The excerpts that follow are adapted from Floral's financial statements for 2010 and 2009.

	February 28,	
Balance Sheet (dollars in millions)	**2010**	**2009**
Assets		
Total current assets	$7,980	$6,900
Property, plant, and equipment	4,830	4,199
Less: Accumulated depreciation	2,126	1,726
Goodwill...	558	519

	Year Ended February 28,	
Statement of Cash Flows (dollars in millions)	**2010**	**2009**
Operating activities:		
Net income	$1,146	$ 981
Noncash items affecting net income:		
Depreciation	460	457
Investing activities:		
Additions to property, plant, and equipment................	(707)	(615)

I Requirements

1. How much was Floral's cost of plant assets at February 28, 2010? How much was the book value of plant assets? Show computations.
2. The financial statements give three evidences that Floral purchased plant assets and goodwill during fiscal year 2010. What are they?
3. Prepare T-accounts for Property, Plant, and Equipment; Accumulated Depreciation; and Goodwill. Then show all the activity in these accounts during 2010. Label each increase or decrease and give its dollar amount. During 2010, Floral sold plant assets that had cost the company $76 million (accumulated depreciation on these assets was $60 million). Assume there were no losses on goodwill during 2010.

P7-68A *(Learning Objective 5: Accounting for natural resources, and the related expense)* Northeastern Energy Company's balance sheet includes the asset Iron Ore. Northeastern Energy paid $2.5 million cash for a lease giving the firm the right to work a mine that contained an estimated 197,000 tons of ore. The company paid $65,000 to remove unwanted buildings from the land and $75,000 to prepare the surface for mining. Northeastern Energy also signed a $37,230 note payable to a landscaping company to return the land surface to its original condition after the lease ends. During the first year, Northeastern Energy removed 33,500 tons of ore, which it sold on account for $35 per ton. Operating expenses for the first year totaled $250,000, all paid in cash. In addition, the company accrued income tax at the tax rate of 32%.

I Requirements

1. Record all of Northeastern Energy's transactions for the year.
2. Prepare the company's income statement for its iron ore operations for the first year. Evaluate the profitability of the company's operations.

P7-69A (*Learning Objectives 4, 7: Reporting plant asset transactions on the statement of cash flows*) At the end of 2009, Solving Engineering Associates (SEA) had total assets of $17.1 billion and total liabilities of $9.7 billion. Included among the assets were property, plant, and equipment with a cost of $4.4 billion and accumulated depreciation of $3.2 billion.

SEA completed the following selected transactions during 2010: The company earned total revenues of $26.4 billion and incurred total expenses of $21.2 billion, which included depreciation of $1.9 billion. During the year, SEA paid $1.8 billion for new property, plant, and equipment and sold old plant assets for $0.3 billion. The cost of the assets sold was $1.1 billion, and their accumulated depreciation was $0.6 billion.

▌Requirements

1. Explain how to determine whether SEA had a gain or loss on the sale of old plant assets during the year. What was the amount of the gain or loss, if any?
2. Show how SEA would report property, plant, and equipment on the balance sheet at December 31, 2010, after all the year's activity. What was the book value of property, plant, and equipment?
3. Show how SEA would report its operating activities and investing activities on its statement of cash flows for 2010. Ignore gains and losses.

(Group B)

P7-70B (*Learning Objectives 1, 2, 3: Identifying the elements of a plant asset's cost*) Assume Lance Pharmacy, Inc., opened an office in Vero Beach, Florida. Further assume that Lance Pharmacy incurred the following costs in acquiring land, making land improvements, and constructing and furnishing the new sales building:

a.	Purchase price of land, including an old building that will be used for a garage (land market value is $310,000; building market value is $90,000)..	$340,000
b.	Landscaping (additional dirt and earth moving)...................................	8,900
c.	Fence around the land..	31,000
d.	Attorney fee for title search on the land	400
e.	Delinquent real estate taxes on the land to be paid by Lance Pharmacy	5,800
f.	Company signs at entrance to the property	1,400
g.	Building permit for the sales building...	700
h.	Architect fee for the design of the sales building.................................	19,900
i.	Masonry, carpentry, and roofing of the sales building.........................	510,000
j.	Renovation of the garage building..	41,900
k.	Interest cost on construction loan for sales building...........................	9,000
l.	Landscaping (trees and shrubs)	6,300
m.	Parking lot and concrete walks on the property	52,900
n.	Lights for the parking lot and walkways	7,000
o.	Salary of construction supervisor (86% to sales building; 10% to land improvements; and 4% to garage building renovations).............	41,000
p.	Office furniture for the sales building..	79,200
q.	Transportation and installation of furniture..	1,100

Assume Lance Pharmacy depreciates buildings over 30 years, land improvements over 15 years, and furniture over eight years, all on a straight-line basis with zero residual value.

▌Requirements

1. Show how to account for each of Lance Pharmacy's costs by listing the cost under the correct account. Determine the total cost of each asset.
2. All construction was complete and the assets were placed in service on May 2. Record depreciation for the year ended December 31. Round to the nearest dollar.
3. How will what you learned in this problem help you manage a business?

P7-71B (*Learning Objectives 2, 3: Recording plant asset transactions; reporting on the balance sheet*) Rossi Lakes Resort reported the following on its balance sheet at December 31, 2010:

Property, plant, and equipment, at cost:	
Land..	$ 149,000
Buildings	704,000
Less: Accumulated depreciation	(342,000)
Equipment...	401,000
Less: Accumulated depreciation	(268,000)

In early July 2011, the resort expanded operations and purchased additional equipment at a cost of $105,000. The company depreciates buildings by the straight-line method over 20 years with residual value of $89,000. Due to obsolescence, the equipment has a useful life of only 10 years and is being depreciated by the double-declining-balance method with zero residual value.

Requirements

1. Journalize Rossi Lakes Resort's plant asset purchase and depreciation transactions for 2011.
2. Report plant assets on the December 31, 2011, balance sheet.

P7-72B (*Learning Objectives 1, 2, 3, 4: Recording plant asset transactions, exchanges, and changes in useful life*) Tarrier, Inc., has the following plant asset accounts: Land, Buildings, and Equipment, with a separate accumulated depreciation account for each of these except land. Tarrier completed the following transactions:

Jan 2	Traded in equipment with accumulated depreciation of $64,000 (cost of $138,000) for similar new equipment with a cash cost of $179,000. Received a trade-in allowance of $73,000 on the old equipment and paid $106,000 in cash.
Jun 30	Sold a building that had a cost of $645,000 and had accumulated depreciation of $155,000 through December 31 of the preceding year. Depreciation is computed on a straight-line basis. The building has a 40-year useful life and a residual value of $285,000. Tarrier received $135,000 cash and a $350,500 note receivable.
Oct 29	Purchased land and a building for a single price of $340,000. An independent appraisal valued the land at $108,900 and the building at $254,100.
Dec 31	Recorded depreciation as follows:
	Equipment has an expected useful life of 4 years and an estimated residual value of 4% of cost. Depreciation is computed on the double-declining-balance method.
	Depreciation on buildings is computed by the straight-line method. The new building carries a 40-year useful life and a residual value equal to 10% of its cost.

Requirement

1. Record the transactions in Tarrier, Inc.'s journal.

P7-73B (*Learning Objective 2: Explaining the concept of depreciation*) The board of directors of Cooper Structures, Inc., is reviewing the 2010 annual report. A new board member—a wealthy woman with little business experience—questions the company accountant about the depreciation amounts. The new board member wonders why depreciation expense has decreased from $190,000 in 2008 to $174,000 in 2009 to $166,000 in 2010. She states that she could understand the decreasing annual amounts if the company had been disposing of properties each year, but that has not occurred. Further, she notes that growth in the city is increasing the values of company properties. Why is the company recording depreciation when the property values are increasing?

■ **spreadsheet**

P7-74B *(Learning Objectives 1, 2, 3: Computing depreciation by three methods; identifying the cash-flow advantage of accelerated depreciation for tax purposes)* On January 6, 2010, K.P. Scott Co. paid $245,000 for a computer system. In addition to the basic purchase price, the company paid a setup fee of $800, $6,400 sales tax, and $27,800 for a special platform on which to place the computer. K.P. Scott management estimates that the computer will remain in service for five years and have a residual value of $20,000. The computer will process 45,000 documents the first year, with annual processing decreasing by 2,500 documents during each of the next four years (that is, 42,500 documents in 2011; 40,000 documents in 2012; and so on). In trying to decide which dep-reciation method to use, the company president has requested a depreciation schedule for each of the three depreciation methods (straight-line, units-of-production, and double-declining-balance).

❙ Requirements

1. For each of the generally accepted depreciation methods, prepare a depreciation schedule showing asset cost, depreciation expense, accumulated depreciation, and asset book value.
2. K.P. Scott reports to stockholders and creditors in the financial statements using the depreciation method that maximizes reported income in the early years of asset use. For income tax purposes, the company uses the depreciation method that minimizes income tax payments in those early years. Consider the first year K.P. Scott Co. uses the computer. Identify the depreciation methods that meet Scott's objectives, assuming the income tax authorities permit the use of any of the methods.
3. Cash provided by operations before income tax is $155,000 for the computer's first year. The income tax rate is 35%. For the two depreciation methods identified in Requirement 2, compare the net income and cash provided by operations (cash flow). Show which method gives the net-income advantage and which method gives the cash-flow advantage.

P7-75B *(Learning Objectives 2, 4, 7: Analyzing plant asset transactions from a company's financial statements)* Parem, Inc., sells electronics and appliances. The excerpts that follow are adapted from Parem's financial statements for 2010 and 2009.

	February 28,	
Balance Sheet (dollars in millions)	2010	2009
Assets		
Total current assets	$7,986	$6,901
Property, plant, and equipment	4,836	4,198
Less: Accumulated depreciation	2,123	1,727
Goodwill	553	511

	Year Ended February 28,	
Statement of Cash Flows (dollars in millions)	2010	2009
Operating activities:		
Net income	$1,147	$ 989
Noncash items affecting net income:		
Depreciation	458	460
Investing activities:		
Additions to property, plant, and equipment	(716)	(617)

▌Requirements

1. How much was Parem's cost of plant assets at February 28, 2010? How much was the book value of plant assets? Show computations.
2. The financial statements give three evidences that Parem purchased plant assets and goodwill during fiscal year 2010. What are they?
3. Prepare T-accounts for Property, Plant, and Equipment; Accumulated Depreciation; and Goodwill. Then show all the activity in these accounts during 2010. Label each increase or decrease and give its dollar amount. During 2010, Parem sold plant assets that had cost the company $78 million (accumulated depreciation on these assets was $62 million). Assume there were no losses on goodwill during 2010.

P7-76B (*Learning Objective 5: Accounting for natural resources and the related expense*)   South Pacific Energy Company's balance sheet includes the asset Iron Ore. South Pacific Energy paid $2.2 million cash for a lease giving the firm the right to work a mine that contained an estimated 190,000 tons of ore. The company paid $61,000 to remove unwanted buildings from the land and $71,000 to prepare the surface for mining. South Pacific Energy also signed a $24,000 note payable to a landscaping company to return the land surface to its original condition after the lease ends. During the first year, South Pacific Energy removed 31,500 tons of ore, which it sold on account for $31 per ton. Operating expenses for the first year totaled $242,000, all paid in cash. In addition, the company accrued income tax at the tax rate of 25%.

▌Requirements

1. Record all of South Pacific Energy's transactions for the year.
2. Prepare the company's income statement for its iron ore operations for the first year. Evaluate the profitability of the company's operations.

P7-77B (*Learning Objectives 4, 7: Reporting plant asset transactions on the statement of cash flows*)   At the end of 2009, Great Financial Associates (GFA) had total assets of $17.4 billion and total liabilities of $9.9 billion. Included among the assets were property, plant, and equipment with a cost of $4.5 billion and accumulated depreciation of $3.3 billion.

GFA completed the following selected transactions during 2010: The company earned total revenues of $26.1 billion and incurred total expenses of $21.0 billion, which included depreciation of $1.9 billion. During the year, GFA paid $1.6 billion for new property, plant, and equipment and sold old plant assets for $0.4 billion. The cost of the assets sold was $1.2 billion, and their accumulated depreciation was $0.5 billion.

▌Requirements

1. Explain how to determine whether GFA had a gain or loss on the sale of old plant assets during the year. What was the amount of the gain or loss, if any?
2. Show how GFA would report property, plant, and equipment on the balance sheet at December 31, 2010, after all the year's activity. What was the book value of property, plant, and equipment?
3. Show how GFA would report its operating activities and investing activities on its statement of cash flows for 2010. Ignore gains and losses.

APPLY YOUR KNOWLEDGE

Decision Cases

writing assignment ■

Case 1. *(Learning Objectives 2, 3: Measuring profitability based on different inventory and depreciation methods)* Suppose you are considering investing in two businesses, La Petite France Bakery and Burgers Ahoy!. The two companies are virtually identical, and both began operations at the beginning of the current year. During the year, each company purchased inventory as follows:

Jan 4	10,000 units at $4 =	40,000
Apr 6	5,000 units at 5 =	25,000
Aug 9	7,000 units at 6 =	42,000
Nov 27	10,000 units at 7 =	70,000
Totals	32,000	$177,000

During the first year, both companies sold 25,000 units of inventory.

In early January, both companies purchased equipment costing $150,000 that had a 10-year estimated useful life and a $20,000 residual value. La Petite France uses the inventory and depreciation methods that maximize reported income. By contrast, Burgers uses the inventory and depreciation methods that minimize income tax payments. Assume that both companies' trial balances at December 31 included the following:

Sales revenue	$350,000
Operating expenses	50,000

The income tax rate is 40%.

❙ Requirements

1. Prepare both companies' income statements.
2. Write an investment newsletter to address the following questions: Which company appears to be more profitable? Which company has more cash to invest in promising projects? If prices continue rising over the long term, which company would you prefer to invest in? Why? (Challenge)

writing assignment ■

Case 2. *(Learning Objectives 1, 6: Accounting for plant assets and intangible assets)* The following questions are unrelated except that they all apply to plant assets and intangible assets:

1. The manager of Carpet World regularly debits the cost of repairs and maintenance of plant assets to Plant and Equipment. Why would she do that, since she knows she is violating GAAP?
2. The manager of Horizon Software regularly buys plant assets and debits the cost to Repairs and Maintenance Expense. Why would he do that, since he knows this action violates GAAP?
3. It has been suggested that because many intangible assets have no value except to the company that owns them, they should be valued at $1.00 or zero on the balance sheet. Many accountants disagree with this view. Which view do you support? Why?

Ethical Issue

United Jersey Bank of Princeton purchased land and a building for the lump sum of $6.0 million. To get the maximum tax deduction, the bank's managers allocated 80% of the purchase price to the building and only 20% to the land. A more realistic allocation would have been 60% to the building and 40% to the land.

❙ *Requirements*

1. What is the ethical issue in this situation?
2. Who are the stakeholders? What are the possible consequences to each?
3. Analyze the alternatives from the following standpoints: (a) economic, (b) legal, and (c) ethical.
4. What would you do? How would you justify your decision?

Focus on Financials: ■ Amazon.com, Inc.

(***Learning Objectives 2, 3, 6: Analyzing plant assets***) Refer to **Amazon.com, Inc.**'s Consolidated Financial Statements in Appendix A at the end of the book, and answer the following questions:

1. Refer to Note 1 and Note 3 of the Notes to Consolidated Financial Statements. What kinds of assets are included in fixed assets of Amazon.com, Inc?
2. Which depreciation method does Amazon.com, Inc., use for reporting to stockholders and creditors in the financial statements? What type of depreciation method does the company probably use for income tax purposes? Why is this method preferable for tax purposes?
3. Depreciation expense is embedded in the expense amounts listed on the income statement. It is reported on the Consolidated Statements of Cash Flows. How much was Amazon.com, Inc.'s depreciation and amortization expense during 2008? Now refer to Note 3 of the Notes to Consolidated Financial Statements. How much was Amazon.com, Inc.'s accumulated depreciation and amortization at the end of 2008? Explain why accumulated depreciation and amortization exceeds depreciation and amortization expense for the current year.
4. How much did Amazon.com, Inc., spend on fixed assets, including internal-use software and website development, during 2008? In 2007? Evaluate the trend in these capital expenditures as to whether it conveys good news or bad news for Amazon.com, Inc. Explain.
5. Refer to Notes 1 and 4 of the Notes to Consolidated Financial Statements. What are Amazon.com, Inc.'s intangible assets? How does the company account for each of these intangibles over its lifetime?

Focus on Analysis: ■ Foot Locker, Inc.

(***Learning Objectives 2, 4, 7: Explaining plant asset activity***) Refer to the **Foot Locker, Inc.**, Consolidated Financial Statements in Appendix B at the end of this book. This case leads you through a comprehensive analysis of Foot Locker, Inc.'s long-term assets. Its purpose is to show you how to account for plant asset (properties) transactions in summary form.

1. On the statement of cash flows, how much did Foot Locker, Inc., pay for capital expenditures during fiscal 2007? In what section of the cash flows statement do you find this amount? How much cash did Foot Locker, Inc., pay to repay capital leases in fiscal 2007? In what section of the cash flows statement was this recorded?
2. Explain Foot Locker, Inc.'s policy for capitalization of fixed assets. You can find this in Note 1 to the Consolidated Financial Statements (Summary of Significant Accounting Policies).
3. Which depreciation method does Foot Locker, Inc., use? Over what useful life does Foot Locker, Inc., depreciate various types of fixed assets?
4. Were Foot Locker, Inc.'s plant assets proportionately newer or older at the end of fiscal 2007 (versus 2006)? Explain your answer. (Challenge)

Group Project

Visit a local business.

❚ *Requirements*

1. List all its plant assets.
2. If possible, interview the manager. Gain as much information as you can about the business's plant assets. For example, try to determine the assets' costs, the depreciation method the company is using, and the estimated useful life of each asset category. If an interview is impossible, then develop your own estimates of the assets' costs, useful lives, and book values, assuming an appropriate depreciation method.
3. Determine whether the business has any intangible assets. If so, list them and gain as much information as possible about their nature, cost, and estimated useful lives.
4. Write a detailed report of your findings and be prepared to present your results to the class.

For online homework, exercises, and problems that provide you with immediate feedback, please visit www.myaccountinglab.com.

Quick Check Answers

1. *b* {[$1,380/($1,380 + $575 + $345)] × $1,900 = $1,140}
2. *d*
3. *b* ($45,000 − $5,000)/10 × 6/12 = $2,000)
4. *d* [($45,000 − $5,000)/10 × 2 = $8,000; $45,000 = $8,000 = $37,000]
5. *d* [$45,000 × .2 = $9,000; ($45,000 − $9,000) × .2 = $7,200]
6. *b* [($45,000 − $5,000)/5 × 4 = $16,000; $45,000 − $16,000 = $29,000; $36,500 − $29,000 = gain of $7,500]
7. *b* [$24,000 × 2/5 = $9,600; ($24,000 − $9,600) × 2/5 = $5,760; $9,600 + $5,760 = $15,360]
8. *b*
9. *b*
10. *b*
11. *d* [$270,000 × (3,000/90,000) = $30,000]
12. *e*

8

Liabilities

SPOTLIGHT: Southwest Airlines: A Success Story

Southwest Airlines has been a maverick in the airline industry from the start. In recent years, despite turmoil in the industry, Southwest has managed to stay profitable while other airlines have been in bankruptcy or close to it.

The airlines have some interesting liabilities. Southwest's Rapid Rewards program provides free flights to the company's frequent fliers. Southwest accrues frequent-flier liability for this program and reports "Accrued Liabilities" on the company's consolidated balance sheet.

Southwest collects cash in advance and then provides flights for customers later. This creates unearned revenue that Southwest reports as "Unearned Ticket Revenue." The company also has notes payable and bonds payable that it reports under "Long-Term Debt."

Southwest Airlines Co.
Consolidated Balance Sheet (Adapted)
December 31, 2008

(In millions)

Assets			Liabilities and Stockholders' Equity		
Current Assets			Current Liabilities		
Cash		$ 1,368	Accounts payable	$	668
Other current assets		1,525	Accrued liabilities		1,012
Total current assets		2,893	Unearned ticket revenue		963
Equipment and			Current maturities of		
property, net		11,040	long-term debt		163
Other assets		375	Total current liabilities		2,806
			Long-term debt		3,498
			Other long-term liabilities		3,051
			Stockholders' Equity		4,953
Total assets		$14,308	Total liabilities and equity		$14,308

This chapter shows how to account for liabilities—both current and long-term. We begin with current liabilities.

LEARNING OBJECTIVES

1 **Account** for current liabilities and contingent liabilities

2 **Account** for bonds payable

3 **Measure** interest expense

4 **Understand** the advantages and disadvantages of borrowing

5 **Report** liabilities on the balance sheet

CURRENT LIABILITIES

OBJECTIVE

1 Account for current liabilities and contingent liabilities

Current liabilities are obligations due within one year or within the company's normal operating cycle if longer than a year. Obligations due beyond that period of time are classified as *long-term liabilities*.

Current liabilities are of two kinds:

- Known amounts
- Estimated amounts

We look first at current liabilities of a known amount.

Current Liabilities of Known Amount

Current liabilities of known amount include accounts payable, short-term notes payable, sales tax payable, accrued liabilities, payroll liabilities, unearned revenues, and current portion of long-term debt.

Accounts Payable. Amounts owed for products or services purchased on account are *accounts payable*. For example, Southwest Airlines purchases soft drinks and napkins on accounts payable. We have seen many other accounts payable examples in preceding chapters. One of a merchandiser's most common transactions is the credit purchase of inventory. **Best Buy** and **Wal-Mart** buy their inventory on account.

Short-Term Notes Payable.   **Short-term notes payable**, a common form of financing, are notes payable due within one year. **Starbucks** lists its short-term notes payable as *short-term borrowings*. Starbucks may issue short-term notes payable to borrow cash or to purchase assets. On its notes payable, Starbucks must accrue interest expense and interest payable at the end of the period. The following sequence of entries covers the purchase of inventory, accrual of interest expense, and payment of a 10% short-term note payable that's due in one year.

2010			
Jan 1	Inventory	8,000	
	Note Payable, Short-Term		8,000
	Purchase of inventory by issuing a note payable.		

This transaction increases both an asset and a liability.

Assets	=	Liabilities	+	Stockholders' Equity
+ 8,000	=	+ 8,000	+	0

The Starbucks fiscal year ends each September 30. At year-end, Starbucks must accrue interest expense at 10% for January through September:

Sep 30	Interest Expense ($8,000 × .10 × 9/12)	600	
	Interest Payable		600
	Accrual of interest expense at year-end.		

Liabilities increase and equity decreases because of the expense.

Assets	=	Liabilities	+	Stockholders' Equity	–	Expenses
0	=	+ 600				– 600

The balance sheet at year-end will report the Note Payable of $8,000 and the related Interest Payable of $600 as current liabilities. The income statement will report interest expense of $600.

The following entry records the note's payment at maturity on January 1, 2011:

2011			
Jan 1	Note Payable, Short-Term	8,000	
	Interest Payable	600	
	Interest Expense ($8,000 × .10 × 3/12)	200	
	Cash [$8,000 + ($8,000 × .10)]		8,800
	Payment of a note payable and interest at maturity.		

The debits zero out the payables and also record Starbucks' interest expense for October, November, and December.

Sales Tax Payable.   Most states levy a sales tax on retail sales. Retailers collect the tax from customers and thus owe the state for sales tax collected. Suppose one Saturday's sales at a Home Depot store totaled $200,000. Home Depot collected an additional 5% ($10,000) of sales tax. The store would record that day's sales as follows:

Cash ($200,000 × 1.05)	210,000	
Sales Revenue		200,000
Sales Tax Payable ($200,000 × .05)		10,000
To record cash sales and the related sales tax.		

Assets, liabilities, and equity all increase—equity because of the revenues.

Assets	=	Liabilities	+	Stockholders' Equity	+	Revenues
+ 210,000	=	+ 10,000				+ 200,000

Accrued Liabilities (Accrued Expenses).   An **accrued liability** usually results from an expense the business has incurred but not yet paid. Therefore, an accrued expense creates a liability, which explains why it is also called an **accrued expense**.

For example, Southwest Airlines' salary expense and salary payable occur as employees work for the company. Interest expense accrues with the passage of time. There are several categories of accrued expenses:

- Salaries and Wages Payable
- Interest Payable
- Income Taxes Payable

Salaries and Wages Payable is the liability for payroll expenses not yet paid at the end of the period. This category includes salaries, wages, and payroll taxes withheld from employee paychecks. *Interest Payable* is the company's interest payable on notes payable. *Income Taxes Payable* is the amount of income tax the company still owes at year-end.

Payroll Liabilities.   **Payroll**, also called *employee compensation*, is a major expense. For service organizations—such as law firms, real estate companies, and airlines—compensation is *the* major expense, just as cost of goods sold is the largest expense for a merchandising company.

Employee compensation takes many different forms. A *salary* is employee pay stated at a monthly or yearly rate. A *wage* is employee pay stated at an hourly rate. Sales employees earn a *commission*, which is a percentage of the sales the employee has made. A *bonus* is an amount over and above regular compensation. Accounting for all forms of compensation follows the pattern illustrated in Exhibit 8-1 (using assumed figures).

EXHIBIT 8-1 | **Accounting for Payroll Expenses and Liabilities**

Salary Expense	10,000	
Employee Income Tax Payable		1,200
FICA Tax Payable		800
Salary Payable to Employees [take-home pay]		8,000
To record salary expense.		

Every expense accrual has the same effect: Liabilities increase and equity decreases because of the expense. The accounting equation shows these effects.

Assets	=	Liabilities	+	Stockholders' Equity	–	Expenses
		+ 1,200				– 10,000
0	=	+ 800				
		+ 8,000				

Salary expense represents *gross pay* (that is, employee pay before subtractions for taxes and other deductions). Salary expense creates several payroll liabilities:

- *Employee Income Tax Payable* is the employees' income tax that has been withheld from paychecks.
- *FICA Tax Payable* includes the employees' Social Security tax and Medicare tax, which also are withheld from paychecks. (FICA stands for the Federal Insurance Contributions Act, which created the Social Security tax.)
- *Salary Payable* to employees is their net (take-home) pay.

Companies must also pay some *employer* payroll taxes and expenses for employee benefits. Accounting for these expenses is similar to the illustration in Exhibit 8-1.

Unearned Revenues.   *Unearned revenues* are also called *deferred revenues* and *revenues collected in advance.* For all unearned revenue the business has received cash from customers before earning the revenue. The company has a liability—an obligation to provide goods or services to the customer. Let's consider an example.

Southwest Airlines sells tickets and collects cash in advance. Southwest therefore reports Unearned Ticket Revenue for airline tickets sold in advance.[1] At December 31, 2008, Southwest owed customers $963 million of air travel (see page 468). Let's see how Southwest accounts for unearned ticket revenue.

---

[1]Some airlines call this liability "Air Traffic Liability."

Assume that Southwest collects $300 for a round-trip ticket from Dallas to Los Angeles and back. Southwest records the cash collection and related liability as follows:

2010			
Dec 15	Cash	300	
	Unearned Ticket Revenue		300
	Received cash in advance for ticket sales.		

Unearned Ticket Revenue	
	300

Suppose the customer flies to Los Angeles late in December. Southwest records the revenue earned as follows:

2010			
Dec 28	Unearned Ticket Revenue	150	
	Ticket Revenue ($300 × 1/2)		150
	Earned revenue that was collected in advance.		

The liability decreases and the revenue goes up.

Unearned Ticket Revenue			
150		300	
	Bal	150	

Ticket Revenue	
	150

At year-end, Southwest reports

- $150 of unearned ticket revenue (a liability) on the balance sheet
- $150 of ticket revenue on the income statement

The customer returns to Dallas in January 2011, and Southwest records the revenue earned with this journal entry:

2011			
Jan 4	Unearned Ticket Revenue	150	
	Ticket Revenue ($300 × 1/2)		150
	Earned revenue that was collected in advance.		

Now the liability balance is zero because Southwest has earned all the revenue it collected in advance.

Unearned Ticket Revenue			
150		300	
150			
	Bal	0	

Current Portion of Long-Term Debt.   Some long-term debt must be paid in installments. The **current portion of long-term debt** (also called *current maturity* or *current installment*) is the amount of the principal that is payable within one year. At the end of each year, a company reclassifies (from long-term debt to a current liability) the amount of its long-term debt that must be paid next year.

Southwest Airlines reports Current Maturities of Long-Term Debt as a current liability. Southwest also reports a long-term liability for Long-Term Debt, which excludes the current maturities. *Long-term debt* refers to long-term notes payable and bonds payable, which we cover in the second half of this chapter.

Current Liabilities That Must Be Estimated

A business may know that a liability exists but not know its exact amount. The business must report the liability on the balance sheet. Estimated liabilities vary among companies. Let's look first at Estimated Warranty Payable, a liability account that most merchandisers have.

Estimated Warranty Payable.   Many companies guarantee their products under *warranty* agreements. The warranty period may extend for 90 days to a year for consumer products. Automobile companies—General Motors, BMW, and Toyota—accrue liabilities for vehicle warranties.

Whatever the warranty's life, the matching principle demands that the company record the *warranty expense* in the same period that the business records sales revenue. After all, the warranty motivates customers to buy products, so the company must record warranty expense. At the time of the sale, however, the company doesn't know which products are defective. The exact amount of warranty expense cannot be known with certainty, so the business must estimate warranty expense and the related liability.

Assume that **Black & Decker**, which manufactures power tools, made sales of $100,000 subject to product warranties. Assume that in past years between 2% and 4% of products proved defective. Black & Decker could estimate that 3% of sales will require repair or replacement. In this case Black & Decker would estimate warranty expense of $3,000 ($100,000 × 0.03) for the year and make the following entry:

Warranty Expense	3,000	
Estimated Warranty Payable		3,000
To accrue warranty expense.		

Estimated Warranty Payable	
	3,000

Assume that defects add up to $2,800, and Black & Decker will replace the defective products. Black & Decker then records the following:

Estimated Warranty Payable	2,800	
Inventory		2,800
To replace defective products sold under warranty.		

Estimated Warranty Payable		
2,800		3,000
	Bal	200

At the end of the year Black & Decker will report Estimated Warranty Payable of $200 as a current liability. The income statement reports Warranty Expense of $3,000 for the year. Then, next year Black & Decker will repeat this process. The Estimated Warranty Payable account probably won't ever zero out.

If Black & Decker paid cash to satisfy the warranty, then the credit would be to Cash rather than to Inventory. Vacation pay is another expense that must be estimated. And income taxes must be estimated because the final amount isn't determined until early the next year.

Contingent Liabilities

A *contingent liability* is not an actual liability. Instead, it's a potential liability that depends on the future outcome of past events. Examples of contingent liabilities are future obligations that may arise because of lawsuits, tax disputes, or alleged violations of environmental protection laws. The principle of conservatism, discussed in Chapter 6, requires that companies avoid painting too "rosy" a picture of their financial positions. With liabilities, that principle says "When in doubt, disclose. When necessary, accrue." The Financial Accounting Standards Board (FASB) provides these guidelines to account for contingent liabilities:[2]

1. *Accrue* (i.e., make an adjusting journal entry for) a contingent liability if it's *probable* that the loss (or expense) will occur **and** the *amount can be reasonably estimated*. Warranty expense, illustrated on the previous page, is an example. Another example is a lawsuit that has been settled as of the balance sheet date but has not yet been paid.

2. *Disclose* a contingency in a financial statement note if it's *reasonably possible* that a loss (or expense) will occur. Lawsuits in progress are a prime example. Southwest Airlines includes a note in its financial statements to report contingent liabilities from examinations of its past income tax returns by the IRS.

---

[2]The FASB is currently reconsidering its disclosure requirements for contingent liabilities. If the new requirements are adopted, entities will be required to greatly expand disclosures of their loss contingencies. Specifically, *regardless of likelihood*, entities will be required to *disclose* loss contingencies (a) if they are expected to be resolved within the next year; and (b) if, in the opinion of management, they could have a *severe impact* on the entity's financial position, cash flows, or results of operation. An example of such a situation is a lawsuit that could put the company out of business within the next year. Both quantitative (dollar amounts) and qualitative (descriptive) information would be included. In addition, for all amounts *accrued*, the entity would have to include a table and explanations that show how these accruals have changed from the previous period.

> **Note 17, Contingencies**
> The Company is subject to various legal proceedings [...] including [...] examinations by the Internal Revenue Service (IRS). The IRS regularly examines the Company's federal income tax returns and, in the course thereof, proposes adjustments to the Company's federal income tax liability reported on such returns.
> The Company's management does not expect that [...] any of its currently ongoing legal proceedings or [...] any proposed adjustments [...] by the IRS [...] will have a material adverse effect on the Company's financial condition, results of operations or cash flow.

3. There is no need to report a contingent loss that is unlikely to occur. Instead, wait until an actual transaction clears up the situation. For example, suppose **Del Monte Foods** grows vegetables in Nicaragua, and the Nicaraguan government threatens to confiscate the assets of all foreign companies. Del Monte will report nothing about the contingency if the probability of a loss is considered remote.

A contingent liability may arise from lawsuits that claim wrongdoing by the company. The plantiff may seek damages through the courts. If the court or the IRS rules in favor of Southwest, there is no liability. But if the ruling favors the plaintiff, then Southwest will have an actual liability. It would be unethical to omit these disclosures from the financial statements because investors need this information to properly evaluate a company.

The international accounting standard for loss contingencies requires accrual (i.e., journal entries) for **both** probable and possible contingent liabilities.

The IASB is studying its existing standard with a view toward harmonizing it with the changes that are being contemplated by the FASB (discussed in the footnote on p. 474). Regardless of the outcome of the changes that are being proposed by both the IASB and FASB, it is likely that future financial statements of all companies will include **more disclosures of both quantitative and qualitative information** for contingent liabilities than are presently required.

Appendix F summarizes differences between U.S. GAAP and IFRS, cross-referenced by chapter.

Are All Liabilities Reported on the Balance Sheet?

The big danger with liabilities is that you may fail to report a large debt on your balance sheet. What is the consequence of missing a large liability? You will definitely understate your liabilities and your debt ratio. By failing to accrue interest on the liability, you'll probably overstate your net income as well. In short, your financial statements will make you look better than you really are. Any such error, if significant, hurts a company's credibility.

Contingent liabilities are very easy to overlook because they aren't actual debts. How would you feel if you owned stock in a company that failed to report a contingency that put the company out of business? If you had known of the contingency, you could have sold the stock and avoided the loss. In this case, you would hire a lawyer to file suit against the company for negligent financial reporting.

> **COOKING THE BOOKS**
> with Liabilities
> **Crazy Eddie, Inc.**

Accidentally understating liabilities is one thing, but doing it intentionally is quite another. When unethical management decides to cook the books in the area of liabilities, its strategy is to **deliberately understate recorded liabilities**. This can be done by intentionally under-recording the amount of existing liabilities, or by omitting certain liabilities altogether.

Crazy Eddie, Inc., first discussed in Chapter 6, used *multiple tactics* to overstate its financial position from 1984 through 1987. In addition to overstating inventory (thus understating cost of goods sold and overstating income), the management of the company deliberately *understated accounts payable* by issuing fictitious (false) debit memoranda from suppliers (vendors). A debit memo is issued for goods returned to a vendor, such as Sony. When a debit memorandum is issued, accounts payable are debited (reduced), thus reducing current liabilities and increasing the current ratio. Eventually, expenses are also decreased, and profits are correspondingly increased through reduction of expenses. Crazy Eddie, Inc., issued $3 million of fictitious debit memoranda in 1985, making the company's current ratio and debt ratio look better than they actually were, and eventually overstating profits. ▲

SUMMARY OF CURRENT LIABILITIES

Let's summarize what we've covered thus far. A company can report its current liabilities on the balance sheet as follows:

Accounting, Inc.
Balance Sheet
December 31, 2010

Assets		Liabilities	
Current Assets:		Current liabilities:	
Cash		Accounts payable	
Short-term investments		Salary payable*	
Etc.		Interest payable*	
		Income tax payable*	
Property, plant, and equipment:		Unearned revenue	
Land		Estimated warranty payable*	
Etc.		Notes payable, short-term	
		Current portion of long-term debt	
Other assets		Total current liabilities	
		Long-term liabilities	
		Stockholders' Equity	
		Common stock	
		Retained earnings	
Total assets	$XXX	Total liabilities and stockholders equity	$XXX

*These items are often combined and reported in a single total as "Accrued Liabilities" or "Accrued Expenses Payable."

On its income statement this company would report

- *Expenses* related to some of the current liabilities. Examples include Salary Expense, Interest Expense, Income Tax Expense, and Warranty Expense.
- *Revenue* related to the unearned revenue. Examples include Service Revenue and Sales Revenue that were collected in advance.

MID-CHAPTER SUMMARY PROBLEM

Assume that the Estée Lauder Companies, Inc., faced the following liability situations at June 30, 2010, the end of the company's fiscal year. Show how Estée Lauder would report these liabilities on its balance sheet at June 30, 2010.

a. Salary expense for the last payroll period of the year was $900,000. Of this amount, employees' withheld income tax totaled $88,000 and FICA taxes were $61,000. These payroll amounts will be paid in early July.

b. On fiscal-year 2010 sales of $400 million, management estimates warranty expense of 2%. One year ago, at June 30, 2009, Estimated Warranty Payable stood at $3 million. Warranty payments were $9 million during the year ended June 30, 2010.

c. The company pays royalties on its purchased trademarks. Royalties for the trademarks are equal to a percentage of Estée Lauder's sales. Assume that sales in 2010 were $400 million and were subject to a royalty rate of 3%. At June 30, 2010, Estée Lauder owes two-thirds of the year's royalty, to be paid in July.

d. Long-term debt totals $100 million and is payable in annual installments of $10 million each. The interest rate on the debt is 7%, and the interest is paid each December 31.

Answer

Liabilities at June 30, 2010:	
a. Current liabilities:	
Salary payable ($900,000 − $88,000 − $61,000)...............	$ 751,000
Employee income tax payable	88,000
FICA tax payable	61,000
b. Current liabilities:	
Estimated warranty payable..	2,000,000
[$3,000,000 + ($400,000,000 × 0.02) − $9,000,000]	
c. Current liabilities:	
Royalties payable ($400,000,000 × 0.03 × 2/3).................	8,000,000
d. Current liabilities:	
Current installment of long-term debt................................	10,000,000
Interest payable ($100,000,000 × 0.07 × 6/12)..................	3,500,000
Long-term debt ($100,000,000 − $10,000,000).....................	90,000,000

LONG-TERM LIABILITIES: BONDS AND NOTES PAYABLE

Large companies such as Southwest Airlines, Home Depot, and **Toyota** cannot borrow billions from a single lender. So how do corporations borrow huge amounts? They issue (sell) bonds to the public. **Bonds payable** are groups of notes payable issued to multiple lenders, called *bondholders*. Southwest Airlines needs airplanes and can borrow large amounts by issuing bonds to thousands of individual investors, who each lend Southwest a modest amount. Southwest receives the cash it needs, and each investor limits risk by diversifying investments—not putting all the investor's "eggs in one basket." Here we treat bonds payable and notes payable together because their accounting is the same.

Bonds: An Introduction

Each bond payable is, in effect, a note payable. Bonds payable are debts of the issuing company.

Purchasers of bonds receive a bond's certificate, which carries the issuing company's name. The certificate also states the *principal*, which is typically stated in units of $1,000; principal is also called the bond's *face value*, *maturity value*, or *par value*. The bond obligates the issuing company to pay the debt at a specific future time called the *maturity date*.

Interest is the rental fee on borrowed money. The bond certificate states the interest rate that the issuer will pay the holder and the dates that the interest payments are due (generally twice a year). Exhibit 8-2 shows an actual bond certificate.

Issuing bonds usually requires the services of a securities firm, such as Merrill Lynch, to act as the underwriter of the bond issue. The **underwriter** purchases the bonds from the issuing company and resells them to its clients, or it may sell the bonds to its clients and earn a commission on the sale.

EXHIBIT 8-2 | **Bond (Note) Certificate (Adapted)**

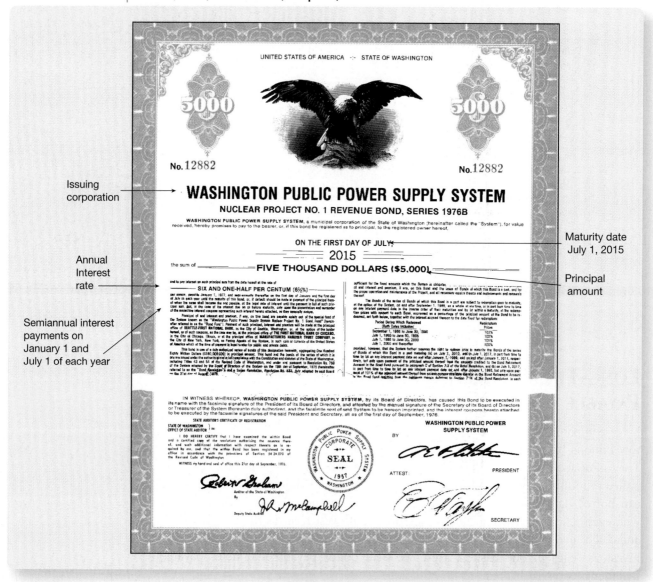

Types of Bonds. All the bonds in a particular issue may mature at the same time (**term bonds**) or in installments over a period of time (**serial bonds**). Serial bonds are like installment notes payable. Some of Southwest Airlines' long-term debts are serial in nature because they are payable in installments.

Secured, or *mortgage*, *bonds* give the bondholder the right to take specified assets of the issuer if the company *defaults*—that is, fails to pay interest or principal. *Unsecured bonds*, called **debentures**, are backed only by the good faith of the borrower. Debentures carry a higher rate of interest than secured bonds because debentures are riskier investments.

Bond Prices. Investors may buy and sell bonds through bond markets. Bond prices are quoted at a percentage of their maturity value. For example,

- A $1,000 bond quoted at 100 is bought or sold for $1,000, which is 100% of its face value.
- The same bond quoted at 101.5 has a market price of $1,015 (101.5% of face value = $1,000 × 1.015).
- A $1,000 bond quoted at 88.375 is priced at $883.75 ($1,000 × 0.88375).

Bond Premium and Bond Discount. A bond issued at a price above its face (par) value is said to be issued at a **premium**, and a bond issued at a price below face (par) value has a **discount**.

Premium on Bonds Payable has a *credit* balance and Discount on Bonds Payable carries a *debit* balance. Bond Discount is therefore a contra liability account.

As a bond nears maturity, its market price moves toward par value. Therefore, the price of a bond issued at a

- premium decreases toward maturity value.
- discount increases toward maturity value.

On the maturity date, a bond's market value exactly equals its face value because the company that issued the bond pays that amount to retire the bond.

The Time Value of Money. A dollar received today is worth more than a dollar to be received in the future. You can invest today's dollar immediately and earn income from it. But if you must wait to receive the dollar, you forgo the interest revenue. Money earns income over time, a fact called the *time value of money*. Let's examine how the *time value of money* affects the pricing of bonds.

Assume that a Southwest Airlines bond with a face value of $1,000 reaches maturity three years from today and carries no interest. Would you pay $1,000 today to purchase this bond? No, because the payment of $1,000 today to receive the same amount in the future provides you with no income on the investment. Just how much would you pay today to receive $1,000 at the end of three years? The answer is some amount *less* than $1,000. Let's suppose that you feel $750 is a good price. By investing $750 now to receive $1,000 later, you earn $250 interest revenue over the three years. The issuing company such as Southwest Airlines, sees the transaction this way: Southwest will pay you $250 interest to use your $750 for three years.

The amount to invest *now* to receive more later is called the **present value** of a future amount. In our example, $750 is the present value, and $1,000 is the future amount.

Our $750 bond price is a reasonable estimate. The exact present value of any future amount depends on

1. the amount of the future payment ($1,000 in our example).
2. the length of time from the investment date to the date when the future amount is to be collected (three years).
3. the interest rate during the period (say 10%).

In this case the present value is very close to $750. Present value is always less than the future amount. We discuss how present value is computed in Appendix C at the end of the book (pp. 885–894).

Bond Interest Rates Determine Bond Prices.   Bonds are always sold at their *market price*, which is the amount investors will pay for the bond. **Market price is the bond's present value**, which equals the present value of the principal payment plus the present value of the cash interest payments. Interest is usually paid semiannually (twice a year). Some companies pay interest annually or quarterly.

Two interest rates work to set the price of a bond:

- The **stated interest rate**, also called the coupon rate, is the interest rate printed on the bond certificate. The stated interest rate determines the amount of cash interest the borrower pays—and the investor receives—each year. Suppose Southwest Airlines bonds have a stated interest rate of 9%. Southwest would pay $9,000 of interest annually on each $100,000 bond. Each semiannual payment would be $4,500 ($100,000 × 0.09 × 6/12).
- The **market interest rate**, or *effective interest rate*, is the rate that investors demand for loaning their money. The market interest rate varies by the minute.

A company may issue bonds with a stated interest rate that differs from the prevailing market interest rate. In fact, the two interest rates often differ.

Exhibit 8-3 shows how the stated interest rate and the market interest rate interact to determine the issue price of a bond payable for three separate cases.

EXHIBIT 8-3 | **How the Stated Interest Rate and the Market Interest Rate Interact to Determine the Price of a Bond**

Issue Price of Bonds Payable

Case A:

Stated interest rate on a bond payable	equals	Market interest rate	Therefore,	Price of face (par, or maturity) value
Example: 9%	=	9%	→	*Par: $1,000 bond issued for $1,000*

Case B:

Stated interest rate on a bond payable	less than	Market interest rate	Therefore,	Discount price (price below face value)
Example: 9%	<	10%	→	*Discount: $1,000 bond issued for a price below $1,000*

Case C:

Stated interest rate on a bond payable	greater than	Market interest rate	Therefore,	Premium price (price above face value)
Example: 9%	>	8%	→	*Premium: $1,000 bond issued for a price above $1,000*

Southwest Airlines may issue 9% bonds when the market rate has risen to 10%. Will the Southwest 9% bonds attract investors in this market? No, because investors can earn 10% on other bonds of similar risk. Therefore, investors will purchase Southwest bonds only at a price less than their face value. The difference between the lower price and face value is a *discount* (Exhibit 8-3). Conversely, if the market interest rate is 8%, Southwest's 9% bonds will be so attractive that investors will pay more than face value to purchase them. The difference between the higher price and face value is a *premium*.

Issuing Bonds Payable at Par (Face Value)

OBJECTIVE

2 **Account** for bonds payable

We start with the most straightforward situation—issuing bonds at their par value. There is no premium or discount on these bonds payable.

Suppose Southwest Airlines has $50,000 of 9% bonds payable that mature in five years. Assume that Southwest issued these bonds at par on January 1, 2010. The issuance entry is

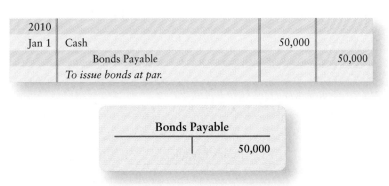

2010			
Jan 1	Cash	50,000	
	Bonds Payable		50,000
	To issue bonds at par.		

Bonds Payable

	50,000

Assets and liabilities increase when a company issues bonds payable.

Assets	=	Liabilities	+	Stockholders' Equity
+ 50,000	=	+ 50,000	+	0

Southwest, the borrower, makes a one-time entry to record the receipt of cash and the issuance of bonds. Afterward, investors buy and sell the bonds through the bond markets. These later buy-and-sell transactions between outside investors do *not* involve Southwest at all.

Interest payments occur each January 1 and July 1. Southwest's entry to record the first semiannual interest payment is

2010			
Jul 1	Interest Expense ($50,000 × 0.09 × 6/12)	2,250	
	Cash		2,250
	To pay semiannual interest.		

The payment of interest expense decreases assets and equity. Bonds payable are not affected.

Assets	=	Liabilities	+	Stockholders' Equity	−	Expenses
− 2,250	=	0	+			− 2,250

At year-end, Southwest accrues interest expense and interest payable for six months (July through December), as follows:

2010			
Dec 31	Interest Expense ($50,000 × 0.09 × 6/12)	2,250	
	Interest Payable		2,250
	To accrue interest.		

Liabilities increase, and equity decreases.

Assets	=	Liabilities	+	Stockholders' Equity	−	Expenses
0	=	+ 2,250	+			− 2,250

On January 1, Southwest will pay the interest, debiting Interest Payable and crediting Cash. Then, at maturity, Southwest pays off the bonds as follows:

2015			
Jan 1	Bonds Payable	50,000	
	Cash		50,000
	To pay bonds payable at maturity.		

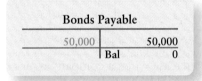

Bonds Payable

50,000	50,000
	Bal 0

Assets	=	Liabilities	+	Stockholders' Equity
− 50,000	=	− 50,000		

Issuing Bonds Payable at a Discount

Market conditions may force a company to issue bonds at a discount. Suppose Southwest Airlines issued $100,000 of 9%, five-year bonds when the market interest rate is 10%. The market price of the bonds drops, and Southwest receives $96,149[3] at issuance. The transaction is recorded as follows:

2010			
Jan 1	Cash	96,149	
	Discount on Bonds Payable	3,851	
	Bonds Payable		100,000
	To issue bonds at a discount.		

---

[3]Appendix C at the end of this book shows how to determine the price of this bond.

The accounting equation shows that Southwest has a net liability of $96,149—not $100,000.

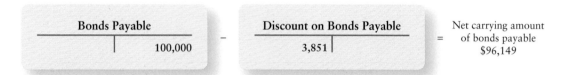

Assets	=	Liabilities	+	Stockholders' Equity
+ 96,149	=	− 3,851	+	0
		+ 100,000		

The bonds payable accounts have a net balance of $96,149 as follows:

Bonds Payable			Discount on Bonds Payable		Net carrying amount
	100,000	−	3,851	=	of bonds payable $96,149

Southwest's balance sheet immediately after issuance of the bonds would report the following:

Total current liabilities..................................	$ XXX
Long-term liabilities:	
Bonds payable, 9%, due 2015....................	$100,000
Less: Discount on bonds payable...............	(3,851) 96,149

Discount on Bonds Payable is a contra account to Bonds Payable, a decrease in the company's liabilities. Subtracting the discount from Bonds Payable yields the *carrying amount* of the bonds. Thus, Southwest's liability is $96,149, which is the amount the company borrowed.

What Is the Interest Expense on These Bonds Payable?

Southwest pays interest on bonds semiannually, which is common practice. Each semiannual *interest payment* is set by the bond contract and therefore remains the same over the life of the bonds:

OBJECTIVE

3 **Measure** interest expense

$$\text{Semiannual interest payment} = \$100,000 \times 0.09 \times 6/12$$
$$= \$4,500$$

But Southwest's *interest expense* increases as the bonds march toward maturity. Remember: These bonds were issued at a discount.

Panel A of Exhibit 8-4 on the following page repeats the Southwest Airlines bond data we've been using. Panel B provides an amortization table that does two things:

- Determines the periodic interest expense (column B)
- Shows the bond carrying amount (column E)

Study the exhibit carefully because the amounts we'll be using come directly from the amortization table. This exhibit shows the *effective-interest method of amortization*, which is the correct way to measure interest expense.

EXHIBIT 8-4 | Debt Amortization for a Bond Discount

Panel A—Bond Data

Issue date—January 1, 2010	Maturity date—January 1, 2015
Face (par or *maturity*) value—$100,000	Market interest rate at time of issue—10% annually, 5% semiannually
Stated interest rate—9%	Issue price—$96,149
Interest paid—4½% semiannually, $4,500 = $100,000 × 0.09 × 6/12	

Panel B—Amortization Table

	A	B	C	D	E
Semiannual Interest Date	Interest Payment (4 1/2% of Maturity Value)	Interest Expense (5% of Preceding Bond Carrying Amount)	Discount Amortization (B – A)	Discount Account Balance (Preceding D – C)	Bond Carrying Amount ($100,000 – D)
Jan 1, 2010				$3,851	$ 96,149
Jul 1	$4,500	$4,807	$307	3,544	96,456
Jan 1, 2011	4,500	4,823	323	3,221	96,779
Jul 1	4,500	4,839	339	2,882	97,118
Jan 1, 2012	4,500	4,856	356	2,526	97,474
Jul 1	4,500	4,874	374	2,152	97,848
Jan 1, 2013	4,500	4,892	392	1,760	98,240
Jul 1	4,500	4,912	412	1,348	98,652
Jan 1, 2014	4,500	4,933	433	915	99,085
Jul 1	4,500	4,954	454	461	99,539
Jan 1, 2015	4,500	4,961*	461	-0-	100,000

*Adjusted for effect of rounding

Notes
- Column A The semiannual interest payments are constant—fixed by the bond contract.
- Column B The interest expense each period = the preceding bond carrying amount × the market interest rate. Interest expense increases as the bond carrying amount (E) increases.
- Column C The discount amortization (C) is the excess of interest expense (B) over interest payment (A).
- Column D The discount balance (D) decreases when amortized.
- Column E The bond carrying amount (E) increases from $96,149 at issuance to $100,000 at maturity.

Interest Expense on Bonds Issued at a Discount

In Exhibit 8-4, Southwest Airlines borrowed $96,149 cash but must pay $100,000 when the bonds mature. What happens to the $3,851 balance of the discount account over the life of the bond issue?

The $3,851 is additional interest expense to Southwest over and above the stated interest that Southwest pays each six months. Exhibit 8-5 graphs the interest expense and the interest payment on the Southwest bonds over their lifetime. Observe that the semiannual interest payment is fixed—by contract—at $4,500. But the amount of interest expense increases as the discount bond marches upward toward maturity.

EXHIBIT 8-5 | **Interest Expense on Bonds Payable Issued at a Discount**

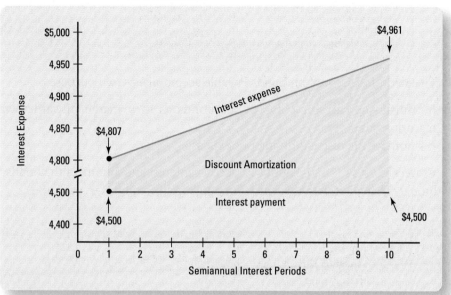

The discount is allocated to interest expense through amortization over the term of the bonds. Exhibit 8-6 illustrates the amortization of the bonds from $96,149 at the start to $100,000 at maturity. These amounts come from Exhibit 8-4, column E (p. 484).

Now let's see how Southwest would account for these bonds issued at a discount. In our example, Southwest issued its bonds on January 1, 2010. On July 1, Southwest made the first semiannual interest payment. But Southwest's interest expense is greater than its payment of $4,500. Southwest's journal entry to record interest expense and the interest payment for the first 6 months follows (with all amounts taken from Exhibit 8-4):

EXHIBIT 8-6 | **Amortizing Bonds Payable Issued at a Discount**

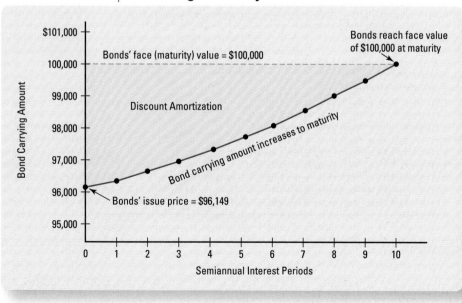

2010			
Jul 1	Interest Expense	4,807	
	Discount on Bonds Payable		307
	Cash		4,500
	To pay semiannual interest and amortize bond discount.		

The credit to Discount on Bonds Payable accomplishes two purposes:

- It adjusts the carrying value of the bonds as they march upward toward maturity value.
- It amortizes the discount to interest expense.

At December 31, 2010, Southwest accrues interest and amortizes the bonds for July through December with this entry (amounts from Exhibit 8-4, page 484):

2010			
Dec 31	Interest Expense	4,823	
	Discount on Bonds Payable		323
	Interest Payable		4,500
	To accrue semiannual interest and amortize bond discount.		

At December 31, 2010, Southwest's bond accounts appear as follows:

Bonds Payable		Discount on Bonds Payable	
	100,000	3,851	307
			323
		Bal 3,221	

Bond carrying amount, $96,779 = $100,000 − $3,221 from Exhibit 8-4, page 484.

STOP & THINK...

What would Southwest Airlines' 2010 income statement and year-end balance sheet report for these bonds?

Answer:

Income Statement for 2010		
Interest expense ($4,807 + $4,823)		$ 9,630
Balance Sheet at December 31, 2010		
Current liabilities:		
Interest payable		$ 4,500
Long-term liabilities:		
Bonds payable	$100,000	
Less: Discount on bonds payable...............	(3,221)	96,779

At maturity on January 1, 2015, the discount will have been amortized to zero, and the bonds' carrying amount will be face value of $100,000. Southwest will retire the bonds by paying $100,000 to the bondholders.

Partial-Period Interest Amounts

Companies don't always issue bonds at the beginning or the end of their accounting year. They issue bonds when market conditions are most favorable, and that may be on May 16, August 1, or any other date. To illustrate partial-period interest, assume **Google Inc.** issues $100,000 of 8% bonds payable at 96 on August 31, 2010. The market rate of interest was 9%, and these bonds pay semiannual interest on February 28 and August 31 each year. The first few lines of Google's amortization table are

Semiannual Interest Date	4% Interest Payment	4 ½% Interest Expense	Discount Amortization	Discount Account Balance	Bond Carrying Amount
Aug 31, 2010				$4,000	$96,000
Feb 28, 2011	$4,000	$4,320	$320	3,680	96,320
Aug 31, 2011	4,000	4,334	334	3,346	96,654

Google's accounting year ends on December 31, so at year-end Google must accrue interest and amortize bond discount for four months (September through December). At December 31, 2010, Google will make this entry:

	2010			
Dec 31	Interest Expense ($4,320 × 4/6)		2,880	
	Discount on Bonds Payable ($320 × 4/6)			213
	Interest Payable ($4,000 × 4/6)			2,667
	To accrue interest and amortize discount at year-end.			

The year-end entry at December 31, 2010, uses 4/6 of the upcoming semiannual amounts at February 28, 2011. This example clearly illustrates the benefit of an amortization schedule.

Issuing Bonds Payable at a Premium

Let's modify the Southwest Airlines bond example to illustrate issuance of the bonds at a premium. Assume that Southwest issues $100,000 of five-year, 9% bonds that pay interest semiannually. If the 9% bonds are issued when the market interest rate is 8%, their issue price is $104,100.[4] The premium on these bonds is $4,100, and Exhibit 8-7 on the following page shows how to amortize the bonds by the effective-interest method. In practice, bond premiums are rare because few companies issue their bonds to pay cash interest above the market interest rate. We cover bond premiums for completeness.

Southwest's entries to record issuance of the bonds on January 1, 2010, and to make the first interest payment and amortize the bonds on July 1, are as follows:

	2010			
Jan 1	Cash		104,100	
	Bonds Payable			100,000
	Premium on Bonds Payable			4,100
	To issue bonds at a premium.			

---

[4]Appendix C at the end of this book shows how to determine the price of this bond.

At the beginning, Southwest's liability is $104,100—not $100,000. The accounting equation makes this clear.

Assets	=	Liabilities	+	Stockholders' Equity
+ 104,100	=	+ 100,000	+	0
		+ 4,100		

2010			
Jul 1	Interest Expense (from Exhibit 8-7)	4,164	
	Premium on Bonds Payable	336	
	Cash		4,500
	To pay semiannual interest and amortize bond premium.		

EXHIBIT 8-7 | Debt Amortization for a Bond Premium

Panel A—Bond Data

Issue date—January 1, 2010	Maturity date—January 1, 2015
Face (par or *maturity*) value—$100,000	Market interest rate at time of issue—8% annually, 4% semiannually
Stated interest rate—9%	Issue price—$104,100
Interest paid—4½% semiannually, $4,500 = $100,000 × 0.09 × 6/12	

Panel B—Amortization Table

	A	B	C	D	E
Semiannual Interest Date	Interest Payment (4 1/2% of Maturity Value)	Interest Expense (4% of Preceding Bond Carrying Amount)	Premium Amortization (A – B)	Premium Account Balance (Preceding D – C)	Bond Carrying Amount ($100,000 + D)
Jan 1, 2010				$4,100	$ 104,100
Jul 1	$4,500	$4,164	$336	3,764	103,764
Jan 1, 2011	4,500	4,151	349	3,415	103,415
Jul 1	4,500	4,137	363	3,052	103,052
Jan 1, 2012	4,500	4,122	378	2,674	102,674
Jul 1	4,500	4,107	393	2,281	102,281
Jan 1, 2013	4,500	4,091	409	1,872	101,872
Jul 1	4,500	4,075	425	1,447	101,447
Jan 1, 2014	4,500	4,058	442	1,005	101,005
Jul 1	4,500	4,040	460	545	100,545
Jan 1, 2015	4,500	3,955*	545	-0-	100,000

*Adjusted for effect of rounding

Notes
- Column A The semiannual interest payments are constant—fixed by the bond contract.
- Column B The interest expense each period = the preceding bond carrying amount × the market interest rate. Interest expense decreases as the bond carrying amount (E) decreases.
- Column C The premium amortization (C) is the excess of interest payment (A) over interest expense (B).
- Column D The premium balance (D) decreases when amortized.
- Column E The bond carrying amount (E) decreases from $104,100 at issuance to $100,000 at maturity.

Immediately after issuing the bonds at a premium on January 1, 2010, Southwest would report the bonds payable on the balance sheet as follows:

Total current liabilities..............................		$ XXX
Long-term liabilities:		
Bonds payable.......................................	$100,000	
Premium on bonds payable...................	4,100	104,100

A premium is *added* to the balance of bonds payable to determine the carrying amount.

In Exhibit 8-7 Southwest borrowed $104,100 cash but must pay back only $100,000 at maturity. The $4,100 premium is a reduction in Southwest's interest expense over the term of the bonds. Exhibit 8-8 graphs Southwest's interest payments (column A from Exhibit 8-7) and interest expense (column B).

EXHIBIT 8-8 | **Interest Expense on Bonds Payable Issued at a Premium**

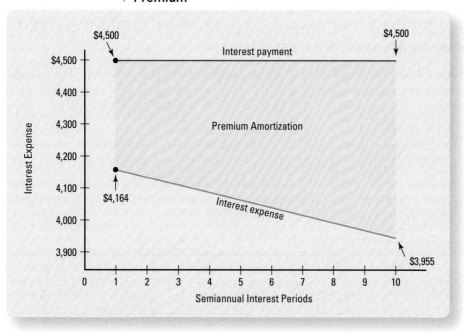

Through amortization the premium decreases interest expense each period over the term of the bonds. Exhibit 8-9 on the following page diagrams the amortization of the bonds from the issue price of $104,100 to maturity value of $100,000. All amounts are taken from Exhibit 8-7.

EXHIBIT 8-9 | Amortizing Bonds Payable Issued at a Premium

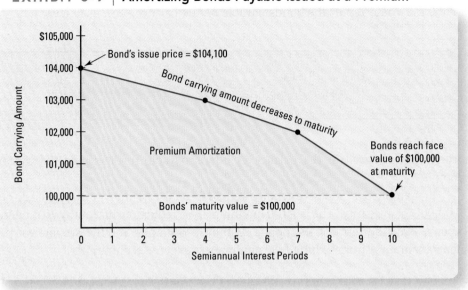

The Straight-Line Amortization Method: A Quick and Dirty Way to Measure Interest Expense

There's a less precise way to amortize bond discount or premium. The *straight-line amortization method* divides a bond discount (or premium) into equal periodic amounts over the bond's term. The amount of interest expense is the same for each interest period.

Let's apply the straight-line method to the Southwest Airlines bonds issued at a discount and illustrated in Exhibit 8-4 (p. 484). Suppose Southwest's financial vice president is considering issuing the 9% bonds at $96,149. To estimate semiannual interest expense on the bonds, the executive can use the straight-line amortization method for the bond discount, as follows:

Semiannual cash interest payment ($100,000 × 0.09 × 6/12)...............	$4,500
+ Semiannual amortization of discount ($3,851 ÷ 10)..........................	385
= Estimated semiannual interest expense	$4,885

The straight-line amortization method uses these same amounts every period over the term of the bonds.

Southwest's entry to record interest and amortization of the bond discount under the straight-line amortization method would be

2010			
Jul 1	Interest Expense	4,885	
	Discount on Bonds Payable		385
	Cash		4,500
	To pay semiannual interest and amortize bond discount.		

Generally accepted accounting principles (GAAP) permit the straight-line amortization method only when its amounts differ insignificantly from the amounts determined by the effective-interest method.

Should We Retire Bonds Payable Before Their Maturity?

Normally, companies wait until maturity to pay off, or *retire*, their bonds payable. But companies sometimes retire bonds early. The main reason for retiring bonds early is to relieve the pressure of making high interest payments. Also, the company may be able to borrow at a lower interest rate.

Some bonds are **callable**, which means that the issuer may *call*, or pay off, those bonds at a prearranged price (this is the *call price*) whenever the issuer chooses. The call price is often a percentage point or two above the par value, perhaps 101 or 102. Callable bonds give the issuer the benefit of being able to pay off the bonds whenever it is most favorable to do so. The alternative to calling the bonds is to purchase them in the open market at their current market price.

Southwest Airlines has $300 million of debenture bonds outstanding. Assume the unamortized discount is $30 million. Lower interest rates may convince management to pay off these bonds now. Assume that the bonds are callable at 101. If the market price of the bonds is 99, will Southwest call the bonds at 101 or purchase them for 99 in the open market? Market price is the better choice because the market price is lower than the call price. Let's see how to account for an early retirement of bonds payable. Retiring the bonds at 99 results in a loss of $27 million, computed as follows:

	Millions
Par value of bonds being retired	$300
Less: Unamortized discount	(30)
Carrying amount of the bonds being retired	270
Market price ($300 × .99)	297
Loss on retirement of bonds payable	$ 27

Gains and losses on early retirement of bonds payable are reported as Other income (loss) on the income statement.

Convertible Bonds and Notes

Some corporate bonds may be converted into the **issuing** company's common stock. These bonds are called **convertible bonds** (or **convertible notes**). For investors these bonds combine the safety of (a) assured receipt of interest and principal on the bonds with (b) the opportunity for gains on the stock. The conversion feature is so attractive that investors usually accept a lower interest rate than they would on non-convertible bonds. The lower cash interest payments benefit the issuer. If the market price of the issuing company's stock gets high enough, the bondholders will convert the bonds into stock.

Suppose Southwest Airlines has convertible notes payable of $100 million. If Southwest's stock price rises high enough, the noteholders will convert the notes into the company's common stock. Conversion of the notes payable into stock will decrease Southwest's liabilities and increase its equity.

Assume the noteholders convert the notes into 4 million shares of Southwest Airlines common stock ($1 par) on May 14. Southwest makes the following entry in its accounting records:

May 14	Notes Payable	100,000,000	
	Common Stock (4,000,000 × $1 par)		4,000,000
	Paid-in Capital in Excess of		
	Par—Common		96,000,000
	To record conversion of notes payable.		

The accounting equation shows that liabilities decrease and equity goes up.

Assets	=	Liabilities	+	Stockholders' Equity
0	=	– 100,000,000		+ 4,000,000 + 96,000,000

The carrying amount of the notes ($100 million) ceases to be debt and becomes stockholders' equity. Common Stock is recorded at its *par value*, which is a dollar amount assigned to each share of stock. In this case, the credit to Common Stock is $4,000,000 (4,000,000 shares × $1 par value per share). The extra carrying amount of the notes payable ($96,000,000) is credited to another stockholders' equity account, Paid-in Capital in Excess of Par—Common. We'll be using this account in various ways in the next chapter.

Financing Operations with Bonds or Stock?

OBJECTIVE

4 **Understand** the advantages and disadvantages of borrowing

Managers must decide how to get the money they need to pay for assets. There are three main ways to finance operations:

■ By retained earnings
■ By issuing stock
■ By issuing bonds (or notes) payable

Each strategy has its advantages and disadvantages.

1. ***Financed by retained earnings*** means that the company already has enough cash to purchase the needed assets. There's no need to issue more stock or to borrow money. This strategy is low-risk to the company.

2. ***Issuing stock*** creates no liabilities or interest expense and is less risky to the issuing corporation. But issuing stock is more costly, as we shall see.

3. *Issuing bonds or notes payable* does not dilute control of the corporation. It often results in higher earnings per share because the earnings on borrowed money usually exceed interest expense. But creating more debt increases the risk of the company.

Earnings per share (EPS) is the amount of a company's net income for each share of its stock. EPS is the single most important statistic for evaluating companies because EPS is a standard measure of operating performance that applies to companies of different sizes and from different industries.

Suppose Southwest Airlines needs $500,000 for expansion. Assume Southwest has net income of $300,000 and 100,000 shares of common stock outstanding. Management is considering two financing plans. Plan 1 is to issue $500,000 of 6% bonds payable, and plan 2 is to issue 50,000 shares of common stock for $500,000. Management believes the new cash can be invested in operations to earn income of $200,000 before interest and taxes.

Exhibit 8-10 shows the earnings-per-share advantage of borrowing. As you can see, Southwest's EPS amount is higher if the company borrows by issuing bonds (compare lines 9 and 10). Southwest earns more on the investment ($102,000) than the interest it pays on the bonds ($30,000). This is called **trading on the equity**, or using **leverage**. It is widely used to increase earnings per share of common stock.

EXHIBIT 8-10 | Earnings-Per-Share Advantage of Borrowing

	Plan 1		Plan 2	
	Borrow $500,000 at 6%		Issue 50,000 Shares of Common Stock for $500,000	
1 Net income before expansion		$300,000		$300,000
2 Expected project income before interest and income tax	$200,000		$200,000	
3 Less interest expense ($500,000 × .06)	(30,000)		0	
4 Expected project income before income tax	170,000		200,000	
5 Less income tax expense (40%)	(68,000)		(80,000)	
6 Expected project net income		102,000		120,000
7 Total company net income		$402,000		$420,000
8 Earnings per share after expansion:				
9 Plan 1 Borrow ($402,000/100,000 shares)		$4.02		
10 Plan 2 Issue Stock ($420,000/150,000 shares)				$2.80

In this case borrowing results in higher earnings per share than issuing stock. Borrowing has its disadvantages, however. Interest expense may be high enough to eliminate net income and lead to losses. Also, borrowing creates liabilities that must be paid during bad years as well as good years. In contrast, a company that issues stock can omit its dividends during a bad year. The Decision Guidelines provide some help in deciding how to finance operations.

DECISION GUIDELINES

FINANCING WITH DEBT OR WITH STOCK

El Chico is the leading chain of Tex-Mex restaurants in the United States, begun by the Cuellar family in the Dallas area. Suppose El Chico is expanding into neighboring states. Take the role of Miguel Cuellar and assume you must make some key decisions about how to finance the expansion.

Decision	Guidelines
How will you finance El Chico's expansion?	Your financing plan depends on El Chico's ability to generate cash flow, your willingness to give up some control of the business, the amount of financing risk you are willing to take, and El Chico's credit rating.
Do El Chico's operations generate enough cash to meet all its financing needs?	If yes, the business needs little outside financing. There is no need to borrow. If no, the business will need to issue additional stock or borrow the money.
Are you willing to give up some of your control of the business?	If yes, then issue stock to other stockholders, who can vote their shares to elect the company's directors. If no, then borrow from bondholders, who have no vote in the management of the company.
How much financing risk are you willing to take?	If much, then borrow as much as you can, and you may increase El Chico's earnings per share. But this will increase the business's debt ratio and the risk of being unable to pay its debts. If little, then borrow sparingly. This will hold the debt ratio down and reduce the risk of default on borrowing agreements. But El Chico's earnings per share may be lower than if you were to borrow.
How good is the business's credit rating?	The better the credit rating, the easier it is to borrow on favorable terms. A good credit rating also makes it easier to issue stock. Neither stockholders nor creditors will entrust their money to a company with a bad credit rating.

The Times-Interest-Earned Ratio

We have just seen how borrowing can increase EPS. But too much debt can lead to bankruptcy if the business cannot pay liabilities as they come due. UAL, Inc., the parent company of United Airlines, fell into the debt trap.

The **debt ratio** measures the effect of debt on the company's *financial position* but says nothing about the ability to pay interest expense. Analysts use a second ratio—the **times-interest-earned ratio**—to relate income to interest expense. To compute this ratio, we divide *income from operations* (also called *operating income*) by interest expense. This ratio measures the number of times that operating income can *cover* interest expense. The times-interest-earned ratio is also called the **interest-coverage** *ratio*. A high times-interest-earned ratio indicates ease in paying interest expense; a low value suggests difficulty. Let's see how competing airlines, Southwest and United (UAL), compare on the times-interest-earned ratio (dollar amounts in millions taken from the companies' 2008 financial statements):

Times–interest earned ratio $=$	$\dfrac{\text{Operating income}}{\text{Interest expense}}$
Southwest	$\dfrac{\$449}{\$130} = 3.5 \text{ times}$
United	$\dfrac{\$(4,438)}{\$523} = (8.5) \text{ times}$

Southwest's income from operations covers its interest expense 3.5 times. In contrast, UAL incurred a $4.4 billion loss for 2008, which dwarfs its interest expense by 8.5 times. It is obvious that UAL is experiencing difficulty staying in business. Paying interest on its outstanding debt is just the beginning of its worries.

STOP & THINK...

Which company, Southwest or UAL, would you expect to have the higher debt ratio? Compute the two companies' debt ratios to confirm your opinion. Summarized balance sheets follow at December 31, 2008.

	(In millions)	
	Southwest	**UAL**
Total assets	$14,308	$19,461
Total liabilities	$ 9,355	$21,926
Stockholders' equity	4,953	(2,465)
Total liabilities and equity................	$14,308	$19,461

Answer:

As expected, UAL has a much higher debt ratio than Southwest, as follows (dollar amounts in millions). UAL actually has 13% more liabilities than assets! The company is literally awash in debt, resulting in a negative balance in stockholders' equity as of December 31, 2008. In comparison, although Southwest's leverage, as expressed by the debt ratio, is getting higher (its was 0.521 in 2006) Southwest is still far less leveraged than UAL, or any other major airline, as of December 31, 2008:

		Southwest	**UAL**
Debt ratio $= \dfrac{\text{Total liabilities}}{\text{Total assets}} =$		$\dfrac{\$9,355}{\$14,308}$	$\dfrac{\$21,926}{\$19,461}$
		$= 0.654$	$= 1.13$

Long-Term Liabilities: Leases and Pensions

A **lease** is a rental agreement in which the tenant (**lessee**) agrees to make rent payments to the property owner (**lessor**) in exchange for the use of the asset. Leasing allows the lessee to acquire the use of a needed asset without having to make the large up-front payment that purchase agreements require. Accountants distinguish between two types of leases: operating leases and capital leases.

Types of Leases

Operating leases are sometimes short-term or cancelable. However, often operating lease agreements are noncancelable and require the lessee to commit funds to pay the lessor for use of property for years. They give the lessee the right to use the asset but provide no continuing rights to the asset. Instead, the lessor retains the usual risks and rewards of owning the leased asset. To account for an operating lease, the lessee debits Rent Expense (or Lease Expense) and credits Cash for the amount of the lease payment. Operating leases require the lessee to make rent payments, so an operating lease creates a liability even though that liability does not appear on the lessee's balance sheet. In recent years, Southwest Airlines has begun to lease many of its facilities (hangars, buildings, and equipment, including airplanes) under operating lease agreements. Following is an excerpt from Note 8 of Southwest's 2008 financial statements:

Note 8 Leases (partial)
The majority of the Company's terminal operations space, as well as 82 aircraft, were under operating leases at December 31, 2008. Future minimum lease payments under noncancelable operating leases with initial or remaining terms in excess of one year at December 31, 2008, were (in millions):

2009	$ 376
2010	324
2011	249
2012	203
2013	152
After 2013	728
Total	$2,032

This essentially means that, although the company has merely signed rental agreements for these assets, it has an obligation over several years in an amount exceeding $2 billion to the companies from which it is leasing these assets. Neither the obligation nor the associated assets are included in Southwest's balance sheet.

Capital leases. Sometimes businesses use capital leases to finance the acquisition of some assets. A **capital lease** is a long-term noncancelable debt. How do we distinguish a capital lease from an operating lease? *FASB Statement No. 13* provides the U.S. GAAP guidelines. To be classified as a capital lease, the lease must meet any *one* of the following criteria:

1. The lease transfers title of the leased asset to the lessee at the end of the lease term. Thus, the lessee becomes the legal owner of the leased asset.

2. The lease contains a *bargain purchase option*. The lessee can be expected to purchase the leased asset and become its legal owner.

3. The lease term is 75% or more of the estimated useful life of the leased asset. The lessee uses up most of the leased asset's service potential.

4. The present value of the lease payments is 90% or more of the market value of the leased asset. In effect, the lease payments are the same as installment payments for the leased asset.

If the lease does not meet one of these exact criteria, it is classified as an operating lease by default.

Accounting for a capital lease is much like accounting for the purchase of an asset. The lessee enters the asset into the lessee's long-term asset accounts and records a long-term lease liability at the beginning of the lease term. Thus, the lessee capitalizes the asset even though the lessee may never take legal title to the asset, because the lease agreement makes the lessee assume the risks and rewards of ownership of the assets and the associated obligations.

Most companies lease some of their plant assets. Southwest Airlines leases airplanes under capital leases. At December 31, 2008, Southwest Airlines reported its capital leases in Note 8 of its financial statements, excerpted as follows:

Note 8 Leases (partial)
Southwest's "future minimum lease payments under capital leases [...] as of December 31, 2008, were" (in millions):

Year Ending December 31	Capital Lease Payments	
2009	$ 16	
2010	15	
2011	12	
after 2011	–	
	43	*This is Southwest's*
Less amount representing interest	(4)	*liability under its*
Present value of...lease payments	$ 39 ←	*capital leases.*

The note shows that Southwest must pay a total of $43 million on its capital leases through 2011. The present value of this liability (gross amount less the amount attributable to interest on the liability) is $39 million. The present value is the net amount that's included in the liability figures reported on Southwest's balance sheet.

Do Lessees Prefer Operating Leases or Capital Leases?

Suppose you were the chief financial officer (CFO) of Southwest Airlines. Southwest leases some of its planes. Suppose the leases can be structured either as operating leases or as capital leases. Which type of lease would you prefer for Southwest? Why? Consider what would happen to Southwest's debt ratio if its operating leases in footnote 8 were capitalized, and the related liabilities recognized. Computing Southwest's debt ratio two ways (*operating* leases versus reclassifying them as *capital* leases) will make your decision clear (using Southwest's actual figures in millions):

			Operating Leases as Stated	Operating Leases Reclassified as Capital Leases	
Debt ratio	=	$\dfrac{\text{Total liabilities}}{\text{Total assets}}$ =	$\dfrac{\$9,355}{\$14,308}$	$\dfrac{\$9,355 + \$2,032}{\$14,308 + \$2,032}$ =	$\dfrac{\$11,387}{\$16,340}$
		=	0.654	=	0.697

You can see that a capital lease increases the debt ratio—by about five percentage points for Southwest, but a lot more for UAL and AMR (parent company of American Airlines). By contrast, notice that operating leases don't affect the debt ratio that's reported on the balance sheet. For this reason, companies prefer operating leases. It is easy to see why Southwest's long-term commitment for operating leases, as disclosed in Note 8, far outweighs that of its capital lease agreements.

Ethical Challenge. Because of the relatively mechanical nature of the accounting criteria for capitalization of leases, it is possible under existing U.S. GAAP to purposely structure a company's lease agreements so that they barely miss meeting the third criterion (75% test) or the fourth criterion (90% test) for capitalization. Many U.S. companies have taken advantage of these mechanical rules, quite legally, to their economic advantage, thus obtaining almost all the same economic benefits associated with ownership of long-term assets, but avoiding the detrimental impact that recording those assets and obligations can have on their debt ratios.

In contrast to U.S. GAAP with its mechanical, or "bright line" tests for capitalization of leases, IFRS adopts a much broader approach. Rather than rules, IFRS employs "guidance" that focuses on the overall substance of the transaction, rather than on the mechanical form, and that leaves more to the judgment of the preparer of the financial statement. If, in the judgment of the company's accountants, the lease transfers "substantially all of the risks and rewards of ownership to the lessee," IFRS says the lease should be capitalized. Otherwise, the lease should be expensed as an operating lease.

As of the publication date of this textbook, the FASB and IASB are in discussions about adopting consistent criteria for disclosures of leases on the financial statements of both lessors and lessees. A revised statement is expected sometime in 2010 or 2011. The impact of eventual adoption of IFRS on U.S. financial statements in the area of leases is hard to predict. Switching to current IFRS could result in more or fewer lease agreements being capitalized, depending on the judgment of financial statement preparers. If given the choice, what would you do?

Pensions and Postretirement Liabilities

Most companies have retirement plans for their employees. A **pension** is employee compensation that will be received during retirement. Companies also provide postretirement benefits, such as medical insurance for retired former employees. Because employees earn these benefits by their service, the company records pension and retirement-benefit expense while employees work for the company.

Pensions are one of the most complex areas of accounting. As employees earn their pensions and the company pays into the pension plan, the plan's assets grow. The obligation for future pension payments to employees also accumulates. At the end of each period, the company compares

- the fair market value of the assets in the retirement plans—cash and investments—with
- the plans' *accumulated benefit obligation*, which is the present value of promised future payments to retirees.

If the plan assets exceed the accumulated benefit obligation, the plan is said to be *overfunded*. In this case, the asset and obligation amounts are to be reported only in the notes to the financial statements. However, if the accumulated benefit obligation (the liability) exceeds plan assets, the plan is *underfunded*, and the company must report the excess liability amount as a long-term liability on the balance sheet.

Southwest Airlines' retirement plans don't create large liabilities for Southwest. To illustrate pension liabilities let's see the pension plan of AMR Corp., the parent company of American Airlines.

At December 31, 2007, the retirement plans of AMR Corporation were underfunded. They had

- assets with a fair market value of $9,323 million.
- accumulated benefit obligations totaling $13,123 million.

AMR's balance sheet, therefore, included a Pension and Post-Retirement Liability of $3,800 million ($13,123 – $9,323). This liability was split between current and long-term liabilities, in accordance with the due dates for the obligations.

REPORTING LIABILITIES

Reporting on the Balance Sheet

This chapter began with the liabilities reported on the consolidated balance sheets of Southwest Airlines. Exhibit 8-11 shows a standard way for Southwest to report its long-term debt.

OBJECTIVE

5 Report liabilities on the balance sheet

EXHIBIT 8-11 | **Reporting the Liabilities of Southwest Airlines Co.**

Southwest Airlines Co. Consolidated Balance Sheet (Partial, adapted)		Note 10 Financial Instruments (adapted) Long-term debt consists of (in millions);	
Liabilities (in millions)		Revolving credit facility	$ 400
Current Liabilities:		10.5% notes due 2011	400
Accounts payable	$ 668	Term agreement due 2020	585
Accrued liabilities	1,012	French credit agreements due 2012	26
Unearned ticket revenue	963	6½% notes due 2012	410
Current maturities of long-term debt	163	5¼% notes due 2014	391
Total current liabilities	2,806	5¾% notes due 2016	300
Long-term debt	3,498	5⅛% notes due 2017	358
Other long-term liabilities	3,051	French credit agreements due 2017	87
		Other long-term debt	704
		Total long-term debt	3,661
		Less current maturities	(163)
		Long-term debt	$3,498

Exhibit 8-11 includes Note 10 from Southwest's consolidated financial statements. The note gives additional details about the company's liabilities. Note 10 shows the interest rates and the maturity dates of Southwest's long-term debt. Investors need these data to evaluate the company. The note also reports

- current maturities of long-term debt ($163 million) as a current liability.
- long-term debt (excluding current maturities) of $3,498 million.

Trace these amounts from the Note to the balance sheet. Working back and forth between the financial statements and the related notes is an important part of financial analysis. You now have the tools to understand the liabilities reported on an actual balance sheet.

Reporting the Fair Market Value of Long-Term Debt

Generally accepted accounting principles require companies to report the fair market value of their long-term debt. At December 31, 2008, Southwest Airlines' Note 11 included this excerpt:

> The estimated fair value of the Company's long-term debt was $3,163 million.

Overall, the fair market value of Southwest's long-term debt is about $335 million less than its carrying amount on books ($3,498). Fair market values of publicly-traded debt are based on quoted market prices, which fluctuate with interest rates and overall market conditions. Therefore, at any one time, fair market values for various obligations can either exceed or be less than their carrying amounts.

Reporting Financing Activities on the Statement of Cash Flows

The Southwest Airlines consolidated balance sheet (p. 468) shows that the company finances 65% of its operations with debt. Southwest's debt ratio is 65%. Let's examine Southwest's financing activities as reported on its statement of cash flows. Exhibit 8-12 is an excerpt from Southwest's consolidated statement of cash flows.

EXHIBIT 8-12 | **Consolidated Statement of Cash Flows (partial; adapted) for Southwest Airlines Co.**

Southwest Airlines Co.
Consolidated Statement of Cash Flows (Adapted)

(In millions)	Year Ended December 31, 2008
Cash Flow from Operating Activities:	
Net cash provided by operating activities	$(1,521)
Cash Flow from Investing Activities:	
Net cash used for investing activities	$ (978)
Cash Flow from Financing Activities:	
Issuance of long-term debt	$ 1,491
Payments of long-term debt	(55)
Other financing sources	218
Net cash from financing activities	$ 1,654
Net decrease in Cash	$ (845)

Southwest used more cash from operations than it provided in 2008 by over $1.5 billion. This was largely due to a global economic recession made worse by a four-month spike in fuel prices. During 2008, Southwest's major source of cash ($1,654 million) was from financing, mostly with long-term debt. Southwest borrowed $1.5 billion and paid off only $55 million. You can see that Southwest is greatly increasing its debt position. Borrowing on a long-term basis enabled Southwest to invest $978 million, mostly in equipment, in order to keep growing during turbulent times. The company ended 2008 with a net decrease of $845 (−$1,521 − $978 + $1,654) million in cash.

END-OF-CHAPTER SUMMARY PROBLEM

The **Cessna Aircraft Company** has outstanding an issue of 8% convertible bonds that mature in 2018. Suppose the bonds are dated October 1, 2010, and pay interest each April 1 and October 1.

I Requirements

1. Complete the following effective-interest amortization table through October 1, 2012.

   Bond Data
   Maturity (face) value—$100,000
   Stated interest rate—8%
   Interest paid—4% semiannually, $4,000 ($100,000 × 0.08 × 6/12)
   Market interest rate at the time of issue—9% annually, 4 1/2% semiannually
   Issue price—93.5

	A	B	C	D	E
			Amortization Table		
Semiannual Interest Date	Interest Payment (4% of Maturity Amount)	Interest Expense (4½% of Preceding Bond Carrying Amount)	Discount Amortization (B – A)	Discount Account Balance (Preceding D – C)	Bond Carrying Amount ($100,000 – D)
10-1-10					
4-1-11					
10-1-11					
4-1-12					
10-1-12					

2. Using the amortization table, record the following transactions:
   a. Issuance of the bonds on October 1, 2010.
   b. Accrual of interest and amortization of the bonds on December 31, 2010.
   c. Payment of interest and amortization of the bonds on April 1, 2011.
   d. Conversion of one-third of the bonds payable into no-par stock on October 2, 2012. For no-par stock, transfer the bond carrying amount into the Common Stock account. There is no Additional Paid-in Capital account.
   e. Retirement of two-thirds of the bonds payable on October 2, 2012. Purchase price of the bonds was based on their call price of 102.

Answers

I Requirement 1

	A	B	C	D	E
Semiannual Interest Date	Interest Payment (4% of Maturity Amount)	Interest Expense (4½% of Preceding Bond Carrying Amount)	Discount Amortization (B – A)	Discount Account Balance (Preceding D – C)	Bond Carrying Amount ($100,000 – D)
10-1-10				$6,500	$93,500
4-1-11	$4,000	$4,208	$208	6,292	93,708
10-1-11	4,000	4,217	217	6,075	93,925
4-1-12	4,000	4,227	227	5,848	94,152
10-1-12	4,000	4,237	237	5,611	94,389

❙ *Requirement 2*

a.	2010			
	Oct 1	Cash ($100,000 × 0.935)	93,500	
		Discount on Bonds Payable	6,500	
		Bonds Payable		100,000
		To issue bonds at a discount.		
b.	Dec 31	Interest Expense ($4,208 × 3/6)	2,104	
		Discount on Bonds Payable ($208 × 3/6)		104
		Interest Payable ($4,000 × 3/6)		2,000
		To accrue interest and amortize the bonds.		
c.	2011			
	Apr 1	Interest Expense ($4,208 × 3/6)	2,104	
		Interest Payable	2,000	
		Discount on Bonds Payable ($208 × 3/6)		104
		Cash		4,000
		To pay semiannual interest, part of which was		
		accrued, and amortize the bonds.		
d.	2012			
	Oct 2	Bonds Payable ($100,000 × 1/3)	33,333	
		Discount on Bonds Payable ($5,611 × 1/3)		1,870
		Common Stock ($94,389 × 1/3)		31,463
		To record conversion of bonds payable.		
e.	Oct 2	Bonds Payable ($100,000 × 2/3)	66,667	
		Loss on Retirement of Bonds	5,074	
		Discount on Bonds Payable ($5,611 × 2/3)		3,741
		Cash ($100,000 × 2/3 × 1.02)		68,000
		To retire bonds payable before maturity.		

REVIEW LIABILITIES

Quick Check (Answers are given on page 531.)

1. Which of the following is *not* an estimated liability?
   - **a.** Product warranties
   - **b.** Vacation pay
   - **c.** Income taxes
   - **d.** Allowance for bad debts

2. Recording estimated warranty expense in the current year *best* follows which accounting principle?
   - **a.** Historical cost
   - **b.** Consistency
   - **c.** Full disclosure
   - **d.** Materiality
   - **e.** Matching

3. Crank the Volume grants a 120-day warranty on all stereos. Historically, approximately 1% of all sales prove to be defective. Sales in March are $450,000. In March, $3,800 of defective units are returned for replacement. What entry must Crank the Volume make at the end of March to record the warranty expense?

   a. Debit Warranty Expense and credit Estimated Warranty Payable, $3,800.

   b. Debit Warranty Expense and credit Estimated Warranty Payable, $4,500.

   c. Debit Warranty Expense and credit Cash, $4,500.

   d. No entry is needed at March 31.

4. Expedition Camera Co. was organized to sell a single product that carries a 45-day warranty against defects. Engineering estimates indicate that 4% of the units sold will prove defective and require an average repair cost of $25 per unit. During Expedition's first month of operations, total sales were 900 units; by the end of the month, 15 defective units had been repaired. The liability for product warranties at month-end should be

   a. $1,275.   d. $900.

   b. $375.   e. none of these.

   c. $525.

5. A contingent liability should be recorded in the accounts

   a. if the amount can be reasonably estimated.

   b. if the amount is due in cash within one year.

   c. if the related future event will probably occur.

   d. Both b and c

   e. Both a and c

6. An unsecured bond is a

   a. mortgage bond.   d. serial bond.

   b. debenture bond.   e. term bond.

   c. registered bond.

7. The Discount on Bonds Payable account

   a. is expensed at the bond's maturity.   d. is a contra account to Bonds Payable.

   b. is a miscellaneous revenue account.   e. is an expense account.

   c. has a normal credit balance.

8. The discount on a bond payable becomes

   a. a reduction in interest expense over the life of the bonds.

   b. a liability in the year the bonds are sold.

   c. additional interest expense over the life of the bonds.

   d. a reduction in interest expense the year the bonds mature.

   e. additional interest expense the year the bonds are sold.

9. A bond that matures in installments is called a

   a. term bond.   d. zero coupon.

   b. secured bond.   e. callable bond.

   c. serial bond.

10. The carrying value of Bonds Payable equals

    a. Bonds Payable + Accrued Interest.

    b. Bonds Payable + Discount on Bonds Payable.

    c. Bonds Payable – Premium on Bonds Payable.

    d. Bonds Payable – Discount on Bonds Payable.

11. A corporation issues bonds that pay interest each May 1 and November 1. The corporation's December 31 adjusting entry may include a

    a. credit to Discount on Bonds Payable.   d. debit to Interest Payable.

    b. credit to Cash.   e. debit to Cash.

    c. credit to Interest Expense.

Use this information to answer questions 12–16.

McCabe Corporation issued $550,000 of 7% 10-year bonds. The bonds are dated and sold on January 1, 2011. Interest payment dates are January 1 and July 1. The bonds are issued for $512,408 to yield the market interest rate of 8%. Use the effective-interest method for questions 12–15.

12. What is the amount of interest expense that McCabe Corporation will record on July 1, 2011, the first semiannual interest payment date? (All amounts rounded to the nearest dollar.)

    a. $20,496   c. $19,250
    b. $38,500   d. $22,000

13. What is the amount of discount amortization that McCabe Corporation will record on July 1, 2011, the first semiannual interest payment date?

    a. $0   c. $1,246
    b. $2,562   d. $1,504

14. What is the total cash payment for interest for each 12-month period? (All amounts rounded to the nearest dollar.)

    a. $22,000   c. $40,993
    b. $38,500   d. $44,000

15. What is the carrying amount of the bonds on the January 1, 2012 balance sheet?

    a. $514,950   c. $512,408
    b. $513,654   d. $516,167

16. Using straight-line amortization, the carrying amount of McCabe Corporation's bonds at December 31, 2011, is

    a. $513,654.   c. $514,950.
    b. $512,408.   d. $516,167.

Accounting Vocabulary

accrued expense (p. 470) An expense incurred but not yet paid in cash. Also called *accrued liability*.

accrued liability (p. 470) A liability for an expense that has not yet been paid. Also called *accrued expense*.

bonds payable (p. 477) Groups of notes payable issued to multiple lenders called *bondholders*.

callable bond (p. 491) Bonds that are paid off early at a specified price at the option of the issuer.

capital lease (p. 496) Lease agreement in which the lessee assumes, in substance, the risks and rewards of asset ownership. In the United States, a lease is assumed to be a capital lease if it meets any one of four criteria: (1) The lease transfers title of the leased asset to the lessee. (2) The lease contains a bargain purchase option. (3) The lease term is 75% or more of the estimated useful life of the leased asset. (4) The present value of the lease payments is 90% or more of the market value of the leased asset.

convertible bonds (or notes) (p. 491) Bonds or notes that may be converted into the issuing company's common stock at the investor's option.

current portion of long-term debt (p. 473) The amount of the principal that is payable within one year.

debentures (p. 479) Unsecured bonds—bonds backed only by the good faith of the borrower.

discount (on a bond) (p. 479) Excess of a bond's face (par) value over its issue price.

earnings per share (EPS) (p. 493) Amount of a company's net income per share of its outstanding common stock.

interest-coverage ratio (p. 494) Another name for the *times-interest-earned ratio*.

lease (p. 495) Rental agreement in which the tenant (lessee) agrees to make rent payments to the property owner (lessor) in exchange for the use of the asset.

lessee (p. 495) Tenant in a lease agreement.

lessor (p. 495) Property owner in a lease agreement.

leverage (p. 493) Using borrowed funds to increase the return on equity. Successful use of leverage means earning more income on borrowed money than the related interest expense, thereby increasing the earnings for the owners of the business. Also called *trading on the equity*.

market interest rate (p. 480) Interest rate that investors demand for loaning their money. Also called *effective interest rate*.

operating lease (p. 496) A lease in which the lessee does not assume the risks or rewards of asset ownership.

payroll (p. 470) Employee compensation, a major expense of many businesses.

pension (p. 498) Employee compensation that will be received during retirement.

premium (on a bond) (p. 479) Excess of a bond's issue price over its face (par) value.

present value (p. 479) Amount a person would invest now to receive a greater amount at a future date.

serial bonds (p. 479) Bonds that mature in installments over a period of time.

short-term notes payable (p. 469) Note payable due within one year.

stated interest rate (p. 480) Interest rate that determines the amount of cash interest the borrower pays and the investor receives each year.

term bonds (p. 479) Bonds that all mature at the same time for a particular issue.

times-interest-earned ratio (p. 494) Ratio of income from operations to interest expense. Measures the number of times that operating income can cover interest expense. Also called the *interest-coverage ratio*.

trading on the equity (p. 493) Earning more income on borrowed money than the related interest expense, thereby increasing the earnings for the owners of the business. Also called *leverage*.

underwriter (p. 478) Organization that purchases the bonds from an issuing company and resells them to its clients or sells the bonds for a commission, agreeing to buy all unsold bonds.

ASSESS YOUR PROGRESS

Short Exercises

S8-1 (*Learning Objective 1: Accounting for a note payable*) Franklin Sports Authority purchased inventory costing $5,000 by signing an 8% short-term note payable. The purchase occurred on September 30, 2010. Franklin pays annual interest each year on September 30. Journalize the company's (a) purchase of inventory, (b) accrual of interest expense on June 30, 2011, which is the year-end, and (c) payment of the note plus interest on September 30, 2011. (Round your answers to the nearest whole number.)

S8-2 (*Learning Objective 1: Reporting a short-term note payable and the related interest in the financial statements*) This short exercise works with Short Exercise 8-1.

1. Refer to the data in Short Exercise 8-1. Show what the company would report on its balance sheet at June 30, 2011, and on its income statement for the year ended on that date.
2. What single item will the financial statements for the year ended June 30, 2012, report? Identify the financial statement, the item, and its amount.

S8-3 (*Learning Objective 1: Accounting for warranty expense and estimated warranty payable*) Trekster USA guarantees automobiles against defects for five years or 55,000 miles, whichever comes first. Suppose Trekster USA can expect warranty costs during the five-year period to add up to 6% of sales. Assume that Trekster USA dealer in Atlanta, Georgia, made sales of $483,000 during 2010. Trekster USA received cash for 30% of the sales and took notes receivable for the remainder. Payments to satisfy customer warranty claims totaled $19,000 during 2010.

1. Record the sales, warranty expense, and warranty payments for Trekster USA.
2. Post to the Estimated Warranty Payable T-account. The beginning balance was $11,000. At the end of 2010, how much in estimated warranty payable does Trekster USA owe to its customers?

S8-4 (*Learning Objective 1: Applying GAAP; reporting warranties in the financial statements*) Refer to the data given in Short Exercise 8-3. What amount of warranty expense will Trekster USA report during 2010? Which accounting principle addresses this situation? Does the warranty expense for the year equal the year's cash payments for warranties? Explain the relevant accounting principle as it applies to measuring warranty expense.

S8-5 *(Learning Objective 1: Interpreting a company's contingent liabilities)* Marley-David, Inc., the motorcycle manufacturer, included the following note in its annual report:

> **NOTES TO CONSOLIDATED FINANCIAL STATEMENTS**
> **7 (In Part): Commitments and Contingencies**
> The Company self-insures its product liability losses in the United States up to $3.2 million (catastrophic coverage is maintained for individual claims in excess of $3.2 million up to $25.2 million). Outside the United States, the Company is insured for product liability up to $25.2 million per individual claim and in the aggregate.

1. Why are these *contingent* (versus *real*) liabilities?
2. In the United States, how can the contingent liability become a real liability for Marley-David? What are the limits to the company's product liabilities in the United States?
3. How can a contingency outside the United States become a real liability for the company? How does Marley-David's potential liability differ for claims outside the United States?

S8-6 *(Learning Objective 2: Pricing bonds)* Compute the price of the following bonds:

a. $300,000 issued at 75.75
b. $300,000 issued at 102.75
c. $300,000 issued at 94.50
d. $300,000 issued at 104.50

S8-7 *(Learning Objective 2: Determining bond prices at par, discount, or premium)* Determine whether the following bonds payable will be issued at maturity value, at a premium, or at a discount:

a. The market interest rate is 5%. Carlisle Corp. issues bonds payable with a stated rate of 4 1/2%.
b. Oiler, Inc., issued 7% bonds payable when the market rate was 6 3/4%.
c. Toronto Corporation issued 5% bonds when the market interest rate was 5%.
d. Ontario Company issued bonds payable that pay stated interest of 6%. At issuance, the market interest rate was 7 1/4%.

S8-8 *(Learning Objective 2: Journalizing basic bond payable transactions; bonds issued at par)* Deer Corp. issued 15-year bonds payable with a face amount of $80,000, when the market interest rate was 5.5%. Assume that the accounting year of Deer ends on December 31. Journalize the following transactions for Deer. Include an explanation for each entry.

a. Issuance of the bonds payable at par on July 1, 2010.
b. Accrual of interest expense on December 31, 2010 (rounded to the nearest dollar).
c. Payment of cash interest on January 1, 2011.
d. Payment of the bonds payable at maturity. (Give the date.)

S8-9 *(Learning Objectives 2, 3: Issuing bonds payable; amortizing bonds by the effective-interest method)* GIT, Inc., issued $600,000 of 5%, 12-year bonds payable at a price of 77 on March 31, 2010. The market interest rate at the date of issuance was 8%, and the GIT bonds pay interest semiannually.

1. Prepare an effective-interest amortization table for the bonds through the first three interest payments. Round amounts to the nearest dollar.
2. Record GIT, Inc.'s issuance of the bonds on March 31, 2010, and payment of the first semiannual interest amount and amortization of the bond discount on September 30, 2010. Explanations are not required.

S8-10 *(Learning Objectives 2, 3: Accounting for bonds payable; analyzing data on long-term debt)* Use the amortization table that you prepared for GIT's bonds in Short Exercise 8-9 to answer the following questions:

1. How much cash did GIT borrow on March 31, 2010? How much cash will GIT pay back at maturity on March 31, 2022?

2. How much cash interest will GIT pay each six months?

3. How much interest expense will GIT report on September 30, 2010, and on March 31, 2011? Why does the amount of interest expense increase each period?

S8-11 (*Learning Objectives 2, 3: Determining bonds payable amounts; amortizing bonds by the straight-line method*)   Sunset Drive-Ins Ltd. borrowed money by issuing $5,000,000 of 3% bonds payable at 36.5 on July 1, 2010. The bonds are 10-year bonds and pay interest each January 1 and July 1.

1. How much cash did Sunset receive when it issued the bonds payable?

2. How much must Sunset pay back at maturity? When is the maturity date?

3. How much cash interest will Sunset pay each six months?

4. How much interest expense will Sunset report each six months? Assume the straight-line amortization method.

S8-12 (*Learning Objectives 2, 3: Issuing bonds payable; accruing interest; amortizing bonds by the straight-line method*)   Sunset Drive-Ins Ltd. issued a $500,000, 8%, 10-year bond payable on July 1, 2010, at a price of 94. Also assume that Sunset's accounting year ends on December 31. Journalize the following transactions for Sunset Drive-Ins Ltd., including an explanation for each entry:

a. Issuance of the bond payable on July 1, 2010.

b. Accrual of interest expense and amortization of bonds on December 31, 2010. (Use the straight-line amortization method, and round amounts to the nearest dollar.)

c. Payment of the first semiannual interest amount on January 1, 2011.

S8-13 (*Learning Objective 4: Computing earnings-per-share effects of financing with bonds versus stock*)   Speedtown Marina needs to raise $3 million to expand the company. Speedtown Marina is considering the issuance of either:

- $3,000,000 of 8% bonds payable to borrow the money, or
- 100,000 shares of common stock at $30 per share.

Before any new financing, Speedtown Marina expects to earn net income of $300,000, and the company already has 100,000 shares of common stock outstanding. Speedtown Marina believes the expansion will increase income before interest and income tax by $500,000. The income tax rate is 35%.

   Prepare an analysis to determine which plan is likely to result in the higher earnings per share. Based solely on the earnings-per-share comparison, which financing plan would you recommend for Speedtown Marina?

S8-14 (*Learning Objective 4: Computing the times-interest-earned ratio*)   Houle Plumbing Products Ltd. reported the following data in 2010 (in billions):

writing assignment ■

	2010
Net operating revenues................	$29.7
Operating expenses	24.7
Operating income........................	5.0
Nonoperating items:	
Interest expense.......................	(1.6)
Other	(0.1)
Net income.................................	$ 3.3

   Compute Houle's times-interest-earned ratio, and write a sentence to explain what the ratio value means. Would you be willing to lend Houle $1 billion? State your reason.

S8-15 (*Learning Objective 5: Reporting liabilities, including capital lease obligations*)
Like Home, Inc., includes the following selected accounts in its general ledger at
December 31, 2010:

Bonds payable	$400,000
Equipment	112,000
Current portion of bonds payable	51,000
Notes payable, long-term	300,000
Interest payable (due March 1, 2011)	1,000
Accounts payable	36,000
Discount on bonds payable (all long-term)	12,000
Accounts receivable	27,000

Prepare the liabilities section of Like Home, Inc.'s balance sheet at December 31, 2010,
to show how the company would report these items. Report total current liabilities and
total liabilities.

Exercises

All of the A and B exercises can be found within MyAccountingLab, an online homework
and practice environment. Your instructor may ask you to complete these exercises using
MyAccountingLab.

(Group A)

E8-16A (*Learning Objective 1: Accounting for warranty expense and the related
liability*) The accounting records of From the Earth Ceramics included the following balances at the end of the period:

Estimated Warranty Payable		Sales Revenue		Warranty Expense	
	Beg bal 3,000		161,000		

In the past, From the Earth's warranty expense has been 7% of sales. During 2010 the business paid $8,000 to satisfy the warranty claims.

❚ Requirements

1. Journalize From the Earth's warranty expense for the period and the company's cash payments to satisfy warranty claims. Explanations are not required.
2. Show what From the Earth will report on its income statement and balance sheet for
   this situation.
3. Which data item from Requirement 2 will affect From the Earth's current ratio? Will
   From the Earth's current ratio increase or decrease as a result of this item?

E8-17A *(Learning Objective 1: Recording and reporting current liabilities)* TransWorld Publishing completed the following transactions for one subscriber during 2010:

Oct 1	Sold a one-year subscription, collecting cash of $1,400, plus sales tax of 8%.
Nov 15	Remitted (paid) the sales tax to the state of Massachusetts.
Dec 31	Made the necessary adjustment at year-end.

I Requirement

1. Journalize these transactions (explanations not required). Then report any liability on the company's balance sheet at December 31, 2010.

E8-18A *(Learning Objective 1: Reporting payroll expense and liabilities)* Perform Talent Search has an annual payroll of $200,000. In addition, the company incurs payroll tax expense of 8%. At December 31, Perform owes salaries of $8,100 and FICA and other payroll tax of $800. The company will pay these amounts early next year. Show what Perform will report for the foregoing on its income statement and year-end balance sheet.

E8-19A *(Learning Objective 1: Recording note payable transactions)* Assume that Crandell Company completed the following note-payable transactions.

2010	
May 1	Purchased delivery truck costing $83,000 by issuing a one-year, 6% note payable.
Dec 31	Accrued interest on the note payable.
2011	
May 1	Paid the note payable at maturity.

I Requirements

1. How much interest expense must be accrued at December 31, 2010? (Round your answer to the nearest whole dollar.)
2. Determine the amount of Crandell's final payment on May 1, 2011.
3. How much interest expense will Crandell report for 2010 and for 2011? (Round your answer to the nearest whole dollar.)

E8-20A *(Learning Objective 1: Accounting for income tax)* At December 31, 2010, Souza Real Estate reported a current liability for income tax payable of $180,000. During 2011, Souza earned income of $1,200,000 before income tax. The company's income tax rate during 2011 was 36%. Also during 2011, Souza paid income taxes of $370,000.

How much income tax payable did Souza Real Estate report on its balance sheet at December 31, 2011? How much income tax expense did Souza report on its 2011 income statement?

E8-21A *(Learning Objectives 1, 5: Analyzing liabilities)* Mountainside Manors, Inc., builds environmentally sensitive structures. The company's 2010 revenues totaled $2,760 million, and at December 31, 2010, the company had $650 million in current assets. The December 31, 2010 and 2009, balance sheets reported the liabilities and stockholders' equity as follows:

At year-end (In millions)	2010	2009
Liabilities and Stockholders' Equity		
Current Liabilities		
Accounts payable	$ 138	$ 179
Accrued expenses	155	172
Employee compensation and benefits...................	38	20
Current portion of long-term debt........................	9	24
Total Current Liabilities...................................	340	395
Long-Term Debt	1,494	1,323
Post-Retirement Benefits Payable	122	123
Other Liabilities	12	8
Stockholders' Equity	2,027	1,784
Total Liabilities and Stockholders' Equity..............	$3,995	$3,633

Ⅰ Requirements

1. Describe each of Mountainside Manors, Inc.'s liabilities and state how the liability arose.
2. What were the company's total assets at December 31, 2010? Was the company's debt ratio at the end of 2010 high, low, or in a middle range?

E8-22A *(Learning Objective 1: Reporting a contingent liability)* Roden Security Systems' revenues for 2010 totaled $6.3 million. As with most companies, Roden is a defendant in lawsuits related to its products. Note 14 of the Roden Annual Report for 2010 reported:

14. Contingencies
The company is involved in various legal proceedings.... It is the Company's policy to accrue for amounts related to these legal matters if it is probable that a liability has been incurred and an amount is reasonably estimable.

Ⅰ Requirements

1. Suppose Roden's lawyers believe that a significant legal judgment against the company is reasonably possible. How should Roden report this situation in its financial statements?
2. Suppose Roden's lawyers believe it is probable that a $1.5 million judgment will be rendered against the company. Report this situation in Roden's financial statements. Journalize any entry requirements by GAAP. Explanations are not required.

E8-23A *(Learning Objectives 1, 5: Reporting current and long-term liabilities)* Assume that McKinley Electronics completed these selected transactions during June 2010:

a. Sales of $2,200,000 are subject to estimated warranty cost of 7%. The estimated warranty payable at the beginning of the year was $34,000, and warranty payments for the year totaled $50,000.
b. On June 1, McKinley Electronics signed a $55,000 note payable that requires annual payments of $13,750 plus 6% interest on the unpaid balance each June 2.

c. Music For You, Inc., a chain of music stores, ordered $125,000 worth of CD players. With its order, Music For You, Inc., sent a check for $125,000 in advance, and McKinley shipped $70,000 of the goods. McKinley will ship the remainder of the goods on July 3, 2010.

d. The June payroll of $260,000 is subject to employee withheld income tax of $30,000 and FICA tax of 7.65%. On June 30, McKinley pays employees their take-home pay and accrues all tax amounts.

▌ Requirement

1. Report these items on McKinley Electronics' balance sheet at June 30, 2010.

E8-24A (*Learning Objectives 2, 3: Issuing bonds payable (discount); paying and accruing interest; amortizing the bonds by the straight-line method*) On January 31, Driftwood Logistics, Inc., issued 10-year, 6% bonds payable with a face value of $13,000,000. The bonds were issued at 94 and pay interest on January 31 and July 31. Driftwood Logistics, Inc., amortizes bonds by the straight-line method. Record (a) issuance of the bonds on January 31, (b) the semiannual interest payment and amortization of bond discount on July 31, and (c) the interest accrual and discount amortization on December 31.

E8-25A (*Learning Objectives 2, 3: Measuring cash amounts for a bond payable (premium); amortizing the bonds by the straight-line method*) Federal Bank has $500,000 of 7% debenture bonds outstanding. The bonds were issued at 103 in 2010 and mature in 2030.

▌ Requirements

1. How much cash did Federal Bank receive when it issued these bonds?
2. How much cash in *total* will Federal Bank pay the bondholders through the maturity date of the bonds?
3. Take the difference between your answers to Requirements 1 and 2. This difference represents Federal Bank's total interest expense over the life of the bonds.
4. Compute Federal Bank's annual interest expense by the straight-line amortization method. Multiply this amount by 20. Your 20-year total should be the same as your answer to Requirement 3.

E8-26A (*Learning Objectives 2, 3: Issuing bonds payable (discount); recording interest payments and the related bond amortization*) Goal Sports Ltd. is authorized to issue $3,000,000 of 10%, 10-year bonds payable. On December 31, 2010, when the market interest rate is 12%, the company issues $2,400,000 of the bonds and receives cash of $2,128,800. Goal Sports Ltd. amortizes bond discounts by the effective-interest method. The semiannual interest dates are June 30 and December 31.

▌ Requirements

1. Prepare a bond amortization table for the first four semiannual interest periods.
2. Record issuance of the bonds payable on December 31, 2010, the first semiannual interest payment on June 30, 2011, and the second payment on December 31, 2011.

E8-27A (*Learning Objectives 2, 3: Issuing bonds payable (premium); recording interest accrual and payment and the related bond amortization*) On June 30, 2010, the market interest rate is 4%. Score Sports Ltd. issues $800,000 of 5%, 30-year bonds payable at 117.38. The bonds pay interest on June 30 and December 31. Score Sports Ltd. amortizes bonds by the effective-interest method.

▌ Requirements

1. Prepare a bond amortization table for the first four semiannual interest periods.
2. Record the issuance of bonds payable on June 30, 2010, the payment of interest on December 31, 2010, and the payment of interest on June 30, 2011.

■ spreadsheet

■ spreadsheet

■ spreadsheet

E8-28A *(Learning Objective 3: Creating a bond amortization schedule (discount))* Dracut Co. issued $100,000 of 8% (0.08), 10-year bonds payable on January 1, 2010, when the market interest rate was 10% (0.10). The company pays interest annually at year-end. The issue price of the bonds was $87,711.

I Requirement

1. Create a spreadsheet model to prepare a schedule to amortize the bonds. Use the effective-interest method of amortization. (Round to the nearest dollar).

E8-29A *(Learning Objective 2: Recording conversion of notes payable)* Coastalview Imaging Ltd. issued $3,300,000 of 6% notes payable on December 31, 2010, at a price of 95. The notes' term to maturity is 20 years. After four years, the notes may be converted into Coastalview common stock. Each $1,000 face amount of notes is convertible into 50 shares of $1 par common stock. On December 31, 2015, note holders exercised their right to convert all the notes into common stock.

I Requirements

1. Without making journal entries, compute the carrying amount of the notes payable at December 31, 2015, immediately before the conversion. Coastalview Imaging Ltd. uses the straight-line method to amortize bonds.
2. All amortization has been recorded properly. Journalize the conversion transaction at December 31, 2015.

E8-30A *(Learning Objective 4: Measuring the times-interest-earned ratio)* Companies that operate in different industries may have very different financial ratio values. These differences may grow even wider when we compare companies located in different countries.

Compare three leading companies on their current ratio, debt ratio, and times-interest-earned ratio. Compute three ratios for Company A, Company N, and Company S.

(Amounts in millions or billions)	Company A	Company N	Company S
Income data			
Total revenues..............................	$9,723	¥7,311	€136,431
Operating income.........................	291	222	5,581
Interest expense............................	42	31	671
Net income..................................	27	15	441
Asset and liability data			
(Amounts in millions or billions)			
Total current assets	431	5,932	170,140
Long-term assets	139	39	45,315
Total current liabilities................	197	2,197	72,400
Long-term liabilities	137	2,341	110,737
Stockholders' equity....................	236	1,433	32,318

Based on your computed ratio values, which company looks the least risky?

writing assignment ■

E8-31A *(Learning Objective 4: Analyzing alternative plans for raising money)* First Bank Financial Services is considering two plans for raising $800,000 to expand operations. Plan A is to borrow at 10%, and plan B is to issue 200,000 shares of common stock at $4.00 per share. Before any new financing, First Bank Financial Services has net income of $600,000 and 200,000 shares of common stock outstanding. Assume you own most of First Bank Financial Services' existing stock. Management believes the company can use the new funds to earn additional income of $800,000 before interest and taxes. First Bank Financial Services' income tax rate is 25%.

Requirements

1. Analyze First Bank Financial Services situation to determine which plan will result in higher earnings per share.
2. Which plan results in the higher earnings per share? Which plan allows you to retain control of the company? Which plan creates more financial risk for the company? Which plan do you prefer? Why? Present your conclusion in a memo to First Bank Financial Services board of directors.

(Group B)

E8-32B (*Learning Objective 1: Accounting for warranty expense and the related liability*)   The accounting records of Made from Clay Ceramics included the following balances at the end of the period:

Estimated Warranty Payable		Sales Revenue		Warranty Expense	
	Beg bal 4,000		160,000		

In the past, Made from Clay's warranty expense has been 4% of sales. During 2010 the business paid $5,000 to satisfy the warranty claims.

Requirements

1. Journalize Made from Clay's warranty expense for the period and the company's cash payments to satisfy warranty claims. Explanations are not required.
2. Show what Made from Clay will report on its income statement and balance sheet for this situation.
3. Which data item from Requirement 2 will affect Made from Clay's current ratio? Will Made from Clay's current ratio increase or decrease as a result of this item?

E8-33B (*Learning Objective 1: Recording and reporting current liabilities*)   Trevor Publishing completed the following transactions for one subscriber during 2010:

Oct 1	Sold a one-year subscription, collecting cash of $1,300, plus sales tax of 9%.
Nov 15	Remitted (paid) the sales tax to the state of Massachusetts.
Dec 31	Made the necessary adjustment at year-end.

Requirement

1. Journalize these transactions (explanations not required). Then report any liability on the company's balance sheet at December 31.

E8-34B (*Learning Objective 1: Reporting payroll expense and liabilities*)   Potvin Talent Search has an annual payroll of $160,000. In addition, the company incurs payroll tax expense of 9%. At December 31, Potvin owes salaries of $7,900 and FICA and other payroll tax of $850. The company will pay these amounts early next year.

Show what Potvin will report for the foregoing on its income statement and year-end balance sheet.

E8-35B (*Learning Objective 1: Recording note payable transactions*)   Assume that Concilio Company completed the following note-payable transactions:

2010	
Mar 1	Purchased delivery truck costing $82,000 by issuing a one-year, 5% note payable.
Dec 31	Accrued interest on the note payable.
2011	
Mar 1	Paid the note payable at maturity.

▍Requirements

1. How much interest expense must be accrued at December 31, 2010? (Round your answer to the nearest whole dollar.)
2. Determine the amount of Concilio's final payment on March 1, 2011.
3. How much interest expense will Concilio report for 2010 and for 2011? (Round your answer to the nearest whole dollar.)

E8-36B (*Learning Objective 1: Accounting for income tax*)   At December 31, 2010, Saglio Real Estate reported a current liability for income tax payable of $190,000. During 2011, Saglio earned income of $1,500,000 before income tax. The company's income tax rate during 2011 was 25%. Also during 2011, Saglio paid income taxes of $300,000.

How much income tax payable did Saglio Real Estate report on its balance sheet at December 31, 2011? How much income tax expense did Saglio report on its 2011 income statement?

writing assignment ■   **E8-37B** (*Learning Objectives 1, 5: Analyzing liabilities*)   New Planet Structures, Inc., builds environmentally sensitive structures. The company's 2010 revenues totaled $2,815 million, and at December 31, 2010, the company had $654 million in current assets. The December 31, 2010 and 2009, balance sheets reported the liabilities and stockholders' equity as follows.

At Year-end (In millions)	2010	2009
Liabilities and Stockholders' Equity		
Current Liabilities		
Accounts payable	$ 145	$ 183
Accrued expenses	161	182
Employee compensation and benefits..................	31	15
Current portion of long-term debt.......................	3	9
Total Current Liabilities......................................	340	389
Long-Term Debt	1,488	1,317
Post-Retirement Benefits Payable	129	135
Other Liabilities...	11	7
Stockholders' Equity	2,030	1,776
Total Liabilities and Stockholders' Equity..............	$3,998	$3,624

▍Requirements

1. Describe each of New Planet Structures, Inc.'s liabilities and state how the liability arose.
2. What were the company's total assets at December 31, 2010? Was the company's debt ratio at the end of 2010 high, low, or in a middle range?

E8-38B (*Learning Objective 1: Reporting a contingent liability*) Peterson Security Systems' revenues for 2010 totaled $26.2 million. As with most companies, Peterson is a defendant in lawsuits related to its products. Note 14 of the Peterson Annual Report for 2010 reported the following:

> **14. Contingencies**
> The company is involved in various legal proceedings.... It is the Company's policy to accrue for amounts related to these legal matters if it is probable that a liability has been incurred and an amount is reasonably estimable.

Requirements

1. Suppose Peterson's lawyers believe that a significant legal judgment against the company is reasonably possible. How should Peterson report this situation in its financial statements?
2. Suppose Peterson's lawyers believe it is probable that a $2.5 million judgment will be rendered against the company. Report this situation in Peterson's financial statements. Journalize any entry required by GAAP. Explanations are not required.

E8-39B (*Learning Objectives 1, 5: Reporting current and long-term liabilities*) Assume Five Mile Electronics completed these selected transactions during September 2010.

    a. Sales of $2,150,000 are subject to estimated warranty cost of 5%. The estimated warranty payable at the beginning of the year was $33,000, and warranty payments for the year totaled $57,000.

    b. On September 1, Five Mile Electronics signed a $40,000 note payable that requires annual payments of $10,000 plus 4% interest on the unpaid balance each September 2.

    c. Music For You, Inc., a chain of music stores, ordered $110,000 worth of CD players. With its order, Music For You, Inc., sent a check for $110,000, and Five Mile Electronics shipped $90,000 of the goods. Five Mile Electronics will ship the remainder of the goods on October 3, 2010.

    d. The September payroll of $240,000 is subject to employee withheld income tax of $30,000 and FICA tax of 7.65%. On September 30, Five Mile Electronics pays employees their take-home pay and accrues all tax amounts.

Requirement

1. Report these items on Five Mile Electronics' balance sheet at September 30, 2010.

E8-40B (*Learning Objectives 2, 3: Issuing bonds payable (discount); paying and accruing interest; amortizing the bonds by the straight-line method*) On January 31, Daughtry Logistics, Inc., issued five-year, 5% bonds payable with a face value of $11,000,000. The bonds were issued at 95 and pay interest on January 31 and July 31. Daughtry Logistics, Inc., amortizes bond discounts by the straight-line method. Record (a) issuance of the bonds on January 31, (b) the semiannual interest payment and amortization of bond discount on July 31, and (c) the interest accrual and discount amortization on December 31.

E8-41B (*Learning Objectives 2, 3: Measuring cash amounts for a bond payable (premium); amortizing the bonds by the straight-line method*) Commonwealth Bank has $400,000 of 9% debenture bonds outstanding. The bonds were issued at 104 in 2010 and mature in 2030.

Requirements

1. How much cash did Commonwealth Bank receive when it issued these bonds?
2. How much cash in *total* will Commonwealth Bank pay the bondholders through the maturity date of the bonds?
3. Take the difference between your answers to Requirements 1 and 2. This difference represents Commonwealth Bank's total interest expense over the life of the bonds.
4. Compute Commonwealth Bank's annual interest expense by the straight-line amortization method. Multiply this amount by 20. Your 20-year total should be the same as your answer to Requirement 3.

■ spreadsheet

E8-42B *(Learning Objectives 2, 3: Issuing bonds payable (discount); recording interest payments and the related bond amortization)* First Place Sports Ltd. is authorized to issue $1,000,000 of 9%, 10-year bonds payable. On December 31, 2010, when the market interest rate is 10%, the company issues $800,000 of the bonds and receives cash of $750,232. First Place Sports amortizes bonds by the effective-interest method. The semiannual interest dates are June 30 and December 31.

❙ Requirements

1. Prepare a bond amortization table for the first four semiannual interest periods.
2. Record issuance of the bonds payable on December 31, 2010, the first semiannual interest payment on June 30, 2011, and the second payment on December 31, 2011.

■ spreadsheet

E8-43B *(Learning Objectives 2, 3: Issuing bonds payable (premium); recording interest accrual and payment and the related bond amortization)* On June 30, 2010, the market interest rate is 9%. Team Sports Ltd. issues $3,200,000 of 10%, 10-year bonds payable at 106.5. The bonds pay interest on June 30 and December 31. Team Sports Ltd. amortizes bonds by the effective-interest method.

❙ Requirements

1. Prepare a bond amortization table for the first four semiannual interest periods.
2. Record the issuance of bonds payable on June 30, 2010, the payment of interest on December 31, 2010, and the payment of interest on June 30, 2011.

■ spreadsheet

E8-44B *(Learning Objective 3: Creating a bond amortization schedule (discount))* Tewksbury Co. issued $720,000 of 11% (0.11), 10-year bonds payable on January 1, 2010, when the market interest rate was 12% (0.12). The company pays interest annually at year-end. The issue price of the bonds was $679,318.

❙ Requirement

1. Create a spreadsheet model to prepare a schedule to amortize the bonds. Use the effective-interest method of amortization. (Round to the nearest dollar.)

E8-45B *(Learning Objective 2: Recording conversion of notes payable)* Worldview Imaging Ltd. issued $3,600,000 of 9% notes payable on December 31, 2010, at a price of 94. The notes' term maturity is 10 years. After four years, the notes may be converted into Worldview common stock. Each $1,000 face amount of notes is convertible into 60 shares of $1 par common stock. On December 31, 2015, noteholders exercised their right to convert all the notes into common stock.

❙ Requirements

1. Without making journal entries, compute the carrying amount of the notes payable at December 31, 2015, immediately before conversion. Worldview uses the straight-line method to amortize bonds.
2. All amortization has been recorded properly. Journalize the conversion transaction at December 31, 2015.

E8-46B *(Learning Objective 4: Measuring the times-interest-earned ratio)* Companies that operate in different industries may have very different financial ratio values. These differences may grow even wider when we compare companies located in different countries.

Compare three leading companies on their current ratio, debt ratio, and times-interest-earned ratio. Compute three ratios for Company F, Company L, and Company V.

(Amounts in millions or billions)	Company F	Company L	Company V
Income data			
Total revenues...........................	$9,728	¥7,312	€136,377
Operating income.......................	294	229	5,627
Interest expense.........................	43	29	687
Net income.................................	25	12	443
Asset and liability data			
(Amounts in millions or billions)			
Total current assets....................	433	5,414	147,378
Long-term assets	137	731	61,153
Total current liabilities...............	227	2,237	72,600
Long-term liabilities...................	107	2,310	110,907
Stockholders' equity...................	236	1,598	25,024

Based on your computed ratio values, which company looks the least risky?

E8-47B (*Learning Objective 4: Analyzing alternative plans for raising money*) First Federal Financial Services is considering two plans for raising $600,000 to expand operations. Plan A is to borrow at 5%, and plan B is to issue 100,000 shares of common stock at $6.00 per share. Before any new financing, First Federal Financial Services has net income of $400,000 and 100,000 shares of common stock outstanding. Assume you own most of First Federal Financial Services existing stock. Management believes the company can use the new funds to earn additional income of $550,000 before interest and taxes. First Federal Financial Services' income tax rate is 40%.

writing assignment ■

I Requirements

1. Analyze First Federal Financial Services situation to determine which plan will result in the higher earnings per share.
2. Which plan results in the higher earnings per share? Which plan allows you to retain control of the company? Which plan creates more financial risk for the company? Which plan do you prefer? Why? Present your conclusion in a memo to First Federal Financial Services board of directors.

Challenge Exercises

E8-48 (*Learning Objectives 1, 5: Reporting current liabilities*) The top management of Pratt Marketing Services examines the following company accounting records at August 29, immediately before the end of the year, August 31:

Total current assets	$ 324,700
Noncurrent assets........................	1,067,500
	$1,392,200
Total current liabilities................	$ 193,400
Noncurrent liabilities	253,400
Owners' equity............................	945,400
	$1,392,200

Suppose Pratt's management wants to achieve a current ratio of 2.25. How much in current liabilities should Pratt's pay off within the next two days in order to achieve its goal?

E8-49 *(Learning Objectives 2, 3, 5: Refinancing old bonds payable with new bonds)* Great Brands completed one of the most famous debt refinancings in history. A debt refinancing occurs when a company issues new bonds payable to retire old bonds. The company debits the old bonds payable and credits the new bonds payable.

Great Brands had $140 million of 5 3/4% bonds payable outstanding, with 21 years to maturity. Great retired these old bonds by issuing $77 million of new 11% bonds payable to the holders of the old bonds and paying the bondholders $8 million in cash. Great issued both groups of bonds at face value. At the time of the debt refinancing, Great Brands had total assets of $497 million and total liabilities of $357 million. Net income for the most recent year was $6.2 million on sales of $1 billion.

❙ Requirements

1. Journalize the debt refinancing transaction.
2. Compute annual interest expense for both the old and the new bond issues.
3. Why did Great Brands refinance the old bonds 5 3/4% payable with the new 11% bonds? Consider interest expense, net income, and the debt ratio.

writing assignment ■

E8-50 *(Learning Objectives 2, 3: Analyzing bond transactions)* This (adapted) advertisement appeared in the *Wall Street Chronicle*.

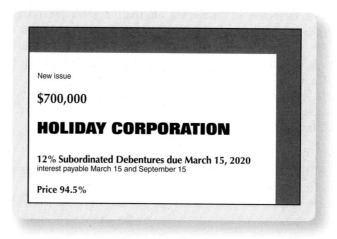

New issue

$700,000

HOLIDAY CORPORATION

12% Subordinated Debentures due March 15, 2020
interest payable March 15 and September 15

Price 94.5%

(Note: A *subordinated debenture* is an unsecured bond payable whose rights are less than the rights of other bondholders.)

❙ Requirements

1. Journalize Holiday's issuance of these bonds payable on March 15, 2010. No explanation is required, but describe the transaction in detail, indicating who received cash, who paid cash, and how much.
2. Why is the stated interest rate on these bonds so high?
3. Compute the semiannual cash interest payment on the bonds.
4. Compute the semiannual interest expense under the straight-line amortization method.
5. Compute both the first-year (from March 15, 2010, to March 15, 2011) and the second-year interest expense (March 15, 2011, to March 15, 2012) under the effective-interest amortization method. The market rate of interest at the date of issuance was 13%. Why is interest expense greater in the second year?

Quiz

Test your understanding of accounting for liabilities by answering the following questions. Select the best choice from among the possible answers given.

Q8-51 For the purpose of classifying liabilities as current or noncurrent, the term *operating cycle* refers to
a. the average time period between business recessions.
b. the time period between date of sale and the date the related revenue is collected.
c. the time period between purchase of merchandise and the conversion of this merchandise back to cash.
d. a period of one year.

Q8-52 Failure to accrue interest expense results in
a. an understatement of net income and an understatement of liabilities.
b. an understatement of net income and an overstatement of liabilities.
c. an overstatement of net income and an overstatement of liabilities.
d. an overstatement of net income and an understatement of liabilities.

Q8-53 FastscarsWarehouse operates in a state with a 5.5% sales tax. For convenience, Fastscars Warehouse credits Sales Revenue for the total amount (selling price plus sales tax) collected from each customer. If Fastscars Warehouse fails to make an adjustment for sales taxes,
a. net income will be overstated and liabilities will be understated.
b. net income will be understated and liabilities will be overstated.
c. net income will be understated and liabilities will be understated.
d. net income will be overstated and liabilities will be overstated.

Q8-54 What kind of account is Unearned Revenue?
a. Asset account
b. Liability account
c. Expense account
d. Revenue account

Q8-55 An end-of-period adjusting entry that debits Unearned Revenue most likely will credit
a. an asset.
b. a liability.
c. a revenue.
d. an expense.

Q8-56 Alexander, Inc., manufactures and sells computer monitors with a three-year warranty. Warranty costs are expected to average 7% of sales during the warranty period. The following table shows the sales and actual warranty payments during the first two years of operations:

Year	Sales	Warranty Payments
2010	$450,000	$ 3,150
2011	750,000	30,000

Based on these facts, what amount of warranty liability should Alexander, Inc., report on its balance sheet at December 31, 2011?
a. $33,150
b. $30,000
c. $84,000
d. $50,850

Q8-57 Yesterday's Fashions has a debt that has been properly reported as a long-term liability up to the present year (2010). Some of this debt comes due in 2010. If Yesterday's Fashions continues to report the current position as a long-term liability, the effect will be to
a. overstate net income.
b. understate total liabilities.
c. overstate the current ratio.
d. understate the debt ratio.

Q8-58 A bond with a face amount of $10,000 has a current price quote of 104.885. What is the bond's price?
a. $10,488.50
b. $1,048,850
c. $1,048.85
d. $10,104.89

Q8-59 Bond carrying value equals Bonds Payable
a. minus Premium on Bonds Payable.
b. plus Discount on Bonds Payable.
c. minus Discount on Bonds Payable.
d. plus Premium on Bonds Payable.
e. Both a and b
f. Both c and d

Q8-60 What type of account is *Discount on Bonds Payable* and what is its normal balance?
a. Adjusting amount;   Credit
b. Reversing account;   Debit
c. Contra liability;   Credit
d. Contra liability;   Debit

Questions 61–64 use the following data:

Spring Company sells $200,000 of 12%, 10-year bonds for 96 on April 1, 2010. The market rate of interest on that day is 12.5%. Interest is paid each year on April 1.

Q8-61 The entry to record the sale of the bonds on April 1 would be

a.	Cash	192,000	
	Discount on Bonds Payable	8,000	
	Bonds Payable		200,000
b.	Cash	200,000	
	Discount on Bonds Payable		8,000
	Bonds Payable		192,000
c.	Cash	200,000	
	Bonds Payable		200,000
d.	Cash	192,000	
	Bonds Payable		192,000

Q8-62 Spring Company uses the straight-line amortization method. The amount of interest expense on April 1 of each year will be
a. $24,000.
b. $25,000.
c. $24,800.
d. $32,000.
e. none of these.

Q8-63 Write the adjusting entry required at December 31, 2010.

Q8-64 Write the journal entry requirements at April 1, 2011.

Q8-65 McPartlin Corporation issued $300,000 of 10%, 10-year bonds payable on January 1, 2010, for $236,370. The market interest rate when the bonds were issued was 14%. Interest is paid semiannually on January 1 and July 1. The first interest payment is July 1, 2010. Using the effective-interest amortization method, how much interest expense will McPartlin record on July 1, 2010?

a. $15,500

b. $15,000

c. $14,500

d. $21,000

e. $16,546

Q8-66 Using the facts in the preceding question, McPartlin's journal entry to record the interest expense on July 1, 2010 will include a

a. debit to Bonds Payable.

b. credit to Discount on Bonds Payable.

c. credit to Interest Expense.

d. debit to Premium on Bonds Payable.

Q8-67 Amortizing the discount on bonds payable

a. reduces the semiannual cash payment for interest.

b. is necessary only if the bonds were issued at more than face value.

c. reduces the carrying value of the bond liability.

d. increases the recorded amount of interest expense.

Q8-68 The journal entry on the maturity date to record the payment of $500,000 of bonds payable that were issued at a $50,000 discount includes

a. a debit to Bonds Payable for $500,000.

b. a credit to Cash for $550,000.

c. a debit to Discount on Bonds Payable for $50,000.

d. all of the above.

Q8-69 Is the payment of the face amount of a bond on its maturity date regarded as an operating activity, an investing activity, or a financing activity?

a. Financing activity

b. Investing activity

c. Operating activity

Problems

All of the A and B problems can be found within MyAccountingLab, an online homework and practice environment. Your instructor may ask you to complete these problems using MyAccountingLab.

MyAccountingLab

(Group A)

P8-70A (*Learning Objective 1: Measuring current liabilities*)   Big Wave Marine experienced these events during the current year.

   a. December revenue totaled $120,000, and in addition, Big Wave collected sales tax of 5%. The tax amount will be sent to the state of Florida early in January.

   b. On August 31, Big Wave signed a six-month, 4% note payable to purchase a boat costing $85,000. The note requires payment of principal and interest at maturity.

   c. On August 31, Big Wave received cash of $2,400 in advance for service revenue. This revenue will be earned evenly over six months.

   d. Revenues of $850,000 were covered by Big Wave's service warranty. At January 1, estimated warranty payable was $11,600. During the year, Big Wave recorded warranty expense of $34,000 and paid warranty claims of $34,800.

   e. Big Wave owes $70,000 on a long-term note payable. At December 31, 12% interest for the year plus $35,000 of this principal are payable within one year.

▌Requirement

1. For each item, indicate the account and the related amount to be reported as a current liability on the Big Wave Marine balance sheet at December 31.

P8-71A (*Learning Objective 1: Recording liability-related transactions*)   The following transactions of Harmony Music Company occurred during 2010 and 2011:

2010	
Mar 3	Purchased a piano (inventory) for $70,000, signing a six-month, 4% note payable.
May 31	Borrowed $75,000 on a 4% note payable that calls for annual installment payments of $15,000 principal plus interest. Record the short-term note payable in a separate account from the long-term note payable.
Sep 3	Paid the six-month, 4% note at maturity.
Dec 31	Accrued warranty expense, which is estimated at 3.0% of sales of $190,000.
31	Accrued interest on the outstanding note payable.
2011	
May 31	Paid the first installment and interest for one year on the outstanding note payable.

▌Requirement

1. Record the transactions in Harmony's journal. Explanations are not required.

P8-72A (*Learning Objectives 2, 3: Recording bond transactions (at par); reporting bonds payable on the balance sheet*)   The board of directors of Monitors Plus authorizes the issue of $9,000,000 of 10%, five-year bonds payable. The semiannual interest dates are May 31 and November 30. The bonds are issued on May 31, 2010, at par.

▌Requirements

1. Journalize the following transactions:
   a. Issuance of half of the bonds on May 31, 2010.
   b. Payment of interest on November 30, 2010.
   c. Accrual of interest on December 31, 2010.
   d. Payment of interest on May 31, 2011.
2. Report interest payable and bonds payable as they would appear on the Monitors Plus balance sheet at December 31, 2010.

P8-73A (*Learning Objectives 2, 3, 5: Issuing bonds at a discount; amortizing by the straight-line method; reporting bonds payable on the balance sheet*)   On February 28, 2010, Marlin Corp. issues 8%, 10-year bonds payable with a face value of $900,000. The bonds pay interest on February 28 and August 31. Marlin Corp. amortizes bonds by the straight-line method.

▌Requirements

1. If the market interest rate is 7% when Marlin Corp. issues its bonds, will the bonds be priced at par, at a premium, or at a discount? Explain.
2. If the market interest rate is 9% when Marlin Corp. issues its bonds, will the bonds be priced at par, at a premium, or at a discount? Explain.
3. Assume that the issue price of the bonds is 99. Journalize the following bonds payable transactions.
   a. Issuance of the bonds on February 28, 2010.
   b. Payment of interest and amortization of the bonds on August 31, 2010.
   c. Accrual of interest and amortization of the bonds on December 31, 2010.
   d. Payment of interest and amortization of the bonds on February 28, 2011.
4. Report interest payable and bonds payable as they would appear on the Marlin Corp. balance sheet at December 31, 2010.

P8-74A (*Learning Objectives 2, 3: Accounting for bonds payable at a discount; amortizing by the straight-line method*)

❙ Requirements

1. Journalize the following transactions of Laporte Communications, Inc.:

2010		
Jan	1	Issued $7,000,000 of 9%, 10-year bonds payable at 96.
Jul	1	Paid semiannual interest and amortized bonds by the straight-line method on the 9% bonds payable.
Dec	31	Accrued semiannual interest expense and amortized bonds by the straight-line method on the 9% bonds payable.
2011		
Jan	1	Paid semiannual interest.
2020		
Jan	1	Paid the 9% bonds at maturity.

2. At December 31, 2010, after all year-end adjustments, determine the carrying amount of Laporte Communications bonds payable, net.
3. For the six months ended July 1, 2010, determine for Laporte Communications, Inc.:
   a. Interest expense
   b. Cash interest paid

What causes interest expense on the bonds to exceed cash interest paid?

P8-75A (*Learning Objectives 2, 3, 5: Analyzing a company's long-term debt; reporting long-term debt on the balance sheet (effective-interest method)*)   The notes to the Helping Charities financial statements reported the following data on December 31, Year 1 (end of the fiscal year):

❙ spreadsheet

Note 6. Indebtedness		
Bonds payable, 7% due in Year 7	$3,000,000	
Less: Discount..	(138,686)	$2,861,314
Notes payable, 6%, payable in amounts of $55,000 annual installments starting in Year 5...............		330,000

Helping Charities amortizes bonds by the effective-interest method and pays all interest amounts at December 31.

❙ Requirements

1. Answer the following questions about Helping Charities' long-term liabilities:
   a. What is the maturity value of the 7% bonds?
   b. What are Helping Charities' annual cash interest payments on the 7% bonds?
   c. What is the carrying amount of the 7% bonds at December 31, year 1?
2. Prepare an amortization table through December 31, Year 4, for the 7% bonds. The market interest rate on the bonds was 8%. (Round all amounts to the nearest dollar.) How much is Helping Charities' interest expense on the 7% bonds for the year ended December 31, Year 4?
3. Show how Helping Charities would report the 7% bonds payable and the 6% notes payable at December 31, Year 4.

■ **spreadsheet**

P8-76A (*Learning Objectives 2, 3, 5: Issuing convertible bonds at a discount; amortizing by the effective-interest method; converting bonds; reporting the bonds payable on the balance sheet*)   On December 31, 2010, Mugaboo Corp. issues 7%, 10-year convertible bonds payable with a maturity value of $3,000,000. The semiannual interest dates are June 30 and December 31. The market interest rate is 8%, and the issue price of the bonds is 93.165. Mugaboo Corp. amortizes bonds by the effective-interest method.

I *Requirements*

1. Prepare an effective-interest method amortization table for the first four semiannual interest periods.
2. Journalize the following transactions:
    a. Issuance of the bonds on December 31, 2010. Credit Convertible Bonds Payable.
    b. Payment of interest and amortization of the bonds on June 30, 2011.
    c. Payment of interest and amortization of the bonds on December 31, 2011.
    d. Conversion by the bondholders on July 1, 2012, of bonds with face value of $1,200,000 into 40,000 shares of Mugaboo Corp.'s $1-par common stock.
3. Show how Mugaboo Corp. would report the remaining bonds payable on its balance sheet at December 31, 2012.

writing assignment ■

P8-77A (*Learning Objective 4: Financing operations with debt or with stock*)   Paulus Sporting Goods is embarking on a massive expansion. Assume plans call for opening 25 new stores during the next three years. Each store is scheduled to be 40% larger than the company's existing locations, offering more items of inventory, and with more elaborate displays. Management estimates that company operations will provide $1.5 million of the cash needed for expansion. Paulus must raise the remaining $6.5 million from outsiders. The board of directors is considering obtaining the $6.5 million either through borrowing or by issuing common stock.

I *Requirement*

1. Write a memo to Paulus' management discussing the advantages and disadvantages of borrowing and of issuing common stock to raise the needed cash. Which method of raising the funds would you recommend?

P8-78A (*Learning Objectives 4, 5: Reporting liabilities on the balance sheet; calculating the times-interest-earned ratio*)   The accounting records of Barnstable Foods, Inc., include the following items at December 31, 2010:

Mortgage note payable, current	$ 94,000		Accumulated depreciation, equipment	$164,000
Accumulated pension benefit obligation	465,000		Discount on bonds payable (all long-term)	27,000
Bonds payable, long-term	1,200,000		Operating income	400,000
Mortgage note payable, long-term	319,000		Equipment	745,000
Bonds payable, current portion	400,000		Pension plan assets (market value)	405,000
Interest expense	222,000		Interest payable	72,000

I *Requirements*

1. Show how each relevant item would be reported on the Barnstable Foods, Inc., classified balance sheet, including headings and totals for current liabilities and long-term liabilities.
2. Answer the following questions about Barnstable's financial position at December 31, 2010:
    a. What is the carrying amount of the bonds payable (combine the current and long-term amounts)?
    b. Why is the interest-payable amount so much less than the amount of interest expense?
3. How many times did Barnstable cover its interest expense during 2010?

(Group B)

P8-79B (*Learning Objective 1: Measuring current liabilities*)   Sea Breeze Marine experienced these events during the current year.

    a. December revenue totaled $110,000, and in addition, Sea Breeze collected sales tax of 8%. The tax amount will be sent to the state of Georgia early in January.

    b. On August 31, Sea Breeze signed a six-month, 4% note payable to purchase a boat costing $82,000. The note requires payment of principal and interest at maturity.

    c. On August 31, Sea Breeze received cash of $1,200 in advance for service revenue. This revenue will be earned evenly over six months.

    d. Revenues of $750,000 were covered by Sea Breeze's service warranty. At January 1, estimated warranty payable was $11,400. During the year, Sea Breeze recorded warranty expense of $30,000 and paid warranty claims of $34,600.

    e. Sea Breeze owes $85,000 on a long-term note payable. At December 31, 10% interest for the year plus $25,000 of this principal are payable within one year.

Requirement

1. For each item, indicate the account and the related amount to be reported as a current liability on the Sea Breeze Marine balance sheet at December 31.

P8-80B (*Learning Objective 1: Recording liability-related transactions*)   The following transactions of Soft Sounds Music Company occurred during 2010 and 2011:

2010		
Mar 3	Purchased a piano (inventory) for $30,000, signing a six-month, 10% note payable.	
May 31	Borrowed $75,000 on a 6% note payable that calls for annual installment payments of $15,000 principal plus interest. Record the short-term note payable in a separate account from the long-term note payable.	
Sep 3	Paid the six-month, 10% note at maturity.	
Dec 31	Accrued warranty expense, which is estimated at 1.5% of sales of $196,000.	
31	Accrued interest on the outstanding note payable.	
2011		
May 31	Paid the first installment and interest for one year on the outstanding note payable.	

Requirement

1. Record the transactions in Soft Sounds Music Company's journal. Explanations are not required.

P8-81B (*Learning Objectives 2, 3: Recording bond transactions (at par); reporting bonds payable on the balance sheet*)   The board of directors of Pictures Plus authorizes the issue of $6,000,000 of 8%, 15-year bonds payable. The semiannual interest dates are May 31 and November 30. The bonds are issued on May 31, 2010, at par.

Requirements

1. Journalize the following transactions:

    a. Issuance of half of the bonds on May 31, 2010.

    b. Payment of interest on November 30, 2010.

    c. Accrual of interest on December 31, 2010.

    d. Payment of interest on May 31, 2011.

2. Report interest payable and bonds payable as they would appear on the Pictures Plus balance sheet at December 31, 2010.

P8-82B (*Learning Objectives 2, 3, 5: Issuing bonds at a discount; amortizing by the straight-line method; reporting notes payable on the balance sheet*)   On February 28, 2010, Mackerel Corp. issues 6%, 20-year bonds payable with a face value of $1,800,000. The bonds pay interest on February 28 and August 31. Mackerel Corp. amortizes bonds by the straight-line method.

❙ *Requirements*

1. If the market interest rate is 5% when Mackerel Corp. issues its bonds, will the bonds be priced at par, at a premium, or at a discount? Explain.
2. If the market interest rate is 7% when Mackerel Corp. issues its bonds, will the bonds be priced at par, at a premium, or at a discount? Explain.
3. Assume that the issue price of the bonds is 96. Journalize the following bond transactions.
   a. Issuance of the bonds on February 28, 2010.
   b. Payment of interest and amortization of the bonds on August 31, 2010.
   c. Accrual of interest and amortization of the bonds on December 31, 2010, the year-end.
   d. Payment of interest and amortization of the bonds on February 28, 2011.
4. Report interest payable and bonds payable as they would appear on the Mackerel Corp. balance sheet at December 31, 2010.

P8-83B (*Learning Objectives 2, 3: Accounting for bonds payable at a discount; amortizing by the straight-line method*)

❙ *Requirements*

1. Journalize the following transactions of Lamore Communications, Inc.:

2010		
Jan	1	Issued $4,000,000 of 7%, 10-year bonds payable at 96.
Jul	1	Paid semiannual interest and amortized the bonds by the straight-line method on the 7% bonds payable.
Dec 31		Accrued semiannual interest expense and amortized the bonds by the straight-line method on the 7% bonds payable.
2011		
Jan	1	Paid semiannual interest.
2020		
Jan	1	Paid the 7% bonds at maturity.

2. At December 31, 2010, after all year-end adjustments, determine the carrying amount of Lamore Communications bonds payable, net.
3. For the six months ended July 1, 2010, determine the following for Lamore Communications Inc:
   a. Interest expense   b. Cash interest paid

What causes interest expense on the bonds to exceed cash interest paid?

❙ **spreadsheet**

P8-84B (*Learning Objectives 2, 3, 5: Analyzing a company's long-term debt; reporting the long-term debt on the balance sheet (effective-interest method)*)   The notes to the Helpful Charities financial statements reported the following data on December 31, Year 1 (end of the fiscal year):

Note 6. Indebtedness		
Bonds payable, 4% due in Year 7	$6,000,000	
Less: Discount	(304,542)	$5,695,458
Notes payable, 7%, payable in $60,000		
annual installments starting in Year 5		360,000

Helpful Charities amortizes bonds by the effective-interest method and pays all interest amounts at December 31.

I Requirements

1. Answer the following questions about Helpful Charities long-term liabilities:
   a. What is the maturity value of the 4% bonds?
   b. What is Helpful Charities' annual cash interest payment on the 4% bonds?
   c. What is the carrying amount of the 4% bonds at December 31, Year 1?
2. Prepare an amortization table through December 31, Year 4, for the 4% bonds. The market interest rate on the bonds was 5%. Round all amounts to the nearest dollar. How much is Helpful Charities' interest expense on the 4% bonds for the year ended December 31, Year 4?
3. Show how Helpful Charities would report the 4% bonds and the 7% notes payable at December 31, Year 4.

P8-85B (*Learning Objectives 2, 3, 5: Issuing convertible bonds at a discount; amortizing by the effective-interest method; converting bonds; reporting the bonds payable on the balance sheet*) On December 31, 2010, Rugaboo Corp. issues 9%, 10-year convertible bonds payable with a maturity value of $2,000,000. The semiannual interest dates are June 30 and December 31. The market interest rate is 10%, and the issue price of the bonds is 93.779. Rugaboo Corp. amortizes bonds by the effective-interest method.

■ spreadsheet

I Requirements

1. Prepare an effective-interest method amortization table for the first four semiannual interest periods.
2. Journalize the following transactions:
   a. Issuance of the bonds on December 31, 2010. Credit Convertible Bonds Payable.
   b. Payment of interest and amortization of the bonds on June 30, 2011.
   c. Payment of interest and amortization of the bonds on December 31, 2011.
   d. Conversion by the bondholders on July 1, 2012, of bonds with face value of $800,000 into 90,000 shares of Rugaboo Corp. $1-par common stock.
3. Show how Rugaboo Corp. would report the remaining bonds payable on its balance sheet at December 31, 2012.

P8-86B (*Learning Objective 4: Financing operations with debt or with stock*) Fitzpatrick Sporting Goods is embarking on a massive expansion. Assume plans call for opening 30 new stores during the next four years. Each store is scheduled to be 45% larger than the company's existing locations, offering more items of inventory, and with more elaborate displays. Management estimates that company operations will provide $1.75 million of the cash needed for expansion. Fitzpatrick must raise the remaining $7 million from outsiders. The board of directors is considering obtaining the $7 million either through borrowing or by issuing common stock.

writing assignment ■

I Requirement

1. Write a memo to Fitzpatrick's management discussing the advantages and disadvantages of borrowing and of issuing common stock to raise the needed cash. Which method of raising the funds would you recommend?

P8-87B (*Learning Objectives 4, 5: Reporting liabilities on the balance sheet; calculating the times-interest-earned ratio*) The accounting records of Brilliant Foods, Inc., include the following items at December 31, 2010:

Mortgage note payable,		Accumulated depreciation,	
current	$ 95,000	equipment	$165,000
Accumulated pension		Discount on bonds payable	
benefit obligation	460,000	(all long-term)	23,000
Bonds payable, long-term............	200,000	Operating income................	360,000
Mortgage note payable,		Equipment..........................	746,000
long-term	313,000	Pension plan assets	
Bonds payable, current portion ...	500,000	(market value)................	410,000
Interest expense..........................	224,000	Interest payable...................	72,000

❙ Requirements

1. Show how each relevant item would be reported on the Brilliant Foods, Inc., classified balance sheet, including headings and totals for current liabilities and long-term liabilities.
2. Answer the following questions about Brilliant's financial position at December 31, 2010:
   a. What is the carrying amount of the bonds payable (combine the current and long-term amounts)?
   b. Why is the interest-payable amount so much less than the amount of interest expense?
3. How many times did Brilliant cover its interest expense during 2010?

APPLY YOUR KNOWLEDGE

Decision Cases

Case 1. (*Learning Objective 2: Exploring an actual bankruptcy*) In 2002, **Enron Corporation** filed for Chapter 11 bankruptcy protection, shocking the business community: How could a company this large and this successful go bankrupt? This case explores the causes and the effects of Enron's bankruptcy.

At December 31, 2000, and for the four years ended on that date, Enron reported the following (amounts in millions):

Balance Sheet (summarized)				
Total assets				$65,503
Total liabilities				54,033
Total stockholders' equity				11,470
Income Statements (excerpts)				
	2000	1999	1998	1997
Net income	$979*	$893	$703	$105

*Operating income = $1,953
Interest expense = $838

Unknown to investors and lenders, Enron also controlled hundreds of partnerships that owed vast amounts of money. These special-purpose entities (SPEs) did not appear on the Enron financial statements. Assume that the SPEs' assets totaled $7,000 million and their liabilities stood at $6,900 million; assume a 10% interest rate on these liabilities.

During the four-year period up to December 31, 2000, Enron's stock price shot up from $17.50 to $90.56. Enron used its escalating stock price to finance the purchase of the SPEs by guaranteeing lenders that Enron would give them Enron stock if the SPEs could not pay their loans.

In 2001, the SEC launched an investigation into Enron's accounting practices. It was alleged that Enron should have been including the SPEs in its financial statements all along. Enron then restated net income for years up to 2000, wiping out nearly $600 million of total net income (and total assets) for this four-year period. Enron's stock price tumbled, and the guarantees to the SPEs' lenders added millions to Enron's liabilities (assume the full amount of the SPEs' debt). To make matters worse, the assets of the SPEs lost much of their value; assume that their market value is only $500 million.

❙ Requirements

1. Compute the debt ratio that Enron reported at the end of 2000. Recompute this ratio after including the SPEs in Enron's financial statements. Also compute Enron's times-interest-earned ratio both ways for 2000. Assume that the changes to Enron's financial position occurred during 2000.
2. Why does it appear that Enron failed to include the SPEs in its financial statements? How do you view Enron after including the SPEs in the company's financial statements? (Challenge)

Case 2. *(Learning Objective 4: Analyzing alternative ways of raising $5 million)* Business is going well for **Park 'N Fly**, the company that operates remote parking lots near major airports. The board of directors of this family-owned company believes that Park 'N Fly could earn an additional $1.5 million income before interest and taxes by expanding into new markets. However, the $5 million that the business needs for growth cannot be raised within the family. The directors, who strongly wish to retain family control of the company, must consider issuing securities to outsiders. The directors are considering three financing plans.

Plan A is to borrow at 6%. Plan B is to issue 100,000 shares of common stock. Plan C is to issue 100,000 shares of nonvoting, $3.75 preferred stock ($3.75 is the annual dividend paid on each share of preferred stock).[5] Park 'N Fly presently has net income of $3.5 million and 1 million shares of common stock outstanding. The company's income tax rate is 35%.

❙ Requirements

1. Prepare an analysis to determine which plan will result in the highest earnings per share of common stock.
2. Recommend a plan to the board of directors. Give your reasons.

Ethical Issues

Issue 1. **Microsoft Corporation** is the defendant in numerous lawsuits claiming unfair trade practices. Microsoft has strong incentives not to disclose these contingent liabilities. However, GAAP requires that companies report their contingent liabilities.

❙ Requirements

1. Why would a company prefer not to disclose its contingent liabilities?
2. Identify the parties involved in the decision and the potential consequences to each.
3. Analyze the issue of whether to report contingent liabilities from lawsuits from the following standpoints:
    a. economic
    b. legal
    c. ethical
4. What impact will future changes in accounting standards, both at the U.S. level and the international level, likely have on the issue of disclosure of loss contingencies?

Issue 2. WHEN IS A LEASE A CAPITAL IDEA? Laurie Gocker, Inc., entered into a lease arrangement with Nathan Morgan Leasing Corporation for an industrial machine. Morgan's primary business is leasing. The cash purchase price of the machine is $1,000,000. Its economic life is six years.

Gocker's balance sheet reflects total assets of $10 million and total liabilities of $7.5 million. Among the liabilities is a $2.5 million long-term note outstanding at Last National Bank. The note carries a restrictive covenant that requires the company's debt ratio to be no higher than 75%. The company's revenues have been falling of late and the shareholders are concerned about profitability.

Gocker and Morgan are engaging in negotiations for terms of the lease. Some relevant other facts:

1. Morgan wants to take possession of the machine at the end of the initial lease term.
2. The term may run from four to five years, at Gocker's discretion.
3. Morgan estimates the machine will have no residual value, and Gocker will not purchase it at the end of the lease term.
4. The present value of minimum lease payments on the machine is $890,000.

❙ Requirements

1. What is (are) the ethical issue(s) in this case?
2. Who are the stakeholders? Analyze the consequences for each stakeholder from the following standpoints: (a) economic, (b) legal, and (c) ethical.

---

[5]For a discussion of preferred stock, see Chapter 9.

3. How should Gocker structure the lease agreement?
4. How will the analysis of this case change when IFRS are adopted in the United States? Would your decision be different? Why or why not?

Focus on Financials: ■ Amazon.com, Inc.

(*Learning Objectives 1, 2, 5: Analyzing current and contingent liabilities*) Refer to **Amazon.com, Inc.**'s consolidated financial statements in Appendix A at the end of this book.

1. Did accounts payable for Amazon.com, Inc., increase or decrease in 2008? What was the amount? What might have caused this change?
2. Examine Note 12—Income Taxes—in the Notes to Consolidated Financial Statements. Income tax provision is another title for income tax expense. What was Amazon.com, Inc.'s income tax provision in 2008? How much did the company pay in federal income taxes? How much was income taxes payable as of December 31, 2008? In general, why were these amounts different? (Challenge)
3. Did Amazon.com, Inc., borrow more or pay off more long-term debt during 2008? How can you tell? (Challenge)
4. Examine Note 7—Commitments and Contingencies—in the Notes to Consolidated Financial Statements. Describe some of Amazon.com, Inc.'s contingent liabilities as of December 31, 2008.
5. How would you rate Amazon.com, Inc.'s overall debt position—risky, safe, or average? Compute the ratio at December 31, 2008, that answers this question.

Focus on Analysis: ■ Foot Locker, Inc.

(*Learning Objectives 1, 2, 3, 5: Analyzing current liabilities and long-term debt*) **Foot Locker, Inc.**'s consolidated financial statements in Appendix B at the end of this book report a number of liabilities. Show amounts in thousands.

1. The current liability section of Foot Locker, Inc.'s Consolidated Balance Sheet as of February 2, 2008 (the end of fiscal 2007) lists accrued and other liabilities totaling $268 million. Find the details of this total in the Notes to Consolidated Financial Statements. What are the four principal items comprising this total? (Challenge)
2. Refer to Note 15 of the Notes to Consolidated Financial Statements—Long-Term Debt and Obligations under Capital Leases. Why do you think the company has combined these two totals? Summarize the contents of this section of the balance sheet as of the end of the fiscal 2007 year, as well as the changes that have occurred during fiscal 2007. When do the company's long-term liabilities of $221 million mature? (Challenge)
3. How would you rate Foot Locker, Inc.'s overall debt position at the end of fiscal 2007—risky, safe, or average? Compute the ratios that enable you to answer this question. (Challenge)
4. Access Foot Locker, Inc.'s most recent financial statements from its Web site (www.footlocker.com). You will find a link called "about us" under the customer service section of the website, which will lead you to the latest financial statements filed with the SEC. What has happened to Foot Locker, Inc.'s debt position since the end of fiscal 2007? Why?

Group Projects

Project 1.   Consider three different businesses:

1. A bank
2. A magazine publisher
3. A department store

For each business, list all of its liabilities—both current and long-term. Then compare the three lists to identify the liabilities that the three businesses have in common. Also identify the liabilities that are unique to each type of business.

Project 2.   Alcenon Corporation leases the majority of the assets that it uses in operations. Alcenon prefers operating leases (versus capital leases) in order to keep the lease liability off its balance sheet and maintain a low debt ratio.

Alcenon is negotiating a 10-year lease on an asset with an expected useful life of 15 years. The lease requires Alcenon to make 10 annual lease payments of $20,000 each, with the first payment due at the beginning of the lease term. The leased asset has a market value of $135,180. The lease agreement specifies no transfer of title to the lessee and includes no bargain purchase option.

Write a report for Alcenon's management to explain what conditions must be present for Alcenon to be able to account for this lease as an operating lease.

For online homework, exercises, and problems that provide you with immediate feedback, please visit www.myaccountinglab.com.

Quick Check Answers

1. *d*

2. *e*

3. *b* ($450,000 × 0.01 = $4,500)

4. *c* [900 × 0.04 × $25 = warranty expense of $900; repaired $25 × 15 = $375; year-end liability = $525 ($900 - $375)]

5. *e*

6. *b*

7. *d*

8. *c*

9. *c*

10. *d*

11. *a*

12. *a* ($512,408 × 0.08 × 6/12 = $20,496)

13. *c* [Int. exp. = $20,496 Int. payment = $19,250 ($550,000 × 0.07 × 6/12) $20,496 – $19,250 = $1,246]

14. *b* ($550,000 × 0.07 = $38,500)

15. *a* (See Amortization Schedule)

Date	Interest Payment	Interest Expense	Discount Amortiz.	Bond Carry Amt.
1/1/2011				$512,408
7/1/2011	$19,250	$20,496	$1,246	513,654
1/1/2012	19,250	20,546	1,296	514,950

16. *d* {$512,408 + [($550,000 – $512,408) × 1/10] = $516,167}

9

Stockholders' Equity

SPOTLIGHT: DineEquity: Where IHOP meets Applebee's

It's late and you have a history exam tomorrow morning at 8. Where do you go for a quick bite? Either IHOP or Applebee's may be your choice, because both of these popular restaurants locate near college campuses.

IHOP started in 1958 and first offered the company's stock to the public in 1991. Now IHOP operates 1,350 restaurants in 49 states. In November 2007, IHOP bought Applebee's International, the world's largest casual dining restaurant, with more than 1,900 restaurants. To help finance the transaction, IHOP issued some new preferred stock. In May 2008, IHOP changed its corporate name to DineEquity. These events bring together two leading restaurant chains under one umbrella, creating the largest full-service franchise restaurant corporation in the world. In 2007, the corporation racked up sales of $484 million. However, Applebee's operating losses, combined with a long and deep business recession, have forced DineEquity to incur big losses for the past fiscal year, and have distorted its rate of return on stockholders' equity (ROE), as will be discussed later.

In this chapter we'll show you how to account for the issuance of corporate capital stock to investors. We'll also cover the other elements of stockholders' equity—Additional Paid-in Capital, Retained Earnings, and Treasury Stock, plus dividends and stock splits. By the time you finish this chapter, you may be hungry for a stack of IHOP pancakes or a steak from Applebee's. Or you may go out and buy some DineEquity stock. The consolidated balance sheet on the next page is for December 31, 2007, the last year before IHOP changed its name to DineEquity.

IHOP Corp.
Consolidated Balance Sheet (Adapted)
December 31, 2007

(In thousands, except number of shares)

Assets
Current assets:

Total current assets	$ 433,678
Long-term receivables	288,452
Property and equipment, net	1,139,616
Goodwill..	730,728
Other intangibles, net...	1,011,457
Other assets...	227,231
Total assets...	$3,831,162

Liabilities and Stockholders' Equity
Current liabilities:

	Total current liabilities	$ 381,340
	Long-term debt	2,432,129
	Other long-term liabilities	621,270
1	Perpetual Preferred stock, series A, $1 par value,	
	220,000 shares authorized; 190,000 shares issued	
	and outstanding	187,050
2	Stockholders' equity:	
3	Preferred stock, series B, $1 par value, 10,000,000 shares	
	authorized; 35,000 shares issued and outstanding:	
	35,000 shares..	35
4	Common stock, $.01 par value, 40,000,000 shares authorized;	
	23,359,664 shares issued and 17,105,469 shares outstanding	230
5	Additional paid-in capital	184,710
6	Retained earnings..	338,790
7	Treasury stock, at cost (6,254,195 shares).............	(277,654)
8	Other equity..	(36,738)
9	Total stockholders' equity	209,373
	Total liabilities and stockholders' equity	$3,831,162

Chapters 4 to 8 discussed accounting for assets and liabilities. By this time, you should be familiar with all the assets and liabilities listed on IHOP's balance sheet. Let's focus now on IHOP's stockholders' equity. In this chapter we discuss some of the decisions a company faces when:

- paying dividends
- issuing stock
- buying back its stock

Let's begin with the organization of a corporation.

LEARNING OBJECTIVES

1 **Explain** the features of a corporation

2 **Account** for the issuance of stock

3 **Describe** how treasury stock affects a company

4 **Account** for dividends

5 **Use** stock values in decision making

6 **Compute** return on assets and return on equity

7 **Report** equity transactions on the statement of cash flows

WHAT'S THE BEST WAY TO ORGANIZE A BUSINESS?

Anyone starting a business must decide how to organize the company. Corporations differ from proprietorships and partnerships in several ways.

Separate Legal Entity.   A corporation is a business entity formed under state law. It is a distinct entity, an artificial person that exists apart from its owners, the **stockholders**, or **shareholders**. The corporation has many of the rights that a person has. For example, a corporation may buy, own, and sell property. Assets and liabilities in the business belong to the corporation and not to its owners. The corporation may enter into contracts, sue, and be sued.

Nearly all large companies, such as DineEquity, **Toyota**, and **Wal-Mart**, are corporations. Their full names may include *Corporation* or *Incorporated* (abbreviated *Corp.* and *Inc.*) to indicate that they are corporations, for example, DineEquity Corp. and Williams-Sonoma, Inc. Corporations can also use the word *Company*, such as Ford Motor Company.

Continuous Life and Transferability of Ownership.   Corporations have *continuous lives* regardless of changes in their ownership. The stockholders of a corporation may buy more of the stock, sell the stock to another person, give it away, or bequeath it in a will. The transfer of the stock from one person to another does not affect the continuity of the corporation. In contrast, proprietorships and partnerships terminate when their ownership changes.

Limited Liability.   Stockholders have **limited liability** for the corporation's debts. They have no personal obligation for corporate liabilities. The most that a stockholder can lose on an investment in a corporation's stock is the cost of the investment. Limited liability is one of the most attractive features of the corporate form of organization. It enables corporations to raise more capital from a wider group of investors than proprietorships and partnerships can. By contrast, proprietors and partners are personally liable for all the debts of their businesses.[1]

---

[1]Unless the business is organized as a limited-liability company (LLC) or a limited-liability partnership (LLP).

OBJECTIVE

1 **Explain** the features of a corporation

Separation of Ownership and Management. Stockholders own the corporation, but the *board of directors*—elected by the stockholders—appoints officers to manage the business. Thus, stockholders may invest $1,000 or $1 million in the corporation without having to manage it.

Management's goal is to maximize the firm's value for the stockholders. But the separation between owners and managers may create problems. Corporate officers may run the business for their own benefit and not for the stockholders. For example, the CEO of **Tyco Corporation** was accused of looting Tyco of $600 million. The CFO of **Enron Corporation** set up outside partnerships and paid himself millions to manage the partnerships—unknown to Enron stockholders. Both men went to prison.

Corporate Taxation. Corporations are separate taxable entities. They pay several taxes not borne by proprietorships or partnerships, including an annual franchise tax levied by the state. The franchise tax keeps the corporate charter in force. Corporations also pay federal and state income taxes.

Corporate earnings are subject to **double taxation** on their income to the extent they are distributed to shareholders in the form of dividends.

- First, corporations pay income taxes on their corporate income.
- Then stockholders pay income tax on the cash dividends received from corporations. Proprietorships and partnerships pay no business income tax. Instead, the business' tax falls solely on the owners.

Government Regulation. Because stockholders have only limited liability for corporation debts, outsiders doing business with the corporation can look no further than the corporation if it fails to pay. To protect a corporation's creditors and stockholders, both federal and state governments monitor corporations. The regulations mainly ensure that corporations disclose the information that investors and creditors need to make informed decisions. Accounting provides much of this information.

Exhibit 9-1 summarizes the advantages and disadvantages of the corporate form of business organization.

EXHIBIT 9-1 | Advantages and Disadvantages of the Corporation

Advantages	Disadvantages
1. Can raise more capital than a proprietorship or partnership can	1. Separation of ownership and management
2. Continuous life	2. Corporate taxation
3. Ease of transferring ownership	3. Government regulation
4. Limited liability of stockholders	

ORGANIZING A CORPORATION

The creation of a corporation begins when its organizers, called the *incorporators*, obtain a charter from the state. The charter includes the authorization for the corporation to issue a certain number of shares of stock. A share of stock is the basic unit of ownership for a corporation. The incorporators

- pay fees,
- sign the charter,

- file documents with the state, and
- agree to a set of **bylaws**, which act as the constitution for governing the company.

The corporation then comes into existence.

Ultimate control of the corporation rests with the stockholders who elect a **board of directors** that sets company policy and appoints officers. The board elects a **chairperson**, who usually is the most powerful person in the organization. The chairperson of the board of directors has the title chief executive officer (CEO). The board also designates the **president**, who is the chief operating officer (COO) in charge of day-to-day operations. Most corporations also have vice presidents in charge of sales, manufacturing, accounting and finance (the chief financial officer, or CFO), and other key areas. Exhibit 9-2 shows the authority structure in a corporation.

EXHIBIT 9-2 | Authority Structure in a Corporation

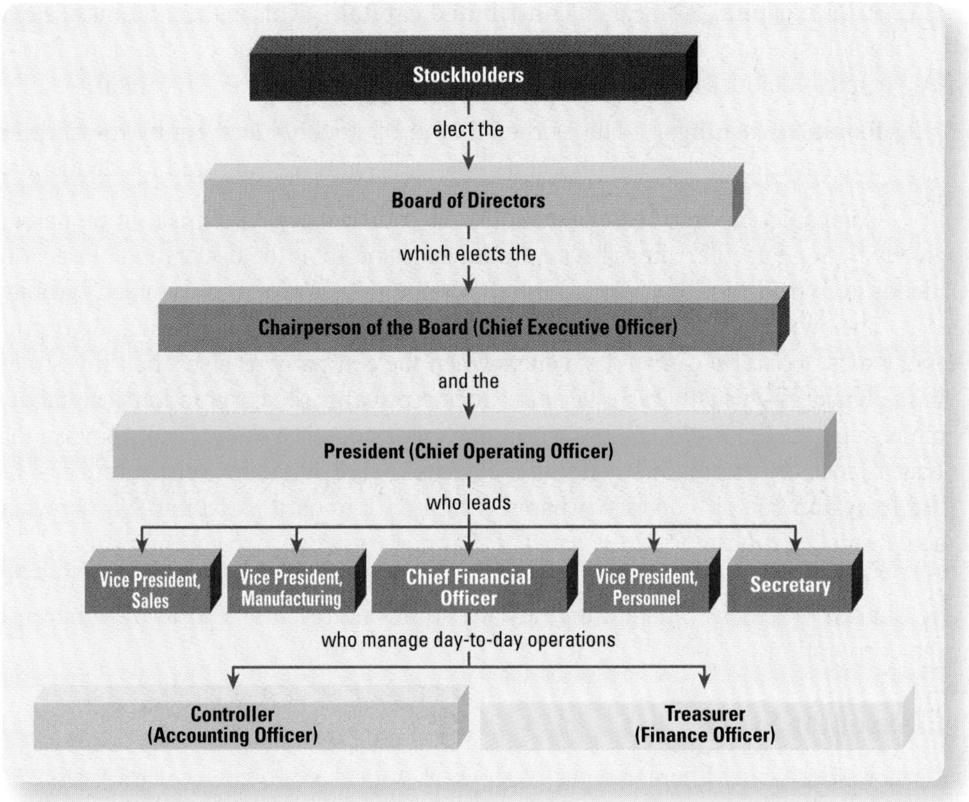

Stockholders' Rights

Ownership of stock entitles stockholders to four basic rights, unless a specific right is withheld by agreement with the stockholders:

1. *Vote.* The right to participate in management by voting on matters that come before the stockholders. This is the stockholder's sole voice in the management of the corporation. A stockholder gets one vote for each share of stock owned.

2. *Dividends.* The right to receive a proportionate part of any dividend. Each share of stock in a particular class receives an equal dividend.

3. *Liquidation.* The right to receive a proportionate share of any assets remaining after the corporation pays its liabilities in liquidation. Liquidation means to go

out of business, sell the assets, pay all liabilities, and distribute any remaining cash to the owners.

4. *Preemption.* The right to maintain one's proportionate ownership in the corporation. Suppose you own 5% of a corporation's stock. If the corporation issues 100,000 new shares, it must offer you the opportunity to buy 5% (5,000) of the new shares. This right, called the *preemptive right*, is usually withheld from the stockholders.

Stockholders' Equity

As we saw in Chapter 1, **stockholders' equity** represents the stockholders' ownership interest in the assets of a corporation. Stockholders' equity is divided into two main parts:

1. **Paid-in capital**, also called **contributed capital.** This is the amount of stockholders' equity the stockholders have contributed to the corporation. Paid-in capital includes the stock accounts and any additional paid-in capital.

2. **Retained earnings.** This is the amount of stockholders' equity the corporation has earned through profitable operations and has not used for dividends.

Companies report stockholders' equity by source. They report paid-in capital separately from retained earnings because most states prohibit the declaration of cash dividends from paid-in capital. Thus, cash dividends are declared from retained earnings.

The owners' equity of a corporation is divided into shares of **stock**. A corporation issues *stock certificates* to its owners when the company receives their investment in the business—usually cash. Because stock represents the corporation's capital, it is often called *capital stock*. The basic unit of capital stock is a *share*. A corporation may issue a stock certificate for any number of shares—1, 100, or any other number—but the total number of *authorized* shares is limited by charter. Exhibit 9-3 shows an actual stock certificate for 288 shares of Central Jersey Bancorp common stock.

Stock in the hands of a stockholder is said to be *outstanding*. The total number of shares of stock outstanding at any time represents 100% ownership of the corporation.

Classes of Stock

Corporations issue different types of stock to appeal to a variety of investors. The stock of a corporation may be either

- Common or preferred
- Par or no-par

Common and Preferred. Every corporation issues **common stock**, the basic form of capital stock. Unless designated otherwise, the word *stock* is understood to mean "common stock." Common stockholders have the four basic rights of stock ownership, unless a right is specifically withheld. The common stockholders are the owners of the corporation. They stand to benefit the most if the corporation succeeds because they take the most risk by investing in common stock.

Preferred stock gives its owners certain advantages over common stockholders. Preferred stockholders receive dividends before the common stockholders and they also receive assets before the common stockholders if the corporation liquidates. Owners of preferred stock also have the four basic stockholder rights, unless a right

EXHIBIT 9-3 | Stock Certificate

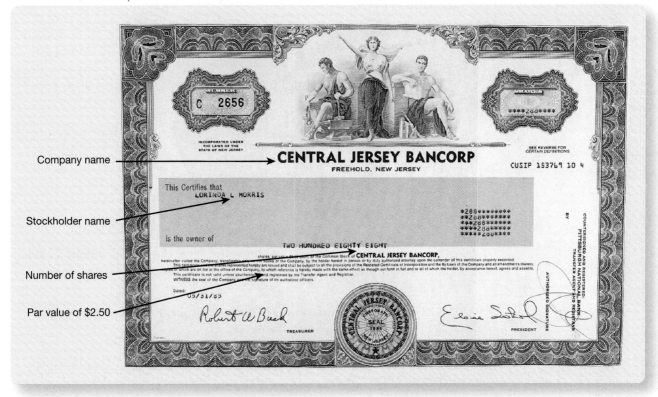

Company name → **CENTRAL JERSEY BANCORP**
FREEHOLD, NEW JERSEY

Stockholder name → LORINDA L MORRIS

Number of shares → TWO HUNDRED EIGHTY EIGHT

Par value of $2.50

is specifically denied. Companies may issue different classes of preferred stock (Class A and Class B or Series A and Series B, for example). Each class of stock is recorded in a separate account. The most preferred stockholders can expect to earn on their investments is a fixed dividend.

Preferred stock is a hybrid between common stock and long-term debt. Like interest on debt, preferred stock pays a fixed dividend. But unlike interest on debt, the dividend is not required to be paid unless the board of directors declares the dividend. Also, companies have no obligation to pay back true preferred stock. Preferred stock that must be redeemed (paid back) by the corporation is a liability masquerading as a stock.

Preferred stock is rare. A recent survey of 600 corporations revealed that only 9% of them had preferred stock (Exhibit 9-4 on the following page). All corporations have common stock. The balance sheet of IHOP Corp. (p. 534) shows that IHOP actually has two classes of preferred stock: Series A and Series B. Both of these classes of stock were issued in November 2007, in connection with IHOP's acquisition of Applebee's International Corp. The Class A preferred stock, recorded at a net amount of $187,050,000 ($190,000,000 par value less $2,950,000 issuance costs) is called "perpetual preferred stock." It has so many features that are like long-term debt (i.e., fixed but potentially increasing dividend amounts, cumulative as to dividends) that the company actually classifies it between the long-term debt and stockholders' equity sections of the balance sheet, rather than in stockholders' equity per se. IHOP also has authorized 10 million shares of Series B $1 convertible preferred stock. As of December 31, 2007, 35,000 of these shares have been issued and are outstanding. The company received approximately $35 million for these shares. We will explain the meanings of the terms "cumulative" and "convertible" later.

EXHIBIT 9-4 | Preferred Stock

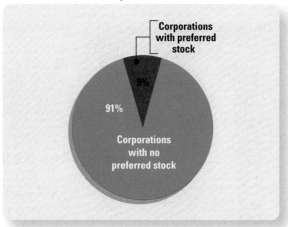

Exhibit 9-5 shows some of the similarities and differences among common stock, preferred stock, and long-term debt.

EXHIBIT 9-5 | Comparison of Common Stock, Preferred Stock, and Long-Term Debt

	Common Stock	Preferred Stock	Long-Term Debt
1. Obligation to repay principal	No	No	Yes
2. Dividends/interest	Dividends are not tax-deductible	Dividends are not tax-deductible	Interest expense is tax-deductible
3. Obligation to pay dividends/interest	Only after declaration	Only after declaration	At fixed rates and dates

Par Value and No-Par. Stock may be par-value stock or no-par stock. **Par value** is an arbitrary amount assigned by a company to a share of its stock. Most companies set the par value of their common stock low to avoid legal difficulties from issuing their stock below par. Most states require companies to maintain a minimum amount of stockholders' equity for the protection of creditors, and this minimum is often called the corporation's legal capital. For corporations with par-value stock, **legal capital** is the par value of the shares issued.

The par value of **PepsiCo** common stock is $0.0166 (1 2/3 cents) per share. **Best Buy** common stock carries a par value of $1 per share, and **IHOP**'s common stock has par value of $0.01 per share. Par value of preferred stock is sometimes higher. IHOP's December 31, 1997, balance sheet lists Series B preferred stock with $1 par value.

No-par stock does not have par value. But some no-par stock has a **stated value**, which makes it similar to par-value stock. The stated value is an arbitrary amount similar to par value. In a recent survey, only 9% of the companies had no-par stock outstanding. Apple, Inc., Krispy Kreme Doughnuts, and Sony have no-par stock.

ISSUING STOCK

OBJECTIVE

2 **Account** for the issuance of stock

Large corporations such as **IHOP**, **PepsiCo**, and **Microsoft** need huge quantities of money to operate. Corporations may sell stock directly to the stockholders or use the service of an *underwriter*, such as the investment banking firms **UBS** and **Goldman**

Sachs. Companies often advertise the issuance of their stock to attract investors. *The Wall Street Journal* is the most popular medium for such advertisements, which are also called *tombstones*. Exhibit 9-6 is a reproduction of IHOP's tombstone, which appeared in *The Wall Street Journal*.

EXHIBIT 9-6 | **Announcement of Public Offering of IHOP Stock (Adapted)**

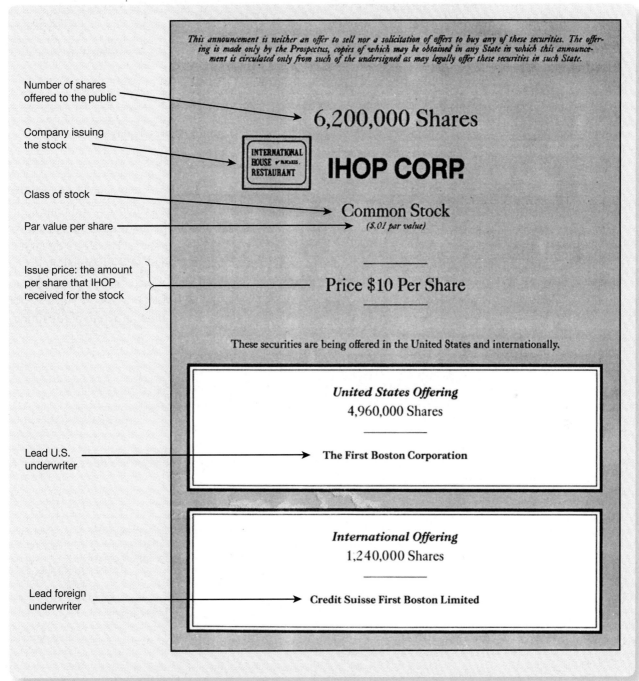

The lead underwriter of IHOP's public offering was First Boston Corporation. Outside the United States, Credit Suisse First Boston Limited led the way. Several other domestic brokerage firms and investment bankers sold IHOP stock to their clients. In its initial public offering (Exhibit 9-6), IHOP sought to raise $62 million of capital (6.2 million shares at the offering price of $10 per share). Let's see how a stock issuance works.

Common Stock

Common Stock at Par.   Suppose IHOP's common stock had carried a par value equal to its issuance price of $10 per share. The entry for issuance of 6.2 million shares of stock at par would be

Jan 8	Cash (6,200,000 × $10)	62,000,000	
	Common Stock		62,000,000
	To issue common stock.		

IHOP's assets and stockholders' equity increase by the same amount.

Assets	=	Liabilities	+	Stockholders' Equity
+ 62,000,000	=	0		+ 62,000,000

Common Stock Above Par.   Most corporations set par value low and issue common stock for a price above par. Rather than $10 as in the assumed example above, IHOP's common stock has a par value of $0.01 (1 cent) per share. The $9.99 difference between issue price ($10) and par value ($0.01) is additional paid-in capital. Both the par value of the stock and the additional amount are part of paid-in capital.

Because the entity is dealing with its own stockholders, a sale of stock is not gain, income, or profit to the corporation. This situation illustrates one of the fundamentals of accounting:

> **A company neither earns a profit nor incurs a loss when it sells its stock to, or buys its stock from, its own stockholders.**

With par value of $0.01, IHOP's actual entry to record the issuance of common stock looked something like this:

Jul 23	Cash (6,200,000 × $10)	62,000,000	
	Common Stock (6,200,000 × $0.01)		62,000
	Paid-in Capital in Excess of Par—Common		
	(6,200,000 × $9.99)		61,938,000
	To issue common stock.		

Both assets and equity increase by the same amount.

Assets	=	Liabilities	+	Stockholders' Equity
+ 62,000,000	=	0		+ 62,000
				+ 61,938,000

Another title for Paid-in Capital in Excess of Par—Common is Additional Paid-in Capital, as used by IHOP Corporation (p. 534, line 5). At the end of the year, IHOP could report stockholders' equity on its balance sheet as follows:

Stockholders' Equity

Common stock, $0.01 par, 40 million shares authorized, 6.2 million shares issued	$ 62,000
Paid-in capital in excess of par	61,938,000
Total paid-in capital	62,000,000
Retained earnings	338,790
Total stockholders' equity	$62,338,790

All the transactions in this section include a receipt of cash by the corporation as it issues *new* stock. The transactions we illustrate are different from those reported in the daily news. In those transactions, one stockholder sold stock to another investor. The corporation doesn't record those transactions because they were between two outside parties.

STOP & THINK...

Examine IHOP's balance sheet at December 31, 2007 (p. 534). Answer these questions about IHOP's actual stock transactions (amounts in thousands, except per share):

1. What was IHOP's total paid-in capital at December 31, 2007?
2. How many shares of common stock had IHOP issued through the end of 2007 (in thousands)?
3. What was the average issue price of the IHOP common stock that the company had issued through the end of 2007?

Answers:

		December 31, 2007
1.	Total paid-in capital (in thousands)	$35 + $230 + $184,710 = $184,975
2.	Number of shares of common stock issued (in thousands)	23,360

3.
$$\frac{\text{Average issue price}}{\text{of common stock through the end of 2007}} = \frac{\text{Total received from issuance of common stock}}{\text{Common shares issued}} = \frac{\$230 + (\$184,710 - \$34,215^1) = \$150,725}{23,360}$$
$$= \$6.45 \text{ per share}$$

[1]A total of $34,215 in additional paid-in capital came from the issuance of the series B preferred stock. It must be subtracted to compute the total received from issuance of common stock.

IHOP has issued its common stock at an average price of $6.45 per share.

No-Par Common Stock. To record the issuance of no-par stock, the company debits the asset received and credits the stock account for the cash value of the asset received. Suppose Apple, Inc., issues 855 million shares of no-par common stock for $4,355 million. Apple's stock issuance entry is (in millions)

Aug 14	Cash	4,355	
	Common Stock		4,355
	To issue no-par common stock.		

Assets	=	Liabilities	+	Stockholders' Equity
+ 4,355	=	0		+ 4,355

Apple's charter authorizes the company to issue 1,800 million shares of no-par stock, and the company has approximately $5,629 in retained earnings. Apple, Inc., reports stockholders' equity on the balance sheet as follows (in millions):

Stockholders' Equity	
Common stock, no par, 1,800 shares authorized, 855 shares issued..................	$4,355
Retained earnings...	5,629
Total stockholders' equity	$9,984

You can see that a company with true no-par stock has no Additional Paid-in Capital account.

No-Par Common Stock with a Stated Value. Accounting for no-par stock with a stated value is identical to accounting for par-value stock. The excess over stated value is credited to Additional Paid-in Capital.

Common Stock Issued for Assets Other Than Cash. When a corporation issues stock and receives assets other than cash, the company records the assets received at their current market value and credits the stock and additional paid-in capital accounts accordingly. The assets' prior book value isn't relevant because the stockholder will demand stock equal to the market value of the asset given. On November 12, Kahn Corporation issued 15,000 shares of its $1 par common stock for equipment worth $4,000 and a building worth $120,000. Kahn's entry is

Nov 12	Equipment	4,000	
	Building	120,000	
	Common Stock (15,000 × $1)		15,000
	Paid-in Capital in Excess of Par—Common		
	($124,000 – $15,000)		109,000
	To issue no-par common stock in exchange for equipment		
	and a building.		

Assets and equity both increase by $124,000.

Assets	=	Liabilities	+	Stockholders' Equity
+ 4,000 + 120,000	=	0		+ 15,000 + 109,000

Common Stock Issued for Services. Sometimes a corporation will issue shares of common stock in exchange for services rendered, either by employees or outsiders. In this case, no cash is exchanged. However, the transaction is recognized at fair market value. The corporation usually recognizes an expense for the fair market value of the services rendered. Common stock is increased for its par value (if any) and additional paid-in capital is increased for any difference. For example, assume that Kahn Corporation engages an attorney to represent the company on a legal matter. The attorney bills the corporation $25,000 for services, and agrees to accept 2,500 shares of $1 par common stock, rather than cash, in settlement of the fee. The fair market value of the stock is $10 per share. The journal entry to record the transaction is

Legal Expense	25,000	
Common Stock		2,500
Paid-in Capital in Excess of Par—Common ($25,000 – $2,500)		22,500

In this case, retained earnings (stockholders' equity) is eventually decreased by $25,000, and paid-in capital (stockholders' equity) is increased for the same amount.

A Stock Issuance for Other Than Cash Can Create an Ethical Challenge

Generally accepted accounting principles require a company to record its stock at the fair market value of whatever the corporation receives in exchange for the stock. When the corporation receives cash, there is clear evidence of the value of the stock because cash is worth its face amount. But when the corporation receives an asset other than cash, the value of the asset can create an ethical challenge.

A computer whiz may start a new company by investing computer software. The software may be market-tested or it may be new. The software may be worth millions or worthless. The corporation must record the asset received and the stock given with a journal entry such as the following:

Software	500,000	
Common Stock		500,000
Issued stock in exchange for software.		

If the software is really worth $500,000, the accounting records are okay. But if the software is new and untested, the assets and equity may be overstated.

Suppose your computer-whiz friend invites you to invest in the new business and shows you this balance sheet:

Gee-Whiz Computer Solutions, Inc.
Balance Sheet
December 31, 2011

Assets		Liabilities	
Computer software	$500,000		$ -0-
		Stockholders' Equity	
		Common stock...........................	500,000
Total assets...........................	$500,000	Total liabilities and equity...........	$500,000

Companies like to report large asset and equity amounts on their balance sheets. That makes them look prosperous and creditworthy. Gee-Whiz looks debt-free and appears to have a valuable asset. Will you invest in this new business? Here are two takeaway lessons:

- Some accounting values are more solid than others.
- Not all financial statements mean exactly what they say—unless they are audited by independent CPAs.

Preferred Stock

Accounting for preferred stock follows the same pattern we illustrated for common. When a company issues preferred stock, it credits Preferred Stock at its par value, with any excess credited to Paid-in Capital in Excess of Par—Preferred.

There may be separate accounts for paid-in capital in excess of par for preferred and common stock, but not necessarily. Some companies, such as DineEquity (formerly IHOP), combine paid-in capital in excess of par from both preferred and common stock transactions into one account. Accounting for no-par preferred follows the pattern for no-par common stock. When reporting stockholders' equity on the balance sheet, a corporation lists its accounts in this order:

- preferred stock
- common stock
- additional paid-in capital
- retained earnings

as illustrated for IHOP on page 534.

In Chapter 8 we saw how to account for convertible bonds payable (p. 491). Companies also issue convertible preferred stock. The preferred stock is usually convertible into the company's common stock at the discretion of the preferred stockholders. For example, in November 2007, IHOP issued 35,000 shares of Class B preferred stock. This stock is convertible into shares of DineEquity (formerly IHOP) stock according to a formula based on the relative values of preferred and common stock, during the first five years after issuance. On the 5th anniversary (November 2012), all the shares automatically convert into shares of the company's common stock, without any action on the part of the stockholder. The journal entry to record the transaction was

2007	Cash	34,250,000	
	Preferred Stock, Series B		35,000
	Additional Paid-in Capital		34,215,000
	Issued 35,000 shares of series B preferred stock.		

Whenever the common stock's market price gets high enough—or the preferred's market price gets low enough—holders of convertible preferred will convert their stock into common. Here are some representative journal entries for convertible preferred stock, using assumed amounts:

2008	Cash	50,000	
	Convertible Preferred Stock		50,000
	Issued convertible preferred stock.		

2010	Convertible Preferred Stock	50,000	
	Common Stock		8,000
	Paid-in Capital in Excess of Par—Common		42,000
	Investors converted preferred into common.		

As you can see, we merely remove Preferred Stock from the books and give the new Common Stock the prior book value of the preferred.

MID-CHAPTER SUMMARY PROBLEM

1. Test your understanding of the first half of this chapter by deciding whether each of the following statements is true or false.
   a. The policy-making body in a corporation is called the board of directors.
   b. The owner of 100 shares of preferred stock has greater voting rights than the owner of 100 shares of common stock.
   c. Par-value stock is worth more than no-par stock.
   d. Issuance of 1,000 shares of $5 par-value stock at $12 increases contributed capital by $12,000.
   e. The issuance of no-par stock with a stated value is fundamentally different from issuing par-value stock.
   f. A corporation issues its preferred stock in exchange for land and a building with a combined market value of $200,000. This transaction increases the corporation's owners' equity by $200,000 regardless of the assets' prior book values.
   g. Preferred stock is a riskier investment than common stock.

2. Adolfo Company has two classes of common stock. Only the Class A common stockholders are entitled to vote. The company's balance sheet included the following presentation:

Stockholders' Equity

Capital stock:	
Class A common stock, voting, $1 par value,	
authorized and issued 1,260,000 shares..................	$ 1,260,000
Class B common stock, nonvoting, no par value,	
authorized and issued 46,200,000 shares................	11,000,000
	12,260,000
Additional paid-in capital..	2,011,000
Retained earnings...	872,403,000
	$886,674,000

❙ Requirements

a. Record the issuance of the Class A common stock. Use the Adolfo account titles.
b. Record the issuance of the Class B common stock. Use the Adolfo account titles.
c. How much of Adolfo's stockholders' equity was contributed by the stockholders? How much was provided by profitable operations? Does this division of equity suggest that the company has been successful? Why or why not?
d. Write a sentence to describe what Adolfo's stockholders' equity means.

Answers

1. a. True   b. False   c. False   d. True   e. False   f. True   g. False
2. a.

Cash	3,271,000	
Class A Common Stock		1,260,000
Additional Paid-in Capital		2,011,000
To record issuance of Class A common stock.		

b.

Cash	11,000,000	
Class B Common Stock		11,000,000
To record issuance of Class B common stock.		

c. Contributed by the stockholders: $14,271,000 ($12,260,000 + $2,011,000). Provided by profitable operations: $872,403,000.

This division suggests that the company has been successful because most of its stockholders' equity has come from profitable operations.

d. Adolfo's stockholders' equity of $886,674,000 means that the company's stockholders own $886,674,000 of the business's assets.

AUTHORIZED, ISSUED, AND OUTSTANDING STOCK

It's important to distinguish among three distinctly different numbers of a company's stock. The following examples use IHOP's actual data from page 534.

- **Authorized stock** is the maximum number of shares the company can issue under its charter. As of December 31, 2007, IHOP was authorized to issue 40 million shares of common stock.
- **Issued stock** is the number of shares the company has issued to its stockholders. This is a cumulative total from the company's beginning up through the current date. As of December 31, 2007, IHOP had issued 23,359,664 shares of its common stock.
- **Outstanding stock** is the number of shares that the stockholders own (that is, the number of shares outstanding in the hands of the stockholders). Outstanding stock is issued stock minus treasury stock. At December 31, 2007, IHOP had 17,105,469 shares of common stock outstanding, computed as follows:

Issued shares (line 4)	23,359,664
Less: Treasury shares (line 7)...............	(6,254,195)
Outstanding shares (line 4)..................	17,105,469

Now let's learn about treasury stock.

TREASURY STOCK

A company's own stock that it has issued and later reacquired is called **treasury stock**.[2] In effect, the corporation holds this stock in its treasury. Many public companies spend millions of dollars each year to buy back their own stock. Corporations purchase their own stock for several reasons:

OBJECTIVE

3 **Describe** how treasury stock affects a company

1. The company has issued all its authorized stock and needs some stock for distributions to employees under stock purchase plans.

2. The business wants to increase net assets by buying its stock low and hoping to resell it for a higher price.

3. Management wants to avoid a takeover by an outside party.

---

[2]In this text, we illustrate the *cost* method of accounting for treasury stock because it is used most widely. Other methods are presented in intermediate accounting courses.

4. Management wants to increase its reported earnings per share (EPS) of common stock (net income/number of common shares outstanding). Purchasing shares removes them from outstanding shares, thus decreasing the denominator of this fraction and increasing EPS. We cover the computation of EPS in more depth in Chapter 11.

How is Treasury Stock Recorded?

Treasury stock is recorded at cost (the market value of the stock on the date of the purchase) without regard to stock's par value. Treasury stock is a *contra stockholders' equity* account. Therefore, the treasury stock account carries a debit balance, the opposite of the other equity accounts. It is reported beneath the retained earnings account on the balance sheet as a negative amount.

To understand the way treasury stock transactions work, it is helpful to analyze the changes that occur in the treasury stock account during the year. Let's start with the company's stockholders' equity at the end of the previous year, December 31, 2006 (we use rounded amounts in thousands, except for shares):

IHOP, Inc. Stockholders' Equity December 31, 2006	
Common stock..	$ 227
Additional paid-in capital............................	131,748
Retained earnings...	358,975
Treasury stock (4,944,459 shares)...............	(201,604)
Other equity..	(133)
Total stockholders' equity...........................	$289,213

Notice that, up to the end of 2006, IHOP had spent $201,604,000 to repurchase 4,944,459 shares of its own stock throughout the company's history. The average price it paid for the shares was therefore about $40.77 ($201,604,000/4,944,459). Assume that during 2007, IHOP paid $76,050,000 to purchase 1,309,736 additional shares of its common stock as treasury stock. Therefore, it paid $58.065 per share for the stock ($76,050,000/1,309,736 shares). IHOP would record the purchase of treasury stock as follows (in thousands):

2007			
Nov 12	Treasury Stock	76,050	
	Cash		76,050
	Purchased treasury stock.		

Assets	=	Liabilities	+	Stockholders' Equity
– 76,050	=	0		– 76,050

Notice that treasury stock is recorded at cost, which is the market price of the stock on the day IHOP purchased it ($58.065 per share). The financial statement impact of the transaction is to decrease cash as well as stockholders' equity by $76,050,000.

Now let's examine the stockholders' equity section of IHOP on December 31, 2007. In addition to purchasing treasury stock, the company issued both preferred stock and common stock during 2007. It also reported a net loss for 2007 and had some other reductions in retained earnings. The stockholders' equity account balances (rounded amounts in thousands, except for shares) at December 31, 2007, follow. For now, focus only on the treasury stock account:

IHOP, Inc.
Stockholders' Equity
December 31, 2007

Preferred stock	$ 35
Common stock	230
Paid-in capital in excess of par	184,710
Retained earnings	338,790
Less Treasury stock (at cost) 6,254,195 shares	(277,654)
Other equity	(36,738)
Total stockholders' equity	$ 209,373

The treasury stock purchase increased the contra account treasury stock by $76,050,000. Therefore, it decreased IHOP's stockholders' equity by $76,050,000. The new number of treasury shares is now 6,254,195 (4,944,459 + 1,309,736). The new average purchase price of treasury shares is $44.39, reflecting the higher amount paid for the newly acquired shares.

In summary, the purchase of treasury stock has the opposite effect of issuing stock:

- Issuing stock *grows* assets and equity.
- Purchasing treasury stock *shrinks* assets and equity.

Treasury stock is so named because it is held in the company treasury awaiting resale. Now let's see how to account for the resale of treasury stock.

Resale of Treasury Stock

Reselling treasury stock grows assets and equity exactly as issuing new stock does. Suppose that, on July 22, 2008, IHOP resells all of the treasury stock it purchased in 2007 for $100,000,000. The sale increases assets and equity by the full amount of cash received. Notice that the company **never records gains or losses on transactions involving its own treasury stock**. Rather, amounts received in excess of amounts originally paid for treasury stock are recorded as paid-in capital from treasury stock transactions, thus bypassing the income statement. If amounts received from resale of treasury stock were less than amounts originally paid, the difference would be debited to paid-in capital to the extent of that balance, and after that, to retained earnings. IHOP would record this sale of treasury stock as follows (in thousands):

2008			
Jul 22	Cash	100,000	
	Treasury Stock		76,050
	Paid-in Capital from Treasury Stock Transactions		
	(or Additional Paid-in Capital—Common)		23,950
	Sold treasury stock.		

Assets	=	Liabilities	+	Stockholders' Equity
+ 100,000	=	0		+ 76,050
				+ 23,950

If IHOP had sold the treasury stock for a price below cost, then IHOP could have debited Retained Earnings for the difference.

Issuing Treasury Stock as Compensation

Sometimes companies supplement their employee salaries by granting them stock rather than cash. If, in the preceding example, IHOP had chosen to distribute $100,000,000 in stock as compensation, the account debited would have been salary expense, rather than cash. The credit side of the transaction would have been the same.

Summary of Treasury-Stock Transactions

There are only two types of treasury-stock transactions:

- Buying treasury stock. Assets and equity *decrease* by an amount equal to the cost of treasury stock purchased.
- Selling treasury stock. Assets and equity *increase* by an amount equal to the sale price of the treasury stock sold.

Retirement of Stock

A corporation may purchase its own stock and *retire* it by canceling the stock certificates. Companies retire their preferred stock to avoid paying dividends on the preferred stock. The retired stock cannot be reissued. When a company retires its stock, the journal entry credits Cash and debits the stock account and any additional paid-in capital on the stock. Retirements of common stock are rare.

RETAINED EARNINGS, DIVIDENDS, AND SPLITS

The Retained Earnings account carries the balance of the business's net income, less its net losses and less any declared dividends that have been accumulated over the corporation's lifetime. *Retained* means "held onto." Successful companies grow by reinvesting back into the business the assets they generate through profitable operations. IHOP Corp. is an example. Take another look at its stockholders' equity as of December 31, 2007 (p. 534). Notice that the Retained Earnings account ($338,790,000) is the largest account balance in stockholders' equity as of the end of 2007. In fact, because historically the company has spent so much money on treasury stock, retained earnings actually *exceeds* total stockholders' equity ($209,373,000) as of the end of 2007.

The Retained Earnings account is not a reservoir of cash for paying dividends to the stockholders. In fact, the corporation may have a large balance in Retained Earnings but not have enough cash to pay a dividend. Cash and Retained Earnings are two entirely separate accounts with no particular relationship. Retained Earnings says nothing about the company's Cash balance.

A *credit* balance in Retained Earnings is normal, indicating that the corporation's lifetime earnings exceed lifetime losses and dividends. A *debit* balance in Retained Earnings arises when a corporation's lifetime losses and dividends exceed lifetime earnings. Called a **deficit**, this amount is subtracted to determine total stockholders' equity. In a recent survey, 15.5% of companies had a retained earnings deficit (Exhibit 9-7).

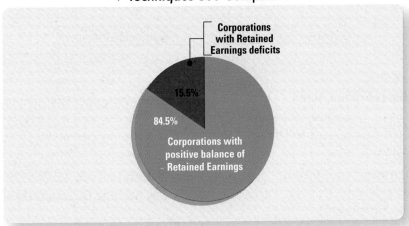

EXHIBIT 9-7 | **Retained Earnings of the *Accounting Trends & Techniques 600* Companies**

Should the Company Declare and Pay Cash Dividends?

A **dividend** is a distribution by a corporation to its stockholders, usually based on earnings. Dividends usually take one of three forms:

- Cash
- Stock
- Noncash assets

OBJECTIVE

4 **Account** for dividends

In this section we focus on cash dividends and stock dividends because noncash dividends are rare. For a noncash asset dividend, debit Retained Earnings and credit the asset (for example, Long-Term Investment) for the current market value of the asset given.

Cash Dividends

Most dividends are cash dividends. Finance courses discuss how a company decides on its dividend policy. Accounting tells a company if it can pay a dividend. To do so, a company must have both

- Enough Retained Earnings   and   ■ Enough Cash to *pay*
  to *declare* the dividend   the dividend

A corporation declares a dividend before paying it. Only the board of directors has the authority to declare a dividend. The corporation has no obligation to pay a dividend until the board declares one, but once declared, the dividend becomes a legal liability of the corporation. There are three relevant dates for dividends (using assumed amounts):

1. ***Declaration date, June 19.*** On the declaration date, the board of directors announces the dividend. Declaration of the dividend creates a liability for the corporation. Declaration is recorded by debiting Retained Earnings and crediting Dividends Payable. Assume a $50,000 dividend.

Jun 19	Retained Earnings³	50,000	
	Dividends Payable		50,000
	Declared a cash dividend.		

Liabilities increase, and equity goes down.

Assets	=	Liabilities	+	Stockholders' Equity
0	=	+ 50,000		− 50,000

2. *Date of record, July 1.* As part of the declaration, the corporation announces the record date, which follows the declaration date by a few weeks. The stockholders on the record date will receive the dividend. There is no journal entry for the date of record.

3. *Payment date, July 10.* Payment of the dividend usually follows the record date by a week or two. Payment is recorded by debiting Dividends Payable and crediting Cash.

Jul 10	Dividends Payable	50,000	
	Cash		50,000
	Paid cash dividend.		

Both assets and liabilities decrease. The corporation shrinks.

Assets	=	Liabilities	+	Stockholders' Equity
− 50,000	=	− 50,000		

The net effect of a dividend declaration and its payment, as shown in steps 1, 2, and 3, is a decrease in assets and a corresponding decrease in stockholders' equity.

Analyzing the Stockholder's Equity Accounts

By knowing accounting you can look at a company's comparative year-to-year financial statements and tell a lot about what the company did during the current year. For example, IHOP reported the following for Retained Earnings (in thousands):

	December 31,	
	2007	2006
Retained earnings...............	$338,790	$358,975

What do these figures tell you about IHOP's results of operations during 2007—was it a net income or a net loss? How can you tell? Remember that

- Net income is the only item that increases retained earnings;
- Net losses decrease retained earnings;
- Dividends decrease retained earnings; and
- Other adjustments to retained earnings are usually relatively minor and relatively rare.

---

³ In the early part of this book, we debited a Dividends account to clearly identify the purpose of the payment. From here on, we follow the more common practice of debiting the Retained Earnings account for dividend declarations.

In most cases, if you know the amount of either net income or dividends, but not both, and if you know both beginning and ending balances of retained earnings, you can figure out the amount you don't know by analyzing the Retained Earnings account.

For example, let's assume that IHOP's net income for 2007 had been $10,000,000, and that there were no other changes besides dividends. How much in dividends did the company pay?

If you know accounting—if you know IHOP's net income (assumed to be $10,000,000), you can compute IHOP's dividend declarations during 2007, as follows (in thousands):

		Retained Earnings		
			Beg bal	358,975
Dividends	?		Net income	10,000
			End bal	338,790

Dividends (x) would have been $30,185 ($358,975 + $10,000 − x = $338,790; x = $30,185). It really helps to be able to use accounting in this way!

Unfortunately, in IHOP's case, 2007 wasn't that simple. Every change to IHOP's retained earnings in 2007 was negative:

1. The company incurred a net loss of $480,000.

2. It paid dividends on common stock in the amount of $17,293,000, and dividends on preferred stock in the amount of $1,742,000 (total $19,035,000).

3. It had to make two other relatively minor negative adjustments to retained earnings that totaled $670,000.

Therefore, an analysis of IHOP's ending balance in retained earnings as of December 31, 2007 is as follows (in thousands):

		Retained Earnings		
Net loss	480		Beg bal	358,975
Dividends	19,035			
Other adj	670			
			End bal	338,790

Dividends on Preferred Stock

As shown in the previous section, IHOP paid dividends on its preferred stock in 2007 in the amount of $1,742,000. When a company has issued both preferred and common stock, the preferred stockholders receive their dividends first. The common stockholders receive dividends only if the total dividend is large enough to pay the preferred stockholders first.

Avant Garde, Inc., has 100,000 shares of $1.50 preferred stock outstanding in addition to its common stock. The $1.50 designation means that the preferred stockholders receive an annual cash dividend of $1.50 per share. In 2010, Avant Garde declares an annual dividend of $500,000. The allocation to preferred and common stockholders is:

Preferred dividend (100,000 shares × $1.50 per share)............	$150,000
Common dividend (remainder: $500,000 − $150,000)	350,000
Total dividend...	$500,000

If Avant Garde declares only a $200,000 dividend, preferred stockholders receive $150,000, and the common stockholders get the remainder, $50,000 ($200,000 − $150,000).

Two Ways to Express the Dividend Rate on Preferred Stock.

Dividends on preferred stock are stated either as a

- Percent of par value   or   ■ Dollar amount per share

For example, preferred stock may be "6% preferred," which means that owners of the preferred stock receive an annual dividend equal to 6% of the stock's par value. If par value is $100 per share, preferred stockholders receive an annual cash dividend of $6 per share (6% of $100). Alternatively, the preferred stock may be "$3 preferred," which means that the preferred stockholders receive an annual dividend of $3 per share regardless of the stock's par value. The dividend rate on no-par preferred stock is stated in a dollar amount per share.

Dividends on Cumulative and Noncumulative Preferred Stock.

The balance sheet classification of preferred stock, as well as the allocation of dividends, may be complex if the preferred stock is *cumulative*. IHOP's balance sheet (p. 534), for example, reflects that it has issued 190,000 shares of Series A, $1 par value cumulative preferred stock. The cumulative feature gives this series of preferred stock sufficient debt features that the company has opted to report the $187 million carrying value immediately after long-term liabilities, but has omitted it from stockholders' equity. Why? Corporations sometimes fail to pay a dividend to preferred stockholders. This is called *passing the dividend*, and the passed dividends are said to be *in arrears*. The owners of **cumulative preferred stock** must receive all dividends in arrears plus the current year's dividend before any dividends go to the common stockholders. In this sense, cumulative dividends almost take on the flavor of accrued interest on long-term debt, but not quite. Although cumulative dividends must be paid before other dividends, they must still be declared by the company's board of directors.

In contrast, interest on long-term debt doesn't have to go through a formal approval process by the board. Nevertheless, the similarity of cumulative dividends on preferred stock with interest on long-term debt are one feature that justify classifying such instruments as debt, rather than equity financing. Hence, IHOP has recorded the Series A preferred stock between its long-term debt and stockholders' equity. It doesn't quite fit in either section, so it is classified between them. *In most states preferred stock is cumulative unless it is specifically labeled as noncumulative.*

Here's an example of how cumulative dividends work. The preferred stock of Avant Garde, Inc., is cumulative. Suppose Avant Garde passed the preferred dividend of $150,000 in 2010. Before paying dividends to common in 2011, Avant Garde must first pay preferred dividends of $150,000 for both 2010 and 2011, a total of $300,000. On September 6, 2011, Avant Garde declares a $500,000 dividend. The entry to record the declaration is

Sep 6	Retained Earnings	500,000	
	Dividends Payable, Preferred ($150,000 × 2)		300,000
	Dividends Payable, Common ($500,000 − $300,000)		200,000
	To declare a cash dividend.		

If the preferred stock is *noncumulative*, the corporation is not obligated to pay dividends in arrears—until the board of directors declares the dividend.

Stock Dividends

A **stock dividend** is a proportional distribution by a corporation of its own stock to its stockholders. Stock dividends increase the stock account and decrease Retained Earnings. Total equity is unchanged, and no asset or liability is affected.

The corporation distributes stock dividends to stockholders in proportion to the number of shares they already own. If you own 300 shares of IHOP common stock and IHOP distributes a 10% common stock dividend, you get 30 (300 × .10) additional shares. You would then own 330 shares of the stock. All other IHOP stockholders would also receive 10% more shares, leaving all stockholders' ownership unchanged.

In distributing a stock dividend, the corporation gives up no assets. Why, then, do companies issue stock dividends? A corporation may choose to distribute stock dividends for these reasons:

1. **To continue dividends but conserve cash.** A company may need to conserve cash and yet wish to continue dividends in some form. So the corporation may distribute a stock dividend. Stockholders pay no income tax on stock dividends.

2. **To reduce the per-share market price of its stock.** Distribution of a stock dividend usually causes the stock's market price to fall because of the increased number of outstanding shares that result from it. The objective is to make the stock less expensive and therefore attractive to more investors.

Generally accepted accounting principles (GAAP) label a stock dividend of 25% or less as *small* and suggest that the dividend be recorded at the market value of the shares distributed. Suppose DineEquity (formerly IHOP) declared a 10% common stock dividend in 2011. At the time, assume DineEquity had 20,000,000 shares of common stock outstanding, and DineEquity's stock is trading for $10 per share. DineEquity would record this stock dividend as follows:

2011			
May 19	Retained Earnings[4] (20,000,000 shares of common outstanding × 0.10 stock dividend × $10 market value per share of common)	20,000,000	
	Common Stock (20,000,000 × 0.10 × $0.01 per value per share)		20,000
	Paid-in Capital in Excess of Par—Common		19,980,000
	Distributed a 10% stock dividend.		

The accounting equation clearly shows that a stock dividend has no effect on total assets, liabilities, or equity. The increases in equity offset the decreases, and the net effect is zero.

Assets	=	Liabilities	+	Stockholders' Equity
0	=	0		− 20,000,000
				+ 20,000
				+ 19,980,000

---

[4]Many companies debit Additional Paid-in Capital for their stock dividends.

GAAP identifies stock dividends above 25% as *large* and permits large stock dividends to be recorded at par value. For a large stock dividend, therefore, IHOP would debit Retained Earnings and credit Common Stock for the par value of the shares distributed in the dividend.

Stock Splits

A **stock split** is an increase in the number of shares of stock authorized, issued, and outstanding, coupled with a proportionate reduction in the stock's par value. For example, if the company splits its stock 2 for 1, the number of outstanding shares is doubled and each share's par value is halved. A stock split, like a large stock dividend, decreases the market price of the stock—with the intention of making the stock more attractive in the market. Most leading companies in the United States—including **IBM**, **PepsiCo**, and **Best Buy**—have split their stock.

The market price of a share of Best Buy common stock has been approximately $50. Assume that Best Buy wishes to decrease the market price to approximately $25 per share. Best Buy can split its common stock 2 for 1, and the stock price will fall to around $25. A 2-for-1 stock split means that

- the company will have twice as many shares of stock authorized, issued, and outstanding after the split as it had before.
- each share's par value will be cut in half.

Before the split, Best Buy had approximately 500 million shares of $0.10 (10 cents) par common stock issued and outstanding. Compare Best Buy's stockholders' equity before and after a 2-for-1 stock split:

Best Buy Co., Inc., Stockholders' Equity (Adapted)

Before **2-for-1 Stock Split**	(In millions)	After **2-for-1 Stock Split**	(In millions)
Common stock, $0.10 par, 1,000 shares authorized, 500 shares issued.........	$ 50	Common stock, $0.05 par, 2,000 shares authorized, 1,000 shares issued......	$ 50
Additional paid-in capital....................	643	Additional paid-in capital....................	643
Retained earnings..............................	4,304	Retained earnings...............................	4,304
Other equity...	260	Other...	260
Total stockholders' equity..................	$5,257	Total stockholders' equity..................	$5,257

All account balances are the same after the stock split as before. Only three Best Buy items are affected:

- Par value per share drops from $0.10 to $0.05.
- Shares *authorized* double from 1,000 to 2,000 (both in millions).
- Shares *issued* double from 500 to 1,000 (both in millions).

Total equity doesn't change, nor do any assets or liabilities.

Summary of the Effects on Assets, Liabilities, and Stockholders' Equity

We've seen how to account for the basic stockholders' equity transactions:

- Issuance of stock—common and preferred (pp. 540–547)
- Purchase and sale of treasury stock (pp. 549–552)
- Cash dividends (pp. 553–554)
- Stock dividends and stock splits (pp. 557–558)

How do these transactions affect assets, liabilities, and equity? Exhibit 9-8 provides a helpful summary.

EXHIBIT 9-8 | **Effects on Assets, Liabilities, and Equity**

| | Effect on Total | | |
Transaction	Assets =	Liabilities +	Stockholders' Equity
Issuance of stock—common and preferred...................................	Increase	No effect	Increase
Purchase of treasury stock.................	Decrease	No effect	Decrease
Sale of treasury stock	Increase	No effect	Increase
Declaration of cash dividend.............	No effect	Increase	Decrease
Payment of cash dividend.................	Decrease	Decrease	No effect
Stock dividend—large and small	No effect	No effect	No effect*
Stock split	No effect	No effect	No effect

*The stock accounts increase and retained earnings decrease by offsetting amounts that net to zero.

MEASURING THE VALUE OF STOCK

The business community measures *stock values* in various ways, depending on the purpose of the measurement. These values include market value, redemption value, liquidation value, and book value.

OBJECTIVE

5 **Use** stock values in decision making

Market, Redemption, Liquidation, and Book Value

A stock's **market value**, or *market price*, is the price a person can buy or sell 1 share of the stock for. Market value varies with the corporation's net income, financial position, and future prospects, and with general economic conditions. *In almost all cases, stockholders are more concerned about the market value of a stock than any other value.*

DineEquity's stock price has been quoted recently at $31.50 per share. Therefore, if DineEquity were issuing 100,000 shares of its common stock, it would receive cash of $3,150,000 (100,000 shares × $31.50 per share). This is the market value of the stock DineEquity issued.

Preferred stock that requires the company to redeem the stock at a set price is called **redeemable preferred stock**. The company is *obligated* to redeem (pay to retire) the preferred stock. Therefore, redeemable preferred stock is really not stockholders' equity. Instead it's a liability. The price the corporation agrees to pay for the stock, set when the stock is issued, is called the **redemption value**. **Liquidation value** is the amount that a company must pay a preferred stockholder in the event the company liquidates (sells out) and goes out of business.

The **book value** per share of common stock is the amount of owners' equity on the company's books for each share of its stock. If the company has only common stock outstanding, its book value is computed by dividing total equity by the number of shares of common *outstanding*. Recall that *outstanding* stock is *issued* stock minus *treasury* stock. For example, a company with stockholders' equity of $150,000 and 5,000 shares of common stock outstanding has a book value of $30 per share ($150,000 ÷ 5,000 shares).

If the company has both preferred and common outstanding, the preferred stockholders have the first claim to owners' equity. Preferred stock often has a specified redemption value. The preferred equity is its redemption value plus any cumulative preferred dividends in arrears. Book value per share of common is then computed as follows:

$$\text{Book value per share of common stock} = \frac{\text{Total stockholders' equity} - \text{Preferred equity}}{\text{Number of shares of common stock outstanding}}$$

Crusader Corporation's balance sheet reports the following amounts:

Stockholders' Equity	
Preferred stock, 5%, $100 par, 400 shares issued, redemption value $130 per share	$ 40,000
Common stock, $10 par, 5,500 shares issued	55,000
Additional paid-in capital—common	72,000
Retained earnings	88,000
Treasury stock—common, 500 shares at cost	(15,000)
Total stockholders' equity	$240,000

Cumulative preferred dividends are in arrears for four years (including the current year). Crusader's preferred stock has a redemption value of $130 per share. The book-value-per-share computations for Crusader Corporation are:

Preferred Equity	
Redemption value (400 shares × $130)	$52,000
Cumulative dividends ($40,000 × 0.05 × 4 years)	8,000
Preferred equity	$60,000*
Common Equity	
Total stockholders' equity	$240,000
Less preferred equity	(60,000)
Common equity	$180,000
Book value per share [$180,000 ÷ 5,000 shares outstanding (5,500 shares issued minus 500 treasury shares)]	$ 36.00

*If the preferred stock had no redemption value, then preferred equity would be $40,000 + preferred dividends in arrears.

Some investors search for stocks whose market price is below book value. They believe this indicates a good buy. Financial analysts often shy away from companies with a stock price at or below book value. To these investors, such a company is in trouble. As you can see, not all investors agree on a stock value. In fact, wise investors base their decisions on more than a single ratio. In Chapter 13 you'll see the full range of financial ratios, plus a few more analytical techniques.

Relating Profitability to a Company's Stock

OBJECTIVE

6 **Compute** return on assets and return on equity

Investors search for companies whose stocks are likely to increase in value. They're constantly comparing companies. But a comparison of IHOP with a new restaurant chain is not meaningful. IHOP's profits run into the millions, which far exceed a new company's net income. Does this automatically make IHOP a better investment? Not necessarily. To compare companies of different size, investors use some standard profitability measures, including

- return on assets
- return on equity

Return on Assets.   The **rate of return on total assets**, or simply **return on assets (ROA)**, measures a company's use of its assets to earn income for the two groups who finance the business:

- Creditors to whom the corporation owes money. Creditors want interest.
- Stockholders who own the corporation's stock. Stockholders want net income.

The sum of interest expense and net income is the return to the two groups who finance a corporation. This sum is the numerator of the return-on-assets ratio. The denominator is average total assets. ROA is computed as follows, using actual data (in thousands) from the 2007 annual report of IHOP Corp.:

$$\frac{\text{Rate of return}}{\text{on total assets}} = \frac{\text{Net income} + \text{Interest expense}}{\text{Average total assets}}$$

$$= \frac{\$(480) + \$28,654}{\$(3,831,162 + 766,250)/2} = .012$$

Net income and interest expense come from the income statement. Average total assets is computed from the beginning and ending balance sheets. Notice that total assets for 2007 increased by five times over total assets in 2006 (not shown), because of the purchase of Applebee's International. In addition, the tidy net income of $45 million that IHOP earned in 2006 (not shown) has turned into a loss ($480 thousand) when combined with Applebee's results in 2007.

What is a good rate of return on total assets? Ten percent is considered strong in most industries. However, rates of return vary by industry. Some high-technology companies earn much higher returns than do utility companies, groceries, and manufacturers of consumer goods such as toothpaste and paper towels. IHOP's return on assets (1.2%) is very low due to two factors. First, the company's total assets increased by five times when IHOP bought Applebee's in November 2007, thus greatly increasing the denominator of the ROA fraction. In addition, after operating at a profit for many years, the combined entity reflected an operating loss of $480,000 in 2007. This was mostly due to excessive operating costs associated with Applebee's that, by December 31, 2007, management hadn't yet had a chance to trim. Hopefully, within a few years operating as DineEquity, the company can cut these costs and return to profitability.

Return on Equity. **Rate of return on common stockholders' equity**, often called **return on equity (ROE)**, shows the relationship between net income available to common and average common stockholders' equity. Return on equity is computed only on common stock because the return to preferred stockholders is the specified dividend (for example, 5%).

The numerator of return on equity is net income minus preferred dividends. The denominator is *average common stockholders' equity*—total stockholders' equity minus preferred equity. IHOP Corp.'s ROE for 2007 is computed as follows (dollars in thousands):

$$\text{Rate of return on common stockholder's equity} = \frac{\text{Net income (loss)} - \text{Preferred dividends}}{\text{Average common stockholders' equity}}$$

$$= \frac{\$(480) - (1,742)}{\$(289,213 + 175,123^5)/2} = \frac{\$(2,222)}{\$232,168} = (0.957\%)$$

The common stockholders' equity for 2007 is total stockholders' equity of $209,373 less the portion attributable to preferred stock ($35 stock + $34,215 additional paid-in capital) or $175,123 (all amounts in thousands).

IHOP's return on equity (about −1%) is less than its return on assets, which is, in itself, very small (1.2%). This is not a good signal. In contrast, IHOP's ROE for the 2006 year was 15.4%. It appears that the acquisition of Applebee's International in 2007 has, at least in the short run, placed a great deal of pressure on the income of DineEquity, while greatly multiplying the amount of assets under management. ROE is always higher than ROA for a successful company in the long run. Stockholders take a lot more investment risk than bondholders, so the stockholders demand that ROE exceed ROA. They expect the return on their investment to exceed the amount they are having to pay their creditors for borrowed funds. Since ROA is higher in the case of IHOP, that means that the creditors' return on debt—interest—is higher than the return on equity—net income.

The common stockholders of DineEquity cannot permit this situation to persist for a long period of time, or they will sell their stock! It is no wonder that the market price of the company's common stock has fallen from the high $50s to $31.50 per share recently. Common stockholders are going to demand some changes in the way the company is run, cutting costs, finding new ways to increase profitability, and possibly closing a large number of marginally profitable restaurants.

Investors and creditors use ROE in much the same way they use ROA—to compare companies. The higher the rate of return, the more successful the company. In many industries, 15% is considered a good ROE.

The Decision Guidelines feature (p. 565) offers suggestions for what to consider when investing in stock.

---

[5] Ending equity comes from page 534. Beginning equity comes from the 2006 balance sheet, which is not shown.

REPORTING STOCKHOLDERS' EQUITY TRANSACTIONS

OBJECTIVE

7 **Report** equity transactions on the statement of cash flows

Statement of Cash Flows

Many of the transactions we've covered are reported on the statement of cash flows. Equity transactions are *financing activities* because the company is dealing with its owners. Financing transactions that affect both cash and equity fall into three main categories:

- issuance of stock
- treasury stock
- dividends

Issuances of Stock.   During 2007, IHOP Corp. issued preferred stock as well as common stock. This is as a financing activity, as shown in Exhibit 9-9

EXHIBIT 9-9 | **IHOP Corp's Financing Activities (Adapted from the consolidated statement of cash flows)**

Cash Flows from Financing Activities	(In thousands)
Issuance of preferred stock	$222,800
Issuance of common stock	8,928
Purchase of treasury stock	(76,050)
Payment of dividends	(17,293)

Treasury Stock.   During 2007, IHOP purchased treasury stock and reported the payment as a financing activity.

Dividends.   Most companies, including IHOP, pay cash dividends to their stockholders. Dividend payments are a type of financing transaction because the company is paying its stockholders for the use of their money. Stock dividends are not reported on the statement of cash flows because the company pays no cash for them.

In Exhibit 9-9, cash receipts appear as positive amounts and cash payments as negative amounts, denoted by parentheses.

Reporting Stockholders' Equity on the Balance Sheet

Businesses may report stockholders' equity in a way that differs from our examples. We use a detailed format in this book to help you learn all the components of stockholders' equity.

One of the most important skills you will take from this course is the ability to understand the financial statements of real companies. Exhibit 9-10 presents a side-by-side comparison of our general teaching format and the format you are likely to encounter in real-world balance sheets, such as IHOP's. All amounts are assumed for this illustration.

EXHIBIT 9-10 | Formats for Reporting Stockholders' Equity

General Teaching Format	Real-World Format
Stockholders' Equity	**Stockholders' Equity**
Paid-in capital:	Preferred stock, 8%, $10 par, 30,000
Preferred stock, 8%, $10 par, 30,000	shares authorized and issued .... $ 330,000
shares authorized and issued .... $ 300,000	Common stock, $1 par, 100,000 shares
Paid-in capital in excess of	authorized, 60,000 shares issued 60,000
par—preferred 30,000	Additional paid-in capital......................... 2,150,000
Common stock, $1 par, 100,000 shares	Retained earnings..................................... 1,500,000
authorized, 60,000 shares issued 60,000	Less treasury stock, common
Paid-in capital in excess of	(1,400 shares at cost) .... (40,000)
par—common 2,100,000	Total stockholders' equity $4,000,000
Paid-in capital from treasury stock	
transactions, common 20,000	
Paid-in capital from retirement of	
preferred stock 30,000	
Total paid-in capital 2,540,000	
Retained earnings................................... 1,500,000	
Subtotal 4,040,000	
Less treasury stock, common	
(1,400 shares at cost) .... (40,000)	
Total stockholders' equity $4,000,000	

In general:

- Preferred Stock comes first and is usually reported as a single amount
- Common Stock lists par value per share, the number of shares authorized and the number of shares issued. The balance of the Common Stock account is determined as follows:

> Common stock = Number of shares *issued* × Par value per share

- Additional paid-in capital combines Paid-in Capital in Excess of Par plus Paid-in Capital from Treasury Stock Transactions plus Paid-in Capital from Retirement of Preferred Stock. Additional paid-in capital belongs to the common stockholders.
- Outstanding stock equals issued stock minus treasury stock.
- Retained Earnings comes after the paid-in capital accounts.
- Treasury Stock can come last, as a subtraction in arriving at total stockholders' equity.

DECISION GUIDELINES

INVESTING IN STOCK

Suppose you've saved $5,000 to invest. You visit a nearby **Edward Jones** office, where the broker probes for your risk tolerance. Are you investing mainly for dividends or for growth in the stock price? You must make some key decisions.

Investor Decision	Guidelines
Which category of stock to buy for:	
■ A safe investment?	Preferred stock is safer than common, but for even more safety, invest in high-grade corporate bonds or government securities.
■ Steady dividends?	Cumulative preferred stock. However, the company is not obligated to declare preferred dividends, and the dividends are unlikely to increase.
■ Increasing dividends?	Common stock, as long as the company's net income is increasing and the company has adequate cash flow to pay a dividend after meeting all obligations and other cash demands.
■ Increasing stock price?	Common stock, but again only if the company's net income and cash flow are increasing.
How to identify a good stock to buy?	There are many ways to pick stock investments. One strategy that works reasonably well is to invest in companies that consistently earn higher rates of return on assets and on equity than competing firms in the same industry. Also, select industries that are expected to grow.

END-OF-CHAPTER SUMMARY PROBLEM

1. The balance sheet of Trendline Corp. reported the following at December 31, 2010.

Stockholders' Equity

Preferred stock, 4%, $10 par, 10,000 shares authorized and issued (redemption value, $110,000)..................	$100,000
Common stock, no-par, $5 stated value, 100,000 shares authorized, 50,000 shares issued.............................	250,000
Paid-in capital in excess of par or stated value:	
Common stock	239,500
Retained earnings..	395,000
Less: Treasury stock, common (1,000 shares)................	(8,000)
Total stockholders' equity	$976,500

❚ Requirements

    a. Is the preferred stock cumulative or noncumulative? How can you tell?

    b. What is the total amount of the annual preferred dividend?

    c. How many shares of common stock are outstanding?

    d. Compute the book value per share of the common stock. No preferred dividends are in arrears, and Trendline has not yet declared the 2010 dividend.

2. Use the following accounts and related balances to prepare the classified balance sheet of Whitehall, Inc., at September 30, 2011. Use the account format of the balance sheet.

Common stock, $1 par, 50,000 shares authorized, 20,000 shares issued...................	20,000	Long-term note payable	80,000	
		Inventory......................................	85,000	
Dividends payable........................	4,000	Property, plant, and equipment, net	226,000	
Cash...	9,000	Accounts receivable, net..............	23,000	
Accounts payable	28,000	Preferred stock, $3.75, no-par, 10,000 shares authorized, 2,000 shares issued...................	24,000	
Paid-in capital in excess of par—common	115,000			
Treasury stock, common, 1,000 shares at cost...................	6,000	Accrued liabilities.......................	3,000	
		Retained earnings........................	75,000	

Answers

1. a. The preferred stock is cumulative because it is not specifically labeled otherwise.

    b. Total annual preferred dividend: $4,000 ($100,000 × 0.04).

c. Common shares outstanding: 49,000 (50,000 issued − 1,000 treasury).

d. Book value per share of common stock:

Common:	
Total stockholders' equity	$976,500
Less stockholders' equity allocated to preferred	(114,000)*
Stockholders' equity allocated to common	$862,500
Book value per share ($862,500 ÷ 49,000 shares)	$17.60

*Redemption value	$110,000
Cumulative dividend ($100,000 × 0.04)	4,000
Stockholders' equity allocated to preferred	$114,000

2.

Whitehall, Inc.
Balance Sheet
September 30, 2011

Assets		Liabilities	
Current		Current	
Cash	$ 9,000	Account payable	$ 28,000
Accounts receivable, net	23,000	Dividends payable	4,000
Inventory	85,000	Accrued liabilities	3,000
Total current assets	117,000	Total current liabilities	35,000
Property, plant, and equipment, net	226,000	Long-term note payable	80,000
		Total liabilities	115,000
		Stockholders' Equity	
		Preferred stock, $3.75, no par,	
		10,000 shares authorized,	
		2,000 shares issued	$ 24,000
		Common stock, $1 par,	
		50,000 shares authorized,	
		20,000 shares issued	20,000
		Paid-in capital in excess of	
		par—common	115,000
		Retained earnings	75,000
		Treasury stock, common,	
		1,000 shares at cost	(6,000)
		Total stockholders' equity	228,000
		Total liabilities and	
Total assets	$343,000	stockholders' equity	$343,000

REVIEW STOCKHOLDERS' EQUITY

Quick Check (Answers are given on page 601.)

1. Lurvey Company is authorized to issue 50,000 shares of $25 par common stock. On May 30, 2010, Lurvey issued 20,000 shares at $45 per share. Lurvey's journal entry to record these facts should include a
   a. credit to Common Stock for $500,000.
   b. debit to Common Stock for $900,000.
   c. credit to Paid-in Capital in Excess of Par for $900,000.
   d. both a and c.

Questions 2–5 use the following account balances of Machado Co. at August 31, 2010:

Dividends Payable	$ 12,500	Cash	$111,000
Preferred Stock, $150 par	375,000	Common Stock, $5 par	600,000
Paid-in Capital in Excess of Par—		Retained Earnings	325,000
Common	60,000		

2. How many shares of common stock has Machado issued?
   a. 111,000
   c. 120,000
   b. 660,000
   d. Some other amount
3. Machado's total paid-in capital at August 31, 2010, is
   a. $1,347,500.
   c. 1,458,500.
   b. $1,022,500.
   d. $1,035,000.
4. Machado's total stockholders' equity as of August 31, 2010, is
   a. $1,035,000.
   c. $1,458,500.
   b. $1,347,500.
   d. $1,360,000.
5. What would Machado's total stockholders' equity be if Machado had $10,000 of treasury stock?
   a. $1,448,500
   c. $1,350,000
   b. $1,025,000
   d. $1,337,500
6. Syracuse Corporation purchased treasury stock in 2010 at a price of $15 per share and resold the treasury stock in 2011 at a price of $35 per share. What amount should Syracuse report on its income statement for 2011?
   a. $20 gain per share
   c. $35 gain per share
   b. $15 gain per share
   d. $0
7. The stockholders' equity section of a corporation's balance sheet reports

	Discount on Bonds Payable	Treasury Stock
a.	No	Yes
b.	Yes	No
c.	No	No
d.	Yes	Yes

8. The purchase of treasury stock
   a. decreases total assets and increases total stockholders' equity.
   b. decreases total assets and decreases total stockholder's equity.
   c. has no effect on total assets, total liabilities, or total stockholders' equity.
   d. increases one asset and decreases another asset.
9. When does a cash dividend become a legal liability?
   a. It never becomes a liability because it is paid.
   b. On date of payment.
   c. On date of record.
   d. On date of declaration.

10. When do dividends increase stockholders' equity?
    a. On date of declaration.
    b. On date of payment.
    c. Never.
    d. On date of record.

11. Maple Tree Mall, Inc., has 2,500 shares of 2%, $25 par cumulative preferred stock and 125,000 shares of $2 par common stock outstanding. At the beginning of the current year, preferred dividends were four years in arrears. Maple Tree's board of directors wants to pay a $2.50 cash dividend on each share of outstanding common stock in the current year. To accomplish this, what total amount of dividends must Maple Tree declare?
    a. $250,000
    b. $255,000
    c. $256,250
    d. Some other amount

12. Stock dividends
    a. have no effect on total stockholders' equity.
    b. increase the corporation's total liabilities.
    c. reduce the total assets of the company.
    d. are distributions of cash to stockholders.

13. What is the effect of a stock dividend and a stock split on total assets?

	Stock dividend	Stock split
a.	No effect	Decrease
b.	Decrease	Decrease
c.	No effect	No effect
d.	Decrease	No effect

14. A 2-for-1 stock split has the same effect on the number of shares being issued as a
    a. 50% stock dividend.
    b. 200% stock dividend.
    c. 100% stock dividend.
    d. 20% stock dividend.

15. The numerator for computing the rate of return on total assets is
    a. net income.
    b. net income minus preferred dividends.
    c. net income minus interest expense.
    d. net income plus interest expense.

16. The numerator for computing the rate of return on common equity is
    a. net income.
    b. net income minus interest expense.
    c. net income minus preferred dividends.
    d. net income plus preferred dividends.

Accounting Vocabulary

authorized stock (p. 549) Maximum number of shares a corporation can issue under its charter.

board of directors (p. 537) Group elected by the stockholders to set policy for a corporation and to appoint its officers.

book value (of a stock) (p. 560) Amount of owners' equity on the company's books for each share of its stock.

bylaws (p. 537) Constitution for governing a corporation.

chairperson (p. 537) Elected by a corporation's board of directors, usually the most powerful person in the corporation.

common stock (p. 538) The most basic form of capital stock. The common stockholders own a corporation.

contributed capital (p. 538) The amount of stockholders' equity that stockholders have contributed to the corporation. Also called *paid-in capital*.

cumulative preferred stock (p. 556) Preferred stock whose owners must receive all dividends in arrears before the corporation can pay dividends to the common stockholders.

deficit (p. 553) Debit balance in the Retained Earnings account.

dividend (p. 553) Distribution (usually cash) by a corporation to its stockholders.

double taxation (p. 536) Corporations pay income taxes on corporate income. Then, the stockholders pay personal income tax on the cash dividends that they receive from corporations.

issued stock (p. 549) Number of shares a corporation has issued to its stockholders.

legal capital (p. 540) Minimum amount of stockholders' equity that a corporation must maintain for the protection of creditors. For corporations with par-value stock, legal capital is the par value of the stock issued.

limited liability (p. 535) No personal obligation of a stockholder for corporation debts. A stockholder can lose no more on an investment in a corporation's stock than the cost of the investment.

liquidation value (p. 560) The amount a corporation must pay a preferred stockholder in the event the company liquidates and goes out of business.

market value (of a stock) (p. 559) Price for which a person could buy or sell a share of stock.

outstanding stock (p. 549) Stock in the hands of stockholders.

paid-in capital (p. 538) The amount of stockholders' equity that stockholders have contributed to the corporation. Also called *contributed capital*.

par value (p. 540) Arbitrary amount assigned by a company to a share of its stock.

preferred stock (p. 538) Stock that gives its owners certain advantages, such as the priority to receive dividends before the common stockholders and the priority to receive assets before the common stockholders if the corporation liquidates.

president (p. 537) Chief operating officer in charge of managing the day-to-day operations of a corporation.

rate of return on common stockholders' equity (p. 562) Net income minus preferred dividends, divided by average common stockholders' equity. A measure of profitability. Also called *return on equity*.

rate of return on total assets (p. 561) Net income plus interest expense divided by average total assets. This ratio measures a company's success in using its assets to earn income for the persons who finance the business. Also called *return on assets*.

redeemable preferred stock (p. 559) A corporation reserves the right to buy an issue of stock back from its shareholders, with the intent to retire the stock.

redemption value (p. 560) The price a corporation agrees to eventually pay for its redeemable preferred stock, set when the stock is issued.

retained earnings (p. 538) The amount of stockholders' equity that the corporation has earned through profitable operation of the business and has not given back to stockholders.

return on assets (ROA) (p. 561) Another name for *rate of return on total assets*.

return on equity (ROE) (p. 562) Another name for *rate of return on common stockholders' equity*.

shareholders (p. 535) Persons or other entities that own stock in a corporation. Also called *stockholders*.

stated value (p. 540) An arbitrary amount assigned to no-par stock; similar to par value.

stock (p. 538) Shares into which the owners' equity of a corporation is divided.

stock dividend (p. 557) A proportional distribution by a corporation of its own stock to its stockholders.

stockholder (p. 535) A person who owns stock in a corporation. Also called a *shareholder*.

stockholders' equity (p. 538) The stockholders' ownership interest in the assets of a corporation.

stock split (p. 558) An increase in the number of authorized, issued, and outstanding shares of stock coupled with a proportionate reduction in the stock's par value.

treasury stock (p. 549) A corporation's own stock that it has issued and later reacquired.

ASSESS YOUR PROGRESS

Short Exercises

S9-1 (*Learning Objective 1: Explaining advantages and disadvantages of a corporation*) What are two main advantages that a corporation has over a proprietorship and a partnership? What are two main disadvantages of a corporation?

S9-2 (*Learning Objective 1: Describing the authority structure in a corporation*) Consider the authority structure in a corporation, as diagrammed in Exhibit 9-2.

1. What group holds the ultimate power in a corporation?
2. Who is the most powerful person in the corporation? What's the abbreviation of this person's title?
3. Who's in charge of day-to-day operations? What's the abbreviation of this person's title?
4. Who's in charge of accounting and finance? What's the abbreviation of this person's title?

S9-3 (*Learning Objective 1: Describing characteristics of preferred and common stock*)
Answer the following questions about the characteristics of a corporation's stock:

1. Who are the real owners of a corporation?
2. What privileges do preferred stockholders have over common stockholders?
3. Which class of stockholders reap greater benefits from a highly profitable corporation? Explain.

S9-4 (*Learning Objective 1: Organizing a corporation*)   Karen Scanlon and Jennifer Shaw are
opening a Submarine's deli. Scanlon and Shaw need outside capital, so they plan to organize the
business as a corporation. They come to you for advice. Write a memorandum informing them of
the steps in forming a corporation. Identify specific documents used in this process, and name the
different parties involved in the ownership and management of a corporation.

S9-5 (*Learning Objective 2: Describing the effect of a stock issuance on paid-in capital*)
SHOE received $73,000,000 for the issuance of its stock on April 24. The par value of the
SHOE stock was only $73,000. Was the excess amount of $72,927,000 a profit to SHOE? If
not, what was it?

Suppose the par value of the SHOE stock had been $2 per share, $12 per share, or $15
per share. Would a change in the par value of the company's stock affect SHOE's total paid-
in capital? Give the reason for your answer.

S9-6 (*Learning Objective 2: Issuing stock—par value stock and no-par stock*)   At fiscal year-
end 2010, Horris Printer and Delectable Doughnuts reported these adapted amounts on their balance sheets (amounts in millions):

Horris Printer:	
Common stock, 1 cent par value, 2,300 shares issued	$ 23
Additional paid-in capital	17,100

Delectable Doughnuts:	
Common stock, no par value, 63 shares issued	$ 292

Assume each company issued its stock in a single transaction. Journalize each company's
issuance of its stock, using its actual account titles. Explanations are not required.

S9-7 (*Learning Objective 2: Issuing stock to finance the purchase of assets*)   This short exercise
demonstrates the similarity and the difference between two ways to acquire plant assets.

Case A—Issue stock and buy the assets in separate transactions:

Ashley, Inc., issued 12,000 shares of its $20 par common stock for cash of $800,000. In a separate
transaction, Ashley used the cash to purchase a building for $550,000 and equipment for $250,000.
Journalize the two transactions.

Case B—Issue stock to acquire the assets in a single transaction:

Ashley, Inc., issued 12,000 shares of its $20 par common stock to acquire a building valued at
$550,000 and equipment worth $250,000. Journalize this transaction.

Compare the balances in all the accounts after making both sets of entries. Are the account
balances similar or different?

S9-8 (*Learning Objective 2: Preparing the stockholders' equity section of a balance sheet*)   The financial statements of Mountainpeak Employment Services, Inc., reported the following accounts (adapted, with dollar amounts in thousands except for par value):

Paid-in capital in excess of par	$196	Total revenues......................	$1,340
Other stockholders' equity (negative)........	(22)	Accounts payable	440
Common stock, $0.01 par		Retained earnings................	647
400 shares issued..................................	4	Other current liabilities	2,569
Long-term debt	27	Total expenses.....................	806

Prepare the stockholders' equity section of Mountainpeak's balance sheet. Net income has already been closed to Retained Earnings.

S9-9 (*Learning Objective 2: Using stockholders' equity data*)   Use the Mountainpeak Employment Services data in Short Exercise 9-8 to compute Mountainpeak's

    a. Net income.
    b. Total liabilities.
    c. Total assets (use the accounting equation).

S9-10 (*Learning Objective 3: Accounting for the purchase and sale of treasury stock*) Genius Marketing Corporation reported the following stockholders' equity at December 31 (adapted and in millions):

Common stock.................................	$ 225
Additional paid-in capital..................	245
Retained earnings.............................	2,149
Treasury stock..................................	(621)
Total stockholders' equity.................	$1,998

    During the next year, Genius Marketing purchased treasury stock at a cost of $29 million and resold treasury stock for $8 million (this treasury stock had cost Genius Marketing $2 million). Record the purchase and resale of Genius Marketing's treasury stock. Overall, how much did stockholders' equity increase or decrease as a result of the two treasury stock transactions?

S9-11 (*Learning Objective 3: Purchasing treasury stock to fight off a takeover of the corporation*)   Susan Smith Exports, Inc., is located in Birmingham, Alabama. Smith is the only company with reliable sources for its imported gifts. The company does a brisk business with specialty stores such as Bloomingdale's. Smith's recent success has made the company a prime target for a takeover. An investment group in Mobile is attempting to buy 52% of Smith's outstanding stock against the wishes of Smith's board of directors. Board members are convinced that the Mobile investors would sell the most desirable pieces of the business and leave little of value.

At the most recent board meeting, several suggestions were advanced to fight off the hostile takeover bid. The suggestion with the most promise is to purchase a huge quantity of treasury stock. Smith has the cash to carry out this plan.

❚ *Requirements*

    1. Suppose you are a significant stockholder of Susan Smith Exports, Inc. Write a memorandum to explain to the board how the purchase of treasury stock would make it difficult for the Mobile group to take over Smith. Include in your memo a discussion of the effect that purchasing treasury stock would have on stock outstanding and on the size of the corporation.

2. Suppose Smith management is successful in fighting off the takeover bid and later sells the treasury stock at prices greater than the purchase price. Explain what effect these sales will have on assets, stockholders' equity, and net income.

S9-12 (*Learning Objective 4: Accounting for cash dividends*)   Greentea Corporation earned net income of $95,000 during the year ended December 31, 2010. On December 15, Greentea declared the annual cash dividend on its 6% preferred stock (11,000 shares with total par value of $110,000) and a $1.00 per share cash dividend on its common stock (45,000 shares with total par value of $450,000). Greentea then paid the dividends on January 4, 2011.

Journalize for Greentea Corporation:
    a. Declaring the cash dividends on December 15, 2010.
    b. Paying the cash dividends on January 4, 2011.

Did Retained Earnings increase or decrease during 2010? By how much?

S9-13 (*Learning Objective 4: Dividing cash dividends between preferred and common stock*)   Access Garde, Inc., has 200,000 shares of $1.80 preferred stock outstanding in addition to its common stock. The $1.80 designation means that the preferred stockholders receive an annual cash dividend of $1.80 per share. In 2010, Access Garde declares an annual dividend of $500,000. The allocation to preferred and common stockholders is:

Preferred dividend, (200,000 shares × $1.80 per share)............	$360,000
Common dividend (remainder: $500,000 – $360,000)	140,000
Total dividend...	$500,000

Answer these questions about Access Garde's cash dividends.

    1. How much in dividends must Access Garde declare each year before the common stockholders receive any cash dividends for the year?
    2. Suppose Access Garde, Inc., declares cash dividends of $400,000 for 2010. How much of the dividends goes to preferred? How much goes to common?
    3. Is Access Garde's preferred stock cumulative or noncumulative? How can you tell?
    4. Access Garde, Inc., passed the preferred dividend in 2009 and 2010. Then in 2011, Access Garde declares cash dividends of $1,500,000. How much of the dividends goes to preferred? How much goes to common?

S9-14 (*Learning Objective 4: Recording a small stock dividend*)   Centerville Bancshares has 13,000 shares of $3 par common stock outstanding. Suppose Centerville distributes a 15% stock dividend when the market value of its stock is $25 per share.

    1. Journalize Centerville's distribution of the stock dividend on May 11. An explanation is not required.
    2. What was the overall effect of the stock dividend on Centerville's total assets? On total liabilities? On total stockholders' equity?

S9-15 (*Learning Objective 5: Computing book value per share*)   Fools Gold, Inc., has the following stockholders' equity:

Preferred stock, 4%, $5 par,	
33,000 shares authorized and issued....................................	$ 195,000
Common stock, $2 par, 100,000 shares authorized	
63,000 shares issued..	126,000
Additional paid-in capital..	2,170,000
Retained earnings...	1,700,000
Less treasury stock, common (1,400 shares at cost)	(45,000)
Total stockholders' equity...	$4,146,000

That company has passed its preferred dividends for three years including the current year. Compute the book value per share of the company's common stock.

S9-16 *(Learning Objective 6: Computing and explaining return on assets and return on equity)* Give the formula for computing (a) rate of return on total assets (ROA) and (b) rate of return on common stockholders' equity (ROE). Then answer these questions about the rate-of-return computations.

1. Why is interest expense added to net income in the computation of ROA?
2. Why are preferred dividends subtracted from net income to compute ROE?

S9-17 *(Learning Objective 6: Computing return on assets and return on equity for a leading company)* Godhi Corporation's 2010 financial statements reported the following items, with 2009 figures given for comparison (adapted and in millions).

	2010	2009
Balance Sheet		
Total assets	¥10,624	¥9,515
Total liabilities	¥ 7,412	¥6,637
Total stockholders' equity (all common)	3,212	2,878
Total liabilities and equity	¥10,624	¥9,515
Income Statement		
Revenues and other income	¥ 7,633	
Operating expense	7,286	
Interest expense	31	
Other expense	196	
Net income	¥ 120	

Compute Godhi's return on assets and return on common equity for 2011. Evaluate the rates of return as strong or weak. ¥ is the symbol for the Japanese yen.

S9-18 *(Learning Objectives 1, 2, 5: Explaining the features of a corporation's stock)* McGahan Corporation is conducting a special meeting of its board of directors to address some concerns raised by the stockholders. Stockholders have submitted the following questions. Answer each question.

1. Why are common stock and retained earnings shown separately in the shareholders' equity section of the balance sheet?
2. Linda Leary, a McGahan shareholder, proposes to transfer some land she owns to the company in exchange for shares of the company stock. How should McGahan Corporation determine the number of shares of our stock to issue for the land?
3. Preferred shares generally are preferred with respect to dividends and in the event of our liquidation. Why would investors buy our common stock when preferred stock is available?
4. What does the redemption value of our preferred stock require us to do?
5. One of our stockholders owns 200 shares of McGahan stock and someone has offered to buy her shares for their book value. Our stockholder asks us the formula for computing the book value of her stock.

S9-19 *(Learning Objective 7: Measuring cash flows from financing activities)* During 2010, Dwyer Corporation earned net income of $5.8 billion and paid off $2.4 billion of long-term notes payable. Dwyer raised $1.1 billion by issuing common stock, paid $3.5 billion to purchase treasury stock, and paid cash dividends of $1.6 billion. Report Dwyer's *cash flows from financing* activities on the statement of cash flows for 2010.

Exercises

All of the A and B exercises can be found within MyAccountingLab, an online homework and practice environment. Your instructor may ask you to complete these exercises using MyAccountingLab.

(Group A)

E9-20A *(Learning Objective 2: Issuing stock and reporting stockholders' equity)*   Bread & Butter, Inc., is authorized to issue 120,000 shares of common stock and 7,000 shares of preferred stock. During its first year, the business completed the following stock issuance transactions:

Jan 19	Issued 12,000 shares of $2.00 par common stock for cash of $6.00 per share.
Apr 3	Issued 400 shares of $1.00 no-par preferred stock for $54,000 cash.
11	Received inventory valued at $16,000 and equipment with market value of $9,500 for 3,700 shares of the $2.00 par common stock.

❙ Requirements

1. Journalize the transactions. Explanations are not required.
2. Prepare the stockholders' equity section of Bread & Butter's balance sheet. The ending balance of retained earnings is a deficit of $43,000.

E9-21A *(Learning Objective 2: Preparing stockholders' equity section of a balance sheet)* Army Navy Sporting Goods is authorized to issue 10,000 shares of preferred stock and 19,000 shares of common stock. During a two-month period, Army Navy completed these stock-issuance transactions:

Apr 23	Issued 1,700 shares of $1.50 par common stock for cash of $16.50 per share.
May 2	Issued 600 shares of $2.50, no-par preferred stock for $22,000 cash.
12	Received inventory valued at $19,000 and equipment with market value of $41,000 for 3,300 shares of the $1.50 par common stock.

❙ Requirement

1. Prepare the stockholders' equity section of the Army Navy Sporting Goods' balance sheet for the transactions given in this exercise. Retained Earnings has a balance of $45,000. Journal entries are not required.

E9-22A *(Learning Objective 2: Measuring the paid-in capital of a corporation)*   Travel Publishing was recently organized. The company issued common stock to an attorney who provided legal services worth $23,000 to help organize the corporation. Travel also issued common stock to an inventor in exchange for his patent with a market value of $82,000. In addition, Travel received cash both for the issuance of 2,000 shares of its preferred stock at

$120 per share and for the issuance of 22,000 of its common shares at $1 per share. During the first year of operations, Travel earned net income of $50,000 and declared a cash dividend of $29,000. Without making journal entries, determine the total paid-in capital created by these transactions.

E9-23A *(Learning Objectives 2, 3: Preparing stockholders' equity section of a balance sheet)* Patterson Software had the following selected account balances at December 31, 2010 (in thousands, except par value per share).

Inventory....................................	$ 651	Common stock, $0.75 par	
Property, plant, and		per share, 800 shares	
equipment, net	900	authorized, 320 shares	
Paid-in capital in excess of par	899	issued	$ 240
Treasury stock,		Retained earnings................	2,220
100 shares at cost......................	1,150	Accounts receivable, net......	1,000
Other stockholders' equity	(730)*	Notes payable	1,100

*Debit balance

Requirements

1. Prepare the stockholders' equity section of Patterson's balance sheet (in thousands).
2. How can Patterson have a larger balance of treasury stock than the sum of Common Stock and Paid-in Capital in Excess of Par?

E9-24A *(Learning Objectives 2, 3: Recording treasury stock transactions and measuring their effects on stockholders' equity)* Journalize the following transactions of Aliant Productions:

Jan 17	Issued 2,200 shares of $2.50 par common stock at $10 per share.
May 23	Purchased 300 shares of treasury stock at $12 per share.
Jul 11	Sold 200 shares of treasury stock at $20 per share.

What was the overall effect of these transactions on Aliant's stockholders' equity?

E9-25A *(Learning Objectives 2, 3, 4: Recording stock issuance, treasury stock, and dividend transactions)* At December 31, 2010, Northeast Corporation reported the stockholders' equity accounts shown here (with dollar amounts in millions, except per share amounts).

Common stock $2.00 par value per share,	
2,100 million shares issued................	$ 4,200
Capital in excess of par value................	8,400
Retained earnings.................................	250
Treasury stock, at cost	(70)
Total stockholders' equity................	$12,780

Northeast's 2011 transactions included the following:

   a. Net income, $446 million.
   b. Issuance of 8 million shares of common stock for $13.50 per share.
   c. Purchase of 2 million shares of treasury stock for $16 million.
   d. Declaration and payment of cash dividends of $31 million.

❙ Requirement

1. Journalize Northeast's transactions in b, c, and d. Explanations are not required.

E9-26A (*Learning Objectives 2, 3, 4: Reporting stockholders' equity after a sequence of transactions*)   Use the Northeast Corporation data in Exercise 9-25A to prepare the stockholders' equity section of the company's balance sheet at December 31, 2011.

E9-27A (*Learning Objectives 2, 3, 4, 5: Inferring transactions from a company's stockholders' equity*)   Theta Products Company reported the following stockholders' equity on its balance sheet:

Stockholders' Equity (Dollars and shares in millions)	December 31, 2011	2010
Preferred stock—$0.50 par value; authorized 30 shares; Convertible Preferred Stock; issued and outstanding: 2011 and 2010—6 and 12 shares, respectively	$ 3	$ 6
Common stock—$2 per share par value; authorized 1,400 shares; issued: 2011 and 2010—300 and 200 shares, respectively	600	400
Additional paid-in capital	1,950	1,200
Retained earnings	6,270	5,066
Treasury stock, common—at cost 2011—52 shares; 2010—12 shares	(1,144)	(228)
Total stockholders' equity	7,679	6,444
Total liabilities and stockholders' equity	$48,299	$45,294

❙ Requirements

1. What caused Theta's preferred stock to decrease during 2011? Cite all possible causes.
2. What caused Theta's common stock to increase during 2011? Identify all possible causes.
3. How many shares of Theta's common stock were outstanding at December 31, 2011?
4. Theta's net income during 2011 was $1,380 million. How much were Theta's dividends during the year?
5. During 2011, Theta sold no treasury stock. What average price per share did Theta pay for the treasury stock the company purchased during the year?

E9-28A (*Learning Objective 4: Computing dividends on preferred and common stock*)   Huron Manufacturing, Inc., reported the following:

Stockholders' Equity	
Preferred stock, cumulative, $0.50 par, 9%, 40,000 shares issued	$ 20,000
Common stock, $0.10 par, 9,170,000 shares issued	917,000

Huron Manufacturing has paid all preferred dividends through 2007.

❙ Requirement

1. Compute the total amounts of dividends to both preferred and common for 2010 and 2011 if total dividends are $60,000 in 2010 and $120,000 in 2011.

E9-29A (*Learning Objective 4: Recording a stock dividend and reporting stockholders' equity*) The stockholders' equity for Heavenly Desserts Drive-Ins (HD) on December 31, 2010, follows:

Stockholders' Equity	
Common stock, $0.80 par, 2,600,000 shares authorized, 300,000 shares issued......................	$ 240,000
Paid-in capital in excess of par—common..............	307,200
Retained earnings...	7,122,000
Other equity...	(200,000)
Total stockholders' equity.................................	$7,469,200

On May 11, 2011, the market price of HD common stock was $19 per share. Assume HD distributed a 15% stock dividend on this date.

Requirements

1. Journalize the distribution of the stock dividend.
2. Prepare the stockholders' equity section of the balance sheet after the stock dividend.
3. Why is total stockholders' equity unchanged by the stock dividend?
4. Suppose HD had a cash balance of $560,000 on May 12, 2011. What is the maximum amount of cash dividends HD can declare?

E9-30A (*Learning Objectives 2, 3, 4: Measuring the effects of stock issuance, dividends, and treasury stock transactions*) Identify the effects—both the direction and the dollar amount—of these assumed transactions on the total stockholders' equity of Athol Corporation. Each transaction is independent.

a. Declaration of cash dividends of $78 million.
b. Payment of the cash dividend in a.
c. A 25% stock dividend. Before the dividend, 70 million shares of $2.00 par common stock were outstanding; the market value was $8.250 at the time of the dividend.
d. A 50% stock dividend. Before the dividend, 70 million shares of $2.00 par common stock were outstanding; the market value was $15.50 at the time of the dividend.
e. Purchase of 1,900 shares of treasury stock (par value $2.00) at $5.25 per share.
f. Sale of 900 shares of the treasury stock for $7.00 per share. Cost of the treasury stock was $5.25 per share.
g. A 2-for-1 stock split. Prior to the split, 70 million shares of $2.00 par common stock were outstanding.

E9-31A (*Learning Objective 4: Reporting stockholders' equity after a stock split*) Clublink Corp. had the following stockholders' equity at October 31 (dollars in millions, except par value per share):

Stockholders' Equity	
Common stock, $1.50 par, 750 million shares authorized, 420 million shares issued................	$ 630
Additional paid-in capital..	318
Retained earnings...	2,399
Other equity...	(148)
Total stockholders' equity.......................................	$3,199

On December 6, Clublink split its $1.50 par common stock 3-for-1.

I Requirement

1. Prepare the stockholders' equity section of the balance sheet immediately after the split.

E9-32A (*Learning Objective 5: Measuring the book value per share of common stock*)   The balance sheet of Luxury Rug Company reported the following:

Redeemable preferred stock, 4%, $60 par value, redemption value $45,000; outstanding 500 shares...............	$30,000
Common stockholders' equity:	
6,000 shares issued and outstanding	66,000
Total stockholders' equity...	$96,000

I Requirements

1. Compute the book value per share for the common stock, assuming all preferred dividends are fully paid up (none in arrears).
2. Compute the book value per share of the common stock, assuming that three years' cumulative preferred dividends including the current year, are in arrears.
3. Luxury Rug's common stock recently traded at a market price of $6.00 per share. Does this mean that Luxury Rug's stock is a good buy at $6.00?

E9-33A (*Learning Objective 6: Evaluating profitability*)   Luna Inns reported these figures for 2011 and 2010 (in millions):

	2011	2010
Balance sheet		
Total assets	$15,906	$13,700
Common stock and additional paid-in capital	44	390
Retained earnings	11,522	16,490
Other equity...	(3,010)	(9,044)
Income statement		
Operating income...	$ 4,023	$ 3,818
Interest expense	222	269
Net income...	1,525	1,549

I Requirement

1. Compute Luna's return on assets and return on common stockholders' equity for 2011. Do these rates of return suggest strength or weakness? Give your reason.

E9-34A (*Learning Objective 6: Evaluating profitability*)   Littleton Company included the following items in its financial statements for 2010, the current year (amounts in millions):

Payment of long-term debt..........	$17,060	Dividends paid		$ 230
Proceeds from issuance		Interest expense:		
of common stock.....................	8,500	Current year.....................		1,439
Total liabilities:		Preceding year.................		601
Current year-end....................	32,315	Net income:		
Preceding year-end	38,025	Current year.....................		1,878
Total stockholders' equity:		Preceding year.................		2,003
Current year-end....................	23,475	Operating income:		
Preceding year-end	14,033	Current year.....................		4,884
Borrowings...............................	6,580	Preceding year.................		4,006

❙ Requirement

1. Compute Littleton's return on assets and return on common equity during 2010 (the current year). Littleton has no preferred stock outstanding. Do the company's rates of return look strong or weak? Give your reason.

E9-35A (*Learning Objective 7: Reporting cash flows from financing activities*)   Use the Littleton Company data in Exercise E9-34A to show how the company reported cash flows from financing activities during 2010 (the current year). List items in descending order from largest to smallest dollar amount.

(Group B)

E9-36B (*Learning Objective 2: Issuing stock and reporting stockholders' equity*)   Sweet & Sour, Inc., is authorized to issue 110,000 shares of common stock and 5,000 shares of preferred stock. During its first year, the business completed the following stock issuance transactions:

Aug 19	Issued 15,000 shares of $3.50 par common stock for cash of $7.50 per share.	
Nov 3	Issued 400 shares of $2.00 no-par preferred stock for $55,000 cash.	
11	Received inventory valued at $18,000 and equipment with market value of $10,500 for 4,000 shares of the $3.50 par common stock.	

❙ Requirements

1. Journalize the transactions. Explanations are not required.
2. Prepare the stockholders' equity section of Sweet & Sour's balance sheet. The ending balance of retained earnings is a deficit of $47,000.

E9-37B (*Learning Objective 2: Preparing stockholders' equity section of a balance sheet*) Honcho Sporting Goods is authorized to issue 7,000 shares of preferred stock and 16,000 shares of common stock. During a two-month period, Honcho completed these stock-issuance transactions:

Jun 23	Issued 1,500 shares of $2.00 par common stock for cash of $17.50 per share.	
Jul 2	Issued 400 shares of $5.50, no-par preferred stock for $30,000 cash.	
12	Received inventory valued at $15,000 and equipment with market value of $44,000 for 3,700 shares of the $2.00 par common stock.	

❙ Requirement

1. Prepare the stockholders' equity section of the Honcho Sporting Goods balance sheet for the transactions given in this exercise. Retained Earnings has a balance of $46,000. Journal entries are not required.

E9-38B (*Learning Objective 2: Measuring the paid-in capital of a corporation*)   Journey Publishing was recently organized. The company issued common stock to an attorney who provided legal services worth $24,000 to help organize the corporation. Journey also issued common stock to an inventor in exchange for his patent with a market value of $85,000. In addition, Journey received cash both for the issuance of 3,000 shares of its preferred stock at $90 per share and for the issuance of 17,000 shares of its common shares at $18 per share. During the first year of operations, Journey earned net income of $65,000 and declared a cash dividend of $23,000. Without making journal entries, determine the total paid-in capital created by these transactions.

E9-39B (*Learning Objectives 2, 3: Stockholders' equity section of a balance sheet*)   Bukala Software had the following selected account balances at December 31, 2010 (in thousands, except par value per share):

Inventory..	$ 705	Common stock, $0.50 par	
Property, plant, and		per share, 900 shares	
equipment, net	903	authorized, 300 shares	
Paid-in capital in excess of par	897	issued	$ 150
Treasury stock,		Retained earnings................	2,270
140 shares at cost......................	1,610	Accounts receivable, net......	200
Other stockholders' equity	(726)*	Notes payable	1,166

*Debit balance

Requirements

1. Prepare the stockholders' equity section of Bukala Software's balance sheet (in thousands).
2. How can Bukala have a larger balance of treasury stock than the sum of Common Stock and Paid-in Capital in Excess of Par?

E9-40B (*Learning Objectives 2, 3: Recording treasury stock transactions and measuring their effects on stockholders' equity*)   Journalize the following assumed transactions of Applebug Productions:

Mar 16	Issued 2,400 shares of $1.50 par common stock at $7 per share.
Apr 20	Purchased 800 shares of treasury stock at $16 per share.
Aug 8	Sold 600 shares of treasury stock at $17 per share.

What was the overall effect of these transactions on Applebug's stockholders' equity?

E9-41B (*Learning Objectives 2, 3, 4: Recording stock issuance, treasury stock, and dividend transactions*)   At December 31, 2010, Eastern Corporation reported the stockholders' equity accounts shown here (with dollar amounts in millions, except per share amounts).

Common stock $1.50 par value per share,	
1,700 million shares issued................	$ 2,550
Capital in excess of par value...............	7,650
Retained earnings..................................	260
Treasury stock, at cost	(10)
Total stockholders' equity.................	$10,450

Eastern's 2011 transactions included the following:

    a. Net income, $447 million.
    b. Issuance of 9 million shares of common stock for $12.50 per share.
    c. Purchase of 3 million shares of treasury stock for $15 million.
    d. Declaration and payment of cash dividends of $34 million.

▌ Requirement

    1. Journalize Eastern's transactions in b, c, and d. Explanations are not required.

E9-42B (*Learning Objectives 2, 3, 4: Reporting stockholders' equity after a sequence of transactions*) Use the Eastern Corporation data in Exercise 9-41B to prepare the stockholders' equity section of the company's balance sheet at December 31, 2011.

E9-43B (*Learning Objectives 2, 3, 4, 5: Inferring transactions from a company's stockholders' equity*) Supreme Products Company reported the following stockholders' equity on its balance sheet:

Stockholders' Equity	December 31,	
(Dollars and shares in millions)	2011	2010
Preferred stock—$1.50 par value; authorized 40 shares;		
Convertible Preferred Stock; issued and outstanding:		
2011 and 2010—8 and 16 shares, respectively	$ 12	$ 24
Common stock—$4 per share par value; authorized		
1,200 shares; issued: 2011 and 2010—500		
and 400 shares, respectively	2,000	1,600
Additional paid-in capital	2,750	2,000
Retained earnings	6,300	5,025
Treasury stock, common—at cost		
2011—54 shares; 2010—14 shares	(1,242)	(280)
Total stockholders' equity	9,820	8,369
Total liabilities and stockholders' equity	$50,320	$47,215

▌ Requirements

    1. What caused Supreme's preferred stock to decrease during 2011? Cite all possible causes.
    2. What caused Supreme's common stock to increase during 2011? Identify all possible causes.
    3. How many shares of Supreme's common stock were outstanding at December 31, 2011?
    4. Supreme's net income during 2011 was $1,475 million. How much were Supreme's dividends during the year?
    5. During 2011, Supreme sold no treasury stock. What average price per share did Supreme pay for the treasury stock the company purchased during the year?

E9-44B (*Learning Objective 4: Computing dividends on preferred and common stock*) Eerie Manufacturing, Inc., reported the following:

Stockholders' Equity	
Preferred stock, cumulative, $1.50 par, 7%, 50,000 shares issued	$ 75,000
Common stock, $0.20 par, 9,110,000 shares issued	1,822,000

Eerie Manufacturing has paid all preferred dividends through 2007.

❙ Requirement

1. Compute the total amounts of dividends to both preferred and common for 2010 and 2011 if total dividends are $100,000 in 2010 and $200,000 in 2011.

E9-45B (*Learning Objective 4: Recording a stock dividend and reporting stockholders' equity*)   The stockholders' equity for Icy Pop Drive-Ins (IP) on December 31, 2010, follows:

Stockholders' Equity	
Common stock, $0.30 par, 2,200,000 shares authorized, 400,000 shares issued	$ 120,000
Paid-in capital in excess of par—common	409,600
Retained earnings	7,133,000
Other equity	(185,000)
Total stockholders' equity	$7,477,600

On August 15, 2011, the market price of IP common stock was $15 per share. Assume IP distributed a 20% stock dividend on this date.

❙ Requirements

1. Journalize the distribution of the stock dividend.
2. Prepare the stockholders' equity section of the balance sheet after the stock dividend.
3. Why is total stockholders' equity unchanged by the stock dividend?
4. Suppose IP had a cash balance of $590,000 on August 16, 2011. What is the maximum amount of cash dividends IP can declare?

E9-46B (*Learning Objectives 2, 3, 4: Measuring the effects of stock issuance, dividends, and treasury stock transactions*)   Identify the effects—both the direction and the dollar amount—of these assumed transactions on the total stockholders' equity of Dracut Corporation. Each transaction is independent.

a. Declaration of cash dividends of $85 million.
b. Payment of the cash dividend in a.
c. A 5% stock dividend. Before the dividend, 72 million shares of $3.00 par common stock were outstanding; the market value was $9.185 at the time of the dividend.
d. A 30% stock dividend. Before the dividend, 72 million shares of $3.00 par common stock were outstanding; the market value was $13.75 at the time of the dividend.
e. Purchase of 1,800 shares of treasury stock (par value $3.00) at $6.25 per share.
f. Sale of 900 shares of the treasury stock for $9.00 per share. Cost of the treasury stock was $6.25 per share.
g. A 3-for-1 stock split. Prior to the split, 72 million shares of $3.00 par common stock were outstanding.

E9-47B (*Learning Objective 4: Reporting stockholders' equity after a stock split*)   Griffin Corp. had the following stockholders' equity at March 31 (dollars in millions, except par value per share):

Stockholders' Equity	
Common stock, $0.30 par, 500 million shares authorized, 450 million shares issued................	$ 135
Additional paid-in capital...	315
Retained earnings..	2,393
Other equity...	(146)
Total stockholders' equity.................................	$2,697

On May 3, Griffin split its $0.30 par common stock 3-for-1.

❙ Requirement

1. Prepare the stockholders' equity section of the balance sheet immediately after the split.

E9-48B (*Learning Objective 5: Measuring the book value per share of common stock*)   The balance sheet of Eclectic Rug Company reported the following:

Redeemable preferred stock, 10%, $30 par value, redemption value $25,000; outstanding 700 shares................	$ 21,000
Common stockholders' equity:	
10,000 shares issued and outstanding	100,000
Total stockholders' equity	$121,000

❙ Requirements

1. Compute the book value per share for the common stock, assuming all preferred dividends are fully paid up (none in arrears).
2. Compute the book value per share of the common stock, assuming that three years' cumulative preferred dividends, including the current year, are in arrears.
3. Eclectic Rug's common stock recently traded at a market price of $7.10 per share. Does this mean that Eclectic Rug's stock is a good buy at $7.10?

E9-49B (*Learning Objective 6: Evaluating profitability*)   LaSalle Inns reported these figures for 2011 and 2010 (in millions):

	2011	2010
Balance sheet		
Total assets	$16,000	$13,790
Common stock and additional paid-in capital	38	384
Retained earnings	11,528	16,530
Other equity...	(2,962)	(9,112)
Income statement		
Operating income	$ 4,022	$ 3,815
Interest expense	219	273
Net income	1,530	1,544

❙ Requirement

1. Compute LaSalle's return on assets and return on common stockholders' equity for 2011. Do these rates of return suggest strength or weakness? Give your reason.

E9-50B *(Learning Objective 6: Evaluating profitability)* Lawrence Company included the following items in its financial statements for 2010, the current year (amounts in millions):

Payment of long-term debt..........	$17,100	Dividends paid.....................	$ 215
Proceeds from issuance		Interest expense:	
of common stock.....................	8,495	Current year.....................	1,443
Total liabilities:		Preceding year.................	603
Current year-end....................	32,315	Net income:	
Preceding year-end.................	38,031	Current year.....................	1,872
Total stockholders' equity:		Preceding year.................	1,993
Current year-end....................	23,477	Operating income:	
Preceding year-end.................	14,043	Current year.....................	4,876
Borrowings................................	6,590	Preceding year.................	3,996

❙ Requirement

1. Compute Lawrence's return on assets and return on common equity during 2010 (the current year). Lawrence has no preferred stock outstanding. Do the company's rates of return look strong or weak? Give your reason.

E9-51B *(Learning Objective 7: Reporting cash flows from financing activities)* Use the Lawrence data in Exercise E9-50B to show how the company reported cash flows from financing activities during 2010 (the current year). List items in descending order from largest to smallest dollar amount.

Challenge Exercises

E9-52 *(Learning Objectives 2, 3, 4: Reconstructing transactions from the financial statements)* D-4 Networking Solutions began operations on January 1, 2010, and immediately issued its stock, receiving cash. D-4's balance sheet at December 31, 2010, reported the following stockholders' equity:

Common stock, $1 par.....................	$ 51,000
Additional paid-in capital.................	102,000
Retained earnings.............................	35,000
Treasury stock, 850 shares...............	(7,650)
Total stockholders' equity............	$180,350

During 2010, D-4

    a. Issued stock for $3 per share.
    b. Purchased 950 shares of treasury stock, paying $9 per share.
    c. Resold some of the treasury stock.
    d. Earned net income of $58,000 and declared and paid cash dividends. Revenues were $172,000 and expenses totaled $114,000.

❙ Requirement

1. Journalize all of D-4's stockholders' equity transactions during the year. D-4's entry to close net income to Retained Earnings was:

Revenues	172,000	
Expenses		114,000
Retained Earnings		58,000

E9-53 *(Learning Objective 7: Reporting financing activities on the statement of cash flows)* Use the D-4 Networking Solutions data in Exercise 9-52 to show how the company reported cash flows from financing activities during 2010.

E9-54 *(Learning Objectives 2, 3, 4: Explaining the changes in stockholders' equity)* Space Walk Corporation reported the following stockholders' equity data (all dollars in millions except par value per share):

	December 31, 2010	December 31, 2009
Preferred stock	$ 609	$ 740
Common stock, $1 par value	905	889
Additional paid-in capital.....................	1,514	1,482
Retained earnings.................................	20,625	19,100
Treasury stock, common	(2,777)	(2,600)

Space Walk earned net income of $2,980 during 2010. For each account except Retained Earnings, one transaction explains the change from the December 31, 2009, balance to the December 31, 2010, balance. Two transactions affected Retained Earnings. Give a full explanation, including the dollar amount, for the change in each account.

E9-55 *(Learning Objectives 2, 3, 4: Accounting for changes in stockholders' equity)* Clubhouse, Inc., ended 2010 with 7 million shares of $1 par common stock issued and outstanding. Beginning additional paid-in capital was $10 million, and retained earnings totaled $35 million.

- In April 2011, Clubhouse issued 5 million shares of common stock at a price of $3 per share.
- In June, the company distributed a 10% stock dividend at a time when Clubhouse's common stock had a market value of $6 per share.
- Then in September, Clubhouse's stock price dropped to $2 per share and the company purchased 5 million shares of treasury stock.
- For the year, Clubhouse earned net income of $22 million and declared cash dividends of $12 million.

▌ Requirement

1. Complete the following tabulation to show what Clubhouse should report for stockholders' equity at December 31, 2011. Journal entries are not required.

(Amounts in millions)	Common Stock	+	Additional Paid-In Capital	+	Retained Earnings	−	Treasury Stock	=	Total Equity
Balance, Dec 31, 2010......................	$7		$10		$35		0		$52
Issuance of stock									
Stock dividend....................................									
Purchase of treasury stock.................									
Net income...									
Cash dividends...................................									
Balance, Dec 31, 2011.......................									

Quiz

Test your understanding of stockholders' equity by answering the following questions. Select the best choice from among the possible answers given.

Q9-56 Which of the following is a characteristic of a corporation?

a. No income tax   **c.** Limited liability of stockholders

b. Mutual agency   **d.** Both a and b

Q9-57 Spirit World, Inc., issues 280,000 shares of no-par common stock for $9 per share. The journal entry is:

a.	Cash	2,520,000	
	Common Stock		560,000
	Paid-In Capital in Excess of Par		1,960,000
b.	Cash	2,520,000	
	Common Stock		2,520,000
c.	Cash	2,520,000	
	Common Stock		280,000
	Gain on the Sale of Stock		2,240,000
d.	Cash	280,000	
	Common Stock		280,000

Q9-58 Par value

a. represents the original selling price for a share of stock.

b. is established for a share of stock after it is issued.

c. may exist for common stock but not for preferred stock.

d. represents what a share of stock is worth.

e. is an arbitrary amount that establishes the legal capital for each share.

Q9-59 The paid-in capital portion of stockholders' equity does not include

a. Common Stock.

b. Preferred Stock.

c. Retained Earnings.

d. Paid-in Capital in Excess of Par Value.

Q9-60 Preferred stock is least likely to have which of the following characteristics?

a. Extra liability for the preferred stockholders

b. The right of the holder to convert to common stock

c. Preference as to dividends

d. Preference as to assets on liquidation of the corporation

Q9-61 Which of the following classifications represents the most shares of common stock?

a. Authorized shares

b. Outstanding shares

c. Unissued shares

d. Treasury shares

e. Issued shares

Use the following information for Questions Q9-62 to Q9-64:

These account balances at December 31 relate to Sportworld, Inc.:

Accounts Payable	$ 51,500	Paid-in Capital in Excess	
Accounts Receivable	81,550	of Par—Common	$220,000
Common Stock	317,000	Preferred Stock, 10%, $100 Par	85,000
Treasury Stock	5,200	Retained Earnings	71,300
Bonds Payable	3,800	Notes Receivable	12,100

Q9-62 What is total paid-in capital for Sportworld, Inc.?

a. $634,445
b. $622,000
c. $641,345

d. $693,300
e. None of the above

Q9-63 What is total stockholders' equity for Sportworld, Inc.?

a. $688,100
b. $641,345
c. $693,300

d. $698,500
e. None of the above

Q9-64 Sportworld's net income for the period is $119,100 and beginning common stockholders' equity is $681,500. Calculate Sportworld's return on common stockholders' equity.

a. 17.2%
b. 16.4%

c. 18.2%
d. 19.3%

Q9-65 A company paid $24 per share to purchase 600 shares of its common stock as treasury stock. The stock was originally issued at $16 per share. The journal entry to record the purchase of the treasury stock is:

a.	Treasury Stock	14,400	
	Cash		14,400
b.	Treasury Stock	9,600	
	Retained Earnings	4,800	
	Cash		14,400
c.	Treasury Stock	7,200	
	Paid-in Capital in Excess of Par	7,200	
	Cash		14,400
d.	Common Stock	14,000	
	Cash		14,000

Q9-66 When treasury stock is sold for less than its cost, the entry should include a debit to:

a. Paid-in Capital in Excess of Par.
b. Retained Earnings.

c. Gain on Sale of Treasury Stock.
d. Loss on Sale of Treasury Stock.

Q9-67 A company purchased 100 shares of its common stock at $50 per share. It then sells 35 of the treasury shares at $56 per share. The entry to sell the treasury stock includes a

a. credit to Paid-in Capital, Treasury Stock for $210.
b. debit to Retained Earnings for $210.
c. credit to Retained Earnings for $600.
d. credit to Treasury Stock for $1,960.
e. credit to Cash for $1,960.

Q9-68 Stockholders are eligible for a dividend if they own the stock on the date of:

a. record.

b. issuance.

c. declaration.

d. payment.

Q9-69 Luca's Foods has outstanding 600 shares of 7% preferred stock, $100 par value, and 1,600 shares of common stock, $30 par value. Luca's declares dividends of $15,800. The correct entry is:

a.	Dividends Payable, Preferred	4,200	
	Dividends Payable, Common	11,600	
	Cash		15,800
b.	Dividends Expense	15,800	
	Cash		15,800
c.	Retained Earnings	15,800	
	Dividends Payable, Preferred		4,200
	Dividends Payable, Common		11,600
d.	Retained Earnings	15,800	
	Dividends Payable, Preferred		7,900
	Dividends Payable, Common		7,900

Q9-70 A corporation has 40,000 shares of 10% preferred stock outstanding. Also, there are 40,000 shares of common stock outstanding. Par value for each is $100. If a $500,000 dividend is paid, how much goes to the preferred stockholders?

a. None

b. $400,000

c. $50,000

d. $380,000

e. $500,000

Q9-71 Assume the same facts as in question 70. What is the amount of dividends per share on common stock?

a. $1.00

b. $5.50

c. $2.50

d. $12.50

e. None of these

Q9-72 Which of the following is *not* true about a 10% stock dividend?

a. The market value of the stock is needed to record the stock dividend.

b. Total stockholders' equity remains the same.

c. Paid-in Capital increases.

d. Retained Earnings decreases.

e. Par value decreases.

Q9-73 A company declares a 5% stock dividend. The debit to Retained Earnings is an amount equal to

a. the excess of the market price over the original issue price of the shares to be issued.

b. the market value of the shares to be issued.

c. the par value of the shares to be issued.

d. the book value of the shares to be issued.

Q9-74 Which of the following statements is *not* true about a 3-for-1 stock split?

a. The market price of each share of stock will decrease.

b. Total stockholders' equity increases.

c. A stockholder with 10 shares before the split owns 30 shares after the split.

d. Par value is reduced to one-third of what it was before the split.

e. Retained Earnings remains the same.

Q9-75 Antonio Company's net income and interest expense are $27,000 and $3,000, respectively, and average total assets are $600,000. How much is Antonio's return on assets?

a. 5.0%   c. 6.2%

b. 4.5%   d. 4.0%

Problems

MyAccountingLab

> All of these A and B problems can be found within MyAccountingLab (MAL), an online homework and practice environment. Your instructor may ask you to complete these problems using MyAccountingLab.

(Group A)

P9-76A (*Learning Objective 2: Recording corporate transactions and preparing the stockholders' equity section of the balance sheet*)   The partners who own Cohen Canoes Co. wished to avoid the unlimited personal liability of the partnership form of business, so they incorporated as Cohen Canoes Inc. The charter from the state of Utah authorizes the corporation to issue 9,000 shares of $2 no-par preferred stock and 100,000 shares of $5 par common stock. In its first month, Cohen Canoes completed the following transactions:

May 6	Issued 900 shares of common stock to the promoter for assistance with issuance of the common stock. The promotional fee was $22,500. Debit Organization Expense.
9	Issued 10,000 shares of common stock to Ben Cohen and 12,000 shares to Bill Cohen in return for cash equal to the stock's market value of $25 per share. The Cohens were partners in Cohen Canoes Co.
10	Issued 800 shares of preferred stock to acquire a patent with a market value of $20,000.
26	Issued 1,000 shares of common stock for $25 cash per share.

❘ Requirements

1. Record the transactions in the journal.
2. Prepare the stockholders' equity section of the Cohen Canoes, Inc., balance sheet at May 31. The ending balance of Retained Earnings is $55,000.

P9-77A (*Learning Objectives 2, 4: Preparing the stockholders' equity section of the balance sheet*)   Garman Corp. has the following stockholders' equity information:

Garman's charter authorizes the company to issue 8,000 shares of 5% preferred stock with par value of $130 and 600,000 shares of no-par common stock. The company issued 1,600 shares of the preferred stock at $130 per share. It issued 120,000 shares of the common stock for a total of $513,000. The company's retained earnings balance at the beginning of 2010 was $74,000, and net income for the year was $94,000. During 2010, Garman declared the specified dividend on preferred and a $0.20 per-share dividend on common. Preferred dividends for 2009 were in arrears.

❚ Requirement

1. Prepare the stockholders' equity section of Garman Corp.'s balance sheet at December 31, 2010. Show the computation of all amounts. Journal entries are not required.

P9-78A (*Learning Objectives 2, 3, 4: Measuring the effects of stock issuance, treasury stock, and dividend transactions on stockholders' equity*)   Good Foods, Inc., is authorized to issue 5,500,000 shares of $5.00 par common stock.

In its initial public offering during 2010, Good issued 475,000 shares of its $5.00 par common stock for $7.00 per share. Over the next year, Good's stock price increased, and the company issued 380,000 more shares at an average price of $10.00.

During 2012, the price of Good's common stock dropped to $7.25, and Good purchased 58,000 shares of its common stock for the treasury. After the market price of the common stock rose in 2013, Good sold 41,000 shares of the treasury stock for $10.00 per share.

During the five years 2010 to 2015, Good earned net income of $1,010,000 and declared and paid cash dividends of $610,000. Stock dividends of $645,570 were distributed to the stockholders in 2011, with $358,650 credited to common stock and $286,920 credited to additional paid-in capital. At December 31, 2015, total assets of the company are $14,600,000, and liabilities add up to $7,085,500.

❚ Requirement

1. Show the computation of Good's total stockholders' equity at December 31, 2015. Present a detailed computation of each element of stockholders' equity. Use the end-of chapter summary problem on pages 566–567 to format your answer.

P9-79A (*Learning Objectives 2, 4: Analyzing the stockholders' equity and dividends of a corporation*)   Elegant Outdoor Furniture Company included the following stockholders' equity on its year-end balance sheet at February 28, 2011:

Stockholders' Equity	
Preferred stock, 6.5% cumulative—par value $35 per share; authorized 110,000 shares in each class	
Class A—issued 78,000 shares	$ 2,730,000
Class B—issued 89,000 shares	3,115,000
Common stock—$3 par value: authorized 1,200,000 shares, issued 290,000 shares	870,000
Additional paid-in capital—common	5,530,000
Retained earnings	8,390,000
	$20,635,000

❚ Requirements

1. Identify the different issues of stock Elegant Outdoor Furniture Company has outstanding.
2. Give the summary entries to record issuance of all the Elegant stock. Assume that all the stock was issued for cash. Explanations are not required.
3. Suppose Elegant passed its preferred dividends for three years. Would the company have to pay those dividends in arrears before paying dividends to the common stockholders? Give your reason.
4. What amount of preferred dividends must Elegant declare and pay each year to avoid having preferred dividends in arrears?
5. Assume that preferred dividends are in arrears for 2010. Record the declaration of an $860,000 dividend on February 28, 2011. An explanation is not required.

P9-80A (*Learning Objectives 2, 3, 4: Accounting for stock issuance, dividends, and treasury stock*) Moscow Jewelry Company reported the following summarized balance sheet at December 31, 2010:

Assets	
Current assets...	$ 33,600
Property and equipment, net	74,000
Total assets..	$107,600
Liabilities and Equity	
Liabilities	$ 37,300
Stockholders' equity:	
$0.70 cumulative preferred stock, $5 par, 300 shares issued	1,500
Common stock, $4 par, 6,500 shares issued........................	26,000
Paid-in capital in excess of par	17,800
Retained earnings..	25,000
Total liabilities and equity..	$107,600

During 2011, Moscow completed these transactions that affected stockholders' equity:

Feb	13	Issued 5,400 shares of common stock for $5 per share.
Jun	7	Declared the regular cash dividend on the preferred stock.
	24	Paid the cash dividend.
Aug	9	Distributed a 10% stock dividend on the common stock. Market price of the common stock was $6 per share.
Oct	26	Reacquired 500 shares of common stock as treasury stock, paying $7 per share.
Nov	20	Sold 200 shares of the treasury stock for $11 per share.

Requirements

1. Journalize Moscow's transactions. Explanations are not required.
2. Report Moscow's stockholders' equity at December 31, 2011. Net income for 2011 was $28,000.

P9-81A (*Learning Objectives 3, 4: Measuring the effects of dividend and treasury stock transactions on a company*) Assume Dessert Destination of Montana, Inc., completed the following transactions during 2010, the company's 10th year of operations:

Feb	3	Issued 15,000 shares of company stock ($1.00 par) for cash of $435,000.
Mar	19	Purchased 2,600 shares of the company's own common stock at $24 per share.
Apr	24	Sold 1,300 shares of treasury common stock for $32 per share.
Aug	15	Declared a cash dividend on the 18,000 shares of $0.40 no-par preferred stock.
Sep	1	Paid the cash dividends.
Nov	22	Distributed a 8% stock dividend on the 92,000 shares of $1.00 par common stock outstanding. The market value of the common stock was $26 per share.

❚ Requirement

1. Analyze each transaction in terms of its effect on the accounting equation of Dessert Destination of Montana, Inc.

P9-82A (*Learning Objectives 3, 6: Preparing a corporation's balance sheet; measuring profitability*)   The following accounts and related balances of Seagull Designers, Inc., as of December 31, 2010, are arranged in no particular order.

Cash	$55,000	Interest expense	$ 15,600
Accounts receivable, net	34,000	Property, plant, and	
Paid-in capital in excess		equipment, net	364,000
of par—common	20,000	Common stock, $2 par,	
Accrued liabilities	24,000	600,000 shares authorized,	
Long-term note payable	99,000	116,000 shares issued	232,000
Inventory	93,000	Prepaid expenses	13,000
Dividends payable	6,000	Common stockholders'	
Retained earnings	?	equity, December 31, 2009	222,000
Accounts payable	136,000	Net income	32,000
Trademarks, net	4,000	Total assets,	
Preferred stock, $.50,		December 31, 2009	493,000
no-par, 11,000 shares		Treasury stock,	
authorized and issued	29,700	21,000 shares at cost	24,000
Goodwill	13,000		

❚ Requirements

1. Prepare Seagull's classified balance sheet in the account format at December 31, 2010.
2. Compute rate of return on total assets and rate of return on common stockholders' equity for the year ended December 31, 2010.
3. Do these rates of return suggest strength or weakness? Give your reason.

P9-83A (*Learning Objective 7: Analyzing the statement of cash flows*)   The statement of cash flows of Frappe, Inc., reported the following (adapted) for the year ended December 31, 2010:

Cash flows from financing activities (amounts in millions)	
Cash dividends paid	$(1,918)
Issuance of common stock at par value	1,000
Proceeds from issuance of long-term notes payable	54
Purchases of treasury stock	(3,030)
Payments of long-term notes payable	(163)

❚ Requirement

1. Make the journal entry that Frappe would use to record each of these transactions.

(Group B)

P9-84B (*Learning Objective 2: Recording corporate transactions and preparing the stockholders' equity section of the balance sheet*)   The partners who own Liard Canoes Co. wished to avoid the unlimited personal liability of the partnership form of business, so they incorporated as Liard Canoes, Inc. The charter from the state of Texas authorizes the corporation to issue 5,000 shares of $1 no-par preferred stock and 140,000 shares of $5 par common stock. In its first month, Liard Canoes completed the following transactions:

Jan	6	Issued 500 shares of common stock to the promoter for assistance with issuance of common stock. The promotional fee was $7,500. Debit Organization Expense.
	9	Issued 9,000 shares of common stock to Lou Liard and 10,000 shares to Larry Liard in return for cash equal to the stock's market value of $15 per share. The Liards were partners in Liard Canoes, Inc.
	10	Issued 600 shares of preferred stock to acquire a patent with a market value of $12,000.
	26	Issued 1,400 shares of common stock for $15 cash per share.

I Requirements

1. Record the transactions in the journal.
2. Prepare the stockholders' equity section of the Liard Canoes, Inc., balance sheet at January 31. The ending balance of Retained Earnings is $56,000.

P9-85B (*Learning Objectives 2, 4: Preparing the stockholders' equity section of the balance sheet*)   Holman Corp. has the following stockholders' equity information:

Holman's charter authorizes the company to issue 5,000 shares of 8% preferred stock with par value of $110 and 400,000 shares of no-par common stock. The company issued 1,000 shares of the preferred stock at $110 per share. It issued 80,000 shares of the common stock for a total of $512,000. The company's retained earnings balance at the beginning of 2010 was $71,000, and net income for the year was $92,000. During 2010, Holman declared the specified dividend on preferred and a $0.60 per-share dividend on common. Preferred dividends for 2009 were in arrears.

I Requirement

1. Prepare the stockholders' equity section of Holman Corp.'s balance sheet at December 31, 2010. Show the computation of all amounts. Journal entries are not required.

P9-86B (*Learning Objectives 2, 3, 4: Measuring the effects of stock issuance, treasury stock, and dividend transactions on stockholders' equity*)   Hearty Foods, Inc., is authorized to issue 5,000,000 shares of $2.00 par common stock.

In its initial public offering during 2010, Hearty issued 500,000 shares of its $2.00 par common stock for $5.00 per share. Over the next year, Hearty's stock price increased, and the company issued 395,000 more shares at an average price of $9.00.

During 2012, the price of Hearty's common stock dropped to $7.25, and Hearty purchased 61,000 shares of its common stock for the treasury. After the market price of the common stock rose in 2013, Hearty sold 38,000 shares of the treasury stock for $8.00 per share.

During the 5 years 2010 to 2015, Hearty earned net income of $1,150,000 and declared and paid cash dividends of $700,000. Stock dividends of $600,480 were distributed to the stockholders in 2011, with $150,120 credited to common stock and $450,360 credited to additional paid-in capital. At December 31, 2015, total assets of the company are $14,200,000, and liabilities add up to $7,833,250.

Requirement

1. Show the computation of Hearty's total stockholders' equity at December 31, 2015. Present a detailed computation of each element of stockholders' equity. Use the end-of-chapter summary problem on pages 566 and 567 to format your answer.

P9-87B (*Learning Objectives 2, 4: Analyzing the stockholders' equity and dividends of a corporation*) Seasonal Outdoor Furniture Company included the following stockholders' equity on its year-end balance sheet at February 28, 2011:

Stockholders' Equity	
Preferred stock, 4.0% cumulative—par value $20 per share authorized 100,000 shares in each class	
Class A—issued 76,000 shares	$ 1,520,000
Class B—issued 97,000 shares	1,940,000
Common stock—$4 par value: authorized 1,500,000 shares,	
issued 250,000 shares	1,000,000
Additional paid-in capital—common	5,520,000
Retained earnings	8,320,000
	$18,300,000

Requirements

1. Identify the different issues of stock Seasonal Outdoor Furniture Company has outstanding.
2. Give the summary entries to record issuance of all the Seasonal stock. Assume that all the stock was issued for cash. Explanations are not required.
3. Suppose Seasonal passed its preferred dividends for three years. Would the company have to pay these dividends in arrears before paying dividends to the common stockholders? Give your reasons.
4. What amount of preferred dividends must Seasonal declare and pay each year to avoid having preferred dividends in arrears?
5. Assume that preferred dividends are in arrears for 2010. Record the declaration of an $840,000 dividend on February 28, 2011. An explanation is not required.

P9-88B (*Learning Objectives 2, 3, 4: Accounting for stock issuance, dividends, and treasury stock*) London Jewelry Company reported the following summarized balance sheet at December 31, 2010:

Assets	
Current assets	$33,500
Property and equipment, net	63,100
Total assets	$96,600
Liabilities and Equity	
Liabilities	$37,600
Stockholders' equity:	
$0.80 cumulative preferred stock, $15 par, 400 shares issued	6,000
Common stock, $2 par, 6,300 shares issued	12,600
Paid-in capital in excess of par	17,400
Retained earnings	23,000
Total liabilities and equity	$96,600

During 2011, London completed these transactions that affected stockholders' equity:

Feb	13	Issued 5,200 shares of common stock for $6 per share.
Jun	7	Declared the regular cash dividend on the preferred stock.
	24	Paid the cash dividend.
Aug	9	Distributed a 20% stock dividend on the common stock. Market price of the common stock was $7 per share.
Oct	26	Reacquired 900 shares of common stock as treasury stock, paying $8 per share.
Nov	20	Sold 600 shares of the treasury stock for $12 per share.

▌ Requirements

1. Journalize London's transactions. Explanations are not required.
2. Report London's stockholders' equity at December 31, 2011. Net income for 2011 was $25,000.

P9-89B (*Learning Objectives 3, 4: Measuring the effects of dividend and treasury stock transactions on a company*)   Assume Cookie Corner of Wisconsin, Inc., completed the following transactions during 2010, the company's 10th year of operations:

Feb	4	Issued 14,000 shares of company stock ($1.00 par) for cash of $350,000.
Mar	20	Purchased 2,200 shares of the company's own common stock at $21 per share.
Apr	25	Sold 900 shares of treasury stock for $30 per share.
Aug	17	Declared a cash dividend on the 14,000 shares of $0.80 no-par preferred stock.
Sep	4	Paid the cash dividends.
Nov	28	Distributed a 5% stock dividend on the 99,000 shares of $1.00 par common stock outstanding. The market value of the common stock was $22 per share.

▌ Requirement

1. Analyze each transaction in terms of its effect on the accounting equation of Cookie Corner of Wisconsin, Inc.

P9-90B (*Learning Objectives 3, 6: Preparing a corporation's balance sheet; measuring profitability*)   The following accounts and related balances of Hawk Designers, Inc., as of December 31, 2010, are arranged in no particular order.

Cash	$43,000		Interest expense	$ 16,000
Accounts receivable, net	22,000		Property, plant, and	
Paid-in capital in excess			equipment, net	359,000
of par—common	17,000		Common stock, $2 par,	
Accrued liabilities	27,000		300,000 shares authorized,	
Long-term note payable	96,000		117,000 shares issued	234,000
Inventory	94,000		Prepaid expenses	16,000
Dividends payable	12,000		Common stockholders'	
Retained earnings	?		equity, December 31, 2009	225,000
Accounts payable	133,000		Net income	30,000
Trademarks, net	10,000		Total assets,	
Preferred stock, $.50,			December 31, 2009	496,000
no-par, 12,000 shares			Treasury stock, common,	
authorized and issued	32,400		19,000 shares at cost	22,000
Goodwill	11,000			

Requirements

1. Prepare Hawk's classified balance sheet in the account format at December 31, 2010.
2. Compute rate of return on total assets and rate of return on common stockholders' equity for the year ended December 31, 2010.
3. Do these rates of return suggest strength or weakness? Give your reason.

P9-91B *(Learning Objective 7: Analyzing the statement of cash flows)*   The statement of cash flows of Smoothie, Inc., reported the following (adapted) for the year ended December 31, 2010:

Cash flows from financing activities (amounts in millions)	
Cash dividends paid	$(1,890)
Issuance of common stock at par value	1,234
Proceeds from issuance of long-term notes payable	58
Purchases of treasury stock	(3,080)
Payments of long-term notes payable	(162)

Requirement

1. Make the journal entry that Smoothie would use to record each of these transactions.

APPLY YOUR KNOWLEDGE

Decision Cases

Case 1. *(Learning Objective 2: Evaluating alternative ways of raising capital)* Nate Smith and Darla Jones have written a computer program for a video game that may rival Playstation and Xbox. They need additional capital to market the product, and they plan to incorporate their business. Smith and Jones are considering alternative capital structures for the corporation. Their primary goal is to raise as much capital as possible without giving up control of the business. Smith and Jones plan to receive 50,000 shares of the corporation's common stock in return for the net assets of their old business. After the old company's books are closed and the assets adjusted to current market value, Smith's and Jones' capital balances will each be $25,000.

writing assignment ■

The corporation's plans for a charter include an authorization to issue 10,000 shares of preferred stock and 500,000 shares of $1 par common stock. Smith and Jones are uncertain about the most desirable features for the preferred stock. Prior to incorporating, Smith and Jones are discussing their plans with two investment groups. The corporation can obtain capital from outside investors under either of the following plans:

- *Plan 1.*   Group 1 will invest $80,000 to acquire 800 shares of 6%, $100 par nonvoting, preferred stock.
- *Plan 2.*   Group 2 will invest $55,000 to acquire 500 shares of $5, no-par preferred stock and $35,000 to acquire 35,000 shares of common stock. Each preferred share receives 50 votes on matters that come before the stockholders.

Requirements

Assume that the corporation is chartered.

1. Journalize the issuance of common stock to Smith and Jones. Debit each person's capital account for its balance.
2. Journalize the issuance of stock to the outsiders under both plans.
3. Assume that net income for the first year is $120,000 and total dividends are $30,000. Prepare the stockholders' equity section of the corporation's balance sheet under both plans.
4. Recommend one of the plans to Smith and Jones. Give your reasons. (Challenge)

writing assignment ■

Case 2. *(Learning Objective 4: Analyzing cash dividends and stock dividends)* **United Parcel Service (UPS), Inc.**, had the following stockholders' equity amounts on December 31, 2010 (adapted, in millions):

Common stock and additional paid-in capital; 1,135 shares issued...............	$ 278
Retained earnings...	9,457
Total stockholders' equity	$9,735

During 2010, UPS paid a cash dividend of $0.715 per share. Assume that, after paying the cash dividends, UPS distributed a 10% stock dividend. Assume further that the following year UPS declared and paid a cash dividend of $0.65 per share.

Suppose you own 10,000 shares of UPS common stock, acquired three years ago, prior to the 10% stock dividend. The market price of UPS stock was $61.02 per share before the stock dividend.

❙ Requirements

1. How does the stock dividend affect your proportionate ownership in UPS? Explain.
2. What amount of cash dividends did you receive last year? What amount of cash dividends will you receive after the above dividend action?
3. Assume that immediately after the stock dividend was distributed, the market value of UPS's stock decreased from $61.02 per share to $55.473 per share. Does this decrease represent a loss to you? Explain.
4. Suppose UPS announces at the time of the stock dividend that the company will continue to pay the annual $0.715 *cash* dividend per share, even after distributing the *stock* dividend. Would you expect the market price of the stock to decrease to $55.473 per share as in Requirement 3? Explain.

writing assignment ■

Case 3. *(Learning Objectives 2, 3, 4, 5: Evaluating financial position and profitability)* At December 31, 2000, **Enron Corporation** reported the following data (condensed in millions):

Total assets	$65,503
Total liabilities	54,033
Stockholders' equity	11,470
Net income, as reported, for 2000.................	979

During 2001, Enron restated company financial statements for 1997 to 2000, after reporting that some data had been omitted from those prior-year statements. Assume that the startling events of 2001 included the following:

- Several related companies should have been, but were not, included in the Enron statements for 2000. These companies had total assets of $5,700 million, liabilities totaling $5,600 million, and net losses of $130 million.
- In January 2001, Enron's stockholders got the company to give them $2,000 million of 12% long-term notes payable in return for their giving up their common stock. Interest is accrued at year-end.

Take the role of a financial analyst. It is your job to analyze Enron Corporation and rate the company's long-term debt.

❙ Requirements

1. Measure Enron's expected net income for 2001 two ways:
   a. Assume 2001's net income should be the same as the amount of net income that Enron actually reported for 2000. (Given)
   b. Recompute expected net income for 2001 taking into account the new developments of 2001. (Challenge)
   c. Evaluate Enron's likely trend of net income for the future. Discuss *why* this trend is developing. Ignore income tax. (Challenge)

2. Write Enron's accounting equation two ways:
   a. As actually reported at December 31, 2000.
   b. As adjusted for the events of 2001. (Challenge)
3. Measure Enron's debt ratio as reported at December 31, 2000, and again after making the adjustments for the events of 2001.
4. Based on your analysis, make a recommendation to the Debt-Rating Committee of Moody's Investor Services. Would you recommend upgrading, downgrading, or leaving Enron's debt rating undisturbed (currently, it is "high-grade"). (Challenge)

Ethical Issues

Ethical Issue 1. *Note:* This case is based on a real situation.

writing assignment ■

George Campbell paid $50,000 for a franchise that entitled him to market Success Associates software programs in the countries of the European Union. Campbell intended to sell individual franchises for the major language groups of western Europe—German, French, English, Spanish, and Italian. Naturally, investors considering buying a franchise from Campbell asked to see the financial statements of his business.

Believing the value of the franchise to be greater than $50,000, Campbell sought to capitalize his own franchise at $500,000. The law firm of McDonald & LaDue helped Campbell form a corporation chartered to issue 500,000 shares of common stock with par value of $1 per share. Attorneys suggested the following chain of transactions:

   a. A third party borrows $500,000 and purchases the franchise from Campbell.
   b. Campbell pays the corporation $500,000 to acquire all its stock.
   c. The corporation buys the franchise from the third party, who repays the loan.

In the final analysis, the third party is debt-free and out of the picture. Campbell owns all the corporation's stock, and the corporation owns the franchise. The corporation balance sheet lists a franchise acquired at a cost of $500,000. This balance sheet is Campbell's most valuable marketing tool.

❚ Requirements

1. What is the ethical issue in this situation?
2. Who are the stakeholders to the suggested transaction?
3. Analyze this case from the following standpoints: (a) economic, (b) legal, (c) ethical. What are the consequences to each stakeholder?
4. How should the transaction be reported?

Ethical Issue 2. St. Genevieve Petroleum Company is an independent oil producer in Baton Parish, Louisiana. In February, company geologists discovered a pool of oil that tripled the company's proven reserves. Prior to disclosing the new oil to the public, St. Genevieve quietly bought most of its stock as treasury stock. After the discovery was announced, the company's stock price increased from $6 to $27.

writing assignment ■

❚ Requirements

1. What is the ethical issue in this situation? What accounting principle is involved?
2. Who are the stakeholders?
3. Analyze the facts from the following standpoints: (a) economic, (b) legal, and (c) ethical. What is the impact to each stakeholder?
4. What decision would you have made?

Focus on Financials: ■ Amazon.com, Inc.

(*Learning Objectives 2, 3, 6: Analyzing common stock, retained earnings, return on equity, and return on assets*) **Amazon.com's** consolidated financial statements appear in Appendix A at the end of this book.

1. Refer to the Consolidated Balance Sheets and Note 8 (Stockholders' Equity). Describe the classes of stock that Amazon.com, Inc., has authorized. How many shares of each class have been issued? How many are outstanding as of December 31, 2008?

2. Refer to the Consolidated Balance Sheets and the Consolidated Statements of Stockholders' Equity. (Note: The Statement of Stockholders' Equity is discussed in detail in Chapter 11, pages 667 through 675.) How many shares of treasury stock did the company purchase during the year ended December 31, 2008? How much did it pay for it in total? How much per share?

3. Examine Amazon.com's consolidated statement of shareholders' equity. Analyze the change that occurred in the company's Retained Earnings account during the year ended December 31, 2008. Can you trace the change to any of its other financial statements? Is this a good thing or a bad thing? (Note: The Statement of Stockholders' Equity is discussed in detail in Chapter 11, pages 667 through 675.)

4. Compute Amazon.com's return on equity and return on assets for 2008. Which is larger? Is this a sign of financial strength or weakness? Explain.

Focus on Analysis: ■ Foot Locker, Inc.

(*Learning Objectives 2, 3, 4: Analyzing treasury stock and retained earnings*) This case is based on the consolidated financial statements of **Foot Locker, Inc.**, given in Appendix B at the end of this book. In particular, this case uses Foot Locker, Inc.'s consolidated statement of shareholders' equity for the year 2007. (Note: The Statement of Stockholders' Equity is discussed in detail in Chapter 11, pages 667 through 675.)

1. As of the end of fiscal 2007, how many classes of stock does Foot Locker, Inc., have authorized? Issued? Outstanding?

2. During 2007, Foot Locker, Inc., repurchased its treasury stock. How many shares did it purchase? How much did it pay for the stock? How much per share? Compare the price it paid for these shares with the market price of the company's stock at the end of each quarter (see footnote 26). Does it look like the company was getting a "good deal" on the purchase of its stock? Why do you think it did it? (Challenge)

3. Did Foot Locker, Inc., issue any new shares of common stock during fiscal 2007? Briefly explain the reasons. (Challenge)

4. Prepare a T-account to show the beginning and ending balances, plus all the activity in Retained Earnings for fiscal 2007.

Group Project in Ethics

writing assignment ■

The global economic recession that started in 2007 has impacted every business, but it was especially hard on banks, automobile manufacturing, and retail companies. Banks were largely responsible for the recession. Some of the biggest banks made excessively risky investments collateralized by real estate mortgages, and many of these investments soured when the real estate markets collapsed. When banks had to write these investments down to market values, the regulatory authorities notified them that they had inadequate capital ratios on their balance sheets to operate. Banks stopped loaning money. Because stock prices were depressed, companies could not raise capital by selling stock. With both debt and stock financing frozen, many businesses had to close their doors.

Fearing collapse of the whole economy, the central governments of the United States and several European nations loaned money to banks to prop up their capital ratios and keep them open. The government also loaned massive amounts to the largest insurance company in the United States (AIG), as well as to General Motors and Chrysler, to help them stay in business. When asked why, many in government replied "these businesses were too important to fail." In several cases, the U.S. government has taken an "equity stake" in some banks and businesses by taking preferred stock in exchange for the cash infusion.

Because of the recession, corporate downsizing has occurred on a massive scale throughout the world. While companies in the retail sector provide more jobs than the banking and automobile industry combined, the government has not chosen to "bail out" any retail businesses. Each company or industry mentioned in this book has pared down plant and equipment, laid off employees, or restructured operations. Some companies have been forced out of business altogether.

Requirements

1. Identify all the stakeholders of a corporation. A *stakeholder* is a person or a group who has an interest (that is, a stake) in the success of the organization.
2. Do you believe that some entities are "too important to fail?" Should the federal government help certain businesses to stay afloat during economic recessions, and allow others to fail?
3. Identify several measures by which a company may be considered deficient and in need of downsizing. How can downsizing help to solve this problem?
4. Debate the bailout issue. One group of students takes the perspective of the company and its stockholders, and another group of students takes the perspective of the other stakeholders of the company (the community in which the company operates and society at large).
5. What is the problem with the government taking an equity position such as preferred stock in a private enterprise?

For online homework, exercises, and problems that provide you with immediate feedback, please visit www.myaccountinglab.com.

Quick Check Answers

1. *a* (20,000 shares × $25 = $500,000)
2. *c* ($600,000/$5 par = 120,000 shares)
3. *d* ($375,000 + $60,000 + $600,000)
4. *d* ($375,000 + $60,000 + $600,000 + $325,000)
5. *c* ($1,360,000 − $10,000)
6. *d* [No gain or loss (for the income statement) on treasury stock transactions]
7. *a*
8. *b*
9. *d*
10. *c*
11. *d* [First, annual preferred dividend = $1,250 (2,500 × $25 × .02)]. Five years of preferred dividends must be paid (four in arrears plus the current year).
    [($1,250 × 5) + ($125,000 × $2.50 per share common dividend) = $318,750]
12. *a*
13. *c*
14. *c*
15. *d*
16. *c*

10

Long-Term Investments & International Operations

SPOTLIGHT: Intel Holds Several Different Types of Investments

After college you'll start investing through a retirement or savings plan at work, and you may make some investments on your own. The reasons people invest are for current income (interest and dividends) and appreciation of the investment's value (stocks, bonds, and real estate, for example). Some very wealthy individuals invest in order to obtain significant influence over, or even to control, corporate entities.

Businesses like **Intel**, **General Electric**, and **Coca-Cola** invest for the same reasons. In this chapter you'll learn how to account for investments of all types. We use Intel Corporation as our example company because Intel has so many interesting investments. You'll also learn how companies like this do business across international borders, and the impact that business has on their financial statements.

Intel Corporation
Consolidated Balance Sheet (partial; adapted)
December 31, 2007

(In millions)	2007
1 **Assets**	
2 Current assets:	
3 Cash and cash equivalents.....................................	$ 7,307
4 Short-term investments...	5,490
5 Trading assets...	2,566
6 Accounts receivable, net of allowance for	
doubtful accounts of $27	2,576
7 Inventories...	3,370
8 Other current assets...	2,576
9 **Total current assets**.......................................	23,885
10 **Property, plant and equipment, net**..........................	16,918
11 Marketable strategic equity securities	987
12 Other long-term investments....................................	4,398
13 **Goodwill**..	3,916
14 Other long-term assets...	5,547
15 **Total assets**	$55,651

What comes to mind when you think of Intel? Computer processors and microchips? Yes, Intel produces processors and computer chips. But, interestingly, 24.2% ($5,490 + $2,566 + $987 + $4,398/$55,651) of Intel's assets are tied up in investments in other companies. The assets section of Intel's 2007 balance sheet reports these investments on lines 4, 5, 11, and 12. Some of Intel's other asset categories also include investments.

Throughout this course, you've become increasingly familiar with the financial statements of companies such as **Intel**, **Southwest Airlines**, and **Starbucks**. You've seen most of the items that appear in a set of financial statements. One of your learning goals should be to develop the ability to analyze whatever you encounter in real-company statements. This chapter will help you advance toward that goal.

The first half of this chapter shows how to account for long-term investments, including a brief overview of consolidated financial statements. The second half of the chapter covers accounting for international operations.

LEARNING OBJECTIVES

1 **Account** for available-for-sale investments

2 **Use** the equity method for investments

3 **Understand** consolidated financial statements

4 **Account** for long-term investments in bonds

5 **Account** for international operations

6 **Report** investing transactions on the statement of cash flows

STOCK INVESTMENTS: AN OVERVIEW

Investments come in all sizes and shapes—from a few shares of stock to a controlling interest in multiple companies. In earlier chapters, we discussed stocks and bonds from the perspective of the company that issued the securities. In this chapter, we examine *long-term* investments.

To consider investments, we need to define two key terms. The entity that owns the stock of a corporation is the *investor*. The corporation that issued the stock is the *investee*. If you own some shares of Intel common stock, you are an investor and Intel is the investee.

Stock Prices

You can log onto the Internet to learn Intel's current stock price. Exhibit 10-1 presents information on Intel. During the previous 52 weeks, Intel common stock had a high price of $25.29 and a low of $12.06 per share. The annual cash dividend is $0.56 per share. During the previous day, 51.3 million shares of Intel common stock were traded. At day's end the price of the stock closed at $13.36, up $0.15 from the closing price of the preceding day.

EXHIBIT 10-1 | Stock Price Information for Intel Corporation

52-Week						
Hi	Lo	Stock (sym)	Div	Volume	Close	Net Change
$25.29	$12.06	INTC	$0.56	51,305,000	$13.36	+ $0.15

Reporting Investments on the Balance Sheet

An investment is an asset to the investor. The investment may be short-term or long-term. **Short-term investments** in marketable securities are current assets. They can be classified as either *trading, held-to-maturity,* or *available for sale,* depending on management's intent and ability to hold them until they mature. To be listed as short-term on the balance sheet,

- the investment must be *liquid* (readily convertible to cash).
- the investor must intend either to convert the investment to cash within one year or to use it to pay a current liability.

We saw how to account for short-term investments in Chapter 5.

Investments that aren't short-term are listed as **long-term investments**, a category of noncurrent assets. Long-term investments include stocks and bonds that the investor expects to hold for longer than one year. Exhibit 10-2 on the following page shows where short-term and long-term investments appear on the balance sheet.

EXHIBIT 10-2 | **Reporting Investments on the Balance Sheet**

Current Assets:		
Cash	$X	
Short-term investments	X	
Accounts receivable	X	
Inventories	X	
Prepaid expenses	X	
Total current assets		X
Long-term investments [or simply Investments]		X
Property, plant, and equipment		X
Intangible assets		X
Other assets		X

Assets are listed in order of liquidity. Long-term investments are less liquid than current assets but more liquid than property, plant, and equipment. Intel also reports short-term investments immediately after cash (p. 604, lines 4 and 5).

The accounting rules for long-term investments in stock depend on the percentage of ownership by the investor. The accounting methods typically used are shown in Exhibit 10-3.

EXHIBIT 10-3 | **Accounting Methods for Long-Term Investments Based on Level of Ownership**

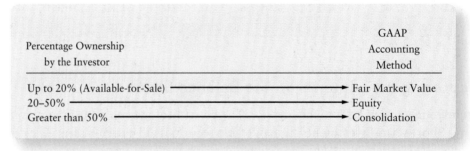

Percentage Ownership by the Investor	GAAP Accounting Method
Up to 20% (Available-for-Sale)	→ Fair Market Value
20–50%	→ Equity
Greater than 50%	→ Consolidation

An investment up to 20% is considered available-for-sale because the investor usually has little or no influence on the investee, in which case the strategy would be to hold the investment, making it available for sale in periods beyond the end of the fiscal year. Ownership between 20% and 50% provides the investor with the opportunity to significantly influence the investee's operating decisions and policies over the long run. An investment above 50% allows the investor a great deal of long-term influence—perhaps control—over the investee company. Let's see how these methods apply to long-term investments in stock.

AVAILABLE-FOR-SALE INVESTMENTS

OBJECTIVE

1 **Account** for available-for-sale investments

Available-for-sale investments are stock investments other than trading securities. They are classified as current assets if the business expects to sell them within the next year. All other available-for-sale investments are classified as long term (Exhibit 10-2).

Accounting for Available-for-Sale Investments

Available-for-sale investments are accounted for at fair market value because the company expects to sell the investment at its market price. *Cost* is used only as the initial amount for recording the investments. These investments are reported on the balance sheet at current **fair market values**.

Suppose Intel purchases 1,000 shares of **Hewlett-Packard** common stock at the market price of $44.00. Intel intends to hold this investment for longer than a year and therefore treats it as an available-for-sale investment. Intel's entry to record the investment is:

2010			
Oct 23	Long-Term Investment (1,000 × $44)	44,000	
	Cash		44,000
	Purchased investment.		

Assets	=	Liabilities	+	Stockholders' Equity
+ 44,000	=	0	+	0
− 44,000				

Assume that Intel receives a $0.20 cash dividend on the Hewlett-Packard stock. Intel's entry to record receipt of the dividend is

2010			
Nov 14	Cash (1,000 × $0.20)	200	
	Dividend Revenue		200
	Received cash dividend.		

Assets	=	Liabilities	+	Stockholders' Equity	+	Revenues
+200	=	0	+			+200

Receipt of a *stock* dividend is different from receipt of a cash dividend. For a stock dividend, the investor records no dividend revenue. Instead, the investor makes a memorandum entry in the accounting records to denote the new number of shares of stock held as an investment. Because the number of shares of stock held has increased, the investor's cost per share decreases. To illustrate, suppose Intel receives a 10% stock dividend from Hewlett-Packard Company. Intel would receive 100 shares (10% of 1,000 shares previously held) and make this memorandum entry in its accounting records:

> **MEMORANDUM—Receipt of stock dividend:** Received 100 shares of Hewlett-Packard common stock in 10% stock dividend. New cost per share is $40.00 (cost of $44,000 ÷ 1,100 shares).

In all future transactions affecting this investment, Intel's cost per share is now $40.00.

What Value of an Investment Is Most Relevant?

Fair market value is the amount that a seller would receive on the sale of an investment to a willing purchaser on a given date. Because of the relevance of fair market values for decision making, available-for-sale investments in stock are reported on the balance sheet at their fair market values. On the balance-sheet date we therefore adjust available-for-sale investments from their last carrying amount to current fair market value. Assume that the fair market value of the Hewlett-Packard common stock is $46,500 on December 31, 2010. In this case, Intel makes the following entry to bring the investment to fair market value.

2010			
Dec 31	Allowance to Adjust Investment to Market		
	($46,500 − $44,000)	2,500	
	Unrealized Gain on Investment		2,500
	Adjusted investment to fair market value.		

The increase in the investment's fair market value creates additional equity for the investor.

Assets	**=**	**Liabilities**	**+**	**Stockholders' Equity**
+ 2,500	=	0		+ 2,500

Allowance to Adjust Investment to Market is a companion account to Long-Term Investment. In this case, the investment's cost ($44,000) plus the Allowance ($2,500) equals the investment fair market value carrying amount ($46,500), as follows:

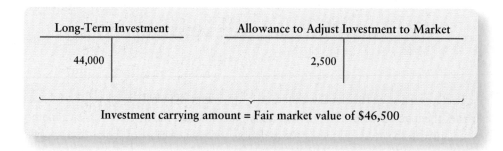

Here the Allowance has a debit balance because the fair market value of the investment increased. If the investment's fair market value declines, the Allowance is credited. In that case the carrying amount is its cost minus the Allowance.

The other side of this adjustment entry is a credit to Unrealized Gain on Investment. If the fair market value of the investment declines, the company debits Unrealized Loss on Investment. *Unrealized* gains and losses result from changes in fair market value, not from sales of investments. For available-for-sale investments, the Unrealized Gain account or the Unrealized Loss account is reported in either of two places in the financial statements:

- *Other comprehensive income*, which can be reported on the *income statement* in a separate section below net income
- *Accumulated other comprehensive income*, which is a separate section of stockholders' equity, below retained earnings, on the *balance sheet*

The following display shows how Intel could report its investment and the related unrealized gain in its financial statements at the end of 2010 (all other figures are assumed for this illustration):

Balance sheet		Income statement		
Assets:				
Total current assets	$ XXX	Revenues		$50,000
Long-term investments—		Expenses, including		
at market value		income tax		36,000
($44,000 + $2,500	46,500	Net income		$14,000
Property, plant, and equipment,		Other comprehensive income:		
net	XXX	Unrealized gain on		
Stockholders' equity:		investments	$ 2,500	
Common stock	1,000	Less Income tax		
Retained earnings	2,000	40%	(1,000)	1,500
Accumulated other		Comprehensive income		$15,500
comprehensive income:				
Unrealized gain on investments	2,500			
Total stockholders' equity	$ 5,500			

The preceding example assumes that the investor holds an investment in only one security of another company. Usually companies invest in a portfolio of securities (more than one). In this case, the periodic adjustment to fair market value must be made for the portfolio as a whole. See the "Stop & Think" exercise at the end of this section (p. 610) for an example.

Selling an Available-for-Sale Investment

The sale of an available-for-sale investment usually results in a *realized* gain or loss. Realized gains and losses measure the difference between the amount received from the sale and the cost of the investment.

Suppose Intel sells its investment in Hewlett-Packard stock for $43,000 during 2011. Intel would record the sale as follows:

2011	Cash	43,000	
May 19	Loss on Sale of Investment	1,000	
	Long-Term Investment (cost)		44,000
	Sold investment.		

Assets	=	Liabilities	+	Stockholders' Equity	−	Losses
+ 43,000	=	0			−	1,000
− 44,000						

Intel would report Loss on Sale of Investments as an "Other" item on the income statement. Then at December 31, 2011, Intel must make adjusting entries to update the Allowance to Adjust Investment to Market and the Unrealized Gain on Investment accounts to their current balances (in this case, these accounts have been reduced to zero since the entire investment was sold). These adjustments are covered in intermediate accounting courses.

STOP & THINK...

Suppose Intel Corporation holds the following available-for-sale securities as long-term investments at December 31, 2011:

Stock	Cost	Current Fair Market Value
The Coca-Cola Company.........	$ 85,000	$71,000
Eastman Kodak Company........	16,000	12,000
	$101,000	$83,000

Show how Intel will report long-term investments on its December 31, 2011, balance sheet.

Answer:

Assets	
Long-term investments, at fair market value	$83,000

When Should We Sell an Investment?

Companies control when they sell investments, and that helps them control when they record gains and losses. Suppose a bad year hits and Intel holds an investment that has appreciated in value. Intel can sell the investment, raise cash, record the gain, and boost reported income.

The cost principle of accounting provides this opportunity to "manage" earnings. If companies had to account for all investments at pure market value, there would be no gain or loss on the sale. Instead, all gains and losses would be recorded when the market value of the asset changes. That would eliminate part of management's ability to "manage" earnings. But the business community may not be ready to fully embrace fair-market-value accounting.

EQUITY-METHOD INVESTMENTS

OBJECTIVE

2 **Use** the equity method for investments

We use the **equity method** to account for investments in which the investor owns 20% to 50% of the investee's stock.

Buying a Large Stake in Another Company

An investor with a stock holding between 20% and 50% of the investee's voting stock may significantly influence the investee. Such an investor can probably affect dividend policy, product lines, and other important matters.

Intel holds equity-method investments in IM Flash Technologies and Clearwire Corporation. These investee companies are often referred to as *affiliates*; thus Clearwire is an affiliate of Intel. And because Intel has a voice in shaping the policy and operations of Clearwire, some measure of Clearwire's profits and losses should be included in Intel's income.

Accounting for Equity-Method Investments

Investments accounted for by the equity method are recorded initially at cost. Suppose Intel pays $400 million for 30% of the common stock of Clearwire Corporation. Intel's entry to record the purchase of this investment follows (in millions):

2010			
Jan 6	Long-Term Investment	400	
	Cash		400
	To purchase equity–method investment.		

Assets	=	Liabilities	+	Stockholders' Equity
+ 400	=	0	+	0
− 400				

The Investor's Percentage of Investee Income.   Under the equity method, Intel, as the investor, applies its percentage of ownership—30%, in our example—in recording its share of the investee's net income and dividends. If Clearwire reports net income of $250 million for the year, Intel records 30% of this amount as follows (in millions):

2010			
Dec 31	Long-Term Investment ($250 $\times$ 0.30)	75	
	Equity-Method Investment Revenue		75
	To record investment revenue.		

Assets	=	Liabilities	+	Stockholders' Equity
+ 75	=	0		+ 75

Because of the close relationship between Intel and Clearwire, Intel the investor, increases the Investment account and records Investment Revenue when Clearwire the investee, reports income. As Clearwire's owners' equity increases, so does the Investment account on Intel's books.

Receiving Dividends Under the Equity Method.   Intel records its proportionate part of cash dividends received from Clearwire. When Clearwire declares and pays a cash dividend of $100 million, Intel receives 30% of this dividend and records this entry (in millions):

2010			
Dec 31	Cash ($100 $\times$ 0.30)	30	
	Long-Term Investment		30
	To receive cash dividend on equity-method investment.		

Assets	=	Liabilities	+	Stockholders' Equity
+ 30	=	0	+	0
− 30				

The Investment account is *decreased* for the receipt of a dividend on an equity-method investment. Why? Because the dividend decreases the investee's owners' equity and thus the investor's investment.

After the preceding entries are posted, Intel's Investment account at December 31, 2010, shows Intel's equity in the net assets of Clearwire (in millions):

Long-Term Investment				
Jan 6	Purchase	400	Dec 31 Dividends	30
Dec 31	Net income	75		
Dec 31	Balance	445		

Intel would report the long-term investment on the balance sheet and the equity-method investment revenue on the income statement as follows:

	Millions
Balance sheet (partial):	
Assets	
Total current assets...	$XXX
Long-term investments, at equity........................	445
Property, plant, and equipment, net....................	XXX
Income statement (partial):	
Income from operations......................................	$XXX
Other revenue:	
Equity-method investment revenue................	75
Net income..	$XXX

Gain or loss on the sale of an equity-method investment is measured as the difference between the sale proceeds and the carrying amount of the investment. For example, Intel's sale of 20% of the Clearwire common stock for $81 million would be recorded as follows:

2011			
Feb 13	Cash	81	
	Loss on Sale of Investment	8	
	Long-Term Investment ($445,000 × 0.20)		89
	Sold 20% of investment.		

Assets	=	Liabilities	+	Stockholders' Equity	–	Losses
+ 81	=	0			–	8
– 89						

Summary of the Equity Method. The following T-account illustrates the accounting for equity-method investments:

Equity-Method Investment	
Original cost	Share of losses
Share of income	Share of dividends
Balance	

CONSOLIDATED SUBSIDIARIES

Companies buy a significant stake in another company in order to *influence* the other company's operations. In this section we cover the situation in which a corporation buys enough of another company to actually *control* that company. Intel's ownership of Intel Capital is an example.

OBJECTIVE

3 **Understand** consolidated financial statements

Why Buy Another Company?

Most large corporations own controlling interests in other companies. A **controlling** (or **majority**) **interest** is the ownership of more than 50% of the investee's voting stock. Such an investment enables the investor to elect a majority of the members of the investee's board of directors and thus control the investee. The investor is called the **parent company**, and the investee company is called the **subsidiary**. For example, **Intel Capital** is a subsidiary of Intel Corporation, the parent. Therefore, the stockholders of Intel control Intel Capital, as diagrammed in Exhibit 10-4.

EXHIBIT 10-4 | **Ownership Structure of Intel Corporation and Intel Capital**

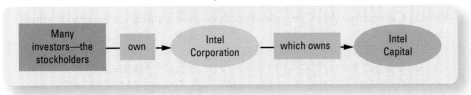

Exhibit 10-5 shows some of the subsidiaries of Intel Corporation.

EXHIBIT 10-5 | **Selected Subsidiaries of Intel**

Intel Capital	Intel Americas, Inc.
Componentes Intel de Costa Rica, S.A.	Intel Europe, Inc.
Intel Asia Holding Limited	Intel Kabushiki Kaisha

Consolidation Accounting

Consolidation accounting is a method of combining the financial statements of all the companies controlled by the same stockholders. This method reports a single set of financial statements for the consolidated entity, which carries the name of the parent company. Exhibit 10-6 summarizes the accounting methods used for stock investments.

EXHIBIT 10-6 | **Accounting Methods for Stock Investment by Percentage of Ownership**

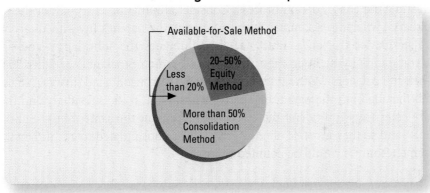

Consolidated statements combine the balance sheets, income statements, and cash-flow statements of the parent company with those of its subsidiaries. The result is a single set of statements as if the parent and its subsidiaries were one company. Investors can gain a better perspective on total operations than they could by examining the reports of the parent and each individual subsidiary.

In consolidated statements the assets, liabilities, revenues, and expenses of each subsidiary are added to the parent's accounts. For example, the balance in Intel Capital's Cash account is added to the balance in the Intel Corporation Cash account and to the cash of all other subsidiaries. The sum of all of the cash amounts is presented as a single amount in the Intel consolidated balance sheet. Each account balance of a subsidiary, such as Intel Capital or Intel Europe, Inc., loses its identity in the consolidated statements, which bear the name of the parent, Intel Corporation. When a subsidiary's financial statements get consolidated into the parent company's statements, the subsidiary's statements are no longer available to the public.

Exhibit 10-7 diagrams a corporate structure for a parent corporation that owns controlling interests in five subsidiaries and an equity-method investment in another investee company.

EXHIBIT 10-7 | **Parent Company with Consolidated Subsidiaries and an Equity-Method Investment**

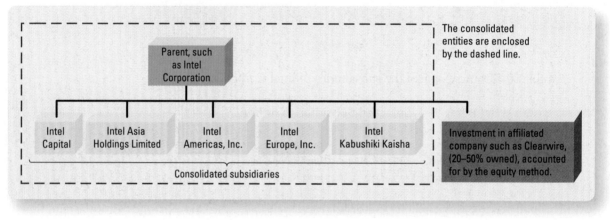

The Consolidated Balance Sheet and the Related Work Sheet

Intel owns all (100%) the outstanding common stock of Intel Capital. Both Intel and Intel Capital keep separate sets of books. Intel, the parent company, uses a work sheet to prepare the consolidated statements of Intel and its consolidated subsidiaries. Then Intel's consolidated balance sheet shows the combined assets and liabilities of both Intel and all its subsidiaries.

Exhibit 10-8 shows the work sheet for consolidating the balance sheets of Parent Corporation and Subsidiary Corporation. We use these hypothetical entities to illustrate the consolidation process. Consider elimination entry (a) for the parent-subsidiary ownership accounts. Entry (a) credits the parent's Investment account to eliminate its debit balance. Entry (a) also eliminates the subsidiary's stockholders' equity accounts by debiting the subsidiary's Common Stock and Retained Earnings for their full balances. Without this elimination, the consolidated financial statements would include both the parent company's investment in the subsidiary and the subsidiary company's equity. But these accounts represent the same thing—Subsidiary's equity—and so they must be eliminated from the consolidated totals. If they weren't, the same resources would be counted twice.

EXHIBIT 10-8 | **Work Sheet for a Consolidated Balance Sheet**

	Parent Corporation	Subsidiary Corporation	Eliminations		Parent and Subsidiary Consolidated Amounts
			Debit	Credit	
Assets					
Cash	12,000	18,000			30,000
Note receivable from Subsidiary	80,000	—		(b) 80,000	—
Inventory	104,000	91,000			195,000
Investment in Subsidiary	150,000	—		(a) 150,000	—
Other assets	218,000	138,000			356,000
Total	564,000	247,000			581,000
Liabilities and Stockholders' Equity					
Accounts payable	43,000	17,000			60,000
Notes payable	190,000	80,000	(b) 80,000		190,000
Common stock	176,000	100,000	(a) 100,000		176,000
Retained earnings	155,000	50,000	(a) 50,000		155,000
Total	564,000	247,000	230,000	230,000	581,000

The resulting Parent and Subsidiary consolidated balance sheet (far-right column) reports no Investment in Subsidiary account. Moreover, the consolidated totals for Common Stock and Retained Earnings are those of Parent Corporation only. Study the final column of the consolidation work sheet.

In this example, Parent Corporation has an $80,000 note receivable from Subsidiary, and Subsidiary has a note payable to Parent. The parent's receivable and the subsidiary's payable represent the same resources—all entirely within the consolidated entity. Both, therefore, must be eliminated and entry (b) accomplishes this.

- The $80,000 credit in the Elimination column of the work sheet zeros out Parent's Note Receivable from Subsidiary.
- The $80,000 debit in the Elimination column zeros out the Subsidiary's Note Payable to Parent.
- The resulting consolidated amount for notes payable is the amount owed to creditors outside the consolidated entity, which is appropriate.

After the work sheet is complete, the consolidated amount for each account represents the total asset, liability, and equity amounts controlled by Parent Corporation.

STOP & THINK...

Examine Exhibit 10-8. Why does the consolidated stockholders' equity ($176,000 + $155,000) *exclude* the equity of Subsidiary Corporation?

Answer:

The stockholders' equity of the consolidated entity is that of the parent only. To include the stockholders' equity of the subsidiary as well as the investment in the subsidiary on the parent's books would be double counting.

Goodwill and Noncontrolling Interest

Goodwill and Noncontrolling (minority) Interest are two accounts that only a consolidated entity can have. *Goodwill*, which we studied in Chapter 7, arises when a parent company pays more to acquire a subsidiary company than the market value of the subsidiary's net assets. As we saw in Chapter 7, goodwill is the intangible asset that represents the parent company's excess payment over and above the fair market value of assets to acquire the subsidiary. GE reports goodwill as an intangible asset on its balance sheet.

Noncontrolling (minority) interest arises when a parent company owns less than 100% of the stock of a subsidiary. For example, General Electric (GE) owns less than 100% of some of the companies it controls. The remainder of the subsidiaries' stock is noncontrolling (minority) interest to GE. Noncontrolling Interest is reported as a separate account in the stockholders' equity section of the consolidated balance sheet of the parent company. The amount of noncontrolling interest in subsidiaries' stock must be clearly identified and labeled as such. GE reports noncontrolling interest in the stockholders' equity section on its balance sheet. By contrast, Intel reports no noncontrolling interest, so that suggests that Intel owns 100% of all its subsidiaries.

Income of a Consolidated Entity

The income of a consolidated entity is the net income of the parent plus the parent's proportion of the subsidiaries' net income. Suppose Parent Company owns all the stock of Subsidiary S-1 and 60% of the stock of Subsidiary S-2. During the year just ended, Parent earned net income of $330,000, S-1 earned $150,000, and S-2 had a net loss of $100,000. Parent Company would report net income of $420,000, computed as follows:

	Net Income (Net Loss) of Each Company		Parent's Ownership of Each Company		Parent's Consolidated Net Income (Net Loss)
Parent Company	$330,000	×	100%	=	$330,000
Subsidiary S-1	150,000	×	100%	=	150,000
Subsidiary S-2	(100,000)	×	60%	=	(60,000)
Consolidated net income					$420,000

COOKING THE BOOKS
with Investments and Debt

Enron Corporation

In 2000, Enron Corporation in Houston, Texas, employed approximately 22,000 people and was one of the world's leading electricity, natural gas, pulp and paper, and communications companies, with reported revenues of nearly $101 billion. *Fortune* had named Enron "America's Most Innovative Company" for six consecutive years. To many outside observers, Enron was the model corporation.

Enron's financial statements showed that the company was making a lot of money, but in reality, most of its profits were merely on paper. Rather than from operations, the great majority of the cash Enron needed to operate on a day-to-day basis came from bank loans. It was very important, therefore, that Enron keep its debt ratio (discussed in Chapter 8) as well as its return on assets (ROA, discussed in Chapter 9) at acceptable levels, so the banks would continue to view the company as creditworthy. Enron's balance sheets contained large misstatements in the liabilities and stockholders' equity sections over a period of years. Many of the offsetting misstatements were in long-term assets. Specifically, Enron owned numerous long-term investments, including power plants, water, broadband cable, and sophisticated, complex, and somewhat dubious derivative financial instruments in such unusual things as the weather! Many of these investments actually had questionable value, but Enron had abused fair market value accounting to estimate them at grossly inflated values.

To create paper profits, Andrew Fastow, Enron's chief financial officer, created a veritable maze of "special purpose entities" (SPEs), financed with bank debt. He then "sold" the dubious investments to the SPEs to get them off Enron's books. Enron recorded millions of dollars in "profits" from these transactions. Fastow then used Enron stock to collateralize the bank debt of the SPEs, making the transactions entirely circular. Unknown to Enron's board of directors, Fastow or members of his own family owned most of these entities, making them related parties to Enron. Enron was, in fact, the owner of the assets, and was, in fact, obligated for the debts of the SPEs since those debts were collateralized with Enron stock. When Enron's fraud was discovered in late 2001, the company was forced to consolidate the assets of the SPEs, as well as all of their bank debt, into its own financial statements. The end result of the restatement so depressed Enron's debt ratio and ROA that the banks refused to loan the company any more money to operate. Enron's energy trading business virtually dried up overnight, and it was bankrupt within 60 days. An estimated $60 billion in shareholder value, and 22,000 jobs, were lost. Enron's CEO, Jeffrey Skilling, its CFO, Andrew Fastow, and Board Chairman Kenneth Lay were all convicted of fraud. Skilling and Fastow both went to prison. Lay died suddenly of a heart attack before being sentenced.

Enron's audit firm, Arthur Andersen, was accused of trying to cover up its knowledge of Enron's practices by shredding documents. The firm was indicted by the U.S. Justice Department in March 2002. Because of the indictment, Andersen lost all of its public clients and was forced out of business. As a result, over 58,000 persons lost their jobs worldwide. A U.S. Supreme Court decision in 2005 eventually led to withdrawal of the indictment, but it came much too late for the once "gold plated" CPA firm. Allegations about the quality of its work on Enron, as well as other well-publicized cases such as Waste Management (p. 427) and WorldCom (p. 415), who were also clients, doomed Arthur Andersen.

Decision Case 1 in Chapter 8 (p. 528) and Decision Case 3 in Chapter 9 (p. 598) illustrate the financial statement impact of Enron's fraudulent transactions.

LONG-TERM INVESTMENTS IN BONDS

The major investors in bonds are financial institutions—pension plans, mutual funds, and insurance companies such as Intel Capital. The relationship between the issuing corporation and the investor (bondholder) may be diagrammed as follows:

OBJECTIVE

4 **Account** for long-term investments in bonds

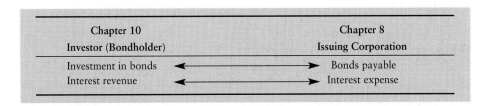

Chapter 10 Investor (Bondholder)		Chapter 8 Issuing Corporation
Investment in bonds	← →	Bonds payable
Interest revenue	← →	Interest expense

An investment in bonds is classified either as short-term (a current asset) or as long-term. Short-term investments in bonds are relatively rare. Here, we focus on long-term investments called **held-to-maturity investments**.

Bond investments are recorded at cost. Years later, at maturity, the investor will receive the bonds' face value. Often bond investments are purchased at a premium or a discount. When there is a premium or discount, held-to-maturity investments are amortized to account for interest revenue and the bonds' carrying amount. Held-to-maturity investments are reported by the *amortized cost method*, which determines the carrying amount.

Suppose Intel Capital purchases $10,000 of 6% CBS bonds at a price of 95.2 on April 1, 2010. The investor intends to hold the bonds as a long-term investment until their maturity. Interest dates are April 1 and October 1. Because these bonds mature on April 1, 2014, they will be outstanding for four years (48 months). In this case the investor paid a discount price for the bonds (95.2% of face value). Intel Capital must amortize the bonds' carrying amount from cost of $9,520 up to $10,000 over their term to maturity. Assume amortization of the bonds by the straight-line method. The following are the entries for this long-term investment:

2010			
Apr 1	Long-Term Investment in Bonds ($10,000 × 0.952)	9,520	
	Cash		9,520
	To purchase bond investment.		
Oct 1	Cash ($10,000 × 0.06 × 6/12)	300	
	Interest Revenue		300
	To receive semiannual interest.		
Oct 1	Long-Term Investment in Bonds [($10,000 – $9,520)/48] × 6	60	
	Interest Revenue		60
	To amortize bond investment.		

At December 31, Intel Capital's year-end adjustments are

2010			
Dec 31	Interest Receivable ($10,000 × 0.06 × 3/12)	150	
	Interest Revenue		150
	To accrue interest revenue.		
Dec 31	Long-Term Investment in Bonds [($10,000 – $9,520)/48] × 3	30	
	Interest Revenue		30
	To amortize bond investment.		

This amortization entry has two effects:

- It increases the Long-Term Investment account on its march toward maturity value.
- It records the interest revenue earned from the increase in the carrying amount of the investment.

The financial statements of Intel Capital at December 31, 2010, would report the following for this investment in bonds:

Balance sheet at December 31, 2010:
Current assets:
    Interest receivable.. $ 150
    Long-term investments in bonds ($9,520 + $60 + $30)............... 9,610
Property, plant, and equipment...................................... X,XXX

Income statement for the year ended December 31, 2010:
Other revenues:
    Interest revenue ($300 + $60 + $150 + $30)..................... $ 540

DECISION GUIDELINES

ACCOUNTING METHODS FOR LONG-TERM INVESTMENTS

These guidelines show which accounting method to use for each type of long-term investment.

Intel has all types of investments—stocks, bonds, 25% interests, and controlling interests. How should Intel account for its various investments?

Type of Long-Term Investment	Accounting Method
Intel owns less than 20% of investee stock	Available-for-sale
Intel owns between 20% and 50% of investee/affiliate stock	Equity
Intel owns more than 50% of investee stock	Consolidation
Intel owns long-term investment in bonds (held-to-maturity investment)	Amortized cost

MID-CHAPTER SUMMARY PROBLEMS

1. Identify the appropriate accounting method for each of the following situations:
   a. Investment in 25% of investee's stock
   b. 10% investment in stock
   c. Investment in more than 50% of investee's stock
2. At what amount should the following available-for-sale investment portfolio be reported on the December 31 balance sheet? All the investments are less than 5% of the investee's stock.

Stock	Investment Cost	Current Market Value
DuPont	$ 5,000	$ 5,500
ExxonMobil	61,200	53,000
Procter & Gamble	3,680	6,230

Journalize any adjusting entry required by these data.

3. Investor paid $67,900 to acquire a 40% equity-method investment in the common stock of Investee. At the end of the first year, Investee's net income was $80,000, and Investee declared and paid cash dividends of $55,000. What is Investor's ending balance in its Equity-Method Investment account? Use a T-account to answer.
4. Parent company paid $85,000 for all the common stock of Subsidiary Company, and Parent owes Subsidiary $20,000 on a note payable. Complete the consolidation work sheet below.

	Parent Company	Subsidiary Company	Eliminations Debit	Eliminations Credit	Consolidated Amounts
Assets					
Cash	7,000	4,000			
Note receivable					
from Parent.........................	—	20,000			
Investment in					
Subsidiary	85,000	—			
Other assets	108,000	99,000			
Total	200,000	123,000			
Liabilities and Stockholders' Equity					
Accounts payable....................	15,000	8,000			
Notes payable.........................	20,000	30,000			
Common stock	120,000	60,000			
Retained earnings	45,000	25,000			
Total.......................................	200,000	123,000			

Answers

1. a. Equity   **b.** Available-for-sale   **c.** Consolidation

2. Report the investments at market value: $64,730, as follows:

Stock	Investment Cost	Current Market Value
DuPont	$ 5,000	$ 5,500
ExxonMobil	61,200	53,000
Procter & Gamble	3,680	6,230
Totals	$69,880	$64,730

Adjusting entry:

Unrealized Loss on Investments ($69,880 – $64,730)	5,150	
Allowance to Adjust Investment to Market		5,150
To adjust investments to current market value.		

3.

Equity-Method Investment			
Cost	67,900	Dividends	22,000**
Income	32,000*		
Balance	77,900		

*$80,000 × .40 = $32,000
**$55,000 × .40 = $22,000

4. Consolidation work sheet:

	Parent Company	Subsidiary Company	Eliminations Debit	Eliminations Credit	Consolidated Amounts
Assets					
Cash	7,000	4,000			11,000
Note receivable from Parent ...	—	20,000		(a) 20,000	—
Investment in Subsidiary.........	85,000	—		(b) 85,000	—
Other assets	108,000	99,000			207,000
Total	200,000	123,000			218,000
Liabilities and Stockholders' Equity					
Accounts payable....................	15,000	8,000			23,000
Notes payable.........................	20,000	30,000	(a) 20,000		30,000
Common stock	120,000	60,000	(b) 60,000		120,000
Retained earnings	45,000	25,000	(b) 25,000		45,000
Total	200,000	123,000	105,000	105,000	218,000

GLOBAL VIEW | ACCOUNTING FOR INTERNATIONAL OPERATIONS

Many U.S. companies do a large part of their business abroad. Intel, General Electric, and PepsiCo, among others, are very active in other countries. In fact, Intel earns 84% of its revenue outside the United States. Exhibit 10-9 shows the percentages of international revenues for these companies.

EXHIBIT 10-9 | Extent of International Business

Company	Percentage of International Revenues
Intel	84%
General Electric	87%
PepsiCo	41%

Accounting for business activities across national boundaries is called *international accounting*. Electronic communication makes international accounting important because investors around the world need the same data to make decisions. Therefore, the accounting in Australia needs to be the same as in Brazil and the United Kingdom. The International Accounting Standards Board (IASB) is working on a uniform set of accounting standards for the whole world. At present, over 130 countries either permit or require the use of international financial reporting standards (IFRS).

U.S. accounting standards are being gradually harmonized with IFRS. As new U.S. standards are being written, they are being made to conform in substance with corresponding IFRS, and vice versa.

In 2008, the U.S. Securities and Exchange Commission (SEC) removed a significant barrier for use of IFRS in the United States when it removed the requirement for foreign-registered companies that prepare their financial statements in accordance with IFRS to provide reconciling schedules with U.S. GAAP. A short time later, the SEC provided a "road map" for U.S. companies to transition from U.S. GAAP to IFRS by 2014. As of the publication date of this textbook, IFRS are expected to supersede U.S. GAAP by 2014.

Recent turmoil in the global credit markets and a global recession, followed by political changes in the United States, may slow the process of abandoning U.S. GAAP in favor of IFRS. Therefore, the exact date for U.S. companies to transition to IFRS is not known. However, because of the advantages of efficiency and consistency provided by a single global set of accounting standards, it is likely that this transition will occur.

As emphasized throughout this text, many U.S. GAAP requirements are already consistent with IFRS. In relevant chapters, we have discussed key differences that remain as of this text's publication date. Appendix F summarizes these differences and cross-references them to discussion in relevant chapters.

Foreign Currencies and Exchange Rates

Most countries use their own national currency. An exception is the European Union nations—France, Germany, Italy, Belgium, and others use a common currency, the *euro*, whose symbol is €. If Intel, a U.S. company, sells computer processors to software developers in France, will Intel receive U.S. dollars or euros? If the transaction is in dollars, the company in France must buy dollars to pay Intel in U.S. currency. If the transaction is in euros, then Intel will collect euros and must sell euros for dollars.

The price of one nation's currency can be stated in terms of another country's monetary unit. This measure of one currency against another is called the **foreign-currency exchange rate**. In Exhibit 10-10, the dollar value of a euro is $1.27. This means that one euro can be bought for $1.27. Other currencies are also listed in Exhibit 10-10.

EXHIBIT 10-10 | **Foreign-Currency Exchange Rates**

Country	Monetary Unit	U.S. Dollar Value	Country	Monetary Unit	U.S. Dollar Value
Brazil...........	Real (R)..............	$0.43	United Kingdom.......	Pound (£).........	$1.44
Canada.........	Dollar ($)..........	0.80	China	Yuan (元)........	0.146
France	Euro (€).............	1.27	Japan.......................	Yen (¥)............	0.012
Germany......	Euro (€).............	1.27	Mexico....................	Peso (P)...........	0.069

Source: *The Wall Street Journal* (February 19, 2009).

We can convert the cost of an item stated in one currency to its cost in a second currency. We call this conversion a *translation*. Suppose an item costs 200 euros. To compute its cost in dollars, we multiply the euro amount by the conversion rate: 200 euros × $1.27 = $254.

Two main factors affect the price (the exchange rate) of a particular currency:

1. the ratio of a country's imports to its exports, and
2. the rate of return available in the country's capital markets.

The Import/Export Ratio. Japanese exports often exceed Japan's imports. Customers of Japanese companies must buy yen (the Japanese unit of currency) to pay for their purchases. This strong demand drives up the price of the yen. In contrast, the United States imports more goods than it exports. Americans must sell dollars to buy the foreign currencies needed to pay for the foreign goods. As the supply of dollars increases, the price of the dollar falls.

The Rate of Return. The rate of return available in a country's capital markets affects the amount of investment funds flowing into the country. When rates of return are high in a politically stable country such as the United States, international investors buy stocks, bonds, and real estate in that country. This activity increases the demand for the nation's currency and drives up its exchange rate.

Currencies are often described as "strong" or "weak." The exchange rate of a **strong currency** is rising relative to other nations' currencies. The exchange rate of a **weak currency** is falling relative to other currencies.

The *Wall Street Journal* listed the exchange rate for the British pound as $1.44 on February 19, 2009. On February 20, that rate may rise to $1.45. We would say that the dollar has weakened against the pound. The pound has become more expensive, and that makes travel in England more expensive for Americans.

Managing Cash in International Transactions. International transactions are common. **D.E. Shipp Belting**, a family-owned company in Waco, Texas, provides an example. Shipp Belting makes conveyor belts used in a variety of industries. Farmers along the Texas–Mexico border use Shipp conveyor belts to process vegetables. Some of these customers are in Mexico, so Shipp makes sales in pesos, the Mexican monetary unit. Shipp Belting purchases inventory from Swiss companies, and some of these transactions are in Swiss francs.

Do We Collect Cash in Dollars or in Foreign Currency? Do We Pay in Dollars or in Foreign Currency?

Consider Shipp Belting's sale of conveyor belts to Artes de Mexico, a vegetable grower in Matamoros, Mexico. The sale can be conducted in dollars or in pesos. If Artes de Mexico agrees to pay in dollars, Shipp avoids the complication of dealing in a foreign currency, and the transaction is the same as selling to M&M Mars across town. But suppose Artes de Mexico orders 1 million pesos (approximately $90,000) worth of conveyor belts from Shipp. Further suppose Artes demands to pay in pesos and Shipp agrees to receive pesos instead of dollars.

Shipp will need to convert the pesos to dollars, so the transaction poses a challenge. What if the peso weakens before Shipp collects from Artes? In that case, Shipp will not collect as many dollars as expected. The following example shows how to account for international sales stated in a foreign currency.

Shipp Belting sells goods to Artes de Mexico for a price of 1 million pesos on July 28. On that date, a peso is worth $0.086. One month later, on August 28, the peso has weakened against the dollar so that a peso is worth only $0.083. Shipp receives 1 million pesos from Artes on August 28, but the dollar value of Shipp's cash receipt is $3,000 less than expected. Shipp ends up earning less than hoped for on the transaction. The following journal entries show how Shipp would account for these transactions:

Jul 28	Accounts Receivable—Artes (1,000,000 pesos × $0.086)	86,000	
	Sales Revenue		86,000
	Sale on account.		

Aug 28	Cash (1,000,000 pesos × $0.083)	83,000	
	Foreign-Currency Transaction Loss	3,000	
	Accounts Receivable—Artes		86,000
	Collection on account.		

If Shipp had required Artes to pay at the time of the sale, Shipp would have received pesos worth $86,000. But by selling on account, Shipp exposed itself to *foreign-currency exchange risk.* Shipp therefore had a $3,000 foreign-currency transaction loss when it received $3,000 less cash than expected. If the peso had increased in value, Shipp would have had a foreign-currency transaction gain.

When a company holds a receivable denominated in a foreign currency, it wants the foreign currency to strengthen so that it can be converted into more dollars. Unfortunately, that did not occur for Shipp Belting.

Purchasing in a foreign currency also exposes a company to foreign-currency exchange risk. To illustrate, assume Shipp Belting buys inventory from Gesellschaft Ltd., a Swiss company. The price is 20,000 Swiss francs. On September 15 Shipp receives the goods, and the Swiss franc is quoted at $0.80. When Shipp pays two weeks later, the Swiss franc has weakened against the dollar—to $0.78. Shipp would record the purchase and payment as follows:

Sep 15	Inventory (20,000 Swiss francs × $0.80)	16,000	
	Accounts Payable—Gesellschaft Ltd.		16,000
	Purchase on account.		

Sep 29	Accounts Payable—Gesellschaft Ltd.	16,000	
	Cash (20,000 Swiss francs × $0.78)		15,600
	Foreign-Currency Transaction Gain		400
	Payment on account.		

The Swiss franc could have strengthened against the dollar, and Shipp would have had a foreign-currency transaction loss. A company with a payable denominated in a foreign currency wants the dollar to get stronger: The payment then costs fewer dollars.

Reporting Gains and Losses on the Income Statement

The Foreign-Currency Transaction Gain account holds gains on transactions settled in a foreign currency. Likewise, the Foreign-Currency Transaction Loss account holds losses on transactions conducted in foreign currencies. Report the *net amount* of these two accounts on the income statement as Other Revenues and Gains, or Other Expenses and Losses, as the case may be. For example, Shipp Belting would combine its $3,000 foreign-currency loss and the $400 gain and report the net loss of $2,600 on the income statement as follows:

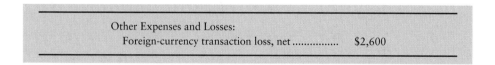

Other Expenses and Losses:
    Foreign-currency transaction loss, net $2,600

These gains and losses fall into the "Other" category because they arise from buying and selling foreign currencies, not from the company's main business (in the case of D.E. Shipp Belting, selling conveyor belts).

Should We Hedge Our Foreign-Currency-Transaction Risk?

One way for U.S. companies to avoid foreign-currency transaction losses is to insist that international transactions be settled in dollars. This requirement puts the burden of currency translation on the foreign party. But this approach may alienate customers and decrease sales. Another way for a company to protect itself is by hedging. **Hedging** means to protect oneself from losing money in one transaction by engaging in a counterbalancing transaction.

A U.S. company selling goods to be collected in Mexican pesos expects to receive a fixed number of pesos. If the peso is losing value, the U.S. company would expect the pesos to be worth fewer dollars than the amount of the receivable—an expected loss situation, as we saw for Shipp Belting.

The U.S. company may have accumulated payables in a foreign currency, such as Shipp's payable to the Swiss company. Losses on pesos may be offset by gains on Swiss francs. Most companies do not have equal amounts of receivables and payables in foreign currency. To obtain a more precise hedge, companies can buy *futures contracts*. These are contracts for foreign currencies to be received in the future. Futures contracts can create a payable to exactly offset a receivable, and vice versa. Many companies that do business internationally use hedging techniques.

Consolidation of Foreign Subsidiaries

A U.S. company with a foreign subsidiary must consolidate the subsidiary's financial statements into its own statements for reporting to the public. The consolidation of a foreign subsidiary poses two special challenges:

1. Some foreign countries require accounting treatments that differ from American accounting principles. For example, the foreign subsidiary's financial statements might be prepared in accordance with international financial reporting standards (IFRS). For reporting to the American public, if those differences are material, the subsidiary's statements must be adjusted to conform to U.S. generally accepted accounting principles (GAAP).

2. The subsidiary's statements may be expressed in a foreign currency. First, we must translate the subsidiary's statements into dollars. Then the two companies' financial statements can be consolidated as illustrated in Exhibit 10-8.

The process of translating a foreign subsidiary's financial statements into dollars usually creates a *foreign-currency translation adjustment*. This item appears in the financial statements of most multinational companies and is reported as part of other comprehensive income on the income statement and as part of stockholders' equity on the consolidated balance sheet.

A translation adjustment arises due to changes in the foreign exchange rate over time. In general,

- *assets* and *liabilities* are translated into dollars at the current exchange rate on the date of the statements.
- *stockholders' equity* is translated into dollars at older, historical exchange rates. Paid-in capital accounts are translated at the historical exchange rate when the subsidiary was acquired. Retained earnings is translated at the average exchange rates applicable over the period that interest in the subsidiary has been held.

This difference in exchange rates creates an out-of-balance condition on the balance sheet. The translation adjustment brings the balance sheet back into balance. Let's see how the translation adjustment works.

Suppose Intel has an Italian subsidiary whose financial statements are expressed in euros (the European currency). Intel must consolidate the Italian subsidiary's financials into its own statements. When Intel acquired the Italian company in 2009, a euro was worth $1.35. When the Italian firm earned its retained income during 2009–2012, the average exchange rate was $1.30. On the balance sheet date in 2012, a euro is worth only $1.20. Exhibit 10-11 shows how to translate the Italian company's balance sheet into dollars.

EXHIBIT 10-11 | Translation of a Foreign-Currency Balance Sheet into Dollars

Italian Imports, Inc., Accounts	Euros	Exchange Rate	Dollars
Assets	800,000	$1.20	$960,000
Liabilities	500,000	1.20	$600,000
Stockholders' equity			
Common stock	100,000	1.35	135,000
Retained earnings	200,000	1.30	260,000
Accumulated other comprehensive income:			
Foreign-currency translation adjustment			(35,000)
	800,000		$960,000

(handwritten: 995,000)

The **foreign-currency translation adjustment** is the balancing amount that brings the dollar amount of liabilities and equity of a foreign subsidiary into agreement with the dollar amount of total assets (in Exhibit 10-11, total assets equal $960,000). Only after the translation adjustment of $35,000 do total liabilities and equity equal total assets stated in dollars.

What caused the negative translation adjustment? The euro weakened after the acquisition of the Italian company.

- When Intel acquired the foreign subsidiary in 2009, a euro was worth $1.35.
- When the Italian company earned its income during 2009 through 2012, the average exchange rate was $1.30.
- On the balance sheet date in 2012, a euro is worth only $1.20.
- Thus, the Italian company's equity (assets minus liabilities) are translated into only $360,000 ($960,000 – $600,000).
- To bring stockholders' equity to $360,000 requires a $35,000 negative adjustment.

In a sense, a negative translation adjustment is like a loss, reported as a contra item in the stockholders' equity section of the balance sheet, as in Exhibit 10-11. The Italian firm's dollar figures in Exhibit 10-11 are what Intel would include in its consolidated balance sheet. The consolidation procedures would follow those illustrated beginning on page 613.

OBJECTIVE

6 **Report** investing
transactions on the
statement of cash flows

IMPACT OF INVESTING ACTIVITIES ON THE STATEMENT OF CASH FLOWS

Investing activities include many types of transactions. In Chapter 7, we covered the purchase and sale of long-term assets such as plant and equipment. In this chapter, we examine investments in stocks and bonds.

Exhibit 10-12 provides excerpts from Intel's 2007 consolidated statement of cash flows. During 2007, Intel sold available-for-sale investments and received $8 billion in cash. Intel bought available-for-sale investments for $11.8 billion and equity-method investments for $1.4 billion. These actual investing activities relate directly to the topics you studied in this chapter.

EXHIBIT 10-12 | **Intel Corporation Statement of Cash Flows (Partial, Adapted)**

Intel Corporation Consolidated Statement of Cash Flows (Partial, Adapted)	
(In billions)	2007
Cash flows provided by (used for) investing activities:	
Sales of available-for-sale investments	$ 8.0
Purchases of available-for-sale investments...................	(11.8)
Additions to property, plant, and equipment...............	(5.0)
Purchases of equity-method investments	(1.4)
Proceeds from selling subsidiary companies	0.3
Net cash (used for) investing activities..............................	$ (9.9)

END-OF-CHAPTER SUMMARY PROBLEM

Translate the balance sheet of the Brazilian subsidiary of **Wrangler Corporation**, a U.S. company, into dollars. When Wrangler acquired this subsidiary, the exchange rate of the Brazilian currency, the real, was $0.40. The average exchange rate applicable to retained earnings is $0.41. The real's current exchange rate is $0.43.

Before performing the translation, predict whether the translation adjustment will be positive or negative. Does this situation generate a foreign-currency translation gain or loss? Give your reasons.

	Reals
Assets...	900,000
Liabilities	600,000
Stockholders' equity:	
Common stock..	30,000
Retained earnings.....................................	270,000
	900,000

Answer

Translation of foreign-currency balance sheet:

This situation will generate a *positive* translation adjustment, which is like a gain. The gain occurs because the real's current exchange rate, which is used to translate net assets (assets minus liabilities), exceeds the historical exchange rates used for stockholders' equity. The calculation follows.

	Reals	Exchange Rate	Dollars
Assets......................................	900,000	0.43	$387,000
Liabilities	600,000	0.43	$258,000
Stockholders' equity:			
Common stock....................	30,000	0.40	12,000
Retained earnings...............	270,000	0.41	110,700
Accumulated other comprehensive income:			
Foreign-currency translation adjustment	—		6,300
	900,000		$387,000

REVIEW LONG-TERM INVESTMENTS AND INTERNATIONAL OPERATIONS

Quick Check (Answers are given on page 651.)

1. Apple's investment in less than 2% of Ford's stock, which Apple expects to hold for three years and then sell, is what type of investment?
   a. Available-for-sale
   b. Equity
   c. Consolidation
   d. Trading

2. Jacques Corporation purchased an available-for-sale investment in 1,500 shares of Home Central stock for $24 per share. On the next balance-sheet date, Home Central stock is quoted at $27 per share. Jacques' *balance sheet* should report
   a. unrealized gain of $36,000.
   b. investments of $40,500.
   c. unrealized loss of $4,500.
   d. investments of $36,000.

3. Use the Jacques Corporation data in question 2. Jacques' *income statement* should report
   a. unrealized loss of $4,500.
   b. investments of $36,000.
   c. unrealized gain of $4,500.
   d. nothing because Jacques hasn't sold the investment.

4. Use the Jacques Corporation data in question 2. Jacques sold the Home Central stock for $45,000 two years later. Jacques' *income statement* should report
   a. investments of $45,000.
   b. unrealized gain of $4,500.
   c. gain on sale of $9,000.
   d. gain on sale of $4,500.

5. Patrick Moving & Storage Co. paid $180,000 for 30% of the common stock of McDonough Co. McDonough earned net income of $50,000 and paid dividends of $20,000. The carrying value of Patrick's investment in McDonough is
   a. $180,000.
   b. $230,000.
   c. $210,000.
   d. $189,000.

6. Tidal, Inc., owns 70% of Granite Corporation, and Granite owns 70% of Shaw Company. During 2010, these companies' net incomes are as follows before any consolidations:
   ■ Tidal $200,000   ■ Granite $64,000   ■ Shaw $55,000
   How much net income should Tidal report for 2010?
   a. $283,300
   b. $200,000
   c. $271,750
   d. $319,000

7. Royalston, Inc., holds an investment in Daley bonds that pay interest each October 31. Royalston's *balance sheet* at December 31 should report
   a. Interest expense.
   b. Interest revenue.
   c. Interest payable.
   d. Interest receivable.

8. You are taking a vacation to Italy, and you buy euros for $1.50. On your return you cash in your unused euros for $1.20. During your vacation
   a. the euro rose against the dollar.
   b. the euro gained value.
   c. the dollar rose against the euro.
   d. the dollar lost value.

9. Coleman County, Texas, purchased earth-moving equipment from a Canadian company. The cost was $1,600,000 Canadian, and the Canadian dollar was quoted at $0.90. A month later, Coleman County paid its debt, and the Canadian dollar was quoted at $0.92. What was Coleman County's cost of the equipment?
   a. $1,472,000
   b. $32,000
   c. $1,632,000
   d. $1,440,000

10. Insight owns numerous foreign subsidiary companies. When Insight consolidates its British subsidiary, Insight should translate the subsidiary's assets into dollars at the
    a. current exchange rate.
    b. average exchange rate during the period Insight owned the British subsidiary.
    c. historical exchange rate when Insight purchased the British company.
    d. none of the above. There's no need to translate the subsidiary's assets into dollars.

Accounting Vocabulary

available-for-sale investments (p. 606) All investments not classified as held-to-maturity or trading securities.

consolidated statements (p. 614) Financial statements of the parent company plus those of majority-owned subsidiaries as if the combination were a single legal entity

controlling (majority) interest (p. 613) Ownership of more than 50% of an investee company's voting stock.

equity method (p. 610) The method used to account for investments in which the investor has 20–50% of the investee's voting stock and can significantly influence the decisions of the investee.

fair market value (p. 607) The amount that a seller would receive on the sale of an investment to a willing purchaser on a given date. Securities and available-for-sale securities are valued at fair market values on the balance sheet date. Other assets may be recorded at fair market value on occasion.

foreign-currency exchange rate (p. 623) The measure of one country's currency against another country's currency.

foreign-currency translation adjustment (p. 627) The balancing figure that brings the dollar amount of the total liabilities and stockholders' equity of the foreign subsidiary into agreement with the dollar amount of its total assets.

hedging (p. 625) To protect oneself from losing money in one transaction by engaging in a counterbalancing transaction.

held-to-maturity investments (p. 617) Bonds and notes that an investor intends to hold until maturity.

long-term investments (p. 605) Any investment that does not meet the criteria of a short-term investment; any investment that the investor expects to hold longer than a year or that is not readily marketable.

noncontrolling (minority) interest (p. 616) A subsidiary company's equity that is held by stockholders other than the parent company (i.e., less than 50%).

parent company (p. 613) An investor company that owns more than 50% of the voting stock of a subsidiary company.

short-term investments (p. 605) Investment that a company plans to hold for 1 year or less. Also called *marketable securities.*

strong currency (p. 623) A currency whose exchange rate is rising relative to other nations' currencies.

subsidiary (p. 613) An investee company in which a parent company owns more than 50% of the voting stock.

weak currency (p. 623) A currency whose exchange rate is falling relative to that of other nations.

ASSESS YOUR PROGRESS

Short Exercises

S10-1 (*Learning Objective 1: Accounting for an available-for-sale investment; recording unrealized gain or loss*)   Ship Your Way completed these long-term available-for-sale investment transactions during 2010:

2010	
Apr 10	Purchased 400 shares of Naradon stock, paying $22 per share. Ship Your Way intends to hold the investment for the indefinite future.
Jul 22	Received a cash dividend of $1.26 per share on the Naradon stock.
Dec 31	Adjusted the Naradon investment to its current market value of $5,200.

1. Journalize Ship Your Way's investment transactions. Explanations are not required.
2. Show how to report the investment and any unrealized gain or loss on Ship Your Way's balance sheet at December 31, 2010. Ignore income tax.

S10-2 (*Learning Objective 1: Accounting for the sale of an available-for-sale investment*) Use the data given in Short Exercise 10-1. On May 21, 2011, Ship Your Way sold its investment in Naradon stock for $27 per share.

1. Journalize the sale. No explanation is required.
2. How does the gain or loss that you recorded here differ from the gain or loss that was recorded at December 31, 2010?

S10-3 (*Learning Objective 2: Accounting for a 40% investment in another company*) Suppose on February 1, 2010, Fall Motors paid $420 million for a 40% investment in Yuza Motors. Assume Yuza earned net income of $50 million and paid cash dividends of $25 million during 2010.

1. What method should Fall Motors use to account for the investment in Yuza? Give your reason.
2. Journalize these three transactions on the books of Fall Motors. Show all amounts in millions of dollars and include an explanation for each entry.
3. Post to the Long-Term Investment T-account. What is its balance after all the transactions are posted?

S10-4 (*Learning Objective 2: Accounting for the sale of an equity-method investment*) Use the data given in Short Exercise 10-3. Assume that in November 2011, Fall Motors sold half its investment in Yuza Motors. The sale price was $155 million. Compute Fall Motors' gain or loss on the sale.

S10-5 (*Learning Objective 3: Understanding consolidated financial statements*) Answer these questions about consolidation accounting:

1. Define "parent company." Define "subsidiary company."
2. How do consolidated financial statements differ from the financial statements of a single company?
3. Which company's name appears on the consolidated financial statements? How much of the subsidiary's shares must the parent own before reporting consolidated statements?

writing assignment ■

S10-6 (*Learning Objective 3: Understanding goodwill and minority interest*) Two accounts that arise from consolidation accounting are goodwill and noncontrolling interest.

1. What is goodwill, and how does it arise? Which company reports goodwill, the parent or the subsidiary? Where is goodwill reported?
2. What is noncontrolling interest, and which company reports it, the parent or the subsidiary? Where is noncontrolling interest reported?

S10-7 (*Learning Objective 4: Working with a bond investment*) Hopter Khan (HK) owns vast amounts of corporate bonds. Suppose HK buys $1,100,000 of Tyconix bonds at a price of 104. The Tyconix bonds pay cash interest at the annual rate of 6% and mature at the end of five years.

1. How much did HK pay to purchase the bond investment? How much will HK collect when the bond investment matures?
2. How much cash interest will HK receive each year from Tyconix?
3. Will HK's annual interest revenue on the bond investment be more or less than the amount of cash interest received each year? Give your reason.
4. Compute HK's annual interest revenue on this bond investment. Use the straight-line method to amortize the investment.

S10-8 (*Learning Objective 4: Recording bond investment transactions*) Return to Short Exercise 10-7, the Hopter Khan (HK) investment in Tyconix bonds. Journalize on HK's books:

a. Purchase of the bond investment on June 30, 2010. HK expects to hold the investment to maturity.
b. Receipt of semiannual cash interest on December 31, 2010.
c. Amortization of the bonds on December 31, 2010. Use the straight-line method.

d. Collection of the investment's face value at the maturity date on June 30, 2015. (Assume the receipt of 2015 interest and the amortization of bonds for 2015 have already been recorded, so ignore these entries.)

S10-9 (*Learning Objective 5: Accounting for transactions stated in a foreign currency*) Suppose Pepson sells soft drink syrup to a Russian company on September 12. Pepson agrees to accept 500,000 Russian rubles. On the date of sale, the ruble is quoted at $0.36. Pepson collects half the receivable on October 18, when the ruble is worth $0.33. Then on November 15, when the foreign-exchange rate of the ruble is $0.39, Pepson collects the final amount.

Journalize these three transactions for Pepson.

S10-10 (*Learning Objective 5: Accounting for transactions stated in a foreign currency*) Ocean Belting sells goods for 1,100,000 Mexican pesos. The foreign-exchange rate for a peso is $0.086 on the date of sale. Ocean Belting then collects cash on April 24, when the exchange rate for a peso is $0.089. Record Ocean's cash collection.

Ocean Belting buys inventory for 28,000 Swiss francs. A Swiss franc costs $0.82 on the purchase date. Record Ocean Belting's payment of cash on October 25, when the exchange rate for a Swiss Franc is $0.87.

In these two scenarios, which currencies strengthened? Which currencies weakened?

S10-11 (*Learning Objective 6: Reporting cash flows*) Companies divide their cash flows into three categories for reporting on the cash flows statement.

1. List the three categories of cash flows in the order they appear on the cash flows statement. Which category of cash flows is most closely related to this chapter?
2. Identify two types of transactions that companies report as cash flows from investing activities.

S10-12 (*Learning Objective 6: Using a statement of cash flows*) Excerpts from The ABC Company statement of cash flows, as adapted, appear as follows:

writing assignment ■

The ABC Company and Subsidiaries Consolidated Statement of Cash Flows (Adapted)		
	Years Ended December 31,	
(In millions)	2011	2009
Operating Activities		
Net cash provided by operating activities..............................	$ 4,222	$ 1,170
Investing Activities		
Purchases of property, plant, and equipment........................	(782)	(743)
Acquisitions and investments, principally trademarks and		
bottling companies..	(665)	(407)
Purchases of investments..	(461)	(522)
Proceeds from disposals of investments................................	475	300
Proceeds from disposals of property, plant, and equipment..............	100	56
Other investing activities..	143	139
Net cash used in investing activities................................	(1,190)	(1,177)
Financing Activities		
Issuances of debt (borrowing)	3,021	3,675
Payments of debt..	(4,017)	(4,279)
Issuances of stock...	172	342
Purchases of stock for treasury...	(280)	(145)
Dividends...	(1,795)	(1,697)
Net cash used in financing activities...............................	(2,899)	(2,104)

As the chief executive officer of The ABC Company, your duty is to write the management letter to your stockholders explaining ABC's major investing activities during 2011. Compare the company's level of investment with previous years and indicate how the company financed its investments during 2011. Net income for 2011 was $3,971 million.

Exercises

All of the A and B exercises can be found within MyAccountingLab, an online homework and practice environment. Your instructor may ask you to complete these exercises using MyAccountingLab.

(Group A)

■ **general ledger**

E10-13A (*Learning Objective 1: Journalizing transactions for an available-for-sale investment*)   Journalize the following long-term available-for-sale investment transactions of Cullen Brothers Department Stores:

- **a.** Purchased 470 shares of Potter Foods common stock at $31 per share, with the intent of holding the stock for the indefinite future.
- **b.** Received cash dividend of $1.70 per share on the Potter investment.
- **c.** At year-end, adjusted the investment account to fair market value of $36 per share.
- **d.** Sold the Potter stock for the market price of $22 per share.

E10-14A (*Learning Objective 1: Accounting for long-term investments*)   Osborn Co. bought 3,400 shares of Stockholm common stock at $35; 660 shares of London stock at $46.50; and 1,200 shares of Glasgow stock at $74—all as available-for-sale investments. At December 31, Hoover's Online reports Stockholm stock at $28.375, London at $48.25, and Glasgow at $68.75.

I *Requirements*

1. Determine the cost and the fair market value of the long-term investment portfolio at December 31.
2. Record Osborn's adjusting entry at December 31.
3. What would Osborn report on its income statement and balance sheet for the information given? Make the necessary disclosures. Ignore income tax.

E10-15A (*Learning Objective 2: Accounting for transactions under the equity method*) Nelson Corporation owns equity-method investments in several companies. Suppose Nelson paid $1,500,000 to acquire a 25% investment in Payton Software Company. Payton Software reported net income of $670,000 for the first year and declared and paid cash dividends of $400,000.

I *Requirements*

1. Record the following in Nelson's journal: (a) purchase of the investment, (b) Nelson's proportion of Payton Software's net income, and (c) receipt of the cash dividends.
2. What is the ending balance in Nelson's investment account?

E10-16A (*Learning Objective 2: Measuring gain or loss on the sale of an equity-method investment*)   Without making journal entries, record the transactions of Exercise 10-15A directly in the Nelson account, Long-Term Investment in Payton Software. Assume that after all the noted transactions took place, Nelson sold its entire investment in Payton Software for cash of $1,100,000. How much is Nelson's gain or loss on the sale of the investment?

E10-17A (*Learning Objective 2: Applying the appropriate accounting method for a 30% investment*)   Ashcroft Financial paid $590,000 for a 30% investment in the common stock of Sonic, Inc. For the first year, Sonic reported net income of $200,000 and at year-end declared and paid cash dividends of $125,000. On the balance-sheet date, the market value of Ashcroft's investment in Sonic stock was $390,000.

❘ Requirements

1. Which method is appropriate for Ashcroft Financial to use in accounting for its investment in Sonic? Why?
2. Show everything that Ashcroft would report for the investment and any investment revenue in its year-end financial statements.

E10-18A (*Learning Objective 3: Preparing a consolidated balance sheet*)   XYZ, Inc., owns Cressida Corp. The two companies' individual balance sheets follow:

■ spreadsheet

XYZ, Inc.
Consolidation Work Sheet

	XYZ, Inc.	Cressida Corp.	Elimination Debit	Elimination Credit
Assets				
Cash	$ 51,000	$ 18,000		
Accounts receivable, net	85,000	58,000		
Note receivable from XYZ	—	40,000		
Inventory	57,000	81,000		
Investment in Cressida	103,000	—		
Plant assets, net	291,000	96,000		
Other assets	22,000	9,000		
Total	$609,000	$302,000		
Liabilities and Stockholders' Equity				
Accounts payable	$ 46,000	$ 29,000		
Notes payable	147,000	35,000		
Other liabilities	79,000	135,000		
Common stock	113,000	81,000		
Retained earnings	224,000	22,000		
Total	$609,000	$302,000		

❘ Requirements

1. Prepare a consolidated balance sheet of XYZ, Inc. It is sufficient to complete the consolidation work sheet.
2. What is the amount of stockholders' equity for the consolidated entity?

E10-19A (*Learning Objective 4: Recording bond investment transactions*)   Assume that on September 30, 2010, Newtex, Inc., paid 98 for 8% bonds of Teague Corporation as a long-term held-to-maturity investment. The maturity value of the bonds will be $30,000 on September 30, 2015. The bonds pay interest on March 31 and September 30.

Requirements

1. What method should Newtex use to account for its investment in the Teague bonds?
2. Using the straight-line method of amortizing the bonds, journalize all of Newtex's transactions on the bonds for 2010.
3. Show how Newtex would report everything related to the bond investment on its balance sheet at December 31, 2010.

writing assignment ■

E10-20A (*Learning Objective 5: Managing and accounting for foreign-currency transactions*) Assume that Computer City Stores completed the following foreign-currency transactions:

Sep	9	Purchased DVD players as inventory on account from Sona, a Japanese company. The price was 800,000 yen, and the exchange rate of the yen was $0.0085.
Oct	18	Paid Sona when the exchange rate was $0.0084.
	22	Sold merchandise on account to CoCo, a French company, at a price of 50,000 euros. The exchange rate was $1.25.
	28	Collected from CoCo when the exchange rate was $1.21.

Requirements

1. Journalize these transactions for Computer City. Focus on the gains and losses caused by changes in foreign-currency rates. (Round your answers to the nearest whole dollar.)
2. On September 10, immediately after the purchase, and on October 23, immediately after the sale, which currencies did Computer City want to strengthen? Which currencies did in fact strengthen? Explain your reasoning.

■ spreadsheet

E10-21A (*Learning Objective 5: Translating a foreign-currency balance sheet into dollars*) Translate into dollars the balance sheet of Utah Leather Goods' Spanish subsidiary. When Utah Leather Goods acquired the foreign subsidiary, a euro was worth $1.01. The current exchange rate is $1.38. During the period when retained earnings were earned, the average exchange rate was $1.18 per euro.

	Euros
Assets.....................................	800,000
Liabilities	550,000
Stockholders' equity:	
Common stock...................	70,000
Retained earnings...............	180,000
	800,000

During the period covered by this situation, which currency was stronger, the dollar or the euro?

E10-22A (*Learning Objective 6: Preparing and using the statement of cash flows*) During fiscal year 2010, Sugar Land Doughnuts reported net loss of $129.6 million. Sugar Land received $1.7 million from the sale of other businesses. Sugar Land made capital expenditures of $10.0 million and sold property, plant, and equipment for $6.9 million. The company purchased long-term investments at a cost of $11.5 million and sold other long-term investments for $2.6 million.

❙ Requirement

1. Prepare the investing activities section of Sugar Land Doughnuts' statement of cash flows. Based solely on Sugar Land Doughnuts' investing activities, does it appear that the company is growing or shrinking? How can you tell?

E10-23A *(Learning Objective 6: Using the statement of cash flows)* At the end of the year, Crown King Properties' statement of cash flows reported the following for investment activities:

Crown King Properties
Consolidated Statement of Cash Flows (Partial)

Cash flows from Investing Activities:	
Notes receivable collected	$ 3,117,000
Purchases of short-term investments......................................	(3,465,000)
Proceeds from sales of equipment	1,599,000*
Proceeds from sales of investments (cost of $470,000).........	487,000
Expenditures for property and equipment............................	(1,741,000)
Net used by investing activities	$ (3,000)

*Cost $5,300,000; Accumulated depreciation, $3,701,000.

❙ Requirement

1. For each item listed, make the journal entry that placed the item on Crown King's statement of cash flows.

(Group B)

E10-24B *(Learning Objective 1: Journalizing transactions for an available-for-sale investment)* Journalize the following long-term available-for-sale investment transactions of Johnson Brothers Department Stores:

■ general ledger

a. Purchased 460 shares of Jefferson Foods common stock at $30 per share, with the intent of holding the stock for the indefinite future.
b. Received cash dividend of $1.20 per share on the Jefferson investment.
c. At year-end, adjusted the investment account to fair market value of $39 per share.
d. Sold the Jefferson stock for the market price of $21 per share.

E10-25B *(Learning Objective 1: Accounting for long-term investments)* Leary Co. bought 3,800 shares of Canada common stock at $38; 640 shares of Chile stock at $47.25; and 1,500 shares of Milan stock at $77—all as available-for-sale investments. At December 31, Hoover's Online reports Canada stock at $29.125, Chile at $49.25, and Milan at $69.50.

❙ Requirements

1. Determine the cost and the market value of the long-term investment portfolio at December 31.
2. Record Leary's adjusting entry at December 31.
3. What would Leary report on its income statement and balance sheet for the information given? Make the necessary disclosures. Ignore income tax.

E10-26B *(Learning Objective 2: Accounting for transactions under the equity method)* Watson Corporation owns equity-method investments in several companies. Suppose Watson paid $1,200,000 to acquire a 35% investment in Smith Software Company. Smith Software reported net income of $650,000 for the first year and declared and paid cash dividends of $440,000.

Requirements

1. Record the following in Watson's journal: (a) purchase of the investment, (b) Watson's proportion of Smith Software's net income, and (c) receipt of the cash dividends.
2. What is the ending balance in Watson's investment account?

E10-27B (*Learning Objective 2: Measuring gain or loss on the sale of an equity-method investment*)   Without making journal entries, record the transactions of Exercise 10-26B directly in the Watson account, Long-Term Investment in Smith Software. Assume that after all the noted transactions took place, Watson sold its entire investment in Smith Software for cash of $3,000,000. How much is Watson's gain or loss on the sale of the investment?

E10-28B (*Learning Objective 2: Applying the appropriate accounting method for a 20% investment*)   Ever Financial paid $560,000 for a 20% investment in the common stock of Laker, Inc. For the first year, Laker reported net income of $220,000 and at year-end declared and paid cash dividends of $105,000. On the balance-sheet date, the market value of Ever's investment in Laker stock was $410,000.

Requirements

1. Which method is appropriate for Ever Financial to use in its accounting for its investment in Laker? Why?
2. Show everything that Ever would report for the investment and any investment revenue in its year-end financial statements.

■ **spreadsheet**

E10-29B (*Learning Objective 3: Preparing a consolidated balance sheet*)   Gamma, Inc., owns Hamlet Corp. These two companies' individual balance sheets follow:

Gamma, Inc.
Consolidation Work Sheet

	Gamma, Inc.	Hamlet Corp.	Elimination Debit	Elimination Credit
Assets				
Cash	$ 50,000	$ 19,000		
Accounts receivable, net	79,000	54,000		
Note receivable from Gamma	—	43,000		
Inventory	55,000	78,000		
Investment in Hamlet	93,000	—		
Plant assets, net	284,000	90,000		
Other assets	24,000	5,000		
Total	$585,000	$289,000		
Liabilities and Stockholders' Equity				
Accounts payable	$ 48,000	$ 27,000		
Notes payable	154,000	31,000		
Other liabilities	80,000	138,000		
Common stock	111,000	78,000		
Retained earnings	192,000	15,000		
Total	$585,000	$289,000		

Requirements

1. Prepare a consolidated balance sheet of Gamma, Inc. It is sufficient to complete the consolidation work sheet.
2. What is the amount of stockholders' equity for the consolidated entity?

E10-30B (*Learning Objective 4: Recording bond investment transactions*) Assume that on September 30, 2010, Baytex, Inc., paid 96 for 7.5% bonds of Collins Corporation as a long-term held-to-maturity investment. The maturity value of the bonds will be $40,000 on September 30, 2015. The bonds pay interest on March 31 and September 30.

▌*Requirements*

1. What method should Baytex use to account for its investment in the Collins bonds?
2. Using the straight-line method of amortizing the bonds, journalize all of Baytex's transactions on the bonds for 2010.
3. Show how Baytex would report everything related to the bond investment on its balance sheet at December 31, 2010.

E10-31B (*Learning Objective 5: Managing and accounting for foreign-currency transactions*) Assume that Tech Know Stores completed the following foreign-currency transactions:

writing assignment ▪

Jul 17	Purchased DVD players as inventory on account from Toshikar, a Japanese company. The price was 700,000 yen, and the exchange rate of the yen was $0.0088.	
Aug 16	Paid Toshikar when the exchange rate was $0.0079.	
19	Sold merchandise on account to Magnificent, a French company, at a price of 20,000 euros. The exchange rate was $1.19.	
30	Collected from Magnificent when the exchange rate was $1.12.	

▌*Requirements*

1. Journalize these transactions for Tech Know. Focus on the gains and losses caused by changes in foreign-currency rates. (Round your answers to the nearest whole dollar.)
2. On July 18, immediately after the purchase, and on August 20, immediately after the sale, which currencies did Tech Know want to strengthen? Which currencies did in fact strengthen? Explain your reasoning.

E10-32B (*Learning Objective 5: Translating a foreign-currency balance sheet into dollars*) Translate into dollars the balance sheet of Wyoming Leather Goods' Spanish subsidiary. When Wyoming Leather Goods acquired the foreign subsidiary, a euro was worth $1.07. The current exchange rate is $1.31. During the period when retained earnings were earned, the average exchange rate was $1.19 per euro.

▪ **spreadsheet**

	Euros
Assets..................................	700,000
Liabilities	500,000
Stockholders' equity:	
Common stock...................	65,000
Retained earnings...............	135,000
	700,000

During the period covered by this situation, which currency was stronger, the dollar or the euro?

E10-33B (*Learning Objective 6: Preparing and using the statement of cash flows*) During fiscal year 2010, Frosted Doughnuts reported net loss of $131.1 million. Frosted received $1.8 million from the sale of other businesses. Frosted made capital expenditures of $10.9 million and sold property, plant, and equipment for $7.2 million. The company purchased long-term investments at a cost of $11.4 million and sold other long-term investments for $2.2 million.

❙ Requirement

1. Prepare the investing activities section of Frosted Doughnuts' statement of cash flows. Based solely on Frosted Doughnuts investing activities, does it appear that the company is growing or shrinking? How can you tell?

E10-34B *(Learning Objective 6: Using the statement of cash flows)* At the end of the year, Elite Properties' statement of cash flows reported the following for investment activities:

Elite Properties	
Consolidated Statement of Cash Flows (Partial)	
Cash flows from Investing Activities:	
Notes receivable collected	$ 3,113,000
Purchases of short-term investments.....................................	(3,453,000)
Proceeds from sales of equipment	1,529,000*
Proceeds from sales of investments (cost of $490,000)..........	498,000
Expenditures for property and equipment............................	(1,720,000)
Net used for investing activities...	$ (33,000)

*Cost $5,200,000; Accumulated depreciation, $3,671,000.

❙ Requirement

1. For each item listed, make the journal entry that placed the item on Elite's statement of cash flows.

Challenge Exercises

E10-35 *(Learning Objectives 1, 2, 3, 5: Accounting for various types of investments)* Suppose ChatNow owns the following investments at December 31, 2010:

a. 100% of the common stock of ChatNow United Kingdom, which holds assets of £1,400,000 and owes a total of £1,200,000. At December 31, 2010, the current exchange rate of the pound (£) is £1 = $2.01. The translation rate of the pound applicable to stockholders' equity is £1 = $1.64. During 2010, ChatNow United Kingdom earned net income of £120,000 and the average exchange rate for the year was £1 = $1.92. ChatNow United Kingdom paid cash dividends of £20,000 during 2010.

b. Investments that ChatNow is holding to sell. These investments cost $1,500,000 and declined in value by $350,000 during 2010, but they paid cash dividends of $23,000 to ChatNow. One year ago, at December 31, 2009, the market value of these investments was $1,500,000.

c. 45% of the common stock of ChatNow Financing Associates. During 2010, ChatNow Financing earned net income of $500,000 and declared and paid cash dividends of $25,000. The carrying amount of this investment was $500,000 at December 31, 2009.

❙ Requirements

1. Which method is used to account for each investment?
2. By how much did each of these investments increase or decrease ChatNow's net income during 2010?
3. For investments b and c, show how ChatNow would report these investments on its balance sheet at December 31, 2010.

E10-36 (*Learning Objectives 1, 6: Explaining and analyzing accumulated other comprehensive income*)   In-the-Box Retail Corporation reported stockholders' equity on its balance sheet at December 31, as follows:

In-the-Box Retail
Balance Sheet (Partial)

Shareholder's Equity:	
Common stock, $1.00 par value—	
600 million shares authorized,	
200 shares issued	$ 200
Additional paid-in capital	1,080
Retained earnings..	6,350
Accumulated other comprehensive (loss)................	(?)
Less: Treasury stock, at cost....................................	(60)

I Requirements

1. Identify the two components that typically make up accumulated other comprehensive income.
2. For each component of accumulated other comprehensive income, describe the event that can cause a *positive* balance. Also describe the events that can cause a *negative* balance for each component.
3. At December 31, 2010, In-the-Box Retail's accumulated other comprehensive loss was $54 million. Then during 2011, In-the-Box Retail had a positive foreign-currency translation adjustment of $24 million and an unrealized loss of $11 million on available-for-sale investments. What was In-the-Box Retail's balance of accumulated other comprehensive income (loss) at December 31, 2011?

Quiz

Test your understanding of long-term investments and international operations by answering the following questions. Select the best choice from among the possible answers given.

Questions 37–39 use the following data:

Assume that Clear Networks owns the following long-term available-for-sale investments:

Company	Number of Shares	Cost per Share	Current Market Value per Share	Dividend per Share
ABC Corp.	1,200	$60	$74	$2.10
Good Food, Inc.	150	11	13	1.40
Lesley Ltd.	700	22	26	0.80

Q10-37 Clear's balance sheet should report

a. investments of $108,950.

b. unrealized loss of $19,900.

c. investments of $89,050.

d. dividend revenue of $3,290.

Q10-38 Clear's income statement should report

a. gain on sale of investment of $19,900.

b. unrealized gain of $19,900.

c. dividend revenue of $3,290.

d. investments of $89,050.

Q10-39 Suppose Clear sells the ABC stock for $73 per share. Journalize the sale.

Q10-40 Dividends received on an equity-method investment

a. decrease the investment account.

b. increase dividend revenue.

c. increase the investment account.

d. increase owners' equity.

Q10-41 The starting point in accounting for all investments is

a. cost.

b. equity value.

c. cost minus dividends.

d. market value on the balance-sheet date.

Q10-42 Consolidation accounting

a. reports the receivables and payables of the parent company only.

b. eliminates all liabilities.

c. combines the accounts of the parent company and those of the subsidiary companies.

d. all of the above.

Q10-43 On January 1, 2010, Microspace, Inc., purchased $80,000 face value of the 5% bonds of Mail Frontier, Inc., at 107. The bonds mature on January 1, 2015. For the year ended December 31, 2015, Microspace received cash interest of

a. $2,000.

b. $3,000.

c. $4,000.

d. $5,000.

Q10-44 Return to Microspace, Inc.'s bond investment in the preceding question. For the year ended December 31, 2013, Microspace received cash interest of $4,000. What was the interest revenue that Microspace earned in this period?

a. $3,000

b. $5,000

c. $2,880

d. $2,000

Q10-45 Providence Systems purchased inventory on account from Megasonic. The price was ¥100,000, and a yen was quoted at $0.0088. Providence paid the debt in yen a month later, when the price of a yen was $0.0093. Providence

a. debited Inventory for $930.

b. recorded a Foreign-Currency Transaction Gain of $50.

c. debited Inventory for $880.

d. none of the above.

Q10-46 One way to hedge a foreign-currency transaction loss is to

a. offset foreign-currency inventory and plant assets.

b. collect in your own currency.

c. pay debts as late as possible.

d. pay in the foreign currency.

Q10-47 Foreign-currency transaction gains and losses are reported on the

a. income statement.

b. consolidation work sheet.

c. balance sheet.

d. statement of cash flows.

Q10-48 Consolidation of a foreign subsidiary usually results in a

a. foreign-currency translation adjustment.

b. gain or loss on consolidation.

c. LIFO/FIFO difference.

d. foreign-currency transaction gain or loss.

Problems

All of the A and B problems can be found within MyAccountingLab, an online home-work and practice environment. Your instructor may ask you to complete these prob-lems using MyAccountingLab.

MyAccountingLab

(Group A)

P10-49A (*Learning Objectives 1, 2: Reporting investments on the balance sheet and the related revenue on the income statement*)   Oregon Exchange Company completed the fol-lowing long-term investment transactions during 2010:

2010	
May 12	Purchased 17,500 shares, which make up 30% of the common stock of Woburn Corporation at total cost of $380,000.
Jul 9	Received annual cash dividend of $1.26 per share on the Woburn investment.
Sep 16	Purchased 900 share of Columbus, Inc., common stock as an available-for-sale investment, paying $41.00 per share.
Oct 30	Received cash dividend of $0.38 per share on the Columbus investment.
Dec 31	Received annual report from Woburn Corporation. Net income for the year was $580,000.

At year-end the fair market value of the Columbus stock is $30,000. The fair market value of the Woburn stock is $658,000.

I Requirements

1. For which investment is fair market value used in the accounting? Why is fair market value used for one investment and not the other?
2. Show what Oregon would report on its year-end balance sheet and income statement for these investment transactions. It is helpful to use a T-account for the Long-Term Investment in Woburn Stock account. Ignore income tax.

P10-50A (*Learning Objectives 1, 2: Accounting for available-for-sale and equity-method investments*)   The beginning balance sheet of Noram Corporation included the following:

■ general ledger

Long-Term Investment in Rockaway Software (equity-method investment)...............	$612,000

Noram completed the following investment transactions during the year:

Mar 16	Purchase 1,400 shares of Canton, Inc., common stock as a long-term available-for-sale investment, paying $13.00 per share.
May 21	Received cash dividend of $1.75 per share on the Canton investment.
Aug 17	Received cash dividend of $86,000 from Rockaway Software.
Dec 31	Received annual reports from Rockaway Software, net income for the year was $520,000. Of this amount Noram's proportion is 21%.

At year-end, the fair market values of Noram's investments are: Canton, $26,600; Rockaway, $698,000.

I Requirements

1. Record the transactions in the journal of Noram Corporation.
2. Post entries to the T-account for Long-Term Investment in Rockaway and determine its balance at December 31.
3. Show how to report the Long-Term Available-for-Sale Investments and the Long-Term Investment in Rockaway accounts on Noram's balance sheet at December 31.

P10-51A (*Learning Objective 3: Analyzing consolidated financial statements*) This problem demonstrates the dramatic effect that consolidation accounting can have on a company's ratios. Fixed Motor Company (Fixed) owns 100% of Fixed Motor Credit Corporation (FMCC), its financing subsidiary. Fixed's main operations consist of manufacturing automotive products. FMCC mainly helps people finance the purchase of automobiles from Fixed and its dealers. The two companies' individual balance sheets are adapted and summarized as follows (amounts in billions):

	Fixed (Parent)	FMCC (Subsidiary)
Total assets	$89.7	$170.7
Total liabilities	$65.1	$156.6
Total stockholders' equity	24.6	14.1
Total liabilities and equity	$89.7	$170.7

Assume that FMCC's liabilities include $1.2 billion owed to Fixed, the parent company.

I Requirements

1. Compute the debt ratio of Fixed Motor Company considered alone.
2. Determine the consolidated total assets, total liabilities, and stockholders' equity of Fixed Motor Company after consolidating the financial statements of FMCC into the totals of Fixed, the parent company.
3. Recompute the debt ratio of the consolidated entity. Why do companies prefer not to consolidate their financing subsidiaries into their own financial statements?

■ spreadsheet

P10-52A (*Learning Objective 3: Consolidating a wholly owned subsidiary*) Assume Rose, Inc., paid $453,000 to acquire all the common stock of Mountain Corporation, and Mountain owes Rose $175,000 on a note payable. Immediately after the purchase on September 30, 2010, the two companies' balance sheets follow.

	Rose	Mountain
Assets		
Cash	$ 60,000	$ 59,000
Accounts receivable, net	194,000	86,000
Note receivable from Mountain	175,000	—
Inventory	305,000	458,000
Investment in Mountain	453,000	—
Plant assets, net	403,000	524,000
Total	$1,590,000	$1,127,000
Liabilities and Stockholders' Equity		
Accounts payable	$ 122,000	$ 67,000
Notes payable	410,000	312,000
Other liabilities	216,000	295,000
Common stock	556,000	268,000
Retained earnings	286,000	185,000
Total	$1,590,000	$1,127,000

Requirement

1. Prepare the worksheet for the consolidated balance sheet of Rose, Inc.

P10-53A *(Learning Objective 4: Accounting for a bond investment purchased at a premium)* Insurance companies and pension plans hold large quantities of bond investments. Sea Insurance Corp. purchased $2,400,000 of 4.0% bonds of Sheehan, Inc., for 110 on January 1, 2010. These bonds pay interest on January 1 and July 1 each year. They mature on January 1, 2014. At October 31, 2010, the market price of the bonds is 108.

Requirements

1. Journalize Sea's purchase of the bonds as a long-term investment on January 1, 2010 (to be held to maturity), receipt of cash interest, and amortization of the bond investment at July 1, 2010. The straight-line method is appropriate for amortizing the bond investment.
2. Show all financial statement effects of this long-term bond investment on Sea Insurance Corp.'s balance sheet and income statement at October 31, 2010.

P10-54A *(Learning Objective 5: Recording foreign-currency transactions and reporting the transaction gain or loss)*   Suppose Turquoise Corporation completed the following international transactions:

■ **general ledger**

May	1	Sold inventory on account to Fiat, the Italian automaker, for €65,000. The exchange rate of the euro was $1.32, and Fiat demands to pay in euros.
	10	Purchased supplies on account from a Canadian company at a price of Canadian $59,000. The exchange rate of the Canadian dollar was $0.77, and the payment will be in Canadian dollars.
	17	Sold inventory on account to an English firm for 134,000 British pounds. Payment will be in pounds, and the exchange rate of the pound was $1.97.
	22	Collected from Fiat. The exchange rate is €1 = $1.35.
Jun	18	Paid the Canadian company. The exchange rate of the Canadian dollar is $0.76.
	24	Collected from the English firm. The exchange rate of the British pound was $1.94.

Requirements

1. Record these transactions in Turquoise's journal and show how to report the transaction gain or loss on the income statement.
2. How will what you learned in this problem help you structure international transactions?

P10-55A *(Learning Objective 5: Measuring and explaining the foreign-currency translation adjustment)*   Assume that Folgate has a subsidiary company based in Japan.

Requirements

1. Translate into dollars the foreign-currency balance sheet of the Japanese subsidiary of Folgate.

	Yen
Assets.....................................	480,000,000
Liabilities	115,000,000
Stockholders' equity:	
Common stock...................	40,000,000
Retained earnings...............	325,000,000
	480,000,000

When Folgate acquired this subsidiary, the Japanese yen was worth $0.0095. The current exchange rate is $0.0110. During the period when the subsidiary earned its income, the average exchange rate was $0.0100 per yen. Before you perform the foreign-currency translation calculations, indicate whether Folgate has experienced a positive or a negative translation adjustment. State whether the adjustment is a gain or a loss, and show where it is reported in the financial statements.

2. To which company does the foreign-currency translation adjustment "belong"? In which company's financial statements will the translation adjustment be reported?

(Group B)

P10-56B (*Learning Objectives 1, 2: Reporting investments on the balance sheet and the related revenue on the income statement*)   Colorado Exchange Company completed the following long-term investment transactions during 2010:

2010	
May 12	Purchased 18,200 shares, which make up 40% of the common stock of Brentwood Corporation at total cost of $330,000.
Jul 9	Received annual cash dividend of $1.24 per share on the Brentwood investment.
Sep 16	Purchased 900 shares of Bangkok, Inc., common stock as an available-for-sale investment, paying $42.00 per share.
Oct 30	Received cash dividend of $0.33 per share on the Bangkok investment.
Dec 31	Received annual report from Brentwood Corporation. Net income for the year was $530,000.

At year-end the fair market value of the Bangkok stock is $30,300. The fair market value of the Brentwood stock is $655,000.

I Requirements

1. For which investment is fair market value used in the accounting? Why is fair market value used for one investment and not the other?
2. Show what Colorado would report on its year-end balance sheet and income statement for these investment transactions. It is helpful to use a T-account for the Long-Term Investment in Brentwood Stock account. Ignore income tax.

P10-57B (*Learning Objectives 1, 2: Accounting for available-for-sale and equity-method investments*)   The beginning balance sheet of Segui Corporation included the following:

Long-Term Investment in NEW Software (equity-method investment)......................	$616,000

Segui completed the following investment transactions during the year:

Mar 16	Purchase 1,600 shares of Hubbardston, Inc., common stock as a long-term available-for-sale investment, paying $12.75 per share.
May 21	Received cash dividend of $1.50 per share on the Hubbardston investment.
Aug 17	Received cash dividend of $85,000 from NEW Software.
Dec 31	Received annual reports from NEW Software, net income for the year was $500,000. Of this amount Segui's proportion is 23%.

At year-end, the fair market values of Segui's investments are: Hubbardston, $26,100; NEW, $701,000.

I *Requirements*

1. Record the transactions in the journal of Segui Corporation.
2. Post entries to the T-account for Long-Term Investment in NEW and determine its balance at December 31.
3. Show how to report the Long-Term Available-for-Sale Investments and the Long-Term Investment in NEW accounts on Segui's balance sheet at December 31.

P10-58B (*Learning Objective 3: Analyzing consolidated financial statements*)   This problem demonstrates the dramatic effect that consolidation accounting can have on a company's ratios. Space Motor Company (Space) owns 100% of Space Motor Credit Corporation (SMCC), its financing subsidiary. Space's main operations consist of manufacturing automotive products. SMCC mainly helps people finance the purchase of automobiles from Space and its dealers. The two companies' individual balance sheets are adapted and summarized as follows (amounts in billions):

	Space (Parent)	SMCC (Subsidiary)
Total assets	$89.5	$170.8
Total liabilities	$65.7	$156.1
Total stockholders' equity................	23.8	14.7
Total liabilities and equity................	$89.5	$170.8

Assume that SMCC's liabilities include $1.7 billion owed to Space, the parent company.

I *Requirements*

1. Compute the debt ratio of Space Motor Company considered alone.
2. Determine the consolidated total assets, total liabilities, and stockholders' equity of Space Motor Company after consolidating the financial statements of SMCC into the totals of Space, the parent company.
3. Recompute the debt ratio of the consolidated entity. Why do companies prefer not to consolidate their financing subsidiaries into their own financial statements?

P10-59B (*Learning Objective 3: Consolidating a wholly owned subsidiary*)   Assume Ronny, Inc., paid $346,000 to acquire all the common stock of Dinette Corporation, and Dinette owes Ronny $192,000 on a note payable. Immediately after the purchase on September 30, 2010, the two companies' balance sheets follow.

■ spreadsheet

	Ronny	Dinette
Assets		
Cash.......................................	$ 54,000	$ 52,000
Accounts receivable, net........................	195,000	89,000
Note receivable from Dinette	192,000	—
Inventory..	278,000	452,000
Investment in Dinette	346,000	—
Plant assets, net.....................................	397,000	457,000
Total..	$1,462,000	$1,050,000
Liabilities and Stockholders' Equity		
Accounts payable	$ 127,000	$ 79,000
Notes payable	399,000	329,000
Other liabilities	249,000	296,000
Common stock..	577,000	259,000
Retained earnings...................................	110,000	87,000
Total...	$1,462,000	$1,050,000

❚ Requirement

1. Prepare the worksheet for the consolidated balance sheet of Ronny, Inc.

P10-60B (*Learning Objective 4: Accounting for a bond investment purchased at a premium*) Insurance companies and pension plans hold large quantities of bond investments. Safe Insurance Corp. purchased $2,700,000 of 8.0% bonds of Sherman, Inc., for 118 on January 1, 2010. These bonds pay interest on January 1 and July 1 each year. They mature on January 1, 2014. At October 31, 2010, the market price of the bonds is 104.

❚ Requirements

1. Journalize Safe's purchase of the bonds as a long-term investment on January 1, 2010 (to be held to maturity), receipt of cash interest, and amortization of the bond investment at July 1, 2010. The straight-line method is appropriate for amortizing the bond investment.
2. Show all financial statement effects of this long-term bond investment on Safe Insurance Corp.'s balance sheet and income statement at October 31, 2010.

■ general ledger

P10-61B (*Learning Objective 5: Recording foreign-currency transactions and reporting the transaction gain or loss*) Suppose Lavender Corporation completed the following international transactions:

May	1	Sold inventory on account to Palermo, the Italian automaker, for €60,000. The exchange rate of the euro was $1.38, and Palermo demands to pay in euros.
	10	Purchased supplies on account from a Canadian company at a price of Canadian $57,000. The exchange rate of the Canadian dollar was $0.78, and the payment will be in Canadian dollars.
	17	Sold inventory on account to an English firm for 148,000 British pounds. Payment will be in pounds, and the exchange rate of the pound was $1.94.
	22	Collected from Palermo. The exchange rate is €1 = $1.41.
Jun	18	Paid the Canadian company. The exchange rate of the Canadian dollar is $0.77.
	24	Collected from the English firm. The exchange rate of the British pound was $1.91.

❚ Requirements

1. Record these transactions in Lavender's journal and show how to report the transaction gain or loss on the income statement.
2. How will what you learned in this problem help you structure international transactions?

P10-62B (*Learning Objective 5: Measuring and explaining the foreign-currency translation adjustment*) Assume that Mason has a subsidiary company based in Japan.

❚ Requirements

1. Translate into dollars the foreign-currency balance sheet of the Japanese subsidiary of Mason.

	Yen
Assets......................................	410,000,000
Liabilities	100,000,000
Stockholders' equity:	
Common stock....................	18,000,000
Retained earnings..............	292,000,000
	410,000,000

When Mason acquired this subsidiary, the Japanese yen was worth $0.0075. The current exchange rate is $0.0090. During the period when the subsidiary earned its income, the average exchange rate was $0.0088 per yen. Before you perform the foreign-currency translation calculations, indicate whether Mason has experienced a positive or a negative translation adjustment. State whether the adjustment is a gain or a loss, and show where it is reported in the financial statements.

2. To which company does the foreign-currency translation adjustment "belong?" In which company's financial statements will the translation adjustment be reported?

APPLY YOUR KNOWLEDGE

Decision Cases

Case 1. (*Learning Objectives 1, 5: Making an investment decision*) Infografix Corporation's consolidated sales for 2010 were $26.6 billion, and expenses totaled $24.8 billion. Infografix operates worldwide and conducts 37% of its business outside the United States. During 2010, Infografix reported the following items in its financial statements (amounts in billions):

Foreign-currency translation adjustments..	$(202)
Unrealized holding _____ on available-for-sale investments.............	(328)

As you consider an investment in Infografix stock, some concerns arise. Answer each of the following questions:

1. What do the parentheses around the two dollar amounts signify?
2. Are these items reported as assets, liabilities, stockholders' equity, revenues, or expenses? Are they normal-balance accounts, or are they contra accounts?
3. Did Infografix include these items in net income? in retained earnings? In the final analysis, how much net income did Infografix report for 2010?
4. Should these items scare you away from investing in Infografix stock? Why or why not? (Challenge)

Case 2. (*Learning Objectives 1, 2, 4: Making an investment sale decision*) Cathy Talbert is the general manager of Barham Company, which provides data-management services for physicians in the Columbus, Ohio, area. Barham Company is having a rough year. Net income trails projections for the year by almost $75,000. This shortfall is especially important. Barham plans to issue stock early next year and needs to show investors that the company can meet its earnings targets.

Barham holds several investments purchased a few years ago. Even though investing in stocks is outside Barham's core business of data-management services, Talbert thinks these investments may hold the key to helping the company meet its net income goal for the year. She is considering what to do with the following investments:

1. Barham owns 50% of the common stock of Ohio Office Systems, which provides the business forms that Barham uses. Ohio Office Systems has lost money for the past two years but still has a retained earnings balance of $550,000. Talbert thinks she can get Ohio's treasurer to declare a $160,000 cash dividend, half of which would go to Barham.
2. Barham owns a bond investment purchased eight years ago for $250,000. The purchase price represents a discount from the bonds' maturity value of $400,000. These bonds mature two years from now, and their current market value is $380,000. Ms. Talbert has checked with a **Charles Schwab** investment representative, and Talbert is considering selling the bonds. Schwab would charge a 1% commission on the sale transaction.

3. Barham owns 5,000 shares of **Microsoft** stock valued at $53 per share. One year ago, Microsoft stock was worth only $28 per share. Barham purchased the Microsoft stock for $37 per share. Talbert wonders whether Barham should sell the Microsoft stock.

❚ Requirement

1. Evaluate all three actions as a way for Barham Company to generate the needed amount of income. Recommend the best way for Barham to achieve its net income goal.

Ethical Issue

writing assignment ■

Media One owns 18% of the voting stock of Web Talk, Inc. The remainder of the Web Talk stock is held by numerous investors with small holdings. Austin Cohen, president of Media One and a member of Web Talk's board of directors, heavily influences Web Talk's policies.

Under the market value method of accounting for investments, Media One's net income increases as it receives dividend revenue from Web Talk. Media One pays President Cohen a bonus computed as a percentage of Media One's net income. Therefore, Cohen can control his personal bonus to a certain extent by influencing Web Talk's dividends.

A recession occurs in 2010, and Media One's income is low. Cohen uses his power to have Web Talk pay a large cash dividend. The action requires Web Talk to borrow in order to pay the dividend.

❚ Requirements

1. What are the ethical issues in the Media One case?
2. Who are the stakeholders? What are the possible consequences to each?
3. What are the alternatives for Austin Cohen to consider? Analyze each alternative from the following standpoints: (a) economic, (b) legal, (c) ethical.
4. If you were Cohen, what would you do?
5. Discuss how using the equity method of accounting for investment would decrease Cohen's potential for manipulating his bonus.

Focus on Financials: ■ Amazon.com, Inc.

(*Learning Objectives 2, 3, 5: Analyzing investments, consolidated subsidiaries, and international operations*) The consolidated financial statements of **Amazon.com, Inc.**, are given in Appendix A at the end of this book.

1. Refer to Note 1—Description of Business and Accounting Policies, under *Investments*. Describe the method of accounting used for investments over which the company can exercise significant influence, but not control. How does the company classify these investments on its balance sheet? How does the company account for these investments on its income statement?
2. Does Amazon.com have any other types of investments other than the ones described in (1)? How does the company account for them? Does it adjust for periodic changes in fair market value of these investments? If so, where do these adjustments appear?
3. Continue looking in Note 1, under the caption *Foreign Currency*. Describe the nature of Amazon.com's business dealings with foreign currencies. What has been the impact of this activity on its financial statements? On which financial statement is the impact of this activity reflected?
4. Which monetary currency was stronger, the U.S. dollar or Amazon.com, Inc.'s foreign currencies, during 2008, 2007, and 2006? Give the basis for your answers.

Focus on Analysis: ■ Foot Locker, Inc.

(Learning Objectives 3, 5: Analyzing consolidated statements and international operations)
This case is based on the consolidated financial statements of **Foot Locker, Inc.,** given in Appendix B at the end of this book. Refer specifically to Note 1, Summary of Significant Accounting Policies.

1. What indicates that Foot Locker, Inc., owns foreign subsidiaries? Identify the item that proves your point and the financial statement on which the item appears.
2. Which currency, the U.S. dollar, or the currency of foreign countries in which Foot Locker did business, was stronger in each fiscal year 2007, 2006, and 2005? Give the evidence to support each answer.
3. At February 2, 2008, did Foot Locker, Inc., have a cumulative net gain or a cumulative net loss from translating its foreign subsidiaries' financial statements into dollars? How can you tell?

Group Project

Pick a stock from The *Wall Street Journal* or other database or publication. Assume that your group purchases 1,000 shares of the stock as a long-term investment and that your 1,000 shares are less than 20% of the company's outstanding stock. Research the stock in *Value Line*, *Moody's Investor Record*, or other source to determine whether the company pays cash dividends and, if so, how much and at what intervals.

I *Requirements*

1. Track the stock for a period assigned by your professor. Over the specified period, keep a daily record of the price of the stock to see how well your investment has performed. Each day, search the Corporate Dividend News in The *Wall Street Journal* to keep a record of any dividends you've received. End the period of your analysis with a month end, such as September 30 or December 31.
2. Journalize all transactions that you have experienced, including the stock purchase, dividends received (both cash dividends and stock dividends), and any year-end adjustment required by the accounting method that is appropriate for your situation. Assume you will prepare financial statements on the ending date of your study.
3. Show what you will report on your company's balance sheet, income statement, and statement of cash flows as a result of your investment transactions.

For online homework, exercises, and problems that provide you with immediate feedback, please visit www.myaccountinglab.com.

Quick Check Answers

1. *a*
2. *b* (1,500 shares x $27 = $40,500)
3. *d*
4. *c* ($45,000 – $36,000)

5. *d* [$180,000 + 0.30 ($50,000 – $20,000) = $189,000]
6. *c* {$200,000 + 0.70 [$64,000 + 0.70($55,000)] = $271,750}

7. *d*
8. *c*
9. *d* ($1,600,000 Canadian × $0.90 = $1,440,000)
10. *a*

11

The Income Statement & the Statement of Stockholders' Equity

SPOTLIGHT: The Gap Encounters Headwinds

The Gap, Inc., is a leading international specialty retailer with a strong portfolio of casual apparel, accessories, and personal care products for men, women, and children under The Gap, Old Navy, Banana Republic, and Piperlime brands. The company is encountering "top line" headwinds. Its revenues have been declining slowly but steadily over the past few years. In spite of successes in controlling costs, revenue declines are eroding profits. In fiscal 2007, the company earned revenues of $15.8 billion and net earnings of $833 million. By the end of 2008 (not reflected in the chapter because the financial statements had not yet been released) a global recession caused revenues (and profit from operations) to plummet still further. In its 2007 annual report, the company stated a commitment to serve the needs of customers while delivering "quality earnings and long-term value to shareholders." When you finish this chapter, you will have a better understanding of both of these terms and how you can use a company's income statement to estimate them.

This chapter rounds out your coverage of the corporate income statement. After studying this chapter, you will have seen all the types of items that typically appear on an income statement. You'll study the components of *net income from continuing operations*, which is the basis for many analysts' predictions about companies' future operations, as well as their current values. You'll also learn about earnings per share, the most often-mentioned statistic in business. Finally, you'll learn about the statement of stockholders' equity, of which a component is the analysis of changes in retained earnings. The knowledge you get from this chapter will help you analyze financial statements and use the information in decision making.

We begin with a basic question: How do we evaluate the quality of a company's earnings? The term *quality of earnings* refers to the characteristics of an earnings number that make it most useful for decision making.

LEARNING OBJECTIVES

1 **Analyze** a corporate income statement

2 **Account** for a corporation's income tax

3 **Analyze** a statement of stockholders' equity

4 **Understand** managers' and auditors' responsibilities for the financial statements

EVALUATING THE QUALITY OF EARNINGS

OBJECTIVE

1 **Analyze** a corporate income statement

A corporation's net income (including earnings per share) receives more attention than any other item in the financial statements. To stockholders, the larger the net income, the greater the likelihood of dividends. In addition, an upward trend in net income generally translates sooner or later to a higher stock price.

Suppose you are considering investing in either the stock of **The Gap, Inc.**, or Brand X Superstore. How do you make the decision? A knowledgeable investor will want to assess each company's **earnings quality**. The higher the quality of earnings in the current period as compared to its recent past, the more likely it is that the company is executing a successful business strategy to generate healthy earnings in the future, which is a key component in its stock price.

There are many components of earnings quality. Among the most prominent are (1) proper revenue and expense recognition, (2) high and improving gross margin/sales ratio, (3) low operating expenses compared to sales, and (4) high and improving operating earnings/sales. To explore the makeup and the quality of earnings, let's examine its various sources. Exhibit 11-1 shows the Consolidated Statements of Earnings of The Gap, Inc., for fiscal years 2007, 2006, and 2005. We'll use this statement as a basis for our discussion of earnings quality.

EXHIBIT 11-1 | **Consolidated Statements of Earnings**

The Gap, Inc.
Consolidated Statements of Earnings

($ and shares in millions except per share amounts)	52 Weeks Ended February 2, 2008	52 Weeks Ended February 3, 2007	52 Weeks Ended January 28, 2006
1 Net sales	$15,763	$15,923	$16,019
2 Cost of goods sold and occupancy expenses	10,071	10,266	10,145
3 Gross profit	5,692	5,657	5,874
4 Operating expenses	4,377	4,432	4,099
5 Interest expense	26	41	45
6 Interest income	(117)	(131)	(93)
7 Earnings from continuing operations before income taxes	1,406	1,315	1,823
8 Income taxes	539	506	692
9 Earnings from continuing operations, net of income taxes	867	809	1,131
10 Loss from discontinued operation, net of income tax benefit	(34)	(31)	(18)
11 Net earnings	$ 833	$ 778	$ 1,113
12 Weighted-average number of shares—basic	791	831	881
13 Weighted-average number of shares—diluted	794	836	902
Basic earnings per share:			
14 Earnings from continuing operations, net of income taxes	$ 1.10	$ 0.97	$ 1.28
15 Loss from discontinued operation, net of income tax benefit	(0.05)	(0.03)	(0.02)
16 Net earnings per share	$ 1.05	$ 0.94	$ 1.26
Diluted earnings per share:			
17 Earnings from continuing operations, net of income taxes	$ 1.09	$ 0.97	$ 1.26
18 Loss from discontinued operation, net of income tax benefit	(0.04)	(0.04)	(0.02)
19 Net earnings per share	$ 1.05	$ 0.93	$ 1.24

Revenue Recognition

The first component of earnings quality, and the top line of the income statement, is proper recognition of net revenue, or *net sales*. You learned a little about revenue in Chapters 3 through 6. The *revenue principle*, discussed in Chapter 3 (p. 140) states that, under accrual accounting, revenue should be recognized when it is *earned*—that is, when the selling business has done everything it has to do to either deliver the product or the service to the customer. In recognizing revenue, several important events have to occur: (1) the seller delivers the product or service to the customer, (2) the customer takes both possession and ownership of the product or service, and (3) the seller either collects cash or is reasonably assured of collecting the cash in the near future. In Chapter 4 (p. 256), you learned the process by which cash collected over the counter is entered into the accounting system. In Chapter 5 (pp. 297 through 305), you learned that credit sales, or sales on account, have to go through the process of collection, that some would ultimately not be collectible, and that a company must make allowances for doubtful accounts. In Chapter 6 (p. 346), you studied the concept of *free on board* (F.O.B.) terms, which governs the issue of who owns the goods during the shipment process, and therefore the timing of revenue. You must understand all of these concepts in order to grasp the meaning of revenue recognition.

Proper revenue recognition in a retail business, like The Gap, Inc., is relatively straightforward. As explained in its Notes to Consolidated Financial Statements, The Gap, Inc., properly recognizes revenue, as well as related cost of goods sold, at the time customers receive the products. In the stores, revenue is recognized at the registers when the customers receive and pay for merchandise. For online sales (which comprise about 5.7% of the total) the company has to estimate how long it takes the merchandise to reach customers by mail or courier. For both over-the-counter and Internet sales, the company estimates an allowance for returns and deducts it from gross sales, to report *net sales*.

Let's examine Exhibit 11-1 and analyze the trend in The Gap's net sales revenue (line 1). Notice that, over the past three years, net sales for the company have been declining by about 1% per year ($16,019, $15,923, and $15,763, respectively). Same-store sales, a key factor in growth for retail stores, have declined each year. Competition from other specialty retailers has contributed to the "top line" decline. This has reflected negatively on the company's earnings and, as a result, on its stock price.

 Although the general definition and principles are the same under U.S. GAAP and IFRS, revenue recognition remains one of the principal areas of difference between U.S. GAAP and IFRS. Over its 70-year existence, U.S. GAAP has built up very specific rules for revenue recognition by industry and type of contract. For example, U.S. GAAP contains detailed guidance on revenue recognition for the computer software and real estate industries. When a sales contract contains multiple elements, revenue may be recognized differently for each element. In the construction industry, revenue may be recognized under either the completed-contract method or the percentage-of-completion method. In contrast, IFRS recognizes revenue based mainly on a single standard that contains general principles applied to all industries and all types of contracts. Whereas IFRS literature on revenue recognition contains about 250 pages, U.S. GAAP in this area contains over 2,500 pages! Fortunately for us, this textbook focuses mostly on the retail sector, in which U.S. GAAP and IFRS for revenue recognition are similar. Later courses will address more complex U.S. GAAP and IFRS revenue recognition differences.

COOKING THE BOOKS
with Revenue

Research has shown that roughly half of all financial statement fraud over the past two decades has involved improper revenue recognition.[1] Following are several of the more significant revenue recognition issues involving fraud from the SEC's files:

- **Recognizing revenue prematurely (before it is earned).** One of the common fraud techniques is **channel stuffing**, where a company may ship inventory to regular customers in excess of amounts ordered. **Bristol-Myers Squibb**, a global pharmaceuticals company, was sued by the SEC in 2004 for channel stuffing during 2000 and 2001. The company allegedly stuffed its distribution channels with excess inventory near the end of every quarter in amounts sufficient to meet company sales targets (tied to executive bonuses), overstating revenue by about $1.5 billion. The company paid a civil fine of $100 million and established a $50 million fund to compensate shareholders for their losses.[2]
- **Providing incentives for customers to purchase more inventory than is needed**, in exchange for future discounts and other benefits.
- **Reporting revenue when significant services are still to be performed or goods delivered.**
- **Reporting sales to fictitious or nonexistent customers.** This may include falsified shipping and inventory records.

Cost of Goods Sold and Gross Profit (Gross Margin)

After revenue, the next two important components in earnings quality are cost of goods sold and resulting gross profit. Before we get to these components, however, it is important to emphasize that, just as it is important to avoid premature or improper revenue recognition, it is equally important to make sure that *all expenses are accurately, completely, and transparently included* in the computation of net income. We saw with the example of the WorldCom fraud in Chapter 7 what can happen when a company manipulates reported earnings by deliberately understating expenses. Without the integrity that comes through full and complete disclosures of all existing expenses, and without matching those expenses against the revenues they are incurred to earn, trends in earnings are at best meaningless, and at worst, downright misleading.

Cost of Goods Sold.   Covered in Chapter 6, cost of goods sold represents the direct cost of the goods sold to customers. In the case of The Gap, Inc., cost of goods sold also includes the cost of occupying the space used to sell the product, or store

---

[1]*CPA Letter* (February 2003). American Institute of Certified Public Accountants. See www.aicpa.org/pubs/cpaltr/feb2003/financial.htm.

[2]Accounting and Auditing Enforcement Release No. 2075, August 4, 2004. *Securities and Exchange Commission v. Bristol-Myers Squibb Company,* 04-3680 DNJ (2004). See www.sec.gov.

rent. As shown on line 2 of Exhibit 11-1, cost of goods sold and occupancy costs represents the largest single operating expense for The Gap, Inc., ranging from 63% to 65% of each revenue dollar. In general, assuming cost of goods sold are accurately measured each period, steadily decreasing cost of goods sold as a percentage of net sales revenue is regarded as a sign of increasing earnings quality. Unfortunately for The Gap, Inc., rather than a steady trend downward, we observe a rather erratic trend, first upward and then downward, from fiscal 2005 through fiscal 2007.

Gross Profit (Gross Margin).   Gross profit (gross margin) represents the difference between net sales and cost of goods sold. Conversely with steadily decreasing cost of goods sold, steadily increasing gross profit as a percentage of net sales revenue is considered a sign of increasing earnings quality. For The Gap, Inc., gross profit was 36.7% in fiscal 2005 (52 weeks ended January 28, 2006). Fiscal 2006 (the 53 weeks ended February 3, 2007) was a particularly tough year for The Gap, Inc. Sales declined by 0.6%, and cost of goods sold and occupancy expenses went up by 1.2%, causing gross profit to fall to 35.5%. By the end of fiscal 2007, the company improved its control over gross margin by cutting costs of goods sold and rental expense. Although the company's net sales fell by another 1% in fiscal 2007, cost of goods sold and occupancy expenses fell by 1.9%, causing gross profit to rise to 36.1%.

Operating and Other Expenses

As implied in the title, operating expenses are the ongoing expenses incurred by the entity, other than direct expenses for merchandise and other costs directly related to sales. The largest operating expenses generally include salaries, wages, utilities, and supplies. Again, given that the entity takes care to accurately measure operating expenses, the lower these costs are relative to sales, the more efficiently and, therefore, the more profitably, we can assume management is operating the business. As shown in line 4 of Exhibit 11-1, operating expenses of The Gap, Inc., have followed a rather erratic pattern in relation to sales over the three-year period. From fiscal 2005 to fiscal 2006, operating expenses increased from $4,099 to $4,432, while revenue slipped from $16,019 to $15,923. In fiscal 2007, company management apparently began to exercise tighter control, and operating expenses thus began to follow the same downward trend as sales, representing an improvement relative to fiscal 2006.

The next two ingredients in operating earnings are interest expense and interest income. Covered in Chapters 8, 5, and 10, respectively, interest expense and interest income represent the charges for borrowed money, and the return earned on invested money. As shown in lines 5 and 6 of Exhibit 11-1, interest expense declined over the three-year period and interest income increased, representing a positive trend.

The next important ingredient of operating earnings is corporate income tax expense, which must be subtracted in arriving at income from continuing operations. The current maximum federal income tax rate for corporations is 35%. State income taxes run about 5% in many states. The Gap, Inc.'s fiscal 2007 income tax expense of $539 amounts to about 38.3% of earnings from continuing operations before income taxes. Thus, we use a rate of 40% to approximate income taxes in our illustrations later in the chapter. Effective tax planning, both by in-house tax staff, and externally, through the counsel of the company's independent outside accountants and attorneys, can help lower the company's tax burden, and can contribute substantially to improved operating profits.

Operating Earnings

Given the integrity that comes with accuracy and transparency of reported revenues and expenses, a trend of high and improving operating earnings in relation to net sales reflects increasing earnings quality. Operating earnings are a function of all of its individual ingredients: revenue, cost of goods sold, gross margin, operating and other expenses, interest income and expense, and income tax expense. Unfortunately for The Gap, Inc., for the reasons outlined previously, the trend in earnings from continuing operations (line 9 of Exhibit 11-1) has fallen short of the goal of high and improving operating earnings. Rather than follow a steady path upward over time, earnings from continuing operations for The Gap, Inc., has followed a rather erratic path downward over the fiscal 2005–fiscal 2007 period.

Which Income Number Predicts Future Profits?

How is income from continuing operations used in investment analysis? Suppose Kimberly Kuhl, an analyst with **Morgan Stanley**, is estimating the value of The Gap, Inc.'s common stock. Kuhl believes that The Gap, Inc., can earn annual income each year equal to its income from continuing operations—$1,406 million for The Gap, Inc.

To estimate the value of The Gap, Inc.'s common stock, financial analysts determine the present value (present value means the value *today*) of The Gap, Inc.'s stream of future income. Blume must use some interest rate to compute the present value. Assume that an appropriate interest rate (i) for the valuation of The Gap, Inc., is 12%. This rate is based on the risk that The Gap, Inc., might not be able to earn annual income of $1,406 million for the indefinite future. The rate is also called the **investment capitalization rate** because it is used to estimate the value of an investment. The higher the risk, the higher the rate, and vice versa. The computation of the estimated value of the stock of The Gap, Inc., is

$$\text{Estimated value of The Gap, Inc., common stock} = \frac{\text{Estimated annual income in the future}}{\text{Investment capitalization rate}} = \frac{\$1,406 \text{ million}}{0.12} = \$11.717 \text{ billion}$$

Kuhl thus estimates that The Gap, Inc., as a company is worth $11.72 billion. She then computes the company's market capitalization. The Gap, Inc.'s balance sheet at February 2, 2008, reports that the company has 734 million shares of common stock outstanding. The market price of The Gap, Inc., common stock at the beginning of February 2008 is about $19 per share. The current market value of The Gap, Inc., as a company (market capitalization) is thus

$$\text{Current market value of the company} = \text{Number of shares of common stock outstanding} \times \text{Current market price per share}$$

$$\$13.946 \text{ billion} = 734 \text{ million} \times \$19$$

The investment decision rule may be

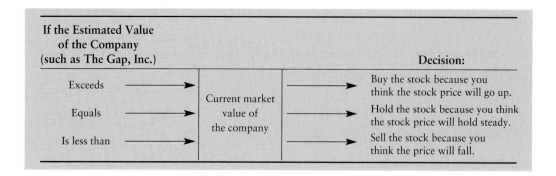

In this case,

			Decision:
Estimated Value of The Gap, Inc. $11.717 billion	Is less than	Current market value of The Gap, Inc. $13.946 billion	Sell the stock
$15.96 per share*	Is less than	$19 per share	

*$11.717 billion/734 million = $15.96

Kuhl believes The Gap, Inc.'s stock price should fall below its current market value of $19 to somewhere in a range near $15.96. Based on this analysis, Morgan Stanley would recommend that investors holding The Gap, Inc., stock should sell it.

Discontinued Operations

Most large companies engage in several lines of business. For example, The Gap, Inc., owns The Gap stores, its mid-line store; as well as **Old Navy**, its less expensive lines; **Banana Republic**, its upscale lines; and **Piperlime**, a specialty line of women's shoes and handbags. **General Electric** makes household appliances and jet engines and owns **NBC**, the media network. We call each identifiable part of a company a segment of the business.

A company may sell a segment of its business. During fiscal 2007 The Gap, Inc., closed its Forth and Towne stores, which were designed to appeal to women 35 and older. The discontinuance of a business segment, either through sale or closure, is viewed as a one-time transaction. The Gap, Inc.'s income statement reports the loss from the closure of Forth and Towne stores under the heading Discontinued Operations (line 10 in Exhibit 11-1). The loss is reported net of the income tax benefit that the company receives from being allowed to deduct it on its corporate income tax return.

Financial analysts typically do *not* include discontinued operations in predictions of future corporate income because the discontinued segments will not continue to generate income for the company.

EXTRAORDINARY ITEMS: ANOTHER IFRS DIFFERENCE

Extraordinary gains and losses, also called **extraordinary items**, are both *unusual* for the company and *infrequent*. Losses from natural disasters (such as earthquakes, floods, and tornadoes) and the expropriation of company assets by a foreign government are extraordinary. The Gap, Inc., had no extraordinary items on its income statement for fiscal year 2007.

Gains and losses due to lawsuits, restructuring, and the sale of plant assets are *not* extraordinary items. These gains and losses are considered normal business occurrences and are reported as Other Gains and Losses. The Gap, Inc., had none of these items on its income statement for fiscal 2007.

International Financial Reporting Standards (IFRS) do not give special treatment to extraordinary items. Instead, items that are "unusual" in nature or "infrequent" in occurrence are combined with operating income and expenses on the income statement. The result of U.S. companies' adoption of IFRS will be that extraordinary items will eventually disappear from the income statement. In fact, due to the narrow definition, extraordinary items are very rare even under current U.S. GAAP.

Accounting Changes

Companies sometimes change from one accounting method to another, such as from double-declining-balance (DDB) to straight-line depreciation, or from first-in, first-out (FIFO) to average cost for inventory. An accounting change makes it difficult to compare one period with preceding periods. Without detailed information, investors can be misled into thinking that the current year is better or worse than the preceding year, when in fact the only difference is a change in accounting method.

Two types of accounting changes are most relevant to introductory accounting:[3]

a. *Changes in accounting estimates* include changing the estimated life of a building or equipment and the collectibility of receivables. For these changes, companies report amounts for the *current and future* periods on the new basis. There is no looking back to the past. A change in depreciation method is treated as a change in estimate.

b. *Changes in accounting principles* include most changes in accounting methods, such as from FIFO to average cost for inventory and from one method to another for a revenue or an expense. For these changes the company reports figures for all periods presented in the income statement—*past as well as current*—on the new basis. The company *retrospectively restates* (looks back and restates) all prior-period amounts that are presented for comparative purposes with the current year, as though the new accounting method had been in effect all along. This lets investors compare all periods that are presented on the same accounting basis. If an accounting change impacts periods prior to the earliest one presented in the current income statement, an adjustment to retained earnings must be made. The Gap, Inc., reports one of these in its Consolidated Statement of Stockholders' Equity, which is covered later in this chapter.

---

[3]FASB Statement No. 154, "Accounting Changes and Error Corrections," May 2005.

Watch Out for Voluntary Accounting Changes That Increase Reported Income

Investment analysts follow companies to see if they meet their forecasted earnings targets. And managers sometimes take drastic action to increase reported earnings. Assume it's late in November and our earnings may fall *below* the target for the year. A reasonable thing to do is to try to increase sales and net income. Managers can also cut expenses. These actions are ethical and honest. Profits earned by these actions are real. Managers can take another action that is honest and legal, but its ethics are questionable. Suppose the company has been using the double-declining-balance method for depreciation. Changing to straight-line depreciation can increase reported income.

Accounting changes are a quick-and-dirty way to create profits when the company can't earn enough from continuing operations. This is why GAAP requires companies to report all accounting changes, along with their effects on earnings—to let investors know where the income came from.

Earnings per Share of Common Stock

The final segment of the income statement reports earnings per share. **Earnings per share (EPS)** is the amount of a company's net income per share of its *outstanding common stock*. EPS is a key measure of a business's success because it shows how much income the company earned for each share of stock. Stock prices are quoted at an amount per share, and investors buy a certain number of shares. EPS is used to help determine the value of a share of stock. EPS is computed as follows:

$$\text{Earnings per share} = \frac{\text{Net income} - \text{Preferred dividends}}{\text{Average number of shares of common stock outstanding}}$$

The corporation lists its various sources of income separately: continuing operations, discontinued operations, and so on. It also lists the EPS figure for each element of net income. Consider the EPS of The Gap, Inc. The final section of Exhibit 11-1 (lines 14 through 19) shows how companies report EPS. Notice that two EPS computations are made: one for "basic" (the currently outstanding shares) and one for "diluted" (which takes into account potential increases in outstanding shares). Companies must first compute a weighted average number of shares outstanding. This computation, which is beyond the scope of this textbook, takes into account the changes that might occur in the number of shares outstanding during the year from such things as treasury stock purchases or reissuances. According to Exhibit 11-1, The Gap, Inc., has a "basic" weighted average of 791 million shares of common stock outstanding.

Basic earnings per share of common stock (791 weighted average shares outstanding) (in millions):	
14 Income from continuing operations ($867/791)	$1.10
15 Loss from discontinued operations, net of tax ($(34)/791)	(0.05)
16 Net income ($833/791)	$1.05

Effect of Preferred Dividends on Earnings per Share.   Recall that EPS is earnings per share of *common* stock. But the holders of preferred stock have first claim on dividends. Therefore, preferred dividends must be subtracted from net income to compute EPS. Preferred dividends are not subtracted from discontinued operations or extraordinary items.

Suppose that The Gap, Inc., had 10,000,000 shares of preferred stock outstanding, each with a $1.00 dividend. The Gap, Inc.'s annual preferred dividends would be $10,000,000 (10,000,000 × $1.00). The $10,000,000 is subtracted from each income subtotal, resulting in the following EPS amounts (recall that The Gap, Inc., has a weighted average of 791 million shares of common stock outstanding):

Basic earnings per share of common stock (791 weighted average
shares outstanding) (in millions):

Income from continuing operations ($867 − $10)/791	$1.08
Loss from discontinued operations ($(34)/791)	(0.05)*
Net income ($833 − $10)/791	$1.03

*rounded up to agree with company's actual financial statements

Earnings per Share Dilution. Some corporations have convertible preferred stock, which may be exchanged for common stock. For example, The Gap, Inc., is authorized to issue 30 million shares of one or more series of common stock, as well as Class B common stock, which is convertible into shares of its current common stock. The company has not yet issued any of these shares, but could, at some date in the future. When preferred is converted to common, the EPS is *diluted*—reduced—because more common shares are divided into net income. Corporations with complex capital structures present two sets of EPS figures:

- EPS based on actual outstanding common shares (*basic* EPS)
- EPS based on outstanding common shares plus the additional shares that can arise from conversion of the preferred stock into common (*diluted* EPS)

The Gap, Inc.'s weighted average diluted number of shares as of February 2, 2008, (the end of fiscal 2007) is 794 million. The computations for diluted EPS are similar to those illustrated previously for basic EPS.

What Should You Analyze to Gain an Overall Picture of a Company?

Two key figures used in financial analysis are

- net income (or income from continuing operations), and
- cash flow from operations.

For a given period, The Gap, Inc.'s net income and net cash flow from operating activities may chart different paths. Accounting income arises from the accrual process as follows:

Total revenues and gains − Total expenses and losses = Net income (or Net loss)

As we have seen, revenues and gains are recorded when they occur, regardless of when the company receives or pays cash.

Net cash flow, on the other hand, is based solely on cash receipts and cash payments. During 2011, a company may have lots of revenues and expenses and a hefty net income. But the company may have weak cash flow because it cannot collect from customers. The reverse may also be true: The company may have abundant cash but little income.

The income statement and the cash flows statement often paint different pictures of the company. Which statement provides better information? Neither: Both statements are needed, along with the balance sheet and statement of stockholders' equity, for an overall view of the business. In Chapter 12 we'll cover the statement of cash flows in detail.

ACCOUNTING FOR CORPORATE INCOME TAXES

OBJECTIVE

2 Account for a corporation's income tax

Corporations pay income tax as individuals do, but corporate and personal tax rates differ. The current federal tax rate on most corporate income is 35%. Most states also levy income taxes on corporations, so most corporations have a combined federal and state income tax rate of approximately 40%.

To account for income tax, the corporation measures

- *Income tax expense*, an expense on the income statement. Income tax expense helps measure net income.
- *Income tax payable*, a current liability on the balance sheet. Income tax payable is the amount of tax to pay the government in the next period.

Accounting for income tax follows the principles of accrual accounting. Suppose at the end of fiscal 2010 The Gap, Inc., reports net income before tax (also called **pretax accounting income**) of $1 billion. The Gap, Inc.'s combined income tax rate is close to 40%. To start this discussion, assume income tax expense and income tax payable are the same. Then The Gap, Inc., would record income tax for the year as follows (amounts in millions):

2011			
Jan 28	Income Tax Expense ($1,000 × 0.40)	400	
	Income Tax Payable		400
	Recorded income tax for the year.		

The Gap, Inc.'s financial statements for fiscal 2010 would report these figures (partial, in millions):

Income statement		**Balance sheet**	
Income before income tax	$1,000	Current liabilities:	
Income tax expense	(400)	Income tax payable	$400
Net income	$ 600		

In general, income tax expense and income tax payable can be computed as follows:*

Income tax expense	=	Income before income tax (from the income statement)	×	Income tax rate		Income tax payable	=	Taxable income (from the *income tax return* filed with the IRS)	×	Income tax rate

*The authors thank Jean Marie Hudson for suggesting this presentation.

The income statement and the income tax return are entirely separate documents:

- The *income statement* reports the results of operations.
- The *income tax return* is filed with the Internal Revenue Service (IRS) to measure how much tax to pay the government in the current period.

For most companies, tax expense and tax payable differ. Some revenues and expenses affect income differently for accounting and for tax purposes. The most common difference between accounting income and **taxable income** occurs when a corporation uses straight-line depreciation in its financial statements and accelerated depreciation for the tax return.

Continuing with the The Gap, Inc., illustration, suppose for fiscal 2010 that it had

- pretax accounting income of $1 billion on its income statement, and
- taxable income of $800 million on its income tax return.

Taxable income is less than accounting income because The Gap, Inc., uses

- straight-line depreciation for accounting purposes (say $100 million), and
- accelerated depreciation for tax purposes (say $300 million).

The Gap, Inc., would record income tax for fiscal 2010 as follows (dollar amounts in millions and an income tax rate of 40%):

2011			
Jan 28	Income Tax Expense ($1,000 × 0.40)	400	
	Income Tax Payable ($800 × 0.40)		320
	Deferred Tax Liability		80
	Recorded income tax for the year.		

Deferred Tax Liability is usually long-term.

The Gap, Inc.'s financial statements for fiscal 2010 will report the following:

Income statement		Balance sheet	
Income before income tax	$1,000	Current liabilities:	
Income tax expense	(400)	Income tax payable	$320
Net income	$ 600	Long-term liabilities:	
		Deferred tax liability	80*

*The beginning balance of Deferred tax liability was zero.

In March 2011, The Gap, Inc., would pay income tax payable of $320 million because this is a current liability. The deferred tax liability can be paid later.

For a given year, Income Tax Payable can exceed Income Tax Expense. This occurs when, because of differences in revenue and expenses for book and tax purposes, taxable income exceeds book income. When that occurs, the company debits a Deferred Tax Asset. The remainder of this topic is reserved for a more advanced course.

CORRECTING RETAINED EARNINGS

Occasionally a company records a revenue or an expense incorrectly. If the error is corrected in a later period, the balance of Retained Earnings is wrong until corrected. Corrections to Retained Earnings for errors of an earlier period are called

prior-period adjustments. The prior-period adjustment appears on the statement of retained earnings.

Assume that NPR Corporation recorded 2010 income tax expense as $30,000, but the correct amount was $40,000. This error understated expenses by $10,000 and overstated net income by $10,000. The government sent a bill in 2011 for the additional $10,000, and this alerted NPR to the mistake.

This accounting error requires a prior-period adjustment. Prior-period adjustments are not reported on the income statement because they relate to an earlier accounting period. This prior-period adjustment would appear on the statement of retained earnings, as shown in Exhibit 11-2, with all amounts assumed:

EXHIBIT 11-2 | **Reporting a Prior-Period Adjustment**

NPR Corporation
Statement of Retained Earnings
Year Ended December 31, 2011

Retained earnings balance, December 31, 2010, as originally reported	$390,000
Prior-period adjustment—debit to correct error in recording income tax expense of 2010	(10,000)
Retained earnings balance, December 31, 2010, as adjusted	380,000
Net income for 2011	110,000
	490,000
Dividends for 2011	(40,000)
Retained earnings balance, December 31, 2011	$450,000

Reporting Comprehensive Income

All companies report net income or net loss on their income statements. As we saw in Chapter 10, companies with unrealized gains and losses on certain investments and foreign-currency translation adjustments also report another income figure. **Comprehensive income** is the company's change in total stockholders' equity from all sources other than from the owners of the business. Comprehensive income includes net income plus

- unrealized gains (losses) on available-for-sale investments, and
- foreign-currency translation adjustments.

These items do not enter into the determination of net income or of earnings per share. Exhibit 11-3 shows the statement of comprehensive earnings presented as a part of the Consolidated Statements of Stockholders' Equity of The Gap, Inc., as of February 2, 2008 (end of fiscal 2007). Comprehensive earnings are listed in the far right column. Notice that they include net earnings of $833 million from the income statement in Exhibit 11-1, plus a foreign currency translation adjustment of $84 million, and two negative adjustments for changes in the fair value of derivative financial instruments (available-for-sale securities) of $18 million each.

EXHIBIT 11-3 | **Consolidated Statements of Stockholders' Equity**

The Gap, Inc.
Consolidated Statements of Stockholders' Equity

($ and shares in millions except per share amounts)	Common Stock Shares	Common Stock Amount	Additional Paid-in Capital	Retained Earnings	Accumulated Other Comprehensive Earnings	Deferred Compensation	Treasury Stock Shares	Treasury Stock Amount	Total	Comprehensive Earnings
1 Balance at February 3, 2007	1,093	$55	$2,631	$8,646	$ 77	—	(279)	$(6,235)	$ 5,174	$804
2 Net earnings				833					833	$833
3 Foreign currency translation					84				84	84
4 Change in fair value of derivative financial instruments, net of tax of $17					(18)				(18)	(18)
5 Reclassification adjustment for realized gains on derivative financial instruments, net of tax of $11					(18)				(18)	(18)
6 Cumulative effect of adoption of FIN 48				(4)					(4)	
7 Issuance of common stock pursuant to stock option and other stock award plans and related tax benefit of $8	7	—	101						101	
8 Amortization of unrecognized share-based compensation, net of estimated forfeiture			49						49	
9 Repurchase of common stock							(89)	(1,700)	(1,700)	
10 Reissuance of treasury stock			2				2	23	25	
11 Cash dividends ($0.32 per share)				(252)					(252)	
12 Balance at February 2, 2008	1,100	$55	$2,783	$9,223	$125	$—	(366)	$(7,912)	$ 4,274	$881

ANALYZING THE STATEMENT OF STOCKHOLDERS' EQUITY

The **statement of stockholders' equity** reports the reasons for all the changes in the stockholders' equity section of the balance sheet during the period.

Take another look at Exhibit 11-3, the Consolidated Statements of Stockholders' Equity for The Gap, Inc. Study its format. There is a column for each element of equity, starting with Common Stock on the left. The second column from the far right reports the total. The top row (line 1) reports beginning balances as of February 3, 2007, taken from last period's statement of stockholders' equity. The rows then report the various transactions that affected equity, starting with net earnings (line 2). The statement ends with the February 2, 2008, balances (line 12). All the amounts on the bottom line appear on the ending balance sheet, given in Exhibit 11-4 on page 669.

OBJECTIVE

3 **Analyze** a statement of stockholders' equity

Let's examine the changes in The Gap, Inc.'s stockholders' equity during fiscal 2007.

Net Income (Line 2).   During 2007, The Gap, Inc., earned net income (net earnings) of $833 million, which increased Retained Earnings. Trace net income from the Consolidated Statements of Earnings (Exhibit 11-1, p. 655) to the Consolidated Statements of Stockholders' Equity (Exhibit 11-3).

Accumulated Other Comprehensive Income (Lines 3 Through 5).   Two categories of other comprehensive income are unrealized gains and losses on available-for-sale investments and the foreign-currency translation adjustment.

At February 2, 2007, The Gap, Inc. had an accumulated other comprehensive earnings from previous years of $77 million (line 1). This was made up of $63 million from foreign currency translation sources, and $14 million from fluctuations in the fair market value of derivative (available-for-sale) securities. During fiscal 2007, it made a foreign-currency translation adjustment that increased accumulated other comprehensive earnings by $84 million (line 3). Also, during fiscal 2007, the company recognized an unrealized loss from the change in fair value of derivative financial instruments (available-for-sale) and made another adjustment to reclassified realized gains from these investments. Two negative adjustments for $18 million each resulted, for a total of $36 million. The company ended fiscal 2007 with accumulated other comprehensive earnings of $125 ($147 million accumulated from foreign currency translation adjustments, netted against a $22 million accumulated unrealized loss from the fluctuations in fair market value of derivative—available-for-sale—investments).

Cumulative Effect of Adoption of New Accounting Principle (Line 6). Earlier in the chapter we discussed the impact of accounting changes on current year financial statements. The normal way to account for changes in accounting principles (or methods) is to report them "retrospectively," meaning that, for each prior period presented in the comparative financial statements of the current year, income is restated to incorporate the new method's impact as if the new principle had been in effect in those years as well. When changes in accounting principle impact income of periods that were prior to the earliest presented, the cumulative impact on those periods is reported as an adjustment to retained earnings in the current period. In Exhibit 11-3, The Gap, Inc., adopted Financial Interpretation (FIN) 48 of the FASB during fiscal 2007. The net impact on net income of prior periods is negative $4 million.

Issuance of Stock (Lines 7 and 8).   During fiscal 2007, The Gap, Inc., in conjunction with its stock option plan to compensate employees, issued 7 million shares of common stock. The impact of the issuance of the stock was to increase additional paid-in capital, and total stockholders' equity, in the amount of $101 million. The company amortized an additional $49 million of previously unrecognized share-based compensation in the amount of $49 million. This topic is beyond the scope of this textbook, and a discussion of it is reserved for future accounting courses.

Treasury Stock Transactions (Lines 9 and 10).   The company repurchased 89 million shares of its own stock for $1.7 billion in fiscal 2007, resulting in a reduction to total stockholders' equity. It then reissued 2 million shares for $25 million, resulting in a reduction in treasury stock in the amount of $23 million and an increase in additional paid-in-capital of $2 million.

Declaration of Cash Dividends (Line 11).   The Gap, Inc., declared cash dividends of $0.32 per share in fiscal 2007. This resulted in a reduction in retained earnings of $252 million.

EXHIBIT 11-4	Stockholders' Equity Section of the Balance Sheet

The Gap, Inc.
Consolidated Balance Sheet (Partial)
February 2, 2008

(In millions)		
Total assets..		$7,838
Total liabilities		$3,564
Stockholders' equity:		
Common stock, $0.05 par, shares issued—1,100		55
Additional paid-in capital		2,783
Retained earnings		9,223
Accumulated other comprehensive income		125
Treasury stock		(7,912)
Total stockholders' equity..		4,274
Total liabilities and stockholders' equity		$7,838

RESPONSIBILITY FOR THE FINANCIAL STATEMENTS

Management's Responsibility

Management issues a report on internal control over financial reporting, along with the company's financial statements. Exhibit 11-5 is an excerpt from the report of management for The Gap, Inc.

OBJECTIVE

4 **Understand** managers' and auditors' responsibilities for the financial statements

EXHIBIT 11-5	Excerpt from Management's Responsibility for Financial Reporting

Management is responsible for establishing and maintaining an adequate system of internal control over financial reporting. Management conducted an assessment of internal control over financial reporting based on the framework established by the Committee of Sponsoring Organizations of the Treadway Commission in *Internal Control—Integrated Framework*. Based on the assessment, management concluded that, as of February 2, 2008, our internal control over financial reporting is effective. The Company's internal control over financial reporting as of February 2, 2008, has been audited by Deloitte & Touche, LLP, an independent registered public accounting firm, as stated in their report which is included herein.

Management declares its responsibility for the internal controls over financial reporting in accordance with the Securities Exchange Act of 1934. Management also states that it has conducted an assessment of internal controls over financial reporting based on the framework established by the Committee of Sponsoring Organizations (COSO) of the Treadway Commission, and has concluded that, as of February 2, 2008, internal controls over financial reporting are effective. In addition, management states that the internal controls of the company have been audited by the company's outside auditors, and refers to their report, an excerpt of which is contained in Exhibit 11-6 in the next section.

Auditor Report

The Securities Exchange Act of 1934 requires companies that issue their stock publicly to file audited financial statements with the SEC. Companies engage outside auditors who are certified public accountants to examine their financial statements as well as their internal controls over financial reporting. The independent auditors decide whether the company's financial statements comply with GAAP. They must also decide whether the internal controls of the company meet certain standards. They then issue a combined audit report on both the financial statements and the company's system of internal controls over financial reporting. Exhibit 11-6 contains this report for The Gap, Inc., and its subsidiaries as of February 2, 2008.

EXHIBIT 11-6 | **Excerpt of Report of Independent Registered Public Accounting Firm**

To the Board of Directors and Stockholders of The Gap, Inc.

We have audited the accompanying consolidated balance sheets of The Gap, Inc. and subsidiaries (the "Company") as of February 2, 2008 and February 3, 2007, and the related consolidated statements of earnings, stockholders' equity, and cash flows for each of the three fiscal years in the period ended February 2, 2008. We also have audited the Company's internal control over financial reporting as of February 2, 2008, based on criteria established by *Internal Control—Integrated Framework* issued by the Committee of Sponsoring Organizations of the Treadway Commission. The Company's management is responsible for these financial statements, for maintaining effective internal control over financial reporting, and for its assessment of the effectiveness of internal control over financial reporting, included in the accompanying Management's Report on Internal Control over Financial Reporting. Our responsibility is to express an opinion on these financial statements and opinion on the Company's internal control over financial reporting based on our audits.

We conducted our audits in accordance with the standards of the Public Company Accounting Oversight Board (United States). Those standards require that we plan and perform the audit to obtain reasonable assurance about whether the financial statements are free from material misstatements and whether effective internal control over financial reporting was maintained in all material respects.....We believe that our audits provide a reasonable basis for our opinions.

A company's internal control over financial reporting is a process designed by, or under the supervision of, the company's...financial officers...and effected by the Company's board of directors...to provide reasonable assurance regarding the reliability of financial reporting and the preparation of financial statements....in accordance with generally accepted accounting principles.

Because of the inherent limitations of internal control over financial reporting, including the possibility of collusion or improper management override of controls, material misstatements due to error or fraud may not be prevented or detected on a timely basis. Also, projections of any evaluation of the effectiveness of internal control over financial reporting to future periods are subject to the risk that the controls may become inadequate because of changes in conditions, or that the degree of compliance with the policies or procedures may deteriorate.

In our opinion, the consolidated financial statement referred to above present fairly, in all material respects, the financial position of The Gap, Inc. and subsidiaries as of February 2, 2008 and February 3, 2007, and the results of their operations and their cash flows for each of the three years in the period ended February 2, 2008, in conformity with accounting principles generally accepted in the United States of America. Also, in our opinion, the Company maintained, in all material respects, effective internal control over financial reporting as of February 2, 2008, based on the criteria established in *Internal Control—Integrated Framework* issued by the Committee of Sponsoring Organizations of the Treadway Commission.

/s/ Deloitte & Touche, LLP

San Francisco, California

March 28, 2008

The audit report is addressed to the board of directors and stockholders of the company. A partner of the auditing firm signs the firm's name to the report. In this case, the auditing firm is the San Francisco office of **Deloitte & Touche, LLP** (limited liability partnership).

The combined audit report on financial statements and internal control over financial reporting typically contains five paragraphs:

- The first paragraph identifies the audited financial statements as well as the company being audited. It also states the responsibility of the company's management as well as the auditor's responsibilities.
- The second paragraph describes how the audit was performed in accordance with generally accepted auditing standards of the Public Company Accounting Oversight Board (an independent regulatory body with SEC oversight). These are the standards used by auditors as the benchmark for evaluating audit quality.
- The third paragraph describes in detail what a system of internal controls is, that it should be designed to provide reasonable assurance that transactions are recorded to permit preparation of financial statements that are fairly presented in conformity with GAAP.
- The fourth paragraph describes inherent limitations in the system of internal controls and, that at best, the system of internal controls can only provide reasonable assurance that financial statements are fairly presented.
- The fifth paragraph expresses the auditor's combined opinion on both the fairness of financial statements, in all material respects, in conformity with GAAP, and the effectiveness of the company's internal controls over financial reporting. Deloitte & Touche, LLP, is expressing an **unqualified (clean) opinion** on both the fairness of the financial statements and the effectiveness of The Gap, Inc.'s internal controls. The unqualified opinion is the highest statement of assurance that an independent certified public accountant can express.

The independent audit adds credibility to the financial statements of a company as well as to its system of internal controls. It is no accident that financial reporting and auditing are more advanced in the United States than anywhere else in the world and that U.S. capital markets are the envy of the world.

DECISION GUIDELINES

USING THE INCOME STATEMENT AND RELATED NOTES IN INVESTMENT ANALYSIS

Suppose you've completed your studies, taken a job, and been fortunate to save $10,000. Now you are ready to start investing. These guidelines provide a framework for using accounting information for investment analysis.

Decision	Factors to Consider		Decision Variable or Model
Which measure of profitability should be used for investment analysis?	Are you interested in accounting income? ———→	Income, including all revenues, expenses, gains, and losses?	Net income (bottom line)
	———————→	Income that can be expected to repeat from year to year?	Income from continuing operations
	Are you interested in cash flows? ——————————————→		Cash flows from operating activities (Chapter 12)

Note: A conservative strategy may use both income and cash flows and compare the two sets of results.

What is the estimated value of the stock?	If you believe the company can earn the income (or ——→ cash flow) indefinitely	$$\text{Estimated value} = \frac{\text{Annual income}}{\text{Investment capitalization rate}}$$
	If you believe the company can earn the income (or ——→ cash flow) for a finite number of years	$$\text{Estimated value} = \text{Annual income} \times \frac{\text{Present value of annuity}}{\text{(See Appendix C)}}$$
How does risk affect the value of the stock?	If the investment is high risk ——→	Increase the investment capitalization rate
	If the investment is low risk ——→	Decrease the investment capitalization rate

END-OF-CHAPTER SUMMARY PROBLEM

The following information was taken from the ledger of Maxim, Inc.:

Prior-period adjustment—		Treasury stock, common	
credit to Retained Earnings	$ 5,000	(5,000 shares at cost)	$ 25,000
Gain on sale of plant assets	21,000	Selling expenses	78,000
Cost of goods sold	380,000	Common stock, no par,	
Income tax expense (saving):		45,000 shares issued	180,000
Continuing operations	32,000	Sales revenue	620,000
Discontinued operations	8,000	Interest expense	30,000
Extraordinary gain	10,000	Extraordinary gain	26,000
Preferred stock, 8%, $100 par,		Income from discontinued	
500 shares issued	50,000	operations	20,000
Dividends	16,000	Loss due to lawsuit	11,000
Retained earnings, beginning,		General expenses	62,000
as originally reported	103,000		

Requirement

1. Prepare a single-step income statement (with all revenues and gains grouped together) and a statement of retained earnings for Maxim, Inc., for the current year ended December 31, 2010. Include the earnings-per-share presentation and show computations. Assume no changes in the stock accounts during the year.

Answers

Maxim, Inc.
Income Statement
Year Ended December 31, 2010

Revenue and gains:		
Sales revenue..		$620,000
Gain on sale of plant assets..		21,000
Total revenues and gains		641,000
Expenses and losses:		
Cost of goods sold	$380,000	
Selling expenses	78,000	
General expenses	62,000	
Interest expense	30,000	
Loss due to lawsuit	11,000	
Income tax expense...	32,000	
Total expenses and losses		593,000
Income from continuing operations...................................		48,000
Discontinued operations, $20,000, less income tax, $8,000		12,000
Income before extraordinary item		60,000
Extraordinary gain, $26,000, less income tax, $10,000		16,000
Net income..		$ 76,000
Earnings per share:*		
Income from continuing operations		
[($48,000 – $4,000)/40,000 shares]		$ 1.10
Income from discontinued operations		
($12,000/40,000 shares)...		0.30
Income before extraordinary item		
[($60,000 – $4,000)/40,000 shares]		1.40
Extraordinary gain ($16,000/40,000 shares)................................		0.40
Net income [($76,000 – $4,000)/40,000 shares]..........................		$ 1.80

*Computations:

$$EPS = \frac{Income - Preferred\ dividends}{Common\ shares\ outstanding}$$

Preferred dividends: $50,000 × 0.08 = $4,000
Common shares outstanding:
  45,000 shares issued – 5,000 treasury shares = 40,000 shares outstanding

Maxim, Inc.
Statement of Retained Earnings
Year Ended December 31, 2010

Retained earnings balance, beginning, as originally reported................	$103,000
Prior-period adjustment—credit	5,000
Retained earnings balance, beginning, as adjusted..............................	108,000
Net income for current year...	76,000
	184,000
Dividends for current year..	(16,000)
Retained earnings balance, ending..	$168,000

REVIEW THE INCOME STATEMENT

Quick Check (Answers are given on page 700.)

1. The quality of earnings suggests that
   a. net income is the best measure of the results of operations.
   b. continuing operations and one-time transactions are of equal importance.
   c. stockholders want the corporation to earn enough income to be able to pay its debts.
   d. income from continuing operations is better than income from one-time transactions.

2. Which statement is true?
   a. Extraordinary items are part of discontinued operations.
   b. Discontinued operations are a separate category on the income statement.
   c. Extraordinary items are combined with continuing operations on the income statement.
   d. All of the above are true.

3. Stafford Corporation earned $5.12 per share of its common stock. Suppose you capitalize Stafford's income at 4%. How much are you willing to pay for a share of Stafford stock?
   a. $125.00   c. $5.12
   b. $20.48   d. $128.00

4. The following is a selected portion of Trendy Trinkets' income statement.

		Year Ended	
	2011	2010	2009
Income (loss) from continuing operations	$(50,000)	$55,000	$145,000
Income (loss) from discontinued operations	(10,000)	(5,000)	1,000
Net income (loss)	$(60,000)	$50,000	$146,000
Earnings (loss) per share from continuing operations:			
Basic	$ (0.33)	$ 0.37	$ 0.92
Earnings (loss) per share from discontinued operations:			
Basic	$ (0.07)	$ (0.03)	$ 0.01
Earnings (loss) per share:			
Basic	$ (0.40)	$ 0.34	$ 0.93

   Trendy Trinkets has no preferred stock outstanding. How many shares of common stock did Trendy Trinkets have outstanding during fiscal year 2011?
   a. 175,000 shares   c. 181,818 shares
   b. 125,000 shares   d. 150,000 shares

5. Why is it important for companies to report their accounting changes to the public?
   a. It is important for the results of operations to be compared between periods.
   b. Most accounting changes increase net income, and investors need to know why the increase in net income occurred.
   c. Some accounting changes are more extraordinary than others.
   d. Accounting changes affect dividends, and investors want dividends.

6. Other comprehensive income
   a. includes unrealized gains and losses on investments.
   b. has no effect on income tax.
   c. affects earnings per share.
   d. includes extraordinary gains and losses.

7. Never Lost Systems earned income before tax of $190,000. Taxable income was $165,000, and the income tax rate was 35%. Never Lost recorded income tax with this journal entry:

a.	Income Tax Expense	66,500	
	Income Tax Payable		57,750
	Deferred Tax Liability		8,750
b.	Income Tax Expense	66,500	
	Income Tax Payable		66,500
c.	Income Tax Payable	66,500	
	Income Tax Expense		57,750
	Deferred Tax Liability		8,750
d.	Income Tax Expense	57,750	
	Income Tax Payable		57,750

8. Deferred Tax Liability is usually

Type of Account	Reported on the
a. Long-term	Income statement
b. Long-term	Balance sheet
c. Short-term	Statement of stockholders' equity
d. Short-term	Income statement

9. The main purpose of the statement of stockholders' equity is to report
   a. reasons for changes in the equity accounts.
   b. results of operations.
   c. financial position.
   d. comprehensive income.

10. An auditor report by independent accountants
   a. gives investors assurance that the company's financial statements conform to GAAP.
   b. is ultimately the responsibility of the management of the client company.
   c. ensures that the financial statements are error-free.
   d. gives investors assurance that the company's stock is a safe investment.

Accounting Vocabulary

channel stuffing (p. 657) A type of financial statement fraud that is accomplished by shipping more to customers (usually around the end of the year) than they ordered, with the expectation that they may return some or all of it. The objective is to record more revenue than the company has actually earned with legitimate sales and shipments.

clean opinion (p. 672) An *unqualified opinion*.

comprehensive income (p. 666) A company's change in total stockholders' equity from all sources other than from the owners of the business.

earnings per share (EPS) (p. 662) Amount of a company's net income per share of its outstanding common stock.

earnings quality (p. 654) The characteristics of an earnings number that make it most useful for decision making. The degree to which earnings are an accurate reflection of underlying economic events for both revenues and expenses, and the extent to which earnings from a company's core operations are improving over time. Assuming that revenues and expenses are measured accurately, high-quality earnings are reflected in steadily improving sales and steadily declining costs over time, so that income from continuing operations follows a high and improving pattern over time.

extraordinary gains and losses (p. 661) Also called *extraordinary items*, these gains and losses are both unusual for the company and infrequent.

extraordinary items (p. 661) An *extraordinary gain or loss*.

investment capitalization rate (p. 659) An earnings rate used to estimate the value of an investment in stock.

pretax accounting income (p. 664) Income before tax on the income statement.

prior-period adjustment (p. 666) A correction to beginning balance of retained earnings for an error of an earlier period.

statement of stockholders' equity (p. 667) Reports the changes in all categories of stockholders' equity during the period.

taxable income (p. 665) The basis for computing the amount of tax to pay the government.

unqualified (clean) opinion (p. 672) An audit opinion stating that the financial statements are reliable.

ASSESS YOUR PROGRESS

Short Exercises

S11-1 (*Learning Objective 1: Analyzing a corporate income statement*) Research has shown that over 50% of financial statement frauds are committed by companies that improperly recognize revenue. What does this mean? Describe the most common ways companies improperly recognize revenue.

writing assignment ■

S11-2 (*Learning Objective 1: Analyzing items on an income statement*) Study the 2010 (not 2011) income statement of Household Imports, Inc., and answer these questions about the company:

Household Imports, Inc.
Consolidated Statement of Operations (Adapted)

	Year Ended 2010	Year Ended 2009
(In thousands except per share amounts)	**2010**	**2009**
1 Net sales	$1,825,775	$1,806,293
Operating costs and expenses:		
2 Cost of sales (including buying and store occupancy costs)	1,121,697	1,045,380
3 Selling, general, and administrative expenses...	549,250	526,550
4 Depreciation and amortization..	55,275	48,750
	1,726,222	1,620,680
5 Operating income (loss)...	99,553	185,613
Nonoperating (income) and expenses:		
6 Interest and investment income	(2,665)	(2,760)
7 Interest expense..	1,785	1,610
	(880)	(1,150)
8 Income (loss) from continuing operations before income taxes...............	100,433	186,763
9 Provision (benefit) for income taxes...	36,384	69,515
10 Income (loss) from continuing operations...	64,049	117,248
11 Discontinued operations:		
12 Income (loss) from discontinued operations (including write		
down of assets held for sale of $7,993 in 2011)...............................	(2,500)	270
13 Income tax savings...	—	—
14 Income (loss) from discontinued operations...	(2,500)	270
15 Net income (loss)..	$ 61,549	$ 117,518
Earnings (loss) per share from continuing operations:		
16 Basic...	$ 0.69	$ 1.52
Earnings (loss) per share from discontinued operations:		
17 Basic...	$ (0.06)	$ 0.00
Earnings (loss) per share:		
18 Basic...	$ 0.63	$ 1.52

1. How much gross profit did Household earn on the sale of its products? How much was income from continuing operations? Net income?

2. At the end of 2010, what dollar amount of net income would most sophisticated investors use to predict Household's net income for 2011 and beyond? Name this item, give its amount, and state your reason.

S11-3 (*Learning Objective 1: Preparing a complex income statement*)   Knowledge King, Inc., reported the following items, listed in no particular order at December 31, 2010 (in thousands):

Other gains (losses)	$ (21,000)	Extraordinary gain	$ 4,000
Net sales revenue	184,000	Cost of goods sold	72,000
Loss on discontinued		Operating expenses	60,000
operations	17,000	Accounts receivable	16,000

Income tax of 30% applies to all items.

   Prepare Knowledge King's income statement for the year ended December 31, 2010. Omit earnings per share.

S11-4 (*Learning Objective 1: Reporting earnings per share*)   Return to the Knowledge King data in Short Exercise 11-3. Knowledge King had 10,000 shares of common stock outstanding during 2010. Knowledge King declared and paid preferred dividends of $1,000 during 2010.

   Report Knowledge King's earnings per share on the income statement. (Round all calculations to two decimal places.)

S11-5 (*Learning Objective 1: Reporting comprehensive income*)   Use the Knowledge King data in Short Exercise S11-3. In addition, Knowledge King had unrealized gains of $1,100 on investments and a $2,400 foreign-currency translation adjustment (a gain) during 2010. Both amounts are net of tax. Start with Knowledge King's net income from S11-3 and show how the company could report other comprehensive income on its 2010 income statement.

   Should Knowledge King report earnings per share for other comprehensive income? State why or why not.

S11-6 (*Learning Objective 1: Valuing a company's stock*)   For fiscal year 2010, Kiwi Computer, Inc., reported net sales of $19,322 million, net income of $1,993 million, and no significant discontinued operations, extraordinary items, or accounting changes. Earnings per share was $2.10. At a capitalization rate of 10%, how much should one share of Kiwi stock be worth? Compare your estimated stock price with the market price of $71.04 as quoted in the newspaper. Based on your estimated market value, should you buy, hold, or sell Kiwi stock?

S11-7 (*Learning Objective 1: Interpreting earnings-per-share data*)   Scorzelli Motor Company has preferred stock outstanding and issued additional common stock during the year.   **writing assignment ■**

1. Give the basic equation to compute earnings per share of common stock for net income.
2. List the income items for which Scorzelli must report earnings-per-share data.
3. What makes earnings per share so useful as a business statistic?

S11-8 (*Learning Objective 1: Using an income statement*)   Christianson Cruise Lines, Inc., reported the following income statement for the year ended December 31, 2010:   **writing assignment ■**

	Millions
Operating revenues	$80,998
Operating expenses	71,300
Operating income	9,698
Other revenue (expense), net	887
Income from continuing operations	10,585
Discontinued operations, net of tax	908
Net income	$11,493

❙ *Requirements*

1. Were Christianson's discontinued operations more like an expense or revenue? How can you tell?
2. Should the discontinued operations of Christianson be included in or excluded from net income? State your reason.
3. Suppose you are working as a financial analyst and your job is to predict Christianson's net income for 2011 and beyond. Which item from the income statement will you use for your prediction? Identify its amount. Why will you use this item?

S11-9 *(Learning Objective 2: Accounting for a corporation's income tax)* Freeman Marine, Inc., had income before income tax of $122,000 and taxable income of $94,000 for 2010, the company's first year of operations. The income tax rate is 30%.

1. Make the entry to record Freeman Marine's income taxes for 2010.
2. Show what Freeman Marine will report on its 2010 income statement starting with income before income tax. Also show what Freeman Marine will report for current and long-term liabilities on its December 31, 2010, balance sheet.

S11-10 *(Learning Objective 3: Reporting a prior-period adjustment)* iPlace, Inc., was set to report the following statement of retained earnings for the year ended December 31, 2010:

iPlace, Inc.
Statement of Retained Earnings
Year Ended December 31, 2010

Retained earnings, December 31, 2009	$ 71,000
Net income for 2010	97,000
Dividends for 2010	(26,000)
Retained earnings, December 31, 2010	$142,000

Before issuing its 2010 financial statements, iPlace learned that net income of 2009 was overstated by $19,000. Prepare iPlace's 2010 statement of retained earnings to show the correction of the error—that is, the prior-period adjustment.

S11-11 (*Learning Objective 3: Using the statement of stockholders' equity*)   Use the statement of stockholders' equity to answer the following questions about Mason Electronics Corporation:

<table>
<tr><td colspan="8">Mason Electronics Corporation
Statement of Stockholders' Equity
For the Year Ended December 31, 2010</td></tr>
<tr><td></td><td></td><td></td><td></td><td></td><td colspan="2">Accumulated Other
Comprehensive Income</td><td></td></tr>
<tr><td></td><td>Common
Stock
$2 Par</td><td>Additional
Paid-in
Capital</td><td>Retained
Earnings</td><td>Treasury
Stock</td><td>Unrealized
Gain
(Loss) on
Investments</td><td>Foreign-
Currency
Translation
Adjustment</td><td>Total
Stockholders'
Equity</td></tr>
<tr><td>1 Balance, December 31, 2009</td><td>$20,000</td><td>$ 140,000</td><td>$185,000</td><td>$(24,000)</td><td>$21,000</td><td>$(11,000)</td><td>$ 331,000</td></tr>
<tr><td>2 Issuance of stock.......................</td><td>40,000</td><td>1,100,000</td><td></td><td></td><td></td><td></td><td>1,140,000</td></tr>
<tr><td>3 Net income ....</td><td></td><td></td><td>93,000</td><td></td><td></td><td></td><td>93,000</td></tr>
<tr><td>4 Cash dividends.........................</td><td></td><td></td><td>(23,000)</td><td></td><td></td><td></td><td>(23,000)</td></tr>
<tr><td>5 Stock dividends—10%..............</td><td>6,000</td><td>78,000</td><td>(84,000)</td><td></td><td></td><td></td><td>0</td></tr>
<tr><td>6 Purchase of treasury stock ....</td><td></td><td></td><td></td><td>(8,000)</td><td></td><td></td><td>(8,000)</td></tr>
<tr><td>7 Sale of treasury stock................</td><td></td><td>7,000</td><td></td><td>5,000</td><td></td><td></td><td>12,000</td></tr>
<tr><td>8 Unrealized gain
   on investments ....</td><td></td><td></td><td></td><td></td><td>6,000</td><td></td><td>6,000</td></tr>
<tr><td>9 Foreign-currency
   translation adjustment...........</td><td></td><td></td><td></td><td></td><td></td><td>3,000</td><td>3,000</td></tr>
<tr><td>10 Balance, December 31, 2010</td><td>$66,000</td><td>$1,325,000</td><td>$171,000</td><td>$(27,000)</td><td>$27,000</td><td>$ (8,000)</td><td>$1,554,000</td></tr>
</table>

1. How much cash did the issuance of common stock bring in during 2010?

2. What was the effect of the stock dividends on Mason's retained earnings? On total paid-in capital? On total stockholders' equity? On total assets?

3. What was the cost of the treasury stock that Mason purchased during 2010? What was the cost of the treasury stock that Mason sold during the year? For how much did Mason sell the treasury stock during 2010?

S11-12 *(Learning Objective 4: Identifying responsibility and standards for the financial statements)* The annual report of Ashburnham Computer, Inc., included the following:

Management's Annual Report on Internal Control over Financial Reporting

The Company's management is responsible for establishing and maintaining adequate control over financial reporting [....] Management conducted an evaluation of the effectiveness of the Company's internal control over financial reporting [....] Based on this evaluation, management has concluded that the Company's internal control over financial reporting was effective as of September 30, 2010....

Report of Independent Registered Public Accounting Firm
The Board of Directors and Shareholders
Ashburnham Computer, Inc.:

We have audited the accompanying consolidated balance sheets of Ashburnham Computer, Inc., and subsidiaries (the Company) as of September 30, 2010, and September 30, 2009, and the related consolidated statements of operations, shareholders' equity, and cash flows for each of the years in the three-year period ended September 30, 2010. These consolidated financial statements are the responsibility of the Company's management. Our responsibility is to express an opinion on these consolidated financial statements based on our audits.
We conducted our audits in accordance with the standards of the Public Company Accounting Oversight Board (United States)....
In our opinion, the consolidated financial statements referred to above present fairly, in all material respects, the financial position of the Company as of September 30, 2010, and September 30, 2009, and the results of their operations and their cash flows for each of the years in the three-year period ended September 30, 2010, in conformity with accounting principles generally accepted in the United States of America.

/S/ SLMA LLP

Portage, Michigan
December 28, 2010

---

1. Who is responsible for Ashburnham's financial statements?
2. By what accounting standard are the financial statements prepared?
3. Identify one concrete action that Ashburnham management takes to fulfill its responsibility for the reliability of the company's financial information.
4. Which entity gave an outside, independent opinion on the Ashburnham financial statements? Where was this entity located, and when did it release its opinion to the public?
5. Exactly what did the audit cover? Give names and dates.
6. By what standard did the auditor conduct the audit?
7. What was the auditor's opinion of Ashburnham's financial statements?

Exercises

> All of the A and B exercises can be found within MyAccountingLab, an online homework and practice environment. Your instructor may ask you to complete these exercises using MyAccountingLab.

(Group A)

E11-13A *(Learning Objective 1: Preparing and using a complex income statement)*   Suppose Dighton Cycles, Inc., reported a number of special items on its income statement. The following data, listed in no particular order, came from Dighton's financial statements (amounts in thousands):

Income tax expense (saving):		Net sales..	$14,000
Continuing operations.................	$295	Foreign-currency translation	
Discontinued operations..............	56	adjustment	320
Extraordinary loss.......................	(2)	Extraordinary loss................................	10
Unrealized gain on		Income from discontinued operations	280
available-for-sale investments.......	35	Dividends declared and paid	600
Short-term investments...................	25	Total operating expenses.......................	12,800

▌Requirement

1. Show how the Dighton Cycles, Inc., income statement for the year ended September 30, 2010, should appear. Omit earnings per share.

E11-14A *(Learning Objective 1: Preparing and using a complex income statement)*   The Regan Books Company accounting records include the following for 2010 (in thousands):

> ■ spreadsheet

Other revenues	$ 2,400
Income tax expense—extraordinary gain	1,600
Income tax expense—income from continuing operations............	2,880
Extraordinary gain..	4,000
Sales revenue...	102,000
Total operating expenses...	97,200

▌Requirements

1. Prepare Regan Books' single-step income statement for the year ended December 31, 2010, including EPS. Regan Books had 1,800 thousand shares of common stock and no preferred stock outstanding during the year.
2. Assume investors capitalize Regan Books' earnings at 5%. Estimate the price of one share of the company's stock.

E11-15A *(Learning Objective 1: Using income data for investment analysis)* During 2010, Prime, Inc., had sales of $7.26 billion, operating profit of $2.20 billion, and net income of $3.30 billion. EPS was $4.80. On March 13, 2011, one share of Prime's common stock was priced at $53.80 on the New York Stock Exchange.

What investment capitalization rate did investors appear to be using to determine the value of one share of Prime stock? The formula for the value of one share of stock uses EPS in the calculation.

E11-16A *(Learning Objective 1: Computing earnings per common share)* Jetty Loan Company's balance sheet reports the following:

Preferred stock, $60 par value, 3%, 12,000 shares issued	$720,000
Common stock, $0.75 par, 1,100,000 shares issued....................	825,000
Treasury stock, common, 90,000 shares at cost	540,000

During 2010 Jetty earned net income of $6,100,000. Compute Jetty's earnings per common share for 2010. (Round EPS to two decimal places.)

E11-17A *(Learning Objective 1: Computing and using earnings per share)* Athens Holding Company operates numerous businesses, including motel, auto rental, and real estate companies. Year 2010 was interesting for Athens, which reported the following on its income statement (in millions):

Net revenues	$3,932
Total expenses and other...	3,358
Income from continuing operations..............................	574
Discontinued operations, net of tax savings	(89)
Income before extraordinary item and cumulative	
effect of accounting change, net of tax...............	485
Extraordinary loss, net of tax savings..........................	(7)
Net income...	$ 478

During 2010, Athens had the following (in millions, except for par value per share):

Common stock, $0.05 par value, 900 shares issued	$ 45
Treasury stock, 300 shares at cost..	(3,649)

❙ Requirement

1. Show how Athens should report earnings per share for 2010. (Round EPS to the nearest cent.)

E11-18A *(Learning Objective 2: Accounting for income tax by a corporation)* For 2010, its first year of operations, Quinn Advertising, Inc., earned pretax accounting income (on the income statement) of $375,000. Taxable income (on the tax return filed with the Internal Revenue Service) is $300,000. The income tax rate is 30%. Record Quinn's income tax for the year. Show what Quinn will report on its 2010 income statement and balance sheet for this situation. Start the income statement with income before tax.

E11-19A *(Learning Objective 2: Accounting for income tax by a corporation)* During 2010, the Alvin Heights Corp. income statement reported income of $330,000 before tax. The company's income tax return filed with the IRS showed taxable income of $280,000. During 2010, Alvin Heights was subject to an income tax rate of 30%.

❙ Requirements

1. Journalize Alvin Heights' income taxes for 2010.
2. How much income tax did Alvin Heights have to pay currently for the year 2010?
3. At the beginning of 2010, Alvin Heights' balance of Deferred Tax Liability was $36,000. How much Deferred Tax Liability did Alvin Heights report on its balance sheet at December 31, 2010?

E11-20A (*Learning Objective 3: Reporting a prior-period adjustment on the statement of retained earnings*) Domicile, Inc., a household products chain, reported a prior-period adjustment in 2010. An accounting error caused net income of 2009 to be overstated by $16 million. Retained earnings at December 31, 2009, as previously reported, stood at $342 million. Net income for 2010 was $96 million, and 2010 dividends were $68 million.

❙ spreadsheet

❙ Requirement

1. Prepare the company's statement of retained earnings for the year ended December 31, 2010. How does the prior-period adjustment affect Domicile's net income for 2010?

E11-21A (*Learning Objective 3: Preparing a statement of stockholders' equity*) At December 31, 2010, Pacheco Mall, Inc., reported stockholders' equity as follows:

Common stock, $1.75 par, 400,000 shares authorized, 310,000 shares issued	$ 542,500
Additional paid-in capital	700,000
Retained earnings	630,000
	$1,872,500

During 2011, Pacheco Mall completed these transactions (listed in chronological order):

a. Declared and issued a 2% stock dividend on the outstanding stock. At the time, Pacheco Mall stock was quoted at a market price of $20 per share.
b. Issued 2,000 shares of common stock at the price of $18 per share.
c. Net income for the year, $342,000.
d. Declared cash dividends of $187,000.

❙ Requirement

1. Prepare Pacheco Mall, Inc.'s statement of stockholders' equity for 2011.

E11-22A (*Learning Objective 3: Using a company's statement of stockholders' equity*) Clean Water Company reported the following items on its statement of shareholders' equity for the year ended December 31, 2010:

	$3 Par Common Stock	Additional Paid-in Capital	Retained Earnings	Accumulated Other Comprehensive Income	Total Shareholders' Equity
Balance, December 31, 2009	$405	$1,695	$3,600	$12	$5,712
Net earnings			950		
Unrealized gain on investments					
Issuance of stock	60	240		5	
Cash dividends			(50)		
Balance, December 31, 2010					

▌Requirements

1. Determine the December 31, 2010, balances in Clean Water's shareholders' equity accounts and total shareholders' equity on this date.
2. Clean Water's total liabilities on December 31, 2010, are $8,000. What is Clean Water's debt ratio on this date?
3. Was there a profit or a loss for the year ended December 31, 2010? How can you tell?
4. At what price per share did Clean Water issue common stock during 2010?

(Group B)

E11-23B (*Learning Objective 1: Preparing and using a complex income statement*) Suppose Searstown Cycles, Inc., reported a number of special items on its income statement. The following data, listed in no particular order, came from Searstown's financial statements (amounts in thousands):

Income tax expense (saving):		Net sales....................................	$13,300
Continuing operations..................	$300	Foreign-currency translation	
Discontinued operations..............	(62)	adjustment	330
Extraordinary loss........................	(8)	Extraordinary loss.................................	14
Unrealized gain on		Income from discontinued operations	310
available-for-sale investments.......	38	Dividends declared and paid	610
Short-term investments....................	50	Total operating expenses.......................	12,400

▌Requirement

1. Show how the Searstown Cycles, Inc., income statement for the year ended September 30, 2010, should appear. Omit earnings per share.

E11-24B (*Learning Objective 1: Preparing and using a complex income statement*) The Beemer Books Company accounting records include the following for 2010 (in thousands):

Other revenues...	$ 2,100
Income tax expense—extraordinary gain	1,440
Income tax expense—income from continuing operations............	4,840
Extraordinary gain...	3,600
Sales revenue..	107,000
Total operating expenses...	97,000

▌Requirements

1. Prepare Beemer Books' single-step income statement for the year ended December 31, 2010, including EPS. Beemer Books had 1,500 thousand shares of common stock and no preferred stock outstanding during the year.
2. Assume investors capitalize Beemer Books earnings at 6%. Estimate the price of one share of the company's stock.

E11-25B (*Learning Objective 1: Using income data for investment analysis*) During 2010, Doppler, Inc., had sales of $7.36 billion, operating profit of $2.10 billion, and net income of $3.10 billion. EPS was $4.20. On April 12, 2011, one share of Doppler's common stock was priced at $54.40 on the New York Stock Exchange.

What investment capitalization rate did investors appear to be using to determine the value of one share of Doppler stock? The formula for the value of one share of stock uses EPS in the calculation.

E11-26B (*Learning Objective 1: Computing earnings per share*)   Tidepool Loan Company's balance sheet reports the following:

Preferred stock, $40 par value, 4%, 9,000 shares issued..............	$ 360,000
Common stock, $2.00 par, 1,000,000 shares issued....................	2,000,000
Treasury stock, common, 200,000 shares at cost........................	1,200,000

During 2010 Tidepool earned net income of $6,000,000. Compute Tidepool's earnings per common share for 2010. (Round EPS to two decimal places.)

E11-27B (*Learning Objective 1: Computing and using earnings per share*)   Helenic Holding Company operates numerous businesses, including motel, auto rental, and real estate companies. Year 2010 was interesting for Helenic, which reported the following on its income statement (in millions):

Net revenues	$3,934
Total expenses and other...	3,357
Income from continuing operations...............................	577
Discontinued operations, net of tax..............................	88
Income before extraordinary item and cumulative	
effect of accounting change, net of tax................	665
Extraordinary gain, net of tax......................................	10
Net income...	$ 675

During 2010, Helenic had the following (in millions, except for par value per share):

Common stock, $0.30 par value, 600 shares issued	$ 180
Treasury stock, 200 shares at cost...	(3,542)

❙ Requirement

1. Show how Helenic should report earnings per share for 2010. (Round EPS to the nearest cent.)

E11-28B (*Learning Objective 2: Accounting for income tax by a corporation*)   For 2010, its first year of operations, Johnson Advertising earned pretax accounting income (on the income statement) of $750,000. Taxable income (on the tax return filed with the Internal Revenue Service) is $650,000. The income tax rate is 35%. Record Johnson's income tax for the year. Show what Johnson will report on its 2010 income statement and balance sheet for this situation. Start the income statement with income before tax.

E11-29B (*Learning Objective 2: Accounting for income tax by a corporation*)   During 2010, Florimax Heights Corp. income statement reported income of $410,000 before tax. The company's income tax return filed with the IRS showed taxable income of $360,000. During 2010, Florimax Heights was subject to an income tax rate of 32%.

❙ Requirements

1. Journalize Florimax Heights' income taxes for 2010.
2. How much income tax did Florimax Heights have to pay for the year 2010?
3. At the beginning of 2010, Florimax Heights' balance of Deferred Tax Liability was $34,000. How much Deferred Tax Liability did Florimax Heights report on its balance sheet at December 31, 2010?

E11-30B (*Learning Objective 3: Reporting a prior-period adjustment on the statement of retained earnings*)   Tidy, Inc., a household products chain, reported a prior-period adjustment in 2010. An accounting error caused net income of 2009 to be understated by $8 million. Retained earnings at December 31, 2009, as previously reported, stood at $343 million. Net income for 2010 was $98 million, and 2010 dividends were $65 million.

❙ *Requirement*

1. Prepare the company's statement of retained earnings for the year ended December 31, 2010. How does the prior-period adjustment affect Tidy's net income for 2010?

E11-31B (*Learning Objective 3: Preparing a statement of stockholders' equity*)   At December 31, 2010, Cox Mall, Inc., reported stockholders' equity as follows:

Common stock, $2.00 par, 600,000 shares authorized, 280,000 shares issued	$ 560,000
Additional paid-in capital.......................................	700,000
Retained earnings..	645,000
	$1,905,000

During 2011, Cox Mall completed these transactions (listed in chronological order):

a. Declared and issued a 1% stock dividend on the outstanding stock. At the time, Cox Mall stock was quoted at a market price of $28 per share.
b. Issued 2,100 shares of common stock at the price of $14 per share.
c. Net income for the year, $343,000.
d. Declared cash dividends of $180,000.

❙ *Requirement*

1. Prepare Cox Mall, Inc.'s statement of stockholders' equity for 2011.

E11-32B (*Learning Objective 3: Using a company's statement of stockholders' equity*) Rockaway Water Company reported the following items on its statement of shareholders' equity for the year ended December 31, 2010:

	$2 Par Common Stock	Additional Paid-in Capital	Retained Earnings	Accumulated Other Comprehensive Income	Total Shareholders' Equity
Balance, December 31, 2009.............	$390	$1,710	$5,000	$9	$7,109
Net earnings.....................................			1,170		
Unrealized gain on investments				2	
Issuance of stock	90	270			
Cash dividends.................................			(50)		
Balance, December 31, 2010.............					

❙ *Requirements*

1. Determine the December 31, 2010, balances in Rockaway Water's shareholders' equity accounts and total stockholders' equity on this date.
2. Rockaway Water's total liabilities on December 31, 2010, are $6,700. What is Rockaway Water's debt ratio on this date?
3. Was there a profit or a loss for the year ended December 31, 2010? How can you tell?
4. At what price per share did Rockaway Water issue common stock during 2010?

Quiz

Test your understanding of the corporate income statement and the statement of stockholders' equity by answering the following questions. Select the best choice from among the possible answers given.

Q11-33 What is the best source of income for a corporation?
a. Discontinued operations
b. Continuing operations
c. Extraordinary items
d. Prior-period adjustments

Michael's Lotion Company reports several earnings numbers on its current-year income statement (parentheses indicate a loss):

Gross profit..............................	$150,000	Income from continuing operations.......	$33,000
Net income...............................	43,000	Extraordinary gains..............................	16,000
Income before income tax	62,000	Discontinued operations.......................	(6,000)

Q11-34 How much net income would most investment analysts predict for Michael's to earn next year?
a. $43,000
b. $16,000
c. $33,000
d. $49,000

Q11-35 Return to the preceding question. Suppose you are evaluating Michael's Lotion Company stock as an investment. You require an 8% rate of return on investments, so you capitalize Michael's earnings at 8%. How much are you willing to pay for all of Michael's stock?
a. $1,875,000
b. $412,500
c. $537,500
d. $775,000

Q11-36 Superior Value Corporation had the following items that were labeled "extraordinary" on its income statement:

Extraordinary flood loss.........................	$100,000
Extraordinary gain on lawsuit................	150,000

Net income from operations, before income tax and before these "extraordinary" items, totals $240,000, and the income tax rate is 30%. Superior Value's "bottom line" net income after tax is
a. $273,000.
b. $203,000.
c. $290,000.
d. $168,000.

Q11-37 Superior Value Corporation in question 36 has 9,000 shares of 7%, $100 par preferred stock, and 200,000 shares of common stock outstanding. Earnings per share for net income is
a. $0.58.
b. $1.20.
c. $1.51.
d. $0.70.

Q11-38 Earnings per share is *not* reported for
a. extraordinary items.
b. discontinued operations.
c. continuing operations.
d. comprehensive income.

Q11-39 Copyhouse Corporation has income before income tax of $160,000 and taxable income of $120,000. The income tax rate is 30%. Copyhouse's income statement will report net income of
a. $142,000.
b. $48,000.
c. $112,000.
d. $36,000.

Q11-40 Copyhouse Corporation in the preceding question must immediately pay income tax of
a. $112,000.
b. $36,000.
c. $48,000.
d. $84,000.

Q11-41 Use the Copyhouse Corporation data in question 39. At the end of its first year of operations, Copyhouse's deferred tax liability is

a. $12,000.

b. $20,000.

c. $36,000.

d. $28,000.

Q11-42 Which of the following items is most closely related to prior-period adjustments?

a. Preferred stock dividends

b. Retained earnings

c. Accounting changes

d. Earnings per share

Q11-43 Examine the statement of stockholders' equity of Mason Electronics Corporation.

Mason Electronics Corporation
Statement of Stockholders' Equity
Year Ended December 31, 2010

	Common Stock $2 Par	Additional Paid-in Capital	Retained Earnings	Treasury Stock	Unrealized Gain (Loss) on Investments	Foreign-Currency Translation Adjustment	Total Stockholders' Equity
					Accumulated Other Comprehensive Income		
1 Balance, December 31, 2009.....	$20,000	$ 140,000	$185,000	$(24,000)	$21,000	$(11,000)	$ 331,000
2 Issuance of stock........................	40,000	1,100,000					1,140,000
3 Net income			93,000				93,000
4 Cash dividends...........................			(23,000)				(23,000)
5 Stock dividend—10%	6,000	78,000	(84,000)				0
6 Purchase of treasury stock				(8,000)			(8,000)
7 Sale of treasury stock................		7,000		5,000			12,000
8 Unrealized gain on investments					6,000		6,000
9 Foreign-currency translation adj......................						3,000	3,000
10 Balance, December 31, 2010	$66,000	$1,325,000	$171,000	$ 27,000	$27,000	$ (8,000)	$1,554,000

What was the market value of each share of the stock that Mason gave its stockholders in the stock dividend?

a. $3,000

b. $28

c. $42,000

d. $56

Q11-44 Which statement is true?

a. Independent auditors prepare the financial statements.

b. Management audits the financial statements.

c. GAAP governs the form and content of the financial statements.

d. The Public Company Oversight Board evaluates internal controls.

Problems

All of the A and B problems can be found within MyAccountingLab, an online homework and practice environment. Your instructor may ask you to complete these problems using MyAccountingLab.

(Group A)

P11-45A (*Learning Objective 1: Preparing a complex income statement*)   The following information was taken from the records of Daughtry Cosmetics, Inc., at December 31, 2010:

Prior-period adjustment—		Dividends on common stock	$24,000	
debit to Retained Earnings	$ 1,000	Interest expense	30,000	
Income tax expense (saving):		Gain on lawsuit settlement	14,000	
Continuing operations	33,980	Dividend revenue	20,000	
Income from discontinued		Treasury stock, common		
operations	8,680	(3,000 shares at cost)	17,000	
Extraordinary loss	(12,280)	General expenses	85,000	
Loss on sale of plant assets	15,000	Sales revenue	610,000	
Income from discontinued		Retained earnings, beginning,		
operations	21,000	as originally reported	195,000	
Preferred stock, 4%, $20 par,		Selling expenses	105,000	
3,000 shares issued	60,000	Common stock, no par,		
Extraordinary loss	29,400	25,000 shares authorized		
Cost of goods sold	324,000	and issued	400,000	

Requirements

1. Prepare Daughtry Cosmetics' single-step income statement, which lists all revenues together and all expenses together, for the fiscal year ended December 31, 2010. Include earnings-per-share data.
2. Evaluate income for the year ended December 31, 2010. Daughtry's top managers hoped to earn income from continuing operations equal to 12% of sales.

P11-46A (*Learning Objective 3: Preparing a statement of retained earnings*)   Use the data in Problem P11-45A to prepare the Daughtry Cosmetics statement of retained earnings for the year ended December 31, 2010. Use the Statement of Retained Earnings for Maxim, Inc., in the End-of-Chapter Summary Problem as a model.

P11-47A (*Learning Objective 1: Using income data to make an investment decision*) Daughtry Cosmetics in Problem P11-45A holds significant promise for carving a niche in its industry. A group of Irish investors is considering purchasing the company's outstanding common stock. Daughtry's stock is currently selling for $43 per share.

A *BetterLife Magazine* story predicted the company's income is bound to grow. It appears that Daughtry can earn at least its current level of income for the indefinite future. Based on this information, the investors think that an appropriate investment capitalization rate for estimating the value of Daughtry's common stock is 5%. How much will this belief lead the investors to offer for Daughtry Cosmetics? Will Daughtry's existing stockholders be likely to accept this offer? Explain your answers.

P11-48A (*Learning Objective 1: Computing earnings per share and estimating the price of a stock*)   Overhaul Experts, Ltd., (OEL) specializes in taking underperforming companies to a higher level of performance. OEL's capital structure at December 31, 2009, included 11,000 shares of $2.30 preferred stock and 125,000 shares of common stock. During 2010, OEL issued common stock and ended the year with 131,000 shares of common stock out-standing. Average common shares outstanding during 2010 were 128,000. Income from con-tinuing operations during 2010 was $220,000. The company discontinued a segment of the business at a loss of $67,000, and an extraordinary item generated a gain of $50,000. All amounts are after income tax.

❙ Requirements

1. Compute OEL's earnings per share. Start with income from continuing operations.
2. Analysts believe OEL can earn its current level of income for the indefinite future. Estimate the market price of a share of OEL common stock at investment capitalization rates of 10%, 12%, and 14%. Which estimate presumes an investment in OEL is the most risky? How can you tell?

P11-49A (*Learning Objective 1: Preparing a corrected income statement, including comprehensive income*)   Jim Heller, accountant for Perfect Pie Foods, was injured in an auto accident. Another employee prepared the following income statement for the fiscal year ended June 30, 2010:

Perfect Pie Foods, Inc.
Income Statement
June 30, 2010

Revenue and gains:		
Sales...		$896,000
Paid-in capital in excess of par—common...........................		15,000
Total revenues and gains...		911,000
Expenses and losses:		
Cost of goods sold..	$387,000	
Selling expenses..	101,000	
General expenses...	93,000	
Sales returns...	23,000	
Unrealized loss on available-for-sale investments.................	13,000	
Dividends paid	16,000	
Sales discounts	12,000	
Income tax expense...	35,000	
Total expenses and losses...		680,000
Income from operations		231,000
Other gains and losses:		
Extraordinary loss...	(42,000)	
Income from discontinued operations	27,000	
Total other gains (losses)...		(15,000)
Net income...		$216,000
Earnings per share		$ 10.80

The individual *amounts* listed on the income statement are correct. However, some *accounts* are reported incorrectly, and some accounts do not belong on the income statement at all. Also, income tax (40%) has not been applied to all appropriate figures. Perfect Pie Foods issued 24,000 shares of common stock back in 2004 and held 4,000 shares as treasury stock all during the fiscal year 2010.

I Requirement

1. Prepare a corrected statement of income (single-step, which lists all revenues together and all expenses together), including comprehensive income, for fiscal year 2010. Include earnings per share.

P11-50A (*Learning Objective 2: Accounting for a corporation's income tax*)   The accounting (not the income tax) records of Crowley Publications, Inc., provide the comparative income statement for 2010 and 2011, respectively:

	2010	2011
Total revenue	$930,000	$1,020,000
Expenses:		
Cost of goods sold	$410,000	$ 440,000
Operating expenses	290,000	300,000
Total expenses before tax	700,000	740,000
Pretax accounting income	$230,000	$ 280,000

Taxable income for 2010 includes these modifications from pretax accounting income:

a. Additional taxable income of $18,000 for accounting income earned in 2011 but taxed in 2010.

b. Additional depreciation expense of $30,000 for MACRS tax depreciation.

The income tax rate is 30%.

I Requirements

1. Compute Crowley's taxable income for 2010.
2. Journalize the corporation's income taxes for 2010.
3. Prepare the corporation's income statement for 2010.

P11-51A (*Learning Objective 3: Using a statement of stockholders' equity*)   Falmouth Food Specialties, Inc., reported the following statement of stockholders' equity for the year ended October 31, 2010:

Falmouth Food Specialties, Inc.
Statement of Stockholders' Equity
For the Year Ended October 31, 2010

(In millions)	Common Stock	Additional Paid-in Capital	Retained Earnings	Treasury Stock	Total
Balance, October 31, 2009	$450	$1,670	$ 911	$(114)	$2,917
Net income			280		280
Cash dividends			(197)		(197)
Issuance of stock (25 shares)	50	200			250
Stock dividend	100	400	(500)		—
Sale of treasury stock		12		13	25
Balance, October 31, 2010	$600	$2,282	$ 494	$(101)	$3,275

❚ Requirements

Answer these questions about Falmouth Food Specialties' stockholders' equity transactions.

1. The income tax rate is 30%. How much income before income tax did Falmouth Food Specialties report on the income statement?
2. What is the par value of the company's common stock?
3. At what price per share did Falmouth Food Specialties issue its common stock during the year?
4. What was the cost of treasury stock sold during the year? What was the selling price of the treasury stock sold? What was the increase in total stockholders' equity?
5. Falmouth Food Specialties' statement of stockholders' equity lists the stock transactions in the order in which they occurred. What was the percentage of the stock dividend? (Round to the nearest percentage.)

(Group B)

P11-52B (*Learning Objective 1: Preparing a complex income statement*)   The following information was taken from the records of Ahern Cosmetics, Inc., at December 31, 2010:

Prior-period adjustment—		Dividends on common stock	$23,000
debit to Retained Earnings.............	$ 3,000	Interest expense.................................	25,000
Income tax expense (saving):		Gain on lawsuit settlement................	9,000
Continuing operations...................	24,450	Dividend revenue	15,000
Income from discontinued		Treasury stock, common	
operations......................................	7,190	(4,000 shares at cost)...............	12,000
Extraordinary loss	(12,910)	General expenses...............................	80,000
Loss on sale of plant assets.....................	13,000	Sales revenue.....................................	560,000
Income from discontinued		Retained earnings, beginning,	
operations......................................	18,000	as originally reported................	193,000
Preferred stock, 10%, $15 par,		Selling expenses.................................	90,000
500 shares issued..........................	7,500	Common stock, no par,	
Extraordinary loss................................	32,000	27,000 shares authorized	
Cost of goods sold.................................	314,000	and issued...............................	380,000

❚ Requirements

1. Prepare Ahern Cosmetics' single-step income statement, which lists all revenues together and all expenses together, for the fiscal year ended December 31, 2010. Include earnings-per-share data.
2. Evaluate income for the year ended December 31, 2010. Ahern's top managers hoped to earn income from continuing operations equal to 14% of sales.

P11-53B (*Learning Objective 3: Preparing a statement of retained earnings*)   Use the data in Problem P11-52B to prepare the Ahern Cosmetics statement of retained earnings for the year ended December 31, 2010. Use the Statement of Retained Earnings for Maxim, Inc., in the End-of-Chapter Summary Problem as a model.

P11-54B (*Learning Objective 1: Using income data to make an investment decision*) Ahern Cosmetics in Problem P11-52B holds significant promise for carving a niche in its industry. A group of Swedish investors is considering purchasing the company's outstanding common stock. Ahern's stock is currently selling for $19 per share.

A *Dollars and Sense* story predicted the company's income is bound to grow. It appears that Ahern can earn at least its current level of income for the indefinite future. Based on this information, the investors think that an appropriate investment capitalization rate for estimating the value of Ahern's common stock is 10%. How much will this belief lead the investors to offer for Ahern Cosmetics? Will Ahern's existing stockholders be likely to accept this offer? Explain your answers.

P11-55B (*Learning Objective 1: Computing earnings per share and estimating the price of a stock*) New Ventures Ltd. (NVL) specializes in taking underperforming companies to a higher level of performance. NVL's capital structure at December 31, 2009, included 12,000 shares of $2.20 preferred stock and 130,000 shares of common stock. During 2010, NVL issued common stock and ended the year with 138,000 shares of common stock outstanding. Average common shares outstanding during 2010 were 134,000. Income from continuing operations during 2010 was $225,000. The company discontinued a segment of the business at a loss of $66,000, and an extraordinary item generated a gain of $48,000. All amounts are after income tax.

❙ Requirements

1. Compute NVL's earnings per share. Start with income from continuing operations.
2. Analysts believe NVL can earn its current level of income for the indefinite future. Estimate the market price of a share of NVL common stock at investment capitalization rates of 9%, 11%, and 13%. Which estimate presumes an investment in NVL is the most risky? How can you tell?

P11-56B (*Learning Objective 1: Preparing a corrected income statement, including comprehensive income*) Jack Hodges, accountant for Edible Pie Foods, was injured in an auto accident. Another employee prepared the following income statement for the fiscal year ended June 30, 2010:

Edible Pie Foods, Inc.
Income Statement
June 30, 2010

Revenue and gains:		
Sales		$894,000
Paid-in capital in excess of par—common		14,000
Total revenues and gains		908,000
Expenses and losses:		
Cost of goods sold	$382,000	
Selling expenses	106,000	
General expenses	95,000	
Sales returns	26,000	
Unrealized loss on available-for-sale investments	12,000	
Dividends paid	17,000	
Sales discounts	14,000	
Income tax expense	33,000	
Total expenses and losses		685,000
Income from operations		223,000
Other gains and losses:		
Extraordinary gain	40,000	
Loss on discontinued operations	(26,000)	
Total other gains (losses)		14,000
Net income		$237,000
Earnings per share		$ 23.70

The individual *amounts* listed on the income statement are correct. However, some *accounts* are reported incorrectly, and some accounts do not belong on the income statement at all. Also, income tax (30%) has not been applied to all appropriate figures. Edible Pie Foods issued 13,000 shares of common stock back in 2004 and held 3,000 shares as treasury stock all during the fiscal year 2010.

▌Requirement

1. Prepare a corrected statement of income (single-step, which lists all revenues together and all expenses together), including comprehensive income for 2010. Include earnings per share.

P11-57B (*Learning Objective 2: Accounting for a corporation's income tax*)   The accounting (not the income tax) records of Consolidated Publications, Inc., provide the comparative income statement for 2010 and 2011, respectively:

	2010	2011
Total revenue	$920,000	$1,010,000
Expenses:		
Cost of goods sold...............................	$470,000	$ 500,000
Operating expenses	270,000	280,000
Total expenses before tax....................	740,000	780,000
Pretax accounting income	$180,000	$ 230,000

Taxable income for 2010 includes these modifications from pretax accounting income:

a. Additional taxable income of $13,000 for accounting income earned in 2011 but taxed in 2010.

b. Additional depreciation expense of $40,000 for MACRS tax depreciation.

The income tax rate is 35%.

▌Requirements

1. Compute Consolidated's taxable income for 2010.
2. Journalize the corporation's income taxes for 2010.
3. Prepare the corporation's income statement for 2010.

P11-58B (*Learning Objective 3: Using a statement of stockholders' equity*)   Franklin Food Specialties Inc. reported the following statement of stockholders' equity for the year ended October 31, 2010:

Franklin Food Specialties, Inc.
Statement of Stockholders' Equity
For the Year Ended October 31, 2010

(In millions)	Common Stock	Additional Paid-in Capital	Retained Earnings	Treasury Stock	Total
Balance, October 31, 2009...........	$440	$1,680	$ 907	$(114)	$2,913
Net income..................................			420		420
Cash dividends.............................			(190)		(190)
Issuance of stock (10 shares)........	10	220			230
Stock dividend.............................	45	990	(1,035)		—
Sale of treasury stock		16		11	27
Balance, October 31, 2010...........	$495	$2,906	$ 102	$(103)	$3,400

▌Requirements

Answer these questions about Franklin Food Specialties' stockholders' equity transactions.

1. The income tax rate is 40%. How much income before income tax did Franklin Food Specialties report on the income statement?

2. What is the par value of the company's common stock?
3. At what price per share did Franklin Food Specialties issue its common stock during the year?
4. What was the cost of treasury stock sold during the year? What was the selling price of the treasury stock sold? What was the increase in total stockholders' equity?
5. Franklin Food Specialties' statement of stockholders' equity lists the stock transactions in the order in which they occurred. What was the percentage of the stock dividend? (Round to the nearest percentage).

APPLY YOUR KNOWLEDGE

Decision Cases

Case 1. (*Learning Objective 1: Evaluating the components of income*) Prudhoe Bay Oil Co. is having its initial public offering (IPO) of company stock. To create public interest in its stock, Prudhoe Bay's chief financial officer has blitzed the media with press releases. One, in particular, caught your eye. On November 19, Prudhoe Bay announced unaudited earnings per share (EPS) of $1.19, up 89% from last year's EPS of $0.63. An 89% increase in EPS is outstanding!

Before deciding to buy Prudhoe Bay stock, you investigated further and found that the company omitted several items from the determination of unaudited EPS, as follows:

- Unrealized loss on available-for-sale investments, $0.06 per share
- Gain on sale of building, $0.05 per share
- Prior-period adjustment, increase in retained earnings $1.10 per share
- Restructuring expenses, $0.29 per share
- Loss on settlement of lawsuit begun five years ago, $0.12 per share
- Lost income due to employee labor strike, $0.24 per share
- Income from discontinued operations, $0.09 per share

Wondering how to treat these "special items," you called your stockbroker at **Merrill Lynch**. She thinks that these items are nonrecurring and outside Prudhoe Bay's core operations. Furthermore, she suggests that you ignore the items and consider Prudhoe Bay's earnings of $1.19 per share to be a good estimate of long-term profitability.

❙ Requirement

1. What EPS number will you use to predict Prudhoe Bay's future profits? Show your work, and explain your reasoning for each item.

Case 2. (*Learning Objective 1: Using the financial statements in investment analysis*) Mike Magid Toyota is an automobile dealership. Magid's annual report includes Note 1— Summary of Significant Accounting Policies as follows:

> **Income Recognition**
>
> **Sales are recognized when cash payment is received or, in the case of credit sales, which represent the majority of . . . sales, when a down payment is received and the customer enters into an installment sales contract. These installment sales contracts . . . are normally collectible over 36 to 60 months. . . .**
>
> **Revenue from auto insurance policies sold to customers are recognized as income over the life of the contracts.**

Bay Area Nissan, a competitor of Mike Magid Toyota, includes the following note in its Summary of Significant Accounting Policies:

> **Accounting Policies for Revenues**
> Sales are recognized when cash payment is received or, in the case of credit sales, which represent the majority of . . . sales, when the customer enters into an installment sales contract. Customer down payments are rare. Most of these installment sales contracts are normally collectible over 36 to 60 months. . . . Revenue from auto insurance policies sold to customers are recognized when the customer signs an insurance contract. Expenses are recognized over the life of the insurance contracts.

Suppose you have decided to invest in an auto dealership and you've narrowed your choices to Magid and Bay Area. Which company's earnings are of higher quality? Why? Will their accounting policies affect your investment decision? If so, how? Mention specific accounts in the financial statements that will differ between the two companies. (Challenge)

Ethical Issue

The income statement of Royal Bank of Singapore reported the following results of operations:

Earnings before income taxes and extraordinary gain	$187,046
Income tax expense	72,947
Earnings before extraordinary gain	114,099
Extraordinary gain, net of income tax	419,557
Net earnings	$533,656

Suppose Royal Bank's management, in violation of International Financial Reporting Standards (IFRS), had reported the company's results of operations in this manner:

Earnings before income taxes	$847,111
Income tax expense	352,651
Net earnings	$494,460

❚ *Requirements*

1. Identify the ethical issue in this situation.
2. Who are the stakeholders?
3. Evaluate the issue from the standpoint of (a) economic, (b) legal or regulatory, and (c) ethical dimensions. What are the possible effects on all stakeholders you identified?
4. Put yourself in the position of the controller of the bank. Your boss, the CEO, tries to pressure you to make the disclosure that violates IFRS. What would you do? What are the potential consequences?

Focus on Financials: ■ Amazon.com, Inc.

(Learning Objective 1: Analyzing income and investments) Refer to the **Amazon.com, Inc.**, consolidated financial statements in Appendix A at the end of this book.

1. Amazon.com, Inc.'s consolidated statements of operations do not mention income from continuing operations. Why not?
2. Take the role of an investor, and suppose you are determining the price to pay for a share of Amazon.com, Inc., stock. Assume you are considering three investment capitalization rates that depend on the risk of an investment in Amazon.com: 5%, 6%, and 7%. Compute your estimated value of a share of Amazon.com, Inc., stock using each of the three capitalization rates. Which estimated value would you base your investment strategy on if you rate Amazon.com, Inc., risky? If you consider Amazon.com, Inc., a safe investment? Use basic earnings per share for 2008.
3. Go to Amazon.com's Web site and compare your computed estimates to its actual stock price. Which of your prices is most realistic? (Challenge)

Focus on Analysis: ■ Foot Locker, Inc.

(Learning Objectives 1, 3: Evaluating the quality of earnings, valuing investments, and analyzing stock outstanding) This case is based on the **Foot Locker, Inc.**, consolidated financial statements in Appendix B at the end of this book.

1. Foot Locker, Inc.'s consolidated statements of operations report only one special item. What is it, and what is its amount for 2007?
2. What is your evaluation of the quality of Foot Locker, Inc.'s earnings? State how you formed your opinion.
3. At the end of 2006, how much would you have been willing to pay for one share of Foot Locker, Inc.'s stock if you had rated the investment as high risk? As low risk? Use even-numbered investment capitalization rates in the range of 4%–10% for your analysis, and use basic earnings per share for continuing operations.
4. Go to Foot Locker, Inc.'s Web site and get the current price of a share of its common stock. Which value that you estimated in Requirement 2 is closest to the company's actual stock price? (Challenge)

Group Project

Select a company and research its business. Search the Internet for articles about this company. Obtain its latest available annual report from the company's Web site or from www.sec.gov. Use the link entitled "Search for Company Filings."

❙ Requirements

1. Based on your group's analysis, come to class prepared to instruct the class on six interesting facts about the company that can be found in its financial statements and the related notes. Your group can mention only the obvious, such as net sales or total revenue, net income, total assets, total liabilities, total stockholders' equity, and dividends, in conjunction with other terms. Once you use an obvious item, you may not use that item again.
2. The group should write a paper discussing the facts that it has uncovered. Limit the paper to two double-spaced word-processed pages.

For online homework, exercises, and problems that provide you with immediate feedback, please visit www.myaccountinglab.com.

Quick Check Answers

1. *d*
2. *b*
3. *d* ($5.12/.04)
4. *d* (($60,000)/(.40)) (rounding causes slight differences for computations of other lines)
5. *a*
6. *a*
7. *a*
8. *b*
9. *a*
10. *a*

12

The Statement of Cash Flows

SPOTLIGHT: Google: The Ultimate Answer Machine

What Internet search engine do you use? It's probably Google, the world's largest search engine. Google was created by Larry Page and Sergey Brin when they were students at Stanford University. From small beginnings, Google has grown to become a global technology leader that has helped transform the way people connect with information. The company generates revenue primarily by delivering cost-effective online advertising. Google maintains an index of billions of Web pages, which it makes freely available via its search engine to anyone with an Internet connection. Recently the market value of Google stock surpassed that of Wal-Mart, the world's largest retailer.

The beauty of Google is that it's so easy to use. Access the Internet at www.google.com, and you can simply enter what you want to find in the search box. You get a whole list of helpful Web sites. The world is literally at your fingertips. Google may be the ultimate answer machine, and lately, it has become a cash machine as well! In 2008, its cash flow from operations exceeded its net income by more than $3.6 billion!

Google Inc.
Consolidated Statement of Cash Flows (Adapted; in millions)
Year Ended December 31, 2008

Cash Flows from Operating Activities		
Net income	$ 4,227	
Adjustments to reconcile net income to net cash provided by operating activities:		
Depreciation and amortization	1,500	
Stock-based compensation, net of taxes	961	
Impairment of equity investments	1,095	
Change in assets and liabilities, net of acquired businesses:		
Accounts receivable	(334)	
Other current assets	(147)	
Accounts payable	(212)	
Accrued expenses and other liabilities	339	
Unearned revenue	41	
Income taxes payable	401	
Other, net	(18)	
Net cash provided by operating activities		$ 7,853
Cash Flows from Investing Activities		
Purchases of property and equipment	$ (2,358)	
Purchases of investments	(15,403)	
Sales of investments	15,762	
Acquisitions of other companies	(3,320)	
Net cash used in investing activities		(5,319)
Cash Flows from Financing Activities (net)		87
Other, net		(46)
Net increase (decrease) in cash and cash equivalents		2,575
Cash and cash equivalents at beginning of year		6,082
Cash and cash equivalents at end of year		$ 8,657

In preceding chapters, we covered cash flows as they related to various topics: receivables, plant assets, and so on. In this chapter, we show you how to prepare and use the statement of cash flows. We begin with the statement format used by the vast majority (98.7%) of companies, called the *indirect method*. We end with the alternate format of the statement of cash flows, the *direct method*, used by 1.3% of companies in a recent survey. After working through this chapter, you can analyze the cash flows of actual companies.

This chapter has three distinct sections:

■ Introduction, beginning on this page
■ Preparing the Statement of Cash Flows: Indirect Method, page 706
■ Preparing the Statement of Cash Flows: Direct Method, page 720

The introduction applies to all the cash-flow topics. Professors who wish to cover only the indirect method can assign the first two parts of the chapter. Those interested only in the direct method can proceed from the introduction, which ends on page 706, to the direct method, on page 720.

LEARNING OBJECTIVES

1 **Identify** the purposes of the statement of cash flows

2 **Distinguish** among operating, investing, and financing cash flows

3 **Prepare** a statement of cash flows by the indirect method

4 **Prepare** a statement of cash flows by the direct method

Basic Concepts: The Statement of Cash Flows

The balance sheet reports financial position, and balance sheets from two periods show whether cash increased or decreased. But that doesn't tell *why* the cash balance changed. The income statement reports net income and offers clues about cash, but the income statement doesn't tell *why* cash increased or decreased. We need a third financial statement.

The **statement of cash flows** reports **cash flows**—cash receipts and cash payments—in other words, where cash came from (receipts) and how it was spent (payments). The statement covers a span of time and therefore is dated "Year Ended December 31, 2010" or "Month Ended June 30, 2011." Exhibit 12-1 illustrates the relative timing of the four basic statements.

OBJECTIVE

1 **Identify** the purposes of the statement of cash flows

EXHIBIT 12-1 | **Timing of the Financial Statements**

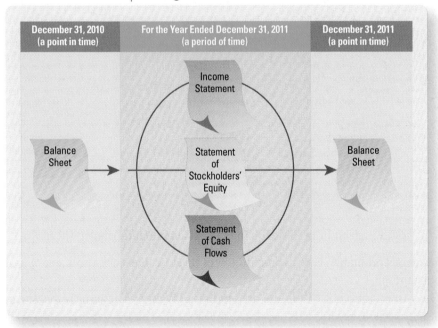

The statement of cash flows serves these purposes:

1. *Predicts future cash flows.* Past cash receipts and payments are reasonably good predictors of future cash flows.
2. *Evaluates management decisions.* Businesses that make wise decisions prosper, and those that make unwise decisions suffer losses. The statement of cash flows reports how managers got cash and how they used cash to run the business.

3. *Determines ability to pay dividends and interest.* Stockholders want dividends on their investments. Creditors demand interest and principal on their loans. The statement of cash flows reports on the ability to make these payments.

4. *Shows the relationship of net income to cash flows.* Usually, high net income leads to an increase in cash, and vice versa. But cash flow can suffer even when net income is high.

On a statement of cash flows, *cash* means more than just cash in the bank. It includes **cash equivalents**, which are highly liquid short-term investments that can be converted into cash immediately. Examples include money-market accounts and investments in U.S. Government securities. Throughout this chapter, the term cash refers to cash and cash equivalents.

How's Your Cash Flow? Telltale Signs of Financial Difficulty

Companies want to earn net income because profit measures success. Without net income, a business sinks. There will be no dividends, and the stock price suffers. High net income attracts investors, but you can't pay bills with net income. That requires cash.

A company needs both net income and strong cash flow. Income and cash flow usually move together because net income generates cash. Sometimes, however, net income and cash flow take different paths. To illustrate, consider Fastech Company:

Fastech Company **Income Statement** Year Ended December 31, 2010	
Sales revenue................	$100,000
Cost of goods sold........	30,000
Operating expenses......	10,000
Net income..................	$ 60,000

Fastech Company **Balance Sheet** December 31, 2010			
Cash.......................	$ 3,000	Total current liabilities............	$ 50,000
Receivables.............	37,000	Long-term liabilities................	20,000
Inventory................	40,000		
Plant assets, net.......	60,000	Stockholders' equity...............	70,000
Total assets.............	$140,000	Total liabilities and equity.......	$140,000

What can we glean from Fastech's income statement and balance sheet?

- Fastech is profitable. Net income is 60% of revenue. Fastech's profitability looks outstanding.
- The current ratio is 1.6, and the debt ratio is only 50%. These measures suggest little trouble in paying bills.
- But Fastech is on the verge of bankruptcy. Can you spot the problem? Can you see what is causing the problem? Three trouble spots leap out to a financial analyst.

1. The cash balance is very low. Three thousand dollars isn't enough cash to pay the bills of a company with sales of $100,000.

2. Fastech isn't selling inventory fast enough. Fastech turned over its inventory only 0.75 times during the year. As we saw in Chapter 6, inventory turnover rates of

3–8 times a year are common. A turnover ratio of 0.75 times means it takes Fastech far too long to sell its inventory, and that delays cash collections.

3. Fastech's days' sales in receivables ratio is 135 days. Very few companies can wait that long to collect from customers.

The takeaway lesson from this discussion is this:

- You need both net income and strong cash flow to succeed in business.

Let's turn now to the different categories of cash flows.

Operating, Investing, and Financing Activities

A business engages in three types of business activities:

- Operating activities
- Investing activities
- Financing activities

OBJECTIVE

2 **Distinguish** among operating, investing, and financing cash flows

Google's statement of cash flows reports cash flows under these three headings, as shown for Google on page 702.

Operating activities create revenues, expenses, gains, and losses—*net income*, which is a product of accrual-basis accounting. The statement of cash flows reports on operating activities. Operating activities are the most important of the three categories because they reflect the core of the organization. *A successful business must generate most of its cash from operating activities.*

Investing activities increase and decrease *long-term assets*, such as computers, land, buildings, equipment, and investments in other companies. Purchases and sales of these assets are investing activities. Investing activities are important, but they are less critical than operating activities.

Financing activities obtain cash from investors and creditors. Issuing stock, borrowing money, buying and selling treasury stock, and paying cash dividends are financing activities. Paying off a loan is another example. Financing cash flows relate to *long-term liabilities* and *owners' equity*. They are the least important of the three categories of cash flows, and that's why they come last. Exhibit 12-2 shows how operating, investing, and financing activities relate to the various parts of the balance sheet.

EXHIBIT 12-2 | **How Operating, Investing, and Financing Cash Flows Affect the Balance Sheet**

Examine Google's statement of cash flows on page 702. Focus on the final line of each section: Operating, Investing, and Financing. Google has very strong cash flows. During 2008, Google's operating activities provided $7.8 billion of cash. Google invested $5.3 billion and received $87 million in financing. These figures show that

- *Operations* are Google's largest source of cash.
- The company is *investing* in the future.
- People are willing to *finance* Google.

Two Formats for Operating Activities

There are two ways to format operating activities on the statement of cash flows:

- **Indirect method**, which reconciles from net income to net cash provided by operating activities. (pp. 706–717)
- **Direct method**, which reports all cash receipts and cash payments from operating activities. (pp. 720–732)

The two methods use different computations, but they produce the same figure for cash from *operating activities*. The two methods do not affect *investing* or *financing activities*. The following table summarizes the differences between the indirect and direct methods:

Indirect Method		Direct Method	
Net income................................	$600	Collections from customers..........	$2,000
Adjustments:		*Deductions:*	
Depreciation, etc.	300	Payments to suppliers, etc.	(1,100)
Net cash provided by		Net cash provided by	
operating activities	$900	operating activities	$ 900

same

We begin with the indirect method because 98 out of 100 companies use it.

PREPARING THE STATEMENT OF CASH FLOWS: INDIRECT METHOD

OBJECTIVE

3 **Prepare** a statement of cash flows by the indirect method

To illustrate the statement of cash flows, we use **The Roadster Factory, Inc. (TRF)**, a dealer in auto parts for sports cars. Proceed as follows to prepare the statement of cash flows by using the indirect method:

Step 1   Lay out the template as shown in Part 1 of Exhibit 12-3. The exhibit is comprehensive. The diagram in Part 2 (p. 708) gives a visual picture of the statement.

Step 2   Use the balance sheet to determine the increase or decrease in cash during the period. The change in cash is the "check figure" for the statement of cash flows. Exhibit 12-4 (p. 709) gives The Roadster

Factory's (TRF's) comparative balance sheet, with cash highlighted. TRF's cash decreased by $8,000 during 2011. *Why* did cash decrease? The statement of cash flows will provide the answer.

Step 3 From the income statement, take net income, depreciation, depletion, and amortization expense, and any gains or losses on the sale of long-term assets. Print these items on the statement of cash flows. Exhibit 12-5 (p. 709) gives TRF's income statement, with relevant items highlighted.

Step 4 Use the income statement and balance sheet data to prepare the statement of cash flows. The statement of cash flows is complete only after you have explained the year-to-year changes in all the balance sheet accounts.

EXHIBIT 12-3 | **Part 1: Template of the Statement of Cash Flows: Indirect Method**

The Roadster Factory, Inc. (TRF)
Statement of Cash Flows
Year Ended December 31, 2011

Cash flows from operating activities
  Net income
    Adjustments to reconcile net income to net cash provided by operating activities:
    + Depreciation/depletion/amortization expense
    + Loss on sale of long-term assets
    − Gain on sale of long-term assets
    − Increases in current assets other than cash
    + Decreases in current assets other than cash
    + Increases in current liabilities
    − Decreases in current liabilities
       Net cash provided by (used for) operating activities
Cash flows from investing activities:
  + Sales of long-term assets (investments, land, building, equipment, and so on)
  − Purchases of long-term assets
  + Collections of notes receivable
  − Loans to others
     Net cash provided by (used for) investing activities
Cash flows from financing activities:
  + Issuance of stock
  + Sale of treasury stock
  − Purchase of treasury stock
  + Borrowing (issuance of notes or bonds payable)
  − Payment of notes or bonds payable
  − Payment of dividends
     Net cash provided by (used for) financing activities
Net increase (decrease) in cash during the year
  + Cash at December 31, 2010
  = Cash at December 31, 2011

Go to "Cash Flows from Operating Activities" on page 710.

EXHIBIT 12-3 | **Part 2: Positive and Negative Items on the Statement of Cash Flows: Indirect Method**

Positive Items	Business Activity	Negative Items

Operating Activities

Positive Items:
- Net Income
- Depreciation/amortization
- Loss on sale of long-term assets
- Decreases in current assets other than cash
- Increases in current liabilities

Negative Items:
- Net loss
- Gain on sale of long-term assets
- Increases in current assets other than cash
- Decreases in current liabilities

Investing Activities

CASH RECEIPTS
- Sale of plant assets
- Sale of investments that are not cash equivalents
- Collections of loans receivable

CASH PAYMENTS
- Acquisition of plant assets
- Purchase of investments that are not cash equivalents
- Making loans to others

Financing Activities

CASH RECEIPTS
- Issuing stock
- Selling treasury stock
- Borrowing money

CASH PAYMENTS
- Payment of dividends
- Purchase of treasury stock
- Payment of principal amounts of debts

EXHIBIT 12-4 | **Comparative Balance Sheet**

The Roadster Factory, Inc. (TRF)
Comparative Balance Sheets
December 31, 2011 and 2010

(In thousands)	2011	2010	Increase (Decrease)	
Assets				
Current:				
Cash..	$ 34	$ 42	$ (8)	⎤
Accounts receivable................	96	81	15	⎥ Changes in current assets—Operating
Inventory	35	38	(3)	⎥
Prepaid expenses.....................	8	7	1	⎦
Notes receivable..........................	21	—	21	⎤ Changes in noncurrent assets—Investing
Plant assets, net of depreciation...	343	219	124	⎦
Total	$537	$387	$150	
Liabilities				
Current:				
Accounts payable....................	$ 91	$ 57	$ 34	⎤
Salary and wage payable.........	4	6	(2)	⎥ Changes in current liabilities—Operating
Accrued liabilities...................	1	3	(2)	⎦
Long-term debt	160	77	83	⎤ Changes in long-term liabilities and paid-in capital accounts—Financing
Stockholders' Equity				⎥
Common stock...........................	162	158	4	⎦
Retained earnings.......................	119	86	33	} Changes due to net income—Operating Change due to dividends—Financing
Total	$537	$387	$150	

EXHIBIT 12-5 | **Income Statement**

The Roadster Factory, Inc. (TRF)
Income Statement
Year Ended December 31, 2011

	(In thousands)	
Revenues and gains:		
Sales revenue...................................	$303	
Interest revenue.............................	2	
Gain on sale of plant assets............	8	
Total revenues and gains............		$313
Expenses:		
Cost of goods sold	$150	
Salary and wage expense................	56	
Depreciation expense	18	
Other operating expense	17	
Income tax expense........................	15	
Interest expense..............................	7	
Total expenses.............................		263
Net income...		$ 50

EXHIBIT 12-6 | **Statement of Cash Flows—Operating Activities by the Indirect Method**

The Roadster Factory, Inc. (TRF) Statement of Cash Flows (Indirect Method) For the Year Ended December 31, 2011		
		(In thousands)
Cash flows from operating activities:		
Net income		$50
Adjustments to reconcile net income to net cash provided by operating activities:		
Ⓐ* Depreciation	$ 18	
Ⓑ Gain on sale of plant assets	(8)	
Increase in accounts receivable.................................	(15)	
Decrease in inventory...	3	
Ⓒ Increase in prepaid expenses	(1)	
Increase in accounts payable	34	
Decrease in salary and wage payable.........................	(2)	
Decrease in accrued liabilities....................................	(2)	27
Net cash provided by operating activities.............		$77

*Adjustments A, B, and C are explained in the following section.

Cash Flows from Operating Activities

Operating activities are related to the transactions that make up net income.[1]

The operating section begins with the net income, taken from the income statement, (Exhibit 12-5) and is followed by "Adjustments to reconcile net income to net cash provided by operating activities." Let's discuss these adjustments.

Ⓐ **Depreciation, Depletion, and Amortization Expenses.** These expenses are added back to net income to convert net income to cash flow. Let's see why. Depreciation is recorded as follows:

Depreciation Expense	18,000	
Accumulated Depreciation		18,000

Depreciation has no effect on cash. But depreciation, like all other expenses, decreases net income. Therefore, to convert net income to cash flows, we add depreciation back to net income. The add-back cancels the earlier deduction.

---

[1] The authors thank Professor Alfonso Oddo for suggesting this summary.

Example: Suppose you had only two transactions, a $1,000 cash sale and depreciation expense of $300. Cash flow from operations is $1,000, and net income is $700 ($1,000 – $300). To go from net income ($700) to cash flow ($1,000), we add back the depreciation ($300). Depletion and amortization are treated like depreciation.

ⓑ **Gains and Losses on the Sale of Assets.** Sales of long-term assets are *investing* activities and there's often a gain or loss on the sale. On the statement of cash flows, the gain or loss is an adjustment to net income. Exhibit 12-6 includes an adjustment for a gain. During 2011, The Roadster Factory sold equipment for $62,000. The book value was $54,000, so there was a gain of $8,000.

The $62,000 cash received from the sale is an investing activity (Exhibit 12-7), and the $62,000 includes the $8,000 gain. Net income also includes the gain, so we must subtract the gain from net cash provided by operations, so that it may be added to the net book value of equipment removed in the investing section ($54,000 + $8,000 = $62,000). (We explain investing activities in the next section.)

A loss on the sale of plant assets also creates an adjustment in the operating section. Since the cash received from the sale of a long-term asset at a loss is less than the asset's book value, the amount of cash received reflects the loss. Losses are deducted from net income. Therefore, in order to show the amount of cash received from the sale of the asset in the investments section, losses are *added back* to net income to compute cash flow from operations.

ⓒ **Changes in the Current Asset and Current Liability Accounts.** Most current assets and current liabilities result from operating activities. For example, accounts receivable result from sales, inventory relates to cost of goods sold, and so on. Changes in the current accounts are adjustments to net income on the cash-flow statement. The reasoning follows:

1. **An increase in another current asset decreases cash.** It takes cash to acquire assets. Suppose you make a sale on account. Accounts receivable are increased, but cash isn't affected yet. Exhibit 12-4 (p. 709) reports that during 2011, The Roadster Factory's Accounts Receivable increased by $15,000. To compute cash flow from operations, we must subtract the $15,000 increase in Accounts Receivable, as shown in Exhibit 12-6. The reason is this: We have *not* collected this $15,000 in cash. Similar logic applies to all the other current assets. If they increase, cash decreases.

2. **A decrease in another current asset increases cash.** Suppose TRF's Accounts Receivable balance decreased by $4,000. Cash receipts caused Accounts Receivable to decrease, so we add decreases in Accounts Receivable and the other current assets to net income.

3. **A decrease in a current liability decreases cash.** Payment of a current liability decreases both cash and the liability, so we subtract decreases in current liabilities from net income. In Exhibit 12-6, the $2,000 decrease in Accrued Liabilities is *subtracted* to compute net cash provided by operations.

4. **An increase in a current liability increases cash.** The Roadster Factory's Accounts Payable increased. That can occur only if cash was not spent to pay this debt. Cash payments are therefore less than expenses and TRF has more cash on hand. Thus, increases in current liabilities increase cash.

EXHIBIT 12-7 | Statement of Cash Flows—Indirect Method

The Roadster Factory, Inc. (TRF)
Statement of Cash Flows (Indirect Method)
For the Year Ended December 31, 2011

		(In thousands)

Cash flows from operating activities:

Net income			$ 50
Adjustments to reconcile net income to net cash provided by operating activities:			
Ⓐ Depreciation		$ 18	
Ⓑ Gain on sale of plant assets		(8)	
Increase in accounts receivable		(15)	
Decrease in inventory		3	
Ⓒ Increase in prepaid expenses		(1)	
Increase in accounts payable		34	
Decrease in salary and wage payable		(2)	
Decrease in accrued liabilities		(2)	27
Net cash provided by operating activities			77

Cash flows from investing activities:

Acquisition of plant assets		$(196)	
Loan to another company		(21)	
Proceeds from sale of plant assets		62	
Net cash used for investing activities			(155)

Cash flows from financing activities:

Proceeds from issuance of long-term debt		$ 94	
Proceeds from issuance of common stock		4	
Payment of long-term debt		(11)	
Payment of dividends		(17)	
Net cash provided by financing activities			70
Net (decrease) in cash			$ (8)
Cash balance, December 31, 2010			42
Cash balance, December 31, 2011			$ 34

Evaluating Cash Flows from Operating Activities. Let's step back and evaluate The Roadster Factory's operating cash flows during 2011. TRF's operations provided net cash flow of $77,000. This amount exceeds net income, which is one sign of a healthy company. Now let's examine TRF's investing and financing activities, as reported in Exhibit 12-7.

Cash Flows from Investing Activities

> Investing activities affect long-term assets, such as Plant Assets, Investments, and Notes Receivable.

Most of the data come from the balance sheet.

Computing Purchases and Sales of Plant Assets. Companies keep a separate account for each plant asset. But for computing cash flows, it is helpful to combine all the plant assets into a single summary account. Also, we subtract accumulated depreciation and use the net figure. It's easier to work with a single plant asset account.

To illustrate, observe that The Roadster Factory's

- balance sheet reports beginning plant assets, net of accumulated depreciation, of $219,000. The ending balance is $343,000 (Exhibit 12-4).
- income statement shows depreciation expense of $18,000 and an $8,000 gain on sale of plant assets (Exhibit 12-5).

TRF's purchases of plant assets total $196,000 (take this amount as given; see Exhibit 12-7). How much, then, are the proceeds from the sale of plant assets? First, we must determine the book value of the plant assets sold, as follows:

Plant Assets, Net

Beginning balance	+	Acquisitions	−	Depreciation	−	Book value of assets sold	=	Ending balance
$219,000	+	$196,000	−	$18,000		−X	=	$343,000
						−X	=	$343,000 − $219,000 − $196,000 + $18,000
						X	=	$54,000

The sale proceeds are $62,000, determined as follows:

Sale proceeds	=	Book value of assets sold	+	Gain	−	Loss
X	=	$54,000	+	$8,000	−	$0
X	=	$62,000				

Trace the sale proceeds of $62,000 to the statement of cash flows in Exhibit 12-7. The Plant Assets T-account provides another look at the computation of the book value of the assets sold.

Plant Assets, Net

Beginning balance	219,000	Depreciation	18,000
Acquisitions	196,000	Book value of assets sold	54,000
Ending balance	343,000		

If the sale resulted in a loss of $3,000, the sale proceeds would be $51,000 ($54,000 − $3,000), and the statement of cash flows would report $51,000 as a cash receipt from this investing activity.

Computing Purchases and Sales of Investments, and Loans and Collections.

The cash amounts of investment transactions can be computed in the manner illustrated for plant assets. Investments are easier because there is no depreciation, as shown in the following equation:

Investments (amounts assumed for illustration only)

Beginning balance	+	Purchases	−	Book value of investments sold	=	Ending balance
$100,000	+	$50,000		−X	=	$140,000
				−X	=	$140,000 − $100,000 − $50,000
				X	=	$10,000

The Investments T-account provides another look (amounts assumed).

Investments			
Beginning balance	100		
Purchases	50	Book value of investments sold	10
Ending balance	140		

The Roadster Factory has a long-term receivable, and the cash flows from loan transactions on notes receivable can be determined as follows (data from Exhibit 12-4):

Notes Receivable								
Beginning balance	+	New loans made	–	Collections	=	Ending balance		
$0	+	X		–0	=	$21,000		
		X			=	$21,000		

Notes Receivable			
Beginning balance	0		
New loans made	21	Collections	0
Ending balance	21		

Exhibit 12-8 summarizes the cash flows from investing activities, highlighted in color.

EXHIBIT 12-8 | **Computing Cash Flows from Investing Activities**

Receipts

From sale of plant assets	Beginning plant assets, net	+	Acquisition cost	–	Depreciation	–	Book value of assets sold	=	Ending plant assets, net
	Cash received	=	Book value of assets sold	+ or –	Gain on sale / Loss on sale				
From sale of investments	Beginning investments	+	Purchase cost of investments	–	Cost of investments sold	=	Ending investments		
	Cash received	=	Cost of investments sold	+ or –	Gain on sale / Loss on sale				
From collection of notes receivable	Beginning notes receivable	+	New loans made	–	Collections	=	Ending notes receivable		

Payments

For acquisition of plant assets	Beginning plant assets, net	+	Acquisition cost	–	Depreciation	–	Book value of assets sold	=	Ending plant assets, net
For purchase of investments	Beginning investments	+	Purchase cost of investments	–	Cost of investments sold	=	Ending investments		
For new loans made	Beginning notes receivable	+	New loans made	–	Collections	=	Ending notes receivable		

Cash Flows from Financing Activities

Financing activities affect liabilities and stockholders' equity, such as Notes Payable, Bonds Payable, Long-Term Debt, Common Stock, Paid-in Capital in Excess of Par, and Retained Earnings. Most of the data come from the balance sheet.

Computing Issuances and Payments of Long-Term Debt. The beginning and ending balances of Long-Term Debt, Notes Payable, or Bonds Payable come from the balance sheet. If either new issuances or payments are known, the other amount can be computed. The Roadster Factory's new debt issuances total $94,000 (take this amount as given; Exhibit 12-7). Debt payments are computed from the Long-Term Debt account (see Exhibit 12-4).

Long-Term Debt (Notes Payable, Bonds Payable)

Beginning balance	+	Issuance of new debt	−	Payments of debt	=	Ending balance
$77,000	+	$94,000		−X	=	$160,000
				−X	=	$160,000 − $77,000 − $94,000
				X	=	$11,000

Long-Term Debt

		Beginning balance	77,000
Payments	11,000	Issuance of new debt	94,000
		Ending balance	160,000

Computing Issuances of Stock and Purchases of Treasury Stock. These cash flows can be determined from the stock accounts. For example, cash received from issuing common stock is computed from Common Stock and Capital in Excess of Par. We use a single summary Common Stock account as we do for plant assets. The Roadster Factory data are

Common Stock

Beginning balance	+	Issuance of new stock	=	Ending balance
$158,000	+	$4,000	=	$162,000

Common Stock

	Beginning balance	158,000
	Issuance of new stock	4,000
	Ending balance	162,000

The Roadster Factory has no treasury stock, but cash flows from purchasing treasury stock can be computed as follows (using assumed amounts):

Treasury Stock (amounts assumed for illustration only)						
Beginning balance	+	Purchase of treasury stock	=	Ending balance		
$16,000	+	$3,000	=	$19,000		

Treasury Stock	
Beginning balance	16,000
Purchase of treasury stock	3,000
Ending balance	19,000

Computing Dividend Declarations and Payments. If dividend declarations and payments are not given elsewhere, they can be computed. For The Roadster Factory, this computation is

Retained Earnings						
Beginning balance	+	Net income	−	Dividend declarations and payments	=	Ending balance
$86,000	+	$50,000		−X	=	$119,000
				−X	=	$119,000 − $86,000 − $50,000
				X	=	$17,000

The T-account also shows the dividend computation.

Retained Earnings			
Dividend declarations and payments	17,000	Beginning balance	86,000
		Net income	50,000
		Ending balance	119,000

Exhibit 12-9 summarizes the cash flows from financing activities, highlighted in color.

EXHIBIT 12-9 | Computing Cash Flows from Financing Activities

Receipts

From borrowing—issuance of long-term debt (notes payable)	Beginning long-term debt (notes payable) + Cash received from issuance of long-term debt − Payment of debt = Ending long-term debt (notes payable)
From issuance of stock	Beginning stock + Cash received from issuance of new stock = Ending stock

Payments

Of long-term debt	Beginning long-term debt (notes payable) + Cash received from issuance of long-term debt − Payment of debt = Ending long-term debt (notes payable)
To purchase treasury stock	Beginning treasury stock + Purchase cost of treasury stock = Ending treasury stock
Of dividends	Beginning retained earnings + Net income − Dividend declarations and payments = Ending retained earnings

STOP & THINK...

Classify each of the following as an operating activity, an investing activity, or a financing activity as reported on the statement of cash flows prepared by the *indirect* method.

a. Issuance of stock

b. Borrowing

c. Sales revenue

d. Payment of dividends

e. Purchase of land

f. Purchase of treasury stock

g. Paying bonds payable

h. Interest expense

i. Sale of equipment

j. Cost of goods sold

k. Purchase of another company

l. Making a loan

Answers:

a. Financing

b. Financing

c. Operating

d. Financing

e. Investing

f. Financing

g. Financing

h. Operating

i. Investing

j. Operating

k. Investing

l. Investing

Noncash Investing and Financing Activities

Companies make investments that do not require cash. They also obtain financing other than cash. Our examples have included none of these transactions. Now suppose The Roadster Factory issued common stock valued at $300,000 to acquire a warehouse. TRF would journalize this transaction as follows:

Warehouse Building	300,000	
Common Stock		300,000

This transaction would not be reported as a cash payment because TRF paid no cash. But the investment in the warehouse and the issuance of stock are important. These noncash investing and financing activities can be reported in a separate schedule under the statement of cash flows. Exhibit 12-10 illustrates noncash investing and financing activities (all amounts are assumed).

EXHIBIT 12-10 | **Noncash Investing and Financing Activities (All Amounts Assumed)**

	Thousands
Noncash Investing and Financing Activities:	
Acquisition of building by issuing common stock	$300
Acquisition of land by issuing note payable	70
Payment of long-term debt by issuing common stock	100
Total noncash investing and financing activities	$470

Now let's apply what you've learned about the statement of cash flows prepared by the indirect method.

MID-CHAPTER SUMMARY PROBLEM

Lucas Corporation reported the following income statement and comparative balance sheets, along with transaction data for 2011:

Lucas Corporation
Income Statement
Year Ended December 31, 2011

Sales revenue		$662,000
Cost of goods sold		560,000
Gross profit		102,000
Operating expenses		
Salary expenses	$46,000	
Depreciation expense— equipment	7,000	
Amortization expense— patent	3,000	
Rent expense	2,000	
Total operating expenses		58,000
Income from operations		44,000
Other items:		
Loss on sale of equipment		(2,000)
Income before income tax		42,000
Income tax expense		16,000
Net income		$ 26,000

Lucas Corporation
Comparative Balance Sheets
December 31, 2011 and 2010

Assets	2011	2010	Liabilities	2011	2010
Current:			Current:		
Cash and equivalents	$ 19,000	$ 3,000	Accounts payable	$ 35,000	$ 26,000
Accounts receivable	22,000	23,000	Accrued liabilities	7,000	9,000
Inventories	34,000	31,000	Income tax payable	10,000	10,000
Prepaid expenses	1,000	3,000	Total current liabilities	52,000	45,000
Total current assets	76,000	60,000	Long-term note payable	44,000	—
Long-term investments	18,000	10,000	Bonds payable	40,000	53,000
Equipment, net	67,000	52,000	**Owners' Equity**		
Patent, net	44,000	10,000	Common stock	52,000	20,000
			Retained earnings	27,000	19,000
			Less: Treasury stock	(10,000)	(5,000)
Total assets	$205,000	$132,000	Total liabilities and equity	$205,000	$132,000

Transaction Data for 2011:

Purchase of equipment	$ 98,000	Issuance of long-term note payable to purchase patent	$ 37,000
Payment of cash dividends	18,000		
Issuance of common stock to retire bonds payable	13,000	Issuance of long-term note payable to borrow cash	7,000
Purchase of long-term investment	8,000	Issuance of common stock for cash	19,000
Purchase of treasury stock	5,000	Sale of equipment (book value, 76,000)	74,000

▮ Requirement

1. Prepare Lucas Corporation's statement of cash flows (indirect method) for the year ended December 31, 2011. Follow the four steps outlined below. For Step 4, prepare a T-account to show the transaction activity in each long-term balance sheet account. For each plant asset, use a single account, net of accumulated depreciation (for example: Equipment, Net).

Step 1 Lay out the template of the statement of cash flows.

Step 2 From the comparative balance sheet, determine the increase in cash during the year, $16,000.

Step 3 From the income statement, take net income, depreciation, amortization, and the loss on sale of equipment to the statement of cash flows.

Step 4 Complete the statement of cash flows. Account for the year-to-year change in each balance sheet account.

Answer

Lucas Corporation
Statement of Cash Flows
Year Ended December 31, 2011

Cash flows from operating activities:		
Net income		$ 26,000
Adjustments to reconcile net income to		
net cash provided by operating activities:		
Depreciation	$ 7,000	
Amortization..	3,000	
Loss on sale of equipment	2,000	
Decrease in accounts receivable.................................	1,000	
Increase in inventories..	(3,000)	
Decrease in prepaid expenses	2,000	
Increase in accounts payable	9,000	
Decrease in accrued liabilities.....................................	(2,000)	19,000
Net cash provided by operating activities.............		45,000
Cash flows from investing activities:		
Purchase of equipment	$(98,000)	
Sale of equipment...	74,000	
Purchase of long-term investment	(8,000)	
Net cash used for investing activities...................		(32,000)
Cash flows from financing activities:		
Issuance of common stock	$ 19,000	
Payment of cash dividends	(18,000)	
Issuance of long-term note payable	7,000	
Purchase of treasury stock..	(5,000)	
Net cash provided by financing activities.............		3,000
Net increase in cash..		**16,000**
Cash balance, December 31, 2010		3,000
Cash balance, December 31, 2011		$ 19,000
Noncash investing and financing activities:		
Issuance of long-term note payable to purchase patent...		$ 37,000
Issuance of common stock to retire bonds payable.........		13,000
Total noncash investing and financing activities.........		$ 50,000

Long-Term Investments	
Bal 10,000	
8,000	
Bal 18,000	

Equipment, Net	
Bal 52,000	
98,000	76,000
	7,000
Bal 67,000	

Patent, Net	
Bal 10,000	
37,000	3,000
Bal 44,000	

Long-Term Note Payable	
	Bal 0
	37,000
	7,000
	Bal 44,000

Bonds Payable	
	Bal 53,000
13,000	
	Bal 40,000

Common Stock	
	Bal 20,000
	13,000
	19,000
	Bal 52,000

Retained Earnings	
	Bal 19,000
18,000	26,000
	Bal 27,000

Treasury Stock	
Bal 5,000	
5,000	
Bal 10,000	

PREPARING THE STATEMENT OF CASH FLOWS: DIRECT METHOD

OBJECTIVE

4 **Prepare** a statement of cash flows by the direct method

The Financial Accounting Standards Board (FASB) prefers the direct method of reporting operating cash flows because it provides clearer information about the sources and uses of cash. But only about 1% of companies use this method because it requires more computations than the indirect method. Investing and financing cash flows are unaffected by the operating cash flows.

To illustrate the statement of cash flows, we use The Roadster Factory, Inc. (TRF), a dealer in auto parts for sports cars. To prepare the statement of cash flows by the direct method, proceed as follows:

Step 1   Lay out the template of the statement of cash flows by the direct method, as shown in Part 1 of Exhibit 12-11. Part 2 (p. 722) gives a visual presentation of the statement.

Step 2 Use the balance sheet to determine the increase or decrease in cash during the period. The change in cash is the "check figure" for the statement of cash flows. The Roadster Factory's comparative balance sheet shows that cash decreased by $8,000 during 2011 (Exhibit 12-4, p. 709). *Why* did cash fall during 2011? The statement of cash flows explains.

EXHIBIT 12-11 | **Part 1: Template of the Statement of Cash Flows—Direct Method**

The Roadster Factory, Inc. (TRF)
Statement of Cash Flows
Year Ended December 31, 2011

Cash flows from operating activities:

  Receipts:

    Collections from customers

    Interest received on notes receivable

    Dividends received on investments in stock

      Total cash receipts

  Payments:

    To suppliers

    To employees

    For interest

    For income tax

      Total cash payments

  Net cash provided by (used for) operating activities

Cash flows from investing activities:

    Sales of long-term assets (investments, land, building, equipment, and so on)

  − Purchases of long-term assets

  + Collections of notes receivable

  − Loans to others

  Net cash provided by (used for) investing activities

Cash flows from financing activities:

    Issuance of stock

  + Sale of treasury stock

  − Purchase of treasury stock

  + Borrowing (issuance of notes or bonds payable)

  − Payment of notes or bonds payable

  − Payment of dividends

  Net cash provided by (used for) financing activities

Net increase (decrease) in cash during the year

  + Cash at December 31, 2010

  = Cash at December 31, 2011

EXHIBIT 12-11 | **Part 2: Cash Receipts and Cash Payments on the Statement of Cash Flows—Direct Method**

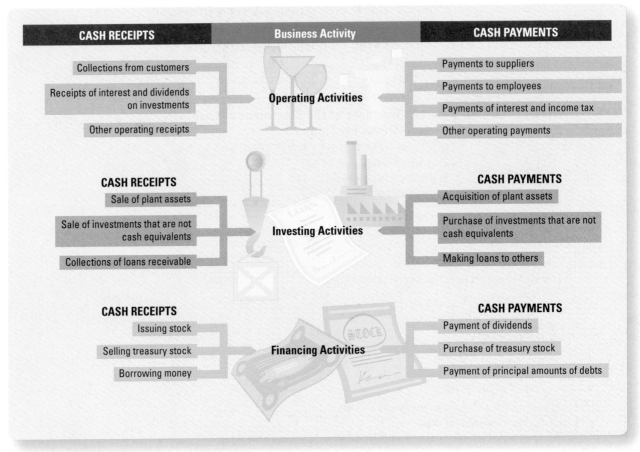

Step 3 Use the available data to prepare the statement of cash flows. The Roadster Factory's transaction data appear in Exhibit 12-12. These transactions affected both the income statement (Exhibit 12-5, p. 709) and the statement of cash flows. Some transactions affect one statement and some affect the other. For example, sales (item 1) are reported on the income statement. Cash collections (item 2) go on the statement of cash flows. Other transactions, such as interest expense and payments (item 11) affect both statements. *The statement of cash flows reports only those transactions with cash effects* (those with an asterisk in Exhibit 12-12). Exhibit 12-13 (on p. 724) gives The Roadster Factory's statement of cash flows for 2011.

Cash Flows from Operating Activities

Operating cash flows are listed first because they are the most important. Exhibit 12-13 shows that The Roadster Factory is sound; operating activities were the largest source of cash.

Cash Collections from Customers   Both cash sales and collections of accounts receivable are reported on the statement of cash flows as "Collections from customers . . . $288,000" in Exhibit 12-13.

Cash Receipts of Interest and Dividends The income statement reports interest revenue and dividend revenue. Only the cash receipts of interest and dividends appear on the statement of cash flows—$2,000 of interest received in Exhibit 12-13.

EXHIBIT 12-12 | Summary of The Roadster Factory's 2011 Transactions

Operating Activities
1. Sales on credit, $303,000
*2. Collections from customers, $288,000
*3. Interest revenue and receipts, $2,000
4. Cost of goods sold, $150,000
5. Purchases of inventory on credit, $147,000
*6. Payments to suppliers, $133,000
7. Salary and wage expense, $56,000
*8. Payments of salary and wages, $58,000
9. Depreciation expense, $18,000
10. Other operating expense, $17,000
*11. Income tax expense and payments, $15,000
*12. Interest expense and payments, $7,000

Investing Activities
*13. Cash payments to acquire plant assets, $196,000
*14. Loan to another company, $21,000
*15. Proceeds from sale of plant assets, $62,000, including $8,000 gain

Financing Activities
*16. Proceeds from issuance of long-term debt, $94,000
*17. Proceeds from issuance of common stock, $4,000
*18. Payment of long-term debt, $11,000
*19. Declaration and payment of cash dividends, $17,000

*Indicates a cash flow to be reported on the statement of cash flows.
Note: Income statement data are taken from Exhibit 12-16, page 727.

Payments to Suppliers Payments to suppliers include all expenditures for inventory and operating expenses except employee pay, interest, and income taxes. *Suppliers* are those entities that provide inventory and essential services. For example, a clothing store's suppliers may include **Tommy Hilfiger, Adidas,** and **Ralph Lauren**. Other suppliers provide advertising, utilities, and office supplies. Exhibit 12-13 shows that The Roadster Factory paid suppliers $133,000.

Payments to Employees This category includes salaries, wages, and other forms of employee pay. Accrued amounts are excluded because they have not yet been paid. The statement of cash flows reports only the cash payments of $58,000.

Payments for Interest Expense and Income Tax Expense Interest and income tax payments are reported separately. The Roadster Factory paid cash for all its interest and income taxes. Therefore, the same amount goes on the income statement and the statement of cash flows. These payments are operating cash flows because the interest and income tax are expenses.

EXHIBIT 12-13 | **Statement of Cash Flows— Direct Method**

The Roadster Factory, Inc. (TRF)
Statement of Cash Flows (Direct Method)
For Year Ended December 31, 2011

	(In thousands)	
Cash flows from operating activities:		
Receipts:		
Collections from customers	$ 288	
Interest received	2	
Total cash receipts		$ 290
Payments:		
To suppliers	$(133)	
To employees	(58)	
For income tax	(15)	
For interest	(7)	
Total cash payments		(213)
Net cash provided by operating activities		77
Cash flows from investing activities:		
Acquisition of plant assets	$(196)	
Loans to another company	(21)	
Proceeds from sale of plant assets	62	
Net cash used for investing activities		(155)
Cash flows from financing activities:		
Proceeds from issuance of long-term debt	$ 94	
Proceeds from issuance of common stock	4	
Payment of long-term debt	(11)	
Payment of dividends	(17)	
Net cash provided by financing activities		70
Net (decrease) in cash		(8)
Cash balance, December 31, 2010		42
Cash balance, December 31, 2011		$ 34

Depreciation, Depletion, and Amortization Expense

These expenses are *not* listed on the direct-method statement of cash flows because they do not affect cash.

Cash Flows from Investing Activities

Investing is critical because a company's investments affect the future. Large purchases of plant assets signal expansion. Meager investing activity means the business is not growing.

Purchasing Plant Assets and Investments and Making Loans to Other Companies. These cash payments acquire long-term assets. The Roadster Factory's first investing activity in Exhibit 12-13 is the purchase of plant assets ($196,000). TRF also made a $21,000 loan and thus got a note receivable.

Proceeds from Selling Plant Assets and Investments and from Collecting Notes Receivable. These cash receipts are also investing activities. The sale of the plant assets needs explanation. The Roadster Factory received $62,000 cash from the sale of plant assets, and there was an $8,000 gain on this transaction. What is the appropriate amount to show on the cash-flow statement? It is $62,000, the cash received from the sale, not the $8,000 gain.

Investors are often critical of a company that sells large amounts of its plant assets. That may signal an emergency. For example, problems in the airline industry have caused some companies to sell airplanes to generate cash.

Cash Flows from Financing Activities

Cash flows from financing activities include the following:

Proceeds from Issuance of Stock and Debt (Notes and Bonds Payable). Issuing stock and borrowing money are two ways to finance a company. In Exhibit 12-13, The Roadster Factory received $4,000 when it issued common stock. TRF also received $94,000 cash when it issued long-term debt (such as a note payable) to borrow money.

Payment of Debt and Purchasing the Company's Own Stock. Paying debt (notes payable) is the opposite of borrowing. TRF reports long-term debt payments of $11,000. The purchase of treasury stock is another example of a use of cash.

Payment of Cash Dividends. Paying cash dividends is a financing activity, as shown by The Roadster Factory's $17,000 payment in Exhibit 12-13. A *stock* dividend has no effect on Cash and is *not* reported on the cash-flow statement.

Noncash Investing and Financing Activities

Companies make investments that do not require cash. They also obtain financing other than cash. Our examples thus far have included none of these transactions. Now suppose that The Roadster Factory issued common stock valued at $300,000 to acquire a warehouse. TRF would journalize this transaction as follows:

Warehouse Building	300,000	
Common Stock		300,000

This transaction would not be reported as a cash payment because TRF paid no cash. But the investment in the warehouse and the issuance of stock are important.

These noncash investing and financing activities can be reported in a separate schedule under the statement of cash flows. Exhibit 12-14 illustrates noncash investing and financing activities (all amounts are assumed).

EXHIBIT 12-14 | **Noncash Investing and Financing Activities (All Amounts Assumed)**

	Thousands
Noncash Investing and Financing Activities:	
Acquisition of building by issuing common stock	$300
Acquisition of land by issuing note payable	70
Payment of long-term debt by issuing common stock	100
Total noncash investing and financing activities	$470

STOP & THINK...

Classify each of the following as an operating activity, an investing activity, or a financing activity. Also identify those items that are not reported on the statement of cash flows prepared by the *direct* method.

a. Net income
b. Payment of dividends
c. Borrowing
d. Payment of cash to suppliers
e. Making a loan
f. Sale of treasury stock
g. Depreciation expense
h. Purchase of equipment

i. Issuance of stock
j. Purchase of another company
k. Payment of a note payable
l. Payment of income taxes
m. Collections from customers
n. Accrual of interest revenue
o. Expiration of prepaid expense
p. Receipt of cash dividends

Answers:

a. Not reported
b. Financing
c. Financing
d. Operating

e. Investing
f. Financing
g. Not reported
h. Investing

i. Financing
j. Investing
k. Financing
l. Operating

m. Operating
n. Not reported
o. Not reported
p. Operating

Now let's see how to compute the operating cash flows by the direct method.

Computing Operating Cash Flows by the Direct Method

To compute operating cash flows by the direct method, we use the income statement and the *changes* in the balance sheet accounts. Exhibit 12-15 diagrams the process. Exhibit 12-16 is The Roadster Factory's income statement, and Exhibit 12-17 is the comparative balance sheet.

EXHIBIT 12-15 | Direct Method of Computing Cash Flows from Operating Activities

RECEIPTS / PAYMENTS	Income Statement Account	Change in Related Balance Sheet Account	
RECEIPTS:			
From customers	Sales Revenue	+ Decrease in Accounts Receivable − Increase in Accounts Receivable	
Of interest	Interest Revenue	+ Decrease in Interest Receivable − Increase in Interest Receivable	
PAYMENTS:			
To suppliers	Cost of Goods Sold	+ Increase in Inventory − Decrease in Inventory	+ Decrease in Accounts Payable − Increase in Accounts Payable
	Operating Expense	+ Increase in Prepaids − Decrease in Prepaids	+ Decrease in Accrued Liabilities − Increase in Accrued Liabilities
To employees	Salary (Wage) Expense	+ Decrease in Salary (Wage) Payable − Increase in Salary (Wage) Payable	
For interest	Interest Expense	+ Decrease in Interest Payable − Increase in Interest Payable	
For income tax	Income Tax Expense	+ Decrease in Income Tax Payable − Increase in Income Tax Payable	

*We thank Professor Barbara Gerrity for suggesting this exhibit.

EXHIBIT 12-16 | Income Statement

The Roadster Factory, Inc. (TRF)
Income Statement
Year Ended December 31, 2011

	(In thousands)	
Revenues and gains:		
Sales revenue	$303	
Interest revenue	2	
Gain on sale of plant assets	8	
Total revenues and gains		$313
Expenses:		
Cost of goods sold	$150	
Salary and wage expense	56	
Depreciation expense	18	
Other operating expense	17	
Income tax expense	15	
Interest expense	7	
Total expenses		263
Net income		$ 50

EXHIBIT 12-17 | **Comparative Balance Sheets**

The Roadster Factory, Inc. (TRF)
Comparative Balance Sheets
December 31, 2011 and 2010

(In thousands)	2011	2010	Increase (Decrease)	
Assets				
Current:				
Cash..............................	$ 34	$ 42	$ (8)	⎫
Accounts receivable................	96	81	15	⎬ Changes in current assets—*Operating*
Inventory	35	38	(3)	⎪
Prepaid expenses	8	7	1	⎭
Notes receivable.........................	21	—	21	⎫ Changes in noncurrent assets—*Investing*
Plant assets, net of depreciation...	343	219	124	⎬
Total	$537	$387	$150	
Liabilities				
Current:				
Accounts payable	$ 91	$ 57	$ 34	⎫
Salary and wage payable.........	4	6	(2)	⎬ Changes in current liabilities—*Operating*
Accrued liabilities...................	1	3	(2)	⎭
Long-term debt	160	77	83	⎫ Changes in long-term liabilities and paid-in capital accounts—*Financing*
Stockholders' Equity				⎬
Common stock..........................	162	158	4	⎭
Retained earnings.......................	119	86	33	⎬ Change due to net income—*Operating* Change due to dividends—*Financing*
Total	$537	$387	$150	

Computing Cash Collections from Customers. Collections start with sales revenue (an accrual-basis amount). The Roadster Factory's income statement (Exhibit 12-16) reports sales of $303,000. Accounts receivable increased from $81,000 at the beginning of the year to $96,000 at year-end, a $15,000 increase (Exhibit 12-17). Based on those amounts, Cash Collections equal $288,000, as follows. We must solve for cash collections (X):

Accounts Receivable				
Beginning balance	+ Sales	− Collections	=	Ending balance
$81,000	+ $303,000	−X	=	$96,000
		−X	=	$96,000 − $81,000 − $303,000
		X	=	$288,000

The T-account for Accounts Receivable provides another view of the same computation.

Accounts Receivable			
Beginning balance	81,000		
Sales	303,000	Collections	288,000
Ending balance	96,000		

Accounts Receivable increased, so collections must be less than sales.

All collections of receivables are computed this way. Let's turn now to cash receipts of interest revenue. In our example, The Roadster Factory earned interest revenue and collected cash of $2,000. The amounts of interest revenue and cash receipts of interest often differ and Exhibit 12-15 shows how to make this computation.

Computing Payments to Suppliers. This computation includes two parts:

- Payments for inventory
- Payments for operating expenses (other than interest and income tax)

Payments for inventory are computed by converting cost of goods sold to the cash basis. We use Cost of Goods Sold, Inventory, and Accounts Payable. First, we must solve for purchases. All the amounts come from Exhibits 12-16 and 12-17.

Cost of Goods Sold							
Beginning inventory	+	Purchases	−	Ending inventory	=	Cost of goods sold	
$38,000	+	X	−	$35,000	=	$150,000	
		X			=	$150,000 − $38,000 + $35,000	
		X			=	$147,000	

Now we can compute cash payments for inventory (Y), as follows:

Accounts Payable							
Beginning balance	+	Purchases	−	Payments for inventory	=	Ending balance	
$57,000	+	$147,000		−Y	=	$91,000	
				−Y	=	$91,000 − $57,000 − $147,000	
				Y	=	$113,000	

The T-accounts show where the data come from. Start with Cost of Goods Sold.

Cost of Goods Sold			
Beg inventory	38,000	End inventory	35,000
Purchases	147,000		
Cost of goods sold	150,000		

Accounts Payable			
Payments for inventory	113,000	Beg bal	57,000
		Purchases	147,000
		End bal	91,000

Accounts Payable increased, so payments for inventory are less than purchases.

Computing Payments for Operating Expenses. Payments for operating expenses other than interest and income tax are computed from three accounts: Prepaid Expenses, Accrued Liabilities, and Other Operating Expenses. All The Roadster Factory data come from Exhibits 12-16 and 12-17.

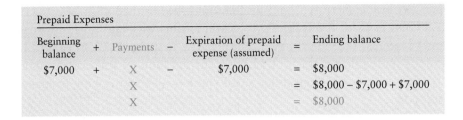

Prepaid Expenses

Beginning balance	+	Payments	−	Expiration of prepaid expense (assumed)	=	Ending balance
$7,000	+	X	−	$7,000	=	$8,000
		X			=	$8,000 − $7,000 + $7,000
		X			=	$8,000

Accrued Liabilities

Beginning balance	+	Accrual of expense at year-end (assumed)	−	Payments	=	Ending balance
$3,000	+	$1,000		−X	=	$1,000
				−X	=	$1,000 − $3,000 − $1,000
				X	=	$3,000

Other Operating Expenses

Accrual of expense at year-end	+	Expiration of prepaid expense	−	Payments	=	Ending balance
$1,000	+	$7,000		X	=	$17,000
				X	=	$17,000 − $1,000 − $7,000
				X	=	$9,000
		Total payments for operating expenses			=	$8,000 + $3,000 + $9,000
					=	$20,000

The T-accounts give another picture of the same data.

Prepaid Expenses				Accrued Liabilities			Other Operating Expenses		
Beg bal	7,000	Expiration of				Beg bal	3,000	Accrual of	1,000
Payments	8,000	prepaid		Payment	3,000	Accrual of		expense at	
		expense 7,000				expense at		year-end	
End bal	8,000					year-end	1,000	Expiration of	
						End bal	1,000	prepaid	
								expense	7,000
								Payments	9,000
								End bal	17,000

Total payments for operating expenses = $20,000($8,000 + $3,000 + $9,000)

Now we can compute Payments to Suppliers as follows:

Payments to Suppliers	=	Payments for Inventory	+	Payments for Operating Expenses
$133,000	=	$113,000	+	$20,000

Computing Payments to Employees. It is convenient to combine all payments to employees into one account, Salary and Wage Expense. We then adjust the expense for the change in Salary and Wage Payable, as shown here:

Salary and Wage Payable

Beginning balance	+	Salary and wage expense	−	Payments	=	Ending balance
$6,000	+	$56,000		−X	=	$4,000
				−X	=	$4,000 − $6,000 − $56,000
				X	=	$58,000

Salary and Wage Payable

Payments to employees	58,000	Beginning balance	6,000
		Salary and wage expense	56,000
		Ending balance	4,000

Computing Payments of Interest and Income Taxes. The Roadster Factory's expense and payment amounts are the same for interest and income tax, so no analysis is required. If the expense and the payment differ, the payment can be computed as shown in Exhibit 12-15.

Computing Investing and Financing Cash Flows

Investing and financing activities are explained on pages 712–716. These computations are the same for both the direct and the indirect methods.

STOP & THINK...

Fidelity Company reported the following for 2011 and 2010 (in millions):

At December 31,	2011	2010
Receivables, net	$3,500	$3,900
Inventory	5,200	5,000
Accounts payable	900	1,200
Income taxes payable	600	700

Year Ended December 31,	2011
Revenues..	$23,000
Cost of goods sold........................	14,100
Income tax expense......................	900

Based on these figures, how much cash did
- Fidelity collect from customers during 2011?
- Fidelity pay for inventory during 2011?
- Fidelity pay for income taxes during 2011?

Answers

		Beginning Receivables	+	Revenues	−	Collections	=	Ending Receivables
Collections from customers	= $23,400:	$3,900	+	$23,000	−	$23,400	=	$3,500

		Cost of Goods Sold	+	Increase in Inventory	+	Decrease in Accounts Payable	=	Payments
Payments for inventory	= $14,600:	$14,100	+	($5,200 − $5,000)	+	($1,200 − $900)	=	$14,600

		Beginning Income Taxes Payable	+	Income Tax Expense	−	Payment	=	Ending Income Taxes Payable
Payment of income taxes	= $1,000:	$700	+	$900	−	$1,000	=	$600

MEASURING CASH ADEQUACY: FREE CASH FLOW

Throughout this chapter, we have focused on cash flows from operating, investing, and financing activities. Some investors want to know how much cash a company can "free up" for new opportunities. **Free cash flow** is the amount of cash available from operations after paying for planned investments in plant assets. Free cash flow can be computed as follows:

$$\text{Free cash flow} = \frac{\text{Net cash provided}}{\text{by operating activities}} - \frac{\text{Cash payments earmarked for}}{\text{investments in plant assets}}$$

PepsiCo, Inc., uses free cash flow to manage its operations. Suppose PepsiCo expects net cash inflow of $2.3 billion from operations. Assume PepsiCo plans to spend $1.9 billion to modernize its bottling plants. In this case, PepsiCo's free cash flow would be $0.4 billion ($2.3 billion − $1.9 billion). If a good investment opportunity comes along, PepsiCo should have $0.4 billion to invest in the other company. **Shell Oil Company** also uses free-cash-flow analysis. A large amount of free cash flow is preferable because it means that a lot of cash is available for new investments. The Decision Guidelines that follow show some ways to use cash-flow and income data for investment and credit analysis.

DECISION GUIDELINES

INVESTORS' AND CREDITORS' USE OF CASH-FLOW AND RELATED INFORMATION

Jan Childres is a private investor. Through years of experience she has devised some guidelines for evaluating both stock investments and bond investments. Childres uses a combination of accrual-accounting data and cash-flow information. Here are her decision guidelines for both investors and creditors.

INVESTORS

Questions	Factors to Consider	Financial Statement Predictor/Decision Model*
1. How much in dividends can I expect to receive from an investment in stock?	Expected future net income	Income from continuing operations**
	Expected future cash balance	Net cash flows from (in order): ■ Operating activities ■ Investing activities ■ Financing activities
	Future dividend policy	Current and past dividend policy
2. Is the stock price likely to increase or decrease?	Expected future net income	Income from continuing operations**
	Expected future cash flows from operating activities	Income from continuing operations** Net cash flow from operating activities
3. What is the future stock price likely to be?	Expected future income from ■ continuing operations, and ■ net cash flow from operating activities	$$\text{Expected future price of a share of stock} = \frac{\text{Net cash flow from operations per share}}{\text{Investment capitalization rate**}}$$ $$\text{Expected future price of a share of stock} = \frac{\text{Expected future earnings per share**}}{\text{Investment capitalization rate**}}$$

CREDITORS

Questions	Factors to Consider	Financial Statement Predictor
Can the company pay the interest and principal at the maturity of a loan?	Expected future net cash flow from operating activities	Income from continuing operations** Net cash flow from operating activities

*There are many other factors to consider in making these decisions. These are some of the more common.
**See Chapter 11.

END-OF-CHAPTER SUMMARY PROBLEM

Adeva Health Foods, Inc., reported the following comparative balance sheet and income statement for 2011.

Adeva Health Foods, Inc.
Comparative Balance Sheets
December 31, 2011 and 2010

	2011	2010
Cash..	$ 19,000	$ 3,000
Accounts receivable................	22,000	23,000
Inventories	34,000	31,000
Prepaid expenses	1,000	3,000
Equipment, net......................	90,000	79,000
Intangible assets	9,000	9,000
	$175,000	$148,000
Accounts payable	$ 14,000	$ 9,000
Accrued liabilities...................	16,000	19,000
Income tax payable	14,000	12,000
Notes payable	45,000	50,000
Common stock.......................	31,000	20,000
Retained earnings...................	64,000	40,000
Treasury stock........................	(9,000)	(2,000)
	$175,000	$148,000

Adeva Health Foods, Inc.
Income Statement
Year Ended December 31, 2011

Sales revenue...	$190,000
Gain on sale of equipment....................	6,000
Total revenue and gains	196,000
Cost of goods sold...............................	85,000
Depreciation expense	19,000
Other operating expenses....................	36,000
Total expenses	140,000
Income before income tax	56,000
Income tax expense	18,000
Net income...	$ 38,000

Assume that **Berkshire Hathaway** is considering buying Adeva. Berkshire Hathaway requests the following cash-flow data for 2011. There were no noncash investing and financing activities.

a. Collections from customers
b. Cash payments for inventory
c. Cash payments for operating expenses
d. Cash payment for income tax
e. Cash received from the sale of equipment. Adeva paid $40,000 for new equipment during the year.

f. Issuance of common stock

g. Issuance of notes payable. Adeva paid off $20,000 during the year.

h. Cash dividends. There were no stock dividends.

Provide the requested data. Show your work.

Answers

a. Analyze Accounts Receivable (let X = Collections from customers):

Beginning	+	Sales	−	Collections	=	Ending
$23,000	+	$190,000	−	X	=	$22,000
				X	=	$191,000

b. Analyze Inventory and Accounts Payable (let X = Purchases, and let Y = Payments for inventory):

Beginning Inventory	+	Purchases	−	Ending Inventory	=	Cost of Goods Sold
$31,000	+	X	−	$34,000	=	$85,000
		X			=	$88,000

Beginning Accounts Payable	+	Purchases	−	Payments	=	Ending Accounts Payable
$9,000	+	$88,000	−	Y	=	$14,000
				Y	=	$83,000

c. Start with Other Operating Expenses, and adjust for the changes in Prepaid Expenses and Accrued Liabilities:

Other Operating Expenses	− Decrease in Prepaid Expenses	+ Decrease in Accrued Liabilities	=	Payments for Operating Expenses
$36,000	− $2,000	+ $3,000	=	$37,000

d. Analyze Income Tax Payable (let X = Payment of income tax):

Beginning	+	Income Tax Expense	−	Payments	=	Ending
$12,000	+	$18,000	−	X	=	$14,000
				X	=	$16,000

e. Analyze Equipment, Net (let X = Book value of equipment sold. Then combine with the gain or loss to compute cash received from the sale.)

Beginning	+	Acquisitions	−	Depreciation	−	Book Value Sold	=	Ending
$79,000	+	$40,000	−	$19,000	−	X	=	$90,000
						X	=	$10,000

Cash Received from Sale	=	Book Value Sold	+	Gain on Sale
$16,000	=	$10,000	+	$6,000

f. Analyze Common Stock (let X = Issuance)

Beginning	+	Issuance	=	Ending
$20,000	+	X	=	$31,000
		X	=	$11,000

g. Analyze Notes Payable (let X = Issuance):

Beginning	+	Issuance	−	Payment	=	Ending
$50,000	+	X	−	$20,000	=	$45,000
		X			=	$15,000

h. Analyze Retained Earnings (let X = Dividends)

Beginning	+	Net Income	−	Dividends	=	Ending
$40,000	+	$38,000	−	X	=	$64,000
				X	=	$14,000

REVIEW STATEMENT OF CASH FLOWS

Quick Check (Answers are given on page 774.)

1. All of the following activities are reported on the statement of cash flows except:
   a. marketing activities.
   c. operating activities.
   b. investing activities.
   d. financing activities.

2. Activities that create long-term liabilities are usually
   a. financing activities.
   b. operating activities.
   c. noncash investing and financing activities.
   d. investing activities.

3. Activities affecting long-term assets are
   a. financing activities.
   c. operating activities.
   b. marketing activities.
   d. investing activities.

4. In 2010, PMW Corporation borrowed $110,000, paid dividends of $34,000, issued 10,000 shares of stock for $45 per share, purchased land for $240,000, and received dividends of $10,000. Net income was $150,000, and depreciation for the year totaled $8,000. How much should be reported as net cash provided by operating activities by the indirect method?

    a. $194,000   c. $234,000
    b. $158,000   d. $134,000

5. Activities that obtain the cash needed to launch and sustain a company are

    a. marketing activities.   c. investing activities.
    b. income activities.   d. financing activities.

6. The exchange of stock for land would be reported as

    a. Exchanges are not reported on the statement of cash flows.
    b. financing activities.
    c. noncash investing and financing activities.
    d. investing activities.

Use the following Montana Company information for questions 7–10.

Net income..	$50,000	Increase in accounts payable	$ 9,000
Depreciation expense	10,000	Acquisition of equipment	35,000
Payment of dividends	1,000	Sale of treasury stock	4,000
Increase in accounts receivable	8,000	Payment of long-term debt	16,000
Collection of long-term notes receivable..........	5,000	Proceeds from sale of land..........	40,000
Loss on sale of land................................	15,000	Decrease in inventories..............	3,000

7. Under the indirect method, net cash provided by operating activities would be

    a. $84,000.   c. $79,000.
    b. $76,000.   d. $89,000.

8. Net cash provided by (used for) investing activities would be

    a. $20,000.   c. $(15,000).
    b. $10,000.   d. $(10,000).

9. Net cash provided by (used for) financing activities would be

    a. $3,000.   c. $(21,000).
    b. $(13,000).   d. $1,000.

10. The cost of land must have been

    a. $40,000.
    b. $55,000.
    c. $25,000.
    d. cannot be determined from the data given.

11. Sweet Treat Ice Cream began the year with $60,000 in accounts receivable and ended the year with $50,000 in accounts receivable. If sales for the year were $700,000, the cash collected from customers during the year amounted to

    a. $690,000.   c. $750,000.
    b. $760,000.   d. $710,000.

12. Nassau Farms, Ltd., made sales of $750,000 and had cost of goods sold of $410,000. Inventory decreased by $10,000 and accounts payable decreased by $12,000. Operating expenses were $180,000. How much was Nassau Farms' net income for the year?

    a. $150,000   c. $148,000
    b. $160,000   d. $340,000

13. Use the Nassau Farms data from question 12. How much cash did Nassau Farms pay for inventory during the year?

    a. $410,000   c. $422,000
    b. $400,000   d. $412,000

Accounting Vocabulary

cash equivalents (p. 704) Highly liquid short-term investments that can be converted into cash immediately.

cash flows (p. 703) Cash receipts and cash payments (disbursements).

direct method (p. 706) Format of the operating activities section of the statement of cash flows; lists the major categories of operating cash receipts (collections from customers and receipts of interest and dividends) and cash disbursements (payments to suppliers, to employees, for interest and income taxes).

financing activities (p. 705) Activities that obtain from investors and creditors the cash needed to launch and sustain the business; a section of the statement of cash flows.

free cash flow (p. 732) The amount of cash available from operations after paying for planned investments in plant assets.

indirect method (p. 706) Format of the operating activities section of the statement of cash flows; starts with net income and reconciles to cash flows from operating activities.

investing activities (p. 705) Activities that increase or decrease the long-term assets available to the business; a section of the statement of cash flows.

operating activities (p. 705) Activities that create revenue or expense in the entity's major line of business; a section of the statement of cash flows. Operating activities affect the income statement.

statement of cash flows (p. 703) Reports cash receipts and cash payments classified according to the entity's major activities: operating, investing, and financing.

ASSESS YOUR PROGRESS

Short Exercises

S12-1 (*Learning Objectives 1, 2, 3: Explaining the purposes of the statement of cash flows*) State how the statement of cash flows helps investors and creditors perform each of the following functions:

   a. Predict future cash flows.
   b. Evaluate management decisions.

writing assignment ■

S12-2 (*Learning Objectives 1, 2, 3: Explaining the purposes of the statement of cash flows*) U.S. Rondeau, Inc., has experienced an unbroken string of nine years of growth in net income. Nevertheless, the company is facing bankruptcy. Creditors are calling all of U.S. Rondeau's loans for immediate payment, and the cash is simply not available. It is clear that the company's top managers overemphasized profits and gave too little attention to cash flows.

▌ *Requirement*

   1. Write a brief memo, in your own words, to explain to the managers of U.S. Rondeau, Inc., the purposes of the statement of cash flows.

S12-3 (*Learning Objective 2: Evaluating operating cash flows—indirect method*)   Examine the statement of cash flows of Clock, Inc.

Clock, Inc.
Consolidated Statement of Cash Flows (Adapted; in millions)
Year Ended December 31, 2010

Cash Flows from Operating Activities		
Net income..	$ 983	
Adjustment to reconcile net income to net cash		
provided by operating activities:		
Depreciation and amortization	278	
Change in assets and liabilities, net of acquired businesses:		
Accounts receivable...	(587)	
Other current assets..	(200)	
Accounts payable	(98)	
Accrued expenses and other liabilities	(298)	
Unearned revenue...	31	
Income taxes payable	(333)	
Other, net	33	
Net cash used in operating activities............................		(191)
Cash Flows from Investing Activities		
Purchase of property and equipment.................................	$ (1,991)	
Purchase of investments	(26,603)	
Sale of investments..	24,108	
Acquisitions of other companies	(454)	
Net cash used in investing activities............................		(4,940)
Cash Flows from Financing Activities		
Proceeds from the issuance of common stock, net..............	$ 1,043	
Other, net..	473	
Net cash provided by financing activities......................		1,516
Other, net..		22
Net increase (decrease) in cash and cash equivalents		(3,593)
Cash and cash equivalents at beginning of year.................		5,194
Cash and cash equivalents at end of year..........................		$ 1,601

Suppose Clock's operating activities *provided*, rather than *used*, cash. Identify three things under the indirect method that could cause operating cash flows to be positive.

S12-4 (*Learning Objectives 1, 2: Using cash-flow data to evaluate performance*)   Top managers of Tranquility Inns are reviewing company performance for 2010. The income statement reports a 25% increase in net income over 2009. However, most of the increase resulted from an extraordinary gain on insurance proceeds from fire damage to a building. The balance sheet shows a large increase in receivables. The cash flows statement, in summarized form, reports the following:

writing assignment ■

Net cash used for operating activities......................	$(50,000)
Net cash provided by investing activities................	30,000
Net cash provided by financing activities	25,000
Increase in cash during 2010..................................	$ 5,000

❙ Requirement

1. Write a memo giving Tranquility Inns' managers your assessment of 2010 operations and your outlook for the future. Focus on the information content of the cash flows data.

S12-5 (*Learning Objective 3: Reporting cash flows from operating activities—indirect method*) Beautiful America Transportation (BAT) began 2010 with accounts receivable, inventory, and prepaid expenses totaling $58,000. At the end of the year, BAT had a total of $55,000 for these current assets. At the beginning of 2010, BAT owed current liabilities of $20,000, and at year-end current liabilities totaled $32,000.

Net income for the year was $12,000. Included in net income were a $2,000 loss on the sale of land and depreciation expense of $8,000.

Show how BAT should report cash flows from operating activities for 2010. BAT uses the *indirect* method.

S12-6 (*Learning Objectives 2, 3: Identifying items for reporting cash flows from operations—indirect method*) Campbell Clinic, Inc., is preparing its statement of cash flows (*indirect* method) for the year ended March 31, 2010. Consider the following items in preparing the company's statement of cash flows. Identify each item as an operating activity—addition to net income (O+) or subtraction from net income (O-), an investing activity (I), a financing activity (F), or an activity that is not used to prepare the cash flows statement by the indirect method (N). Place the appropriate symbol in the blank space.

___	**a.** Increase in accounts payable
___	**b.** Purchase of equipment
___	**c.** Decrease in prepaid expense
___	**d.** Collection of cash from customers
___	**e.** Net income
___	**f.** Retained earnings
___	**g.** Payment of dividends
___	**h.** Decrease in accrued liabilities
___	**i.** Issuance of common stock
___	**j.** Gain on sale of building
___	**k.** Loss on sale of land
___	**l.** Depreciation expense
___	**m.** Increase in inventory
___	**n.** Decrease in accounts receivable

S12-7 (*Learning Objective 3: Computing operating cash flows—indirect method*) Ethan Corporation accountants have assembled the following data for the year ended June 30, 2010.

Net income.............................	$?	Cost of goods sold...................	$116,000
Payment of dividends..............	5,600	Other operating expenses.........	33,000
Proceeds from the issuance		Purchase of equipment.............	43,000
of common stock............	26,000	Increase in current liabilities.....	7,000
Sales revenue...........................	228,000	Payment of note payable..........	32,000
Decrease in current assets		Proceeds from sale of land........	29,000
other than cash...............	35,000	Depreciation expense	11,000
Purchase of treasury stock........	6,000		

Prepare the *operating activities section* of Ethan's statement of cash flows for the year ended June 30, 2010. Ethan uses the *indirect* method for operating cash flows.

S12-8 (*Learning Objective 3: Preparing a statement of cash flows—indirect method*)   Use the data in Short Exercise 12-7 to prepare Ethan Corporation's statement of cash flows for the year ended June 30, 2010. Ethan uses the *indirect* method for operating activities.

S12-9 (*Learning Objective 3: Computing investing cash flows*)   Motorsports of Miami, Inc., reported the following financial statements for 2010:

Motorsports of Miami, Inc.
Income Statement
Year Ended December 31, 2010

(In thousands)	
Service revenue..........................	$770
Cost of goods sold....................	330
Salary expense..........................	40
Depreciation expense	30
Other expenses.........................	170
Total expenses..........................	570
Net income	$200

Motorsports of Miami, Inc.
Comparative Balance Sheets
December 31, 2010 and 2009

(In thousands)

Assets	2010	2009	Liabilities	2010	2009
Current:			Current:		
Cash	$ 28	$ 11	Accounts payable..........	$ 48	$ 43
Accounts receivable	54	43	Salary payable	26	24
Inventory......................	77	89	Accrued liabilities	16	19
Prepaid expenses...........	6	5	Long-term notes payable........	69	54
Long-term investments...........	54	79			
Plant assets, net.....................	229	188	**Stockholders' Equity**		
			Common stock.......................	48	38
			Retained earnings..................	241	237
Total	$448	$415	Total	$448	$415

Compute the following investing cash flows: (Enter all amounts in thousands.)

a. Acquisitions of plant assets (all were for cash). Motorsports of Miami sold no plant assets.
b. Proceeds from the sale of investments. Motorsports of Miami purchased no investments.

S12-10 (*Learning Objective 3: Computing financing cash flows*)   Use the Motorsports of Miami data in Short Exercise 12-9 to compute the following: (Enter all amounts in thousands.)

a. New borrowing or payment of long-term notes payable. Motorsports of Miami had only one long-term note payable transaction during the year.
b. Issuance of common stock or retirement of common stock. Motorsports of Miami had only one common stock transaction during the year.
c. Payment of cash dividends (same as dividends declared).

S12-11 (*Learning Objective 4: Computing operating cash flows—direct method*)   Use the Motorsports of Miami data in Short Exercise 12-9 to compute the following: (Enter all amounts in thousands.)

    a. Collections from customers

    b. Payments for inventory

S12-12 (*Learning Objective 4: Computing operating cash flows—direct method*)   Use the Motorcars of Miami data in Short Exercise 12-9 to compute the following: (Enter all amounts in thousands).

    a. Payments to employees

    b. Payments of other expenses

S12-13 (*Learning Objective 4: Preparing a statement of cash flows—direct method*)   Horse Heaven Horse Farm, Inc., began 2010 with cash of $170,000. During the year, Horse Heaven earned service revenue of $590,000 and collected $480,000 from customers. Expenses for the year totaled $320,000, with $310,000 paid in cash to suppliers and employees. Horse Heaven also paid $136,000 to purchase equipment and a cash dividend of $49,000 to stockholders. During 2010, Horse Heaven borrowed $26,000 by issuing a note payable. Prepare the company's statement of cash flows for the year. Format operating activities by the *direct* method.

S12-14 (*Learning Objective 4: Computing operating cash flows—direct method*)   Middleton Golf Club, Inc., has assembled the following data for the year ended September 30, 2010:

Cost of goods sold............................	$104,000	Payment of dividends	$ 8,000
Payments to suppliers.......................	90,000	Proceeds from issuance	
Purchase of equipment......................	42,000	of common stock	16,000
Payments to employees.....................	75,000	Sales revenue......................................	211,000
Payment of note payable	15,000	Collections from customers................	203,000
Proceeds from sale of land................	61,000	Payment of income tax.......................	14,000
Depreciation expense	6,000	Purchase of treasury stock..................	5,700

       Prepare the *operating activities section* of Middleton Golf Club, Inc.'s statement of cash flows for the year ended September 30, 2010. Middleton uses the *direct* method for operating cash flows.

S12-15 (*Learning Objective 4: Preparing a statement of cash flows—direct method*)   Use the data in Short Exercise 12-14 to prepare Middleton Golf Club, Inc.'s statement of cash flows for the year ended September 30, 2010. Middleton uses the *direct* method for operating activities.

Exercises

All of the A and B exercises can be found within MyAccountingLab, an online homework and practice environment. Your instructor may ask you to complete these exercises using MyAccountingLab.

(Group A)

E12-16A (*Learning Objectives 2, 3: Identifying activities for the statement of cash flows—indirect method*)   Tucker-Breen Investments specializes in low-risk government bonds. Identify each of Tucker-Breen's transactions as operating (O), investing (I), financing (F), noncash investing and financing (NIF), or a transaction that is not reported on the statement of cash flows (N). Indicate whether each item increases (+) or decreases (−) cash. The *indirect* method is used for operating activities.

	a. Sale of long-term investment
	b. Issuance of long-term note payable to borrow cash
	c. Increase in prepaid expenses
	d. Payment of cash dividend
	e. Loss of sale of equipment
	f. Decrease in merchandise inventory
	g. Acquisition of equipment by issuance of note payable
	h. Increase in accounts payable
	i. Amortization of intangible assets
	j. Net income
	k. Payment of long-term debt
	l. Accrual of salary expense
	m. Cash sale of land
	n. Purchase of long-term investment
	o. Acquisition of building by cash payment
	p. Purchase of treasury stock
	q. Issuance of common stock for cash
	r. Decrease in accrued liabilities
	s. Depreciation of equipment

E12-17A (*Learning Objectives 2, 3: Classifying transactions for the statement of cash flows—indirect method*) Indicate whether each of the following transactions records an operating activity, an investing activity, a financing activity, or a noncash investing and financing activity.

a.	Depreciation Expense	11,000		h.	Cash	50,000	
	Accumulated Depreciation		11,000		Accounts Receivable	9,000	
b.	Treasury Stock	7,800			Service Revenue		59,000
	Cash		7,800	i.	Bonds Payable	47,000	
c.	Land	83,000			Cash		47,000
	Cash		83,000	j.	Cash	74,000	
d.	Equipment	19,000			Common Stock		11,000
	Cash		19,000		Capital in Excess of Par		63,000
e.	Salary Expense	24,000		k.	Dividends Payable	17,100	
	Cash		24,000		Cash		17,100
f.	Furniture and Fixtures	24,200		l.	Loss on Disposal of Equipment	1,200	
	Cash		24,200		Equipment, Net		1,200
g.	Building	159,000		m.	Cash	6,900	
	Note Payable, Long-Term		159,000		Long-Term Investment		6,900

E12-18A (*Learning Objective 3: Computing cash flows from operating activities—indirect method*) The accounting records of North East Distributors, Inc., reveal the following:

writing assignment ■

Net income	$38,000	Depreciation	$17,000
Collection of dividend revenue	7,800	Decrease in current liabilities	19,000
Payment of interest	11,000	Increase in current assets	
Sales revenue	13,000	other than cash	24,000
Loss on sale of land	22,000	Payment of dividends	7,800
Acquisition of land	42,000	Payment of income tax	15,000

❙ Requirement

1. Compute cash flows from operating activities by the *indirect* method. Use the format of the operating activities section of Exhibit 12-6. Also evaluate the operating cash flow of North East Distributors. Give the reason for your evaluation.

E12-19A (*Learning Objective 3: Computing cash flows from operating activities—indirect method*)   The accounting records of Wilderness Fur Traders include these accounts:

Cash			
May 1	90,000		
Receipts	440,000	Payments	445,000
May 31	85,000		

Accounts Receivable			
May 1	1,000		
Receipts	540,000	Collections	440,000
May 31	101,000		

Inventory			
May 1	3,000		
Purchases	438,000	Cost of sales	336,000
May 31	105,000		

Equipment			
May 1	185,000		
Acquisition	5,000		
May 31	190,000		

Accumulated Deprec.—Equipment			
		May 1	55,000
		Depreciation	5,000
		May 31	60,000

Accounts Payable			
Payments	327,000	May 1	14,500
		Purchases	438,000
		May 31	125,500

Accrued Liabilities			
		May 1	19,000
Payments	32,000	Receipts	26,000
		May 31	13,000

Retained Earnings			
Quarterly		May 1	63,000
Dividend	16,000	Net Income	20,000
		May 31	67,000

❙ Requirement

1. Compute Wilderness net cash provided by (used for) operating activities during May. Use the *indirect* method. Does Wilderness have trouble collecting receivables or selling inventory? How can you tell?

writing assignment ■   **E12-20A** (*Learning Objective 3: Preparing the statement of cash flows—indirect method*)   The income statement and additional data of Newbury Travel Products, Inc., follow:

Newbury Travel Products, Inc.
Income Statement
Year Ended December 31, 2010

Revenues:		
Service revenue	$283,000	
Dividend revenue	8,000	$291,000
Expenses:		
Cost of goods sold	103,000	
Salary expense	78,000	
Depreciation expense	26,000	
Advertising expense	4,500	
Interest expense	2,600	
Income tax expense...................	8,000	222,100
Net income		$ 68,900

Additional data:

a. Acquisition of plant assets was $212,000. Of this amount, $160,000 was paid in cash and $52,000 by signing a note payable.
b. Proceeds from sale of land totaled $27,000.
c. Proceeds from issuance of common stock totaled $80,000.
d. Payment of long-term note payable was $17,000.
e. Payment of dividends was $13,000.
f. From the balance sheets:

	December 31,	
	2010	2009
Current Assets:		
Cash	$30,000	$10,800
Accounts receivable	42,000	59,000
Inventory................................	30,000	91,000
Prepaid expenses....................	9,400	8,700
Current Liabilities:		
Accounts payable....................	$38,000	$27,000
Accrued liabilities	18,000	99,000

Requirements

1. Prepare Newbury's statement of cash flows for the year ended December 31, 2010, using the *indirect* method.
2. Evaluate Newbury's cash flows for the year. In your evaluation, mention all three categories of cash flows and give the reason for your evaluation.

E12-21A (*Learning Objective 3: Interpreting a statement of cash flows—indirect method*) Consider three independent cases for the cash flows of 579 Pavilion Shoes. For each case, identify from the statement of cash flows how 579 Pavilion Shoes generated the cash to acquire new plant assets. Rank the three cases from the most healthy financially to the least healthy.

	Case A	Case B	Case C
Cash flows from operating activities			
Net income	$ 20,000	$ 20,000	$ 20,000
Depreciation and amortization	9,000	9,000	9,000
Increase in current assets	(22,000)	(2,000)	(11,000)
Decrease in current liabilities	(10,000)	(4,000)	(1,000)
	(3,000)	23,000	17,000
Cash flows from investing activities:			
Acquisition of plant assets	(83,000)	(83,000)	(83,000)
Sales of plant assets	9,000	37,000	90,000
	(74,000)	(46,000)	7,000
Cash flows from financing activities:			
Issuance of stock.............................	97,000	62,000	15,000
Payment of debt..............................	(22,000)	(38,000)	(23,000)
	75,000	24,000	(8,000)
Net increase (decrease) in cash	$ (2,000)	$ 1,000	$ 16,000

E12-22A (*Learning Objectives 3, 4: Computing investing and financing amounts for the statement of cash flows*) Compute the following items for the statement of cash flows:

a. Beginning and ending Plant Assets, Net, are $110,000 and $106,000, respectively. Depreciation for the period was $9,000, and purchases of new plant assets were $33,000. Plant assets were sold at a $4,000 loss. What were the cash proceeds of the sale?

b. Beginning and ending Retained Earnings are $49,000 and $74,000, respectively. Net income for the period was $58,000, and stock dividends were $7,000. How much were cash dividends?

E12-23A *(Learning Objective 4: Computing cash flows from operating activities—direct method)*   The accounting records of Princeton Pharmaceuticals, Inc., reveal the following:

Payment of salaries and wages	$35,000	Net income	$60,000
Depreciation	20,000	Payment of income tax	24,000
Decrease in current liabilities	22,000	Collection of dividend revenue	10,000
Increase in current assets other than cash	23,000	Payment of interest	17,000
Payment of dividends	7,000	Cash sales	33,000
Collection of accounts receivable	50,000	Loss on sale of land	6,000
		Acquisition of land	38,000
		Payment of accounts payable	58,000

❙ Requirement

1. Compute cash flows from operating activities by the *direct* method. Also evaluate Princeton's operating cash flow. Give the reason for your evaluation.

E12-24A *(Learning Objective 4: Identifying items for the statement of cash flows—direct method)*   Selected accounts of Ashley Antiques show the following:

Salary Payable

		Beginning balance	10,000
Payments	30,000	Salary expense	28,000
		Ending balance	8,000

Buildings

Beginning balance	80,000	Depreciation	20,000
Acquisitions	120,000	Book value of building sold	119,000*
Ending balance	61,000		

*Sale price was 150,000.

Notes Payable

		Beginning balance	234,000
Payments	67,000	Issuance of note payable for cash	74,000
		Ending balance	241,000

❙ Requirement

1. For each account, identify the item or items that should appear on a statement of cash flows prepared by the *direct* method. State where to report the item.

E12-25A (*Learning Objective 4: Preparing the statement of cash flows—direct method*)   The   **writing assignment** ■
income statement and additional data of Cobbs Hill, Inc., follow:

Cobbs Hill, Inc. Income Statement Year Ended April 30, 2010		
Revenues:		
Sales revenue......................	$232,000	
Dividend revenue................	11,000	$243,000
Expenses:		
Cost of goods sold..............	108,000	
Salary expense	46,000	
Depreciation expense..........	31,000	
Advertising expense	11,500	
Interest expense	2,100	
Income tax expense.............	9,000	207,600
Net income		$ 35,400

Additional data:

   a. Collections from customers are $13,000 more than sales.
   b. Payments to suppliers are $1,300 less than the sum of cost of goods sold plus adver-
       tising expense.
   c. Payments to employees are $2,000 more than salary expense.
   d. Dividend revenue, interest expense, and income tax expense equal their cash amounts.
   e. Acquisition of plant assets is $143,000. Of this amount, $100,000 is paid in cash and
       $43,000 by signing a note payable.
   f. Proceeds from sale of land total $28,000.
   g. Proceeds from issuance of common stock total $93,000.
   h. Payment of long-term note payable is $17,000.
   i. Payment of dividends is $8,500.
   j. Cash balance, April 30, 2009, was $21,000.

❙ *Requirements*

   1. Prepare Cobbs Hill, Inc.'s statement of cash flows and accompanying schedule of noncash
       investing and financing activities. Report operating activities by the *direct* method.
   2. Evaluate Cobbs Hill's cash flows for the year. In your evaluation, mention all three cate-
       gories of cash flows and give the reason for your evaluation.

E12-26A (*Learning Objective 4: Computing amounts for the statement of cash flows—direct
method*)   Compute the following items for the statement of cash flows:

   a. Beginning and ending Accounts Receivable are $25,000 and $20,000, respectively. Credit
       sales for the period total $62,000. How much are cash collections from customers?
   b. Cost of goods sold is $79,000. Beginning Inventory was $26,000, and ending
       Inventory balance is $29,000. Beginning and ending Accounts Payable are $11,000
       and $9,000, respectively. How much are cash payments for inventory?

(Group B)

E12-27B (*Learning Objectives 2, 3: Identifying activities for the statement of cash flows—indirect method*) Burke-Cassidy Investments specializes in low-risk government bonds. Identify each of Burke-Cassidy's transactions as operating (O), investing (I), financing (F), noncash investing and financing (NIF), or a transaction that is not reported on the statement of cash flows (N). Indicate whether each item increases (+) or decreases (–) cash. The *indirect* method is used for operating activities.

	a. Acquisition of building by cash payment
	b. Decrease in merchandise inventory
	c. Depreciation of equipment
	d. Decrease in accrued liabilities
	e. Payment of cash dividend
	f. Purchase of long-term investment
	g. Issuance of long-term note payable to borrow cash
	h. Increase in prepaid expenses
	i. Accrual of salary expense
	j. Acquisition of equipment by issuance of note payable
	k. Sale of long-term investment
	l. Issuance of common stock for cash
	m. Increase in accounts payable
	n. Amortization of intangible assets
	o. Loss of sale of equipment
	p. Payment of long-term debt
	q. Cash sale of land
	r. Purchase of treasury stock
	s. Net income

E12-28B (*Learning Objectives 2, 3: Classifying transactions for the statement of cash flows—indirect method*) Indicate whether each of the following transactions records an operating activity, an investing activity, a financing activity, or a noncash investing and financing activity.

a.	Cash	85,000		g.	Equipment	15,600	
	Common Stock		14,000		Cash		15,600
	Capital in Excess of Par		71,000	h.	Dividends Payable	18,200	
b.	Furniture and Fixtures	25,600			Cash		18,200
	Cash		25,600	i.	Salary Expense	19,400	
c.	Cash	72,000			Cash		19,400
	Accounts Receivable	15,000		j.	Building	146,000	
	Service Revenue		87,000		Note Payable—Long-Term		146,000
d.	Cash	9,100		k.	Dividends Payable	17,100	
	Long-Term Investment		9,100		Cash		17,100
e.	Loss on Disposal of Equipment	1,500		l.	Depreciation Expense	7,000	
	Equipment, Net		1,500		Accumulated Depreciation		7,000
f.	Land	20,300		m.	Bonds Payable	49,000	
	Cash		20,300		Cash		49,000

E12-29B (*Learning Objective 3: Computing cash flows from operating activities—indirect*   **writing assignment** ■
method)   The accounting records of Central Distributors, Inc., reveal the following:

Net income	$40,000	Depreciation	$15,000
Collection of dividend revenue	6,900	Increase in current liabilities	23,000
Payment of interest	14,000	Decrease in current assets	
Sales revenue	12,000	other than cash	28,000
Loss on sale of land	19,000	Payment of dividends	7,200
Acquisition of land	43,000	Payment of income tax	12,000

❙ Requirement

1. Compute cash flows from operating activities by the *indirect* method. Use the format of the operating activities section of Exhibit 12-6. Also evaluate the operating cash flow of Central Distributors. Give the reason for your evaluation.

E12-30B (*Learning Objective 3: Computing cash flows from operating activities—indirect method*)   The accounting records of Lawrence Fur Traders include these accounts:

Cash			
Oct 1	11,000		
Receipts	537,000	Payments	446,000
Oct 31	102,000		

Accounts Receivable			
Oct 1	8,000		
Receipts	538,000	Collections	537,000
Oct 31	9,000		

Inventory			
Oct 1	4,000		
Purchases	437,000	Cost of sales	434,000
Oct 31	7,000		

Equipment	
Oct 1	188,000
Acquisition	7,000
Oct 31	195,000

Accumulated Deprec.—Equipment			
		Oct 1	52,000
		Depreciation	9,000
		Oct 31	61,000

Accounts Payable			
		Oct 1	14,000
Payments	328,000	Purchases	437,000
		Oct 31	123,000

Accrued Liabilities			
		Oct 1	12,000
Payments	28,000	Receipts	22,000
		Oct 31	6,000

Retained Earnings			
Quarterly		Oct 1	66,000
Dividend	18,000	Net Income	35,000
		Oct 31	83,000

❙ Requirement

1. Compute Lawrence's net cash provided by (used for) operating activities during October. Use the *indirect* method. Does Lawrence have trouble collecting receivables or selling inventory? How can you tell?

writing assignment ■

E12-31B (*Learning Objective 3: Preparing the statement of cash flows—indirect method*) The income statement and additional data of Norton Travel Products, Inc., follow:

Norton Travel Products, Inc.
Income Statement
Year Ended December 31, 2010

Revenues:		
Service revenue	$235,000	
Dividend revenue	8,300	$243,300
Expenses:		
Cost of goods sold	102,000	
Salary expense	62,000	
Depreciation expense	33,000	
Advertising expense	4,300	
Interest expense	2,400	
Income tax expense	7,000	210,700
Net income		$ 32,600

Additional data:

    a. Acquisition of plant assets was $170,000. Of this amount, $140,000 was paid in cash and $30,000 by signing a note payable.

    b. Proceeds from sale of land totaled $48,000.

    c. Proceeds from issuance of common stock totaled $31,000.

    d. Payment of long-term note payable was $16,000.

    e. Payment of dividends was $10,000.

    f. From the balance sheets:

	December 31,	
	2010	**2009**
Current Assets:		
Cash	$32,000	$13,300
Accounts receivable	41,000	57,000
Inventory	48,000	87,000
Prepaid expenses	9,100	8,200
Current Liabilities:		
Accounts payable	$32,000	$17,000
Accrued liabilities	14,000	43,000

▌Requirements

    1. Prepare Norton's statement of cash flows for the year ended December 31, 2010, using the *indirect* method.

    2. Evaluate Norton's cash flows for the year. In your evaluation, mention all three categories of cash flows and give the reason for your evaluation.

E12-32B (*Learning Objective 3: Interpreting a statement of cash flows—indirect method*)
Con-sider three independent cases for the cash flows of 424 Promenade Shoes. For each case, identify from the statement of cash flows how 424 Promenade Shoes generated the cash to acquire new plant assets. Rank the three cases from the most healthy financially to the least healthy.

	Case A	Case B	Case C
Cash flows from operating activities			
Net income	$ 10,000	$ 10,000	$ 10,000
Depreciation and amortization	12,000	12,000	12,000
Increase in current assets	1,000	(5,000)	2,000
Decrease in current liabilities	2,000	(19,000)	3,000
	25,000	(2,000)	27,000
Cash flows from investing activities:			
Acquisition of plant assets	(99,000)	(99,000)	(99,000)
Sales of plant assets	104,000	20,000	33,000
	5,000	(79,000)	(66,000)
Cash flows from financing activities:			
Issuance of stock............................	18,000	105,000	73,000
Payment of debt.............................	(27,000)	(20,000)	(32,000)
	(9,000)	85,000	41,000
Net increase (decrease) in cash	$ 21,000	$ 4,000	$ 2,000

E12-33B (*Learning Objectives 3, 4: Computing investing and financing amounts for the statement of cash flows*) Compute the following items for the statement of cash flows:

a. Beginning and ending Plant Assets, Net, are $102,000 and $97,000, respectively. Depreciation for the period was $12,000, and purchases of new plant assets were $30,000. Plant assets were sold at a $5,000 gain. What were the cash proceeds of the sale?

b. Beginning and ending Retained Earnings are $46,000 and $70,000, respectively. Net income for the period was $48,000, and stock dividends were $11,000. How much were cash dividends?

E12-34B (*Learning Objective 4: Computing cash flows from operating activities—direct method*) The accounting records of One Stop Pharmaceuticals, Inc., reveal the following:

writing assignment ◼

Payment of salaries and wages..........................	$40,000	Net income.................................	$20,000
Depreciation..............................	25,000	Payment of income tax..............	8,000
Increase in current liabilities	27,000	Collection of dividend revenue	7,000
		Payment of interest....................	13,000
Increase in current assets other than cash	28,000	Cash sales..................................	36,000
Payment of dividends	6,000	Gain on sale of land	2,000
Collection of accounts receivable.........................	80,000	Acquisition of land	35,000
		Payment of accounts payable	51,000

❚ *Requirement*

1. Compute cash flows from operating activities by the *direct* method. Also evaluate One Stop's operating cash flow. Give the reason for your evaluation.

E12-35B (*Learning Objective 4: Identifying items for the statement of cash flows—direct method*) Selected accounts of Elizabeth Antiques show the following:

Salary Payable			
		Beginning balance	14,000
Payments	20,000	Salary expense	42,000
		Ending balance	36,000

Buildings			
Beginning balance	100,000	Depreciation	22,000
Acquisitions	155,000	Book value of building sold	117,000*
Ending balance	116,000		

*Sale price was 160,000.

Notes Payable			
		Beginning balance	244,000
Payments	72,000	Issuance of note payable for cash	90,000
		Ending balance	262,000

❙ Requirement

1. For each account, identify the item or items that should appear on a statement of cash flows prepared by the *direct* method. State where to report the item.

E12-36B (*Learning Objective 4: Preparing the statement of cash flows—direct method*) The income statement and additional data of Happy Life, Inc., follow:

Happy Life, Inc.
Income Statement
Year Ended November 30, 2010

Revenues:		
Sales revenue......................	$223,000	
Dividend revenue................	10,500	$233,500
Expenses:		
Cost of goods sold..............	102,000	
Salary expense	42,000	
Depreciation expense...........	19,000	
Advertising expense	14,000	
Interest expense	4,500	
Income tax expense.............	8,000	189,500
Net income		$ 44,000

Additional data:

a. Collections from customers are $16,500 more than sales.
b. Payments to suppliers are $1,200 more than the sum of cost of goods sold plus advertising expense.

c. Payments to employees are $1,700 less than salary expense.

d. Dividend revenue, interest expense, and income tax expense equal their cash amounts.

e. Acquisition of plant assets is $154,000. Of this amount, $108,000 is paid in cash and $46,000 by signing a note payable.

f. Proceeds from sale of land total $21,000.

g. Proceeds from issuance of common stock total $86,000.

h. Payment of long-term note payable is $13,000.

i. Payment of dividends is $9,000.

j. Cash balance, November 30, 2009, was $23,000.

Requirements

1. Prepare Happy Life, Inc.'s statement of cash flows and accompanying schedule of non-cash investing and financing activities. Report operating activities by the *direct* method.

2. Evaluate Happy Life's cash flows for the year. In your evaluation, mention all three categories of cash flows and give the reason for your evaluation.

E12-37B (*Learning Objective 4: Computing amounts for the statement of cash flows—direct method*)   Compute the following items for the statement of cash flows:

a. Beginning and ending Accounts Receivable are $20,000 and $17,000, respectively. Credit sales for the period total $61,000. How much are cash collections from customers?

b. Cost of goods sold is $79,000. Beginning Inventory balance is $28,000, and ending Inventory balance is $24,000. Beginning and ending Accounts Payable are $12,000 and $13,000, respectively. How much are cash payments for inventory?

Challenge Exercises

E12-38 (*Learning Objectives 3, 4: Computing cash-flow amounts*)   Tip Top, Inc., reported the following in its financial statements for the year ended May 30, 2010 (in thousands):

	2010	2009
Income Statement		
Net sales	$23,984	$21,674
Cost of sales	18,026	15,432
Depreciation	266	227
Other operating expenses	3,875	4,254
Income tax expense	536	488
Net income	$ 1,281	$ 1,273
Balance Sheet		
Cash and equivalents	$ 16	$ 15
Accounts receivable	603	614
Inventory	3,140	2,872
Property and equipment, net	4,346	3,436
Accounts payable	1,551	1,371
Accrued liabilities	935	632
Income tax payable	197	193
Long-term liabilities	480	468
Common stock	515	445
Retained earnings	4,427	3,828

❙ Requirement

1. Determine the following cash receipts and payments for Tip Top, Inc., during 2010: (Enter all amounts in thousands.)

    a. Collections from customers

    b. Payments for inventory

    c. Payments for other operating expenses

    d. Payment of income tax

    e. Proceeds from issuance of common stock

    f. Payment of cash dividends

E12-39 (*Learning Objective 3: Using the balance sheet and the statement of cash flows together*)   Delorme Specialties reported the following at December 31, 2010 (in thousands):

	2010	2009
From the comparative balance sheet:		
Property and equipment, net...	$10,950	$9,630
Long-term notes payable..	4,500	3,040
From the statement of cash flows:		
Depreciation...	$ 1,950	
Capital expenditures...	(4,090)	
Proceeds from sale of property and equipment	740	
Proceeds from issuance of long-term note payable.......	1,250	
Payment of long-term note payable.............................	(80)	
Issuance of common stock	389	

❙ Requirement

1. Determine the following items for Delorme Specialties during 2010:

    a. Gain or loss on the sale of property and equipment

    b. Amount of long-term debt issued for something other than cash

Quiz

Test your understanding of the statement of cash flows by answering the following questions. Select the best choice from among the possible answers given.

Q12-40 Paying off bonds payable is reported on the statement of cash flows under

a. noncash investing and financing activities.   **c.** operating activities.

b. investing activities.   **d.** financing activities.

Q12-41 The sale of inventory for cash is reported on the statement of cash flows under

a. financing activities.   **c.** investing activities.

b. noncash investing and financing activities.   **d.** operating activities.

Q12-42 Selling equipment is reported on the statement of cash flows under

a. financing activities.   **c.** noncash investing and financing activities.

b. investing activities.   **d.** operating activities.

Q12-43 Which of the following terms appears on a statement of cash flows—indirect method?

a. Cash receipt of interest revenue   **c.** Depreciation expense

b. Collections from customers   **d.** Payments to suppliers

Q12-44 On an indirect method statement of cash flows, an increase in a prepaid insurance would be

a. added to increases in current assets.   **c.** deducted from net income.

b. included in payments to suppliers.   **d.** added to net income.

Q12-45 On an indirect method statement of cash flows, an increase in accounts payable would be
a. reported in the financing activities section.
b. reported in the investing activities section.
c. added to net income in the operating activities section.
d. deducted from net income in the operating activities section.

Q12-46 On an indirect method statement of cash flows, a gain on the sale of plant assets would be
a. reported in the investing activities section.
b. added to net income in the operating activities section.
c. deducted from net income in the operating activities section.
d. ignored, since the gain did not generate any cash.

Q12-47 Select an activity for each of the following transactions:
1. Paying cash dividends is a/an —————— activity.
2. Receiving cash dividends is a/an —————— activity.

Q12-48 Click Camera Co. sold equipment with a cost of $21,000 and accumulated depreciation of $9,000 for an amount that resulted in a gain of $1,000. What amount should Click report on the statement of cash flows as "proceeds from sale of plant assets"?
a. $10,000   c. $13,000
b. $20,000   d. Some other amount

Questions 49–57 use the following data. Sheehan Corporation formats operating cash flows by the *indirect* method.

Sheehan's Income Statement for 2010

Sales revenue	$177,000	
Gain on sale of equipment	9,000*	$186,000
Cost of goods sold	114,000	
Depreciation	6,500	
Other operating expenses	24,000	144,500
Net income		$ 41,500

*The book value of equipment sold during 2010 was $21,000.

Sheehan's Comparative Balance Sheet at the end of 2010

	2010	2009		2010	2009
Cash	$ 5,500	$ 3,000	Accounts payable	$ 8,000	$ 9,000
Accounts receivable	5,000	13,000	Accrued liabilities	6,000	4,000
Inventory	11,000	10,000	Common stock	18,000	9,000
Plant and equipment, net	97,000	71,000	Retained earnings	86,500	75,000
	$118,500	$97,000		$118,500	$97,000

Q12-49 How many items enter the computation of Sheehan's net cash provided by operating activities?
a. 3   c. 7
b. 2   d. 5

Q12-50 How do Sheehan's accrued liabilities affect the company's statement of cash flows for 2010?

a. Increase in cash used by investing activities.
b. Increase in cash provided by operating activities.
c. Increase in cash used by financing activities.
d. They don't because the accrued liabilities are not yet paid.

Q12-51 How do accounts receivable affect Sheehan's cash flows from operating activities for 2010?

a. Decrease in cash provided by operating activities.
b. Decrease in cash used by investing activities.
c. Increase in cash provided by operating activities.
d. They don't because accounts receivable result from investing activities.

Q12-52 Sheehan's net cash provided by operating activities during 2010 was

a. $53,000.   c. $47,000.
b. $50,000.   d. $44,000.

Q12-53 How many items enter the computation of Sheehan's net cash flow from investing activities for 2010?

a. 5   c. 7
b. 3   d. 2

Q12-54 The book value of equipment sold during 2010 was $21,000. Sheehan's net cash flow from investing activities for 2010 was

a. net cash used of $23,500.
b. net cash used of $53,000.
c. net cash used of $50,000.
d. net cash used of $44,000.

Q12-55 How many items enter the computation of Sheehan's net cash flow from financing activities for 2010?

a. 7   c. 5
b. 3   d. 2

Q12-56 Sheehan's largest financing cash flow for 2010 resulted from

a. payment of dividends.   c. purchase of equipment.
b. sale of equipment.   d. issuance of common stock.

Q12-57 Sheehan's net cash flow from financing activities for 2010 was

a. net cash used of $21,000.   c. net cash provided of $9,000.
b. net cash used of $50,000.   d. net cash used of $44,000.

Q12-58 Sales totaled $820,000, accounts receivable increased by $50,000, and accounts payable decreased by $30,000. How much cash did the company collect from customers?

a. $800,000   c. $770,000
b. $820,000   d. $870,000

Q12-59 Income Tax Payable was $4,500 at the end of the year and $3,000 at the beginning. Income tax expense for the year totaled $59,500. What amount of cash did the company pay for income tax during the year?

a. $62,500   c. $61,000
b. $58,000   d. $59,500

Problems

All of the A and B problems can be found within MyAccountingLab, an online homework and practice environment. Your instructor may ask you to complete these problems using MyAccountingLab.

MyAccountingLab

(Group A)

P12-60A *(Learning Objectives 2, 3: Preparing an income statement, balance sheet, and statement of cash flows—indirect method)* Antique Automobiles of Dallas, Inc., was formed on January 1, 2010. The following transactions occurred during 2010:

On January 1, 2010, Antique issued its common stock for $440,000. Early in January, Antique made the following cash payments:

a. $180,000 for equipment
b. $203,000 for inventory (seven cars at $29,000 each)
c. $17,000 for 2010 rent on a store building

In February, Antique purchased two cars for inventory on account. Cost of this inventory was $80,000 ($40,000.00 each). Before year-end, Antique paid $56,000 of this debt. Antique uses the FIFO method to account for inventory.

During 2010, Antique sold eight vintage autos for a total of $488,000. Before year-end, Antique collected 80% of this amount.

The business employs five people. The combined annual payroll is $125,000, of which Antique owes $7,000 at year-end. At the end of the year, Antique paid income tax of $12,600.

Late in 2010, Antique declared and paid cash dividends of $12,000.

For equipment, Antique uses the straight-line depreciation method, over five years, with zero residual value.

❙ Requirements

1. Prepare Antique Automobiles of Dallas, Inc.'s income statement for the year ended December 31, 2010. Use the single-step format, with all revenues listed together and all expenses together.
2. Prepare Antique's balance sheet at December 31, 2010.
3. Prepare Antique's statement of cash flows for the year ended December 31, 2010. Format cash flows from operating activities by using the *indirect* method.

P12-61A *(Learning Objectives 2, 4: Preparing an income statement, balance sheet, and statement of cash flows—direct method)* Use the Antique Automobiles of Dallas, Inc., data from Problem 12-60A.

❙ Requirements

1. Prepare Antique's income statement for the year ended December 31, 2010. Use the single-step format, with all revenues listed together and all expenses together.
2. Prepare Antique's balance sheet at December 31, 2010.
3. Prepare Antique's statement of cash flows for the year ended December 31, 2010. Format cash flows from operating activities by using the *direct* method.

P12-62A (*Learning Objectives 2, 3: Preparing the statement of cash flows—indirect method*) Morgensen Software Corp. has assembled the following data for the years ending December 31, 2010 and 2009.

	December 31, 2010	December 31, 2009
Current Accounts:		
Current assets:		
Cash and cash equivalents	$120,400	$30,000
Accounts receivable	69,900	64,400
Inventories......................................	8,600	80,000
Prepaid expenses.............................	3,100	1,500
Current liabilities:		
Accounts payable.............................	$ 57,200	$55,800
Income tax payable..........................	18,600	16,700
Accrued liabilities	15,500	27,200

Transaction Data for 2010:

Acquisition of land by issuing long-term note payable	$201,000	Purchase of treasury stock	$10,700
Stock dividends	31,400	Loss on sale of equipment	5,000
Collection of loan.................	10,600	Payment of cash dividends	9,300
Depreciation expense	17,000	Issuance of long-term note payable to borrow cash.....	34,500
Purchase of building.............	97,000	Net income..........................	6,500
Retirement of bonds payable by issuing common stock	64,000	Issuance of common stock for cash	36,500
Purchase of long-term investment.......................	44,600	Proceeds from sale of equipment	81,000
		Amortization expense..........	5,000

❙ Requirement

1. Prepare Morgensen Software Corp.'s statement of cash flows using the *indirect* method to report operating activities. Include an accompanying schedule of noncash investing and financing activities.

writing assignment ■

■ spreadsheet

P12-63A (*Learning Objectives 2, 3: Preparing the statement of cash flows—indirect method*) The comparative balance sheets of Maynard Movie Theater Company at June 30, 2010 and 2009, reported the following:

	June 30, 2010	June 30, 2009
Current assets:		
Cash and cash equivalents	$52,600	$17,000
Accounts receivable	14,500	21,600
Inventories......................................	63,500	61,100
Prepaid expenses.............................	3,100	8,000
Current liabilities:		
Accounts payable.............................	$57,800	$56,200
Accrued liabilities	37,300	17,300
Income tax payable..........................	9,100	10,100

Maynard Movie Theater's transactions during the year ended June 30, 2010, included the following:

Acquisition of land by issuing note payable	$100,000	Sale of long-term investment....	$12,700
Amortization expense............	9,000	Depreciation expense	15,700
Payment of cash dividend......	29,000	Cash purchase of building.....	44,000
Cash purchase of equipment........................	79,000	Net income..........................	54,000
Issuance of long-term note payable to borrow cash.....	42,000	Issuance of common stock for cash....................	24,000
		Stock dividend......................	11,000

Requirements

1. Prepare Maynard Movie Theater Company's statement of cash flows for the year ended June 30, 2010, using the *indirect* method to report cash flows from operating activities. Report noncash investing and financing activities in an accompanying schedule.
2. Evaluate Maynard Movie Theater's cash flows for the year. Mention all three categories of cash flows and give the reason for your evaluation.

P12-64A (*Learning Objectives 2, 3: Preparing the statement of cash flows—indirect method*)   The 2010 and 2009 comparative balance sheets and 2010 income statement of Affordable Supply Corp. follow:

■ spreadsheet

writing assignment ■

Affordable Supply Corp.
Comparative Balance Sheets

	December 31, 2010	December 31, 2009	Increase (Decrease)
Current assets:			
Cash and cash equivalents	$ 17,300	$ 4,000	$ 13,300
Accounts receivable	45,700	44,500	1,200
Inventories....................................	61,400	47,000	14,400
Prepaid expenses...........................	1,800	3,900	(2,100)
Plant assets:			
Land	69,100	22,600	46,500
Equipment, net	53,100	49,500	3,600
Total assets......................................	$248,400	$171,500	$ 76,900
Current liabilities:			
Accounts payable...........................	$ 35,200	$ 26,900	$ 8,300
Salary payable	24,000	13,100	10,900
Other accrued liabilities................	22,100	23,700	(1,600)
Long-term liabilities:			
Notes payable................................	51,000	34,000	17,000
Stockholders' equity:			
Common stock, no-par..................	88,600	65,900	22,700
Retained earnings	27,500	7,900	19,600
Total liabilities and stockholders' equity.....	$248,400	$171,500	$ 76,900

Affordable Supply Corp.
Income Statement
Year Ended December 31, 2010

Revenues:		
Sales revenue		$446,000
Expenses:		
Cost of goods sold	$186,600	
Salary expense	76,000	
Depreciation expense	17,700	
Other operating expense	49,700	
Interest expense	24,100	
Income tax expense	29,000	
Total expenses		383,100
Net income		$ 62,900

Affordable Supply had no noncash investing and financing transactions during 2010. During the year, there were no sales of land or equipment, no payment of notes payable, no retirements of stock, and no treasury stock transactions.

❙ Requirements

1. Prepare the 2010 statement of cash flows, formatting operating activities by using the *indirect* method.
2. How will what you learned in this problem help you evaluate an investment?

writing assignment ■

■ spreadsheet

P12-65A (*Learning Objectives 2, 4: Preparing the statement of cash flows—direct method*) Use the Affordable Supply Corp. data from Problem 12-64A.

❙ Requirements

1. Prepare the 2010 statement of cash flows by using the *direct* method.
2. How will what you learned in this problem help you evaluate an investment?

writing assignment ■

P12-66A (*Learning Objectives 2, 4: Preparing the statement of cash flows—direct method*) Ramirez Furniture Gallery, Inc., provided the following data from the company's records for the year ended May 31, 2010:

a. Credit sales, $584,500
b. Loan to another company, $12,300
c. Cash payments to purchase plant assets, $72,100
d. Cost of goods sold, $312,400
e. Proceeds from issuance of common stock, $7,000
f. Payment of cash dividends, $48,300
g. Collection of interest, $4,600
h. Acquisition of equipment by issuing short-term note payable, $16,000
i. Payments of salaries, $78,000
j. Proceeds from sale of plant assets, $22,600, including $6,900 loss
k. Collections on accounts receivable, $428,500
l. Interest revenue, $3,500
m. Cash receipt of dividend revenue, $8,900
n. Payments to suppliers, $368,000

o. Cash sales, $191,300
p. Depreciation expense, $40,100
q. Proceeds from issuance of note payable, $24,500
r. Payments of long-term notes payable, $83,000
s. Interest expense and payments, $13,400
t. Salary expense, $75,800
u. Loan collections, $11,900
v. Proceeds from sale of investments, $9,500, including $4,400 gain
w. Payment of short-term note payable by issuing long-term note payable, $94,000
x. Amortization expenses, $3,100
y. Income tax expense and payments, $38,300
z. Cash balance: May 31, 2009, $19,100; May 31, 2010, $14,500

Requirements

1. Prepare Ramirez Furniture Gallery, Inc.'s statement of cash flows for the year ended May 31, 2010. Use the *direct* method for cash flows from operating activities. Include an accompanying schedule of noncash investing and financing activities.
2. Evaluate 2010 from a cash-flows standpoint. Give your reasons.

P12-67A (*Learning Objectives 2, 3, 4: Preparing the statement of cash flows—direct and indirect methods*)   To prepare the statement of cash flows, accountants for Daisy Electric Company have summarized 2010 activity in two accounts as follows:

■ spreadsheet

Cash

Beginning balance	49,600	Payments on accounts payable	402,000
Sale of long-term investment	14,600	Payments of dividends	47,900
Collections from customers	661,800	Payments of salaries and wages	143,600
Issuance of common stock	61,000	Payments of interest	26,600
Receipts of dividends	16,900	Purchase of equipment	31,000
		Payments of operating expenses	34,500
		Payment of long-term note payable	41,500
		Purchase of treasury stock	22,400
		Payment of income tax	17,000
Ending Balance	37,400		

Common Stock

	Beginning balance	74,200
	Issuance for cash	61,000
	Issuance to acquire land	80,800
	Issuance to retire note payable	20,000
	Ending balance	236,000

Daisy's 2010 income statement and balance sheet data follow:

Daisy Electric Company
Income Statement
Year Ended December 31, 2010

Revenues:		
Sales revenue		$689,200
Dividend revenue		16,900
Total revenue		706,100
Expenses and losses:		
Cost of goods sold	$334,000	
Salary and wage expense	135,800	
Depreciation expense	19,000	
Other operating expense	23,700	
Interest expense	29,100	
Income tax expense	14,500	
Loss on sale of investments	22,100	
Total expenses and losses		578,200
Net income		$127,900

Daisy Electric Company
Selected Balance Sheet Data
December 31, 2010

	Increase (Decrease)
Current assets:	
Cash and cash equivalents	$(12,200)
Accounts receivable	27,400
Inventories......................................	59,700
Prepaid expenses..............................	600
Long-term investments.............................	(36,700)
Equipment, net..	12,000
Land	80,800
Current liabilities:	
Accounts payable.............................	(8,300)
Interest payable	2,500
Salary payable	(7,800)
Other accrued liabilities....................	(10,200)
Income tax payable...........................	(2,500)
Long-term note payable	(61,500)
Common stock...	161,800
Retained earnings......................................	80,000
Treasury stock...	(22,400)

▌ Requirements

1. Prepare the statement of cash flows of Daisy Electric Company for the year ended December 31, 2010, using the *direct* method to report operating activities. Also prepare the accompanying schedule of noncash investing and financing activities.
2. Use Daisy's 2010 income statement and balance sheet to prepare a supplementary schedule of cash flows from operating activities by using the *indirect* method.

P12-68A (*Learning Objectives 2, 3, 4: Preparing the statement of cash flows—indirect and direct methods*)   The comparative balance sheets of Stephen Summers Design Studio, Inc., at June 30, 2010 and 2009, and transaction data for fiscal 2010 are as follows:

Stephen Summers Design Studio
Comparative Balance Sheets

	June 30, 2010	June 30, 2009	Increase (Decrease)
Current assets:			
Cash	$ 28,900	$ 21,000	$ 7,900
Accounts receivable	48,800	31,700	17,100
Inventories.....................................	78,400	80,700	(2,300)
Prepaid expenses............................	3,100	2,200	900
Long-term investment	10,300	5,600	4,700
Equipment, net..	74,000	73,300	700
Land	33,100	94,500	(61,400)
	$276,600	$309,000	$(32,400)
Current liabilities:			
Notes payable, short-term	$ 14,000	$19,000	$(5,000)
Accounts payable...........................	29,400	40,400	(11,000)
Income tax payable........................	13,200	14,400	(1,200)
Accrued liabilities	3,700	9,400	(5,700)
Interest payable	3,400	2,400	1,000
Salary payable	1,000	4,400	(3,400)
Long-term note payable	47,200	94,000	(46,800)
Common stock..	59,400	52,000	7,400
Retained earnings...................................	105,300	73,000	32,300
	$276,600	$309,000	$(32,400)

Transaction data for the year ended June 30, 2010:

 a. Net income, $80,700
 b. Depreciation expense on equipment, $13,900
 c. Purchased long-term investment, $4,700
 d. Sold land for $54,900, including $6,500 loss
 e. Acquired equipment by issuing long-term note payable, $14,600
 f. Paid long-term note payable, $61,400
 g. Received cash for issuance of common stock, $2,400
 h. Paid cash dividends, $48,400
 i. Paid short-term note payable by issuing common stock, $5,000

▌ Requirements

1. Prepare the statement of cash flows of Stephen Summers Design Studio, Inc., for the year ended June 30, 2010, using the *indirect* method to report operating activities. Also prepare the accompanying schedule of noncash investing and financing activities. All current accounts except short-term notes payable result from operating transactions.
2. Prepare a supplementary schedule showing cash flows from operations by the *direct* method. The accounting records provide the following: collections from customers, $241,700; interest received, $1,700; payments to suppliers, $118,600; payments to employees, $41,900; payments for income tax, $12,900; and payment of interest, $4,900.

(Group B)

P12-69B (*Learning Objectives 2, 3: Preparing an income statement, balance sheet, and statement of cash flows—indirect method*) Sweet Automobiles of Pepperell, Inc., was formed on January 1, 2010. The following transactions occurred during 2010:

On January 1, 2010, Sweet issued its common stock for $350,000. Early in January, Sweet made the following cash payments:

- **a.** $140,000 for equipment
- **b.** $175,000 for inventory (five cars at $35,000 each)
- **c.** $19,000 for 2010 rent on a store building

In February, Sweet purchased six cars for inventory on account. Cost of this inventory was $282,000 ($47,000 each). Before year end, Sweet paid $197,400 of this debt. Sweet uses the FIFO method to account for inventory.

During 2010, Sweet sold six vintage autos for a total of $426,000. Before year-end, Sweet collected 90% of this amount.

The business employs three people. The combined annual payroll is $90,000, of which Sweet owes $5,000 at year-end. At the end of the year, Sweet paid income tax of $14,000.

Late in 2010, Sweet declared and paid cash dividends of $16,000.

For equipment, Sweet uses the straight-line depreciation method, over five years, with zero residual value.

▌ Requirements

1. Prepare Sweet Automobiles of Pepperell, Inc.'s income statement for the year ended December 31, 2010. Use the single-step format, with all revenues listed together and all expenses together.
2. Prepare Sweet's balance sheet at December 31, 2010.
3. Prepare Sweet's statement of cash flows for the year ended December 31, 2010. Format cash flows from operating activities by using the *indirect* method.

P12-70B (*Learning Objectives 2, 4: Preparing an income statement, balance sheet, and statement of cash flows—direct method*) Use the Sweet Automobiles of Pepperell, Inc., data from Problem 12-69B.

▌ Requirements

1. Prepare Sweet's income statement for the year ended December 31, 2010. Use the single-step format, with all revenues listed together and all expenses together.
2. Prepare Sweet's balance sheet at December 31, 2010.
3. Prepare Sweet's statement of cash flows for the year ended December 31, 2010. Format cash flows from operating activities by using the *direct* method.

P12-71B (*Learning Objectives 2, 3: Preparing the statement of cash flows—indirect method*) Neighbor Software Corp. has assembled the following data for the year ended December 31, 2010:

	December 31,	
	2010	2009
Current Accounts:		
Current assets:		
Cash and cash equivalents	$60,000	$26,000
Accounts receivable	22,000	64,100
Inventories.......................................	88,500	85,000
Prepaid expenses...............................	3,200	2,400
Current liabilities:		
Accounts payable..............................	57,700	55,500
Income tax payable...........................	29,000	16,900
Accrued liabilities	15,500	7,600

Transaction Data for 2010:

Acquisition of land by issuing		Purchase of treasury stock	$14,400
long-term note payable	$198,000	Loss on sale of equipment	3,000
Stock dividends	31,600	Payment of cash dividends	18,800
Collection of loan..................	11,000	Issuance of long-term note	
Depreciation expense	17,000	payable to borrow cash.....	34,000
Purchase of building.............	159,000	Net income..........................	58,000
Retirement of bonds payable		Issuance of common stock	
by issuing common stock	71,000	for cash	74,200
Purchase of long-term		Proceeds from sale of	
investment.........................	49,900	equipment	12,900
		Amortization expense..........	6,000

Requirement

1. Prepare Neighbor Software Corp.'s statement of cash flows using the *indirect* method to report operating activities. Include an accompanying schedule of noncash investing and financing activities.

P12-72B (*Learning Objectives 2, 3: Preparing the statement of cash flows—indirect method*)   The comparative balance sheets of Medford Movie Theater Company at June 30, 2010 and 2009, reported the following:

writing assignment ■

■ **spreadsheet**

	June 30,	
	2010	2009
Current assets:		
Cash and cash equivalents	$ 5,800	$16,000
Accounts receivable	14,000	21,700
Inventories.......................................	63,000	60,800
Prepaid expenses...............................	17,200	8,000
Current liabilities:		
Accounts payable..............................	$58,000	$55,900
Accrued liabilities	57,400	47,400
Income tax payable...........................	6,500	10,500

Medford's transactions during the year ended June 30, 2010, included the following:

Acquisition of land by issuing note payable	$115,000	Sale of long-term investment....	$13,400
Amortization expense............	6,000	Depreciation expense	15,600
Payment of cash dividend......	34,000	Cash purchase of building.....	59,000
Cash purchase of		Net income.............................	50,000
equipment	45,600	Issuance of common	
Issuance of long-term note		stock for cash....................	13,000
payable to borrow cash	26,000	Stock dividend......................	9,000

Requirements

1. Prepare Medford Movie Theater Company's statement of cash flows for the year ended June 30, 2010, using the *indirect* method to report cash flows from operating activities. Report noncash investing and financing activities in an accompanying schedule.
2. Evaluate Medford's cash flows for the year. Mention all three categories of cash flows and give the reason for your evaluation.

writing assignment ■

■ spreadsheet

P12-73B (*Learning Objectives 2, 3: Preparing the statement of cash flows—indirect method*)   The 2010 and 2009 comparative balance sheets and 2010 income statement of King Supply Corp. follow:

King Supply Corp.
Comparative Balance Sheets

	December 31, 2010	December 31, 2009	Increase (Decrease)
Current assets:			
Cash and cash equivalents	$ 17,600	$ 5,000	$ 12,600
Accounts receivable	45,500	44,500	1,000
Inventories....................................	79,100	67,500	11,600
Prepaid expenses...........................	2,100	6,000	(3,900)
Plant assets:			
Land	69,100	21,900	47,200
Equipment, net	53,100	49,200	3,900
Total assets....................................	$266,500	$194,100	$ 72,400
Current liabilities:			
Accounts payable...........................	$ 35,800	$ 25,600	$ 10,200
Salary payable	22,000	15,600	6,400
Other accrued liabilities.................	22,900	24,200	(1,300)
Long-term liabilities:			
Notes payable................................	50,000	37,000	13,000
Stockholders' equity:			
Common stock, no-par..................	88,600	64,300	24,300
Retained earnings	47,200	27,400	19,800
Total liabilities and stockholders' equity.....	$266,500	$194,100	$ 72,400

King Supply Corp.
Income Statement
Year Ended December 31, 2010

Revenues:		
Sales revenue		$445,000
Expenses:		
Cost of goods sold	$185,100	
Salary expense	76,400	
Depreciation expense	17,400	
Other operating expense	49,800	
Interest expense	24,800	
Income tax expense	29,500	
Total expenses		383,000
Net income		$ 62,000

King Supply had no noncash investing and financing transactions during 2010. During the year, there were no sales of land or equipment, no payment of notes payable, no retirements of stock, and no treasury stock transactions.

❙ *Requirements*

1. Prepare the 2010 statement of cash flows, formatting operating activities by using the *indirect* method.
2. How will what you learned in this problem help you evaluate an investment?

P12-74B (*Learning Objectives 2, 4: Preparing the statement of cash flows—direct method*)   Use the King Supply Corp. data from Problem P12-73B.

❙ *Requirements*

1. Prepare the 2010 statement of cash flows by using the *direct* method.
2. How will what you learned in this problem help you evaluate an investment?

P12-75B (*Learning Objectives 2, 4: Preparing the statement of cash flows—direct method*)   Dunleavy Furniture Gallery, Inc., provided the following data from the company's records for the year ended December 31, 2010:

a. Credit sales, $567,000
b. Loan to another company, $12,800
c. Cash payments to purchase plant assets, $59,900
d. Cost of goods sold, $382,700
e. Proceeds from issuance of common stock, $7,000
f. Payment of cash dividends, $48,000
g. Collection of interest, $4,200
h. Acquisition of equipment by issuing short-term note payable, $16,500
i. Payments of salaries, $93,700
j. Proceeds from sale of plant assets, $22,300, including $7,000 loss
k. Collections on accounts receivable, $406,000
l. Interest revenue, $3,300
m. Cash receipt of dividend revenue, $4,000
n. Payments to suppliers, $387,200

o. Cash sales, $201,000
p. Depreciation expense, $40,100
q. Proceeds from issuance of note payable, $19,300
r. Payments of long-term notes payable, $69,000
s. Interest expense and payments, $13,700
t. Salary expense, $91,600
u. Loan collections, $12,100
v. Proceeds from sale of investments, $11,200, including $3,800 gain
w. Payment of short-term note payable by issuing long-term note payable, $68,000
x. Amortization expenses, $3,200
y. Income tax expense and payments, $36,800
z. Cash balance: December 31, 2009, $40,000; December 31, 2010, $6,000

writing assignment ■

■ spreadsheet

writing assignment ■

❙ Requirements

1. Prepare Dunleavy Furniture Gallery, Inc.'s statement of cash flows for the year ended December 31, 2010. Use the *direct* method for cash flows from operating activities. Include an accompanying schedule of noncash investing and financing activities.
2. Evaluate 2010 from a cash-flows standpoint. Give your reasons.

■ spreadsheet

P12-76B (*Learning Objectives 2, 3, 4: Preparing the statement of cash flows—direct and indirect methods*) To prepare the statement of cash flows, accountants for Spencer Electric Company have summarized 2010 activity in two accounts as follows:

Cash

Beginning balance	71,500	Payments on accounts payable	399,500
Sale of long-term investment	20,000	Payments of dividends	27,600
Collections from customers	661,600	Payments of salaries and wages	143,300
Issuance of common stock	22,200	Payments of interest	27,100
Receipts of dividends	16,800	Purchase of equipment	31,700
		Payments of operating expenses	34,900
		Payment of long-term note payable	41,300
		Purchase of treasury stock	26,300
		Payment of income tax	18,600
Ending Balance	41,800		

Common Stock

Beginning balance	73,200
Issuance for cash	22,200
Issuance to acquire land	61,700
Issuance to retire note payable	17,000
Ending balance	174,100

Spencer's 2010 income statement and balance sheet data follow:

Spencer Electric Company
Income Statement
Year Ended December 31, 2010

Revenues:		
Sales revenue		$647,200
Dividend revenue		16,800
Total revenue		664,000
Expenses and losses:		
Cost of goods sold	$404,600	
Salary and wage expense	150,500	
Depreciation expense	16,400	
Other operating expense	30,500	
Interest expense	24,900	
Income tax expense	16,100	
Loss on sale of investments................	16,700	
Total expenses and losses		659,700
Net income..		$ 4,300

Spencer Electric Company
Selected Balance Sheet Data
December 31, 2010

	Increase (Decrease)
Current assets:	
Cash and cash equivalents	$(29,700)
Accounts receivable	(14,400)
Inventories.......................................	(12,900)
Prepaid expenses..............................	(6,000)
Long-term investments	(36,700)
Equipment, net..	15,300
Land	61,700
Current liabilities:	
Accounts payable..............................	(7,800)
Interest payable	(2,200)
Salary payable	7,200
Other accrued liabilities....................	(10,400)
Income tax payable...........................	(2,500)
Long-term note payable	(58,300)
Common stock..	100,900
Retained earnings......................................	(23,300)
Treasury stock..	(26,300)

Requirements

1. Prepare the statement of cash flows of Spencer Electric Company for the year ended December 31, 2010, using the *direct* method to report operating activities. Also prepare the accompanying schedule of noncash investing and financing activities.
2. Use Spencer's 2010 income statement and balance sheet to prepare a supplementary schedule of cash flows from operating activities by using the *indirect* method.

P12-77B *(Learning Objectives 2, 3, 4: Preparing the statement of cash flows—indirect and direct methods)*   The comparative balance sheets of Franny Franklin Design Studio, Inc., at June 30, 2010 and 2009, and transaction data for fiscal 2010 are as follows:

Franny Franklin Design Studio
Comparative Balance Sheets

	June 30, 2010	June 30, 2009	Increase (Decrease)
Current assets:			
Cash	$ 28,900	$ 2,400	$ 26,500
Accounts receivable	59,000	22,300	36,700
Inventories....................................	98,200	40,400	57,800
Prepaid expenses...........................	3,500	2,500	1,000
Long-term investment	10,000	5,000	5,000
Equipment, net......................................	74,900	73,600	1,300
Land	58,100	98,900	(40,800)
	$332,600	$245,100	$ 87,500)
Current liabilities:			
Notes payable, short-term	$ 13,200	$20,200	$ (7,000)
Accounts payable...........................	42,300	41,300	1,000
Income tax payable........................	13,300	14,400	(1,100)
Accrued liabilities	97,400	9,300	88,100
Interest payable	3,500	2,500	1,000
Salary payable	400	3,100	(2,700)
Long-term note payable	48,700	94,200	(45,500)
Common stock...	79,700	51,600	28,100
Retained earnings....................................	34,100	8,500	25,600
	$332,600	$245,100	$ 87,500

Transaction data for the year ended June 30, 2010:

a. Net income, $73,400
b. Depreciation expense on equipment, $13,900
c. Purchased long-term investment, $5,000
d. Sold land for $33,800, including $7,000 loss
e. Acquired equipment by issuing long-term note payable, $15,200
f. Paid long-term note payable, $60,700
g. Received cash for issuance of common stock, $21,100
h. Paid cash dividends, $47,800
i. Paid short-term note payable by issuing common stock, $7,000

▍Requirements

1. Prepare the statement of cash flows of Franny Franklin Design Studio, Inc., for the year ended June 30, 2010, using the *indirect* method to report operating activities. Also prepare the accompanying schedule of noncash investing and financing activities. All current accounts except short-term notes payable result from operating transactions.

2. Prepare a supplementary schedule showing cash flows from operations by the *direct* method. The accounting records provide the following: collections from customers, $272,300; interest received, $1,400; payments to suppliers, $130,900; payments to employees, $40,000; payments for income tax, $12,500; and payment of interest, $5,200.

APPLY YOUR KNOWLEDGE

Decision Cases

Case 1. (*Learning Objective 3: Preparing and using the statement of cash flows to evaluate operations*) The 2011 income statement and the 2011 comparative balance sheet of T-Bar-M Camp, Inc., have just been distributed at a meeting of the camp's board of directors. The directors raise a fundamental question: Why is the cash balance so low? This question is especially troublesome since 2011 showed record profits. As the controller of the company, you must answer the question.

writing assignment ■

T–Bar–M Camp, Inc.
Income Statement
Year Ended December 31, 2011

(In thousands)		
Revenues:		
Sales revenue		$436
Expenses:		
Cost of goods sold	$221	
Salary expense	48	
Depreciation expense	46	
Interest expense	13	
Amortization expense	11	
Total expenses		339
Net income		$ 97

T–Bar–M Camp, Inc.
Comparative Balance Sheets
December 31, 2011 and 2010

(In thousands)	2011	2010
Assets		
Cash	$ 17	$ 63
Accounts receivable, net	72	61
Inventories	194	181
Long-term investments	31	0
Property, plant, and equipment	369	259
Accumulated depreciation	(244)	(198)
Patents	177	188
Totals	$ 616	$ 554
Liabilities and Owners' Equity		
Accounts payable	$ 63	$ 56
Accrued liabilities	12	17
Notes payable, long-term	179	264
Common stock, no par	149	61
Retained earnings	213	156
Totals	$ 616	$ 554

I Requirements

1. Prepare a statement of cash flows for 2011 in the format that best shows the relationship between net income and operating cash flow. The company sold no plant assets or long-term investments and issued no notes payable during 2011. There were *no* noncash investing and financing transactions during the year. Show all amounts in thousands.
2. Answer the board members' question: Why is the cash balance so low? Point out the two largest cash payments during 2011. (Challenge)
3. Considering net income and the company's cash flows during 2011, was it a good year or a bad year? Give your reasons.

writing assignment ■ **Case 2.** (*Learning Objectives 1, 2: Using cash-flow data to evaluate an investment*) Applied Technology, Inc., and Four-Star Catering are asking you to recommend their stock to your clients. Because Applied and Four-Star earn about the same net income and have similar financial positions, your decision depends on their statements of cash flows, summarized as follows:

	Applied		Four–Star	
Net cash provided by operating activities:		$ 30,000		$ 70,000
Cash provided by (used for) investing activities:				
Purchase of plant assets	$(20,000)		$(100,000)	
Sale of plant assets	40,000	20,000	10,000	(90,000)
Cash provided by (used for) financing activities:				
Issuance of common stock		—		30,000
Paying off long-term debt		(40,000)		—
Net increase in cash		$ 10,000		$10,000

Based on their cash flows, which company looks better? Give your reasons. (Challenge)

Ethical Issue

writing assignment ■ Columbia Motors is having a bad year. Net income is only $37,000. Also, two important overseas customers are falling behind in their payments to Columbia, and Columbia's accounts receivable are ballooning. The company desperately needs a loan. The Columbia board of directors is considering ways to put the best face on the company's financial statements. Columbia's bank closely examines cash flow from operations. Daniel Peavey, Columbia's controller, suggests reclassifying as long-term the receivables from the slow-paying clients. He explains to the board that removing the $80,000 rise in accounts receivable from current assets will increase net cash provided by operations. This approach may help Columbia get the loan.

I Requirements

1. Using only the amounts given, compute net cash provided by operations, both without and with the reclassification of the receivables. Which reporting makes Columbia look better?
2. Identify the ethical issue(s).
3. Who are the stakeholders?
4. Analyze the issue from the (a) economic, (b) legal, and (c) ethical standpoints. What is the potential impact on all stakeholders?
5. What should the board do?
6. Under what conditions would the reclassification of the receivables be considered ethical?

Focus on Financials: ■ Amazon.com, Inc.

(*Learning Objectives 1, 2, 3, 4: Using the statement of cash flows*) Use **Amazon.com, Inc.'s** consolidated statement of cash flows along with the company's other consolidated financial statements, all in Appendix A at the end of the book, to answer the following questions.

I *Requirements*

1. By which method does Amazon.com, Inc., report cash flows from *operating* activities? How can you tell?

2. Suppose Amazon.com, Inc., reported net cash flows from operating activities by using the direct method. Compute these amounts for the year ended December 31, 2008 (ignore the statement of cash flows, and use only Amazon.com, Inc.'s income statement and balance sheet).

   a. Collections from vendors, customers, and others. Use the information in Note 1—Description of Business and Accounting Policies. Prepare a T-Account for Gross Accounts Receivable. Prepare another T-Account for Allowance for Doubtful Accounts. Calculate the beginning and ending gross amounts of gross accounts receivable by adding the beginning and ending balances of allowance for doubtful accounts ($81 and $64, respectively) to the net accounts receivable at both the beginning and end of the year. Assume that all sales are on account. Also assume that the company uses the percentage of net sales method for estimating doubtful accounts expense, and that the company estimates this amount at 0.5%.

   b. Payments to suppliers. Amazon.com, Inc., calls its Cost of Goods Sold "Cost of Sales." For this computation, use the format provided in Exhibit 12-15. Assume all inventory is purchased on account, and that all cash payments to suppliers are made from accounts payable.

3. Prepare a T-account for Net Fixed Assets (Fixed Assets minus Accumulated Depreciation). In this account, analyze all activity in the fixed assets and accumulated depreciation accounts for 2008. Use the information in Note 3—Fixed Assets to analyze this activity. Assume that Amazon.com, Inc., did not sell any fixed assets during the year. Compare your computation of fixed asset additions with the amount reflected in the investments section of the balance sheet. What is the difference? Where might that difference be reflected in Amazon's Consolidated Statement of Cash Flows? (Challenge)

4. Evaluate 2008 for Amazon.com, Inc., in terms of net income, total assets, stockholders' equity, cash flows from operating activities, and overall results. Be specific. (Challenge)

Focus on Analysis: ∎ Foot Locker, Inc.

(*Learning Objectives 1, 2, 3, 4: Analyzing cash flows*) Refer to the **Foot Locker, Inc.**, consolidated financial statements in Appendix B at the end of this book. Focus on fiscal 2007 (year ended February 2, 2008).

1. What is Foot Locker, Inc.'s main source of cash? Is this good news or bad news to Foot Locker managers, stockholders, and creditors? What is Foot Locker's main use of cash? Good news or bad news? Explain all answers in detail.

2. Explain briefly the three main reasons why net cash provided by operations differs from net income.

3. Did Foot Locker, Inc., buy or sell more fixed assets during fiscal 2007? How can you tell?

4. Identify the largest two items in the financing activities section of the Consolidated Statement of Cash Flows. Explain the company's probable reasoning behind these two expenditures.

Group Projects

Project 1.   Each member of the group should obtain the annual report of a different company. Select companies in different industries. Evaluate each company's trend of cash flows for the most recent two years. In your evaluation of the companies' cash flows, you may use any other information that is publicly available—for example, the other financial statements (income statement, balance sheet, statement of stockholders' equity, and the related notes) and news stories from magazines and newspapers. Rank the companies' cash flows from best to worst and write a two-page report on your findings.

Project 2. Select a company and obtain its annual report, including all the financial statements. Focus on the statement of cash flows and, in particular, the cash flows from operating activities. Specify whether the company uses the direct method or the indirect method to report operating cash flows. As necessary, use the other financial statements (income statement, balance sheet, and statement of stockholders' equity) and the notes to prepare the company's cash flows from operating activities by using the *other* method.

For online homework, exercises, and problems that provide you with immediate feedback, please visit www.myaccountinglab.com.

Quick Check Answers

1. *a*
2. *a*
3. *d*
4. *b* ($150,000 + $8,000)
5. *d*
6. *c*
7. *c* ($50,000 + $10,000 − $8,000 + $15,000 + $9,000 + $3,000)
8. *b* ($5,000 − $35,000 + $40,000)
9. *b* (− $1,000 + $4,000 − $16,000)
10. *b* ($40,000 + $15,000)
11. *d* ($60,000 + $700,000 − $50,000)
12. *b* ($750,000 − $410,000 − $180,000)
13. *d* ($410,000 − $10,000 + $12,000)

13

Financial Statement Analysis

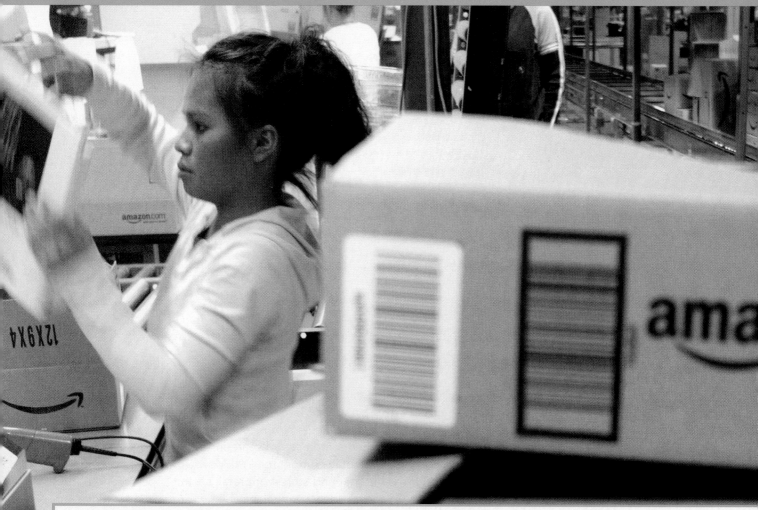

SPOTLIGHT: How Well is Amazon.com Doing?

Throughout this book we have shown how to account for companies such as **Apple, Inc.**, **Starbucks**, **PepsiCo**, **Southwest Airlines**, and **Google**. Only one aspect of the course remains: the overall analysis of financial statements. In this chapter, we cover this process, using the financial statements of Amazon.com, one of the book's focus companies, whose annual report is in Appendix A.

Amazon.com is the largest virtual supermarket on the globe. Since its inception as mostly a bookseller in 1995, the company has become synonymous with Internet retailing, expanding its lines of merchandise to cover almost every conceivable consumer item. Its Web site (www.amazon.com) offers the Earth's biggest selection of merchandise: books; movies, music, and games; computer hardware and software; electronics; home and garden supplies; grocery, health, and beauty products; children's toys and apparel; adult apparel; sports and recreational gear; and auto and industrial tools. In fact, it is hard to think of any consumer item Amazon.com does not sell at competitive prices! How well has Amazon.com been performing during the most severe economic recession in 70 years? We can answer that question by financial statement analysis. We begin with the analysis of Amazon.com, Inc.'s comparative Consolidated Statements of Operations for years ended December 31, 2008, 2007, and 2006. In 2008, Amazon.com earned revenues of about $19.2 billion. Is that positive or negative news? One of several things we can do to answer that question is to compare 2008 results to 2007. We also need to compare Amazon.com's results with those of some of its competitors.

Amazon.com, Inc.
Consolidated Statements of Operations

(In millions, except per share data)	Year ended December 31		
	2008	2007	2006
Net sales	$19,166	$14,835	$10,711
Cost of sales	14,896	11,482	8,255
Gross profit	4,270	3,353	2,456
Operating expenses:			
Fulfillment	1,658	1,292	937
Marketing	482	344	263
Technology and content	1,033	818	662
General and administrative	279	235	195
Other operating expense (income), net	(24)	9	10
Total operating expenses	3,428	2,698	2,067
Income from operations	842	655	389
Interest income	83	90	59
Interest expense	(71)	(77)	(78)
Other income (expense), net	47	(8)	7
Total non-operating income (expense)	59	5	(12)
Income before income taxes	901	660	377
Provision for income taxes	(247)	(184)	(187)
Equity-method investment activity, net of tax	(9)	—	—
Net income	$ 645	$ 476	$ 190
Basic earnings per share	$ 1.52	$ 1.15	$ 0.46

This chapter covers the basic tools of financial analysis. The first part of the chapter shows how to evaluate Amazon.com from year to year and how to compare Amazon.com to other companies who are in the same lines of business. For this comparison we use a retail competitor, **Wal-Mart Stores, Inc.**, a company that operates in both the Internet and store-front retail sectors. The second part of the chapter discusses the most widely used financial ratios. You have seen many of these ratios in earlier chapters—the current ratio, days' sales in receivables, and inventory turnover, return on assets, and return on equity.

By studying all these ratios together,

- You will learn the basic tools of financial analysis.
- You will enhance your business education.

Regardless of your chosen field—marketing, management, finance, entrepreneurship, or accounting—you will find these analytical tools useful as you move through your career.

LEARNING OBJECTIVES

1 **Perform** a horizontal analysis of financial statements

2 **Perform** a vertical analysis of financial statements

3 **Prepare** common-size financial statements

4 **Use** the statement of cash flows for decisions

5 **Compute** the standard financial ratios

6 **Use** ratios in decision making

7 **Measure** the economic value added by operations

How Does an Investor Evaluate a Company?

Investors and creditors cannot evaluate a company by examining only one year's data. This is why most financial statements are comparative, that is, they cover at least two periods, like Amazon.com's Consolidated Statements of Operations that begins this chapter. In fact, most financial analysis covers trends of three to ten years. Since one of the goals of financial analysis is to predict the future, it makes sense to start by mapping the trends of the past. This is particularly true of income statement data such as net sales and net income.

The graphs in Exhibit 13-1 show Amazon.com's three-year trend of net sales and income from operations.

EXHIBIT 13-1 | Representative Financial Data of Amazon.com, Inc.

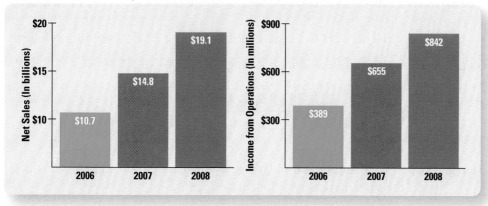

Amazon.com's net sales and income from operations (see Chapter 11 for discussion) both increased at a healthy pace during 2007 and 2008. These are good signs, because they may point the way to growth in company value in future years. How would you predict Amazon.com's net sales and income from operations for 2009 and beyond? Based on the recent past, you would probably extend the net sales line and the income from operations line upward. Let's examine some financial analysis tools. We begin with horizontal analysis.

HORIZONTAL ANALYSIS

OBJECTIVE

1 **Perform** a horizontal analysis of financial statements

Many decisions hinge on the trend of revenues, expenses, income from operations, and so on. Have revenues increased from last year? By how much? Suppose net sales have increased by $50,000. Considered alone this fact is not very helpful, but knowing the long-term *percentage change* in net sales helps a lot. It's better to know that net sales have increased by 20% than to know that the increase is $50,000. It's even better to know that percentage increases in net sales for the past several years have been rising year over year.

The study of percentage changes from year to year is called **horizontal analysis**. Computing a percentage change takes two steps:

1. Compute the dollar amount of the change from one period (the base period) to the next.

2. Divide the dollar amount of change by the base-period amount.

Illustration: Amazon.com, Inc.

Horizontal analysis is illustrated for Amazon.com, Inc., as follows (using the 2007 and 2008 figures, dollars in millions):

	2008	2007	Increase (Decrease) Amount	Increase (Decrease) Percentage
Net sales...............	$19,166	$14,835	$4,331	29.2%

Amazon.com's net sales increased by 29.2% during 2008, computed as follows:

Step 1 Compute the dollar amount of change from 2007 to 2008:

2008		2007		Increase
$19,166	−	$14,835	=	$4,331

Step 2 Divide the dollar amount of change by the base-period amount. This computes the percentage change for the period:

$$\text{Percentage change} = \frac{\text{Dollar amount of change}}{\text{Base-year amount}}$$

$$= \frac{\$4,331}{\$14,835} = 29.2\%$$

Exhibits 13-2 and 13-3 (on the following page) are detailed horizontal analysis for Amazon.com, Inc. The comparative Consolidated Statements of Operations show that net sales increased by 29.2% during 2008. In addition, Amazon.com's net income on the bottom line grew by 35.5%. Why the difference? Amazon.com was successful in increasing net sales while at the same time controlling, or even reducing, rates of increases in some expenses in 2008. In the operating expense category, only marketing expenses grew at a faster pace than net sales. Other operating items actually generated $24 million in income in 2008. Non-operating income items turned in a ten-fold positive change as well. The result was a 35.5% increase in net income after taxes, which is good news for shareholders!

EXHIBIT 13-2 | **Comparative Consolidated Statements of Operations— Horizontal Analysis**

Amazon.com, Inc.
Consolidated Statements of Operations

(In millions, except per share data)	Year ended December 31 2008	Year ended December 31 2007	Increase (decrease) Amount	Increase (decrease) Percentage
Net sales	$19,166	$14,835	$4,331	29.2%
Cost of sales	14,896	11,482	3,414	29.7
Gross profit	4,270	3,353	917	27.3
Operating expenses:				
Fulfillment	1,658	1,292	366	28.3
Marketing	482	344	138	40.1
Technology and content	1,033	818	215	26.3
General and administrative	279	235	44	18.7
Other operating expense (income), net	(24)	9	(33)	–366.7
Total operating expenses	3,428	2,698	730	27.1
Income from operations	842	655	187	28.5
Interest income	83	90	(7)	–7.8
Interest expense	(71)	(77)	6	–7.8
Other income (expense), net	47	(8)	55	687.5
Total non-operating income (expense)	59	5	54	1080.0
Income before income taxes	901	660	241	36.5
Provision for income taxes	(247)	(184)	(63)	34.2
Equity-method investment activity, net of tax	(9)	—		
Net income	$ 645	$ 476	$ 169	35.5%
Basic earnings per share	$ 1.52	$ 1.15	$ 0.37	32.2%

EXHIBIT 13-3 | Comparative Balance Sheets—Horizontal Analysis

Amazon.com, Inc.
Consolidated Balance Sheets

(in millions, except per share data)	December 31, 2008	2007	Increase (decrease) Amount	Percentage
ASSETS				
Current assets:				
Cash and cash equivalents	$2,769	$2,539	$ 230	9.1%
Marketable securities	958	573	385	67.2
Inventories	1,399	1,200	199	16.6
Accounts receivable, net and other	827	705	122	17.3
Deferred tax assets	204	147	57	38.8
Total current assets	6,157	5,164	993	19.2
Fixed assets, net	854	543	311	57.3
Deferred tax assets	145	260	(115)	–44.2
Goodwill	438	222	216	97.3
Other assets	720	296	424	143.2
Total assets	$8,314	$6,485	$1,829	28.2%
LIABILITIES AND STOCKHOLDERS' EQUITY				
Current liabilities:				
Accounts payable	$3,594	$2,795	$ 799	28.6%
Accrued expenses and other	1,093	902	191	21.2
Current portion of long-term debt	59	17	42	247.1
Total current liabilities	4,746	3,714	1,032	27.8
Long-term debt	409	1,282	(873)	–68.1
Other long-term liabilities	487	292	195	66.8
Commitments and contingencies				
Stockholders' equity:				
Preferred stock, $0.01 par value:				
Authorized shares—500				
Issued and outstanding shares—none	—	—		
Common stock, $0.01 par value:				
Authorized shares—5,000				
Issued shares—445 and 431				
Outstanding shares—428 and 416	4	4	—	0.0
Treasury stock, at cost	(600)	(500)	(100)	20.0
Additional paid-in capital	4,121	3,063	1,058	34.5
Accumulated other comprehensive income (loss)	(123)	5	(128)	–2560.0
Accumulated deficit	(730)	(1,375)	645	–46.9
Total stockholders' equity	2,672	1,197	1,475	123.2
Total liabilities and stockholders' equity	$8,314	$6,485	$1,829	28.2%

Studying changes in balance sheet accounts can enhance our total understanding of the current and long-term financial position of the entity. Let's look at a few balance sheet changes. First, cash increased by a healthy 9.1% in 2008, and marketable securities increased by 67.2%. These changes indicate that the company's liquidity has significantly improved. Inventories and accounts receivable increased (16.6% and 17.3%, respectively), but not as fast as net sales (29.2%). Accounts payable increased by about the same rate as net sales (28.6%) indicating that the company's payments of short-term debt has about kept pace with its overall rate of growth in net sales. The aggregate impact of these changes in the current section of the balance sheet indicates that the company is improving in its ability to operate in the short run, which is a healthy sign, especially when one considers that 2008 was a period of deep global economic recession. Long-term assets increased by rates in excess of 50%, indicating that the company is growing. It also appears that the company refinanced some of its long-term debt (likely at lower interest rates), and incurred additional current maturities, which it can well afford to pay off in the near future. The company used some of its excess cash to purchase additional treasury stock from its shareholders. In summary, the net impact of all of these changes reduced its accumulated deficit (from the company's early years) by 46.9%. Overall, it appears that 2008 was a very good year for Amazon.com, Inc., while other companies (especially retailers) were struggling to survive.

STOP & THINK...

Examine Exhibits 13-2 and 13-3. Which items had the largest percentage fluctuations during 2008? Should these fluctuations cause alarm? Explain your reasoning.

Answer:

On the Consolidated Statements of Operations, both for operating and non-operating income and expenses, the category Other Income and Expense had the largest percentage increases (in both categories, net expenses turned to net income, causing huge percentage swings). On the balance sheet, the categories Other Assets, Current Portion of Long-Term Debt, and Accumulated Other Comprehensive Income or Loss experienced huge percentage fluctuations. These fluctuations would *not* cause alarm because the dollar amount of the category is relatively small to begin with, causing year over year percentage changes to look very large. This illustrates the materiality concept, which says to give major consideration to big items and less attention to small (immaterial) items. In this case, these items are immaterial to the analysis of Amazon.com, Inc.

Trend Percentages

Trend percentages are a form of horizontal analysis. Trends indicate the direction a business is taking. How have revenues changed over a five-year period? What trend does net income show? These questions can be answered by trend percentages over a representative period, such as the most recent five years.

Trend percentages are computed by selecting a base year whose amounts are set equal to 100%. The amount for each following year is stated as a percentage of the base amount. To compute a trend percentage, divide an item for a later year by the base-year amount.

$$\text{Trend \%} = \frac{\text{Any year \$}}{\text{Base year \$}}$$

Recall that, in Chapter 11, we established that income from operations is often viewed as the primary measure of a company's earnings quality. This is because operating income represents a company's best predictor of the future net inflows from its core business units. Net income from operations is often used in estimating the current value of the business.

Amazon.com, Inc., showed income from operations for 2003–2008 years as follows:

(In millions)	2008	2007	2006	2005	2004	Base 2003
Income from operations	$842	$655	$389	$432	$440	$270

We want to calculate a trend for the five-year period 2003 through 2008. The first year in the series (2003) is set as the base year. Trend percentages are computed by dividing each year's amount by the 2003 amount. The resulting trend percentages follow (2003 = 100%):

	2008	2007	2006	2005	2004	Base 2003
Income from operations	312	243	144	160	163	100

Income from operations followed a downward trend from 2004 through 2006. In 2007, however, operating income took almost a 100% jump, relative to the base year, and it took another 69% jump in 2008. The most likely cause for these results is that Internet sales were just getting started in 2003. In the early years, people were generally reluctant to use the computer for their purchases because of concerns over Internet security. However, in recent years, improvements in security, as well as the relative convenience and lower cost of shopping from home as opposed to traveling to the store, have made Internet sales boom.

You can perform a trend analysis on any item you consider important. Trend analysis using income statement data is widely used for predicting the future.

Horizontal analysis highlights changes over time. However, no single technique gives a complete picture of a business.

VERTICAL ANALYSIS

OBJECTIVE

2 **Perform** a vertical analysis of financial statements

Vertical analysis shows the relationship of a financial-statement item to its base, which is the 100% figure. All items on the particular financial statement are reported as a percentage of the base. For the income statement, total revenue (sales) is usually the base. Suppose under normal conditions a company's net income is 8% of revenue. A drop to 6% may cause the company's stock price to fall.

Illustration: Amazon.com, Inc.

Exhibit 13-4 shows the vertical analysis of Amazon.com, Inc.'s income statement as a percentage of revenue (net sales). In this case,

$$\text{Vertical analysis } \% = \frac{\text{Each income statement item}}{\text{Total revenue}}$$

EXHIBIT 13-4 | **Comparative Income Statements—Vertical Analysis**

Amazon.com, Inc.
Consolidated Statements of Operations

(In millions, except per share data)	Year ended December 31			
	2008	% of total	2007	% of total
Net sales	$19,166	100.0%	$14,835	100.0%
Cost of sales	14,896	77.7	11,482	77.4
Gross profit	4,270	22.3	3,353	22.6
Operating expenses:				
Fulfillment	1,658	8.7	1,292	8.7
Marketing	482	2.5	344	2.3
Technology and content	1,033	5.4	818	5.5
General and administrative	279	1.5	235	1.6
Other operating expense (income), net	(24)	–0.1	9	0.1
Total operating expenses	3,428	17.9	2,698	18.2
Income from operations	842	4.4	655	4.4
Interest income	83	0.4	90	0.6
Interest expense	(71)	–0.4	(77)	–0.5
Other income (expense), net	47	0.2	(8)	–0.1
Total non-operating income (expense)	59	0.3	5	0.0
Income before income taxes	901	4.7	660	4.4
Provision for income taxes	(247)	–1.3	(184)	–1.2
Equity-method investment activity, net of tax	(9)	0.0	—	
Net income	$ 645	3.4%	$ 476	3.2%

For Amazon.com, Inc., in 2008, the vertical-analysis percentage for cost of sales is 77.7% ($14,896/$19,166), up slightly from 77.4% in 2007. Therefore, the company's gross margin percentage declined slightly from 2007 to 2008, from 22.6% to 22.3%. However, the company was successful in controlling operating costs in 2008 at approximately the same as or slightly lower percentages of net sales than in 2007. Operating expenses declined from 18.2% to 17.9% of net sales, causing income from operations as a percentage of net sales to remain stable at 4.4% over the two years.

Exhibit 13-5 on the following page shows the vertical analysis of Amazon.com's Consolidated Balance Sheets. The base amount (100%) is total assets for each year. The vertical analysis of Amazon.com's balance sheet reveals several things about Amazon.com's financial position at December 31, 2008, relative to 2007:

- Cash increased nicely in 2008, but declined as a percentage of total assets, while marketable (likely trading) securities increased as a percentage of total assets. Amazon.com, Inc., invested its excess cash in short-term investments expected to earn a higher return than interest-bearing cash accounts.
- Inventories as a percentage of total assets fell from 18.5% to 16.8%, indicating that inventory turnover is increasing, because sales (and related cost of sales) are increasing. Accounts receivable increased from 10.9% to 23% of total assets, reflecting an increase in net sales activity. Overall, current assets make up a large percentage of total assets (74.1%, down from 79.6% in 2007).
- The company's debt to total assets (57.1% + 4.9% + 5.9% = 67.9%) improved significantly in 2008 from 81.6% in 2007. Although current liabilities stayed about the same (57%) over the two years, the percentage of total assets financed with long-term

debt declined significantly, reflecting the company's substantially improved cash position and repayment of a good portion of its long-term debt. Amazon.com, Inc., grew substantially healthier from the standpoint of leverage in 2008.

How Do We Compare One Company to Another?

OBJECTIVE

3 **Prepare** common-size
financial statements

Exhibits 13-4 and 13-5 can be modified to report only percentages (no dollar amounts). Such financial statements are called **common-size statements**. In order to perform vertical analysis, you must first convert the financial statements to common-size format.

EXHIBIT 13-5 | **Comparative Balance Sheets—Vertical Analysis**

Amazon.com, Inc.
Consolidated Balance Sheets

	Year ended December 31			
(In millions, except per share data)	2008	% of total	2007	% of total
ASSETS				
Current assets:				
Cash and cash equivalents	$2,769	33.3%	$2,539	39.2%
Marketable securities	958	11.5	573	8.8
Inventories	1,399	16.8	1,200	18.5
Accounts receivable, net and other	827	10.0	705	10.9
Deferred tax assets	204	2.5	147	2.3
Total current assets	6,157	74.1	5,164	79.6
Fixed assets, net	854	10.3	543	8.4
Deferred tax assets	145	1.7	260	4.0
Goodwill	438	5.3	222	3.4
Other assets	720	8.7	296	4.6
Total assets	$8,314	100.0%	$6,485	100.0%
LIABILITIES AND STOCKHOLDERS' EQUITY				
Current liabilities:				
Accounts payable	$3,594	43.2%	$2,795	43.1%
Accrued expenses and other	1,093	13.1	902	13.9
Current portion of long-term debt	59	0.7	17	0.3
Total current liabilities	4,746	57.1	3,714	57.3
Long-term debt	409	4.9	1,282	19.8
Other long-term liabilities	487	5.9	292	4.5
Commitments and contingencies				
Stockholders' equity:				
Preferred stock, $0.01 par value:				
Authorized shares—500				
Issued and outstanding shares—none	—		—	
Common stock, $0.01 par value:				
Authorized shares—5,000				
Issued shares—445 and 431				
Outstanding shares—428 and 416	4	0.05	4	0.1
Treasury stock, at cost	(600)	–7.2	(500)	–7.7
Additional paid-in capital	4,121	49.6	3,063	47.2
Accumulated other comprehensive income (loss)	(123)	–1.5	5	0.1
Accumulated deficit	(730)	–8.8	(1,375)	–21.2
Total stockholders' equity	2,672	32.1	1,197	18.5
Total liabilities and stockholders' equity	$8,314	100.0%	$6,485	100.0%

On a common-size income statement, each item is expressed as a percentage of the revenue (net sales) amount. Total revenue is therefore the *common size*. In the balance sheet, the common size is total assets. A common-size financial statement aids the comparison of different companies because all amounts are stated in percentages, thus expressing the financial results of each comparative company in terms of a common denominator.

STOP & THINK. . .

Calculate the common-size percentages for the following income statement:

Net sales.............................	$150,000
Cost of goods sold................	60,000
Gross profit..........................	90,000
Operating expense................	40,000
Operating income.................	50,000
Income tax expense..............	15,000
Net income..........................	$ 35,000

Answer:

Net sales.............................	100%	(= $150,000 ÷ $150,000)
Cost of goods sold................	40	(= $ 60,000 ÷ $150,000)
Gross profit..........................	60	(= $ 90,000 ÷ $150,000)
Operating expense................	27	(= $ 40,000 ÷ $150,000)
Operating income.................	33	(= $ 50,000 ÷ $150,000)
Income tax expense..............	10	(= $ 15,000 ÷ $150,000)
Net income..........................	23%	(= $ 35,000 ÷ $150,000)

BENCHMARKING

Benchmarking compares a company to some standard set by others. The goal of benchmarking is improvement. Suppose you are a financial analyst for **Goldman Sachs**, a large investment bank. You are considering investing in one of two different retailers, say Amazon.com, Inc., or Wal-Mart Stores, Inc. A direct comparison of these companies' financial statements is not meaningful, in part because Wal-Mart, Inc., is so much larger than Amazon.com. However, you can convert the companies' income statements to common size and compare the percentages. This comparison is meaningful, as we shall see.

Benchmarking Against a Key Competitor

Exhibit 13-6 on the following page presents the common-size income statements of Amazon.com, Inc., benchmarked against Wal-Mart Stores, Inc. The companies are not exactly comparable because of differences in their business models. For example, Wal-Mart has physical stores as well as online retail services. However, if you look at their Web sites, the two companies are very similar, organized in much the same way. They are close enough to illustrate the value of common-size vertical analysis. In this comparison, the results of the two companies are strikingly similar. Amazon.com's cost of sales is 1.2% higher than Wal-Mart's, but its operating expenses are about a percentage point lower. Their net incomes as a percentage of net sales are identical. Of course, Wal-Mart comes out far ahead in terms of total earnings because of its sheer size ($12.7 billion vs. $645 million for Amazon.com).

EXHIBIT 13-6 | **Common-Size Income Statement Compared with a Key Competitor**

Amazon.com, Inc.
Common-Size Income Statement for Comparison with Key Competitor (Adapted)
Year Ended During 2008

	Amazon.com	Wal-Mart
Net sales	100.0%	100.0%
Cost of sales	77.7	76.5
Operating expenses	17.9	18.8
Other expenses (income), net	1.0	1.3
Net income	3.4%	3.4%

OBJECTIVE

4 **Use** the statement of cash flows for decisions

Using the Statement of Cash Flows

This chapter has focused on the income statement and balance sheet. We may also perform horizontal and vertical analyses on the statement of cash flows. To continue our discussion of its role in decision making, let's use Exhibit 13-7, the statement of cash flows of Unix Corporation.

EXHIBIT 13-7 | **Statement of Cash Flows**

Unix Corporation
Statement of Cash Flows
Year Ended June 30, 2010

(In millions)		
Operating activities:		
Net income		$ 35,000
Adjustments for noncash items:		
Depreciation	$ 14,000	
Net increase in current assets other than cash	(24,000)	
Net increase in current liabilities	8,000	(2,000)
Net cash provided by operating activities		33,000
Investing activities:		
Sale of property, plant, and equipment	$ 91,000	
Net cash provided by investing activities		91,000
Financing activities:		
Borrowing	$ 22,000	
Payment of long-term debt	(90,000)	
Purchase of treasury stock	(9,000)	
Payment of dividends	(23,000)	
Net cash used for financing activities		(100,000)
Increase (decrease) in cash		$ 24,000

Analysts find the statement of cash flows more helpful for spotting weakness than for gauging success. Why? Because a *shortage* of cash can throw a company into bankruptcy, but lots of cash doesn't ensure success. The statement of cash flows in Exhibit 13-7 reveals the following:

- Unix's operations provide less cash than net income. That's strange. Ordinarily, cash provided by operations exceeds net income because of the add-back of depreciation and amortization. The increases in current assets and current liabilities should cancel out over time. For Unix Corporation, current assets increased far more than current liabilities during the year. This may be harmless. But it may signal difficulty in collecting receivables or selling inventory. Either event will cause trouble.

- The sale of plant assets is Unix's major source of cash. This is okay if this is a one-time situation. Unix may be shifting from one line of business to another, and it may be selling off old assets. But if the sale of plant assets is the major source of cash for several periods, Unix will face a cash shortage. A company can't sell off its plant assets forever. Soon it will go out of business.

- The only strength shown by the statement of cash flows is that Unix paid off more long-term debt than it did new borrowing. This will improve the debt ratio and Unix's credit standing.

Here are some cash-flow signs of a healthy company:

- Operations are the major *source* of cash (not a *use* of cash).
- Investing activities include more purchases than sales of long-term assets.
- Financing activities are not dominated by borrowing.

MID-CHAPTER SUMMARY PROBLEM

Perform a horizontal analysis and a vertical analysis of the comparative income statement of Hard Rock Products, Inc., which makes metal detectors. State whether 2011 was a good year or a bad year, and give your reasons.

Hard Rock Products, Inc.
Comparative Income Statements
Years Ended December 31, 2011 and 2010

	2011	2010
Total revenues	$275,000	$225,000
Expenses:		
Cost of goods sold	194,000	165,000
Engineering, selling, and administrative expenses	54,000	48,000
Interest expense	5,000	5,000
Income tax expense	9,000	3,000
Other expense (income)	1,000	(1,000)
Total expenses	263,000	220,000
Net income	$ 12,000	$ 5,000

Answer

The horizontal analysis shows that total revenues increased 22.2%. This was greater than the 19.5% increase in total expenses, resulting in a 140% increase in net income.

Hard Rock Products, Inc.
Horizontal Analysis of Comparative Income Statements
Years Ended December 31, 2011 and 2010

	2011	2010	Increase (Decrease) Amount	Increase (Decrease) Percent
Total revenues	$275,000	$225,000	$50,000	22.2%
Expenses:				
Cost of goods sold	194,000	165,000	29,000	17.6
Engineering, selling, and administrative expenses	54,000	48,000	6,000	12.5
Interest expense	5,000	5,000	—	—
Income tax expense	9,000	3,000	6,000	200.0
Other expense (income)	1,000	(1,000)	2,000	—*
Total expenses	263,000	220,000	43,000	19.5
Net income	$ 12,000	$ 5,000	$ 7,000	140.0%

*Percentage changes are typically not computed for shifts from a negative to a positive amount and vice versa.

The vertical analysis on the next page shows decreases in the percentages of net sales consumed by the cost of goods sold (from 73.3% to 70.5%) and by the engineering, selling, and administrative expenses (from 21.3% to 19.6%). Because these two items are Hard Rock's largest dollar expenses, their percentage decreases are quite important. The relative reduction in expenses raised 2011 net income to 4.4% of sales, compared with 2.2% the preceding year. The overall analysis indicates that 2011 was significantly better than 2010.

Hard Rock Products, Inc.
Vertical Analysis of Comparative Income Statements
Years Ended December 31, 2011 and 2010

	2011		2010	
	Amount	Percent	Amount	Percent
Total revenues..............................	$275,000	100.0 %	$225,000	100.0 %
Expenses:				
Cost of goods sold...................	194,000	70.5	165,000	73.3
Engineering, selling, and				
administrative expenses........	54,000	19.6	48,000	21.3
Interest expense	5,000	1.8	5,000	2.2
Income tax expense..................	9,000	3.3	3,000	1.4**
Other expense (income)	1,000	0.4	(1,000)	(0.4)
Total expenses.....................	263,000	95.6	220,000	97.8
Net income.................................	$ 12,000	4.4 %	$ 5,000	2.2 %

**Number rounded up.

Using Ratios to Make Business Decisions

Ratios are a major tool of financial analysis. We have discussed the use of many ratios in financial analysis in various chapters throughout the book. A ratio expresses the relationship of one number to another. Suppose your balance sheet shows current assets of $100,000 and current liabilities of $50,000. The ratio of current assets to current liabilities is $100,000 to $50,000. We can express this ratio as 2 to 1, or 2:1. The current ratio is 2.0.

Many companies include ratios in a special section of their annual reports. RubberMate Corporation displays ratio data in the Summary section. Exhibit 13-8 shows data from that summary section. Investment services—**Moody's, Standard & Poor's, Risk Management Association**, and others—report these ratios.

OBJECTIVE

5 **Compute** the standard financial ratios

EXHIBIT 13-8 | **Financial Summary of RubberMate Corporation (Dollar Amounts in Millions Except per-share Amounts)**

Year Ended December 31	2011	2010	2009
Operating Results			
Net income...	$ 218	$ 164	$ 163
Per common share...	$1.32	$1.02	$1.02
Percent of sales..	10.8%	9.1%	9.8%
Return on average shareholders' equity...............	20.0%	17.5%	19.7%
Financial Position			
Current assets...	$ 570	$ 477	$ 419
Current liabilities	$ 359	$ 323	$ 345
Working capital...	$ 211	$ 154	$ 74
Current ratio...	1.59	1.48	1.21

The ratios we discuss in this chapter are classified as follows:

1. Ability to pay current liabilities
2. Ability to sell inventory and collect receivables
3. Ability to pay long-term debt
4. Profitability
5. Analyze stock as an investment

How much can a computer help in analyzing financial statements for investment purposes? Time yourself as you complete the problems in this chapter. Multiply your efforts by 10 as though you were comparing 10 companies. Now rank these 10 companies on the basis of four or five ratios.

Measuring Ability to Pay Current Liabilities

Working capital is defined as follows:

$$\text{Working capital} = \text{Current assets} - \text{Current liabilities}$$

Working capital measures the ability to pay current liabilities with current assets. In general, the larger the working capital, the better the ability to pay debts. Recall that capital is total assets minus total liabilities. Working capital is like a "current" version of total capital. Consider two companies with equal working capital:

	Company	
	Jones	Smith
Current assets......................	$100,000	$200,000
Current liabilities	50,000	150,000
Working capital	$ 50,000	$ 50,000

Both companies have working capital of $50,000, but Jones' working capital is as large as its current liabilities. Smith's working capital is only one-third as large as current liabilities. Jones is in a better position because its working capital is a higher percentage of current liabilities. Two decision-making tools based on working-capital data are the *current ratio* and the *acid-test ratio*.

Current Ratio. The most common ratio evaluating current assets and current liabilities is the **current ratio**, which is current assets divided by current liabilities. As discussed in Chapter 3, the current ratio measures the ability to pay current liabilities with current assets. Exhibit 13-9 gives the income statement and balance sheet data of Palisades Furniture.

The current ratios of Palisades Furniture, Inc., at December 31, 2011 and 2010, follow, along with the average for the retail furniture industry:

	Formula	*Palisades' Current Ratio*		Industry Average
		2011	2010	
Current ratio =	$\dfrac{\text{Current assets}}{\text{Current liabilities}}$	$\dfrac{\$262,000}{\$142,000} = 1.85$	$\dfrac{\$236,000}{\$126,000} = 1.87$	1.50

EXHIBIT 13-9 | Comparative Financial Statements

Palisades Furniture, Inc.
Comparative Income Statements
Years Ended December 31, 2011 and 2010

	2011	2010
Net sales	$858,000	$803,000
Cost of goods sold	513,000	509,000
Gross profit	345,000	294,000
Operating expenses:		
Selling expenses	126,000	114,000
General expenses	118,000	123,000
Total operating expenses	244,000	237,000
Income from operations	101,000	57,000
Interest revenue	4,000	—
Interest (expense)	(24,000)	(14,000)
Income before income taxes	81,000	43,000
Income tax expense	33,000	17,000
Net income	$ 48,000	$ 26,000

Palisades Furniture, Inc.
Comparative Balance Sheets
December 31, 2011 and 2010

	2011	2010
Assets		
Current Assets:		
Cash	$ 29,000	$ 32,000
Accounts receivable, net	114,000	85,000
Inventories	113,000	111,000
Prepaid expenses	6,000	8,000
Total current assets	262,000	236,000
Long-term investments	18,000	9,000
Property, plant, and equipment, net	507,000	399,000
Total assets	$787,000	$644,000
Liabilities		
Current Liabilities:		
Notes payable	$ 42,000	$ 27,000
Accounts payable	73,000	68,000
Accrued liabilities	27,000	31,000
Total current liabilities	142,000	126,000
Long-term debt	289,000	198,000
Total liabilities	431,000	324,000
Stockholders' Equity		
Common stock, no par	186,000	186,000
Retained earnings	170,000	134,000
Total stockholders' equity	356,000	320,000
Total liabilities and stockholders' equity	$787,000	$644,000

The current ratio decreased slightly but not significantly during 2011. In general, a higher current ratio indicates a stronger financial position. The business has sufficient current assets to maintain its operations. Palisades Furniture's current ratio of 1.85 compares favorably with the current ratios of some well-known companies:

Company	Current Ratio
Wal-Mart Stores, Inc.	0.8
Hewlett-Packard Company................	0.98
eBay	1.70

Note: These figures show that ratio values vary widely from one industry to another.

What is an acceptable current ratio? The answer depends on the industry. The norm for companies in most industries is around 1.50, as reported by the Risk Management Association. Palisades Furniture's current ratio of 1.85 is better than average.

The Limitations of Ratio Analysis

Business decisions are made in a world of uncertainty. As useful as ratios are, they aren't a cure-all. Consider a physician's use of a thermometer. A reading of 102.0° Fahrenheit tells a doctor something is wrong with the patient, but that doesn't indicate what the problem is or how to cure it.

In financial analysis, a sudden drop in the current ratio signals that *something* is wrong, but that doesn't identify the problem. A manager must analyze the figures to learn what caused the ratio to fall. A drop in current assets may mean a cash shortage or that sales are slow. The manager must evaluate all the ratios in the light of factors such as increased competition or a slowdown in the economy.

Legislation, international affairs, scandals, and other factors can turn profits into losses. To be useful, ratios should be analyzed over a period of years to consider all relevant factors. Any one year, or even any two years, may not represent the company's performance over the long term.

Acid-Test Ratio. As discussed in Chapter 5, the **acid-test** (or **quick**) **ratio** tells us whether the entity could pass the acid test of paying all its current liabilities if they came due immediately. The acid-test ratio uses a narrower base to measure liquidity than the current ratio does.

To compute the acid-test ratio, we add cash, short-term investments, and net current receivables (accounts and notes receivable, net of allowances) and divide by current liabilities. Inventory and prepaid expenses are excluded because they are less liquid. A business may be unable to convert inventory to cash immediately.

Palisades Furniture's acid-test ratios for 2011 and 2010 follow:

		Palisades' Acid-Test Ratio		Industry
	Formula	2011	2010	Average
Acid-test ratio =	Cash + Short-term investments + Net current receivables ——————————————— Current liabilities	$\dfrac{\$29,000 + \$0 + \$114,000}{\$142,000} = 1.01$	$\dfrac{\$32,000 + \$0 + \$85,000}{\$126,000} = 0.93$	0.40

The company's acid-test ratio improved during 2011 and is significantly better than the industry average. Compare Palisades' acid test ratio with the values of some leading companies.

Company	Acid-Test Ratio
Best Buy	0.30
DineEquity (IHOP).........	1.41
Foot Locker, Inc.	0.98

An acid-test ratio of 0.90 to 1.00 is acceptable in most industries. How can a company such as Best Buy function with such a low acid-test ratio? Best Buy prices its inventory to turn it over quickly. And most of Best Buy's sales are for cash or credit cards, so the company collects cash quickly. This points us to the next two ratios.

Measuring Ability to Sell Inventory and Collect Receivables

The ability to sell inventory and collect receivables is critical. In this section, we discuss three ratios that measure this ability.

Inventory Turnover.   Companies generally strive to sell their inventory as quickly as possible. The faster inventory sells, the sooner cash comes in.

Inventory turnover, discussed in Chapter 6, measures the number of times a company sells its average level of inventory during a year. A fast turnover indicates ease in selling inventory; a low turnover indicates difficulty. A value of 6 means that the company's average level of inventory has been sold six times during the year, and that's usually better than a turnover of three times. But too high a value can mean that the business is not keeping enough inventory on hand, which can lead to lost sales if the company can't fill orders. Therefore, a business strives for the most *profitable* rate of turnover, not necessarily the *highest* rate.

To compute inventory turnover, divide cost of goods sold by the average inventory for the period. We use the cost of goods sold—*not sales*—in the computation because both cost of goods sold and inventory are stated *at cost*. Palisades Furniture's inventory turnover for 2011 is

Formula	Palisades' Inventory Turnover	Industry Average
Inventory turnover = $\frac{\text{Cost of goods sold}}{\text{Average inventory}}$	$\frac{\$513,000}{\$112,000} = 4.6$	1.50

Cost of goods sold comes from the income statement (Exhibit 13-9). Average inventory is the average of beginning ($111,000) and ending inventory ($113,000). (See the balance sheet, Exhibit 13-9.) If inventory levels vary greatly from month to month, you should compute the average by adding the 12 monthly balances and dividing the sum by 12.

Inventory turnover varies widely with the nature of the business. For example, YUM! Brands, owner of fast food restaurants Pizza Hut, Taco Bell, KFC, and Long John Silver's, has an inventory turnover ratio of 29 times per year because food spoils so quickly. Williams-Sonoma, Inc., on the other hand, turns its inventory over only about 3.7 times per year. Williams-Sonoma keeps enough inventory on hand for customers to make their selections.

To evaluate inventory turnover, compare the ratio over time. A sharp decline suggests the need for corrective action.

Accounts Receivable Turnover. Accounts receivable turnover measures the ability to collect cash from customers. In general, the higher the ratio, the better. However, a receivable turnover that is too high may indicate that credit is too tight, and that may cause you to lose sales to good customers.

To compute accounts receivable turnover, divide net sales by average net accounts receivable. The ratio tells how many times during the year average receivables were turned into cash. Palisades Furniture's accounts receivable turnover ratio for 2011 is

Formula		Palisades' Accounts Receivable Turnover	Industry Average
Accounts receivable turnover	$= \dfrac{\text{Net sales}}{\text{Average net accounts receivable}}$	$\dfrac{\$858,000}{\$99,500} = 8.6$	51.0

Average net accounts receivable is figured by adding beginning ($85,000) and ending receivables ($114,000), then dividing by 2. If accounts receivable vary widely during the year, compute the average by using the 12 monthly balances.

Palisades' receivable turnover of 8.6 times per year is much slower than the industry average. Why the slow collection? Palisades is a hometown store that sells to local people who pay bills over a period of time. Many larger furniture stores sell their receivables to other companies called *factors*. This practice, discussed in Chapter 6, keeps receivables low and receivable turnover high. But companies that factor (sell) their receivables receive less than face value of the receivables. Palisades Furniture follows a different strategy.

Days' Sales in Receivables. Businesses must convert accounts receivable to cash. All else being equal, the lower the receivable balance, the better the cash flow.

The **days'-sales-in-receivables** ratio, also discussed in Chapter 6, shows how many days' sales remain in Accounts Receivable. Compute the ratio by a two-step process:

1. Divide net sales by 365 days to figure average sales per day.

2. Divide average net receivables by average sales per day.

The data to compute this ratio for Palisades Furniture, Inc., are taken from the 2011 income statement and the balance sheet (Exhibit 13-9):

Formula		Palisades' Days' Sales in Accounts Receivable	Industry Average
Days' sales in average accounts receivable:			
1. One day's sales $= \dfrac{\text{Net sales}}{365 \text{ days}}$		$\dfrac{\$858,000}{365 \text{ days}} = \$2,351$	
2. Days' sales in average accounts receivable $= \dfrac{\text{Average net accounts receivable}}{\text{One day's sales}}$		$\dfrac{\$99,500}{\$2,351} = 42 \text{ days}$	7 days

Days' sales in average receivables can also be computed in a single step: $99,500/($858,000/365 days) = 42 days.

Measuring Ability to Pay Debts

The ratios discussed so far relate to current assets and current liabilities. They measure the ability to sell inventory, collect receivables, and pay current bills. Two indicators of the ability to pay total liabilities are the *debt ratio* and the *times-interest-earned ratio*.

Debt Ratio. Suppose you are a bank loan officer and you have received $500,000 loan applications from two similar companies. The first company already owes $600,000, and the second owes only $250,000. Which company gets the loan? Company 2, because it owes less.

This relationship between total liabilities and total assets is called the **debt ratio**. Discussed in Chapters 3 and 8, the debt ratio tells us the proportion of assets financed with debt. A debt ratio of 1 reveals that debt has financed all the assets. A debt ratio of 0.50 means that debt finances half the assets. The higher the debt ratio, the greater the pressure to pay interest and principal. The lower the ratio, the lower the risk.

The debt ratios for Palisades Furniture in 2011 and 2010 follow:

		Palisades' Debt Ratio		Industry
	Formula	2011	2010	Average
Debt ratio =	$\dfrac{\text{Total liabilities}}{\text{Total assets}}$	$\dfrac{\$431,000}{\$787,000} = 0.55$	$\dfrac{\$324,000}{\$644,000} = 0.50$	0.64

Risk Management Association reports that the average debt ratio for most companies ranges around 0.62, with relatively little variation from company to company. Palisades' 0.55 debt ratio indicates a fairly low-risk debt position compared with the retail furniture industry average of 0.64.

Times-Interest-Earned Ratio. Analysts use a second ratio—the **times-interest-earned ratio** (introduced in Chapter 8)—to relate income to interest expense. To compute the times-interest-earned ratio, divide income from operations (operating income) by interest expense. This ratio measures the number of times operating income can *cover* interest expense and is also called the *interest-coverage ratio*. A high ratio indicates ease in paying interest; a low value suggests difficulty.

Palisades' times-interest-earned ratios are

		Palisades' Times-Interest-Earned Ratio		Industry
	Formula	2011	2010	Average
Times-interest-earned ratio =	$\dfrac{\text{Income from operations}}{\text{Interest expense}}$	$\dfrac{\$101,000}{\$24,000} = 4.21$	$\dfrac{\$57,000}{\$14,000} = 4.07$	2.80

The company's times-interest-earned ratio increased in 2011. This is a favorable sign.

Measuring Profitability

The fundamental goal of business is to earn a profit, and so the ratios that measure profitability are reported widely.

Rate of Return on Sales. In business, *return* refers to profitability. Consider the **rate of return on net sales**, or simply *return on sales* (ROS). (The word *net* is usually omitted for convenience.) This ratio shows the percentage of each sales dollar earned as net income. The return-on-sales ratios for Palisades Furniture are

		Palisades' Rate of Return on Sales		Industry
	Formula	2011	2010	Average
Rate of return on sales	$=\dfrac{\text{Net income}}{\text{Net sales}}$	$\dfrac{\$48,000}{\$858,000}=0.056$	$\dfrac{\$26,000}{\$803,000}=0.032$	0.008

Companies strive for a high rate of return on sales. The higher the percentage, the more profit is being generated by sales dollars. Palisades Furniture's return on sales is higher than the average furniture store. Compare Palisades' rate of return on sales to the rates of some leading companies:

Company	Rate of Return on Sales
FedEx....................	0.056
PepsiCo................	0.119
Intel......................	0.141

Rate of Return on Total Assets. Also introduced in Chapter 9, the **rate of return on total assets**, or simply *return on assets* (ROA), measures a company's success in using assets to earn a profit. Creditors have loaned money, and the interest they receive is their return on investment. Shareholders have bought the company's stock, and net income is their return. The sum of interest expense and net income is the return to the two groups that have financed the company. This sum is the numerator of the ratio. Average total assets is the denominator. The return-on-assets ratio for Palisades Furniture is

		Palisades' 2011 Rate of	Industry
	Formula	Return on Total Assets	Average
Rate of return on assets	$=\dfrac{\text{Net income + Interest expense}}{\text{Average total assets}}$	$\dfrac{\$48,000 + \$24,000}{\$715,500}=0.101$	0.078

To compute average total assets, add the beginning and ending balances and divide by 2. Compare Palisades Furniture's rate of return on assets to the rates of these leading companies:

Company	Rate of Return on Assets
General Electric................	0.055
Starbucks	0.066
Google	0.108

Rate of Return on Common Stockholders' Equity. A popular measure of profitability is **rate of return on common stockholders' equity**, often shortened to *return on equity* (ROE). Also discussed in Chapter 9, this ratio shows the relationship between net income and common stockholders' investment in the company—how much income is earned for every $1 invested.

To compute this ratio, first subtract preferred dividends from net income to measure income available to the common stockholders. Then divide income available to common by average common equity during the year. Common equity is total equity minus preferred equity. The 2011 return on common equity for Palisades Furniture is

Formula		Palisades' 2011 Rate of Return on Common Stockholders' Equity	Industry Average
Rate of return on common stockholders' equity	$= \dfrac{\text{Net income} - \text{Preferred dividends}}{\text{Average common stockholders' equity}}$	$\dfrac{\$48,000 - \$0}{\$338,000} = 0.142$	0.121

Average equity uses the beginning and ending balances [($320,000 + $356,000)/2 = $338,000].

Observe that Palisades' return on equity (0.142) is higher than its return on assets (0.101). This is a good sign. The difference results from borrowing at one rate—say, 8%—and investing the funds to earn a higher rate, such as the firm's 14.2% return on equity. This practice is called using **leverage**, or **trading on the equity**. The higher the debt ratio, the higher the leverage. Companies that finance operations with debt are said to *leverage* their positions.

For Palisades Furniture, leverage increases profitability. This is not always the case, because leverage can hurt profits. If revenues drop, debts still must be paid. Therefore, leverage is a double-edged sword. It increases profits during good times but compounds losses during bad times.

Palisades Furniture's rate of return on equity lags behind that of GE, but exceeds those of Google and Starbucks.

Company	Rate of Return on Common Equity
General Electric................	0.158
Google	0.121
Starbucks	0.132

Earnings per Share of Common Stock. Discussed in Chapters 8 and 11, *earnings per share of common stock*, or simply **earnings per share (EPS)**, is the amount of net income earned for each share of outstanding *common* stock. EPS is the most widely quoted of all financial statistics. It's the only ratio that appears on the income statement.

Earnings per share is computed by dividing net income available to common stockholders by the average number of common shares outstanding during the year. Preferred dividends are subtracted from net income because the preferred stockholders have a prior claim to their dividends. Palisades Furniture has no preferred stock and thus has no preferred dividends. The firm's EPS for 2011 and 2010 follows (Palisades has 10,000 shares of common stock outstanding).

	Formula	Palisades' Earnings per Share	
		2011	2010
Earnings per share of common stock	$= \dfrac{\text{Net income} - \text{Preferred dividends}}{\text{Average number of shares of common stock outstanding}}$	$\dfrac{\$48,000 - \$0}{10,000} = \$4.80$	$\dfrac{\$26,000 - \$0}{10,000} = \$2.60$

Palisades Furniture's EPS increased 85% during 2011, and that's good news. The Palisades stockholders should not expect such a significant boost every year. Most companies strive to increase EPS by 10% to 15% annually.

Analyzing Stock Investments

OBJECTIVE

6 **Use** ratios in decision making

Investors buy stock to earn a return on their investment. This return consists of two parts: (1) gains (or losses) from selling the stock and (2) dividends.

Price/Earnings Ratio. The **price/earnings ratio** is the ratio of common stock price to earnings per share. This ratio, abbreviated P/E, appears in *The Wall Street Journal* stock listings and online. It shows the market price of $1 of earnings.

Calculations for the P/E ratios of Palisades Furniture, Inc., follow. The market price of Palisades' common stock was $60 at the end of 2011 and $35 at the end of 2010. Stock prices can be obtained from a company's Web site, a financial publication, or a stockbroker.

	Formula	Palisades' Price/Earnings Ratio	
		2011	2010
P/E ratio	$= \dfrac{\text{Market price per share of common stock}}{\text{Earnings per share}}$	$\dfrac{\$60.00}{\$4.80} = 12.5$	$\dfrac{\$35.00}{\$2.60} = 13.5$

Given Palisades Furniture's 2011 P/E ratio of 12.5, we would say that the company's stock is selling at 12.5 times earnings. Each $1 of Palisades' earnings is worth $12.50 to the stock market.

Dividend Yield. **Dividend yield** is the ratio of dividends per share of stock to the stock's market price. This ratio measures the percentage of a stock's market value returned annually to the stockholders as dividends. *Preferred* stockholders pay special attention to this ratio because they invest primarily to receive dividends.

Palisades Furniture paid annual cash dividends of $1.20 per share in 2011 and $1.00 in 2010. The market prices of the company's common stock were $60 in 2011 and $35 in 2010. The firm's dividend yields on common stock are

	Formula	Dividend Yield on Palisades' Common Stock	
		2011	2010
Dividend yield on common stock*	$= \dfrac{\text{Dividend per share of common stock}}{\text{Market price per share of common stock}}$	$\dfrac{\$1.20}{\$60.00} = 0.020$	$\dfrac{\$1.00}{\$35.00} = 0.029$

*Dividend yields may also be calculated for preferred stock.

An investor who buys Palisades Furniture common stock for $60 can expect to receive around 2% of the investment annually in the form of cash dividends. Dividend yields vary widely, from 5% to 8% for older, established firms (such as **Procter & Gamble** and **General Electric**) down to the range of 0% to 3% for young, growth-oriented companies. **Google**, **Starbucks**, and **eBay** pay no cash dividends.

Book Value per Share of Common Stock.   Book value per share of common **stock** is simply common stockholders' equity divided by the number of shares of common stock outstanding. Common equity equals total equity less preferred equity. Palisades Furniture has no preferred stock outstanding. Calculations of its book value per share of common follow. Recall that 10,000 shares of common stock were outstanding.

	Formula	Book Value per Share of Palisades' Common Stock	
		2011	**2010**
Book value per share of common stock	= $\dfrac{\text{Total stockholders' equity} - \text{Preferred equity}}{\text{Number of shares of common stock outstanding}}$	$\dfrac{\$356{,}000 - \$0}{10{,}000} = \$35.60$	$\dfrac{\$320{,}000 - \$0}{10{,}000} = \$32.00$

Book value indicates the recorded accounting amount for each share of common stock outstanding. Many experts believe book value is not useful for investment analysis because it bears no relationship to market value and provides little information beyond what's reported on the balance sheet. But some investors base their investment decisions on book value. For example, some investors rank stocks by the ratio of market price to book value. The lower the ratio, the more attractive the stock. These investors are called "value" investors, as contrasted with "growth" investors, who focus more on trends in net income.

What does the outlook for the future look like for Palisades Furniture? If the company can stay on the same path it has followed for the past two years, it looks bright. It appears that its earnings per share are solid, and its ROS, ROA, and ROE ratios are all above average for its industry. From the standpoint of liquidity and leverage, it also appears to be in good shape, with higher liquidity, excellent debt and interest coverage, and lower debt ratios than its industry. The company's P/E ratio of 12:1 is relatively low, and it pays a 2% dividend. All of these factors make Palisades Furniture stock look like a good investment.

OTHER MEASURES
Economic Value Added (EVA®)

The top managers of **Coca-Cola**, **Quaker Oats**, and other leading companies use **economic value added (EVA®)** to evaluate operating performance. EVA® combines accounting and finance to measure whether operations have increased stockholder wealth. EVA® can be computed as follows:

OBJECTIVE

7 **Measure** the economic value added by operations

$$\text{EVA}^® = \text{Net income} + \text{Interest expense} - \text{Capital charge}$$

$$\text{Capital charge} = \left(\text{Notes} \atop \text{payable} + { \text{Current} \atop \text{maturities} \atop \text{of long-} \atop \text{term debt}} + {\text{Long-term} \atop \text{debt}} + {\text{Stockholders'} \atop \text{equity}} \right) \times {\text{Cost of} \atop \text{capital}}$$

(Beginning balances)

All amounts for the EVA® computation, except the cost of capital, come from the financial statements. The **cost of capital** is a weighted average of the returns demanded by the company's stockholders and lenders. Cost of capital varies with the company's level of risk. For example, stockholders would demand a higher return from a start-up company than from Amazon.com, Inc., because the new company is untested and therefore more risky. Lenders would also charge the new company a higher interest rate because of its greater risk. Thus, the new company has a higher cost of capital than Amazon.com, Inc.

The cost of capital is a major topic in finance classes. In the following discussions we assume a value for the cost of capital (such as 10%, 12%, or 15%) to illustrate the computation of EVA®.

The idea behind EVA® is that the returns to the company's stockholders (net income) and to its creditors (interest expense) should exceed the company's capital charge. The **capital charge** is the amount that stockholders and lenders *charge* a company for the use of their money. A positive EVA® amount suggests an increase in stockholder wealth, and so the company's stock should remain attractive to investors. If EVA® is negative, stockholders will probably be unhappy with the company and sell its stock, resulting in a decrease in the stock's price. Different companies tailor the EVA® computation to meet their own needs.

Let's apply EVA® to Amazon.com, Inc. The company's EVA® for 2008 can be computed as follows, assuming a 10% cost of capital (dollars in millions):

Amazon.com, Inc.'s EVA® =

(Beginning balances)

	Net income	+	Interest expense	−	(Short-term borrowings	+	Long-term debt	+	Stockholders' equity)	×	Cost of capital
=	$645	+	$71	−	[($3,714	+	$1,574	+	$1,197)	×	0.10]
=	$716			−			$6,485			×	0.10
=	$716			−					$648		
=				$68							

By this measure, Amazon.com, Inc.'s operations added $68 million of value to its stockholders' wealth after meeting the company's capital charge. This performance is considered strong.

Red Flags in Financial Statement Analysis

Recent accounting scandals have highlighted the importance of *red flags* in financial analysis. The following conditions may mean a company is very risky.

- *Earnings Problems.* Have income from continuing operations and net income decreased for several years in a row? Has income turned into a loss? This may be okay for a company in a cyclical industry, such as an airline or a home builder, but a company such as Amazon.com, Inc., may be unable to survive consecutive loss years.

- *Decreased Cash Flow.* Cash flow validates earnings. Is cash flow from operations consistently lower than net income? Are the sales of plant assets a major source of cash? If so, the company may be facing a cash shortage.
- *Too Much Debt.* How does the company's debt ratio compare to that of major competitors and to the industry average? If the debt ratio is much higher than average, the company may be unable to pay debts during tough times. As we saw earlier, Amazon.com, Inc.'s debt ratio of 67.9% in 2008 (while still high) is much improved over its 81.6% debt ratio in 2007.
- *Inability to Collect Receivables.* Are days' sales in receivables growing faster than for other companies in the industry? A cash shortage may be looming. Amazon.com, Inc.'s cash collections are very strong.
- *Buildup of Inventories.* Is inventory turnover slowing down? If so, the company may be unable to move products, or it may be overstating inventory as reported on the balance sheet. Recall from the cost-of-goods-sold model that one of the easiest ways to overstate net income is to overstate ending inventory. Amazon.com, Inc., has no problem here.
- *Trends of Sales, Inventory, and Receivables.* Sales, receivables, and inventory generally move together. Increased sales lead to higher receivables and require more inventory in order to meet demand. Strange movements among these items may spell trouble. Amazon.com, Inc.'s relationships look normal.

Efficient Markets

An **efficient capital market** is one in which market prices fully reflect all information available to the public. Because stock prices reflect all publicly accessible data, it can be argued that the stock market is efficient. Market efficiency has implications for management action and for investor decisions. It means that managers cannot fool the market with accounting gimmicks. If the information is available, the market as a whole can set a "fair" price for the company's stock.

Suppose you are the president of Anacomp Corporation. Reported earnings per share are $4, and the stock price is $40—so the P/E ratio is 10. You believe Anacomp's stock is underpriced. To correct this situation, you are considering changing your depreciation method from accelerated to straight-line. The accounting change will increase earnings per share to $5. Will the stock price then rise to $50? Probably not; the company's stock price will probably remain at $40 because the market can understand the accounting change. After all, the company merely changed its method of computing depreciation. There is no effect on Anacomp's cash flows, and the company's economic position is unchanged: An efficient market interprets data in light of their true underlying meaning.

In an efficient market, the search for "underpriced" stock is fruitless unless the investor has relevant *private* information. But it is unlawful as well as unethical to invest on the basis of *inside* information. An appropriate strategy seeks to manage risk, diversify investments, and minimize transaction costs. Financial analysis helps mainly to identify the risks of various stocks and then to manage the risk.

The Decision Guidelines feature summarizes the most widely used ratios.

DECISION GUIDELINES

USING RATIOS IN FINANCIAL STATEMENT ANALYSIS

Lane and Kay Collins operate a financial services firm. They manage other people's money and do most of their own financial-statement analysis. How do they measure companies' ability to pay bills, sell inventory, collect receivables, and so on? They use the standard ratios we have covered throughout this book.

Ratio	Computation	Information Provided
Measuring ability to pay current liabilities:		
1. Current ratio	$$\frac{\text{Current assets}}{\text{Current liabilities}}$$	Measures ability to pay current liabilities with current assets
2. Acid-test (quick) ratio	$$\frac{\text{Cash} + \frac{\text{Short-term}}{\text{investments}} + \frac{\text{Net current}}{\text{receivables}}}{\text{Current liabilities}}$$	Shows ability to pay all current liabilities if they come due immediately
Measuring ability to sell inventory and collect receivables:		
3. Inventory turnover	$$\frac{\text{Cost of goods sold}}{\text{Average inventory}}$$	Indicates saleability of inventory—the number of times a company sells its average level of inventory during a year
4. Accounts receivable turnover	$$\frac{\text{Net credit sales}}{\text{Average net accounts receivable}}$$	Measures ability to collect cash from credit customers
5. Days' sales in receivables	$$\frac{\text{Average net accounts receivable}}{\text{One day's sales}}$$	Shows how many days' sales remain in Accounts Receivable—how many days it takes to collect the average level of receivables
Measuring ability to pay long-term debt:		
6. Debt ratio	$$\frac{\text{Total liabilities}}{\text{Total assets}}$$	Indicates percentage of assets financed with debt
7. Times-interest-earned ratio	$$\frac{\text{Income from operations}}{\text{Interest expense}}$$	Measures the number of times operating income can cover interest expense
Measuring profitability:		
8. Rate of return on net sales	$$\frac{\text{Net income}}{\text{Net sales}}$$	Shows the percentage of each sales dollar earned as net income
9. Rate of return on total assets	$$\frac{\text{Net income} + \text{Interest expense}}{\text{Average total assets}}$$	Measures how profitably a company uses its assets
10. Rate of return on common stockholders' equity	$$\frac{\text{Net income} - \text{Preferred dividends}}{\text{Average common stockholders' equity}}$$	Gauges how much income is earned with the money invested by the common shareholders
11. Earnings per share of common stock	$$\frac{\text{Net income} - \text{Preferred dividends}}{\text{Average number of shares of common stock outstanding}}$$	Gives the amount of net income earned for each share of the company's common stock outstanding

Ratio	Computation	Information Provided
Analyzing stock as an investment:		
12. Price/earnings ratio	$$\frac{\text{Market price per share of common stock}}{\text{Earnings per share}}$$	Indicates the market price of $1 of earnings
13. Dividend yield	$$\frac{\begin{array}{c}\text{Dividend per share of}\\\text{common (or preferred) stock}\end{array}}{\begin{array}{c}\text{Market price per share of}\\\text{common (or preferred) stock}\end{array}}$$	Shows the percentage of a stock's market value returned as dividends to stockholders each period
14. Book value per share of common stock	$$\frac{\text{Total stockholders' equity} - \text{Preferred equity}}{\text{Number of shares of common stock outstanding}}$$	Indicates the recorded accounting amount for each share of common stock outstanding

END-OF-CHAPTER SUMMARY PROBLEM

The following financial data are adapted from the annual reports of Lampeer Corporation:

Lampeer Corporation
Four-Year Selected Financial Data
Years Ended January 31, 2010, 2009, 2008, and 2007

Operating Results*	2010	2009	2008	2007
Net Sales	$13,848	$13,673	$11,635	$9,054
Cost of goods sold and occupancy expenses excluding depreciation and amortization......................	9,704	8,599	6,775	5,318
Interest expense	109	75	45	46
Income from operations...............	338	1,445	1,817	1,333
Net earnings (net loss)	(8)	877	1,127	824
Cash dividends............................	76	75	76	77
Financial Position				
Merchandise inventory	1,677	1,904	1,462	1,056
Total assets	7,591	7,012	5,189	3,963
Current ratio................................	1.48:1	0.95:1	1.25:1	1.20:1
Stockholders' equity....................	3,010	2,928	2,630	1,574
Average number of shares of common stock outstanding (in thousands)	860	879	895	576

*Dollar amounts are in thousands.

❙ Requirement

1. Compute the following ratios for 2008 through 2010, and evaluate Lampeer's operating results. Are operating results strong or weak? Did they improve or deteriorate during the three-year period? Your analysis will reveal a clear trend.

a. Gross profit percentage*
b. Net income as a percentage of sales
c. Earnings per share

d. Inventory turnover
e. Times-interest-earned ratio
f. Rate of return on stockholders' equity

*Refer to Chapter 6 if necessary.

Answer

	2010	2009	2008
1. Gross profit percentage	$\dfrac{\$13{,}848 - \$9{,}704}{\$13{,}848} = 29.9\%$	$\dfrac{\$13{,}673 - \$8{,}599}{\$13{,}673} = 37.1\%$	$\dfrac{\$11{,}635 - \$6{,}775}{\$11{,}635} = 41.8\%$
2. Net income as a percentage of sales	$\dfrac{\$(8)}{\$13{,}848} = (0.06)\%$	$\dfrac{\$877}{\$13{,}673} = 6.4\%$	$\dfrac{\$1{,}127}{\$11{,}635} = 9.7\%$
3. Earnings per share	$\dfrac{\$(8)}{860} = \$(0.01)$	$\dfrac{\$877}{879} = \$1.00$	$\dfrac{\$1{,}127}{895} = \$1.26$
4. Inventory turnover	$\dfrac{\$9{,}704}{(\$1{,}677 + \$1{,}904)/2} = 5.4 \text{ times}$	$\dfrac{\$8{,}599}{(\$1{,}904 + \$1{,}462)/2} = 5.1 \text{ times}$	$\dfrac{\$6{,}775}{(\$1{,}462 + \$1{,}056)/2} = 5.4 \text{ times}$
5. Times-interest-earned ratio	$\dfrac{\$338}{\$109} = 3.1 \text{ times}$	$\dfrac{\$1{,}445}{\$75} = 19.3 \text{ times}$	$\dfrac{\$1{,}817}{\$45} = 40.4 \text{ times}$
6. Rate of return on stockholders' equity	$\dfrac{\$(8)}{(\$3{,}010 + \$2{,}928)/2} = (0.3\%)$	$\dfrac{\$877}{(\$2{,}928 + \$2{,}630)/2} = 31.6\%$	$\dfrac{\$1{,}127}{(\$2{,}630 + \$1{,}574)/2} = 53.6\%$

Evaluation: During this period, Lampeer's operating results deteriorated on all these measures except inventory turnover. The gross profit percentage is down sharply, as are the times-interest-earned ratio and all the return measures. From these data it is clear that Lampeer could sell its merchandise, but not at the markups the company enjoyed in the past. The final result, in 2010, was a net loss for the year.

REVIEW FINANCIAL STATEMENT ANALYSIS

Quick Check (Answers are given on page 841.)

Analyze the Oullette Company financial statements by answering the questions that follow. Oullette owns a chain of restaurants.

Oullette Company
Consolidated Statements of Income (Adapted)
Years Ended December 31, 2011 and 2010

(In millions, except per share data)	2011	2010
Revenues..		
Sales by Company-operated restaurants....................................	$13,200	11,100
Revenues from franchised and affiliated restaurants.................	4,500	3,700
Total revenues...	17,700	14,800
Food and paper (Cost of goods sold).......................................	3,300	3,108
Payroll and employee benefits..	3,200	3,000
Occupancy and other operating expenses.................................	2,900	2,800
Franchised restaurants—occupancy expenses...........................	949	850
Selling, general, and administrative expenses...........................	1,820	1,730
Other operating expense, net...	510	855
Total operating expenses	12,679	12,343
Operating income..	5,021	2,457
Interest expense...	370	345
Other nonoperating expense, net..	140	168
Income before income taxes	4,511	1,944
Income tax expense...	1,820	820
Net income..	$ 2,691	$ 1,124
Per common-share basic:		
Net income...	$ 2.69	$ 1.15
Dividends per common share	$ 0.50	$ 0.24

Oulette Company
Consolidated Balance Sheets
December 31, 2011 and 2010

(In millions, except per share data)	2011	2010
Assets		
Current Assets		
Cash and equivalents	$ 690	$ 455
Accounts and notes receivable	780	840
Inventories, at cost, not in excess of market	140	120
Prepaid expense and other current assets	580	440
Total current assets	2,190	1,855
Other Assets		
Investments in affiliates	1,150	1,055
Goodwill, net	1,780	1,590
Miscellaneous	990	1,100
Total other assets	3,920	3,745
Property and Equipment		
Property and equipment, at cost	28,800	26,500
Accumulated depreciation and amortization	(8,850)	(7,900)
Net property and equipment	19,950	18,600
Total assets	$26,060	$24,200
Liabilities and Stockholders' Equity		
Current liabilities		
Accounts payable	$ 520	$ 675
Income taxes	70	14
Other taxes	230	180
Accrued interest	189	196
Accrued restructuring and restaurant closing costs	110	385
Accrued payroll and other liabilities	890	795
Current maturities of long-term debt	365	305
Total current liabilities	2,374	2,550
Long-term debt	8,700	9,500
Other long-term liabilities and minority interests	690	520
Deferred income taxes	1,005	1,015
Stockholders' Equity		
Preferred stock, no par value; authorized—140.0 million shares; issued—none	—	—
Common stock, $0.01 par value; authorized—2.0 billion shares; issued—1,400 million shares	14	14
Additional paid-in capital	1,786	1,662
Unearned ESOP compensation	(85)	(101)
Retained earnings	21,741	19,550
Accumulated other comprehensive income (loss)	(815)	(1,570)
Common stock in treasury, at cost; 400 and 420 million shares	(9,350)	(8,940)
Total stockholders' equity	13,291	10,615
Total liabilities and stockholders' equity	$26,060	$24,200

1. Horizontal analysis of Oullette's income statement for 2011 would show which of the following for Selling, General, and Administrative expenses?
   a. 0.95
   b. 1.05
   c. 0.68
   d. None of the above

2. Vertical analysis of Oullette's income statement for 2011 would show which of the following for Selling, General, and Administrative expenses?
   a. 0.103
   b. 0.144
   c. 0.138
   d. None of the above

3. Which item on Oullette's income statement has the most favorable trend during 2010–2011?
   a. Food and paper costs
   b. Total revenues
   c. Payroll and employee benefits
   d. Net income

4. On Oullette's common-size balance sheet, Goodwill would appear as
   a. $1,780 million.
   b. up by 11.9%.
   c. 0.068.
   d. 10.06% of total revenues.

5. A good benchmark for Oullette Company would be
   a. Volvo.
   b. Microsoft.
   c. Whataburger.
   d. All of the above.

6. Oullette's inventory turnover for 2011 was
   a. 17 times.
   b. 61 times.
   c. 25 times.
   d. 72 times.

7. Oullette's acid-test ratio at the end of 2011 was
   a. 0.62.
   b. 2.83.
   c. 0.92.
   d. 0.06.

8. Oullette's average collection period for accounts and notes receivables is
   a. 32 days.
   b. 2 days.
   c. 17 days.
   d. 1 day.

9. The average debt ratio for most companies is 0.64. Oullette's total debt position looks
   a. risky.
   b. middle-ground.
   c. safe.
   d. cannot tell from the financials.

10. Oullette's return on total revenues for 2011 was
    a. $2.69.
    b. $1.16.
    c. 10.33%.
    d. 15.2%.

11. Oullette's return on stockholders' equity for 2011 was
    a. 15.2%.
    b. 22.5%.
    c. 10.33%.
    d. $2,691 million.

12. On May 31, 2011, Oullette's common stock sold for $30 per share. At that price, how much did investors say $1 of the company's net income was worth?
    a. $1.00
    b. $30.00
    c. $11.15
    d. $10.99

13. On May 31, 2011, Oullette's common stock sold for $30 per share and dividends per share were $0.50. Compute Oullette's dividend yield during 2011.
    a. 2.9%
    b. 4.1%
    c. 1.7%
    d. 5.0%

14. How much EVA® did Oullette generate for investors during 2011? Assume the cost of capital was 5%.
    a. $2,040 million
    b. $1,943 million
    c. $3,061 million
    d. $2,691 million

Accounting Vocabulary

accounts receivable turnover (p. 794) Measures a company's ability to collect cash from credit customers. To compute accounts receivable turnover, divide net credit sales by average net accounts receivable.

acid-test ratio (p. 792) Ratio of the sum of cash plus short-term investments plus net current receivables to total current liabilities. Tells whether the entity can pay all its current liabilities if they come due immediately. Also called the *quick ratio*.

benchmarking (p. 785) The comparison of a company to a standard set by other companies, with a view toward improvement.

book value per share of common stock (p. 799) Common stockholders' equity divided by the number of shares of common stock outstanding. The recorded amount for each share of common stock outstanding.

capital charge (p. 800) The amount that stockholders and lenders charge a company for the use of their money. Calculated as (Notes payable + Loans payable + Long-term debt + Stockholders' equity) × Cost of capital.

common-size statement (p. 784) A financial statement that reports only percentages (no dollar amounts).

cost of capital (p. 800) A weighted average of the returns demanded by the company's stockholders and lenders.

current ratio (p. 790) Current assets divided by current liabilities. Measures a company's ability to pay current liabilities with current assets.

days' sales in receivables (p. 794) Ratio of average net accounts receivable to one day's sales. Indicates how many days' sales remain in Accounts Receivable awaiting collection. Also called the *collection period*.

debt ratio (p. 795) Ratio of total liabilities to total assets. States the proportion of a company's assets that is financed with debt.

dividend yield (p. 798) Ratio of dividends per share of stock to the stock's market price per share. Tells the percentage of a stock's market value that the company returns to stockholders as dividends.

earnings per share (EPS) (p. 797) Amount of a company's net income earned for each share of its outstanding common stock.

economic value added (EVA®) (p. 799) Used to evaluate a company's operating performance. EVA combines the concepts of accounting income and corporate finance to measure whether the company's operations have increased stockholder wealth. EVA = Net income + Interest expense − Capital charge.

efficient capital market (p. 801) A capital market in which market prices fully reflect all information available to the public.

horizontal analysis (p. 778) Study of percentage changes in comparative financial statements.

inventory turnover (p. 793) Ratio of cost of goods sold to average inventory. Indicates how rapidly inventory is sold.

leverage (p. 797) Earning more income on borrowed money than the related interest expense, thereby increasing the earnings for the owners of the business. Also called *trading on the equity*.

price/earnings ratio (p. 798) Ratio of the market price of a share of common stock to the company's earnings per share. Measures the value that the stock market places on $1 of a company's earnings.

quick ratio (p. 792) Another name for the *acid-test ratio*.

rate of return on common stockholders' equity (p. 797) Net income minus preferred dividends, divided by average common stockholders' equity. A measure of profitability. Also called *return on equity*.

rate of return on net sales (p. 796) Ratio of net income to net sales. A measure of profitability. Also called *return on sales*.

rate of return on total assets (p. 796) Net income plus interest expense, divided by average total assets. This ratio measures a company's success in using its assets to earn income for the persons who finance the business. Also called *return on assets*.

return on equity (p. 797) Another name for *rate of return on common stockholders' equity*.

times-interest-earned ratio (p. 795) Ratio of income from operations to interest expense. Measures the number of times that operating income can cover interest expense. Also called the *interest-coverage ratio*.

trading on the equity (p. 797) Another name for *leverage*.

trend percentages (p. 781) A form of horizontal analysis that indicates the direction a business is taking.

vertical analysis (p. 782) Analysis of a financial statement that reveals the relationship of each statement item to a specified base, which is the 100% figure.

working capital (p. 790) Current assets minus current liabilities; measures a business's ability to meet its short-term obligations with its current assets.

ASSESS YOUR PROGRESS

Short Exercises

S13-1 (*Learning Objective 1: Performing horizontal analysis of revenues and net income*)   Fitzgerald Corporation reported the following amounts on its 2010 comparative income statement:

(In thousands)	2010	2009	2008
Revenues......................	$10,473	$9,998	$9,111
Total expenses..............	5,822	5,422	5,110

Perform a horizontal analysis of revenues and net income—both in dollar amounts and in percentages—for 2010 and 2009.

S13-2 (*Learning Objective 1: Performing trend analysis of sales and net income*)   Fenton, Inc., reported the following sales and net income amounts:

(In thousands)	2010	2009	2008	2007
Sales..........................	$10,020	$8,960	$8,740	$8,490
Net income................	620	530	420	330

Show Fenton's trend percentages for sales and net income. Use 2007 as the base year.

S13-3 (*Learning Objective 2: Performing vertical analysis to correct a cash shortage*)   Craft Software reported the following amounts on its balance sheets at December 31, 2010, 2009, and 2008:

	2010	2009	2008
Cash....................................	$ 7,500	$ 2,195	$ 1,990
Receivables, net..................	35,000	21,950	23,880
Inventory............................	260,000	193,160	147,260
Prepaid expenses	10,000	17,560	11,940
Property, plant, and equipment, net	187,500	204,135	212,930
Total assets	$500,000	$439,000	$398,000

Sales and profits are high. Nevertheless, Craft is experiencing a cash shortage. Perform a vertical analysis of Craft Software's assets at the end of years 2010, 2009, and 2008. Use the analysis to explain the reason for the cash shortage.

S13-4 (*Learning Objective 3: Comparing common-size income statements of two companies*)   Hartigan, Inc., and Pintal Corporation are competitors. Compare the two companies by converting their condensed income statements to common size.

(In millions)	Hartigan	Pintal
Net sales..	$10,800	$8,752
Cost of goods sold...	6,469	6,065
Selling and administrative expenses.................	3,110	1,698
Interest expense...	54	35
Other expenses...	32	44
Income tax expense	432	210
Net income...	$ 703	$ 700

Which company earned more net income? Which company's net income was a higher percentage of its net sales? Explain your answer.

S13-5 (*Learning Objectives 5, 6: Evaluating the trend in a company's current ratio*) Examine the financial data of Jacob Corporation.

Year Ended December 31	2010	2009	2008
Operating Results			
Net income..	$ 220	$ 120	$ 119
Per common share...	$1.23	$0.93	$0.63
Percent of sales..	15.6%	17.6%	19.6%
Return on average stockholders' equity................	14.0	17.0	20.0
Financial Position			
Current assets...	$ 550	$ 445	$ 435
Current liabilities	$ 360	$ 333	$ 356
Working capital	$ 190	$ 112	$ 79
Current ratio...	1.53	1.34	1.22

Show how to compute Jacob's current ratio for each year 2008 through 2010. Is the company's ability to pay its current liabilities improving or deteriorating?

S13-6 (*Learning Objectives 5, 6: Evaluating a company's acid-test ratio*) Use the Gagnon, Inc., balance sheet data on the following page.

❚ Requirements

1. Compute Gagnon, Inc.'s acid-test ratio at December 31, 2010 and 2009.
2. Use the comparative information from the table on the bottom of page 811 for Horner, Inc., Isaacson Company, and Jona Companies Limited. Is Gagnon, Inc.'s acid-test ratio for 2010 and 2009 strong, average, or weak in comparison?

Gagnon, Inc.
Balance Sheets (Adapted)
December 31, 2010 and 2009

(Dollar amounts in millions)	2010	2009	Increase (Decrease) Amount	Increase (Decrease) Percentage
Assets				
Current Assets				
Cash and cash equivalents	$1,203	$ 903	$ 300	33.2 %
Short-term investments	7	84	(77)	(91.7)
Receivables, net	246	256	(10)	(3.9)
Inventories	91	81	10	12.3
Prepaid expenses and other assets	203	343	(140)	(40.8)
Total current assets	1,750	1,667	83	5.0
Property, plant, and equipment, net	3,619	3,396	223	6.6
Intangible assets	1,089	841	248	29.5
Other assets	824	718	106	14.8
Total assets	$7,282	$6,622	$ 660	10.0 %
Liabilities and Stockholders' Equity				
Current Liabilities				
Accounts payable	$ 977	$ 884	$ 93	10.5 %
Income tax payable	39	69	(30)	(43.5)
Short-term debt	121	115	6	5.2
Other	70	73	(3)	(4.1)
Total current liabilities	1,207	1,141	66	5.8
Long-term debt	3,544	2,982	562	18.8
Other liabilities	1,177	1,046	131	12.5
Total liabilities	5,928	5,169	759	14.7
Stockholders' Equity				
Common stock	—	—	—	—
Retained earnings	1,513	1,629	(116)	(7.1)
Accumulated other comprehensive (loss)	(159)	(176)	17	9.7
Total stockholders' equity	1,354	1,453	(99)	(6.8)
Total liabilities and stockholders' equity	$7,282	$6,622	$ 660	10.0 %

Company	Acid-Test Ratio
Horner, Inc. (Utility)	0.73
Isaacson Company (Department store)	0.68
Jona Companies Limited (Grocery store)	0.72

S13-7 (*Learning Objectives 5, 6: Computing and evaluating inventory turnover and days' sales in receivables*)   Use the Gagnon 2010 income statement below and balance sheet from Short Exercise 13-6 to compute the following:

Gagnon, Inc.
Statements of Income (Adapted)
Year Ended December 31, 2010 and 2009

(Dollar amounts in millions)	2010	2009
Revenues	$9,500	$9,068
Expenses:		
Food and paper (Cost of goods sold)	2,200	2,236
Payroll and employee benefits	2,138	2,001
Occupancy and other operating expenses	2,778	2,745
General and administrative expenses	1,171	1,135
Interest expense	150	133
Other expense (income), net	11	(29)
Income before income taxes	1,052	847
Income tax expense	273	251
Net income	$ 779	$ 596

a. Gagnon's rate of inventory turnover for 2010.
b. Days' sales in average receivables during 2010. (Round dollar amounts to one decimal place.)

Do these measures look strong or weak? Give the reason for your answer.

S13-8 (*Learning Objectives 5, 6: Measuring ability to pay long-term debt*)   Use the financial statements of Gagnon, Inc., in Short Exercises 13-6 and 13-7.

❙ Requirements

1. Compute the company's debt ratio at December 31, 2010.
2. Compute the company's times-interest-earned ratio for 2010. For operating income, use income before both interest expense and income taxes. You can simply add interest expense back to income before taxes.
3. Is Gagnon's ability to pay liabilities and interest expense strong or weak? Comment on the value of each ratio computed for questions 1 and 2.

S13-9 (*Learning Objectives 5, 6: Measuring profitability*)   Use the financial statements of Gagnon, Inc., in Short Exercises 13-6 and 13-7 to compute these profitability measures for 2010. Show each computation.

a. Rate of return on sales.
b. Rate of return on total assets.
c. Rate of return on common stockholders' equity.

S13-10 (*Learning Objective 5: Computing EPS and the price/earnings ratio*)   The annual report of Tri-State Cars, Inc., for the year ended December 31, 2010, included the following items (in millions):

Preferred stock outstanding, 6%	$400
Net income	$500
Number of shares of common stock outstanding	100

Requirements

1. Compute earnings per share (EPS) and the price/earnings ratio for Tri-State Cars' stock. Round to the nearest cent. The price of a share of Tri-State Car stock is $57.12.
2. How much does the stock market say $1 of Tri-State Cars' net income is worth?

S13-11 (*Learning Objective 5: Using ratio data to reconstruct an income statement*) A skeleton of Athol Country Florist's income statement appears as follows (amounts in thousands):

Income Statement

Net sales	$7,500
Cost of goods sold	(a)
Selling expenses	1,511
Administrative expenses	328
Interest expense	(b)
Other expenses	154
Income before taxes	1,046
Income tax expense	(c)
Net income	$ (d)

Use the following ratio data to complete Athol Country Florist's income statement:

a. Inventory turnover was 4 (beginning inventory was $784; ending inventory was $762).

b. Rate of return on sales is 0.10.

S13-12 (*Learning Objective 5: Using ratio data to reconstruct a balance sheet*) A skeleton of Athol Country Florist's balance sheet appears as follows (amounts in thousands):

Balance Sheet

Cash	$ 85		Total current liabilities	$1,900
Receivables	(a)		Long-term debt	(e)
Inventories	762		Other long-term liabilities	720
Prepaid expenses	(b)			
Total current assets	(c)			
Plant assets, net	(d)		Common stock	185
Other assets	2,100		Retained earnings	3,465
Total assets	$7,300		Total liabilities and equity	$ (f)

Use the following ratio data to complete Athol Country Florist's balance sheet:

a. Debt ratio is 0.50.

b. Current ratio is 1.30.

c. Acid-test ratio is 0.40.

writing assignment ■

S13-13 (*Learning Objective 6: Analyzing a company based on its ratios*) Take the role of an investment analyst at Merrimack Lowell. It is your job to recommend investments for your client. The only information you have is the following ratio values for two companies in the graphics software industry.

Ratio	Graphit.net	Data Doctors
Days' sales in receivables............................	44	50
Inventory turnover.....................................	6	10
Gross profit percentage	69%	60%
Net income as a percent of sales................	13%	14%
Times interest earned	17	11
Return on equity.......................................	36%	28%
Return on assets.......................................	15%	20%

Write a report to the Merrimack Lowell investment committee. Recommend one company's stock over the other. State the reasons for your recommendation.

S13-14 (*Learning Objective 7: Measuring economic value added*) Compute economic value added (EVA®) for Beverly Software. The company's cost of capital is 5%. Net income was $770 thousand, interest expense $409 thousand, beginning long-term debt $700 thousand, and beginning stockholders' equity was $3,060 thousand. Round all amounts to the nearest thousand dollars.

Should the company's stockholders be happy with the EVA®?

Exercises

All of the A and B exercises can be found within MyAccountingLab, an online homework and practice environment. Your instructor may ask you to complete these exercises using MyAccountingLab.

(Group A)

E13-15A (*Learning Objective 1: Computing year-to-year changes in working capital*) What were the dollar amount of change and the percentage of each change in Wilderness Lodge's working capital during 2010 and 2009? Is this trend favorable or unfavorable?

	2010	2009	2008
Total current assets	$270,000	$320,000	$340,000
Total current liabilities	125,000	160,000	170,000

■ **spreadsheet**

E13-16A (*Learning Objective 1: Performing horizontal analysis of an income statement*) Prepare a horizontal analysis of the comparative income statements of Sensible Music Co. Round percentage changes to the nearest one-tenth percent (three decimal places).

Sensible Music Co.
Comparative Income Statements
Years Ended December 31, 2010 and 2009

	2010	2009
Total revenue	$852,000	$912,000
Expenses:		
Cost of goods sold	$402,000	$408,000
Selling and general expenses	232,000	261,000
Interest expense	9,200	10,500
Income tax expense	83,000	84,000
Total expenses	726,200	763,500
Net income	$125,800	$148,500

E13-17A *(Learning Objective 1: Computing trend percentages)*   Compute trend percentages for Palm Valley Sales & Service's total revenue, and net income for the following five-year period, using year 0 as the base year. Round to the nearest full percent.

(In thousands)	Year 4	Year 3	Year 2	Year 1	Year 0
Total revenue	$1,414	$1,203	$1,101	$999	$1,020
Net income	104	99	86	74	88

Which grew faster during the period, total revenue or net income?

E13-18A *(Learning Objective 2: Performing vertical analysis of a balance sheet)*   Fore Golf Company has requested that you perform a vertical analysis of its balance sheet to determine the component percentages of its assets, liabilities, and stockholders' equity.

Fore Golf Company
Balance Sheet
December 31, 2010

Assets

Total current assets	$ 43,000
Property, plant, and equipment, net	117,000
Other assets	38,000
Total assets	$198,000

Liabilities

Total current liabilities	$ 49,000
Long-term debt	109,000
Total liabilities	158,000

Stockholders' Equity

Total stockholders' equity	40,000
Total liabilities and stockholders' equity	$198,000

■ spreadsheet

E13-19A (*Learning Objective 3: Preparing a common-size income statement*)   Prepare a comparative common-size income statement for Sensible Music Co., using the 2010 and 2009 data of Exercise 13-16A and rounding to four decimal places.

writing assignment ■

E13-20A (*Learning Objective 4: Analyzing the statement of cash flows*)   Identify any weaknesses revealed by the statement of cash flows of California Fruit Growers, Inc.

California Fruit Growers, Inc.
Statement of Cash Flows
For the Current Year

Operating activities:		
Income from operations..		$ 61,000
Add (subtract) noncash items:		
Depreciation	$ 11,000	
Net increase in current assets other than cash	(52,000)	
Net decrease in current liabilities		
exclusive of short-term debt..........................	(19,000)	(60,000)
Net cash provided by operating activities..........		1,000
Investing activities:		
Sale of property, plant, and equipment		115,000
Financing activities:		
Issuance of bonds payable	$ 113,000	
Payment of short-term debt	(174,000)	
Payment of long-term debt	(86,000)	
Payment of dividends..	(38,000)	
Net cash used for financing activities...............		(185,000)
Increase (decrease) in cash		$ (69,000)

■ spreadsheet

E13-21A (*Learning Objective 5: Computing five ratios*)   The financial statements of Smith News, Inc., include the following items:

	Current Year	Preceding Year
Balance sheet:		
Cash	$ 26,000	$ 32,000
Short-term investments	14,000	20,000
Net receivables	50,000	73,000
Inventory......................................	94,000	76,000
Prepaid expenses..........................	9,000	8,000
Total current assets	193,000	209,000
Total current liabilities.................	129,000	96,000
Income statement:		
Net credit sales	$490,000	
Cost of goods sold	274,000	

❙ *Requirement*

1. Compute the following ratios for the current year:

   a. Current ratio
   b. Acid-test ratio
   c. Inventory turnover
   d. Accounts receivable turnover
   e. Days' sales in average receivables

(Round your answers to a through d to two decimal points. Round your answer to e to the nearest whole number.)

E13-22A (*Learning Objectives 5, 6: Analyzing the ability to pay current liabilities*)   Dorman Furniture Company has requested that you determine whether the company's ability to pay its current liabilities and long-term debts improved or deteriorated during 2010. To answer this question, compute the following ratios for 2010 and 2009:

a. Current ratio

c. Debt ratio

b. Acid-test ratio

d. Times-interest-earned ratio

writing assignment ■

■ **spreadsheet**

Summarize the results of your analysis in a written report.

	2010	2009
Cash	$ 21,000	$ 53,000
Short-term investments	32,000	15,000
Net receivables	117,000	127,000
Inventory	243,000	272,000
Prepaid expenses	18,000	4,000
Total assets	500,000	531,000
Total current liabilities	247,000	312,000
Long-term debt	27,000	134,000
Income from operations	191,000	160,000
Interest expense	39,000	45,000

E13-23A (*Learning Objectives 5, 6: Analyzing profitability*)   Compute four ratios that measure the ability to earn profits for Harmon Decor, Inc., whose comparative income statements follow:

Harmon Decor, Inc. **Comparative Income Statements** **Years Ended December 31, 2010 and 2009**		
	2010	2009
Net sales	$100,000	$90,000
Cost of goods sold	53,000	46,000
Gross profit	47,000	44,000
Selling and general expenses	20,000	18,000
Income from operations	27,000	26,000
Interest expense	3,000	2,000
Income before income tax	24,000	24,000
Income tax expense	8,000	7,000
Net income	$ 16,000	$17,000

Additional data:

	2010	2009	2008
Total assets	$104,000	$100,000	$83,000
Common stockholders' equity	$ 72,000	$ 70,000	$69,000
Preferred dividends	$ 3,000	$ 2,000	$ 1,000
Common shares outstanding during the year	10,000	9,000	4,000

Did the company's operating performance improve or deteriorate during 2010?

writing assignment ■

E13-24A (*Learning Objectives 5, 6: Evaluating a stock as an investment*)   Evaluate the common stock of Regal Distributing Company as an investment. Specifically, use the three common stock ratios to determine whether the common stock increased or decreased in attractiveness during the past year.

	2010	2009
Net income..	$ 83,000	$ 60,000
Dividends to common	22,000	23,000
Total stockholders' equity at year-end...............	300,000	510,000
(includes 90,000 shares of common stock)		
Preferred stock, 5%...	80,000	80,000
Market price per share of common		
stock at year-end	$ 24.50	$ 17.50

E13-25A (*Learning Objective 7: Using economic value added to measure corporate performance*)   Two companies with different economic-value-added (EVA®) profiles are Barton Oil Pipeline Incorporated and Crompton Bank Limited. Adapted versions of the two companies' financial statements are presented here (in millions):

	Barton Oil Pipeline Inc.	Crompton Bank Limited
Balance sheet data:		
Total assets	$ 4,338	$14,000
Interest-bearing debt	$ 1,257	$ 13
All other liabilities............................	2,675	2,605
Stockholders' equity	406	11,382
Total liabilities and equity................	$ 4,338	$14,000
Income statement data:		
Total revenue	$11,007	$ 3,819
Interest expense.................................	76	7
Net income..	$ 180	$ 1,219

I Requirements

1. Before performing any calculations, which company do you think represents the better investment? Give your reason.
2. Compute the EVA® for each company and then decide which company's stock you would rather hold as an investment. Assume both companies' cost of capital is 8.5%.

(Group B)

E13-26B (*Learning Objective 1: Computing year-to-year changes in working capital*)   What were the dollar amount of change and the percentage of each change in Ricardo Lodge's working capital during 2010 and 2009? Is this trend favorable or unfavorable?

	2010	2009	2008
Total current assets	$400,000	$300,000	$240,000
Total current liabilities	190,000	150,000	120,000

■ **spreadsheet**

E13-27B (*Learning Objective 1: Performing horizontal analysis of an income statement*)   Prepare a horizontal analysis of the comparative income statements of Fashion Music Co. Round percentage changes to the nearest one-tenth percent (three decimal places).

Fashion Music Co.
Comparative Income Statements
Years Ended December 31, 2010 and 2009

	2010	2009
Total revenue	$1,080,000	$919,000
Expenses:		
Cost of goods sold	$ 479,000	$400,450
Selling and general expenses	289,000	269,000
Interest expense	24,500	14,500
Income tax expense	106,500	86,850
Total expenses	899,000	770,800
Net income	$181,000	$148,200

E13-28B (*Learning Objective 1: Computing trend percentages*)   Compute trend percentages for Andover Valley Sales & Service's total revenue, and net income for the following five-year period, using year 0 as the base year. Round to the nearest full percent.

(in thousands)	Year 4	Year 3	Year 2	Year 1	Year 0
Total revenue	$1,433	$1,251	$1,067	$1,008	$1,022
Net income	120	112	81	69	83

Which grew faster during the period, total revenue or net income?

E13-29B (*Learning Objective 2: Performing vertical analysis of a balance sheet*)   Epsilon Golf Company has requested that you perform a vertical analysis of its balance sheet to determine the component percentages of its assets, liabilities, and stockholders' equity.

Epsilon Golf Company
Balance Sheet
December 31, 2010

Assets	
Total current assets	$ 45,000
Property, plant, and equipment, net	210,000
Other assets	42,000
Total assets	$297,000
Liabilities	
Total current liabilities..	$ 53,000
Long-term debt...	111,000
Total liabilities..	164,000
Stockholders' Equity	
Total stockholders' equity.....................................	133,000
Total liabilities and stockholders' equity..............	$297,000

E13-30B (*Learning Objective 3: Preparing a common-size income statement*)   Prepare a comparative common-size income statement for Fashion Music Co. using the 2010 and 2009 data of Exercise 13-27B and rounding to four decimal places.

■ **spreadsheet**

writing assignment ■

E13-31B (*Learning Objective 4: Analyzing the statement of cash flows*) Identify any weaknesses revealed by the statement of cash flows of Massachusetts Chowder Distributors, Inc.

Massachusetts Chowder Distributors, Inc.
Statement of Cash Flows
For the Current Year

Operating activities:		
Income from operations...		$ 77,000
Add (subtract) noncash items:		
Depreciation	$ 30,000	
Net increase in current assets other than cash	(61,000)	
Net decrease in current liabilities		
exclusive of short-term debt..........................	(22,000)	(53,000)
Net cash provided by operating activities.........		24,000
Investing activities:		
Sale of property, plant, and equipment		126,000
Financing activities:		
Issuance of bonds payable	$ 99,000	
Payment of short-term debt	(166,000)	
Payment of long-term debt	(90,000)	
Payment of dividends..	(50,000)	
Net cash used for financing activities..............		(207,000)
Increase (decrease) in cash		$ (57,000)

■ spreadsheet

E13-32B (*Learning Objective 5: Computing five ratios*) The financial statements of Advent News, Inc., include the following items:

	Current Year	Preceding Year
Balance sheet:		
Cash	$ 65,000	$ 91,000
Short-term investments	13,000	25,000
Net receivables	79,000	82,000
Inventory......................................	93,000	75,000
Prepaid expenses..........................	6,000	12,000
Total current assets	256,000	285,000
Total current liabilities.................	133,000	97,000
Income statement:		
Net credit sales	$494,000	
Cost of goods sold	277,000	

▌ Requirement

1. Compute the following ratios for the current year:

   a. Current ratio
   b. Acid-test ratio
   c. Inventory turnover
   d. Accounts receivable turnover
   e. Days' sales in average receivables

(Round your answers to a through d to two decimal points. Round your answer to e to the nearest whole number.)

E13-33B (*Learning Objectives 5, 6: Analyzing the ability to pay current liabilities*)   Jalbert Furniture Company has requested that you determine whether the company's ability to pay its current liabilities and long-term debts improved or deteriorated during 2010. To answer this question, compute the following ratios for 2010 and 2009. (Round your answers to two decimal places.)

writing assignment ■

■ **spreadsheet**

    a. Current ratio   **c.** Debt ratio
    b. Acid-test ratio   **d.** Times-interest-earned ratio

Summarize the results of your analysis in a written report.

	2010	2009
Cash	$ 27,000	$ 47,000
Short-term investments	33,000	4,000
Net receivables	120,000	135,000
Inventory	238,000	271,000
Prepaid expenses	22,000	8,000
Total assets	590,000	510,000
Total current liabilities	187,000	332,000
Long-term debt	147,000	84,000
Income from operations	191,000	169,000
Interest expense	41,000	43,000

E13-34B (*Learning Objectives 5, 6: Analyzing profitability*)   Compute four ratios that measure the ability to earn profits for Jarvis Decor, Inc., whose comparative income statements follow:

Jarvis Decor, Inc. **Comparative Income Statements** **Years Ended December 31, 2010 and 2009**		
	2010	2009
Net sales	$254,000	$217,000
Cost of goods sold	125,000	111,000
Gross profit	129,000	106,000
Selling and general expenses	50,000	46,000
Income from operations	79,000	60,000
Interest expense	7,000	6,000
Income before income tax	72,000	54,000
Income tax expense	25,000	19,000
Net income	$ 47,000	$ 35,000

Additional data:

	2010	2009	2008
Total assets	$249,000	$239,000	$227,000
Common stockholders' equity	$106,000	$104,000	$102,000
Preferred dividends	$ 17,000	$ 15,000	$ 13,000
Common shares outstanding during the year	19,000	17,000	11,000

Did the company's operating performance improve or deteriorate during 2010?

E13-35B (*Learning Objectives 5, 6: Evaluating a stock as an investment*) Evaluate the common stock of Basic Distributing Company as an investment. Specifically, use the three common stock ratios to determine whether the common stock increased or decreased in attractiveness during the past year.

	2010	2009
Net income..	$ 91,000	$ 99,000
Dividends to common	28,000	13,000
Total stockholders' equity at year-end................	565,000	515,000
(includes 80,000 shares of common stock)		
Preferred stock, 6%...	90,000	90,000
Market price per share of common		
stock at year-end	$ 24.00	$ 25.16

E13-36B (*Learning Objective 7: Using economic value added to measure corporate performance*) Two companies with different economic-value-added (EVA®) profiles are Houle Oil Pipeline, Inc., and Johnson Bank Limited. Adapted versions of the two companies' financial statements are presented here (in millions):

	Houle Oil Pipeline, Inc.	Johnson Bank Limited
Balance sheet data:		
Total assets	$ 4,338	$14,451
Interest-bearing debt	$ 1,250	$ 5
All other liabilities............................	2,900	2,585
Stockholders' equity..........................	188	11,861
Total liabilities and equity...............	$ 4,338	$14,451
Income statement data:		
Total revenue	$10,991	$ 3,697
Interest expense................................	80	7
Net income..	$ 200	$ 1,197

❙ Requirements

1. Before performing any calculations, which company do you think represents the better investment? Give your reason.
2. Compute the EVA® for each company and then decide which company's stock you would rather hold as an investment. Assume both companies' cost of capital is 11.0%. (Round your EVA® calculation to the nearest whole number.)

Challenge Exercises

E13-37 *(Learning Objectives 2, 3, 5: Using ratio data to reconstruct a company's balance sheet)*   The following data (dollar amounts in millions) are taken from the financial statements of Floor 1 Industries, Inc.:

Total liabilities	$12,600
Preferred stock	$ 0
Total current assets	$11,900
Accumulated depreciation	$ 1,700
Debt ratio	60%
Current ratio	1.70

I Requirement

1. Complete the following condensed balance sheet. Report amounts to the nearest million dollars.

	(In millions)
Current assets	☐
Property, plant, and equipment	☐
Less: Accumulated depreciation	☐ ☐
Total assets	☐
Current liabilities	☐
Long-term liabilities	☐
Stockholders' equity	☐
Total liabilities and stockholders' equity	☐

E13-38 *(Learning Objectives 2, 3, 5: Using ratio data to reconstruct a company's income statement)*   The following data (dollar amounts in millions) are from the financial statements of County Corporation:

Average stockholders' equity	$3,400
Interest expense	$ 800
Preferred stock	$ 0
Operating income as a percent of sales	20%
Rate of return on stockholders' equity	10%
Income tax rate	30%

❙ *Requirement*

1. Complete the following condensed income statement. Report amounts to the nearest million dollars.

Sales...	☐
Operating expense..................	☐
Operating income..................	☐
Interest expense....................	☐
Pretax income	☐
Income tax expense...............	☐
Net income...........................	☐

Quiz

Use the Hialeah Bell Corporation financial statements that follow to answer questions 13–39 through 13–50.

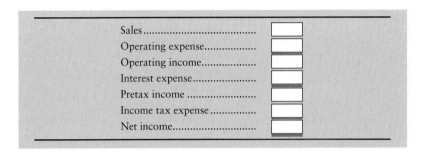

Hialeah Bell Corporation Consolidated Statements of Income (In millions, except per share amounts)			
	Year ended December 31,		
	2010	2009	2008
Net revenue...	$42,788	$35,299	$30,968
Cost of goods sold....................................	34,000	29,111	26,061
Gross profit	8,788	6,188	4,907
Operating expenses:			
Selling, general, and administrative......	3,341	3,000	2,581
Research, development, and			
engineering.....................................	574	556	542
Special charges...................................	—	—	502
Total operating expenses	3,915	3,556	3,625
Operating income...........................	4,873	2,632	1,282
Investment and other income (loss), net	170	212	(78)
Income before income taxes.................	5,043	2,844	1,204
Income tax expense.....................................	1,100	912	472
Net income......................................	$ 3,943	$ 1,932	$ 732
Earnings per common share:			
Basic...	$ 1.33	$ 0.94	$ 0.42

Hialeah Bell Corporation
Consolidated Statements of Financial Position
(In millions)

	December 31, 2010	December 31, 2009
Assets		
Current assets:		
Cash and cash equivalents..................................	$ 4,301	$ 4,138
Short-term investments.....................................	830	512
Accounts receivable, net...................................	3,402	2,401
Inventories	427	410
Other	1,638	1,213
Total current assets	10,598	8,674
Property, plant, and equipment, net	1,517	932
Investments..	6,613	5,323
Other noncurrent assets......................................	301	144
Total assets...	$19,029	$15,073
Liabilities and Stockholders' Equity		
Current liabilities:		
Accounts payable	$ 7,702	$ 6,002
Accrued and other	3,676	3,044
Total current liabilities......................................	11,378	9,046
Long-term debt...	301	302
Other noncurrent liabilities.................................	1,701	1,167
Commitments and contingent liabilities (Note 7)......	—	—
Total liabilities	13,380	10,515
Stockholders' equity:		
Preferred stock and capital in excess of $0.02 par value; shares issued and outstanding: none	—	—
Common stock and capital in excess of $0.05 par value; shares authorized: 6,000; shares issued: 3,240 and 2,989, respectively...........	7,801	7,004
Treasury stock, at cost; 175 and 124 shares, respectively...	(6,333)	(4,404)
Retained earnings...	4,321	2,054
Other comprehensive loss..................................	(104)	(50)
Other..	(36)	(46)
Total stockholders' equity	5,649	4,558
Total liabilities and stockholders' equity	$19,029	$15,073

Q13-39 During 2010, Hialeah Bell's total assets

a. increased by $9,390 million.
b. increased by 26.2%.
c. both a and b.
d. increased by 20.8%.

Q13-40 Hialeah Bell's current ratio at year end 2010 is closest to

a. 1.2.
b. 9,390.
c. 20.8.
d. 0.9.

Q13-41 Hialeah Bell's acid-test ratio at year-end 2010 is closest to

a. $0.68.
b. $0.75.
c. $8,533 million.
d. 0.45.

Q13-42 What is the largest single item included in Hialeah Bell's debt ratio at December 31, 2010?

a. Cash and cash equivalents
b. Investments
c. Accounts payable
d. Common stock

Q13-43 Using the earliest year available as the base year, the trend percentage for Hialeah Bell's net revenue during 2010 was

a. 121%.
b. up by 21.2%.
c. up by $11,820 million.
d. 138%.

Q13-44 Hialeah Bell's common-size income statement for 2010 would report cost of goods sold as

a. 79.5%.
b. Up by 16.8%.
c. 130.5%.
d. $34,000 million.

Q13-45 Hialeah Bell's days' sales in average receivables during 2010 was

a. 29 days.
b. 117 days.
c. 21 days.
d. 25 days.

Q13-46 Hialeah Bell's inventory turnover during fiscal year 2010 was

a. 130 times.
b. 81 times.
c. 41 times.
d. very slow.

Q13-47 Hialeah Bell's long-term debt bears interest at 11%. During the year ended December 31, 2010, Bell's times-interest-earned ratio was

a. 137 times.
b. 144 times.
c. 147 times.
d. 150 times.

Q13-48 Hialeah Bell's trend of return on sales is

a. worrisome.
b. declining.
c. improving.
d. stuck at 20.8%.

Q13-49 How many shares of common stock did Hialeah Bell have outstanding, on average, during 2010? Hint: Compute earnings per share.

a. 2,947 million
b. 5,258 million
c. 5,244 million
d. 2,965 million

Q13-50 Book value per share of Hialeah Bell's common stock outstanding at December 31, 2010, was

a. $5,649.
b. $1.84.
c. $1.96.
d. $2.08.

Problems

MyAccountingLab®

> All of the A and B problems can be found within MyAccountingLab, an online homework and practice environment. Your instructor may ask you to complete these problems using MyAccountingLab.

(Group A)

■ spreadsheet

P13-51A (*Learning Objectives 1, 5, 6: Computing trend percentages, return on sales, and comparison with the industry*) Net sales, net income, and total assets for Amble Shipping, Inc., for a five-year period follow:

(In thousands)	2010	2009	2008	2007	2006
Net sales.................	$902	$800	$492	$313	$303
Net income................	42	39	15	39	33
Total assets	305	268	256	221	203

Requirements

1. Compute trend percentages for each item for 2007 through 2010. Use 2006 as the base year and round to the nearest percent.

2. Compute the rate of return on net sales for 2008 through 2010, rounding to three decimal places.

3. How does Amble Shipping's return on net sales compare with that of the industry? In the shipping industry, rates above 5% are considered good, and rates above 7% are outstanding.

P13-52A (*Learning Objectives 3, 5, 6: Preparing common-size statements; analyzing profitability; making comparisons with the industry*)   Top managers of McDonough Products, Inc., have asked for your help in comparing the company's profit performance and financial position with the average for the industry. The accountant has given you the company's income statement and balance sheet and also the following data for the industry:

writing assignment ■

■ **spreadsheet**

McDonough Products, Inc.
Income Statement Compared with Industry Average
Year Ended December 31, 2010

	McDonough	Industry Average
Net sales.............................	$700,000	100.0%
Cost of goods sold.................	490,000	57.3
Gross profit..........................	210,000	42.7
Operating expenses	175,000	29.4
Operating income..................	35,000	13.3
Other expenses......................	7,000	2.5
Net income	$ 28,000	10.8%

McDonough Products, Inc.
Balance Sheet Compared with Industry Average
December 31, 2010

	McDonough	Industry Average
Current assets..........................	$471,200	72.1%
Fixed assets, net	114,700	19.0
Intangible assets, net	21,080	4.8
Other assets.............................	13,020	4.1
Total	$620,000	100.0%
Current liabilities	$240,560	47.2%
Long-term liabilities	135,160	21.0
Stockholders' equity.................	244,280	31.8
Total	$620,000	100.0%

Requirements

1. Prepare a common-size income statement and balance sheet for McDonough Products. The first column of each statement should present McDonough Products' common-size statement, and the second column should show the industry averages.

2. For the profitability analysis, compute McDonough Products' (a) ratio of gross profit to net sales (b) ratio of operating income to net sales, and (c) ratio of net income to net sales. Compare these figures with the industry averages. Is McDonough Products' profit performance better or worse than the average for the industry?

3. For the analysis of financial position, compute McDonough Products' (a) ratios of current assets and current liabilities to total assets and (b) ratio of stockholders' equity to total assets. Compare these ratios with the industry averages. Is McDonough Products' financial position better or worse than the average for the industry?

writing assignment ■

P13-53A (*Learning Objective 4: Using the statement of cash flows for decision making*) You are evaluating two companies as possible investments. The two companies, similar in size, are commuter airlines that fly passengers up and down the West Coast. All other available information has been analyzed and your investment decision depends on the statements of cash flows.

	2011	2010
Friendly Airlines		
Statements of Cash Flows		
Years Ended November 30, 2011 and 2010		
Operating activities:		
Net income (net loss)	$ (48,000)	$121,000
Adjustments for noncash items:		
Total	60,000	(10,000)
Net cash provided by operating activities	12,000	111,000
Investing activities:		
Purchase of property, plant, and		
equipment...	$ (51,000)	$(106,000)
Sale of long-term investments	44,000	7,000
Net cash provided by (used for)		
investing activities.................................	(7,000)	(99,000)
Financing activities:		
Issuance of short-term notes payable	$ 150,000	$ 165,000
Payment of short-term notes payable........	(186,000)	(139,000)
Payment of cash dividends........................	(39,000)	(70,000)
Net cash used for financing activities........	(75,000)	(44,000)
Increase (decrease) in cash.................................	$ (70,000)	$ (32,000)
Cash balance at beginning of year.....................	80,000	112,000
Cash balance at the end of year.........................	$ 10,000	$ 80,000

Cloudview, Inc.
Statements of Cash Flows
Years Ended September 30, 2011 and 2010

	2011	2010
Operating activities:		
Net income...	$ 200,000	$ 146,000
Adjustments for noncash items:		
Total...	51,000	60,000
Net cash provided by operating activities.....	251,000	206,000
Investing activities:		
Purchase of property, plant,		
and equipment......................................	$(299,000)	$(462,000)
Sale of property, plant, and equipment	52,000	90,000
Net cash used for investing activities	(247,000)	(372,000)
Financing activities:		
Issuance of long-term notes payable..........	$ 150,000	$ 99,000
Payment of short-term notes payable........	(72,000)	(20,000)
Net cash provided by financing activities......	78,000	79,000
Increase (decrease) in cash.................................	$ 82,000	$ (87,000)
Cash balance at beginning of year......................	133,000	220,000
Cash balance at end of year...............................	$ 215,000	$ 133,000

Requirement

1. Discuss the relative strengths and weaknesses of Friendly and Cloudview. Conclude your discussion by recommending one of the companies' stocks as an investment.

P13-54A (*Learning Objectives 5, 6: Computing effects of business transactions on selected ratios*)   Financial statement data of Greatland Engineering include the following items:

Cash	$ 25,000	Accounts payable	$101,000
Short-term investments..............	38,000	Accrued liabilities.....................	37,000
Accounts receivable, net	82,000	Long-term notes payable...........	160,000
Inventories	149,000	Other long-term liabilities	37,000
Prepaid expenses	6,000	Net income................................	96,000
Total assets	674,000	Number of common	
Short-term notes payable...........	41,000	shares outstanding	52,000

❙ *Requirements*

1. Compute Greatland's current ratio, debt ratio, and earnings per share. (Round all ratios to two decimal places.)
2. Compute the three ratios after evaluating the effect of each transaction that follows. Consider each transaction *separately*.
   a. Borrowed $135,000 on a long-term note payable.
   b. Issued 40,000 shares of common stock, receiving cash of $360,000.
   c. Paid short-term notes payable, $28,000.
   d. Purchased merchandise of $44,000 on account, debiting Inventory.
   e. Received cash on account, $16,000.

P13-55A (*Learning Objectives 5, 6: Using ratios to evaluate a stock investment*) Comparative financial statement data of Bloomfield Optical Mart follow:

Bloomfield Optical Mart
Comparative Income Statements
Years Ended December 31, 2010 and 2009

	2010	2009
Net sales...	$690,000	$590,000
Cost of goods sold..............................	375,000	283,000
Gross profit...	315,000	307,000
Operating expenses	126,000	141,000
Income from operations	189,000	166,000
Interest expense..................................	36,000	50,000
Income before income tax	153,000	116,000
Income tax expense............................	40,000	53,000
Net income	$113,000	$ 63,000

Bloomfield Optical Mart
Comparative Balance Sheets
December 31, 2010 and 2009

	2010	2009	2008*
Current assets:			
Cash	$ 38,000	$ 40,000	
Current receivables, net	217,000	149,000	$140,000
Inventories...	298,000	285,000	181,000
Prepaid expenses..	9,000	25,000	
Total current assets...	562,000	499,000	
Property, plant, and equipment, net	284,000	276,000	
Total assets...	$846,000	$775,000	710,000
Total current liabilities	$281,000	$267,000	
Long-term liabilities..	241,000	236,000	
Total liabilities	522,000	503,000	
Preferred stockholders' equity, 5%, $10 par...............	70,000	70,000	
Common stockholders' equity, no par........................	254,000	202,000	195,000
Total liabilities and stockholders' equity	$846,000	$775,000	

*Selected 2008 amounts.

Other information:

1. Market price of Bloomfield common stock: $82.20 at December 31, 2010, and $52.96 at December 31, 2009.
2. Common shares outstanding: 20,000 during 2010 and 18,000 during 2009.
3. All sales on credit.

I Requirements

1. Compute the following ratios for 2010 and 2009:
    a. Current ratio
    b. Inventory turnover
    c. Times-interest-earned ratio
    d. Return on assets
    e. Return on common stockholders' equity
    f. Earnings per share of common stock
    g. Price/earnings ratio
2. Decide whether (a) Bloomfield's financial position improved or deteriorated during 2010 and (b) the investment attractiveness of Bloomfield's common stock appears to have increased or decreased.
3. How will what you learned in this problem help you evaluate an investment?

P13-56A *(Learning Objectives 5, 6, 7: Using ratios to decide between two stock investments;* *measuring economic value added)* Assume that you are considering purchasing stock as an investment. You have narrowed the choice to DVR.com and Express Shops and have assembled the following data.

writing assignment ■

Selected income statement data for the current year:

	DVR	Express
Net sales (all on credit)..................	$602,000	$517,000
Cost of goods sold.........................	449,000	382,000
Income from operations	88,000	73,000
Interest expense............................	—	16,000
Net income.....................................	61,000	39,000

Selected balance sheet and market price data at *end* of current year:

	DVR	Express
Current assets:		
Cash	$ 22,000	$ 38,000
Short-term investments	10,000	14,000
Current receivables, net	182,000	167,000
Inventories...	210,000	181,000
Prepaid expenses...	21,000	8,000
Total current assets	445,000	408,000
Total assets..	981,000	935,000
Total current liabilities	362,000	333,000
Total liabilities	673,000	700,000
Preferred stock, 5%, $150 par		30,000
Common stock, $1 par (100,000 shares).................	100,000	
$5 par (15,000 shares)...................		75,000
Total stockholders' equity	308,000	235,000
Market price per share of common stock	$ 6.10	$ 55.00

Selected balance sheet data at *beginning* of current year:

	DVR	Express
Balance sheet:		
Current receivables, net...	$144,000	$195,000
Inventories	205,000	199,000
Total assets..	853,000	908,000
Long-term debt	—	299,000
Preferred stock, 5%, $150 par..................................		30,000
Common stock, $1 par (100,000 shares).................	100,000	
$5 par (15,000 shares)..................		75,000
Total stockholders' equity..	260,000	221,000

Your strategy is to invest in companies that have low price/earnings ratios but appear to be in good shape financially. Assume that you have analyzed all other factors and that your decision depends on the results of ratio analysis.

Requirements

1. Compute the following ratios for both companies for the current year and decide which company's stock better fits your investment strategy.
   a. Acid-test ratio
   b. Inventory turnover
   c. Days' sales in average receivables
   d. Debt ratio
   e. Times-interest-earned ratio
   f. Return on common stockholders' equity
   g. Earnings per share of common stock
   h. Price/earnings ratio
2. Compute each company's economic-value-added (EVA®) measure and determine whether the companies' EVA®s confirm or alter your investment decision. Each company's cost of capital is 10%.

(Group B)

■ spreadsheet

P13-57B (*Learning Objectives 1, 5, 6: Computing trend percentages, return on common equity, and comparison with the industry*)   Net sales, net income, and total assets for Amaze Shipping, Inc., for a five-year period follow:

(In thousands)	2010	2009	2008	2007	2006
Net sales...	$616	$503	$358	$309	$300
Net income.......................................	33	30	45	34	27
Total assets.....................................	300	268	255	231	204

Requirements

1. Compute trend percentages for each item for 2007 through 2010. Use 2006 as the base year and round to the nearest percent.
2. Compute the rate of return on net sales for 2008 through 2010, rounding to three decimal places.
3. How does Amaze Shipping's return on net sales compare with that of the industry? In the shipping industry, rates above 5% are considered good, and rates above 7% are outstanding.

writing assignment ■

■ spreadsheet

P13-58B (*Learning Objectives 3, 5, 6: Preparing common-size statements; analyzing profitability; making comparisons with the industry*)   Top managers of Walsh Products, Inc., have asked for your help in comparing the company's profit performance and financial position with the average for the industry. The accountant has given you the company's income statement and balance sheet and also the following data for the industry:

Walsh Products, Inc.
Income Statement Compared with Industry Average
Year Ended December 31, 2010

	Walsh	Industry Average
Net sales..................................	$900,000	100.0%
Cost of goods sold..................	648,000	57.3
Gross profit............................	252,000	42.7
Operating expenses	216,000	29.4
Operating income...................	36,000	13.3
Other expenses.......................	13,500	2.5
Net income	$ 22,500	10.8%

Walsh Products, Inc.
Balance Sheet Compared with Industry Average
December 31, 2010

	Walsh	Industry Average
Current assets............................	$408,100	72.1%
Fixed assets, net	99,640	19.0
Intangible assets, net	20,140	4.8
Other assets..............................	2,120	4.1
Total	$530,000	100.0%
Current liabilities	$205,640	47.2%
Long-term liabilities	112,360	21.0
Stockholders' equity.................	212,000	31.8
Total	$530,000	100.0%

Requirements

1. Prepare a common-size income statement and balance sheet for Walsh Products. The first column of each statement should present Walsh Products' common-size statement, and the second column should show the industry averages.
2. For the profitability analysis, compute Walsh Products' (a) ratio of gross profit to net sales (b) ratio of operating income to net sales, and (c) ratio of net income to net sales. Compare these figures with the industry averages. Is Walsh Products' profit performance better or worse than the average for the industry?
3. For the analysis of financial position, compute Walsh Products' (a) ratios of current assets and current liabilities to total assets and (b) ratio of stockholders' equity to total assets. Compare these ratios with the industry averages. Is Walsh Products' financial position better or worse than the average for the industry?

P13-59B (*Learning Objective 4: Using the statement of cash flows for decision making*)   You   **writing assignment ■**
are evaluating two companies as possible investments. The two companies, similar in size, are commuter airlines that fly passengers across the United States of America. All other available information has been analyzed and your investment decision depends on the statements of cash flows.

Zoom Airlines
Statements of Cash Flows
Years Ended May 31, 2011 and 2010

	2011	2010
Operating activities:		
Net income (net loss)	$(78,000)	$160,000
Adjustments for noncash items:		
Total	88,000	(33,000)
Net cash provided by operating activities	10,000	127,000
Investing activities:		
Purchase of property, plant, and		
equipment	$ (70,000)	$(110,000)
Sale of long-term investments	73,000	22,000
Net cash provided by (used for)		
investing activities	3,000	(88,000)
Financing activities:		
Issuance of short-term notes payable	$ 111,000	$ 138,000
Payment of short-term notes payable........	(191,000)	(100,000)
Payment of cash dividends........................	(50,000)	(79,000)
Net cash used for financing activities........	(130,000)	(41,000)
Increase (decrease) in cash.................................	$(117,000)	$ (2,000)
Cash balance at beginning of year.....................	125,000	127,000
Cash balance at end of year...............................	$ 8,000	$125,000

Skyview, Inc.
Statements of Cash Flows
Years Ended May 31, 2011 and 2010

	2011	2010
Operating activities:		
Net income	$ 150,000	$ 110,000
Adjustments for noncash items:		
Total	69,000	49,000
Net cash provided by operating activities	219,000	159,000
Investing activities:		
Purchase of property, plant, and equipment ...	$(334,000)	$(470,000)
Sales of property, plant, and equipment........	65,000	84,000
Net cash used for investing activities	(269,000)	(386,000)
Financing activities:		
Issuance of long-term notes payable..........	$ 182,000	$ 125,000
Payment of short-term notes payable........	(80,000)	(12,000)
Net cash provided by financing activities.......	102,000	113,000
Increase (decrease) in cash.................................	$ 52,000	$(114,000)
Cash balance at beginning of year.....................	101,000	215,000
Cash balance at end of year...............................	$ 153,000	$ 101,000

❚ Requirement

1. Discuss the relative strengths and weaknesses of Zoom and Skyview. Conclude your discussion by recommending one of the companies' stocks as an investment.

P13-60B (*Learning Objectives 5, 6: Computing effects of business transactions on selected ratios*) Financial statement data of Trinton Engineering include the following items:

Cash	$ 26,000	Accounts payable	$106,000
Short-term investments	34,000	Accrued liabilities	34,000
Accounts receivable, net	87,000	Long-term notes payable	165,000
Inventories	145,000	Other long-term liabilities	32,000
Prepaid expenses	8,000	Net income	98,000
Total assets	677,000	Number of common	
Short-term notes payable	48,000	shares outstanding	47,000

❚ Requirements

1. Compute Trinton's current ratio, debt ratio, and earnings per share. (Round all ratios to two decimal places.)
2. Compute the three ratios after evaluating the effect of each transaction that follows. Consider each transaction *separately*.
   a. Borrowed $115,000 on a long-term note payable.
   b. Issued 20,000 shares of common stock, receiving cash of $365,000.
   c. Paid short-term notes payable, $26,000.
   d. Purchased merchandise of $45,000 on account, debiting Inventory.
   e. Received cash on account, $19,000.

P13-61B (*Learning Objectives 5, 6: Using ratios to evaluate a stock investment*) Comparative financial statement data of Rourke Optical Mart follow:

writing assignment ■

Rourke Optical Mart
Comparative Income Statements
Years Ended December 31, 2010 and 2009

	2010	2009
Net sales	$688,000	$593,000
Cost of goods sold	376,000	283,000
Gross profit	312,000	310,000
Operating expenses	131,000	144,000
Income from operations	181,000	166,000
Interest expense	31,000	50,000
Income before income tax	150,000	116,000
Income tax expense	42,000	47,000
Net income	$108,000	$ 69,000

Rourke Optical Mart
Comparative Balance Sheets
December 31, 2010 and 2009

	2010	2009	2008*
Current assets:			
Cash	$ 32,000	$ 36,000	
Current receivables, net	211,000	154,000	$134,000
Inventories	291,000	288,000	188,000
Prepaid expenses	6,000	30,000	
Total current assets	540,000	508,000	
Property, plant, and equipment, net	288,000	278,000	
Total assets	$828,000	$786,000	704,000
Total current liabilities	$280,000	$293,000	
Long-term liabilities	240,000	231,000	
Total liabilities	520,000	524,000	
Preferred stockholders' equity, 3%, $5 par	65,000	65,000	
Common stockholders' equity, no par	243,000	197,000	198,000
Total liabilities and stockholders' equity	$828,000	$786,000	

*Selected 2008 amounts.

Other information:

1. Market price of Rourke common stock: $78.12 at December 31, 2010, and $59.10 at December 31, 2009.
2. Common shares outstanding: 19,000 during 2010 and 17,000 during 2009.
3. All sales on credit.

⎮ Requirements

1. Compute the following ratios for 2010 and 2009:
   a. Current ratio
   b. Inventory turnover
   c. Times-interest-earned ratio
   d. Return on common stockholders' equity
   e. Earnings per share of common stock
   f. Price/earnings ratio
2. Decide whether (a) Rourke's financial position improved or deteriorated during 2010 and (b) the investment attractiveness of Rourke's common stock appears to have increased or decreased.
3. How will what you learned in this problem help you evaluate an investment?

writing assignment ■

P13-62B (*Learning Objectives 5, 6, 7: Using ratios to decide between two stock investments; measuring economic value added*)   Assume that you are considering purchasing stock as an investment. You have narrowed the choice to CDROM.com and E-shop Stores and have assembled the following data.

Selected income statement data for current year:

	CDROM	E-Shop
Net sales (all on credit)	$597,000	$516,000
Cost of goods sold	455,000	388,000
Income from operations	89,000	70,000
Interest expense	—	13,000
Net income	68,000	39,000

Selected balance sheet and market price data at the *end* of the current year:

	CDROM	E-Shop
Current assets:		
Cash	$ 24,000	$ 41,000
Short-term investments	5,000	15,000
Current receivables, net	185,000	165,000
Inventories	219,000	187,000
Prepaid expenses	21,000	11,000
Total current assets	454,000	419,000
Total assets	978,000	928,000
Total current liabilities	363,000	332,000
Total liabilities	663,000	693,000
Preferred stock: 6%, $150 par		30,000
Common stock, $1 par (100,000 shares)	100,000	
$5 par (10,000 shares)		50,000
Total stockholders' equity	315,000	235,000
Market price per share of common stock	$ 8.84	$ 70.68

Selected balance sheet data at the *beginning* of the current year:

	CDROM	E-Shop
Balance sheet:		
Current receivables, net	$143,000	$190,000
Inventories	202,000	195,000
Total assets	843,000	914,000
Long-term debt	—	300,000
Preferred stock, 6%, $150 par		30,000
Common stock, $1 par (100,000 shares)	100,000	
$5 par (10,000 shares)		50,000
Total stockholders' equity	259,000	220,000

Your strategy is to invest in companies that have low price/earnings ratios but appear to be in good shape financially. Assume that you have analyzed all other factors and that your decision depends on the results of ratio analysis.

❚ *Requirements*

1. Compute the following ratios for both companies for the current year and decide which company's stock better fits your investment strategy.
   a. Acid-test ratio
   b. Inventory turnover
   c. Days' sales in average receivables
   d. Debt ratio
   e. Times-interest-earned ratio
   f. Return on common stockholders' equity
   g. Earnings per share of common stock
   h. Price/earnings ratio
2. Compute each company's economic-value-added (EVA®) measure and determine whether the companies' EVA®s confirm or alter your investment decision. Each company's cost of capital is 12%.

APPLY YOUR KNOWLEDGE

Decision Cases

Case 1. (*Learning Objectives 5, 6: Assessing the effects of transactions on a company*) Suppose **AOL Time Warner, Inc.**, is having a bad year in 2011, as the company has incurred a $4.9 billion net loss. The loss has pushed most of the return measures into the negative column and the current ratio dropped below 1.0. The company's debt ratio is still only 0.27. Assume top management of AOL Time Warner is pondering ways to improve the company's ratios. In particular, management is considering the following transactions:

1. Sell off the cable television segment of the business for $30 million (receiving half in cash and half in the form of a long-term note receivable). Book value of the cable television business is $27 million.
2. Borrow $100 million on long-term debt.
3. Purchase treasury stock for $500 million cash.
4. Write off one-fourth of goodwill carried on the books at $128 million.
5. Sell advertising at the normal gross profit of 60%. The advertisements run immediately.
6. Purchase trademarks from **NBC**, paying $20 million cash and signing a one-year note payable for $80 million.

❙ Requirements

1. Top management wants to know the effects of these transactions (increase, decrease, or no effect) on the following ratios of AOL Time Warner:
   a. Current ratio
   b. Debt ratio
   c. Times-interest-earned ratio (measured as [net income + interest expense]/interest expense)
   d. Return on equity
   e. Book value per share of common stock
2. Some of these transactions have an immediately positive effect on the company's financial condition. Some are definitely negative. Others have an effect that cannot be judged as clearly positive or negative. Evaluate each transaction's effect as positive, negative, or unclear. (Challenge)

writing assignment ■

Case 2. (*Learning Objectives 5, 6: Analyzing the effects of an accounting difference on the ratios*) Assume that you are a financial analyst. You are trying to compare the financial statements of **Caterpillar, Inc.**, with those of **CNH Global**, an international company that uses international financial reporting standards (IFRS). Caterpillar, Inc., uses the last-in, first-out (LIFO) method to account for its inventories. IFRS does not permit CNH Global to use LIFO. Analyze the effect of this difference in accounting method on the two companies' ratio values. For each ratio discussed in this chapter, indicate which company will have the higher (and the lower) ratio value. Also identify those ratios that are unaffected by the FIFO/LIFO difference. Ignore the effects of income taxes, and assume inventory costs are increasing. Then, based on your analysis of the ratios, summarize your conclusions as to which company looks better overall.

writing assignment ■

Case 3. (*Learning Objectives 2, 5, 6: Identifying action to cut losses and establish profitability*) Suppose you manage Outward Bound, Inc., a Vermont sporting goods store that lost money during the past year. To turn the business around, you must analyze the company and industry data for the current year to learn what is wrong. The company's data follow:

Outward Bound, Inc.
Common-Size Balance Sheet Data

	Outward Bound	Industry Average
Cash and short-term investments	3.0%	6.8%
Trade receivables, net	15.2	11.0
Inventory	64.2	60.5
Prepaid expenses	1.0	0.0
Total current assets	83.4%	78.3%
Fixed assets, net	12.6	15.2
Other assets	4.0	6.5
Total assets	100.0%	100.0%
Notes payable, short-term, 12%	17.1%	14.0%
Accounts payable	21.1	25.1
Accrued liabilities	7.8	7.9
Total current liabilities	46.0	47.0
Long-term debt, 11%	19.7	16.4
Total liabilities	65.7	63.4
Common stockholders' equity	34.3	36.6
Total liabilities and stockholders' equity	100.0%	100.0%

Outward Bound, Inc.
Common-Size Income Statement Data

	Outward Bound	Industry Average
Net sales	100.0%	100.0%
Cost of sales	(68.2)	(64.8)
Gross profit	31.8	35.2
Operating expense	(37.1)	(32.3)
Operating income (loss)	(5.3)	2.9
Interest expense	(5.8)	(1.3)
Other revenue	1.1	0.3
Income (loss) before income tax	(10.0)	1.9
Income tax (expense) saving	4.4	(0.8)
Net income (loss)	(5.6)%	1.1%

❚ Requirement

1. On the basis of your analysis of these figures, suggest four courses of action Outward Bound might take to reduce its losses and establish profitable operations. Give your reason for each suggestion. (Challenge)

Ethical Issue

Turnberry Golf Corporation's long-term debt agreements make certain demands on the business. For example, Turnberry may not purchase treasury stock in excess of the balance of retained earnings. Also, long-term debt may not exceed stockholders' equity, and the current ratio may not fall below 1.50. If Turnberry fails to meet any of these requirements, the company's lenders have the authority to take over management of the company.

Changes in consumer demand have made it hard for Turnberry to attract customers. Current liabilities have mounted faster than current assets, causing the current ratio to fall to 1.47. Before releasing financial statements, Turnberry management is scrambling to improve the current ratio. The controller points out that the company owns an investment that is currently classified as long-term. The investment can be classified as either long-term or short-term, depending on management's intention. By deciding to convert an investment to cash within one year, Turnberry can classify the investment as short-term—a current asset. On the controller's recommendation, Turnberry's board of directors votes to reclassify long-term investments as short-term.

❚ Requirements

writing assignment ■

1. What is the accounting issue in this case? What ethical decision needs to be made?
2. Who are the stakeholders?
3. Analyze the potential impact on the stakeholders from the following standpoints: (a) economic, (b) legal, and (c) ethical.
4. Shortly after the financial statements are released, sales improve; so, too, does the current ratio. As a result, Turnberry management decides not to sell the investments it had reclassified as short term. Accordingly, the company reclassifies the investments as long term. Has management acted unethically? Give the reasoning underlying your answer.

Focus on Financials: ■ Amazon.com, Inc.

writing assignment ■

(Learning Objectives 4, 5, 6: Computing standard financial ratios; using the statement of cash flows; measuring liquidity and profitability; analyzing stock as an investment) Use the consolidated financial statements and the data in **Amazon.com, Inc.'s** annual report (Appendix A at the end of the book) to evaluate the company's comparative performance for 2008 versus 2007. Does the company appear to be improving or declining in the following dimensions?

❚ Requirements

1. The ability to pay its current liabilities
2. The ability to sell inventory and collect receivables
3. The ability to pay long-term debts
4. Profitability
5. Cash flows from operations
6. The potential of the company's stock as a long-term investment (Challenge)

Focus on Analysis: ■ Foot Locker, Inc.

writing assignment ■

(Learning Objectives 1, 5, 6: Analyzing trend data; computing the standard financial ratios and using them to make decisions) Use the **Foot Locker, Inc.**, consolidated financial statements in Appendix B at the end of this book to address the following questions.

1. Perform a trend analysis of Foot Locker's net sales, gross profit, operating income, and net income. Use 2005 as the base year, and compute trend figures for 2006 and 2007.
2. Find Foot Locker, Inc.'s annual report for 2008 at www.sec.gov. Also perform research at a popular investment Web site such as www.msnmoney.com or www.yahoofinance.com to update the information from part 1. (Challenge)
3. What in your opinion is the company's outlook for the future? Would you buy the company's stock as an investment? Why or why not? (Challenge)

Group Projects

Project 1. Select an industry you are interested in, and use the leading company in that industry as the benchmark. Then select two other companies in the same industry. For each category of ratios in the Decision Guidelines feature on pages 802 and 803, compute at least two ratios for all three companies. Write a two-page report that compares the two companies with the benchmark company.

writing assignment ■

Project 2. Select a company and obtain its financial statements. Convert the income statement and the balance sheet to common size and compare the company you selected to the industry average. **Risk Management Association's** *Annual Statement Studies*, **Dun & Bradstreet's** *Industry Norms & Key Business Ratios*, and **Prentice Hall's** *Almanac of Business and Industrial Financial Ratios* by Leo Troy, publish common-size statements for most industries.

For online homework, exercises, and problems that provide you with immediate feedback, please visit www.myaccountinglab.com.

Quick Check Answers

1. *b* ($1,820/$1,730)
2. *a* ($1,820/$17,700)
3. *d* ($2,691 − $1,124)/$1,124 = 139.4%
4. *c* ($1,780/$26,060)
5. *c*
6. *c* $\left[\dfrac{\$3,300}{(\$140 + \$120)/2}\right] = 25.4 \approx 25$ times
7. *a* [($690 + $780)/ $2,374 = 0.62]
8. *c* $\left[\dfrac{\$780 + \$840/2}{\$17,700/365}\right] = 16.9 \approx 17$ days
9. *c* (Debt ratio is ($26,060 − $13,291)/$26,060 = 0.49. This debt ratio is lower than the average for most companies, given in the chapter as 0.64.)
10. *d* ($2,691/$17,700 = 0.152)
11. *b* $\left[\dfrac{\$2,691}{(\$13,291 + 10,615)/2}\right] = 0.225$
12. *c* ($30/$2.69)
13. *c* ($0.50/$30)
14. *a* [$2,691 + $370 − ($305 + $9,500 + $10,615) × 0.05] = $2,040

2   0   0   8

ANNUAL   REPORT

Report of Ernst & Young LLP, Independent Registered Public Accounting Firm

The Board of Directors and Stockholders
Amazon.com, Inc.

We have audited the accompanying consolidated balance sheets of Amazon.com, Inc. as of December 31, 2008 and 2007, and the related consolidated statements of operations, stockholders' equity, and cash flows for each of the three years in the period ended December 31, 2008. Our audits also included the financial statement schedule listed in the Index at Item 15(a)(2). These financial statements and schedule are the responsibility of the Company's management. Our responsibility is to express an opinion on these financial statements and schedule based on our audits.

We conducted our audits in accordance with the standards of the Public Company Accounting Oversight Board (United States). Those standards require that we plan and perform the audit to obtain reasonable assurance about whether the financial statements are free of material misstatement. An audit includes examining, on a test basis, evidence supporting the amounts and disclosures in the financial statements. An audit also includes assessing the accounting principles used and significant estimates made by management, as well as evaluating the overall financial statement presentation. We believe that our audits provide a reasonable basis for our opinion.

In our opinion, the financial statements referred to above present fairly, in all material respects, the consolidated financial position of Amazon.com, Inc. at December 31, 2008 and 2007, and the consolidated results of its operations and its cash flows for each of the three years in the period ended December 31, 2008, in conformity with U.S. generally accepted accounting principles. Also, in our opinion, the related financial statement schedule, when considered in relation to the basic financial statements taken as a whole, presents fairly in all material respects the information set forth therein.

As discussed in Note 1 to the consolidated financial statements, the Company adopted FASB Interpretation No. 48 *Accounting for Uncertainty in Income Taxes*, effective January 1, 2007, and FASB No. 157 *Fair Value Measurements*, effective January 1, 2008.

We also have audited, in accordance with the standards of the Public Company Accounting Oversight Board (United States), the effectiveness of Amazon.com, Inc.'s internal control over financial reporting as of December 31, 2008, based on criteria established in Internal Control—Integrated Framework issued by the Committee of Sponsoring Organizations of the Treadway Commission and our report dated January 29, 2009 expressed an unqualified opinion thereon.

/s/ Ernst & Young LLP

Seattle, Washington
January 29, 2009

AMAZON.COM, INC.

CONSOLIDATED STATEMENTS OF CASH FLOWS
(in millions)

	Year Ended December 31,		
	2008	2007	2006
CASH AND CASH EQUIVALENTS, BEGINNING OF PERIOD	$ 2,539	$1,022	$ 1,013
OPERATING ACTIVITIES:			
Net income	645	476	190
Adjustments to reconcile net income to net cash from operating activities:			
Depreciation of fixed assets, including internal-use software and website development, and other amortization	287	246	205
Stock-based compensation	275	185	101
Other operating expense (income), net	(24)	9	10
Losses (gains) on sales of marketable securities, net	(2)	1	(2)
Other expense (income), net	(34)	12	(6)
Deferred income taxes	(5)	(99)	22
Excess tax benefits from stock-based compensation	(159)	(257)	(102)
Changes in operating assets and liabilities:			
Inventories	(232)	(303)	(282)
Accounts receivable, net and other	(218)	(255)	(103)
Accounts payable	812	928	402
Accrued expenses and other	247	429	241
Additions to unearned revenue	449	244	206
Amortization of previously unearned revenue	(344)	(211)	(180)
Net cash provided by operating activities	1,697	1,405	702
INVESTING ACTIVITIES:			
Purchases of fixed assets, including internal-use software and website development	(333)	(224)	(216)
Acquisitions, net of cash acquired, and other	(494)	(75)	(32)
Sales and maturities of marketable securities and other investments	1,305	1,271	1,845
Purchases of marketable securities and other investments	(1,677)	(930)	(1,930)
Net cash provided by (used in) investing activities	(1,199)	42	(333)
FINANCING ACTIVITIES:			
Proceeds from exercises of stock options	11	91	35
Excess tax benefits from stock-based compensation	159	257	102
Common stock repurchased	(100)	(248)	(252)
Proceeds from long-term debt and other	87	24	98
Repayments of long-term debt and capital lease obligations	(355)	(74)	(383)
Net cash provided by (used in) financing activities	(198)	50	(400)
Foreign-currency effect on cash and cash equivalents	(70)	20	40
Net increase in cash and cash equivalents	230	1,517	9
CASH AND CASH EQUIVALENTS, END OF PERIOD	$ 2,769	$2,539	$ 1,022
SUPPLEMENTAL CASH FLOW INFORMATION:			
Cash paid for interest	$ 64	$ 67	$ 86
Cash paid for income taxes	53	24	15
Fixed assets acquired under capital leases and other financing arrangements	148	74	69
Fixed assets acquired under build-to-suit leases	72	15	—
Conversion of debt	605	1	—

See accompanying notes to consolidated financial statements.

AMAZON.COM, INC.

CONSOLIDATED STATEMENTS OF OPERATIONS
(in millions, except per share data)

	Year Ended December 31,		
	2008	**2007**	**2006**
Net sales	$19,166	$14,835	$10,711
Cost of sales	14,896	11,482	8,255
Gross profit	4,270	3,353	2,456
Operating expenses (1):			
Fulfillment	1,658	1,292	937
Marketing	482	344	263
Technology and content	1,033	818	662
General and administrative	279	235	195
Other operating expense (income), net	(24)	9	10
Total operating expenses	3,428	2,698	2,067
Income from operations	842	655	389
Interest income	83	90	59
Interest expense	(71)	(77)	(78)
Other income (expense), net	47	(8)	7
Total non-operating income (expense)	59	5	(12)
Income before income taxes	901	660	377
Provision for income taxes	(247)	(184)	(187)
Equity-method investment activity, net of tax	(9)	—	—
Net income	$ 645	$ 476	$ 190
Basic earnings per share	$ 1.52	$ 1.15	$ 0.46
Diluted earnings per share	$ 1.49	$ 1.12	$ 0.45
Weighted average shares used in computation of earnings per share:			
Basic	423	413	416
Diluted	432	424	424

(1) Includes stock-based compensation as follows:

Fulfillment	$ 61	$ 39	$ 24
Marketing	13	8	4
Technology and content	151	103	54
General and administrative	50	35	19

See accompanying notes to consolidated financial statements.

AMAZON.COM, INC.

CONSOLIDATED BALANCE SHEETS
(in millions, except per share data)

	December 31,	
	2008	**2007**
ASSETS		
Current assets:		
Cash and cash equivalents	$2,769	$ 2,539
Marketable securities	958	573
Inventories	1,399	1,200
Accounts receivable, net and other	827	705
Deferred tax assets	204	147
Total current assets	6,157	5,164
Fixed assets, net	854	543
Deferred tax assets	145	260
Goodwill	438	222
Other assets	720	296
Total assets	$8,314	$ 6,485
LIABILITIES AND STOCKHOLDERS' EQUITY		
Current liabilities:		
Accounts payable	$3,594	$ 2,795
Accrued expenses and other	1,093	902
Current portion of long-term debt	59	17
Total current liabilities	4,746	3,714
Long-term debt	409	1,282
Other long-term liabilities	487	292
Commitments and contingencies		
Stockholders' equity:		
Preferred stock, $0.01 par value:		
Authorized shares—500		
Issued and outstanding shares—none	—	—
Common stock, $0.01 par value:		
Authorized shares—5,000		
Issued shares—445 and 431		
Outstanding shares—428 and 416	4	4
Treasury stock, at cost	(600)	(500)
Additional paid-in capital	4,121	3,063
Accumulated other comprehensive income (loss)	(123)	5
Accumulated deficit	(730)	(1,375)
Total stockholders' equity	2,672	1,197
Total liabilities and stockholders' equity	$8,314	$ 6,485

See accompanying notes to consolidated financial statements.

AMAZON.COM, INC.

CONSOLIDATED STATEMENTS OF STOCKHOLDERS' EQUITY

(in millions)

	Common Stock Shares	Common Stock Amount	Treasury Stock	Additional Paid-In Capital	Accumulated Other Comprehensive Income (Loss)	Accumulated Deficit	Total Stockholders' Equity
Balance at January 1, 2006	416	4	$ —	$2,263	$ 6	$(2,027)	$ 246
Net income						190	190
Foreign currency translation losses, net of tax					(13)		(13)
Change in unrealized losses on available-for-sale securities, net of tax					4		4
Amortization of unrealized loss on terminated Euro Currency Swap, net of tax					2		2
Comprehensive income							183
Exercise of common stock options	6			35			35
Repurchase of common stock	(8)		(252)				(252)
Excess tax benefits from stock-based compensation				102			102
Stock-based compensation and issuance of employee benefit plan stock				117			117
Balance at December 31, 2006	414	4	(252)	2,517	(1)	(1,837)	431
Net income						476	476
Foreign currency translation losses, net of tax					(3)		(3)
Change in unrealized losses on available-for-sale securities, net of tax					8		8
Amortization of unrealized loss on terminated Euro Currency Swap, net of tax					1		1
Comprehensive income							482
Change in accounting principle				2		(14)	(12)
Unrecognized excess tax benefits from stock-based compensation				4			4
Exercise of common stock options and conversion of debt	8			92			92
Repurchase of common stock	(6)		(248)				(248)
Excess tax benefits from stock-based compensation				257			257
Stock-based compensation and issuance of employee benefit plan stock				191			191
Balance at December 31, 2007	416	4	(500)	3,063	5	(1,375)	1,197
Net income						645	645
Foreign currency translation losses, net of tax					(127)		(127)
Change in unrealized losses on available-for-sale securities, net of tax					(1)		(1)
Comprehensive income							517
Unrecognized excess tax benefits from stock-based compensation				(8)			(8)
Exercise of common stock options and conversion of debt	14			624			624
Repurchase of common stock	(2)		(100)				(100)
Excess tax benefits from stock-based compensation				154			154
Stock-based compensation and issuance of employee benefit plan stock				288			288
Balance at December 31, 2008	428	4	$(600)	$4,121	$(123)	$ (730)	$2,672

See accompanying notes to consolidated financial statements.

AMAZON.COM, INC.

NOTES TO CONSOLIDATED FINANCIAL STATEMENTS

Note 1—DESCRIPTION OF BUSINESS AND ACCOUNTING POLICIES

Description of Business

Amazon.com opened its virtual doors on the World Wide Web in July 1995 and we offer Earth's Biggest Selection. We seek to be Earth's most customer-centric company for three primary customer sets: consumer customers, seller customers and developer customers. We serve our consumer customers through our retail websites and focus on selection, price, and convenience. We offer programs that enable seller customers to sell their products on our websites and their own branded websites and to fulfill orders through us. We serve developer customers through Amazon Web Services, which provides access to technology infrastructure that developers can use to enable virtually any type of business. In addition, we generate revenue through co-branded credit card agreements and other marketing and promotional services, such as online advertising.

We have organized our operations into two principal segments: North America and International. See "Note 13—Segment Information."

Principles of Consolidation

The consolidated financial statements include the accounts of the Company, its wholly-owned subsidiaries, and those entities (relating primarily to *www.amazon.cn*) in which we have a variable interest. Intercompany balances and transactions have been eliminated.

Use of Estimates

The preparation of financial statements in conformity with U.S. GAAP requires estimates and assumptions that affect the reported amounts of assets and liabilities, revenues and expenses, and related disclosures of contingent liabilities in the consolidated financial statements and accompanying notes. Estimates are used for, but not limited to, valuation of investments, receivables valuation, sales returns, incentive discount offers, inventory valuation, depreciable lives of fixed assets, internally-developed software, valuation of acquired intangibles and goodwill, income taxes, stock-based compensation, and contingencies. Actual results could differ materially from those estimates.

Earnings per Share

Basic earnings per share is calculated using our weighted-average outstanding common shares. Diluted earnings per share is calculated using our weighted-average outstanding common shares including the dilutive effect of stock awards as determined under the treasury stock method.

Our convertible debt instrument is excluded from the calculation of diluted earnings per share as its effect under the if-converted method is anti-dilutive. See "Note 5—Long-Term Debt."

The following table shows the calculation of diluted shares (in millions):

	Year Ended December 31,		
	2008	**2007**	**2006**
Shares used in computation of basic earnings per share	423	413	416
Total dilutive effect of outstanding stock awards (1)	9	11	8
Shares used in computation of diluted earnings per share	432	424	424

AMAZON.COM, INC.

NOTES TO CONSOLIDATED FINANCIAL STATEMENTS—(Continued)

(1) Calculated using the treasury stock method that assumes proceeds available to reduce the dilutive effect of outstanding stock awards, which include the exercise price of stock options, the unrecognized deferred compensation of stock awards, and assumed tax proceeds from excess stock-based compensation deductions.

Treasury Stock

We account for treasury stock under the cost method and include treasury stock as a component of stockholders' equity.

Cash and Cash Equivalents

We classify all highly liquid instruments, including money market funds that comply with Rule 2a-7 of the Investment Company Act of 1940, with an original maturity of three months or less at the time of purchase as cash equivalents.

Inventories

Inventories, consisting of products available for sale, are accounted for using the FIFO method, and are valued at the lower of cost or market value. This valuation requires us to make judgments, based on currently-available information, about the likely method of disposition, such as through sales to individual customers, returns to product vendors, or liquidations, and expected recoverable values of each disposition category. Based on this evaluation, we adjust the carrying amount of our inventories to lower of cost or market value.

We provide fulfillment-related services in connection with certain of our sellers' programs. In those arrangements, as well as all other product sales by other sellers, the seller maintains ownership of the related products. As such, these amounts are not included in our consolidated balance sheets.

Accounts Receivable, Net, and Other

Included in "Accounts receivable, net, and other" on our consolidated balance sheets are amounts primarily related to vendor receivables and customer receivables. At December 31, 2008 and 2007, vendor receivables, net, were $400 million and $280 million, and customer receivables, net, were $311 million and $296 million.

Allowance for Doubtful Accounts

We estimate losses on receivables based on known troubled accounts, if any, and historical experience of losses incurred. The allowance for doubtful customer and vendor receivables was $81 million and $64 million at December 31, 2008 and 2007.

Internal-use Software and Website Development

Costs incurred to develop software for internal use are required to be capitalized and amortized over the estimated useful life of the software in accordance with Statement of Position (SOP) 98-1, *Accounting for the Costs of Computer Software Developed or Obtained for Internal Use*. Costs related to design or maintenance of internal-use software are expensed as incurred. For the years ended 2008, 2007, and 2006, we capitalized $187 million (including $27 million of stock-based compensation), $129 million (including $21 million of stock-based compensation), and $123 million (including $16 million of stock-based compensation) of costs associated with internal-use software and website development. Amortization of previously capitalized amounts was $143 million, $116 million, and $86 million for 2008, 2007, and 2006.

AMAZON.COM, INC.

NOTES TO CONSOLIDATED FINANCIAL STATEMENTS—(Continued)

Depreciation of Fixed Assets

Fixed assets include assets such as furniture and fixtures, heavy equipment, technology infrastructure, internal-use software and website development. Depreciation is recorded on a straight-line basis over the estimated useful lives of the assets (generally two years or less for assets such as internal-use software, two or three years for our technology infrastructure, five years for furniture and fixtures, and ten years for heavy equipment). Depreciation expense is generally classified within the corresponding operating expense categories on our consolidated statements of operations, and certain assets are amortized as "Cost of sales."

Leases and Asset Retirement Obligations

We account for our lease agreements pursuant to Statement of Financial Accounting Standards (SFAS) No. 13, *Accounting for Leases*, which categorizes leases at their inception as either operating or capital leases depending on certain defined criteria. On certain of our lease agreements, we may receive rent holidays and other incentives. We recognize lease costs on a straight-line basis without regard to deferred payment terms, such as rent holidays that defer the commencement date of required payments. Additionally, incentives we receive are treated as a reduction of our costs over the term of the agreement. Leasehold improvements are capitalized at cost and amortized over the lesser of their expected useful life or the life of the lease, without assuming renewal features, if any, are exercised. We account for build-to-suit lease arrangements in accordance with EITF 97-10, *The Effect of Lessee Involvement in Asset Construction,* to the extent we are involved in the construction of structural improvements prior to commencement of a lease.

In accordance with SFAS No. 143, *Accounting for Asset Retirement Obligations,* we establish assets and liabilities for the present value of estimated future costs to return certain of our leased facilities to their original condition. Such assets are depreciated over the lease period into operating expense, and the recorded liabilities are accreted to the future value of the estimated restoration costs.

Goodwill

We evaluate goodwill for impairment annually and when an event occurs or circumstances change to suggest that the carrying amount may not be recoverable. Impairment of goodwill is tested at the reporting unit level by comparing the reporting unit's carrying amount, including goodwill, to the fair value of the reporting unit. The fair values of the reporting units are estimated using discounted projected cash flows. If the carrying amount of the reporting unit exceeds its fair value, goodwill is considered impaired and a second step is performed to measure the amount of impairment loss, if any. We conduct our annual impairment test as of October 1 of each year, and have determined there to be no impairment in 2008 or 2007. There were no events or circumstances from the date of our assessment through December 31, 2008 that would impact this conclusion.

See "Note 4—Acquisitions, Goodwill, and Acquired Intangible Assets."

Other Assets

Included in "Other assets" on our consolidated balance sheets are amounts primarily related to marketable securities restricted for longer than one year, the majority of which are attributable to collateralization of bank guarantees and debt related to our international operations; acquired intangible assets, net of amortization; deferred costs; certain equity investments; and intellectual property rights.

AMAZON.COM, INC.

NOTES TO CONSOLIDATED FINANCIAL STATEMENTS—(Continued)

Investments

The initial carrying cost of our investments is the price we paid. Investments are accounted for using the equity method of accounting if the investment gives us the ability to exercise significant influence, but not control, over an investee. The total of these investments in equity-method investees, including identifiable intangible assets, deferred tax liabilities and goodwill, are classified on our consolidated balance sheets as "Other assets" and our share of the investees' earnings or losses along with amortization of the related intangible assets, if any, as "Equity-method investment activity, net of tax" on our consolidated statements of operations.

All other equity investments consist of investments for which we do not have the ability to exercise significant influence. Under the cost method of accounting, investments in private companies are carried at cost and are adjusted only for other-than-temporary declines in fair value, distributions of earnings, and additional investments. For public companies that have readily determinable fair values, we classify our equity investments as available-for-sale and, accordingly, record these investments at their fair values with unrealized gains and losses, net of tax, included in "Accumulated other comprehensive income (loss)," a separate component of stockholders' equity.

We generally invest our excess cash in investment grade short to intermediate term fixed income securities and AAA-rated money market funds. Such investments are included in "Cash and cash equivalents," or "Marketable securities" on the accompanying consolidated balance sheets, are classified as available-for-sale, and reported at fair value with unrealized gains and losses included in "Accumulated other comprehensive income (loss)." The weighted average method is used to determine the cost of Euro-denominated securities sold, and the specific identification method is used to determine the cost of all other securities.

We periodically evaluate whether declines in fair values of our investments below their cost are other-than-temporary. This evaluation consists of several qualitative and quantitative factors regarding the severity and duration of the unrealized loss as well as our ability and intent to hold the investment until a forecasted recovery occurs. Factors considered include quoted market prices; recent financial results and operating trends; other publicly available information; implied values from any recent transactions or offers of investee securities; or other conditions that may affect the value of our investments.

Long-Lived Assets

Long-lived assets, other than goodwill, are reviewed for impairment whenever events or changes in circumstances indicate that the carrying amount of the assets might not be recoverable. Conditions that would necessitate an impairment assessment include a significant decline in the observable market value of an asset, a significant change in the extent or manner in which an asset is used, or any other significant adverse change that would indicate that the carrying amount of an asset or group of assets may not be recoverable.

For long-lived assets used in operations, impairment losses are only recorded if the asset's carrying amount is not recoverable through its undiscounted, probability-weighted future cash flows. We measure the impairment loss based on the difference between the carrying amount and estimated fair value.

Long-lived assets are considered held for sale when certain criteria are met, including when management has committed to a plan to sell the asset, the asset is available for sale in its immediate condition, and the sale is probable within one year of the reporting date. Assets held for sale are reported at the lower of cost or fair value less costs to sell. Assets held for sale were not significant at December 31, 2008 or 2007.

AMAZON.COM, INC.

NOTES TO CONSOLIDATED FINANCIAL STATEMENTS—(Continued)

Accrued Expenses and Other

Included in "Accrued expenses and other" at December 31, 2008 and 2007 were liabilities of $270 million and $230 million for unredeemed gift certificates. We recognize revenue from a gift certificate when a customer redeems it. If a gift certificate is not redeemed, we recognize revenue when it expires or, for a certificate without an expiration date, when the likelihood of its redemption becomes remote, generally two years from date of issuance.

Unearned Revenue

Unearned revenue is recorded when payments are received in advance of performing our service obligations and is recognized over the service period. Current unearned revenue is included in "Accrued expenses and other" and non-current unearned revenue is included in "Other long-term liabilities" on our consolidated balance sheets. Current unearned revenue was $191 million and $91 million at December 31, 2008 and 2007. Non-current unearned revenue was $46 million and $19 million at December 31, 2008 and 2007.

Income Taxes

Income tax expense includes U.S. and international income taxes. We do not provide for U.S. taxes on our undistributed earnings of foreign subsidiaries, totaling $328 million at December 31, 2008, since we intend to invest such undistributed earnings indefinitely outside of the U.S. If such amounts were repatriated, determination of the amount of U.S. income taxes that would be incurred is not practicable due to the complexities associated with this calculation.

Deferred income tax balances reflect the effects of temporary differences between the carrying amounts of assets and liabilities and their tax bases and are stated at enacted tax rates expected to be in effect when taxes are actually paid or recovered. At December 31, 2008, our deferred tax assets, net of deferred tax liabilities and valuation allowance, were $349 million, which includes $165 million relating to net operating loss carryforwards that were primarily attributed to stock-based compensation. The majority of our net operating loss carryforwards begin to expire in 2021 and thereafter.

SFAS No. 109, *Accounting for Income Taxes,* requires that deferred tax assets be evaluated for future realization and reduced by a valuation allowance to the extent we believe a portion will not be realized. We consider many factors when assessing the likelihood of future realization of our deferred tax assets, including our recent cumulative earnings experience and expectations of future taxable income by taxing jurisdiction, the carry-forward periods available to us for tax reporting purposes, and other relevant factors. In accordance with SFAS No. 109, we allocate our valuation allowance to current and long-term deferred tax assets on a pro-rata basis.

Effective January 1, 2007, we adopted the provisions of FIN No. 48, *Accounting for Uncertainty in Income Taxes—an Interpretation of FASB Statement No. 109.* FIN 48 contains a two-step approach to recognizing and measuring uncertain tax positions (tax contingencies) accounted for in accordance with SFAS No. 109. The first step is to evaluate the tax position for recognition by determining if the weight of available evidence indicates it is more likely than not that the position will be sustained on audit, including resolution of related appeals or litigation processes, if any. The second step is to measure the tax benefit as the largest amount which is more than 50% likely of being realized upon ultimate settlement. We consider many factors when evaluating and estimating our tax positions and tax benefits, which may require periodic adjustments and which may not accurately forecast actual outcomes. Our policy is to include interest and penalties related to our tax contingencies in income tax expense. Implementation of FIN 48 was not material.

AMAZON.COM, INC.

NOTES TO CONSOLIDATED FINANCIAL STATEMENTS—(Continued)

Fair Value of Financial Instruments

Effective January 1, 2008, we adopted SFAS No. 157, except as it applies to the nonfinancial assets and nonfinancial liabilities subject to FSP No. 157-2. SFAS No. 157 clarifies the definition of fair value, prescribes methods for measuring fair value, establishes a fair value hierarchy based on the inputs used to measure fair value, and expands disclosures about fair value measurements. The three-tier fair value hierarchy, which prioritizes the inputs used in the valuation methodologies, is:

Level 1—Valuations based on quoted prices for identical assets and liabilities in active markets.

Level 2—Valuations based on observable inputs other than quoted prices included in Level 1, such as quoted prices for similar assets and liabilities in active markets, quoted prices for identical or similar assets and liabilities in markets that are not active, or other inputs that are observable or can be corroborated by observable market data.

Level 3—Valuations based on unobservable inputs reflecting our own assumptions, consistent with reasonably available assumptions made by other market participants. These valuations require significant judgment.

Revenue

We recognize revenue from product sales or services rendered when the following four revenue recognition criteria are met: persuasive evidence of an arrangement exists, delivery has occurred or services have been rendered, the selling price is fixed or determinable, and collectability is reasonably assured. Additionally, revenue arrangements with multiple deliverables are divided into separate units of accounting if the deliverables in the arrangement meet the following criteria: the delivered item has value to the customer on a standalone basis; there is objective and reliable evidence of the fair value of undelivered items; and delivery of any undelivered item is probable.

We evaluate the criteria outlined in EITF Issue No. 99-19, *Reporting Revenue Gross as a Principal Versus Net as an Agent*, in determining whether it is appropriate to record the gross amount of product sales and related costs or the net amount earned as commissions. Generally, when we are primarily obligated in a transaction, are subject to inventory risk, have latitude in establishing prices and selecting suppliers, or have several but not all of these indicators, revenue is recorded gross. If we are not primarily obligated and amounts earned are determined using a fixed percentage, a fixed-payment schedule, or a combination of the two, we generally record the net amounts as commissions earned.

Product sales and shipping revenues, net of promotional discounts, rebates, and return allowances, are recorded when the products are shipped and title passes to customers. Retail sales to customers are made pursuant to a sales contract that provides for transfer of both title and risk of loss upon our delivery to the carrier. Return allowances, which reduce product revenue, are estimated using historical experience. Revenue from product sales and services rendered is recorded net of sales taxes. Amounts received in advance for subscription services, including amounts received for Amazon Prime and other membership programs, are deferred and recognized as revenue over the subscription term. For our products with multiple elements, where a standalone value for each element cannot be established, we recognize the revenue and related cost over the estimated economic life of the product.

We periodically provide incentive offers to our customers to encourage purchases. Such offers include current discount offers, such as percentage discounts off current purchases, inducement offers, such as offers for future discounts subject to a minimum current purchase, and other similar offers. Current discount offers, when

AMAZON.COM, INC.

NOTES TO CONSOLIDATED FINANCIAL STATEMENTS—(Continued)

accepted by our customers, are treated as a reduction to the purchase price of the related transaction, while inducement offers, when accepted by our customers, are treated as a reduction to purchase price based on estimated future redemption rates. Redemption rates are estimated using our historical experience for similar inducement offers. Current discount offers and inducement offers are presented as a net amount in "Net sales."

Commissions and per-unit fees received from sellers and similar amounts earned through other seller sites are recognized when the item is sold by seller and our collectability is reasonably assured. We record an allowance for estimated refunds on such commissions using historical experience.

Shipping Activities

Outbound shipping charges to customers are included in "Net sales" and were $835 million, $740 million, and $567 million for 2008, 2007, and 2006. Outbound shipping-related costs are included in "Cost of sales" and totaled $1.5 billion, $1.2 billion, and $884 million for 2008, 2007, and 2006. The net cost to us of shipping activities was $630 million, $434 million, and $317 million for 2008, 2007 and 2006.

Cost of Sales

Cost of sales consists of the purchase price of consumer products and content sold by us, inbound and outbound shipping charges, packaging supplies, and costs incurred in operating and staffing our fulfillment and customer service centers on behalf of other businesses. Shipping charges to receive products from our suppliers are included in our inventory, and recognized as "Cost of sales" upon sale of products to our customers. Payment processing and related transaction costs, including those associated with seller transactions, are classified in "Fulfillment" on our consolidated statements of operations.

Vendor Agreements

We have agreements to receive cash consideration from certain of our vendors, including rebates and cooperative marketing reimbursements. We generally presume amounts received from our vendors are a reduction of the prices we pay for their products and, therefore, we reflect such amounts as either a reduction of "Cost of sales" on our consolidated statements of operations, or, if the product inventory is still on hand, as a reduction of the carrying value of inventory. Vendor rebates are typically dependent upon reaching minimum purchase thresholds. We evaluate the likelihood of reaching purchase thresholds using past experience and current year forecasts. When volume rebates can be reasonably estimated, we record a portion of the rebate as we make progress towards the purchase threshold.

When we receive direct reimbursements for costs incurred by us in advertising the vendor's product or service, the amount we receive is recorded as an offset to "Marketing" on our consolidated statements of operations.

Fulfillment

Fulfillment costs represent those costs incurred in operating and staffing our fulfillment and customer service centers, including costs attributable to buying, receiving, inspecting, and warehousing inventories; picking, packaging, and preparing customer orders for shipment; payment processing and related transaction costs, including costs associated with our guarantee for certain seller transactions; and responding to inquiries from customers. Fulfillment costs also include amounts paid to third parties that assist us in fulfillment and customer service operations. Certain of our fulfillment-related costs that are incurred on behalf of other businesses are classified as cost of sales rather than fulfillment.

AMAZON.COM, INC.

NOTES TO CONSOLIDATED FINANCIAL STATEMENTS—(Continued)

Foreign Currency

We have the following internationally-focused websites: *www.amazon.co.uk, www.amazon.de, www.amazon.fr, www.amazon.co.jp, www.amazon.ca,* and *www.amazon.cn.* Net sales generated from internationally-focused websites, as well as most of the related expenses directly incurred from those operations, are denominated in the functional currencies of the resident countries. Additionally, the functional currency of our subsidiaries that either operate or support these international websites is the same as the local currency of the United Kingdom, Germany, France, Japan, Canada, and China. Assets and liabilities of these subsidiaries are translated into U.S. Dollars at period-end exchange rates, and revenues and expenses are translated at average rates prevailing throughout the period. Translation adjustments are included in "Accumulated other comprehensive income (loss)," a separate component of stockholders' equity, and in the "Foreign currency effect on cash and cash equivalents," on our consolidated statements of cash flows. Transaction gains and losses arising from transactions denominated in a currency other than the functional currency of the entity involved are included in "Other income (expense), net" on our consolidated statements of operations. See "Note 11—Other Income (Expense), Net."

Gains and losses arising from intercompany foreign currency transactions are included in net income. In connection with the remeasurement of intercompany balances, we recorded gains of $23 million, $32 million and $50 million in 2008, 2007 and 2006.

Note 2—CASH, CASH EQUIVALENTS, AND MARKETABLE SECURITIES

As of December 31, 2008 and 2007 our cash, cash equivalents, and marketable securities primarily consisted of cash, government and government agency securities, AAA-rated money market funds and other investment grade securities. Such amounts are recorded at fair value. The following table summarizes, by major security type, our cash, cash equivalents and marketable securities (in millions):

	December 31, 2008			
	Cost or Amortized Cost	Gross Unrealized Gains	Gross Unrealized Losses (1)	Total Estimated Fair Value
Cash	$ 355	$—	$—	$ 355
Money market funds	1,682	—	—	1,682
Foreign government and agency securities	1,120	8	—	1,128
Corporate debt securities (2)	194	2	(2)	194
U.S. government and agency securities	589	5	—	594
Asset-backed securities	62	—	(4)	58
Other fixed income securities	23	—	—	23
Equity securities	2	—	(1)	1
	$4,027	$ 15	$ (7)	$4,035
Less: Long-term marketable securities (3)				(308)
Total cash, cash equivalents, and marketable securities				$3,727

AMAZON.COM, INC.

NOTES TO CONSOLIDATED FINANCIAL STATEMENTS—(Continued)

| | December 31, 2007 | | | |
	Cost or Amortized Cost	Gross Unrealized Gains	Gross Unrealized Losses (1)	Total Estimated Fair Value
Cash	$ 813	$—	$—	$ 813
Money market funds	1,558	—	—	1,558
Foreign government and agency securities	358	—	(1)	357
Corporate debt securities (2)	128	1	(1)	128
U.S. government and agency securities	326	5	—	331
Asset-backed securities	106	1	(1)	106
Other fixed income securities	4	—	—	4
Equity securities	5	7	—	12
	$3,298	$ 14	$ (3)	$3,309
Less: Long-term marketable securities (3)				(197)
Total cash, cash equivalents, and marketable securities				$3,112

---

(1) As of December 31, 2008, the cost and fair value of investments with loss positions was $761 million and $753 million. As of December 31, 2007, the cost and fair value of investments with loss positions was $550 million and $547 million. We evaluated the nature of these investments, credit worthiness of the issuer, and the duration of these impairments to determine if an other-than-temporary decline in fair value has occurred and concluded that these losses were temporary. Investments that have continuously been in loss positions for more than twelve months have gross unrealized losses of $2 million and $2 million as of December 31, 2008 and 2007.

(2) Corporate debt securities include investments in financial, insurance, and corporate institutions. No single issuer represents a significant portion of the total corporate debt securities portfolio.

(3) We are required to pledge or otherwise restrict a portion of our marketable securities as collateral for standby letters of credit, guarantees, debt, and real estate lease agreements. We classify cash and marketable securities with use restrictions of twelve months or longer as non-current "Other assets" on our consolidated balance sheets. See "Note 7—Commitments and Contingencies."

The following table summarizes contractual maturities of our cash equivalent and marketable fixed-income securities as of December 31, 2008 (in millions):

	Amortized Cost	Estimated Fair Value
Due within one year	$3,089	$3,090
Due after one year through five years	578	589
	$3,667	$3,679

Gross gains of $9 million, $2 million, and $18 million and gross losses of $7 million, $3 million and $16 million were realized on sales of available-for-sale marketable securities, including Euro-denominated securities, for 2008, 2007, and 2006. Realized gains and losses are included in "Other income (expense), net" on our consolidated statements of operations.

AMAZON.COM, INC.

NOTES TO CONSOLIDATED FINANCIAL STATEMENTS—(Continued)

Note 3—FIXED ASSETS

Fixed assets, at cost, consisted of the following (in millions):

	December 31, 2008	December 31, 2007
Gross Fixed Assets:		
Fulfillment and customer service	$ 564	$ 464
Technology infrastructure	348	196
Internal-use software, content, and website development	331	285
Construction in progress (1)	87	15
Other corporate assets	79	63
Gross fixed assets	1,409	1,023
Accumulated Depreciation :		
Fulfillment and customer service	254	216
Technology infrastructure	82	74
Internal-use software, content, and website development	159	146
Other corporate assets	60	44
Total accumulated depreciation	555	480
Total fixed assets, net	$ 854	$ 543

(1) We capitalize construction in progress and record a corresponding long-term liability for certain lease agreements, including our Seattle, Washington corporate office space subject to leases scheduled to begin in 2010 and 2011. See "Note 6—Other Long-Term Liabilities" and "Note 7—Commitments and Contingencies" for further discussion.

Depreciation expense on fixed assets was $311 million, $258 million, and $200 million, which includes amortization of fixed assets acquired under capital lease obligations of $50 million, $40 million, and $26 million for 2008, 2007, and 2006. Gross assets remaining under capital leases were $304 million and $150 million at December 31, 2008 and 2007. Accumulated depreciation associated with capital leases was $116 million and $64 million at December 31, 2008 and 2007.

AMAZON.COM, INC.

NOTES TO CONSOLIDATED FINANCIAL STATEMENTS—(Continued)

Note 4—ACQUISITIONS, GOODWILL, AND ACQUIRED INTANGIBLE ASSETS

In 2008, we acquired certain companies for an aggregate purchase price of $432 million. For each acquisition, the purchase price has been allocated to the tangible assets, liabilities assumed, and identifiable intangible assets acquired based on estimated fair values on the acquisition date. The excess of purchase price over the fair value of the net assets acquired is classified as "Goodwill" on our consolidated balance sheets.

The following summarizes the allocation of the purchase price for companies acquired in 2008 (in millions):

Goodwill	$210
Internal-use software	31
Other assets, net	104
Deferred tax liabilities net	(75)
Intangible assets (1):	
Marketing-related	12
Contract-based	60
Technology and content	2
Customer-related	88
	$432

(1) Acquired intangible assets have estimated useful lives of between 2 and 13 years.

We acquired certain companies during 2007 for an aggregate purchase price of $33 million, resulting in goodwill of $21 million and acquired intangible assets of $18 million. We also made principal payments of $13 million on acquired debt in connection with one of these acquisitions.

We acquired certain companies during 2006 for an aggregate purchase price of $50 million, resulting in goodwill of $33 million and acquired intangible assets of $17 million.

The results of operations of each of the businesses acquired in 2008, 2007, and 2006 have been included in our consolidated results from each transaction closing date forward. The effect of these acquisitions on consolidated net sales and operating income during 2008, 2007, and 2006 was not significant.

At December 31, 2008 and December 31, 2007, approximately 22% and 36% of our acquired goodwill related to our International segment.

Note 5—LONG-TERM DEBT

Our long-term debt is summarized as follows:

	December 31,	
	2008	**2007**
	(in millions)	
6.875% PEACS due February 2010	$335	$ 350
4.75% Convertible Subordinated Notes	—	899
Other long-term debt	133	50
	468	1,299
Less current portion of long-term debt	(59)	(17)
	$409	$1,282

In 2008, we called for redemption of the remaining principal amount of $899 million of our outstanding 4.75% Convertible Subordinated Notes. Holders elected to convert $605 million in principal amount of the 4.75% Convertible Subordinated Notes, and we issued 7.8 million shares of our common stock as a result; we redeemed the remaining $294 million of the called principal amount for cash.

AMAZON.COM, INC.

NOTES TO CONSOLIDATED FINANCIAL STATEMENTS—(Continued)

Note 6—OTHER LONG-TERM LIABILITIES

Our other long-term liabilities are summarized as follows:

	December 31,	
	2008	2007
	(in millions)	
Tax contingencies	$144	$ 98
Long-term capital lease obligations	124	62
Construction liabilities	87	15
Other	132	117
	$487	$292

Tax Contingencies

As of December 31, 2008 and 2007, we have provided tax reserves for tax contingencies of approximately $144 million and $98 million for U.S. and foreign income taxes, which primarily relate to restructuring of certain foreign operations and intercompany pricing between our subsidiaries. See "Note 12—Income Taxes" for discussion of tax contingencies.

Capital Leases

Certain of our equipment fixed assets, primarily related to technology, have been acquired under capital leases. Long-term capital lease obligations were as follows:

	December 31, 2008
	(in millions)
Gross capital lease obligations	$219
Less imputed interest	(23)
Present value of net minimum lease payments	196
Less current portion	(72)
Total long-term capital lease obligations	$124

Construction Liabilities

We capitalize construction in progress and record a corresponding long-term liability for certain lease agreements, including our Seattle, Washington corporate office space subject to leases scheduled to begin in 2010 and 2011.

In accordance with EITF No. 97-10, for build-to-suit lease arrangements where we are involved in the construction of structural improvements prior to the commencement of the lease or take some level of construction risk, we are considered the owner of the assets during the construction period under U.S. GAAP.

Accordingly, as the landlord incurs the construction project costs, the assets and corresponding financial obligation are recorded in "Fixed assets, net" and "Other long-term liabilities" on our consolidated balance sheet. Once the construction is completed, if the lease meets certain "sale-leaseback" criteria in accordance with SFAS No. 98, *Accounting for Leases*, we will remove the asset and related financial obligation from the balance sheet and treat the building lease as an operating lease. If upon completion of construction, the project does not meet the "sale-leaseback" criteria, the leased property will be treated as a capital lease for financial reporting purposes.

The remainder of our other long-term liabilities primarily include deferred tax liabilities, unearned revenue, asset retirement obligations, and deferred rental liabilities.

AMAZON.COM, INC.

NOTES TO CONSOLIDATED FINANCIAL STATEMENTS—(Continued)

Note 7—COMMITMENTS AND CONTINGENCIES

Commitments

We lease office and fulfillment center facilities and fixed assets under non-cancelable operating and capital leases. Rental expense under operating lease agreements was $158 million, $141 million, and $132 million for 2008, 2007, and 2006.

In December 2007, we entered into a series of leases and other agreements for the lease of corporate office space to be developed in Seattle, Washington with initial terms of up to 16 years commencing on completion of development in 2010 and 2011 and options to extend for two five year periods. At December 31, 2008, under the agreements we committed to occupy approximately 1,360,000 square feet of office space. In addition, we have the right to occupy up to an additional approximately 330,000 square feet subject to a termination fee, estimated to be up to approximately $10 million, if we elect not to occupy the additional space. We also have an option to lease up to an additional approximately 500,000 square feet at rates based on fair market values at the time the option is exercised, subject to certain conditions. In addition, if interest rates exceed a certain threshold, we have the option to provide financing for some of the buildings.

The following summarizes our principal contractual commitments, excluding open orders for inventory purchases that support normal operations, as of December 31, 2008:

	Year Ended December 31,					Thereafter	Total
	2009	2010	2011	2012	2013		
	(in millions)						
Operating and capital commitments:							
Debt principal (1)	$ 59	$335	$ 41	$ 33	$—	$ —	$ 468
Debt interest (1)	30	28	5	1	—	—	64
Capital leases, including interest	86	77	44	7	4	1	219
Operating leases	146	127	105	93	84	261	816
Other commitments (2)(3)	96	143	88	84	76	1,005	1,492
Total commitments	$417	$710	$283	$218	$164	$1,267	$3,059

(1) Under our 6.875% PEACS, the principal payment due in 2010 and the annual interest payments fluctuate based on the Euro/U.S. Dollar exchange ratio. At December 31, 2008, the Euro to U.S. Dollar exchange rate was 1.3974. Due to changes in the Euro/U.S. Dollar exchange ratio, our remaining principal debt obligation under this instrument since issuance in February 2000 has increased by $99 million as of December 31, 2008. The principal and interest commitments at December 31, 2008 reflect the partial redemption of the 6.875% PEACS and full redemption of the 4.75% Convertible Subordinated Notes.

AMAZON.COM, INC.

NOTES TO CONSOLIDATED FINANCIAL STATEMENTS—(Continued)

(2) Includes the estimated timing and amounts of payments for rent, operating expenses, and tenant improvements associated with approximately 1,360,000 square feet of corporate office space being developed in Seattle, Washington and also includes the $10 million termination fee related to our right to occupy up to an additional approximately 330,000 square feet. The amount of space available and our financial and other obligations under the lease agreements are affected by various factors, including government approvals and permits, interest rates, development costs and other expenses and our exercise of certain rights under the lease agreements.

(3) Excludes $166 million of such tax contingencies for which we cannot make a reasonably reliable estimate of the amount and period of payment, if at all. See Item 8 of Part II, "Financial Statements and Supplementary Data—Note 12—Income Taxes."

Pledged Securities

We are required to pledge or otherwise restrict a portion of our cash and marketable securities as collateral for standby letters of credit, guarantees, debt, and real estate leases. We classify cash and marketable securities with use restrictions of twelve months or longer as non-current "Other assets" on our consolidated balance sheets. The balance of pledged securities at December 31, 2008 consisted of $308 million included in "Other assets." The amount required to be pledged for certain real estate lease agreements changes over the life of our leases based on our credit rating and changes in our market capitalization (common shares outstanding multiplied by the closing price of our common stock). Information about collateral required to be pledged under these agreements is as follows:

	Standby and Trade Letters of Credit and Guarantees	Debt (1)	Real Estate Leases (2)	Total
		(in millions)		
Balance at December 31, 2007	$138	$ 60	$13	$211
Net change in collateral pledged	—	100	(3)	97
Balance at December 31, 2008	$138	$160	$10	$308

(1) Represents collateral for certain debt related to our international operations.

(2) At December 31, 2007, our market capitalization was $22.0 billion. The required amount of collateral to be pledged will increase by $5 million if our market capitalization is equal to or below $18.0 billion and by an additional $6 million if our market capitalization is equal to or below $13.0 billion.

Legal Proceedings

The Company is involved from time to time in claims, proceedings and litigation, including the following:

In June 2001, Audible, Inc., our subsidiary acquired in March 2008, was named as a defendant in a securities class-action filed in United States District Court for the Southern District of New York related to its initial public offering in July 1999. The lawsuit also named certain of the offering's underwriters, as well as Audible's officers and directors as defendants. Approximately 300 other issuers and their underwriters have had similar suits filed against them, all of which are included in a single coordinated proceeding in the Southern District of New York. The complaints allege that the prospectus and the registration statement for Audible's offering failed to disclose that the underwriters allegedly solicited and received "excessive" commissions from investors and that some investors allegedly agreed with the underwriters to buy additional shares in the aftermarket in order to inflate the price of the Company's stock. Audible and its officers and directors were named in the suits pursuant to Section 11 of the Securities Act of 1933, Section 10(b) of the Securities Exchange Act of 1934, and other related provisions. The complaints seek unspecified damages, attorney and expert fees,

AMAZON.COM, INC.

NOTES TO CONSOLIDATED FINANCIAL STATEMENTS—(Continued)

and other unspecified litigation costs. The Court has directed that the litigation proceed with a number of "focus cases" rather than all of the consolidated cases at once. Audible's case is not one of these focus cases. We dispute the allegations of wrongdoing in the complaint against Audible and its officers and directors and intend to vigorously defend ourselves in this matter.

Beginning in March 2003, we were served with complaints filed in several different states, including Illinois, by a private litigant, Beeler, Schad & Diamond, P.C., purportedly on behalf of the state governments under various state False Claims Acts. The complaints allege that we (along with other companies with which we have commercial agreements) wrongfully failed to collect and remit sales and use taxes for sales of personal property to customers in those states and knowingly created records and statements falsely stating we were not required to collect or remit such taxes. In December 2006, we learned that one additional complaint was filed in the state of Illinois by a different private litigant, Matthew T. Hurst, alleging similar violations of the Illinois state law. All of the complaints seek injunctive relief, unpaid taxes, interest, attorneys' fees, civil penalties of up to $10,000 per violation, and treble or punitive damages under the various state False Claims Acts. It is possible that we have been or will be named in similar cases in other states as well. We dispute the allegations of wrongdoing in these complaints and intend to vigorously defend ourselves in these matters.

In May 2004, Toysrus.com LLC filed a complaint against us for breach of contract in the Superior Court of New Jersey. The complaint alleged that we breached our commercial agreement with Toysrus.com LLC by selling, and by permitting other third parties to sell, products that Toysrus.com LLC alleged it has an exclusive right to sell on our website. We disputed the allegations in the complaint and brought counterclaims alleging breach of contract and seeking damages and declaratory relief. The trial of both parties' claims concluded in November 2005. In March 2006, the Court entered a judgment in favor of Toysrus.com LLC, terminating the contract but declining to award damages to either party. We are pursuing an appeal of the lower court's rulings terminating the contract, declining to award us damages, and denying our motion to compel Toysrus.com to pay certain fees incurred during the wind-down period.

In December 2005, Registrar Systems LLC filed a complaint against us and Target Corporation for patent infringement in the United States District Court for the District of Colorado. The complaint alleges that our website technology, including the method by which Amazon.com enables customers to use Amazon.com account information on websites that Amazon.com operates for third parties, such as Target.com, infringes two patents obtained by Registrar Systems purporting to cover methods and apparatuses for a "World Wide Web Registration Information Processing System" (U.S. Patent Nos. 5,790,785 and 6,823,327) and seeks injunctive relief, monetary damages in an amount no less than a reasonable royalty, prejudgment interest, costs, and attorneys' fees. We dispute the allegations of wrongdoing in this complaint and intend to vigorously defend ourselves in this matter. In September 2006, the Court entered an order staying the lawsuit pending the outcome of the Patent and Trademark Office's re-examination of the patents in suit.

In August 2006, Cordance Corporation filed a complaint against us for patent infringement in the United States District Court for the District of Delaware. The complaint alleges that our website technology, including our 1-Click ordering system, infringes a patent obtained by Cordance purporting to cover an "Object-Based Online Transaction Infrastructure" (U.S. Patent No. 6,757,710) and seeks injunctive relief, monetary damages in an amount no less than a reasonable royalty, treble damages for alleged willful infringement, prejudgment interest, costs, and attorneys' fees. In response, we asserted a declaratory judgment counterclaim in the same action alleging that a service that Cordance has advertised its intent to launch infringes a patent owned by us entitled "Networked Personal Contact Manager" (U.S. Patent No. 6,269,369). We dispute Cordance's allegations of wrongdoing and intend to vigorously defend ourselves in this matter.

AMAZON.COM, INC.

NOTES TO CONSOLIDATED FINANCIAL STATEMENTS—(Continued)

In October 2007, Digital Reg of Texas, LLC filed a complaint against our subsidiary, Audible, Inc., and several other defendants in the United States District Court for the Eastern District of Texas. The complaint alleges that Audible's digital rights management technology infringes a patent obtained by Digital Reg purporting to cover a system for "Regulating Access to Digital Content" (U.S. Patent No. 6,389,541) and seeks injunctive relief, monetary damages, enhanced damages for alleged willful infringement, prejudgment and post-judgment interest, costs and attorneys' fees. We dispute the allegations of wrongdoing and intend to vigorously defend ourselves in the matter.

In December 2008, Quito Enterprises, LLC filed a complaint against us for patent infringement in the United States District Court for the Southern District of Florida. The complaint alleges that our website technology infringes a patent obtained by Quito purporting to cover a "Personal Feedback Browser for Obtaining Media Files" (U.S. Patent No. 5,890,152) and seeks injunctive relief and monetary damages. We dispute the allegations of wrongdoing and intend to vigorously defend ourselves in this matter.

In January 2009, we learned that the United States Postal Service, including the Postal Service Office of Inspector General, is investigating our compliance with Postal Service rules, and we are cooperating.

Depending on the amount and the timing, an unfavorable resolution of some or all of these matters could materially affect our business, results of operations, financial position, or cash flows.

See also "Note 12—Income Taxes."

Inventory Suppliers

During 2008, no vendor accounted for 10% or more of our inventory purchases. We do not have long-term contracts or arrangements with most of our vendors to guarantee the availability of merchandise, particular payment terms, or the extension of credit limits.

Note 8—STOCKHOLDERS' EQUITY

Preferred Stock

We have authorized 500 million shares of $0.01 par value Preferred Stock. No preferred stock was outstanding for any period presented.

Stock Conversion Activity

Holders of our 4.75% Convertible Subordinated Notes elected to convert a total of $605 million in outstanding principal amount under called redemptions during 2008, and we issued 7.8 million shares of common stock as a result of such elections.

Stock Repurchase Activity

We repurchased 2.2 million shares of common stock for $100 million in 2008 under the $1 billion repurchase program authorized by our Board of Directors in February 2008. We repurchased 6.3 million shares of common stock for $248 million in 2007, and 8.2 million shares of common stock for $252 million in 2006, under the $500 million repurchase program authorized by our Board of Directors in August 2006.

AMAZON.COM, INC.

NOTES TO CONSOLIDATED FINANCIAL STATEMENTS—(Continued)

Note 9—OTHER COMPREHENSIVE INCOME (LOSS)

The changes in the components of other comprehensive income (loss) were as follows:

	Year Ended December 31,		
	2008	2007	2006
	(in millions)		
Net income	$ 645	$476	$190
Net change in unrealized gains/losses on available-for-sale securities	(1)	8	4
Foreign currency translation adjustment, net of tax	(127)	(3)	(13)
Amortization of net unrealized losses on terminated Euro Currency Swap, net of tax	—	1	2
Other comprehensive income (loss)	(128)	6	(7)
Comprehensive income	$ 517	$482	$183

Accumulated balances within other comprehensive income (loss) were as follows:

	December 31,	
	2008	2007
	(in millions)	
Net unrealized losses on foreign currency translation, net of tax	$(128)	$(1)
Net unrealized gains on available-for-sale securities, net of tax	6	7
Net unrealized losses on terminated Euro Currency Swap, net of tax	(1)	(1)
Total accumulated other comprehensive income (loss)	$(123)	$ 5

AMAZON.COM, INC.

NOTES TO CONSOLIDATED FINANCIAL STATEMENTS—(Continued)

Note 10—OTHER OPERATING EXPENSE (INCOME), NET

Other operating expense (income), net, was $(24) million, $9 million and $10 million in 2008, 2007 and 2006. The increase in other operating income in 2008 compared to the comparable prior years is primarily attributable to the $53 million non-cash gain recognized on the sale in 2008 of our European DVD rental assets, partially offset by increased amortization of intangible assets. Other operating expense in 2007 and 2006 was primarily attributable to amortization of intangible assets.

Note 11—OTHER INCOME (EXPENSE), NET

Other income (expense), net, was $47 million, $(8) million, and $7 million in 2008, 2007 and 2006, and consisted primarily of gains and losses on sales of marketable securities, foreign currency transaction gains and losses, and other miscellaneous losses.

Foreign currency transaction gains and losses primarily relate to remeasurement of our 6.875% PEACS and remeasurement of intercompany balances.

Note 12—INCOME TAXES

In 2008, 2007 and 2006 we recorded net tax provisions of $247 million, $184 million, and $187 million. A majority of this provision is non-cash. We have current tax benefits and net operating losses relating to excess stock-based compensation that are being utilized to reduce our U.S. taxable income. As such, cash taxes paid were $53 million, $24 million, and $15 million for 2008, 2007, and 2006.

The components of the provision for income taxes, net were as follows:

	Year Ended December 31,		
	2008	**2007**	**2006**
	(in millions)		
Current taxes:			
U.S. and state	$227	$275	$162
International	25	8	3
Current taxes	252	283	165
Deferred taxes	(5)	(99)	22
Provision for income taxes, net	$247	$184	$187

AMAZON.COM, INC.

NOTES TO CONSOLIDATED FINANCIAL STATEMENTS—(Continued)

Item 9. *Changes in and Disagreements with Accountants On Accounting and Financial Disclosure*

None.

Item 9A. *Controls and Procedures*

Evaluation of Disclosure Controls and Procedures

We carried out an evaluation required by the 1934 Act, under the supervision and with the participation of our principal executive officer and principal financial officer, of the effectiveness of the design and operation of our disclosure controls and procedures, as defined in Rule 13a-15(e) of the 1934 Act, as of December 31, 2008. Based on this evaluation, our principal executive officer and principal financial officer concluded that, as of December 31, 2008, our disclosure controls and procedures were effective to provide reasonable assurance that information required to be disclosed by us in the reports that we file or submit under the 1934 Act is recorded, processed, summarized, and reported within the time periods specified in the SEC's rules and forms and to provide reasonable assurance that such information is accumulated and communicated to our management, including our principal executive officer and principal financial officer, as appropriate to allow timely decisions regarding required disclosures.

Management's Report on Internal Control over Financial Reporting

Management is responsible for establishing and maintaining adequate internal control over financial reporting, as defined in Rule 13a-15(f) of the 1934 Act. Management has assessed the effectiveness of our internal control over financial reporting as of December 31, 2008 based on criteria established in Internal Control—Integrated Framework issued by the Committee of Sponsoring Organizations of the Treadway Commission. As a result of this assessment, management concluded that, as of December 31, 2008, our internal control over financial reporting was effective in providing reasonable assurance regarding the reliability of financial reporting and the preparation of financial statements for external purposes in accordance with generally accepted accounting principles. Ernst & Young has independently assessed the effectiveness of our internal control over financial reporting and its report is included below.

Changes in Internal Control Over Financial Reporting

There were no changes in our internal control over financial reporting during the quarter ended December 31, 2008 that materially affected, or are reasonably likely to materially affect, our internal control over financial reporting.

Limitations on Controls

Our disclosure controls and procedures and internal control over financial reporting are designed to provide reasonable assurance of achieving their objectives as specified above. Management does not expect, however, that our disclosure controls and procedures or our internal control over financial reporting will prevent or detect all error and fraud. Any control system, no matter how well designed and operated, is based upon certain assumptions and can provide only reasonable, not absolute, assurance that its objectives will be met. Further, no evaluation of controls can provide absolute assurance that misstatements due to error or fraud will not occur or that all control issues and instances of fraud, if any, within the Company have been detected.

FOOT LOCKER, INC.

2007 ANNUAL REPORT   OUR BRAND IDENTITY

Foot Locker

Lady Foot Locker

kids Foot Locker

CHAMPS

Eastbay

FOOTACTION

Item 8. Consolidated Financial Statements and Supplementary Data

MANAGEMENT'S REPORT

The integrity and objectivity of the financial statements and other financial information presented in this annual report are the responsibility of the management of the Company. The financial statements have been prepared in conformity with U.S. generally accepted accounting principles and include, when necessary, amounts based on the best estimates and judgments of management.

The Company maintains a system of internal controls designed to provide reasonable assurance, at appropriate cost, that assets are safeguarded, transactions are executed in accordance with management's authorization and the accounting records provide a reliable basis for the preparation of the financial statements. The system of internal accounting controls is continually reviewed by management and improved and modified as necessary in response to changing business conditions. The Company also maintains an internal audit function to assist management in evaluating and formally reporting on the adequacy and effectiveness of internal accounting controls, policies and procedures.

The Company's financial statements have been audited by KPMG LLP, the Company's independent registered public accounting firm, whose report expresses their opinion with respect to the fairness of the presentation of these financial statements.

The Audit Committee of the Board of Directors, which comprises solely independent non-management directors who are not officers or employees of the Company, meets regularly with the Company's management, internal auditors, legal counsel and KPMG LLP to review the activities of each group and to satisfy itself that each is properly discharging its responsibility. In addition, the Audit Committee meets on a periodic basis with KPMG LLP, without management's presence, to discuss the audit of the financial statements as well as other auditing and financial reporting matters. The Company's internal auditors and independent registered public accounting firm have direct access to the Audit Committee.

MATTHEW D. SERRA,
Chairman of the Board,
President and Chief Executive Officer

ROBERT W. MCHUGH,
Senior Vice President and
Chief Financial Officer

March 31, 2008

REPORT OF INDEPENDENT REGISTERED PUBLIC ACCOUNTING FIRM

The Board of Directors and Shareholders of
Foot Locker, Inc.:

We have audited the accompanying consolidated balance sheets of Foot Locker, Inc. and subsidiaries as of February 2, 2008 and February 3, 2007, and the related consolidated statements of operations, comprehensive income, shareholders' equity, and cash flows for each of the years in the three-year period ended February 2, 2008. These consolidated financial statements are the responsibility of the Company's management. Our responsibility is to express an opinion on these consolidated financial statements based on our audits.

We conducted our audits in accordance with the standards of the Public Company Accounting Oversight Board (United States). Those standards require that we plan and perform the audit to obtain reasonable assurance about whether the financial statements are free of material misstatement. An audit also includes examining, on a test basis, evidence supporting the amounts and disclosures in the financial statements, assessing the accounting principles used and significant estimates made by management, as well as evaluating the overall financial statement presentation. We believe that our audits provide a reasonable basis for our opinion.

In our opinion, the consolidated financial statements referred to above present fairly, in all material respects, the financial position of Foot Locker, Inc. and subsidiaries as of February 2, 2008 and February 3, 2007, and the results of their operations and their cash flows for each of the years in the three-year period ended February 2, 2008 in conformity with U.S. generally accepted accounting principles.

As discussed in the Notes to Consolidated Financial Statements, effective February 4, 2007, the Company adopted Statement of Financial Accounting Standards Interpretation ("FIN") No. 48, "Accounting for Uncertainty in Income Taxes." Effective February 3, 2007, the Company adopted Statement of Financial Accounting Standards ("SFAS") No 158, "Employers' Accounting for Defined Benefit Pension and Other Post Retirement Plans – An Amendment of FASB Statements No. 87, 88, 106, and 132(R)." In addition, effective January 29, 2006, the Company adopted SFAS No. 123(R), "Share-Based Payment," and SFAS No. 151, "Inventory Costs – An Amendment of ARB No. 43, Chapter 4," as well as changed their method for quantifying errors based on SEC Staff Accounting Bulletin No. 108, "Considering the Effects of Prior Year Misstatements when Quantifying Misstatements in Current Year Financial Statements."

We also have audited, in accordance with the standards of the Public Company Accounting Oversight Board (United States), the effectiveness of Foot Locker, Inc.'s internal control over financial reporting as of February 2, 2008, based on criteria established in Internal Control – Integrated Framework issued by the Committee of Sponsoring Organizations of the Treadway Commission (COSO), and our report dated March 31, 2008 expressed an unqualified opinion on the effectiveness of internal control over financial reporting.

KPMG LLP

New York, New York
March 31, 2008

* This green rule signifies a gap in the information printed in the full Annual Report.

CONSOLIDATED STATEMENTS OF OPERATIONS

	2007	2006	2005
	(in millions, except per share amounts)		
Sales	$ 5,437	$ 5,750	$ 5,653
Costs and expenses			
Cost of sales	4,017	4,014	3,944
Selling, general and administrative expenses	1,176	1,163	1,129
Depreciation and amortization	166	175	171
Impairment charges and store closing program costs	128	17	—
Interest expense, net	1	3	10
	5,488	5,372	5,254
Other income	(1)	(14)	(6)
	5,487	5,358	5,248
(Loss) Income from continuing operations before income taxes	(50)	392	405
Income tax (benefit) expense	(99)	145	142
Income from continuing operations	49	247	263
Income on disposal of discontinued operations, net of income tax expense (benefit) of $1, $1, and $(3), respectively	2	3	1
Cumulative effect of accounting change, net of income tax benefit of $ —	—	1	—
Net income	$ 51	$ 251	$ 264
Basic earnings per share:			
Income from continuing operations	$ 0.32	$ 1.59	$ 1.70
Income from discontinued operations	0.01	0.02	0.01
Cumulative effect of accounting change	—	0.01	—
Net income	$ 0.33	$ 1.62	$ 1.71
Diluted earnings per share:			
Income from continuing operations	$ 0.32	$ 1.58	$ 1.67
Income from discontinued operations	0.01	0.02	0.01
Cumulative effect of accounting change	—	—	—
Net income	$ 0.33	$ 1.60	$ 1.68

See Accompanying Notes to Consolidated Financial Statements.

CONSOLIDATED STATEMENTS OF COMPREHENSIVE INCOME

	2007	2006	2005
		(in millions)	
Net income	$ 51	$ 251	$ 264
Other comprehensive income, net of tax			
Foreign currency translation adjustment:			
Translation adjustment arising during the period, net of tax	60	27	(25)
Cash flow hedges:			
Change in fair value of derivatives, net of income tax	1	—	2
Reclassification adjustments, net of income tax	—	—	(1)
Net change in cash flow hedges:	1	—	1
Minimum pension liability adjustment:			
Minimum pension liability adjustment, net of deferred tax expense of $-, $120 and $10 million, respectively	—	181	15
Pension and postretirement plan adjustments, net of income tax benefit of $11 million	(20)	—	—
Unrealized loss on available-for-sale securities	(2)	—	—
Comprehensive income	$ 90	$459	$ 255

See Accompanying Notes to Consolidated Financial Statements.

CONSOLIDATED BALANCE SHEETS

	2007	2006
	(in millions)	
ASSETS		
Current assets		
Cash and cash equivalents	$ 488	$ 221
Short-term investments	5	249
Merchandise inventories..	1,281	1,303
Other current assets	290	261
	2,064	2,034
Property and equipment, net	521	654
Deferred taxes	243	109
Goodwill	266	264
Intangible assets, net..	96	105
Other assets	58	83
	$ 3,248	$ 3,249
LIABILITIES AND SHAREHOLDERS' EQUITY		
Current liabilities		
Accounts payable	$ 233	$ 256
Accrued and other liabilities	268	246
Current portion of long-term debt and obligations under capital leases............	—	14
	501	516
Long-term debt and obligations under capital leases	221	220
Other liabilities.	255	218
Total liabilities	977	954
Shareholders' equity...	2,271	2,295
	$ 3,248	$ 3,249

See Accompanying Notes to Consolidated Financial Statements.

CONSOLIDATED STATEMENTS OF SHAREHOLDERS' EQUITY

	2007 Shares	2007 Amount	2006 Shares	2006 Amount	2005 Shares	2005 Amount
			(shares in thousands, amounts in millions)			
Common Stock and Paid-In Capital						
Par value $0.01 per share, 500 million shares authorized						
Issued at beginning of year	157,810	$ 653	157,280	$ 635	156,155	$ 608
Restricted stock issued under stock option and award plans	513	—	—	(3)	225	—
Forfeitures of restricted stock	—	—	—	—	—	2
Share-based compensation expense..........................	—	10	—	10	—	6
Issued under director and employee stock plans, net of tax	674	13	530	11	900	19
Issued at end of year	158,997	676	157,810	653	157,280	635
Common stock in treasury at beginning of year	(2,107)	(47)	(1,776)	(38)	(64)	(2)
Reissued under employee stock plans..........................	—	—	122	3	90	2
Restricted stock issued under stock option and award plans	—	—	157	3	—	—
Forfeitures/cancellations of restricted stock...................	(25)	—	(30)	(1)	(135)	(2)
Shares of common stock used to satisfy tax withholding obligations	(95)	(2)	(241)	(6)	(49)	(1)
Stock repurchases	(2,283)	(50)	(334)	(8)	(1,590)	(35)
Exchange of options.......................................	(13)	—	(5)	—	(28)	—
Common stock in treasury at end of year	(4,523)	(99)	(2,107)	(47)	(1,776)	(38)
	154,474	577	155,703	606	155,504	597
Retained Earnings						
Balance at beginning of year		1,785		1,601		1,386
Cumulative effect of adjustments resulting from the adoption of SAB 108, net of tax (see note 3)		—		(6)		—
Cumulative effect of adjustments resulting from the adoption of FIN 48, net of tax (see note 1)		1		—		—
Adjusted balance at beginning of year.........................		1,786		1,595		1,386
Net income..		51		251		264
Cash dividends declared on common stock $0.50, $0.40 and $0.32 per share, respectively..............		(77)		(61)		(49)
Balance at end of year		1,760		1,785		1,601
Accumulated Other Comprehensive Loss						
Foreign Currency Translation Adjustment						
Balance at beginning of year		37		10		35
Translation adjustment arising during the period, net of tax		60		27		(25)
Balance at end of year		97		37		10
Cash Flow Hedges						
Balance at beginning of year		—		—		(1)
Change during year, net of tax		1		—		1
Balance at end of year		1		—		—
Minimum Pension Liability Adjustment						
Balance at beginning of year		—		(181)		(196)
Change during year, net of tax		—		181		15
Balance at end of year		—		—		(181)
Pension Adjustments						
Balance at beginning of year		(133)		—		—
Adoption of SFAS No. 158.................................		—		(133)		—
Change during year, net of tax		(29)		—		—
Balance at end of year		(162)		(133)		—
Unrealized loss on available-for-sale securities		(2)		—		—
Total Accumulated Other Comprehensive Loss		(66)		(96)		(171)
Total Shareholders' Equity................................		$ 2,271		$ 2,295		$ 2,027

See Accompanying Notes to Consolidated Financial Statements.

CONSOLIDATED STATEMENTS OF CASH FLOWS

	2007	2006	2005
		(in millions)	
From Operating Activities			
Net income	$ 51	$ 251	$ 264
Adjustments to reconcile net income to net cash provided by operating activities of continuing operations:			
Income on disposal of discontinued operations, net of tax	(2)	(3)	(1)
Non-cash impairment charges and store closing program costs	124	17	—
Cumulative effect of accounting change, net of tax.	—	(1)	—
Depreciation and amortization	166	175	171
Share-based compensation expense	10	10	6
Deferred income taxes	(129)	21	24
Change in assets and liabilities:			
Merchandise inventories	55	(38)	(111)
Accounts payable and other accruals	(36)	(103)	14
Qualified pension plan contributions	—	(68)	(26)
Income taxes.	—	(3)	(8)
Other, net	44	(69)	16
Net cash provided by operating activities of continuing operations.	283	189	349
From Investing Activities			
Acquisitions	—	—	1
Gain from lease termination.	1	4	—
Gain from insurance recoveries	1	4	3
Purchases of short-term investments.	(1,378)	(1,992)	(2,798)
Sales of short-term investments	1,620	2,041	2,767
Capital expenditures	(148)	(165)	(155)
Proceeds from investment and note.	21	—	—
Net cash provided by (used in) investing activities of continuing operations.	117	(108)	(182)
From Financing Activities			
Reduction in long-term debt	(7)	(86)	(35)
Repayment of capital lease	(14)	(1)	—
Dividends paid on common stock.	(77)	(61)	(49)
Issuance of common stock.	9	9	12
Treasury stock reissued under employee stock plans.	—	3	2
Purchase of treasury shares	(50)	(8)	(35)
Tax benefit on stock compensation	1	2	—
Net cash used in financing activities of continuing operations	(138)	(142)	(105)
Net Cash Used In operating activities of Discontinued Operations	—	(8)	—
Effect of Exchange Rate Fluctuations on Cash and Cash Equivalents	5	1	2
Net Change in Cash and Cash Equivalents	267	(68)	64
Cash and Cash Equivalents at Beginning of Year	221	289	225
Cash and Cash Equivalents at End of Year	$ 488	$ 221	$ 289
Cash Paid During the Year:			
Interest	$ 18	$ 20	$ 21
Income taxes	$ 52	$ 133	$ 93

See Accompanying Notes to Consolidated Financial Statements.

NOTES TO CONSOLIDATED FINANCIAL STATEMENTS

1.   **Summary of Significant Accounting Policies**

Cash and Cash Equivalents

The Company considers all highly liquid investments with original maturities of three months or less, including commercial paper and money market funds, to be cash equivalents. Amounts due from third party credit card processors for the settlement of debit and credit cards transactions are included as cash equivalents as they are generally collected within three business days. Cash equivalents at February 2, 2008 and February 3, 2007 were $472 million and $208 million, respectively.

Short-Term Investments

The Company accounts for its short-term investments in accordance with SFAS No. 115, "Accounting for Certain Investments in Debt and Equity Securities." At February 2, 2008, the Company's auction rate security was classified as available-for-sale, and accordingly is reported at fair value. Auction rate securities are perpetual preferred or long-dated securities whose dividend/coupon resets periodically through a Dutch auction process. A Dutch auction is a competitive bidding process designed to determine a rate for the next term. As of February 2, 2008, the carrying value of the Company's short-term investment of $7 million was reduced by $2 million. The unrealized loss of $2 million was recorded to accumulated comprehensive loss without tax benefit. There were no unrealized gains or losses recognized in 2006 and 2005. Realized losses recognized in 2007 were not significant.

Merchandise Inventories and Cost of Sales

Merchandise inventories for the Company's Athletic Stores are valued at the lower of cost or market using the retail inventory method. Cost for retail stores is determined on the last-in, first-out (LIFO) basis for domestic inventories and on the first-in, first-out (FIFO) basis for international inventories. The retail inventory method is commonly used by retail companies to value inventories at cost and calculate gross margins due to its practicality. Under the retail method, cost is determined by applying a cost-to-retail percentage across groupings of similar items, known as departments. The cost-to-retail percentage is applied to ending inventory at its current owned retail valuation to determine the cost of ending inventory on a department basis. The Company provides reserves based on current selling prices when the inventory has not been marked down to market. Merchandise inventories of the Direct-to-Customers business are valued at the lower of cost or market using weighted-average cost, which approximates FIFO. Transportation, distribution center and sourcing costs are capitalized in merchandise inventories. In 2006, the Company adopted SFAS No. 151, "Inventory Costs- An Amendment of ARB 43, Chapter 4." This standard amends the guidance to clarify that abnormal amount of idle facility expense, freight, handling costs, and wasted materials (spoilage) should be recognized as current-period charges. With the adoption of this standard the Company no longer capitalized the freight associated with transfers between its store locations. The Company maintains an accrual for shrinkage based on historical rates.

Cost of sales is comprised of the cost of merchandise, occupancy, buyers' compensation and shipping and handling costs. The cost of merchandise is recorded net of amounts received from vendors for damaged product returns, markdown allowances and volume rebates, as well as cooperative advertising reimbursements received in excess of specific, incremental advertising expenses. Occupancy reflects the amortization of amounts received from landlords for tenant improvements.

Property and Equipment

Property and equipment are recorded at cost, less accumulated depreciation and amortization. Significant additions and improvements to property and equipment are capitalized. Maintenance and repairs are charged to current operations as incurred. Major renewals or replacements that substantially extend the useful life of an asset are capitalized and depreciated. Owned property and equipment is depreciated on a straight-line basis over the estimated useful lives of the assets: maximum of 50 years for buildings and 3 to 10 years for furniture, fixtures and equipment. Property and equipment under capital leases and improvements to leased premises are generally amortized on a straight-line basis over the shorter of the estimated useful life of the asset or the remaining lease term. Capitalized software reflects certain costs related to software developed for internal use that are capitalized and amortized. After substantial completion of the project, the costs are amortized on a straight-line basis over a 2 to 7 year period. Capitalized software, net of accumulated amortization, is included in property and equipment and was $22 million at February 2, 2008 and $29 million at February 3, 2007.

Recoverability of Long-Lived Assets

In accordance with SFAS No. 144, "Accounting for the Impairment or Disposal of Long-Lived Assets" ("SFAS No. 144"), an impairment loss is recognized whenever events or changes in circumstances indicate that the carrying amounts of long-lived tangible and intangible assets with finite lives may not be recoverable. Management's policy in determining whether an impairment indicator exists, a triggering event, comprises measurable operating performance criteria at the division level, as well as qualitative measures. The Company considers historical performance and future estimated results, which are predominately identified from the Company's three-year strategic plans, in its evaluation of potential store-level impairment and then compares the carrying amount of the asset with the estimated future cash flows expected to result from the use of the asset. If the carrying amount of the asset exceeds the estimated expected undiscounted future cash flows, the Company measures the amount of the impairment by comparing the carrying amount of the asset with its estimated fair value. The estimation of fair value is measured by discounting expected future cash flows at the Company's weighted-average cost of capital. The Company estimates fair value based on the best information available using estimates, judgments and projections as considered necessary.

Goodwill and Intangible Assets

The Company accounts for goodwill and other intangibles in accordance with SFAS No. 142, "Goodwill and Other Intangible Assets," which requires that goodwill and intangible assets with indefinite lives be reviewed for impairment if impairment indicators arise and, at a minimum, annually.

The Company performs its annual impairment review as of the beginning of each fiscal year. The fair value of each reporting unit is determined using a combination of market and discounted cash flow approaches. During the third and fourth quarters of 2007, the Company performed reviews of its U.S. Athletic stores' goodwill, as a result of the SFAS No. 144 recoverability analysis. These analyses did not result in an impairment charge. Separable intangible assets that are deemed to have finite lives will continue to be amortized over their estimated useful lives. Intangible assets with finite lives primarily reflect lease acquisition costs and are amortized over the lease term.

Derivative Financial Instruments

All derivative financial instruments are recorded in the Consolidated Balance Sheets at their fair values. Changes in fair values of derivatives are recorded each period in earnings, other comprehensive gain or loss, or as a basis adjustment to the underlying hedged item, depending on whether a derivative is designated and effective as part of a hedge transaction. The effective portion of the gain or loss on the hedging derivative instrument is reported as a component of other comprehensive income/loss or as a basis adjustment to the underlying hedged item and reclassified to earnings in the period in which the hedged item affects earnings.

The effective portion of the gain or loss on hedges of foreign net investments is generally not reclassified to earnings unless the net investment is disposed of. To the extent derivatives do not qualify as hedges, or are ineffective, their changes in fair value are recorded in earnings immediately, which may subject the Company to increased earnings volatility. The changes in the fair value of the Company's hedges of net investments in various foreign subsidiaries is computed using the spot method.

Fair Value of Financial Instruments

The fair value of financial instruments is determined by reference to various market data and other valuation techniques as appropriate. The carrying value of cash and cash equivalents, and other current receivables and payables approximates fair value due to the short-term nature of these assets and liabilities. Quoted market prices of the same or similar instruments are used to determine fair value of long-term debt and forward foreign exchange contracts. Discounted cash flows are used to determine the fair value of long-term investments and notes receivable if quoted market prices on these instruments are unavailable.

Income Taxes

On February 4, 2007, the Company adopted FASB Interpretation No. 48, "Accounting for Uncertainty in Income Taxes" ("FIN 48"). Interpretation No. 48 clarifies the accounting for uncertainty in income taxes recognized in an enterprise's financial statements in accordance with Statement of Financial Accounting Standards No. 109, "Accounting for Income Taxes." FIN 48 prescribes a recognition threshold and measurement standard for the financial statement recognition and measurement of a tax position taken or expected to be taken in a tax return. Upon the adoption of FIN 48, the Company recognized a $1 million increase to retained earnings to reflect the change of its liability for the unrecognized income tax benefits as required. At February 4, 2007, the total amount of gross unrecognized tax benefits was $33 million. The Company recognizes interest and penalties related to unrecognized tax benefits in income tax expense.

The Company determines its deferred tax provision under the liability method, whereby deferred tax assets and liabilities are recognized for the expected tax consequences of temporary differences between the tax bases of assets and liabilities and their reported amounts using presently enacted tax rates. Deferred tax assets are recognized for tax credits and net operating loss carryforwards, reduced by a valuation allowance, which is established when it is more likely than not that some portion or all of the deferred tax assets will not be realized. The effect on deferred tax assets and liabilities of a change in tax rates is recognized in income in the period that includes the enactment date.

A taxing authority may challenge positions that the Company adopted in its income tax filings. Accordingly, the Company may apply different tax treatments for transactions in filing its income tax returns than for income tax financial reporting. The Company regularly assesses its tax position for such transactions and records reserves for those differences when considered necessary.

Provision for U.S. income taxes on undistributed earnings of foreign subsidiaries is made only on those amounts in excess of the funds considered to be permanently reinvested.

Pension and Postretirement Obligations

The discount rate selected to measure the present value of the Company's U.S. benefit obligations as of February 2, 2008 was derived using a cash flow matching method whereby the Company compares the plans' projected payment obligations by year with the corresponding yield on the Citibank Pension Discount Curve. The cash flows are then discounted to their present value and an overall discount rate is determined. The discount rate selected to measure the present value of the Company's Canadian benefit obligations as of February 2, 2008 was developed by using the plan's bond portfolio indices which match the benefit obligations.

Insurance Liabilities

The Company is primarily self-insured for health care, workers' compensation and general liability costs. Accordingly, provisions are made for the Company's actuarially determined estimates of discounted future claim costs for such risks for the aggregate of claims reported and claims incurred but not yet reported. Self-insured liabilities totaled $17 million and $16 million at February 2, 2008 and February 3, 2007. The Company discounts its workers' compensation and general liability using a risk-free interest rate. Imputed interest expense related to these liabilities was $1 million in each of 2007, 2006 and 2005.

Accounting for Leases

The Company recognizes rent expense for operating leases as of the possession date for store leases or the commencement of the agreement for a non-store lease. Rental expense, inclusive of rent holidays, concessions and tenant allowances are recognized over the lease term on a straight-line basis. Contingent payments based upon sales and future increases determined by inflation related indices cannot be estimated at the inception of the lease and accordingly, are charged to operations as incurred.

Foreign Currency Translation

The functional currency of the Company's international operations is the applicable local currency. The translation of the applicable foreign currency into U.S. dollars is performed for balance sheet accounts using current exchange rates in effect at the balance sheet date and for revenue and expense accounts using the weighted-average rates of exchange prevailing during the year. The unearned gains and losses resulting from such translation are included as a separate component of accumulated other comprehensive loss within shareholders' equity.

Recent Accounting Pronouncements Not Previously Discussed Herein

In September 2006, the FASB issued SFAS No. 157, "Fair Value Measurements" ("SFAS No. 157") which is effective for fiscal years beginning after November 15, 2007 and for interim periods within those years. This statement defines fair value, establishes a framework for measuring fair value and expands the related disclosure requirements. However, the FASB issued FASB Staff Positions ("FSP") 157-1 and 157-2. FSP 157-1 amends SFAS No. 157 to exclude FASB No. 13, "Accounting for Leases," and its related interpretive accounting pronouncements that address leasing transactions, while FSP-2 delays the effective date of SFAS No. 157 for all nonfinancial assets and nonfinancial liabilities, except those that are recognized or disclosed at fair value in the financial statements on a recurring basis, until fiscal years beginning after November 15, 2008. The Company does not believe that this standard will significantly affect the Company's financial position or results of operations.

In February 2007, the FASB issued SFAS No. 159, "The Fair Value Option for Financial Assets and Financial Liabilities—Including an Amendment of FASB Statement No. 115." This statement permits, but does not require, entities to measure many financial instruments at fair value. The objective is to provide entities with an opportunity to mitigate volatility in reported earnings caused by measuring related assets and liabilities differently without having to apply complex hedge accounting provisions. The Company does not believe that this standard will significantly affect the Company's financial position or results of operations.

In December 2007, the FASB issued SFAS No. 141 (Revised 2007), "Business Combinations," ("SFAS No. 141(R)"). This standard will significantly change the accounting for business combinations. Under SFAS No. 141(R), an acquiring entity will be required to recognize all the assets acquired and liabilities assumed in a transaction at the acquisition-date fair value with limited exceptions. SFAS No. 141(R) also includes a substantial number of new disclosure requirements. SFAS No. 141(R) applies prospectively to business combinations for which the acquisition date is on or after the beginning of the first annual reporting period beginning on or after December 15, 2008.

In December 2007, the FASB issued SFAS No. 160, "Noncontrolling Interests in Consolidated Financial Statements - An Amendment of ARB No. 51" ("SFAS No. 160"), which establishes new accounting and reporting standards for the noncontrolling interest in a subsidiary and for the deconsolidation of a subsidiary. Specifically, this statement requires the recognition of a noncontrolling interest (minority interest) as equity in the consolidated financial statements and separate from the parent's equity. SFAS No. 160 is effective for fiscal years, and interim periods within those fiscal years, beginning on or after December 15, 2008. This standard does not currently affect the Company.

2. Impairment of Long-Lived Assets and Store Closing Program

During 2007, the Company concluded that triggering events had occurred at its U.S. retail store divisions, comprising Foot Locker, Lady Foot Locker, Kids Foot Locker, Footaction, and Champs Sports. Accordingly, the Company evaluated the long-lived assets of those operations for impairment and recorded non-cash impairment charges of $117 million primarily to write-down long-lived assets such as store fixtures and leasehold improvements for 1,395 stores at the Company's U.S. store operations pursuant to SFAS No. 144.

Additionally, in the third quarter of 2007, the Company identified 66 unproductive stores for closure. Accordingly, the Company evaluated the recoverability of long-lived assets considering the revised estimated future cash flows. The Company recorded an additional non-cash impairment charge of $7 million as a result of this analysis. Of the total stores identified for closure in the third quarter of 2007, 13 will remain in operation as the Company was able to negotiate more favorable lease terms. Exit costs related to 33 stores which closed during 2007, comprising primarily lease termination costs of $4 million, were recognized in accordance with SFAS No. 146, "Accounting for Costs Associated with Exit or Disposal Activities." During 2008, the Company currently expects to close the remaining 20 unproductive stores prior to normal lease expiration, depending on the Company's success in negotiating agreements with its landlords. The lease exit costs associated with these remaining closures is expected to total $5 million to $10 million. These charges will be recorded during 2008 in accordance with SFAS No. 146. The cash impact of the 2008 store closings is expected to be minimal, as the related cash lease costs are expected to be offset by associated inventory reductions. Under SFAS No. 144, store closings may constitute discontinued operations if migration of customers and cash flows are not expected. The Company has concluded that no store closings have met the criteria for discontinued operations treatment.

Included in the Athletic Stores division profit for 2006 is an impairment charge of $17 million related to the Company's European operations to write-down long-lived assets in 69 stores to their estimated fair value. During 2006, division profit declined primarily due to the fashion shift from higher priced marquee footwear to lower priced low-profile footwear styles and a highly competitive retail environment, particularly for the sale of low-profile footwear styles. The charge was comprised primarily of stores located in the U.K. and France.

6. Short-Term Investments

The Company's auction rate security investments are accounted for as available-for-sale securities. The following represents the composition of the Company's auction rate securities by underlying investment.

	2007	2006
	(in millions)	
Tax exempt municipal bonds	$ —	$ 44
Equity securities	5	205
	$ 5	$ 249

With the liquidity issues experienced in the global credit and capital markets, the Company's preferred stock auction rate security, having a face value of $7 million, has experienced failed auctions. The Company determined that a temporary impairment has occurred and therefore has recorded a charge of $2 million, with no tax benefit, to accumulated other comprehensive loss as of February 2, 2008. This security will continue to accrue interest at the contractual rate and will be auctioned every 90 days until the auction succeeds. Based on the relatively small size of this investment and the Company's ability to access cash and other short-term investments, and expected operating cash flows, we do not anticipate the lack of liquidity on this investment will affect our ability to operate our business as usual.

7. Merchandise Inventories

	2007	2006
	(in millions)	
LIFO inventories	$ 907	$ 967
FIFO inventories	374	336
Total merchandise inventories	$1,281	$1,303

The value of the Company's LIFO inventories, as calculated on a LIFO basis, approximates their value as calculated on a FIFO basis.

8. Other Current Assets

	2007	2006
	(in millions)	
Net receivables	$ 50	$ 59
Prepaid expenses and other current assets	34	36
Prepaid rent	65	62
Prepaid income taxes	70	67
Deferred taxes	53	21
Investments	—	14
Northern Group note receivable	14	1
Current tax asset	1	—
Fair value of derivative contracts	3	1
	$290	$ 261

9. **Property and Equipment, Net**

	2007	2006
	(in millions)	
Land...	$ 3	$ 3
Buildings:		
Owned	30	30
Furniture, fixtures and equipment:		
Owned	1,117	1,139
Leased	—	14
	1,150	1,186
Less: accumulated depreciation	(903)	(870)
	247	316
Alterations to leased and owned buildings, net of accumulated amortization	274	338
	$ 521	$ 654

13. **Accrued and Other Liabilities**

	2007	2006
	(in millions)	
Pension and postretirement benefits	$ 4	$ 4
Incentive bonuses	5	12
Other payroll and payroll related costs, excluding taxes	52	46
Taxes other than income taxes	44	46
Property and equipment...	23	24
Customer deposits[1]	34	33
Income taxes payable...	7	2
Fair value of derivative contracts	—	2
Current deferred tax liabilities	13	4
Sales return reserve	4	4
Current portion of repositioning and restructuring reserves	—	1
Current portion of reserve for discontinued operations......................	14	3
Other operating costs...	68	65
	$268	$246

[1]   Customer deposits include unredeemed gift cards and certificates, merchandise credits and, deferred revenue related to undelivered merchandise, including layaway sales.

15. Long-Term Debt and Obligations under Capital Leases

In May 2004, the Company obtained a 5-year, $175 million amortizing term loan from the bank group participating in its existing revolving credit facility to finance a portion of the purchase price of the Footaction stores. The interest rate on the LIBOR-based, floating-rate loan was 5.4 percent on February 2, 2008 and 6.5 percent on February 3, 2007. The loan requires minimum principal payments each May, equal to a percentage of the original principal amount of 10 percent in 2006, 15 percent in years 2007 and 2008 and 50 percent in year 2009. Closing and upfront fees totaling approximately $1 million were paid for the term loan and these fees are being amortized using the interest rate method as determined by the principal repayment schedule. During 2007, 2006 and 2005 the Company repaid $2 million, $50 million, and $35 million, respectively, with the outstanding amount of $88 million due in 2009.

The Company purchased and retired $38 million of the $200 million 8.50 percent debentures payable in 2022 at a $2 million discount from face value during 2006. During 2007, the Company purchased and retired an additional $5 million bringing the outstanding amount to $129 million as of February 2, 2008. The Company has various interest rate swap agreements, which convert $100 million of the 8.50 percent debentures from a fixed interest rate to a variable interest rate, which are collectively classified as a fair value hedge. The net fair value of the interest rate swaps at February 2, 2008 was an asset of $4 million, which was included in other assets, the carrying value of the 8.50 percent debentures was increased by the corresponding amount. The net fair value of the interest rate swaps at February 3, 2007 was a liability of $4 million, which was included in other liabilities, the carrying value of the 8.50 percent debentures was decreased by the corresponding amount.

During 2007, the Company's $14 million Industrial Revenue Bond, which was accounted for as a capital lease matured. Accordingly, the Company repaid this amount.

Following is a summary of long-term debt and obligations under capital leases:

	2007	2006
	(in millions)	
8.50% debentures payable 2022	$133	$130
$175 million term loan	88	90
Total long-term debt	221	220
Obligations under capital leases	—	14
	221	234
Less: Current portion	—	14
	$221	$220

Maturities of long-term debt in future periods are:

	Long-Term Debt
	(in millions)
2008	$ —
2009	88
2010 -2012	—
Thereafter	133
Less: Current portion	—
	$ 221

Appendix C

TIME VALUE OF MONEY: FUTURE VALUE AND PRESENT VALUE

The following discussion of future value lays the foundation for our explanation of present value in Chapter 8 but is not essential. For the valuation of long-term liabilities, some instructors may wish to begin on page 889 of this appendix.

The term *time value of money* refers to the fact that money earns interest over time. *Interest* is the cost of using money. To borrowers, interest is the expense of renting money. To lenders, interest is the revenue earned from lending. We must always recognize the interest we receive or pay. Otherwise, we overlook an important part of the transaction. Suppose you invest $4,545 in corporate bonds that pay 10% interest each year. After one year, the value of your investment has grown to $5,000. The difference between your original investment ($4,545) and the future value of the investment ($5,000) is the amount of interest revenue you will earn during the year ($455). If you ignored the interest, you would fail to account for the interest revenue you have earned. Interest becomes more important as the time period lengthens because the amount of interest depends on the span of time the money is invested.

Let's consider a second example, this time from the borrower's perspective. Suppose you purchase a machine for your business. The cash price of the machine is $8,000, but you cannot pay cash now. To finance the purchase, you sign an $8,000 note payable. The note requires you to pay the $8,000 plus 10% interest one year from the date of purchase. Is your cost of the machine $8,000, or is it $8,800 [$8,000 plus interest of $800 ($8,000 × .10)]? The cost is $8,000. The additional $800 is interest expense and not part of the cost of the machine.

Future Value

The main application of future value is the accumulated balance of an investment at a future date. In our first example, the investment earned 10% per year. After one year, $4,545 grew to $5,000, as shown in Exhibit C-1.

EXHIBIT C-1 | **Future Value: An Example**

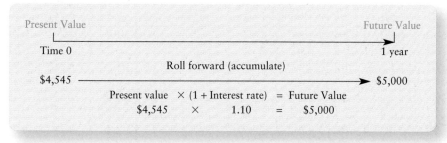

If the money were invested for five years, you would have to perform five such calculations. You would also have to consider the compound interest that your investment is earning. *Compound interest* is not only the interest you earn on your principal amount, but also the interest you receive on the interest you have already earned. Most business applications include compound interest. The following table shows the interest revenue earned on the original $4,545 investment each year for five years at 10%:

End of Year	Interest	Future Value
0	—	$4,545
1	$4,545 × 0.10 = $455	5,000
2	5,000 × 0.10 = 500	5,500
3	5,500 × 0.10 = 550	6,050
4	6,050 × 0.10 = 605	6,655
5	6,655 × 0.10 = 666	7,321

Earning 10%, a $4,545 investment grows to $5,000 at the end of one year, to $5,500 at the end of two years, and $7,321 at the end of five years. Throughout this appendix we round off to the nearest dollar.

Future-Value Tables

The process of computing a future value is called *accumulating* because the future value is *more* than the present value. Mathematical tables ease the computational burden. Exhibit C-2, Future Value of $1, gives the future value for a single sum (a present value), $1, invested to earn a particular interest rate for a specific number of periods. Future value depends on three factors: (1) the amount of the investment,

EXHIBIT C-2 | Future Value of $1

Future Value of $1

Periods	4%	5%	6%	7%	8%	9%	10%	12%	14%	16%
1	1.040	1.050	1.060	1.070	1.080	1.090	1.100	1.120	1.140	1.160
2	1.082	1.103	1.124	1.145	1.166	1.188	1.210	1.254	1.300	1.346
3	1.125	1.158	1.191	1.225	1.260	1.295	1.331	1.405	1.482	1.561
4	1.170	1.216	1.262	1.311	1.360	1.412	1.464	1.574	1.689	1.811
5	1.217	1.276	1.338	1.403	1.469	1.539	1.611	1.762	1.925	2.100
6	1.265	1.340	1.419	1.501	1.587	1.677	1.772	1.974	2.195	2.436
7	1.316	1.407	1.504	1.606	1.714	1.828	1.949	2.211	2.502	2.826
8	1.369	1.477	1.594	1.718	1.851	1.993	2.144	2.476	2.853	3.278
9	1.423	1.551	1.689	1.838	1.999	2.172	2.358	2.773	3.252	3.803
10	1.480	1.629	1.791	1.967	2.159	2.367	2.594	3.106	3.707	4.411
11	1.539	1.710	1.898	2.105	2.332	2.580	2.853	3.479	4.226	5.117
12	1.601	1.796	2.012	2.252	2.518	2.813	3.138	3.896	4.818	5.936
13	1.665	1.886	2.133	2.410	2.720	3.066	3.452	4.363	5.492	6.886
14	1.732	1.980	2.261	2.579	2.937	3.342	3.798	4.887	6.261	7.988
15	1.801	2.079	2.397	2.759	3.172	3.642	4.177	5.474	7.138	9.266
16	1.873	2.183	2.540	2.952	3.426	3.970	4.595	6.130	8.137	10.748
17	1.948	2.292	2.693	3.159	3.700	4.328	5.054	6.866	9.276	12.468
18	2.026	2.407	2.854	3.380	3.996	4.717	5.560	7.690	10.575	14.463
19	2.107	2.527	3.026	3.617	4.316	5.142	6.116	8.613	12.056	16.777
20	2.191	2.653	3.207	3.870	4.661	5.604	6.728	9.646	13.743	19.461

(2) the length of time between investment and future accumulation, and (3) the interest rate. Future-value and present-value tables are based on $1 because unity (the value 1) is so easy to work with.

In business applications, interest rates are always stated for the annual period of one year unless specified otherwise. In fact, an interest rate can be stated for any period, such as 3% per quarter or 5% for a six-month period. The length of the period is arbitrary. For example, an investment may promise a return (income) of 3% per quarter for six months (two quarters). In that case, you would be working with 3% interest for two periods. It would be incorrect to use 6% for one period because the interest is 3% compounded quarterly, and that amount differs from 6% compounded semiannually. *Take care in studying future-value and present-value problems to align the interest rate with the appropriate number of periods.*

Let's see how a future-value table like the one in Exhibit C-2 is used. The future value of $1.00 invested at 8% for one year is $1.08 ($1.00 × 1.080, which appears at the junction of the 8% column and row 1 in the Periods column). The figure 1.080 includes both the principal (1.000) and the compound interest for one period (0.080).

Suppose you deposit $5,000 in a savings account that pays annual interest of 8%. The account balance at the end of one year will be $5,400. To compute the future value of $5,000 at 8% for one year, multiply $5,000 by 1.080 to get $5,400. Now suppose you invest in a 10-year, 8% certificate of deposit (CD). What will be the future value of the CD at maturity? To compute the future value of $5,000 at 8% for 10 periods, multiply $5,000 by 2.159 (from Exhibit C-2) to get $10,795. This future value of $10,795 indicates that $5,000, earning 8% interest compounded annually, grows to $10,795 at the end of 10 years. Using Exhibit C-2, you can find any present amount's future value at a particular future date. Future value is especially helpful for computing the amount of cash you will have on hand for some purpose in the future.

Future Value of an Annuity

In the preceding example, we made an investment of a single amount. Other investments, called *annuities*, include multiple investments of an equal periodic amount at fixed intervals over the duration of the investment. Consider a family investing for a child's education. The Dietrichs can invest $4,000 annually to accumulate a college fund for 15-year-old Helen. The investment can earn 7% annually until Helen turns 18—a three-year investment. How much will be available for Helen on the date of the last investment? Exhibit C-3 shows the accumulation—a total future value of $12,860.

EXHIBIT C-3 | Future Value of an Annuity

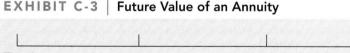
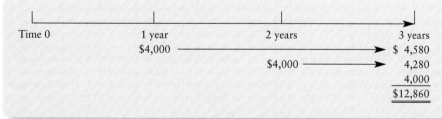

The first $4,000 invested by the Dietrichs grows to $4,580 over the investment period. The second amount grows to $4,280, and the third amount stays at $4,000 because it has no time to earn interest. The sum of the three future values

($4,580 + $4,280 + $4,000) is the future value of the annuity ($12,860), which can also be computed as follows:

End of Year	Annual Investment	Interest	Increase for the Year	Future Value of Annuity
0	—	—	—	0
1	$4,000	—	$4,000	$ 4,000
2	4,000	+ ($4,000 × 0.07 = $280) =	4,280	8,280
3	4,000	+ ($8,280 × 0.07 = $580) =	4,580	12,860

These computations are laborious. As with the Future Value of $1 (a lump sum), mathematical tables ease the strain of calculating annuities. Exhibit C-4, Future Value of Annuity of $1, gives the future value of a series of investments, each of equal amount, at regular intervals.

What is the future value of an annuity of three investments of $1 each that earn 7%? The answer, 3.215, can be found at the junction of the 7% column and row 3 in Exhibit C-4. This amount can be used to compute the future value of the investment for Helen's education, as follows:

Amount of each periodic investment	×	Future value of annuity of $1 (Exhibit C-4)	×	Future value of investment
$4,000	×	3.215	×	$12,860

EXHIBIT C-4 | Future Value of Annuity of $1

Future Value of Annuity of $1

Periods	4%	5%	6%	7%	8%	9%	10%	12%	14%	16%
1	1.000	1.000	1.000	1.000	1.000	1.000	1.000	1.000	1.000	1.000
2	2.040	2.050	2.060	2.070	2.080	2.090	2.100	2.120	2.140	2.160
3	3.122	3.153	3.184	3.215	3.246	3.278	3.310	3.374	3.440	3.506
4	4.246	4.310	4.375	4.440	4.506	4.573	4.641	4.779	4.921	5.066
5	5.416	5.526	5.637	5.751	5.867	5.985	6.105	6.353	6.610	6.877
6	6.633	6.802	6.975	7.153	7.336	7.523	7.716	8.115	8.536	8.977
7	7.898	8.142	8.394	8.654	8.923	9.200	9.487	10.089	10.730	11.414
8	9.214	9.549	9.897	10.260	10.637	11.028	11.436	12.300	13.233	14.240
9	10.583	11.027	11.491	11.978	12.488	13.021	13.579	14.776	16.085	17.519
10	12.006	12.578	13.181	13.816	14.487	15.193	15.937	17.549	19.337	21.321
11	13.486	14.207	14.972	15.784	16.645	17.560	18.531	20.655	23.045	25.733
12	15.026	15.917	16.870	17.888	18.977	20.141	21.384	24.133	27.271	30.850
13	16.627	17.713	18.882	20.141	21.495	22.953	24.523	28.029	32.089	36.786
14	18.292	19.599	21.015	22.550	24.215	26.019	27.975	32.393	37.581	43.672
15	20.024	21.579	23.276	25.129	27.152	29.361	31.772	37.280	43.842	51.660
16	21.825	23.657	25.673	27.888	30.324	33.003	35.950	42.753	50.980	60.925
17	23.698	25.840	28.213	30.840	33.750	36.974	40.545	48.884	59.118	71.673
18	25.645	28.132	30.906	33.999	37.450	41.301	45.599	55.750	68.394	84.141
19	27.671	30.539	33.760	37.379	41.446	46.018	51.159	63.440	78.969	98.603
20	29.778	33.066	36.786	40.995	45.762	51.160	57.275	72.052	91.025	115.380

This one-step calculation is much easier than computing the future value of each annual investment and then summing the individual future values. In this way, you can compute the future value of any investment consisting of equal periodic amounts at regular intervals. Businesses make periodic investments to accumulate funds for equipment replacement and other uses—an application of the future value of an annuity.

Present Value

Often a person knows a future amount and needs to know the related present value. Recall Exhibit C-1, in which present value and future value are on opposite ends of the same time line. Suppose an investment promises to pay you $5,000 at the *end* of one year. How much would you pay *now* to acquire this investment? You would be willing to pay the present value of the $5,000 future amount.

Like future value, present value depends on three factors: (1) the *amount of payment (or receipt)*, (2) the length of *time* between investment and future receipt (or *payment*), and (3) the *interest rate*. The process of computing a present value is called *discounting* because the present value is *less* than the future value.

In our investment example, the future receipt is $5,000. The investment period is one year. Assume that you demand an annual interest rate of 10% on your investment. With all three factors specified, you can compute the present value of $5,000 at 10% for one year:

$$\text{Present value} = \frac{\text{Future value}}{1 + \text{Interest rate}} = \frac{\$5,000}{1.10} = \$4,545$$

By turning the data around into a future-value problem, we can verify the present-value computation:

Amount invested (present value)	$4,545
Expected earnings ($4,545 × 0.10)...	455
Amount to be received one year from now (future value)...............	$5,000

This example illustrates that present value and future value are based on the same equation:

$$\text{Future value} = \text{Present value} \times (1 + \text{Interest rate})$$
$$\text{Present value} = \frac{\text{Future value}}{1 + \text{Interest rate}}$$

If the $5,000 is to be received two years from now, you will pay only $4,132 for the investment, as shown in Exhibit C-5 on the following page. By turning the data around, we verify that $4,132 accumulates to $5,000 at 10% for two years:

Amount invested (present value)	$4,132
Expected earnings for first year ($4,132 × 0.10)...........................	413
Value of investment after one year	4,545
Expected earnings for second year ($4,545 × 0.10)	455
Amount to be received two years from now (future value)...........	$5,000

EXHIBIT C-5 | **Present Value: An Example**

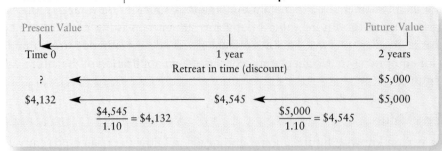

You would pay $4,132—the present value of $5,000—to receive the $5,000 future amount at the end of two years at 10% per year. The $868 difference between the amount invested ($4,132) and the amount to be received ($5,000) is the return on the investment, the sum of the two interest receipts: $413 + $455 = $868.

Present-Value Tables

We have shown the simple formula for computing present value. However, figuring present value "by hand" for investments spanning many years is time-consuming and presents too many opportunities for arithmetic errors. Present-value tables ease our work. Let's reexamine our examples of present value by using Exhibit C-6, Present Value of $1, given below.

EXHIBIT C-6 | **Present Value of $1**

				Present Value of $1					
Periods	4%	5%	6%	7%	8%	10%	12%	14%	16%
1	0.962	0.952	0.943	0.935	0.926	0.909	0.893	0.877	0.862
2	0.925	0.907	0.890	0.873	0.857	0.826	0.797	0.769	0.743
3	0.889	0.864	0.840	0.816	0.794	0.751	0.712	0.675	0.641
4	0.855	0.823	0.792	0.763	0.735	0.683	0.636	0.592	0.552
5	0.822	0.784	0.747	0.713	0.681	0.621	0.567	0.519	0.476
6	0.790	0.746	0.705	0.666	0.630	0.564	0.507	0.456	0.410
7	0.760	0.711	0.665	0.623	0.583	0.513	0.452	0.400	0.354
8	0.731	0.677	0.627	0.582	0.540	0.467	0.404	0.351	0.305
9	0.703	0.645	0.592	0.544	0.500	0.424	0.361	0.308	0.263
10	0.676	0.614	0.558	0.508	0.463	0.386	0.322	0.270	0.227
11	0.650	0.585	0.527	0.475	0.429	0.350	0.287	0.237	0.195
12	0.625	0.557	0.497	0.444	0.397	0.319	0.257	0.208	0.168
13	0.601	0.530	0.469	0.415	0.368	0.290	0.229	0.182	0.145
14	0.577	0.505	0.442	0.388	0.340	0.263	0.205	0.160	0.125
15	0.555	0.481	0.417	0.362	0.315	0.239	0.183	0.140	0.108
16	0.534	0.458	0.394	0.339	0.292	0.218	0.163	0.123	0.093
17	0.513	0.436	0.371	0.317	0.270	0.198	0.146	0.108	0.080
18	0.494	0.416	0.350	0.296	0.250	0.180	0.130	0.095	0.069
19	0.475	0.396	0.331	0.277	0.232	0.164	0.116	0.083	0.060
20	0.456	0.377	0.312	0.258	0.215	0.149	0.104	0.073	0.051

For the 10% investment for one year, we find the junction of the 10% column and row 1 in Exhibit C-6. The figure 0.909 is computed as follows: 1/1.10 = 0.909. This work has been done for us, and only the present values are given in the table. To figure the present value for $5,000, we multiply 0.909 by $5,000. The result is $4,545, which matches the result we obtained by hand.

For the two-year investment, we read down the 10% column and across row 2. We multiply 0.826 (computed as 0.909/1.10 = 0.826) by $5,000 and get $4,130, which confirms our earlier computation of $4,132 (the difference is due to rounding in the present-value table). Using the table, we can compute the present value of any single future amount.

Present Value of an Annuity

Return to the investment example near the bottom of page 889 of this appendix. That investment provided the investor with only a single future receipt ($5,000 at the end of two years). *Annuity investments* provide multiple receipts of an equal amount at fixed intervals over the investment's duration.

Consider an investment that promises *annual* cash receipts of $10,000 to be received at the end of three years. Assume that you demand a 12% return on your investment. What is the investment's present value? That is, what would you pay today to acquire the investment? The investment spans three periods, and you would pay the sum of three present values. The computation follows.

Year	Annual Cash Receipt	Present Value of $1 at 12% (Exhibit C-6)	Present Value of Annual Cash Receipt
1	$10,000	0.893	$ 8,930
2	10,000	0.797	7,970
3	10,000	0.712	7,120
Total present value of investment..............			$24,020

The present value of this annuity is $24,020. By paying this amount today, you will receive $10,000 at the end of each of the three years while earning 12% on your investment.

This example illustrates repetitive computations of the three future amounts, a time-consuming process. One way to ease the computational burden is to add the three present values of $1 (0.893 + 0.797 + 0.712) and multiply their sum (2.402) by the annual cash receipt ($10,000) to obtain the present value of the annuity ($10,000 × 2.402 = $24,020).

An easier approach is to use a present-value-of-an-annuity table. Exhibit C-7 on the following page shows the present value of $1 to be received periodically for a given number of periods. The present value of a three-period annuity at 12% is 2.402 (the junction of row 3 and the 12% column). Thus, $10,000 received annually at the end of each of three years, discounted at 12%, is $24,020 ($10,000 × 2.402), which is the present value.

EXHIBIT C-7 | **Present Value Annuity of $1**

Present Value of Annuity of $1									
Periods	4%	5%	6%	7%	8%	10%	12%	14%	16%
1	0.962	0.952	0.943	0.935	0.926	0.909	0.893	0.877	0.862
2	1.886	1.859	1.833	1.808	1.783	1.736	1.690	1.647	1.605
3	2.775	2.723	2.673	2.624	2.577	2.487	2.402	2.322	2.246
4	3.630	3.546	3.465	3.387	3.312	3.170	3.037	2.914	2.798
5	4.452	4.329	4.212	4.100	3.993	3.791	3.605	3.433	3.274
6	5.242	5.076	4.917	4.767	4.623	4.355	4.111	3.889	3.685
7	6.002	5.786	5.582	5.389	5.206	4.868	4.564	4.288	4.039
8	6.733	6.463	6.210	5.971	5.747	5.335	4.968	4.639	4.344
9	7.435	7.108	6.802	6.515	6.247	5.759	5.328	4.946	4.608
10	8.111	7.722	7.360	7.024	6.710	6.145	5.650	5.216	4.833
11	8.760	8.306	7.887	7.499	7.139	6.495	5.938	5.453	5.029
12	9.385	8.863	8.384	7.943	7.536	6.814	6.194	5.660	5.197
13	9.986	9.394	8.853	8.358	7.904	7.103	6.424	5.842	5.342
14	10.563	9.899	9.295	8.745	8.244	7.367	6.628	6.002	5.468
15	11.118	10.380	9.712	9.108	8.559	7.606	6.811	6.142	5.575
16	11.652	10.838	10.106	9.447	8.851	7.824	6.974	6.265	5.669
17	12.166	11.274	10.477	9.763	9.122	8.022	7.120	6.373	5.749
18	12.659	11.690	10.828	10.059	9.372	8.201	7.250	6.467	5.818
19	13.134	12.085	11.158	10.336	9.604	8.365	7.366	6.550	5.877
20	13.590	12.462	11.470	10.594	9.818	8.514	7.469	6.623	5.929

Present Value of Bonds Payable

The present value of a bond—its market price—is the present value of the future principal amount at maturity plus the present value of the future stated interest payments. The principal is a *single amount* to be paid at maturity. The interest is an *annuity* because it occurs periodically.

Let's compute the present value of the assumed 9% five-year bonds of **Southwest Airlines** (discussed on pages 482–483). The face value of the bonds is $100,000, and they pay 4½%—stated (cash) interest semiannually (that is, twice a year).[1] At issuance, the market interest rate is expressed as 10% annually, but it is computed at 5% semiannually. Therefore, the effective interest rate for each of the 10 semiannual periods is 5%. We thus use 5% in computing the present value (PV) of the maturity and of the interest. The market price of these bonds is $96,149, as follows:

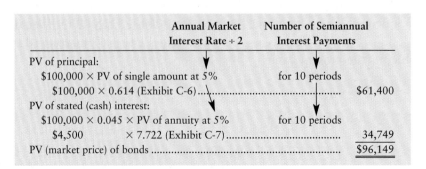

	Annual Market Interest Rate ÷ 2	Number of Semiannual Interest Payments	
PV of principal:			
$100,000 × PV of single amount at 5%		for 10 periods	
$100,000 × 0.614 (Exhibit C-6)			$61,400
PV of stated (cash) interest:			
$100,000 × 0.045 × PV of annuity at 5%		for 10 periods	
$4,500 × 7.722 (Exhibit C-7)			34,749
PV (market price) of bonds			$96,149

[1]For a definition of stated interest rate, see page 480.

The market price of the Southwest bonds shows a discount because the contract (stated) interest rate on the bonds (9%) is less than the market interest rate (10%).

Let's consider a premium price for the 9% Southwest bonds. Assume that the market interest rate is 8% (rather than 10%) at issuance. The effective interest rate is thus 4% for each of the 10 semiannual periods:

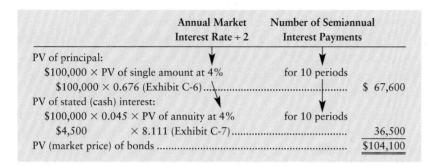

	Annual Market Interest Rate ÷ 2	Number of Semiannual Interest Payments	
PV of principal:			
$100,000 × PV of single amount at 4%		for 10 periods	
$100,000 × 0.676 (Exhibit C-6)			$ 67,600
PV of stated (cash) interest:			
$100,000 × 0.045 × PV of annuity at 4%		for 10 periods	
$4,500 × 8.111 (Exhibit C-7)			36,500
PV (market price) of bonds			$104,100

We discuss accounting for these bonds on pages 483–486. It may be helpful for you to reread this section ("Present Value of Bonds Payable") after you've studied those pages.

Capital Leases

How does a lessee compute the cost of an asset acquired through a capital lease? (See page 496 for the definition of *capital leases*.) Consider that the lessee gets the use of the asset but does *not* pay for the leased asset in full at the beginning of the lease. A capital lease is therefore similar to an installment purchase of the leased asset. The lessee must record the leased asset at the present value of the lease liability. The time value of money must be weighed.

The cost of the asset to the lessee is the sum of any payment made at the beginning of the lease period plus the present value of the future lease payments. The lease payments are equal amounts occurring at regular intervals—that is, they are annuity payments.

Consider a 20-year building lease that requires 20 annual payments of $10,000 each, with the first payment due immediately. The interest rate in the lease is 10%, and the present value of the 19 future payments is $83,650 ($10,000 × PV of annuity at 10% for 19 periods, or 8.365 from Exhibit C-7). The lessee's cost of the building is $93,650 (the sum of the initial payment, $10,000, plus the present value of the future payments, $83,650). The lessee would base its accounting for the leased asset (and the related depreciation) and for the lease liability (and the related interest expense) on the cost of the building that we have just computed.

Appendix Problems

PC-1. For each situation, compute the required amount.

a. **Kellogg Corporation** is budgeting for the acquisition of land over the next several years. Kellogg can invest $100,000 today at 9%. How much cash will Kellogg have for land acquisitions at the end of five years? At the end of six years?

b. **Davidson, Inc.,** is planning to invest $50,000 each year for five years. The company's investment adviser believes that Davidson can earn 6% interest without taking on too much risk. What will be the value of Davidson's investment on the date of the last deposit if Davidson can earn 6%? If Davidson can earn 8%?

PC-2. For each situation, compute the required amount.

a. **Intel Corporation** operations are generating excess cash that will be invested in a special fund. During 2009, Intel invests $5,643,341 in the fund for a planned advertising campaign on a new product to be released six years later, in 2015. If Intel's investments can earn 10% each year, how much cash will the company have for the advertising campaign in 2015?

b. Intel will need $10 million to advertise a new type of chip in 2015. How much must Intel invest in 2009 to have the cash available for the advertising campaign? Intel's investments can earn 10% annually.

c. Explain the relationship between your answers to a and b.

PC-3. Determine the present value of the following notes and bonds:

1. Ten-year bonds payable with maturity value of $500,000 and stated interest rate of 12%, paid semiannually. The market rate of interest is 12% at issuance.
2. Same bonds payable as in number 1, but the market interest rate is 14%.
3. Same bonds payable as in number 1, but the market interest rate is 10%.

PC-4. On December 31, 2010, when the market interest rate is 8% Libby, Libby, & Short, a partnership, issues $400,000 of 10-year, 7.25% bonds payable. The bonds pay interest semiannually.

❙ Requirements

1. Determine the present value of the bonds at issuance.
2. Assume that the bonds are issued at the price computed in Requirement 1. Prepare an effective-interest-method amortization table for the first two semiannual interest periods.
3. Using the amortization table prepared in Requirement 2, journalize issuance of the bonds and the first two interest payments and amortization of the bonds.

PC-5. St. Mere Eglise Children's Home needs a fleet of vans to transport the children to singing engagements throughout Normandy. **Renault** offers the vehicles for a single payment of €630,000 due at the end of four years. **Peugeot** prices a similar fleet of vans for four annual payments of €150,000 at the end of each year. The children's home could borrow the funds at 6%, so this is the appropriate interest rate. Which company should get the business, Renault or Peugeot? Base your decision on present value, and give your reason.

PC-6. American Family Association acquired equipment under a capital lease that requires six annual lease payments of $40,000. The first payment is due when the lease begins, on January 1, 2010. Future payments are due on January 1 of each year of the lease term. The interest rate in the lease is 16%.

❙ Requirement

1. Compute the association's cost of the equipment.

Answers

PC-1   a. 5 yrs. $153,900
            6 yrs. $167,700
        b. 6% $281,850
            8% $293,350
PC-2   a. $10,000,000
        b. $5,640,000
PC-3   1. $500,100   2. $446,820   3. $562,360
PC-4   1. $379,455   2. Bond
            carry. amt. at 12-31-11 $380,838
PC-5   Renault PV €498,960
        Peugeot PV €519,750
PC-6   Cost $170,960

Appendix D

TYPICAL CHARTS OF ACCOUNTS FOR DIFFERENT TYPES OF BUSINESSES

A Simple Service Corporation

Assets	Liabilities	Stockholders' Equity
Cash	Accounts Payable	Common Stock
Accounts Receivable	Notes Payable, Short-Term	Retained Earnings
Allowance for Uncollectible Accounts	Salary Payable	Dividends
Notes Receivable, Short-Term	Wages Payable	**Revenues and Gains**
Interest Receivable	Payroll Taxes Payable	
Supplies	Employee Benefits Payable	Service Revenue
Prepaid Rent	Interest Payable	Interest Revenue
Prepaid Insurance	Unearned Service Revenue	Gain on Sale of Land (Furniture,
Notes Receivable, Long-Term	Notes Payable, Long-Term	Equipment, or Building)
Land		**Expenses and Losses**
Furniture		
Accumulated Depreciation—Furniture		Salary Expense
Equipment		Payroll Tax Expense
Accumulated Depreciation—Equipment		Employee Benefits Expense
Building		Rent Expense
Accumulated Depreciation—Building		Insurance Expense
		Supplies Expense
		Uncollectible Account Expense
		Depreciation Expense—Furniture
		Depreciation Expense—Equipment
		Depreciation Expense—Building
		Property Tax Expense
		Interest Expense
		Miscellaneous Expense
		Loss on Sale (or Exchange) of Land
		(Furniture, Equipment, or Building)

Service Partnership

Same as service corporation, except for owners' equity

Owners' Equity

Partner 1, Capital
Partner 2, Capital
.
.
.
Partner N, Capital

Partner 1, Drawing
Partner 2, Drawing
.
.
.
Partner N, Drawing

A Complex Merchandising Corporation

Assets	Liabilities	Stockholders' Equity
Cash	Accounts Payable	Preferred Stock
Short-Term Investments	Notes Payable, Short-Term	Paid-in Capital in Excess of
Accounts Receivable	Current Portion of Bonds	Par—Preferred
Allowance for Uncollectible	Payable	Common Stock
Accounts	Salary Payable	Paid-in Capital in Excess of
Notes Receivable, Short-Term	Wages Payable	Par—Common
Interest Receivable	Payroll Taxes Payable	Paid-in Capital from Treasury
Inventory	Employee Benefits Payable	Stock Transactions
Supplies	Interest Payable	Paid-in Capital from
Prepaid Rent	Income Tax Payable	Retirement of Stock
Prepaid Insurance	Unearned Sales Revenue	Retained Earnings
Notes Receivable, Long-Term	Notes Payable, Long-Term	Unrealized Gain (or Loss)
Investments in Subsidiaries	Bonds Payable	on Investments
Investments in Stock	Lease Liability	Foreign Currency Translation
(Available-for-Sale	Minority Interest	Adjustment
Securities)		Treasury Stock
Investments in Bonds (Held-to-		
Maturity Securities)		
Other Receivables, Long-Term		
Land		
Land Improvements		
Furniture and Fixtures		
Accumulated Depreciation—		
Furniture and Fixtures		
Equipment		
Accumulated Depreciation—		
Equipment		
Buildings		
Accumulated Depreciation—		
Buildings		
Franchises		
Patents		
Leaseholds		
Goodwill		

Revenues and Gains

Sales Revenue
Interest Revenue
Dividend Revenue
Equity-Method Investment
  Revenue
Unrealized Holding Gain on
  Trading Investments
Gain on Sale of Investments
Gain on Sale of Land
  (Furniture and Fixtures,
  Equipment, or Buildings)
Discontinued Operations—
  Gain
Extraordinary Gains

Expenses and Losses

Cost of Goods Sold
Salary Expense
Wage Expense
Commission Expense
Payroll Tax Expense
Employee Benefits Expense
Rent Expense
Insurance Expense
Supplies Expense
Uncollectible Account Expense
Depreciation Expense—Land
  Improvements
Depreciation Expense—
  Furniture and Fixtures
Depreciation Expense—
  Equipment
Depreciation Expense—
  Buildings
Organization Expense
Amortization Expense—
  Franchises
Amortization Expense—
  Leasholds
Amortization Expense—
  Goodwill
Income Tax Expense
Unrealized Holding Loss on
  Trading Investments
Loss on Sale of Investments
Loss on Sale (or Exchange) of
  Land (Furniture and
  Fixtures, Equipment, or
  Buildings)
Discontinued Operations—
  Loss
Extraordinary Losses

A Manufacturing Corporation

Same as merchandising corporation, except for Assets

Assets

Inventories:
  Materials Inventory
  Work-in-Process Inventory
  Finished Goods Inventory
Factory Wages
Factory Overhead

Appendix E

SUMMARY OF GENERALLY ACCEPTED ACCOUNTING PRINCIPLES (GAAP)

Every technical area has professional associations and regulatory bodies that govern the practice of the profession. Accounting is no exception. In the United States, generally accepted accounting principles (GAAP) are influenced most by the Financial Accounting Standards Board (FASB). The FASB has five full-time members and a large staff. Its financial support comes from professional associations such as the American Institute of Certified Public Accountants (AICPA).

The FASB is an independent organization with no government or professional affiliation. The FASB's pronouncements, called *Statements of Financial Accounting Standards*, specify how to account for certain business transactions. Each new *Standard* becomes part of GAAP, the "accounting law of the land." In the same way that our laws draw authority from their acceptance by the people, GAAP depends on general acceptance by the business community. Throughout this book, we refer to GAAP as the proper way to do financial accounting.

The U.S. Congress has given the Securities and Exchange Commission (SEC), a government organization that regulates the trading of investments, ultimate responsibility for establishing accounting rules for companies that are owned by the general investing public. However, the SEC has delegated much of its rule-making power to the FASB. Exhibit E-1 outlines the flow of authority for developing GAAP.

EXHIBIT E-1 | **Flow of Authority for Developing GAAP**

United States Congress → Securities and Exchange Commission → Financial Accounting Standards Board → Pronouncements that make up generally accepted accounting principles (GAAP)

The Objective of Financial Reporting

The basic objective of financial reporting is to provide information that is useful in making investment and lending decisions. The FASB believes that accounting information can be useful in decision making only if it is *relevant* and if it *faithfully represents* economic reality.

Relevant information is useful in making predictions and for evaluating past performance—that is, the information has feedback value. For example, PepsiCo's disclosure of the profitability of each of its lines of business is relevant for investor evaluations of the company. To be relevant, information must be timely. To faithfully represent, the information must be complete, neutral (free from bias), and without material error (accurate). Accounting information must focus on the *economic substance* of a transaction, event, or circumstance, which may or may not always be the same as its legal form. Faithful represenation makes the information *reliable* to users.

Exhibit 1-3 on page 7 of Chapter 1 presents the objectives of accounting, its fundamental and enhancing qualitative characteristics, as well as its contraints. These characteristics and contraints combine to shape the concepts and principles that make up GAAP. Exhibit E-2 summarizes the assumptions, concepts, and principles that accounting has developed to provide useful information for decision making.

EXHIBIT E-2 | **Summary of Important Accounting Concepts, Principles, and Financial Statements**

Assumptions, Concepts, Principles, and Financial Statements	Quick Summary	Text Reference
Assumptions and Concepts		
Entity assumption	Accounting draws a boundary around each organization to be accounted for.	Chapter 1, page 8
Continuity (going concern) assumption	Accountants assume the business will continue operating for the foreseeable future.	Chapter 1, page 9
Stable-monetary-unit assumption	Accounting information is expressed primarily in monetary terms that ignore the effects of inflation.	Chapter 1, page 10
Time-period concept	Ensures that accounting information is reported at regular intervals.	Chapter 3, page 140
Conservatism concept	Accountants report items in the financial statements in a way that avoids overstating assets, owners' equity, and revenues and avoids understating liabilities and expenses.	Chapter 6, page 359
Materiality	A constraint of accounting. Accountants perform strictly proper accounting only for items that are significant to the company's financial statements.	Chapter 1, page 8
Cost	A constraint of accounting, meaning that the cost of producing information should not exceed the expected benefits to users.	Chapter 1, page 8
Principles		
Historical cost principle	Assets, services, revenues, and expenses are recorded at their actual historical cost.	Chapter 1, page 9
Revenue principle	Tells accountants when to record revenue (only after it has been earned) and the amount of revenue to record (the cash value of what has been received).	Chapter 3, page 140, and Chapter 11
Matching principle	Directs accountants to (1) identify and measure all expenses incurred during the period and (2) match the expenses against the revenues earned during the period. The goal is to measure net income.	Chapter 3, page 141
Consistency principle	Businesses should use the same accounting methods from period to period.	Chapter 6, page 358
Disclosure principle	A company's financial statements should report enough information for outsiders to make informed decisions about the company.	Chapter 6, page 358
Financial Statements		
Balance sheet	Assets = Liabilities + Owners' Equity at a point in time.	Chapter 1
Income statement	Revenues and gains − Expenses and losses = Net income or net loss for the period	Chapters 1 and 11
Statement of cash flows	Cash receipts − Cash payments = Increase or decrease in cash during the period, grouped under operating, investing, and financing activities	Chapters 1 and 12
Statement of retained earnings	Beginning retained earnings + Net income (or − Net loss) − Dividends = Ending retained earnings	Chapters 1 and 11
Statement of stockholders' equity	Shows the reason for the change in each stockholders' equity account, including retained earnings.	Chapter 11
Financial statement notes	Provide information that cannot be reported conveniently on the face of the financial statements. The notes are an integral part of the statements.	Chapter 11

Appendix F

SUMMARY OF DIFFERENCES BETWEEN U.S. GAAP AND IFRS CROSS REFERENCED TO CHAPTER

The following table describes some of the current differences between U.S. GAAP and International Financial Reporting Standards (IFRS) that relate to topics (by chapter) covered in this textbook. The U.S. Securities and Exchange Commission (SEC) has adopted a timetable whereby U.S. public companies may adopt IFRS by 2014. Because of a global economic recession and a crisis in the financial markets, a significant number of informed persons believe that this time table may be delayed. Nevertheless, most people believe that the integration of GAAP and IFRS will eventually become a reality. The last column of the table explains what *could* happen if the U.S. GAAP of today were to switch to IFRS as they currently exist. This will help you assess the impact of these changes on U.S. financial statements.

Accounts	Topic	U.S. GAAP Position	IFRS Position	Implications of Switch to IFRS
Inventory and Cost of Goods Sold Chapter 6	Inventory costing	Companies can choose to use LIFO inventory costing, if desired. Approximately 30% of U.S. companies currently use LIFO for its tax benefits.	LIFO is not allowed under any circumstances.	LIFO could be eliminated. Companies could still choose to use FIFO, average, or specific identification methods.
	Lower-of-cost-or market (LCM)	Market is usually determined to be replacement cost. LCM write-downs cannot be reversed.	Market is always net realizable value (fair market value). LCM write-downs can be reversed under certain conditions.	LCM write-downs may become less common, as selling prices are usually greater than replacement costs. Some write-downs might be reversed over time.
Property, Plant, and Equipment Chapter 7	Asset impairment and revaluation	If long-term assets are impaired, they are written down. Write-downs may not be reversed.	Long-term assets may be written up or down, based on fair market value (appraisals). Adjustments may be potentially reversed.	The cost principle might not apply to long-term assets as strongly. Assets could be evaluated by independent appraisers and adjusted either up or down.
Research and Development Chapter 7	Development costs	All research and development costs are expensed. Only exception is for computer software development costs, which can be capitalized and amortized over future sales revenues.	All research is expensed, but all development costs are capitalized and amortized over future sales revenues.	Standards already developed by U.S. GAAP might be extended to apply to all development costs, not just computer software development.
Intangible Assets Chapter 7	Capitalization and recognition of intangible assets on balance sheet	Only recognized when purchased. Internally developed not recognized.	Recognized if future benefit is probable and reliably measurable (same criteria as recognition of contingencies). May be purchased or internally developed.	More intangible assets could be recognized on balance sheet. Adjusted for amortization or impairment over time.
Contingent Liabilities Chapter 8	Recording of contingent liabilities	Accrued (recorded in journal entry) if probable and reliably measurable. Contingent liabilities that are possible are disclosed in notes to financial statements.	Both probable and possible contingent liabilities are recorded in journal entries.	More liabilities will likely be recorded, regardless of the outcome of proposals being studied by FASB and IASB.

Accounts	Topic	U.S. GAAP Position	IFRS Position	Implications of Switch to IFRS
Contingent Liabilities Chapter 8	Disclosure of contingencies	The FASB has proposed that the standard for disclosure of loss contingencies be increased to include all such matters that are expected to be resolved in the near term (i.e., within the next year) and that could have a severe impact (higher than material, disruptive to the business). In addition, the proposal requires a quantitative tabular reconciliation of accrued loss contingencies that includes increases or decreases in such amounts during the most recent year.	IASB is studying its present requirements with a view to increase required disclosures in the next few years.	More liabilities will likely be recorded, regardless of the outcome of proposals being studied by the FASB and IASB.
Lease Liabilities Chapter 8	Classification of leases	To be classified as a capital lease, one of four quantitative "bright line" tests must be met. If not, lease is classified as an operating lease by default.	Guidance focuses on the overall substance of the transaction. Classification as capital lease depends on whether lease transfers substantially all risks and rewards of ownership to lessee. More judgment required on the part of preparer. No quantitative guidelines exist.	More leases could be classified as capital leases, resulting in more frequent recognition of long-term assets as well as long-term liabilities.
Revenue Chapter 11	Revenue recognition	Many different ways to recognize revenues, depending on the industry and the type of contract.	Revenue recognition based mainly on a single standard that contains general principles applied to different types of transactions.	It will standardize the way in which revenues are recognized, resulting in changes in the timing of revenue recognition.
Extraordinary Items Chapter 11	Recording of extraordinary items	Allows separate disclosure of extraordinary items (unusual in nature and infrequent in occurrence) after income from continuing operations.	Extraordinary items do not have special treatment. Even "unusual and infrequent" items are reported in income from continuing operations.	Extraordinary items may disappear from the income statement, to be reclassified as "ordinary" revenues and expenses.
Interest Revenue and Interest Expense Chapter 12	Indirect method cash flows statement presentation Direct method cash flows statement presentation	Interest revenue and interest expense are part of net income, and as such are included in operating activities (as part of net income) on an indirect method cash flows statement. Interest is not reported under investing activities.	Interest revenue and interest expense are removed from net income (as an adjustment, similar to the adjustment for depreciation expense) in the operating activities section of the indirect method cash flows statement. Interest income is reported under financing activities, and interest expense is reported under investing activities for both direct and indirect methods.	Interest revenue and interest expense reclassified to different sections of the cash flows statement.

Company Index

Glindex

A

Above par common stock, 542–543

Accelerated depreciation method. A depreciation method that writes off a relatively larger amount of the asset's cost nearer the start of its useful life than the straight-line method does, 420–421, 424–426

Account format. A balance-sheet format that lists assets on the left and liabilities and stockholders' equity on the right, 91, 168

Account numbers, list of, 90

Account payable. A liability backed by the general reputation and credit standing of the debtor, 14

Accounting. The information system that measures business activities, processes that information into reports and financial statements, and communicates the results to decision makers. *See also* Assumptions; Principles of accounting.
  defined, 3
  differences, effects on ratio analysis, 838
  financial, 4–5
  guidelines. *See* FASB; GAAP; IFRS.
  management, 5
  method changes, income statement, 661–662
  objectives of, 7
  ratios, 169–173
  vs. bookkeeping, 3

Accounting equation. The most basic tool of accounting: Assets = Liabilities + Owners' Equity, 13–15

Accounting information
  comparability, 8
  constraints on, 8
  cost of, 8
  faithful representation, 7
  focus on economic substance, 8
  global, consistent reporting. *See* IFRS.
  materiality, 8
  relevance, 7
  required characteristics, 7–8
  timeliness, 8
  understandability, 8
  verifiability, 8

Accounting information, users of
  creditors, 4
  external, 4–5
  individuals, 4
  internal, 4–5
  investors, 4
  nonprofit organizations, 4
  regulatory bodies, 4

Accounts. Records of the changes that have occurred in a particular asset, liability, or stockholders' equity during a period. The basic summary device of accounting. *See also* Trial balance.
  accrued liabilities, 66
  analyzing, 88–89
  assets, 65–66
  balance, defined, 78
  buildings, 66
  by business type, 895–896
  cash, 65
  chart of, 90
  common stock, 66
  contra, 80
  defined, 65
  dividends, 67, 80
  equipment, 66
  expenses, 67, 80
  fixtures, 66
  furniture, 66
  increasing/decreasing. *See* Debits and credits.
  land, 66
  liabilities, 66
  merchandise inventory, 65
  negative equity, 80
  notes payable, 66
  notes receivable, 65
  owners' equity, 66
  payable, 66
  posting, 81–82. *See also* Journals; Ledger.
  prepaid expenses, 65
  receivable, 65
  retained earnings, 66
  revenues, 67
  stockholders' equity, 79–80

Accounts payable
  current liabilities, 469
  defined, 66
  in financial statements, 14

Accounts receivable. *See also* Notes receivable; Receivables.
  accounts for, 65
  as assets, 22
  control accounts, 296
  defined, 296
  internal controls over cash, 297
  risk of not collecting, 297
  subsidiary records, 296

Accounts receivable turnover. Measures a company's ability to collect cash from credit customers. To compute accounts receivable turnover, divide net credit sales by average net accounts receivable, 313, 794

Accrual. An expense or a revenue that occurs before the business pays or receives cash. An accrual is the opposite of a deferral, 144

Accrual accounting. Accounting that records the impact of a business event as it occurs, regardless of whether the transaction affected cash.
  account-format balance sheets, 168
  accounting ratios, 169–173
  adjusting accounts, 144
  assets, classifying, 167
  assets, reporting, 167–168
  balance sheets, formats, 168
  balance sheets, preparing, 157–159
  cash flows, 140
  classified balance sheets, 167–168
  current assets, 167
  current liabilities, 167
  current ratio, 170
  debt ratio, 170–171
  defined, 139
  ethical issues, 142–143
  expenses, matching against revenue, 141–142
  expenses, recording, 141–142
  financial statements, preparing, 157–159
  GAAP requirements for, 139
  income statements, formats, 169
  income statements, preparing, 157–159
  liabilities, classifying, 167
  liabilities, reporting, 167–168
  liquidity, 167
  long-term assets, 167
  long-term liabilities, 167
  matching principle, 141–142
  multi-step income statements, 169
  operating cycle, 167
  report-format balance sheets, 168
  revenue, matching against expenses, 141–142
  revenue, recording, 140–141
  revenue principle, 140–141
  revenue recognition, 141
  single-step income statements, 169
  statement of retained earnings, preparing, 157–159
  time-period concept, 140
  transactions, effects on ratios, 171–173
  updating accounts. *See* Adjusting accounts.
  vs. cash-basis accounting, 139

Accrued expense. An expense incurred but not yet paid in cash. Also called *accrued liability*, 150, 470. *See also* Accrued liability.

Accrued liabilities accounts, 66